# 1984 Annual Edition
## West's Federal Taxation:

# Comprehensive Volume

# 1984 Annual Edition
# West's Federal Taxation:
# Comprehensive Volume

---

*General Editors*

WILLIAM H. HOFFMAN, JR., J. D., Ph.D., C.P.A.
EUGENE WILLIS, Ph.D., C.P.A.

---

Contributing Authors

D. LARRY CRUMBLEY, Ph.D., C.P.A.
Texas A & M University

STEVEN C. DILLEY, J.D., Ph.D., C.P.A.
Michigan State University

PATRICA C. ELLIOTT, D.B.A., C.P.A.
University of New Mexico

WILLIAM H. HOFFMAN, Jr., J.D., Ph.D., C.P.A.
University of Houston

JEROME S. HORVITZ, J.D., LL.M. in Taxation
University of Houston

MARILYN PHELAN, J.D., D.B.A., C.P.A.
Texas Tech University

WILLIAM A. RAABE, Jr., Ph.D., C.P.A.
University of Wisconsin-Milwaukee

BOYD C. RANDALL, J.D., Ph.D.
Brigham Young University

W. EUGENE SEAGO, J.D., Ph.D., C.P.A.
Virginia Polytechnic Institute and State University

JAMES E. SMITH, Ph.D., C.P.A.
College of William and Mary

WILLIS C. STEVENSON, Ph.D., C.P.A.
University of Wisconsin-Madison

EUGENE WILLIS, Ph.D., C.P.A.
University of Illinois at Urbana

**WEST PUBLISHING CO.**
ST. PAUL • NEW YORK • LOS ANGELES • SAN FRANCISCO

Copy editor and indexer: Deborah Smith
Text composition: York Graphic Services

COPYRIGHT © 1983 by WEST PUBLISHING CO.
                         50 West Kellogg Boulevard
                         P.O. Box 3526
                         St. Paul, Minnesota 55165

Library of Congress Cataloging in Publication Data

Main entry under title:
  West's Federal Taxation.
  includes index.
  1.  Income tax—United States—Law
I.  Hoffman, William H.   II.  Willis, Eugene
  **ISBN** 0-314-74883-0     KF6369.W47     343'.73'052

1984 ANNUAL EDITION

1st Reprint—1983

# PREFACE

Simply stated, *West's Federal Taxation: Comprehensive Volume* is an abridged version of *West's Federal Taxation: Individual Income Taxes* and *West's Federal Taxation: Corporations, Partnerships, Estates, and Trusts.* In condensing all of this material to a manageable form, it was necessary to utilize our editorial license to pick and choose. Thus, a great deal of useful, but not essential, information had to be pruned in order to arrive at the final product. What to cover or not to cover in any abridgement process is, understandably so, a judgment call. We can only hope that we acted correctly in making most of our decisions.

The *Comprehensive Volume* is designed primarily to service the needs of those who offer only one course in Federal taxation. In many such cases, a broad scope of coverage could be the ultimate objective. Although the income taxation of individuals should be stressed, it is conceivable that some may wish to devote significant classroom time to other areas of Federal taxation. For example, the allocation of course coverage might be structured as follows: 60 percent to the individual income tax (i. e., Chapters 1–11) and 40 percent to the tax treatment of corporations, partnerships, etc. (i. e., Chapters 12–22).

For those who encounter time constraints and/or want to emphasize some areas and not others, the last half of the text (Chapters 12–22) possesses potential for selectivity. Thus, if one wanted to cover corporations (Chapters 12–16) and tax practice (Chapter 21) and not the other subjects (Chapters 17–20, and 22), he or she can proceed accordingly without disrupting the flow of the material. In this regard, there exists flexibility for a number of different combinations for partial coverage of the last half of the text (e. g., for a "light" coverage of corporations resort to Chapters 12 and 13 while for a "heavy" concentration assign Chapters 12–16).

If the *Comprehensive Volume* is to be used in whole (or in part) for a one-course tax offering, the pace of coverage of the subject matter may have to be accelerated. In recognition of this fact, we have followed certain guidelines.

—Although not eliminated entirely, the research orientation has been kept to a minimum. By restricting judicial analysis and controlling the number of footnotes, the reader is spared some measure of distraction. The result is a quicker coverage of the textual material.

—In an accelerated setting, there is a decided constraint placed on the amount of problem solving that can be expected from the reader. We have, therefore, made every effort to limit the quantity of the problem materials. In this connection, we hope that the integrity of the quality of such materials is maintained.

For those users who feel the need for some material on research methodology, the last chapter in the text on WORKING WITH THE TAX LAW is available. In place of the usual problem materials, this chapter also includes numerous research projects, arranged by chapter numbers, dealing with the subject matter treated in the text.

The *Comprehensive Volume* includes the latest tax developments, among which are the Tax Equity and Fiscal Responsibility Act of 1982 (TEFRA), the Subchapter S Revision Act of 1982 and the Social Security Amendments of 1983.

In addition to the usual updating to reflect the changes in the tax law, the 1984 Annual Edition incorporates a new *Instructor's Guide*. The "IG" contains the following materials:

—Instructor's Summaries which can be used as lecture outlines and provide the instuctor with teaching aids and information not contained in the text.

—An extensive set of Examination Questions with solutions thereto.

The *Solutions Manual* continues to contain the answers to the Discussion Questions, Problems, Research Problems, and Comprehensive Tax Return Problems.

As is the case with any new literary undertaking, we will welcome user comments. Please rest assured that any such comments will not be taken lightly and, hopefully, will lead to improvement in later editions of *West's Federal Taxation: Comprehensive Volume*.

William H. Hoffman, Jr.

May, 1983                                              Eugene Willis

# CONTENTS IN BRIEF

|  |  |  | Page |
|---|---|---|---|
|  | PREFACE | v |
| **CHAPTER** 1 | AN INTRODUCTION TO TAXATION | 1-1 |
| **CHAPTER** 2 | TAX DETERMINATION, PERSONAL AND DEPENDENCY EXEMPTIONS, AN OVERVIEW OF PROPERTY TRANSACTIONS | 2-1 |
| **CHAPTER** 3 | GROSS INCOME: CONCEPTS AND INCLUSIONS | 3-1 |
| **CHAPTER** 4 | GROSS INCOME EXCLUSIONS | 4-1 |
| **CHAPTER** 5 | DEDUCTIONS AND LOSSES: IN GENERAL | 5-1 |
| **CHAPTER** 6 | DEDUCTIONS AND LOSSES: CERTAIN BUSINESS EXPENSES AND EMPLOYEE EXPENSES | 6-1 |
| **CHAPTER** 7 | DEDUCTIONS AND LOSSES: CERTAIN ITEMIZED DEDUCTIONS | 7-1 |
| **CHAPTER** 8 | TAX CREDITS | 8-1 |
| **CHAPTER** 9 | PROPERTY TRANSACTIONS: DETERMINATION OF GAIN OR LOSS, BASIS CONSIDERATIONS AND NONTAXABLE EXCHANGES | 9-1 |
| **CHAPTER** 10 | PROPERTY TRANSACTIONS: CAPITAL GAINS AND LOSSES, SECTION 1231, AND RECAPTURE PROVISIONS | 10-1 |
| **CHAPTER** 11 | SPECIAL TAX COMPUTATIONS | 11-1 |
| **CHAPTER** 12 | TAXATION OF CORPORATIONS: ORGANIZATION AND CAPITAL STRUCTURE | 12-1 |
| **CHAPTER** 13 | CORPORATE DISTRIBUTIONS NOT IN COMPLETE LIQUIDATION | 13-1 |
| **CHAPTER** 14 | CORPORATE DISTRIBUTIONS IN COMPLETE LIQUIDATION AND AN OVERVIEW OF CORPORATE REORGANIZATIONS | 14-1 |
| **CHAPTER** 15 | CORPORATE ACCUMULATIONS | 15-1 |
| **CHAPTER** 16 | SUBCHAPTER S CORPORATIONS | 16-1 |
| **CHAPTER** 17 | PARTNERSHIPS | 17-1 |
| **CHAPTER** 18 | THE FEDERAL ESTATE TAX | 18-1 |
| **CHAPTER** 19 | THE FEDERAL GIFT TAX AND CERTAIN STATE TRANSFER TAXES | 19-1 |

  Page

**CHAPTER 20**    INCOME TAXATION OF TRUSTS AND ES-
                    TATES .............................    20-1
**CHAPTER 21**    TAX ADMINISTRATION AND PRACTICE ..    21-1
**CHAPTER 22**    WORKING WITH THE TAX LAW .........    22-1
                    APPENDIXES............................    A-1
                    SUBJECT INDEX ........................    I-1

# TABLE OF CONTENTS

## CHAPTER 1.  AN INTRODUCTION TO TAXATION

Page

HISTORY OF U.S. TAXATION ........................... 1-1
Early Periods ........................................... 1-1
Revenue Acts ........................................... 1-2
Historical Trends ....................................... 1-3

CRITERIA USED IN THE SELECTION OF A TAX BASE .. 1-3

THE TAX STRUCTURE ................................. 1-4
Tax Rates ............................................... 1-4
Adjustments to Tax Base and Incidence of Taxation ......... 1-5

MAJOR TYPES OF TAXES ............................... 1-5
Property Taxes .......................................... 1-5
Transaction Taxes ....................................... 1-9
Death Taxes ............................................ 1-11
Gift Taxes .............................................. 1-12
Income Taxes ........................................... 1-12
Employment Taxes ...................................... 1-15
Other Taxes ............................................ 1-18

THE WHYS OF THE TAX LAW ......................... 1-19
Economic Considerations ................................ 1-19
Social Considerations ................................... 1-23
Equity Considerations .................................. 1-24
Political Considerations ................................. 1-29
Influence of the Internal Revenue Service ................. 1-30
Influence of the Courts.................................. 1-32
Summary................................................ 1-34

PROBLEM MATERIALS.................................. 1-34

## CHAPTER 2.  TAX DETERMINATION, PERSONAL AND DEPENDENCY EXEMPTIONS, AN OVERVIEW OF PROPERTY TRANSACTIONS

TAX FORMULA ......................................... 2-2
Some of the Components ................................. 2-2
Application of the Tax Formula .......................... 2-5
Zero Bracket Amount.................................... 2-6
Unused Zero Bracket Amount ........................... 2-8

Page

PERSONAL AND DEPENDENCY EXEMPTIONS............ 2-11
  Personal Exemptions ..................................... 2-11
  Dependency Exemptions ................................. 2-12

TAX DETERMINATION................................. 2-17
  Tax Table Method ....................................... 2-17
  Tax Rate Schedule Method .............................. 2-17
  Computation of Net Taxes Payable or Refund Due ......... 2-18

FILING CONSIDERATIONS ............................. 2-20
  Filing Requirements..................................... 2-20
  Filing Status........................................... 2-22

GAINS AND LOSSES FROM PROPERTY
  TRANSACTIONS—IN GENERAL ....................... 2-26

GAINS AND LOSSES FROM PROPERTY
  TRANSACTIONS—CAPITAL GAINS AND LOSSES....... 2-27
  Definition of a Capital Asset............................ 2-27
  Computation of Net Capital Gains and Losses ............. 2-28
  Capital Gains Deduction and Alternative Tax ............. 2-28
  Treatment of Capital Losses ............................ 2-29

TAX PLANNING CONSIDERATIONS ..................... 2-30
  Shifting Income to Lower Bracket Family Members ......... 2-30
  Alternating Between Itemized Deductions and the Zero Bracket
    Amount ............................................. 2-30
  Dependency Exemptions ................................ 2-31
  Filing Status........................................... 2-34

PROBLEM MATERIALS................................ 2-35

## CHAPTER 3.   GROSS INCOME:
## CONCEPTS AND INCLUSIONS

GROSS INCOME—WHAT IS IT? ......................... 3-1
  General Definition....................................... 3-1
  Comparison of Accounting and Taxable Income ............. 3-2
  Form of Receipt ........................................ 3-2
  Exceptions to the Income Realization Doctrine............. 3-3

YEAR OF INCLUSION ................................. 3-4
  Annual Accounting Period............................... 3-4
  Accounting Methods ..................................... 3-5
  Exceptions Applicable to Cash Basis Taxpayers............. 3-7
  Exceptions Applicable to Accrual Basis Taxpayers .......... 3-10

| | Page |
|---|---|
| INCOME SOURCES. | 3-12 |
| Personal Services. | 3-12 |
| Income From Property | 3-13 |
| Income From Partnerships, S Corporations, Trusts, and Estates | 3-14 |
| Income in Community Property States. | 3-14 |
| ITEMS SPECIFICALLY INCLUDED IN GROSS INCOME. | 3-16 |
| Alimony and Separate Maintenance Payments | 3-16 |
| Income From Annuities | 3-18 |
| Prizes and Awards. | 3-19 |
| Group-Term Life Insurance | 3-19 |
| Unemployment Compensation | 3-21 |
| TAX PLANNING CONSIDERATIONS | 3-21 |
| Tax Deferral | 3-22 |
| Shifting Income to Relatives | 3-23 |
| Accounting for Community Property. | 3-24 |
| Employee Annuities | 3-24 |
| Alimony. | 3-25 |
| PROBLEM MATERIALS. | 3-25 |

## CHAPTER 4. GROSS INCOME: EXCLUSIONS

| | |
|---|---|
| ITEMS SPECIFICALLY EXCLUDED FROM GROSS INCOME | 4-1 |
| STATUTORY AUTHORITY | 4-1 |
| ADMINISTRATIVE POLICY | 4-2 |
| SUMMARY OF PRINCIPAL EXCLUSIONS. | 4-2 |
| GIFTS AND INHERITANCES | 4-3 |
| LIFE INSURANCE PROCEEDS | 4-4 |
| Interest on Life Insurance Proceeds. | 4-5 |
| EMPLOYEE DEATH BENEFITS. | 4-5 |
| SCHOLARSHIPS AND FELLOWSHIPS | 4-6 |
| Educational Assistance Payments by Employers | 4-7 |
| COMPENSATION FOR INJURIES AND SICKNESS | 4-8 |
| Damages | 4-8 |
| Workers' Compensation | 4-10 |
| Accident and Health Insurance Benefits | 4-10 |

Page

EMPLOYER-SPONSORED ACCIDENT AND
HEALTH PLANS . . . . . . . . . . . . . . . . . . . . . . . . . . . . . . . . . . .   4-11

MEDICAL REIMBURSEMENT PLANS. . . . . . . . . . . . . . . . . . . . .   4-12

DISABILITY AND SICK PAY . . . . . . . . . . . . . . . . . . . . . . . . . .   4-12
   Disability Pay. . . . . . . . . . . . . . . . . . . . . . . . . . . . . . . . . . . . . .   4-12

MEALS AND LODGING FURNISHED FOR THE
CONVENIENCE OF THE EMPLOYER . . . . . . . . . . . . . . . . . .   4-13

OTHER EMPLOYEE FRINGE BENEFITS. . . . . . . . . . . . . . . . .   4-15

FOREIGN EARNED INCOME . . . . . . . . . . . . . . . . . . . . . . . . . .   4-17

INTEREST ON CERTAIN STATE AND LOCAL
GOVERNMENT OBLIGATIONS . . . . . . . . . . . . . . . . . . . . . . .   4-18

INTEREST EXCLUSION FOR INDIVIDUALS . . . . . . . . . . . . .   4-18
   All-Savers Certificates . . . . . . . . . . . . . . . . . . . . . . . . . . . . . . .   4-19
   Net Interest Exclusion . . . . . . . . . . . . . . . . . . . . . . . . . . . . . . .   4-19

DIVIDEND EXCLUSION FOR INDIVIDUALS . . . . . . . . . . . . .   4-19
   Nonqualifying Dividends and Those Requiring Special Treat-
   ment. . . . . . . . . . . . . . . . . . . . . . . . . . . . . . . . . . . . . . . . . . . . . .   4-20
   Stock Dividends and Dividend Reinvestment Plans. . . . . . . . .   4-21

TAX BENEFIT RULE. . . . . . . . . . . . . . . . . . . . . . . . . . . . . . . . . .   4-22

INCOME FROM DISCHARGE OF INDEBTEDNESS . . . . . . . .   4-23

TAX PLANNING CONSIDERATIONS. . . . . . . . . . . . . . . . . . . .   4-24
   Gifts and Inheritances . . . . . . . . . . . . . . . . . . . . . . . . . . . . . . . .   4-25
   Interest on Life Insurance Proceeds Paid to a Surviving Spouse   4-25
   Compensation for Injuries and Sickness. . . . . . . . . . . . . . . . . . .   4-26
   Employee Benefits. . . . . . . . . . . . . . . . . . . . . . . . . . . . . . . . . . . .   4-26

PROBLEM MATERIALS. . . . . . . . . . . . . . . . . . . . . . . . . . . . . . . .   4-27

### CHAPTER 5.  DEDUCTIONS AND LOSSES: IN GENERAL

GENERAL TESTS FOR DEDUCTIBILITY . . . . . . . . . . . . . . . . .   5-1
   Scheme of the Treatment of Deductions and Losses. . . . . . . . .   5-1
   Ordinary and Necessary Expenses. . . . . . . . . . . . . . . . . . . . . . .   5-5
   Reasonableness Requirement . . . . . . . . . . . . . . . . . . . . . . . . . . .   5-6

DISALLOWANCE POSSIBILITIES . . . . . . . . . . . . . . . . . . . . . . .   5-6
   Public Policy Limitation. . . . . . . . . . . . . . . . . . . . . . . . . . . . . . .   5-7
   Political Contributions and Lobbying Activities . . . . . . . . . . . . .   5-9

Page

Hobby Losses . . . . . . . . . . . . . . . . . . . . . . . . . . . . . . . . . . . . . . . 5-10

Expenditures Incurred for Taxpayer's Benefit or
Taxpayer's Obligation. . . . . . . . . . . . . . . . . . . . . . . . . . . . . . . . . 5-13

Disallowance of Personal Expenditures . . . . . . . . . . . . . . . . . . . . 5-14

Disallowance of Deductions for Unrealized Losses . . . . . . . . . . . 5-15

Disallowance of Deductions for Capital Expenditures . . . . . . . . 5-15

Transactions Between Related Parties . . . . . . . . . . . . . . . . . . . . . 5-17

Substantiation Requirements . . . . . . . . . . . . . . . . . . . . . . . . . . . . 5-19

Expenses and Interest Relating to Tax-Exempt Income . . . . . . 5-20

TAX PLANNING CONSIDERATIONS . . . . . . . . . . . . . . . . . . . . . . 5-22

Unreasonable Compensation. . . . . . . . . . . . . . . . . . . . . . . . . . . . . 5-22

Personal Expenditures . . . . . . . . . . . . . . . . . . . . . . . . . . . . . . . . . 5-22

Related Taxpayers. . . . . . . . . . . . . . . . . . . . . . . . . . . . . . . . . . . . . 5-22

Shifting Deductions. . . . . . . . . . . . . . . . . . . . . . . . . . . . . . . . . . . . 5-23

Hobby Losses . . . . . . . . . . . . . . . . . . . . . . . . . . . . . . . . . . . . . . . . 5-23

PROBLEM MATERIALS. . . . . . . . . . . . . . . . . . . . . . . . . . . . . . . . . 5-24

## CHAPTER 6. DEDUCTIONS AND LOSSES: CERTAIN BUSINESS EXPENSES AND EMPLOYEE EXPENSES

BAD DEBTS. . . . . . . . . . . . . . . . . . . . . . . . . . . . . . . . . . . . . . . . . . . 6-1

Allowable Methods . . . . . . . . . . . . . . . . . . . . . . . . . . . . . . . . . . . . 6-3

Determining Reserve Additions . . . . . . . . . . . . . . . . . . . . . . . . . . 6-3

Election of Methods. . . . . . . . . . . . . . . . . . . . . . . . . . . . . . . . . . . . 6-4

Business Versus Nonbusiness Bad Debts . . . . . . . . . . . . . . . . . . . 6-4

Summary of Bad Debt Provisions . . . . . . . . . . . . . . . . . . . . . . . . 6-6

Loans Between Related Parties . . . . . . . . . . . . . . . . . . . . . . . . . . 6-7

WORTHLESS SECURITIES. . . . . . . . . . . . . . . . . . . . . . . . . . . . . . 6-7

Securities in Affiliated Corporations . . . . . . . . . . . . . . . . . . . . . . 6-7

Small Business Stock . . . . . . . . . . . . . . . . . . . . . . . . . . . . . . . . . . 6-8

CASUALTY AND THEFT LOSSES . . . . . . . . . . . . . . . . . . . . . . . . 6-8

Events That Are Not Casualties . . . . . . . . . . . . . . . . . . . . . . . . . 6-8

Theft Losses . . . . . . . . . . . . . . . . . . . . . . . . . . . . . . . . . . . . . . . . . 6-9

When to Deduct Casualty Losses. . . . . . . . . . . . . . . . . . . . . . . . . 6-9

Measuring the Amount of Loss . . . . . . . . . . . . . . . . . . . . . . . . . . 6-9

RESEARCH AND EXPERIMENTAL EXPENDITURES . . . . . . . 6-11

NET OPERATING LOSSES. . . . . . . . . . . . . . . . . . . . . . . . . . . . . . 6-12

Carryback and Carryover Periods . . . . . . . . . . . . . . . . . . . . . . . . 6-13

Computation of the Net Operating Loss. . . . . . . . . . . . . . . . . . . . 6-14

**Page**

DEPRECIATION, AMORTIZATION, COST RECOVERY,
    AND DEPLETION .................................... 6-14
    Depreciation ......................................... 6-15
    Qualifying Property ................................. 6-16
    Other Depreciation Considerations ........................ 6-16

ACCELERATED COST RECOVERY SYSTEM (ACRS) ...... 6-19
    General Considerations ............................... 6-19
    Personalty: Recovery Periods and Methods ................ 6-20
    Realty: Recovery Periods and Methods ..................... 6-24
    Straight-Line Election Under ACRS ..................... 6-25
    Election to Expense Assets ............................ 6-26
    Other Aspects of ACRS ............................... 6-27

DEPLETION ............................................. 6-28
    Intangible Drilling and Development Costs (IDC) .......... 6-28
    Depletion Methods .................................... 6-28

REPORTING PROCEDURES ............................. 6-31

CLASSIFICATION OF EMPLOYMENT-RELATED EXPENSES 6-31
    Self-Employed Versus Employee Status ................... 6-31
    Deductions For or From AGI ........................... 6-32
    Special Treatment for Outside Salespersons ............... 6-33
    Reimbursed Expenses ................................. 6-34

TRANSPORTATION EXPENSES ........................... 6-36
    Qualified Expenditures ................................ 6-36
    Computation of Automobile Expenses ..................... 6-38

TRAVEL EXPENSES .................................... 6-38
    Definition of Travel Expenses .......................... 6-38
    Away-From-Home Requirement .......................... 6-39
    Combined Business and Pleasure Travel .................. 6-39
    Foreign Convention Expenses ........................... 6-40

MOVING EXPENSES .................................... 6-40
    General Requirements ................................. 6-40
    Distance Test ........................................ 6-41
    Time Requirements .................................... 6-41
    When Deductible ..................................... 6-42
    Classification of Moving Expenses ...................... 6-42

EDUCATION EXPENSES ................................. 6-44
    General Requirements ................................. 6-44

Page

Requirements Imposed by Law or by the Employer
for Retention of Employment ........................... 6-45
Maintaining or Improving Existing Skills ................. 6-45
Classification of Specific Items ........................... 6-46

ENTERTAINMENT EXPENSES .......................... 6-46
Classification of Expenses .............................. 6-47
Restrictions Upon Deductibility ......................... 6-47

OTHER EMPLOYEE EXPENSES ......................... 6-50
Office in the Home ..................................... 6-50
Miscellaneous Employee Expenses ...................... 6-51

REPORTING PROCEDURES ............................. 6-51
Other Deductions for Adjusted Gross Income .............. 6-52

TAX PLANNING CONSIDERATIONS ..................... 6-52
Documentation of Related-Taxpayer Loans,
Casualty Losses, and Theft Losses...................... 6-52
Depreciation, ACRS, and Amortization ................... 6-52
Immediate Expensing Election ........................... 6-54
Straight-Line Election Under ACRS ..................... 6-55
Depletion .............................................. 6-55
Shifting Deductions Between Employer
and Employee......................................... 6-55
Moving Expenses....................................... 6-56
Education Expenses .................................... 6-56
Entertainment ......................................... 6-57

PROBLEM MATERIALS................................. 6-58

## CHAPTER 7. DEDUCTIONS AND LOSSES: CERTAIN ITEMIZED DEDUCTIONS

GENERAL CLASSIFICATION OF EXPENSES.............. 7-1

MEDICAL EXPENSES ................................... 7-2
General Requirements .................................. 7-2
Capital Expenditures for Medical Purposes................ 7-3
Transportation Expenses ................................ 7-4
Amounts Paid for Medical Insurance Premiums ............ 7-4
Expenditures for Medicine and Drugs 7-6
Summary and Comparison of Rules for 1982, 1983, and 1984. 7-7
Reimbursement for Medical Expenses Paid in Prior Years ... 7-7

   Page

TAXES . . . . . . . . . . . . . . . . . . . . . . . . . . . . . . . . . . . . . . . . . . . . . . . . .   7-9
    Deductibility as a Tax . . . . . . . . . . . . . . . . . . . . . . . . . . . . . . . . .   7-9
    Property Taxes, Assessments, and Apportionment of
        Taxes . . . . . . . . . . . . . . . . . . . . . . . . . . . . . . . . . . . . . . . . . . .   7-10
    Income Taxes . . . . . . . . . . . . . . . . . . . . . . . . . . . . . . . . . . . . . . . .   7-12
    General Sales Taxes . . . . . . . . . . . . . . . . . . . . . . . . . . . . . . . . . . .   7-13
    Filing Requirements . . . . . . . . . . . . . . . . . . . . . . . . . . . . . . . . . . .   7-14

INTEREST . . . . . . . . . . . . . . . . . . . . . . . . . . . . . . . . . . . . . . . . . . . . . . .   7-14
    Allowed and Disallowed Items . . . . . . . . . . . . . . . . . . . . . . . . . . . .   7-14
    Restrictions on Deductibility and Timing
        Considerations . . . . . . . . . . . . . . . . . . . . . . . . . . . . . . . . . . . . .   7-15
    Classification of Interest Expense . . . . . . . . . . . . . . . . . . . . . . . . .   7-16
    Disallowance Possibilities . . . . . . . . . . . . . . . . . . . . . . . . . . . . . . .   7-17
    Installment Purchases—Interest Not Separately Stated . . . . . .   7-19

CHARITABLE CONTRIBUTIONS . . . . . . . . . . . . . . . . . . . . . . . . .   7-19
    Rationale for Deductibility . . . . . . . . . . . . . . . . . . . . . . . . . . . . . .   7-19
    Criteria for a "Gift" . . . . . . . . . . . . . . . . . . . . . . . . . . . . . . . . . . . .   7-19
    Qualified Organizations . . . . . . . . . . . . . . . . . . . . . . . . . . . . . . . . .   7-20
    Time of Payment . . . . . . . . . . . . . . . . . . . . . . . . . . . . . . . . . . . . . . .   7-20
    Valuation Problems . . . . . . . . . . . . . . . . . . . . . . . . . . . . . . . . . . . . .   7-21
    Limitations on Charitable Deductions . . . . . . . . . . . . . . . . . . . . .   7-21
    Summary of Rules . . . . . . . . . . . . . . . . . . . . . . . . . . . . . . . . . . . . . .   7-27
    Filing Requirements . . . . . . . . . . . . . . . . . . . . . . . . . . . . . . . . . . . .   7-27

TAX PLANNING CONSIDERATIONS . . . . . . . . . . . . . . . . . . . . . .   7-30
    Effective Utilization of Excess Itemized Deductions . . . . . . . . . .   7-30
    Utilization of Medical Deductions . . . . . . . . . . . . . . . . . . . . . . . .   7-30
    Planning With Sales Tax . . . . . . . . . . . . . . . . . . . . . . . . . . . . . . . .   7-32
    Protecting the Interest Deduction . . . . . . . . . . . . . . . . . . . . . . . .   7-33
    Assuring the Charitable Contribution Deduction . . . . . . . . . . . .   7-34

PROBLEM MATERIALS . . . . . . . . . . . . . . . . . . . . . . . . . . . . . . . . . .   7-35


               CHAPTER 8.  TAX CREDITS

TAX POLICY CONSIDERATIONS . . . . . . . . . . . . . . . . . . . . . . . . .   8-1

SPECIFIC BUSINESS-RELATED TAX CREDIT
        PROVISIONS . . . . . . . . . . . . . . . . . . . . . . . . . . . . . . . . . . . . . . . .   8-2
    Investment Tax Credit . . . . . . . . . . . . . . . . . . . . . . . . . . . . . . . . . .   8-2
    Targeted Jobs Credit . . . . . . . . . . . . . . . . . . . . . . . . . . . . . . . . . . . .   8-12
    Tax Credit for Rehabilitation Expenditures . . . . . . . . . . . . . . . . .   8-14

Page

Research and Experimentation Credit . . . . . . . . . . . . . . . . . . . . 8-15
Employee Stock Ownership Credit . . . . . . . . . . . . . . . . . . . . . . . 8-18

OTHER TAX CREDITS . . . . . . . . . . . . . . . . . . . . . . . . . . . . . . . . . 8-20
Energy Tax Credits . . . . . . . . . . . . . . . . . . . . . . . . . . . . . . . . . . . 8-20
Earned Income Credit . . . . . . . . . . . . . . . . . . . . . . . . . . . . . . . . . 8-22
Tax Credit for the Elderly . . . . . . . . . . . . . . . . . . . . . . . . . . . . . 8-23
Foreign Tax Credit . . . . . . . . . . . . . . . . . . . . . . . . . . . . . . . . . . . 8-25
Credit for Child and Dependent Care Expenses . . . . . . . . . . . . 8-26
Political Campaign Contributions . . . . . . . . . . . . . . . . . . . . . . . 8-28
Priority of Credits . . . . . . . . . . . . . . . . . . . . . . . . . . . . . . . . . . . 8-29

TAX PLANNING CONSIDERATIONS . . . . . . . . . . . . . . . . . . . . . 8-30
Investment Credit . . . . . . . . . . . . . . . . . . . . . . . . . . . . . . . . . . . 8-30
Reduced Credit Election . . . . . . . . . . . . . . . . . . . . . . . . . . . . . . 8-31
Jobs Tax Credit . . . . . . . . . . . . . . . . . . . . . . . . . . . . . . . . . . . . . 8-31
Energy Tax Credit . . . . . . . . . . . . . . . . . . . . . . . . . . . . . . . . . . . 8-31
Foreign Tax Credits . . . . . . . . . . . . . . . . . . . . . . . . . . . . . . . . . 8-32
Research and Experimental Expenditures . . . . . . . . . . . . . . . . . 8-32
Credit for Child and Dependent Care Expenses . . . . . . . . . . . . 8-33

PROBLEM MATERIALS . . . . . . . . . . . . . . . . . . . . . . . . . . . . . . . . 8-34

## CHAPTER 9. PROPERTY TRANSACTIONS: DETERMINATION OF GAIN OR LOSS, BASIS CONSIDERATIONS, AND NONTAXABLE EXCHANGES

DETERMINATION OF GAIN OR LOSS . . . . . . . . . . . . . . . . . . . . . 9-1
Realized Gain or Loss . . . . . . . . . . . . . . . . . . . . . . . . . . . . . . . . 9-1
Recognized Gain or Loss . . . . . . . . . . . . . . . . . . . . . . . . . . . . . . 9-4
Nonrecognition of Gain or Loss . . . . . . . . . . . . . . . . . . . . . . . . 9-5

BASIS CONSIDERATIONS . . . . . . . . . . . . . . . . . . . . . . . . . . . . . . 9-6
Determination of Cost Basis . . . . . . . . . . . . . . . . . . . . . . . . . . . 9-6
Gift Basis . . . . . . . . . . . . . . . . . . . . . . . . . . . . . . . . . . . . . . . . . . 9-7
Property Acquired from a Decedent . . . . . . . . . . . . . . . . . . . . . 9-10
Wash Sale . . . . . . . . . . . . . . . . . . . . . . . . . . . . . . . . . . . . . . . . . 9-11
Conversion of Property From Personal Use to
    Business or Income-Producing Use . . . . . . . . . . . . . . . . . . . . 9-12

NONTAXABLE EXCHANGES . . . . . . . . . . . . . . . . . . . . . . . . . . . . 9-13

LIKE-KIND EXCHANGES . . . . . . . . . . . . . . . . . . . . . . . . . . . . . . 9-15
Like-Kind Property . . . . . . . . . . . . . . . . . . . . . . . . . . . . . . . . . . 9-15

Page

Must Be an Exchange .................................. 9-16
Boot ................................................. 9-16
Basis of Property Received ............................ 9-17

INVOLUNTARY CONVERSIONS ......................... 9-19
General Scheme....................................... 9-19
Involuntary Conversion Defined....................... 9-20
Computing the Amount Realized....................... 9-20
Replacement Property ................................ 9-21
Time Limitation on Replacement...................... 9-22
Nonrecognition of Gain .............................. 9-22
Involuntary Conversion of a Personal Residence ........... 9-24
Reporting Considerations............................. 9-24

SALE OF A RESIDENCE—§ 1034 ....................... 9-25
Replacement Period................................... 9-25
Principal Residence................................... 9-27
Nonrecognition of Gain Requirements .................... 9-27
Capital Improvements ................................ 9-28
Basis of the New Improvements....................... 9-29
Reporting Procedures ................................ 9-30

SALE OF A RESIDENCE—§ 121 ........................ 9-31
Requirements......................................... 9-31
Relationship to Other Provisions ...................... 9-32
Computation Procedure .............................. 9-32

OTHER NONRECOGNITION PROVISIONS ................ 9-33
Exchange of Stock for Property—§ 1032 .................. 9-33
Exchange of Certain Insurance Policies—§ 1035 ............ 9-33
Exchange of Stock for Stock of the Same
    Corporation—§ 1036.............................. 9-33
Certain Reacquisitions of Real Property—§ 1038............ 9-34

TAX PLANNING CONSIDERATIONS ...................... 9-34
Sale of Securities Prior to Year-End ..................... 9-34
Wash Sales .......................................... 9-34
Cost Identification and Documentation Considerations....... 9-35
Selection of Property for Making Gifts .................... 9-35
Selection of Property for Making Bequests ................ 9-35
Like-Kind Exchanges ................................. 9-36
Involuntary Conversions ............................. 9-36
Sale of a Personal Residence.......................... 9-36

PROBLEM MATERIALS................................. 9-38

# CHAPTER 10. PROPERTY TRANSACTIONS: CAPITAL GAINS AND LOSSES, SECTION 1231, AND RECAPTURE PROVISIONS

Page

GENERAL CONSIDERATIONS ............................ 10-1
    Rationale for Favorable Capital Gain Treatment ........... 10-1
    General Scheme of Taxation .............................. 10-1

WHAT IS A CAPITAL ASSET? ........................... 10-2
    Definition of a Capital Asset ............................ 10-2
    Statutory Expansions .................................... 10-3

SALE OR EXCHANGE ..................................... 10-5
    Worthless Securities ..................................... 10-5
    Special Rule—Retirement of Corporate Obligations ........ 10-6
    Options ................................................. 10-6
    Patents ................................................. 10-7
    Franchises .............................................. 10-8
    Lease Cancellation Payments ............................. 10-9

HOLDING PERIOD ....................................... 10-9
    Review of Various Holding Period Rules .................. 10-10
    Special Rules for Short Sales ........................... 10-11

TAX TREATMENT OF CAPITAL GAINS AND LOSSES
    OF NONCORPORATE TAXPAYERS .................... 10-13
    Treatment of Capital Gains ............................. 10-13
    Treatment of Capital Losses ............................ 10-15
    Reporting Procedures ................................... 10-17

TAX TREATMENT OF CAPITAL GAINS AND LOSSES
    OF CORPORATE TAXPAYERS ......................... 10-17

SECTION 1231 ASSETS .................................. 10-17
    Relationship to § 1221 .................................. 10-17
    Justification for Favorable Tax Treatment ................. 10-18
    Property Included ....................................... 10-19
    Excluded Property ...................................... 10-20
    General Procedure for § 1231 Computation ................ 10-20

SECTION 1245 RECAPTURE .............................. 10-25
    Section 1245 Property ................................... 10-25
    Section 1245 Potential .................................. 10-26
    Observations on § 1245 ................................. 10-27

SECTION 1250 RECAPTURE PRIOR TO
    ERTA OF 1981 ........................................ 10-27
    Section 1250 Potential .................................. 10-27
    Computing Recapture .................................... 10-28

Page

ACRS RULES FOR RECAPTURE—REAL PROPERTY...... 10-29

CONSIDERATIONS COMMON TO §§ 1245 AND 1250...... 10-31

Exceptions.................................................. 10-31

SPECIAL RECAPTURE PROVISIONS...................... 10-32

Recapture of Investment Credit Basis Reduction............ 10-32

Gain From Sale of Depreciable Property Between
Certain Related Parties.................................. 10-32

Residential Rental Housing................................ 10-33

Rehabilitation Expenditures for Low-Income Rental
Housing................................................. 10-34

Farm Recapture Provisions............................... 10-35

Intangible Drilling Costs................................. 10-35

REPORTING PROCEDURES............................... 10-36

TAX PLANNING CONSIDERATIONS...................... 10-36

Maximizing Benefits...................................... 10-36

Spreading Gains......................................... 10-37

Year-End Planning....................................... 10-37

Stock Sales............................................... 10-38

Planning for Capital Asset Status........................ 10-38

Effect of Capital Asset Status in Other Than
Sale Transactions....................................... 10-39

Timing of § 1231 Gain................................... 10-40

Timing of Recapture..................................... 10-40

Postponing and Shifting Recapture....................... 10-41

Avoiding Recapture...................................... 10-41

Economic Considerations................................. 10-41

ACRS Straight-Line Election to Avoid Recapture.......... 10-41

PROBLEM MATERIALS................................. 10-42

## CHAPTER 11.  SPECIAL TAX COMPUTATIONS

SPECIAL METHODS FOR COMPUTING THE TAX........ 11-2

Income Averaging........................................ 11-2

Alternative Minimum Tax................................. 11-6

Computation of the Alternative Minimum Tax.............. 11-8

ACCOUNTING PERIODS................................. 11-13

In General............................................... 11-13

Making the Election..................................... 11-14

Changes in the Accounting Period........................ 11-14

Page

Taxable Periods of Less Than One Year.................... 11-15
Requirement to Annualize Taxable Income................. 11-15

ACCOUNTING METHODS ............................... 11-16
Permissible Methods....................................... 11-16
Cash Receipts and Disbursements Method—Cash Basis ..... 11-17
Accrual Method ......................................... 11-19
Hybrid Method.......................................... 11-20
Change of Method ...................................... 11-20

SPECIAL ACCOUNTING METHODS ..................... 11-21
Long-Term Contracts .................................... 11-21
Installment Method...................................... 11-23
Installment Method—Dealers in Personal Property ......... 11-24
Electing Out of the Installment Method.................... 11-30

INVENTORIES .......................................... 11-32
Determining Inventory Cost .............................. 11-33
The LIFO Election....................................... 11-35

TAX PLANNING CONSIDERATIONS...................... 11-38
Income Averaging ....................................... 11-38
Minimum Tax............................................ 11-39
Accounting Periods ...................................... 11-40
Changes in Accounting Methods .......................... 11-40
Installment Method...................................... 11-41
LIFO.................................................... 11-41

PROBLEM MATERIALS................................. 11-42

## CHAPTER 12. TAXATION OF CORPORATIONS: ORGANIZATION AND CAPITAL STRUCTURE

The Tax Treatment of Various Business Forms ............. 12-1
What Is a Corporation? ................................. 12-3

AN INTRODUCTION TO THE INCOME TAXATION
OF CORPORATIONS..................................... 12-6
An Overview of Corporate Versus Individual
    Income Tax Treatment ............................... 12-6
Specific Provisions Compared ............................ 12-8
Capital Gains and Losses................................ 12-8
Charitable Contributions................................. 12-10
Net Operating Losses .................................... 12-13
Deductions Available Only to Corporations................ 12-14

Page

DETERMINING THE CORPORATE INCOME TAX
   LIABILITY .............................................. 12-17
   Corporate Income Tax Rates............................. 12-17
   Corporate Tax Preferences and the Minimum Tax.......... 12-18
   Payment and Filing Requirements for Corporations ........ 12-19
   Reconciliation of Taxable Income and Financial Net Income.. 12-21

ORGANIZATION OF AND TRANSFERS TO
   CONTROLLED CORPORATIONS ....................... 12-22
   In General............................................. 12-22
   Transfer of Property ................................... 12-24
   Stock and Securities ................................... 12-24
   Control of the Transferee Corporation..................... 12-25
   Assumption of Liabilities—§ 357.......................... 12-26
   Recapture Considerations ............................... 12-28
   Tax Benefit Rule ...................................... 12-30

CAPITAL STRUCTURE OF A CORPORATION ............. 12-31
   Capital Contributions................................... 12-31
   Debt in the Capital Structure............................ 12-32

TAX PLANNING CONSIDERATIONS..................... 12-33
   Corporate Versus Noncorporate Forms of Business
     Organization........................................ 12-33
   The Association Route .................................. 12-35
   Working With § 351 .................................... 12-36

PROBLEM MATERIALS................................. 12-40

**CHAPTER 13. CORPORATE DISTRIBUTIONS
NOT IN COMPLETE LIQUIDATION**

DIVIDEND DISTRIBUTIONS ............................ 13-1
   Taxable Dividends—In General ........................... 13-1
   Earnings and Profits (E & P)—§ 312 ..................... 13-2
   Property Dividends ..................................... 13-6
   Constructive Dividends ................................. 13-8
   Consequences to the Corporation of a Property Dividend..... 13-10
   Stock Dividends and Stock Rights........................ 13-13

STOCK REDEMPTIONS—EXCHANGE TREATMENT....... 13-16
   Historical Background and Overview ...................... 13-16
   Stock Attribution Rules ................................. 13-17
   Not Essentially Equivalent to a Dividend Stock
     Redemptions—§ 302(b)(1) ............................ 13-17
   Substantially Disproportionate Redemptions—§ 302(b)(2) .... 13-19

Page

Complete Termination of a Shareholder's Interest
Redemptions—§ 302(b)(3) ............................ 13-20
Redemptions to Pay Death Taxes—§ 303.................. 13-20
Effect on the Corporation Redeeming Its Stock ............. 13-21

OTHER CORPORATE DISTRIBUTIONS                          13-22

SUMMARY OF TAX CONSEQUENCES OF CORPORATE
DISTRIBUTIONS .........................'.................. 13-22

TAX PLANNING CONSIDERATIONS...................... 13-24
Corporate Distributions ............................... 13-24
Constructive Dividends ............................... 13-26
Stock Redemptions ................................... 13-27

PROBLEM MATERIALS............................... 13-28

## CHAPTER 14. CORPORATE DISTRIBUTIONS IN COMPLETE LIQUIDATION AND AN OVERVIEW OF CORPORATE REORGANIZATIONS

COMPLETE LIQUIDATIONS—AN OVERVIEW............. 14-1
Summary of the Tax Consequences Applicable to
Complete Liquidations ............................... 14-1
Liquidations, Stock Redemptions and Dividend
Distributions—A Comparison of the Effects
Upon Shareholders ................................... 14-5

EFFECT ON THE DISTRIBUTING CORPORATION ........ 14-6
Distributions In Kind Under § 336 ...................... 14-6
Sales by the Liquidating Corporation—The 12-Month Liquida-
tion of § 337 ......................................... 14-8

EFFECT ON THE SHAREHOLDER—THE GENERAL
RULE .................................................. 14-15
The General Rule—§ 331 .............................. 14-15

EFFECT ON THE SHAREHOLDER—COMPLETE
LIQUIDATION PURSUANT TO § 333 ................... 14-15
Qualifying Electing Shareholders ......................... 14-16
Making the Election and the One-Month Requirement ...... 14-16
Computation of Gain Under § 333........................ 14-17
Basis of Property Received Pursuant to § 333.............. 14-18
Effect on the Distributing Corporation .................... 14-20

LIQUIDATION OF A SUBSIDIARY....................... 14-20
Basis of Property Received by the Parent Corporation ....... 14-21

Page

EFFECT ON THE SHAREHOLDER—COLLAPSIBLE
  CORPORATIONS UNDER § 341 ........................ 14-25
  The Problem ........................................ 14-25
  The Statutory Solution .............................. 14-26

CORPORATE REORGANIZATIONS ...................... 14-26
  Summary of the Different Types of Reorganizations ........ 14-27
  General Consequences of Tax-Free Reorganizations ........ 14-28

TAX PLANNING CONSIDERATIONS ..................... 14-30
  Effect on the Corporation ............................. 14-30
  Effect on the Shareholder ............................ 14-33

PROBLEM MATERIALS ................................ 14-35


**CHAPTER 15.  CORPORATE ACCUMULATIONS**

PENALTY TAX ON UNREASONABLE
  ACCUMULATIONS ................................... 15-2
  The Element of Intent ............................... 15-3
  Imposition of the Tax and the Accumulated
    Earnings Credit ................................... 15-3
  Reasonable Needs of the Business ..................... 15-4
  Mechanics of the Penalty Tax ........................ 15-9

PERSONAL HOLDING COMPANY PENALTY TAX ........ 15-11
  Definition of a Personal Holding Company ............... 15-12
  Calculation of the PHC tax .......................... 15-16

TAX PLANNING CONSIDERATIONS ..................... 15-20
  The § 531 Tax ...................................... 15-20
  The § 541 Tax ...................................... 15-24

PROBLEM MATERIALS ................................ 15-27


**CHAPTER 16.  SUBCHAPTER S CORPORATIONS**

GENERAL CONSIDERATIONS ........................... 16-1
  Advantages of the Corporate Form ..................... 16-1
  Disadvantages of the Corporate Form .................. 16-2
  Subchapter S in Perspective .......................... 16-2

QUALIFICATION ...................................... 16-3
  Definition of a Small Business Corporation .............. 16-3
  Making the Election ................................. 16-5
  Loss of the Election ................................. 16-7

Page

OPERATIONAL RULES................................. 16-12
  Computation of Taxable Income........................ 16-12
  Order of Cash and Property Distributions................. 16-15
  Corporate Treatment of Certain Property Distributions...... 16-16
  The Shareholder's Tax Basis........................... 16-17
  Net Operating Loss.................................. 16-18
  Tax Treatment of Long-Term Capital Gains .............. 16-20
  Partnership Rules Apply to Fringe Benefits .............. 16-22
  Other Operational Rules ............................. 16-23

TAX PLANNING CONSIDERATIONS...................... 16-24
  Determining When the Election Is Advisable.............. 16-24
  Making a Proper Election ............................. 16-26
  Preserving the Election .............................. 16-26
  Planning the Operation of the Corporation ............... 16-27

PROBLEM MATERIALS................................. 16-29

## CHAPTER 17.  PARTNERSHIPS

Nature of Partnership Taxation .......................... 17-2
What Is a Partnership? ................................. 17-3
Exclusion From Partnership Taxation ..................... 17-4
Who Is a Partner?..................................... 17-4

PARTNERSHIP FORMATION............................. 17-4
  Contribution to Partnership ........................... 17-5
  Basis of Partnership Interest .......................... 17-7
  Partnership's Basis in Contributed Property............... 17-12

PARTNERSHIP OPERATION ............................. 17-13
  Measuring and Reporting Partnership Income ............. 17-14
  Allocating Partnership Income......................... 17-17
  Basis Adjustments and Limitations on Losses ............. 17-22
  Taxable Years of Partner and Partnership................. 17-24
  Transactions Between Partner and Partnership............. 17-27

PARTNERSHIP DISTRIBUTIONS ......................... 17-30
  Nonliquidating Distributions .......................... 17-31

TAX PLANNING CONSIDERATIONS...................... 17-32
  Selecting the Partnership Form ........................ 17-32
  Formation and Operation ............................. 17-34

PROBLEM MATERIALS................................. 17-36

## CHAPTER 18.  THE FEDERAL ESTATE TAX

| | Page |
|---|---|
| Nature of the Death Tax | 18-1 |
| GROSS ESTATE | 18-4 |
| Property Owned by the Decedent—§ 2033 | 18-4 |
| Dower and Curtesy Interests—§ 2034 | 18-5 |
| Adjustments for Gifts Made Within Three Years of Death—§ 2035 | 18-6 |
| Transfers With a Retained Life Estate—§ 2036 | 18-8 |
| Revocable Transfers—§ 2038 | 18-9 |
| Annuities—§ 2039 | 18-11 |
| Joint Interest—§ 2040 | 18-15 |
| Proceeds of Life Insurance—§ 2042 | 18-17 |
| TAXABLE ESTATE | 18-19 |
| Expenses, Indebtedness, and Taxes—§ 2053 | 18-19 |
| Losses—§ 2054 | 18-21 |
| Transfers to Charity—§ 2055 | 18-21 |
| Marital Deduction—§ 2056 | 18-22 |
| COMPUTING AND PAYING THE TAX | 18-24 |
| In General | 18-24 |
| The Unified Transfer Tax Credit—§ 2010 | 18-25 |
| Credit for State Death Taxes—§ 2011 | 18-26 |
| Credit for Gift Taxes—§ 2012 | 18-27 |
| Credit for Tax on Prior Transfers—§ 2013 | 18-27 |
| Credit for Foreign Death Taxes—§ 2014 | 18-28 |
| The Federal Estate Tax Return | 18-29 |
| TAX PLANNING CONSIDERATIONS | 18-30 |
| Proper Handling of Estate Tax Deductions | 18-30 |
| PROBLEM MATERIALS | 18-32 |

## CHAPTER 19.  THE FEDERAL GIFT TAX AND CERTAIN STATE TRANSFER TAXES

| | |
|---|---|
| THE FEDERAL GIFT TAX | 19-1 |
| In General | 19-1 |
| Transfers in General | 19-6 |
| Joint Ownership | 19-8 |
| Life Insurance | 19-10 |
| Certain Property Settlements—§ 2516 | 19-11 |

Page

Deductions and Exclusions .................................. 19-11
Procedural Matters .......................................... 19-18

TAX PLANNING CONSIDERATIONS ...................... 19-25
Selecting the Right Property for Lifetime Giving........... 19-25

CERTAIN STATE TRANSFER TAXES .................... 19-21
In General.................................................. 19-21
State Death Taxes .......................................... 19-21
State Gift Taxes............................................ 19-23

PROBLEM MATERIALS................................. 19-30

## CHAPTER 20.  INCOME TAXATION OF TRUSTS AND ESTATES

Introduction—An Overview of Subchapter J................ 20-1
What Is a Trust? ............................................ 20-2
Trust Beneficiaries ......................................... 20-2
What Is an Estate? ......................................... 20-3

NATURE OF TRUSTS AND ESTATE TAXATION ......... 20-3
Filing Requirements........................................ 20-4
Accounting Periods and Methods.......................... 20-4
Tax Rate and Personal Exemption......................... 20-5
The Conduit Concept ...................................... 20-5

TAXABLE INCOME OF TRUSTS AND ESTATES ......... 20-6
Gross Income .............................................. 20-6
Income in Respect of a Decedent ......................... 20-8
Ordinary Deductions....................................... 20-9
Deduction of Losses........................................ 20-11
Charitable Contributions................................... 20-12
Deduction for Distributions to Beneficiaries .............. 20-14
Tax Credits................................................ 20-15

TAXATION OF BENEFICIARIES ......................... 20-15
Distributable Net Income................................... 20-16
Distributions by Simple Trusts............................. 20-18
Distributions by Estates and Complex Trusts.............. 20-19
Separate Share Rule....................................... 20-21

CHARACTER OF INCOME............................... 20-22
Allocation of Classes of Income............................ 20-22
Special Allocations ........................................ 20-23
Deductions Related to Classes of Income ................. 20-23

Page

THE THROWBACK RULE . . . . . . . . . . . . . . . . . . . . . . . . . . . . . . . . 20-24

TAX PLANNING CONSIDERATIONS . . . . . . . . . . . . . . . . . . . . . . 20-25

    Income Tax Planning for Estates . . . . . . . . . . . . . . . . . . . . . . . . . 20-25

    Income Tax Planning With Trusts . . . . . . . . . . . . . . . . . . . . . . . 20-27

PROBLEM MATERIALS . . . . . . . . . . . . . . . . . . . . . . . . . . . . . . . . . . 20-27

## CHAPTER 21.   TAX ADMINISTRATION AND PRACTICE

TAX ADMINISTRATION . . . . . . . . . . . . . . . . . . . . . . . . . . . . . . . . . 21-1

    IRS Procedure—Individual Rulings . . . . . . . . . . . . . . . . . . . . . . 21-1

    IRS Procedure—Additional Issuances . . . . . . . . . . . . . . . . . . . . . 21-3

    The Audit Process . . . . . . . . . . . . . . . . . . . . . . . . . . . . . . . . . . . . 21-4

    The Taxpayer Appeal Process . . . . . . . . . . . . . . . . . . . . . . . . . . . 21-8

    Interest . . . . . . . . . . . . . . . . . . . . . . . . . . . . . . . . . . . . . . . . . . . . 21-10

    Penalties . . . . . . . . . . . . . . . . . . . . . . . . . . . . . . . . . . . . . . . . . . . 21-14

    Administrative Powers of the IRS . . . . . . . . . . . . . . . . . . . . . . . . 21-20

    The Statute of Limitations . . . . . . . . . . . . . . . . . . . . . . . . . . . . . 21-22

TAX PRACTICE . . . . . . . . . . . . . . . . . . . . . . . . . . . . . . . . . . . . . . . . 21-26

    The Tax Practitioner . . . . . . . . . . . . . . . . . . . . . . . . . . . . . . . . . . 21-26

    Ethical Considerations—"Statements on
    Responsibilities in Tax Practice" . . . . . . . . . . . . . . . . . . . . . . 21-29

TAX PLANNING CONSIDERATIONS . . . . . . . . . . . . . . . . . . . . . . 21-34

    Strategy in Seeking an Administrative Ruling . . . . . . . . . . . . . . 21-34

    Considerations in Handling an IRS Audit . . . . . . . . . . . . . . . . . 21-35

    Penalties . . . . . . . . . . . . . . . . . . . . . . . . . . . . . . . . . . . . . . . . . . . 21-36

PROBLEM MATERIALS . . . . . . . . . . . . . . . . . . . . . . . . . . . . . . . . . . 21-37

## CHAPTER 22.   WORKING WITH THE TAX LAW

TAX SOURCES . . . . . . . . . . . . . . . . . . . . . . . . . . . . . . . . . . . . . . . . . 21-1

    Statutory Sources of the Tax Law . . . . . . . . . . . . . . . . . . . . . . . . 22-1

    Administrative Sources of the Tax Law . . . . . . . . . . . . . . . . . . . . 22-5

    Judicial Sources of the Tax Law . . . . . . . . . . . . . . . . . . . . . . . . . . 22-7

WORKING WITH THE TAX LAW—TAX RESEARCH . . . . . . 22-15

    Identifying the Problem . . . . . . . . . . . . . . . . . . . . . . . . . . . . . . . . 22-15

    Locating the Appropriate Tax Law Sources . . . . . . . . . . . . . . . . 22-18

    Assessing the Validity of the Tax Law Source . . . . . . . . . . . . . 22-19

    Arriving at the Solution or at Alternative Solutions . . . . . . . . . 22-21

Page

WORKING WITH THE TAX LAW—TAX PLANNING ...... 22-22

Nontax Considerations.................................... 22-22

Tax Evasion and Tax Avoidance ......................... 22-23

Follow-up Procedures .................................... 22-23

Tax Planning—A Practical Application ................... 22-24

PROBLEM MATERIALS................................... 22-24

## APPENDIXES

App.

A.    Tax Rate Schedules and Tax Tables .................. A-1

B.    Tax Forms......................................... B-1

C.    Glossary of Tax Terms ............................. C-1

D–1.  Table of Code Sections Cited....................... D-1

D–2.  Table of Proposed Regulations and Regulations
        Cited.......................................... D-11

D–3.  Table of Revenue Procedures and Revenue
        Rulings Cited ................................. D-13

E.    Comprehensive Tax Return Problems.................. E-1

F.    Table of Cases Cited .............................. F-1

**Subject Index** ....................................... I-1

# 1984 Annual Edition
## West's Federal Taxation:

# Comprehensive Volume

# Chapter 1

# An Introduction to Taxation

Before dealing with specific tax provisions, it is desirable to review the historical development of the Federal tax law and to understand the underlying rationale for our tax system. To this end, an initial review is made of the historical and economic aspects of the tax law. This chapter also includes a discussion of the major types of taxes.

Also, at the outset one should stress that the Federal tax law does not have as its sole objective the raising of revenue. Although the fiscal needs of the government are of obvious importance, other considerations do exist which explain certain portions of the law. Economic, social, equity, and political factors also play a significant role. Added to these factors is the marked impact the Internal Revenue Service and the courts have had and will continue to have on the evolution of Federal tax law. These matters will be treated in this chapter, and wherever appropriate, the discussion will be tied to subjects covered later in the text.

## HISTORY OF U. S. TAXATION

### EARLY PERIODS

An income tax was first enacted in 1634 by the English colonists in the Massachusetts Bay Colony. In 1861, the first U. S. Federal income tax was enacted to provide revenues for the Civil War. Although these

Federal income taxes were repealed after the end of the war, they proved to be a major source of revenue. Income taxes during the Civil War period provided $376 million of revenue for the Federal government.

In 1894, another Federal income tax law was enacted despite considerable political opposition and the question of the constitutionality of an income tax during this period. The U. S. Constitution provided that ". . . No Capitation, or other direct, Tax shall be laid, unless in Proportion to the Census or Enumeration herein before directed to be taken." The question before the courts was whether an income tax was both a direct tax and unapportioned, since the Constitution required that a direct tax be apportioned among the states in proportion to their populations. In *Pollock v. Farmers' Loan and Trust Co.*, the Supreme Court held that the 1894 income tax law was unconstitutional, since it was a direct tax and unapportioned.[1] In addition, the Supreme Court held that the law was invalid, since it attempted to tax income from municipal obligations. At that time it was felt that the Federal government did not have the right to levy a tax that is imposed on the borrowing power of political subdivisions.

Before the Sixteenth Amendment, which permitted income taxation, was ratified, Congress enacted a corporate income tax in 1909. This corporate tax was upheld by the courts since it was a special form of excise tax and not a direct tax.[2] The corporate tax provision was of little significance because the Revenue Act of 1913 provided for both individual and corporate taxes.

## REVENUE ACTS

Due to an interpretation of the U. S. Constitution by the Supreme Court, it was necessary to amend the Constitution to permit the enactment of a Federal income tax. Following ratification of the Sixteenth Amendment, Congress enacted the Revenue Act of 1913. Under this Act, a flat one percent tax was levied upon the income of corporations. Individuals paid a normal tax rate of one percent on taxable income after deducting a personal exemption of $3,000 for a single individual and $4,000 for a married taxpayer. Surtax rates of one to six percent were applied to high income taxpayers.

Various revenue acts were passed during the period from 1913 to 1939. In 1939, all of these revenue laws were codified into the Internal Revenue Code of 1939. In 1954, a similar codification of the revenue law took place. The current law consists of the Internal Revenue Code of 1954 as amended by numerous revenue laws passed since 1954.

---

**1.** *Pollock v. Farmers' Loan & Trust Co.*, 3 AFTR 2602, 15 S.Ct. 912 (USSC, 1895). See Chapter 22 for an explanation as to how judicial decisions are cited.
**2.** *Flint v. Stone Tracy Co.*, 3 AFTR 2834, 31 S.Ct. 342 (USSC, 1911).

## HISTORICAL TRENDS

The income tax has proved to be a major source of revenue for the Federal government. Figure I contains a breakdown of the major revenue sources. If social insurance taxes and contributions are excluded from the total budget receipts, income tax collections from individuals and corporations amount to approximately 48 percent of the total receipts.

**Figure I**
FEDERAL BUDGET RECEIPTS—1982[3]

| | |
|---|---:|
| Individual income taxes | 41% |
| Corporation income taxes | 7 |
| Social insurance taxes and contributions | 27 |
| Excise taxes | 5 |
| Borrowing | 15 |
| Other | 5 |
| | 100% |

The need for revenues to finance the war effort during WW II converted the income tax into a "mass tax." For example, in 1939, less than six percent of the U. S. population was subject to the Federal income tax. In 1945, over 74 percent of the population was subject to the Federal income tax.[4]

Certain changes in the income tax law are of particular significance in understanding the Federal income tax law. In 1943, Congress passed the Current Tax Payment Act, which provided for the first pay-as-you-go tax system.[5] Many of these changes to the income tax law were necessary to provide a means for raising substantial revenues in the form of a mass tax upon individuals and corporations.

# CRITERIA USED IN THE SELECTION OF A TAX BASE

Adam Smith first identified certain criteria or "canons of taxation" which are still being considered when questions are raised relative to the desirability of a particular type of tax or tax structure. These canons of taxation follow:[6]

---

**3.** *The United States Budget in Brief,* Office of Management and Budget (Washington, D.C., 1982).

**4.** Goode, Richard, *The Individual Income Tax* (Washington, D.C.: Brookings Institution, 1964), pp. 2–4.

**5.** A pay-as-you-go feature of an income tax system compels employers to withhold for taxes a specified portion of an employee's wages. For persons with income from other than wages, periodic (e. g., quarterly) payments may have to be made to the taxing authority (e. g., the Internal Revenue Service) for estimated taxes that will be due for the year.

**6.** *The Wealth of Nations,* Book V, Chapter II, Part II (New York: Dutton, 1910).

—*Equality*. Each taxpayer enjoys fair or equitable treatment by paying taxes in proportion to his or her income level. Ability to pay a tax is the measure of how equitably a tax is distributed among taxpayers.

—*Convenience*. Administrative simplicity has long been valued as an important consideration in formulating tax policy. If a tax is easily assessed and collected and the costs of administration are low, it should be favored. The withholding (pay-as-you-go) system has been advocated because of its convenience for taxpayers. It should be noted, however that our Federal income tax laws have become increasingly complex despite outcries from tax specialists, politicians, business executives, et al., regarding the need for administrative simplicity.

—*Certainty*. A "good" tax structure exists if the taxpayer can readily predict when, where, and how a tax will be levied. A business may need to know the likely tax consequences of a particular type of business transaction. Some degree of certainty is built into our present tax system. For example, the Treasury Department generally writes detailed Regulations following the enactment of a tax change. In addition, the IRS may issue advance rulings on the tax consequences of a proposed transaction.

—*Economy*. A "good" tax system is one which requires only nominal collection costs by the government and involves minimal compliance costs on the part of the taxpayer. Each year the Annual Report of the Commissioner of the IRS indicates that the government's cost to collect Federal taxes amounts to less than one-half of one percent of the revenue which is collected. On the other hand, due to the complexity of our existing tax structure, taxpayer compliance costs are probably substantial.

# THE TAX STRUCTURE

## TAX RATES

Tax rates are applied to the tax base to determine a taxpayer's liability. The tax rates may be proportional or progressive.

A tax is proportional if the rate of tax remains constant for any given income level.

**Example 1.**   T has $10,000 of taxable income and pays a tax of $2,000 or 20%. Y's taxable income is $20,000 and the tax on this amount is $4,000 or 20%. If this constant rate is applied throughout the rate structure, the tax is proportional.

The Federal income tax, Federal gift and estate taxes, and most state income tax rate structures are progressive. In the case of the

Federal income tax, a higher percentage rate of tax is applied as taxable income increases.

> **Example 2.** If T, a married individual filing jointly, has taxable income of $10,000, the tax is $934 for an effective tax rate of 9.34%. If, however, T's taxable income was $20,000, the tax would be $2,899 for an effective tax rate of 14.495%. The tax is progressive since higher rates are applied to greater amounts of taxable income.

## ADJUSTMENTS TO TAX BASE AND INCIDENCE OF TAXATION

The degree to which the total tax burden is shared by various segments of society is difficult to assess. Assumptions must be made concerning who absorbs the burden for payment of the tax. For example, the corporate tax rate structure is a stair-step progression (e. g., for 1983 15 percent of the first $25,000 of taxable income, 18 percent of the next $25,000, 30 percent of taxable income in excess of $50,000 up to $75,000, 40 percent in excess of $75,000 up to $100,000, and 46 percent of amounts over $100,000). Since dividend payments to shareholders are not deductible and such amounts are generally taxable income to shareholders, a form of double taxation on the same income is being levied. Concern over double taxation is valid to the extent that corporations are *not* able to shift the corporate tax to the consumer through higher commodity prices. If it can be shifted, the corporate tax becomes merely a consumption tax which is borne by the ultimate purchasers of goods.

The U. S. Federal income tax rate structure for individuals appears to be highly progressive (e. g., rates range from 0 to 50 percent). However, if adjustments to the tax base are taken into account, a different pattern may emerge. Wealthy individuals with high incomes are able to take advantage of certain tax benefits (e. g., tax-sheltered investments, charitable contributions of money and other property, and recognition of long-term capital gains). Studies have indicated that the effective tax rates for Federal and state taxes are generally proportional for almost 90 percent of the population.[7]

# MAJOR TYPES OF TAXES

## PROPERTY TAXES

Normally referred to as "ad valorem" taxes because they are based on value, property taxes are a tax on wealth, or capital. In this regard, they have much in common with death taxes and gift taxes discussed later in this chapter. Although property taxes do not tax income, the

---

7. Joseph Pechman and Benjamin Okner, *Who Bears the Tax Burden?* (Washington, D.C., The Brookings Institution, 1974).

income actually derived (or the potential for any such income) may be relevant insofar as it affects the value of the property being taxed.

Property taxes fall into two categories: those imposed on realty and those imposed on personalty. Both have added importance, since they usually generate a deduction for Federal income tax purposes (see Chapter 7).

*Ad Valorem Taxes on Realty.* Property taxes on realty are exclusively within the province of the states and their local political subdivisions (e. g., cities, counties, school districts). They represent a major source of revenue for local governments, but their importance at the state level has waned over the past few years.[8] The trend has been for the states to look to other types of taxes (e. g., sales, income, severance) to meet their fiscal needs. Most of the revenue derived from property taxes on realty is used to provide essential governmental services (e. g., police and fire protection, public education, waste disposal, utility sources).

Particularly in those jurisdictions that do not impose ad valorem taxes on personalty, what is included in the definition of realty could have an important bearing on which assets are or are not subject to tax. Primarily a question of state property law, realty generally includes real estate and any capital improvements thereto that comprise "fixtures." Simply stated, a fixture is something so permanently attached to the real estate that its removal will cause irreparable damage.[9] A built-in bookcase might well be a fixture, whereas a typical movable bookcase would not. Certainly items like electrical wiring and plumbing when installed in a building have ceased to be personalty and have become realty.

Some of the characteristics of ad valorem taxes on realty are highlighted below:

—Exemption is provided for property owned by the Federal government. Similar immunity usually is extended to property owned by state and local governments and by certain charitable organizations.

—Some states provide for lower valuations on property dedicated to agricultural use or other special uses (e. g., wildlife sanctuaries).

—Some states provide for partial exemption from taxation of the homestead portion of the property.[10]

---

**8.** The furor in California over Proposition 13 (and similar proposals in other states) reflects that the ad valorem tax on realty is not without controversy. It may be that continued taxpayer opposition and resistance will cause such taxes to decline in significance in the years to come.

**9.** *Black's Law Dictionary,* fifth edition (St. Paul, Minn.: West Publishing Co., 1979), p. 574.

**10.** Modern homestead laws normally operate to protect some or all of a personal residence (including a farm or ranch) from the actions of creditors pursuing claims against the owner.

—Some jurisdictions extend immunity from tax for a specified period of time (i. e., "tax holiday") for new or relocated businesses.

—Common in recent years, some states have enacted legislation preventing upward reassessment in value for a specified period of time (unless the property is disposed of during the "freeze" period).

Unlike the ad valorem tax on personalty (see below), the tax on realty is difficult to avoid. Since real estate is impossible to hide, a high degree of taxpayer compliance is not surprising. The only avoidance possibility that generally is available lies with the assessed value of the property. For this reason, both the assessed value of the property and, particularly, a reassessed value upward are not without their share of controversy and litigation. For these purposes, at least, everyone is convinced that his or her property is worth less than that belonging to neighbors or near-neighbors.

The four methods currently in use for assessing the value of real estate are summarized below:

1. Actual purchase or construction price.

2. Contemporaneous sales prices or construction costs of comparable properties.

3. Cost of reproducing a building, less allowance for depreciation and obsolescence from the time of actual construction.

4. Capitalization of income from rental property.

Because all of these methods suffer faults and lead to inequities, a combination of one or more is not uncommon.[11] Nevertheless, the history of the ad valorem tax on realty has been marked by inconsistent results in its application due to a lack of competent tax administration and definitive guidelines as to assessment procedures. In recent years, however, significant inroads toward improvement have taken place.[12]

*Ad Valorem Tax on Personalty.* Personalty can be defined as all assets that are not realty. At the outset, it may be well to make the distinction between the classification of an asset (i. e., realty or personalty) and the use to which it is placed. Both realty and personalty

---

11. Due to rising real estate values and construction costs, the use of actual purchase or construction price (method 1), for example, places the purchaser of a new home at a definite disadvantage with the owner who acquired similar property years ago. As another illustration, suppose the capitalization of income (method 4) deals with property that is subject to rent controls?

12. Some jurisdictions have computerized their valuation reassessment procedures so as to have immediate effect on all property located within any such jurisdiction. This has to be a definite move toward equity in tax treatment when one compares the probable result of the previous approach (e. g., because of personnel shortages in tax assessors, one-tenth of the property within the jurisdiction is revalued every ten years).

can be either business use or personal use property. Examples of this distinction include a residence (realty that is personal use), an office building (realty that is business use), surgical instruments (personalty that is business use), and regular wearing apparel (personalty that is personal use).[13]

Personalty can be also classified as tangible property or intangible property. For ad valorem tax purposes, intangible personalty includes stocks, bonds, and various other securities (e. g., bank shares).

Generalizations concerning the ad valorem tax on personalty are listed below:

—Particularly with personalty devoted to personal use (e. g., jewelry, household furnishings) taxpayer compliance ranges from poor to zero. In some jursidictions, enforcement of the tax on these items is not even attempted. In the case of automobiles devoted to personal use, many jurisdictions have converted from value as the tax base to arbitrary license fees based on the weight of the vehicle. Recently, some jurisdictions are taking into consideration the age factor (e. g., automobiles six years or older are not subject to the ad valorem tax as they are presumed to have little, if any, value).

—In the case of personalty devoted to business use (e. g., inventories, trucks, machinery, equipment) taxpayer compliance and enforcement procedures are measurably better.

—Assessed values of personalty may run lower than in the case of realty.

—Which jurisdiction possesses the authority to tax movable personalty (e. g., railroad rolling stock) always has been and continues to be a troublesome issue.

—The ad valorem tax on intangibles, although it still exists in some jurisdictions, largely has fallen into disfavor. Undoubtedly the lack of effective enforcement capability on the part of the taxing authorities has contributed to this decline in use. As in the case of jewelry, ownership of stocks and bonds is information that is difficult to obtain without a substantial investment of time and money. In many cases, this use of time and money is not warranted by the revenue generated from the tax on intangibles.

---

**13.** The distinction, important for ad valorem and for Federal income tax purposes, becomes confused when personalty often is referred to as "personal" property to distinguish it from "real" property. Obviously, such designation does not give a complete picture of what is involved. The description "personal" residence, however, is clearer since one can identify a residence as being realty. What is meant, in this case, is realty that is personal use property.

## TRANSACTION TAXES

Characteristically imposed at the manufacturer's, wholesaler's, or retailer's level, transaction taxes cover a wide range of transfers. Like many other types of taxes (e. g., income taxes, death taxes, and gift taxes), transaction taxes usually are not peculiarly within the exclusive province of any level of taxing authority (i. e., Federal, state, local government). As the description implies, these levies place a tax on the transfers of property and normally are determined by a percentage rate multiplied by the value involved.

*Federal Excise Taxes.* Long one of the mainstays of the Federal tax system, Federal excise taxes had declined in relative importance until recently. It may be that the trend is changing, however, with the enactment of the Crude Oil Windfall Profit Tax Act of 1980. (This legislation imposes a temporary excise tax on the production of domestic crude oil after February 29, 1980. Furthermore, in late 1982 Congress substantially increased the Federal excise taxes on such items as tobacco products, fuel and gasoline sales, telephone usage, and air travel passenger tickets.) Other Federal excise taxes include:[14]

—Manufacturers' excise taxes on trucks, trailers, tires, firearms, sporting equipment, and coal, and the gas guzzler tax on automobiles.[15]

—Alcohol taxes.

—Miscellaneous taxes (e.g., the tax on wagering).

The list of transactions covered, although seemingly impressive, has diminished over the years. At one time, for example, there was a Federal excise tax on admission to amusement facilities (e. g., theaters) and on the sale of such "luxury" items as leather goods, furs, jewelry, and cosmetics.

When reviewing the list of both Federal and state excise taxes, one should recognize the possibility that the tax laws involved may be trying to influence social behavior. Quite obviously, for example, the gas guzzler tax is intended as an incentive for the automobile companies to build cars that are fuel efficient in performance. Since alcohol and tobacco are considered by many to be harmful to a person's health, why not increase their cost with the imposition of excise taxes and thereby discourage their use? Unfortunately, there exists little evidence to support a high level of correlation between the imposition of an excise tax and consumer behavior. This is particularly true

---

**14.** Most excise taxes are contained in § § 4041–4998 of the Internal Revenue Code of 1954. Alcohol and tobacco taxes, however, are in § § 5001–5872. The Crude Oil Windfall Profit Tax Act of 1980 was incorporated in new § § 4986–4998. See Chapter 22 for an explanation of how provisions of the Internal Revenue Code of 1954 are cited.
**15.** The gas guzzler tax is imposed on the manufacturers of automobiles and progresses in amount as the mileage ratings per gallon of gas decrease. See § 4064.

where the rate of the excise tax is modest and the demand for the commodity being taxed is relatively inelastic.

*State Excise Taxes.* Many state and local excise taxes parallel the Federal version. Thus, all states tax the sale of gasoline, liquor, and tobacco products; however, the rates vary significantly. In the case of gasoline products, for example, compare the 12 cents per gallon imposed by the state of Washington with the 5 cents per gallon levied by the state of Texas. For tobacco sales, contrast the one mill per cigarette in effect in North Carolina with the 7½ cents per 10 cigarettes applicable in New York. In the latter situation, is it surprising that the smuggling of cigarettes from North Carolina for resale in New York is so widespread? Here might be a situation where an excise tax probably encourages criminal conduct more than it discourages consumer use.

Other excise taxes found at some state and local levels include those on admission to amusement facilities, hotel occupancy and the rental of various other facilities, the sale of playing cards and oleomargarine products, and the sale of prepared foods. Most states impose a transaction tax on the transfer of property that requires the recording of documents (e. g., real estate sales).[16] Some extend the tax to the transfer of stocks and other securities.

*General Sales Taxes.* The distinction between an excise tax and a general sales tax is easy to make.[17] One is restricted to a particular transaction (e. g., the 9 cents per gallon Federal excise tax on the sale of gasoline), while the other covers a multitude of transactions (e. g., a 5 percent tax on *all* retail sales). In actual practice, however, the distinction is not always that clear. Some state statutes might exempt certain transactions from the application of the general sales taxes (e. g., sales of food to be consumed off the premises, sales of certain medicines and drugs). Also, it is not uncommon to find that rates vary depending on the commodity involved. In many states, for example, preferential rates are allowed for the sale of agricultural equipment or different rates (either higher or lower than the general rate) apply to the sale of automobiles. With many of these special exceptions and classifications of rates, a general sales tax can take on the appearance of a collection of individual excise taxes.

Every state that imposes a general sales tax levied on the consumer also has a use tax.[18] To prevent the avoidance of a sales tax, a use tax is a necessary complement.

---

**16.** This type of tax has much in common with the stamp tax levied by Great Britain on the American colonies during the pre-Revolutionary period in U. S. history.

**17.** As noted in Chapter 7, the distinction is very important for Federal income tax purposes. General sales taxes on the purchase of property intended for personal use are normally deductible while excise taxes usually are not.

**18.** The states without either tax are Alaska, Delaware, Montana, New Hampshire, and Oregon.

> **Example 3.** T resides in a jurisdiction that imposes a 5% general sales tax but lives near a state that has no tax at all. T purchases for $10,000 an automobile from a dealer located in the neighboring state. Has T saved $500 in sales taxes? The state use tax is designed to pick up the difference between the tax paid in another jurisdiction and what would have been paid in the state where T resides.

The use tax may be difficult to enforce for many purchases and is, therefore, often avoided. In the case of an automobile (see Example 3), however, it probably would be imposed when T registers the car in his or her home state.

Local general sales taxes, over and above those levied by the state, are common.[19] It is not unusual to find taxpayers living in the same state who pay different general sales taxes due to the situs of their residence.

> **Example 4.** R and S, two individuals, both live in a state that has a general sales tax of 3%. S, however, resides in a city that imposes an additional general sales tax of 2%. In spite of the fact that R and S live in the same state, one is subject to a rate of 3% while the other pays a tax of 5%.

*Severance Taxes.* An important source of revenue for many states is derived from severance taxes. These transaction taxes are based on the notion that the state has an interest in its natural resources (e. g., oil, gas, iron ore, coal), and therefore, their extraction is an occasion for the imposition of a tax.

## DEATH TAXES

A death tax is a tax on the right to transfer property or to receive property upon the death of the owner. Consequently, a death tax falls into the category of an excise tax. If the death tax is imposed on the right to pass property at death, it is classified as an estate tax. If it taxes the right to receive property from a decedent, it is termed an inheritance tax. Typical of other types of excise taxes, the value of the property transferred measures the base for determining the amount of the death tax.

Of the two, inheritance tax and estate tax, the Federal government imposes only an estate tax. State governments, however, levy inheritance taxes, estate taxes, or both. Death taxes are discussed in Chapter 18.

---

19. The existence of a local (e. g., city, county) sales tax becomes important when working with the Optional State Sales Tax Tables (see Appendix A) issued by the IRS. These tables, discussed in Chapter 7, provide a way to determine one of the deductions a taxpayer may be entitled to for Federal income tax purposes.

## GIFT TAXES

Like a death tax, a gift tax is an excise tax levied on the right to transfer property. In this case, however, the tax is directed to transfers made during the owner's life and not at death. Also, a gift tax only applies to transfers that are not supported by full and adequate consideration.

> **Example 5.** D sells to his daughter property worth $20,000 for $1,000. Although property worth $20,000 has been transferred, only $19,000 represents a gift, since this is the portion not supported by full and adequate consideration.

*The Federal Gift Tax.* First enacted in 1932, the purpose of the Federal gift tax was to complement the estate tax. Without any tax applicable to lifetime transfers by gift, it would be possible, of course, to avoid the estate tax and escape taxation entirely.

Only taxable gifts are subject to the gift tax. For this purpose, a taxable gift is measured by the fair market value of the property on the date of transfer less the annual exclusion of $10,000 per donee and, in some cases, less the marital deduction, which allows tax-free transfers between spouses.[20] Each donor is allowed an annual exclusion of $10,000 per year for each donee.[21]

*State Gift Taxes.* The states imposing a state gift tax are Colorado, Delaware, Louisiana, New York, North Carolina, Oregon, Rhode Island, South Carolina, Tennessee, and Wisconsin.

Most of these laws provide for lifetime exemptions and annual exclusions. Unlike the Federal version, the amount of tax depends on the relationship between the donor and the donee. Like state inheritance taxes, larger exemptions and lower rates apply when the donor and donee are closely related to each other.

Gift taxes are discussed in Chapter 19.

## INCOME TAXES

Income taxes are levied by the Federal government, most states, and some local governments. Needless to say, the trend in recent years has been to place greater reliance on this method of taxation. The trend is not consistent with what is happening in other countries, and in this sense, our system of taxation is somewhat different.[22]

---

**20.** The marital deduction is available for gifts between husband and wife.

**21.** § 2503(b). The purpose of the annual exclusion is to avoid the need of having to report and pay a tax on "modest" gifts. The absence of the exclusion could create for the Internal Revenue Service a real problem of taxpayer noncompliance.

**22.** At least in the Common Market countries of Western Europe, the value added tax (i. e., VAT) has gained in acceptance as a major source of revenue. Although variously classified, VAT seems more like a national sales tax, since it taxes the increment in value as goods move through production and manufacturing stages to the market place. VAT has its proponents in the U. S. as a partial solution to high Federal income tax rates and increases in employment taxes. Its incorporation as part of our tax system in the near future, however, appears doubtful.

Income taxes generally are imposed on individuals, corporations, and certain fiduciaries (estates and trusts). Most jurisdictions attempt to assure their collection by requiring certain pay-as-you-go procedures (e. g., withholding requirements as to employees and estimated tax prepayments for other taxpayers).

On occasion, Congress has seen fit to impose additional taxes on income. Such impositions were justified either by economic considerations[23] or by special circumstances resulting from wartime conditions.[24]

*Federal Income Taxes.* Chapters 2 through 11 deal with the application of the Federal income tax to individuals. The procedure for determining the Federal income tax applicable to individuals is summarized in Figure II.

**Figure II**

| | |
|---|---|
| Income (broadly conceived) | $  xx,xxx |
| Less:  Exclusions (income that is not subject to tax) | x,xxx |
| Gross income (income that is subject to tax) | $  xx,xxx |
| Less:  Business deductions (usually referred to as deductions *for* adjusted gross income) | x,xxx |
| Adjusted gross income | $  xx,xxx |
| Less:  Certain personal deductions (usually referred to as *itemized deductions* or as deductions *from* adjusted gross income) in excess of the zero bracket amount | x,xxx |
| Personal and dependency exemptions | x,xxx |
| Taxable income | $  x,xxx |
| Tax on taxable income (see tax rate schedules or table in Appendix A) | $      xxx |
| Less:  Tax credits (including Federal income tax withheld and other prepayments of Federal income taxes) | xxx |
| Tax due (or refund) | $      xx |

As explained in Chapter 2, the zero bracket amount represents a deduction allowed to every taxpayer and varies from $3,400 allowed to married persons filing together (i. e., joint return) to $1,700 for married persons filing apart (i. e., separate returns), with $2,300 permitted for single (unmarried) taxpayers. (Note: The zero bracket

---

**23.**  During the period from April 1, 1968, to July 1, 1970, taxpayers were subject to a surcharge of 10% on the amount of their regular income tax liability. This led to the strange result that taxpayers, so to speak, had to pay an income tax on their income tax. The justification for the special tax was to place restraints on what was regarded to be an overactive economy, to curtail inflation, and to reduce the Federal deficit.
**24.**  During World War II and the Korean conflict, an excess-profits tax was imposed in addition to the regular Federal income tax. The tax was aimed at the profiteering that occurs when the economy is geared to the production of war materials.

amount has not been separately deducted in Figure II, since the Tax Table and the Tax Rate Schedules are structured such that the respective amounts are taken into account.) The personal exemptions are $1,000 apiece and are allowed for the taxpayer and spouse, for age (65 or over), and for blindness. An exemption of $1,000 is allowed for each dependent of the taxpayer. Both personal and dependency exemptions are explained in Chapter 2.

The rules for the application of the Federal corporate income tax do not require the computation of adjusted gross income and do not provide for the zero bracket amount and personal and dependency exemptions. All allowable deductions of a corporation fall into the business-expense category. In effect, therefore, the taxable income of a corporation is the difference between gross income (net of exclusions) and deductions.

Once the taxable income of a corporation is determined, however, any income tax liability is computed under a set of rates separate from those applicable to individuals. But unlike the tax rates that apply to individuals, the corporate tax rates are progressive only to a mild extent. The rates applicable to 1983 are as follows:[25]

| Rate Applicable | Amount of Taxable Income |
|---|---|
| 15% | first $25,000 |
| 18 | above $25,000 through $50,000 |
| 30 | above $50,000 through $75,000 |
| 40 | above $75,000 through $100,000 |
| 46 | over $100,000 |

Corporate taxation is discussed in detail in Chapters 12 through 16.

*State Income Taxes.*   All but the following states impose an income tax on individuals: Alaska, Florida, Nevada, South Dakota, Texas, Washington, and Wyoming. New Hampshire and Tennessee have an income tax, but its application is limited to dividend and interest income.

Some of the characteristics of state income taxes are summarized below:

—Except for New Hampshire and Tennessee, all states require some form of withholding procedures. In North Dakota, such procedures apply only to nonresident taxpayers.

—Slightly less than one-half allow a deduction for Federal income taxes.

---

**25.**  The 15% rate (applicable to the first $25,000 of taxable income) was reduced from 16% in 1982; likewise, the 18% rate (applicable to taxable income above $25,000 through $50,000) was reduced from 19% in 1982.

—Most use as the tax base the income determination made for Federal income tax purposes.

—The due date for filing is generally the same as that for the Federal income tax (i. e., the fifteenth day of the fourth month following the close of the tax year).

—Most states have their own set of rates and exemptions, but some determine the tax as a flat percentage of the Federal income tax liability.

Nearly all states have an income tax applicable to corporations.[26] For corporations that do business or derive income from more than one state, this could lead to the multiple taxation of the same income or, in some cases, to no taxation at all. To the extent that income and expenses cannot be specifically allocated to sources within any one state, it may be necessary to apportion these items among the states involved.[27] Various formulas, or a combination thereof, are available to carry out any required apportionment.[28]

Cities imposing an income tax include, but are not limited to, Baltimore, Cincinnati, Cleveland, Detroit, Kansas City (Mo.), New York, Philadelphia, and St. Louis.

## EMPLOYMENT TAXES

Classification as an employee usually leads to the imposition of employment taxes on the employer and to the requirement that the employer withhold specified amounts for income taxes. The material that follows concentrates on the two major employment taxes: FICA (Federal Insurance Contributions Act—commonly referred to as the Social Security tax) and FUTA (Federal Unemployment Tax Act). Both taxes can be justified by social and public welfare considerations: FICA offers some measure of retirement security while FUTA provides a modest source of income in the event of loss of employment.

Employment taxes come into play only if two conditions are satisfied. First, is the individual involved an "employee" (as opposed to "self-employed")? The difference between an employee and a self-employed person is discussed in Chapter 6.[29] Second, if the individual involved is an employee, is he or she covered under FICA or FUTA?

---

**26.** It is difficult to determine those that do not because a state franchise tax sometimes is based, in part, on the income earned by the corporation. See the subsequent discussion of state franchise taxes.

**27.** Passive income (e. g., rents, dividends, gains from the sales of investments, interest) which is not considered business income usually is assigned for tax purposes to the state where such income-producing property is located.

**28.** Business income may be allocated, for income taxation, among the various states based on a percentage of property owned in the state, on the amount of payroll there, on sales within the state, or on some other reasonable basis.

**29.** See also Circular E, Employer's Tax Guide, issued by the IRS as Publication 15.

*FICA Taxes.* The tax rates and wage base under FICA are not constant, and as reflected in Figure III, the increases over the years are quite apparent.[30]

**Figure III**

FICA RATES AND BASE

| Year | Percent | Base Amount | Maximum Tax |
|------|---------|-------------|-------------|
| 1978 | 6.05% | $ 17,700 | $ 1,070.85 |
| 1979 | 6.13% | 22,900 | 1,403.77 |
| 1980 | 6.13% | 25,900 | 1,587.67 |
| 1981 | 6.65% | 29,700 | 1,975.05 |
| 1982 | 6.70% | 32,400 | 2,170.80 |
| 1983 | 6.70% | 35,700 | 2,391.90 |
| 1984 | 7.00% | —* | —** |
| 1985 | 7.05% | — | — |
| 1986–87 | 7.15% | — | — |
| 1988–89 | 7.51% | — | — |
| 1990 on | 7.65% | — | — |

\* Not yet determined by Congress
\*\* Cannot be computed until the wage base is set by Congress

In at least two situations it is possible for an employee to have paid excess FICA taxes.

**Example 6.** During 1983, T changed employers in the middle of the year and from each job he earned $30,000 (all of which was subject to FICA). As a result, each employer withheld $2,010 (6.7% × $30,000) for a total of $4,020. Since T has overpaid his share of the FICA taxes by $1,628.10 [$4,020 (amount paid) − $2,391.90 (maximum tax from Figure III)] he should claim this amount as a tax credit when filing an income tax return for 1983.[31]

**Example 7.** During 1983, E earned $30,000 from her regular job and $10,000 from a part-time job (all of which was subject to FICA). As a result, one employer withheld $2,010 (6.7% × $30,000), while the other employer withheld $670 (6.7% × $10,000) for a total of $2,680. Since E has overpaid her share of the FICA taxes by $288.10 ($2,680 − $2,391.90), she should claim this amount as a tax credit when filing an income tax return for 1983.

In both Examples 6 and 7 it was not possible for the employee to prevent the overwithholding from taking place. In both cases, however, the employee was able to obtain a credit for the excess withheld.

---

**30.** The provisions of the Internal Revenue Code dealing with FICA are contained in §§ 3101–3126.

**31.** The effect of a tax credit would be to reduce any income tax T might owe or, possibly, to generate a tax refund.

The mere fact that a husband and wife both are employed does not, by itself, result in over-withholding of FICA taxes.[32]

**Example 8.** During 1983, H and W (husband and wife) both are employed and each earns wages subject to FICA of $20,000. Accordingly, each has FICA withheld of $1,340 [6.7% × $20,000 (wages earned)] for a total of $2,680. Since neither spouse paid FICA in excess of $2,391.90 (see Figure III), there is no over-withholding.

The frequency with which an employer must make payments to the IRS depends on the monthly total of three items: income tax withheld from the employees, FICA taxes withheld from the employees, and the employer's matching share of the FICA taxes. But regardless of whether or not monthly deposits are required, each employer must file a Form 941, Employer's Quarterly Federal Tax Return, on a quarterly basis.[33] It is important that Form 941 contain the employer's identification number.[34]

The failure to make deposits and to file required employment tax returns on time could result in the imposition by the IRS of various penalties. Additionally, employers are liable for any taxes that should have been, but were not, withheld from their employees.[35]

*FUTA Taxes.* The purpose of FUTA is to provide funds that the states can use to pay unemployment benefits. This leads to the somewhat unusual situation of one tax being handled by both Federal and state governments. The end product of such joint administration is to compel the employer to observe a double set of rules. Thus, state and Federal returns must be filed and payments made to both governmental units.

FUTA applies at a rate of 3.5 percent (beginning January 1, 1983, until December 31, 1984) on the first $7,000 of covered wages paid during the year to each employee.[36] The Federal government allows a credit for FUTA paid (or allowed under a merit rating system) to the state. The credit cannot exceed 2.7 percent of the covered wages. Thus, the amount required to be paid to the IRS could be as low as 0.8 percent (i. e., 3.5 percent − 2.7 percent).

States follow a policy of reducing the unemployment tax on employers who experience stability in employment. Thus, an employer

---

**32.** However, if a spouse works for his or her spouse, none of the amounts paid are subject to either FICA or FUTA.

**33.** For further information on deposit and filing requirements see Circular E (cited in Footnote 29).

**34.** An identification number is obtained by filing Form SS–4, Application for Employer Identification Number.

**35.** § 3403.

**36.** The provisions of the Internal Revenue Code dealing with FUTA are contained in § § 3301–3311.

with little or no turnover among employees might find that the state rate could drop as low as 0.1 percent or, in some states, even to zero. The reason for the merit rating credit is obvious. Steady employment means the state will have lower unemployment benefits to pay.

FUTA is to be distinguished from FICA in the sense that the incidence of taxation falls entirely upon the employer. A few states, however, levy a special tax on employees either to provide disability benefits or supplemental unemployment compensation, or both.[37]

Also distinguishable from FUTA are various union negotiated plans funded by employers that provide for additional or extended unemployment compensation to workers that have been laid off. Common in certain seasonal industries (e. g., automobile production), these plans are not part of the tax structure but are private sector compensation arrangements.

Every employer subject to FUTA must make an annual accounting to the IRS by filing Form 940, Employer's Annual Federal Unemployment Tax Return, on or before January 31 of the following year. The return should be accompanied by the portion of FUTA due and payable to the IRS. State filing and payment requirements also must be satisfied.

## OTHER TAXES

In order to complete the overview of the U. S. tax system, some missing links need to be covered which do not fit into the classifications discussed elsewhere in this chapter.

*Federal Customs Duties.*   One tax that has not yet been mentioned is the tariff on certain imported goods.[38] Generally referred to as customs duties or levies, this tax, together with selective excise taxes, provided most of the revenues needed by the Federal government during the nineteenth century and even to the advent of World War I in the early twentieth century. Considering present times, it is remarkable to note that tariffs and excise taxes alone paid off the national debt in 1835 and enabled the U. S. Treasury to pay a surplus of $28 million to the states.

In recent years, tariffs have served the nation more as an instrument for carrying out protectionist policies than as a means of generating revenue. Thus, a particular U. S. industry might be saved, so the argument goes, from economic disaster by placing customs duties on the importation of foreign goods that can be sold at lower prices.

---

37.   These states are Alaska, California, New Jersey, New York, and Rhode Island. Alabama has such a provision, but it comes into play only if the state's unemployment fund falls below a certain level.
38.   Less-developed countries that place principal reliance on one or more major commodities (e. g., oil, coffee) are prone to favor *export* duties as well.

The protectionist would contend that the tariff, therefore, neutralizes the competitive edge held by the producer of the foreign goods.[39]

*Miscellaneous State and Local Taxes.* Most states impose a franchise tax on corporations. Basically, a franchise tax is one levied on the right to do business in the state. The base used for the determination of the tax, of course, varies from state to state. Although corporate income considerations may come into play, this tax most often is based on the capitalization of the corporation (either with or without certain long-term indebtedness).

Closely akin to the franchise tax are occupational taxes applicable to various trades or businesses: a liquor store license, for example, or a taxicab permit or a fee to practice the various professions (e. g., law, medicine, accounting). Most of these are not significant revenue producers and fall more into the category of licenses rather than taxes. The revenue derived is used to defray the cost incurred by the jurisdiction in regulating the business or profession in the interest of the public good.

# THE WHYS OF THE TAX LAW

The Federal tax law is a mosaic of statutory provisions, administrative pronouncements, and court decisions. Anyone who has attempted to work with this body of knowledge would have to admit to its disturbing complexity. For the person who has to trudge through a myriad of rule upon rule to find the solution to a tax problem, it may be of some consolation to know that the law's complexity can generally be explained. Whether sound or not, there is a reason for the formulation of every rule. Knowing these reasons, therefore, is a considerable step toward understanding the Federal tax law. The remainder of this chapter deals with economic, social, equity, and political factors which play a role in the development of tax law. Also discussed is the impact of the Internal Revenue Service and the courts on the evolution of tax law.

## ECONOMIC CONSIDERATIONS

The use of the tax system in an effort to accomplish economic objectives appears to have become increasingly popular in recent years. Generally, it involves utilization of tax legislation to amend the Inter-

---

**39.** Protectionist policies seem more appropriate for less-developed countries whose industrial capacity has not yet matured. In a world where a developed country should have everything to gain from the encouragement of international free trade, such policies may be of dubious value. History proves that tariffs often lead to retaliatory action on the part of the nation(s) affected.

nal Revenue Code[40] and looks toward measures designed to help control the economy or to encourage certain activities and businesses.

*Control of the Economy.* One of the better known provisions of the tax law which purports to aid in controlling the economy is the investment tax credit. By providing a tax credit for investment in qualified property, so the logic goes, businesses will be encouraged to expand.[41] The resulting expansion stimulates the economy and generates additional employment. As a safety valve against over-expansion, the investment credit can be suspended for a period of time or completely terminated.[42]

A further incentive towards capital formation is the degree to which a capital investment can be recovered with a tax benefit. For many years the tax law had recognized this consideration with provisions allowing accelerated methods of depreciation when writing off the cost of most tangible personalty (e. g., machinery, equipment) acquired for use in a trade or business. The Economic Recovery Tax Act of 1981 (ERTA) goes much further by generally allowing shorter recovery periods and more generous recovery amounts under a newly established accelerated cost recovery system (ACRS). Additionally, beginning in 1982, taxpayers are allowed to expense certain capital asset acquisitions. In other words, limited amounts (up to $5,000 in 1983) may be deducted in the year the asset(s) is purchased and placed in service. Thus, the taxpayer derives an immediate tax benefit from the property acquisition and does not have to await (under ACRS) recoupment of cost over a prescribed period of time.

> **Example 9.** In 1983 T purchases a machine for $5,000 for use in his trade or business. The machine is classified as five-year property under ACRS. At T's election, he may expense the $5,000 in 1983 rather than capitalize the amount and deduct its cost over a five-year period.

Of more immediate impact on the economy is a change in the tax rate structure. By lowering tax rates, taxpayers are able to retain more spendable funds. An increase in tax rates, moreover, carries the opposite effect. An illustration of this approach was the passage of the Revenue Act of 1978. Among the many changes provided by this legislation was a decrease (from 48 percent to 46 percent) in the maximum

---

**40.** The Internal Revenue Code is a compilation of Federal tax legislation.

**41.** Keep in mind that a dollar of tax credit generally means a dollar of income tax savings.

**42.** Since the investment tax credit first was enacted in 1962, it has been suspended once and repealed once. The credit was reinstated in 1971, and its benefits were expanded under the Tax Reduction Act of 1975 and the Revenue Act of 1978. Some restriction of the credit, however, did occur as the result of the Tax Equity and Fiscal Responsibility Act of 1982 (TEFRA). Except for the TEFRA retrenchment, which was more motivated by budgetary constraints, all of these changes were justified in terms of the effect they would have on the nation's economy.

rate of tax applicable to corporations. Also modified was the amount of taxable income (from the excess of $50,000 to the excess of $100,000) to which the maximum rate applies.

The Economic Recovery Tax Act of 1981 indicates that Congress has every intention of pursuing rate reduction as a means of stimulating the economy. The new law includes a multistage, across-the-board reduction in income tax rates to be phased in over a period from 1981–1983.

*Encouragement of Certain Activities.* Without passing judgment on the wisdom of any such choices, it is quite clear that the tax law does encourage certain types of economic activity or segments of the economy. If, for example, one assumes that technological progress is fostered, the favorable treatment allowed research and development expenditures can be explained. Under the tax law such expenditures can be deducted in the year incurred or, as an alternative, capitalized and amortized over a period of 60 months or more. In terms of timing the tax saving, such options usually are preferable to a capitalization of the cost with a write-off over the estimated useful life of the asset created.[43]

The Economic Recovery Tax Act of 1981 further recognized the need to stimulate, through the use of the tax laws, technological progress. In addition to the favorable write-off treatment noted above, certain incremental research and development costs now qualify for a 25 percent tax credit (see Chapter 8).

The encouragement of technological progress can also explain why the tax law places the inventor in an advantageous position. Not only can patents qualify as capital assets, but under certain conditions their disposition automatically carries favorable long-term capital gain treatment.

Is it desirable to encourage the conservation of energy resources? Considering the world energy situation and our own reliance on foreign oil production, the answer to this question has to be obvious. The concern over energy usage was a prime consideration that led to the enactment in 1978 of the Energy Tax Act. The result of this legislation was to make available to taxpayers various tax savings (in the form of tax credits) for energy conservation expenditures made on personal residence and business property.

Are ecological considerations a desirable objective? If they are, this explains why the tax law permits a 60-month amortization period for costs incurred in the installation of pollution-control facilities.

Is it wise to stimulate U. S. exports of goods and services abroad? Considering the pressing and continuing problem of a deficit in the U. S. balance of payments, the answer should be clear. Along this line,

---

**43.** If the asset developed has no estimated useful life, no write-off would be available without the two options allowed by the tax law.

Congress has created a unique type of organization designed to encourage domestic exports of goods. Called DISCs (i. e., Domestic International Sales Corporations), such corporations are allowed, under prescribed conditions, to defer for income tax purposes the recognition of a percentage of their income derived from foreign sales. Also in an international setting, Congress has deemed it advisable to establish incentives for those U. S. citizens who accept employment overseas. Under the Economic Recovery Tax Act of 1981, such persons receive generous tax breaks through special treatment of their foreign-source income and certain housing costs.

An item previously mentioned can be connected to the encouragement of U. S. foreign trade. Because one of this country's major exportable products is its technology, can it not be said that the special favoritism accorded to research and development expenditures (see above) also serves to foster international trade?

*Encouragement of Certain Industries.* No one can question the proposition that a sound agricultural base is necessary for a well-balanced national economy. Undoubtedly this can explain why farmers are accorded special treatment under the Federal tax system. Among these benefits are the following: the election to expense rather than capitalize soil and water conservation expenditures, fertilizers, and land-clearing costs; the possibility of obtaining favorable long-term capital gain treatment on the disposition of livestock held for draft, breeding, or dairy purposes; the availability of the investment tax credit on certain farm structures; and, the election to defer the recognition of gain on the receipt of crop insurance proceeds.

The economic difficulties recently encountered by certain financial institutions (viz., savings and loan associations) can explain, in part, the special tax treatment allowed any All-Savers Certificates purchased through 1982. Under the Economic Recovery Tax Act of 1981, the interest from such certificates (up to $2,000 on a joint return) is not taxed. One should note in passing, moreover, that the "all-savers" certificates have as a further objective the encouragement of the residential construction industry which, in recent years, has fallen upon hard times. Thus, so the argument goes, more savings lead to additional mortgage funds which, in turn, stimulate home construction.

*Encouragement of Small Business.* At least in the U. S., there exists a consensus that what is good for small business is good for the economy as a whole. Without evaluating the validity of this assumption, it has led to a definite bias in the tax law favoring small business. How else can one explain why the owner of a family business can elect to write off a capital expenditure for 1983 of up to $5,000 while Exxon is limited to the same amount?

In the corporate tax area, several provisions can be explained by their motivation to benefit small business. One provision permits the shareholders of a small business corporation to make a special election that generally will avoid the imposition of the corporate income tax.[44] Furthermore, such an election enables the corporation to pass through to its shareholders any of its operating losses and investment tax credits.[45]

The tax rates applicable to corporations tend to favor small business insofar as size is relative to the amount of taxable income generated in any one year. Since the full corporate tax rate of 46 percent applies only to taxable income in excess of $100,000, corporations that stay within these limits are subject to lower effective tax rates.

> **Example 10.**  For calendar year 1983, X Corporation has taxable income of $100,000 and Y Corporation has taxable income of $200,000. Based on this information, the corporate income tax is $25,750 for X Corporation and $71,750 for Y Corporation. By comparison, then, X Corporation is subject to an effective tax rate of 25.75% (i. e., $25,750/$100,000) while Y Corporation is subject to a rate of 35.875% (i. e., $71,750/$200,000).

Another provision specifically designed to aid small business is the new LIFO inventory procedure. Enacted in 1981, such procedures are available only to those businesses with average gross receipts of less than two million dollars.[46]

## SOCIAL CONSIDERATIONS

Some of the tax laws can be explained by looking to social considerations. This is particularly the case when dealing with the Federal income tax of individuals. Notable examples and the rationale behind each are summarized below:

> —The nontaxability of certain benefits provided to employees through accident and health plans financed by employers. It would appear socially desirable to encourage such plans, since they provide medical benefits in the event of an employee's illness or injury.

> —The nontaxability to the employee of premiums paid by an employer for group-term insurance covering the life of the employee. These arrangements can be justified on social grounds in that they provide funds for the family unit to help it readjust following the loss of wages caused by the employee's death.

---

**44.**  Known as the Subchapter S election, the subject is discussed in Chapter 16.
**45.**  In general, an operating loss can benefit only the corporation incurring the loss through a carryback or carryforward to profitable years. Consequently, the shareholders of the corporation usually cannot take advantage of any such loss.
**46.**  LIFO inventory and small business accounting are discussed in Chapter 11.

—The tax treatment to the employee of contributions made by an employer to qualified pension or profit sharing plans.[47] The contribution and any income it generates will not be taxed to the employee until the funds are distributed. Private retirement plans should be encouraged, since they supplement the subsistence income level the employee otherwise would have under the Social Security system.[48]

—The deduction allowed for contributions to qualified charitable organizations.[49] The deduction attempts to shift some of the financial and administrative burden of socially desirable programs from the public (the government) to the private (the citizens) sector.

—The tax credit allowed for amounts spent to furnish care for certain minor or disabled dependents to enable the taxpayer to seek or maintain gainful employment.[50] Who could deny the social desirability of encouraging taxpayers to provide care for their children while they work?

—The disallowance of a tax deduction for certain expenditures deemed to be contrary to public policy. This disallowance extends to such items as fines, penalties, illegal kickbacks, and bribes to government officials.[51] Social considerations dictate that these activities should not be encouraged by the tax law. Permitting the deduction would supposedly encourage these activities.

Many other examples could be included, but the conclusion would be unchanged: Social considerations do explain a significant part of the Federal tax law.


## EQUITY CONSIDERATIONS

The concept of equity is, of course, relative. Reasonable persons can, and often do, disagree about what is fair or unfair. In the tax area, moreover, equity is most often tied to a particular taxpayer's personal situation. To illustrate, it may be difficult for Ms. Jones to understand

---

**47.**  These arrangements also benefit the employer by allowing a tax deduction when the contribution is made to the qualified plan.

**48.**  The same rationale explains the availability of similar arrangements for self-employed persons (the H.R. 10 or Keogh type of plan).

**49.**  The charitable contribution deduction is discussed in Chapter 7.

**50.**  See Chapter 8.

**51.**  Disclosures involving large corporations with international operations have highlighted this policy. It is interesting to note that the Tax Equity and Fiscal Responsibility Act of 1982, Congress singled out for special treatment those persons who deal in illegal drug operations. Such persons will no longer be able to deduct any related business expenses (except the cost of goods sold in arriving at taxable income. One must question, however, what deterrent (if any) this provision will have on illegal drug trafficking.

why none of the rent she pays on her apartment is deductible when her brother, Mr. Jones, is able to deduct a large portion of the monthly payments he makes on his personal residence in the form of interest and taxes.[52]

In the same vein, compare the tax treatment of a corporation with that of a partnership. Although the two businesses may be of equal size, similarly situated, and competitors in production of goods or services, they are not comparably treated under the tax law. The corporation is subject to a separate Federal income tax; the partnership is not. Whether the differences in tax treatment logically can be justified in terms of equity is beside the point. The point is that the tax law can and does make a distinction between these business forms.

Equity, then, is not what appears fair or unfair to any one taxpayer or group of taxpayers. It is, instead, what the tax law recognizes. Some recognition of equity does exist, however, and offers an explanation of part of the law. The concept of equity appears in tax provisions that alleviate the effect of multiple taxation, postpone the recognition of gain when the taxpayer lacks the ability or wherewithal to pay the tax, and mitigate the effect of the application of the annual accounting period concept.

*Alleviating the Effect of Multiple Taxation.* The income earned by a taxpayer may be subject to taxes imposed by different taxing authorities. If, for example, the taxpayer is a resident of New York City, income might generate Federal, state of New York, and city of New York income taxes. To compensate for this apparent inequity, the Federal tax law allows a taxpayer to claim a deduction for state and local income taxes. The deduction, however, does not neutralize the effect of multiple taxation, since the benefit derived depends on the taxpayer's Federal income tax bracket.[53]

Equity considerations can explain the Federal tax treatment of certain income from foreign sources. Since double taxation results when the same income is subject to both foreign and U.S. income taxes, the tax law permits the taxpayer to choose between a credit or a deduction for the foreign taxes paid.

*The Wherewithal to Pay Concept.* Quite simply, the wherewithal to pay concept recognizes the inequity of taxing a transaction when the taxpayer lacks the means with which to pay the tax. It is particularly suited to situations in which the taxpayer's economic position has not changed significantly as a result of the transaction.

**Example 11.** T owns unimproved land held as an investment. The land cost T $60,000 and has a fair market value of $100,000.

---

52. The encouragement of home ownership can also be justified on both economic and social grounds.

53. A tax credit, rather than a deduction, would eliminate the effects of multiple taxation on the same income.

This land is exchanged for a building (worth $100,000) which T will use in his business.[54]

**Example 12.** T owns a warehouse which she uses in her business. At a time when the warehouse has an adjusted cost of $60,000, it is destroyed by fire. T collects the insurance proceeds of $100,000 and, within two years of the end of the year in which the fire occurred, uses all of the proceeds to purchase a new warehouse.[55]

In both of the above examples, T had an economic gain of $40,000 [i. e., $100,000 (fair market value of the property received) − $60,000 (cost of the property given up)]. It would seem inequitable to force the taxpayer to recognize any of this gain for two reasons. First, without disposing of the property or interest acquired, the taxpayer would be hard-pressed to pay the tax. Second, the taxpayer's economic situation has not changed significantly.

*Mitigating the Effect of the Annual Accounting Period Concept.* For purposes of effective administration of the tax law, it is necessary for all taxpayers to report to and settle with the Federal government at periodic intervals. Otherwise taxpayers would remain uncertain as to their tax liabilities, and the government would have difficulty judging revenues and budgeting expenditures. The period selected for final settlement of most tax liabilities, in any event an arbitrary determination, is one year. At the close of each year, therefore, a taxpayer's position becomes finalized for that particular year. Referred to as the annual accounting period concept, its effect is to divide, for tax purposes, each taxpayer's life into equal annual intervals.

The finality of the annual accounting period concept could lead to dissimilarity in tax treatment for taxpayers who are, from a long-range standpoint, in the same economic position. Compare, for example, two individual taxpayers, C and D. Over a five-year period, C has annual income of $10,000 for the first four years and $100,000 in the fifth year. During the same period, D has income of $28,000 per year. Which taxpayer is better off? Considering the progressive nature of the Federal income tax, D's overall tax liability will be much less than that incurred by C. Is this a fair result in view of the fact that each taxpayer earned the same total income (i. e., $140,000) over the five-year period? It is easy to see, therefore, why the income averaging provision of the tax law can be explained on the basis of equitable

---

**54.** The nontaxability of like-kind exchanges applies to the exchange of property held for investment or used in a trade or business for property to be similarly held or used. See Chapter 9.

**55.** The nontaxability of gains realized from involuntary conversions applies when the proceeds received by the taxpayer are reinvested within a prescribed period of time in property similar or related in service or use to that converted. Involuntary conversions take place as a result of casualty losses, theft losses, and condemnations by a public authority.

considerations.[56] Keep in mind, however, that the income averaging provision does not violate the annual accounting period concept but merely operates to mitigate its effect. By income averaging, C would compute the tax on the $100,000 received in the fifth year by a special and favorable procedure without disturbing the finality of any of the returns filed or the taxes paid for the preceding four years.

The same reasoning used to support income averaging can be applied to explain the special treatment accorded by the tax law to net operating losses, excess capital losses, and excess charitable contributions.[57] Carryback and carryover procedures help mitigate the effect of limiting a loss or a deduction to the accounting period in which it was realized. With such procedures, a taxpayer might be able to salvage a loss or a deduction that might otherwise be wasted.

**Example 13.** R and S are two sole proprietors and have experienced the following results during the past four years:

| | Profit (or Loss) | |
| Year | R | S |
|---|---|---|
| 1980 | $ 50,000 | $ 150,000 |
| 1981 | 60,000 | 60,000 |
| 1982 | 70,000 | 70,000 |
| 1983 | 50,000 | (50,000) |

Although R and S have the same profit of $230,000 over the period from 1980–1983, the finality of the annual accounting period concept places S at a definite disadvantage for tax purposes. The net operating loss procedure, therefore, offers S some relief by allowing him to apply some or all of his 1983 loss to the earlier profitable years (in this case 1980). Thus, he would be in a position with a net operating loss carryback to obtain a refund for some of the taxes he paid on the $150,000 profit reported for 1980.

Mitigation of the annual accounting period concept also explains in part the preferential treatment the tax law accords to long-term capital gains. Often the gain from the disposition of an asset is attributable to appreciation that has developed over a long period of time. In view of the impracticality of taxing such appreciation as it occurs, the law looks to the year of realization as the taxable event.[58] Long-term capital gain treatment, therefore, represents a rough means of achieving relief from the bunching effect of forcing a gain to be recognized in the tax year of realization.

---

56. See Chapter 11.
57. The tax treatment of these items is discussed in Chapters 6, 7, and 10.
58. Postponing the recognition of gain until the year it is realized is consistent with the wherewithal to pay concept. It would be difficult, for example, to pay a tax on the appreciation of an asset before its sale or other disposition has provided the necessary funds.

**Example 14.** In 1981, T (a calendar year individual) acquired as an investment shares in X Corporation at a cost of $20,000. The stock had a value of $22,000 as of December 31, 1981, and $25,000 on December 31, 1982. In 1983, T sells the stock for $30,000. Since it is neither practical nor appropriate for the taxpayer to recognize the appreciation as it develops (i. e., $2,000 for 1981, $3,000 for 1982, and $5,000 for 1983), the full $10,000 gain [$30,000 (selling price) − $20,000 (cost)] must be reported for 1983. Consequently, T is provided some measure of relief from this concentration of gain in the year of sale through the availability of the long-term capital gain deduction.[59]

The installment method of recognizing gain on the sale of property allows a taxpayer to spread tax consequences over the payout period.[60] The harsh effect of taxing all the gain in the year of sale is thereby avoided. The installment method can also be explained by the wherewithal to pay concept, since recognition of gain is tied to the collection of the installment notes received from the sale of the property. Tax consequences, then, tend to correspond to the seller's ability to pay the tax.

**Example 15.** In 19X2, T sold real estate (cost of $40,000) for $100,000. Under the terms of the sale, T receives two notes from the purchaser, each for $50,000 (plus interest). One note is payable in 19X3 and the other note in 19X4. Without the installment method, T would have to recognize and pay a tax on the gain of $60,000 for the year of the sale (i. e., 19X2). A rather harsh result since none of the sale proceeds will be received until 19X3 and 19X4. With the installment method and presuming the notes are paid when each comes due, T recognizes half of the gain (i. e., $30,000) in 19X3 and the remaining half in 19X4.

The annual accounting period concept has been modified to apply to situations in which taxpayers may have difficulty in accurately assessing their tax positions by year-end. In many such cases, the law permits taxpayers to treat transactions taking place in the next year as having occurred in the prior year.

**Example 16.** T, a calendar year individual taxpayer, is a participant in an H.R. 10 (Keogh) retirement plan. (See Appendix C for a definition of a Keogh plan.) Under the plan, T contributes 15% of her net self-employment income, such amount being deducti-

---

**59.** As a general rule, only 40% of long-term capital gains are subject to the Federal income tax. Thus, if a taxpayer has a long-term capital gain for the year of $10,000 only $4,000 of this amount is subject to the income tax. See Chapter 10.

**60.** Under the installment method, each payment received by the seller represents both a return of basis (the nontaxable portion) and profit from the sale (the taxable portion).

ble for Federal income tax purposes. On April 10, 1983, T determines that her net self-employment income for calendar year 1982 was $40,000, and consequently, she contributes $6,000 (15% × $40,000) to the plan. Even though the $6,000 contribution was made in 1983, the law permits T to claim it as a deduction for tax year 1982. Requiring T to make the contribution by December 31, 1982, in order to obtain the deduction for that year would place the burden on her of arriving at an accurate determination of net self-employment income long before her income tax return needs to be prepared and filed.

## POLITICAL CONSIDERATIONS

A large segment of the Federal tax law is made up of statutory provisions. Since these statutes are enacted by Congress, is it any surprise that political considerations do influence tax law? For purposes of discussion, the effect of political considerations on the tax law is divided into the following topics: special interest legislation, political expediency situations, and state and local government influences.

*Special Interest Legislation.* There is no doubt that certain provisions of the tax law can largely be explained by looking to the political influence some pressure groups have had on Congress. Is there any other realistic reason why, for example, prepaid subscription and dues income are not taxed until earned while prepaid rents are taxed to the landlord in the year received?

Along the same line are those tax provisions sponsored by individual members of Congress at the obvious instigation of a particularly influential constituent. In one case, for example, the effective date in proposed legislation that would reinstate the investment tax credit was moved back several months. It was well-known by all that the members of Congress initiating the change had a constituent with substantial capital expenditures that otherwise would not have qualified for the credit.

Special interest legislation is not necessarily to be condemned if it can be justified on economic, social, or some other utilitarian grounds. At any rate, it is an inevitable product of our political system.

*Political Expediency Situations.* Various tax reform proposals rise and fall in favor depending upon the shifting moods of the American public. That Congress is sensitive to popular feeling is an accepted fact. There are, therefore, certain provisions of the tax law that can be explained on the basis of political expediency existing at the time of enactment.

Measures which deter more affluent taxpayers from obtaining so-called preferential tax treatment have always had popular appeal and, consequently, the support of Congress. Provisions such as the minimum tax, the imputed interest rules, and the limitation on the deductibility of interest on investment indebtedness can be explained on this basis.[61]

Other changes partially founded on the basis of political expediency include the lowering of individual income tax rates, increasing the amount of the dependency exemption, and instituting the earned income credit.

*State and Local Influences.*   Political considerations have played a major role in the nontaxability of interest received on state and local obligations. In view of the furor that has been raised by state and local political figures every time any kind of modification of this tax provision has been proposed, one might well regard it as next to sacred.

Somewhat less apparent has been the influence state law has had in shaping our present Federal tax law. Of prime import in this regard has been the effect of the community property system employed in eight states.[62] At one time the tax position of the residents of these states was so advantageous that many common law states actually adopted community property systems.[63] Needless to say, the political pressure placed on Congress to correct the disparity in tax treatment was considerable. To a large extent this was accomplished in the Revenue Act of 1948 which extended many of the community property tax advantages to residents of common law jurisdictions.[64] Thus, common law states avoided the trauma of discarding the time-honored legal system familiar to everyone.

## INFLUENCE OF THE INTERNAL REVENUE SERVICE

The influence of the IRS is recognized in many areas beyond its obvious role in the issuance of the administrative pronouncements which make up a considerable portion of our tax law. In its capacity as the protector of the national revenue, the IRS has been instrumental in

---

**61.**   See Chapters 7 and 11.

**62.**   The eight states with community property systems are Louisiana, Texas, New Mexico, Arizona, California, Washington, Idaho, and Nevada. The rest of the states are classified as common law jurisdictions. The difference between common law and community property systems centers around the property rights possessed by married persons. In a common law system, each spouse owns whatever he or she earns. Under a community property system, one-half of the earnings of each spouse is considered owned by the other spouse. Assume, for example, H and W are husband and wife and their only income is the $40,000 annual salary H receives. If they live in New York (a common law state), the $40,000 salary belongs to H. If, however, they live in Texas (a community property state), the $40,000 salary is divided equally, in terms of ownership, between H and W.

**63.**   Such states included Michigan, Oklahoma, and Pennsylvania.

**64.**   The major advantage extended was the provision allowing married taxpayers to file joint returns and compute the tax liability as if the income had been earned one-half by each spouse. This result is automatic in a community property state since half of the income earned by one spouse belongs to the other spouse. The income-splitting benefits of a joint return are incorporated as part of the tax rates applicable to married taxpayers. See Chapter 2.

securing the passage of much legislation designed to curtail the most flagrant tax avoidance practices (to close tax loopholes). In its capacity as the administrator of the tax laws, the IRS has sought and obtained legislation to make its job easier (to attain administrative feasibility).

*The IRS as Protector of the Revenue.* Innumerable examples can be given of provisions in the tax law which stemmed from the direct influence of the IRS when it was applied to preclude the use of a loophole as a means of avoiding the tax consequences intended by Congress. Working within the letter of existing law, ingenious taxpayers and their advisers devise techniques which accomplish indirectly what cannot be accomplished directly. As a consequence, legislation is enacted to close the loophole that taxpayers have located and exploited. Some tax law can be explained in this fashion and is discussed in the chapters to follow.

In addition, the IRS has secured from Congress legislation of a more general nature which enables it to make adjustments based on the substance, rather than the formal construction, of what a taxpayer has done. One such provision permits the IRS to make adjustments to a taxpayer's method of accounting when the method used by the taxpayer "does not clearly reflect income."[65]

*Administrative Feasibility.* Some of the tax law is justified on the grounds that it simplifies the task of the IRS in collecting the revenue and administering the law. With regard to collecting the revenue, the IRS long ago realized the importance of placing taxpayers on a pay-as-you-go basis. Elaborate withholding procedures apply to wages, while the tax on other types of income may be paid at periodic intervals throughout the year. Examples of recent extensions of the withholding-at-the-source procedure can be found in the changes made by Congress in the Tax Equity and Fiscal Responsibility Act of 1982 (e. g., most interest, dividends, and some pensions are now covered). The IRS has been instrumental in convincing the courts that accrual basis taxpayers should pay taxes on prepaid income in the year received and not when earned. The approach may be contrary to generally accepted accounting principles, but it is consistent with the wherewithal to pay concept.

Of considerable aid to the IRS in collecting revenue are the numerous provisions which impose interest and penalties on taxpayers for noncompliance with the tax law. Provisions such as the penalties for failure to pay a tax or to file a return that is due, the negligence penalty for intentional disregard of rules and regulations, and various penalties for civil and criminal fraud serve as deterrents to taxpayer noncompliance.

**Example 17.** At the instigation of the IRS, Congress in the Economic Recovery Tax Act of 1981 increased the civil penalty for

---

65. § 446(b).

furnishing false withholding information on a Form W–4 from $50 to $500. Apparently, the IRS was concerned that many employees were listing mythical dependents (e. g., 19) so that no income tax would be withheld from their wages. The imposition of the stiffer penalty is an obvious effort to deter noncompliance with the pay-as-you-go withholding procedures.

**Example 18.** T, a tax protester, files an income tax return but does not reflect any financial information thereon on the grounds that the Federal income tax is unconstitutional. Under a new provision contained in the Tax Equity and Fiscal Responsibility Act of 1982, T's return will be treated as "frivolous," and T will be subject to a penalty of $500 for his actions. This penalty will be imposed in addition to other penalties that normally would result (e. g., failure to pay, negligence).

One of the keys to an effective administration of our tax system is the audit process conducted by the IRS. To carry out this function, the IRS is aided by provisions which reduce the chance of taxpayer error or manipulation and, therefore, simplify the audit effort that is necessary. An increase in the amount of the zero bracket amount, for example, reduces the number of individual taxpayers who will choose the alternative of itemizing their excess personal deductions.[66] With fewer deductions to check, therefore, the audit function is simplified.[67]

The audit function of the IRS has been simplified by provisions of the tax law dealing with the burden of proof. Suppose, for example, the IRS audits a taxpayer and questions a particular deduction. Who has the burden of proving the propriety of the deduction? Except in the case of criminal fraud, the burden is always on the taxpayer.

## INFLUENCE OF THE COURTS

In addition to interpreting statutory provisions and the administrative pronouncements issued by the IRS, the Federal courts have influenced tax law in two other respects.[68] First, the courts have

---

**66.**  For a discussion of the zero bracket amount, see Chapter 2.

**67.**  The same justification was given by the IRS when it proposed to Congress the $100 limitation on personal casualty and theft losses. Imposition of the limitation eliminated many casualty and theft loss deductions and, as a consequence, saved the IRS considerable audit time. The further curtailment of casualty and theft loss deductions certainly will follow as a result of recent statutory changes. The Tax Equity and Fiscal Responsibility Act of 1982, in addition to retaining the $100 feature, limits deductible losses to those in excess of 10% of a taxpayer's adjusted gross income. See Chapter 6.

**68.**  A great deal of case law is devoted to ascertaining Congressional intent. The courts, in effect, ask: What did Congress have in mind when it enacted a particular tax provision?

formulated certain judicial concepts which serve as guides in the application of various tax provisions. Second, certain key decisions have led to changes in the Internal Revenue Code. Understanding this influence helps to explain some of our tax law.

*Judicial Concepts Relating to Tax.* A leading tax concept developed by the courts deals with the interpretation of statutory tax provisions which operate to benefit taxpayers. The courts have established the rule that these relief provisions are to be narrowly construed against taxpayers if there is any doubt about their application. Suppose, for example, T wants to treat an expenditure as deductible for income tax purposes but has not literally satisfied the statutory requirements covering the deduction. Because income tax deductions are relief provisions favoring taxpayers, chances are the courts will deny T this treatment.

Important in this area is the arm's length concept. Particularly in dealings between related parties, transactions may be tested by looking to whether the taxpayers acted in an "arm's length" manner. The question to be asked is: Would unrelated parties have handled the transaction in the same way?

**Example 19.** The sole shareholder of a corporation leases property to it for a monthly rental of $500. To test whether the corporation should be allowed a rent deduction for this amount, the IRS and the courts will apply the arm's length concept. Would the corporation have paid $500 a month in rent if the same property had been leased from an unrelated party (rather than from the sole shareholder)?

*Judicial Influence on Statutory Provisions.* Some court decisions have been of such consequence that Congress has incorporated them into statutory tax law. One illustration of this influence appears below.

**Example 20.** In 19X0, T claimed a loss of $100,000 for stock in Z Corporation that had become worthless during the year. Because of the absence of any offsetting gains, the loss deduction produced no income tax savings for T either in 19X0 or in future years. In 19X5, T institutes a lawsuit against the former officers of Z Corporation for their misconduct which resulted in the corporation's failure and, thereby, led to T's $100,000 loss. In settlement of the suit, the officers pay $50,000 to T. The IRS argued that the full $50,000 should be taxed as gain to T. Because the stock in Z Corporation was written off in 19X0 as being worthless, it had a zero value for tax purposes. The $50,000 recovery received by T on the stock was, therefore, all gain. Although the position of the IRS was logical and conformed to the tax statutes as they then existed, it was not equitable. The court stated that T should not be taxed on the recovery of an amount previously deducted unless the deduction produced a tax savings. Since the $100,000 loss deduction in 19X0 produced no tax benefit, none of the $50,000 received in 19X5 results in gain.

The decision reached by the courts in Example 20, known as the tax benefit rule, has since become part of the statutory tax law.[69]

## SUMMARY

In addition to its obvious revenue raising objective, the Federal tax law has developed in response to several other factors:

- —*Economic considerations.*  Here, the emphasis is on tax provisions which help regulate the economy and encourage certain activities and types of businesses.

- —*Social considerations.*  Some tax provisions are designed to encourage (or discourage) certain socially desirable (or undesirable) practices.

- —*Equity considerations.*  Of principal concern in this area are tax provisions which alleviate the effect of multiple taxation, recognize the wherewithal to pay concept, and mitigate the effect of the annual accounting period concept.

- —*Political considerations.*  Of significance in this regard are tax provisions which represent special interest legislation, reflect political expediency situations, and exhibit the effect of state law.

- —*Influence of the IRS.*  Many tax provisions are intended to aid the IRS in the collection of the revenue and in the administration of the tax law.

- —*Influence of the Courts.*  Court decisions have established a body of judicial concepts relating to tax law and have, on occasion, led Congress to enact statutory provisions to either clarify or negate their effect.

These factors explain various tax provisions and, thereby, help in understanding why the tax law developed to its present state.

## PROBLEM MATERIALS

### Questions for Class Discussion

1. When and why was the first Federal income tax enacted in the U. S.?

2. Why did the Supreme Court hold that the 1894 income tax was unconstitutional?

---

**69.** See Chapter 4.

3. What is the difference between the Internal Revenue Code of 1939 and the Internal Revenue Code of 1954, as amended?

4. Why are most individuals currently subject to Federal income tax, whereas in 1939 less than 6% of the U. S. population was required to pay Federal income taxes?

5. Do you feel that our Federal government could continue to collect the same amount of tax from its taxpayers if the pay-as-you-go tax system were abolished? Why?

6. Discuss Adam Smith's canons of taxation. Are these criteria for a "good" tax system still appropriate in today's economy?

7. Several proposals have been introduced in Congress that would institute a Federal value added tax (i. e., VAT). Such proposals would impose a tax on the increment in value that is added at each stage of the manufacturing process and would be levied on the party adding such value. Evaluate VAT in terms of Adam Smith's canons of taxation.

8. How would you characterize the Federal income and estate and gift tax rate structure (i. e., progressive or proportional)?

9. T lives in a jurisdiction that does impose an ad valorem tax on realty but does not have such a tax on personalty. She just recently installed an automatic sprinkler system in the warehouse she operates for lease. What, if any, could be her concern with regard to taxation?

10. T buys a new home for $150,000, its cost of construction plus the usual profit margin for the builder. The new home is located in a neighborhood largely developed 10 years ago when the homes sold for approximately $50,000 each. Assuming the homes of his neighbors are worth (in current values) in the vicinity of $150,000, could T be at a disadvantage with regard to the ad valorem tax on realty?

11. T, a farmer, lives in a county where a significant amount of property is owned by the Federal government (for use as a military installation) and the state (for use as an experimental agricultural station). If the county assesses and collects an ad valorem tax on realty, what might be T's position?

12. A jurisdiction that is in need of additional (and substantial) revenue is considering imposing an ad valorem tax on personalty devoted to personal use. The tax also would cover intangible property. Any comment on the jurisdiction's realistic expectations on revenue production?

13. "There exists every indication to believe that the revenue yield, on a relative basis, from Federal excise taxes will continue to diminish in the years to come." Do you agree or disagree with this statement? Why?

14. T pays $15.90 for a ticket to attend a theatrical production of *Evita*. If $1.90 of the price is for taxes, what are the possibilities in terms of their classification? What type of jurisdiction(s) probably imposed the taxes?

15. Nevada, a state where gambling is legalized and heavily regulated, does not have many of the taxes common to other states. For example, Nevada does not have corporate and individual income taxes, death taxes, and gift taxes. However, it does impose a general sales tax, a gambling tax, and a casino entertainment tax.

(a) Is there any rationale underlying this scheme of taxation?

(b) Is the state of Nevada "missing the boat" by not having some type of death tax? Why?

16. Alaska and Texas are leading producers of oil and gas, and neither imposes an individual income tax. Is there any correlation between these two facts? Explain.

17. The retail purchase price of cigarettes in Kentucky and North Carolina is lower than in other states. Why?

18. Why should some states see fit to impose a tax on oleomargarine products?

19. "There is no national general sales tax." Explain this statement.

20. Why might a person who purchases a product from an establishment located in jurisdiction X desire to take delivery in jurisdiction Y? Would it matter whether or not the person resided in jurisdiction X? Explain.

21. "There is no Federal inheritance tax." Do you agree or disagree with this statement?

22. An employee who has more than one job during the year always will have excess FICA withholdings. Do you agree? Why or why not?

23. In connection with FUTA, what purpose is served by a state merit rating system?

24. Compare FICA and FUTA in connection with each of the following:

(a) Incidence of taxation.

(b) Justification for taxation.

(c) Reporting and filing requirements.

(d) Rates and base involved.

25. Although the FICA taxes an employee pays are not deductible, any Social Security benefits the employee receives will not be subject to the Federal income tax. As a result, tax equity is achieved (i. e., no deduction and no income tax). Do you have any comment on this assumption? What might be a better approach toward achieving tax equity?

26. T, a sole proprietor, is considering incorporating his business. One of the advantages he sees of using the corporate form is the substitution of FICA taxes (6.7% for the employee's portion) for self-employment taxes (9.35%). Is T thinking clearly? Explain.

27. T, an individual taxpayer and a resident of Rhode Island, is considering retiring to a warmer climate. At present, T has in mind either Florida or Arizona. What tax factors might affect his decision in making a choice between these two states?

28. During 1983, T is employed by X Corporation on a full-time basis with a salary of $50,000. He also has a part-time job with Y Corporation for which he earns $10,000.

(a) Since T's main salary clearly exceeds the FICA maximum, there is no need for Y Corporation to withhold any amounts for this purpose. Please comment.

(b) In any event, Y Corporation will be entitled to recover its share of FICA contributions made on behalf of T. Please comment.

29. Give examples of specific provisions of the tax law which are intended to help control the national economy.

30. In what way does the tax law attempt to encourage technological progress?

31. Suppose Congress decided to use the tax laws to further encourage the installation of pollution-control equipment.

(a) What type of tax benefit would you suggest?

(b) What might be more effective, a tax deduction or a tax credit? Explain.

32. In what way does the tax law encourage home ownership?

33. In what manner does the tax law favor agriculture? Why?

34. Congress has enacted an income tax credit for the cost of home insulation and certain other energy-saving items. What objective, if any, does such legislation accomplish?

35. Discuss the probable justification for the following provisions of the tax law:

(a) Multiple tax rates for corporate income tax purposes.

(b) The election permitting certain corporations to avoid the corporate income tax.

(c) A provision which allows railroads to amortize the cost of tunnel bores over a period of 50 years.

(d) A provision which makes nontaxable certain benefits furnished to employees through accident and health plans financed by employers.

(e) Nontaxable treatment for an employee as to premiums paid by an employer for group-term insurance covering the life of the employee.

(f) The tax treatment to the employee of contributions made by an employer to qualified pension or profit sharing plans.

(g) The deduction allowed for contributions to qualified charitable organizations.

36. The Tax Reform Act of 1976 provided a tax credit for amounts spent to furnish care for certain minor or disabled dependents to enable the taxpayer to seek or maintain gainful employment.

(a) What justification can you see for this credit?

(b) Prior to the Tax Reform Act of 1976, the child and disabled dependent care provision of the tax law allowed only a tax deduction for such expenses. Why, do you suppose, did Congress convert the deduction into a credit?

37. T owns and operates a trucking firm. During the year his employees incur a substantial number of fines for violating the 55 mile per hour highway speed limitation. T considers these fines as a necessary expense of running the business, as he knows his firm cannot make a profit by observing the posted speed limitation. Are these fines deductible for income tax purposes? Why or why not?

38. A provision of the Code allows a taxpayer a deduction for Federal income tax purposes for state and local income taxes paid. Does the provision eliminate the effect of multiple taxation of the same income? Why or why not? In this connection, consider the following:

    (a) Taxpayer, an individual, has itemized deductions less than the zero bracket amount.

    (b) Taxpayer is in the 30% tax bracket for Federal income tax purposes. The 50% tax bracket.

    (c) The state imposing the income tax allows a deduction for Federal income taxes paid.

39. Provide examples of the wherewithal to pay concept operating to insulate a transaction from Federal income tax consequences.

40. Explain the annual accounting period concept. Why is it necessary?

41. Under the tax law, wagering losses are deductible only to the extent of wagering gains during the same year.

    (a) How can this rule be explained?

    (b) Suppose T, an individual and calendar year taxpayer, wins $40,000 at the races in 1982 but loses the same amount in 1983. How would T be treated for tax purposes? How does T's tax position compare with that of S who wins and loses the same amount but within the same year?

42. T leases a building from L for 20 years. During the term of the lease, T makes significant capital improvements to the property which revert to L on the termination of the lease. Several years after the lease has terminated, L sells the building for a profit, a portion of which is attributable to the value of the improvements made by T.

    (a) Should the improvements made by T be taxed to L?

    (b) If so, when (i. e., at the time when made, on the termination of the lease, on the sale of the property)?

43. State the manner in which the annual accounting period concept is mitigated by the tax provisions relating to:

    (a) Income averaging.

    (b) Net operating loss carrybacks and carryovers.

    (c) Excess charitable contribution carryovers.

    (d) Long-term capital gains.

    (e) Installment sales.

44. H and W are husband and wife and live in Indiana (a common law state). During the year they earn wages as follows: $20,000 for H and $26,000 for W. If H and W file a joint return, their tax will be determined by a schedule based on the tax for $23,000 multiplied by two.

    (a) Why is the tax schedule applicable to married taxpayers filing a joint return determined in this manner?

    (b) Suppose H and W lived in California (a community property state) and filed separate returns. How would the result compare with that reached under part (a)?

45. T, an individual taxpayer, files a Federal income tax return for the year in which he reports income on a cash basis and expenditures on an accrual basis.

   (a) What was T trying to accomplish in reporting as income only the amounts actually received while claiming deductions for amounts due but unpaid?

   (b) Does the IRS have any defense against T's approach? Explain.

46. In what way does the wherewithal to pay concept aid the IRS in the collection of tax revenue?

47. On her income tax return for the year, T claims as a deduction certain charitable contributions that she did not make. When you question her about this she responds:

   (a) "How is the IRS going to prove that I did not make these contributions?"

   (b) "Even if the IRS disallows the deductions, the worst that can happen is that I will owe the same amount of tax I would have paid anyway."

   Comment on T's misconceptions about the tax law.

48. Describe how administrative feasibility is achieved for the IRS by each of the following tax provisions:

   (a) The zero bracket amount allowed to individual taxpayers.

   (b) The $100 and 10% nondeductible limitations on personal casualty and theft losses.

49. Under current tax law, a donor generally can make a gift of $10,000 per year to a donee wthout having to file a Federal gift tax return and pay a Federal gift tax. How does this provision simplify the administrative responsibility of the IRS for enforcement of the tax laws?

50. The tax law allows a taxpayer to avoid the recognition of gain on the sale of a personal residence if the proceeds are reinvested in a newly constructed home and such home is occupied within 24 months. What would be the tax result if a taxpayer was unable to occupy the new home within 24 months due to some causal factor beyond his or her control (e. g., a strike by the construction trade unions that prevents the home from being completed)? Why?

51. "The Federal income tax is more frequently evaded by self-employed taxpayers than by those who are employed."

   (a) Do you agree with this statement? Why or why not?

   (b) If the statement is true, how might the problem be resolved?

52. T, an employee and a calendar year taxpayer, lives in a state that imposes a state income tax. During 1982 (through the withholding procedure), T pays state income taxes of $1,800. Of this amount, $400 is refunded to T in 1983 by the state as being in excess of the tax that she owed. How should the $400 state income tax refund be handled for Federal income tax purposes? In answering this question evaluate the following alternatives:

   (a) T should limit the deduction for state income taxes on her 1982 Federal income tax return to $1,400.

(b) T should offset the $400 refund against any state income tax paid in 1983.

(c) T should disregard the $400 refund.

(d) Should T include any of the $400 refund in her income for 1983?

53.  The Tax Equity and Fiscal Responsibility Act of 1982 contains a provision requiring states that impose an income tax to issue to taxpayers and the IRS information returns on any refunds paid during the year. Why do you think this provision was enacted?

54.  When told that a certain portion of the dividends he receives from his stock investments will be withheld at the source, T remarks: "What difference does it make, since I have to pay tax on them anyway?" Any comment?

# Chapter 2

# Tax Determination, Personal and Dependency Exemptions, An Overview of Property Transactions

To understand how the Federal income tax applies to individuals, it is necessary to look into the manner in which the tax is determined. To this end, Chapter 2 reviews and develops further some of the components of the tax formula, introduces and explains the concept of the zero bracket amount, and explains the steps involved in the computation of the tax using both the Tax Table and the Tax Rate Schedules.

The role of the deduction for personal and dependency exemptions in the determination of the income tax liability of individuals is covered in this chapter. Justification for these exemptions, as well as the rules governing their application, is included in the discussion.

When property is sold or otherwise disposed of, the result could affect the determination of income tax liability. Although the area of property transactions is covered in detail in Chapters 9 and 10, an understanding of certain basic concepts is helpful in working with some of the materials to follow. The concluding portion of this chapter, therefore, furnishes an overview of the area. Here, the distinction is made between realized and recognized gain or loss, the classification of such gain or loss (i. e., ordinary or capital), and its treatment for income tax purposes.

# TAX FORMULA

Most individuals will compute taxable income using the tax formula shown in Figure I.[1]

**Figure I**

TAX FORMULA

| | | |
|---|---|---|
| Income (broadly conceived) | | $ xx,xxx |
| Less: Exclusions | | x,xxx |
| Gross income | | $ xx,xxx |
| Less: Deductions *for* adjusted gross income | | x,xxx |
| Adjusted gross income | | $ xx,xxx |
| Less: Excess itemized deductions— | | |
| Total itemized deductions | $ x,xxx | |
| Minus: Zero bracket amount | x,xxx | x,xxx |
| Personal and dependency exemptions (number of exemptions × $1,000) | | x,xxx |
| Taxable income | | $ xx,xxx |

Before illustrating the application of the tax formula, a brief introduction to the components of the formula is necessary.

## SOME OF THE COMPONENTS

*Income (broadly conceived).* This includes all income of the taxpayer, both taxable and nontaxable. It is essentially equivalent to gross receipts, but it does not include a return of capital or receipt of borrowed funds.

*Exclusions.* For various reasons[2] Congress has chosen to exclude certain types of income from the income tax base. The principal income exclusions are discussed in Chapter 4. A partial list of these exclusions is shown in Figure II.

**Figure II**

PARTIAL LIST OF EXCLUSIONS FROM GROSS INCOME

| | |
|---|---|
| Accident insurance proceeds | Compensatory damages |
| Annuities (to a limited extent) | Cost-of-living allowance (for |
| Bequests | military) |
| Casualty insurance proceeds | Damages for personal injury or |
| Child support payments | sickness |

---

**1.** Some taxpayers are required to compute an unused zero bracket amount in determining taxable income. These taxpayers will use a different tax formula, as shown in Example 5 (to be used by certain dependent children) or Example 7 (to be used by married taxpayers filing separate returns and by all other taxpayers who are required to compute an unused zero bracket amount).

**2.** See Chapter 4 for a discussion of the reasons for some of the principal exclusions from income.

**Figure II** (*continued*)

Death benefits (up to $5,000)
Disability benefits
Disability pensions (to a limited
  extent)
Federal Employee's Compensation
  Act payments
Fellowship grants (to a limited
  extent)
Gifts
Group-term life insurance,
  premium paid by employer
  (coverage not over $50,000)
Health insurance proceeds not
  deducted as a medical
  expense
Inheritances
Life insurance paid on death

Meals and lodging (furnished for
  employer's convenience)
Military allowances
Minister's dwelling rental value
  allowance
Moving and storage expenses
  paid by employer
Railroad retirement benefits
Relocation payments
Scholarship grants (to a limited
  extent)
Social Security benefits
Unemployment compensation (to
  a limited extent)
Veterans' benefits
Welfare payments
Worker's compensation

*Gross Income.* Gross income is defined broadly in the Code as "all income from whatever source derived."[3] It includes, but is not limited to, the items shown in the partial list in Figure III. It does not include unrealized gains. Gross income is discussed in Chapters 3 and 4.

**Figure III**
PARTIAL LIST OF GROSS INCOME ITEMS

Alimony
Amounts recovered after being
  deducted in prior years
Annuities
Awards
Back pay
Bargain purchase from employer
Bonuses
Breach of contract damages
Business income
Christmas bonus from employer
Clergy fees and contributions
Commissions
Compensation for services
Contributions to members of the
  clergy
Death benefits in excess of $5,000
Debts forgiven
Director's fees
Dividends (subject to a limited
  exclusion)*
Embezzled funds

Employee awards
Employee bonuses
Employee benefits (except certain
  fringe benefits)
Employee stock options
Estate and trust income
Farm income
Fees
Free tour
Gains from illegal activities
Gains from sale of property
Gambling winnings
Group-term life insurance,
  premium paid by employer
  (coverage over $50,000)
Hobby income
Incentive awards
Interest
Jury duty fees
Living quarters, meals (unless
  furnished for employer's
  convenience)

* For 1983 certain dividends are excluded from gross income of up to $100 ($200 on a joint return).

---

3.  § 61(a).

**Figure III** (*continued*)

| | |
|---|---|
| Mileage allowance | Retirement pay |
| Military pay (unless combat pay) | Rewards |
| Notary fees | Royalties |
| Partnership income | Salaries |
| Pensions | Severance pay |
| Prizes | Strike and lockout benefits |
| Professional fees | Supplemental unemployment |
| Punitive damages |   benefits |
| Reimbursement for moving | Tips and gratuities |
|   expenses | Travel allowance |
| Rents | Wages |

*Deductions for Adjusted Gross Income.*   There are two categories of deductions for individual taxpayers: (1) deductions *for* adjusted gross income and (2) deductions *from* adjusted gross income. Deductions for adjusted gross income include ordinary and necessary expenses incurred in a trade or business, certain employee business expenses, moving expenses, alimony paid, payments to an individual retirement account, forfeited interest penalty for premature withdrawal of time deposits, the capital gain deduction, and others.[4] Deductible employee business expenses include employment-related expenses for travel and transportation. The principal deductions *for* adjusted gross income are discussed in Chapters 5 and 6.

*Adjusted Gross Income.*   This is an important subtotal which serves as the basis for computing percentage limitations on certain itemized deductions, such as medical expenses and charitable contributions.

*Itemized deductions.*   As a general rule, personal expenditures are disallowed as deductions in arriving at taxable income. However, Congress has chosen to allow certain specified expenses as itemized deductions, even though they are personal in nature. In addition, taxpayers are allowed to itemize expenses related to (1) the production or collection of income; (2) the management of property held for the production of income; and (3) the determination, collection, or refund of any tax.[5] Itemized deductions (discussed in Chapter 7) include, but are not limited to, the expenses listed in Figure IV.

**Figure IV**

PARTIAL LIST OF ITEMIZED DEDUCTIONS

Medical expenses in excess of 5% (3% before 1983) of adjusted gross income
State and local income taxes
Real estate taxes
General sales taxes
Personal property taxes

---

4.   § 62.
5.   § 212.

**Figure IV** (*continued*)

Interest on home mortgage
Interest on credit and charge cards
Interest (in general)
Charitable contributions
Casualty and theft losses
Miscellaneous expenses:
      Union dues
      Professional dues and subscriptions
      Certain educational expenses
      Tax return preparation fee
      Investment counsel fees

*Zero Bracket Amount.* The zero bracket amount is a specified amount set by Congress which is dependent on the filing status of the taxpayer.[6] The effect of the zero bracket amount is to exempt a taxpayer's income, up to the specified amount, from Federal income tax liability.

| Filing Status | Zero Bracket Amount[7] |
| --- | --- |
| Single | $ 2,300 |
| Married, filing jointly | 3,400 |
| Surviving spouse[8] | 3,400 |
| Head of household | 2,300 |
| Married, filing separately | 1,700 |

*Excess Itemized Deductions.* Taxpayers are allowed to deduct itemized deductions in excess of the zero bracket amount (see Example 3). Taxpayers whose itemized deductions are less than the zero bracket amount will compute their tax using the zero bracket amount rather than itemizing (see Example 4).

*Exemptions.* Exemptions of $1,000 each are allowed for the taxpayer, the taxpayer's spouse, and for each dependent of the taxpayer. Additional exemptions are allowed taxpayers and their spouses who are age 65 or older and/or blind.

## APPLICATION OF THE TAX FORMULA

The tax formula shown in Figure I is illustrated in the following example.

**Example 1.** J, age 25, is single and has no dependents. She is a high school teacher and earned a $16,000 salary in 1983. Her other income consisted of a $1,000 prize won in a sweepstakes contest she had entered and $500 interest on municipal bonds

---

**6.** Filing status is discussed in a later section of this chapter.

**7.** § 63(d).

**8.** This filing status is described on the tax return as "Qualifying widow(er) with dependent child," but is commonly referred to as "surviving spouse" status.

received as a graduation gift in 1980. During 1983 she incurred deductible travel expenses of $100 while attending the annual state teacher's convention. Her itemized deductions, which consisted mostly of interest on the mortgage on her condominium, were $2,750. J's taxable income for 1983 would be computed as follows:

| | | |
|---|---:|---:|
| Income (broadly conceived): | | |
| Salary | | $ 16,000 |
| Prize | | 1,000 |
| Interest on municipal bonds | | 500 |
| | | $ 17,500 |
| Less: Exclusion— | | |
| Interest on municipal bonds | | 500 |
| Gross income | | $ 17,000 |
| Less: Deduction *for* adjusted gross income— | | |
| Travel expenses | | 100 |
| Adjusted gross income | | $ 16,900 |
| Less: Excess itemized deductions— | | |
| Total itemized deductions | $ 2,750 | |
| Minus: Zero bracket amount | 2,300 | 450 |
| Personal and dependency exemptions | | |
| (1 × $1,000) | | 1,000 |
| Taxable income | | $ 15,450 |

The structure of the individual income tax return (Form 1040, Form 1040A or Form 1040EZ) differs somewhat from the tax formula illustrated above. On the tax return, gross income generally is the starting point in computing taxable income. Exclusions, with few exceptions, are not reported on the tax return at all. Examples of these exceptions which are reported on the tax return are the exclusions for dividends and for disability income (see Form 1040 in Appendix B).

## ZERO BRACKET AMOUNT

*General Rule.* As a general rule, taxpayers compute their taxable income using the full zero bracket amount. If itemized deductions exceed the zero bracket amount, taxable income is computed as shown in Example 2.

**Example 2.** H and W are married taxpayers who file a joint return. They have itemized deductions of $5,000 and four personal and dependency exemptions. Assuming they have adjusted gross income of $20,000, their taxable income is computed as follows:

| | | |
|---|---:|---:|
| Adjusted gross income[9] | | $ 20,000 |
| Less:   Excess itemized deductions— | | |
|      Total itemized deductions | $ 5,000 | |
|      Minus:   Zero bracket amount | 3,400 | 1,600 |
|    Personal and dependency exemptions | | |
|      (4 × $1,000) | | 4,000 |
| Taxable income | | $ 14,400 |

If itemized deductions are less than the zero bracket amount, the taxpayer will compute taxable income using the zero bracket amount rather than itemizing.

**Example 3.** Assume the same facts as in the previous example except that H and W have total itemized deductions of only $3,000.

| | | |
|---|---:|---:|
| Adjusted gross income | | $ 20,000 |
| Less:   Excess itemized deductions— | | |
|      Total itemized deductions | $ 3,000 | |
|      Minus:   Zero bracket amount | 3,400 | –0–[10] |
|    Personal and dependency exemptions | | |
|      (4 × $1,000) | | 4,000 |
| Taxable income | | $ 16,000 |

*Structure of the Tax Table and Rate Schedules.* To fully understand the role of the zero bracket amount, it is necessary to understand the structure of the Tax Table and Tax Rate Schedules.[11]

Careful study of the tax formula shows that the zero bracket amount is not subtracted from adjusted gross income in arriving at taxable income. Instead, the zero bracket amount is subtracted from total itemized deductions in computing excess itemized deductions.

If the zero bracket amount is not subtracted in computing taxable income, how does the taxpayer benefit from the zero bracket amount? The answer is that the zero bracket amount is built into the Tax Table and Tax Rate Schedules, which has the effect of exempting the taxpayer's income, up to the specified zero bracket amount, from Federal income tax liability.

---

**9.** For convenience, adjusted gross income is used as the starting point in this and certain other examples throughout the text. Adjusted gross income is computed as shown in Figure I.

**10.** Since the taxpayer's total itemized deductions are less than the zero bracket amount, the taxpayer will not itemize. Thus, taxable income equals adjusted gross income minus exemptions.

**11.** Individuals must compute their tax using either the Tax Table or the Tax Rate Schedules. Procedures for using the Tax Table and Tax Rate Schedules are discussed under TAX DETERMINATION later in this chapter. Some taxpayers are eligible to compute their tax using a special method, income averaging (see Chapter 11).

**Example 4.** R, age 20, is single and has no dependents. In 1982, he earned $3,300. R has no itemized deductions, so his taxable income is $2,300 (i. e., gross income of $3,300 minus R's $1,000 personal exemption). Examination of the Tax Table in Appendix A confirms that R's tax liability is $0.

In the past, Congress has attempted to set the tax-free amount (represented by the zero bracket amount) approximately equal to an estimated poverty level,[12] although it has not always been consistent in doing so.

Through the personal exemption, Congress has exempted an additional $1,000 of income for every taxpayer. The combined effect of the zero bracket amount and the personal exemption is demonstrated in the previous example.

## UNUSED ZERO BRACKET AMOUNT

The following taxpayers are ineligible to use the full zero bracket amount and are required to make a special computation which might result in an *unused zero bracket amount:*[13]

—A married individual filing a separate return where either spouse itemizes deductions.

—A nonresident alien.

—A U. S. citizen who is entitled to exemption under § 931 for income from U. S. possessions.

—A dependent child who is either under 19 or a full-time student, who may be claimed as a dependent on his or her parents' return, and who has unearned income of $1,000 or more (e. g., dividends or interest).

The special computation is required because of the structure of the Tax Table and Tax Rate Schedules. For various reasons, Congress has chosen to limit the zero bracket amount for the taxpayers listed above. Because the Tax Table and Tax Rate Schedules have the full zero bracket amount built in, the portion of the zero bracket amount not allowed must be added to adjusted gross income in arriving at taxable income. The portion of the zero bracket amount which is disallowed is called the unused zero bracket amount. Two situations which require the special computation limiting the zero bracket amount are discussed in the following two sections.

---

**12.** S.Rep.No.92–437, 92nd Cong., 1st Sess., 1971, p. 54. Another purpose of the zero bracket amount was discussed in Chapter 1 under the heading of "Administrative Feasibility." The size of the zero bracket amount has a direct bearing on the number of taxpayers who are in a position to itemize excess deductions *from* adjusted gross income. A reduction of the number of such taxpayers, in turn, requires less audit effort on the part of the IRS.

**13.** § 63(e).

*Dependent Child.* The zero bracket is limited for a child who may be claimed as a dependent[14] on his or her parents' tax return and who has unearned income of $1,000 or more.[15] The unused zero bracket amount in this case is equal to the child's zero bracket amount[16] minus the greater of the child's itemized deductions or the child's earned income. Earned income includes salaries, wages, and other forms of compensation. Unearned income includes dividends, interest, and distributions from trusts established for the benefit of the child.

**Example 5.** K is a full-time student who is supported by her parents and is claimed by them as a dependent on their tax return for 1983. K earned $1,800 from a part-time job and has dividend income of $1,200 (after the $100 dividend exclusion). K's itemized deductions amounted to $600. Her taxable income would be computed as follows:

| | | |
|---|---:|---:|
| Adjusted gross income ($1,800 + $1,200) | | $ 3,000 |
| Plus:   Unused zero bracket amount— | | |
|       Zero bracket amount | $ 2,300 | |
|         Minus:   The greater of— | | |
|             Itemized deductions ($600) or | | |
|             Earned income ($1,800) | 1,800 | 500 |
| Total | | $ 3,500 |
| Less:   Personal and dependency exemptions | | |
|             (1 × $1,000) | | 1,000 |
| Taxable income | | $ 2,500 |

The unused zero bracket amount computation is not required if the dependent child has itemized deductions or earned income in excess of his or her zero bracket amount. In such case, the child's taxable income is computed according to the tax formula in Figure I.

Example 5 shows that the zero bracket amount of a dependent child who does not itemize will be limited to the amount of earned income (or itemized deductions, if greater). If it were not for this limitation, up to $3,300 of income could be shifted tax-free from a parent to a child.

**Example 6.** G is a wealthy taxpayer who is in the 50% marginal tax bracket. (The highest rate of tax paid by a taxpayer is referred to as his or her marginal tax rate.) In an attempt to reduce his income tax, G transfers cash to a savings account in the name of S, his son. The bank pays interest of $3,300 to S in 1982. G fully supports S, age 6, and claims S as a dependent on

---

**14.**   The requirements for claiming a child as a dependent are discussed later in this chapter.

**15.**   § 63(e)(1)(D).

**16.**   A dependent child's zero bracket amount is $2,300 if single or $1,700 if married filing a separate return.

his tax return. Will the $3,300 be tax-free to S? The answer is *no*, because S must compute an unused zero bracket amount in arriving at taxable income. Assuming S has no itemized deductions and no earned income, taxable income for 1982 is computed as follows:

| | | | |
|---|---|---|---|
| Adjusted gross income | | | $ 3,300 |
| Plus: Unused zero bracket amount— | | | |
|     Zero bracket amount | | $ 2,300 | |
|       Minus: The greater of— | | | |
|           Itemized deductions ($0) or | | | |
|           Earned income ($0) | | –0– | 2,300 |
| Total income | | | $ 5,600 |
| Less: Personal and dependency exemptions | | | |
|       (1 × $1,000) | | | 1,000 |
| Taxable income | | | $ 4,600 |

The Tax Table in Appendix A shows that the tax on S's income is $308.[17]

*Married Taxpayers Filing Separately.*  The unused zero bracket amount computation also is required of a married taxpayer filing a separate return when either spouse itemizes deductions.[18] The unused zero bracket amount is equal to that portion of the zero bracket amount that exceeds the taxpayer's itemized deductions.[19] This computation differs from the unused zero bracket amount computation of a dependent child in that earned income is of no significance in computing the unused zero bracket amount.

> **Example 7.** H and W are married individuals who file separate returns. H itemizes deductions on his separate return. W's adjusted gross income is $15,000, and she has itemized deductions of $1,400. W's taxable income would be computed as follows:
>
> | | | |
> |---|---|---|
> | Adjusted gross income | | $ 15,000 |
> | Plus: Unused zero bracket amount— | | |
> |     Zero bracket amount | $ 1,700 | |
> |       Minus: Itemized deductions | 1,400 | 300 |
> | Total | | $ 15,300 |
> | Less: Personal and dependency exemptions | | |
> |       (1 × $1,000) | | 1,000 |
> | Taxable income | | $ 14,300 |

The unused zero bracket amount must be added to adjusted gross income, since the zero bracket amount of $1,700 is built into the

---

17. A dependent child who is claimed as an exemption on his or her parents' tax return is also allowed to claim an exemption on his or her own return. See discussion later in this chapter.
18. § 63(e)(1)(A).
19. § 63(e)(2).

Tax Table and W is required to itemize her deductions of $1,400 rather than make use of the zero bracket amount. This computation is designed to prevent the double benefit which would result if one spouse were allowed to itemize all deductions of the family while the other spouse used the zero bracket amount.

If the itemized deductions of a married taxpayer filing separately exceed the zero bracket amount, there is no unused zero bracket amount. Instead, taxable income is computed as shown in the tax formula in Figure I.

# PERSONAL AND DEPENDENCY EXEMPTIONS

The use of exemptions in the tax system is based in part on the concept that a taxpayer with a small amount of income should be exempt from income taxation. Every individual taxpayer is allowed an exemption which frees $1,000 of income from tax. A broader justification for the use of exemptions is the wherewithal to pay concept. Thus, even larger amounts of income are freed from tax by allowing exemptions for dependents of the taxpayer and additional exemptions if the taxpayer or the taxpayer's spouse is age 65 or over, blind, or both.

## PERSONAL EXEMPTIONS

The Code provides a $1,000 personal exemption for the taxpayer and an additional $1,000 exemption for the spouse if a joint return is filed.[20] However, when separate returns are filed, a married taxpayer cannot claim a $1,000 exemption for his or her spouse unless the spouse has no gross income and is not claimed as the dependent of another taxpayer.

The determination of marital status generally is made at the end of the taxable year except when a spouse dies during the year. If spouses enter into a legal separation under a decree of divorce or separate maintenance prior to the end of the year, they are considered to be unmarried at the end of the taxable year.

**Example 8.** The effect of death or divorce upon marital status is illustrated below:

|  | | Marital Status for 19X1 |
|---|---|---|
| 1. | W is the widow of H who dies on January 3, 19X1. | They are considered to be married for purposes of filing the 19X1 return. |
| 2. | W and H entered into a divorce decree which is effective on December 31, 19X1. | They are considered to be unmarried for purposes of filing the 19X1 return. |

---

**20.**  § 151(b). For several years prior to 1979 the personal and dependency exemptions were $750.

In addition to the regular $1,000 exemptions for a taxpayer and his spouse, additional exemptions are permitted if either has attained the age of 65 prior to the end of the year and/or if either is blind.[21]

**Example 9.** The exemptions available to H and W (married and filing a joint return) are illustrated below:

|  | Regular Exemptions | Additional Exemptions |
|---|---|---|
| —H and W are married and file a joint return. | $ 2,000 | |
| —H is 66 years old and W is 62. | $ 2,000 | $ 1,000 |
| —H and W file a joint return; W is not totally blind, but she has a doctor's statement that her visual acuity does not exceed 20/200 in her better eye with corrective lenses. She is, however, considered to be blind for purposes of the personal exemptions.[22] | $ 2,000 | $ 1,000 |

Note that personal exemptions for blindness and for age 65 or over are applicable only to the taxpayer and spouse and not to dependents of the taxpayer (e. g., a taxpayer who supports an aged parent cannot claim more than one dependency exemption for the parent).

## DEPENDENCY EXEMPTIONS

The Code also allows an individual to claim a dependency exemption of $1,000 for each eligible dependent. To qualify as a dependent, the following five tests must be met:

—Support.

—Relationship or member of the household.

—Gross income.

—Joint return.

—Citizenship or residency.

*Support Test.* Over one-half of the support of a dependent must be furnished by the taxpayer. Support includes food, shelter, clothing, medical and dental care, education, etc.[23] In testing for the 50 percent requirement, expenditures of nontaxable amounts such as Social Secu-

---

**21.** § § 151(c) and (d). For tax purposes, a person becomes 65 on the day before the 65th birthday. Thus, a taxpayer whose sixty-fifth birthday is January 1, 19X2, is considered to be age 65 for the tax year 19X1.

**22.** § 151(d)(3).

**23.** Reg. § 1.152–1(a)(2). If property or lodging is provided, the amount of support is measured by its fair market value.

rity payments are included.[24] However, a scholarship received by a student is not included for purposes of computing whether the taxpayer furnished more than one-half of the child's support.[25]

> **Example 10.**  H contributed $2,500 (consisting of food, clothing, and medical care) toward the support of his son, S, who earned $1,500 from a part-time job and received a $2,000 scholarship to attend a local university. Assuming that the other dependency tests are met, H may claim S as a dependent, since he has contributed more than one-half of S's support. The $2,000 scholarship is not included as support for purposes of this test.

> **Example 11.**  S contributed $1,000 to his father's support during 1983. His father received $800 in Social Security benefits and $300 of dividend income before deducting the $100 dividend exclusion. All of these amounts were used for his support during the year. Since the Social Security payments expended for support are considered in the determination of whether the support test has been met, S cannot claim his father as a dependent because he has not contributed more than one-half of the total support.

If a dependent does not spend funds which have been received from any source, such unexpended amounts are not counted for purposes of the support test (e. g., Social Security benefits received by the dependent are not considered if such amounts are not spent on items considered "support").[26]

> **Example 12.**  S contributed $3,000 to her father's support during the year. In addition, her father received $2,400 in Social Security benefits, $200 of interest, and wages of $600. The Social Security benefits, interest, and wages were deposited in the father's savings account and were not used for his support. Thus, the Social Security benefits, interest, and wages are not considered as support provided by her father, and S may claim her father as a dependent if the other tests are met.

Capital expenditures such as furniture, appliances, and automobiles, are included in total support if the item does, in fact, constitute support.[27]

> **Example 13.**  F purchased a television set costing $150 for his minor daughter. The television set was placed in the child's bedroom and was used exclusively by her. F should include the cost of the television set in determining the support of his daughter.

---

**24.**  Reg. § 1.152–1(a)(2)(ii).
**25.**  Reg. § 1.152–1(c).
**26.**  Rev.Rul. 57–344, 1957–2 C.B. 112; Rev.Rul. 58–419, 1958–2 C.B. 57.
**27.**  *Your Federal Income Tax,* IRS Publication 17 (Rev. Nov. 82), p. 19.

**Example 14.** F paid $6,000 for an automobile which was titled and registered in his name. F's minor son is permitted to use the automobile equally with F. Since F did not give the automobile to his son, the $6,000 cost is not includible as a support item. However, the out-of-pocket operating expenses for the benefit of the child are includible as support.[28]

One exception to the support test, which is based on the existence of a multiple support agreement, permits one of a group of taxpayers who furnishes more than one-half of the support of a dependent to claim a dependency exemption even when no one person provides more than 50 percent of the support.[29] Any individual who contributed more than 10 percent of the support is entitled to claim the exemption if each person in the group who contributed more than 10 percent files a written consent. This provision frequently enables one of the children of aged dependent parents to claim an exemption when none of the children meets the 50 percent support test. Each person who is a party to the multiple support agreement must meet all other requirements (except the support requirement) for claiming the dependent. A person who does not meet the relationship or member of household requirement, for instance, could not claim the dependency exemption under a multiple support agreement, even though he or she contributed more than 10 percent of the dependent's support.

**Example 15.** M, who resides with her son, received $2,000 from various sources during 19X2; this constituted her entire support for the year. The support was received from the following:

|  | Amount | Percent of Total |
| --- | --- | --- |
| A, a son | $ 960 | 48 |
| B, a son | 200 | 10 |
| C, a daughter | 600 | 30 |
| D, a friend | 240 | 12 |
|  | $ 2,000 | 100 |

If they file a multiple support agreement, either A or C may claim M as a dependent. B may not claim M as a dependent because he did not contribute more than 10 percent of her support, nor would B's consent be required in order for A and C to file a multiple support agreement. D does not meet the relationship or member of household test and therefore cannot be a party to the multiple support agreement. The decision as to who claims M will rest with A and C. It is possible for C to claim M as a dependent even though A furnished more of M's support.

---

28. Ibid.
29. § 152(c).

A second exception to the 50 percent support requirement can occur in the case of children of divorced or separated parents. Special rules have been established to help resolve disputes and uncertainty relative to the dependency status of these children.[30] Generally, the parent having custody of the child for the greater portion of the year is entitled to the dependency exemption. However, the noncustodial parent may be entitled to the dependency exemption in either of the following situations:

—The noncustodial parent contributed at least $600 support for each child claimed as a dependent, and the divorce or separate maintenance decree or a written agreement between the parents provides that the noncustodial parent is to receive the dependency exemption.

—The noncustodial parent provides $1,200 or more support for each child, and the custodial parent cannot clearly establish that he or she provided more than one-half of the total support.[31] In such cases, each parent is entitled to receive an itemized statement of the expenditures made by the other parent.

> **Example 16.** H and W obtain a divorce decree in 19X8. In 19X9, their two children are in the custody of W. H contributed $700 of child support for each child. Absent any written agreement relative to the dependency exemptions, W should be entitled to the exemptions.

> **Example 17.** Assume the same facts as in Example 16 except that H contributed $3,000 of child support for each child and the divorce decree gives the exemptions to H. H is entitled to the two dependency exemptions since his contribution exceeded the $600 minimum.

*Relationship or Member of the Household Test.* The dependent must be either a relative of the taxpayer or a member of the taxpayer's household. The Code contains a detailed listing of the various blood and marriage relationships which are permitted. Note, however, that the relationship test is met if the dependent is a relative of either spouse, and a relationship, once established by marriage, continues regardless of subsequent changes in marital status.

The following individuals may be claimed as dependents of the taxpayer if the other tests for dependency are met.[32]

---

**30.**  § 152(e); Reg. § 1.152–4.

**31.**  § 152(e)(2)(B)(1). Contrast the result reached in *Lynne T. Robinson,* 37 TCM 140, T.C. Memo. 1978–21 with that in *Nancy Boyd Martin,* 37 TCM 202, T.C. Memo. 1978–37.

**32.**  § 152(a). However, under § 152(b)(5) a taxpayer may not claim someone who is a member of his or her household as a dependent if their relationship is in violation of local law. In a recent case, the dependency exemption was denied because the taxpayer's relationship to the person claimed as a dependent constituted "cohabitation," a crime under applicable state law. *Cassius L. Peacock, III,* 37 TCM 177, T.C. Memo. 1978–30.

1. A son or daughter of the taxpayer, or a descendant of either.

2. A stepson or stepdaughter of the taxpayer.

3. A brother, sister, stepbrother, or stepsister of the taxpayer.

4. The father or mother of the taxpayer, or an ancestor of either.

5. A stepfather or stepmother of the taxpayer.

6. A son or daughter of a brother or sister of the taxpayer.

7. A brother or sister of the father or mother of the taxpayer.

8. A son-in-law, daughter-in-law, father-in-law, mother-in-law, brother-in-law, or sister-in-law of the taxpayer.

9. An individual (other than an individual who at any time during the taxable year was the spouse of the taxpayer) who, for the taxable year of the taxpayer, has as his or her principal place of abode the home of the taxpayer and is a member of the taxpayer's household.

The following rules are also prescribed in the Code:

—A legally adopted child is treated as a natural child.

—A foster child qualifies if the child has his or her principal place of abode in the taxpayer's household.

*Gross Income Test.* The dependent's gross income must be less than $1,000 unless the dependent is a child under 19 or a full-time student.[33] A parent who provides over one-half of the support of a child who is under 19 at the end of the year or who is a full-time student may claim a $1,000 dependency exemption for such child. In addition, the child is entitled to claim a personal exemption on his or her own income tax return, if one is filed. A child is defined as a son, stepson, daughter, stepdaughter, adopted son, or adopted daughter and may include a foster child.[34] For the child to qualify as a student for purposes of the dependency exemption, he or she must be a full-time student for at least five months of the year at an educational institution.[35] This exception to the gross income test, for dependent children who are under 19 or full-time students is intended to permit a child or college student to earn money from part-time or summer jobs without penalizing the parent with the loss of the dependency exemption.

*Joint Return Test.* If a dependent is married, the supporting taxpayer (e. g., the father of a married child) is not permitted a dependency exemption if the married individual files a joint return with his or her spouse.[36] An exception to this rule is provided, however, if neither the dependent nor the dependent's spouse is required to file a

---

**33.** § 151(e).

**34.** Reg. § 1.151–3(a).

**35.** Reg. § 1.151–3(b) and (c).

**36.** § 151(e)(2).

return but does so solely to claim a refund of tax withheld (i. e., if the dependent and spouse each had gross income of less than $1,000).[37]

*Citizenship or Residency Test.*  A dependent generally must be either a U. S. citizen or a resident of the U. S. or a country which is contiguous to the U. S.[38]

# TAX DETERMINATION

Most taxpayers will compute their tax using the Tax Table.[39] Those who are not allowed to use the Tax Table will compute their tax using the Tax Rate Schedules.

## TAX TABLE METHOD

Taxpayers who are eligible to use the Tax Table will (1) compute taxable income (as shown in Figure I) and (2) determine their tax by reference to the Tax Table. Since the 1983 Tax Table was not available at the date of publication of this text, the 1982 Tax Table will be used for purposes of illustration in all examples throughout the text in which tax is determined by the Tax Table method. It is expected that the structure of the Tax Table and the method of computing tax will remain in effect in 1983 and future years. However, the Economic Recovery Tax Act of 1981 contains provisions for a 10 percent rate reduction in 1983, so the Tax Table will be revised to reflect this reduction.

> **Example 18.**  J is single and has taxable income of $15,450. She will determine her tax on taxable income of $15,450 using the Tax Table method. J's tax from the 1982 Tax Table (reproduced in Appendix A) is $2,458.

## TAX RATE SCHEDULE METHOD

Certain taxpayers are not eligible to use the Tax Table for computing their tax.[40]

—An estate or trust.

—An individual who uses income averaging (discussed in Chapter 11).

—An individual who files a short period return.

---

**37.**  Rev.Rul. 54–567, 1954–2 C.B. 108; Rev.Rul. 65–34, 1965–1 C.B. 86.

**38.**  § 152(b)(3); *Pir M. Toor,* 36 TCM 1616, T.C. Memo. 1977–399.

**39.**  According to Treasury Department estimates, 96% of individual taxpayers would be able to use the Tax Table introduced in the Tax Reduction and Simplification Act of 1977. This percentage should increase as a result of the provisions in the Economic Recovery Tax Act of 1981 which expand the coverage of the table.

**40.**  § 3(b).

—Those taxpayers whose taxable income exceeds the maximum amounts in the Tax Table. (In 1982, taxpayers with taxable income of $50,000 or more must use the Tax Rate Schedules rather than the Tax Table.)

The 1983 Tax Rate Schedules (reproduced in Appendix A) will be used to illustrate the computation of tax using the Tax Rate Schedule method.

**Example 19.** Z had taxable income of $65,300 in 1983. Because his taxable income is not less than $50,000, Z is not eligible to use the Tax Table. Therefore, he must compute his tax using the Tax Rate Schedule method. Since Z is single and has no dependents, he will use 1983 Tax Rate Schedule X (see Appendix A):

| | |
|---|---:|
| Tax on $55,300 | $ 17,123 |
| Plus:   Tax at 50%* on $10,000 of taxable income in excess of $45,300 | 5,000 |
| Total tax | $ 22,123 |

\* This is the taxpayer's marginal tax rate.

## COMPUTATION OF NET TAXES PAYABLE OR REFUND DUE

The pay-as-you-go feature of the Federal income tax system requires payment of all or part of the taxpayer's income tax liability during the year. These payments take the form of Federal income tax withheld by employers or estimated tax paid by the taxpayer or both. These amounts are applied against the tax from the Tax Table or Tax Rate Schedules to determine whether the taxpayer will get a refund or pay additional tax.

Employers are required to withhold income tax on compensation paid to their employees and to pay this tax over to the government. The employer notifies the employee of the amount of income tax withheld on Form W–2, Wage and Tax Statement. The employee should receive this form by January 31 after the year in which the income tax is withheld.

Estimated tax must be paid by taxpayers who receive income that is not subject to withholding or income from which not enough tax is being withheld. These individuals must file Form 1040–ES, Declaration of Estimated Tax for Individuals, and pay in quarterly installments the income tax and self-employment tax estimated to be due.

In the belief that significant amounts of dividend and interest income go unreported, Congress has enacted provisions requiring withholding (at a 10 percent rate) on certain dividend and interest payments. These new provisions, included in the Tax Equity and Fiscal Responsibility Act (TEFRA) of 1982, take effect for dividends and interest paid after June 30, 1983. See Chapter 11 for a more thorough discussion.

The income tax from the Tax Table or the Tax Rate Schedules is reduced first by the individual's tax credits. There is an important distinction between tax credits and tax deductions. Tax credits reduce the tax liability dollar-for-dollar. Tax deductions reduce taxable income on which the tax liability is based.

> **Example 20.** X is a taxpayer in the 40% marginal tax bracket. As a result of a $100 contribution to the campaign fund of Senator Z, she is entitled to a $50 tax credit for political contributions (see Chapter 8 for details). X also contributed $100 to the American Cancer Society and included this amount in her itemized deductions. The credit for political contributions results in a $50 reduction of X's tax liability for the year. The contribution to the American Cancer Society results in a $40 reduction in X's tax liability ($100 contribution deduction times 40% marginal rate).

Tax credits are discussed in Chapter 8. Some of the more common credits are listed below:

—Credit for contributions to candidates for public office.

—Credit for child and dependent care expenses.

—Credit for the elderly.

—Investment tax credit.

—Foreign tax credit.

—Targeted jobs credit.

—Energy credits for individuals.

Computation of an individual's net tax payable or refund due is illustrated in the following examples.

> **Example 21.** Y, age 30, is a single taxpayer with no dependents. During 1982, Y had the following: taxable income, $21,200; income tax withheld, $3,000; estimated tax payments, $900; and credit for political contributions, $50. X's net tax payable is computed as follows:

| | | |
|---|---:|---:|
| Income tax (from 1982 Tax Table, Appendix A) | | $ 4,132 |
| Less: Tax credits and prepayments— | | |
| Credit for political contributions | $ 50 | |
| Income tax withheld | 3,000 | |
| Estimated tax payments | 900 | 3,950 |
| Net taxes payable or (refund due) | | $ 182 |

> **Example 22.** Assume the same facts as in Example 21 except that income tax withheld was $3,300. X's refund due is computed as follows:

| | | |
|---|---:|---:|
| Income tax | | $ 4,132 |
| Less:  Tax credits and prepayments— | | |
| Credit for political contributions | $    50 | |
| Income tax withheld | 3,300 | |
| Estimated tax payments | 900 | 4,250 |
| Net taxes payable or (refund due) | | $   (118) |

# FILING CONSIDERATIONS

Under the category of filing considerations, the following questions need to be resolved:

—Is the taxpayer required to file an income tax return?

—If so, which form should be used?

—When and how should the return be filed?

—In computing the tax liability, which column of the Tax Table or which Tax Rate Schedule should be used?

The first three of these questions are discussed below under the heading of FILING REQUIREMENTS. The last question is treated under the category of FILING STATUS.

## FILING REQUIREMENTS

An individual must file a tax return if certain minimum amounts of gross income have been received. A self-employed individual with net earnings from a business or profession of $400 or more must file a tax return regardless of the amount of his or her gross income. Also required to file is an individual who receives any advance earned income credit payments (see Chapter 8) from his or her employer during the year. The other filing requirements for 1983 are as follows:[41]

| | |
|---|---:|
| Single (legally separated, divorced, or married and living apart from spouse) and under 65 | $ 3,300 |
| Single (legally separated, divorced, or married and living apart from spouse) and 65 or over | 4,300 |
| Single (can be claimed as a dependent on parents' return) with taxable dividends, interest, or other unearned income of $1,000 or more | 1,000 |
| Qualified surviving spouse [i. e., widow(er) with dependent child] under 65 | 4,400 |
| Qualified surviving spouse [i. e., widow(er) with dependent child] 65 or over | 5,400 |
| Married couple filing jointly, living together at the end of the year (or at date of death of spouse), and both under 65 | 5,400 |
| Married couple filing jointly, living together at the end of the year (or at date of death of spouse), and one spouse 65 or over | 6,400 |

---

41.  § 6012(a).

Married couple filing jointly, living together at
the end of the year (or at date of death of spouse),
and both 65 or over                                              7,400
Married individual filing a separate return              1,000

The filing requirements reflect the zero bracket amount and the allowable personal exemptions (including additional exemptions for taxpayers 65 or older). For example, a single taxpayer under age 65 must file a tax return in 1983 if gross income is $3,300 or greater ($2,300 zero bracket amount plus $1,000 personal exemption).

Even though an individual's gross income is below the required amounts and he or she does not, therefore, owe any tax, it may be necessary to file a return to obtain a tax refund of amounts which have been withheld. A return is also necessary to obtain the benefits of the earned income credit allowed to taxpayers with little or no tax liability. Chapter 8 discusses the earned income credit.

Individual taxpayers file a return on either Form 1040, Form 1040A, or Form 1040EZ. (See Appendix B.) Form 1040A is a short form used by many taxpayers who have uncomplicated situations. An individual may be required to use Form 1040 rather than Form 1040A if:[42]

—Taxable income is $50,000 or more.

—The taxpayer has income other than wages, salaries, tips, unemployment compensation, dividends, or interest.

—The taxpayer claims credits other than credits for political contributions or the earned income credit.

—The taxpayer is required to use the Tax Rate Schedules.

—The taxpayer claims any deduction for adjusted gross income or the disability income exclusion.

—The taxpayer itemizes deductions.

Form 1040EZ, a new form for taxpayers with uncomplicated tax situations, has been introduced for 1982. This form, which has only 11 lines, may be used by taxpayers who are single, have no dependents, and who

—do not claim exemptions for being 65 or over, or for being blind.

—have taxable income of less than $50,000.

—had only wages, salaries, and tips and had interest income of $400 or less.

—had no dividend income.

—had no interest from an All-Savers Certificate.

---

42. *Your Federal Income Tax,* IRS Publication 17 (Rev. Nov. 82), pp. 5–6. *Your Federal Income Tax* lists 23 reasons a taxpayer may not use Form 1040A, including those noted here.

Taxpayers who cannot use Form 1040EZ will use either Form 1040 or Form 1040A.

Tax returns of individuals are due on or before the fifteenth day of the fourth month following the close of the tax year. For the calendar year taxpayer, therefore, the usual filing date is on or before April 15 of the following year.[43] When the due date falls on a Saturday, Sunday, or legal holiday, the last day for filing falls on the next business day. If the return is mailed to the proper address with sufficient postage and is postmarked on or before the due date, it is deemed to be timely filed.

If a taxpayer is unable to file his or her return by the specified due date, a four-month extension of time can be obtained by filing Form 4868, Application for Automatic Extension of Time to File U. S. Individual Income Tax Return.[44] Further extensions of time may be granted by the IRS upon a showing by the taxpayer of good cause. For this purpose, Form 2688, Application for Extension of Time to File U. S. Individual Income Tax Return, should be used. Although obtaining an extension excuses a taxpayer from a penalty for failure to file, it does not insulate against the penalty for failure to pay.[45] If more tax is owed, therefore, the filing of Form 4868 (see above) should be accompanied by an additional remittance to cover the balance due.

The return should be sent or delivered to the Regional Service Center of the IRS for the area where the taxpayer lives.[46]

If it is necessary to file an amended return (e. g., due to a failure to report income or to claim a deduction or tax credit), Form 1040X is filed by individual taxpayers and is generally filed within three years of the filing date of the original return or within two years from the time the tax was paid, whichever is later.[47]

## FILING STATUS

Effective in 1979, the Tax Rate Schedules were widened for all individuals and rate reductions were provided in certain brackets. The Economic Recovery Tax Act of 1981 provided further tax cuts across all brackets, with a reduction of the top rate from 70 percent to 50 percent taking effect in 1982. The Act included a multistage, across-the-board reduction in individual income tax rates, phased in as follows:

---

**43.** § 6072(a).

**44.** Reg. § 1.6081-4.

**45.** For an explanation of these penalties, see Chapter 20.

**46.** The Regional Service Centers and the geographical area each covers can be found in *Your Federal Income Tax,* IRS Publication 17 (Rev. Nov. 82), p. 13.

**47.** See Rev.Rul. 81-269, I.R.B. No. 46, 13 for the date that the period of limitation for assessment of tax will expire when the date prescribed for filing the original return is a Saturday, Sunday, or legal holiday.

| Rate Reduction | Effective Date |
|----------------|-----------------|
| 5% | October 1, 1981 |
| 10% | July 1, 1982 |
| 10% | July 1, 1983 |

These reductions in tax liability are accompanied by a series of with-holding adjustments that will correspond to the rate changes.

The amount of tax will vary considerably depending on which filing status applies. This is illustrated in the following example.

**Example 23.** These amounts of tax appear in the 1982 Tax Table for a taxpayer (or taxpayers in the case of a joint return) with $20,000 of taxable income (see Appendix A).

| Filing Status | Amount of Tax |
|---------------|---------------|
| Single | $ 3,760 |
| Married, filing joint return | $ 2,899 |
| Married, filing separate return | $ 4,607 |
| Head of household | $ 3,469 |

*Rate Schedules and Tax Table for Married Individuals.* The joint return [Tax Rate Schedule Y, Code § 1(a)] was originally enacted to establish equity for married taxpayers in common law states because married taxpayers in community property states are able to split their income. Therefore, under the joint return Tax Rate Schedule, the progressive rates are constructed based on the assumption that income is earned equally by the two spouses. If married individuals elect to file separate returns, both must use a different Tax Rate Schedule [§ 1(d)] which is applied to married taxpayers filing separately. It is generally advantageous for married individuals to file a joint return, since the combined amount of tax is lower. However, special circumstances (e. g., significant medical expenses incurred by one spouse subject to the five percent limitation may warrant the use of the separate-return election. Note also that the Code places some limitations on deductions, credits, etc., when married individuals file separately.

The joint return rates also apply for two years following the death of one spouse providing the surviving spouse maintains a household for a dependent child.[48]

**Example 24.** H dies leaving W with a dependent child. For the year of H's death, W files a joint return with H (presuming the consent of H's executor is obtained). For the next two years, W, as a surviving spouse, may use the joint return rates (i. e., Schedule Y). (Note: In subsequent years, W may use the head-of-household rates if she maintains a household as her home which is the domi-cile of the child.)

---

48. § 2(a).

*Rate Schedules and Tax Table for Unmarried Individuals.* Unmarried individuals who maintain a household for dependents are entitled to use the head-of-household rates.[49] The head-of-household rates are approximately two-thirds of the way (in terms of progression) between the joint return Tax Rate Schedule and the Tax Rate Schedule for unmarried individual taxpayers. As a general rule, to qualify for head-of-household rates, an unmarried taxpayer must maintain a household as his or her home which is the domicile of a relative as defined in § 152(a).[50] Over one-half of the cost of maintaining the household must be furnished by the unmarried taxpayer. However, certain unmarried relatives (i. e., a son, stepson, daughter, stepdaughter, or a descendant of a son or daughter) need not qualify as a dependent of the taxpayer.

> **Example 25.** M maintains a household in which her nondependent, unmarried son and she reside. Since the son is not married, M qualifies for the head-of-household rates (i. e., Tax Rate Schedule Z). (Note: If the son is married, he must qualify as M's dependent in order for M to use the head-of-household rates.)

Head-of-household status also may be claimed if the taxpayer maintains a separate home for his or her parent or parents who also qualify as dependents.[51]

> **Example 26.** S, an unmarried individual, lives in New York City and maintains a household in Detroit for his dependent parents. S may use the favorable head-of-household rates (i. e., Tax Rate Schedule Z) even though his parents do not reside in his New York home.

*Mitigation of the Marriage Penalty.* In 1971, Congress liberalized the rate schedule for single taxpayers (Schedule X) so that the tax paid by a single individual will not exceed 120 percent of the comparable rates for married individuals. Generally, it is advantageous from a tax standpoint to enter into marriage. However, where the former single individuals' incomes are approximately equal, the opposite may be the case (see Example 27).

It is questionable whether Congress considered this result when it liberalized the rates for single individuals. This situation has been offset, in part, by the 1977 changes in the zero bracket amount. The zero bracket amount for single taxpayers is now $2,300; in 1976 the ceiling limitation was $2,400 for such individuals. The zero bracket amount for married individuals filing jointly, however, has been increased to $3,400 from a ceiling of $2,800 in 1976.

The Economic Recovery Tax Act of 1981 provided further relief

---

**49.** § 2(b).
**50.** § 2(b)(1)(A)(i).
**51.** § 2(b)(1)(B).

from this obviously undesirable result by providing a deduction for working couples. This deduction, called the two-earner married couples deduction, is equal to a percentage of the first $30,000 of qualified earnings of the spouse with the lesser earnings.[52] The deduction is available both to couples who claim itemized deductions and to those who do not (i. e., it is a deduction *for* adjusted gross income). The table below summarizes the transitional phase-in of the percentage and the maximum deduction allowed:

| Year | Percentage for Computing Deduction | Maximum Deduction Allowed |
|---|---|---|
| 1982 | 5% | $ 1,500 |
| 1983 and thereafter | 10% | 3,000 |

The deduction will benefit married persons who both work and whose combined income is allocated between them more evenly than 80%:20%. Together with the across-the-board tax rate cut, it is expected that the new deduction will reduce the present marriage penalty by at least 50 percent.

The following examples illustrate the effect of the deduction for two-earner married couples. In Example 27, tax is computed assuming there is no deduction for a married couple filing jointly. Example 28 takes the new two-earner married couples deduction into consideration. The tax in these examples is computed using the 1982 Tax Rate Schedules (see Appendix A).

**Example 27.** The computation of tax for single and married individuals at the same income level is illustrated below. Assume that in 1983 H and W each have gross income of $25,000 with no itemized deductions or deductions *for* adjusted gross income. Also assume that there is no deduction for two-earner married couples.

| | | Tax Liability (Using 1983 Tax Rate Schedules) | |
|---|---|---|---|
| | | If Unmarried | Married Filing Jointly |
| H's taxable income | $ 24,000 | $ 4,509 | |
| W's taxable income | 24,000 | 4,509 | |
| Total | $ 48,000 | $ 9,018 | $ 11,214 |

The marriage penalty without the two-earner married couples deduction is $2,196 (i. e., $11,214 − $9,018).

---

52. § 221. Income items which are not "qualified earnings" are set out in § 221(b)(2)(A).

**Example 28.** Assuming the same facts as in Example 27, under the ERTA provisions, H and W are entitled to a two-earner married couples deduction of $2,500 (i. e., 10% of $25,000). Thus, their taxable income on a joint return is $45,500 [i. e., $50,000 − $2,500 (two-earner married couples deduction) − $2,000 (exemptions)] and their tax is $10,229. The marriage penalty under the ERTA provisions will be reduced to $1,211 (i. e., $10,229 − $9,018). Example 27 shows a marriage penalty of $2,196 without the two-earner married couples deduction. The reduction in the marriage penalty is $985.

## GAINS AND LOSSES FROM PROPERTY TRANSACTIONS—IN GENERAL

Gains and losses from property transactions discussed in detail in Chapters 9 and 10. Because of their importance in the tax system, however, they will be introduced briefly at this point.

On the sale or other disposition of property, gain or loss may result. Such gain or loss has an effect on the income tax position of the party making the sale or other disposition when the *realized* gain or loss is *recognized* for tax purposes. Without realized gain or loss, generally, there can be no recognized gain or loss. The concept of realized gain or loss can be expressed as follows:

Amount realized from the sale

− Adjusted basis of the property

Realized gain or loss

The amount realized is the selling price of the property less any costs of disposition (e. g., brokerage commissions) incurred by the seller. Simply stated, adjusted basis of the property is determined as set forth below:

Cost (or other original basis) at date of acquisition[53]

Add:   Capital additions

Subtract:   Depreciation (if appropriate)[54] and other capital recoveries

Adjusted basis at date of sale or other disposition

All realized gains are recognizable (i. e., taxable) unless some specific provision of the tax law provides otherwise (see Chapter 9 dealing with certain nontaxable exchanges). Realized losses may or

---

**53.**   Cost usually means purchase price plus expenses incident to the acquisition of the property and incurred by the purchaser (e. g., brokerage commissions). For the basis of property acquired by gift or inheritance and other basis rules, see Chapter 9.
**54.**   See Chapter 6.

may not be recognizable (i. e., deductible) for tax purposes, depending on the circumstances involved. Usually, losses realized from the disposition of personal use property (i. e., property neither held for investment nor used in a trade or business) are not recognizable.

**Example 29.** During the current year, T (age 50) sells his personal residence (adjusted basis of $40,000) for $100,000. The proceeds from the sale of the residence are not reinvested in a new principal residence, and T moves into a high-rise apartment.[55] T also sells one of his personal automobiles (adjusted basis of $8,000) for $5,000. T's realized gain of $60,000 from the sale of the personal residence is, under these circumstances, recognizable. On the other hand, the $3,000 realized loss on the sale of the automobile is not recognized and will not provide T with any deductible tax benefit.

Once it has been determined that the disposition of property results in a recognizable gain or loss, the next step is to classify such gain or loss as capital or ordinary. Although ordinary gain is fully taxable and ordinary loss is fully deductible, the same may not hold true for capital gains and capital losses.

# GAINS AND LOSSES FROM PROPERTY TRANSACTIONS— CAPITAL GAINS AND LOSSES

The sale or exchange of capital assets receives special treatment under the income tax law. Preferential long-term capital gain treatment is accorded to the sale or exchange of capital assets which have been held for more than one year. These favorable long-term capital gain provisions are intended to encourage the formation of private capital investment.

## DEFINITION OF A CAPITAL ASSET

Capital assets are defined in the Code as any property held by the taxpayer other than property listed in § 1221. This list includes inventory, accounts receivable, depreciable property or real estate used in a business, etc. Thus, the sale or exchange of assets in these categories usually receives ordinary income or loss treatment. Note, however that the sale or exchange of § 1231 assets (i. e., assets that are not capital assets, such as machinery, equipment, land, and buildings used in business) may result in favorable long-term capital gain treatment under certain circumstances (see Chapter 10).

---

**55.** If T had reinvested the sale proceeds in a new principal residence, the exchange might have been nontaxable due to the application of § 1034. See Chapter 9.

**Example 30.**  C owns a pizza parlor. During 19X1, C sells two automobiles. The first automobile, used as a pizza delivery car, was sold at a loss of $1,000. Because this automobile is an asset used in his business (i. e., a § 1231 asset), C has an ordinary loss deduction of $1,000, rather than a capital loss deduction. The second automobile, which C had owned for two years, was C's personal car. It was sold for a gain of $800. The personal car is a capital asset. Therefore, C has a capital gain of $800.

The principal capital assets held by an individual taxpayer include assets held for personal (as opposed to business) use, such as a personal residence or an automobile, and assets held for investment purposes (e. g., corporate securities and land).

## COMPUTATION OF NET CAPITAL GAINS AND LOSSES

Short-term capital gains and losses (i. e., those on assets held for one year or less) are offset initially, and long-term capital losses are used to offset long-term capital gains. Any net short-term capital losses are used then to offset net long-term capital gains. The same offsetting process is used if a taxpayer has net long-term capital losses and net short-term capital gains.

**Example 31.**  In 1983, T has the following capital gains and losses: short-term losses of $4,000, short-term gains of $3,000, long-term gains of $6,000, and long-term losses of $2,000. T has net short-term capital losses of $1,000 ($4,000 − $3,000) and net long-term capital gains of $4,000 ($6,000 − $2,000). The $1,000 net short-term capital loss is used to offset the $4,000 net long-term capital gain resulting in an excess of net long-term capital gain over net short-term capital loss of $3,000.

## CAPITAL GAINS DEDUCTION AND ALTERNATIVE TAX

Only the amount of net long-term capital gains in excess of net short-term capital losses receives preferential tax treatment. This excess is defined in § 1222 as *net capital gain.* Individuals receive a deduction equal to 60 percent of the net capital gain. Net short-term capital gains are included in gross income in full and do not receive preferential treatment.

**Example 32.**  N has the following capital gains and losses during 1983: long-term gains of $8,000, long-term losses of $3,000, short-term gains of $2,000, and short-term losses of $6,000. The long-term gains and losses are netted, resulting in net long-term capital gain of $5,000 (i. e., $8,000 − $3,000). The short-term gains and losses are netted, resulting in net short-term capital loss of $4,000. The $1,000 of net long-term capital gain in excess of net short-term capital loss (i. e., $5,000 − $4,000) is the *net* *capital gain.* N includes the entire $1,000 in gross income and deducts $600 ($1,000 net capital gain times 60% net capital gain deduction) as a deduction for adjusted gross income.

**Example 33.** During 1983, F had short-term capital gains of $2,500 and short-term capital losses of $1,000. The short-term gains and losses are netted, resulting in net short-term capital gain of $1,500. Net short-term capital gains do not receive preferential treatment (i. e., there is no net capital gain deduction). The entire $1,500 is included in F's gross income.

Under current law, the maximum *effective* tax rate on net capital gain is 20 percent. This effective tax rate is computed by multiplying the 40 percent of net capital gain included in computing taxable income (i. e., 100 percent minus the 60 percent net capital gain deduction) times the 50 percent maximum marginal tax rate for individuals. For taxpayers who are in a tax bracket below 50 percent, the effective rate on net capital gain can be computed by multiplying their marginal rate by 40 percent. For example, a taxpayer in the 30 percent bracket would pay an effective rate of 12 percent (30 percent times the 40 percent net capital gain remaining after the 60 percent deduction). It is apparent why capital gains are so important in an individual's tax planning.

Corporate taxpayers are not eligible for the long-term capital gain deduction. Net capital gains are included in income in full under the regular tax computation. However, a corporation is entitled to compute its tax under an alternative tax computation which effectively subjects net capital gain to a maximum rate of 28 percent (30 percent for years prior to 1979). See Chapter 12 for a discussion of the corporate capital gain tax rules.

## TREATMENT OF CAPITAL LOSSES

Capital losses are first offset against capital gains. If an individual taxpayer has net capital losses, they are deductible as a deduction *for* adjusted gross income, limited to a maximum of $3,000 per year. Any unused amounts are carried over for an indefinite period. Net short-term capital losses are deductible on a dollar-for-dollar basis. However, $2 of net long-term capital loss must be used to obtain a $1 deduction against ordinary income.

**Example 34.** In 19X2, T has $1,000 of net long-term capital losses and $2,000 of net short-term capital losses. T's other income is $100,000. T's capital loss deduction for 19X2 is $2,500, which consists of $2,000 short-term capital loss (deductible in full) and $500 long-term capital loss (½ × $1,000). T's benefit from the long-term capital loss of $1,000 is only $500. The full $1,000 loss is used up, and none is carried forward to 19X3.

When a taxpayer has both short-term and long-term capital losses, the short-term losses must be used first in absorbing the $3,000 limitation.

**Example 35.** R has short-term capital losses of $2,500 and long-term capital losses of $5,000 in 19X2. R's other income is $50,000. R uses the losses as follows:

| | |
|---|---:|
| Short-term loss | $ 2,500 |
| Long-term loss ($1,000 used because of 2-for-1 reduction) | 500 |
| Maximum 19X2 capital loss deduction | $ 3,000 |

The remaining long-term capital loss of $4,000 (i. e., $5,000 loss minus $1,000 used in 19X2) may be carried over for an indefinite period. See Chapter 10 for a detailed discussion of capital loss carryovers.

Corporate taxpayers may offset capital losses only against capital gains. Capital losses in excess of capital gains may not be used to reduce ordinary income of a corporation. A corporation's unused capital losses are subject to a carryback and carryover. Capital losses are initially carried back three years and then carried forward five years to offset capital gains that arise in those years. See Chapter 10 for a discussion of capital losses of individual and corporate taxpayers.

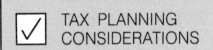 TAX PLANNING CONSIDERATIONS

### SHIFTING INCOME TO LOWER BRACKET FAMILY MEMBERS

The following example illustrates one of the basic principles of income tax planning—shifting of income from high bracket to low bracket family members.

**Example 36.** Referring to Example 6, had G's action resulted in any income tax savings? It has, for two reasons. First, because S is entitled to an exemption on his own tax return, $1,000 of the $3,300 interest income is sheltered from income tax. Second, if G had continued to hold the rental property, he would have paid income tax of 50% on $3,300. Thus, G's tax on this rental income would have been $1,650 (50% of $3,300) compared to $308 of income tax which will be paid by S.

### ALTERNATING BETWEEN ITEMIZED DEDUCTIONS AND THE ZERO BRACKET AMOUNT

When total itemized deductions are approximately equal to the zero bracket amount from year to year, it is possible for cash basis taxpayers, by proper timing of payments, to obtain a deduction for excess itemized deductions in one year and make use of the zero bracket amount in the next year, thereby obtaining a larger benefit over the two-year period than otherwise would be available.

**Example 37.** T, an unmarried cash basis and calendar year taxpayer, qualifies as a head of household for income tax purposes. For tax years 1983 and 1984, T's itemized deductions are as follows:

|  | 1983 | 1984 |
|---|---|---|
| Church contribution | $ 1,200 | $ 1,200 |
| Other itemized deductions | | |
| (e. g., interest, taxes) | 900 | 900 |
| Total itemized deductions | $ 2,100 | $ 2,100 |

As presently structured, in neither year will T be able to benefit from these itemized deductions, since they do not exceed the zero bracket amount applicable to a head of household (i. e., $2,300). Thus, T's benefit for both years totals $4,600 (i. e., $2,300 + $2,300), all based on the zero bracket amount.

**Example 38.** Assume the same facts as in Example 37 except that in late 1983 T prepays the church contribution for 1984. With this change, T's position for both years becomes:

|  | 1983 | 1984 |
|---|---|---|
| Church contribution | $ 2,400 | $ –0– |
| Other itemized deductions | 900 | 900 |
| Total itemized deductions | $ 3,300 | $ 900 |

Under these circumstances, T would claim itemized deductions of $3,300 for 1983 and make use of the zero bracket amount of $2,300 for 1984. A comparison of the total benefit of $5,600 (i. e., $3,300 + $2,300) with the result reached in Example 37 of $4,600 (i. e., $2,300 + $2,300) clearly shows the advantage of this type of planning.

## DEPENDENCY EXEMPTIONS

*The Joint Return Test.* In order for a taxpayer to be able to claim a married person as a dependent, such person must not file a joint return with his or her spouse. If a joint return has been filed, however, the damage might be undone if separate returns are substituted on a timely basis (i. e., on or before the due date of the return).

**Example 39.** While preparing a client's 1983 income tax return on April 10, 1984, the tax practitioner discovered that the client's daughter filed a joint 1983 return with her husband in late January of 1984. Presuming the daughter otherwise qualifies as the client's dependent, the exemption will not be lost if she and her husband file separate returns on or before April 15, 1984.

Keep in mind that the filing of a joint return will not be fatal to the dependency exemption if the parties are filing solely to recover income tax withholdings and neither is required to file a return. In determining whether a return has to be filed, the appropriate test is the one applicable to married persons filing separately (i. e., either spouse has gross income of $1,000 or more). The application of these rules can be interesting when contrasting common law and community property jurisdictions.

**Example 40.** In 1983, T furnished 80% of the support of his son (S) and daughter-in-law (D). During the year, D earned $1,800 from a part-time job, and as a result, D and S filed a joint return in order to obtain a refund of the income tax withheld. All parties reside in New York (a common law state). Presuming the joint return stands (refer to Example 39), T cannot claim either S or D as his dependent. Although D and S filed a joint return to recover D's withholdings, D was required to file (i. e., she had gross income of $1,000 or more).

**Example 41.** Assume the same facts as in Example 40 except that all parties reside in Arizona (a community property state). Under these circumstances, T may claim both S and D as dependents. Not only have they filed a joint return to recover D's withholdings, but neither was required to file. Recall that in a community property state (unless otherwise altered by agreement between spouses, if permitted by state law), half of the wages of a spouse are attributable to the other spouse. Thus, S and D each will be treated as having earned $900, or less than the $1,000 gross income filing requirement for married persons filing separate returns.

*The Gross Income Test.* The exception to the gross income test for a person under the age of 19 or a full-time student applies only to a child of the taxpayer. The term "child" is limited to a son, stepson, daughter, stepdaughter, adopted son, or adopted daughter and may include a foster child.

**Example 42.** Assume the same facts as in Example 40 except that S and D (the son and daughter-in-law) do not file a joint return. Further assume that D (the person who had gross income of $1,800) is a full-time student. Even though T may claim S as a dependent, D does not qualify, since she has gross income of $1,000 or more. The student exception to the gross income test does not apply because D is not a "child" of T.

As was true with Example 41, the residence of the parties in a common law or a community property state can produce different results.

**Example 43.** In 1983, T furnishes 60% of the support of his son (S) and daughter-in-law (D), both over the age of 19. During the year, D earns $3,000 from a part-time job, while S is unemployed and not a full-time student. All parties reside in New Jersey (a common law state). T may claim S as a dependent, but D does not qualify due to the gross income test.

**Example 44.** Assume the same facts as in Example 43 except that all parties reside in Washington (a community property state). T may not claim either S or D as dependents due to the application of the gross income test. Each spouse is treated as having gross income of $1,500 (i. e., one-half of $3,000) which is not below the $1,000 restriction.

*The Support Test.* Adequate records of expenditures for support should be maintained in the event a dependency exemption is questioned on audit by the IRS. The maintenance of adequate records is particularly important in situations involving children of divorced or separated parents and for exemptions arising from multiple support agreements.

It may be desirable to provide in a divorce decree or separation agreement that the noncustodial parent is entitled to the dependency exemption if the noncustodial parent is in a higher tax bracket, because the relative benefits from the dependency exemptions are thereby increased.

*Relationship to the Deduction for Medical Expenses.* Generally, medical expenses are deductible only if they are paid on behalf of the taxpayer, his or her spouse, and their dependents. Since deductibility may rest on dependency status, planning becomes important in arranging multiple support agreements.

**Example 45.** During 1983, M will be supported by her two sons ($S_1$ and $S_2$) and her daughter (D), each to furnish approximately one-third of the required support. If the parties decide that the dependency exemption should be claimed by the daughter under a multiple support agreement, any medical expenses incurred by M should be paid by D.

In planning the decision under a multiple support agreement, one should take into account which of the parties is most likely to exceed the five percent and one percent limitations in effect in 1983 (see

Chapter 7 for further discussion, including explanation of the TEFRA changes in the limitations). In Example 45, for instance, D might be a poor choice if she and her family do not expect to incur many medical and drug expenses of their own.

One exception exists to permit the deduction of medical expenses paid on behalf of someone who is not a spouse or a dependent. If the person could be claimed as a dependent *except* for the gross income or joint return tests, the medical expenses, nevertheless, are deductible.

> **Example 46.** In 1983, T pays for all of the medical expenses of her uncle (U) and her married son (S). U otherwise qualifies as T's dependent except that he had gross income of $1,200. Also, S otherwise qualifies as a dependent except that he filed a joint return with his wife. Even though T may not claim dependency exemptions for U and S, she can claim the medical and drug expenses she paid on their behalf.

## FILING STATUS

When married persons file separate returns, the following unfavorable tax consequences materialize:

—Each spouse is limited to a zero bracket amount of $1,700.

—Both spouses must be consistent in choosing the zero bracket amount or the alternative of itemizing deductions *from* adjusted gross income.

—The highest of all the tax rates relating to individual taxpayers apply.

—The earned income credit and the child care credit (see Chapter 8) are not available.

Section 143(b) mitigates these harsh results by allowing a married taxpayer to be treated as single for income tax purposes if all of the following conditions are satisfied:

1. A separate return is filed.

2. The taxpayer furnished more than one-half of the cost of maintaining his or her home during the year.

3. The other spouse did not live in the home at any time during the year.

4. The home was, for more than six months of the year, the principal residence of the taxpayer's child or stepchild who qualifies as a dependent.

If the last condition is satisfied for the *entire* year, the taxpayer will qualify as a head of household as well. Otherwise, he or she must use the rates applicable to single persons. This provision is commonly referred to as the abandoned spouse rule.

**Example 47.** W's husband left her and their three-year-old son in 1981. She had taxable income of $20,000 in 1982. W met requirements 1 through 4, and in addition, she maintained a household which was the principal residence of the child for the entire taxable year. Therefore, W was eligible to file as a head of household in 1982. Her tax using the 1982 Tax Table is $3,469. If she had not met the abandoned spouse requirements, she would have been required to file as a married person filing separately and her tax would have been $4,607. Filing as a head of household saved W $1,138 ($4,607 − $3,469).

**Example 48.** Assume the same facts as in Example 47 except that the child lived with his father for three months during 1981. Since W met the abandoned spouse requirements, she was eligible to file as a single taxpayer rather than as a married taxpayer filing separately. She did not qualify as a head of household, since the child did not live with her for the *entire* year.

## PROBLEM MATERIALS

### Questions for Class Discussion

1. How is taxable income computed? Describe the components of the tax formula.

2. Explain how certain individuals may reduce their income taxes by making use of the zero bracket amount in one year and itemizing their deductions in another year. (Assume that income earned and itemized deductions incurred are relatively stable during such years.)

3. Why is it necessary for dependent children (who are under 19 or are full-time students) to add back any unused zero bracket amounts to their adjusted gross income in the computation of taxable income?

4. What is the rationale for permitting personal and dependency exemptions?

5. What tests must be met to qualify as a dependent of another person?

6. If an individual who may qualify as a dependent does not spend funds which he or she has earned (e. g., wages or Social Security benefits), are such unexpended amounts included in the support test? Are such amounts included in the gross income test?

7. What is the difference between a personal exemption and a dependency exemption?

8. Why are Social Security payments included as support while scholarships are specifically excluded?

9. Under what circumstances are capital expenditures, which are incurred for the benefit of a dependent, included in the computation of support?

10. Is a dependent son, a full-time student or under 19 years of age, who earns $1,000 or more permitted a personal exemption for himself even though the supporting parent claims a dependency exemption for him?

11. Assuming the same facts as in question 10, would the supporting parent be able to claim a dependency exemption if the child were 19 years old and not attending school on a full-time basis?

12. What is a multiple support agreement? When is it necessary to file such an agreement with the IRS? ( *Page 2-14* ) .

13. Why are special rules relating to dependency exemptions for children of divorced or separated spouses necessary?

14. Under what conditions are individuals ineligible to use the Tax Table?

15. Under certain conditions, a married taxpayer is eligible to file as a single taxpayer. What are these conditions?

16. Are head-of-household rates preferable to the rates for single taxpayers?

17. How was the marriage tax partially rectified by the 1981 changes in the tax law?

18. T and S are engaged to be married. Each has gross income of approximately $20,000 for 1982. Assume that they plan to make use of the zero bracket amount and have no dependency exemptions or tax credits. What is the overall effect on the total Federal income taxes that would be paid if they marry prior to the end of 1982? Use the 1982 Tax Table in your computations.

19. Will married individuals always benefit from using the joint return rate schedules? Why?

20. Is it possible to itemize one's deductions if an individual uses the Tax Table?

21. When is it desirable to file a tax return even though the filing of such return is not required?

22. Under what circumstances is an individual not eligible to file Form 1040A? Form 1040EZ?

23. If an individual fails to claim a deduction or tax credit on a tax return which has previously been filed with the IRS, what remedy is available?

24. During the current year, T has a realized gain of $10,000 and a realized loss of $10,000 from the sale of various properties. Since T figures that losses should offset gains, he plans to report none of these transactions on his Federal income tax return. Do you agree with T's approach? Why or why not?

25. Ten years ago, T purchased a personal residence for $45,000. In the current year, she sells the residence for $150,000. T's friends tell her she has a recognized gain from the sale of $105,000. Do you agree with the friend's comment? Elaborate.

26. Discuss the reasons for according preferential treatment to long-term capital gains.

27. Why is it important to determine whether an asset is an ordinary asset or capital asset?

28. Are corporate taxpayers eligible for the long-term capital gain deduction? Explain.

29. Discuss the tax treatment of an individual who has both net short-term capital gains and net long-term capital gains.

30. If an individual has net long-term capital losses of $1,500 and net short-term capital losses of $1,500, what amount is deductible? Assume the individual has sufficient amounts of other income.

31. If a corporation has net short-term capital losses of $20,000 and net long-term capital gains of $6,000, what amounts are deductible by the corporation? How are any unused losses treated?

32. T and S, two individual and unrelated taxpayers, have the following gains and losses from the sale of capital assets over a two-year period:

|  | T | S |
| --- | --- | --- |
| For tax year 1982— | | |
|   Long-term capital gain | $ 3,000 | $ –0– |
|   Short-term capital loss | 3,000 | 3,000 |
| For tax year 1983— | | |
|   Long-term capital gain | –0– | 3,000 |

Presuming both taxpayers are in the same tax bracket in both years, does one have a better tax position than the other? Why or why not?

33. In early 1983, T, an individual taxpayer, incurred a long-term capital loss of $6,000. In late 1983, he consults you concerning the advisability of selling some securities for a short-term capital gain of $6,000. Since T has heard that short-term capital gains yield ordinary income and do not qualify for the 60% long-term capital gain deduction, he is hesitant about making the sale. What is your advice on this matter?

## Problems

Note: Because the 1983 Tax Table was not available at the date of publication of this text, all problems requiring use of the Tax Table are written for 1982. Problems requiring use of the Tax Rate Schedules are written for 1983. The 1983 Tax Rate Schedules and 1982 Tax Table are reproduced in Appendix A.

34. Compute T's taxable income and tax before credits and prepayments for 1982 under the following circumstances:

(a) T is married and files a joint return with his spouse. They have two dependent children. T and his spouse have adjusted gross income of $15,000 and $3,600 of itemized deductions.

(b) T is unmarried and has no dependents. He has adjusted gross income of $20,000 and itemized deductions of $2,700.

(c) T is a full-time college student who is supported by his parents. He earned $2,100 from a part-time job and had interest income of $600. T's itemized deductions amounted to $500.

(d) T is a full-time college student who is supported by his parents. He earned $1,100 from a part-time job and had interest income of $1,600. T's itemized deductions amounted to $500.

35. Compute T's taxable income and tax before credits and prepayments for 1983 in the following situations:

(a) T is married, files separately, and claims two dependent children. T's adjusted gross income is $60,000, and he claims itemized deductions of $8,700. T's spouse also itemizes her deductions.

(b) Assume the same facts as (a) except that T's itemized deductions are only $1,500.

36. Which of the following individuals will be required to determine his or her income tax from the Tax Rate Schedules rather than from the Tax Table?
    (a) T, single, with no dependents, earned $10,000 and had itemized deductions of $2,400.
    (b) H and W are married and file a joint return. They have eight children whom they claim as dependents. His salary was $76,000 and their itemized deductions were $4,500.
    (c) B, a bachelor, age 36, earned $57,000. His itemized deductions were $6,400. He had no dependents.
    (d) P, single, age 45, earned $58,000 and had itemized deductions of $5,100. She has no dependents. Because of her unusually high earnings, P elects to compute her tax using the income averaging method.

37. Select the appropriate Tax Table or Tax Rate Schedule and compute the tax before prepayments or credits for the taxpayers in parts (a), (b), and (c) of Problem 37. If you choose the Tax Table method, use the 1982 Tax Table. If you select the Tax Rate Schedule method, use the 1983 Tax Rate Schedules.

38. X is single, age 30, and has no dependents. In 1982, X earned $20,000, had deductible employee business expenses of $500, and had itemized deductions of $3,800. Compute X's adjusted gross income, taxable income, and tax before prepayments or credits in 1982.

39. T earned $75,000 in 1983. He had deductible employee business expenses of $2,000 and total itemized deductions of $9,200. Compute T's taxable income and tax before prepayments and credits for 1983.

40. R is a wealthy executive who is in the 50% marginal tax bracket. He is considering transferring title in a duplex he owns to his son, S, age 6. S has no income and is claimed as a dependent by R. Net rental income from the duplex is $3,000 a year, which S will be encouraged to place in a savings account. How much income tax will the family save in 1982 if R transfers title in the duplex to S? Use the 1982 Tax Table.

41. In each of the following independent cases determine the number of personal and dependency exemptions T may claim. Assume any dependency test not mentioned has been met. Unless otherwise specified, T is not married and is not entitled to a personal exemption for old age or blindness.

    Case 1.  T provides 80% of the support of an uncle who does not live with him. The uncle has gross receipts of $1,100 from rental property. Expenses attributable to this income amounting to $200 are paid by the uncle.

    Case 2.  T provides 80% of the support of his nephew (age 17) who lives with him. During the year, the nephew has gross income of $1,000 and is a full-time student.

    Case 3.  Assume the same facts as in Case 2 except that the $1,000 was paid to the nephew as a scholarship.

    Case 4.  T provides over 50% of the support of his son, S, and his son's wife, D. S is a full-time student at a university. During 19X1, D earned

$1,950 on which income taxes were withheld. On January 31, 19X2, D filed a separate return for tax year 19X1. All parties reside in New York.

*Case 5.* Assume the same facts as in Case 4 except that all parties reside in California.

*Case 6.* During 19X1, T gave his father, F (age 68), cash of $1,000 and a used automobile (cost of $2,000). F's total expenditures for food, lodging, and clothing for 19X1 amount to $3,000 ($1,000 received from T and $2,000 withdrawn from F's savings account). F meets the test for blindness, although he possesses an unrestricted driver's license. F dies on June 3, 19X1.

*Case 7.* T and his two brothers each provide 15% of the support of their mother. The mother derives the remainder of her support from a Social Security benefit of $1,300.

42. Determine the correct number of personal and dependency exemptions in each of the following situations:

(a) T, age 66 and disabled, is a widower who maintains a home for his unmarried daughter who is 24 years old. The daughter earned $3,000 and attends college on a part-time basis. T provides more than 50% of her support.

(b) T, a bachelor age 45, provides more than 50 percent of the support of his father, age 70. T's father had gross income of $900 from a part-time job.

(c) T, age 45, is married and has two dependent foster children who live with him and are totally supported by T. One of the foster children, age 14, had $1,100 of gross income. T and his spouse file a joint return.

(d) T, age 67, is married and has a married daughter, age 24. T's daughter attended college on a full-time basis and was supported by T. The daughter filed a joint return with her spouse; and T filed a joint return with his spouse, age 62.

43. Compute the number of personal and dependency exemptions in the following independent situations:

(a) T, a single individual, provides 60% of the support of his mother, age 69. She received $800 in dividend income and $1,500 in Social Security benefits.

(b) T, a married individual filing a joint return, provides 100% of the support of his son, age 21, who is a part-time student. T's son earned $2,000 during the year from part-time employment.

(c) T, who is divorced, provides $2,000 child support for his child who is living with her mother. The divorce decree provides that the non-custodial parent is to receive the dependency exemption.

44. Has T provided more than 50% support in the following situations?

(a) T paid $6,000 for an automobile which was titled in his name. His 19-year-old son uses the automobile approximately 50% of the time while attending a local college on a full-time basis. The son earned $4,000 from a part-time job which was used to pay his college and living expenses. The value of the son's room and board which was provided by T amounted to $1,200.

(b) T contributed $4,000 to his mother's support during the year. His mother received $5,000 in Social Security benefits which were placed in her savings account for future use.

(c) Assume the same facts in (b) except that T's mother used the funds for her support during the year.

45. X, Y, and Z contribute to the support of their father, age 72, who is blind. Their father lives with each of the children for approximately four months during the year. The father's total living costs amounted to $4,000 and consisted of the following:

| | |
|---|---:|
| Pension from a qualified plan | $ 300 |
| Social Security payments | 1,400 |
| Support from X | 1,050 |
| Support from Y | 1,050 |
| Support from Z | 200 |
| | $ 4,000 |

(a) Which, if any, of these individuals may claim the father as a dependent (assume no multiple support agreement is filed)?

(b) If X, Y, and Z file a multiple support agreement, who is entitled to the dependency exemption?

46. Which of the following individuals is required to file a tax return for 1983? Should any of these individuals file a return even if such filing is not required? Why?

(a) T is married and files a joint return with his spouse. Their combined gross income was $6,000.

(b) T is a dependent child under age 19 who received $1,000 in wages from a part-time job and $1,100 of dividend income.

(c) T is single and is 67 years old. His gross income from wages was $4,800.

(d) T is a self-employed single individual with gross income of $12,000 from an unincorporated business. Business expenses amounted to $11,800.

47. Which of the following individuals may use the short Form 1040A?

(a) T's gross income is solely from wages. His taxable income was $70,000 during the year.

(b) T is a self-employed individual whose income was $30,000 from professional services as an accountant. He also received taxable dividends of $2,000.

(c) T earned wages of $14,000 and received $250 interest from a savings account. T itemizes his deductions during the year.

48. Which of the following individuals may use Form 1040EZ?

(a) G, who is single, age 67, had taxable income of $42,000. Her gross income included a salary of $48,000 and interest on a savings account of $350.

(b) S, age 32, is divorced. She had taxable income of $26,000. She contributed $1,500 toward the support of B, her son, who lives with F, her former husband. F contributed $1,000 toward B's support. The divorce decree is silent as to which parent may claim the exemption for B. S will claim the exemption if she is allowed to.

(c) M, age 40, is married to W, who left him two years ago and has not returned. Her whereabouts are unknown. M had taxable income of $31,000, which consisted entirely of salary.

(d) K is single, age 29. She had taxable income of $32,500, which included her salary plus interest of $300. She does not claim any dependents.

49. Can T use Tax Rate Schedule Z (head of household) in 19X3?

(a) T's wife died in 19X2. T maintained a household for his two dependent children during 19X3. Over one-half of the cost of the household was provided by T.

(b) T is unmarried and lives in an apartment. He supported his aged parents who live in a separate home. T provides over one-half of the funds used to maintain his parents' home. T also claimed his parents as dependents, since he provided more than one-half of their support during the year.

(c) T is unmarried and maintains a household (over one-half of the cost) for his 18-year-old married daughter and her husband. His daughter filed a joint return with her husband solely for the purpose of obtaining a refund of income taxes that were withheld.

50. Indicate in each of the following situations which of the Tax Rate Schedules that T should use for calendar year 1983. (Assume that T is not eligible to use the Tax Table.)

(a) T, the mother and sole support of her three minor children, was abandoned by her husband in late 1982.

(b) T is a widower whose wife died in 1982. T furnishes all of the support of his household which includes two dependent children.

(c) T furnishes all of the support of his parents who live in their own home in a different city. T's parents qualify as his dependents. T is not married.

(d) T's household includes an unmarried stepchild, age 18, who has a gross income of $6,000 during the year. T furnishes all of the maintenance of the household. T is not married.

51. G, single with no dependents, was paid a salary of $60,000 in 1983. During the year, he sustained a loss of $4,000 from the sale of stock he had owned for 11 months. The stock paid no dividends in 1983. He also sold land held as an investment for three years for a $7,000 gain. G had itemized deductions of $2,900. For 1983, compute G's

(a) Adjusted gross income.

(b) Taxable income.

(c) Income tax before prepayments and credits.

52. H, single with no dependents, had a short-term capital loss of $2,600 in 1982. He earned a salary of $15,000 and had itemized deductions of $2,100.

(a) Compute H's taxable income for 1982.

(b) Assume the same facts as in (a) except that H also had a $1,400 long-term capital loss in 1982. Compute H's taxable income and capital loss carryforward to 1983.

53.  J, single with no dependents, had a short-term capital gain of $1,000 and a long-term capital gain of $2,000 in 1983. He also earned a salary of $18,000 and had itemized deductions of $2,800. Compute J's taxable income for 1983.

54.  T is a cash basis, calendar year taxpayer. For the years 19X1 and 19X2 he expects adjusted gross income of $20,000 and the following itemized deductions:

|                                   |          |
| --------------------------------- | -------- |
| Church pledge                     | $ 1,200  |
| Interest on home mortgage         | 1,500    |
| Other (sales taxes, etc.)         | 700      |

Assuming the zero bracket amount for each year is $3,400, discuss the tax consequences of the following alternatives:

(a) In 19X2, T pays his church pledge for 19X1 and 19X2 ($1,200 for each year).

(b) T does nothing different (i. e., deductions from adjusted gross income for each year are $3,400).

## Cumulative Problems

55.  J and K, both age 25, are husband and wife. J is a computer programmer and earned $24,000 during 1982. K is a student at State University medical school. They have one child, L, who was born on June 30, 1982. K had taken the summer off from school and returned in the fall. J and K hired a neighbor to care for L during the day from September through December. As a result of the payments made for child care, they are entitled to a tax credit for child and dependent care expenses of $133. J received $10,000 of taxable income from a trust her father had established to pay for her education. In addition, she was awarded a $3,000 scholarship by the medical school in 1982.

In examining their records, you find that J and K are entitled to the following itemized deductions:

|                                                                  |          |
| ---------------------------------------------------------------- | -------- |
| Medical expenses (in excess of 3% of adjusted gross income)      | $   600  |
| State and local income taxes                                     | 550      |
| Real estate taxes on their condominium                           | 1,140    |
| General sales taxes                                              | 260      |
| Interest on mortgage on their condominium                        | 3,100    |
| Charitable contributions                                         | 400      |
| Tax return preparation fee                                       | 100      |
|                                                                  | $ 6,150  |

Income tax withheld by J's employer was $2,600. In addition, J and K made estimated tax payments of $2,200 during 1982.

Compute (a) taxable income and (b) net tax payable or refund due for J and K on a joint return.

56. H and W, husband and wife, file a joint return for the tax year 1983. H, who is 66 years old, is a restaurant manager. W, who is 54, is manager of a beauty shop. During 1983, H and W received the following amounts:

| | |
|---|---:|
| H's salary | $ 32,000 |
| W's salary | 29,000 |
| Bonus from W's employer | 3,000 |
| Net capital gain (excess of net long-term capital gain over net short-term capital loss) on the sale of 50 shares of stock | 10,000 |
| Interest on bonds issued by the City of Chicago | 700 |
| Life insurance proceeds received on the death of H's mother | 50,000 |
| Property inherited from H's mother | 80,000 |

In examining the records of H and W, you find the following items of possible tax consequence (all applicable to 1983):

(a) H attended a convention of restaurant managers in July and incurred $400 travel expenses for which he was not reimbursed by his employer.

(b) H and W subscribe to several professional journals; they paid $140 for these subscriptions.

(c) In April, H and W paid you $100 for preparing their 1982 tax return.

(d) H and W had other itemized deductions, not including any amount mentioned above, of $7,600.

(e) Federal income tax withheld by their employers totaled $11,000; in addition, they made estimated tax payments of $2,100.

(f) H and W are entitled to a political contribution credit of $100 for a contribution they made to the campaign fund of J, a friend of theirs who was elected mayor.

H and W have a son, S, who lived with them during 1983, except for nine months during which he was away at college. S, age 27, is a law student and plans to graduate in 1984. During the summer, S worked and earned $1,100. He used his earnings for school expenses. His parents contributed $2,700 toward his support.

Compute the following amounts for H and W: (a) gross income, (b) adjusted gross income, (c) taxable income, and (d) net tax payable or refund due.

## Tax Form Problems

57. Harold Green, age 41, is married to Joan Green, age 38. They have two dependent children, Anthony, age 15, and Lisa, age 13. The Greens live at 121 Barberry Court, Franklin, Anystate, 02816. Harold is a factory worker and earned $14,200 in 1982. Joan worked part-time as a department store clerk and earned $5,200. Their only other income was $500 interest on a joint savings account. Their employers withheld income tax of $2,228 in 1982. They had itemized deductions of $2,800. Harold and Joan file a joint return. Compute their net tax payable or refund due using Form 1040A. On the form, disregard any blanks for which no information is provided.

58.  Walter Hankins, age 20, is a full-time student at State University. He is single and is claimed as a dependent by his parents, who provided over half of his support. Walter earned $1,500 working part-time at a department store during 1982. In addition, Walter received $1,200 of taxable income from a trust set up by his grandfather to help pay his college expenses. Walter's itemized deductions for 1982 were $700. His adjusted gross income (from Form 1040, line 31) was $2,700. Walter's Social Security number is 111-01-0001. Compute Walter's tax, before prepayments and credits, for 1982, using lines 32a through 37 of Form 1040.

59.  Fred Kennedy, age 40, is married to Irene Kennedy, age 39. They have two dependent children, Deanna, age 14, and Brenda, age 12. During 1982 they had the following items of income:

| | |
|---|---:|
| Fred's salary | $ 14,000 |
| Irene's salary | $ 12,000 |
| Interest on a joint bank account | $     480 |

Fred incurred deductible employee business expenses (reported on Form 2106) of $250. They had excess itemized deductions (from Schedule A, line 41) of $2,630. Fred and Irene are entitled to a credit for contributions to a candidate for public office of $100. Their employers withheld Federal income tax of $2,780 in 1982. Compute the Kennedys' net tax payable or refund due on Form 1040. They file a joint return.

Chapter 3

# Gross Income:
# Concepts and
# Inclusions

Computation of the income tax liability of an individual or a corporation begins with the determination of "gross income." Section 61 provides an all-inclusive definition of gross income: "Gross income means all income from whatever source derived." Section 61 supplements this definition with a list of items (not all-inclusive) which are includible in gross income (e. g., compensation for services, rents, interest, dividends, alimony). Other Code sections contain specific rules for particular types of income.

Congress has provided that certain items are exempt from taxation. These items include interest on certain governmental obligations (state and municipal bonds). The exemptions appear in §§ 101–129 of the Code and are discussed in Chapter 4.

## GROSS INCOME—WHAT IS IT?

### GENERAL DEFINITION

Section 61(a) of the Internal Revenue Code defines the term "gross income" as follows:

> Except as otherwise provided in this subtitle, gross income means all income from whatever source derived.

Since the sweeping scope of the definition is apparent, the Supreme Court has stated:

The starting point in all cases dealing with the question of the scope of what is included in "gross income" begins with the basic premise that the purpose of Congress was to use the full measure of its taxing power.[1]

The § 61 clause, "Except as otherwise provided in this subtitle," refers to sections of the Code in which Congress has exempted certain types of income from the tax base. Such exclusions are discussed in Chapter 4.

## COMPARISON OF ACCOUNTING AND TAXABLE INCOME

Although income tax rules frequently parallel financial accounting measurement concepts, differences do exist. Of major significance, for example, is the fact that unearned (i. e., prepaid) income received by an accrual basis taxpayer is taxed in the year of receipt. For financial accounting purposes, of course, such prepayments are not treated as income until earned.[2] Because of this and other differences, many corporations report financial accounting income which is substantially different from the amounts reported for tax purposes. (See Chapter 12, Reconciliation of Taxable Income and Accounting Income.)

## FORM OF RECEIPT

Gross income is not limited to cash received. "It includes income realized in any form, whether in money, property, or services. Income may be realized [and recognized], therefore, in the form of services, meals, accommodations, stock or other property, as well as in cash."[3]

**Example 1.** An employee realizes income if his or her employer allows him or her to use the company car for vacation. Income realized by the employee is equal to the rental value of a car for the trip.

**Example 2.** A stockholder realizes income (i. e., a constructive dividend) when a corporation sells him or her property for less than its market value. The income is the difference between the market value of the property and the price paid by the stockholder.

**Example 3.** A debtor generally realizes income if debt is discharged for less than the amount due the creditor.

---

1. *James v. U. S.,* 61–1 USTC ¶ 9449, 7 AFTR2d 1361, 81 S.Ct. 1052 (USSC, 1961).
2. Similar differences exist in the deduction area. Goodwill, for example, can be amortized for financial accounting purposes but cannot be deducted under the Federal income tax.
3. Reg. § 1.61–1(a).

## EXCEPTIONS TO THE INCOME REALIZATION DOCTRINE

*Indirect Economic Benefits to Employee.* Over the years the courts have developed an exception to the rule that any economic gain realized by the taxpayer is recognized as taxable income. Benefits received by the employee when the goods or services were actually provided for the convenience of the employer and when the employee had no control over their receipt are not taxable income.

In 1954, Congress enacted § 119 (discussed in Chapter 4), which excludes the value of meals and lodging from the employee's income. Similar reasoning can be applied to indirect economic benefits received by employees in a number of situations not addressed by § 119. For example, the employee has no taxable income from the following:

—An employer requires the employee to attend a convention in Hawaii to perform significant services.

—The employee is required to undergo an annual physical examination, the cost of which is paid by the employer.

—The employer furnishes uniforms that must be worn on the job.

—The employee consumes food and beverages while entertaining a customer, and the expenses are paid by the employer.

—The employer provides the employee with an expensive automobile for visiting customers.

It takes very little imagination to envision various significant nontaxable fringe benefits available to employees. However, the expenditure must serve a business purpose of the employer, other than to compensate the employee, if the benefit is to be considered a tax-free item.

*The Recovery of Capital Doctrine.* The Constitution grants Congress the power to tax "income" but does not define the term. Because the Constitution does not define income, it would seem that Congress could simply tax gross receipts. And while Congress can allow certain deductions, none are constitutionally required. However, the Supreme Court has held that there can be no income subject to tax until the taxpayer has recovered the capital invested.[4]

> . . . We must withdraw from the gross proceeds an amount sufficient to restore the capital value that existed at the commencement of the period under consideration.

In its simplest application, the recovery of capital doctrine means a seller can reduce the gross receipts (i. e., selling price) by the adjusted basis in the property sold.[5] This net amount, in the language of the Code, is gross income. But the doctrine also has subtle implications.

---

**4.** *Doyle v. Mitchell Brothers Co.,* 1 USTC ¶ 17, 1 AFTR 235, 38 S.Ct. 467 (USSC, 1916).

**5.** For a definition of adjusted basis see the Glossary of Tax Terms in Appendix C.

**Example 4.** In 19X3, B paid $5,000 additional taxes because his accountant did not maintain proper documentation of expenses. B's loss was only temporary, because he collected the $5,000 from the accountant after threatening a negligence suit. The $5,000 received from the accountant is not income, because it merely replaces the capital taken by the tax collector as a result of the accountant's negligence. B also lost one day's pay, $100, for time spent at the local office of the IRS protesting the additional taxes. The accountant cheerfully reimbursed B for his loss of wages. The $100 is not a recovery of capital, because no capital was formed until either the income or its substitute (payment from the accountant) was received.

**Example 5.** Z Corporation recovered $150,000 as damages inflicted by a competitor on the goodwill of the corporation. The goodwill was the product of fast and efficient services to its customers, and no cost of the asset was reflected on the corporation's balance sheet. Because the company has no capital invested in its goodwill, the $150,000 is taxable.

**Example 6.** In 19X1, the taxpayer, C, purchased an acre of land for $10,000. In 19X2, Alma Electric Company paid C $1,000 for a permanent easement to run an underground cable across his property. The easement prevents C from making certain uses of his property (e. g., it affected where a house could be located and where trees could be planted), but C can still make some use of the property. The costs of the interests in the property C gave up for the $1,000 cannot be determined; therefore, C may treat the $1,000 as a recovery of his original cost of the property and reduce his basis to $9,000. If C later sells the property for more than $9,000 he will recognize a gain.

In Example 6, the amount received for the easement was treated as a recovery of capital, because the costs of the different interests in the property relinquished could not be determined.

# YEAR OF INCLUSION

## ANNUAL ACCOUNTING PERIOD

The annual accounting period is a basic component of our tax system. All taxable entities may use a calendar year to report income. Those who keep adequate books and records may use a fiscal year (i. e., a period of 12 months ending on the last day of any month other than December) or a 52-53 week year which ends on the same day of the week nearest the last day of the same month each year.[6] A retailer considering a 52–53 week year might choose a year ending in Janu-

---

6. §§ 441(a) and (d).

ary so that he or she can properly account for Christmas returns and on a Saturday so that inventory can be taken on Sunday. Automobile dealers often select a fiscal year ending in September, since the taxable year corresponds with their natural business year (i. e., the change in car models).

Since the lifetime earnings of a taxable entity must be divided into these 12-month intervals and a progressive tax rate schedule must be applied to the taxable income for each interval, it is often of more than just academic interest to determine the period into which a particular item of income is allocated. Determining this period is important because (1) Congress may change the tax rate schedule, (2) the entity's income may rise or fall between years so that placing the income in a particular year may mean that the income is taxed at a different marginal rate, or (3) the entity may undergo a change in its status and a different tax rate schedule may apply (e. g. an individual might marry or a proprietorship may incorporate).

## ACCOUNTING METHODS

The year an item of income is subject to tax often depends upon which acceptable accounting method the taxpayer regularly employs. Most individuals and many businesses use the cash receipts and disbursements method of accounting, whereas most corporations use the accrual method. Section 1.446 of the Regulations requires the accrual method for determining purchases and sales when a taxpayer maintains inventory. Therefore, some businesses employ a hybrid method which reflects a combination of the cash and accrual methods of accounting.

In addition to these overall accounting methods, a taxpayer may choose to spread the gain from the sale of property over the collection periods by electing the installment method of income recognition; contractors may either spread profits from contracts over the periods in which the work is done (the percentage of completion method) or defer all profit until the year in which the project is completed (the completed contract method).

The Commissioner has the power to prescribe the accounting method to be used by the taxpayer. Section 446(b) grants the Commissioner broad powers to determine if the accounting method used clearly reflects income:

> Exceptions—If no method of accounting has been regularly used by the taxpayer, or *if the method used does not clearly reflect income, the computation of taxable income shall be made under such method as, in the opinion of the Secretary or his delegate, does clearly reflect income.*

Also, a change in the method of accounting requires the consent of the Commissioner.[7]

---

7. § 446(e).

*Cash Receipts Method.* Under the cash receipts method, property or services received are included in the taxpayer's gross income in the year of actual or "constructive" receipt by the taxpayer or agent, regardless of whether the income was earned in that year. The receipt of income need not be reduced to cash in the same year; rather, all that is necessary for income recognition is that property or services received have a fair market value—a cash equivalent. Thus, if a cash basis taxpayer receives a note in payment for services, he or she has income in the year of receipt equal to the value of the note. However, a creditor's mere promise to pay (e. g., an account receivable), with no supporting note, is not usually considered to have a fair market value. Thus, the cash basis taxpayer defers income recognition until the account receivable is collected.

> **Example 7.** D, an accountant, reports his income by the cash method. In 19X1, he performed an audit for X and billed the client $5,000 which was collected in 19X2. In 19X1, D also performed an audit for Y, and because of Y's precarious financial position, D required Y to issue an $8,000 secured negotiable note in payment of the fee. The note had a fair market value of $6,000. D collected $8,000 on the note in 19X2. D's gross income for the two years is as follows:

|  | 19X1 | 19X2 |
|---|---|---|
| Fair market value of note received from Y | $ 6,000 | |
| Cash received: | | |
| From Y on account receivable | | $ 5,000 |
| From X on note receivable | | 8,000 |
| Less: Recovery of capital | | (6,000) |
| Total gross income | $ 6,000 | $ 7,000 |

*Accrual Method.* Under accrual accounting, an item is generally included in the gross income for the year in which it is earned, regardless of when the income is collected. The income is earned when (1) all the events have occurred which fix the right to receive such income and (2) the amount thereof can be determined with reasonable accuracy.[8]

Generally, the taxpayer's rights to the income accrue when title to property passes to the buyer or the services are performed for the customer or client.[9] If the rights to the income have accrued but are subject to a potential refund claim (e. g., under a product warranty), the income is reported in the year of sale and a deduction is allowed in subsequent years when actual claims accrue.

---

**8.** Reg. § 1.451–1(a).
**9.** *Lucas v. North Texas Lumber Co.,* 2 USTC ¶ 484, 8 AFTR 10276, 50 S.Ct. 184 (USSC, 1929).

Where the taxpayer's rights to the income are being contested (e. g., a contractor who fails to meet specifications), the year in which the income is subject to tax depends upon whether payment has been received. If payment has not been received, no income is recognized until the claim has been settled; only then is the right to the income established. However, if the payment is received before the dispute is settled, the court-made claim of right doctrine requires the taxpayer to recognize the income in the year of receipt.

**Example 8.** A contractor completed a building in 19X1 and presented a bill to the customer. The customer refused to pay the bill and claimed that the contractor had not met specifications. A settlement with the customer was not reached until 19X2. Assuming the customer had a valid claim, no income would accrue to the contractor until 19X2. If the customer paid for the work and then filed suit for damages, the contractor could not defer the income.

The measure of accrual basis income is generally the amount the taxpayer has a right to receive. Unlike the cash basis, the fair market value of the customer's obligation is irrelevant in measuring accrual basis income.

**Example 9.** Assume the same facts as in Example 7 except D is an accrual basis taxpayer. D must recognize $13,000 ($8,000 + $5,000) income in 19X1, when his rights to the income accrued.

## EXCEPTIONS APPLICABLE TO CASH BASIS TAXPAYERS

*Constructive Receipt.* The doctrine of constructive receipt places certain limits upon the ability of cash basis taxpayers to arbitrarily shift income from one year to another in an effort to minimize total taxes.

A taxpayer who is entitled to receive income made available to him or her cannot "turn his or her back" on it. A taxpayer is not permitted to defer income for December services by refusing to accept payment until January.

Some examples of the application of the constructive receipt doctrine follow:

**Example 10.** A salary check received by T on December 31, 19X8, but after banking hours, was taxable in 19X8. The check was property with a market value.

**Example 11.** T, the controlling shareholder of a corporation, accrued a bonus to himself on December 31, 19X8, but he waited until the following year to have the check written. Since T could control when the payment was to be made, the bonus was constructively received on December 31, 19X8.

**Example 12.** T is a member of a barter club. In 19X1 T performed services for other club members and earned 1,000 points. Each point entitles him to $1 in goods and services sold by other members of the club, and the points can be used at any time. In 19X2, T exchanged his points for a new color TV. T must recognize $1,000 income in 19X1 when the 1,000 points were credited to his account.

**Example 13.** On December 31, 19X8, an employer issued a bonus check to an employee but asked him to hold it for a few days until the company could make deposits to cover the check. The income was not constructively received on December 31, 19X8, since the issuer did not have sufficient funds in its account to pay the debt.

**Example 14.** Interest coupons which have matured and are payable, but which have not been cashed, are constructively received in the taxable year during which the coupons mature, unless it can be shown that there are no funds available for the payment of the interest.

**Example 15.** Interest on bank savings accounts and dividends on savings and loan deposits (treated as interest for tax purposes) are income to the depositor for the tax year when credited to his or her account.

**Example 16.** Dividends on stock are not taxed until the check is received if the corporation, as a regular business policy, mails year-end dividends so that they cannot be received by the shareholder until January.

*Series E and Series EE Bonds.* Certain U. S. Government savings bonds [Series E (before 1980) and Series EE (after 1979)] are issued at a discount and are redeemable for fixed amounts which increase at stated intervals. No interest payments are actually made; rather, the difference between the purchase price and the amount received on redemption is the bondholder's interest income from the investment.

The income from these savings bonds is generally deferred until they are redeemed or mature. There are three maturity dates: the original maturity date (at which time the bond can be redeemed for its face amount), an extended maturity date (at which time the bond can be redeemed for more than its face amount), and a final maturity date (at which time the total interest accumulated must be reported in income unless the bond is exchanged for a new Series HH bond within one year of the final maturity date). As discussed above, no such deferral is available for corporate bonds or savings accounts. The savings bonds may, therefore, be especially attractive to taxpayers who are in high tax brackets but approaching retirement years and expect to be in lower tax brackets. The bonds can be used to shift income to the low bracket years.

The date of *final* maturity will soon come (or has already come) for the earliest issues of Series E bonds (i. e., those issued during the period May 1, 1941, through April 30, 1952). For these bonds, the final maturity date is 40 years after the date of issue. Series E bonds issued after April 30, 1952, and through November 30, 1965, will reach final maturity 30 years after the issue date. Suppose the taxpayer at the time he or she purchased the bonds was overly pessimistic about his or her earnings in the years of final maturity and unaware of the consequences of 30 or 40 years' interest becoming taxable on the date of reckoning (*final* maturity).

> **Example 17.** In May 1944, R purchased Series E bonds with a total face amount of $10,000 at a cost of $7,500. At *final* maturity in 1984, R will receive $32,760 and will have taxable income of $25,260 ($32,760 − $7,500).

Fortunately, the government has provided R a means of further deferring the tax. If these early issue Series E bonds are exchanged *within one year of the final maturity date* for new Series HH bonds, the accumulated interest will be deferred until the Series HH bonds are redeemed, reach final maturity, or otherwise are disposed of. In the meantime, interest is paid at semiannual intervals on the Series HH bonds and must be included in income as received. One important advantage of the rollover of Series E into Series HH bonds is that it allows the taxpayer to choose the year in which to report his or her income from the Series E bonds.

Of course, the deferral feature of government bonds issued at a discount is not an advantage if the investor has insufficient income to be subject to tax as the income accrues. In fact, the deferral may work to the investor's disadvantage if he or she has other income in the year the bonds mature or the bunching of the bond interest into one tax year creates a tax liability. But U. S. Government bonds also have a provision for these investors. A cash basis taxpayer can elect to include in gross income the annual increment in redemption value.[10] The election is frequently useful for minors who have less than enough income to offset their personal exemption and receive the bonds as gifts.

When the election is made to report the income from the bonds on an annual basis, it applies to all such obligations the taxpayer owns at the time of the election and all such securities acquired subsequent to the election. A change in the method of reporting the income from the bonds requires permission of the IRS.

*Crop Insurance Proceeds.* Another exception to the general rules of cash basis accounting is a provision which allows farmers to defer

---

**10.** § 454(a).

the recognition of crop insurance proceeds until the tax year following the year in which the crop was destroyed, if the crop would ordinarily have been sold in the following year.[11] This provision protects the farmer from reporting the income from two years in one tax year.

> **Example 18.** T, a cash basis farmer, completes his harvest in October 19X1 but does not collect the sales proceeds until January 19X2. In March 19X2, T plants a crop which is destroyed in August 19X2. He collects the crop insurance proceeds in September of 19X2. Under the usual applications of accounting, the income from the 19X1 harvest and the 19X2 crop insurance would be reported in 19X2. However, T may elect under § 451(d) to defer the 19X2 income from the insurance until 19X3.

*Amounts Received Under an Obligation to Repay.* The receipt of funds now but with an obligation to make repayment in the future is the essence of borrowing. Because the taxpayer's assets and liabilities increase by the same amount, no income is realized when the borrowed funds are received. Because amounts paid to the taxpayer by mistake and customer deposits are often classified as borrowed funds, receipt of the funds is not a taxable event.

> **Example 19.** A customer erroneously paid a utility bill twice. The utility company does not recognize income from the second payment because it has a liability to the customer.

> **Example 20.** A lessor received a damage deposit from a tenant. No income would be recognized by the lessor prior to forfeiture of the deposit because the lessor has an obligation to repay the deposit if no damage occurs. However, if the deposit is in fact a prepayment of rent, it is taxed in the year of receipt, as discussed below.

## EXCEPTIONS APPLICABLE TO ACCRUAL BASIS TAXPAYERS

*Prepaid Income.* For financial reporting purposes, advance payments received from customers are reflected as prepaid income and as a liability of the seller. However, for tax purposes, the prepaid income often is taxed in the year of receipt. For example, if a tenant pays the January rent in the preceding December, an accrual or cash basis landlord must report the income as earned in December for tax purposes.

Taxpayers have repeatedly argued that deferral of income until it is actually earned properly matches revenues and expenses; moreover, a proper matching of income with the expenses of earning the income is necessary to "clearly reflect" income, as required by the Code. The Commissioner responds that § 446(b) grants him broad

---

11.  § 451(d).

powers to determine whether an accounting method "clearly reflects" income. He further argues that generally accepted financial accounting principles should not dictate tax accounting for prepaid income because of the practical problems of collecting federal revenues. Collection of the tax is simplest in the year the taxpayer receives the payment from the customer or client.

Over a 40-year period of litigation, the Commissioner had less than complete success in the courts. In cases involving prepaid income from services to be performed at the demand of customers (e. g., dance lessons to be taken at any time in a 24-month period), the Commissioner's position has been upheld.[12] In these cases, the taxpayer's argument that deferral of the income was necessary to match the income with expenses was not persuasive, because the taxpayer did not know precisely when each customer would demand services and, thus, when the expenses would be incurred. However, taxpayers have had some success in the courts when the services were performed on a fixed schedule (e. g., a baseball team's season-ticket sales). In some cases involving the sale of goods, taxpayers have successfully argued that the prepayments were mere deposits or in the nature of loans.

Against this background of mixed results in the courts, Congressional intervention, and taxpayers' strong resentment to the IRS's position on prepaid income, in 1971, the IRS modified its rules, as explained below.

*Deferral of Advance Payments for Goods.* Under Reg. § 1.451–5 a taxpayer can elect to defer advance payments for goods under the following conditions:

1. The goods are not on hand on the last day of the year.
2. The amount collected is less than the seller's cost of the goods.
3. The taxpayer's method of accounting for the sale is the same for tax and financial reporting purposes.

The first two conditions would be satisfied in the commonly encountered situation where the buyer makes a partial payment but the seller is out of stock.

*Deferral of Advance Payments for Services.* Revenue Procedure 71–21[13] permits an accrual basis taxpayer to defer advance payments for services to be performed by the end of the tax year following the year of receipt. No deferral is allowed if the taxpayer may be required to perform the services, under the agreement, after the tax year following the year of receipt of the advance payment.

---

12. *Automobile Club of Michigan v. U. S.*, 57–1 USTC ¶ 9593, 50 AFTR 1967, 77 S.Ct. 707 (USSC, 1957); *American Automobile Association v. U. S.*, 61–2 USTC ¶ 9517, 7 AFTR2d 1618, 81 S.Ct. 1727 (USSC, 1961); *Schlude v. Comm.*, 63–1 USTC ¶ 9284, 11 AFTR2d 7517501, 83 S.Ct. 601 (USSC, 1963).
13. 1971–2 C.B. 549.

**Example 21.** X Corporation, an accrual basis taxpayer, sells its services under 12-month, 18-month, and 24-month contracts. The corporation services each customer every month. In April of 19X8, X Corporation sold the following customer contracts:

| Length of Contract | Total Proceeds |
| --- | --- |
| 12 months | $ 6,000 |
| 18 months | 3,600 |
| 24 months | 2,400 |

Fifteen hundred dollars of the $6,000 may be deferred ($3/12 \times \$6,000$), and $1,800 of the $3,600 may be deferred because it will not be earned until 19X9. However, the entire $2,400 received on the 24-month contracts is taxable in the year of receipt, since a part of the income will still be unearned by the end of the tax year following the year of receipt.

Revenue Procedure 71–72 does not apply to prepaid rent, prepaid interest, or amounts received under guarantee or warranty contracts. Thus, the income will still be taxed in the year of receipt if collected before the income is actually earned. However, there is a special condition on the definition of the term "rents":

> "Rent" does not include payments for the use or occupancy of rooms or other space where significant services are also rendered to the occupant . . . .

The effect of the definition is to allow hotels, motels, tourist homes, and convalescent homes to defer the recognition of income under the rules discussed above.

In summary, Revenue Procedure 71–21 will result in conformity of tax and financial accounting in a very limited number of prepaid income cases. It is not apparent why prepaid rents and interest cannot be deferred, why revenues under some service contracts may be spread over two years, and why revenues under longer service contracts must be reported in one year. Revenue Procedure 71–21 will lessen the number of controversies involving prepaid income, but a consistent policy has not yet evolved.

# INCOME SOURCES

## PERSONAL SERVICES

It is a well-established principle of taxation that the income from personal services must be included in the gross income of the person who performs the services. In the case of a child, § 53 specifically provides that amounts earned from his or her personal services must be included in the child's gross income, even though the income is paid to other persons (e. g., the parents).

## INCOME FROM PROPERTY

Income from property (e. g., interest, dividends, rent) must be included in the gross income of the owner of the property. If a father clips interest coupons from bonds shortly before the interest payment date and gives the coupons to his son, the interest will still be taxed to the father.[14] Also, a father who assigns rents from rental property to his son will be taxed on the rent, since he retains ownership of the property.

Who is to pay the tax on income accrued at the time of the transfer of income-producing property, and when does the income accrue? The position of the IRS is that in the case of a gift, interest accrues on a daily basis; but the cash basis donor does not recognize the income until it is collected by the donee.[15]

> **Example 22.** F, a cash basis taxpayer, gave S $10,000 face amount bonds with an 8% stated rate of interest. The gift was made on November 30, and the interest is payable each January 1. When S collects the interest in January, F must recognize $732 interest income (8% × $10,000 × 334/365). The son will recognize $68 interest income ($800 − $732).

When there is a sale of property which has accrued interest, a portion of the selling price is treated as interest and is taxed to the seller in the year of sale.

Dividends, unlike interest, do not accrue on a daily basis because the declaration of the dividend is at the discretion of the board of directors of the corporation. Generally, the dividends are taxed to the person who is entitled to receive them, the stockholder of record as of the corporation's record date.[16] However, the Tax Court has held that a donor does not shift the dividend income to the donee if a gift of stock is made after the date of declaration but before the date of record.[17] The income has sufficiently materialized as of the declaration date to tax the dividend to the donor of the stock.

> **Example 23.** On June 20, 19X1, the board of directors of Z Corporation declares a $10 per share dividend. The dividend is payable on June 30, 19X1, to shareholders of record on June 25, 19X1. As of June 20, 19X1, M owned 200 shares of Z Corporation's stock. On June 21, 19X1, M sold 100 of the shares to N for their fair market value and gave 100 of the shares to S. Assume both N and S are stockholders of record as of June 25, 19X1. N (the purchaser) will be taxed on $1,000, since he is entitled to receive the

---

14. *Helvering v. Horst,* 40–2 USTC ¶ 9787, 24 AFTR 1058, 61 S.Ct. 144 (USSC, 1940).
15. Rev.Rul. 72–312, 1972–1 C.B. 22.
16. Reg. § 1.61–9(c).
17. *M. G. Anton,* 34 T.C. 842 (1960). The record date is the cutoff for determining the shareholders who are entitled to receive the dividend.

dividend. However, M (the donor) will be taxed on the $1,000 received by S (the donee), because the gift was made after the declaration date of the dividend.

## INCOME FROM PARTNERSHIPS, S CORPORATIONS, TRUSTS, AND ESTATES

Each partner must report his or her distributive share of the partnership's income and deductions for the partnership's tax year ending within or with his or her tax year.[18] The income must be reported by each partner as if earned even if such amounts are not actually distributed.

> **Example 24.** T owned a one-half interest in the capital and profits of T & S Company (a partnership). For tax year 19X1, the partnership earned revenue of $150,000 and had operating expenses of $80,000. During the year, T withdrew from his capital account $2,500 per month (for a total of $30,000). For 19X1, T must report $35,000 as his share of the partnership's profits [½ × ($150,000 − $80,000)] even though he received a distribution of only $30,000.

A small business corporation may elect to be taxed as a partnership; thus, the shareholders pay the tax on the corporation's income.[19] The electing corporation is referred to as an "S corporation." Generally, the shareholder reports his or her proportionate share of the corporation's income and deductions for the year, whether or not any distributions are actually made by the corporation.

> **Example 25.** Assume the same facts as in Example 24 except that T & S Company is an S corporation. T's income for the year is his share of the net taxable income earned by the corporation, i. e., $35,000, rather than the amount actually distributed to him.

The beneficiaries of estates and trusts generally are taxed on the income earned by the estates or trusts that is actually distributed or required to be distributed to them.[20] Any of the income not taxed to the beneficiaries is taxable to the estate or trust.

## INCOME IN COMMUNITY PROPERTY STATES

State law in Louisiana, Texas, New Mexico, Arizona, California, Washington, Idaho, and Nevada is based upon a community property system. The basic difference between common law and community property systems centers around the property rights possessed by married persons.

---

18. For a further discussion see Chapter 15.
19. For a further discussion see Chapter 14.
20. §§ 652(a) and 662(a).

Under a community property system, all property is deemed to be either separately owned by the spouse or belonging to the marital community. Property may be held separately by a spouse if it was acquired prior to marriage or received by gift or inheritance following marriage. Otherwise, any property is deemed to be community property. For Federal tax purposes, each spouse is taxable on one-half the income from property belonging to the community.

The laws of Texas, Louisiana, and Idaho distinguish between separate property and the income it produces. In these states, the income from separate property belongs to the community. Accordingly, for Federal income tax purposes, each spouse is taxed on one-half the income. In the remaining community property states, separate property produces separate income that the owner-spouse must report as his or her Federal taxable income.

What appears to be income, however, may really represent a recovery of capital. A return of capital and gain realized on separate property retains its identity as separate property. Items such as nontaxable stock dividends, royalties from mineral interests, and gains and losses from the sale of property take on the same classification as the assets to which they relate.

> **Example 26.** H and W are husband and wife and reside in a community property state. Among other transactions during the year, the following occurred:
>
> —Nontaxable stock dividend received by W on stock that was given to her by her mother after marriage.
>
> —Gain of $10,000 on the sale of unimproved land purchased by H prior to his marriage.
>
> —Oil royalties of $15,000 from a lease W acquired after marriage with her separate funds.
>
> Since the stock dividend was distributed on stock held by W as separate property, it also is her separate property. The same result occurs as to the oil royalties W receives. All of the proceeds from the sale of unimproved land (including the gain of $10,000) are H's separate property.

Income from personal services (e. g., salaries, wages, income from a professional partnership) is generally treated as one-half earned by each spouse in all community property states.

> **Example 27.** H and W are married but file separate returns. H received $25,000 salary and $300 taxable interest on a savings account he established in his name. The deposits to the savings account were made from H's salary earned since the marriage. W collected $2,000 taxable dividends on stock she inherited from her father. W's gross income is compared below under three assumptions as to the state of residency of the couple.

|  | California | Texas | Common Law States |
|---|---|---|---|
| Dividends | $ 2,000 | $ 1,000 | $ 2,000 |
| Salary | 12,500 | 12,500 | –0– |
| Interest | 150 | 150 | –0– |
|  | $ 14,650 | $13,650 | $ 2,000 |

# ITEMS SPECIFICALLY INCLUDED IN GROSS INCOME

The general principles of gross income determination (discussed above) as applied by the IRS and the courts have on occasion yielded results that Congress found unacceptable. Thus, Congress has set forth more specific rules for determining the gross income from certain sources. Some of these special rules are clustered in §§ 66–86 of the Code.

## ALIMONY AND SEPARATE MAINTENANCE PAYMENTS

Alimony payments are taxable to the recipient and deductible by the payor if such payments are periodic payments: (1) made pursuant to a decree of divorce or separate maintenance or (2) made pursuant to a written separation agreement or pursuant to a decree of support.[21] The payments must be in "discharge of a legal obligation arising from the marital or family relationship."

> **Example 28.**  The terms of the divorce decree require H to make monthly alimony payments of $1,000 to W. If H makes a *voluntary* payment of $2,000 per month, the $1,000 excess is neither deductible by H nor includible in W's gross income.

*Property Settlements.*  The divorce decree or separation agreement often includes a division of the property accumulated during marriage as well as a provision to provide for future support. The property division is not considered to be alimony, since a property settlement is a mere redistribution of property rights between the individual spouses. Conversely, payments for future support are in discharge of the husband's legal obligation and therefore qualify as alimony. Despite the fact that property settlements do not qualify as alimony, a transfer of property owned by a husband to his wife (or vice versa) may be a taxable event. If the value of the transferred property exceeds its basis, the transferor (husband) recognizes gain on the exchange.[22]

Often, the settlement provides for a lump-sum payment of a principal amount. Since a lump sum is not a "periodic payment," none of it

---

21.  § 71; § 215 grants the payor a deduction for the periodic alimony paid.
22.  *U. S. v. Davis* 62–2 USTC ¶ 9509, 9 AFTR2d 1625, 82 S.Ct. 1190 (USSC, 1962).

can be considered alimony. However, § 71 specifies that if the principal sum is paid in installments, it will still be treated as alimony provided (1) the principal sum is paid over a period ending more than 10 years from the date of the agreement or (2) the payments are subject to a contingency such as the death of either spouse, remarriage of the recipient, or change in the economic status of either spouse, and the payments are in the nature of alimony or an allowance for support (rather than a property settlement).

> **Example 29.**  The divorce decree provides that H is to pay W a principal sum of $60,000 payable in the amount of $1,000 per month for five years. If W dies before the end of the fifth year, W's estate is to receive the balance of the payments. The payments are not "periodic" and are not income to W or deductible by H.

> **Example 30.**  The separation agreement requires H to pay W a principal sum of $108,000 in the amount of $1,000 per month for nine years or until W's remarriage, whichever occurs first. The payments satisfy H's obligation of support. Since the payments are subject to a contingency and in the nature of a support payment, they are "periodic."

> **Example 31.**  The separation agreement provides that W will receive $1,000 per month for five years in satisfaction of H's obligation of support. The payments are not treated as alimony, since they are neither subject to a contingency nor paid over more than 10 years.

If the installment payments are to extend for more than 10 years, only payment of up to 10 percent of the principal sum can be considered alimony in any one year.

> **Example 32.**  The decree of divorce provides that H is to pay W a principal sum in installments of $15,000 per year for five years and $5,000 per year for the next 10 years. The total amount to be received, $125,000, is considered a principal sum. Therefore, in each of the first five years W must include in income $12,500 (10% of $125,000). W must include the entire $5,000 per year in the sixth through the fifteenth year. Comparable treatment is accorded to H.

*Child Support.*  Amounts expended for the support of a dependent child of the taxpayer represent a nondeductible personal expense, regardless of whether the payments are made in the typical family setting or pursuant to a decree of divorce or a separation agreement. Undoubtedly, the need for funds to support a child must enter into the bargaining between a husband and wife contemplating divorce or separation. The Supreme Court has held that unless the decree or agreement specifically provides for child support payments, none of the payments actually made will be regarded as such.[23] Therefore, the agreement should specifically identify the portion of the payment which is for child support.

> **Example 33.**  The divorce agreement provides that H is required to make periodic alimony payments of $500 per month. However, when H's and W's child reaches age 21, marries, or dies (whichever should occur first), the payments will be reduced to $300 per month. W has custody of the child. Although it is reasonable to infer that $200 ($500 − $300) is for child support, because no payments are specified as for child support, the $500 is alimony.

## INCOME FROM ANNUITIES

The tax accounting problem associated with annuities is one of apportioning the amounts received between recovery of capital and income.

> **Example 34.**  In 19X1, T purchased an annuity for $15,000 which he intended as a source of retirement income. In 19X3, when the cash value of the annuity was $17,000, T collected $1,000 on the contract. Is the $1,000 gross income, recovery of capital, or a combination of capital and income?

The statutory solution to this problem depends upon whether the payments began before or after the "annuity starting date" and when the policy was acquired.

*Collections Before the Annuity Starting State.*  Generally, an annuity contract specifies a date on which monthly or annual payments will begin—the "annuity starting date." Often the contract will also allow the annuitant to collect a limited amount before the starting date.

For contracts issued before August 14, 1982, prestarting date collections are treated first as a recovery of capital. Thus, in Example 34, if the $1,000 was received before the starting date, the $1,000 would be a nontaxable recovery of T's investment. For contracts issued after August 13, 1982, the order of distribution is reversed: prestarting date collections are first considered income to the extent of the increase in the cash value of the contract. Thus, the $1,000 prestarting date collection by T in Example 34 would be income if the policy was purchased after August 13, 1982, because the increase in values ($17,000 − $15,000 = $2,000) exceeded the amount received.

The new rules were enacted in 1982 because Congress perceived abuse of the recovery of capital rule. Formerly, although individuals could purchase annuity contracts that guaranteed an annual increase

---

**23.**  *Comm. v. Lester,* 61–1 USTC ¶ 9463, 7 AFTR2d 1445, 81 S.Ct. 1343 (USSC, 1961).

in cash value and withdraw the equivalent of interest on the contract, no income was recognized. This is no longer possible. Moreover, the individual must recognize income from borrowing on the contract (e. g., the individual pledges the contract as security for a loan) as well as from an actual distribution.

*Collections On and After the Annuity Starting Date.* The annuitant can exclude from income (as a recovery of capital) the proportion of each payment that the investment in the contract bears to the expected return under the contract.

The expected return is the annual amount to be paid to the annuitant multiplied by the number of years the payments will be received. The payment period may be fixed, i. e., a "term certain" or based on the life expectancy of the individual, as determined from tables published in the Regulations.[24]

**Example 35.** The taxpayer purchased an annuity from an insurance company for $60,000. He was to receive $500 per month for life, and his life expectancy was 15 years from the annuity starting date. Thus, his expected return is $500 \times 12 \times 15 = $90,000.

$$\frac{\$60,000}{\$90,000} \times \$6,000 = \$4,000$$

The $4,000 is a nontaxable return of capital, and $2,000 is taxable income.

The exclusion ratio remains the same and continues to be applied to annuity payments even if the annuitant outlives his life expectancy. Thus, if in Example 35 the taxpayer lived 20 years after the payments began, he could still exclude two-thirds of each payment from income even though the entire investment was recovered after 15 years. On the other hand, if he lived less than 15 years, the annuitant would have been taxed on some amounts that were actually a return of capital.

## PRIZES AND AWARDS

Under § 74, the fair market value of prizes and awards (other than fellowships and scholarships that are exempted under § 117, to be discussed subsequently) is includible in income. Therefore, TV giveaway prizes, door prizes, and awards from an employer to an employee in recognition of achievement are fully taxable to the recipient.

An exception is provided if the award is received in recognition of religious, charitable, scientific, educational, artistic, literary, or civic achievement. In such cases, the recipient must be selected without

---

24.   § 72(c)(3); Reg. § 1.72–9.

any action on his or her part to enter a contest or proceeding, and the recipient must not be required to render substantial future services as a condition to receiving the prize or award. Awards such as the Nobel and the Pulitzer prizes qualify for the exclusion.

The definition of "artistic" achievement has been narrowly construed by the Courts. Thus, athletes have been unsuccessful in their attempts to exclude from income outstanding player awards as recognition for artistic achievement.

## GROUP-TERM LIFE INSURANCE

Prior to the passage of § 79 in 1964, the premiums paid by employers for group-term life insurance on the life of employees were totally excluded from the employee's income. Some companies took undue advantage of the exclusion by providing large amounts of group-term insurance for executives. Current law, therefore, sanctions an exclusion only for the premiums paid on the first $50,000 of group-term life protection. For each $1,000 of coverage in excess of $50,000, the employee must include the following amounts of premiums paid by the employer in gross income:

*Uniform Premiums for $1,000 of Group-Term*
*Life Insurance Protection*

| Attained Age Last Day of the Employee's Tax Year | Cost Per $1,000 of Protection for One-Month Period |
|---|---|
| Under 30 | 8 cents |
| 30–34 | 10 cents |
| 35–39 | 14 cents |
| 40–44 | 23 cents |
| 45–49 | 40 cents |
| 50–54 | 68 cents |
| 55–59 | $1.10 |
| 60–64 | $1.63 |

**Example 36.** XYZ Corporation has a group-term life insurance policy with coverage equal to the employee's annual salary. Mr. A, age 52, is president of the Corporation and receives an annual salary of $75,000. Mr. A must include $204 in gross income from the insurance protection for the year.

$$\frac{(\$75,000 - \$50,000)}{\$1,000} \times (.68) \times (12 \text{ months}) = \$204$$

Generally, the amount that must be included in income, computed from the preceding table, is much less than the price an individual would pay for the same amount of protection. Thus, even the excess coverage provides some tax-favored income for employees when group-term life coverage in excess of $50,000 is desirable.

The benefits under § 79 are available only to employees. Proprietors and partners are not employees; therefore, the premiums paid on the life of the proprietor or a partner are not deductible by them. In addition, to prevent a company from providing coverage solely to a selected few highly paid officers or shareholders, the Regulations generally require broad scale coverage of employees to satisfy the "group" requirement. For example, shareholder-employees would not constitute a qualified group. If premium coverage were confined solely to this group, the $50,000 exclusion on group-term life insurance coverage for each employee would not apply.

## SOCIAL SECURITY BENEFITS

Beginning in 1984 as much as one half of social security retirement benefits must be included in gross income. Under § 86, the taxable amount of social security benefits is the lesser of:

1.  .50 (social security benefits), or
2.  .50 [modified adjusted gross income + .50 (social security benefits) − base amount]

"Modified adjusted gross income" is, generally, the taxpayer's adjusted gross income from all sources (other than social security), plus the two-earner married couple's deduction and plus any tax exempt interest received. The "base amount" is

—$32,000 for married taxpayers who file a joint return

—$0 for married taxpayers who do not live apart for the entire year but file separate returns

—$25,000 for all other taxpayers

For example, a married couple with adjusted gross income of $40,000, no two-earner deduction, no tax exempt interest and $11,000 of social security benefits must include one-half of the benefits in gross income. This works out as the lesser of 1. or 2. below:

1.  .50($11,000) = $5,500
2.  .50[$40,000 + .50($11,000) − $32,000] = .50 ($13,000) = $6,750

If the couple's adjusted gross income was $15,000 and social security benefits totaled $5,000, none of the benefits would be taxable, since .50[$15,000 + .50($5,000) − $32,000] = $0.

## UNEMPLOYMENT COMPENSATION

In 1978, Congress addressed the unemployment compensation issue and enacted § 85. The section provides that unemployment benefits are taxable only if the recipient's adjusted gross income exceeds certain levels. The taxable portion (i. e., excess unemployment compensation) is computed by the following formula for a single individual:

Taxable portion = 50% × [(Net unemployment benefits* + Adjusted gross income without including benefits + Disability income deducted in arriving at adjusted gross income) − $12,000]

*Net Unemployment Benefits are total benefits received less any overpayments of benefits during the tax year that were paid back during the tax year.

In the case of a married individual filing a joint return, $18,000 is substituted for $12,000 in the preceding formula. If the married individual files a separate return, zero is substituted for $12,000.

**Example 37.** T is a bricklayer. He was unemployed during January and February when a severe cold spell halted construction activities. T received $800 in unemployment benefits, and he and his wife had adjusted gross income of $21,000, before unemployment benefits, for the year. They received no disability income.

Taxable portion = 50% [($800 + $21,000 − $18,000] = $1,900. Since the taxable portion is greater than the unemployment benefits ($1,900 > $800), the taxpayer includes $800 in gross income.

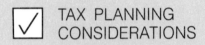

## TAX PLANNING CONSIDERATIONS

The materials in this chapter focused on the all-inclusive concept of gross income. With the exception of the discussion of the employee's indirect benefits of the employer's mandates (e. g., "you must go to the trade show in Hawaii at my expense, you must take clients to nice restaurants at my expense, and you must visit customers in the company's Mercedes"), not much was discussed concerning ways to minimize taxable income. However, a few observations about tax planning can be drawn as to when the income is to be recognized and decisions need to be made concerning who will pay the tax on the income.

### TAX DEFERRAL

Since deferred taxes are tantamount to interest-free loans, the deferral of taxes is a worthy goal of the tax planner. However, the tax planner must also consider the marginal tax rates for the years the income is shifted from and to. For example, a one-year deferral of income from a year in which the taxpayer's marginal rate was 30 percent to a year in which his or her marginal tax rate will be 50 percent would not be advisable if the taxpayer expects to earn less than a 20 percent after-tax return on the deferred tax dollars.

The taxpayer can often defer the recognition of income from appreciated property by postponing the event triggering realization

(i. e., the final closing on a sale or exchange of property). If the taxpayer needs cash, obtaining a loan by using the appreciated property as collateral may be the least costly alternative.

Series E and EE bonds may be purchased for long-term deferrals of income. As was discussed in the chapter, Series E bonds can be exchanged for new Series HH bonds and further postpone the tax. In situations where the taxpayer's goal is merely to shift income one year into the future, bank certificates of deposit are useful tools. If the maturity date is one year or less, the original issue discount does not have to be amortized. Time certificates are especially useful for a taxpayer who realizes an unusually large gain from the sale of property in one year (and thus is in a high marginal tax bracket) but expects his or her income to be less the following year.

The timing of income from services can often be controlled through the use of the cash method of accounting. Although taxpayers are somewhat constrained by the constructive receipt doctrine ("they cannot turn their backs on income"), seldom will customers and clients offer to pay before they are asked. The usual lag between billings and collections (e. g., December's billings collected in January) will result in a continuous deferring of some income until the last year of operations. A salaried individual approaching retirement may contract with his or her employer, before the services are rendered, to receive a portion of compensation in the lower tax bracket retirement years.

Moreover, a cash basis taxpayer has some control over the year in which he or she deducts expenses. At year-end, the taxpayer may pay all outstanding expenses or pay and deduct the expenses in the following year. The choice would be made on the basis of the taxpayer's expected marginal tax brackets in the two years.

In the case of the accrual basis taxpayer who receives advance payments from customers, the transactions should be structured to avoid payment of tax on income prior to the time the income is actually earned. Revenue Procedure 71–21 provides the guidelines for deferring the tax on prepayments for services, and Reg. § 1.451–5 provides the guidelines for deferrals on sales of goods. In addition, with respect to both the cash and accrual basis taxpayer, income can sometimes be deferred by stipulating that the payments are deposits rather than prepaid income. For example, a landlord should require an equivalent damage deposit rather than prepayment of the last month's rent under the lease.

## SHIFTING INCOME TO RELATIVES

The tax liability of a family can be minimized by shifting income from higher- to lower-bracket family members. This can be accomplished through gifts of income-producing property. Furthermore, in many cases, the shifting of income can be accomplished with no negative effect on the family's investment plans.

> **Example 38.** Mr. Brown, who is in the 40% marginal tax bracket, is saving for his eight-year-old child's college education. At his current level of income, he can save $100 per month. If he invests the savings at 16% interest, his after-tax yield is only 9.6% ((1 − .40) × 16%) and he will accumulate $20,000 at the end of 10 years. In contrast, his child can earn up to $1,000 per year with no tax liability; thus, if the savings are given to the child, he can earn 16% after-tax return on the first $1,000 interest each year. By this method, the child's savings will total $29,200 at the end of 10 years.

The Uniform Gifts to Minors Act, a model law adopted by all states (but with some variations among the states), facilitates income shifting. Under the Act, a gift of intangibles (e. g., bank accounts, stocks, bonds, life insurance contracts) can be made to a minor but with an adult serving as custodian. Usually, a parent who makes the gift is also named as custodian. The state laws allow the custodian to sell or redeem and reinvest the principal and to accumulate or distribute the income, practically at the custodian's discretion, provided there is no commingling of the child's income with the parent's property. Thus, the parent can give appreciated securities to the child, and the donor custodian can then sell the securities and reinvest the proceeds, thereby shifting both the gain and annual income to the child.

U. S. Government bonds (Series E and EE) may be purchased by the parent for his or her children. When this is done, the children should file a return and elect to report the income on the accrual basis.

> **Example 39.** F (father) pays $7,500 for Series E bonds and immediately gives them to S (son), who will enter college the same year the bonds originally mature. The bonds have a maturity value of $10,000. S elects to report the annual increment in redemption value as income for each year the bonds are held. The first year the increase is $250, and S includes that amount in his gross income. If S had no other income, no tax will be due on the $250 bond interest, since such amounts will be more than offset by S's personal exemption. The following year, the increment is $260, and S includes this amount in income. Thus, over the life of the bonds, S will include $2,500 in income ($10,000 − $7,500), none of which will result in a tax liability, assuming S has no other income. However, if the election had not been made, S would be required to include $2,500 in income on the bonds in the year of original maturity, if redeemed as planned; and this amount of income might result in a tax liability.

## ACCOUNTING FOR COMMUNITY PROPERTY

The classification of income as community or separate property becomes important when either of two events occurs:

—Husband and wife, married taxpayers, file separate income tax returns for the year.

—Husband and wife obtain a divorce and therefore have to file separate returns for the year (refer to Chapter 2).

For planning purposes, it behooves married persons to keep track of the source of income (i. e., community or separate). To be in a position to do this effectively when income-producing assets are involved, it may be necessary to distinguish between separate and community property.[25]

## EMPLOYEE ANNUITIES

Qualified pension and profit sharing plans often allow employees options for receiving retirement benefits (e. g., payments for life or for a fixed number of years). If the employee has made substantial contributions to the plan, the rule that allows the employee to treat payments first as a return of capital should be factored into the decision.

> **Example 40.** T has contributed $15,000 to his employer's qualified plan. At retirement, T has two options for receiving his benefits and the before-tax present values of the options are the same: (1) $4,400 per year for 15 years or (2) $5,500 per year for 10 years.
>
> The exclusion ratio for alternative (1) is $15,000 \div ($4,400 \times 15$ years) = .2222. Thus, the annual exclusion is $.2222 \times $4,400 = $978$. Under alternative (2), T will recover his cost in the first three years, $3 \times $5,500 = $16,500 > $15,000$. Therefore, the first $15,000 received will be a nontaxable recovery of capital.
>
> Assuming T does not expect his marginal tax rate to increase, alternative (2) should be accepted, because the before-tax present values of the alternatives are the same, the recovery of capital exclusion is used more quickly under (2), and, thus, the tax deferral is greater.

## ALIMONY

The person making the alimony payments favors a divorce settlement which includes provision for deductible alimony payments. On the

---

**25.** Being able to distinguish between separate and community property is crucial to the determination of a property settlement incident to a divorce. It also is vital in the estate tax area (Chapter 18), since the surviving wife's or husband's share of the community property is not included in the gross estate of the deceased spouse.

other hand, the recipient prefers that the payments do not qualify as alimony. If the payor is in a higher tax bracket than the recipient, both parties may benefit, after-tax, by increasing the payments and constructing them so that they qualify as "periodic."

> **Example 41.** H and W are in the process of reaching a divorce agreement. W has asked for $100,000 to be paid in four equal annual installments of $25,000 each. W is in a 30% marginal tax bracket. H, who is in a 50% marginal bracket, agrees on the total amount but would like the agreement to stipulate that the payments cease in the event W remarries before the end of the four years (so that the payments will qualify as alimony). W agrees to accept the remarriage contingency provided she receives $40,000 each year for four years. Under the $25,000 per year alternative. W would have $25,000 per year in nontaxable income at an after-tax cost to H of $25,000 per year. Under the $40,000 per year alternative, she would receive $28,000 [(1 − .30) × $40,000] at an after-tax cost to H of $20,000 [(1 − .50) × $40,000].
>
> The parties should be aware of the potential tax consequences of property transfers at divorce. Generally, if property owned by one spouse is transferred to the other spouse, the transferor must recognize a gain (fair market value less basis).

## PROBLEM MATERIALS

### Questions for Class Discussion

1. Comment on the following formula: Accounting income ± Adjustments = Taxable income.

2. In 19X1, a farmer incurred costs of $2,000 to raise corn with a market value of $3,000. In 19X2 he fed the corn to his hogs and they gained 5,000 pounds. At the end of 19X2 the farmer sold the hogs for $0.75 per pound. When did the farmer realize income from the above?

3. Does a taxpayer realize income when making a gift? no

4. What are some nontaxable fringe benefits an employer can provide employees?

5. Does an attorney realize income upon preparation of a medical doctor's will in exchange for a "free" physical examination? Explain.

6. Does a taxpayer realize income from an award received from the court as the result of a slander suit? Explain. no

7. What are the possible consequences of shifting taxable income from one tax year to the next?

8. Under what conditions must the taxpayer use the accrual method of accounting?

9. Can a taxpayer use the cash method to report interest income and the accrual method to report dividend income? no

10. A corporation pays all of its monthly salaried employees on the last Friday in each month. What would be the tax consequences to the employees if the date of payment were changed to the first Monday of the following month?

11. What are some possible tax advantages from the use of the cash method of accounting?

12. What is the constructive receipt doctrine?

13. When is income that has been received, but which is being contested, subject to tax?

14. What alternatives are available for reporting interest income from Series E or Series EE U. S. Government bonds?

15. Compare the accounting and tax treatment of income collected by an accrual basis taxpayer prior to the time it is earned.

16. The taxpayer is in the wholesale hardware business. His customers pay for the goods at the time they place the order. Often, the taxpayer is out of stock on particular items and must back order the goods. When this occurs, the taxpayer usually retains the customer's payment, orders the goods from the manufacturer, and ships them to the customer within a month. At the end of the year there were several unfilled orders. Is it possible to defer the recognition of income from the receipt of advance payments on the unfilled orders? No- 3 Conditions to be met (Failed 2nd test).

17. F, a cash basis taxpayer, gave bonds to S in 19X1. At the time of the gift, the accrued interest on the bonds was $500 and the interest was payable in 19X2. Does F realize taxable income in 19X1 as a result of the gift?

18. Who pays the tax on dividends when the stock was given away after the date of declaration but prior to the date of record? — owner

19. Who pays the tax on the income of (a) a corporation and (b) an estate?

20. When is it essential for the tax adviser to understand the community property system?

21. Critique this comment. "I was a tax practitioner in Texas for 25 years, so I know community property laws."

22. What are the tax advantages of group-term life insurance?

23. What are the possible income tax consequences of a divorce agreement for the husband and wife if they have minor children?

24. What special tax treatment is afforded an individual who collects on an employee annuity?

25. What conditions must be satisfied for a prize to be excluded from income?

## Problems

26. Determine the taxpayer's income for tax purposes in each of the following cases:

borrowed Money is not income

(a) R borrowed $30,000 from the First National Bank. R was required to deliver to the bank stocks with a value of $30,000 and a cost of $10,000. The stocks were to serve as collateral for the loan.

(b) P owned a lot on Sycamore Street which measured 100 feet by 100 feet. His cost of the lot is $10,000. The City condemned a 10-foot strip

($8,000 basis).    (Casualty loss).

decrease in basis

of the land so that it could widen the street. P received a $2,000 con-
demnation award.          *Recovery of Capital*

(c) M owned land zoned for residential use only. Its cost was $5,000, and it
had a market value of $7,000. M spent $500 and several hundred hours
petitioning the county supervisors to change the zoning to A–1 Commercial. The value of the property immediately increased to $20,000
when the county approved the zoning change.

27.  (a) N had $500 in a savings account which yielded $50 per year interest.
He was paying about $60 per year in service charges on his checking
account. A bank officer told N that the bank has a new plan and if N
maintained at least a $500 balance in his checking account, he would
not have to pay any bank service charges. N transferred $500 from his
savings to his checking account, and as a result, N avoided $65 of
bank service charges. Has N realized taxable income?

(b) M uses the same bank as N, but he normally maintains a checking
account balance in excess of $500. Thus, he did not have to transfer
savings to his checking account to take advantage of the free checking. Has M realized taxable income?

28.  XYZ, Inc. is a dance studio and sells lessons for cash, on open account
and for notes receivable. During 19X1 the company's cash receipts from
customers totaled $150,000:

| | |
|---|---:|
| Cash sales | $ 90,000 |
| Collections on accounts receivable | 35,000 |
| Collections on notes receivable | 25,000 |
| Total cash receipts | $ 150,000 |

The balances in accounts and notes receivable at the beginning and end
of the year were as follows:

| | 1-1-X1 | 12-31-X1 |
|---|---|---|
| Accounts receivable | $ 15,000 | $ 24,000 |
| Notes receivable | 20,000 | 15,000 |

The fair market value of the notes is equal to 80% of their book value. There
were no bad debts for the year and all notes were for services performed
during the year.

Compute the corporation's gross income:

(a) Using the cash basis of accounting.

(b) Using the accrual basis of accounting.

29.  When would a cash basis taxpayer recognize income in each of the following independent situations?

(a) The taxpayer's payroll check is mailed from the home office on December 31 and is delivered to her in a local office on January 3 of the
following year.

(b) The taxpayer, who was entitled to a $10,000 bonus on December 15 of
the current year, asked his employer to place the bonus in an escrow
account on his behalf. The taxpayer would be unable to withdraw the
bonus until age 65 (in 10 years). If the taxpayer dies before age 65, the
$10,000 will be paid to his heirs.

(c) A medical doctor had several Blue Cross claims which, if mailed in by the end of November, would be paid in December. However, he told his office manager not to process the claims until December 1 so that payment would not be received until January of the following year.

30. What would be the tax effects to cash basis employees of the following transactions?

    (a) The employer's computer made an error and printed T two payroll checks for the week ended December 28, 19X1. The checks were automatically deposited to T's bank account on December 29, 19X1. T discovered the error in January 19X2, informed the employer of the mistake, and paid the company the excess amount received.

    (b) On December 31, an employee received a $500 advance for estimated traveling expenses for the following January. The employee actually spent $480 in January and retained the $20 to apply to February expenses.

31. What would be the tax effects of the following transactions on an accrual basis taxpayer?

    (a) On December 15, 19X1, B signed a contract to purchase land from T. Payment for the land was to be made on closing, January 15, 19X2. During the interval between the contract and the closing dates, B's attorney was to verify that T had good title to the land. The closing was completed on January 15, 19X2.

    (b) M collected $1,500 for services rendered the client in 19X1. Late in 19X1 the client complained that the work was not done in accordance with contract specifications. Also in 19X1, the parties agreed to allow an arbitrator to settle the dispute. In January 19X2 the arbitrator ordered M to refund $500 to the client.

32. The XYZ Apartments, an accrual basis taxpayer, requires each new tenant to make a $200 deposit upon signing a lease. If the tenant breaks the lease, the deposit is forfeited. Also, when a tenant moves (upon expiration of the lease), the apartment is inspected and any damages are deducted from the deposit. During the current year, XYZ collected $15,000 in deposits from new tenants, withheld $9,000 for damages and forfeitures from old tenants, and refunded $5,000. What are the effects of these items on XYZ's taxable income? Assume the same facts except the $15,000 collected was for a payment of the last month's rent under the lease. Would the $15,000 be taxable in the year of receipt?

33. T, age 22, recently graduated from college. For several years, he has been reporting as income the annual increment in redemption value of his U. S. Government Series E savings bonds. Now that T is employed full-time and will be in a much higher marginal tax bracket, he would like to defer the income on new Series EE bonds purchased. Can T elect to report the income from new bonds purchased in the years they are redeemed?

34. (a) An automobile dealer has several new cars in inventory but often does not have the right combination of body style, color, and accessories. In some cases, the dealer makes an offer to sell a car at a certain price, accepts a deposit, and then orders the car from the manufacturer. When the car is received from the manufacturer, the sale is closed and the dealer receives the balance of the sales price. At the end of the

current year, the dealer has deposits totaling $8,200 for cars that have not been received from the manufacturer. When is the $8,200 subject to tax?

(b) T Corporation, an exterminating company, is a calendar year taxpayer. It contracts to service homeowners once a month under a one- or two-year contract. On April 1 of the current year, the company sold a customer a one-year contract for $60. How much of the $60 is taxable in the current year if the company is an accrual basis taxpayer? If the $60 is payment on a two-year contract, how much is taxed in the year the contract is sold?

(c) X, an accrual basis taxpayer, owns an amusement park whose fiscal year ends September 30. To increase business during the fall and winter months, X sold passes that would allow the holder to ride "free" during the months of October through March. During the month of September $6,000 was collected from the sale of passes for the upcoming fall and winter. When will the $6,000 be taxable to X?

(d) The taxpayer is in the office equipment rental business and uses the accrual basis of accounting. In December he collected $5,000 in rents for the following January. When is the $5,000 taxable?

35. During 19X3, F makes the following transfers:

| Description of Asset | Nature and Date of Transfer |
|---|---|
| A corporate bond (acquired in 19X2) in the face amount of $20,000 which pays interest of $900 on January 1 and June 30 of each year | Gift to S (F's son) on March 31, 19X3 |
| 100 shares of stock in Z Corporation | Gift to S on October 5, 19X3 |
| 100 shares of stock in Z Corporation (cost of $7,000) | Sale to S for $12,000 on October 5, 19X3 |

On October 1, 19X3, the board of directors of Z Corporation declared a dividend of $1 per share payable on October 15 to shareholders of record as of October 10.

Presuming F and S use the cash method of accounting for tax purposes, how would these transactions affect the gross income of each for 19X3?

36. F is a famous and wealthy entertainer. What would be the tax consequences to F in the following cases:

(a) F's agent contracted for F to perform on a university campus. After the concert, F told the university personnel to make the check payable to the university's scholarship fund.

(b) F agreed to give a concert at the university. The proceeds of the concert were to go to the university's scholarship fund. When F agreed to perform the concert he waived his usual fee.

(c) F fell under deep religious conviction and took a vow of poverty. In the future he would work for the church and receive only meals, lodging, and minimal expense money. The church contracted for all of F's concert performances.

37. T owns 100% of the stock of T, Inc., an S corporation. For 19X1, the corporation earned $100,000 taxable income but paid only $30,000 dividends to T. T is also a beneficiary of a trust. The trustee can distribute or withhold income "according to the needs of the beneficiary." In 19X1, the trust earned $20,000 but distributed only $5,000 to T, because he had adequate income from other sources. What is T's taxable income from the S corporation and trust for 19X1?

38. Mr. and Mrs. X are in the process of negotiating their divorce agreement. What would be the tax consequences to Mr. X and Mrs. X if the following, considered individually, become part of the agreement:

    (a) Mrs. X is to receive $1,000 per month until she dies or remarries. She also is to receive $500 per month for 12 years for her one-half interest in their personal residence. She paid for her one-half interest out of her earnings.

    (b) Mrs. X is to receive a principal sum of $50,000 as part of a property settlement, plus $1,600 per month. The payments will cease if she dies or remarries but will continue for not more than 60 months.

    (c) Mrs. X is to receive a principal sum of $100,000. Of this amount $50,000 is to be paid in the year of the divorce and $5,000 per year will be paid to her in each of the following 10 years.

    (d) Mrs. X is to receive the family residence (value of $120,000 and basis of $75,000). The home was jointly owned by Mr. and Mrs. X. In exchange for the residence, Mrs. X relinquished all of her rights to property accumulated during the marriage. She also is to receive $1,000 per month until her death or remarriage but for a period of not longer than 10 years.

39. Under the terms of their divorce agreement, H is to transfer common stocks (cost of $25,000, market value of $60,000) to W in satisfaction of her property rights. W is also to receive $15,000 per year until her death or remarriage. W originally asked for $9,000 alimony and $5,000 child support. It was the understanding between H and W that she would use $5,000 of the amount received for the support of the children. How will the terms of the agreement affect H's taxable income?

40. T purchased an annuity from an insurance company for $12,000 on Jaunary 1, 19X1. The annuity was to pay him $1,500 per year for life. At the time he purchased the contract his life expectancy was 10 years.

    (a) Determine T's taxable income from the annuity in the first year.

    (b) Assume he lives 20 years after purchasing the contract. What would be T's taxable income in the nineteenth year?

    (c) Same as (a) except the annuity was received from a qualified pension plan and T had contributed $3,000 toward the cost of the annuity.

41. T purchased an annuity for $50,000. Determine the tax consequences of the following transactions under the assumptions stated:

    (a) The contract was purchased in 1981, and monthly payments were to begin in 1985. In 1984, when the cash value of the contract was $55,000, T pledged the annuity as collateral for a $20,000 loan.

    (b) Same as (a) except the annuity contract was purchased in 1983.

42. Indicate whether the following items result in taxable income to the recipient. If the item is not taxable, explain why.

(a) S won the Miss Centerville beauty contest and received a $1,000 cash prize. *yes*

(b) L won the master's mile run. As the winner, L received a $1,000 cash prize paid by a philanthropist who sponsored the race to encourage running. *yes*

(c) C, a part-time student, received a $500 award from his employer for being named to the Dean's list. The employer frequently makes such payments to encourage employees to further their education. *nontaxable*

(d) Mr. and Mrs. D are married and file a joint return. In 19X3, they had adjusted gross income of $19,000 before considering unemployment benefits of $1,800.

43. Mr. Y, a tax accountant, is happily married, but he is not sure he can continue to afford marital bliss. His gross income is approximately $70,000 per year. Itemized deductions total $10,000. His wife has no income, and they have two children in college—his major cause for concern over family finances. Under Y's plan, he and his wife would be divorced. Mrs. Y would receive $25,000 per year in alimony but would continue to live with him. Mr. Y would also have custody of the children. After the children graduate from college, Mr. and Mrs. Y would remarry.

(a) How much income tax would Mr. Y's plan save? (Use the 1983 Tax Rate Schedules in your computations.)

(b) Can you improve upon Mr. Y's plan?

## Cumulative Problem

44. T is single, age 42, and is employed as a plumber. In 1983, T earned wages of $36,000 and a bonus of $2,000 under his employer's incentive plan. He received the bonus check on December 30, 1983, but did not deposit it in his bank account until January 3, 1984. He held the check until January 3, because he did not want to report it as income in 1983.

T's mother, age 68, lives in a small house he bought for her in Florida. She has no income of her own and is totally dependent on T for her support. In order to provide his mother with some spending money, T assigned to her the income from some corporate bonds he owns. The interest received by T's mother was $1,050. T retained ownership of the bonds but surrendered all rights to the interest on the bonds.

Over the years, T and his physician, Z, have become good friends. During 1983, T incurred doctor bills of $350. Instead of paying Z in cash, T did the plumbing work for a new bar Z had installed in his basement in September 1983. T and Z agreed that the value of T's services was equal to the $350 in medical bills.

In September 1983, T sold 100 shares of corporate stock for $3,100. He had acquired the stock four years ago for $1,600.

T's itemized deductions for 1983 total $5,800. His employer withheld income tax of $7,600, and T made estimated tax payments of $200.

Compute the following for T:

(a) Adjusted gross income.

(b) Taxable income.

(c) Net tax payable or refund due.

## Chapter 4

# Gross Income: Exclusions

## ITEMS SPECIFICALLY EXCLUDED FROM GROSS INCOME

Chapter 3 discussed the concepts and judicial doctrines that affect the determination of gross income. As was demonstrated, the § 61 definition of gross income is all-inclusive. Chapter 4 focuses on specific items that Congress or, in some cases, the IRS has chosen to exclude from the tax base.

## STATUTORY AUTHORITY

Sections 101 through 129 provide the authority for excluding specific items from gross income. In addition, other exclusions are scattered throughout the Code. Each exclusion has its own legislative history and reason for enactment. Certain exclusions are intended as a form of indirect welfare payments. Other exclusions prevent double taxation of income or provide incentives for socially desirable activities (i. e., nontaxable scholarships for educational activities).

In some cases, exclusions have been enacted by Congress to rectify the effects of judicially imposed decisions. For example, § 109 was enacted to exclude the value of improvements made by a lessee from the lessor's income upon termination of the lease. Previously, the Supreme Court held that such amounts were taxable income. In this court decision, the lessor was required to include the fair market value of the improvements in income upon the termination of the lease despite the fact that there had been no sale or disposition of the property. Congress provided relief in this situation by deferring the value of the improvements until the property was sold, unless the improvements were made by the lessee in lieu of rent.[1]

Section 123 was enacted to counter a district court's decision in *Arnold v. U. S.*[2] In *Arnold*, the court included in gross income insurance proceeds paid to the taxpayer as reimbursement for temporary housing expenses incurred as a result of a fire in the taxpayer's home. Similar payments made by a government agency to families displaced by urban renewal projects had been held nontaxable in a previous Revenue Ruling.[3] Dissatisfied with the results in *Arnold*, Congress exercised its authority by exempting from tax the insurance proceeds received in circumstances similar to that case. The exclusion is described in § 123.

# ADMINISTRATIVE POLICY

Administrative actions of the IRS, expressed through the issuance of interpretive Rulings and Regulations, occasionally have resulted in the exclusion of an item from gross income. For example, the IRS has excluded "supper money" paid to employees who work after regular hours.[4] Apparently, in the view of the Commissioner, these payments are in part a return of the after-tax contributions made by the individual and in part a welfare or annuity payment from the government. In addition, the IRS has excluded welfare payments as essentially in the nature of gifts.[5]

# SUMMARY OF PRINCIPAL EXCLUSIONS

Figure I contains a listing of the principal exclusions from gross income.

### Figure I
### PRINCIPAL EXCLUSIONS FROM GROSS INCOME

1. Donative Items
   Gifts, bequests, inheritances, and employee death benefits (§ § 102 and 101(b))
   Life insurance proceeds paid by reason of death (§ 101)
   Scholarships and fellowships (§ 117)
   Certain prizes and awards (§ 74(b))
2. Personal and Welfare Items
   Injury or sickness payments (§ 104)
   Public assistance payments (Rev.Rul. 71–425, 1971–2 C.B. 76)
   Amounts received under insurance contracts for certain living expenses (§ 123)

---

1. § 109.
2. 68–2 USTC ¶ 9590, 22 AFTR2d 5661, 289 F. Supp. 206 (D.Ct.N.Y. 1968).
3. Rev.Rul. 60–279, 1960–2 C.B. 11.
4. O.D. 514, 2 C.B. 90 (1921).
5. Rev.Rul. 71–425, 1971–2 C.B. 76.

3.  Wage and Salary Supplements
    (a) Fringe benefits:
        Accident and health benefits (§ § 105 and 106)
        Disability pay (§ 105).·
        Lodging and meals furnished for the convenience of the employer (§ 119)
        Rental value of parsonages (§ 107)
        Employer contributions to employee group-term life insurance (§ 79)
        Employee discounts and the use of the employer's facilities and services
        Amounts received under qualified group legal service plans (§ 120)
        Qualified transportation provided by employer (§ 124)
        Cafeteria plans (§ 125)
        Educational assistance payments to employees (§ 127)
        Child or dependent care (§ 129)
    (b) Military Benefits
        Combat pay (§ 112)
        Mustering-out pay (§ 113)
    (c) Foreign earned income (§ 911)
4.  Investor Items
        Interest on All-Savers Certificates and net interest exclusions (§ 128)
        Interest on state and local government obligations (§ 103)
        Dividend exclusion (§ 116)
        Stock dividends from public utilities reinvestment plans (§ 305(e))
5.  Benefits for the Elderly
        Social Security benefits (except in the case of certain higher income taxpayers)
        Gain from the sale of personal residence for elderly taxpayers (§ 121)
6.  Other
        Recovery of a prior year's deduction which yielded no tax benefits (§ 111)

# GIFTS AND INHERITANCES

Beginning with the Income Tax Act of 1913 and continuing to the present, Congress has allowed the recipient of a gift to exclude the value of the property from gross income.[6] The exclusion applies to gifts made during the life of the donor (*inter vivos* gifts) and transfers that take effect upon the death of the donor (bequests and inheritances). However, as discussed in Chapter 3, the recipient of a gift of income-producing property is subject to tax on the income subsequently earned from the property.

In numerous cases, "gifts" are made in a business setting. For example, a salesman gives a purchasing agent free samples; an employee receives cash from her employer on retirement; a corporation makes payments to employees who were victims of a natural disaster; a corporation makes a cash payment to a former employee's widow. In these and similar instances, it is frequently unclear whether a gift was made or the payments represent compensation for past, present, or future services.

The courts have defined a gift as "a voluntary transfer of property by one to another without adequate [valuable] consideration or compensation therefrom." If the payment is intended to be for services

---

**6.** § 102(a).

4-4 Gross Income: Exclusions Ch. 4

rendered it is not a gift, even though the payment is made without legal or moral obligation and the payor receives no economic benefit from the transfer. To qualify as a gift, the payment must be made "out of affection, respect, admiration, charity or like impulses." Thus, the cases on this issue have been decided on the basis of the donor's intent.

In a landmark case, *Comm. v. Duberstein,*[7] the taxpayer, (Duberstein) received a Cadillac from a business acquaintance. Duberstein had supplied the businessman with the names of potential customers with no expectation of compensation. The Supreme Court concluded:

> . . . despite the characterization of the transfer of the Cadillac by the parties [as a gift] and the absence of any obligation, even of a moral nature, to make it, it was at the bottom a recompense for Duberstein's past service, or an inducement for him to be of further service in the future.

Therefore, Duberstein was required to include the fair market value of the automobile in gross income.

Similarly, a bequest may be taxable if it represents a disguised form of compensation for services.

**Example 1.** An attorney entered into an agreement whereby the client would bequeath to the attorney certain securities in consideration for services rendered during the client's life. The value of the securities on the date of the client's death is taxable income to the attorney.

## LIFE INSURANCE PROCEEDS

Generally, insurance proceeds paid to the beneficiary on the death of the insured are exempt from income tax.[8] Insurance proceeds are excluded from income because their payment is similar to the receipt of a nontaxable inheritance. In addition, social policy considerations suggest that favorable tax treatment should be granted to the beneficiaries of life insurance following the death of the insured, who is frequently the sole provider for the family. It should be noted, however, that life insurance proceeds are generally subject to the Federal estate tax.

Section 101(a)(2) provides an exception to the general rule that life insurance proceeds are excluded from income. This exception is applicable to a life insurance contract that has been transferred for valuable consideration to another individual who assumes ownership rights. The insurance proceeds are income to the assignee to the ex-

---

7. 60–2 USTC ¶ 9515, 5 AFTR2d 1626, 80 S.Ct. 1190 (USSC, 1960).
8. § 101(a). Certain *flexible premium contracts* issued before 1984 are not eligible for the exclusion. See § 101(f).

tent that the proceeds exceed the amount paid for the policy plus any subsequent premiums paid.

> **Example 2.** A pays premiums of $500 for an insurance policy in the face amount of $1,000 upon the life of B and, subsequently, transfers the policy to C for $600. C receives the proceeds of $1,000 on the death of B. The amount which C can exclude from gross income is limited to $600 plus any premiums paid by C subsequent to the transfer.

The Code, however, provides exceptions to the rule illustrated in the preceding example. The four exceptions include transfers to:

—A partner of the insured.

—A partnership in which the insured is a partner.

—A corporation in which the insured is an officer or shareholder.

—A transferee whose basis in the policy is determined by reference to the transferor's basis.

## INTEREST ON LIFE INSURANCE PROCEEDS

Investment earnings arising from the reinvestment of life insurance proceeds are generally subject to income tax. However, § 101(d) provides favorable tax advantages for a surviving spouse who elects to receive the insurance proceeds in installments. The surviving spouse may exclude the first $1,000 of interest income collected on the proceeds each year.

> **Example 3.** Mrs. T was the beneficiary of her husband's $100,000 life insurance policy. She elected to receive the principal in 10 installments of $10,000 each plus interest on the unpaid principal. The first year she received $13,600 which included $3,600 interest. She must recognize interest income of $2,600.

The $1,000 interest exclusion offers a potential tax advantage if the election is made to receive the proceeds in the form of installment payments; however, it may be possible to earn a greater after-tax return by investing the lump-sum proceeds in other types of investments (e. g., stocks or tax-free municipal bonds).

# EMPLOYEE DEATH BENEFITS

Frequently an employer will make payments to a deceased employee's widow, children, or other beneficiaries, even though there is no legal or moral obligation to make such payments. Thus, the question arises as to whether the employer's payments may be treated as a gift by the recipient.

Section 101(b) attempts to eliminate or reduce controversy in this area by providing an automatic exclusion of the first $5,000 paid by the employer to the employee's beneficiaries "by reason of the death of the employee." The $5,000 exclusion must be apportioned among the beneficiaries on the basis of each beneficiary's percentage of the total death benefits received. When the employer's payments exceed $5,000, the beneficiaries may still be able to exclude the entire amount received as a gift if they are able to show gratuitous intent on the part of the employer.

The exclusion is not applicable to amounts that the employee had a nonforfeitable right to receive immediately before his death (i. e., accrued salary or commissions.) Because such nonforfeitable amounts would be payable regardless of the employee's death, the payments are not considered to be made "by reason of the death of the employee." However, lump-sum distributions to an employee's beneficiaries from a qualified pension, profit sharing, or stock bonus plan are not treated as nonforfeitable for purposes of the death benefit exclusion. In the case of a distribution (not a lump-sum distribution) from a qualified plan, the $5,000 exclusion applies only if the employee's rights to such amounts were forfeitable.[9]

> **Example 4.** The X Corporation has a profit sharing plan for the benefit of its employees. For each year of the employee's service to the firm, 10% of the employee's accumulated share of the profit sharing trust becomes nonforfeitable. If death occurs prior to completion of 10 years of service, the employee's beneficiaries receive 100% of the accumulated benefits in a lump-sum distribution. At the time of his death, Y had completed six years of service with X Corporation. His accumulated share of the profit sharing trust was $10,000, of which $6,000 (6 years × .10 × $10,000) was nonforfeitable. If the plan were not "qualified," the beneficiaries would be entitled to exclude only $4,000 (i. e., the $10,000 they received less the $6,000 that was nonforfeitable at the time of the employee's death). However, if the profit sharing plan were qualified, $5,000 could be excluded if payment were made in a lump sum.

If payments in excess of $5,000 are treated as compensation and are taxable income of the beneficiaries, such amounts are deductible by the employer as ordinary and necessary business expenses.

# SCHOLARSHIPS AND FELLOWSHIPS

The Regulations define a scholarship as "an amount paid or allowed to, or for the benefit of, a student, whether an undergraduate or a graduate, to aid such individual in pursuing his studies."[10] A fellow-

---

**9.** See Chapter 6 for further discussion of qualified plans.
**10.** Reg. § 1.117–3(a).

ship is "an amount paid or allowed to, or for the benefit of, an individual in the pursuit of study or research."[11] The term "fellowship" includes amounts received to cover the expenses of travel, research, clerical help, and equipment as well as the individual's general living expenses (provided the expenses are related to the individual's studies).[12] However, the payments are compensation and are therefore taxable if they represent payment for past, present, or future services or are primarily for the benefit of the grantor.[13]

Many graduate students receive payments for teaching or assisting in research. Generally, the payments are compensation for services and, therefore, taxable. However, in some degree programs, all students are required to do some teaching or research (e. g., an internship in education or research in the physical sciences). In these cases, the requirements to perform services will not prevent the payment from being excluded as a scholarship; but an institution cannot bring all of its payments to graduate students under the scholarship exclusion by simply making some teaching or research a requirement for a degree. The primary purpose of the payment must be to further the education and training of the recipient rather than "to serve the interest of the grantor." Whether this test is satisfied is "basically a question of fact."

A hospital's payments to interns and residents are often the subject of litigation under the fellowship provision. Generally, the payments are considered compensation if the interns' duties are geared to the operational needs of the hospital rather than the interns' research and study needs.

## EDUCATIONAL ASSISTANCE PAYMENTS BY EMPLOYERS

Amounts paid which do not qualify as scholarships or fellowships under § 117 are includible in income under § 61. However, such amounts may still qualify as expenses incurred in the trade or business of the employee (rather than a personal expense). In such event, the employee receives an offsetting deduction against the taxable income. Many employers provide for tuition reimbursements for their employees. When the courses relate to the work performed by the employee, the IRS has ruled that such expenditures are deductible by the employee as educational expenditures; and, therefore, it is not necessary for the employer to report the tuition reimbursements as wages for purposes of Federal employment taxes or for inclusion on the employee's Form W–2.

---

**11.**　Reg. § 1.117–3(c).

**12.**　§ 117(a)(2).

**13.**　Reg. § 1.117–4(c). Rev.Rul. 68–20, 1968–1 C.B. 55 held that a scholarship awarded to a contestant in a beauty pageant was compensation for participating in the televised pageant and for performing subsequent services for the sponsor.

Educational expenses, such as the cost of obtaining an under-graduate or professional school education, are considered personal expenses and are not deductible by an employee. Thus, as a general rule, if the employer pays for the employee's basic education, the employee's gross income is increased by the amount paid by the employer.

Section 127 provides an exception to this rule which is effective for taxable years beginning after December 31, 1978, and before January 1, 1984. If the employer has a written policy to reimburse educational expenses and the plan does not discriminate in favor of employees who are officers, owners, or highly compensated individuals, the employee can exclude the reimbursement from income. Under one test, a plan will be considered discriminatory if more than five percent of the employer's annual costs are for the benefit of highly compensated individuals or of those individuals who own more than a five percent interest in the business. However, partners and proprietors are treated as employees. Thus, payments on behalf of these owners will be excluded provided that the plan otherwise qualifies.

The exclusion applies to reimbursement for books, tuition, supplies, and fees but does not apply to the cost of meals, lodging, or transportation. Moreover, employer reimbursements for otherwise qualifying expenses are not excludible if the employee has an option to receive other forms of compensation.

> **Example 5.** XYZ Corporation maintains a nondiscriminatory educational assistance plan for the exclusive benefit of its employees. T, an employee, is reimbursed for the following educational expenses: $2,000 tuition, $100 books and fees, and $500 lodging and transportation costs. The reimbursement for tuition, fees, and books amounting to $2,100 is excluded from T's gross income (assuming the requirements of § 127 are otherwise met). However, the $500 reimbursement for lodging and transportation is includible in T's gross income. All of the above expenditures are deductible by the XYZ Corporation, assuming they qualify as ordinary and necessary business expenses under § 162.

# COMPENSATION FOR INJURIES AND SICKNESS

## DAMAGES

A person who suffers physical or emotional harm caused by another is often entitled to monetary damages. The legal theory of damages is that the amount awarded is intended "to make the plaintiff [the injured party] whole as before the injury."[14] It follows that if the dam-

---

14. *C. A. Hawkins,* 6 B.T.A. 1023(1928).

ages received were subject to tax, the after-tax amount received would be less than the actual damages incurred and the injured party would not be "whole as before the injury."

Thus, Congress has specifically excluded from income "the amount of any damages received (whether by suit or agreement) on account of personal injuries or sickness."[15] The courts have applied the exclusion to any personal wrong committed against the taxpayer (e. g., breach of promise to marry, invasion of privacy, libel, slander, battery).

The injured party may also suffer a loss of income as a result of the personal wrong (e. g., loss of wages while hospitalized following an automobile accident). Generally, damages received to replace a loss of income are subject to tax, just as the income replaced would have been subject to tax.[16]

In addition to compensatory damages for the personal harm and loss of income, the plaintiff in some cases may seek punitive damages—an amount awarded to punish the defendant for gross negligence or intentional infliction of harm. Generally, punitive damages are treated the same as the compensating damages. Thus, punitive damages awarded in a claim for personal injury are nontaxable,[17] but punitive damages awarded in a claim for loss of income are taxable.[18]

It is not always simple to classify damages received as taxable or nontaxable. Often a claim is settled or a jury awards a total amount, and the amount paid for each type of damage is not specified. In such cases, the IRS refers to the written claim to determine the amount received for each item. Amounts received for ascertainable damages, i.e., medical expenses and property damages, are deemed to have been first recovered and the balance of the amount received is apportioned among the other claims.[19]

> **Example 6.** J was walking on a sidewalk when she was struck by a car driven by T, a known member of the underworld. T was driving under the influence of alcohol and attempting to evade a police officer at the time of the collision.

> J filed a claim against T as follows:

| | | |
|---|---|---|
| Medical expenses incurred | $    2,000 | (nontaxable) |
| Loss of future income | 30,000 | (taxable) |
| Pain and suffering | 10,000 | (nontaxable) |
| Punitive damages | 60,000 | (apportioned) |
| Total | $ 102,000 | |

---

15.  § 104(a)(2).
16.  *Glenshaw Glass Co. v. Comm.*, 55–1 USTC ¶ 9308, 47AFTR 162, 75 S.Ct. 473(USSC 1955).
17.  Rev.Rul. 75–45, 1975–1 C.B. 47.
18.  *Supra,* Footnote 40.
19.  Rev.Rul. 58–418, 1958–2 C.B. 18; Rev.Rul. 75–230, 1975–1 C.B.

Before trial, J settled with T and received $38,000 without an itemization of the payment. Of this amount, $2,000 was received for ascertainable medical expenses and is not taxable. The types of damages to which the $36,000 amount relates are not directly ascertainable. Therefore, the IRS requires an allocation between nontaxable pain and suffering and taxable compensatory damages for loss of income as follows:

$$\frac{\$30,000 \text{ loss of income}}{\$30,000 \text{ loss of income} + \$10,000 \text{ pain and suffering}} \times \$36,000$$

$$= \$27,000 \text{ taxable amount}$$

## WORKERS' COMPENSATION

State workers' compensation laws require the employer to pay fixed amounts for specific job-related injuries. The state laws were enacted so that the employee will not have to go through the ordeal of a lawsuit (and possibly not collect damages because of some defense available to the employer) to recover the damages. Although the payments are intended in part to compensate for a loss of future income, Congress has nevertheless specifically exempted workers' compensation benefits.[20]

## ACCIDENT AND HEALTH INSURANCE BENEFITS

Section 104(a)(3) excludes from income the benefits collected under an accident and health insurance policy purchased by the taxpayer. Moreover, unlike damages received from another party (discussed above), benefits collected under the taxpayer's insurance policy are exempted even though the payments are a substitute for income.

> **Example 7.**  B purchased a medical and disability insurance policy. The insurance company paid B $200 per week to replace wages he lost while in the hospital. Although the payments serve as a substitute for income, the amounts received are tax-exempt benefits collected under B's insurance policy.

> **Example 8.**  B's injury resulted in a partial paralysis of his left foot. He received $5,000 from his accident insurance company for the injury. The $5,000 accident insurance proceeds are tax-exempt.

> **Example 9.**  B's injury was caused by T. B threatened to file a lawsuit seeking damages for his personal injuries. T paid B $3,000 in settlement of the controversy. The $3,000 damages received are nontaxable.

---

**20.**  § 104(a)(1).

A different set of rules applies if the accident and health insurance protection was purchased by the individual's employer, as discussed below.

## EMPLOYER-SPONSORED ACCIDENT AND HEALTH PLANS

Congress encourages employers to provide employees and their dependents with accident and health and disability insurance plans. The premiums are deductible by the employer and excluded from the employee's income.[21] Although § 105(a) provides the general rule that the employee has taxable income when he or she collects the insurance benefits, § § 105(b) through (d) provide several exceptions.

§ 105(b)  Excludes payments received for medical care of the employee, spouse, and dependents except to the extent such amounts relate to medical expenses which were deducted by the taxpayer in a prior year.

§ 105(c)  Excludes payments for the permanent loss or the loss of the use of a member or function of the body or the permanent disfigurement of the employee, spouse, or a dependent.

§ 105(d)  Excludes "disability pay," subject to certain limitations.

**Example 10.**  Employee D incurred $2,000 medical expenses in 19X1. D claimed the medical expenses as an itemized deduction on his 19X1 return. D's adjusted gross income for 19X1 was $30,000, and he had no other medical expenses. Because only medical expenses in excess of 5% of adjusted gross income may be claimed as an itemized deduction on D's 19X1 return, the expense reduced taxable income by only $500 [$2,000 − .05($30,000) = $500]. In 19X2, D received a $2,000 reimbursement from his employer-sponsored health insurance plan.

The general rule of Section 105(b) excludes the $2,000 from D's income. However, because D deducted the medical expenses on his return, the exception in § 105(b) applies. D is required to include in 19X2 gross income the $500 deducted on his 19X1 return.

**Example 11.**  Employee E lost an eye in an automobile accident that was unrelated to his work. As a result of the accident, E incurred $2,000 of medical expenses, which he deducted on his return. He collected $10,000 from an accident insurance policy carried by his employer. The benefits were paid according to a schedule of amounts that varied with the part of the body injured (e. g., $10,000 for loss of an eye, $20,000 for loss of a hand).

---

21.  § 106.

Because the payment was for loss of a *member or function of the body,* § 105(c) applies and the $10,000 is excluded from income. Moreover, § 105(b) does not apply, because the payment was not specifically for medical care. Thus, the $2,000 deducted is not included in gross income under § 105(b).

# MEDICAL REIMBURSEMENT PLANS

In lieu of, and in some cases in addition to, providing the employee with insurance coverage for hospital and medical expenses, the employer may agree to reimburse the employee for these expenses. The amounts received through the insurance coverage (i. e., "insured" plan benefits) are excluded from income under § 105 (as discussed above). Unfortunately in terms of cost considerations, the insurance companies that issue these types of policies usually require a broad coverage of employees. An alternative would be to have a plan that is not funded with insurance (i. e., a "self-insured" arrangement). Here, the employer can single out a group of employees (e. g.; management level only) for sole coverage under the plan. Obviously, such plans might prove to be discriminatory in their effect.

Congress addressed itself to this problem with the enactment of § 105(h). This provision requires the employee to include in gross income the medical benefits received from a "self-insured" arrangement if the plan discriminates in favor of "highly-compensated individuals."

> **Example 12.** F Corporation carries a Blue Cross medical care policy (i. e., an insured plan) that covers all employees and their dependents. Further, F Corporation has a self-insured arrangement, whereby it reimburses its management-level employees for any medical expenses not absorbed by the Blue Cross policy.
>
> T is the president and major stockholder of F Corporation. During the current year, the corporation paid $600 Blue Cross premiums for T and his dependents. T incurred and paid $1,500 medical expenses. He was fully reimbursed for these expenses as follows: $1,200 from Blue Cross and $300 from F Corporation.
>
> The reimbursement from F Corporation is taxable under § 105(h). The Blue Cross premiums are excluded from gross income under § 106 and the Blue Cross reimbursement is excluded under § 105(b).

# DISABILITY

## DISABILITY PAY

An employee or former employee who is under age 65 and is permanently and totally disabled is allowed a limited exclusion of wage and salary continuation benefits received from the employer before 1984. For the disability to be considered permanent, the physical or mental impairment must be expected to result in death or the disability must have lasted or be expected to last for a continuous period of not less than 12 months.

The exclusion is limited to $100 per week. In addition, if the taxpayer's adjusted gross income (including disability payments) is more than $15,000, the excludible amount is reduced on a dollar-for-dollar basis.[22]

> **Example 13.** T, age 58, is totally and permanently disabled in 1983. His retirement disability pension from his company amounted to $200 per week. In addition, T had $8,000 gross income from other sources (e. g., taxable dividends, interest).

| Gross Income: | |
|---|---:|
| Disability pension ($200 × 52 weeks) | $ 10,400 |
| Other taxable income | 8,000 |
| | 18,400 |
| Deductions for adjusted gross income | –0– |
| Adjusted gross income | 18,400 |
| | |
| Excluded amount—Limit $100 per week | 5,200 |
| Less: Ceiling amount ($18,400–$15,000) | 3,400 |
| Allowable exclusion from income | $ 1,800 |

The exclusion does not apply to payments received after 1983.

# MEALS AND LODGING FURNISHED FOR THE CONVENIENCE OF THE EMPLOYER

As was discussed in Chapter 3, income can take any form, including meals and lodging. However, § 119 excludes from income the value of meals and lodging under the following conditions:

—The meals and lodging are *furnished* by the employer, on the employer's *business premises,* for the *convenience of the employer*.

—In the case of lodging, the employee is *required* to accept the lodging as a condition of employment.

Each of these requirements has been strictly construed by the courts.

The IRS and some courts have reasoned that a partner is not an employee, and therefore, the exclusion does not apply to the partner. However the Tax Court and the Fifth Circuit Court have ruled in favor of the taxpayer on this issue.[23]

---

**22.** § 105(d)(1)(5).

**23.** Rev.Rul. 80, 1953–1 CB 62; *Comm. v. Doak,* 56–2 UST ¶ 9708, 49 AFTR 1491, 234 F.2d 704(CA–4, 1956); *Moran v. Comm.,* 56–2 USTC ¶ 9789, 50 AFTR 64, 236 F.2d 53(CA–8, 1956); *Robinson v. U. S.,* 60–1 USTC ¶ 9152, 273 F.2d 503 (CA–3, 1960). *Briggs v. U. S.,* 56–2 USTC ¶ 10020, 50 AFTR 667, 238 F.2d 53 (CA–10, 1956). But see *G. A. Papineau,* 16 T.C. 130(1956). *Armstrong v. Phinney,* 68–1, USTC ¶ 9355, 21 AFTR2d 1260, 394 F.2d 661 (CA–5, 1968).

The Supreme Court held a cash meal allowance was ineligible for the exclusion because the employer did not actually furnish the meals.[24] Similarly, one court denied the exclusion where the employer paid for the food and supplied the cooking facilities, but the employee prepared the meal.[25]

The *on the business premises of the employer* requirement, applicable to both meals and lodging, has resulted in much litigation. The Regulations define business premises as simply "the place of employment of the employee."[26] Generally, the closer the lodging to the business operations, the more likely the convenience of the employer is served.

The *convenience of the employer* test is intended to focus the analysis on the employer's motivation for furnishing the meals and lodging, rather than on the benefits received by the employee. If the employer furnishes the meals and lodging primarily to enable the employee to properly perform his or her duties, it does not matter that the employee considers these benefits to be a part of his compensation.

The employer *required* test, applicable to lodging but not meals, overlaps with the convenience of the employer test. The employer requires that the employee live on the premises, apparently, so that he or she can properly perform the duties of the job. But making meals available at no charge may induce a sufficient number of employees to remain on the premises to meet the employer's operational needs as illustrated in Reg. § 1.119–1(d):

—A hospital provides a free cafeteria for its staff. The employees are not required to eat on the premises, but the hospital's business purpose in providing the meals is to induce employees to stay on the premises in case an emergency arises. The value of the meals may be excluded from income.

The Regulation gives the following additional examples in which the tests for excluding meals are satisfied:

—A waitress is required to eat her meals on the premises during the busy lunch and breakfast hours.

—A bank furnishes a teller meals on the premises to limit the time the employee is away from his or her booth during the busy hours.

—A worker is employed at a construction site in a remote part of Alaska. The employer must furnish meals and lodging due to the inaccessibility of other facilities.

---

**24.** *Comm. v. Kowalski*, 77–2 USTC ¶ 9748, 40 AFTR2d 6128, 98 S.Ct. 315 (USSC. 1977).

**25.** *Tougher v. Comm.*, 71–1 USTC ¶ 9398, 27 AFTR2d 1301, 441 F.2d 1148 (CA–9, 1971).

**26.** Reg. 1.119–1(c)(1).

# OTHER EMPLOYEE FRINGE BENEFITS

In 1976 and 1978 Congress enacted various exclusions that have become popular forms of nontaxable fringe benefits. These provisions are summarized below:

—The employee does not have to include in gross income the value of child and dependent care services paid for by the employer and incurred to enable the employee to work. In the case of married couples, the exclusion generally cannot exceed the earned income of either spouse.[27]

—Any benefit received by employees from coverage under qualified group legal service plans provided by the employer is excluded.

**Example 14.** X Corporation provides its employees with free legal services. In this connection, it pays a law firm an annual retainer to furnish these services. Under § 120, neither the cost of the retainer nor the value of any services so rendered will be taxed to the employees.

Note that this provision parallels the treatment of medical reimbursement plans pursuant to § § 105 and 106 (discussed above).

—Qualified transportation provided by employers will be nontaxable to the employees. As mentioned in Chapter 6, commuting expenses (i. e., the cost of going from home to work and back) normally are personal in nature and, therefore, are not deductible. Thus, if these expenses were furnished by the employer, income resulted to the employees. Section 124 now enables employers to furnish commuting-van services for employees without the recognition of income by them.

—Until recently, if an employee was granted a choice between cash and a nontaxable fringe benefit, the better view was that the option of cash made the fringe benefit taxable. Section 125 permits this option (called "cafeteria" plans) if certain conditions are met.

**Example 15.** Y Corporation offers its employees a choice of a cash payment of $1,800 or coverage in its group-term life insurance and medical reimbursement plans. An employee who accepts the cash alternative, of course, will be taxed on the $1,800. By way of contrast, an employee choosing participation in the fringe benefit program will be accorded the typical exclusion

---

**27.** § 129, effective for tax years beginning after December 31, 1981. The exclusion applies to the same types of expenses which, if they were paid by the employee (and not reimbursed by the employer), would be eligible for the Credit for Child and Dependent Care Expense, discussed in Chapter 8.

from gross income. Cafeteria plans provide tremendous flexibility in tailoring the employee-pay package to fit individual needs. Some employees (usually the younger group) prefer cash, while others (usually the older group) will opt for the fringe benefit programs.

The financing of these fringe benefits will result in a tax deduction to the employer. Nevertheless, requirements for extensive coverage of employees are imposed in order for the plans to qualify. Therefore, even considering the tax deduction that is generated, cost considerations will play a role in which, if any, of these fringe benefits an employer decides to adopt.

Other employee benefits that are not generally includible in gross income are discounts on the employer's merchandise, free parking, payment of the employee's dues in vocational or professional organizations, supper money, and nonbusiness use of the employer's facilities where no additional cost is incurred by the employer.

> **Example 16.** Z Airlines allows its employees to fly on a standby basis on any scheduled flight at no charge. Since the seats the employees occupy would otherwise be empty, the airline incurs no additional cost due to employee use. Consequently, the IRS will not require the employee to include the fair market value of the transportation in his or her gross income.

It should be recalled that in cases such as employee discounts, the value received by the employee probably is within the ambit of § 61 (gross income broadly defined), but the IRS, as a matter of policy, has chosen not to enforce inclusion in gross income where the benefits are made available to all employees.[28]

One fringe benefit that has been subject to repeated attacks by the IRS is loans to employees at less than the market rate of interest (or at no interest at all). The Tax Court has refused to impose a tax on the difference between the market rate of interest and the rate, if any, actually charged to the employee. However, the Tax Court's rationale for its position is not that the employee did not realize any income but rather that the income realized (actually imputed) is offset by an allowable deduction for interest deemed paid.[29]

> **Example 17.** X Corporation loaned its president $100,000 for one year but did not charge any interest, although the market

---

**28.** In the late 1970s, the IRS indicated it intended to issue new regulations which would tax fringe benefits such as illustrated in Example 16. But in 1978 and again in 1981, Congress established a statutory barrier prohibiting any fringe benefit regulations before 1984.

**29.** *J. Simpson Dean,* 35 T.C. 1083 (1961), *nonacq.* 1973–2 C.B. 4. Also see, *Max Zager,* 72 T.C. 1009 (1979) which involved a borrower who was an employee-shareholder. But see, *W. C. Hardee vs U. S.,* 82–2 USTC ¶ 9459, 50 AFTR 2d 82–5079, where the Court of Claims, trial division, refused to follow the Tax Court and required the taxpayer to include the imputed interest in his gross income.

rate for interest on such loans was 14%. According to the IRS, the president must recognize income of $14,000. The Tax Court holds that if the $14,000 interest is included in income, the president would be entitled to a deduction of $14,000 for the interest deemed paid. Thus, the imputed income and deduction offset each other.

## FOREIGN EARNED INCOME

A U. S. citizen is generally subject to U. S. tax on his or her income regardless of its geographic origin. The income may also be subject to tax in the foreign country, and thus, the taxpayer must carry a double tax burden. Out of a sense of fairness, and to encourage U. S. citizens to work abroad (so that exports might be increased), Congress has provided alternative forms of relief from taxes on foreign earned income. The taxpayer can elect to either (1) include the foreign income in his or her taxable income and then claim a credit for foreign taxes paid or (2) exclude the foreign earnings from his or her U. S. gross income.[30] The foreign tax credit option is discussed in Chapter 8, but as apparent from the discussion below, most taxpayers will choose the exclusion.

Foreign earned income consists of the earnings from the individual's personal services rendered in a foreign country (other than as an employee of the U. S. Government). To qualify for the exclusion, the taxpayer must be either a bona fide resident of the foreign country or present in the country for 330 days during any twelve consecutive months.

The exclusion is limited to $75,000 in 1982 and increases by $5,000 per year until 1986, when it reaches $95,000. For married persons, both of whom have foreign earned income, the exclusion is computed separately for each spouse. Also, the community property rules do not apply (i. e., the community property spouse is not deemed to have earned one-half of the other spouse's foreign earned income). A taxpayer who is present in the country for less than the entire year must compute the maximum exclusion on a daily basis (e. g., in 1983, $80,000 divided by the number of workdays present).

In addition to the exclusion for foreign earnings, the reasonable housing costs incurred by the taxpayer and the taxpayer's family in a foreign country in excess of a base amount may also be excluded from gross income. The base amount is 16 percent of the U. S. Government pay scale for a GS–14 (Step 1) employee, which varies from year to year.

As previously mentioned, the taxpayer may elect to include the foreign earned income in federal adjusted gross income and claim a credit (an offset against U. S. tax) for the foreign tax paid. The credit

---

**30.** § 911(a). These rules became effective January 1, 1982, and substantially changed the foreign earned income exclusion. Once the election is made to exclude income, it cannot be revoked without the consent of the IRS. See § 911(e).

alternative may be advantageous if the individual's foreign earned income far exceeds the excludible amount so that the foreign taxes paid exceed the U. S. tax on the amount excluded. However, once an election is made, it applies to all subsequent years, unless affirmatively revoked. Moreover, the revocation is effective for the year of the change and the four subsequent years.[31]

## INTEREST ON CERTAIN STATE AND LOCAL GOVERNMENT OBLIGATIONS

At the time the Sixteenth Amendment was ratified by the states, there was some question as to whether the Federal government possessed the constitutional authority to tax interest on state and local government obligations. Taxing the interest on these obligations was thought to violate the doctrine of intergovernmental immunity in that the tax would impair the state and local government's ability to finance its operations. Thus, interest on state and local government obligations was specifically exempted from Federal income taxation. The exemption is still part of our tax laws, but most commentators agree that the exclusion of such interest is based upon political rather than constitutional requirements.

Obviously, the exclusion of the interest reduces the cost of borrowing for the state and local governments. A taxpayer in the 50 percent marginal tax bracket requires only a four percent yield on a tax-exempt bond to obtain the same after-tax income as a taxable bond paying eight percent interest [$4\% \div (1 - .5) = 8\%$].

However, the lower cost for the state and local government is more than offset by the revenue loss of the Federal government. Also, tax-exempt interest is considered to be a substantial loophole for the very wealthy. For this reason, bills have been proposed to Congress calling for Federal government subsidies to those state and local governments which voluntarily choose to issue taxable bonds. Under these proposals, the tax-exempt status of existing bonds would not be eliminated.

The current exempt status applies solely to the obligations of state and local governments (e. g., interest on bonds and notes). Thus, income received from the accrual of interest on an overpayment of state income tax is fully taxable. Nor does the exemption apply to gains on the sale of tax-exempt securities.

## INTEREST EXCLUSION FOR INDIVIDUALS

In recent years, Congress has created some new interest exclusions for individuals in addition to the exclusion for interest on state and

---

**31.** § 911(e).

local government bonds which applies to all taxpayers and has always been a part of our tax laws. The purpose of the exclusions is to encourage savings and thereby reduce the general rate of inflation and, in particular, reduce interest rates charged borrowers.

## ALL-SAVERS CERTIFICATES

These certificates were issued by banks and other financial institutions in 1981 and 1982. Each individual was entitled to a $1,000 ($2,000 on a joint return) lifetime exclusion of interest received on the certificates before 1984.

## NET INTEREST EXCLUSION

By the end of 1983, the last of the All-Savers Certificates will have been redeemed. For 1984, we revert to pre-1981 law and all interest (except from state and local obligations) will be taxable. Beginning in 1985, an individual will be allowed to exclude a portion of his or her interest income, with the exclusion limited to the lesser of (1) $450 ($900 on a joint return) or (2) 15 percent of the taxpayer's interest income reduced by his or her interest expense (other than home mortgage interest).[32]

# DIVIDEND EXCLUSION FOR INDIVIDUALS

Section 116 provides some relief from the double taxation of corporate income (i. e., the income is initially subject to the corporate income tax and the subsequent dividend distributions are taxed to the shareholders). Unmarried individuals and married individuals who file separate returns may exclude the first $100 of dividends received from domestic (U. S.) corporations during the year. On a joint return, a maximum of $200 of dividends may be excluded, regardless of which spouse owns the stock on which the dividends are paid.

> **Example 18.** Mr. and Mrs. A received dividends in the current year as follows:

| | Dividends Received on Stock Owned By | | | |
| --- | --- | --- | --- | --- |
| | Mr. A | Mrs. A | Jointly | Total |
| X Corporation | $ 40 | $ 150 | | $ 190 |
| Y Corporation | | 90 | | 90 |
| Z Corporation | | | $ 30 | 30 |
| | $ 40 | $ 240 | $ 30 | $ 310 |

---

32. New § 128 replacing the All-Savers Certificates provisions (also § 128).

On a joint return, Mr. and Mrs. A would report $310 minus a $200 exclusion. On a separate return, Mr. A would report $55 [$40 + 1/2($30)] of dividends, but because the total is less than $100, none would be taxable. Mrs. A would report $255 [$240 + 1/2($30)] of dividends and a $100 exclusion on a separate return. Thus, their total taxable income is $155 on separate returns but only $110 on a joint return.

## NONQUALIFYING DIVIDENDS AND THOSE REQUIRING SPECIAL TREATMENT

A dividend is a payment to a shareholder in respect of his or her stock. The dividend exclusion does not apply to some items which are frequently referred to as dividends:

—Dividends received on deposits with savings and loan associations, credit unions, and banks are actually interest (a contractual rate paid for the use of money).

—Patronage dividends paid by cooperatives (i. e., for farmers) are rebates made to the users and are considered reductions in the cost of items purchased from the association. The rebates are usually made after year-end (after the cooperative has determined whether it has met its expenses) and are apportioned among members on the basis of their purchases.

—Mutual insurance companies pay "dividends" on unmatured life insurance policies that are considered rebates of premiums.

—Shareholders in mutual investment funds are allowed to report as capital gains their proportionate share of the fund's gains realized and distributed. The capital gain and ordinary income portions are reported on the Form 1099 which the fund supplies its shareholders each year.

Dividends to shareholders are taxable only to the extent the payments are made from either the corporation's current earnings and profits (in many cases the same as before-tax net income per books) or its accumulated earnings and profits (in many cases the same as retained earnings per books).[33] Distributions to shareholders that exceed earnings and profits are treated as a nontaxable recovery of capital and reduce the shareholder's basis in the stock. Once the shareholder's basis is reduced to zero, any subsequent distributions in excess of the corporation's earnings and profits are taxed as capital gains.[34]

---

**33.**   § 316(a).
**34.**   § 301(c).

## STOCK DIVIDENDS AND DIVIDEND REINVESTMENT PLANS

When a corporation issues a simple stock dividend (e. g., common stock issued to common stockholders), the shareholder has merely received additional shares to represent the same total investment; thus, the shareholder does not realize income. However, if the shareholder has the option of receiving either cash or stock in the corporation, then the individual realizes taxable income whether he or she receives stock or cash. If the taxpayer elects to receive the stock, he or she could be deemed in constructive receipt of the cash rejected. Under § 305(b)(1), the stock dividend is taxable and the amount of income is the value of the stock received, rather than the cash the shareholder rejected.

In recent years, many public utilities corporations have adopted dividend policies that allow the shareholder to choose between cash or additional shares of stock. These stocks in lieu of cash schemes are commonly referred to as "dividend reinvestment plans." Dividends from these plans received by individuals are eligible for an exclusion of $750 per year ($1,500 on a joint return).[35] The exclusion is elective (made by indicating on the tax return that the election is being made). If the individual elects to exclude the value of the stock from income, the taxpayer's cost basis in the stock is zero. The proceeds from the sale of the stock are taxed as ordinary income if the sale occurs within one year after receipt of the dividend. A sale more than one year after receipt of the stock will produce a long-term capital gain equal to the proceeds.

> **Example 19.** In 1983, individuals C and D each received shares of stock under a public utility dividend reinvestment plan. C and D each received stock with a value of $200. C elected to exclude his dividends from income, but D included her dividends in gross income for 1983. In 1985, C and D each sold the shares received in 1983 for $300. C's and D's long-term capital gain for 1985 would be computed as follows:
>
> |                         | C       | D       |
> | ----------------------- | ------- | ------- |
> | Sales price             | $ 300   | $ 300   |
> | Basis                   | –0–     | 200     |
> | Long-term capital gain  | $ 300   | $ 100   |

The exclusion is available from 1982–85. As the short life of the dividend reinvestment plan exclusion indicates, Congress is experimenting. The objective of the exclusion is to assist public utilities in meeting capital needs for the future. The availability of the exclusion

---

**35.**   § 305(e).

allows public utilities to remain competitive in the capital markets without having to distribute cash to shareholders and thus permits the industry to expand through internally generated funds.

# TAX BENEFIT RULE

Generally, if a taxpayer obtains a deduction for an item in one year and later recovers a portion of the prior deduction, the recovery produces taxable income in the year it is received.[36]

> **Example 20.** A taxpayer who uses the direct charge-off method[37] for bad debts deducted as a loss a $1,000 receivable from a customer when it appeared the amount would never be collected. The following year, the customer paid $800 on the receivable. The taxpayer must report as income the $800 in the year it is received.

However, § 111 provides that no income is recognized upon the recovery of a deduction or the portion of a deduction that did not yield a tax benefit in the year it was taken. Thus, if the taxpayer in the above example had no tax liability in the year of the deduction (e. g., the excess itemized deductions, the zero bracket amount, and personal exemptions exceeded adjusted gross income), the recovery would be partially or totally excluded from income in the year of the recovery.

The Code specifically mentions "bad debts, prior taxes and delinquency amounts" as items subject to the tax benefit rule. However, due to a Supreme Court decision,[38] the Regulations have been expanded to make § 111 applicable to recoveries "with respect to all losses, expenditures, and accruals made the basis of deductions from gross income for prior taxable years."[39]

> **Example 21.** T, a cash basis taxpayer, received a state income tax refund in 19X2 relating to her 19X1 state income taxes. The refunded amount was deductible on T's 19X1 Federal income tax return (assuming T itemized her deductions in 19X1). Thus, the state income tax refund must be included in T's gross income for 19X2. If T used the zero bracket amount in 19X1, the refund is not includible in gross income because she did not receive a tax benefit in 19X1.[40]

---

**36.** § 111(a). See the Glossary of Tax Terms (Appendix C) for a discussion of the term "tax benefit rule" and its application to medical expenses.
**37.** See Chapter 6 for a discussion of bad debts.
**38.** *Dobson v. Comm.*, 44–1 USTC ¶ 9108, 31 AFTR 773, 64 S.Ct. 239 (USSC, 1944).
**39.** Reg. § 1.111–1(a).
**40.** Itemized deductions are discussed in Chapter 7, and the zero bracket amount was discussed in Chapter 2.

# INCOME FROM DISCHARGE
## OF INDEBTEDNESS

*taxable.*

A transfer of appreciated property in satisfaction of a debt is an event which triggers the realization of income. The transaction is treated as a sale of the appreciated property followed by a payment of the debt.[41]

Frequently the transfer occurs as a result of foreclosure by the creditor. But in many cases, the creditor will not foreclose and will even forgive a portion of the debt to insure the vitality of the debtor.

> **Example 22.** X Corporation is unable to meet the mortgage payments on its factory building. Both the corporation and the mortgage holder are aware of the depressed market for industrial property in the area. Foreclosure would only result in the creditor's obtaining unsalable property. To improve X Corporation's financial position and thus improve its chances of obtaining the additional credit from other lenders necessary for survival, the creditor agrees to forgive all amounts past due and to reduce the principal amount of the mortgage.

Prior case law had held that the reduction in indebtness was a taxable event. The rationale of these cases was that the debt adjustment was a transaction that increased the taxpayer's net worth. However, the courts also developed numerous exceptions to this general rule.

The Bankruptcy Tax Act of 1980 established an almost uniform rule of nonrecognition of income from the discharge of indebtedness. The gain realized but not recognized (i.e., the reduction in indebtedness) is applied against the taxpayer's basis (cost less depreciation) in assets.[42] Thus, the gain is merely deferred until the assets are sold (or depreciated). Moreover, no income recognition or basis adjustments are required if payment of the indebtedness would yield a deduction (e. g., accrued interest owed by a cash basis taxpayer).[43]

*allows deferral of recognition of income*

> **Example 23.** X Corporation issued bonds for $1,000,000. Two years later, the corporation repurchased the bonds on the open market for $900,000. X Corporation, realized a $100,000 gain on the retirement of the debt. The corporation may exclude the gain from income and reduce the bases in assets by $100,000.

---

**41.**  *Crane v. Commissioner,* 47–1 USTC ¶ 9217, 35 AFTR 776, 67 S.Ct. 1047 (USSC, 1947).

**42.**  § 1017. Forthcoming regulations will explain how the total nonrecognized gain will be allocated among assets. Insolvent and bankrupt taxpayers have additional options for allocating the gain to tax attributes other than bases (e. g., net operating loss carryovers and investment credit). § 108(b).

**43.**  § 108(e)(2).

The few remaining discharge of indebtedness situations that are subject to special treatment are:

1.  A reduction in the debt as the result of a gift by the creditor to the debtor.
2.  Cancellation by a shareholder of the corporation's indebtedness to him or her.
3.  The discharge of a solvent individual's nonbusiness indebtedness.

The first exception is rarely applicable in a business setting, because businesspeople generally do not gratuitously forgive debts. While a businessman or woman, may settle debts for less than the original amount, the settlement is usually due to the debtor's adverse financial condition or to a dispute as to the correct amount of the liability rather than due to "love, affection or generosity."

A shareholder's cancellation of the corporation's indebtedness to him or her (the second exception) is considered a contribution of capital to the corporation. However, if the shareholder's basis in the receivable from the corporation is less than the amount owed (e. g., accrued interest receivable by a cash basis shareholder), discharge is treated under the general rules discussed above (i. e., the corporation would reduce its bases in assets by the amount of the accrued interest payable).

The final exception is very narrow but has a frequently encountered application. The debtor must be solvent (i. e., the fair market value of the taxpayer's assets exceeds his or her liabilities) after the debt is forgiven. Also, the liability cannot have been incurred in a trade or business (i. e., the funds must have been used for personal or investment, rather than trade or business, purposes). The most common situation where this exception will apply is shareholders borrowing from their controlled corporations. If the shareholder does not provide convincing evidence that he or she intended to repay the debt, the IRS will treat the debt as cancelled. The shareholder is deemed to have received a taxable dividend equal to the amount owed to the corporation.

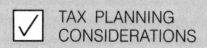

## ☑ TAX PLANNING CONSIDERATIONS

The present law excludes certain types of economic gains from taxation. Therefore, tax planning techniques may be useful to assist taxpayers in obtaining the maximum benefits from the exclusion of such gains. Below are some of the tax planning opportunities made available by the exclusions described in the preceding sections of this chapter.

## GIFTS AND INHERITANCES

Family tax planning is largely concerned with shifting income-producing property among family members. The gift and inheritance exclusions facilitate these intrafamily transfers.

It should be recognized that the exclusions apply only to the recipient of the gift. The donor generally recognizes no income from the gift, because he or she realizes nothing; however, the donor may be subject to a gift tax on the transfer.[44] In a recent Supreme Court decision, the gift tax and income tax rules overlapped and the donor was required to recognize income.[45]

> **Example 24.** F gave S stock with a cost of $30,000 and a value of $300,000. S accepted the property on the condition that he would pay F's $40,000 gift tax on the transfer. F was required to recognize a $10,000 gain ($40,000 − $30,000) from the transfer of appreciated property in satisfaction of his liability.

Income must also be recognized if the donee assumes a mortgage in excess of the donor's basis in the property.

## INTEREST ON LIFE INSURANCE PROCEEDS PAID TO A SURVIVING SPOUSE

A $1,000 annual interest exclusion is available to a surviving spouse who collects life insurance proceeds in installments. Although the exclusion is an apparent sweetener, whether the installment option is preferable depends upon the interest rate paid by the insurance company, alternative rates of return, and the spouse's marginal tax bracket.

> **Example 25.** Mrs. T is the beneficiary of her husband's $50,000 life insurance policy. She can elect to receive the face amount of the policy or $7,500 ($2,500 interest) per year for 10 years which will yield 8% before-tax interest. Assume she can invest the $50,000 in savings certificates yielding 12% and is in the 30% marginal tax bracket. Mrs. T's effective tax rate on the installment payments is 18% [[($2,000 − $1,000) ÷ $2,500] × .30 = .18], and thus her after-tax rate of return is 6.56% [(1 − .18)(.08)]. The after-tax rate of return on the time certificates is 8.4% [(1 − .30)(.12)]. Therefore, the insurance company will have to present some reasons other than rate of return on investment to make the installment payments the preferable option.

---

44. See Chapters 11–13 of *West's Federal Taxation: Corporations Partnerships, Estates, and Trusts* for a detailed discussion of the gift tax.
45. *Diedrich v. Comm.,* 82–1 USTC ¶ 9419, 50 AFTR2d 82–5053, 102 S.Ct. 2414(USSC, 1982).

## COMPENSATION FOR INJURIES AND SICKNESS

In arranging an out-of-court settlement of a suit involving personal injury and loss of income, the taxpayer should be aware that damages to the person are excluded from income. However, the portion of the settlement representing loss of income is fully taxable. Often the payor is an insurance company and is indifferent as to how the total amount is allocated (except the company may not be liable for punitive damages). Thus, the taxpayer should negotiate for a favorable allocation to the personal injury portion.

## EMPLOYEE BENEFITS

Generally, employees view accident and health insurance, as well as life insurance, as necessities. Employees can obtain group coverage at much lower rates than individuals would have to pay for the same protection. Moreover, premiums paid by the employer can be excluded from gross income. Because of the exclusion, employees will have a greater after-tax and after-insurance income if the employer pays a lower salary but also pays the insurance premiums.

> **Example 26.** Individual A receives a salary of $30,000. The company has group insurance benefits, but A was required to pay his own premiums as follows:

| | |
|---|---:|
| Hospitalization and medical insurance | $ 1,400 |
| Term life insurance ($30,000) | 200 |
| Disability insurance | 400 |
| | $ 2,000 |

> To simplify the analysis, assume A's average and marginal tax rate on income is 25%. After paying taxes of $7,500 (.25 × $30,000) and $2,000 for insurance, A has $20,500 ($30,000 − $7,500 − $2,000) for his other living needs.
>     If A's employer reduced A's pay by $2,000 (to $28,000) but paid A's insurance premiums, A's tax liability would be only $7,000 ($28,000 × .25). Thus, A would have $21,000 ($28,000 − $7,000) to meet his living needs other than insurance. The change in the compensation plan would save $500 ($21,000 − $20,500).

Similarly, the employer's payment of the employee's child care and group legal services are attractive nontaxable employee fringe benefits.
    The meals and lodging exclusion enables the employee to receive from his or her employers what he or she ordinarily must purchase with after-tax dollars. While the requirements that the employee live and take his or her meals on the employer's premises limit the tax

planning opportunities, in certain situations, the exclusion is an important factor in the employer's compensation (e. g., hotels, motels, restaurants, farms, and ranches).

It should be recognized that the exclusion of benefits discussed above are generally available only to employees. Proprietors and partners must pay tax on the same benefits their employees receive tax-free. By incorporating and becoming an employee of the corporation, the former proprietor or partner can also receive these tax-exempt benefits. Thus, the availability of employee benefits is a consideration in the decision to incorporate.

*Nonstatutory Fringe Benefits.* Generally, an employer can provide a variety of incidental benefits which, if made available to all employees, will not be taxable income. Examples of these benefits are company-provided recreational facilities, travel passes for airline employees, and limited personal use of company telephones. However, it should be recognized that the tax treatment of nonstatutory fringe benefits may be changed in the near future and abuses of the exclusion will not be tolerated by the IRS.

## PROBLEM MATERIALS

### Questions for Class Discussion

1. What are the possible tax consequences to an owner of land when a tenant constructs a permanent building on the property?

2. Who pays the tax on a gift of the income from a certain piece of property? The donee or the donor?    *(owner of the property — up to the date of the gift.)*

3. What is a gift?

4. (a) Mr. A served as chairman of the local school board. Upon completion of his term in office, the organization awarded him a silver serving tray in recognition of his outstanding service to the organization. The value of the tray is $200. Is Mr. A required to include the value of the tray in his income?

   (b) Assume the employees took up a collection and purchased the tray for Mr. A.

5. How does the employee death benefit provision reduce the tax problems of the family of a deceased employee?

6. What types of payments made by the employer to the family of a deceased employee would not be eligible for the employee death benefit exclusion?    *first $5,000 paid by emp. by reason of death of emp.*

7. Under what conditions are life insurance proceeds subject to taxation?

8. How do the tax laws influence a survivor's choice of a settlement option under a life insurance policy on the life of his or her deceased spouse?

9. If a taxpayer receives damages to compensate for injuries suffered in an automobile accident, the payment is generally excludible from taxable income. Is the tax treatment of payments for personal injury and damages to property consistent?    *NO— gain is recognized generally an amt the diff between the basis and*

*all amt. for bodily injury is income.*

10. What nontaxable fringe benefits are available to employees that are not available to partners and proprietors?

11. What are the possible tax consequences for a corporation that establishes a medical expense reimbursement plan covering only one employee who also owns all of the corporation's outstanding stock? *— disguised dividend.*

12. How does one determine if meals and lodging supplied by the employer are to serve a valid business purpose? Is the tax treatment of meals and lodging affected if the employer advertises that the meals and lodging provided are one of the employees' fringe benefits?

13. What special tax treatment is available to U. S. citizens who work abroad?

14. What would be the social and economic consequences of eliminating the tax exemption now granted for interest on state and local government bonds?

15. What is the purpose of the § 116 exclusion? *— double taxation of dividend.*

16. What are the tax consequences of recovering an amount deducted on a previous year's tax return?

## Problems

17. Determine whether the following may be excluded from gross income as gifts, bequests, scholarships, prizes, or life insurance proceeds.

    (a) Uncle told Nephew, "Come live with me and take care of me in my old age and you can have all my property after my death." Nephew complied with Uncle's request. Uncle's will made Nephew sole beneficiary of the estate.

    (b) Uncle told Nephew, "If you study hard and make the Dean's list this year, I will pay your tuition for the following year." Nephew made the Dean's list, and Uncle paid the tuition.

    (c) D cashed in her life insurance contract and collected $10,000. She had paid premiums totaling $7,000.

18. R Company has a qualified pension plan with survivor's benefits. Mr. K was employed by R company at the time of his death. He had contributed $4,000 to the plan, and his nonforfeitable benefits were valued at $15,000. Mrs. K had the option of receiving $21,000 in a lump sum or an annuity of $2,400 per year for 20 years. The present value of the annuity was also $21,000.

    (a) Assuming Mrs. K elected the lump-sum option, compute her taxable income from receipt of the $21,000.

    (b) Assuming Mrs. K elected the annuity option, compute her taxable income from collection of the first $2,400.

19. T died during 1983 at age 64. T was hospitalized for the six weeks before his death, and he continued to receive his regular salary of $200 per week. Total salary received during the year until his death was $9,000, with the last paycheck being paid to his spouse. T and his wife had other income of $6,000 for the year, before considering the following data:

    (a) At the time of T's death, T had accumulated $20,000 in a qualified employee retirement plan to which he had contributed $5,000. None of

T's benefits were forfeitable. T's wife elected to collect the benefits as an annuity of $150 per week and received $1,050 in the year T died.

(b) The employer also paid T's wife $2,000 "in appreciation of T's past services to the company."

(c) T's wife also was the beneficiary of T's $10,000 life insurance policy and elected to leave the proceeds with the insurance company. She received $155 interest on the proceeds in the calendar year of T's death.

Compute Mr. and Mrs. T's adjusted gross income assuming a joint return was filed in the year of T's death.

20. Several years ago, R transferred his life insurance policy to a partnership in which he was a partner. The partnership was to receive the proceeds of the policy at the time of his death. When the partnership's basis in the policy was $25,000, and after R had ceased to work in the partnership on a full-time basis, the partnership was incorporated. The incorporation was a nontaxable event, and in exchange for his interest in the partnership, R received interest-bearing long-term notes (due in 10 years). R did not participate in the corporation's business affairs. Several years later when the corporation's basis in the policy was $35,000 due to additional premiums paid, R died and the corporation used the proceeds of the policy ($60,000) to retire R's notes for $5,000 (less than their face amount). What are the tax consequences to the corporation of collection on the policy and retirement of the notes?

21. T served as the manager of an orphanage in 19X8. In this connection he had the following transactions:

(a) He received no salary from his job but was given room and board (valued at $3,600) on the premises. No other person was employed by the orphanage, which is a tax-exempt organization.

(b) The orphanage paid $300 in tuition for a night course T took at a local university. The course was in the field of philosophy and dealt with the meaning of life. The payment was authorized by the orphanage's trustees in a written resolution.

(c) The orphanage paid $500 of the premiums on T's life insurance policy and all of his medical expenses of $1,800. Again, the payment was made pursuant to a resolution approved by the trustees.

(d) T received $1,000 as a cash award in recognition of his services to the orphanage. The award is given each year by a local civic organization to a "great humanitarian."

Determine the effect of these transactions on T's gross income.

22. In addition to receiving the items mentioned in Problem 21, T enjoyed the following further benefits:

(a) He received $5,000 under the terms of a will. The decedent was a benefactor of the orphanage, and her will provided that the manager of the orphanage was to receive the funds in lieu of a salary.

(b) Merchandise worth $250 was obtained by T in exchange for trading stamps. The stamps were received by T when he purchased food for the orphanage with funds obtained from donations by the general public. The merchandise was retained by T for his own personal use.

(c) Because of his low income, T qualified for the food stamp program. Food stamps valued in the amount of $600 were received by T and given to his sister.

(d) A creditor forgave T $1,200 of debt. Although T was solvent, his cash flow was insufficient to repay the debt. The creditor forgave the debt because he felt that anyone who was devoting his time and efforts to such a worthy cause (the orphanage) should not have to worry about personal indebtedness.

What effect, if any, would these transactions have on T's gross income?

23. A, age 40, is an officer of the XYZ Company, which provided the following fringe benefits in 1983:

(a) Group-term life insurance protection of $80,000. *(30 par)*

(b) Group hospitalization insurance, $1,080. *not taxable*

(c) Reimbursement of $2,800 from an uninsured medical reimbursement plan maintained exclusively for highly compensated employees. *(includible)* *discriminatory plan*

(d) Salary continuation payments for $3,000 while A was hospitalized for an illness. *taxable*

(e) In addition, $1,800 was collected from a wage continuation policy purchased by A. *not taxable.*

Which items are includible in gross income? *a.c.d.*

24. Which of the following payments for damages would be taxable?

(a) A corporation received $100,000 from a competitor for infringement of its patent rights.

(b) A woman is paid $60,000 because her personal files were incorporated in a biography without her consent.

(c) A client is paid $12,000 by an investment counselor as reimbursement for a loss resulting from the counselor's poor advice.

25. B was a partner in a very successful law firm when she developed emphysema. She was not able to work after Friday, April 1. B died October 1 after collecting her full share of the partnership profits, totaling $15,000, for the period January through September. What is B's disability pay exclusion?

26. R was injured in an accident that was not related to his employment. He incurred $10,000 in medical expenses and collected $7,500 on a medical insurance policy he purchased. He also collected $9,500 in medical benefits under his employer's group plan. Originally, the doctor diagnosed R's injury as requiring no more than three months of disability. Because of subsequent complications, R was unable to return to work until 14 months after the accident. While away from the job, R collected $200 per week on his employer's wage continuation plan. R also owned an insurance policy which paid him $100 per week while he was disabled. What are the tax consequences of the receipts of the

(a) $17,000 medical benefits? *excluded*

(b) $300 per week to replace his wages?

27. Does the taxpayer recognize taxable income in the following situations?
(a) A is a registered nurse working in a community hospital. She is not required to take her lunch on the hospital premises, but she can eat in

the cafeteria at no charge. The hospital adopted this policy to encourage employees to stay on the premises and be available in case of emergencies. During the year, A ate most of her meals on the premises. The total value of those meals was $750.

(b) J is the manager of a hotel. His employer will allow him either to live in one of the rooms rent-free or to receive a $200 per month cash allowance for rent. J elected to live in the hotel.

(c) S is a forest ranger and lives in his employer's cabin in the forest. He is required to live there, and because there are no restaurants nearby, the employer supplies S with groceries that he cooks and eats on the premises.

(d) T is a partner in the ABC Ranch (a partnership). He is the full-time manager of the ranch, and there is a business purpose for his living on the ranch.

28. Analyze the following in terms of the meals and lodging exclusions.

(a) During the busy season when employees are required to work 10- to 12-hour days, the employees receive $5 per day as supper money. The employees eat in local restaurants. *Excluded.*

(b) The N Corporation maintains a dining room for its executives so that good business use can be made of the lunch hour. However, executives are not required to eat in the company's dining room. *excludible.*

(c) The S Corporation pays for its executives' business meals at the Capital City Club. The company also pays for the executives to stay overnight at the club when they work too late to return home at night.

29. During 1983, A received $60 in dividends on stock she owned in AT Company. A's spouse also owned shares in the same corporation and received $120 in dividends. They jointly owned stock in another domestic corporation which paid $50 in dividends and stock in a French corporation which paid $40 in dividends. They also have a joint account in a savings and loan association which paid $80 in dividends, and A collected a $30 dividend on her life insurance policy.

(a) Calculate the § 116 exclusion for Mr. and Mrs. A on a joint tax return, assuming they reside in a common law state.

(b) Calculate the § 116 exclusion if Mr. and Mrs. A file separate returns.

30. Determine a cash basis taxpayer's gross income for 19X2 from the following transactions:

(a) Redemption of Series E U. S. savings bonds for $8,750. The cost of these bonds was $6,250, and no income previously had been recognized on the bonds.

(b) Sale of state of New York bonds for $10,500 plus $200 in accrued interest. The bonds cost $10,000.

(c) Receipt of $1,680 from the state of New York which represented a state income tax refund for tax year 19X0 of $1,500 plus $180 in interest. The taxpayer had itemized deductions of $7,000 on the 19X0 Federal income tax return which reported over $60,000 in taxable income.

31. In a previous year, the cash basis taxpayer took a deduction for an $8,000 commission paid to a broker who supposedly located a customer for the

taxpayer's products. Actually, the customer did not have the necessary capital to buy the taxpayer's product, and the broker was aware of this at the time he collected his commission. In the current year, following the threat of a suit, the broker refunded the commission. The taxpayer is in a higher marginal tax bracket in the current year than he was in the year the commission was deducted. Can he obtain any relief under § 111?

32. During 1984, H (husband) and W (wife) had dividends and other receipts from investments as follows:

July 2     H received two shares of AM Company common stock as a stock dividend. H had the option of receiving $150 cash.

Sept. 30    H received two shares of CE Corporation common stock under a dividend reinvestment plan. He had the option of receiving $150 cash, which was the value of the shares received.

Oct. 15     H sold two shares of CE stock for $160. The shares were received in December 1983 and treated as dividends received under a public utilities reinvestment plan on his 1983 return.

Dec. 15     H and W received $70 cash dividends from B Manufacturing Company on stock owned jointly by H and W.

Dec. 31     W collected $120 dividends from CD Company, a Canadian corporation.

Dec. 31     W received notice from the bank that $120 had been credited to her savings account. She did not withdraw the interest.

Compute gross income for H and W on a joint return.

33. In 1976, J, a cash basis taxpayer, purchased land for $10,000 and constructed a commercial building at a cost of $100,000 financed with a 20-year mortgage. By the end of 1983, J had deducted $50,000 in depreciation on the building; thus, his basis in the properties was $60,000 ($10,000 + $100,000 − $50,000). The balance on the mortgage was $75,000 plus $3,000 accrued interest at the end of 1983, and the taxpayer estimates $78,000 as the approximate value of the property. However, it often takes several years to sell commercial properties in the area. J's tenant has moved out, and $5,000 in mortgage payments are overdue ($3,000 interest and $2,000 principal).

     J believes he can negotiate a debt adjustment with the mortgage holder, and he asks your advice regarding the tax consequences of the following proposals:

(a) J surrenders the property in satisfaction of the debt.

(b) The mortgage holder would forgive J of the $5,000 due and further reduce the principal to $70,000.

## Cumulative Problem

34. H was divorced from F on May 12, 1982. On September 6, 1983, he married W, with whom he files a joint return for 1983.

H is 49 and is employed as an electrical engineer. His salary for 1983 was $45,000. W is 30 and earned $25,200 as a marriage counselor in 1983.

The decree of divorce required H to pay F a principal sum of $100,000 in installments of $12,000 a year for the first five years and $8,000 a year for the next five years and one month. He was also required to pay $200 a month in child support for D, their daughter, age 11. F was granted custody of D and can document that she provided $2,000 of support for D.

H's employer provided him with group-term life insurance coverage in the amount of $90,000, which was equal to twice his salary for 1983.

W's employer provided her with free parking in a parking garage adjacent to their office building. The monthly charge to the general public is $50.

H received dividends of $40 on stock he owned before marriage, and W received dividends of $50 on her separately owned stock. They received dividends of $100 on jointly owned stock which they had acquired after marriage. H and W live in a common law state.

Combined itemized deductions for H and W in 1983 were $6,400, not including state income taxes withheld by their employers. H's employer withheld $810 for state income taxes, and W's employer withheld $430. W received a refund of 1982 state income taxes of $250. She had deducted state income taxes withheld as an itemized deduction on her 1982 return.

Compute income tax, before prepayments or credits, for H and W for 1983.

## Tax Form Problems

35. Florence Flatt retired on permanent and total disability in 1979. If she had not been disabled, she would have been required to retire at age 70 on June 21, 1986. She received $7,200 of disability benefits during 1982. In addition, she received unearned income of $9,000, including interest and dividends of $500. Compute her disability income exclusion on Form 2440.

36. Keith Olson retired on June 30, 1979, and started receiving pension payments of $300 a month on July 15, 1979. During 1982, Keith received $3,600 in pension payments. He had contributed $9,315 to the employer-employee financed pension fund. Compute his taxable pension for 1982 on lines 15 and/or 16 of Form 1040.

## Cumulative Tax Return Problem

37. T, age 45, is married and has two dependent children. In 1982, he had the following transactions:

| | | |
|---|---|---|
| 1. | Salary received from his employer | $ 60,000 |
| 2. | Interest received on state of Nebraska General Obligation Bonds | 8,000 |
| 3. | Group-term life insurance premiums paid by his employer (coverage of $40,000) | 80 |
| 4. | Annual increment in the redemption value of Series E Government savings bonds (T has not previously included the accrued amounts in gross income) | 400 |

5. Taxable dividends received from U. S. companies (held jointly). Of the $5,900 in dividends, $1,000 was mailed by a company on December 31, 1982, and received by T on January 2, 1983        5,900

6. Alimony payments made to T's former wife under a divorce decree        6,000

7. Itemized deductions        6,800

8. Federal income tax withheld and quarterly estimated tax payments        14,000

Required:

(a) Determine T's adjusted gross income and taxable income for 1982. Preparation of pages 1 and 2 of Form 1040 and Schedule B is suggested. Assume that T files a joint return with his wife, who has no other items of income or deductions.

(b) Determine T's tax liability and net tax payable (or refund due) for 1982.

# Chapter 5

# Deductions and Losses: In General

## GENERAL TESTS FOR DEDUCTIBILITY

Following the discussion of gross income and inclusions and exclusions from gross income, it is necessary to review deductions and losses. Understanding the manner in which expense items are classified is a necessary prelude to the discussion of specific tax rules. Therefore, this chapter includes the initial discussion of the classification of expenses under the tax law.

As previously discussed, § 61 provides an all-inclusive definition of gross income. Deductions, however, must be specifically provided for in the statute.[1] The courts have established the doctrine that an item is not deductible unless a specific Code section provides for its deduction (i. e., whether and to what extent deductions shall be allowed depends on "legislative grace")[2].

### SCHEME OF THE TREATMENT OF DEDUCTIONS AND LOSSES

There are three Code sections dealing with deductions and losses that have widespread applicability and as such, can be compared with Code § 61. These Code sections are § § 162, 165, and 212.

Section 162 allows a deduction for "all the ordinary and necessary expenses paid or incurred during the taxable year in carrying on any

---

**1.** § 63(b).
**2.** *New Colonial Ice Co. v. Helvering,* 4 USTC ¶ 1292, 13 AFTR 1180, 54 S.Ct. 788 (USSC, 1934).

trade or business . . . " Section 165 provides a deduction for losses incurred in a trade or business, losses incurred in any transaction entered into for a profit (even though it is not a trade or business), and casualty losses. Section 212 allows deductions for expenses incurred in the production or collection of income; for expenses incurred in the management, conservation, or maintenance of property held for the production of income; and for expenses in connection with the determination, collection, or refund of any tax.

Section 162 deductions (i. e., trade or business deductions) are deductions *for* adjusted gross income, and can be taken whether or not one itemizes. Section 212 deductions, on the other hand, are itemized deductions with the sole exception of expenses incurred in producing rental or royalty income, which are deductions *for* adjusted gross income. Section 165 deductions can be either *for* adjusted gross income or itemized. For example, a business casualty loss is deductible *for* adjusted gross income; a personal casualty loss is an itemized deduction.

The relationship between the three general expense classifications (Sections 162, 165, and 212) and Section 62 is crucial in determining where a deduction is taken on the income tax return. Section 62 specifies which deductions are *for* adjusted gross income and includes (in addition to trade or business deductions) certain employee business expenses, the long-term capital gains deduction, rent and royalty expenses, alimony, and certain other expenses. The employee business expenses that are deductible *for* adjusted gross income are travel and transportation expenses (whether or not reimbursed), all expenses of an outside salesperson, and other reimbursed expenses. All other employee business expenses (e. g., unreimbursed dues and subscriptions) are itemized deductions. Contributions to retirement plans (Keogh plans and Individual Retirement Accounts) are deductions *for* adjusted gross income. Moving expenses incurred in connection with a job in a new location are also deductions *for* adjusted gross income. Employee expenses which are deductions *for* adjusted gross income are discussed in detail in Chapter 10.

These three general expense classifications are supplemented by many Code sections dealing with specific expenses, such as interest (§ 163), taxes (§ 164), and bad debts (§ 166). Such expenses are discussed later in this chapter and in following chapters.

*Trade or Business Expenses.* Section 162(a) permits a deduction for all "ordinary and necessary" expenses paid or incurred in carrying on a trade or business. These include (among others) reasonable salaries paid for personal services, traveling expenses incurred while away from home overnight in the pursuit of a business, and expenses for the use of business property.

The term "trade or business" is not defined in the Code or Regulations, and the courts have not provided a satisfactory definition. Therefore, it is usually necessary to ask one or more of the following questions to determine whether an item qualifies as a trade or business expense:

—Was the use of the particular item related to a business activity? If funds are borrowed for use in a business, the interest should be deductible as a business expense. However, if the funds were used to acquire passive investments (e. g., stocks and taxable bonds), the interest expense is an itemized deduction.

—Was the expenditure incurred with the intent to realize a profit or to produce income? Expenses in excess of the income from raising horses (for example) would not be deductible if the activity were conducted as a personal hobby.

—Were the taxpayer's operation or management activities extensive enough to indicate the carrying on of a trade or business?

Certain employee expenses are treated as § 162 expenses, since employment status is regarded as a trade or business. See Chapter 6 for further discussion.

Section 162 excludes the following items from classification as a trade or business expense:

—Charitable contributions or gifts.

—Illegal bribes and kickbacks and certain treble damage payments.

—Fines and penalties.

The Tax Equity and Fiscal Responsibility Act of 1982 relaxed the rules on so-called grease payments by making the payment deductible unless it is unlawful under the Foreign Corrupt Practices Act of 1977. Formerly, any bribe was disallowed if it was paid to a foreign official and if it was illegal under the laws of the United States. The former law ignored the fact that bribes are accepted business practice in certain foreign countries and that U. S. businesses had to engage in such practices to do business abroad.

*Business and Nonbusiness Losses.* Section 165 provides for a deduction for losses sustained which are not compensated for by insurance, to the extent of the adjusted basis of the property involved.

For individual taxpayers, the losses which result in a deduction are limited to losses incurred in a trade or business or in a transaction entered into for profit. The only personal losses allowed are those that are the result of a casualty. Casualty losses include, but are not limited to, fire, storm, shipwreck, and theft (see Chapter 6 for a further discussion of this area). Deductible personal casualty losses are reduced by $100 per casualty and by 10 percent of adjusted gross income. The excess is an itemized deduction.

*Expenses Attributable to the Production or Collection of Income.* Section 212 provides for the deductibility of ordinary and necessary expenses which are paid or incurred:

—For the production or collection of income.

—For the management, conservation, or maintenance of property held for the production of income.

—In connection with the determination (including preparation), collection, or refund of any tax.

According to this definition, the following items would not be deductible:

—Expenses related to the management, conservation, or maintenance of a personal residence.

—Expenses related to tax-exempt income.

—Hobby, sport, or recreation-related expenses.

Investment-related expenses (e. g., safe deposit box rentals) are deductible under § 212 as deductions attributable to the production of investment income. Investment related expenses, however, are generally treated as itemized deductions. Rent and royalty expenses are deductible *for* adjusted gross income.[3]

To qualify for a deduction under § 212, it is not necessary for the property to be currently producing taxable income. For example, a taxpayer who holds a former residence with the expectation of realizing appreciation in the market value may be entitled to expense deductions such as maintenance and depreciation even though the property is not held for rental purposes.

> **Example 1.** T moves into a new residence. Since real estate values in the area are rising rapidly, T decides to rent the former residence in anticipation of future appreciation. T rents the property on a break-even basis (i. e., the rent is equal to cash outlay). T is entitled to deduct depreciation, maintenance, and other related expenses.

*Classification of Deductible Expenses.* For individual taxpayers, deductions are either (1) *for* adjusted gross income or (2) *from* adjusted gross income (i. e., itemized deductions). Corporations are not subject to this separate classification scheme since the term "adjusted gross income" does not appear in the corporate tax formula.[4] In the computation of taxable income for corporate taxpayers, items of expense are either deductible or not deductible (e. g., certain corporate expenses which are unreasonable would not be deductible).

The most frequently encountered deductions *for* adjusted gross income of individual taxpayers include:

—Expenses of a trade, business, or profession (usually reported on Schedule C of Form 1040).

---

3.  § 62(5).
4.  See the discussion of corporate taxation in Chapter 12.

—Expenses attributable to the production or collection of income or to the management, conservation, or maintenance of property held for the production of income are deducted *from* adjusted gross income (i. e., itemized deductions) with the sole exception of rent and royalty expenses, which are deductible *for* adjusted gross income.

—Certain employment-related expenses (i. e., traveling expenses including meals and lodging while away from home, transportation, moving, and employee expenses which are reimbursed by the employer).

—Alimony payments.

Some of the more frequently encountered deductions *from* adjusted gross income (itemized deductions) include the following:

—Contributions to qualified charitable organizations.

—Medical expenses in excess of five percent (three percent before 1983) of adjusted gross income.

—State and local taxes (e. g., sales, real estate, and state and local income taxes).

—Investment-related expenses (e. g., safe deposit box rental and investment counsel or custodian fees).

The distinction between *for* and *from* adjusted gross income is significant, since many tax calculations are based on the amount of adjusted gross income (e. g., medical expenses and contribution deduction limitations). Further, if an item is deductible *from* adjusted gross income as an itemized deduction, a taxpayer would not be able to benefit from such deduction if the zero bracket amount is used.

**Example 2.** T is married and files a joint return with his spouse in 1983. He and his wife have adjusted gross income of $30,000 and have $2,400 of itemized deductions during the year. In December, T asks you whether he should pay his real estate taxes of $400 in December or wait until the following January. Since the zero bracket amount for 1983 is $3,400 and the real estate taxes are deductible only as itemized deductions, T would obtain no tax benefit from paying the real estate taxes in December and should, therefore, make the payment in January of the following year. Recall, from Chapter 2, the tax planning opportunities in timing these deductions.

## ORDINARY AND NECESSARY EXPENSES

The terms "ordinary" and "necessary" are found in both § § 162 and 212. Section 162 governs the deductibility of trade or business expenses. To be deductible under this provision of the Code, a trade or business expense must be "ordinary and necessary," and in addition, salaries must be "reasonable" in amount.

The words "ordinary and necessary" are not defined in the Code or Regulations. An expenditure must be both ordinary and necessary, but many expenses which are necessary are *not* ordinary. The courts have held that an expense is necessary if a prudent business-person would incur the same expense which is expected to be appropriate and helpful in the taxpayer's business.[5]

## REASONABLENESS REQUIREMENT

Section 162(a)(1) refers to reasonableness solely with respect to salaries and other compensation for personal services.

What constitutes reasonableness is a "question of fact." If an expense is unreasonable, the excess amount is not allowed as a deduction. The question of reasonableness generally arises with respect to closely-held corporations where there is no separation of ownership and management. In such cases, transactions between the shareholders and the company may result in the disallowance of excessive salaries and rent expense to the corporation. If the excessive payments for salaries and rents bear a close relationship to the percentage of stock ownership of the recipients, such amounts are treated as dividends to the shareholders and are not deductible by the corporation. However, deductions for reasonable salaries will not be disallowed on the sole ground that the corporation has paid insubstantial portions of its earnings as dividends to its shareholders.

> **Example 3.** XYZ Corporation is closely-held in equal ownership interests by X, Y, and Z. The company has been highly profitable for several years and has not paid dividends. X, Y, and Z are key officers of the company, and each receives a salary of $200,000. Salaries for similar positions in comparable companies average only $100,000. Amounts paid to X, Y, and Z in excess of $100,000 may be deemed unreasonable; and a total of $300,000 in salary deductions may be disallowed. The excess amounts may be treated as dividends rather than salary income to X, Y, and Z because such amounts are proportional to stock ownership.

# DISALLOWANCE POSSIBILITIES

The tax law includes several provisions for the disallowance of certain types of expenses. Without specific restrictions in the tax law, taxpayers might be able to deduct certain items which in reality are personal, nondeductible expenditures. For example, specific tax rules are provided to determine whether an expenditure is for trade or business purposes or whether it is related to a personal hobby and is therefore nondeductible.

---

5.  *Welch v. Helvering*, 3 USTC ¶ 1164, 12 AFTR 1456, 54 S.Ct. 8 (USSC, 1933).

Certain disallowance provisions represent a codification and/or extension of prior court decisions (e. g., the courts had denied deductions for payments which were deemed to be in violation of public policy). Thus, the tax law was changed to provide specific authority for the disallowance of such deductions.

The following material includes a detailed discussion of specific disallowance provisions in the tax law.

## PUBLIC POLICY LIMITATION

*Justification for Denying Deductions.* The courts have developed the principle that a payment which is in violation of public policy is not a necessary expense and is therefore not deductible.[6] If the law were to permit such deductions, the government would, in effect, be subsidizing a taxpayer's wrongdoing. As a result of these judicial interpretations, § 162 now denies a deduction for bribes and kickbacks (only if the payments violate the U. S. Foreign Corrupt Practices Act of 1977 in the case of foreign bribes and kickbacks), for fines and penalties paid to a government for violation of law, and for two-thirds of the treble damage payments made to claimants resulting from violation of the antitrust law. Section 162(c) states that no deduction is permitted for a kickback which is illegal under state law (if such state law is generally enforced) and which subjects the payor to a criminal penalty or the loss of license or privilege to engage in a trade or business.

> **Example 4.** During the year T, an insurance salesman, paid $5,000 to U, a real estate broker. The payment represented 20% of the commissions earned by T from policies referred by U. Under state law, the splitting of commissions by an insurance salesperson is an act of misconduct which could warrant a revocation of the salesperson's license. Thus, the payments of $5,000 by T to U are not deductible if the state law is generally enforced.

> **Example 5.** Y Company, a moving company, consistently loads its trucks with weights in excess of the limits allowed by state law because the additional revenue more than offsets the fines levied. Because the fines are in violation of public policy (and therefore not a necessary expense), they are not deductible.

*Legal Expenses Incurred in Defense of Civil or Criminal Penalties.* Generally, legal expenses are deductible (*for* adjusted gross income) as ordinary and necessary business expenses if incurred in connection with a trade or business activity. Legal expenses may also be deductible (*for* adjusted gross income) under § 212 as expenses

---

6. *Tank Truck Rentals, Inc. v. Comm.*, 58–1 USTC ¶ 9366, 1 AFTR2d 1154, 78 S.Ct. 507 (USSC, 1958).

incurred in conjunction with rental property which is held for the production of income or (*from* adjusted gross income) as fees for tax advice relative to the preparation of the taxpayer's income tax returns. If legal expenses are incurred for personal reasons (e. g., to obtain a divorce), the expenses are not deductible.

Legal fees pursuant to a criminal defense are deductible if the crime is associated with the taxpayer's trade or business activity.[7] Previously, the position of the IRS was that the legal fees were deductible only if the taxpayer was successful in the criminal suit.

In determining whether legal expenses are deductible, the taxpayer must be able to show that the origin and character of the claim are directly related to a trade or business or an income-producing activity. Otherwise, the legal expenses are personal and nondeductible.

**Example 6.** T, a financial officer of X Corporation, incurred legal expenses in connection with the defense in a criminal indictment for evasion of X Corporation's income taxes. T may deduct her legal expenses because she is deemed to be in the trade or business of being an executive, and such legal action impairs her ability to conduct this business activity.

*Expenses Relating to an Illegal Business.* The usual expenses of operating an illegal business (e. g., a numbers racket) are deductible. However, those expenses that are contrary to public policy (e. g., fines, bribes to public officials) are not deductible.[8]

**Example 7.** S owns and operates an illegal gambling establishment. In connection with this activity, he had the following expenses during the year:

| | |
|---|---:|
| Rent | $ 60,000 |
| Payoffs to the police | 40,000 |
| Depreciation on equipment | 100,000 |
| Wages | 140,000 |
| Interest | 30,000 |
| Criminal fines | 50,000 |
| Illegal kickbacks | 10,000 |
| Total | $ 430,000 |

All of the usual expenses (i. e., rent, depreciation, wages, and interest) are deductible, while the expenses that are contrary to public policy (i. e., payoffs, fines, and kickbacks) are not deductible. Of the $430,000 spent, therefore, $330,000 is deductible while $100,000 is not.

---

7. *Comm. v. Tellier,* 66–1 USTC ¶ 9319, 17 AFTR2d 633, 86 S.Ct. 1118 (USSC, 1966).
8. *Comm. v. Sullivan,* 58–1 USTC ¶ 9368, 1 AFTR2d 1158, 78 S.Ct. 512 (USSC 1958).

An exception was made under TEFRA (new § 280E) for expenses paid with regard to illegal trafficking in drugs. Drug dealers are no longer allowed a deduction for ordinary and necessary business expenses incurred in such a business. A deduction for cost of goods sold is still allowed, however.

> **Example 8.** If S (in Example 7) were in the business of drug dealing, none of the expenses would be deductible except those that constituted cost of goods sold.

## POLITICAL CONTRIBUTIONS AND LOBBYING ACTIVITIES

*Political Contributions.* Generally, no business deduction is permitted for direct or indirect payments for political purposes.[9] Historically, the government has been reluctant to grant favorable tax treatment to business expenditures for political purposes because of the possible abuses and the need to prevent undue influence upon the political process. However, since 1971 a tax benefit has been allowed for political contributions. For years after 1978, a direct tax credit is allowed. The credit is equal to one-half of the contribution but is limited to $50 ($100 on a joint return). Tax credits are discussed in Chapter 8.

*Lobbying Expenditures.* A deduction for certain expenses incurred in the influence of legislation is allowed provided that the proposed legislation is of direct interest to the taxpayer.[10] A "direct" interest exists if the legislation is of such a nature that it will, or may reasonably be expected to, affect the trade or business of the taxpayer. Any dues and expenses paid to an organization which consists of individuals with a common direct interest in proposed legislation also are deductible. A "common direct" interest exists where an organization consists of persons with the same direct interests in legislation or proposed legislation. However, no deduction is allowed for any expenses incurred to influence the public on legislative matters or for any political campaign.

> **Example 9.** T, a contractor, drove to his state capitol to testify against proposed legislation that would affect building codes. T believes that the proposed legislation is unnecessary and not in the best interest of his company. The expenses are deductible because the legislation is of direct interest to T's company. If T later journeyed to another city to make a speech concerning the legislation at a Lion's Club meeting, the expenditures would not be deductible because the expenses were incurred to influence the public on legislative matters.

---

**9.** § 276.
**10.** § 162(e)(1)(A).

## HOBBY LOSSES

*Rationale for § 183.* Deductions under § 162 for business expenses and § 212 for expenses attributable to the production of income are permitted only if the taxpayer can show that the business or investment activity was entered into for the purpose of making a profit and not for personal pleasure. Certain activities may have profit-seeking or personal attributes depending upon individual circumstances (e. g., raising horses and operating a farm which is used as a weekend residence). Since personal losses are not deductible, while losses attributable to profit-seeking activities may be deducted and used to offset a taxpayer's other income, it was necessary to develop tax rules to prevent possible tax avoidance.

*General Rules.* If a taxpayer (an individual or a Subchapter S corporation) can show that an activity has been conducted with the intent to earn a profit, any losses from the activity are fully deductible and § 183 is not applicable. The hobby loss rules apply only if the activity is not engaged in for profit. Section 183 provides that hobby expenses are deductible only to the extent of hobby income.

The Regulations stipulate the following relevant factors which are to be considered in making the determination of the nature of an activity—profit-seeking or a hobby.

—Whether the activity is conducted in a businesslike manner.

—The expertise of the taxpayer or his or her advisers.

—The time and effort expended.

—The expectation that the assets of the activity will appreciate in value.

—The previous success of the taxpayer in the conduct of similar activities.

—The history of income or losses from the activity.

—The relationship of profits earned to losses incurred.

—The financial status of the taxpayer (e. g., if the taxpayer does not have substantial amounts of other income, this fact may indicate that the activity is engaged in for profit).

—Elements of personal pleasure or recreation in the activity.

*Presumptive Rule of § 183.* The Code provides a rebuttable presumption that an activity is profit-seeking if it shows a profit in at least two of any five consecutive years (seven years for activities involving horses) ending with the taxable year in question.[11] For example, if these profitability tests have been met, the activity is presumed to be a trade or business rather than a personal hobby. In effect, the IRS bears the burden of proving that the activity is personal rather than trade or business related.

---

11. § 183(d).

A taxpayer can elect to postpone this presumption until five or seven years from the time the activity began by filing a statement with the Internal Revenue Service within three years of the commencement of the activity. This election automatically extends the statute of limitations. The extension of the statute of limitations is necessary, because otherwise the normal three-year statute of limitations might run out before the taxpayer has had two gain years to meet the presumption of § 183.

> **Example 10.** T began an activity in 1982 and incurred losses in 1982, 1983, and 1984. If the activity earns profits in 1985 and 1986, T would be presumed to be in a trade or business. However, if T later showed losses in 1985 and 1986, the IRS would be barred from collecting deficiencies resulting from losses disallowed in 1982 because the normal statute of limitations is three years. Therefore, the election (which can be in T's favor) extends the statute at least two years to allow the IRS to collect deficiencies if T does not later show a profit in two out of five years. This gives T two more years in which to show a profit and meet the presumption that he is in a trade or business.

> **Example 11.** N is an executive for a large corporation and is paid a salary of $200,000. His wife is a collector of antiques. Several years ago she opened an antique shop in a local shopping center and spends most of her time buying and selling antiques. She occasionally earns a small profit from this activity but more frequently incurs substantial losses. If such losses are business related, they are fully deductible against N's salary income if a joint return is filed.
>
> —As a tax adviser, you should initially determine if the antique "business" has met the two of five years profit test in § 183.
>
> —If the presumption is not met, the activity may nevertheless qualify as a business if the taxpayer can show that the intent is to engage in a profit-seeking activity. It is not necessary to show actual profits.
>
> —Attempts should be made to fit the operation within the nine criteria which are prescribed in the Regulations and listed above.

If an activity is deemed to be a hobby, the expenses are deductible only to the extent of the income from the hobby. However, certain expenses may be allowable under other sections of the Code without regard to the nature of the activity. For example, interest expense is deductible under § 163. Since the total expense deductions of the hobby cannot exceed income, the Code provides that the otherwise deductible items must be deducted first in computing the overall limitation.

**Example 12.** T, the vice-president of an oil company, decides to pursue painting in his spare time. During the current year T incurs the following expenses:

| | |
|---|---:|
| Correspondence study course | $    350 |
| Art supplies | 200 |
| Cost of converting attic in family residence to a studio | 3,000 |
| Interest on $3,000 borrowed from a bank—the proceeds were used to convert the attic to a studio | 240 |
| Fees paid to models | 450 |

During the year T sold three paintings to close friends for $100 each. In the event the activity is deemed a hobby, the $240 of interest expense (which is fully deductible without regard to the nature of the activity) must first be offset against the $300 of income. Thus, only $60 of other hobby expenses are deductible. The net result is that T must include $300 in his gross income and may deduct $240 of interest and $60 of other expenses *for* adjusted gross income. The remaining expenditures are not deductible. If the interest expenses exceed the amount of hobby income, such excess amounts would be deductible *from* adjusted gross income (as itemized deductions) if the activity is deemed a hobby.

*Rental of Vacation Homes.* § 280A places restrictions on taxpayers who rent residences (including vacation homes) for part of the tax year. The following rules apply, depending on the extent to which the home is rented during a particular year:

1. If the residence is rented for less than 15 days, all rentals are excluded from gross income and rent expenses are disallowed. However, the taxpayer may still claim deductions for real estate taxes, interest, etc., which would otherwise be deductions *from* adjusted gross income (itemized deductions).

2. If the dwelling is not used more than 14 days for personal use (or more than 10 percent of the total days rented), it is not considered a residence and the allocations and limitations discussed in item 3 do not apply.

3. If the residence is rented for 15 or more days and is used for personal purposes for the greater of (1) more than 14 days or (2) more than 10 percent of the rental days (the usual case), deductions are applied *for* adjusted gross income and may be limited as are hobby loss expenses.

**Example 13.** S rents her vacation home for two months and lives in the home for one month (a total of three months—one-third personal and two-thirds rental). Rules outlined in 3 apply. S's gross rental income is $3,000. For the entire year, the real estate taxes are $800, S's mortgage interest expense is $1,900, utilities and maintenance expense equals $1,200, and depreciation is $900. These amounts are deductible in this specific order:

| | |
|---|---:|
| Gross income | $ 3,000 |
| Deduct: Taxes and interest (⅔ × $2,700) | 1,800 |
| Remainder to apply to rental operating expenses and depreciation | $ 1,200 |
| Deduct: Utilities and maintenance (⅔ × $1,200) | 800 |
| Balance applicable to depreciation | $ 400 |
| Deduct: Depreciation (⅔ × $900 = $600 but is limited to above balance) | 400 |
| Net income | $ 0 |

The personal use portion of taxes and interest (one-third in this case) is deductible if the taxpayer elects to itemize (see Chapter 7); the personal use portion of utilities, maintenance, and depreciation is not deductible in any case. Also note that the basis of the property is not reduced by the depreciation not allowed [$200 ($600 − $400)] because of the above limitation. (See Chapter 9 for discussion of reduction in basis for depreciation allowed or allowable.)

The Revenue Act of 1978 amended § 280A(d) to resolve the problem of whether or not a taxpayer's primary residence was subject to the above rules in the year it was converted to rental property. The deduction for expenses of the property incurred during a qualified rental period are no longer subject to the personal use test of the vacation home rules. A "qualified rental period" is a consecutive period of 12 or more months and begins or ends in the taxable year in which the *residence* is rented to other than a related party [as defined in § 267(c)(4)] or is held for rental at a fair rental price. If the property is sold before 12 months, the qualified rental period is the actual time rented.

## EXPENDITURES INCURRED FOR TAXPAYER'S BENEFIT OR TAXPAYER'S OBLIGATION

Generally, an expense must be incurred for the taxpayer's benefit or arise from the taxpayer's obligation; an individual cannot claim a tax deduction for the payment of the expenses of another individual.

**Example 14.** During the current year, F pays the interest on his son, T's, home mortgage. Neither F nor T can take a deduction for the interest paid because the obligation is not F's and his son did not pay the interest. The tax result might have been more favorable if F had made a cash gift to T and let him pay the interest. The interest then could have been deducted by the son and (depending upon other gifts and the amount involved), F may not have been liable for any gift taxes. A deduction would have been created with no cash difference to the family. One exception to this rule is the payment of medical expenses for a dependent. Such expenses are deductible by the payor.

**Example 15.**  T's daughter, D, is a full-time student at a university. During the year she earned $4,000 from a part-time job. D would qualify as T's dependent but for the fact that he contributed only 40% of D's support. Any of D's medical expenses paid by her father would not be deductible by T, since these expenses are not for his benefit nor are they his obligation. However, if T contributed more than 50% of D's support to qualify D as his dependent, such expenses would be deductible under the exception noted in Example 14.

## DISALLOWANCE OF PERSONAL EXPENDITURES

Section 262 states that "except as otherwise expressly provided in this chapter, no deduction shall be allowed for personal, living, or family expenses." Thus, an individual must be able to identify a particular section of the Code which sanctions the deductibility of an otherwise personal nondeductible expenditure (e. g., charitable contributions, § 170; medical expenses, § 213; moving expenses, § 217). In addition, an individual may deduct ordinary and necessary expenses paid or incurred (1) for the production or collection of income; (2) for the management, conservation, or maintenance of property held for the production of income; or (3) as expenses in connection with the determination, collection, or refund of any tax.[12]

Sometimes the character of a particular expenditure is not easily determined.

**Example 16.**  During the current year, H pays $1,500 in legal fees and court costs to obtain a divorce from his wife, W. Involved in the divorce action is a property settlement which concerns the disposition of income-producing property owned by H. In a similar situation, the Tax Court[13] held that H could not deduct any of the $1,500 costs. "Although fees primarily related to property division concerning his income-producing property, they weren't ordinary and necessary expenses paid for conservation or maintenance of property held for production of income. Legal fees incurred in defending against claims that arise from taxpayer's marital relationship aren't deductible expenses regardless of possible consequences on taxpayer's income-producing property."

---

**12.**  § 212.
**13.**  *Harry H. Goldberg,* 29 TCM 74, T.C. Memo., 1970–27.

The IRS has clarified the issue of the deduction of legal fees incurred in connection with a divorce.[14] To be deductible, an expense must relate solely to tax advice in a divorce proceeding. For example, legal fees attributable to the determination of dependency exemptions of children, the creation of a trust to make periodic alimony payments, or determination of the tax consequences of a property settlement are deductible if the fees are distinguishable from the general legal fees incurred in obtaining a divorce.

## DISALLOWANCE OF DEDUCTIONS FOR UNREALIZED LOSSES

One of the basic concepts in the tax law is that a deduction can be taken only when a loss has actually been realized. For example, a drop in the market price of securities held by the taxpayer does not result in a loss until the securities are actually sold or exchanged at the lower price. Furthermore, any deductible loss is limited to the taxpayer's cost basis in the asset.

**Example 17.** Early this year T purchased a home in a new residential subdivision for $50,000. Shortly thereafter, heavy spring rains led to severe flooding which indicated that the subdivision's drainage facilities were inadequate. Because the subdivision now has a reputation for poor drainage, T estimates that he could receive only $30,000 on the sale of his home. He has the written appraisal reports of several reputable real estate brokers to support the $20,000 loss in value. Although § 165 allows a deduction for casualty losses, this loss is based on actual physical loss and not the decline in value that may be a "fluctuation in market value not attributable to any actual physical depreciation."[15]

If T later sells his house for $30,000, he will have a $20,000 nondeductible loss. The loss is not deductible because the house is a personal asset, and the decline in value is not the result of a casualty. Casualty losses are discussed in Chapter 6.

## DISALLOWANCE OF DEDUCTIONS FOR CAPITAL EXPENDITURES

The Code specifically disallows a deduction for "any amount paid out for new buildings or for permanent improvements or betterments made to increase the value of any property or estate."[16] The Regulations further define capital expenditures to include those expenditures which add to the value or prolong the life of property or adapt

---

14. Rev.Rul. 72–545, 1972–2 C.B. 179.
15. *Joe B. Thornton,* 47 T.C. 1 (1966).
16. § 263(a).

the property to a new or different use.[17] Incidental repairs and maintenance of the property are not capital expenditures and can be deducted as ordinary and necessary business expenses. Repairing a roof is a deductible expense, but replacing a roof is a capital expenditure subject to depreciation deductions over its useful life. The tune-up of a delivery truck is an expense; a complete overhaul is probably a capital expenditure.

*Exceptions.*   There are several exceptions to the general rule regarding capitalization of expenditures. Taxpayers can elect to expense certain mineral developmental costs and intangible drilling costs.[18] Certain farm capital expenditures (such as soil and water conservation, fertilizer, and land clearing costs) and certain research and experimental expenditures may be immediately expensed.[19]

In addition, § 179 now permits an immediate write-off of certain amounts of depreciable property. These provisions are discussed more fully in Chapter 6.

*Capitalization Versus Expense.*   When an expenditure is capitalized rather than expensed, the deduction is at best deferred and at worst lost forever. Although an immediate tax benefit for a large cash expenditure is lost, the cost can be deducted in increments over a longer period of time. If the expenditure is for some improvement that has an ascertainable life, it can be capitalized and depreciated or amortized over that life. Costs that can be amortized include copyrights and patents. However, there are many other expenditures, such as land and payments made for goodwill, that cannot be amortized or depreciated. Goodwill has an indeterminate life, and land is not a depreciable asset since its value does not generally decline.

> **Example 18.**   T purchased a prime piece of land located in an apartment zoned area. T paid $500,000 for the property which had an old, but usable, apartment building on it. T immediately had the building demolished at a cost of $100,000. The $500,000 purchase price and the $100,000 demolition costs must be capitalized, and the basis of the land is $600,000. Since land is a nondepreciable asset, no deduction is allowed. More favorable tax treatment might result if T rented the apartments in the old building for a period of time to attempt to establish that there was no intent to demolish the building. If T's attempt is successful, it might be possible to allocate a substantial portion of the original purchase price of the property to the building (a depreciable asset). When the building is later demolished, any remaining adjusted cost basis can be taken as an ordinary (§ 1231) loss. See Chapter 10 for a discussion of the treatment of § 1231 assets.

---

17.  Reg. § 1.263(a)–1(b).
18.  § § 263(c) and 616.
19.  § § 174, 175, 180, and 182.

**Example 19.** During the year, T pays $3,000 in legal fees incurred in connection with the defense of a will contest suit. In an action brought by her brothers, T was successful in protecting the inheritance left to her by her mother. T must capitalize the $3,000 of legal fees unless the contested items were income items which must be included in her gross income when received. The capitalized fees are, of course, not deductible by her.

In some cases a taxpayer might prefer to capitalize rather than expense a particular item if the property is depreciable. An immediate deduction may create a net operating loss which (unless utilized) expires in 15 years. No tax benefit (or a smaller tax benefit) would be derived from an immediate deduction. The same expenditure, if capitalized and depreciated over a longer future period, could be offset against taxable income later (or against higher tax bracket income in future years), resulting in a greater tax benefit.

## TRANSACTIONS BETWEEN RELATED PARTIES

The Code places restrictions on the recognition of gains and losses between related parties. Because of relationships created by birth, marriage, and business, there would be endless possibilities for engaging in various types of financial transactions which would produce tax savings with no real economic substance or change. For example, a wife could sell property to her husband at a loss and deduct the loss on their joint return, and her husband could hold the asset indefinitely. This illustrates the creation of an artificial loss. Such "sham" transactions have resulted in a complex set of laws designed to eliminate these abuses.

*Losses.* Section 267 provides for the disallowance of any "losses from sales or exchanges of property . . . directly or indirectly," between related persons. Upon the subsequent sale of such property to a nonrelated party, any gain recognized is reduced by the loss which was previously disallowed.

**Example 20.** F sells common stock with a basis of $1,000 to his son, T, for $800. T sells the stock several years later for $1,100. F's $200 loss is disallowed upon the sale to T, and only $100 of gain is taxable to T upon the subsequent sale.

**Example 21.** F sells common stock with a basis of $1,000 to his son, T, for $800. T sells the stock to an unrelated party for $900. T's gain of $100 is eliminated due to F's previously disallowed loss of $200. Note that the offset may result in only partial tax benefit upon the subsequent sale. If the property had not been transferred to T, F could have recognized a $100 loss upon the subsequent sale to the unrelated party ($1,000 basis − $900 selling price).

**Example 22.** F sells common stock with a basis of $1,000 to an unrelated third party for $800. F's son repurchased the same stock in the market on the same day for $800. The $200 loss is not allowed, because the transaction is an indirect sale between related parties.

*Unpaid Expenses and Interest.* Section 267 also operates to prevent related taxpayers from engaging in tax avoidance schemes in which one related taxpayer uses the accrual method of accounting and the other is on the cash basis. For example, an accrual basis closely-held corporation could borrow funds from a cash basis individual shareholder. At the end of the year, the corporation would accrue and deduct the interest, but the cash basis lender would not recognize interest income, since no interest had been paid. Section 267 specifically disallows a deduction to the accruing taxpayer unless the interest is paid within two and one-half months after the end of the lender's taxable year. This rule applies to interest as well as to other expenses, such as salaries and bonuses. Section 267 is particularly burdensome for owner-employees of closely-held corporations, since the accrual basis corporation will never be entitled to the deduction if the payment is not made within the two and one-half month period. This stipulation remains in effect even if the payment is made during a subsequent period, and the cash basis individual is required to include the payment in income.

*Relationships and Constructive Ownership.* Section 267 operates to disallow losses and deductions only between related parties. Losses or deductions generated by similar transactions with an unrelated party are allowed. Related parties include the following:

—Siblings and half-siblings, spouse, ancestors (i. e., parents, grandparents), and lineal descendants (i. e., children, grandchildren) of the taxpayer.

—A corporation owned more than 50 percent (directly or indirectly) by the taxpayer.

—Two corporations owned more than 50 percent (directly or indirectly) by the taxpayer if either corporation is a personal holding company or a foreign personal holding company.

—A series of other complex relationships between trusts, corporations, and individual taxpayers.

The law provides that constructive ownership rules are applied to determine whether the taxpayers are "related."[20] Constructive ownership rules state that stock owned by certain relatives or related entities is deemed to be owned by the taxpayer for loss and expense deduction disallowance purposes. For example, a taxpayer is deemed to own not only his or her stock but the stock owned by his or her lineal descendants, ancestors, brothers and sisters or half-brothers

---

**20.** § 267(c).

or -sisters, and spouse. The taxpayer is also deemed to own his or her proportionate share of stock owned by any partnership, corporation, estate, or trust of which he or she is a member. Additionally, an individual is deemed to own any stock owned, directly or indirectly, by his or her partner. However, constructive ownership by an individual of the partnership's and the other partner's shares does not extend to the individual's spouse or other relatives.

> **Example 23.** The stock of V Corporation is owned 20% by T, 30% by T's father, 30% by T's mother, and 20% by T's sister. On July 1 of the current year, T loaned $10,000 to V Corporation at 7% annual interest, principal and interest payable on demand. V Corporation uses the accrual basis, and T uses the cash basis for tax purposes. Both are on a calendar year. Since T is deemed to own the 80% owned by her parents and sister, she constructively owns 100% of V Corporation. If the corporation accrues but does not pay the interest within the taxable year or within two and one-half months thereafter (i. e., by March 15 of next year), no deduction is allowed to V. If T were an accrual basis taxpayer or if payment were actually or constructively received by T, the deduction would be allowed.

## SUBSTANTIATION REQUIREMENTS

The tax law is built on a voluntary system: Taxpayers file their tax returns, report income and take deductions to which they are entitled, and pay their taxes through the withholding method (on salaries and wages) or by making estimated tax payments throughout the year. Some events throughout the year should be documented as they occur. For example, it is generally advisable to receive a pledge payment statement from one's church, in addition to a cancelled check, for proper documentation of a charitable contribution. Other types of deductible expenditures may require receipts or some other type of support.

Some areas of deductible expenditures such as business entertainment, gifts, and travel have been subject to abuse. Prior to 1962, taxpayers could rely on the so-called Cohan rule which provided that a taxpayer could deduct travel or entertainment expenses based on an approximation of the actual amounts if the exact amount was not determinable. In *Cohan v. Comm.*, the Court permitted a partial deduction for entertainment expenses of a playwright who kept no records.[21] The law now provides that no deduction will be allowed for any travel, entertainment, or business gift expenditure unless properly substantiated by "sufficient evidence corroborating [the taxpayer's] own statements" of the following information:[22]

---

**21.** *Cohan v. Comm.*, 2 USTC ¶ 489, 8 AFTR 10552, 39 F.2d 540 (CA–2, 1930).
**22.** § 274(d).

—The amount of the expense.

—The time and place of travel or entertainment (or date of gift).

—The business purpose of such expense.

—The business relationship of the taxpayer to the person entertained (or receiving the gift).

"Adequate records" can be a diary, account book, or other expense record, provided the record is made at or near the time of the expenditure. Furthermore, documentary evidence (e. g., receipts, paid bills) is required for lodging and any other expenditure of $25 or more.

**Example 24.** B had entertainment expenses which were substantiated only by credit card receipts. The receipts established the time, place, and amount of the expenditure. Because neither the business relationship nor the business purpose was established, the deduction may be disallowed.

**Example 25.** D had entertainment expenses which were substantiated by a diary showing the time, place, amount of the expenditure, business relationship, and business purpose. However, since he had no receipts, any expenditures of $25 or more may be disallowed.

Specific rules for deducting travel and entertainment expenses are discussed in Chapter 6.

## EXPENSES AND INTEREST RELATING TO TAX-EXEMPT INCOME

Since certain income, such as interest on municipal bonds, is tax-exempt and § 212 allows one to deduct expenses incurred for the production of income, it might be possible to make money at the expense of the government by excluding interest income and deducting interest expense.

**Example 26.** P, a taxpayer in the 50% bracket, purchased $100,000 of 12% municipal bonds. At the same time she used the bonds as collateral on a bank loan of $100,000 at 18% interest. A positive cash flow would result from the tax benefit as follows:

| | |
|---|---:|
| Cash paid out on loan | ($ 18,000) |
| Cash received from bonds | 12,000 |
| Tax savings from deducting interest expense (50% of $18,000 interest expense) | 9,000 |
| Net positive cash flow | $ 3,000 |

*Specific Disallowance Under the Law.* In order to eliminate the possibility outlined above, § 265 specifically disallows as a deduction the expenses of producing tax-exempt income. Interest on any indebtedness incurred or continued to purchase or carry tax-exempt obligations (including All-Savers Certificates) is disallowed under § 265. There is an exception for nonbanking financial institutions.

*Judicial Interpretations.* It is often difficult to show a direct relationship between borrowing and investment in tax-exempt securities. Suppose, for example, that a taxpayer borrows money, adds it to existing funds, buys inventory and stocks, then later sells the inventory and buys municipal bonds. A series of transactions such as these can completely obscure any relationship between the loan and the tax-exempt investment. One solution would be to disallow any interest on any debt to the extent that any tax-exempt securities were held. This kind of approach would preclude individuals from deducting part of their home mortgage interest if they owned an All-Savers Certificate. Obviously, the law was not intended to go to such extremes. As a result, judicial interpretations have tried to show reasonableness in the disallowance of interest deductions under § 265.

In one case,[23] a company used municipal bonds as collateral on short-term loans to meet seasonal liquidity needs. The Court disallowed the interest deduction on the grounds that the company could predict its seasonal liquidity needs and therefore knew it would have to borrow the money to continue to carry the tax-exempt securities. The same company *was* allowed an interest deduction on a building mortgage, even though tax-exempt securities it owned could have been sold to pay off the mortgage. The Court reasoned that short-term liquidity needs would have been impaired if the tax-exempt securities were sold and bore no relationship to the long-term financing of a construction project.

In another case,[24] the Court disallowed an interest deduction to a company that refused to sell tax-exempt securities it had received from the sale of a major asset, which necessitated large borrowings to finance the operation. The Court found that the primary reason that the company would not sell its bonds to reduce its bank debt was the tax savings. Other business reasons existed for holding the municipal bonds, but the dominant reason was for the tax savings. Moreover, there was a direct relationship between the bonds and the debt because they both arose from the same transaction.

**Example 27.** In January of the current year, T borrowed $100,000 at 8% interest which she used to purchase 5,000 shares of stock in P Corporation. In July of the same year, she sold the stock for $120,000 and reinvested the proceeds in City of Denver

---

**23.** *The Wisconsin Cheeseman, Inc. v. U. S.,* 68–1 USTC ¶ 9145, 21 AFTR2d 383, 388 F.2d 420 (CA–7, 1968).

**24.** *Illinois Terminal Railroad Co. v. U. S.,* 67–1 USTC ¶ 9374, 19 AFTR2d 1219, 375 F.2d 1016 (Ct.Cls., 1967).

bonds, the income from which is tax-exempt. Assuming the $100,000 loan remained outstanding throughout the entire year, the interest attributable to the period in which the bonds were held cannot be deducted.

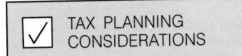

## TAX PLANNING CONSIDERATIONS

### UNREASONABLE COMPENSATION

In substantiating the reasonableness of a shareholder-employee's compensation, an internal comparison test is sometimes useful. If it can be shown that employees who are nonshareholders receive the same (or more) compensation as shareholder-employees in comparable positions, it is evident that compensation is not unreasonable.

Another possibility is to demonstrate that the shareholder-employee has been underpaid in prior years. For example the shareholder-employee may have agreed to take a less-than-adequate salary during the unprofitable formative years of the business, provided this "postponed" compensation will be paid in later, more profitable years. This agreement should be documented, if possible, in the corporate minutes.

It is important to keep in mind that in testing for reasonableness, it is the *total* pay package that must be taken into account. One must look at all fringe benefits or perks, such as contributions by the corporation to a qualified pension plan (even though those amounts are not immediately available to the covered employee-shareholder).

### PERSONAL EXPENDITURES

Section 262 disallows a deduction for legal fees that are personal in nature. Legal fees are deductible under § 212(3), however, to the extent such services represent the rendering of tax advice (e. g., the tax consequences of a property settlement or child support payments). Therefore, it is advisable to request an itemization of attorney's fees to substantiate a partial deduction for the tax-related amounts.

### RELATED TAXPAYERS

If an accrual basis corporation accrues salary, bonus, interest, etc. to a related shareholder-employee, the corporation must be careful to pay these amounts within two and one-half months of the end of the year. Payments not made within the two and one-half month period are not allowed as a deduction in any year, even though the payments are subsequently made. If a company is unable to pay the accrued amounts (or does not do so because of an oversight), it may still be possible to show that the amounts have been constructively received in the year of accrual. In such event, the shareholder-employee should include the accrued amounts in income in the year of accrual, and the corporation should claim a deduction in the same period. A corporation which is temporarily short of funds should consider borrowing money to pay the accrued amounts to insure against loss of the deduction.

Note that an extension of time to file an income tax return does not also extend the two and one-half month period for payment of accrued items to related shareholder-employees.

**Example 28.** In February, Y Corporation was granted an extension of time to file its corporate tax return to June 15, 1984 (rather than March 15). An accrued bonus of $20,000 to an employee-shareholder was paid on June 1, 1984. Y Corporation cannot deduct the bonus on its calendar-year 1983 return, nor can it deduct the bonus in 1984 when paid, even though the employee-shareholder must include it in his 1984 return.

## SHIFTING DEDUCTIONS

Taxpayers should manage their obligations to avoid the loss of a deduction. Deductions can be shifted among family members, depending upon who makes the payment. For example, a father buys a car for his daughter and both sign the note. If either one makes the payment, that person gets the deduction for the interest. If the note is signed by the daughter only and her father makes the payment, neither is entitled to a deduction.

## HOBBY LOSSES

To demonstrate that an activity has been entered into for the purpose of making a profit (i. e., not a hobby), a taxpayer should treat the activity like a business. The business should engage in advertising, use business letterhead stationery, and maintain a business phone.

If a taxpayer's activity earns a profit in two out of five consecutive years, the presumption is that the activity is engaged in for profit. It may be possible for a cash basis taxpayer to meet these requirements by timing the payment of expenses or the receipt of revenues. The payment of certain expenses incurred prior to the end of the year may be made in the following year, or the billing of year-end sales may be delayed so that collections are received in the following year.

It should be kept in mind that the two-out-of-five year rule under § 183 is not absolute. All it does is shift the presumption. If a profit is not made in two out of five years, the losses may still be allowed if the taxpayer can show that they are due to the nature of the business. For example, success in artistic or literary endeavors can take a long time. Also, due to the present state of the economy, full-time farmers and ranchers are unable to show a profit; how can one expect a part-time farmer or rancher to do so?

On the other hand, merely satisfying the two-out-of-five year rule does not guarantee that one is automatically "home free" either. Consider, for example, the following situation:

| Year | Gain (loss) |
|------|-------------|
| 1980 | $(50,000) |
| 1981 | (35,000) |
| 1982 | (60,000) |
| 1983 | 200 |
| 1984 | 125 |

Under these circumstances, the Internal Revenue Service should have a relatively easy time of showing that the operation is not much of a business.

## PROBLEM MATERIALS

### Questions for Class Discussion

1. T and S are unrelated individual single taxpayers, and each has gross income of $20,000 and deductions of $3,000 for the current year. However, T's deductions are *for* adjusted gross income while S's are *from* adjusted gross income. Are these taxpayers in the same position? Why or why not?

2. Are the following items deductible *for* adjusted gross income, deductible *from* adjusted gross income, or nondeductible personal items?

    (a) Unreimbursed travel expenses of an employee. – for.

    (b) Alimony payments. — for

    (c) Charitable contributions. — from

    (d) Medical expenses. — from

    (e) Safe deposit box rentals. – from.

    (f) Repairs made on a personal residence. — Not deductible.

    (g) Expenses related to tax-exempt municipal bonds. – not deductible.

    *Capital exp –*

3. Discuss the implications of "reasonable" compensation. Does it make a difference if the corporation is owned by the taxpayer and his or her immediate family? What are the tax consequences to the corporation and shareholder-employee?

4. Is a taxpayer permitted to deduct bribes, kickbacks, or fines and penalties? Why or why not? NO

5. Are legal expenses deductible if they are incurred to obtain a divorce? Are they deductible if they are incurred in connection with a trade or business? —yes Why is this distinction made?

6. Are lobbying expenses deductible? Explain.

7. What factors should be considered to determine whether an activity is a legitimate business activity or a hobby? *for profit - not for personal pleasure Page 5-10.*

8. If a taxpayer is unable to meet the requirements of § 183 relative to earning a profit in at least two of five consecutive years, is it possible to qualify the activity as a business? Why or why not?

9. Why has the Code placed restrictions upon deductions relating to the rental of vacation homes?

10. What would be the tax manipulation possibilities if a taxpayer could deduct items paid by him but for the benefit of a parent who does not qualify as a dependent?

11. Why is a loss limited to a taxpayer's basis (even where the fair market value is much higher) or actual outlay?

12. Distinguish between deductible repairs and capital expenditures. Is the distinction dependent upon the dollar amount involved? *no*

13. Discuss the reasons for the disallowance of losses between related parties. Would it make any difference if a parent sold stock to an unrelated third party and the child repurchased the same number of shares of the stock in the market the same day?

14. What is constructive ownership? Discuss.

15. Discuss the substantiation requirements for deductible expenditures, particularly those for travel and entertainment.

16. Is a deduction permitted for the interest payments on the borrowed funds used to acquire tax-exempt securities? Why?

17. Discuss the tracing problems which are encountered in the enforcement of the restrictions of § 265 which disallow a deduction for the expenses of producing tax-exempt income.

## Problems

18. K inherited some money from his aunt which he subsequently invested in the stock market. K has an office (complete with ticker tape and secretary) where he spends eight hours a day buying and selling securities. He does not have a broker's license and does not buy or sell for anyone other than himself. K incurred office expenses of $9,000 and earned investment income of $286,000. Can he deduct the expenses as trade or business expenses under § 162?

19. T operates a trucking company in Kansas and Nebraska. T's financial records indicate quite clearly that he can stay in business (on a profitable basis) only if his trucks operate at 65 miles per hour during the runs. In the current year T's firm was fined $10,000 by the Kansas and Nebraska authorities for violations of the 55 mile per hour speed limit. Comment on the deductibility of the fines. *(no deduction)*

20. T owns a restaurant that has a limited liquor license (beer and wine only) under state law. He travels to the capital to testify against a proposed bill that would eliminate such limited licenses. Is his travel expense deductible? *yes.*

21. L is a housewife who makes pottery items at home for sale to friends. She had the following income and expenses for the year: — *no*

| | |
|---|---|
| Sales | $ 1,000 |
| Expenses: | |
| Materials | 400 |
| Advertising | 250 |
| Travel | 350 |
| Classes in ceramics | 500 |
| | $ 1,500 |
| Net loss | $ (500) |

Comment on whether her activities constitute a "trade or business."

22. Taxpayer is engaged in horse breeding activities in addition to his regular executive position with a large corporation. He had three years of operations with losses of $120,000, $100,000, and $130,000, respectively. Upon audit by the IRS, he demands a chance at the presumption period of two out of seven years. In the fourth and fifth years, he sustained losses of $90,000 and $126,000. In the sixth and seventh years, he showed net profits of $1,500 and $1,000, respectively.

    (a) Is he "safe" under § 183?

    (b) Can he claim the statute of limitations bars the loss disallowances for the earlier years?

23. During the current year, P's vacation home was used as follows: one month of occupancy by P, four months of rental to unrelated parties, and seven months of vacancy. Further information concerning the property is summarized below:

| | |
|---|---|
| Rental income | $ 4,500 |
| Expenses: | |
| Real estate taxes | $ 1,000 |
| Interest on mortgage | 2,500 |
| Utilities and maintenance | 1,200 |
| Repairs | 400 |
| Landscaping | 1,700 |
| Depreciation | 3,000 |

Compute P's net rental income or loss and the amount(s) that can be itemized on his income tax return.

24. Indicate whether each expenditure below is deductible by F, who paid the items in question:

    (a) Interest on his dependent son's auto loan. *no*

    (b) Medical expenses of his mother who furnishes 60% of her own support. *no*

    (c) Property taxes on his wife's summer home. They are filing a joint return. *yes*

    (d) Business lunches for F's clients. *yes*

25. H obtained a divorce in 19X6 and paid the following fees:

| | |
|---|---:|
| Court costs and legal fees of obtaining divorce | $ 200 |
| Rewriting of will | 150 |
| Detective fees paid for obtaining evidence of infidelity | 500 |
| Legal fees to determine who may claim the children as dependents | 500 |
| Legal fees to determine the basis of settlement property | 1,500 |

How much can H deduct on his 19X6 return?

26. P made the following expenditures in 19X6 in connection with her business property. Identify the items which are (a) deductible in 19X6, (b) depreciable capital expenditures, and (c) nondepreciable capital expenditures.

| | |
|---|---:|
| Purchase of 10 acres for a parking lot | $ 15,000 |
| Paving of parking lot | 6,000 |
| Overhaul of delivery truck | 1,200 |
| Tune-up of second delivery truck | 180 |
| Purchase of goodwill | 3,000 |
| Interest on loan on 10 acres | 900 |
| Replacement of furnace in factory | 4,500 |
| Repair of hail-damaged roof tiles | 1,350 |

27. J sold stock (basis of $20,000) to her brother, B, for $16,000.

    (a) What are the tax consequences to J? — non-ded-

    (b) What are the tax consequences to B if he later sells the stock for $21,000? (she can disallow your loss J had. So taxable gain of $1,000.

    (c) If B sells it for $14,000? — non ded.

    (d) If B sells it for $18,000? — no Reco. gain or loss.

28. What is R's constructive ownership of X Corporation, given the following information?

| | |
|---|---:|
| Shares owned by R | 450 |
| Shares owned by S, R's uncle | 300 |
| Shares owned by T, R's partner | 15 |
| Shares owned by U, a partnership owned by R and T equally | 150 |
| Shares owned by V, R's granddaughter | 285 |
| Shares owned by unrelated parties | 300 |

29. J is the sole owner of X Corporation (an accrual basis taxpayer). X Corporation owes J $125,000 and accrues $10,000 of interest expense on December 31, 19X8.

    (a) What are the tax consequences to J and X Corporation if the interest is paid on January 15, 19X9?

    (b) On March 20, 19X9?

30. T, a college professor, receives a nontaxable research grant of $3,600 and her regular salary of $21,600 during a year in which she takes a sabbatical leave. In connection with the leave, she incurs $2,100 in travel expenses, all of which would normally be deductible. How much of a deduction will she be allowed for the travel expenses?

## Cumulative Problem

31. Z, age 36, is married to M. They have no dependents. Z is employed as manager of a large apartment complex. His salary for 1983 was $30,000, and he was provided with an apartment free of rent. The apartment he lives in would rent for $400 a month. His contract with his employer requires him to live on the premises. M earned $18,000 as an office manager.

In July 1983, M was injured in an automobile accident. In November, she received a settlement for damages of $20,000 from the other driver's insurance company. As a result of her injuries, M incurred medical expenses of $2,500. In September, she received reimbursement of $2,500 from the insurance company under an accident and health policy provided by her employer.

Over the years, Z had developed a close working relationship with B, who owns a moving company. On his recommendation, several tenants hired B to move them. As an expression of his appreciation, on December 24, 1983, B gave Z a stereo system for which he had paid $1,500 on December 23.

Z and M had the following interest items in 1983:

> $200—interest received from United States Series H savings bonds
> $100—interest credited to their savings account but not withdrawn
>        in 1983
> $250—interest received on City of Miami general obligation bonds

On April 14, Z sold some stock to pay Federal income tax they owed for 1982. The stock, which he had acquired on January 12, 1983, for $1,000, was sold for $1,500. On November 8, 1983, he sold 50 shares of stock for $43 a share. He had acquired the stock on February 16, 1982, for $27 a share. Z and M received $600 dividends on their stock investments in 1983.

Z made a preliminary computation of their tax liability late in December and realized they needed to take some action to reduce their taxable income. His first move was to sell 100 shares of stock to his father, with the understanding that he would buy the stock back in January 1984. He sold the stock, which had been acquired on August 23, 1983, at $36 a share for $2,000. His next action was to delay depositing his December 1983, salary check until January 4, 1984. His net pay for December, after withholding and other deductions, was $1,731.

In examining their receipts, canceled checks, and other documents, you have ascertained that Z and M have various itemized deductions of $4,300, not including any amount described below:

(a) In connection with their stock investments, Z paid an investment counselor $300 in 1983. He also rented a safe deposit box, in which he kept their stocks, for $50.

(b) Z's father was ill for three months in 1983 and was unable to work. To help his father during this time, Z made three of his father's mortgage payments, which included interest of $950.

Z and M file a joint return. You are to compute their taxable income for 1983.

# Chapter 6

# Deductions and Losses:
# Certain Business
# Expenses and
# Employee Expenses

Working with the tax formula for individuals requires the proper classification of items which are deductible *for* adjusted gross income and items which are deductions *from* adjusted gross income (itemized deductions). Business expenses and losses, discussed in this chapter, are reductions of gross income to arrive at the taxpayer's adjusted gross income. The one exception, however, might be casualty losses, which could be either deductions *for* adjusted gross income or deductions *from*, depending on the circumstances.

This chapter also covers employee expenses. The Code provides that certain employee expenses are deductible *for* adjusted gross income and treated as expenses incurred in a trade or business. Other types of employee expenses are deductible *from* adjusted gross income (itemized deductions). Consideration is given first to the proper classification of employee expenses before discussing specific items.

Itemized deductions (in excess of the zero bracket amount) and a taxpayer's personal and dependency exemptions are subtracted *from* adjusted gross income in the determination of taxable income. Itemized deductions are discussed in Chapter 7; the zero bracket amount and the personal and dependency exemptions were discussed in Chapter 2.

## BAD DEBTS

If a taxpayer sells goods or provides services on credit and the account receivable subsequently becomes worthless, a bad debt deduction is permitted only if income arising from the creation of the debt (accounts receivable) was previously included in income. No deduction is allowed, for example, for a bad debt arising from the sale of a product or service when the taxpayer is on the cash basis, because no income is reported until the cash has been collected. A bad debt deduction for a cash basis taxpayer would amount to a double deduction, because the expenses of the product or service rendered are deducted when payments are made to suppliers and to employees.

**Example 1.** T, an individual engaged in the practice of accounting, performed accounting services for X for which he charged $8,000 ($7,700 for services and $300 materials). X never paid the bill, and his whereabouts are unknown.

If T is an accrual basis taxpayer, the $8,000 would be included in income when the services were performed. The $300 would be a business expense when the costs were incurred. When it is determined that X's account will not be collected, the $8,000 will be expensed as a bad debt.

If T is a cash basis taxpayer, the $8,000 would not be included in income until payment is received. However, the $300 would be a business expense at the time the expense was incurred. When it is determined that X's account will not be collected, the $8,000 will not be a bad debt expense, since it was never recognized as income.

A deduction is allowed for any debt which becomes wholly worthless or partially worthless during the taxable year.[1] The taxpayer must be able to demonstrate to the satisfaction of the IRS the amount which is worthless and the amount charged off on the taxpayer's books. If the debt previously deducted as partially worthless becomes totally worthless in a future year, only the remainder not previously deducted can be written off.

One of the more difficult tasks is determining if and when a bad debt is, in fact, worthless, since the loss is deductible solely in the year of partial or total worthlessness. Legal proceedings need not be initiated against the debtor when the surrounding facts indicate that such action will not result in collection.

**Example 2.** In 19X1, J loaned $1,000 to K, who agreed to repay the loan in two years. In 19X3, K disappeared after the note became delinquent. If a reasonable investigation by J indicates that he cannot find K or a suit against her would not result in collection, he can deduct the $1,000 in 19X3.

Bankruptcy is generally an indication of at least partial worthlessness of a debt. Bankruptcy may create worthlessness before the

---

1.   § 166(a); Reg. § 1.166–3.

settlement date. If this is the case, the deduction must be taken in the year of worthlessness, not in the later year upon settlement.

A taxpayer may use the reserve for bad debts method or the specific charge-off method in accounting for bad debts. However, a deduction for partial worthlessness of a bad debt is permitted only if the specific charge-off method is being used. Under the reserve for bad debts method, a deduction is allowed for a reasonable addition to the reserve.

## ALLOWABLE METHODS

A taxpayer using the specific charge-off method receives a deduction when a specific debt becomes either partially or wholly worthless. The taxpayer must satisfy the IRS that a debt is partially worthless and must demonstrate the amount of worthlessness. In the case of total worthlessness, a deduction is allowed for the entire amount in the year the debt becomes worthless. The amount of the deduction depends on the taxpayer's basis in the bad debt. If the debt arose from the sale of services or products and the face amount was previously included in income, this amount is deductible. If the taxpayer purchased the debt, the deduction is equal to the amount the taxpayer paid for the debt instrument.

Under the reserve method of accounting for bad debts, the taxpayer's deduction is based on a "reasonable addition" to the reserve. This may be contrasted with the specific charge-off method. A taxpayer using this method bases the bad debt deduction on the actual write-off of specific accounts. What constitutes a "reasonable addition" to the reserve is largely a matter of judgment and depends on individual facts and circumstances. If the taxpayer's estimated bad debts are more (or less) than actual losses, the reserve must be adjusted downward (or upward) in the future year.

## DETERMINING RESERVE ADDITIONS

The courts have generally applied a formula approach for determining a "reasonable addition" to the bad debt reserve. The IRS frequently uses an approach which was derived from the *Black Motor Co.* case.[2] The formula approach is based on a weighted average of the ratio of bad debts to accounts and notes receivable for the current year and preceding five years. This percentage is then applied to the ending balance of accounts and notes receivable to determine the required amount in the reserve at the end of the year. The bad debt deduction represents the amount necessary to bring the reserve up to its required balance at the end of the year.

---

**2.** *Black Motor Co. v. Comm.*, 42–1 USTC ¶ 9265, 28 AFTR 1193, 125 F.2d 977 (CA–6, 1942).

### Example 3.   Black Motor Co. formula approach

1. $\dfrac{\text{Bad debts—current year plus five preceding years}}{\begin{array}{c}\text{Total accounts and notes receivable at the end}\\\text{of each of these years}\end{array}}$   $\dfrac{20,000}{500,000} = 4\%$

2. 4% × accounts and notes receivable at the end of
   the current year ($80,000)                                    $ 3,200*

3. Beginning balance in the reserve for doubtful ac-
   counts                                                                       $ 3,000
   + Recoveries of previous accounts written off                 300
   − Write-off of specific accounts during the year            (600)
   + Bad debt deduction (addition to reserve)                    500
   Ending balance in the reserve                                    $ 3,200

*This amount represents the required balance in the reserve at the end of the year.

It should be noted that the formula approach is not mandatory; individual facts and circumstances must be taken into account. In addition, the IRS now agrees that the formula outlined above is not controlling and that the bad debt addition may be more or less depending on the facts and circumstances.

## ELECTION OF METHODS

Subject to the approval of the IRS, a taxpayer may elect to use either the reserve or specific charge-off method of accounting. However, the taxpayer can elect the reserve method without the consent of the IRS if the election is made in the first taxable year that a bad debt occurs. The election is subject to the approval of the District Director upon examination of the return. Once an election is made, that method must be followed in all future years unless the taxpayer receives permission to change. A request for a change in method must generally be made within 180 days of the start of the tax year for which the change is sought.[3]

If a taxpayer desires to change to the reserve method, only 10 percent of the initial reserve amount is deductible in the year of change. The remaining 90 percent of the initial reserve deduction must be spread over the next succeeding nine years. Spreading the deduction over a 10-year period is required to prevent the "bunching" of deductions in one year.

## BUSINESS VERSUS NONBUSINESS BAD DEBTS

A nonbusiness bad debt is a debt unrelated to the taxpayer's trade or business either when it was created or when it became worthless. The nature of a debt depends on whether the lender was engaged in the business of lending money or if there is a proximate relationship between the creation of the debt and the lender's trade or business.

---

3.   § 466(e); Reg. § 1.446–1(e)(3).

The use to which the borrowed funds are put by the debtor is of no consequence. Loans to relatives or friends are the most common type of nonbusiness bad debt.

> **Example 4.** J loaned his friend, S, $1,500. S used the money to start a business which subsequently failed. Even though proceeds of the loan were used in a business, the loan is a nonbusiness bad debt because the business was S's, not J's.

> **Example 5.** J loaned another friend, T, $500. T was unable to repay J because of financial difficulties. The loss is attributable to a nonbusiness bad debt.

The distinction between a business bad debt and a nonbusiness bad debt is important: A business bad debt is deductible as an ordinary loss in the year incurred, whereas a nonbusiness bad debt is always treated as a short-term capital loss.[4] Thus, regardless of the age of a nonbusiness bad debt, the deduction is of limited benefit due to the capital loss limitations on deductibility in any one year. In addition, no deduction is allowed for the partial worthlessness of a nonbusiness bad debt, and no deduction is permitted if the lender receives a partial recovery of the debt. However, the taxpayer is entitled to deduct the net amount of the loss upon final settlement of the debt.

The following are illustrations of business bad debts adapted from the Regulations.

> **Example 6.** In 19X1, L sold his business but retained a claim (i. e., note or account receivable) against B. The claim became worthless in 19X2. L's loss is treated as a business bad debt because the debt was created in the conduct of L's former trade or business. Business bad debt treatment is accorded to L despite the fact that he was holding the note as an investor and was no longer in a trade or business when the claim became worthless.

> **Example 7.** In 19X1, L died and left his business assets to his son, S. One of the business assets inherited by S was a claim against B which became worthless in S's hands in 19X3. S's loss is a business bad debt, since "the loss is sustained as a proximate incident to the conduct of the trade or business in which he is engaged at the time the debt becomes worthless."

The nonbusiness bad debt provisions are not applicable to corporations; it is assumed that any loans made by a corporation are related to its trade or business.

---

4. § 166(d)(1)(B).

## SUMMARY OF BAD DEBT PROVISIONS

**Figure I**

BAD DEBT DEDUCTIONS

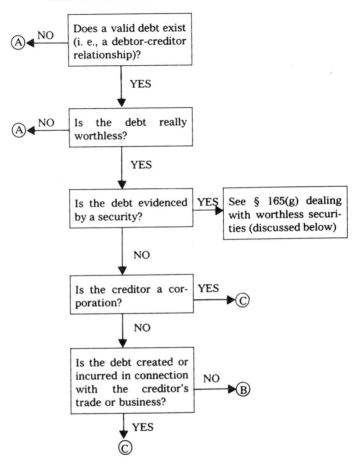

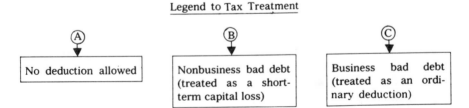

Legend to Tax Treatment

## LOANS BETWEEN RELATED PARTIES

Loans between relatives always raise the issue of whether the loan was bona fide or was a gift. The Regulations state that a bona fide debt arises from a debtor-creditor relationship based on a valid and enforceable obligation to pay a fixed or determinable sum of money. Thus, individual circumstances must be examined to determine whether advances between related parties are gifts or loans. Some considerations are these: Was a note properly executed? Is there collateral? What collection efforts were made? What was the intent of the parties?

> **Example 8.** L loans $2,000 to his widowed mother for an operation. L's mother owns no property and is not employed, and her only income consists of the Social Security benefits. No note is issued for the loan, no provision for interest is made, and no repayment date is mentioned. In the current year, L's mother dies leaving no estate. Assuming the loan is not repaid, L cannot take a deduction for a nonbusiness bad debt, because the facts indicate that no debtor-creditor relationship existed.

# WORTHLESS SECURITIES

A loss is allowed under § 165 for a security that becomes worthless during the year.[5] Such securities are usually shares of stock or some form of indebtedness, and the losses generated are usually treated as capital losses which are deemed to have occurred on the last day of the taxable year. (even if it occured in Jan.)

> **Example 9.** T, a calendar year taxpayer, owns stock in X Corporation (a publicly held company). The stock was acquired as an investment on November 30 of last year at a cost of $5,000. On July 1 of this year, the stock became worthless. Since the stock is deemed to have become worthless as of December 31 of this year, T has a capital loss from an asset held for 13 months (i. e., a long-term capital loss).

## SECURITIES IN AFFILIATED CORPORATIONS

Special treatment is provided for corporations that own securities in affiliated companies.[6] Ordinary loss treatment is granted for such worthless securities if the corporate holder owns 80 percent of the voting power of all classes of stock and at least 80 percent of each class of nonvoting stock of the affiliated company.

---

**5.** § 165(g).
**6.** § 165(g)(3).

## SMALL BUSINESS STOCK

The general rule is that shareholders receive capital gain or loss treatment upon the sale or exchange of stock. However, it is possible to receive an ordinary loss deduction if the loss is sustained on small business stock—"§ 1244 stock." Only individuals are eligible to receive the ordinary loss treatment under § 1244, and the loss is limited to $50,000 ($100,000 for married individuals filing jointly) per year. The corporation must meet certain qualifications (such as capitalization not exceeding $1,000,000) for the worthlessness of § 1244 stock to be treated as an ordinary—rather than a capital—loss.

# CASUALTY AND THEFT LOSSES

An individual may deduct a loss under § 165(c) in the following circumstances: (1) the loss is incurred in a trade or business; (2) the loss is incurred in a transaction entered into for profit; and (3) the loss is caused by fire, storm, shipwreck, or other casualty or by theft.[7] A casualty is defined as the complete or partial destruction of property resulting from an event due to some sudden, unexpected, or unusual cause. The property need not be business-related to qualify as a casualty loss. Examples of casualties include hurricanes, tornadoes, floods, storms, shipwrecks, fires, auto accidents, mine cave-ins, sonic booms, and vandalism. Weather that causes damages (drought, for example) must be unusual and severe for the particular region. Damage must be to the taxpayer's property to qualify as a casualty loss.

The deduction for a casualty loss in the case of an automobile accident can be taken only if the damage was not caused by the taxpayer's willful act or willful negligence.

## EVENTS THAT ARE NOT CASUALTIES

Not all "acts of God" are treated as casualty losses for income tax purposes. A casualty must be sudden, unexpected, or unusual. Progressive deterioration (such as erosion due to wind or rain) is not a casualty, because it does not meet the suddenness test.

Examples of nonsudden events are in the area of disease and insect damages. In the past, some courts have held that termite damage over periods of up to 15 months after infestation constituted a sudden event and was, therefore, deductible as a casualty loss. On the other hand, when the damage was caused by termites over periods of several years, some courts have disallowed a casualty loss deduction. Despite the existence of some judicial support for the deductibility of termite damage as a casualty loss, the current position of the IRS is that termite damage is not deductible.

---

7. § 165(c)(3).

## THEFT LOSSES

Theft includes, but is not necessarily limited to, larceny, embezzlement, and robbery. Theft does not include misplaced items.

Theft losses are computed like other casualty losses (discussed below), but the timing for recognition of the loss differs. A theft loss is taken in the year of discovery, not the year of the theft (unless, of course, the discovery occurs in the same year as the theft). If, in the year of the discovery, a claim exists (e. g., against an insurance company) and there is a reasonable expectation of recovering the fair market value of the asset from the insurance company, no deduction is permitted. If, in the year of settlement, the recovery is less than the asset's fair market value, a partial deduction may be available.

## WHEN TO DEDUCT CASUALTY LOSSES

*Disaster Area Losses.* Generally, a casualty loss is deducted in the year the loss occurs. An exception is allowed for casualties sustained in an area designated as a disaster area by the President of the United States.[8] In such cases, the taxpayer may elect to treat the loss as having occurred in the taxable year immediately preceding the taxable year in which the disaster actually occurred. The law was amended in 1972 to provide this immediate relief to flood victims in the form of accelerated tax benefits.

No casualty loss is permitted if there exists a reimbursement claim with a "reasonable prospect of [full] recovery." If the taxpayer has a partial claim, only part of the loss can be claimed in the year of the casualty and the remainder is deducted in the year the claim is settled.

If a taxpayer receives subsequent reimbursement for a casualty loss previously sustained and deducted, an amended return is not filed. Instead, the taxpayer must include the reimbursement in gross income on the return for the year in which it is received (to the extent that the previous deduction resulted in tax benefit).

## MEASURING THE AMOUNT OF LOSS

The computation of a casualty loss deduction depends on whether the property subject to the loss is held for personal use or is business property. Property which is held for the production of income (e. g., rent property) is treated similarly to business use property. After the loss is computed on property held for personal use, a $100 statutory floor is used to reduce the allowable deduction.[9] To the extent of this $100 of loss, the taxpayer receives no relief for damages to property which is held for personal use. The $100 statutory floor does not apply to casualty losses on business property. The $100 floor applies sepa-

---

**8.** § 165(h).
**9.** § 165(c)(3).

rately to each casualty and applies to the entire loss from each casualty (e. g., if a storm damages both a taxpayer's residence and automobile, only $100 is subtracted from the total amount of the loss).

TEFRA has added a substantial new floor that will apply to the deduction of nonbusiness casualty and theft losses for tax years beginning after 1982. This new floor, added by amended § 165(h), is equal to 10 percent of adjusted gross income. It will apply after reduction by the current floor of $100 for each loss.

> **Example 10.** T, whose adusted gross income is $20,000, suffers a casualty loss of $2,500 in 1983. T's deduction is $400 [$2,500 (casualty loss) − $100 (floor per casualty) − $2,000 (10% of adjusted gross income)].

This change will not only reduce the amount of the deduction for those taxpayers who have significant casualty losses but also eliminate casualty loss deductions for most taxpayers.

Taxpayers who suffer qualified disaster area losses can elect to deduct such losses in the year preceding the year of occurrence. However, TEFRA provides that taxpayers cannot avoid the new 10 percent floor by electing to deduct 1983 disaster area losses in 1982. New § 165(i) provides that any such losses in 1983 may be deducted in 1982, but they will be subject to the new 10 percent floor.

Any insurance recovery reduces the loss for both business and personal use casualties. In fact, a taxpayer may realize a gain on a casualty if the insurance proceeds exceed the cost basis of the property. Chapter 10 discusses the treatment of net casualty gains and losses.

The lower of (1) the adjusted basis of the property or (2) the difference between the fair market value of the property before the casualty and the fair market value immediately after the casualty measures the amount of the deduction for partial losses to both business and personal use property and for the complete destruction of personal use property. If business property or property which is held for the production of income (e. g., rental property) is completely destroyed, the measure of the deduction is always the adjusted basis of the property at the time of the destruction. The deduction for the loss of property that is part business and part personal must be computed separately for the business portion and the personal portion. The $100 floor is then deducted from the personal use portion only.

> **Example 11.** In 1983, T, who had adjusted gross income of $25,000, suffered the following casualty losses:

| | | Fair Market Value of Asset | |
| Asset | Adjusted Basis | Before the Casualty | After the Casualty |
|---|---|---|---|
| A | $ 2,500 | $ 2,300 | $ −0− |
| B | 1,800 | 1,600 | 500 |
| C | 900 | 200 | −0− |
| D | 100 | 700 | 400 |

Assets A and B were held for personal use; C and D were used in T's business at the time of the casualty. Assume no insurance recovery is expected and the losses to Assets A and B are from different casualties.

Losses on the various assets are computed as follows:

Asset A: $2,200 ($2,300, the lesser of adjusted basis or loss in value, minus the $100 floor). Personal use casualty losses are generally treated as itemized deductions.

Asset B: $1,000 ($1,100, the lesser of adjusted basis or loss in value, minus the $100 floor).

Asset C: $900. The complete destruction of a business asset results in a deduction of the adjusted basis of the property regardless of its fair market value.

Asset D: $100 (the lesser of adjusted basis or loss in value).

The losses on the personal use assets are combined, then reduced by 10% of adjusted gross income. This results in a personal casualty loss of $700 [$2,200 (loss on Asset A) + $1,000 (loss on Asset B) − $2,500 (10% of $25,000 AGI)]. Personal casualty losses are generally treated as itemized deductions (see Chapter 10 for exceptions).

Losses on the business assets ($900 loss on Asset C, $100 loss on Asset D) are deductions *for* adjusted gross income. They are not reduced by either the $100 floor per casualty or the 10 percent floor.

Generally, an appraisal before and after the casualty is needed to measure the amount of the loss.

# RESEARCH AND EXPERIMENTAL EXPENDITURES

Section 174 sets forth the treatment accorded to "research and experimental expenditures." The Regulations define research and experimental expenditures as:

All such costs incident to the development of an experimental or pilot model, a plant process, a product, a formula, an invention, or similar property, and the improvement of already existing property of the type mentioned. The term does not include expenditures such as those for the ordinary testing or inspection of materials or products for quality control or those for efficiency surveys, management studies, consumer surveys, advertising, or promotions.

Expenses in connection with the acquisition or improvement of land or depreciable property are not research and experimental expenditures; they increase the basis of the land or depreciable property. However, depreciation on a building used for research may be a research and experimental expenditure.

The law permits three alternatives for the handling of research and experimental expenditures. These expenditures may be expensed in the year paid or incurred or they may be deferred and amortized. If neither of these two methods is elected, the research and experimental costs must be capitalized. If the costs are capitalized, a deduction may not be available until the research project is abandoned or is deemed worthless. Since many products resulting from research projects do not have a definite and limited useful life, a taxpayer should ordinarily elect to write off the expenditures immediately or to defer and amortize them. It is generally preferable to elect an immediate write-off of the research expenditures due to the time value of the tax deduction. A new credit for research and experimentation was introduced in ERTA. The credit amounts to 25 percent of certain excess research and experimentation expenditures made after June 30, 1981, and before 1986.[10] The credit is discussed more fully in Chapter 8.

# NET OPERATING LOSSES

The requirement that every taxpayer file an annual income tax return (whether on a calendar year or a fiscal year) may result in certain inequities for taxpayers who experience cyclical patterns of income or expense. Inequities result from the application of a progressive rate structure to amounts of taxable income applied on an annual basis. A net operating loss in a particular tax year would produce no tax benefit if the Code did not include provisions for the carryback and carryforward of such losses to profitable years.

> **Example 12.** J has a business which realizes the following taxable income or (loss) over a five-year period: 19X1, $50,000; 19X2, ($30,000); 19X3, $100,000; 19X4, ($200,000); and 19X5, $380,000. She is married and files a joint return. P, on the other hand, has a taxable income pattern of $60,000 every year. He, too, is married and files a joint return. A comparison of their five-year tax bills follows:

| Year | J's Tax | P's Tax |
|------|---------|---------|
| 19X1 | $  12,104 | $ 16,014 |
| 19X2 | –0– | 16,014 |
| 19X3 | 34,190 | 16,014 |
| 19X4 | –0– | 16,014 |
| 19X5 | 174,002 | 16,014 |
|      | $ 220,206* | $ 80,070* |

> *The computation of tax is made without regard to any tax credits, income averaging or net operating loss benefits. Rates applicable to 1983 are used to compute the tax.

---

10.  § 44F.

Even though J and P realized the same total income ($300,000) over the five-year period, J had to pay taxes of $220,206, while P paid taxes of $80,070.

To provide partial relief from this inequitable tax treatment, deduction is allowed for net operating losses.[11] This provision permits the offset of net operating losses for any one year against taxable income of other years. A net operating loss is intended as a relief provision for business income and losses; therefore, only losses from the operation of a trade or business (or profession), casualty losses, or losses from the confiscation of a business by a foreign government can create a net operating loss. In other words, a salaried individual with itemized deductions and personal exemptions in excess of income is not permitted to deduct such excess amounts as a net operating loss. On the other hand, a personal casualty loss is treated as a business loss and can, therefore, create (or increase) a net operating loss for a salaried individual.

## CARRYBACK AND CARRYOVER PERIODS

A net operating loss must be applied initially to the three taxable years preceding the year of the loss. It is carried first to the third prior year, then the second prior year, then the immediately preceding tax year (or until used up). If the loss is not fully used in the carryback period, it must be carried forward to the first year after the loss year, and then forward to the second, third, etc., year after the loss year. For years ending after 1975, the carryover period is 15 years. If a loss is sustained in 1981, it is used in this order: 1978, 1979, 1980, 1982, 1983, 1984, 1985, 1986, 1987, 1988, 1989, 1990, 1991, 1992, 1993, 1994, 1995, and 1996.

For taxable years ending after December 31, 1975, a taxpayer can elect not to carry back a net operating loss to any of the three prior years. In such case, the loss is available as a carryforward to the next year. A taxpayer would make the election if it is to his or her tax advantage. For example, a taxpayer might be in a very low marginal tax bracket in the carryback years but expect to be in a high marginal tax bracket in future years. Therefore, it would be to the taxpayer's tax advantage to use the net operating loss to offset income in years when the marginal tax rate is high rather than use it when the marginal tax rate is relatively low. The election might also be advantageous if the taxpayer has taken investment tax credit in the carryback years. If the net operating loss is carried back and the tax liability reduced or eliminated, the benefit of the investment tax credit could be lost because of the expiration of its carryover time limit.

If the loss is being carried to a preceding year, an amended return

---

11. § 172.

is filed on Form 1040X or a quick refund claim is filed on Form 1045. In any case, a refund of taxes previously paid is requested. When the loss is carried forward, the current return shows a net operating loss deduction for the prior year's loss.

Where there are net operating losses in two or more years, the rule is always to use the earliest loss first until it is completely absorbed; then the later loss(es) can be used until they also are absorbed or lost. Thus, one year's return could show net operating loss carryovers from two or more years; each loss is computed and applied separately.

## COMPUTATION OF THE NET OPERATING LOSS

Since the net operating loss provisions apply solely to business-related losses, certain adjustments must be made to reflect a taxpayer's "economic" loss. The required adjustments for corporate taxpayers are usually insignificant, because a corporation's taxable loss is generally similar to its economic loss. However, individual taxpayers are allowed deductions for such items as personal and dependency exemptions, itemized deductions, and long-term capital gains which do not reflect actual business-related economic losses. The details of this computation are beyond the scope of this text.

# DEPRECIATION, AMORTIZATION, COST RECOVERY, AND DEPLETION

The Internal Revenue Code provides for a deduction for the consumption of the cost of an asset. This deduction takes the form of depreciation, cost recovery, amortization, or depletion. However, before discussing each cost consumption method, it may be well to review the difference between the classification of an asset (i. e., realty or personalty) and the use to which it is placed (i. e., business or personal). Personalty can be defined as all assets that are not realty. Both realty and personalty can be either business use or personal use property. Examples of this distinction include a residence (realty that is personal use), an office building (realty that is business use), a dump truck (personalty that is business use), and regular wearing apparel (personalty that is personal use).

A further distinction is made between tangible and intangible property. Tangible property is any property with physical substance (e. g., equipment, buildings), while intangible property lacks such substance (e. g., goodwill, patents).

A write-off of the cost (or other adjusted basis) of an asset is known as the process of depreciation, cost recovery, depletion, or amortization. Depreciation and cost recovery relate to tangible property, depletion refers to certain natural resources (e. g., oil, coal, gravel), and amortization concerns intangible property. As noted later, a write-off for income tax purposes is not allowed when an asset lacks a determinable useful life (e. g., land, goodwill) or when it is not business use property.

## DEPRECIATION

Section 167 permits a depreciation deduction in the form of a reasonable allowance for the exhaustion, wear and tear, and obsolescence of business property and property which is held for the production of income (e. g., rental property held by an investor).[12] Obsolescence refers to normal technological change due to reasonably foreseeable economic conditions. If rapid or abnormal obsolescence occurs, a taxpayer may change to a shorter estimated useful life if there is a "clear and convincing basis for the redetermination." The rules discussed in this section apply to property acquired before January 1, 1981. The depreciation rules, which were completely overhauled by ERTA and modified further by TEFRA, are discussed later in this chapter under Accelerated Cost Recovery System (ACRS).

The taxpayer must adopt a reasonably consistent plan for depreciating the cost or other basis of assets over the estimated useful life of the property (e. g., the taxpayer cannot arbitrarily defer or accelerate the amount of depreciation from one year to another). In addition, the basis of the depreciable property must be reduced by the depreciation allowed and not less than the allowable amount.[13] For example, if the taxpayer does not claim any depreciation on property during a particular year, the basis of the property is nevertheless reduced by the amount of depreciation which should have been deducted.

> **Example 13.** On January 1, 19X1, T paid $6,000 for a truck to be used in his business. He chose a four-year estimated useful life, no salvage value, and straight-line depreciation. Thus, the allowable depreciation deduction was $1,500 per year. However, depreciation actually taken was as follows:
>
> | | |
> |------|--------|
> | 19X1 | $ 1,500 |
> | 19X2 | –0– |
> | 19X3 | –0– |
> | 19X4 | 1,500 |
>
> The adjusted basis of the truck must be reduced by the full amount of allowable depreciation of $6,000 ($1,500 × 4 years) despite the fact that T claimed only $3,000 depreciation during the four-year period. Therefore, if T sold the truck at the end of 19X4 for $1,000, a $1,000 gain would be recognized, since the adjusted cost basis of the truck is zero.

---

**12.** § 167(a); Reg. § 1.167(a)–1(a).
**13.** § 1016(a)(2); Reg. § 1.167(a)–10(a).

## QUALIFYING PROPERTY

As mentioned earlier, the use rather than the character of property determines whether a depreciation deduction is permitted. Property must be used in a trade or business or held for the production of income to qualify as depreciable.

> **Example 14.** T is a self-employed CPA who uses her automobile for both personal and business purposes. A depreciation deduction is permitted only for the portion of the property which is used in business. If the automobile were acquired at a cost of $12,000 and T's mileage during the year was 10,000 miles, of which 3,000 miles was for business, only 30% of the cost, or $3,600, would be subject to depreciation.

The basis for depreciation is generally the adjusted cost basis used to determine gain if the property is sold or disposed of.[14] However, if personal use assets are converted to business or income-producing use, the basis for depreciation is the lower of the adjusted basis or fair market value when the property is converted.

> **Example 15.** T acquires a personal residence in 19X1 for $30,000. In 19X4, he converts the property to rental use when the fair market value is only $25,000. The basis for depreciation is $25,000, since the fair market value is less than the adjusted basis. The $5,000 decline in value is deemed to be personal (since it occurred while the property was held for personal use) and therefore nondeductible.

The Regulations provide that tangible property is depreciable only to the extent that the property is subject to wear and tear, to decay or decline from natural causes, to exhaustion, and to obsolescence. Thus, land and inventory are not depreciable but land improvements are depreciable (e. g., paved surfaces, fences, landscaping.

Depreciation or amortization of intangible property is not permitted unless the property has a definite and limited useful life. For example, patents and copyrights have a definite and limited legal life and are therefore eligible for amortization. Goodwill is not amortizable, since its life extends for an unlimited period.

## OTHER DEPRECIATION CONSIDERATIONS

Under pre-1981 depreciation rules, taxpayers had to take into account the salvage value (assuming there was a salvage value) of an asset in calculating depreciation. An asset could not be depreciated below its salvage value.

However, the Code permitted a taxpayer to disregard salvage

---

14. § 167(g).

value for amounts up to 10 percent of the basis in the property.[15] This rule applied to tangible personal property (other than livestock) with an estimated useful life of three years or more.

Another consideration before ERTA was the choice of depreciation methods allowed. The Code provided for the following alternative depreciation methods for property placed in service before January 1, 1981:[16]

— The straight-line (SL) method (cost basis less salvage ÷ the estimated useful life).

— The declining-balance (DB) method using a rate not to exceed twice the straight-line rate. Common methods included 200 percent DB (double-declining balance), 150 percent DB, and 125 percent DB. Salvage value is not taken into account under any of the declining-balance methods. However, no further depreciation can be claimed once net book value (i. e., cost minus depreciation) and salvage value are the same.

— Any other consistent method which did not result in greater total depreciation being claimed during the first two-thirds of the useful life than would have been allowable under the double-declining balance method. Permissible methods included sum-of-the-years' digits (i. e., SYD), machine-hours, and the unit-of-production method.

**Example 16.** T acquired a new automobile on January 1, 1980, to be used in his business. The asset cost $10,000 with an estimated salvage value of $2,000 and a four-year estimated useful life. The following amounts of depreciation could be deducted depending on the method of depreciation which is used (note that pre-ERTA rules continue to apply for the entire useful life of assets acquired by the owner before 1981):

|  | 1980 | 1981 | 1982 | 1983 |
|---|---|---|---|---|
| 1.  Straight-line:<br>$10,000 cost less ($2,000<br>salvage reduced by 10%<br>of cost) ÷ 4 years | $ 2,250 | $ 2,250 | $ 2,250 | $ 2,250 |
| 2.  Double-declining balance: |  |  |  |  |
| a.   $10,000 × 50% (twice<br>the straight-line rate) | $ 5,000 |  |  |  |
| b.   ($10,000 − $5,000) × 50% |  | $ 2,500 |  |  |
| c.   ($10,000 − $5,000 − $2,500)<br>× 50% |  |  | $ 1,250 |  |
| d.   ($10,000 − $5,000 − $2,500 −<br>$1,250) × 50% |  |  |  | $   250[17] |

---

**15.**  § 167(f).
**16.**  § 167(b).
**17.**  Total depreciation taken cannot exceed cost minus estimated salvage value (i.e., $1,000 in this example).

|  | 1981 | 1982 | 1983 | 1984 |
|---|---|---|---|---|
| 3.  Sum-of-the-years' digits:* | | | | |
| $10,000 cost less ($2,000 | | | | |
| salvage reduced by 10% | | | | |
| of cost) or $9,000 | | | | |
| a.  $9,000 × 4/10 | $ 3,600 | | | |
| b.  $9,000 × 3/10 | | $ 2,700 | | |
| c.  $9,000 × 2/10 | | | $ 1,800 | |
| d.  $9,000 × 1/10 | | | | $   900 |

*The-sum-of-the-years' digits method formula is:

$$\text{Cost minus salvage} \times \frac{\text{remaining life at the beginning of the year}}{\text{sum-of-the-years' digits of the estimated life}}$$

In this example, the denominator for SYD is $1 + 2 + 3 + 4$, or 10. The numerator is 4 for year 1 (i. e., the number of years left at the beginning of year 1), 3 for year 2, etc. The denominator can be calculated by the following formula:

$$S = \frac{Y(Y + 1)}{2} \text{ where } Y = \text{estimated useful life}$$

$$\text{e. g., } S = \frac{4(4 + 1)}{2} = 10$$

The Tax Reform Act of 1969 placed certain restrictions on the use of accelerated methods for new and used realty placed in service prior to January 1, 1981. These restrictions were imposed to reduce the opportunities for using real estate investments as tax shelters; the use of accelerated depreciation frequently resulted in the recognition of ordinary tax losses on economically profitable real estate ventures.

The following methods were permitted for commercial and residential real property acquired prior to ERTA:[18]

|  | Nonresidential Real Property (commercial and industrial buildings, etc.) | Residential Real Property (two-family houses, etc.) |
|---|---|---|
| New property acquired after July 24, 1969, and prior to January 1, 1981 | 150% DB, SL | 200% DB, SYD, 150% DB, or SL |
| Used property acquired after July 24, 1969, and prior to January 1, 1981 | SL | 125% DB (if estimated useful life is 20 years or greater) or SL |

Restrictions on the use of accelerated methods were not imposed on new tangible personalty (e. g., machinery, equipment, and automobiles). However, 200 percent declining-balance and sum-of-the-years' digits were not permitted for used tangible personal property. The 150 percent declining-balance method was permitted for used tangible

---

**18.**  § 167(j).

personalty which had a useful life of at least three years. Since the acquisition of used property did not result in any net addition to gross private investment in our economy, Congress chose not to provide as rapid accelerated depreciation for used property. It should be noted that accelerated methods (i. e., 200 percent declining-balance and sum-of-the-years' digits) were permitted for new residential real property. Presumably, the desire to stimulate construction of new housing units justified the need for such accelerated methods.

Another consideration for pre-ERTA property was the additional first-year depreciation allowed. This so-called bonus depreciation was limited to 20 percent of the cost of new or used tangible depreciable personalty, with a ceiling $10,000 of basis ($20,000 if a joint return was filed). Thus, the maximum deduction per year was $2,000 ($4,000 on a joint return). Bonus depreciation was replaced by a direct write-off under ERTA (discussed later in this chapter).

A pre-ERTA consideration which often caused disagreement between taxpayers and the IRS was the determination of a useful life for a depreciable asset. One source of information was the company's previous experience and policy with respect to asset maintenance and utilization. Another source was the guideline lives issued by the IRS.[19] In 1971, the IRS guideline life system was modified and liberalized by the enactment of the Asset Depreciation Range (ADR) system. The ADR rules were extremely complex and have been eliminated by ERTA.

# ACCELERATED COST RECOVERY SYSTEM (ACRS)

## GENERAL CONSIDERATIONS

The depreciation rules prior to ERTA were designed to allocate depreciation deductions over the period the asset is used in business so that the deductions for the cost of an asset are matched with the income produced by the asset (the so-called matching concept).

Often this led to controversies between taxpayers and the IRS concerning the estimated useful life of an asset, and it delayed the tax benefit to be derived from the recoupment of a capital investment in the form of a deduction for depreciation.

One way to resolve the estimated useful life problem was to utilize the Asset Depreciation Range (ADR) system. But many assets were not eligible for ADR, or taxpayers saw fit not to elect the system. In such cases, useful lives were determined according to the facts and

---

**19.**   Rev.Proc. 77–10, 1977–1 C.B. 548.

circumstances pertaining to each asset or by agreement between the taxpayer and the IRS.

ERTA replaced the ADR system for property placed in service after December 31, 1980, with the accelerated cost recovery system (ACRS). Under ACRS, the cost of an asset is recovered over a predetermined period generally shorter than the useful life of the asset or the period the asset is used to produce income.[20] The change was designed to encourage investment, improve productivity, and simplify the law and its administration.

*Eligible Property Under ACRS.*  Assets used in a trade or business or for the production of income are depreciable if they are subject to wear and tear, decay, decline from natural causes, or obsolescence. Assets that do not decline in value on a predictable basis or that do not have a determinable useful life (e. g., land, goodwill, stock) are not depreciable.

Under ERTA, most tangible depreciable property (real and personal) is covered by ACRS. However, ACRS does not apply to (1) property not depreciated in terms of years (e. g., units-of-production method) except for certain railroad property or (2) property that is amortized (e. g., leasehold improvements and certain rehabilitation expenditures).

## PERSONALTY: RECOVERY PERIODS AND METHODS

ACRS provides that the cost of eligible personalty (and certain realty) is recovered under 3, 5, 10, or 15 years. The classification of property by recovery period is as follows:

3 years . . . . . Autos, light-duty trucks, R & D equipment, race horses over 2 years old and other horses over 12 years old, and personalty with an ADR midpoint life of 4 years or less.

5 years . . . . . Most other equipment except long-lived public utility property. Also includes single-purpose agricultural structures and petroleum storage facilities, which are designated as § 1245 property under the law.

10 years . . . . . Public utility property with an ADR midpoint life greater than 18 but not greater than 25 years; burners and boilers using coal as a primary fuel if used in a public utility power plant and if replacing or converting oil- or gas-fired burners or boilers; railroad tank cars; mobile homes; and realty with an ADR midpoint life of 12.5 years or less (e. g., theme park structures).

---

**20.**  § 168.

15 years . . . . .  Public utility property with an ADR midpoint life exceeding 25 years (except certain burners and boilers using coal as a primary fuel).

Under ACRS, taxpayers have the choice of using (1) the straight-line method over the regular or optional (see below) recovery period or (2) a prescribed accelerated method over the regular recovery period. These two methods are both part of the ACRS system enacted in new § 168. However, § 168 does not provide a convenient name for either of the two methods. Hereafter, the straight-line method will be referred to as the optional (or elective) straight-line method. The method using percentages prescribed in the Code will be referred to as the statutory percentage method.

The accelerated cost recovery system (ACRS) as originally enacted in ERTA contained cost recovery schedules designed to take effect in a three-step process. The first cost recovery schedule, intended for property placed in service in 1981 through 1984, is based on the 150 percent declining balance method, with a switch to straight-line to maximize acceleration. This schedule is shown in Figure II. The cost recovery schedule for 1985 reflected the 175 percent declining-balance method, and the schedule for property placed in service after 1985 reflected the 200 percent declining balance method.

## Figure II

### ACRS STATUTORY PERCENTAGES
### FOR PROPERTY OTHER THAN 15-YEAR REAL PROPERTY

**For Property Placed in Service After December 31, 1980, and Before January 1, 1985**

The applicable percentage for the class of property is:

| If the recovery year is: | 3-year | 5-year | 10-year | 15-year public utility |
|---|---|---|---|---|
| 1 | 25 | 15 | 8 | 5 |
| 2 | 38 | 22 | 14 | 10 |
| 3 | 37 | 21 | 12 | 9 |
| 4 | | 21 | 10 | 8 |
| 5 | | 21 | 10 | 7 |
| 6 | | | 10 | 7 |
| 7 | | | 9 | 6 |
| 8 | | | 9 | 6 |
| 9 | | | 9 | 6 |
| 10 | | | 9 | 6 |
| 11 | | | | 6 |
| 12 | | | | 6 |
| 13 | | | | 6 |
| 14 | | | | 6 |
| 15 | | | | 6 |

Under TEFRA, the step-up in recovery rates reflected in the 1985 and post-1985 cost recovery schedules will not occur. Instead, the current cost recovery schedule reflecting the 150 percent declining-balance method will remain in effect.

The reasons why Congress made this change are twofold. First, there was recognition that the accelerated write-offs coupled with the immediate benefits of the investment credit may have been too generous, in some cases providing benefits greater than those which would result from immediate expensing of the entire cost of the asset. Second, there was concern that some taxpayers might be motivated to postpone acquisitions to take advantage of the faster write-offs in 1985 and thereafter, thus slowing economic recovery.

The rates to be used in computing the deduction under the statutory percentage method are prescribed in § 168, which was added by ERTA and modified by TEFRA, as discussed previously. These rates are shown in Figure II. The rates are based on the 150 percent declining-balance method, using the half-year convention and an assumption of zero salvage value.

**Example 17.** In December 1983, T buys the following business assets: $34,000 of machinery, $6,000 of office furniture, and $16,000 of light-duty trucks. The machinery and office furniture are five-year properties, and the trucks are three-year properties. Her depreciation deductions using the statutory percentage method are as follows:

**1983**

| | |
|---|---|
| 25% of $16,000 (trucks) | $  4,000 |
| 15% of $40,000 (machine and furniture) | 6,000 |
| | $ 10,000 |

**1984**

| | |
|---|---|
| 38% of $16,000 | $  6,080 |
| 22% of $40,000 | 8,800 |
| | $ 14,880 |

**1985**

| | |
|---|---|
| 37% of $16,000 | $  5,920 |
| 21% of $40,000 | 8,400 |
| | $ 14,320 |

**1986**

| | |
|---|---|
| 21% of $40,000 | $  8,400 |

**1987**

| | |
|---|---|
| 21% of $40,000 | $  8,400 |

Note that in 1983, T got a half year's depreciation deduction although she held the property only one month (since the half-year convention is reflected in the percentages in Figure II). For three-year property, the statutory percentage rate is computed as follows: $\frac{1}{3} = 33\frac{1}{3}\%$ (straight-line rate), $33\frac{1}{3}\%$ (straight-line rate) $\times$ 150% = 50% (150% declining-balance rate), and 50% (150% declining-balance rate) $\times$ $\frac{1}{2}$ (half-year convention) = 25% statutory-percentage rate for year one. The first-year statutory percentages for other classes of property (5-year, 10-year, and 15-year classes) are computed in the same manner. However, the table reflects percentages which have been rounded to the nearest whole number.

As another means of insuring that ACRS write-offs coupled with the investment credit do not provide tax benefits better than immediate expensing, TEFRA requires that the basis for depreciation be reduced by one-half the amount of the credit taken.[21] This requirement applies to property placed in service after 1982.

> **Example 18.** In 1983, T purchases a machine, which is five-year ACRS property, for $10,000. T takes a $1,000 investment credit on the property (10% of $10,000). Under the new TEFRA provision, the basis of the property must be reduced by $500 [½ of $1,000 (investment credit)]. Thus, T's cost recovery allowance will be based on $9,500 [$10,000 (cost) − $500 (reduction for investment credit)].

The 50 percent basis reduction rule applies to the following: regular investment credit property, energy credit property, and certified historic property. The basis of properties to which the 15 or 20 percent rehabilitation credit applies must be reduced by the full amount of the credit.[22]

As an alternative to reducing the basis of the property, a taxpayer may elect to take a reduced investment credit. Under this election, the investment credit is eight percent (rather than 10 percent) for recovery property that is not three-year property and four percent (instead of six percent) for three-year property.[23]

Upon sale of the asset in the future, the reduction in basis will be treated as depreciation for purposes of applying the recapture provisions. However, the basis of the property disposed of will be increased by one-half the amount of any investment credit to be recaptured. This increase occurs immediately prior to the disposition (or other event) which triggers recapture of depreciation.[24]

---

**21.** § 48(q)(1).
**22.** § 48(q)(3).
**23.** § 48(q)(4).
**24.** § 48(q)(5).

## REALTY: RECOVERY PERIODS AND METHODS

Under ACRS, realty is assigned a 15-year recovery period. Component depreciation generally is no longer allowed. Given a new 15-year recovery period, real estate (e. g., rental property) is immediately more attractive as an investment than under the old law.

Real property other than low-income housing can be depreciated using the 175 percent declining-balance method, changing to the straight-line method to maximize acceleration. Low-income housing is depreciated using the 200 percent declining-balance method, changing to straight-line.[25]

Statutory percentages for real property are shown in Figure III,

**Figure III**

ACRS STATUTORY PERCENTAGES FOR 15-YEAR REAL PROPERTY

*15–year Real Property Table (other than low-income housing)*

| Year | Month Placed in Service | | | | | | | | | | | |
|---|---|---|---|---|---|---|---|---|---|---|---|---|
| | 1 | 2 | 3 | 4 | 5 | 6 | 7 | 8 | 9 | 10 | 11 | 12 |
| 1st | 12% | 11% | 10% | 9% | 8% | 7% | 6% | 5% | 4% | 3% | 2% | 1% |
| 2d | 10% | 10% | 11% | 11% | 11% | 11% | 11% | 11% | 11% | 11% | 11% | 12% |
| 3d | 9% | 9% | 9% | 9% | 10% | 10% | 10% | 10% | 10% | 10% | 10% | 10% |
| 4th | 8% | 8% | 8% | 8% | 8% | 8% | 9% | 9% | 9% | 9% | 9% | 9% |
| 5th | 7% | 7% | 7% | 7% | 7% | 7% | 8% | 8% | 8% | 8% | 8% | 8% |
| 6th | 6% | 6% | 6% | 6% | 7% | 7% | 7% | 7% | 7% | 7% | 7% | 7% |
| 7th | 6% | 6% | 6% | 6% | 6% | 6% | 6% | 6% | 6% | 6% | 6% | 6% |
| 8th | 6% | 6% | 6% | 6% | 6% | 6% | 6% | 6% | 6% | 6% | 6% | 6% |
| 9th | 6% | 6% | 6% | 6% | 5% | 6% | 5% | 5% | 5% | 6% | 6% | 6% |
| 10th | 5% | 6% | 5% | 6% | 5% | 5% | 5% | 5% | 5% | 5% | 6% | 5% |
| 11th | 5% | 5% | 5% | 5% | 5% | 5% | 5% | 5% | 5% | 5% | 5% | 5% |
| 12th | 5% | 5% | 5% | 5% | 5% | 5% | 5% | 5% | 5% | 5% | 5% | 5% |
| 13th | 5% | 5% | 5% | 5% | 5% | 5% | 5% | 5% | 5% | 5% | 5% | 5% |
| 14th | 5% | 5% | 5% | 5% | 5% | 5% | 5% | 5% | 5% | 5% | 5% | 5% |
| 15th | 5% | 5% | 5% | 5% | 5% | 5% | 5% | 5% | 5% | 5% | 5% | 5% |
| 16th | — | — | 1% | 1% | 2% | 2% | 3% | 3% | 4% | 4% | 4% | 5% |

*15–year Real Property Low-Income Housing Table*

| Year | Month Placed in Service | | | | | | | | | | | |
|---|---|---|---|---|---|---|---|---|---|---|---|---|
| | 1 | 2 | 3 | 4 | 5 | 6 | 7 | 8 | 9 | 10 | 11 | 12 |
| 1st | 13% | 12% | 11% | 10% | 9% | 8% | 7% | 6% | 4% | 3% | 2% | 1% |
| 2d | 12% | 12% | 12% | 12% | 12% | 12% | 12% | 13% | 13% | 13% | 13% | 13% |
| 3d | 10% | 10% | 10% | 10% | 11% | 11% | 11% | 11% | 11% | 11% | 11% | 11% |
| 4th | 9% | 9% | 9% | 9% | 9% | 9% | 9% | 9% | 10% | 10% | 10% | 10% |
| 5th | 8% | 8% | 8% | 8% | 8% | 8% | 8% | 8% | 8% | 8% | 8% | 9% |
| 6th | 7% | 7% | 7% | 7% | 7% | 7% | 7% | 7% | 7% | 7% | 7% | 7% |
| 7th | 6% | 6% | 6% | 6% | 6% | 6% | 6% | 6% | 6% | 6% | 6% | 6% |
| 8th | 5% | 5% | 5% | 5% | 5% | 5% | 5% | 5% | 5% | 5% | 6% | 6% |
| 9th | 5% | 5% | 5% | 5% | 5% | 5% | 5% | 5% | 5% | 5% | 5% | 5% |
| 10th | 5% | 5% | 5% | 5% | 5% | 5% | 5% | 5% | 5% | 5% | 5% | 5% |
| 11th | 4% | 5% | 5% | 5% | 5% | 5% | 5% | 5% | 5% | 5% | 5% | 5% |
| 12th | 4% | 4% | 4% | 5% | 4% | 5% | 5% | 5% | 5% | 5% | 5% | 5% |
| 13th | 4% | 4% | 4% | 4% | 4% | 4% | 5% | 4% | 5% | 5% | 5% | 5% |
| 14th | 4% | 4% | 4% | 4% | 4% | 4% | 4% | 4% | 4% | 5% | 4% | 4% |
| 15th | 4% | 4% | 4% | 4% | 4% | 4% | 4% | 4% | 4% | 4% | 4% | 4% |
| 16th | — | — | 1% | 1% | 2% | 2% | 2% | 3% | 3% | 3% | 4% | 4% |

25. § 168(b)(2).

which contains rates for low-income housing as well as other 15-year real estate.

Since the half-year convention does not apply to 15-year real property, these tables are structured differently from those in Figure II. The cost recovery deduction for 15-year real property is based on the month of acquisition rather than on the half-year convention.

**Example 19.**  T purchased a warehouse for $100,000 on January 1, 1983. The first year's cost recovery allowance using the statutory percentage method is $12,000 (12% of $100,000). Cost recovery deductions for 1984, 1985, and 1986 are, respectively, $10,000, $9,000, and $8,000.

**Example 20.**  Assume the same facts as in Example 19 except the property is low-income housing. Cost recovery deductions for 1983 through 1986 are $13,000, $12,000, $10,000, and $9,000, respectively.

## STRAIGHT-LINE ELECTION UNDER ACRS

Under ACRS, taxpayers may elect to write off an asset using the straight-line method rather than the statutory percentage method. The straight-line recovery period may be equal to the prescribed recovery period under the statutory percentage method or it may be a longer period. Allowable straight-line recovery periods for each class of property are summarized below:

    3-year property........... 3, 5, or 12 years
    5-year property........... 5, 12, or 25 years
    10-year property........... 10, 25, or 35 years
    15-year property........... 15, 35, or 45 years

If the straight-line option is elected, the half-year convention is applied in computing the cost recovery deduction in the case of property other than 15-year real property. There is no cost recovery deduction in the year of disposition of property other than 15-year real property.

**Example 21.**  J acquired a light-duty truck (three-year property) on March 1, 1983, at a cost of $10,000. J elects to write off the cost of the truck using the optional straight-line method with a recovery period of five years. Because the half-year convention applies, J can deduct only $1,000 (($10,000 ÷ 5) × ½) in 1983.

**Example 22.**  Assume the same facts as in Example 21. If J disposes of the truck at any time during 1984, the adjusted basis will be $9,000 ($10,000 cost − $1,000 cost recovery deduction in 1983). No cost recovery deduction is allowed for 1984, the year of disposition.

The half-year convention does not apply in the case of 15-year real property for which the straight-line option is elected. Nor is the cost recovery deduction disallowed in the year of disposition. The first year's deduction and the deduction for the year of disposition are computed on the basis of the number of months the property was held during the year.

> **Example 23.** K acquired a store building on October 1, 1983, at a cost of $150,000. K elects the straight-line method using a recovery period of 15 years. K's cost recovery deduction for 1983 is $2,500 (($150,000 ÷ 15) × $\frac{3}{12}$).

> **Example 24.** Assume the same facts as in Example 23 and that K disposes of the asset on September 30, 1985. K's cost recovery deduction for 1985 would be $7,500 (($150,000 ÷ 15) × $\frac{9}{12}$).

For each class of property other than 15-year real estate, the straight-line election applies to all assets in a particular class that are placed in service during the year for which the election is made, and later to the entire recovery period for those vintage assets. The election may be changed for property of the same class placed in service in other taxable years. By contrast, the straight-line election for 15-year real property may be made on a property-by-property basis within the same year.

## ELECTION TO EXPENSE ASSETS

Prior to ERTA, taxpayers were allowed additional first-year (or "bonus") depreciation of 20 percent of up to $10,000 ($20,000 on a joint return) of qualifying § 179 property. ERTA repeals § 179 as presently worded and substitutes new § 179. Entitled "Election to Expense Certain Depreciable Business Assets," the new § 179 permits an immediate write-off based on the following amounts and phase-in period:[26]

| Year | Amount of Write-off |
| --- | --- |
| 1982–1983 | $  5,000 |
| 1984–1985 | 7,500 |
| 1986 and thereafter | 10,000 |

Thus, such amounts need not be capitalized and depreciated. However, no investment tax credit will be allowed for items expensed under new § 179. The election applies to purchased tangible personal property used in a trade or business.

> **Example 25.** T acquires machinery (five-year property) on February 1, 1983, at a cost of $40,000 and elects to expense $5,000

---

26.  § 179(b)(1). The amount shown is per taxpayer, per year.

under the § 179 provisions. T takes $3,500 investment credit on the machine [10% of $35,000 ($40,000 cost − $5,000 § 179 expense not eligible for investment credit)]. T's statutory percentage cost recovery deduction for 1983 is $4,987.50 [$35,000 ($40,000 cost − $5,000 expensed) − $1,750 (½ × 3,500 investment credit) × .15]. Thus, T's total write-off in 1983 is $9,987.50 ($5,000 expense + $4,987.50 cost recovery deduction).

## OTHER ASPECTS OF ACRS

Because the ACRS deduction may be larger than the depreciation deduction under pre-1981 rules, there was concern that in an attempt to change pre-1981 property into post-1980 recovery property, some taxpayers might engage in transactions that did not result in an actual ownership change. To prevent this, ACRS contains antichurning rules that prevent the use of ACRS on property that is churned. Hence, the taxpayer must use pre-1981 depreciation rules on churned property.

ACRS does not apply to personal property acquired after 1980 if the property was owned or used during 1980 by the taxpayer or a related person.

> **Example 26.** T began renting a tractor to use in his farming business in 1979. T used the tractor until 1982, at which time he purchased it. T is not entitled to use ACRS, because he used the tractor in 1980. Instead, he must use the pre-1981 depreciation rules.

In addition, ACRS does not apply to real property if:

1. The property was owned by the taxpayer or a related person at any time during 1980.

2. The taxpayer leaves the property to a person, or a person related to such person, who owned the property at any time during 1980.

3. The property is acquired in nonrecognition transactions such as certain like-kind exchanges or involuntary conversions (see Chapter 9). However, this applies only to the extent that the basis of the property includes an amount representing the adjusted basis of other property owned by the taxpayer or a related person during 1980.

> **Example 27.** In 1983, J made a nontaxable like-kind exchange. He gave up an apartment building, held since 1978, with an adjusted basis of $300,000 and a fair market value of $400,000. He also gave $200,000 in cash. In exchange, J received an apartment building worth $600,000. The basis of the new building is $500,000, but only $200,000 (cash paid) of the basis is subject to the ACRS rules.

A person is considered related to a previous user or owner if there exists a family or fiduciary relationship or if there exists ownership of 10 percent of a corporation or partnership.

# DEPLETION

In developing an oil or gas well, four types of expenditures must be made by the producer. The first type is the payment for the natural resource (the oil under the ground). Because natural resources are physically limited, these costs are recovered through depletion. The second type occurs when the property is made ready for drilling: clearing the property, erecting derricks, and the cost of labor, etc. in drilling the hole. These costs, called intangible drilling and development costs, generally have no salvage value and are a lost cost if the well is dry. The third type of costs covers tangible assets such as tools, pipes, and engines. These costs are capital in nature and must be capitalized and recovered through depreciation. Finally, there are costs incurred after the well is producing, including such items as labor, fuel, and supplies. They are clearly operating expenses which are deductible currently when incurred (on the accrual basis) or when paid (on the cash basis).

The expenditures for depreciable assets and operating expenses pose no unusual problems for producers of natural resources. The tax treatment of depletable costs and intangible drilling and development costs is quite a different matter.

## INTANGIBLE DRILLING AND DEVELOPMENT COSTS (IDC)

Intangible drilling and development costs can be handled in one of two ways at the option of the taxpayer. They can be either charged off as an expense in the year in which they are incurred or capitalized and written off through depletion. The election is made in the first year that such expenditures are incurred either by taking a deduction on the return or by adding them to the depletable basis. No formal statement of intent is required, and once made, the election is binding on both the taxpayer and the Commissioner for all such expenditures in the future. If the taxpayer fails to make the election to expense such costs on the original timely filed return the first year such expenditures are incurred, an automatic election to capitalize them has been made and is irrevocable.

## DEPLETION METHODS

Wasting assets (e. g., oil, gas, coal, gravel) are subject to depletion, which simply is a form of depreciation applicable to natural resources. Land generally cannot be depleted.

The owner of an interest in the wasting asset is entitled to deduct depletion. An owner is one who has an economic interest in the property. An economic interest requires the acquisition of an interest in the minerals in place and the receipt of income from the extraction or severance of such minerals. Like depreciation, depletion is a deduction *for* adjusted gross income.

There are two methods of calculating depletion: cost and percentage. Cost depletion can be used on any wasting asset (and is the only method allowed for timber). Percentage depletion is subject to a number of limitations, particularly as to oil and gas deposits. Depletion should be calculated both ways, and generally the method that results in the largest deduction is used. The choice between cost and percentage depletion is an annual election.

*Cost Depletion.* Cost depletion is determined by using the adjusted basis of the asset.[27] Such basis is divided by the estimated recoverable units of the asset (e. g., barrels, tons) to arrive at the depletion per unit. The depletion per unit then is multiplied by the number of units sold (*not* the units produced) during the year to arrive at the cost depletion allowed. Cost depletion, therefore, resembles the units-of-production method of calculating depreciation.

> **Example 28.** On January 1, 19X1, T purchased the rights to a mineral interest for $1,000,000. At that time, the remaining recoverable units in the mineral interest were estimated to be 200,000. Under these circumstances, the depletion per unit becomes $5 [$1,000,000 (adjusted basis) ÷ 200,000 (estimated recoverable units)]. If during the year 60,000 units were mined and 25,000 were sold, the cost depletion would be $125,000 [$5 (depletion per unit) × 25,000 (units sold)].

If later it is discovered that the original estimate was incorrect, the depletion per unit must be redetermined based on the revised estimate.[28]

*Percentage Depletion.* Percentage depletion (also referred to as statutory depletion) is a specified percentage provided for in the Code. The percentage varies in accordance with the type of mineral interest involved. A sample of such percentages is shown in Figure IV. The rate is applied to the gross income from the property, but in no event may percentage depletion exceed 50 percent of the taxable income from the property before the allowance for depletion.

> **Example 29.** Assuming gross income of $100,000, a depletion rate of 22%, and other expenses relating to the property of $60,000, the depletion allowance is determined as follows:

---

**27.** § 612.
**28.** § 611(a).

| | |
|---|---:|
| Gross income | $ 100,000 |
| Less:  Other expenses | 60,000 |
| Taxable income before depletion | $  40,000 |
| Depletion allowance [the lesser of $22,000 | |
| (22% × $100,000) or $20,000 (50% × $40,000)] | 20,000 |
| Taxable income after depletion | $   20,000 |

The adjusted basis of the property would be reduced by $20,000, the depletion allowed. If the other expenses had been only $55,000, the full $22,000 could have been deducted and the adjusted basis would have been reduced by $22,000.

Note that percentage depletion is based on a percentage of the gross income from the property and makes no reference to cost. When percentage depletion is used, it is therefore possible to deduct more

**Figure IV**

SAMPLE OF PERCENTAGE DEPLETION RATES

#### 22% Depletion

| | |
|---|---|
| Antimony | Nickel |
| Beryllium | Platinum |
| Cadmium | Sulfur |
| Cobalt | Tin |
| Lead | Titanium |
| Manganese | Tungsten |
| Mercury | Uranium |
| Molybdenum | Zinc |

#### 15% Depletion

| | |
|---|---|
| Copper mines | Oil shale |
| Gold mines | Silver mines |
| Iron mines | |

#### 14% Depletion

| | |
|---|---|
| Borax | Magnesium carbonates |
| Calcium carbonates | Marble |
| Dolomite | Phosphate rock |
| Feldspar | Potash |
| Gilsonite | Quartzite |
| Granite | Slate |
| Limestone | Soapstone |

#### 10% Depletion

| | |
|---|---|
| Coal | Perlite |
| Lignite | Sodium chloride |

#### 5% Depletion

| | |
|---|---|
| Gravel | Pumice |
| Peat | Sand |

than the original cost of the property. If percentage depletion is used, however, the adjusted basis of the property (for computing cost depletion) must be reduced by the amount of percentage depletion taken until basis reaches zero.

# REPORTING PROCEDURES

Sole proprietors engaged in a business should file a Schedule C, Profit or (Loss) From Business or Profession, to accompany the Form 1040. Schedule C is reproduced in Appendix B.

# CLASSIFICATION OF EMPLOYMENT-RELATED EXPENSES

## SELF-EMPLOYED VERSUS EMPLOYEE STATUS

In many instances it is difficult to distinguish between an individual who is self-employed and one who is performing services as an employee. Expenses of self-employed individuals are deductible as trade or business expenses (*for* adjusted gross income). However, if the expenses are incurred as the result of an employment relationship, they are deductible subject to limitations in the Code relative to employee expenses.

Generally, an employer-employee relationship exists when the employer has the right to specify the end result and the ways and means by which the end result is to be attained. Thus, an employee is subject to the will and control of the employer with respect to not only what shall be done but also how it shall be done.[29] If the individual is subject to the direction or control of another only to the extent of the end result (e. g., the preparation of a taxpayer's return by an independent CPA) but not as to the means of accomplishment, an employee relationship does not exist.

> **Example 30.** D is a lawyer whose major client accounts for 60% of her billings. She does the routine legal work and income tax returns at her client's request. She is paid a monthly retainer in addition to amounts charged for extra work. D is a self-employed individual. Even though most of her income is from one client, she still has the right to determine how the end result of her work is attained.

> **Example 31.** E is a lawyer hired by D to assist her in the performance of services for the client mentioned in Example 30. E is under D's supervision; D reviews E's work; and D pays E an hourly fee. E is an employee of D.

---

**29.** Reg. § 31.3401(c)–(1)(b).

A self-employed individual is required to file Schedule C of Form 1040, and all allowable expenses related to the Schedule C activity are deductions *for* adjusted gross income.[30]

## DEDUCTIONS FOR OR FROM AGI

The Code specifies those employee expenses which are deductible *for* adjusted gross income as follows:[31]

1. Reimbursed expenses.
2. Expenses for travel away from home.
3. Transportation expenses.
4. Expenses of outside salespersons.
5. Moving expenses.

All other employee expenses are deductions *from* adjusted gross income which can be deducted only if the employee-taxpayer itemizes his or her deductions. Certain activities require an apportionment of expenses among these two categories (*for* and *from* AGI).

The distinction between *for* and *from* AGI is important because no benefit is received for an item which is deductible *from* adjusted gross income if a taxpayer's itemized deductions are less than the zero bracket amount. In addition, certain deductions are based on the amount of adjusted gross income (e. g., medical expenses are deductible to the extent they exceed five percent of adjusted gross income).

Besides the employee expenses listed above, the only deductions allowed *for* adjusted gross income are specified in § 62, as follows:

1. Trade or business deductions (more fully defined in § 162).
2. The long-term capital gains deduction.
3. Losses from the sale or exchange of property (no losses are allowed for personal use property).
4. Deductions attributable to rents and royalties.
5. Certain deductions of life tenants and income beneficiaries of property.
6. Certain retirement plan contributions of a self-employed individual (e. g., a Keogh plan).
7. Pension plans of electing small business corporations.
8. Certain retirement plan contributions of an employee (e. g., an IRA).
9. A portion of certain lump-sum distributions from certain pension plans.
10. Interest forfeited due to early withdrawal of deposits.

---

**30.** § § 62(1) and 162(a).
**31.** § 62(2).

11. Alimony paid.

12. A deduction for two-earner married couples (§ 221 added by ERTA).

13. Certain charitable contributions (§ 63(i) added by ERTA).

Code § 212 specifies the deductible expenses for the production of income which are itemized (*from* AGI) deductions, as follows:

1. Ordinary and necessary expenses paid or incurred for the production or collection of income (except expenses related to rent and royalty income, which are deductions *for* adjusted gross income).

2. Expenses for the management, conservation, or maintenance of property held for the production of income.

3. Expenses in connection with the determination, collection, or refund of any tax.

Other itemized deductions (medical expenses, charitable contributions, interest, taxes, etc.) are discussed in Chapter 7.

## SPECIAL TREATMENT FOR OUTSIDE SALESPERSONS

If an employee qualifies as an outside salesperson, all employment-related expenses are deductible *for* adjusted gross income and may be claimed even if the taxpayer uses the zero bracket amount.[32]

Congress apparently considers that an outside salesperson's activities resemble those of a self-employed individual more than they resemble those of an employee and therefore should receive comparable treatment.

*Definition of an Outside Salesperson.* An outside salesperson is one who solicits business away from an employer's place of business on a full-time basis.[33] An employee who performs service or delivery functions from an employer's place of business is not an outside salesperson. However, outside salesperson status is not lost if the employee performs incidental tasks (such as writing up orders or picking up mail or phone messages) at the employer's office.

The question of whether an employee is an outside salesperson has been the subject of extensive litigation. Each case has been decided on its own merits, and quite often, different interpretations have been given to similar fact patterns.

**Example 32.** The following are illustrations of employees who qualify as outside salespersons, since the performance of office duties is incidental to their primary outside sales job:

—G is a real estate agent who reports to his office on a daily basis to check new listings, current sales, etc.

---

**32.** § 62(2)(D).
**33.** Reg. § 1.62–1(h).

—R is an employee who sells burglar alarm systems to local businesses. She checks in to her office periodically to obtain new leads and to write up orders.

The following are illustrations of employees who are not outside salespersons since the nature of their jobs is primarily service or delivery rather than sales:

—B is a bread deliveryman who makes regular rounds after picking up fresh bread at his employer's bakery. He uses the company office to do his daily accounting and cash checkout.

—Q is a television repairman who is dispatched from his employer's shop to perform service repair calls for customers.

## REIMBURSED EXPENSES

It has been stressed in this chapter that certain expenses of an employee are deductions *for* adjusted gross income: travel, transportation, and moving expenses, and the expenses of an outside salesperson. Other expenses of an employee, such as professional dues and subscriptions, entertainment, and uniforms, must be deducted *from* adjusted gross income. If reimbursement is received, the expense deduction will be *for* adjusted gross income.

Reimbursements are included in an employee's gross income. Congress apparently felt that because the reimbursements were income, an offsetting deduction should be allowed. Therefore, the law allows an employee to deduct any bona fide employee expense *for* adjusted gross income if that expense is reimbursed by the employer.[34] An employee who receives reimbursement for employee expenses is allowed to offset the expenses incurred against the reimbursement (income) whether or not the election to itemize is made.

When reimbursements are present, there are three distinct possibilities: (1) the expenses and the reimbursement are equal, (2) the reimbursement exceeds the expenses, or (3) the expenses exceed the reimbursement. The treatment of these possibilities depends on whether the employee has made an "adequate accounting" to the employer.

*Recordkeeping Requirements.* An adequate accounting means that the employee has submitted a record (with receipts and other substantiation) to the employer with the following pertinent facts: amount, place and date of expenditure, and the business purpose and business relationship of the expenditure. The use of a reasonable per diem (currently $44 per day except in an area where the Federal government allows its employees a higher per diem) and mileage allowance (currently 20 cents per mile) does constitute an adequate accounting unless the employer and employee are related. Any em-

---

34.   § 62(2)(A).

ployee who does not adequately account to his or her employer must submit a detailed statement with his or her return showing expense categories, reimbursements, etc. The following situations may be encountered:

—Expenses and reimbursements are equal. If an adequate accounting has been made, the employee may omit both the reimbursement and the expenses from the tax return.

—Reimbursements exceed expenses. If an adequate accounting has been made, the employee may report the excess as miscellaneous income and ignore expenses and reimbursements up to the amount of the expenses.

—Expenses exceed reimbursements. Regardless of whether an adequate accounting is made to the employer, if the employee deducts the excess expenses, a statement of all expenses (by category) and all reimbursements must be attached to the income tax return.

**Example 33.** M, an employee of an unrelated corporation, incurred the following expenses which were carefully documented and submitted for complete reimbursement:

| | | |
|---|---|---:|
| Travel: | | |
| | Transportation | $ 1,600 |
| | Meals and lodging | 980 |
| Other: | | |
| | Dues and subscriptions | 70 |
| | Entertainment | 350 |
| Total reimbursed | | $ 3,000 |

M can ignore both the reimbursement and the expenditures on her tax return because she made an adequate accounting to her employer.

**Example 34.** Assume the same facts as in Example 33 except that M did not make an adequate accounting to her employer but instead received an expense account allowance of $5,000. The $5,000 is included in M's gross income, and the expenses must be reported on her return.

*Allocation Problems.* A further problem exists when reimbursements are intended to cover all employee expenses and the total reimbursement is less than the total expense. Travel and transportation are deductible *for* adjusted gross income, whether or not they are reimbursed. Other expenses of an employee (except an outside salesperson) are deductible *for* adjusted gross income only to the extent that they are reimbursed. When all expenses are partially reimbursed, the whole problem is solved by using a simple pro rata procedure. All travel and transportation expenses are deductible *for* adjusted gross income, but only the pro rata share of other expenses that have been reimbursed is deductible *for* adjusted gross income. The remaining expenses (the unreimbursed other expenses) are itemized deductions. The formula for computing the other expenses deductible *for* adjusted gross income is:[35]

$$\frac{\text{Total other expenses}}{\text{Total expenses (including travel + transportation)}} \times \text{Reimbursement}$$

**Example 35.** Assume an employee incurs a total of $3,750 in business expenses consisting of transportation expenses of $500; meals and lodging away from home of $2,500; and dues, subscriptions, and entertainment expenses amounting to $750. The reimbursement which is intended to cover all of the expenses amounts to $2,500. The deductions *for* and *from* adjusted gross income are computed as follows:

| | | |
|---|---:|---:|
| Travel (100%) | $ 2,500 | |
| Transportation (100%) | 500 | |
| Other $\left(\dfrac{\$750}{\$3,750} \times \$2,500\right)$ | 500 | |
| Deductible *for* AGI | $ 3,500 | |
| Less: Reimbursements | 2,500 | |
| Net deductible *for* AGI | | $ 1,000 |
| Total other | $ 750 | |
| Less: Deducted *for* AGI | 500 | |
| Deductible *from* AGI | | 250 |
| Total deductible | | $ 1,250 |

# TRANSPORTATION EXPENSES

## QUALIFIED EXPENDITURES

An employee is permitted a deduction *for* adjusted gross income for transportation expenses paid in connection with services performed as an employee.[36] Transportation expense includes only the cost of transporting the employee from one place to another in the course of employment when the employee is not "away from home" in a travel status. Such costs include taxi fares, automobile expenses, tolls, and parking.

Commuting from home to one's place of employment is a personal, nondeductible expense. The fact that one employee drives 30 miles to work and another employee walks six blocks is of no significance.

---

**35.** Reg. § 1.62–1(f).
**36.** § 62(2)(C).

**Example 36.** G is employed by the X Corporation. He drives 22 miles each way to work. One day G drove to a customer's office from his place of work. It was a 14-mile round trip to the customer's office. G can take a deduction for 14 miles of business transportation. The remaining 44 miles are a nondeductible commuting expense.

There are several exceptions to the general rule which disallows a deduction for commuting expenses. An employee who uses an automobile to transport heavy tools to work and who otherwise would not drive to work will be allowed a deduction. However, the deduction is allowed only for the additional costs incurred to transport work implements. Additional costs are those exceeding the cost of commuting by the same mode of transportation without the tools (e. g., the rental of a trailer but *not* the expenses of operating the automobile). The Supreme Court has held that a deduction is permitted only if the taxpayer can show that he or she would not have used the automobile were it not necessary to transport tools or equipment.[37]

Another exception is provided for an employee who has a second job. The expenses of getting from one job to another are deductible. If the employee goes home between jobs, the deduction is limited to the lesser of (1) the cost of the transportation (or mileage) between the two jobs or (2) the actual expenditure.

**Example 37.** In the current year, T holds two jobs, a full-time job with B Corporation and a part-time job with C Corporation. During the 250 days T works (adjusted for weekends, vacation, and holidays), she customarily leaves home at 7:30 a.m. and drives 30 miles to the B Corporation plant where she works until 5:00 p.m. After dinner at a nearby cafe, T drives 20 miles to C Corporation and works from 7:00 to 11:00 p.m. The distance from the second job to T's home is 40 miles. Only 20 miles (the distance between jobs) is allowed as a deduction.

Transportation expenses associated with temporary or minor assignments beyond the general area of the tax home are a final exception to the rule that commuting expenses are nondeductible. Thus, a bank manager who must spend an occasional day at a remote branch office in the suburbs can deduct transportation expenses (or mileage) as an employee expense.

**Example 38.** V works for a firm in downtown Denver, and he commutes to work. V occasionally works in a customer's office. On one such occasion, he drove directly to the customer's office (a round-trip distance from his home of 40 miles). He did not go into his office, which is a 52-mile round-trip distance. None of his mileage is deductible.

---

37. *Fausner v. Comm.*, 73-2 USTC ¶ 9515, 32 AFTR2d 73–5202, 93 S.Ct. 2820 (USSC, 1973).

**Example 39.** T drove 10 miles to his office and then drove home after making a stop at his customer's office on business (which was a total distance of 26 miles). T can deduct the cost attributable to 6 miles (the distance in excess of his normal round-trip commuting mileage).

## COMPUTATION OF AUTOMOBILE EXPENSES

Basically, a taxpayer has two choices in computing automobile expenses. The actual operating cost, which includes depreciation, gas, oil, repairs, licenses, and insurance, may be used. Records should be kept which detail the automobile's personal and business use. Only the percentage (based upon the ratio of business miles to total miles) which is allocable to business transportation and travel is allowed as a deduction.

Use of the automatic mileage method is the second alternative. The deduction is based upon 20 cents per mile for the first 15,000 business miles driven. Eleven cents per mile is allowed for any miles in excess of 15,000. Parking fees, tolls, and the investment tax credit are allowed in addition to expenses computed using the automatic mileage method.

Generally, a taxpayer may elect either method for any particular year. However, certain restrictions apply.

# TRAVEL EXPENSES

## DEFINITION OF TRAVEL EXPENSES

A deduction *for* adjusted gross income is allowed for travel expenses related to a trade or business or employment.[38] Travel expenses are more broadly defined in the Code than are transportation expenses. Travel expenses include, in addition to transportation expenses, meals and lodging that are not lavish or extravagant under the circumstances while away from home in the pursuit of a trade or business (including that of being an employee). Transportation expenses are deductible even though the taxpayer is not away from home; a deduction for travel expenses is available only if the taxpayer is away from his or her tax home. Travel expenses also include reasonable laundry and incidental expenses. Entertainment expenses are not a travel expense even if incurred while traveling. They are treated as an "other employee expense" and, unless fully reimbursed, are an itemized deduction.

---

38.   § § 62(2)(B) and 162(a)(2).

## AWAY-FROM-HOME REQUIREMENT

The crucial test of the deductibility of travel expenses is whether the employee is "away from home overnight." "Overnight" need not be a 24-hour period, nor from dusk to dawn, but it must be a period substantially longer than an ordinary day's work and require rest, sleep, or a relief-from-work period. A one-day or intracity business trip is not travel; therefore, meals and lodging are not deductible.

The employee must be away from home for a temporary period. If the taxpayer-employee is reassigned to a new post for an indefinite period of time, that new post becomes his or her "tax home". Temporary indicates that the assignment's termination is expected within a reasonably short period of time. The position of the IRS is that the tax home is the business location, post, or station of the taxpayer. Thus, travel expenses are not deductible if a taxpayer is reassigned for an indefinite period and does not move his or her place of residence to the new location. The IRS rule of thumb is that reassignments for one year or more are indefinite. The courts are in conflict regarding what constitutes a person's "home" for tax purposes. Some courts have held that the test is whether it is reasonable to expect the taxpayer to move to the new job location, while other courts, including the Tax Court, have accepted the view of the IRS. As a result of this uncertainty, the IRS has established criteria which it will attempt to apply in making the determination of a person's tax home.

> **Example 40.** H is employed as a long-haul truck driver. He stores his clothes, etc., at his parents' home and stops there for periodic visits. The rest of the time, H is on the road, sleeping in his truck and in motels. His meals, lodging, laundry, and incidental expenses are not deductible because he has no tax home from which he can be absent.

> **Example 41.** T is employed as a short-distance hauler. His wife and children live in Chicago. T makes trips of both long and short duration. These short trips are often one-day trips in the surrounding area. His meals on a one-day trip are not deductible. If he makes a 10-day trip to Florida, he is "away from home" and his meals are deductible.

## COMBINED BUSINESS AND PLEASURE TRAVEL

To be deductible, travel expenses need not be incurred in the performance of specific job functions. For example, travel expenses incurred in attending a professional convention are deductible by an employee, if attendance is connected with services as an employee. Thus, an employee of a CPA firm could deduct travel expenses incurred in attending a meeting of the American Institute of Certified Public Accountants. Unfortunately, this deduction has been abused in the past by persons who claimed a tax deduction for what was essentially a personal vacation. As a result, several provisions have been enacted to govern deductions associated with combined business-pleasure trips. If the business-pleasure trip is within the United States (i. e., the trip is from one point in the U. S. to another point in the U. S.), the transportation expenses are deductible only if the trip is primarily business. If the trip is primarily for pleasure, no transportation expenses can be taken as a deduction. Even if the trip is primarily for pleasure (or other personal reasons), any expenses incurred at the destination that are properly allocable to business are deductible.

> **Example 42.** J traveled from Seattle to New York on a combined business-pleasure trip. She spent five days conducting business and three days sightseeing and seeing shows. Her plane and taxi fare amounted to $560. Her meals, lodging, and incidental expenses amounted to $120 per day. Since the trip was primarily business (five days versus three days), the transportation is fully deductible. Only $600 of the other expenses (five days) is deductible.

### FOREIGN CONVENTION EXPENSES

Certain restrictions are imposed on the deductibility of expenses paid or incurred to attend conventions located outside the North American area. For this purpose, the North American area includes the United States, its possessions (including the Trust Territory of the Pacific Islands), Canada, and Mexico. The expenses will be disallowed unless the taxpayer establishes that the meeting is directly related to a trade or business or to an activity described in § 212 (i. e., for the production or collection of income or for the management, conservation, or maintenance of property held for the production of income). Disallowance also will occur unless the taxpayer shows that it is as reasonable for the meeting to be held in a foreign location as within the North American area. No deduction is in order for conventions, seminars, or other meetings held on cruise ships.

# MOVING EXPENSES

### GENERAL REQUIREMENTS

Moving expenses are deductible *for* adjusted gross income (see Form 3903).[39] Reimbursements from employers must be included in gross income under § 82. To be eligible for a moving expense deduction, a taxpayer must meet two basic tests: distance and time.[40]

---

39.   § § 62(8) and 217(a).
40.   § 217(c).

## DISTANCE TEST

The distance test requires that the taxpayer's new job location must be at least 35 miles farther from the taxpayer's old residence than the old residence was from the former place of employment. In this regard, the minimum distance requirement does not apply to the location of the new residence. This eliminates a moving deduction for taxpayers who purchase a new home in the same general area without changing place of employment or accept a new job in the same general area as the old job location. If a new job does not necessitate moving or if the move is for personal reasons (e. g., a better neighborhood), the taxpayer is not permitted a tax deduction.

> **Example 43.** J was permanently transferred to a new job location. J has met the distance requirements for a moving expense deduction. (Refer to the diagram below.) The distance from J's former home to his new job (80 miles) exceeds the distance from his former home to his old job (30 miles) by more than 35 miles. If J was not employed prior to the move, his new job must be at least 35 miles from his former residence. In this instance, the distance requirements also would be met if J had not been previously employed.

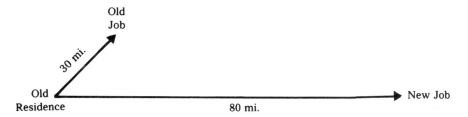

## TIME REQUIREMENTS

To be eligible for a moving expense deduction, the employee must be employed on a full-time basis at the new location for 39 weeks in the 12-month period following the move. If the taxpayer is a self-employed individual, he or she must work (either as a self-employed individual or as an employee of another) in the new location for 78 weeks during the next two years. (The first 39 weeks must be in the first 12 months.) The time requirement is suspended if the taxpayer dies, becomes disabled, or is discharged or transferred by the new employer through no fault of the employee.

It is obvious that an employee might not be able to meet the 39-week requirement by the end of the tax year. For this reason, there are two alternatives allowed. The taxpayer can take the deduction in the year the expenses were incurred even though the 39-week test has not been met. If the taxpayer later fails to meet the test, the income of the first year that the test cannot be met (i. e., the following year) must be increased by an amount equal to the deduction previously claimed for moving expenses. The second alternative is to wait until the test is met and then file an amended tax return for the prior year.

## WHEN DEDUCTIBLE

The general rule is that expenses of a cash basis taxpayer are deductible only in the year of payment. However, if reimbursement is received from the employer, an election may be made to deduct the moving expenses in the year subsequent to the move in the following circumstances.

—The moving expenses are incurred and paid in 1982, and the reimbursement is received in 1983.

—The moving expenses are incurred in 1982 and are paid in 1983 (on or before the due date including extensions for filing the 1982 return), and the reimbursement is received in 1982.

The election to deduct moving expenses in the year the reimbursement is received is made by claiming the deduction on the return, amended return, or claim for refund for the taxable year the reimbursement is received.

The moving expense deduction is allowed regardless of whether the employee is transferred by the existing employer, is employed by a new employer, moves to a new area and obtains employment, or switches from self-employed status to employee status (or vice versa). The moving expense deduction is also allowed if an individual is unemployed prior to obtaining employment in a new area.

**Example 44.** The following taxpayers moved during the year:

—A is transferred by her employer from Wichita to Santa Barbara.

—B obtains a job with a new employer in Phoenix, terminates his employment in Omaha, and moves to Phoenix.

—C terminates his employment in New York, moves to Miami, and obtains a job in Miami.

—D resigns her position in Chicago, moves to San Diego, and opens a small business in the area.

—E graduates from college in Boston, obtains a job in Portland, and moves to the new location.

Assuming the distance and time requirements are met, all of the above individuals may deduct moving expenses.

## CLASSIFICATION OF MOVING EXPENSES

There are five classes of moving expenses, and different limitations and qualifications apply to each class. Direct moving expenses include:

1.   The expense of moving household and personal belongings. This class includes fees paid to a moving company for packing, storing, and moving possessions and the rental of a truck if the taxpayer moves his or her own belongings. Also included is the cost of moving household pets. Reasonableness is the only limit on these direct expenses.

2.   Travel to the new residence. This includes the cost of transportation, meals, and lodging of the taxpayer and the members of the taxpayer's household en route, but does not include the cost of moving servants or others who are not members of the household. The taxpayer can elect to take actual auto expenses (no depreciation is allowed) or the automatic mileage method. In this case, moving expense mileage is limited to nine cents per mile for each car.

Indirect moving expenses include the following:

3.   House-hunting trips. Expenses of traveling (including meals and lodging) to the new place of employment to look for a home are deductible only if the job has been secured in advance of the house-hunting trip. The dollar limitation is explained below.

4.   Temporary living expenses. Meals and lodging expenses incurred while living in temporary quarters in the general area of the new job while waiting to move into a new residence are deductible within certain dollar limits (see below). However, these living expenses are limited to any consecutive 30-day period commencing after employment is secured.

5.   Certain residential buying and selling expenses. Buying and selling expenses include those that would normally be offset against the selling price of a home and those expenses incurred in buying a new home. Examples are commissions, escrow fees, legal expenses, points paid to secure a mortgage, transfer taxes, and advertising. Also deductible are costs involved in settling an old lease or acquiring a new lease or both. "Fixing up" expenses, damage deposits, prepaid rent, and the like are not deductible. The dollar limits are discussed below.

Indirect moving expenses are limited to a total of $3,000. Furthermore, house-hunting and temporary living expenses may not exceed $1,500 in the aggregate.[41] Again, direct moving expenses are unlimited.

Items 1.[42] + 2.    = No limit
Items 3. + 4.      = $1,500 limit
Items 3. + 4. + 5. = $3,000 limit

_ded. limited to $1500_

---

41.   § 217(b)(3)(A).
42.   The numbers refer to the types of moving expenses outlined above.

**Example 45.** T, an employee of X Corporation, is hired by Y Corporation at a substantial increase in salary. T is hired in February 19X1 and is to report for work in March 19X1. The new job requires a move from Los Angeles to New York City. Pursuant to the move, T incurs the following expenses:

| | |
|---|---|
| February 19X1 house-hunting trip | $   600 |
| Temporary living expenses in New York City incurred by T and family from March 10–30, 19X1, while awaiting the renovation of their new apartment | 1,000 |
| Penalty for breaking lease on Los Angeles apartment | 2,400 |
| Charge for packing and moving household goods | 4,200 |
| Travel expense during move (March 5–10) | 700 |

Assuming there is no reimbursement of any of these expenses by T's new employer, she can deduct the following amount:

| | | | |
|---|---|---|---|
| Moving household goods | | | $ 4,200 |
| Travel expense | | | 700 |
| House-hunting trip | $   600 | | |
| Temporary living expense | 1,000 | | |
| | $ 1,600 | | |
| Limited to: | | $ 1,500 | |
| Lease penalty | | 2,400 | |
| | | $ 3,900 | |
| Limited to: | | | 3,000 |
| Moving expense deduction allowed | | | $ 7,900 |

A statement should be attached to the tax return showing the detailed calculations of the ceiling limitations, reimbursements, change in job locations, etc. Form 3903 may be used for this purpose.

# EDUCATION EXPENSES

## GENERAL REQUIREMENTS

An employee may deduct expenses incurred for education as ordinary and necessary business expenses provided such items were incurred either (1) to maintain or improve existing skills required in the present job or (2) to meet the express requirements of the employer or the requirements imposed by law to retain his or her employment status. This provision for deductibility of education expenses should be distinguished from the exclusion possibility in cases where these expenses are incurred by an employee and either reimbursed or paid for directly by the employer. Called educational assistance payments, these exclusions must satisfy the requirements of § 127. A deduction would be precluded in those cases in which the employee's educational expenses have been reimbursed or paid by the employer. For a further discussion of educational assistance payments by employers, refer to Chapter 4.

*Exceptions.* Education expenses are not deductible under any conditions if the education either (1) is required to meet the minimum educational standards for qualification in the taxpayer's existing job or (2) qualifies the taxpayer for a new trade or business. Thus, fees incurred for professional qualification exams (the bar exam, for example) and fees for review courses (such as a CPA review course) are not deductible. If the education incidentally results in a promotion or raise, the deduction can still be taken so long as the education maintained and improved existing skills and did not qualify a person for a new trade or business. A change in duties is not always fatal to the deduction if the new duties involve the same general work. For example, the IRS has ruled that a practicing dentist's educational expenses incurred to become an orthodontist are deductible.

## REQUIREMENTS IMPOSED BY LAW OR BY THE EMPLOYER FOR RETENTION OF EMPLOYMENT

Teachers often qualify under the provision that permits the deduction of the educational expenses if they are required by the employer or if the requirements are imposed by law. Many states require a minimum of a bachelor's degree and a specified number of additional courses to retain a teaching job. In addition, some public school systems have imposed a master's degree requirement and have required teachers to make satisfactory progress toward a master's degree in order to keep their position. An instructor with a master's degree who is teaching at a college where the degree required for a permanent post is a doctorate is not permitted to deduct the expenses of obtaining a PhD.; the instructor is obtaining the minimum education required for that position.

## MAINTAINING OR IMPROVING EXISTING SKILLS

The "maintaining or improving existing skills" requirement in the Code has been difficult for both taxpayers and the courts to interpret. For example, a business executive may be permitted to deduct the costs of obtaining an M.B.A. on the grounds that the advanced management education is undertaken to maintain and improve existing management skills. However, if the business executive incurred the expenses to obtain a law degree, the expenses would not be deductible, because they constitute training for a new trade or business. For example, the Regulations deny the deduction by a self-employed accountant of expenses relating to law school. In addition, several courts have disallowed deductions to IRS agents for the cost of obtaining a law degree, since the degree was not required to retain employment; the education qualified the agent for a new profession. Clearly, the executive mentioned previously would be eligible to deduct the costs of specialized, nondegree management courses which were taken for continuing education or to maintain or improve existing skills.

## CLASSIFICATION OF SPECIFIC ITEMS

Education expenses include books, tuition, typing, and transportation (e. g., from the office to night school) and travel (e. g., meals and lodging while away from home at summer school). Transportation and travel are deductible *for* adjusted gross income (whether or not reimbursed), and all other educational expenses are deductions *from* adjusted gross income (unless such expenses are reimbursed by the employer or incurred by a self-employed individual or an outside salesperson).

> **Example 46.**   T holds a bachelor of education degree. T is a teacher of secondary education in the Los Angeles, California, school system. Last year the school board changed its minimum education requirement for new teachers by prescribing five years of college training instead of four. Under a grandfather clause, teachers who have only four years of college (such as T) would continue to qualify if they show satisfactory progress toward a graduate degree. Pursuant to this new requirement, T enrolls at the University of Southern California and takes three graduate courses. T's unreimbursed expenses for this purpose are as follows:
>
> | | |
> |---|---:|
> | Books and tuition | $   250 |
> | Meals and lodging while in travel status (June–August) | 1,150 |
> | Laundry while in travel status | 220 |
> | Transportation | 600 |

T can claim the meals and lodging, laundry, and transportation as a deduction *for* adjusted gross income (as a travel expense). The books and tuition are deductible *from* adjusted gross income on Schedule A of Form 1040 if T itemizes her deductions.

# ENTERTAINMENT EXPENSES

In 1962 Congress enacted § 274 of the Code to place restrictions on the deductibility of entertainment expenses. This provision was in response to the alleged abuses by business executives and other employees of entertainment expense deductions. The law now contains strict recordkeeping requirements and provides restrictive tests for the deduction of certain types of entertainment expenses.

## CLASSIFICATION OF EXPENSES

Entertainment expenses may be categorized as follows: those *directly related to* business and those *associated with* business.[43] Directly related expenses are related to an actual business meeting or discussion. These expenses may be contrasted with entertainment expenses that are often incurred to promote goodwill. To obtain a deduction for directly related entertainment, it is not necessary to show that actual benefit resulted from the expenditure as long as there was a "reasonable" expectation of benefit. To qualify as directly related, the expense should be incurred in a clear business setting. If there is little possibility of engaging in the active conduct of a trade or business due to the nature of the social facility, it may be difficult to qualify the expenditure as "directly related to" business.

Expenses associated with, rather than directly related to, business entertainment must serve a specific business purpose, such as obtaining new business or continuing existing business. These expenditures qualify only if the expenses directly precede or follow a bona fide business discussion. Entertainment occurring on the same day as the business discussion meets the test.

## RESTRICTIONS UPON DEDUCTIBILITY

*Business Meals.*   Section 274(e) allows the deduction of certain entertainment expenses that would, otherwise, not be deductible. The cost of meals or beverages served in surroundings which are conducive to a business discussion (the so-called quiet business meal rule) is deductible. There is no requirement that business actually be discussed. The taxpayer need only demonstrate a business relationship for the entertainment and a reasonable expectation of business benefit. This quiet business meal rule also extends to the furnishing of meals or beverages at business programs, conventions, etc. (e. g., a dental equipment supplier may purchase meals or buy drinks for dentists at a convention).

> **Example 47.**   T, a sales representative, took a customer to dinner at a local restaurant. After dinner, T took the customer to a nearby nightclub where they had drinks and watched a floor show. The cost of dinner is deductible because it meets the "directly related" test. This is true whether or not business was actually discussed because of the "quiet business meal" rule. The cost of entertainment at the nightclub is also deductible, since it meets the "associated with" test (i. e., the nightclub entertainment directly followed the business dinner, which meets the "directly related" test).

---

**43.**   § 274(a)(1)(A).

**Example 48.** S, a sales representative, took a customer to a nightclub where they had drinks and watched a floor show. Business was not discussed during the evening. The expenses incurred by S are not deductible. The entertainment does not satisfy the "associated with" test, since it did not precede or follow a bona fide business discussion (nor does it meet the "quiet business meal" requirement). Contrast this result with the result in Example 47, where both the "directly related" and "associated with" tests were met.

*Entertainment Facilities.* If certain conditions were met, prior to 1979 all or part of the cost of maintaining an entertainment facility (e. g., hunting lodge, fishing camp, yacht, country club) could be deducted as a business expense. In this connection, the amount deductible included such items as depreciation, maintenance and repairs, and annual membership dues. Apparently fearful that taxpayer abuse was taking place, Congress narrowed the categories of entertainment facilities that qualify for the deduction. As to amounts paid or incurred after December 31, 1978, only "dues or fees to any social, athletic, or sporting club or organization" can be considered.

To obtain a deduction for the dues paid or incurred to maintain a club membership, a "primary use" test is imposed. Unless it can be shown that over 50 percent of the use of the facility was for business purposes, no deduction is permitted. In meeting the primary use test, the following rules govern:

—Consider only the days the facility is used. Thus, days of nonuse do not enter into the determination.

—A day of both business and personal use counts as a day of business use.

—Business use includes entertainment that is *associated with* and *directly related to.*

But even if the primary use test is satisfied, only the portion of the dues attributable to the *directly related to* entertainment qualify for the deduction. For this purpose, however, quiet business meals are treated as *directly related to* entertainment.

**Example 49.** T is the sales manager of an insurance agency and as such is expected to incur entertainment expenditures in connection with the sale of insurance to existing and potential clients. None of these expenses are reimbursed by his employer. During the year, T paid the following amounts to the Leesville Country Club:

| | |
|---|---:|
| Membership fee (refundable upon termination of membership) | $ 2,000 |
| Annual dues | 1,200 |
| Meals and other charges relating to business use | 900 |
| Meals and other charges relating to personal use | 400 |

The club was used 120 days for purposes *directly related to* business and 80 days for personal use. The club was not used at all during the remaining days of the year. Since the facility was used for business more than 50% of the time (i. e., 120 days out of 200 days), the "primary use" test is satisfied. The portion of the annual dues that can be deducted is $720 (120/200 = 60% × $1,200). None of the membership fee is deductible, since it is refundable. In summary, a total deduction of $1,620 [$720 (club dues) + $900 (meals and other charges relating to business use)] is allowed.

*Recordkeeping Requirements.* Prior to 1962, the courts frequently permitted a deduction for entertainment expenses under the Cohan rule. Under this rule, deduction of a portion of the taxpayer's expenses was permitted where the exact amount could not be determined due to incomplete records.[44]

Section 274(d) now provides that no deduction is permitted unless adequate substantiation is maintained including:

—The amount of the expense.

—The time and place of the expense.

—The business purpose.

—The business relationship.

It is not necessary to report the expenses and employer reimbursements on the employee's tax return if the reimbursement is equal to the expenses and if the employee furnishes adequate accounting to the employer. The employee is only required to state on the return that the reimbursements did not exceed the allowable expenses. In all other cases, it is necessary to submit a statement with the return (i. e., when the reimbursements exceed the allowable expenses or when the expenses exceed the reimbursement and the taxpayer deducts such excess amounts on the return, the excess must be included in income). In all cases involving a shareholder-employee relationship (i. e., where the employee owns more than 10% of the employer corporations's stock), a statement of the employee's expenses must be submitted with the tax return.

*Business Gifts.* Business gifts are deductible to the extent of $25 per donee per year.[45] An exception is made for gifts costing $4 or less (e. g., pens with the employee's or company's name on them) or promotional materials. Such items are not treated as business gifts (subject to the $25 limitation). In addition, incidental costs such as engraving on jewelry, nominal charges for giftwrapping, mailing, and delivery

---

**44.** *Cohan v. Comm.,* 2 USTC ¶ 489, 8 AFTR 10552, 39 F.2d 540 (CA–2, 1930); in Rev.Rul. 75–169, 1975–1 C.B. 59, the IRS held that due to the passage of § 274(d) no deduction will be allowed on the basis of the Cohan rule or unsupported testimony.
**45.** § 274(b)(1).

are not included in the cost of the gift for purposes of applying the $25 per gift limitation. Excluded from the $25 limit are gifts or awards to employees for length of service, etc., that are under $400. Prior to August 13, 1981, the limit for awards to employees was $100.

If the taxpayer is an outside salesperson or if the expenses are reimbursed by an employer, employee gifts are deductible *for* adjusted gross income; in all other cases, the deduction is *from* adjusted gross income and can be taken only if the employee itemizes deductions.

# OTHER EMPLOYEE EXPENSES

## OFFICE IN THE HOME

No deduction is permitted for an office in the home unless a portion of the residence is used exclusively on a regular basis (1) as the principal place of business for any trade or business of the taxpayer or (2) as a place of business which is used by patients, clients, or customers.[46] Employees must meet an additional test: The use must be for the convenience of the employer as opposed to being merely "appropriate and helpful."

The exclusive use requirement means that a specific part of the home must be used solely for business purposes. Since the office in the home must be used exclusively for business, a deduction, if permitted, will require an allocation of total expenses of operating the home between business and personal use based on floor space or number of rooms.

Even if the taxpayer meets the above requirements, the allowable business expenses may not exceed the gross income from the business activity reduced by an allocable portion of expense deductions which would otherwise qualify as personal itemized deductions (e. g., mortgage interest and real estate taxes).

> **Example 50.** T is a self-employed CPA who maintains an office in his home which is devoted exclusively to client work. Clients regularly visit this office. The gross income from his practice was $2,000 during 19X1. The portion of mortgage interest and real estate taxes allocated to business use amounted to $1,500; an allocable portion of maintenance expenses, utilities, maid service, and depreciation on the house was $1,000. As shown below, his other business expenses of $1,000 are limited, therefore, to $500 which is the excess of gross income of $2,000 over the allocable portion of T's itemized deductions of $1,500.

---

46.   § 280A(c)(1), as amended by P.L. 97–119.

|  |  |  |
|---|---|---|
| Gross income from self-employment | $ 2,000 |  |
| Less: Allocable portion of itemized deduction items – interest and taxes | 1,500 | – deductible as itemized deductions |
| Balance of deductions | $   500 |  |

## MISCELLANEOUS EMPLOYEE EXPENSES

Other employee expenses which are deductible include special clothing and its upkeep, union dues, professional expenses such as dues and attendance of professional meetings, and employment agency fees for seeking employment in the same trade or business whether or not a new job is secured. These deductions are *for* adjusted gross income only if the employee is an outside salesperson, if the expenses are travel or transportation, or if they are reimbursed. In all other cases, they are deductions *from* adjusted gross income.

To be deductible, special clothing must be both specifically required as a condition of employment and not generally adaptable to regular wear (e. g., a police officer's uniform is not suitable for off-duty activities) or continually used to the extent that the clothing takes the place of regular clothing (e. g., military uniforms).

Regulation § 1.212–1(f) disallows a deduction for job-hunting expenses. The current position of the IRS, however, is that expenses incurred in seeking employment (e. g., travel, employment agency fees) are deductible if the taxpayer is seeking employment in the same trade or business in which he or she is currently employed (or, if unemployed, there has been no substantial lack of continuity since the last job and the search for a new position) even if the attempts to secure the job are unsuccessful. However, no deduction is allowed for persons seeking their first job or seeking employment in a new trade or business (whether or not successful).

Other employee expenses which are not deductible include regular clothes, commuting expenses, and any other expenditures of a personal nature.

# REPORTING PROCEDURES

Form 2106 is used for reporting employee business expenses. Keep in mind that no reporting would be required where the employee renders an adequate accounting to the employer and is reimbursed fully for all legitimate expenses. Form 2106 also need not be used where the reimbursement is less than the amount spent but the employee chooses to forego the excess deduction. Form 2106 is reproduced in Appendix B.

## OTHER DEDUCTIONS FOR ADJUSTED GROSS INCOME

ERTA provides for two new deductions *for* adjusted gross income. New Code Section 221 allows a deduction for two-earner married couples (discussed in Chapter 2).

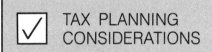

## DOCUMENTATION OF RELATED-TAXPAYER LOANS, CASUALTY LOSSES, AND THEFT LOSSES

Since non-bona fide loans between related taxpayers may be treated as gifts, adequate documentation is needed to substantiate a bad debt deduction if the loan subsequently becomes worthless. Documentation should include proper execution of the note (legal form) and the establishment of a bona fide purpose for the loan. In addition, it is desirable to stipulate a reasonable rate of interest and a fixed maturity date.

Since a theft loss is not permitted for misplaced items, a loss should be documented by a police report and evidence of the value of the property (e. g., appraisals, pictures of the property, newspaper clippings). Similar documentation of the value of property should be provided to support a casualty loss deduction because the amount of loss is measured by the decline in fair market value of the property.

Casualty loss deductions must be reported on Form 4684 (see Appendix B).

## DEPRECIATION, ACRS, AND AMORTIZATION

If a taxpayer starts a new business and initial losses are anticipated, or if a net operating loss is going to expire in the next few years, the taxpayer should consider the use of cost recovery and amortization methods which produce smaller deductions in the early years. The taxpayer might elect under § 174 to capitalize and amortize research and experimental costs over a period of not less than 60 months instead of electing the expense method. In addition, it may be preferable to elect straight-line ACRS instead of the statutory percentage ACRS method. The straight-line election of ACRS allows the taxpayer to use a longer life than the prescribed life under ACRS, thereby decreasing the early years' deductions.

Depreciation schedules should be reviewed annually for possible retirements, abandonments, obsolescence, and changes in estimated useful lives.

**Example 51.** An examination of the depreciation schedule of X Company reveals the following:

—Asset A has been abandoned when it was discovered that the cost of repairs would be in excess of the cost of replacement. Asset A had an adjusted basis of $3,000.

—Asset D was being depreciated over a period of 10 years, but a revised estimate shows that its estimated remaining life is only two years. Its original cost was $60,000 and had been depreciated under the straight-line method for three years. It was a pre-ERTA asset and was not subject to ACRS provisions.

—Asset J had become obsolete this year. At that point, its adjusted basis was $8,000.

The depreciation expense on Asset D should be $21,000 [$60,000 (cost) − $18,000 (accumulated depreciation) = $42,000 ÷ 2 (remaining estimated useful life)]. Assets A and J should be written off for an additional expense of $11,000 ($3,000 + $8,000).

Because of the deductions for depreciation, interest, and ad valorem property taxes, investments in real estate can be highly attractive. In figuring the economics of such investments, one should be sure to take into account any tax savings that result.

**Example 52.** In early January 1980, T (an individual in the 50% marginal tax bracket) purchased rental property for $125,000 (of which $20,000 was allocated to the land and $105,000 to the building). The building had an estimated useful life of 25 years and no anticipated salvage value. T made a down payment of $25,000 and assumed the seller's mortgage for the balance. Under the mortgage agreement, monthly payments of $1,000 are required and are applied toward interest, taxes, insurance, and principal. As the property already was occupied, T continued to receive rent of $1,200 per month from the tenant.

During the first year of ownership, T's expenses were as follows:

| | |
|---|---:|
| Interest | $ 10,000 |
| Taxes | 800 |
| Insurance | 1,000 |
| Repairs and maintenance | 2,200 |
| Depreciation (under the straight-line method) | 4,200 |
| Total | $ 18,200 |

The deductible loss from the rental property is computed below:

| | |
|---|---:|
| Rental income ($1,200 × 12 months) | $ 14,400 |
| Less expenses (see above) | 18,200 |
| Net loss | $ 3,800 |

But what is T's overall position for the year when the tax benefit of the loss is taken into account? Considering just the cash intake and outlay, this is summarized as follows:

| | | |
|---|---:|---:|
| Intake— | | |
| Rental income | $ 14,400 | |
| Tax savings [50% (income tax bracket) ×  $3,800 (loss from the property)] | 1,900 | $ 16,300 |
| Outlay— | | |
| Mortgage payments ($1,000 × 12 months) | $ 12,000 | |
| Repairs and maintenance | 2,200 | 14,200 |
| Net cash benefit | | $ 2,100 |

## IMMEDIATE EXPENSING ELECTION

In taking the expensing election under ACRS, timing is of utmost importance. A mere purchase at December 31 is not enough, as the asset has to be placed in service during the year. A similar, and usually more significant, problem arises in terms of the availability of the investment tax credit (see Chapter 8).

The taxpayer should carefully consider the benefits of current expensing under § 179 with the ACRS statutory percentage method. To do this, the taxpayer must consider the tax savings generated by the alternatives. Current expensing may initially seem to be the best. However, no investment credit may be taken on any amount which has been expensed under § 179. In addition, if the investment credit is taken, the basis of the property must be reduced by 50% of the investment credit unless the taxpayer elects to reduce the credit by two percent. Example 53 compares the tax savings generated by the alternatives.

**Example 53.** Assume that in 1983 a taxpayer invests $5,000 in personal property. Since the comparison is of cash flow from tax savings over a period of time, the time value of money must be considered. Assume 15% is the appropriate rate. The present value of the tax savings generated if (1) the capital asset is expensed immediately, (2) ACRS and the total investment credit is taken, or (3) ACRS and the reduced investment credit is taken, are compared in the following table:

Three-year Class Property

| Marginal Tax Rate | Section 179 Expensing | ACRS AND ITC 6% ITC | ACRS AND ITC 4% ITC |
|---|---|---|---|
| 20% | $ 870 | $ 986 | $ 922 |
| 30% | 1,304 | 1,349 | 1,296 |
| 40% | 1,739 | 1,712 | 1,670 |
| 50% | 2,174 | 2,075 | 2,044 |

Five-year Class Property

| Marginal Tax Rate | Section 179 Expensing | ACRS AND ITC | |
|---|---|---|---|
| | | 10% ITC | 8% ITC |
| 20% | $ 870 | $1,061 | $1,007 |
| 30% | 1,304 | 1,374 | 1,337 |
| 40% | 1,739 | 1,688 | 1,667 |
| 50% | 2,174 | 2,011 | 1,996 |

The figures show that with respect to both three-year and five-year class property, the taxpayer should elect ACRS with the full investment credit if his or her marginal tax rate is 30% or less. However, if the marginal tax rate is 40% or more, the taxpayer is better off to elect to expense the $5,000 under § 179.

## STRAIGHT-LINE ELECTION UNDER ACRS

The straight-line election of ACRS allows a taxpayer to use a longer life than the prescribed life under ACRS. A taxpayer who has a net operating loss which is going to expire in the current year may elect to depreciate property with a three-year life over five or 12 years, thereby decreasing the current year's deductions, increasing the net income, and as a result, using up an NOL that would otherwise be lost forever. The write-off of the basis of the property is merely deferred to later years.

## DEPLETION

Since the election to use the cost or percentage depletion method is an annual election, a taxpayer can use cost depletion (if higher) until the basis is exhausted, then switch to percentage depletion in the following years.

**Example 54.** Assume the following facts for T:

| | |
|---|---|
| Remaining depletable basis | $ 11,000 |
| Gross income (10,000 units) | 100,000 |
| Expenses (other than depletion) | 30,000 |
| Depletion per unit | 4 |

Since cost depletion is limited to the basis of $11,000 and the percentage depletion is $22,000, T would choose the latter. His basis is then reduced to zero, but in future years, he can continue to take percentage depletion, since percentage depletion is taken without reference to the remaining basis.

## SHIFTING DEDUCTIONS BETWEEN EMPLOYER AND EMPLOYEE

In a closely-held corporation, there is an opportunity for the employee-shareholder to shift deductions from the corporation to the employee if proper advance planning is done. Typically, the share-holder-employee incurs travel and entertainment expenses in the course of employment. The corporation gets the deduction if it reimburses the employee-shareholder. Suppose the employee is in a higher tax bracket than the corporation so that the deduction is more valuable on the employee-shareholder's return. If the employer simply pays the expenses and fails to get reimbursed by the corporation, both the employee and the corporation lose the deduction, since the employee could have been reimbursed by the corporation and the corporation did not make the payment (refer to Chapter 5).

However, if there is a resolution by the corporation that employees are expected to absorb such expenses out of their salaries, the employee can take the deduction. Note that such a corporate resolution must be made before such expenses are incurred so that the tax planning (and the corporate resolution establishing this policy) takes place before the beginning of the year.

## MOVING EXPENSES

Commissions on the sale of a personal residence may either be treated as indirect moving expenses subject to the overall ceiling limitations or be deducted from the selling price of the residence in arriving at the amount realized. Generally, it is preferable to deduct the commissions as moving expenses, since a deduction from the selling price of the house merely reduces the capital gain on the sale (or increases a nondeductible loss). In addition, such capital gains may be postponed if a new residence is acquired within the prescribed time period and certain other requirements of the Code are met. Postponement of gain rules for the sale of a personal residence are discussed in Chapter 9. Consideration should be given to the fact that sale-related expenses which are not used as moving expenses (due to the ceiling limitations) may be deducted from the selling price of the residence.

Persons who retire and move to a new location incur personal, nondeductible moving expenses. However, if the retired person accepts a full-time job in the new location prior to moving, the moving expenses become deductible.

> **Example 55.**  J retired from the practice of public accounting in New York and moved to Las Cruces, New Mexico, where he became an instructor in accounting at New Mexico State University. If he had acquired the new job prior to the move, his moving expenses would be deductible. Otherwise, they were personal in nature and, therefore, nondeductible.

## EDUCATION EXPENSES

Educational expenses are treated as nondeductible personal items unless the individual is employed or is engaged in a trade or business.

A temporary leave of absence for further education is one way to reasonably assure that the taxpayer is still qualified, even if a full-time student. It has been held that an individual is qualified for the education expense deduction even though he or she resigned from his or her job, returned to school full time for two years, and accepted another job in the same field upon graduation. The Court held that he or she had merely suspended active participation in his or her field. In another instance, a nurse had been inactive in her field for 13 years and returned to school to study biology; she was not in a trade or business and the expenses were not deductible. To secure the deduction, an individual should be advised to arrange his or her work situation to preserve employee or business status.

Travel as a form of education is allowed under Reg. § 1.162–5(d) only to "the extent [that] such expenditures are attributable to a period of travel that is directly related to the duties of the individual in his employment. . . ." The travel must directly maintain or improve existing skills, and the major portion of the travel must be primarily for education. General travel that is primarily for pleasure or only indirectly enhances one's existing skills is not deductible. Thus, it is particularly important to document educational travel activities.

## ENTERTAINMENT

Proper documentation of expenditures is essential due to the strict recordkeeping requirements and the restrictive tests which must be met. For example, credit card receipts as the sole source of documentation may be inadequate to substantiate the business purpose and business relationship. Taxpayers should be advised to maintain detailed records of amounts, time, place, business purpose, and business relationships.

"Associated with" or goodwill entertainment is not deductible unless a business discussion is conducted immediately before or after the entertainment and there is a business purpose for such entertainment. Taxpayers should be advised to arrange for a business discussion before or after such entertainment and to provide documentation of the business purpose (e. g., to obtain new business from a prospective customer).

Since a 50 percent test is imposed for the deductibility of country club dues, it may be necessary to accelerate business use or reduce personal use of a club facility. The 50 percent test is made on a daily use basis; therefore, detailed records should be maintained to substantiate business versus personal use.

**Example 56.** T confers with his CPA on December 5 and finds that he has used the country club 30 days for business and 33 days for personal use. On the advice of his CPA, T schedules four business lunches between December 5 and December 31 and refrains from using the club for personal purposes until January of the following year. Because of this action, T will meet the 50 percent test and will be permitted a deduction for a portion of the club dues.

---

## PROBLEM MATERIALS

---

### Questions for Class Discussion

1. Dr. T, an individual and cash basis taxpayer engaged in the general practice of dentistry, performed extensive bridge and crown work on Mr. S. for which he charged $3,500 ($2,500 for services and $1,000 for materials and lab work). Since Mr. S never paid the bill and has left for parts unknown, Dr. T feels that he is entitled to a bad debt deduction of $3,500. Comment on Dr. T's tax position on this matter.

2. Compare and contrast the reserve and the direct charge-off methods. Which method is generally preferred by most businesses? Why? _— Reserve M._

3. Discuss the difference(s) between business and nonbusiness bad debts? How is the distinction determined? How is each treated on the return?

4. Under what circumstances may a worthless security be treated as an ordinary loss? _If this security is in Sec 1244._

5. What acts of God give rise to a casualty loss? Which ones do not? Discuss.

6. How is a personal casualty loss computed? A business casualty loss? What effect do insurance proceeds have on both types of losses?

7. What are research and experimental expenditures? Discuss the alternative ways they may be handled for tax purposes.

8. What is the rationale behind the net operating loss deduction? Who benefits from this provision?

9. What depreciation methods can be used for the following assets which were acquired after 1969 and before January 1, 1981?

    (a) Used machinery and equipment used in the business.

    (b) New apartment building held for investment.

    (c) Land held for business use.

    (d) Used apartment building held for investment. _— 125% used life is 25 yrs or more_

    (e) New factory used for business. _— 150%, 125% or S.L._

    (f) New automobile used in the business. _— 200%, 150%, SYD or st line_

10. Discuss the § 179 election to expense assets. Should all taxpayers who qualify make the election?

11. If a taxpayer does not claim depreciation in one year, can an excess amount be claimed during a subsequent year? How is the basis for depreciable property affected by the failure to claim depreciation during any one year?

12. XYZ Corporation acquired the assets of ABC Company for $1,000,000 in cash. The book value of the tangible assets was $400,000; their fair market value was $600,000. XYZ Corporation was willing to pay $400,000 for the ABC Company's goodwill, since the company's operations have been ex-

tremely profitable. For accounting purposes, XYZ Corporation will amortize the goodwill over a period of 40 years as prescribed by Accounting Principles Board Opinion No. 17. Is this procedure acceptable for income tax purposes? Explain.

13. Why is a patent subject to amortization while goodwill is not amortizable?

14. Why would a taxpayer elect the optional straight-line method for an asset acquired after 1980?

15. Briefly discuss the differences between cost depletion and percentage depletion.

16. T owns a barber shop with four chairs, one of which he operates himself. The other three chairs are worked by other persons. What factors should be taken into account in determining whether or not the other barbers are T's employees or independent contractors?

17. What difference does it make if an individual's expenses are classified as employment-related versus expenses from self-employment?

18. One employee commutes one block to work; another employee travels 60 miles to his place of employment. Does the distance traveled have any effect upon the deductibility of these transportation expenses?

19. Distinguish between the terms "transportation" expense and "travel" expense.

20. A taxpayer has two jobs. He drives 40 miles to his first job. The distance from the first job to the second is 32 miles. During the year he worked 200 days at both jobs. On 150 days, he drove from his first job to the second job; on the remaining 50 days, he drove home (40 miles) and then to the second job (42 miles). How much can he deduct?

21. What requirements must be met for an employee to deduct office-in--the-home expenses? — Principal place of any one of tax p. business.

22. If an employee takes a combined business/pleasure trip, what portion of the expenses are deductible?

23. Does the outside salesperson classification apply if an employee performs service or delivery functions (e. g., television repair or milk delivery)? no.

24. What is the reason for imposing time and distance requirements to determine the deductibility of moving expenses?

25. Why is a taxpayer permitted a deduction *for* adjusted gross income for reimbursed expenses which would be treated as itemized deductions if no reimbursement were received?

26. What tax return reporting procedures must be followed by an employee under the following circumstances:

    (a) Expenses and reimbursements are equal and an adequate accounting is made to the employer.

    (b) Reimbursements exceed expenses and an adequate accounting is made to the employer.

    (c) Expenses exceed reimbursements and no accounting is made to the employer.

27. Why is it sometimes necessary to make an allocation of expenses when reimbursements cover all types of employee expenses?

28. Why are educational travel and transportation expenses deductions *for* adjusted gross income and all other unreimbursed educational expenses deductions *from* adjusted gross income?

29. Discuss whether each of the following employees will be allowed a deduction for education expenses. Why or why not?

*maintain or improve existing skill*

(a) A, a CPA who attended night school in order to take computer courses to improve her auditing skills. *yes*

(b) B, a CPA who is a tax specialist attended night law school to gain a greater expertise in the tax area. *No*

(c) C, a computer programmer who attended night school to become a computer analyst for her present employer. *Yes*

(d) D, an elementary school teacher who took courses in art appreciation during the summer. D had no art training, and art is taught in his school. It was not a requirement of the employer. *yes*

(e) E, a marketing manager who took a Dale Carnegie course. *yes*

(f) F, a homemaker who took a Dale Carnegie course. *— no*

(g) G, a retired Army officer, who returns to school for business courses to prepare for a civilian job. *— no*

(h) What if G (above) took the courses after he had obtained a civilian business position? *not enough info — yes or no*

30. S and T are employees of different companies who attend a local college at night on a part-time basis. S personally absorbs all of her education costs while T is reimbursed for his by his employer. For income tax purposes, which of these taxpayers might be in a better position? (Refer to the discussion of § 127 in Chapter 4.)

31. Discuss the difference between "directly related to" and "associated with" entertainment.

32. To what extent may a taxpayer make business gifts to a business associate? To an employee? To a superior? *$25. Cash —*

## Problems

33. M loaned T $10,000 on April 1, 19X4. In 19X5 T filed for bankruptcy. At that time it was revealed that T's creditors could expect to receive 60¢ on the dollar. In February 19X6 final settlement was made and M received $3,000. How much loss can M deduct and in which year? How is it treated on M's return?

34. Determine the amount of the addition to the reserve for bad debts of J Company as of December 31, 19X6, using the *Black Motor Co.* formula and given the following information:

(a) Net bad debts for the current year and five preceding years is $60,000.

(b) Total accounts and notes receivable outstanding at the end of the year are as follows:

| | |
|---|---|
| 19X1 | $ 167,000 |
| 19X2 | 183,000 |
| 19X3 | 150,000 |

|      |         |
|------|---------|
| 19X4 | 133,000 |
| 19X5 | 200,000 |
| 19X6 | 167,000 |

(c) Beginning balance in the reserve for bad debts in 19X6 is $20,000.

(d) In 19X6 recoveries of previous accounts written off equal $3,333.

(e) Specific write-offs during 19X6 equal $13,328.

35.  T, a single taxpayer, bought stocks for $65,000 on June 3, 19X8. On May 15, 19X9, the company went bankrupt and the stock became worthless.

(a) Does the taxpayer have a deduction?

(b) When?

(c) What is the character of the loss?

36.  K owned an acre of land in Kansas upon which he had his home, two rental houses, an apartment building, and his construction company. A tornado hit the area and destroyed one of the rental houses, damaged the apartment building, and destroyed some of his construction equipment. The tenant of his other rental house moved out for fear of another tornado and K lost $450 in rent. The local real estate appraiser told K his personal residence (with an adjusted basis of $52,500) had been worth $75,000 until the disaster and was now worth only $45,000 (although it was undamaged) because it had been established that the house was in a tornado path. Other losses were as follows:

| Item | Adjusted Basis | FMV Before | FMV After | Insurance Proceeds |
|------|----------------|------------|-----------|--------------------|
| House # 1 | $  34,500 | $  43,500 | $  –0– | $ 37,500 |
| Apartment house | 100,000 | 225,000 | 180,000 | 31,500 |
| Equipment | 90,000 | 112,500 | –0– | 75,000 |

(a) Determine the amount of the casualty loss K can take on his tax return.

(b) Assuming the loss occurred on March 3, 19X7, and that the area was designated by the President as a disaster area, what options are open to K with respect to the timing of the loss?

37.  X Company acquired an automobile for use in its business on January 1, 1979, for $9,000. No depreciation was taken in 1979 or 1980, since the company had net operating losses and wanted to "save" the deductions for later years. In 1981 the company claimed a three-year life for the automobile (and no salvage value) and deducted $3,000 of depreciation using a straight-line rate. On January 1, 1982, the automobile was sold for $4,500. Calculate the gain or loss on the sale of the automobile in 1982.

38.  T, who is single, acquired a new machine for $30,000 on January 1, 1979. Assuming bonus depreciation is taken, calculate the total depreciation deduction allowed in the first year if the estimated useful life is 10 years (salvage value of $4,000) under each of the following methods:

(a) 200% declining-balance.

(b) Sum-of-the-years' digits.

(c) 150% declining-balance. —— 6200

(d) Straight-line. —— 5651

39. Assume the same facts as in Problem 38, except that T acquired the new machine on March 2, 1983 and claimed $2,000 of investment credit on the machine. What is the maximum amount that T can write off in 1983?

40. In January 1980, K, who is single, acquired a machine for use in his trade or business. Information concerning the machine follows:

| | |
|---|---|
| Cost of equipment | $ 100,000 |
| Estimated useful life | 20 years |
| Salvage value | $ 26,000 |

Calculate the first year's depreciation expense using the straight-line, sum-of-the-years' digits, and double-declining balance methods based on the assumption that additional first-year depreciation is claimed.

41. K acquired a machine on September 5, 1983, for $100,000. The machine has a recovery period of five years. Calculate K's write-off for 1983 assuming:

(a) K elects the straight-line method over the longest permissible recovery period and does not elect immediate expensing under § 179. K claims $10,000 of investment tax credit on the machine.

(b) K elects immediate expensing under § 179 and does not elect the straight-line recovery method. K claims $9,500 of investment tax credit on the machine.    13,538 + 5000 = 18,538 dep'ded.

(c) K does not elect immediate expensing under § 179, nor does he elect the straight-line recovery method. However, K does claim $10,000 of investment tax credit on the machine.    95000 x 15% = 14,250.

42. C acquired a building on July 1, 1983, at a cost of $200,000.    ×    6% tax table = 12,000

(a) Calculate C's cost recovery allowance for 1983, assuming the building is a warehouse and that C does not elect the straight-line recovery method.

(b) Calculate C's cost recovery allowance for 1983, assuming the building is low-income housing and that C does not elect the straight-line re-covery method.    7% = 14,000

43. T acquired a mineral interest during the year for $5,000,000. A geological survey estimated that 250,000 tons of the mineral remain in the deposit. During the year 70,000 tons were mined and 45,000 tons were sold. Cal-culate the depletion allowance based on the cost method.

44. X had gross income from a gravel pit of $60,000. Assuming the depletion rate allowed by law is 5% and other expenses relating to the property are $40,000, calculate X's depletion allowance under the percentage method.

45. During 1982, T bought the following business assets:

| | |
|---|---|
| Factory machinery (5-year recovery period) | $ 50,000 |
| Light-duty trucks (3-year recovery period) | 20,000 |

Calculate T's cost recovery allowances for 1982 and 1983:

(a) Using the statutory percentage method, assuming T does not make the § 179 election but does make the reduced investment credit election.

(b) Using the statutory percentage method, assuming T does make the § 179 election but does make the reduced investment credit election.

(c) Using the optional straight-line method over the shortest permissible cost recovery period. Assume T does not make the § 179 election but does make the reduced investment credit election.

46. B incurred the following expenses on a business trip: (It was 100% business, and the taxpayer was away from home overnight.)

| | |
|---|---|
| Airfare | $ 1,082 |
| Taxi | 30 |
| Meals | 75 |
| Room | 105 |
| Entertainment | 40 |
| Laundry | 25 |

None of the expenses are reimbursed by B's employer. How much can be deducted, and is the deduction *for* or *from* adjusted gross income if B is not an outside salesperson?

47. J is a salesman for the XYZ Company. He solicits orders from commercial businesses within the general vicinity of the company office, which is also his tax home. When business is slow, he promotes the company's residential products by making house-to-house calls within the general area. The company provides a desk for J which he occasionally uses to write up an order. On Friday of each week, J goes to the company office to pick up his mail. J incurred the following unreimbursed expenses during 1983:

—Automobile (e. g., depreciation, gas, oil)—$5,000.

—Luncheons for clients—$3,000.

J maintains that he "never" eats lunch unless he entertains a client.

 (a) Is J classified as an outside salesperson?

 (b) Is J entitled to a tax deduction for these expenses? If so, is the deduction *for* adjusted gross or *from* adjusted gross income?

48. P is employed by L Corporation. She drives 12 miles each way to work. After work, she drove by a customer's home to drop off a rush order. The total distance from the office to her home via the customer's home was 20 miles. What, if any, transportation expense can she deduct?

49. T incurred the following employee expenses (he is not an outside salesperson):

| | |
|---|---|
| Travel while away from home | $ 2,000 |
| Transportation | 1,000 |
| Entertainment of customers | 900 |
| Professional dues | 600 |
| Telephone for business use | 500 |

T's employer allowed him $4,000 to cover all of these expenses. Calculate T's deduction *for* and *from* adjusted gross income.

50. T uses his automobile 70% for business and 30% for personal travel. Dur-

ing the year, T traveled a total of 25,000 miles. How much can he deduct using the automatic mileage method?

51. J took a trip from Los Angeles to New York. He spent three days conducting business and seven days vacationing and visiting friends. The expenses incurred were as follows:

*75% personal ✓*

| | | |
|---|---|---|
| Air fare | $   600 | — *no* |
| Meals and lodging | 1,200 | — *3 days (1200×3)=* |
| Entertainment of clients | 400 | — *from AGI.* |
| | $ 2,200 | |

What expenses, if any, can J deduct on his tax return? Is the deduction *for* or *from* AGI?

52. D, a college professor, accepted a position with the GAO in Washington, D.C. The assignment was designated as temporary and was for a 15-month period. The professor left his wife and children in Cleveland and rented an apartment in Washington during the period of employment. He incurred the following expenses, none of which were reimbursed by his employer:

(a) Air fare—weekend trips between Washington and Cleveland to visit his family—$7,000.

(b) Rent—Washington apartment—$5,000.

(c) Meals, laundry, etc., in Washington—$4,000.

(d) Entertainment of fellow employees and supervisor in the GAO—$2,000.

Which, if any, of these expenses are deductible by D? Are they deductions *for* adjusted gross income or *from* adjusted gross income?

53. T incurred the following expenses when she was transferred from San Francisco to Dallas:

| | |
|---|---|
| Loss on the sale of old residence | $ 7,000 |
| Moving company's charges | 2,100 |
| House-hunting trip | 1,200 |
| Temporary living expenses for 60 days | 3,000 |
| Brokers' fees on residences bought and sold | 5,000 |
| Charges for fitting drapes in new residence | 800 |
| Total | $ 19,100 |

(a) How much can T deduct, assuming no reimbursement?

(b) What would be T's tax consequences if the employer reimburses her for all of the expenses?

54. T is a tax specialist for a large CPA firm. During the year, he enrolled in the following course of study to continue his education and incurred the following expenses:

—Business school courses in taxation—enrolled as a nondegree special student—with tuition of $1,500 and transportation expenses of $150.

—Special courses offered by the Kansas Society of CPAs for continuing education. Tuition totaled $1,000 and transportation expenses were $200.

—CPA exam review and CPA license fee. Fees amounted to $800 plus transportation expenses of $100.

(a) Which, if any, of these expenses are deductible by T? *For* adjusted gross income or *from* adjusted gross income?

(b) What would your answer be if T took course work on a Ph.D. in accounting with the eventual expectation of becoming a college professor?

55. T belongs to a country club which he uses for both business and personal purposes. Assuming none of his expenses are reimbursed, how much can he deduct on his tax return in the two cases outlined below?

| | | |
|---|---|---|
| Annual dues | | $ 5,000 |
| Business meals "directly related to" | | 400 |
| Business meals "associated with" | | 300 |
| Business meals "quiet business meals" | | 350 |
| Personal meals and charges | | 2,000 |
| Case (a) Days directly related to business | 80 | |
| Days associated with business | 30 | |
| Days for quiet business meals | 30 | |
| Days for personal use | 150 | |
| Case (b) Days directly related to business | 60 | |
| Days associated with business | 70 | |
| Days for quiet business meals | 20 | |
| Days for personal use | 75 | |

56. J is an accountant with the XYZ Company. He is also a self-employed tax consultant with several clients and earns $12,000 per year from his outside consulting. He has an office in his home which is used exclusively for meeting with his consulting clients and for work performed for these clients. Based on square footage, he estimates that total expenses amount to $3,500, including $1,500 of taxes and interest on his home mortgage.

(a) Can J take a deduction for an office in the home? If so, how is it reported and how much can be deducted?

(b) If the office was also used for work he brought home from his regular job, how would your answer to (a) differ? Assume it was used 80% for the consulting business and 20% for his regular job.

## Cumulative Problem

57. Y is single, age 40, and has no dependents. She is employed half-time as a legal secretary. In addition, she owns and operates a typing service located in the campus area of Florida State University. She is a cash basis taxpayer. During 1983, Y had the following receipts.

(a) $10,000 salary as a legal secretary.

(b) $32,000 gross receipts from her typing service business.

(c) $500 cash dividend from Buffalo Mining Company, a Canadian corporation.

(d) $1,000 Christmas bonus from her employer for outstanding work as a legal secretary.

(e) $10,000 life insurance proceeds on the death of her sister.

(f) $5,000 check given by her wealthy aunt.

(g) $100 won in a bingo game.

Y had various business deductions of $18,680, not including any of the items below.

(h) $4,000 net operating loss carryover from 1982; this is the remaining amount of a $10,000 net operating loss, $6,000 of which has been carried back to 1979, 1980, and 1981.

After examining Y's records, you have determined that she has various itemized deductions of $3,100, not including any of the following amounts.

(i) $5,000 fair market value of silverware stolen from her home by a burglar. She had paid $4,000 for the silverware eight years ago. She was reimbursed $1,500 by her insurance company, having neglected to increase the insurance coverage as the price of silver increased.

(j) $2,100 she had loaned to a friend, K, a year ago. K declared bankruptcy in August 1983 and was unable to repay the loan.

You are to compute Y's taxable income for 1983.

## Tax Form Problems

58.    Steven R. Chandler, Social Security number 215-04-1786, is single. In October 1982, Steve was transferred by his employer from Louisville, Kentucky, to Pittsburgh, Pennsylvania. Steve incurred the following expenses in connection with the move:

| | |
|---|---:|
| Premove house-hunting trip | $    800 |
| Temporary living expenses in Pittsburgh while waiting for his furniture to arrive (15 days) | 900 |
| Travel expenses from old residence to new residence | 130 |
| Broker's commission on sale of old residence | 1,800 |
| Cost of moving household goods (reimbursed by employer, with reimbursement included on Steve's Form W–2) | 1,400 |
| Down payment on new residence | 10,000 |

Steve expects to meet the 39-week, full-time work test. Compute Steve's moving expense deduction using Form 3903.

59.    Richard Fuller is a professor of accounting at State University who travels extensively in presenting continuing professional education courses for the university. He is paid by the university for these engagements. Richard is reimbursed in full for his airplane fare, and is reimbursed at the rate of 15¢ a mile for automobile expenses. His reimbursement for meals and lodging is limited to $50 a day. During 1982, Richard incurred the following business-related expenses:

|                             |          |
|-----------------------------|----------|
| Airplane fares              | $ 1,750  |
| Meals and lodging (20 days) | 1,360    |

He drove his automobile 16,000 miles on business, but did not keep records of his automobile expenses, except for parking fees and tolls, which totaled $90 in 1982.

In order to keep abreast of recent developments in accounting, Richard attended a three-day workshop sponsored by the American Institute of Certified Public Accountants in June 1982 at his own expense. In connection with this workshop, he incurred the following expenses:

|                    |        |
|--------------------|--------|
| Airplane fare      | $ 319  |
| Meals and lodging  | 186    |
| Enrollment fee     | 300    |

Compute Richard's deduction for employee business expenses for 1982, using Form 2106.

## Chapter 7

# Deductions and Losses: Certain Itemized Deductions

## GENERAL CLASSIFICATION OF EXPENSES

Personal expenditures are specifically disallowed by § 262 as deductions in arriving at taxable income. Personal expenses may be contrasted with business expenses which are incurred in the production or expectation of profit. Business expenditures are adjustments to gross income in arriving at adjusted gross income and are placed on Schedule C of Form 1040. Certain nonbusiness expenses are also deductible in arriving at adjusted gross income (e. g., expenses attributable to rents and royalties and forfeited interest on a time savings deposit).

This chapter is principally concerned with expenses which are essentially personal in nature but which are deductible due to specific legislative sanction (e. g., contributions, medical expenses, and certain state and local taxes). If the Code does not specifically state that a personal type of expense is deductible, no deduction is permitted. Allowable personal types of expenses are deductible *from* adjusted gross income in arriving at taxable income to the extent that they exceed the zero bracket amount. At this point, it may be helpful to review the tax formula for individuals, which appears in Chapters 1 and 2.

In certain instances, it is unclear to taxpayers whether an item is deductible under a specific section of the Code or if the item is personal and nondeductible. For example, the following expenditures have been held to be personal, nondeductible expenses: the construction of a bomb shelter; the cost of a chauffeur to drive a taxpayer to and from his place of business; the expenses of an executive's vacation, although incurred for reconditioning and health restoration.

# MEDICAL EXPENSES

TEFRA has made several changes in the computation of the medical-expense deduction. These changes, which generally become effective after 1982, are discussed in later sections of this chapter. A comparison of the 1982, 1983 and 1984 rules is presented in Example 9.

## GENERAL REQUIREMENTS

Medical expenses paid for the care of the taxpayer, spouse, and dependents are allowed under § 213 as an itemized deduction to the extent the expenses are "not compensated for by insurance or otherwise . . ." [i. e., not reimbursed to the taxpayer or paid to anyone else (such as to a doctor or a hospital) by hospital, health, or accident insurance or by an employer]. Further, the medical expense deduction is limited to the amount of such expenses that exceeds five percent (three percent before 1983) of the taxpayer's adjusted gross income. The rationale for allowing a medical deduction solely for amounts in excess of such limits is based on social considerations. Since five percent of adjusted gross income is considered by Congress to be a normal yearly expenditure, only amounts in excess of this percentage are deductible.

The term "medical care" includes expenditures incurred for the "diagnosis, cure, mitigation, treatment, or prevention of disease."[1] The term also includes expenditures incurred for "affecting any structure or function of the body."[2] A taxpayer cannot deduct medical expenses that have both therapeutic benefits and personal enjoyment unless the expenditure is necessary and is the only method of treating the illness. The IRS has ruled that the cost of a program to stop smoking is not deductible as a medical expense because the cost is incurred for the purpose of improving the taxpayer's general health and not for the purpose of curing any specific ailment or disease. A similar ruling has been issued denying the cost of a weight reduction program.

The deductibility of nursing home expenses depends on the medical condition of the patient and the nature of the services rendered. If an individual enters a home for the aged for personal or family considerations and not because he or she requires medical or nursing attention, deductions are allowed only for the costs which are attributable to the medical and nursing care (i. e., meals and lodging normally are not considered a cost of medical care).

---

1. Reg. § 1.213–1(e).
2. § 213(e)(1)(A).

**Example 1.** T is totally disabled and has a chronic heart ailment. His children have decided to place T in a nursing home which is equipped to provide medical and nursing care facilities. Total nursing home expenses amount to $15,000 per year. Of this amount, $4,500 is directly attributable to medical and nursing care. Since T is in need of significant medical and nursing care and is placed into the facility primarily for this purpose, all $15,000 of the nursing home costs are deductible. Only $4,500 of the expenses would be deductible if T were placed in the home primarily for personal or family considerations.

Tuition expenses of a dependent at a special school may be deductible as a medical expense. The cost of medical care includes the expenses of a special school for a mentally or physically handicapped individual if his condition is such that the resources of the school for alleviating such infirmities are a principal reason for his presence there. If this is the case, the cost of meals and lodging, in addition to the tuition, is a proper medical expense deduction.

**Example 2.** T's daughter, D, attended public school through the seventh grade. Because D was a poor student, she was tested by a clinical psychologist who diagnosed an organic problem which created a learning disability. D was enrolled in a private school so that she would receive individual attention. Since this school has no special program for students with learning disabilities, nor does it provide special medical treatment, the expenses related to D's attendance are not deductible under § 213(a) as medical expenses.

## CAPITAL EXPENDITURES FOR MEDICAL PURPOSES

Normally, capital expenditures for medical purposes are adjustments to basis and are not deductible, because the Code makes no provision for depreciation relative to these capital improvements. However, a capital expenditure for a permanent improvement and expenditures made for its operation or maintenance may both qualify as medical expenses. Some examples of capital expenditures for medical purposes are swimming pools (if the taxpayer does not have access to a neighborhood pool), air conditioners (if they do not become permanent improvements), dust elimination systems, elevators, and a room built to house an iron lung. These expenditures are medical in nature if they are incurred as a medical necessity upon the advice of a physician, the facility is used primarily by the taxpayer alone, and the expense is reasonable. A capital improvement which otherwise qualifies as a medical expenditure is deductible to the extent that the expenditure exceeds the increase in value of the related property. It should also be noted that the appraisal costs would also be deductible under § 212(3), since such amounts are expenses incurred in the determination of the taxpayer's tax liability.

**Example 3.** The taxpayer is advised by his physician to install an elevator in his residence so that the taxpayer's wife, who is afflicted with heart disease, will not be required to climb the stairs. If the cost of installing the elevator is $3,000 and the increase in the value of the residence is determined to be only $1,700, $1,300 is deductible as a medical expense. Additional utility costs to operate the elevator should also be deductible as medical expenses.

## TRANSPORTATION EXPENSES

Expenditures for a taxi, airplane, train, etc., to and from a point of treatment are deductible as medical expenses. However, the amount allowable as a deduction for "transportation primarily for and essential to medical care" does not include meals and lodging while away from home receiving medical treatment. Note, however, that some courts have allowed a medical deduction for the cost of meals and lodging incurred "in transit" to reach the place of medical treatment if it is necessary to travel to another location to receive treatment.

The IRS currently allows a deduction of nine cents a mile for the use of an automobile in traveling for medical treatment.

**Example 4.** T was ordered by his doctor to receive specialized medical care which could only be rendered in a hospital in Boston. T resides in Columbus, Ohio, and incurred transportation costs of $300 to reach the Boston hospital. The transportation costs of $300 are deductible as medical expenses because the expenditure was "primarily for and essential to medical care." The $100 for meals and lodging incurred "in transit" to reach the place of medical treatment should be deductible because the location of the treatment center was not selected purely for personal purposes.

## AMOUNTS PAID FOR MEDICAL INSURANCE PREMIUMS

In years before 1983, one-half of the amount paid for medical care insurance for the taxpayer, spouse, or a dependent was not subject to the three percent limitation for total medical expenses. Such amounts were fully deductible up to $150 per year. Premiums paid in excess of $150 (if any) were included with other medical expenses and were subject to the overall three percent limitation rules.

If amounts are paid under an insurance contract to cover loss of life, limb, sight, etc., no amount can be deducted unless the coverage for medical care is separately stated in the contract.

**Example 5.** H and W filed a joint return for 1982. Their adjusted gross income was $20,000. H and W incurred and paid a total of $700 for health insurance premiums. Such premiums are specifically for medical care coverage. H and W incurred other medical expenses of $800 which were not compensated by insurance. The allowable deduction under § 213 for medical expenses paid in 1982 is $900, computed as follows:[3]

| | | |
|---|---:|---:|
| (1) Lesser of $350 ($700 insurance premiums × ½) or $150 | | $ 150 |
| (2) Payments for medical care (including $700 of insurance premiums and $800 of other medical expenses) | $ 1,500 | |
| (3) Less:   Insurance premiums not subject to the three percent limitation | 150 | |
| (4) Medical expenses to be taken into account under three percent limitation | $ 1,350 | |
| (5) Less:   Three percent of $20,000 (adjusted gross income) | 600 | |
| (6) Amount of (4) in excess of (5) allowable as a deduction for 19X7 | | 750 |
| (7) Allowable medical expense deduction for 19X7 [(1) plus (6)] | | $ 900 |

**Example 6.**  Assume the same facts as in the previous example except that H and W incurred and paid only $200 for health insurance premiums and other medical expenses amount to $20.

| | | |
|---|---:|---:|
| (1) Deductible health insurance premiums not subject to three percent limitation—$200 × ½ | | $ 100 |
| (2) Payments for medical care subject to three percent limitation: | | |
|     Insurance premiums not deductible above | $ 100 | |
|     Other medical expenses | 20 | |
| (3) Less:   Three percent of adjusted gross income ($20,000 × 3 %) | $ 120 | |
| | 600 | |
| (4) Deductions allowable under the three percent limit | | –0– |
| (5) Allowable medical expense deduction | | $ 100 |

Beginning in 1983, medical insurance premiums will not be treated as a separate item. Instead, premiums will be included with other medical expenses and subject to the five percent of AGI limit scheduled to take effect in 1983. Thus, in Example 6, if the year were 1983, there would be no deduction for medical insurance premiums, since total expenses including the premiums do not exceed the percentage limitation [i. e. $220 (total medical expenses including medical insurance premiums) does not exceed $1,000 (five percent of adjusted gross income)]. (See Example 9 for a comparison of the 1982 and post-1982 rules for computing the medical expense deduction.)

---

3.   Reg. § 1.213–1(a)(5)(ii).

## EXPENDITURES FOR MEDICINE AND DRUGS

For years before 1984, Section 213(b) has permitted a deduction for expenses incurred for medicine and drugs to the extent that such amounts were in excess of one percent of adjusted gross income (and if total medical expenses exceeded the percentage floor). The one percent floor on medicine and drugs is eliminated effective 1984. Through 1983, the term "medicine and drugs" includes those drugs that are "legally procured" and are purchased either with or without a prescription. However, expenditures for such items as toothpaste, shaving lotion, face creams, deodorants, and hand lotions are not deductible. Amounts paid for vitamins, iron supplements, and similar items are deductible if recommended by a doctor. Beginning in 1984, the definition of medicine and drugs will be limited to prescription drugs and insulin.

> **Example 7.** In 1983, T moved from Rhode Island to southern Louisiana where the climate is semitropical, and T immediately began to suffer from heat rash. T's dermatologist recommended a special nonprescription soap. The cost of the soap is deductible as a medicine.

For years before 1984, if the total amount paid for medicine and drugs exceeded one percent of adjusted gross income, the excess was added to other medical expenses for computing the medical expense deduction. Beginning in 1984, the total cost of such items will be added to other medical expenses.

> **Example 8.** The taxpayer, a single individual with no dependents, had adjusted gross income of $12,000 for the calendar year 1982. During 1982, he paid a doctor $600 for medical services, a hospital $200 for hospital care, and a pharmacy $200 for medicine and drugs. These payments were not compensated by insurance. The deduction allowable under § 213 for the calendar year 1982 is $520:

| Payments for medical care in 1982: | | |
|---|---:|---:|
| Doctor | | $ 600 |
| Hospital | | 200 |
| Medicine and drugs | $ 200 | |
| Less: One percent of $12,000 (adjusted gross income) | 120 | 80 |
| Total medical expenses taken into account | | $ 880 |
| Less: Three percent of $12,000 (adjusted gross income) | | 360 |
| Allowable deduction for 1982 | | $ 520 |

To help understand how the medical expense deduction operates, the reader should examine Schedule A of Form 1040. If in Example 8 the taxpayer also had incurred $700 for health insurance premiums, the allowable deduction under § 213 would be reported on Schedule A as reflected on the following page.

## SUMMARY AND COMPARISON OF RULES FOR 1982, 1983, AND 1984

The medical deduction rules will change in 1983 and again in 1984. Starting in 1983, the floor on medical expense deductions will be increased from 3 percent to 5 percent of adjusted gross income. The separate one percent floor on drugs will be retained in 1983 but eliminated in 1984. Beginning in 1983, the separate deduction for one-half of medical insurance premiums will be eliminated. Premiums will be combined with other medical expenses. When the one percent floor on drugs is eliminated in 1984, the definition of drugs will be limited to prescription drugs and insulin.

> **Example 9.** Mr. and Mrs. T, who have an adjusted gross income of $40,000, have the following expenses:

| | |
|---|---:|
| Medical insurance premiums | $ 500 |
| Prescription drugs | 300 |
| Other drugs | 140 |
| Other medical expense | 2,000 |

The medical deduction would vary depending on the tax year as follows:

| | 1982 | 1983 | 1984 |
|---|---:|---:|---:|
| Premiums | $ 150 | | |
| Prescription drugs | 300 | $ 300 | $ 300 |
| Other drugs | 140 | 140 | |
| Total | 440 | 440 | |
| 1% of AGI | (400) | (400) | |
| Balance | 40 | 40 | |
| Balance of premiums | 350 | 500 | 500 |
| Other medical | 2,000 | 2,000 | 2,000 |
| Total | 2,390 | 2,540 | |
| 3% of AGI | (1,200) | | |
| 5% of AGI | | (2,000) | (2,000) |
| Balance | $1,190 | $ 540 | $ 800 |
| Deduction | $1,340 | $ 540 | $ 800 |

## REIMBURSEMENT FOR MEDICAL EXPENSES PAID IN PRIOR YEARS

When a taxpayer receives an insurance reimbursement for medical expenses deducted in a previous year, the reimbursement must be included in gross income in the year of receipt. Taxpayers are not permitted to include expenses for which reimbursement is anticipated

| Schedules A&B (Form 1040)<br>Department of the Treasury<br>Internal Revenue Service (0) | Schedule A—Itemized Deductions<br>(Schedule B is on back)<br>▶ Attach to Form 1040.   ▶ See Instructions for Schedules A and B (Form 1040). | OMB No. 1545-0074<br>1982<br>07 |
|---|---|---|

Name(s) as shown on Form 1040            Your social security number

| Medical and Dental Expenses<br><br>(Do not include expenses reimbursed or paid by others.)<br><br>(See page 17 of Instructions.) | | | |
|---|---|---|---|
| 1 Medicines and drugs . . . . . . . | **1** | 200 | |
| 2 Write 1% of Form 1040, line 33 . . . . | **2** | 120 | |
| 3 Subtract line 2 from line 1. If line 2 is more than line 1, write zero . | **3** | 80 | |
| 4 Total insurance premiums you paid for medical and dental care . | **4** | 700 | |
| 5 Other medical and dental expenses: | | | |
| a Doctors, dentists, nurses, hospitals, etc . . . . . . . . | **5a** | 800 | |
| b Transportation . . . . . . . . . . . . . . | **5b** | | |
| c Other (list—include hearing aids, dentures, eyeglasses, etc.) | | | |
| ▶ ------------------------------------------- | | | |
| ------------------------------------------- | **5c** | | |
| 6 Add lines 3 through 5c . . . . . . . . . . . . . . | **6** | 1,580 | |
| 7 Multiply amount on Form 1040, line 33, by 3% (.03) . . . . . | **7** | 360 | |
| 8 Subtract line 7 from line 6. If line 7 is more than line 6, write zero . | **8** | 1,220 | |
| 9 Write one-half of amount on line 4, but not more than $150 . . | **9** | 150 | |
| 10 COMPARE amounts on line 8 and line 9, and write the LARGER amount here . . ▶ | **10** | | 1,220 |

in the computation of the medical expenses for the year such expenses are incurred. Reimbursements in the following year are included in gross income only to the extent that the expenses were deductible in the prior year. If the taxpayer used the zero bracket amount in the year the expenses were incurred rather than itemizing deductions, any reimbursement received in a subsequent year will not be included in gross income. The expenses incurred would not reduce the taxpayer's taxable income for the prior year (i. e., the taxpayer would receive no tax benefit from the deduction).

The following rules apply to reimbursements for medical expenses:

—If the amount of the reimbursement is equal to or less than the amount which was deducted in a prior year, the entire amount is includible in gross income.

—If the amount of the reimbursement is greater than the amount which is deducted, the portion of the reimbursement received which is equal to the deduction taken shall be included in gross income.

**Example 10.** T has adjusted gross income of $20,000 for 1982. He was injured in a car accident and paid $1,200 for hospitalization expenses and $800 for doctor bills. T also incurred medical expenses of $600 for his wife and child. In 1983 T was reimbursed $800 by his insurance company for his car accident. His deduction for medical expenses in 1982 would be computed as follows:

| | |
|---|---|
| Hospitalization | $ 1,200 |
| Bills for doctor's services | 800 |
| Medical expenses for dependents | 600 |
|     Total | $ 2,600 |
| Less:   3% of $20,000 | 600 |
| Medical expense deduction (assuming T itemizes his deductions) | $ 2,000 |

If medical care reimbursement had occurred in 1982, the medical expense deduction would have been only $1,200. Since the reimbursement was made in a subsequent year, $800 would be included in gross income for 1983. If T used the zero bracket amount in 1982, the $800 reimbursement would not be included in 1983 gross income because no tax benefit resulted in 1982.

# TAXES

The deduction of state and local taxes paid or accrued by a taxpayer is permitted by § 164. The Committee Reports indicate that the deduction for state and local taxes was created to relieve the burden of multiple taxes upon the same source of revenue. Further, the Committee Reports state that without provision for the deductibility of all non-Federal taxes, state and local governments might be forced to impose additional taxes to generate operating revenues.

## DEDUCTIBILITY AS A TAX

One must make a distinction between a "tax" and a "fee," since fees are not deductible unless incurred as an ordinary and necessary business expense under § 162 or as an expense in the production of income under § 212.

The IRS has defined a tax as follows:

> A tax is an enforced contribution exacted pursuant to legislative authority in the exercise of taxing power, and imposed and collected for the purpose of raising revenue to be used for public or governmental purposes, and not as payment for some special privilege granted or service rendered. Taxes are, therefore, distinguished from various other contributions and charges imposed for particular purposes under particular powers or functions of the government. In view of such distinctions, the question whether a particular contribution or charge is to be regarded as a tax depends upon its real nature.[4]

Thus, in accordance with the above definition, fees for dog licenses, automobile inspection, automobile titles and registration, hunting and fishing licenses, bridge and highway tolls, drivers' licenses, parking meter deposits, postage, etc., are not considered to be currently deductible unless incurred as a business expense under § 162 or for the production of income under § 212.

Section 164 lists the following taxes to be deductible whether paid or accrued during the taxable year:[5]

---

4. Rev.Rul. 57–345, 1957–2 C.B. 132 and Rev.Rul. 70–622, 1970–2 C.B. 41.
5. § 164(a) and Reg. § 1.164–1. The deduction for state and local taxes on gasoline, diesel, and other motor fuel consumed in vehicles used for personal purposes was eliminated by the Revenue Act of 1978.

—State, local, and foreign real property taxes.

—State and local personal property taxes.

—State, local, and foreign income taxes.

—State and local general sales taxes.

—The windfall profit tax.

The following taxes cannot be deducted:[6]

—Federal income taxes, including Social Security and railroad retirement taxes paid by the employee.

—Estate, inheritance, legacy, succession, and gift taxes.

—Foreign income taxes, if the taxpayer claims a foreign tax credit.

—Taxes on real property to the extent that such taxes are to be apportioned and treated as imposed on another taxpayer.

## PROPERTY TAXES, ASSESSMENTS, AND APPORTIONMENT OF TAXES

*Property Taxes.* State, local, and foreign taxes on real and personal property are generally deductible only by the person against whom the tax is imposed. Cash basis taxpayers may deduct these taxes in the year of actual payment, and accrual basis taxpayers may deduct them in the year which fixes the right to deductibility.

Personal property taxes must be ad valorem (i. e., assessed in relation to the value of the property) to be deductible. Therefore, a motor vehicle tax based on weight, model year, and horsepower is not an ad valorem tax. However, a tax based on value and other criteria may qualify in part.

> **Example 11.** State X imposes a motor vehicle registration tax on 4% of the value of the vehicle plus 40 cents per hundredweight. A, a resident of the state, owns a car having a value of $4,000 and weighing 3,000 pounds. A pays an annual registration fee of $172. Of this amount, $160 (4% of $4,000) would be deductible as a personal property tax. The remaining $12 based on the weight of the car, would not be deductible.

*Assessments for Local Benefits.* As a general rule, real property taxes do not include taxes assessed for local benefits, since such assessments tend to increase the value of the property (e. g., special assessments for streets, sidewalks, curbing, and other like improvements). A taxpayer cannot deduct the cost of a new sidewalk (relative to a personal residence), even though the construction was required by the city and the sidewalk may have provided an inci-

---

**6.** § 164(c)(2) and Reg. § 1.164–2(a) through (e).

dental benefit to the public welfare. Such assessments are added to the adjusted cost basis of the taxpayer's property.

Assessments for local benefits are deductible as a tax if they are made for maintenance or repair or for meeting interest charges with respect to such benefits. In such cases, the burden is on the taxpayer to show the allocation of the amounts assessed for the different purposes. If the allocation cannot be made, none of the amount paid is deductible.

*Apportionment of Taxes on Real Property Between Seller and Purchaser.* The real estate taxes for the entire year are apportioned between the buyer and seller on the basis of the number of days the property was held by each in the year of sale.[7] This apportionment is required without regard to whether the tax is paid by the buyer or the seller or is prorated pursuant to the purchase agreement. The rationale for apportioning the taxes between the buyer and seller is based on administrative convenience of the IRS in determining who is entitled to deduct the real estate taxes in the year of sale. In making the apportionment, the assessment date and the lien date are disregarded.

> **Example 12.** The real property tax year in County R is April 1 to March 31. S, the owner on April 1, 19X6, of real property located in County R, sells the real property to B on June 30, 19X6. B owns the real property from June 30, 19X6, through March 31, 19X7. The tax for the real property tax year April 1, 19X6, through March 31, 19X7, is $365. For purposes of § 164(a), $90 (90/365 × $365, April 1 to June 29 of 19X6) of the real property tax is treated as imposed upon S, the seller, and $275 (275/365 × $365, June 30, 19X6, to March 31, 19X7) of such tax is treated as imposed upon B, the purchaser.

If the actual real estate taxes are not prorated between the buyer and seller as part of the purchase agreement, adjustments are required in the determination of the amount realized by the seller and the adjusted cost basis of the property to the buyer.[8] If the buyer pays the entire amount of the tax, he or she has, in effect, paid the seller's portion of the real estate tax and has therefore paid more for the property than the actual selling price. Thus, the amount of real estate tax which is apportioned to the seller (for tax purposes) is added to the buyer's adjusted cost basis. The seller must increase the amount realized on the sale by the same amount.

> **Example 13.** S sells real estate on June 30, 19X6, for $50,000. The buyer, B, pays the real estate taxes of $1,000 for the calendar year. Of the real estate taxes, $500 is apportioned to and is de-

7.   § 164(d).
8.   § § 1001(b)(2) and 1012; Reg. § § 1.1001–1(b) and 1.1012–1(b).

ductible by the seller, S, and $500 of the taxes is deductible by B. The buyer has, in effect, paid S's real estate taxes of $500 and has therefore paid $50,500 for the property. B's basis is increased to $50,500, and the amount realized by S from the sale is increased to $50,500.

The opposite result occurs if the seller (rather than the buyer) pays the real estate taxes. In this case, the seller reduces the amount realized from the sale by the amount which has been apportioned to the buyer. The buyer is required to reduce his or her adjusted cost basis by a corresponding amount.

> **Example 14.** S sells property for $50,000 on June 30, 19X6. While S held the property, he paid the real estate taxes for the calendar year in the amount of $1,000. Although S paid the entire $1,000 of real estate tax, $500 of that amount is apportioned to B and is therefore deductible by B. The effect is that the buyer, B, has paid only $49,500 for the property. The amount realized by S, the seller, is reduced by $500, and the buyer reduces his cost basis in the property to $49,500.

## INCOME TAXES

State, local, or foreign income taxes are not deductible *for* adjusted gross income unless the taxes are incurred in a trade or business or for the production of income. Personal use taxes are deductible only *from* AGI as itemized deductions. It is the position of the IRS that state income taxes imposed upon an individual are deductible only as itemized deductions even if the taxpayer's sole source of income is from business, rents, or royalties.

Cash basis taxpayers are entitled to deduct state income taxes withheld by the employer in the year such amounts are withheld. In addition, estimated state income tax payments are deductible in the year the payment is made by cash basis taxpayers even if the payments relate to a prior or subsequent year. If the taxpayer overpays the state income taxes due to excessive withholdings or estimated tax payments, the refund which is received must be included in gross income of the following year to the extent that the deduction provided a tax benefit in the prior year.

> **Example 15.** T is a cash basis taxpayer who had $800 state income tax withheld during 19X7. In addition, she made quarterly estimated payments amounting to $400 in 19X7. These payments and withholdings of $1,200 were deducted on T's 19X7 return which was filed in April 19X8. However, if her actual liability for the 19X7 state income tax was only $1,000, the $200 refund received in 19X8 would be included in gross income on T's Federal income tax return for 19X8.

## GENERAL SALES TAXES

State and local sales taxes are deductible by the consumer providing the tax is separately stated and imposed upon the consumer (i. e., the tax is added to the sales price and collected or charged as a separate item). Whether a state or local tax is imposed on the retailer or consumer depends on state and local law. In most instances, state and local sales taxes are deemed to be passed on to the consumer and are therefore deductible.

The tax will be considered separately stated, to meet the requirement noted above, if it clearly appears that at the time of sale to the consumer the tax was added to the sales price and collected or charged as a separate item. It is not necessary that the consumer be furnished with a sales slip, bill, invoice, or other statement on which the tax is separately stated.

To aid the taxpayer, the IRS issues optional state sales tax tables. These tables are reprinted in Appendix A. It should be noted that the tables can be used only if deductions are being itemized on Schedule A of Form 1040.

The state sales tax tables are based on the taxpayer's adjusted gross income plus nontaxable items such as tax-exempt interest and Social Security benefits. The table does not include sales taxes on specified major purchases, including automobiles, boats, airplanes, and materials for a new home (if the tax is separately stated on the invoice). In addition, the tables generally do not make any provision for county and local sales taxes. Thus, sales tax on specified major purchase items and county and local sales taxes, if not included in the table amount, must be added to the amount which is derived from the sales tax table.

**Example 16.** T has a wife and two dependent children and was a resident of Ohio during 1982. His adjusted gross income was $28,000. T received $2,100 of income which was nontaxable during the year (i. e., tax-exempt interest). He had no major purchases during the year. County and local sales taxes are levied at a rate of 2%. T's sales tax deduction using the optional sales tax tables is computed as follows:

| | | |
|---|---|---|
| Adjusted gross income | $ 28,000 | |
| Add: Nontaxable income | 2,100 | |
| Base for sales tax table (total available income) | $ 30,100 | |
| Tax per table | | $ 301 |
| Add: County and local sales taxes | | |
| $\frac{2\%}{4\%}\left(\frac{\text{local and county rate}}{\text{Ohio rate}}\right) \times \$301$ | | 151 |
| Total sales tax deduction | | $ 452 |

If the taxpayer's records indicate that more taxes were paid than the amount shown in the tables, the larger amount may be deducted.

However, a taxpayer has the burden of proving that he or she is entitled to the amount claimed as a sales tax deduction. If there is no evidence to indicate that the amount allowed by the IRS is incorrect, the allowance stated in the optional tables will be approved.

## FILING REQUIREMENTS

Deductible state and local taxes are reported on Schedule A of Form 1040. For example, if the taxpayer had incurred $1,200 of state and local income taxes, $600 of real estate taxes on his residence, general sales taxes of $420 (as determined by the state sales tax tables), and personal property taxes of $275, these items would appear on Schedule A as noted below.

| Taxes (See page 18 of Instructions.) | | | |
|---|---|---|---|
| 11 State and local income . . . . . . . . . . . . . . . . | 11 | 1,200 | |
| 12 Real estate . . . . . . . . . . . . . . . . | 12 | 600 | |
| 13 a General sales (see sales tax tables) . . . . . . . . . | 13a | 420 | |
| b General sales on motor vehicles . . . . . . . . . . | 13b | | |
| 14 Other (list—include personal property) ▶ _____ | 14 | 275 | |
| 15 Add lines 11 through 14. Write your answer here . . . . . . . . . . . ▶ | 15 | 2,495 | |

# INTEREST

A deduction for interest has been allowed since the enactment of the income tax law in 1913. Despite its long history of Congressional acceptance, the interest deduction continues to be one of the most controversial areas in the tax law.

The controversy centers around the propriety of deducting interest charges for the purchase of consumer goods and services and interest on borrowings which are used to acquire investments (i. e., investment interest). Currently, various limitations are imposed on the deductibility of prepaid interest and the deduction of interest on funds which are used to acquire investment property. In addition, no deduction is permitted for interest on debt incurred to purchase or carry tax-exempt securities.

$10,000+

## ALLOWED AND DISALLOWED ITEMS

Interest has been defined by the Supreme Court as compensation for the use or forbearance of money.[9] The general rule permits a deduction for all interest paid or accrued within the taxable year on in-

---

**9.** *Old Colony Railroad Co. v. Comm.,* 3 USTC ¶ 880, 10 AFTR 786, 52 S.Ct. 211 (USSC, 1936).

debtedness.[10] This general rule is modified by other Code provisions which disallow or restrict certain interest deductions.[11] Generally, a deduction is allowed for the following:

—Mortgage interest.

—Loan origination fees (i. e., points paid by the buyer of a principal residence).

—Mortgage prepayment penalty.

—Finance charges separately stated.

—Bank credit card plan interest.

—Note discount interest.

—Penalty for late payment of utility bills.

Generally, a deduction is not allowed for:

—Points if paid by a seller.

—Service charges.

—Credit investigation fees.

—Loan placement fees paid by a seller of property.

—Nonredeemable ground rents.

—Interest relative to tax-exempt income.

—Interest paid to carry single premium life insurance.

—Premiums paid on the purchase of a convertible bond arising from the conversion feature.

## RESTRICTIONS ON DEDUCTIBILITY AND TIMING CONSIDERATIONS

*Taxpayer's Obligation.* Interest is deductible if the related debt represents a bona fide obligation for which the taxpayer is liable.[12] Thus, a taxpayer is not allowed a deduction for interest paid on behalf of another individual. To insure the deduction of interest, both debtor and creditor must intend that the loan be repaid. Intent of the parties can be especially crucial between related parties such as a shareholder and a closely-held corporation. A stockholder may not deduct interest paid by the corporation on his or her behalf. Likewise, a husband cannot deduct interest paid on his wife's property if they file separate returns.

*Time of Deduction.* Generally, interest must be paid to secure a deduction unless the taxpayer uses the accrual method of accounting. Under the accrual method, interest is deductible ratably over the life of the loan.

---

**10.** § 163(a).

**11.** § § 163(b) and (d), 264 through 267 and 483.

**12.** *Arcade Realty Co.*, 35 T.C. 256 (1960).

**Example 17.** T borrows $1,000 on November 1, 19X6. The loan is payable in 90 days at 6% interest. On February 1, 19X7, T pays the $1,000 note and interest amounting to $15. The accrued portion ($\frac{2}{3} \times \$15 = \$10$) of the interest is deductible by T in 19X6 only if he is an accrual basis taxpayer. Otherwise, the entire amount of interest ($15) is deductible in 19X7.

*Prepaid Interest.* The Tax Reform Act of 1976 effectively imposes accrual method requirements on cash basis taxpayers relative to interest prepayments which extend beyond the end of the taxable year.[13] Such payments must be capitalized and allocated to the subsequent periods to which the interest payments relate. These restrictions do not apply to points (loan origination fees) paid by the purchaser of a principal residence if charging points is customary and the points do not exceed a normal rate.[14] These changes were intended to prevent cash basis taxpayers from "manufacturing" tax deductions prior to the end of the year by entering into prepayment of interest agreements.

## CLASSIFICATION OF INTEREST EXPENSE

Whether interest is deductible *for* adjusted gross income or as an itemized deduction depends on whether the indebtedness has a business, investment, or personal purpose. If the indebtedness is incurred in relation to a business or for the production of rent or royalty income, the interest is deductible *for* adjusted gross income.[15] However, if the indebtedness is incurred for personal use, the deduction must be reported as an itemized deduction on Schedule A of Form 1040. Schedule A deductions are allowed only if the taxpayer has itemized deductions in excess of the zero bracket amount. See Appendix B, Form 1040. Business expenses appear on Schedule C of Form 1040.

The courts have established that the use to which the borrowed funds are put, not the security behind the obligation, governs the nature of the debt (i. e., business or nonbusiness).

**Example 18.** If T mortgages his home to raise money for his business, the interest is deductible as a business expense. However, if the funds were used to purchase security investments, the interest expense would be deductible only if T elects to itemize his deductions on Schedule A of Form 1040.

The interest expense deduction is reported on Schedule A of Form 1040. Thus, if the taxpayer has interest expense from his home mortgage of $3,500, interest charge of $110 from credit cards, and $1,150

---

**13.** § 461(g).
**14.** § 461(g)(2).
**15.** § 62(1) and (5).

interest expense from his car loan, these interest charges would appear on Schedule A as shown below.

| Interest Expense | | | |
|---|---|---|---|
| (See page 19 of Instructions.) | 16 a Home mortgage interest paid to financial institutions . . . . | 16a | 3,500 |
| | b Home mortgage interest paid to individuals (show that person's name and address) ▶------------------------------------------------ | | |
| | ------------------------------------------- | 16b | |
| | 17 Credit cards and charge accounts . . . . . . . . . | 17 | 110 |
| | 18 Other (list) ▶----------------------------------------- | | |
| | -------------------------------------------- | 18 | 1,150 |
| | 19 Add lines 16a through 18. Write your answer here . . . . . . . . . . ▶ | 19 | 4,760 |

## DISALLOWANCE POSSIBILITIES

*Related Parties.*  There is nothing to prevent the deduction of interest paid to a related party as long as the payment actually took place and meets the usual requirement for deduction as stated above. Recall from Chapter 5 that there is a special rule for related taxpayers which is applicable when the debtor uses the accrual basis and the related creditor is on the cash basis. If this rule is applicable, interest which has been accrued but not paid at the end of the debtor's tax year must be paid within two and one-half months. Otherwise, no interest deduction is permitted to the accrual basis debtor even if such amounts are paid following the expiration of the two and one-half month period.

*Tax-Exempt Securities.*  Section 265 provides that no deduction is allowed for interest on debt incurred to purchase or carry tax-exempt securities. A major problem has been for the courts to determine what is meant by the words "to purchase or carry." Refer to Chapter 5 for a detailed discussion of these complex issues.

*Interest on Investment Indebtedness.*  High-income taxpayers frequently borrow funds which are then used to acquire low income-producing assets (e. g., vacant land held for appreciation or low-yield high growth stocks). The deduction of interest expense coupled with little or no offsetting ordinary income and the eventual sale of the assets at favorable long-term capital gain rates would result in substantial tax benefits. Congress, therefore, has placed limitations on the deductibility of interest when funds are borrowed for the purpose of purchasing or continuing to hold investment property.[16] The limitations do not apply to corporate taxpayers or to interest expense which is incurred for business use. After 1975, interest that can be deducted is limited to the following:

    —$10,000 plus

    —The amount of net investment income (if any)

---

16.  § 163(d).

Amounts which are disallowed may be carried over and treated as investment interest of the succeeding year. Investment income is defined as the gross income from interest, dividends, rents, royalties, net short-term capital gains attributed to the property held for investment, and ordinary income from the recapture of depreciation under § 1245 and § 1250. Investment expenses are deducted from investment income in arriving at net investment income.

**Example 19.** T had net investment income of $15,000 and paid $60,000 of investment interest. His deduction in the current year is $25,000. This interest deduction is calculated as follows:

| | |
|---|---|
| Floor | $ 10,000 |
| Net investment income | 15,000 |
| Current year deduction | $ 25,000 |

T would be allowed a carryover of $35,000.

Form 4952, Investment Interest Expense Deduction, is used to calculate the current deduction and the amount of any carryover. For individuals, if the investment interest expense pertains to rental property, it is reported in Part I of Schedule E, Supplemental Income Schedule; otherwise it is reported in the interest expense section of Schedule A.

*Interest Paid for Services.* It is common practice in the mortgage loan business to charge a fee for finding, placing, or processing a mortgage loan. Such fees are often called points and are expressed as a percentage of the loan amount. In periods of tight money, it may be necessary to pay points to obtain the necessary financing. To qualify as deductible interest, the points must be considered compensation to a lender solely for the use or forbearance of money. The points cannot be a form of service charge or payment for specific services if they are to qualify as deductible interest. Points paid by the seller are not deductible because the debt on which they are paid is not the debt of the seller. Points paid by the seller are treated as a reduction of the selling price of the property. If the points are paid by the buyer and are for the use or forbearance of money, the "points" are immediately deductible if they are not prepaid interest which must be capitalized and amortized.

The 1968 Federal Truth in Lending Act, which requires disclosure of finance charges as an annual percentage, has simplified the determination of whether a charge is interest or a fee for servicing the account. The IRS has now ruled that the following charges are deductible as interest: finance charges on gasoline credit cards, on department store purchases, and on bank credit cards.

## INSTALLMENT PURCHASES—INTEREST NOT SEPARATELY STATED

Whenever a taxpayer enters into a contract to purchase personal property (furniture, household appliances, etc.) that requires installment payments and there is a separately stated carrying charge but the interest is not separately stated, then interest is imputed (charged) at six percent according to Code Section 163(b). This interest is imputed to the contract regardless of whether payments are made when due or are in default. They are still deductible. The six percent interest charge allowable as an itemized deduction is considerably lower than installment interest presently charged by bank credit cards. Undoubtedly, Congress will update the imputed interest figure to a more realistic amount. This calculation is, however, seldom necessary as a result of the requirement that finance charges be disclosed as an annual percentage (see the preceding discussion of the 1968 Federal Truth in Lending Act).

# CHARITABLE CONTRIBUTIONS

## RATIONALE FOR DEDUCTIBILITY

Section 170 permits the deduction of contributions made to qualified domestic organizations by individuals and corporations. Contributions to qualified charitable organizations serve certain social welfare needs and therefore relieve the government of the cost of providing these needed services to the community.

## CRITERIA FOR A "GIFT"

Section 170(c) defines "charitable contribution" as a gift made to a qualified organization. The major elements needed to qualify a contribution as a gift are a donative intent, the absence of consideration, and acceptance by the donee. Consequently, the taxpayer has the burden of establishing that the transfer was made from motives of "disinterested generosity" as established by the courts.[17] As one can imagine, this test is quite subjective and has led to problems of interpretation. For example, a taxpayer engaged in a trade or business may attempt to qualify an expenditure as an ordinary and necessary business expense under § 162 rather than as a charitable contribution, since contributions are subject to certain ceiling limitations.

> **Example 20.** X is a travel agent and has for a number of years conducted most of his business with clients who are charitable

*Qualified Charitable Contribution*

---

17. *Comm. v. Duberstein,* 60–2 USTC ¶ 9515, 5 AFTR2d 1626, 80 S.Ct. 1190 (USSC, 1960).

organizations as described under § 170. At the end of each year, payments were made directly to these organizations, the amount of which depended directly on the volume and profitability of the business relationship. These payments are not charitable contributions but are business expenses under § 162; therefore, the charitable contribution limitations do not apply.

## QUALIFIED ORGANIZATIONS

To be deductible, a contribution must be made to one of the following organizations:[18]

—A state or possession of the United States or any subdivisions thereof.

—A corporation, trust, or community chest, fund, or foundation that is situated in the United States and is organized and operated exclusively for religious, charitable, scientific, literary, or educational purpose or for the prevention of cruelty to children or animals.

—A veterans' organization.

—A fraternal organization operating under the lodge system.

—A cemetery company.

The IRS publishes a list of organizations which have applied for and received tax-exempt status under § 501 of the Code.[19] This publication is updated frequently and may be helpful to determine if a gift has been made to a qualifying charitable organization.

Gifts made to needy individuals are generally not deductible; therefore, a deduction will not be permitted if a gift is received by a donee in an individual capacity rather than as a representative of a qualifying organization.

## TIME OF PAYMENT

The Code permits a contribution deduction generally in the year the payment is made. This requirement extends to both cash and accrual basis individuals.[20] An accrual basis corporation, however, is permitted a deduction if the contribution is made within two and one-half months of the close of the taxable year and if the board of directors authorizes such payment prior to the end of the taxable year.[21]

---

**18.**   § 170(c).

**19.**   Although this *Cumulative List of Organizations* (IRS Publication 78) may be helpful, it is not required that a qualified organization be listed. Not all organizations that qualify are listed in this publication (e. g., American Red Cross, University of Cleveland).

**20.**   § 170(a)(1). Also see *infra,* Footnote 107.

**21.**   § 170(a)(2).

A contribution is ordinarily deemed to have been made on the delivery of the property to the donee. For example, if a gift of securities (properly endorsed) is made to a qualified charitable organization, the gift is considered complete on the day of delivery or mailing. However, if the donor delivers the certificate to his bank broker or to the issuing corporation, the gift is considered complete on the date that the stock is transferred on the books of the corporation.

## VALUATION PROBLEMS

Property donated to a charity is generally valued at fair market value at the time the gift is made. The Code and Regulations give very little guidance on the measurement of the fair market value except to say, "The fair market value is the price at which the property would change hands between a willing buyer and a willing seller, neither being under any compulsion to buy or sell and both having reasonable knowledge of relevant facts."[22] The IRS has established guidelines for appraising contributed property, and many established charities offer appraisal services to donors. Contributed property that has a value of $200 or more must be fully described, and a statement of how the property was valued must accompany the taxpayer's return.

## LIMITATIONS ON CHARITABLE DEDUCTIONS

*In General.* Charitable contributions are subject to certain overall ceiling limitations (i. e., contributions for individuals are limited to 50 percent of the taxpayer's adjusted gross income, and in some cases, a 30 percent ceiling limitation is imposed for contributions of capital gain property).[23] Certain contributions of individuals are subject to either a 50 percent or 20 percent limitation for contributions to certain private foundations. The distinction between the ceiling limitations for private foundations is discussed below. Corporations are subject to an overall limitation of 10 percent of taxable income computed without regard to the contributions made and certain other adjustments.[24]

In addition, the contribution of certain types of property (e. g., inventory) may result in a deduction of less than the fair market value of such property.

*Ordinary Income Property.* Ordinary income property is any property which, if sold, will result in the recognition of ordinary income. The term includes inventory for sale in the taxpayer's trade

---

**22.** Reg. § 1.170–1(c)(1).
**23.** Under § 170(b) the ceiling limitations apply to the taxpayer's contribution base. Pursuant to § 170(b)(1)(E), the contribution base is defined as adjusted gross income (computed without regard to any net operating loss carryback to the taxable year).
**24.** § 170(b)(2).

or business, a work of art created by the donor, a manuscript prepared by the donor, and a capital asset held by the donor for less than the required holding period for long-term capital gain treatment. Also included is property that results in the recognition of ordinary income due to the recapture of depreciation. If ordinary income property is contributed, the deduction is equal to the fair market value of the property less the amount of ordinary income which would have been reported if the property were sold (i. e., in most instances, the deduction is limited to the cost basis of the property to the donor).

> **Example 21.**  T owned stock in Conservation Corporation which he donated to a local university on May 1, 19X7. T had purchased the stock for $2,500 on April 3, 19X7, and the stock had a value of $3,600 when he made the donation. Since the property has not been held for a sufficient period to meet the long-term capital gain requirements, a short-term capital gain of $1,100 would have been recognized had the property been sold. Since short-term capital gain property is treated as ordinary income property, T's charitable contribution deduction is limited to the extent of its adjusted basis of $2,500.

A special exception was added by the Tax Reform Act of 1976 which permits a corporation to contribute inventory (ordinary income property) to a public charity or private operating foundation (50 percent charities) and receive a deduction equal to the adjusted basis of the property, plus one-half of the difference between the fair market value and the adjusted basis of the property. In no event may the deduction exceed twice the adjusted basis of the property.

To qualify for this exception, the inventory must be used by the charity in its exempt purpose for the care of children, the ill, or the needy.

The limitations on ordinary income property were intended to prevent taxpayers from obtaining undue advantage from the contribution of substantially appreciated ordinary income property. For example, a taxpayer (in a 50 percent bracket) who contributed inventory with a fair market value of $100 and an adjusted basis of $40 would receive a tax benefit of $50 (50% × $100) and have a net profit, in effect, of $10 if these limitations did not apply. Application of these rules limits the deduction to $70 [$40 + ½ ($100 − $40)] and thus limits the tax benefit to $35 ($70 × 50%).

*Capital Gain Property.*  Capital gain property is any property that would have resulted in the recognition of long-term capital gain if the property had been sold by the donor. If capital gain property is contributed to a private foundation as defined in § 509(a), the taxpayer must reduce the contribution by 40 percent of the long-term capital gain which would have been recognized if the property had been sold at its fair market value. This reduction was imposed because a taxpayer is not taxed on the appreciated portion of the contributed property at long-term capital gain rates (i. e., 40 percent of the long-term capital gain would have been subject to tax at ordinary rates if the property were sold rather than contributed to the private foundation). It should be noted, however, that contributions of capital gain property to public charities are not generally reduced by 40 percent of the capital gain element.

> **Example 22.** T purchases stock for $800 on January 1, 1975, and donates it to a private foundation on June 21, 1979, when it is worth $2,000. T's charitable contribution is $1,520 [$2,000 − (40% × $1,200 appreciation)].

> **Example 23.** Assume the same facts as in the previous example except that T contributed the stock to a public charity (e. g., the YMCA, his church, or a university). T's charitable contribution would be $2,000, since these limitations apply only to private foundations.

Special rules apply to capital gain property which is tangible personalty. If tangible personalty is contributed to a public charity such as a museum, church, or university, the charitable deduction is reduced by 40 percent of the long-term capital gain if the property is put to an unrelated use. A taxpayer in this instance must establish that the property is not in fact being put to an unrelated use by the donee and that at the time of the contribution, it was reasonable to anticipate that the property would not be put to an unrelated use. In the case of a contribution of personalty to a museum, if the work of art is the kind of art normally retained by the museum, it will be reasonable for a donor to anticipate that the work of art will not be put to an unrelated use (even if the object is later sold or exchanged).

> **Example 24.** T contributes a Picasso, for which he paid $20,000, to a local museum. It had a value of $30,000 at the time of the donation. The painting was displayed by the museum for a period of two years and subsequently sold for $50,000. The charitable contribution is not reduced by 40% of the unrealized appreciation [40% × ($30,000 − $20,000)], since the painting was put to a related use even though it was later sold by the museum.

*Contribution of Services.* No deduction is allowed under § 170 for a contribution of one's services to a qualified charitable organization. However, unreimbursed expenses related to the services rendered may be deductible. For example, the cost of a uniform (without general utility) which is required to be worn while performing services may be deductible. Deductions are also permitted for transportation and reasonable expenses for meals and lodging while away from home incurred in performance of the donated services.

> **Example 25.** If a delegate representing her church in San Francisco, California, travels to a national meeting in Denver,

Colorado, the transportation, meals, and lodging would be deductible if the meeting was solely for religious reasons.

*Fifty Percent Ceiling Limitation.* Contributions made to public charities may not exceed 50 percent of an individual's adjusted gross income for the year.[25] Excess contributions may be carried over to the next five years.[26] The 50 percent ceiling on contributions applies to the following types of public charities:[27]

—A church or a convention or association of churches.

—An educational organization which maintains a regular faculty and curriculum.

—A hospital or medical school.

—An organization supported by the government which holds property or investments for the benefit of a college or university.

—A governmental unit which is Federal, state, or local.

—An organization normally receiving a substantial part of its support from the public or a governmental unit.

—Certain types of private foundations.

*Twenty Percent Ceiling.* Contributions to most private foundations are limited generally to 20 percent of adjusted gross income. However, a 50 percent limitation generally applies to private foundations that have broad public support. If substantial contributions are also made to public (50 percent) charities, the limitation to private charities categorized as 20 percent organizations may be less than 20 percent.

The deduction for contributions in these cases is the lesser of 20 percent of the taxpayer's contribution base (generally adjusted gross income) or 50 percent × adjusted gross income less the amount of charitable contributions qualifying for the 50 percent deduction ceiling. The excess, if any, cannot be carried over.[28]

> **Example 26.** T has adjusted gross income of $15,000. He contributes $5,000 to a local university which is a 50% charity and $4,000 to the XYZ Foundation for the deaf, which is a private foundation. T's contribution deduction is $7,500 (the sum of the $5,000 contribution to the university and $2,500 of the $4,000 contribution to the XYZ Foundation). The lesser of $3,000 (20% × $15,000) or $2,500 [(50% × $15,000) − $5,000] is allowed for the contribution to the XYZ Foundation.

---

**25.** § 170(b).
**26.** § 170(d)(1).
**27.** § 170(b)(1)(A).
**28.** § 170(b)(1)(B).

*Thirty Percent Ceiling.* To prevent possible abuse when a taxpayer contributes appreciated property, specific rules apply to limit the deduction. For example, if capital gain property does not come under the 20 percent limitation for contributions to a private foundation, it is subject to a 30 percent limitation based on the taxpayer's adjusted gross income.[29] Consequently, any capital asset or § 1231 asset that would result in a long-term capital gain if sold is subject to the 30 percent limitation. When applying the limitation rules, contributions to which the 30 percent limit is applicable are the last to be considered.[30]

> **Example 27.** T has adjusted gross income for the taxable year of $20,000. T contributes cash of $6,000 and stock with a cost basis of $3,000 and fair market value of $7,000, which has been held for two years, to a local university. Since the appreciated stock is a capital asset which has been donated to a public charity, it is subject to the 30% limitation of $6,000 (30% of $20,000). Since this contribution plus the cash contribution exceeds 50% of adjusted gross income ($10,000), the actual deduction must be limited to $10,000 or $6,000 cash plus $4,000 in appreciated stock. The $3,000 unused capital gain property contribution can be carried over (subject to the 30 percent rule) to subsequent years.

Under the law, a taxpayer may elect to reduce the deduction for donated capital gain property by 40 percent of the difference between its fair market value and its adjusted cost basis.[31] In making this election, a taxpayer may receive a larger deduction in the year the contributions are made due to the higher ceiling (i. e., 50 percent in lieu of 30 percent). However, if the property is substantially appreciated, the election will result in a reduction of the contributions which might otherwise be carried forward to subsequent years.

*Excess Contributions Carryover.* Excess contributions to public charities subject to the 50 percent limitation may be carried over for five years.[32] Excess contributions under the 30 percent ceiling are also carried over but are subject to the 30 percent ceiling limitation in the carryover years. In a carryover year, the contributions made during such year are first applied before any carryover amounts are deducted.[33]

> **Example 28.** T, in 19X1, contributes $20,000 cash to a public charity. Her adjusted gross income for 19X1 is $30,000. Since T's contribution ceiling is $15,000 (50% of $30,000), she may carry

---

**29.**　§ 170(b)(1)(D). See the discussion of § 1231 in Chapter 10.

**30.**　§ 170(b)(1)(C)(i).

**31.**　§ 170(e)(1).

**32.**　§ 170(d)(1).

**33.**　§ 170(d)(1)(A).

over $5,000 to 19X2, then, if any remains, to 19X3, etc., through 19X6.

**Example 29.** Assume the same facts as in the previous example plus for the following information related to 19X2–19X6:

|  | 19X1 | 19X2 | 19X3 | 19X4 |
|---|---|---|---|---|
| Adjusted gross income | $ 30,000 | $ 25,000 | $ 35,000 | $ 40,000 |
| Contributions subject to the 50 percent limitations | 20,000 | 20,000 | 10,000 | 10,000 |
| Deductible contributions: | | | | |
| Current year | 15,000 | 12,500 | 10,000 | 10,000 |
| Carryovers from: | | | | |
| 19X1 | | | 5,000 | |
| 19X2 | | | 2,500 | 5,000 |
| Unused carryovers from: | | | | |
| 19X1 | 5,000 | | — | — |
| 19X2 | | 7,500 | 5,000 | — |
| Total deduction | $ 15,000 | $ 12,500 | $ 17,500 | $ 15,000 |

*Direct Charitable Contributions.* Because the zero bracket amount has increased over the past few years, individual taxpayers have found it more difficult to accumulate enough itemized deductions to exceed the zero bracket amount. Consequently, the incentive to make charitable contributions has been reduced. To restore some of this incentive, Congress enacted new Code Section 170(i).

According to this new provision, a "direct charitable contribution" as defined under new Code Section 63(i) will be allowed as a deduction *from* adjusted gross income even by taxpayers who do not itemize. It will be phased in over a five-year period, with a ceiling limitation (i. e., the maximum amount of the contribution that qualifies) for the first three years. The phase-in is scheduled as follows:

| Year | Percentage Allowed | Ceiling Limitation |
|---|---|---|
| 1982 | 25% | $ 100 |
| 1983 | 25% | $ 100 |
| 1984 | 25% | $ 300 |
| 1985 | 50% | None |
| 1986 | 100% | None |
| 1987 | —Provision Expires— | |

**Example 30.** X and Y are married and file a joint return for 1983. They have $500 in interest expenses, $250 in medical expenses after the application of the percentage limitation, and $200 in charitable contributions. Because these expenses do not exceed $3,400 (the zero bracket amount for a joint return), X and Y are not in a position to itemize deductions. However, $25 [$100

ceiling limitation times 25% (percentage allowed)] is permitted as a direct charitable contribution and is deducted *from* adjusted gross income.

The ceiling limitation is not doubled for a married person filing a joint return. Thus, a single taxpayer comes under the same ceiling limitation as a married taxpayer filing a joint return. In the case of a married individual filing a separate return, the ceiling limitation is $50 for tax years beginning in 1982 and 1983 and $150 for tax year 1984. There is no ceiling limitation for tax years beginning in 1985 and 1986. For tax years beginning *after* 1986 the provision for a direct charitable contribution deduction is terminated. Also, there is no carryover provision for excess direct charitable contributions beyond the applicable ceiling limitation.

## SUMMARY OF RULES

Figure I reflects a summary of the rules applicable to the contribution of appreciated property by individuals. (Note: The rules for the direct charitable contribution have been omitted from the chart.)

## FILING REQUIREMENTS

The deduction for contributions (other than direct charitable contributions) is made as an itemized deduction on Schedule A of Form 1040. Cash contributions which are supported by receipts, cancelled checks, etc., are totaled and listed together on Schedule A. Those cash contributions not supported by cancelled checks or receipts are to be detailed as to payee and amount. Other-than-cash contributions (such as contributions of property or mileage at nine cents per mile incurred in performing charitable work) are reported separately from cash contributions. If the taxpayer makes a gift of property in excess of $200, the Regulations require that the taxpayer state the name of each organization to which a contribution was made, the amount of the contribution, and its date. In addition, it is necessary to provide a description of the property; the manner of its acquisition; the fair market value of the property at the time of the gift; the basis of the property; and the terms of any agreement relating to the contribution.

To illustrate the use of Schedule A, assume a taxpayer made the following contributions to qualified charitable organizations during the year:

| | |
|---|---|
| Payment of a church pledge (cancelled checks retained) | $ 2,800 |
| Donations of cash to door-to-door solicitors—$5 to the March of Dimes, $15 to the Salvation Army Christmas Drive | 20 |

**Figure I[95*]**

## DETERMINING THE DEDUCTION FOR CONTRIBUTIONS OF APPRECIATED PROPERTY BY INDIVIDUALS

| If the sale of the contributed property by the donor would result in: | and the property is contributed to: | the contribution is measured by: | but the deduction is limited to: | with: |
|---|---|---|---|---|
| 1. Long-term capital gain | a 50 percent organization | fair market value of the property | 30 percent of adjusted gross income | a 5-year carryover |
| 2. Ordinary income only | a 50 percent organization | the basis of the property | 50 percent of adjusted gross income | a 5-year carryover |
| 3. Long-term capital gain (and the property is tangible personal property put to an unrelated use by the donee) | a 50 percent organization | fair market value minus 40 percent of the appreciation on the property | 50 percent of adjusted gross income | a 5-year carryover |
| 4. A portion of ordinary income | a 50 percent organization | fair market value minus ordinary income which would result | 50 percent of adjusted gross income | a 5-year carryover |
| 5. Long-term capital gain (and the reduced deduction is elected) | a 50 percent organization | fair market value minus 40 percent of the appreciation on the property | 50 percent of adjusted gross income | a 5-year carryover (but no carryover for amount by which deduction is reduced) |

| | | | | |
|---|---|---|---|---|
| 6. Long-term capital gain | a 20 percent organization or for the use of a 20 percent or 50 percent organization | fair market value minus 40 percent of the appreciation on the property | the lesser of: 1. 20 percent of adjusted gross income 2. 50 percent of adjusted gross income minus other contributions to 50 percent organizations | no carryover |
| 7. Long-term capital gain (and the property is tangible personal property put to an unrelated use by the donee) | a 20 percent organization or for the use of a 20 percent or 50 percent organization | fair market value minus 40 percent of the appreciation on the property | the lesser of: 1. 20 percent of adjusted gross income 2. 50 percent of adjusted gross income minus other contributions to 50 percent organizations | no carryover |
| 8. Ordinary income only | a 20 percent organization or for the use of a 20 percent or 50 percent organization | the basis of the property | the lesser of: 1. 20 percent of adjusted gross income 2. 50 percent of adjusted gross income minus other contributions to 50 percent organizations | no carryover |
| 9. A portion of ordinary income | a 20 percent organization or for the use of a 20 percent or 50 percent organization | fair market value minus ordinary income which would result from sale of the property | the lesser of: 1. 20 percent of adjusted gross income 2. 50 percent of adjusted gross income minus other contributions to 50 percent organizations | no carryover |

**95.** Adopted with permission of the author and the publisher (*The Accounting Review*) from Eugene Willis, "The Amount of a Charitable Contribution of Property," *The Accounting Review* (April 1977), p. 498.

*Under the Economic Recovery Act of 1981, corporations can make charitable contributions of research property. This provision is omitted from this illustration and is discussed in *West's Federal Taxation: Corporations, Partnerships, Estates, and Trusts.*

Donation of used clothing and certain
household effects (e. g., chairs, table,
baby furniture) to Goodwill Industries.
The property cost $1,200 and had an
estimated fair market value of $300. Re-
ceipts acknowledging the donations
are available.                                                300

Presuming there is no problem with the percentage limitations, the completed portion of Schedule A that is relevant is reproduced below.

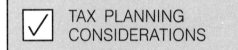

| Contributions<br>(See page 19 of<br>Instructions.) | 20 a Cash contributions. (If you gave $3,000 or more to any one or-<br>ganization, report those contributions on line 20b.) . . . . | 20a | 2,820 | |
|---|---|---|---|---|
| | b Cash contributions totaling $3,000 or more to any one organi-<br>zation. (Show to whom you gave and how much you gave.)<br>▶ | | | |
| | | 20b | | |
| | 21 Other than cash (see page 19 of Instructions for required statement) . . . | 21 | 300 | |
| | 22 Carryover from prior years . . . . . . . . . . . . | 22 | | |
| | 23 Add lines 20a through 22. Write your answer here . . . . . . . . . . ▶ | 23 | 3,120 | |

## ✓ TAX PLANNING CONSIDERATIONS

## EFFECTIVE UTILIZATION OF EXCESS ITEMIZED DEDUCTIONS

Since an individual may use the zero bracket amount in one year and itemize his or her deductions in another year, it is frequently possible to obtain maximum benefit by shifting itemized deductions from one year to another. For example, if a taxpayer's itemized deductions and the zero bracket amount are approximately the same for each year of a two-year period, the taxpayer should use the zero bracket amount in one year and shift itemized deductions (to the extent permitted by law) to the other year. The individual could, for example, prepay a church pledge for a particular year or avoid paying end-of-the-year medical expenses to shift the deduction to the following year.

## UTILIZATION OF MEDICAL DEDUCTIONS

Because of the percentage limitations on medical and drug expenses, taxpayers may find it worthwhile to delay the processing of year-end medical insurance reimbursement claims.

**Example 31.**  Prior to paying $2,000 for an operation carried out in November of 1983, T had medical expenses for the year of $800. In late December of 1983, she files a claim with the insurance company to recover the amount allowed to her under the policy covering her medical care. In January of 1983, T receives a check from the company in the amount of $2,000. For tax year 1983, T has adjusted gross income of $30,000 and has itemized deductions in excess of the zero bracket amount. Under these circumstances, T has a medical expense deduction of $1,300 [i. e., ($800 + $2,000) − (5% × $30,000)]. Under the application of the tax benefit rule, she must, however, include in her gross income for 1984, $1,300 of the $2,000 reimbursement received in January.

In Example 31 what did the taxpayer accomplish? By delaying the filing of the claim for reimbursement, T obtained the benefit of an additional deduction of $1,300 for 1983. Although this amount has to be reported as income in 1984, she obtains the advantage of a tax savings for one year. The advisability of her actions presumes that her income tax bracket in 1984 will not increase significantly over the 1983 level.

When a taxpayer anticipates that his or her medical and drug expenses will approximate the five percent and one percent limitations, much might be done to generate a deductible excess. Any of the procedures described below can help build a deduction by the end of the year:

—Purchase some or all of the drugs that the taxpayer, spouse, and dependents will need in the following year. In this connection, it is the year of payment and not the year of use that controls the timing of the deduction. Keep in mind that most patent medicines (i. e., those obtainable without a prescription) qualify for the deduction.

—Incur the obligation for or have carried out needed dental work. Orthodontic treatment, for example, may have been recommended for a member of taxpayer's family.

—Have certain remedial surgery that may have been postponed from prior years (e. g., tonsillectomies, vasectomies, correction of hernias, hysterectomies).

—Make or incur the obligation for capital improvements to taxpayer's personal residence recommended by a physician (e. g., an air filtration system to alleviate a respiratory disorder).

As an aid to taxpayers who might experience temporary cash-flow problems at the end of the year, the use of bank credit cards is deemed to be payment for purposes of timing the deductibility of charitable and medical expenses.

**Example 32.** On December 12, 19X1, T (a calendar year taxpayer) purchases two pairs of prescription contact lenses and one pair of prescribed orthopedic shoes for a total of $305. These purchases are separately charged to T's credit card. On January

6, 19X2, T receives his credit card statement containing these charges and makes payment shortly thereafter. The purchases are deductible as medical expenses in the year charged (i. e., 19X1) and not in the year the account is settled (i. e., 19X2).

Recognizing which expenditures qualify for the medical deduction also may be crucial to exceeding the percentage limitations.

**Example 33.** T employs E (an unrelated party) to care for her incapacitated and dependent mother. E is not a trained nurse but spends approximately one-half of the time performing nursing duties (e. g., administering injections and providing physical therapy) and the rest of the time doing household chores. An allocable portion of E's wages that T pays (including the employer's portion of FICA taxes) qualifies as a medical expense.[35]

To assure a deduction for the entire cost of a nursing home for an aged dependent, it is helpful if the transfer of the individual to the home is for medical reasons which are recommended by a doctor. In addition, the nursing home facilities should be adequate to provide the necessary medical and nursing care. To assure a deduction for all of the nursing care expenses, it is necessary to show that the individual was placed in the home due to required medical care rather than for personal or family considerations.

For tax years beginning after 1982, the separate deductions for one-half (up to $150) of medical insurance expenses is repealed. After 1982, any medical premium expense will be limited by the five percent floor. Since the benefit for deducting medical premiums will be limited, individuals will probably turn more to commercial insurance, since contributions made by employers are excluded from gross income under § 106.

Proper documentation is required to substantiate medical expenses. The taxpayer should keep all receipts of credit card or other charge purchases of medical services and supplies, cash register receipts, etc. In addition medical transportation mileage should be recorded.

## PLANNING WITH SALES TAXES

In a year of major purchases such as remodeling or building a new house, individuals should record actual sales tax payments, since such amount may be in excess of the figure provided by the optional sales tax table issued by the IRS. If a new home or addition is planned, it is possible to receive a sales tax deduction for the building materials

---

**35.** These expenditures might qualify for the child and disabled dependent care tax credit discussed in Chapter 8.

if the tax is separately stated and is billed to the taxpayer. If the optional sales tax tables are used, the deduction for building materials should be added to the amount determined by the tables.

## PROTECTING THE INTEREST DEDUCTION

Although the deductibility of prepaid interest by a cash basis taxpayer has been severely restricted, a notable exception is contained in § 461(g)(2). Under this provision, points paid to obtain financing for the purchase or improvement of a principal residence may be deductible in the year of payment. However, such points must actually be paid by the taxpayer obtaining the loan and must represent a charge for the use of money. It has been held that points paid from the mortgage proceeds do not satisfy the payment requirement. Also, the portion of the points attributable to service charges does not represent deductible interest. For taxpayers financing home purchases or improvements, planning usually should be directed toward avoiding these two hurdles to immediate deductibility.

There may be instances when a taxpayer wishes to elect to capitalize points if the points plus other itemized deductions do not exceed the taxpayer's zero bracket amount.

> **Example 34.** X purchases a home on December 15, 19X1, for $95,000 with a 30-year mortgage of $65,000 financed by the Greater Metropolis National Bank. X pays two points as a processing fee in addition to interest allocated to the period from December 15 until December 31, 19X1, at an annual rate of 14%. Since X does not have enough itemized deductions to exceed the zero bracket amount for 19X1, this taxpayer should elect to capitalize the interest expense by amortizing the points over 30 years. In this instance X, would deduct $43.33 for 19X1 as an interest expense [$1,300 (two points) divided by 30 years].

Interest is not deductible unless the party making the payment is the party who has the obligation to do so. A proper structuring of the loan agreement may avoid the possible loss of the deduction.

> **Example 35.** As a college graduation present, M makes a down payment on a new automobile for her daughter, D. As there is some doubt as to D's ability to make the earlier monthly payments, M makes herself co-liable on the car loan issued by the finance company. Under these circumstances, M will be entitled to the interest deduction on any car payments she makes. Had the loan listed only D as being liable, the interest portion of any payments made by M would be nondeductible. In that case, the loan is D's, not M's, obligation.

## ASSURING THE CHARITABLE CONTRIBUTION DEDUCTION

For a charitable contribution deduction to be available, the recipient must be a qualified charitable organization. Sometimes the mechanics of how the contribution is carried out can determine whether or not a deduction results.

> **Example 36.** T wants to donate $5,000 to her church's mission in Seoul, Korea. In this regard, she considers three alternatives:
>
> 1. Send the money directly to the mission.
>
> 2. Give the money to her church with the understanding that it is to be passed on to the mission.
>
> 3. Give the money directly to the missionary in charge of the mission who is currently in the U. S. on a fund-raising trip.
>
> If T wants to obtain a deduction for the contribution, she would be well advised to choose alternative (2). A direct donation to the mission [alternative (1)] would not be deductible because the mission is a foreign charity. A direct gift to the missionary [alternative (3)] does not comply since an individual cannot be a qualified charity for income tax purposes.

When making donations of other than cash, the type of property chosen can have decided implications in measuring the amount, if any, of the deduction.

> **Example 37.** T desires to give $60,000 in value to her church in some form other than cash. In this connection, she considers four alternatives:
>
> 1. Stock held as an investment with a cost basis of $100,000 and a fair market value of $60,000.
>
> 2. Stock held as an investment for more than one year with a cost basis of $10,000 and a fair market value of $60,000.
>
> 3. One year's rent-free use of a building which normally leases for $5,000 a month.
>
> 4. A valuable stamp collection held as an investment and owned for more than one year with a cost basis of $10,000 and a fair market value of $60,000. The church plans to sell the collection if and when it is donated.
>
> Alternative (1) is ill-advised as the subject of the gift. Even though T would obtain a deduction of $60,000, she would forego the potential loss of $40,000 that would be recognized if the property had been sold. Alternative (2) makes good sense, since the deduction still is $60,000 and none of the $50,000 of appreciation that has occurred must be recognized as income. Alternative (3) yields no deduction at all and would not, therefore, appear to be a

wise choice.[36] Alternative (4) involves tangible personalty which the recipient does not plan to use. As a result, 40% of the appreciation involved, or $20,000 [40% × ($60,000 − $10,000)], becomes nondeductible. Thus, the amount of the deduction would be limited to $40,000 ($60,000 − $20,000).

In the case of property transfers (particularly real estate) the ceiling limitations on the amount of the deduction allowed in any one year (i. e., 20 percent, 30 percent, or 50 percent of adjusted gross income—as the case may be) could be a factor to take into account. With proper planning, donations can be controlled to stay within the limitations and therefore avoid the need for a carryover of unused charitable contributions.

> **Example 38.** T desires to donate a tract of unimproved land, held as an investment, to the University of Maryland (a qualified charitable organization). The land has been held for more than one year and has a current fair market value of $300,000 and a basis to T of $50,000. T's adjusted gross income for the current year is estimated to be $200,000, and he expects much the same for the next few years. In the current year he deeds (i. e., transfers) an undivided one-fifth interest in the real estate to the university.

What has T accomplished for income tax purposes? In the current year he will be allowed a charitable contribution deduction of $60,000 [i. e., ⅕ (or 20%) × $300,000] which will be within the applicable limitation of adjusted gross income (30% × $200,000). Presuming no other charitable contributions for the year, T has avoided the possibility of a carryover. In future years, T can arrange donations of undivided interests in the real estate to stay within the bounds of the percentage limitations. The only difficulty with this approach is the necessity of having to revalue the real estate each year before the donation, since the amount of the deduction is based on the fair market value of the interest contributed at the time of the contribution.

## PROBLEM MATERIALS

### Questions for Class Discussion

1. "Medical care insurance premiums are independently deductible and, therefore, are not subject to the percentage limitation." Comment on the validity of this statement.

2. T, a self-employed individual taxpayer, prepared his own income tax return for the past year and asked you to check it over for accuracy. A review by

---

**36.** Due to abuse on the part of taxpayers, the Tax Reform Act of 1969 eliminated any deduction for allowing a charitable organization free or bargain use of property.

you indicates that he failed to claim certain business entertainment expenses.

(a) Would the correction of this omission affect the amount of medical expenses T can deduct? Explain. *yes*

(b) Would it matter if T were employed rather than self-employed? *yes*

3. If a taxpayer incurred medical expenses of $500 and deducted such amounts in 19X1, how would a $300 insurance reimbursement be treated if received in 19X2? Received in 19X1? What if the taxpayer had no excess itemized deductions in 19X1 and received the $300 reimbursement in 19X2? *not includible.* *included in g.I* *limited to $200*

4. What is an ad valorem tax? Why should a distinction be made between an ad valorem tax (based on value) and a tax based on other factors such as weight, year, model?

5. Why is it necessary to make an apportionment of real estate taxes between the buyer and the seller of a home in the year of sale? What effect does the apportionment have upon the adjusted basis of the property to the buyer if the seller pays the real estate taxes? *apportionment of taxes between seller & buyer*

6. If a taxpayer overpays his or her state income tax due to excessive withholdings or estimated tax payments, how is the refund check treated when received in the subsequent year? Are the excess amounts paid deductible in the current year?

7. If a taxpayer's records indicate that state sales taxes in excess of the amount allowed per the sales tax tables were paid, is such excess amount deductible? Do the IRS sales tax tables include major purchase items such as automobiles and appliances? Is it necessary to make adjustments for local and county sales taxes? Why? *yes* *yes*

8. Which of the following is generally deductible as interest:

   (a) Bank credit card interest. — *yes*

   (b) Service charges. *no*

   (c) Points paid by the seller of property. *no*

   (d) Finance charges separately stated. *yes*

   (e) Late payment fees on the payment of utility bills. *yes*

9. Discuss the special problems that arise with respect to the deductibility of interest on a debt between related parties. How does § 267 of the Code relate to this problem?

10. Is it permissible for the purchaser of a home to deduct mortgage points? *yes*

11. How and why does the tax treatment of interest expense differ when borrowed funds are used for business versus nonbusiness purposes? *yes - for AGI* *Pers - Itemi ded*

12. Why has Congress imposed limitations on the deductibility of interest when funds are borrowed for the purpose of purchasing or continuing to hold investment property?

13. What is ordinary income property? If inventory with an adjusted cost basis of $60 and fair market value of $100 is contributed to a public charity, how much is deductible? (Assume that the inventory is not used by the charity for the care of children, the ill, or the needy.)

14. What is capital gain property? What tax treatment is required if capital gain property is contributed to a private foundation? To a public charity? What difference does it make if the contribution is tangible personalty and it is put to a use unrelated to the donee's business?

15. An accountant normally charges $50 an hour when preparing financial statements for clients. If the accountant performs accounting services for a church without charge, can the value of the donated services be deducted on his or her tax return?

16. Compare the deductibility of contributions made to private foundations with contributions made to public charities (i. e., with respect to percentage limitations and carryover rules).

17. Discuss the filing requirements for contributions of property in excess of $200.

## Problems

18. H and W are married and together have adjusted gross income of $24,000. They have no dependents and they filed a joint return in 1983. Each pays $450 for hospitalization insurance. During the year, they paid the following amounts for medical care: $1,900 in doctor and dentist bills and hospital expenses and $310 for medicine and drugs. An insurance reimbursement for hospitalization was received in December 1983 for $700. Determine the deduction allowable under § 213 for medical expenses paid in 1983. $970

19. H and W, who have a dependent child, C, were both under 65 years of age at the close of calendar year 1983, and filed a joint return for that year. During the year 1983, H's mother, M, attained the age of 65 and qualified as a dependent of H. The adjusted gross income in 1983 of H and W was $14,000. During 1983, H and W paid the following amounts for medical care: $700 for doctors and hospital expenses and $145 for medicine and drugs for themselves, $375 for doctors and hospital expenses and $70 for medicine and drugs for C, and $500 for doctors and hospital expenses and $125 for medicine and drugs for M. No insurance reimbursements were received for these expenses. How much is allowed as a deduction for medical expenses for the taxable year 1983?

20. Upon the advice of his physician, T, a heart patient, installs an elevator in his personal residence at a cost of $8,000. The elevator has a cost recovery period of five years. A neighbor who is in the real estate business charges T $40 for an appraisal which places the value of the residence at $50,000 before the improvement and $55,000 after. The value increases because T lives in a region where many older people retire and therefore would find the elevator an attractive feature in a home. As a result of the operation of the elevator, T noticed an increase of $55 in his utility bills for the current year. Disregarding percentage limitations, which of the above expenditures qualify as a medical deduction?

21. During the year, T incurs the following expenses in connection with his dependent father:

| | |
|---|---:|
| Meals and lodging to Green Acres Rest Home | $ 5,600 |
| Drugs (patent medicines) | 280 |
| Operation to correct a heart disorder (paid to the attending physician and the hospital) | 6,800 |

*Convalescent Home*

(a) Under what conditions would the payments to Green Acres Rest Home qualify as medical care expenses? $12,680

(b) In the event the payments to Green Acres Rest Home do not qualify, are the other payments deductible? *drugs, & op. exces 5% AGI*

22. T uses the cash method of accounting and lives in a state that imposes an income tax (including withholding from wages). On April 14, 19X2, he files his state return for 19X1 paying an additional $500 in income taxes. During 19X2, his withholdings for state income tax purposes amount to $2,750. On April 13, 19X3, T files his state return for 19X2 claiming a refund of $125. The refund is received by T on August 3, 19X3.

    (a) If T itemizes his deductions, how much may he claim as a deduction for state income taxes on his Federal return for calendar year 19X2 (filed in April 19X3)?

    (b) How will the refund of $125 received in 19X3 be treated for Federal income tax purposes?

23. In County Z the real property tax year is the calendar year. The real property tax becomes a personal liability of the owner of real property on January 1 in the current real property tax year 19X1. The tax is payable on July 1, 19X1. On May 1, 19X1, A sells his house to B, who uses the cash method of accounting, but B reports his income on the basis of a fiscal year ending July 31. On July 1, 19X1, B pays the entire real estate tax for the year ending December 31, 19X1. How much of the real estate tax for 19X1 is considered to be imposed on B?

24. X is married, has two dependent children, and files a joint return with his wife. During 1982, their adjusted gross income was $35,000, which included 40% of a $2,000 net capital gain (i. e., $800 was included). He also had $2,000 of tax-exempt interest income. X acquired a new automobile during the year; and he paid $550 of state, county, and local sales tax on the purchase. X is a resident of Texas, which imposes a 4% general state sales tax. County and local sales taxes (not included in the table) amount to a total of 2% of consumer purchases.

    (a) Calculate X's sales tax deductions using the table in Appendix A.

    (b) If X's actual payments of sales tax were greater than the amount determined above, which amount should be deducted?

25. X is married and files a joint tax return for 19X5. X has investment interest expense of $95,000 for a loan made to him in 19X5 to purchase a parcel of unimproved land. His income from investments (dividends, capital gains, and interest) totaled $15,000 and investment expenses amounted to $2,500. Consequently, his net investment income is $12,500 ($15,000 less $2,500). X also has $3,000 as a net long-term capital gain from the sale of another parcel of unimproved land. Calculate X's investment interest deduction for 19X5.

26. A, B, and C are equal owners in the X Corporation. All three shareholders make loans to X Corporation in 19X1 and receive interest-bearing notes. A and B are brothers, and C is their uncle. All three owners are on the cash method of accounting, while X Corporation is on the accrual method. A, B, C, and X Corporation use a calendar year for tax purposes. Can X Corporation deduct the interest payments made to A, B, and C on April 1, 19X2, for 19X1?

27. Dr. X, a famous heart surgeon practicing in Chicago, performs heart surgery in charitable hospitals around the state during one day of each week. He incurs $250 per week in travel and related expenses pursuant to the rendition of these services. He receives no compensation for the services, nor is he reimbursed for the travel expenses. Assume his professional fees average $3,000 per operation and that he normally performs two operations each day. Based on these facts, what is Dr. X's charitable contribution deduction for the year?

28. Determine the amount of the charitable deduction allowed in each of the following situations:

    (a) Donation of X Corporation stock (a publicly traded corporation) to taxpayer's church. The stock cost the taxpayer $2,000 four months ago and has a fair market value of $3,000 on the date of the donation.

    (b) Donation of a painting to the Salvation Army. The painting cost the taxpayer $2,000 five years ago and has a fair market value of $3,500 on the date of the donation.

    (c) The local branch of the American Red Cross uses a building rent-free for half of the current year. The building normally rents for $500 a month.

    (d) Donation by a cash basis farmer to a church of a quantity of grain worth $900. The grain was raised by the farmer in the preceding year at a cost of $650, all of which was deducted for income tax purposes.

29. T, an individual with an adjusted gross income of $60,000 in 19X3, contributed 100 shares of IBM stock to a local college. The adjusted basis of the IBM stock was $250 per share, and its fair market value was $400 per share on the date of the gift. The stock was acquired in 19X1 and contributed to the college in 19X3.

    (a) Calculate the amount of the gift which qualifies for the charitable contribution deduction.

    (b) How are excess amounts, if any, treated?

30. An individual taxpayer, M, had adjusted gross income of $30,000. She contributed $12,000 to a public charity and $9,000 to a private foundation in 19X1.

    (a) Calculate the total contribution deduction for 19X1.

    (b) How are any excess amounts treated?

31. On December 30, 19X1, T purchased four tickets to a charity ball sponsored by the City of Mobile and for the benefit of underprivileged children. Each ticket cost $100 and had a fair market value of $25. On the same day as their purchase, T gave the tickets to the minister of her church for the personal use by his family. At the time of the gift of the tickets, T pledged $1,000 to the building fund of her church. The pledge was satisfied by check dated December 31, 19X1, but not mailed until January 3, 19X2.

    (a) Presuming T is a cash basis and calendar year taxpayer, how much can be deducted as a charitable contribution for 19X1?

    (b) Would the amount of the deduction be any different if T is an accrual basis taxpayer? Explain.

32. Classify each of the independent expenditures appearing below as nondeductible (ND) items, business (*dfor*) deductions, or itemized (*dfrom*) deductions. (Note: In many cases, it may be necessary to refer to the materials contained in the earlier chapters of the text.)

(a) Interest on home mortgage accrued by a cash basis taxpayer. ND

(b) State income taxes paid by a sole proprietor of a business. D From

(c) Subscription to *The Wall Street Journal* paid by a vice-president of a bank and not reimbursed by her employer. D From

(d) Automobile mileage for attendance at weekly church services. ND

(e) Street paving assessment paid to the county by a homeowner. ND

(f) Speeding ticket paid by the owner-operator of a taxicab. ND

(g) Interest and taxes paid by the owner of residential rental property. d for

(h) Business entertainment expenses (properly substantiated) paid by a self-employed taxpayer. d for

(i) State and Federal excise taxes on tobacco paid by a self-employed taxpayer who gave his clients cigars as Christmas presents. The business gifts were properly substantiated and under $25 each. d for

(j) State and Federal excise taxes on cigarettes purchased by a heavy smoker for personal consumption. ND

(k) Federal excise taxes (i. e., nine cents per gallon) on the purchase of gasoline for use in the taxpayer's personal automobile. ND

(l) Theft loss of personal jewelry worth $300 but which originally cost $75. dfrom

(m) Maternity clothing purchased by a taxpayer who is pregnant. ND

(n) Stretch bandage purchased by a taxpayer with a "trick" knee. dfrom

(o) An electric toothbrush purchased by a taxpayer whose dentist recommended its use to alleviate a gum disorder. dfrom

(p) Medical expenses paid by an employer on behalf of an employee. dfor

(q) Interest paid by a taxpayer on a loan obtained to build an artist studio in his personal residence. Assume that taxpayer's art activities are classified as a hobby. From

(r) Assume the same facts as in q, (except that the art activities are classified as a trade or business.) For

## Cumulative Problems

33. A and N, both 27, are married with one dependent child. They file a joint return. A and N had the following receipts in 1983.

| | | |
|---|---|---:|
| (1) | A's salary. | $ 20,000 |
| (2) | N's salary. | 15,000 |
| (3) | Dividends on domestic stock owned by A | 200 |
| (4) | Reimbursement of 1983 medical bills by insurance company. | 1,600 |
| (5) | Expense allowance from A's employer to cover business expenses incurred by A. | 750 |
| (6) | Selling price of a parcel of land they had held for two years as an investment (basis was $5,000). | 7,000 |
| (7) | Reimbursement by A's employer of A's dues in a professional organization related to A's work. | 150 |

(8) Dividends received on X Corporation stock owned by N before marriage (A and N live in a common law state). X Corporation is a domestic corporation. 200

(9) Dividends on Y Corporation stock (jointly owned). Y Corporation is a domestic corporation. 100

(10) Interest on corporate coupon bonds owned by N's father, who clipped the coupons shortly before the interest payment date and gave them to N. 500

(11) Payment to A by insurance company of disability benefits under a medical and disability insurance policy; A, who was injured and unable to work for four weeks, had acquired and paid the premiums on the policy. 800

(12) Refund of Federal income tax withheld in 1982. 400

A and N had receipts and other documentary evidence for the following disbursements made in 1983:

(13) Business expenses incurred by A [see (5) for reimbursement information] included business travel, $600, and business entertainment, $400. $ 1,000

(14) Contribution to United Way. 520

(15) Premiums for health insurance coverage. 400

(16) Prescription drugs and medicines. 420

(17) Nonprescription drugs and medicines. 60

(18) Doctor bills. 800

(19) Hospital bills. 2,200

(20) Contact lenses for N. 150

(21) Interest on home mortgage. 3,000

(22) Interest on charge accounts. 120

(23) Real property taxes on their residence. 729

(24) State sales tax on new automobile purchased in December 1983 (A and N live in West Virginia). 325

(25) State income tax paid in April 1983, when they filed their state income tax return for 1982. 70

(26) Fee for preparation of 1982 tax returns. 100

(27) Professional dues and subscriptions for N. 85

A's personal automobile was totaled in November 1983 when it caught fire because of a leak in the fuel line. A had paid $2,200 for the auto two years ago. Its fair market value on the date of the fire was $1,400. A carried only liability insurance on the auto and received no reimbursement from his insurance company. He sold the auto to a salvage company for $500.

Federal income tax withheld by their employers totaled $5,033, and state income tax withheld totaled $700. Estimated federal tax payments were $400. They are entitled to a political contributions credit of $100.

Compute taxable income for 1983 for A and N. Assume A does not render an adequate accounting to his employer but has the records necessary to substantiate employee expenses.

34. H and W are married taxpayers, age 44 and 42, respectively, who file a joint return. In 1983, H was employed as an assistant manager of a depart-

ment store at a salary of $26,000. W is a high school teacher and earned $16,000. W has two children, ages 13 and 15, from a previous marriage. The children reside with H and W throughout the school year and reside with F, W's former husband, during the summer. Pursuant to the divorce decree, F pays $100 per month per child for each of the nine months during which W has custody of the children, but the decree is silent as to which parent may claim the exemptions. F says that he spends $200 a month supporting each child during the three summer months when the children live with him. W can document that she and H provided support of $1,600 for each child in 1983.

In August H and W decided to add a "mother-in-law" suite to their home to provide more comfortable accommodations for W's mother who had moved in with them the preceding February after the death of W's father. Not wanting to borrow the money for this addition at the current high interest rates, H and W sold 400 shares of stock for $30 a share and used the $12,000 to cover construction costs. They had purchased the stock four years ago for $20 a share. They received dividends of $100 on the jointly owned stock prior to the sale.

W's mother is 66 years old and drew $3,600 in Social Security benefits during the year, of which she gave H and W $1,200 to use toward household expenses and deposited $2,400 in her personal savings account. H and W estimate that they spent a minimum of $1,500 of their own money for food, clothing, medical expenses, and other items for M, not counting the rental value of the portion of the house she occupies.

H and W received $1,600 interest on some municipal bonds they had bought in 1983. H had heard from a friend that municipal bonds were paying good rates and that municipal bond interest was not taxable. To finance the purchase of the bonds, he borrowed $20,000 from the bank at 10% interest, figuring the deduction for interest would save him enough to make the investment worthwhile. He paid the bank $2,000 interest during 1983.

Other interest paid during the year included $3,530 on their home mortgage and $106 on various charge accounts.

W's favorite uncle died in October and willed W 50 shares of stock worth $25 per share. She received a dividend of $2 a share on the stock late in the year.

In December 1983, H was riding a snowmobile he had just acquired for $4,200. In his eagerness to try it out, he neglected two things: First, he had forgotten to insure it. Second, he had not taken time to read the operating instructions. As a result of his lack of familiarity with the snowmobile, he lost control of it as he was headed toward a large, concrete barn. Fortunately, H was able to jump off before the crash and escaped injury. The barn was not damaged. The snowmobile, however, was demolished. H sold it back to the dealer for parts for $200.

W incurred travel expenses of $600 while attending a teacher's convention. On the second day of the convention, she attended a workshop for which she paid an enrollment fee of $50. The school district which employs her does not reimburse her for either travel expenses or educational expenses.

H and W paid doctor and hospital bills of $2,800 and were reimbursed by their insurance company for $1,400. Medicines and drugs cost them $600, and premiums on their health insurance policy were $450. Included in the amounts paid for hospital bills was $800 for W's mother; and of the $600 spent for medicines and drugs, $300 was for W's mother.

Taxes paid during the year included $1,120 property taxes on their home, sales tax of $325 on the purchase of a new automobile, and state income taxes (withheld) of $840. In March 1983, H and W received a refund on their 1982 state income taxes of $140. They reside in Wisconsin. They had itemized deductions on their 1982 return and had received a tax benefit for the full amount of state income taxes reported.

H and W contribute $20 a week to their church and have cancelled checks for these contributions totaling $1,040. In addition, H's employer withheld $260 from his check, per his instructions, as a contribution to United Way. H and W also have a receipt from the Salvation Army for some used clothing the family had contributed. H and W estimated the value of the clothes at $200.

H and W had $5,773 of Federal income tax withheld in 1983, and paid estimated Federal income tax of $800.

Compute taxable income for H and W for 1983.


## Cumulative Tax Return Problem

35. T, age 45, is married and has two dependent children. In 1982, he incurred the following:

| | |
|---|---:|
| (1) Salary received from his employer | $ 60,000 |
| (2) Cost of art supplies. T took up painting as a hobby and plans to sell the paintings to friends and art galleries but had no willing purchasers during 1982. | 1,000 |
| (3) Contribution of 20 shares of X Corporation stock to his church (fair market value of $1,000, cost of $400, and acquired in 1976). | 1,000 |
| (4) T's wife had a diamond ring which was stolen by her maid in April 1982. A police report was filed but the ring was not recovered. It is not covered by insurance, and the maid was not prosecuted. The ring had been recently appraised at $2,000, which was also its original cost. | 2,000 |
| (5) Travel and auto expenses incurred in connection with T's employment (none of which were reimbursed) | 2,500 |

(6) T and his family moved from Nashville to Providence during the year and incurred the following unreimbursed expenses:

| | | |
|---|---:|---:|
| Moving van | $ 2,500 | |
| Temporary relocation and house-hunting expenses | 1,800 | |
| Selling commissions on the former home | 3,500 | 7,800 |

(7) T paid and incurred the following personal expenses:

| | |
|---|---:|
| Medical and dental bills for the family | 1,500 |
| Hospital insurance premiums | 500 |
| State and local taxes | 4,500 |

Required:

Determine T's adjusted gross income and taxable income for 1982, assuming that a joint return is filed and that there are no other items of income or deduction. Preparation of pages 1 and 2 and Schedules A and B of Form 1040 and Forms 3903 and 2106 is suggested.

# Chapter 8

# Tax Credits

## TAX POLICY CONSIDERATIONS

In recent years, Congress has increased its reliance on tax credits as a means of implementing tax policy objectives. This trend is evidenced by numerous provisions in recent tax acts which either modify old credits (such as the investment tax credit, child and dependent care credit, rehabilitation credit, and the targeted jobs credit) or introduce new credits (including the payroll-based ESOP credit and the research and experimentation credit).

A tax credit should not be confused with an income tax deduction. Certain deductions for individuals are permitted as deductions from gross income in arriving at adjusted gross income (e. g., business expenses or certain unreimbursed employee expenses). Additionally, individuals are permitted to deduct nonbusiness personal and investment-related expenses *from* adjusted gross income. A tax credit is generally worth substantially more to a taxpayer, since the credit is directly offset against the tax liability; however, a deduction merely reduces taxable income.

**Example 1.** T has paid a 15% Canadian withholding tax in the amount of $3,000 on royalties for books published in that country. This item qualifies as either a business deduction or a tax credit. T's marginal tax rate is 50%. Use of the tax as a deduction produces a $1,500 tax reduction ($3,000 × 50%). However, a tax credit would provide a $3,000 tax reduction.

Tax credits generally are used by Congress to achieve social or economic objectives or to provide equity for different types of taxpayers. For example, the investment tax credit, introduced by the Kennedy administration in 1962, was expected to encourage growth in the economy, improve the competitive position of American industry at home and abroad, and help alleviate the nation's balance of payments problem.[1]

One reason for the increased popularity of tax credits as a means of implementing tax policy is that tax credits provide benefits on a more equitable basis when compared with tax deductions.

> **Example 2.** Assume Congress wishes to encourage a certain type of expenditure. One way to accomplish this objective would be to allow a tax credit of 25% for such expenditures. Another way to accomplish this objective would be to allow an itemized deduction for the expenditures. Assume taxpayer A's marginal tax rate is 15%, while taxpayer B's marginal rate is 50%. The tax benefits available to each taxpayer, for a $1,000 expenditure, are summarized below.

|  | Taxpayer A | Taxpayer B |
|---|---|---|
| Tax benefit if a 25% credit is allowed | $ 250 | $ 250 |
| Tax benefit if an itemized deduction is allowed | $ 150 | $ 500 |

These results make it clear that tax credits provide benefits on a more equitable basis than tax deductions. This is even more apparent considering the fact that the deduction approach would benefit only those taxpayers who itemize deductions, while the credit approach benefits all taxpayers who make the specified expenditure.

# SPECIFIC BUSINESS-RELATED TAX CREDIT PROVISIONS

## INVESTMENT TAX CREDIT

The investment tax credit was initially enacted in 1962 and has been a significant fiscal policy tool for controlling the economy. The tax credit on the purchase of certain types of business property presumably acts to encourage expansion and investment. The resulting expansion stimulates the economy and generates additional employment.

---

1. Summary of remarks of the Secretary of the Treasury, quoted in S. Rep. No. 1881, 87th Cong., 2nd Sess., reported in 1962–3 C.B. 707.

The investment credit has been suspended, reinstated, repealed, and reenacted in response to varying economic conditions and political pressures. In addition, many specific operational and definitional rules have been modified.

These changes in the tax law have created a nightmare for tax practitioners. Both suspension and reenactment of the investment credit have necessitated the adoption of special transitional rules relative to qualification and to the carryback and carryover of unused credits. Further complications have been created by modifications of what constitutes qualified investment credit property. As a result of these changes, the Code contains numerous provisions relative to specific suspension and reenactment years and other transitional rules.

*Amount of the Credit.*  The Economic Recovery Tax Act of 1981 (ERTA) made several significant changes in the investment tax credit area, some of which were necessary to conform to the new accelerated cost recovery system (ACRS) rules. Under the ACRS provisions, an asset is assigned a recovery period of three, five, ten, or fifteen years, depending on the nature of the asset (refer to Chapter 6). The investment credit for property placed in service after 1980 is based on the recovery period under ACRS, as shown below.[2]

| Recovery Period (in years) | Percentage of Credit |
|---|---|
| 3 | 6 |
| 5, 10, and 15 | 10 |

The limitation on used property qualifying for the credit is $125,000 for 1981 through 1984 and $150,000 beginning in 1985.[3]

**Example 3.**  In 1983, T acquired and placed in service the following assets: automobile, $9,000; light-duty truck, $12,000; office furniture, $2,500; and an airplane, $120,000. T's tentative investment credit would be computed as follows:

| Qualifying Property | Cost | Recovery Period | Percentage of Credit | Investment Tax Credit |
|---|---|---|---|---|
| Automobile | $    9,000 | 3 years | 6% | $      540 |
| Light-duty truck | $   12,000 | 3 years | 6% | 720 |
| Office furniture | $    2,500 | 5 years | 10% | 250 |
| Airplane | $ 120,000 | 5 years | 10% | 12,000 |
| Tentative investment credit | | | | $ 13,510 |

---

2.   § 46(c).
3.   § 48(c)(2).

The amount computed above is described as a tentative investment credit because the allowable credit for any year is subject to certain ceiling limitations (see Example 6).

*Reduced Credit Election.* The Tax Equity and Fiscal Responsibility Act of 1982 contained two major provisions to reduce the rate of cost recovery. First, the step-up in rates for computing cost recovery allowances, scheduled to be phased in after 1984, has been eliminated (see Chapter 6). Second, taxpayers are required to reduce the basis for depreciation by 50 percent of the amount of the credit taken.[4] This basis reduction requirement applies to property placed in service after 1982.

> **Example 4.** In 1983, T purchases a machine, which is five-year ACRS property, for $10,000. T takes a $1,000 investment credit on the property (10% of $10,000). Under the new TEFRA provision, the basis of the property must be reduced by $500 [½ of $1,000 (investment credit)]. Thus, T's cost recovery allowance will be based on $9,500 [$10,000 (cost) − $500 (reduction for investment credit)].

The 50 percent basis reduction rule applies to the following: regular investment credit property, energy credit property, and certified historic property. The basis of properties to which the 15 or 20 percent rehabilitation credit applies must still be reduced by the full amount of the credit.

As an alternative to reducing the basis of the property, a taxpayer may elect to take a reduced investment credit. Under this election, the investment credit is eight percent (rather than 10 percent) for recovery property that is not three-year property, and four percent (instead of six percent) for three-year property.[5]

Upon sale of the asset in the future, the reduction in basis will be treated as depreciation for purposes of applying the recapture provisions. However, the basis of the property disposed of will be increased by one-half the amount of the investment credit to be recaptured. This increase occurs immediately before the disposition (or other event) that triggers recapture of depreciation.[6]

Computation of the investment credit under the reduced credit election is illustrated in Example 5.

> **Example 5.** Assume the same facts as in Example 3 except that T elects to take the reduced investment credit to avoid reducing the basis of the properties acquired. T's investment credit decreases from $13,510 (without the election) to $10,640 as shown below:

---

4. § 48(q)(1).
5. § 48(q)(4).
6. § 48(q)(5).

| Qualifying Property | Cost | Recovery Period | Percentage of Credit | Investment Tax Credit |
|---|---|---|---|---|
| Automobile | $ 9,000 | 3 years | 4% | $ 360 |
| Light-duty truck | $ 12,000 | 3 years | 4% | 480 |
| Office furniture | $ 2,500 | 5 years | 8% | 200 |
| Airplane | $ 120,000 | 5 years | 8% | 9,600 |
| Tentative investment credit | | | | $ 10,640 |

*Ceiling Limitations.* The maximum allowable investment credit beginning in 1983 is 100 percent of the first $25,000 of tax liability plus 85 percent of the tax liability in excess of $25,000.[7] The limitation is imposed on the amount of the tax liability computed in the regular manner without regard to any minimum tax (§ 56) or other special taxes, such as the accumulated earnings tax, which have been imposed. This regular tax liability is reduced by certain tax credits (e. g., the foreign tax credit) to compute the limitation. Controlled corporate groups are required to apportion the basic $25,000 limitation. The basic limitation for married taxpayers filing separately is $12,500 unless one of the spouses is not entitled to the investment credit.[8]

**Example 6.** T acquired $600,000 of qualified investment credit property (with a five-year recovery period) in 1983. His tax liability, without regard to special taxes, was $50,000. The computation of unused investment credit is illustrated below:

| | 1983 |
|---|---|
| Qualified investment credit ($600,000 × 10%) | $ 60,000 |
| Total credit allowed [$25,000 + (85% × $25,000)] | 46,250 |
| Unused investment credit | $ 13,750 |

*Treatment of Unused Investment Credits.* Unused credits are initially carried back three years (to the earliest year in the sequence) and are applied to reduce any amounts in excess of the ceiling during these years. Thus, the taxpayer may receive a refund of tax from the benefits of such carryback. Any remaining unused credits are then carried forward for 15 years.[9] Carryovers from pre-1971 years are permitted a 10-year carryover and are used up before applying the regular credits for the carryover year. For 1976 and later years, a FIFO method is applied to the carryovers, carrybacks, and utilization of credits earned during a particular year. The oldest credits are used first in determining the amount of investment credit.

---

7. § 46(a)(3)(B).
8. § 46(a)(5).
9. § 46(b).

The FIFO method minimizes the potential for a loss of investment credit benefit due to the expiration of credit carryovers, since the earliest years are used before the current credit for the taxable year.

**Example 7.** This example illustrates the use of investment credit carryovers:

| | | |
|---|---:|---:|
| —Investment credit carryovers: | | |
| 1980 | $ 4,000 | |
| 1981 | 6,000 | |
| 1982 | 2,000 | |
| Total carryovers | $ 12,000 | |
| —1983 investment credit: | | |
| 10 % × $400,000 qualified investment in 5-year property | | $ 40,000 |
| —Total credit allowed in 1983 (based on tax liability) | $ 50,000 | |
| Less:  Utilization of carryovers | | |
| 1980 | 4,000 | |
| 1981 | 6,000 | |
| 1982 | 2,000 | |
| —Remaining credit allowed | $ 38,000 | |
| Applied against: | | |
| 1983 investment credit | | (38,000) |
| 1983 unused amount carried forward to 1984 | | $  2,000 |

*Recapture of Investment Tax Credit.*  The amount of the investment tax credit is based on the recovery period of the qualifying property (see Example 3). However, if property is disposed of (or ceases to be qualified investment credit property) prior to the end of the recovery period, the taxpayer must recapture all or a portion of the investment credit originally taken.[10] The amount of investment tax credit which is recaptured in the year of premature disposition (or disqualification as investment credit property) is added to the taxpayer's regular tax liability for that year. Recapture provisions were created to prevent taxpayers from assigning an artificially long useful life to qualified investment credit property in order to maximize the credit.

The portion of the credit recaptured is a specified percentage of the credit which was taken by the taxpayer.[11] This percentage is based on the period the investment credit property was held by the taxpayer, as shown in Figure I:

---

10.  § 47(a)(5).
11.  § 47(a)(5).

**Figure I**

| If the Property Is Held For | The Recapture Percentage Is | |
|---|---|---|
| | For 15-year, 10-year, and 5-year Property | For 3-year Property |
| Less than 1 year | 100 | 100 |
| One year or more but less than 2 years | 80 | 66 |
| Two years or more but less than 3 years | 60 | 33 |
| Three years or more but less than 4 years | 40 | 0 |
| Four years or more but less than 5 years | 20 | 0 |
| Five years or more | 0 | 0 |

**Example 8.** T acquired an automobile (three-year recovery property) for $10,000 on January 3, 1982, and took an investment tax credit of $600 (6% of $10,000) in that year. T also acquired office furniture (five-year recovery property) on January 3, 1982, at a cost of $5,000. T's investment tax credit on the office furniture was $500 (10% of $5,000). T sold both pieces of property in June 1983. Since T held the assets more than one year but less than two, he is required to recapture $396 (66% of $600) of investment tax credit on the automobile and $400 on the office furniture (80% of $500). The effect of the recapture requirement is to increase T's 1983 tax liability by the $796 of investment tax credit recaptured ($396 + $400).

Recapture of investment credit generally is triggered by the following:

—Disposition of property through sale, exchange, or sale-and-leaseback transactions.

—Retirement or abandonment of property or conversion to personal use.

—Gifts of § 38 property.

—Transfers to partnerships and corporations unless certain conditions are met.

—Like-kind exchanges (certain exceptions are provided).

Exceptions are provided for in the Code to prevent inequities. The following transactions illustrate some situations to which the recapture provisions are not applicable:

—A transfer of property to an estate by reason of death.

—A transfer pursuant to certain tax-free reorganizations.

—A liquidation of a subsidiary corporation where the assets are transferred to the parent without receiving a change in basis.

Prior to the Economic Recovery Tax Act of 1981, the investment tax credit was computed differently. As a result, the recapture provisions were also different. Even though the 1981 Act changed the investment credit and recapture rules for property placed in service after 1980, the pre-1981 recapture rules continue to apply to premature dispositions of property placed in service before 1981. The pre-1981 rules are covered in a later section of this chapter (see Example 14 and related discussion).

*Qualifying Property.* Qualifying property (called § 38 property) for 1971 and subsequent years includes the following types of property which is placed in service during the year.[12]

—Tangible personal property (other than an air-conditioning or heating unit) which is depreciable and has a useful life of at least three years.

—Other tangible depreciable property (excluding buildings and their structural components) with a useful life of at least three years if used in manufacturing, production, or extraction, or in furnishing transportation or certain public utility services.

—New elevators and escalators.

—Coin-operated vending and washing machines and dryers.

—Livestock (excluding horses).

The credit is also available for:

—Assets accessory to a business (e. g., grocery store counters, printing presses).

—Assets of a mechanical nature, even though located outside a building (e. g., gasoline pumps).

—Single-purpose livestock and horticulture structures or enclosures.

—Pollution control facilities. Generally, for years after 1978, 100 percent of the credit is available for the portion of the basis of the property that is being rapidly amortized over 60 months. In 1977 and 1978, only 50 percent of such property was eligible for the investment credit; and for years prior to 1977, none of the basis of rapidly amortized pollution control facilities was eligible.

The investment credit is not permitted for the following types of property.

—Intangible property (e. g., patents, copyrights).

—Buildings and their structural components including central air-conditioning, plumbing, and wiring units.

---

12. § 48(a).

—Property (other than coin-operated vending and washing machines and dryers) used primarily for nontransient lodging (such as the operation of an apartment building).

—Certain property used outside of the U. S.

—Foreign-produced property whenever temporary import surcharge is in effect (as determined by the President of the U. S.).

—Property such as rehabilitation expenditures for low-income housing, certain child care facility expenditures when a special 60-month amortization provision is elected.

—Certain property leased by noncorporate lessors.

—Generally, boilers fueled by oil or gas.

It is sometimes difficult to determine whether an item is tangible personal property and therefore eligible for the investment credit or whether such property constitutes a structural component of a building which is not eligible. An item is generally considered to be tangible personal property if it can be removed without causing structural damage to the building. For example, movable partitions are considered tangible personal property if the partitions can be moved without causing injury to the building. Window air-conditioning units no longer are qualified due to specific changes in the Energy Act of 1978 dealing with conservation issues. Also, cinderblock walls, doors, rest rooms, plumbing, office partitions, and electrical wiring do not qualify because they are of a permanent nature.

A functional use test has also been applied to determine whether a special-purpose structure qualifies for the investment credit. For example, the IRS has held that safety equipment units that service an entire building are structural components and therefore do not qualify. But comparable equipment which is necessary and used directly in the production process or the operation of a machine will qualify as tangible personal property.

Section 1.48–1 of the Regulations contains detailed rules and examples to assist in determining eligible and excluded property and should be referred to for resolving specific questions.

*Computation of Qualified Investment.*     Qualified investment credit property is the aggregate of new § 38 property which is placed in service during the year. Used § 38 property is included in the above calculation, but the maximum amount of cost is limited to $125,000.[13] The cost basis of § 38 property is determined under the general rules for determining the basis of property (e. g., basis includes installation and freight costs which are properly included in the depreciable basis of the property). If new § 38 property is acquired in a like-kind exchange, the cost basis of the newly acquired property is equal to the

---

**13.**     § 48(c)(2). For 1980, the limitation was $100,000. The $125,000 limitation applies to 1981 through 1984. It will be increased to $150,000 for years after 1984.

adjusted basis of the property exchanged plus any cash paid. Special rules apply to used property. Its cost is equal to the basis of the property, except that basis is not determined by reference to the adjusted basis of the property being replaced. Apportionment and limitation rules are provided for married individuals filing separately, controlled corporate groups, and partnerships.

> **Example 9.** In 1983, T acquired used machinery (which was five-year recovery property) for use in his business. The cost of such property was $200,000. Only $125,000 of the machinery qualifies for the investment credit due to the limitation on used property.

> **Example 10.** T traded in an automobile used in his business for a new business automobile which had a fair market value of $7,000. T paid the dealer $4,000. The basis of the automobile exchanged was $1,000. Since the transaction qualifies as a like-kind exchange (see Chapter 9), the basis of the new automobile is equal to the basis of the old automobile plus cash paid ($1,000 + $4,000). The cost for investment credit purposes is also $5,000.

> **Example 11.** Assume the same facts as in Example 10 except that T acquired a used automobile. Although the adjusted basis of the used automobile is $5,000, its cost in computing the qualified investment for investment credit purposes is only $4,000 because the $1,000 basis in the replaced automobile is not included.

*Special Rules and Exceptions.* Special rules are provided for public utilities. In general, such companies are permitted a 10 percent credit (formerly four percent) and the maximum ceiling limitations (subject to phase-out beginning in 1977) are 100 percent (formerly 50 percent) of the tax liability.[14] Utilities were granted special treatment due to their recent economic difficulties and the need for raising significant amounts of new capital to provide for replacement and capital expansion requirements.

For tax years beginning before 1983, an 11 percent credit could be claimed by all taxpayers in lieu of the regular 10 percent rate if the extra amount was contributed to an employee stock ownership plan.[15] For years beginning after 1976, an additional credit of one-half of one percent was permitted if additional amounts of employer securities were transferred to the plan and an equal amount was contributed by employees. If additional amounts were contributed, however, certain requirements had to be met in order to prevent recapture.

The Economic Recovery Tax Act of 1981 repealed these provisions

---

**14.** § 46(a)(7).

**15.** § 46(a)(1)(B).

for additional investment tax credit for contributions to employee stock ownership plans after 1982. Beginning in 1983, the maximum investment tax credit rate is 10 percent. A separate credit was enacted for contributions to employee stock ownership plans after 1982 (see discussion of the payroll-based ESOP credit later in this chapter).

A taxpayer may now elect to claim the investment credit for progress payments for property that is under construction for two or more years if the property will be new § 38 property in the hands of the taxpayer when placed in service.[16] Previously, the credit was not available until the property was placed in service. Special transitional rules are provided if this election is made.

*Investment Credit At-Risk Limitation.* Prior to 1981, there was no at-risk limitation on the allowance of investment credits. However, the Economic Recovery Tax Act of 1981 contained an at-risk limitation which applies to business activities, the losses from which are subject to limitation under the at-risk rules of § 465.[17]

> **Example 12.** T, whose business is subject to the at-risk rules of § 465, bought a machine (five-year recovery property) for $100,000 in 1983. He paid $10,000 cash and negotiated a nonrecourse note of $90,000 for the remainder. Prior to 1981, T's investment tax credit would have been $10,000 (10% of the entire cost of $100,000). However, the at-risk provisions will limit T's investment tax credit to $1,000 (10% of the $10,000 T has at risk), since T is not at risk for the nonrecourse debt. (See Appendix C, Glossary of Tax Terms, for definition of nonrecourse debt).

If the taxpayer's at-risk amount increases during the term of the loan, additional investment credit is allowed based on the increase. On the other hand, if the amount at-risk decreases, the investment credit recapture provisions will apply to the amount of the decrease.

The at-risk limitations under § 465 are extremely complex and are beyond the scope of this text. Therefore, the preceding discussion of the investment credit at-risk provisions is necessarily brief.

*Computation of Investment Credit Under Pre-ERTA Rules.* Under pre-ERTA rules (i. e., for years prior to 1981), the full amount of the investment credit was allowed (subject to certain limitations) for the acquisition of qualified property with a useful life of seven years or longer. The taxpayer was required to use the same useful life for investment credit purposes which was used for computing depreciation.[18] For property with a useful life of less than seven years, the

---

16.  § 46(d).
17.  § 46(c)(8).
18.  § 46(c)(2).

following percentages were applied to determine the amount of "qualified investment":

—66⅔% for a useful life of five or six years.

—33⅓% for a useful life of three or four years.

**Example 13.** The computation of the investment credit under pre-ERTA rules is illustrated below:

| Qualified Property | Useful Life | Adjusted Cost Basis | Percent | Qualified Investment |
|---|---|---|---|---|
| Office equipment | 7 | $ 10,000 | 100 | $ 10,000 |
| Factory machinery | 6 | 30,000 | 66 ⅔ | 20,000 |
| Automobiles | 3 | 18,000 | 33 ⅓ | 6,000 |
| Total qualified investment | | | | $ 36,000 |
| × Investment tax credit rate | | | | 10% |
| = Tentative investment credit | | | | $ 3,600 |

*Recapture of Investment Credit Under Pre-ERTA Rules.* Pre-ERTA provisions for recapture of the investment credit were, like the current rules, triggered by premature dispositions (or disqualifying use) of property on which the credit was taken. If investment credit property was prematurely disposed of or ceased to be qualified investment property, investment credit which was previously taken was recaptured in part or in full.[19]

**Example 14.** The pre-ERTA recapture of investment credit is illustrated below:

| | |
|---|---|
| Investment credit on machinery—Cost of $10,000, assigned a seven-year estimated useful life in 1977 ($10,000 × 10%) | $ 1,000.00 |
| The machinery was sold in 1983 after six years. Recomputed credit (66⅔% × $10,000 × 10%). | (666.67) |
| Recaptured amount—included in the 1983 tax | $ 333.33 |

These pre-ERTA recapture provisions still apply to property placed in service prior to 1981. Thus, pre-1981 investment credit property which is disposed of prematurely or ceases to be qualifying investment credit property will be subject to recapture as shown in Example 14. Recapture for all investment credit property, whether subject to the old or the new provisions, is reported on Form 4255. A more detailed discussion of the pre-ERTA recapture provisions is contained in the instructions for Form 4255 (see Appendix B).

---

**19.** § 47(a)(1).

## TARGETED JOBS CREDIT

The targeted jobs credit was enacted to encourage employers to hire individuals from one or more of seven target groups (including handicapped individuals, economically disadvantaged youths, Vietnam-era veterans, and ex-convicts).[20] The credit, which was scheduled to expire after December 31, 1981, was extended by ERTA through December 31, 1984, by the Tax Equity and Fiscal Responsibility Act of 1982.

The targeted jobs credit is equal to 50 percent of the first $6,000 of wages (per eligible employee) for the first year of employment and 25 percent of such wages for the second year. To qualify for the credit, an unemployed individual must be certified by a local jobs service office of a state employment security agency. The former rules which permitted retroactive certification after the employee had been hired have been amended to require certification (or a written request for certification) before the individual begins work. This provision was enacted to insure that employers could claim the credit only for new workers and not for employees who were already on the job before the employer learned of the availability of the credit. The intent, obviously, is to allow the credit for new jobs rather than existing jobs.

Under prior law, qualified wages of first-year employees were limited to 30 percent of the total Federal unemployment insurance wages paid for all employees. This ceiling limitation has been repealed. However, the provision which limits the credit to 90 percent of the employer's tax liability (after being reduced by certain specified tax credits) still applies. Unused credits may be carried back to the preceding three years and carried forward to the succeeding 15 years.[21] In addition, the employer's tax deduction for wages is reduced by the amount of the credit.[22]

> **Example 15.** In 1983, T Company hires four handicapped individuals (certified to be eligible employees for the targeted jobs credit). Each of these employees is paid wages of $7,000 during 1983. Assuming the limitation applicable to the jobs credit does not apply (i. e., the 90 percent limit referred to above), T Company's targeted jobs credit is $12,000 [($6,000 × 50%) × 4 employees]. If the tax credit is taken, T Company must reduce its deduction for wages paid by $12,000.

*TEFRA Changes in Targeted Jobs Credit.* Involuntarily terminated CETA employees have been eliminated as a targeted group. Wages paid to these CETA employees continue to qualify for the credit, however, if the employee was hired before 1983.[23] However, a

---

**20.**  § 51.
**21.**  § 53(b) as amended by ERTA.
**22.**  § 280C.
**23.**  § 51(d).

new group—qualified summer youth employees—has been added. The purpose of this provision is to encourage employers to hire certified 16- or 17-year-old economically disadvantaged youths for summer jobs. The credit is allowed on wages for services during any 90-day period between May 1 and September 15, and applies to certified employees hired on or after May 1, 1983.[24] The maximum wages eligible for the credit are $3,000 per summer employee, and the rate of the credit is 85 percent. Thus, the maximum credit per employee is $2,550 ($3,000 × .85).[25] If the employee continues employment after the 90-day period as a member of another targeted group, the amount of wages subject to the regular targeted jobs credit must be reduced by the wages paid to the employee as a qualified summer employee.

> **Example 16.** X Corporation employs T as a qualified summer youth employee beginning May 5, 1983. After 90 days, T continues his employment as a member of a second targeted group. T was paid $3,000 as a qualified summer employee, for which X Corporation is allowed a $2,550 targeted jobs credit. As a member of the second targeted group, T is paid another $5,000. Of the $8,000 total paid to T, only $6,000 qualifies for the targeted jobs credit. This amount must be reduced by the $3,000 wages paid under the qualified summer employee program. Thus, X Corporation will be allowed an additional credit of $1,500 [($6,000 − $3,000) × .50)]. X Corporation's total targeted jobs credit based on wages paid to T in 1983 will be $4,050 ($2,550 + $1,500).

## TAX CREDIT FOR REHABILITATION EXPENDITURES

Prior to 1982, taxpayers were allowed a tax credit of 10 percent for expenditures to rehabilitate industrial and commercial buildings *or* a special 60-month amortization period for expenditures to rehabilitate certified historic structures. Effective for 1982 and future years, a new credit is substituted for these provisions. Its operating features are summarized below:[26]

| Rate of the Credit for Rehabilitation Expenses | Nature of the Property |
| --- | --- |
| 15% | Industrial and commercial buildings at least 30 years of age |
| 20% | Industrial and commercial buildings at least 40 years of age |
| 25% | Residential and nonresidential certified historic structures |

---

**24.** § 51(d)(12).
**25.** § 51(d)(12).
**26.** § 46(a)(2)(F).

The 60-month amortization election has been repealed.[27] In addition, the taxpayer is required to depreciate the rehabilitated property over a 15-year period using the straight-line method in order to qualify for the credit.[28] The basis of a rehabilitated building, other than a certified historic structure, must be reduced for the full rehabilitation credit which is taken.[29] In the case of certified historic structures placed in service after 1982, the basis must be reduced by 50 percent of the credit taken. No basis reduction was required for certified historic structures placed in service before 1983.

> **Example 17.**  T spent $50,000 to rehabilitate a 40-year-old office building. T is allowed a credit of $10,000 (20% of $50,000) for rehabilitation expenditures. T must reduce the basis of the building by the $10,000 credit and depreciate the building over a 15-year period using the straight-line method.

To qualify for the credit, buildings must be substantially rehabilitated. A building has been substantially rehabilitated if qualified rehabilitation expenditures exceed the greater of (1) the adjusted basis of the property or (2) $5,000.[30]

The rehabilitation credit must be recaptured if the rehabilitated property is disposed of prematurely or if it ceases to be qualifying property. The amount recaptured will be based on a holding period requirement of five years.[31]

The percentage recaptured is based on the period the property was qualified rehabilitation property. These percentages are shown in Figure I in the "15-year, 10-year, and 5-year" column. In effect, for each year the property is held, the taxpayer earns a credit of 20 percent of the credit originally claimed. Thus, the credit earned each year amounts to three percent (15% times 20%), four percent (20% times 20%) or five percent (25% times 20%) depending on the nature of the property rehabilitated.

## RESEARCH AND EXPERIMENTATION CREDIT

In order to encourage research and experimentation, usually described as research and development (i. e., R&D), § 44F provides a new credit of 25 percent for certain qualifying expenditures. The credit, however, applies only to the extent that the current-year expenditures exceed the average amount of research expenditures in a base period (usually, the preceding three taxable years). Subject to

---

**27.**  § 1981 Act § 212(d)(1) repealing § 191.
**28.**  § 48(g)(2)(B)(i).
**29.**  § 48(g)(5)(A).
**30.**  § 48(g)(1)(C).
**31.**  § 47(a)(5).

certain exceptions, this new provision adopts the same definition of research as used for purposes of the special income tax deduction rules under existing § 174.[32]

Research expenditures qualifying for the credit consist of (1) "in-house" expenditures for research wages and supplies, plus certain lease or other charges for research use of computers, laboratory equipment, etc.; (2) 65 percent of amounts paid (e. g., to a research firm or university) for contract research; and (3) 65 percent of corporate grants for basic research to be performed by universities or certain scientific research organizations (or of grants to certain funds organized to make basic research grants to universities). The new credit applies to research expenditures made after June 30, 1981, and before 1986.

Qualified research and experimentation expenditures not only are eligible for the 25 percent credit but also can be expensed in the year incurred (or amortized over 60 months if the taxpayer chooses).[33]

**Example 18.** X Corporation incurred incremental research and experimentation expenditures of $100,000. Assuming X Corporation is in the 46% marginal tax bracket and elects to expense the $100,000, the corporation will receive a $71,000 tax benefit for the incremental research and experimentation costs:

| | |
|---|---:|
| Research and experimentation credit ($100,000 × 25%) | $ 25,000 |
| Tax savings from deductions ($100,000 × 46%) | 46,000 |
| Total tax benefit | $ 71,000 |

Incremental research expenditures are defined as the excess of qualified research expenses for the year over the base period research expenses.[34] Generally the term "base period research expense" means the average of qualified research expenditures for the three years immediately preceding the taxable year for which the computation is being made.

**Example 19.** Y Corporation incurs qualified research and experimentation expenditures as follows: $70,000 in 1985, $50,000 in 1984, $40,000 in 1983, and $30,000 in 1982. Incremental research expenses for 1985 are computed as follows:

---

32. § 44F.
33. § 174. Also refer to discussion of rules for deduction of research and development expenditures in Chapter 6.
34. § 44F(a).

|  |  |
|---|---|
| Expenses in 1985 | $ 70,000 |
| Minus:  Average base period expenses | |
| [($50,000 + $40,000 + $30,000) ÷ 3] | 40,000 |
| Incremental expenses | $  30,000 |

Y Corporation would be entitled to a credit of $7,500 (25% of $30,000) in 1985 (subject to a specified ceiling limitation to be discussed later).

To limit the credit available for taxpayers who have incurred only small amounts of research and experimentation costs during the base period, a special rule provides that in no event shall the base period research expenses be less than 50 percent of research expenses in the determination year.

**Example 20.**  Assume the same facts as in Example 19 except that qualified research and experimentation expenses in 1985 were $100,000. Incremental research and experimentation expenditures eligible for the credit are computed as follows:

|  |  |
|---|---|
| Expenses in 1985 | $ 100,000 |
| Minus:  Base period expenses (50% of | |
| $100,000, since average ex- | |
| penses for the base period are | |
| less than 50% of 1985 expenses) | 50,000 |
| Incremental expenses | $  50,000 |

The research and experimentation credit is nonrefundable, that is, it may not exceed the tax for the year reduced by certain specified credits.[35] Any unused credit is carried back three years and forward 15 years.

Until the issuance of regulations or other interpretive pronouncements, it is difficult to determine the types of research activities for which Congress intended to allow the credit. According to § 44F(d), the term "qualified research" has the same meaning as the term "research or experimental" has under existing § 174. However, § 174 does not specifically define the term "research or experimental." Fortunately, the Regulations under § 174 provide some guidance as to the type of research which is covered:

> The term research or experimental expenditures, as used in section 174, means expenditures incurred in connection with the taxpayer's trade or business which represent re-

---

**35.**  § 44F(g)(1). The credits which reduce the tax are those having a lower section number designation than § 44F [except for credits allowable under § 31 (tax withheld on wages), § 39 (certain uses of gasoline, special fuels, and lubricating oil), and § 43 (earned income credit)].

search and development costs in the experimental or laboratory sense. The term includes generally all such costs incident to the development of an experimental or pilot model, a plant process, a product, a formula, an invention, or similar property, and the improvement of already existing property of the type mentioned. The term does not include expenditures such as those for the ordinary testing or inspection of materials or products for quality control or those for efficiency surveys, management studies, consumer surveys, advertising, or promotions.

Additional guidance is provided in the Congressional committee reports which accompanied the Economic Recovery Tax Act of 1981. According to the House report,[36] the credit is allowed for research and experimental expenditures incurred (1) to develop a new business item, (2) to improve significantly an existing business item, and (3) to apply the results of the activities noted in (1) or (2).

## EMPLOYEE STOCK OWNERSHIP CREDIT

Section 44G provides a payroll-based credit for contributions to employee stock ownership plans (commonly referred to as ESOPs).[37] The existing investment-based additional tax credit for contributions to ESOPs is repealed after 1982. Beginning in 1983, a tax credit is allowed based on a percentage of the employer's payroll to be phased in as follows:

| Year | Percentage of Employer's Payroll |
|------|----------------------------------|
| 1983–1984 | 0.5% |
| 1985–1987 | 0.75% |
| After 1987 | None unless extended |

The rationale behind these modifications of the ESOP rules is that current law falls short in spurring ESOP contributions among labor-intensive corporations. Such businesses normally do not make substantial qualified investments in machinery and equipment and therefore are not eligible for large investment tax credits.

The amount of the credit is equal to the lesser of (1) the value of employee securities transferred to the tax credit ESOP for the taxable year or (2) the applicable percentage of the amount of compensation paid or accrued to all employees under a tax credit ESOP during the taxable year.

---

**36.** H. Rep. 97–215 (Aug. 1, 1981).
**37.** § 44G(a)(1).

The maximum allowable employee stock ownership credit is 100 percent of the first $25,000 of employer's tax liability plus 90 percent of the employer's tax liability in excess of $25,000. Tax liability in this regard is defined as the employer's regular tax liability for the year reduced by the total tax credits allowed by Code sections numbered below § 44G (with the exception of those credits provided for by § § 31, 39, and 43).

Excess employee stock ownership credit can be carried back to each of the three preceding taxable years (including taxable years ending before 1983) then carried forward to each of the 15 taxable years following the unused credit year. Any unused credit carryover which would expire at the end of the last taxable year to which it may be carried is allowed as a deduction.

There are special rules for companies whose rates are regulated (e. g., public utilities) limiting the use of the credit to the degree the credit will influence the rate-setting process.

The employee stock ownership credit is available if the corporation meets certain requirements:

1.  The corporation's plan must meet the § 409A requirements (qualifications for tax credit employee stock ownership plans).

2.  No more than one-third of the employer contributions for the taxable year can be allocated to a group of employees consisting of officers, shareholders owning more than 10 percent of the voting stock or 10 percent of total value of all stock, and highly compensated individuals as described in § 415(c)(6)(B)(iii) (for 1981, those employees whose annual compensation exceeds $83,000).

3.  The corporation must make timely transfers of the employer securities (within 30 days after the due date for filing the tax return for the taxable year).

**Example 21.** In 1983, XYZ Corporation, which files on the calendar year, transfers $4,000 of their corporate stock to their employee stock ownership plan. XYZ Corporation paid gross wages and salaries of $1,200,000 of which $900,000 was paid to employees who qualify under the plan. The credit determined by applying the applicable percentage to qualified compensation is $4,500 (.5% × $900,000). The employee stock ownership credit is limited to the lesser of the value of employer securities transferred to the plan ($4,000) or the amount determined by applying the applicable percentage to qualified compensation ($4,500). Provided that XYZ Corporation has a regular tax liability of at least $4,000 and no other credits to consider, it will be able to currently use the allowable credit of $4,000.

# OTHER TAX CREDITS

## ENERGY TAX CREDITS

*Residential.* Section 44C provides individual homeowners and renters with two separate tax credits: one for energy conservation expenditures (installation of insulation and other energy-conserving components) and the other for renewable energy source property.[38] All such expenditures must be made for property installed in or on the taxpayer's principal residence. The total credit allowed for the tax year is the sum of the two energy credits.

In addition to the installation of insulation, energy-conserving components include the following:

—Specially designed furnace replacement burners.

—A device for modifying flue openings to increase the efficiency of the heating system.

—Furnace ignition systems which replace a gas pilot light.

—Storm or thermal windows or doors (exterior).

—Energy-saving setback thermostats.

—Caulking or weatherstripping of exterior doors or windows.

—Meters which display the cost of energy usage.

The tax credit for energy conservation expenditures is 15 percent of the first $2,000 of qualifying expenditures, and the maximum credit is $300.

Renewable energy source property expenditures include those for solar, wind, or geothermal energy devices. For years after 1979, the credit is equal to 40 percent of qualifying expenditures up to $10,000, subject to an overall ceiling limitation of $4,000.[39]

Expenditures made on or after April 20, 1977, through 1985 will qualify for the credit. No credit is allowed if the credit computed amounts to less than $10. The credits are nonrefundable; but if the total credit exceeds the taxpayer's tax liability, the excess amount is allowed as a credit carryover (but no carryover is allowed to tax years beginning after December 31, 1987).

> **Example 22.** In 1983, T installs the following energy-conserving materials and equipment in his principal residence: insulation, $1,200; storm doors, $800; caulking and weatherstripping, $400. (Assume no energy credits were claimed in prior years.) These expenditures qualify for the residential energy credit. However, T's credit is limited to $300 (15% of the first $2,000 of qualifying expenditures). Because the total expenditures amount to $2,400, the excess expenditures of $400 are not eligible for the credit. If T's tax liability (before deduction of the credit) is only

---

**38.**   § 44C(a).

**39.**   § 44C(b)(2).

Max Credit $300

$200, a tax credit of $200 is allowed in 1983, and $100 of the credit will be carried over to 1984.

If a taxpayer acquires another principal residence to replace a former residence during the period the credits are in effect, both credits (energy conservation and renewable energy source) start anew.

For purposes of determining the amount of the residential energy tax credit for a tax year, the maximum qualifying expenditures must be reduced by the amount of the expenditures that qualified for the energy tax credit in previous years.

> **Example 23.** In 1981, K had qualified residential renewable energy source expenditures of $6,000. A credit of $2,400 (40% × $6,000) is allowed for that year. In 1983, K incurs additional renewable energy source expenditures of $5,000 on the same residence. The maximum amount of renewable energy source expenditures which qualify in 1983 is $4,000 ($10,000 − $6,000). Thus, of the $5,000 of expenditures in 1983, $4,000 is subject to the 40% credit (for a total residential energy credit in 1983 of $1,600). K receives no energy tax credit for the remaining $1,000 of 1983 expenditures, and no further renewable energy source expenditures by K on the same residence are eligible for the tax credit.

If any of the energy conservation expenditures or the renewable energy source expenditures result in an addition to the basis (see Chapter 9) of the residence, the amount of such addition is reduced by the energy tax credit allowed.[40]

Form 5695, Energy Credits, is used to claim the energy credits (see Appendix B).

*Business.* Energy tax credits are also extended to businesses to create incentives for conservation and to penalize increased use of oil or gas. The investment credit provisions have been amended to include additional tax credits of 10 to 15 percent for certain energy property. If the property also qualifies as investment credit property, a total credit of 20 to 25 percent is allowed. Qualifying energy property generally must be completed or acquired new after September 30, 1978, and before 1986.

The business energy tax credit applies to the following:

—Solar, wind, or geothermal property (10 percent for the period from October 1, 1978, through 1979, and 15 percent for periods after 1979 through 1985).

—Ocean thermal property (15 percent for periods after 1979 and through 1985 only).

—Small-scale hydroelectric generating property (11 percent for periods after 1979 and through 1985 only).

---

**40.** § 1016(a)(21).

—Intercity busses (10 percent for periods after 1979 and through 1985 only).

—Biomass property (e. g., boiler, burners, and related pollution control, and fuel-handling equipment) (10 percent for periods from October 1, 1978, through 1985).

—Certain other business energy property not included in the above categories (10 percent for periods from October 1, 1978, through 1985).

The business energy credit is limited to 100 percent of tax liability. It is deducted after the regular investment credit and is subject to the same carryover rules as the regular investment credit. Until January 1, 1980, the credit for solar and wind energy property was refundable and treated as a prepayment of income tax. This refundable feature has been repealed for years after 1979. Also, any such business energy tax credit applicable to qualified solar and wind energy property after 1979 and carried back to years before 1980 is not eligible to be refunded.

If property is disposed of prior to the end of its useful life, the credit is recaptured in the same manner as the investment credit. This additional energy credit differs from the regular investment credit, however, in that it is available for qualifying property even though the property is considered a structural component of a building or otherwise not eligible for the regular investment credit.

## EARNED INCOME CREDIT

The earned income credit was originally enacted in 1975 and has been made permanent by the Revenue Act of 1978. For 1979 and subsequent years, the earned income credit is 10 percent of the first $5,000 of earned income.[41] If an individual's adjusted gross income is greater than $6,000, the earned income credit of $500 is reduced by 12.5 percent of the amount of adjusted gross income (or, if greater, earned income) that exceeds $6,000.[42]

> **Example 24.** In 1983, T who otherwise qualifies for the earned income credit, receives wages of $7,200 and has $700 of unreimbursed employee expenses which are deductible in arriving at adjusted gross income. T's earned income credit is $500 (10% × $5,000 earned income) reduced by $150 [12.5% × ($7,200 earned income − $6,000)]. Thus, T's earned income credit is $350 ($500 − $150) for 1983.

It is not necessary to compute the earned income credit. As part of the simplification process, the IRS has issued an Earned Income Credit Table for the determination of the appropriate amount of

---

41. § 43(c)(2).
42. § § 43(a) and (b).

earned income credit. The table is constructed in income increments of $50 from $0 through $5,000 and from $6,000 through $9,999. This table, along with a worksheet, is included in the instructions to both Form 1040 and Form 1040A and is reproduced in Appendix C.

If adjusted gross income is $6,000 or less, the appropriate earned income credit is found in the table on the same line and to the right of the taxpayer's earned income amount.

If adjusted gross income is greater than $6,000, three steps are required:

1. Determine the earned income credit by locating the appropriate amount of income that represents the taxpayer's earned income.

2. Determine the earned income credit by locating the appropriate amount that represents the taxpayer's adjusted gross income.

3. Claim the allowed earned income credit by taking the smaller of the Step 1 amount or the Step 2 amount.

To be eligible for the credit, the taxpayer must be either (1) married and entitled to a dependency exemption for a child; (2) a surviving spouse; or (3) a head of household with an unmarried (need not be a dependent) child, stepchild, or grandchild or a married (must be a dependent) child, stepchild, or grandchild. Such child, stepchild, or grandchild must reside with the taxpayer in the United States. Married individuals must file a joint return to receive the benefits of the credit.

The earned income credit is a form of negative income tax (i. e., a refundable credit for taxpayers who do not have a tax liability). Beginning July 1, 1979, an eligible individual may elect to receive advance payments of the earned income credit from his or her employer (rather than to receive the credit from the IRS upon filing of the tax return.[43] If this election is made, the taxpayer must file a certificate of eligibility (Form W–5) with his or her employer and *must* file a tax return for the year the income is earned.[44]

## TAX CREDIT FOR THE ELDERLY

Retirement income credit provisions were originally enacted in 1954 to provide tax relief for certain elderly taxpayers who were not receiving substantial benefits from tax-free Social Security payments. In 1976, the retirement income credit provisions were substantially modified to include earned income (e. g., salaries and professional fees) as well as retirement income (e. g., dividends and interest). The credit is 15 percent of the taxpayer's income subject to specific ceiling limitations as indicated below.

---

43. § 3507.
44. § 6012(a)(8).

Unfortunately, many elderly taxpayers receive Social Security benefits in excess of the ceiling limitations and therefore are ineligible to receive the credit. The revised eligibility requirements and the tax computation are highly complicated. Therefore, the Code permits an individual to elect to have the IRS compute his or her tax and the amount of the tax credit.[45]

The credit is based on an initial ceiling amount of $2,500 (designated as the § 37 amount) for a single taxpayer. This initial ceiling amount is reduced by (1) Social Security, railroad retirement, and certain excluded pension benefits and (2) one-half of the taxpayer's adjusted gross income in excess of $7,500. The remainder is multiplied by 15 percent to compute the credit.

The § 37 amount is also $2,500 for married taxpayers filing a joint return when only one spouse is 65 or older. This increases to $3,750 for married taxpayers filing jointly when both spouses are 65 or older. For married individuals filing separately, the § 37 amount is $1,875.

The adjusted gross income factor of $7,500 for single taxpayers mentioned above is increased to $10,000 for married taxpayers filing jointly. This amount is $5,000 for married taxpayers filing separately.

Beginning in 1984, individuals under age 65 are eligible for this credit only if they retired with a permanent and total disability and have disability income from a public or private employer on account of that disability. For these individuals, the initial § 37 amounts are twice the amounts discussed previously (e. g., $7,500 rather than $3,750 on a joint return where both spouses are eligible). This initial amount, however, is limited to disability income. In other respects, the new rules follow the law in effect for 1983. A related provision repeals the disability income exclusion for taxable years beginning after December 31, 1983.

*Special Rules.* A multitude of special rules is provided by the Code:

— If both spouses are 65 or older and file a joint return, a ceiling amount of $3,750 is permitted for the combined retirement income of both spouses. To qualify for the credit, married taxpayers generally must file a joint return. However, if the married individuals live apart, under certain conditions they may each claim a maximum base for the tax credit of $1,875 on separate returns.

— Special rules for determining the credit are provided for taxpayers who receive pensions from a Federal, state, or local government retirement system.[46]

— The maximum amount of the credit is reduced by FICA and

---

**45.** § 6014.
**46.** § 37.

railroad retirement benefits received and by pension amounts which are excludible from gross income.

—All types of taxable income qualify for the tax credit (e. g., salaries, wages, and investment income).

**Example 25.** H and his wife W are both over 65 and received FICA benefits of $2,000 in 1983. On a joint return, H and W reported adjusted gross income of $12,000.

| | | |
|---|---:|---:|
| Initial § 37 amount | | $ 3,750.00 |
| Less: FICA benefits | $ 2,000 | |
| (One-half of the excess of adjusted gross income of $12,000 over $10,000) | 1,000 | (3,000.00) |
| Balance subject to credit | | $ 750.00 |
| Tax credit allowed ($750 × 15%) | | $ 112.50 |

## FOREIGN TAX CREDIT

Both individual taxpayers and corporations may claim a foreign tax credit on income earned and subject to tax in a foreign country or U. S. possession. As an alternative to the credit, a taxpayer may claim a deduction under § 164 of the Code. In most instances, the tax credit is advantageous, since it is a direct offset against the tax liability.

The purpose of the foreign tax credit is to eliminate double taxation, since income earned in a foreign country is subject to both U. S. and foreign taxes. However, the operation of the ceiling limitation formula may result in some form of double taxation or taxation at rates in excess of U. S. rates when the foreign tax rate is in excess of U. S. rates. In addition, recent changes in the law now place added restrictions upon the benefits of the credit.

*Computation.* For years ending after 1975, taxpayers are required to compute the foreign tax credit based upon an "overall" limitation. Formerly, a taxpayer could elect to compute the credit on a "per country" basis. The per country method is still available for taxpayers with income from U. S. possessions.

**Example 26.** Computation of the foreign tax credit follows: in 1983, T Corporation has $10,000 of income from Country Y, which imposes a 15% tax, and $20,000 from Country Z, which imposes a 50% tax. T Corporation has taxable income of $70,000 from within the U. S. The U. S. tax before the credit is $25,750. Overall limitation:

$$\frac{\text{Foreign income}}{\text{Total U. S. taxable income}} = \frac{\$30,000}{\$100,000} \times \$25,750 = \qquad \underline{\$\ 7,725}$$

The foreign tax credit, therefore, is the lesser of the foreign taxes imposed ($11,500) or the overall limitation ($7,725). In this case, $7,725 is the amount allowed.

Unused foreign tax credits may be carried back two years and then forward five years. Special transitional rules are applied for carryovers from pre-1976 years for taxpayers who were using the per country limitation method.[47]

Form 1116, Computation of Foreign Tax Credit, is used to compute the limitation on the amount of foreign tax credit.

The foreign earned income exclusion is discussed in Chapter 4, and expenses of employees working outside the United States are discussed in Chapter 7.

## CREDIT FOR CHILD AND DEPENDENT CARE EXPENSES

This credit was enacted to benefit taxpayers who incur employment-related expenses for child or dependent care. The credit is a specified percentage of expenses incurred to enable the taxpayer to work or to seek employment. Expenses on which the credit is based are subject to limitations (see Examples 27 and 28).

Provisions related to child and dependent care expenses have been changed frequently in recent years, with a noticeable trend toward liberalization. Originally child and dependent care expenses were treated as itemized deductions, subject to limitations on the amount of the deduction and on the level of adjusted gross income of the taxpayer. Liberalization initially took the form both of increases in the amounts of expenses which could be deducted and of increases in the allowable level of adjusted gross income taxpayers could have before becoming ineligible to take the deduction. A major shift in the treatment of these expenses occurred when the deduction was replaced by a credit. More recent provisions liberalize the treatment of child and dependent care expenses by increasing both the rate and the base for the credit as well as expanding the definition of qualifying expenses.

*Eligibility.* An individual must maintain a household for a dependent under age 15 or a dependent or spouse who is physically or mentally incapacitated.[48] Generally, married taxpayers must file a joint return to obtain the credit.

*Eligible Employment-Related Expenses.* Eligible expenses include amounts paid for household services and care of a qualifying individual which are incurred to enable the taxpayer to be employed. Child and dependent care expenses include expenses incurred in the home, such as payments for a housekeeper. The Economic Recovery Tax Act of 1981 broadened the definition of out-of-the-home expenses that qualify for the credit. Under prior law, out-of-the-home expenses qualified only if such expenses were incurred for the care of a depend-

---

**47.** § 904(e)(2).
**48.** § 44A.

ent under age 15. Beginning in 1982, out-of-the-home expenses that qualify for the credit include those for the care of a dependent under the age of 15 and those incurred for an older dependent or spouse who is physically or mentally incapacitated as long as he or she regularly spends at least eight hours each day in the taxpayer's household. This makes the credit available to taxpayers who keep handicapped or older children and elderly relatives in the home, instead of institutionalizing them, to receive a tax benefit. The out-of-the-home expenses incurred for services provided by a dependent care center will qualify only if the center complies with all applicable laws and regulations of a state or unit of local government.

Child care payments to a relative are eligible for the credit unless the relative is a dependent or is a child (under 19) of the taxpayer.

The total employment-related expenses are limited to an individual's earned income. For married taxpayers, this limitation applies to the spouse with the least amount of earned income.

Special rules are provided for taxpayers with nonworking spouses who are disabled or are full-time students. If a nonworking spouse is physically or mentally disabled or is a full-time student, such spouse is deemed to have earned income of $200 per month if there is one qualifying individual in the household (or $400 per month if there are two or more qualifying individuals in the household).

*Allowable Amounts.* In general, the credit is equal to 30 percent of employment-related expenses up to $2,400 for one qualifying individual and $4,800 for two or more individuals.[49] The 30 percent rate is reduced one percent for each $2,000 (or fraction thereof) of additional adjusted gross income in excess of $10,000 (but not below 20 percent). The following chart shows the applicable percentage for taxpayers with adjusted gross income greater than $10,000.

| Adjusted Gross Income in Excess of | Applicable Credit Percentage |
|---|---|
| $ 10,000 | 29% |
| 12,000 | 28% |
| 14,000 | 27% |
| 16,000 | 26% |
| 18,000 | 25% |
| 20,000 | 24% |
| 22,000 | 23% |
| 24,000 | 22% |
| 26,000 | 21% |
| 28,000 | 20% |

**Example 27.** H and W are married and file a joint return. They have two children under 15 and incurred $6,000 of child care expenses (for a housekeeper) during the year. H and W were fully

---

**49.** § 44A.

employed with H earning $10,000 and W earning $3,000. They have no other income or deductions *for* AGI. The maximum amount of child care expenses for two or more dependents is $4,800, but this amount is further limited by the earned income of W (the spouse with the least amount). In this case, the amount allowed as child care expenses would be $3,000 (earned income of W). H and W have combined AGI of $13,000, which reduces their applicable credit percentage to 28% (see chart above). H and W would be entitled to a tax credit of $840 (28% × $3,000) for the tax year.

**Example 28.** W has two children under 15 and worked full-time while her spouse, H, was attending college for 10 months during the year. W earned $10,000 and incurred $5,000 of child care expenses. H is deemed to be fully employed and to have earned $400 for each of the 10 months (or a total of $4,000). Since H and W have adjusted gross income of $10,000, they will not have to make an adjustment to the maximum credit rate of 30%. H and W are limited to $4,000 in qualified child care expenses (the lesser of $4,800 or $4,000). They are entitled to a tax credit of $1,200 (30% × $4,000) for the year.

The credit should be claimed by completing and filing Form 2441, Credit for Child and Dependent Care Expenses. A copy of this form appears in Appendix B.

## POLITICAL CAMPAIGN CONTRIBUTIONS

Individuals are eligible to receive a tax credit for one-half of qualifying political contributions made after 1978. This credit is subject to an overall limit of $50 ($100 on a joint return.)[50]

**Example 29.** T files a joint return for 1983 and makes qualifying political contributions of $400. T's tax credit for 1983 is $100 (one-half of $400, subject to an overall limit of $100, since a joint return is filed). If T had made qualifying political contributions of only $150, the credit allowed would be limited to $75 (one-half of $150). In this latter case, the overall limitation does not apply.

Contributions qualify for the credit if they are made to the following persons or organizations:[51]

—A candidate for nomination to any Federal, state, or local office.

—A political campaign committee sponsoring such individual.

—A national, state, or local committee of a national political party.

---

**50.** § 41(b)(1).
**51.** § 41(c).

## PRIORITY OF CREDITS

Certain credits are refundable while others are nonnrefundable. Refundable credits include tax withheld on wages, the credit for nonhighway use of certain funds, and the earned income credit. These credits are refunded to the taxpayer even if the amount of the credit (or credits) exceeds the taxpayer's tax liability.

> **Example 30.** T, who is single, had taxable income of $20,000 in 1982. His income tax from the 1982 Tax Table (see Appendix A) is $3,760. During 1982, T's employer withheld income tax of $3,850. T is entitled to a refund of $90, since the credit for tax withheld on wages is a refundable credit.

Nonrefundable credits are not refunded if they exceed the taxpayer's liability.

> **Example 31.** T is single, age 67, and retired. T's taxable income for 1982 is $2,500, and the tax on this amount is $26. T's tax credit for the elderly is $65. This credit can be used to reduce T's tax liability to zero, but it will not result in a refund, even though the credit ($65) exceeds the tax liability ($26). This result occurs because the tax credit for the elderly is a nonrefundable credit.

Some nonrefundable credits, such as the investment tax credit, are subject to carryover provisions if they exceed the amount allowable as a credit in a given year. Other nonrefundable credits, such as the tax credit for the elderly (see Example 31), are not subject to carryover provisions and are lost if they exceed the limitations. Because some nonrefundable credits are subject to carryover provisions while others are not, it is important to determine the order in which credits are offset against the tax liability. A specific order of priority is given in various sections of the Code as shown below:

—Tax credit for the elderly.

—Foreign tax credit.

—Investment tax credit.

—Political contributions credit.

—Child and dependent care credit.

—Targeted jobs credit.

—Residential energy credit.

—Alternative fuel source credit.

—Alcohol fuels credit.

—Research and experimentation credit.

—Payroll-based ESOP credit.

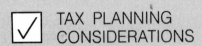

## TAX PLANNING CONSIDERATIONS

### INVESTMENT CREDIT

The optimal utilization of investment credits, including unused carry-overs, should be considered by management in the formulation of capital expenditure and project abandonment decisions. Companies that are frequently subject to the ceiling limitations should be particularly aware of the potential for losing part or all of the tax benefits from investment credits due to the expiration of loss carryovers. It should also be noted that if a company incurs net operating losses which are carried back to prior years, the previously allowed investment credits for such prior years may be scaled down or lost.

For capital expenditure planning purposes, it is important to note that certain expenditures within a project may not qualify for the investment credit (e. g., land, buildings, and structural components). It may be possible to design a capital project so that certain components qualify for the credit. For example, movable partitions are considered tangible personal property if the partitions can be removed without causing injury to the building. Also, note that the cost of used property is subject to a limitation of $125,000. Furthermore, the full amount of the investment tax credit is available for pollution control facility costs for years after 1978.

One common misconception taxpayers have about the investment tax credit concerns timing considerations. The mere purchase and transfer of ownership of eligible property will not be sufficient to make the credit available. In some cases, moreover, even the delivery of the property does not qualify the purchaser for the credit. The critical point is when the property is placed in service. According to the IRS, this occurs when "it is placed in a condition or state of readiness and availability for a specifically assigned function."[52]

> **Example 32.** In December of 1982, T (a calendar year taxpayer) purchased six electric typewriters for use in his business. The typewriters were not delivered by the manufacturer until February of 1983. Any investment tax credit that results from this acquisition must be claimed in tax year 1983.

> **Example 33.** In July of 1982, R Corporation (a calendar year taxpayer) purchase a lathe for use in its business. Since the lathe required special construction procedures to meet the agreed-upon specifications, it is not delivered to R Corporation until December of 1982. After several test runs were conducted during January

---

**52.** Reg. § 1.46–3(d)(1)(ii).

and various modifications made, the lathe was operational and available for use in February of 1983. Because the lathe will not be deemed to have been placed in service until 1983, this is the year that R Corporation should claim any investment tax credit.

## REDUCED CREDIT ELECTION

A taxpayer who elects to take a reduced investment credit avoids reducing the basis of the asset by 50 percent of the investment credit. The trade-off if the election is made is lower investment credit in the year of acquisition in exchange for higher cost recovery allowances over the life of the asset.

> **Example 34.** T Corporation acquires a heavy-duty truck (five-year recovery property) for $20,000 in 1983. If the reduced credit election is not made, the credit will be $2,000 (10% of $20,000). The basis of the property will be $19,000. If the reduced credit election is made, T's credit will be $1,600 (8% of $20,000), and the basis of the property will be $20,000.

It is clear that present value analysis should be considered in deciding whether to make the reduced credit election. Factors which must be built into this analysis include (1) T Corporation's marginal tax bracket and (2) the time value of money.

## JOBS TAX CREDIT

Employers should evaluate their personnel needs relative to the targeted jobs tax credit. To be eligible for the credit, an expanding work force is required. Also, the decision whether to hire eligible employees should take into account the fact that the benefits of the targeted jobs tax credit are less than the full amount of the credit, because the employer's wage deduction is reduced by the amount of the credit.

The new credit for qualified summer youth employees should be utilized when appropriate. The 85 percent rate is higher than the 50 percent rate for the regular targeted jobs credit. Thus, a greater tax credit will result if employees who are members of other targeted groups can be hired initially under the qualified summer youth employee program.

## ENERGY TAX CREDITS

Individual homeowners and renters who are faced with rapidly increasing home heating costs should investigate potential cost saving benefits (include tax credits) from energy conservation measures. While the ceiling limitations (i. e., 15 percent of the first $2,000 of qualifying energy conservation expenditures, subject to a maximum total credit of $300) may restrict the potential tax benefits, many states permit comparable tax credits for state income taxes. In addition, alternative energy sources (e. g., solar heat) should be considered because this form of credit has been increased to 40 percent of qualifying expenditures up to $10,000 with an overall ceiling limitation of $4,000.

Business capital budgeting decisions should take into account the availability of tax credits for qualifying energy-related expenditures. The business energy credits generally have been increased from 10 to 15 percent, and the definition of qualifying property has been expanded for years after 1979.

## FOREIGN TAX CREDITS

Individuals who intend to take a job assignment in a foreign country and companies who have international operations should take into account the related income tax effect. Companies should consider the adoption of an equitable reimbursement policy for employees who are given a foreign assignment. Otherwise, such individuals may be subject, in part, to the effects of double taxation.

An expatriate taxpayer may elect either to take the foreign tax credit or the foreign earned income exclusion. It is obvious that the taxpayer should elect the credit if the rate of tax in the foreign country is higher than the rate of tax in the United States. On the other hand, the exclusion should be elected if the U. S. rate is higher than the tax rate in the foreign country. Once the election is made, however, it is binding on future years. Thus, it is necessary that the expatriate taxpayer predict his or her future job track. If the taxpayer is likely to be assigned to a country with a rate higher than the U. S. rate, the credit should be elected. If it is expected that future assignments will be in countries with low tax rates, the exclusion should be elected.

## RESEARCH AND EXPERIMENTAL EXPENDITURES

Research and experimental expenditures are fully deductible if the taxpayer so elects under § 174. Prior to the Economic Recovery Tax Act of 1981 (ERTA), there was no particular motivation to segregate these expenditures from other expenditures. For example, salaries incurred in research and experimental activities could be left in the salaries account and deducted as salaries expense.

To provide a basis for the new research and experimentation credit added by ERTA, taxpayers should consider establishing a separate account for accumulating research and experimentation expenditures. It is likely that many businesses, particularly small businesses, do not currently have such an account.

Taxpayers should also study the new credit provisions carefully to determine the types of activities for which the credit is allowed. The Congressional committee reports are a good source of information. As an example, the committee reports point out that the credit is allowed for certain research and experimentation expenses incurred to develop computer software. This might be of particular interest, for instance, to accounting firms which are faced with developing new software to cope with the ERTA changes in the tax law.

## CREDIT FOR CHILD AND DEPENDENT CARE EXPENSES

Upper-middle and upper income level taxpayers, who were formerly ineligible for a child care deduction due to the ceiling limitations, may now qualify for the tax credit. Thus, if a nonworking spouse is considering full-time employment or if the nonworking spouse is attending college on a full-time basis, the availability of the child care credit should not be overlooked.

If the taxpayer incurs employment-related expenses that also qualify as medical expenses (e. g., a nurse is hired to provide in-the-home care for an ill and incapacitated dependent parent), such expenses may be either deducted as a medical expense (subject to the five percent limitation) or utilized in determining the child and dependent care credit. If the choice is to take the dependent care credit and the employment-related expenses exceed the limitation ($2,400, $4,800, or earned income, as the case may be) the excess may be considered a medical expense. If, however, the choice is made to deduct such qualified employment-related expenses as medical expenses, any portion that is not deductible because of the five percent limitation may not be used in computing the child and dependent care credit.

**Example 35.** T, a single individual, has the following tax position for tax year 1983:

| | | |
|---|---:|---:|
| Gross income from wages | | $ 30,000 |
| Deductions *for* adjusted gross income | | –0– |
| Adjusted gross income | | 30,000 |
| Itemized deductions *from* adjusted gross income— | | |
| Other than medical expenses | $ 2,300 | |
| Medical expenses | 6,000 | 8,300 |

All of T's medical expenses were incurred to provide nursing care for her disabled father while she was working. The father lives with T and qualifies as her dependent.

What should T do in this situation? One approach would be to use $2,400 of the nursing care expenses to obtain the maximum dependent care credit allowed. Under § 44A this would be $480 (20% × $2,400). The balance of these expenses should be claimed under § 213. After a reduction of 5% of adjusted gross income, this would produce a medical expense deduction of $2,100 [$3,600 (remaining medical expenses) − (5% × $30,000)].

Another approach would be to claim the full $6,000 as a medical expense and forego the § 44A credit. After the 5% adjustment of $1,500 (5% × $30,000), a deduction of $4,500 remains.

The choice, then, is between a credit of $480 plus a deduction of $2,100 and a credit of $0 plus a deduction of $4,500. Which is better, of course, depends upon the relative tax savings involved.

## PROBLEM MATERIALS

### Questions for Class Discussion

1. Discuss the underlying rationale of the enactment of the following tax credits:

   (a) Investment credit.

   (b) Foreign tax credit.

   (c) Tax credit for the elderly.

   (d) Earned income credit.

   (e) Credit for child and dependent care expenses.

   (f) Targeted jobs credit.

   (g) Energy tax credit.

2. Which of the following is correct?

   (a) The investment credit is not available for the purchase of buildings used in a trade or business.

   (b) The recovery period for investment credit property must be the same as that used for cost recovery purposes.

   (c) Investment credit is allowed for a year in which the corporation incurs a net operating loss.

   (d) Unused investment credits are carried back three years and are generally carried forward for 15 years.

   (e) Conversion of qualified investment credit property to personal use may result in recapture of the credit in part or in full.

3. Why has the investment credit been enacted, suspended, reinstated, repealed, and subsequently reenacted since 1962? What problems does this create for taxpayers and tax specialists?

4. What general limitations are imposed upon the amount of investment credit which may be taken in any one year?

5. The FIFO method is now applied to investment credit carryovers, carrybacks, and the utilization of credits generated during a particular year. What effect does the FIFO method have on the utilization of investment credit carryovers?

6. What limitations have been placed upon used investment credit property? Why did Congress impose such limitations?

7. How is the investment credit computed if new § 38 property is acquired in a like-kind exchange? If used § 38 property is acquired?

8. If investment credit property is prematurely disposed of or ceases to be qualified property, how is the tax liability affected in the year of the disposition?

9. What factors should a taxpayer consider in deciding whether to make the reduced investment credit election?

10. What happens if a three-year recovery period is initially assigned to investment credit property and the property is actually held for seven years?

11. Is a tax credit worth more than a tax deduction? Why?

12. Discuss the general requirements for obtaining the jobs tax credit.

13. What is the purpose of the targeted jobs credit for summer youth employees? Do all youths qualify?

14. May an employer take both the regular targeted jobs credit and the credit for qualified summer youth employees for the same employee? Explain.

15. "The tax benefit of the credit for rehabilitation expenditures on certified historic structures has been reduced somewhat by the Tax Equity and Fiscal Responsibility Act of 1982." Do you agree or disagree? Explain.

16. The tax treatment of rehabilitation expenditures has been liberalized by ERTA. What are the significant changes with regard to these expenditures?

17. What provisions in the tax law were enacted to encourage technological development in the United States?

18. The investment-based additional tax credit for contributions to employee stock ownership plans (ESOPs) will be replaced by a new payroll-based credit beginning in 1983. Explain the key features of the new payroll-based credit and why Congress felt the change was necessary.

19. Distinguish between the terms "energy conservation expenditures" and "renewable energy source property" for the purpose of computing the amount of residential energy tax credits. Are these two residential energy tax credits computed separately or are they subject to one overall computation and ceiling limitation rule?

20. Is the earned income credit a form of negative income tax? Why?

21. Which of the following is correct?

    (a) Individuals who receive substantial Social Security payments are usually not eligible for the tax credit for the elderly, since the FICA payments effectively eliminate the base upon which the credit is computed.

    (b) A taxpayer may claim a foreign tax credit under § 901 or a deduction under § 164.

    (c) Taxpayers are now required to compute the foreign tax credit on a "per country" basis.

22. Discuss the requirements for obtaining a tax credit for child and dependent care expenses.

23. Would a high income level individual generally receive greater benefit from a deduction or a credit?

## Problems

24.  In 1983, XYZ Corporation made the following purchases:

|  | Recovery Period | Cost Basis |
| --- | --- | --- |
| New factory building | 15 | $ 600,000 |
| Land for future building site | — | 400,000 |
| New auto and trucks used in business | 3 | 100,000 |
| Used equipment | 5 | 150,000 |
| Plant machinery (new) | 5 | 300,000 |

XYZ Corporation's tax liability (before investment credit) was $50,000 for 1983. Assume XYZ Corporation does not make the reduced credit election.

Compute the following:

(a) Tentative investment credit for 1983.

(b) The credit allowed in 1983.

(c) The 1983 cost recovery allowance for the plant machinery using the statutory percentage method.

25.  Assume the same facts as in Problem 24 except that XYZ Corporation makes the reduced credit election.

Compute the following.

(a) Tentative investment credit for 1983.

(b) The credit allowed in 1983.

(c) The 1983 cost recovery allowance for the plant machinery using the statutory percentage method.

26.  XYZ Corporation acquired the following new properties during 1983:

|  | Recovery Period | Cost Basis |
| --- | --- | --- |
| Office equipment | 5 years | $ 140,000 |
| Trucks | 3 years | 150,000 |
| Factory building | 15 years | 410,000 |
|  |  | $ 700,000 |

XYZ's tax liability for 1983 was $35,000 (before investment credit). XYZ has an unused investment credit of $18,000 from 1982 which is carried over to 1983. Assume XYZ Corporation does not make the reduced credit election.

(a) Calculate the amount of tentative investment credit for 1983.

(b) Calculate the amount of investment credit carryover to 1984 and identify the years to which the carryover relates.

27.  During 1983, T sells for $10,000 some investment credit property acquired four and one-half years ago at a cost of $15,000. An investment credit of $1,500 was claimed (based on an estimated life of 10 years) in the year the property was acquired. At the time of its disposition the property has an adjusted basis of $12,000.

(a) How much, if any, of the original credit must be recaptured?

(b) Suppose the property was sold by the executor of T's estate four months after T's death. Would investment credit recapture be required?

28. XYZ Corporation acquired used machinery for use in its business. Its cost was $200,000, and it had a recovery period of five years. XYZ also acquired a new machine by paying the vendor $40,000 and trading in an old machine which had an adjusted cost basis of $20,000. The new machine had a fair market value of $70,000, and a five-year recovery period. XYZ's tax liability in 1983 (before being reduced by the investment credit) was $25,500. Assume the XYZ Corporation does not make the reduced credit election.

(a) Calculate the tentative investment credit for 1983.

(b) Calculate the amount of investment credit allowed during 1983.

(c) How does the tax law treat any unused investment credit amounts during the year?

29. T is a CPA who uses his automobile totally for business purposes. On January 1, 1980, he acquired a new Lincoln for $12,000 and estimated it would have a five-year life. T claimed investment credit on the car on his tax return for 1980. On April 1, 1983, T acquired a new automobile for use in his business and kept the Lincoln for use as a second car for his wife.

(a) Calculate the amount of investment credit recapture, if any, for tax year 1983.

(b) Would your answer be different if T traded in the Lincoln on the new car?

(c) Would your answer be different if T gave the car to his son?

30. B claimed the investment tax credit on the following property acquired in 1981:

| Asset | Recovery Period | Cost |
|-------|-----------------|------|
| Truck | 3 years | $ 20,000 |
| Machinery | 5 years | $ 80,000 |

*[handwritten: 6% = 1200; 10% = 8000; @ 59200]*

(a) Compute B's tentative investment tax credit for 1981.

(b) Assume B sells both assets in 1983 after holding them for two full years. What is the amount of investment tax credit B must recapture in 1983.

(c) Assume the same facts as in (b) and that B also sells a machine acquired in 1978 after holding it for five full years. In 1978, B had claimed an investment credit based on a useful life of seven years and cost of $30,000. What is the total amount of investment tax credit B must recapture in 1983?

31. X Company hired four handicapped individuals (qualifying for the targeted jobs credit) in 1983. Each of these individuals received wages of $7,000 during 1982. X Company's tax liability for 1983 (after deducting certain tax credits) amounted to $40,000.

(a) Calculate the amount of the jobs tax credit for 1983.

(b) Assume X Company paid total wages of $120,000 to its employees during the year. How much of this amount is deductible in 1983 if the jobs credit is elected?

(c) Calculate the amount of T's jobs credit if the company's tax liability is only $2,000 in 1983.

32. On May 15, 1983, Y Corporation hired four handicapped individuals (A, B, C, and D) all of whom qualified Y Corporation for the targeted jobs credit. A and B also were certified as qualified summer youth employees. D moved out-of-state in September, quitting his job after earning $4,000 in wages. A, B, and C all continued as employees of Y Corporation. During 1983, each earned $6,500. A and B each earned $3,500 during their first 90 days of employment. Compute Y Corporation's targeted jobs credit, without regard to the ceiling limitation, for 1983. Also compute Y's deduction for wages paid to A, B, C, and D during 1983.

33. Assume the same facts as in Problem 32 and that A, B, and C continue working for Y Corporation in 1984. Each is paid $12,000 wages during the year. What is Y Corporation's targeted jobs credit in 1984?

34. T acquired a 30-year-old office building for $50,000 and spent $60,000 to rehabilitate it. The building was placed in service on January 1, 1982. Compute T's credit for rehabilitation expenditures, basis in the building, and cost recovery allowance for 1982.

35. P incurred research and experimentation expenses as follows:

| | |
|---|---|
| 1983 | $ 100,000 |
| 1982 | 80,000 |
| 1981 | 60,000 |
| 1980 | 40,000 |

(a) Compute P's credit for research and experimentation expenditures in 1983.

(b) Assume the same facts as above except that P incurs $160,000 research and experimentation expenses in 1984. Compute P's research and experimentation credit for 1984.

36. T incurred the following expenditures on his principal residence in 1981 and 1982.

| | 1981 | 1982 |
|---|---|---|
| Caulking and weatherstripping | $ 400 | $ 200 |
| Insulation | 100 | –0– |
| Storm doors | –0– | 300 |
| Solar heating system | 6,000 | 8,000 |

(a) Calculate the amount of T's allowable residential energy credits for 1981 and 1982 (assuming no energy credits in prior years).

(b) How much unused energy tax credit is available for 1983 and subsequent years?

37. T incurred the following expenditures with respect to her principal residence in 1983:

Insulation materials to reduce heating bills, $2,000.

Storm windows and doors, $1,200.

New roof, $3,000.

(a) Which of the above expenditures qualify for the residential energy credit?

(b) Calculate the amount of T's allowable residential energy credit for 1983 (assuming no energy credits in prior years).

(c) If T's energy credit exceeds the amount of the tax liability, is a carry-over of any unused amounts allowed? Explain.

38. Which of the following individuals qualify for the earned income credit for 1983?

(a) T is single and has no dependents. His income consisted of $6,000 wages and taxable interest of $1,000. T's adjusted gross income is $7,000.

(b) T maintains a household for a dependent unmarried child and is eligible for head-of-household rates. Her income consisted of $6,000 salary and $500 taxable interest. T incurred $400 unreimbursed employment-related expenses, and her adjusted gross income is $6,100.

(c) T is married and files a joint return with his wife. They have no dependents. Their combined income consisted of $6,000 salary and $600 taxable interest. Adjusted gross income is $6,600.

39. T, a widower, lives in an apartment with three minor children whom he supports. T earned $7,600 during 1983. He incurred $1,000 of unreimbursed employee business expenses and uses the zero bracket amount. Calculate the amount, if any, of T's earned income credit.

40. H, age 67, and W, age 66, are married retirees who received the following income and retirement benefits during 1983:

| | |
|---|---:|
| Fully taxable pension income from H's former employer | $  9,000 |
| Dividends and interest (after exclusion) | 2,000 |
| FICA payments | 4,000 |
| | $ 15,000 |

Assume H and W file a joint return, have no deductions *for* adjusted gross income, and do not itemize. Are they eligible for the tax credit for the elderly? If so, calculate the amount of the credit.

41. H, age 67, and W, age 66, are married retirees who received the following income and retirement benefits during 1983:

| | |
|---|---:|
| Fully taxable pension from H's former employer | $  3,000 |
| Dividends and interest (after exclusion) | 8,000 |
| FICA payments | 1,750 |
| | $ 12,750 |

Assume H and W file a joint return and have no deductions *for* adjusted gross income. Are they eligible for the tax credit for the elderly? If so, calculate the amount of the credit assuming their actual tax liability (before credits) is $400.

42. X, a U. S. citizen, had taxable income of $50,000 from sources within the U. S. and $10,000 foreign income from investments in France. X paid a tax of $1,200 to the French government. X files a joint return with his wife, and they have two minor children. X and his spouse use the zero bracket amount and have no other items of income or deductions. Compute the net tax payable if X elects to take the foreign tax credit in 1983.

43. XYZ Corporation is a U. S. corporation which has foreign operations (a division) in England. XYZ had U. S. taxable income of $200,000, which included $100,000 from the foreign division. XYZ paid foreign taxes of $60,000. XYZ's U. S. tax liability was $71,750 before deducting any foreign tax credit. Compute the amount of XYZ Corporation's foreign tax credit for 1983.

44. H and W are married and have two dependent children under age 15. W works full time and earned $27,000 during 1983 (and had no deductions *for* AGI) while her husband attended college on a full-time basis for the entire year. They incurred child care expenses of $4,000 during the year, filed a joint return, and used the zero bracket amount. Calculate the amount, if any, of their child care credit for 1983.

45. In 1983, W hired a domestic worker to enable her to be employed on a full-time basis. W made salary payments of $7,000 to the housekeeper during the year and earned $6,000 from her employer. W's husband earned $58,000 from his employer. They have two dependent children under 15, elected the zero bracket amount, and filed a joint return. Compute the amount of child and dependent care credit, if any, for the current year.

46. H and W maintain a household for two minor children under age 15. H is employed on a full-time basis; W held a part-time job during the entire year. H's gross earned income was $30,000, and W earned $3,500. H incurred $2,000 unreimbursed employee expenses (automobile travel while attending job-related meetings). H and W incurred $7,000 of child care expenses. H and W file a joint return for 1983 and have itemized deductions of $6,000.

    (a) Calculate the amount, if any, of the credit for child care expenses.

    (b) Calculate the amount, if any, of the credit if H and W have only one child.

47. During 1983, X made a political campaign contribution of $600 to her next-door neighbor who was running for a local political office in the community. X had adjusted gross income of $110,000, itemized deductions of $12,000, and personal and dependency exemptions of $3,000. X files a joint return with her spouse.

    (a) Compute the amount of the tax credit without regard to any ceiling limitations.

    (b) Compute the amount of the tax credit allowed in 1983.

## Cumulative Problems

48. H and W are married, ages 38 and 36, and file a joint return. Their household includes S, their 10-year-old son, and F, who is H's 76-year-old father.

F is very ill and has been confined to bed for most of the year. He has no income of his own and is fully supported by H and W. H and W had the following amounts of income during 1983:

| | |
|---|---:|
| (a) H's wages | $ 9,800 |
| (b) W's salary | 17,200 |
| (c) Interest from First National Bank | 250 |
| (d) Unemployment compensation received by H, who was laid off for five months during 1983 | 4,000 |
| (e) Dividends received on January 3, 1984; the corporation mailed the check on December 31, 1983 | 250 |

The following expenses were incurred by H and W during 1983.

| | |
|---|---:|
| (f) Amounts paid to N, H's niece, for household help and caring for S and F while H and W were working | $ 3,000 |
| (g) Contribution to Senator X's campaign for reelection | 200 |
| (h) Unreimbursed travel expenses incurred by W in connection with her job | 450 |
| (i) Itemized deductions | 4,600 |
| (j) Insulation added to their home to reduce heating costs | 1,200 |
| (k) Federal income taxes withheld by their employers | 3,460 |

Compute net tax payable (or refund due) for H and W for 1983. (Use the 1983 Tax Rate Schedules. The 1983 Tax Table was not available at the date of publication of this text.)

## Form Problem

49. Jim Green is 67 years of age and files a joint return with his wife, Helen, age 65. Their adjusted gross income for 1982 was $11,100, and they received $3,000 in FICA (Social Security) benefits. The amount of their tax from Form 1040 is $410. Compute their credit for the elderly on Schedule R of Form 1040.

## Cumulative Tax Return Problem

50. T acquired a new automobile used solely in his business on January 1, 1982, for $6,000. The recovery period is three years. T and his spouse maintained a household for two dependent children (Julia, age 14, and Laura, age 17) and incurred eligible child care expenses of $6,000 during the year. T had earned income of $40,000 from his business, and Mrs. T had earned income of only $5,000. During the year, T made a political campaign contribution of $500 to the State Committee of the Democratic Party. Mr. and Mrs. T filed a joint return for 1982.

Compute the total amount of tax credit allowed for 1982. Assume that none of the credit is limited by the amount of their tax liability. Preparation of page 2 (Tax Credits section) of Form 1040 and Forms 2441, Credit for Child and Dependent Care Expenses, and 3468, Computation of Investment Credit, is suggested.

# Chapter 9

# Property Transactions:
# Determination of Gain
# or Loss, Basis Considerations,
# and Nontaxable Exchanges

This chapter and the following chapter are concerned with the income tax consequences of property transactions. This term includes the sale or other disposition of property. The questions to be considered with respect to the sale or other disposition of property are:

—Is there a realized gain or loss?

—If so, is the gain or loss recognized?

—If the gain or loss is recognized, is it ordinary or capital?

Chapter 9 is concerned with the determination of realized and recognized gain or loss; Chapter 10 is concerned with determining whether a recognized gain or loss is ordinary or capital.

## DETERMINATION OF GAIN OR LOSS

### REALIZED GAIN OR LOSS

Realized gain or loss is measured by the difference between the amount realized from the sale or other disposition of property and its adjusted basis on the date of disposition. If the amount realized exceeds the property's adjusted basis, the result is a realized gain. Conversely, if the property's adjusted basis exceeds the amount realized, the result is a realized loss.[1]

---

1.  § 1001(a).

**Example 1.** T sells X Corporation stock with an adjusted basis of $3,000 for $5,000. T's realized gain is $2,000. If T had sold the stock for $2,000, he would have had a $1,000 realized loss.

*Sale or Other Disposition.* The term "sale or other disposition" is defined broadly in the tax law and includes virtually any disposition of property. Thus, transactions such as trade-ins, casualties, condemnations, thefts, and bond retirements are treated as dispositions of property. The most common disposition of property arises from a sale or exchange. The key factor in determining whether a disposition has taken place usually is whether an identifiable event has occurred as opposed to a mere fluctuation in the value of the property.

**Example 2.** T sells X Corporation stock, which cost $3,000, for $5,000 on December 1, 19X2. This is a disposition, and T realizes a $2,000 gain in 19X2.

**Example 3.** T exchanges X Corporation stock, which cost $3,000, for another taxpayer's S Corporation stock worth $5,000 on December 1, 19X2. This is a disposition, and T realizes a $2,000 gain in 19X2.

**Example 4.** T does not dispose of the X Corporation stock, and it has appreciated in value by $2,000 during 19X2. T has no realized gain, since mere fluctuation in value is not a disposition or identifiable event for tax purposes. For the same reason, if the stock had declined in value, T would not have a realized loss.

*Amount Realized.* The amount realized from a sale or other disposition of property is the sum of any money received plus the fair market value of other property received. The amount realized also includes amounts representing real property taxes treated under § 164(d) as imposed on the taxpayer (i. e., the seller) if they are to be paid by the buyer.[2] The reason for including these taxes in the amount realized is that their payment by the purchaser is, in effect, an additional amount paid to the seller of the property. The seller is relieved of paying the taxes in addition to receiving money or other property.

The amount realized also includes any liability on the property disposed of, such as a mortgage debt, if the buyer assumes the mortgage or the property is sold subject to the mortgage.[3]

**Example 5.** T sells property on which there is a mortgage of $20,000 to U for $50,000 cash. T's amount realized from the sale

---

2. § 1001(b)(2). Refer to Chapter 7 for a discussion of this subject.
3. *Crane v. Comm.,* 47–1 USTC ¶ 9217, 35 AFTR 776, 67 S.Ct. 1047 (USSC, 1947).

is $70,000 if the mortgage is assumed by U or if U takes the property subject to the mortgage.

The fair market value of property received in a sale or other disposition has been defined by the courts as the price at which property will change hands between a willing seller and a willing buyer when neither is compelled to sell or buy. Fair market value is determined by considering the relevant factors in each case. An expert appraiser is often required to evaluate these factors in arriving at fair market value. When the fair market value of the property received cannot be determined, the value of the property surrendered may be used.[4]

Finally, the amount realized is reduced by selling expenses such as advertising, commissions, and legal fees relating to the disposition. The amount realized is the net amount received directly or indirectly by the taxpayer from the disposition of property regardless of whether it is in the form of cash.

*Adjusted Basis.* The adjusted basis of the property disposed of is its original basis adjusted to the date of disposition.[5] Original basis is the cost or other basis of the property on the date it is acquired by the taxpayer. Capital additions increase and recoveries of capital decrease the original basis so that on the date of disposition the adjusted basis reflects the unrecovered cost or other basis of the property. Adjusted basis is determined as follows:

Cost (or other adjusted basis) on date of acquisition + Capital additions − Capital recoveries = Adjusted basis on date of disposition

*Capital Additions.* Capital additions include the cost of capital improvements and betterments made to the property by the taxpayer.[6] These expenditures are distinguishable from expenditures for the ordinary repair and maintenance of the property which are neither capitalized nor added to the original basis (refer to Chapter 5). The latter expenditures are deductible in the current taxable year if they are related to business or income-producing property.[7] Amounts representing real property taxes treated under § 164(d) as imposed on the seller but paid or assumed by the buyer are part of the cost of the property. Any liability on property transferred to the taxpayer upon purchase is also included in the original basis of the property.

*Capital Recovery.* The original basis of depreciable property is reduced by the annual depreciation (or cost recovery) charges while

---

4. *U. S. v. Davis*, 62–2 USTC ¶ 9509, 9 AFTR2d 1625, 82 S.Ct. 1190 (USSC, 1962).
5. § 1011(a).
6. § 1016(a).
7. Refer to the discussion of capital expenditures versus repairs in Chapter 5.

the property is held by the taxpayer.[8] The amount of depreciation which is subtracted from the original basis is the greater of the allowed or allowable depreciation on an annual basis. In most circumstances, the allowed and allowable depreciation amounts are usually the same.

Allowed depreciation is the amount actually deducted on the taxpayer's return. Allowable depreciation is the amount the taxpayer should have deducted given the useful life and salvage value of the property and the method of depreciation used.[9] The application of the greater of allowed or allowable rule is illustrated as follows:

> **Example 6.** T purchased depreciable property (which was not ACRS recovery property) on January 2, 19X2, at a cost of $100,000. The property had a 10-year useful life and no salvage value. T used the straight-line method of depreciation and deducted the following amounts of depreciation for taxable years 19X2 through 19X4:
>
> | | |
> |------|----------|
> | 19X2 | $ 10,000 |
> | 19X3 | 10,000 |
> | 19X4 | None |
>
> T sold the property on January 2, 19X5, for $90,000. T reported a gain of $10,000 on the 19X5 tax return (amount realized of $90,000 less adjusted basis of $80,000). The proper gain is $20,000. The reason is that the adjustment for depreciation is $30,000, the greater of allowed or allowable depreciation on an annual basis. Thus, the adjusted basis is $70,000 when the property is sold, and the gain is $20,000 ($90,000 − $70,000).[10]

## RECOGNIZED GAIN OR LOSS

Recognized gain is the amount of the realized gain that is included in the taxpayer's gross income.[11] A recognized loss, on the other hand, is the amount of a realized loss that is deductible for tax purposes.[12] As a

---

**8.** § 1016(a)(2). The term "depreciation" as used in this discussion is intended to encompass the term "cost recovery allowance" as introduced in the Economic Recovery Tax Act of 1981.

**9.** Reg. § 1.1016–3(a)(1)(ii). If no depreciation deductions have been taken by the taxpayer, the amount allowable is determined by using the straight-line method of depreciation. Reg. § 1.1016–3(a)(2)(i).

**10.** The taxpayer could file an amended return and claim depreciation not taken for any taxable years within the statute of limitations, which is generally three years from the date the original return was filed. § 6511(a) and Reg. § 301.6511(a)–1.

**11.** § 61(a)(3) and Reg. § 1.61–6(a).

**12.** § 165(a) and Reg. § 1.165–1(a).

general rule, the entire amount of a realized gain or loss is recognized.[13]

Figure I summarizes the realized gain or loss and recognized gain or loss concepts:

**Figure I**
RECOGNIZED GAIN OR LOSS

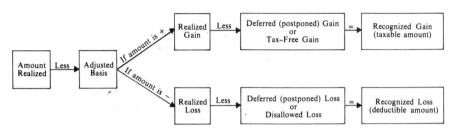

## NONRECOGNITION OF GAIN OR LOSS

In certain cases, a realized gain or loss is not recognized upon the sale or other disposition of property. One of the exceptions to the recognition of gain or loss involves nontaxable exchanges, which are covered later in the chapter. Additional exceptions include losses realized upon the sale, exchange, or condemnation of personal use assets (as opposed to business or income-producing property), and gains realized upon the sale of a residence by taxpayers 55 years of age or older. In addition, realized losses from the sale or exchange of business or income-producing property (as opposed to personal use assets) between certain related parties are not recognized.[14]

The sale of a residence by taxpayers 55 years of age and older is covered later in the chapter. The nonrecognition of realized losses from sales or exchanges between related parties is also discussed subsequently in the chapter.

*Sale, Exchange, and Condemnation of Personal Use Assets.* As indicated above, a realized loss from the sale, exchange, or condemnation of personal use assets (e. g., a personal residence or an automobile which is not used for business or income-producing purposes) is not recognized for tax purposes. An exception is provided to this rule for casualty or theft losses from personal use assets. In contrast, any gain realized from the sale or other disposition of personal use assets is, generally, fully taxable. The following examples illustrate the tax consequences of the sale of personal use assets.

---

**13.**   § 1001(c) and Reg. § 1.1002–1(a).
**14.**   § 267(a)(1).

**Example 7.** T sells an automobile, which is held exclusively for personal use, with an adjusted basis of $5,000 for $6,000. T has a $1,000 realized and recognized gain.

**Example 8.** T sells the automobile in the prior example for $4,000. T has a $1,000 realized loss, but the loss is not recognized.

# BASIS CONSIDERATIONS

## DETERMINATION OF COST BASIS

The basis of property is generally its cost.[15] Cost is the amount paid for the property in cash or other property. This general rule follows logically from the recovery of cost doctrine. That is, the cost or other basis of property is to be recovered tax-free by the taxpayer.

A bargain purchase of property is an exception to the general rule for determining basis. A bargain purchase may result when an employer transfers property to an employee, as compensation for services, at less than its fair market value or when a corporation transfers property to a shareholder, as a dividend, at less than its fair market value. The basis of property acquired in a bargain purchase is its fair market value.

**Example 9.** T buys a machine from her employer for $10,000 on December 30, 19X2. The fair market value of the machine is $15,000. T must include the $5,000 difference between cost and the fair market value of the machine in gross income for the taxable year 19X2. The bargain element represents additional compensation to T. T's basis for the machine is $15,000, the machine's fair market value.

*Identification Problems.* Cost identification problems are frequently encountered in securities transactions. For example, the Regulations require that the taxpayer must adequately identify the particular stock which has been sold. A problem arises when the taxpayer has purchased separate lots of stock on different dates or at different prices and cannot adequately identify the lot from which a particular sale takes place. In this case, the stock is presumed to come from the first lot or lots purchased (i. e., a FIFO presumption). When securities are left in the custody of a broker, it may be necessary to provide specific instructions and receive written confirmation as to which securities are being sold.

**Example 10.** T purchases 100 shares of S Corporation stock on July 1, 19X2, for $5,000 ($50 a share), and another 100 shares of the same stock on July 1, 19X3, for $6,000 ($60 a share). She sells 50 shares of the stock on January 2, 19X4. The cost of the stock sold, assuming T cannot adequately identify the shares, is $50 a

---

**15.** § 1012.

share or $2,500. This is the cost she will compare to the amount realized in determining the gain or loss from the sale.

*Allocation Problems.* When a taxpayer acquires multiple assets in a lump-sum purchase, it is necessary to allocate the total cost among the individual assets. Allocation is necessary because some of the assets acquired may be depreciable (e. g., buildings) and others not (e. g., land), a portion of the assets acquired may be sold, or some of the assets may be capital or § 1231 assets which receive special tax treatment upon subsequent sale or other disposition. A lump-sum cost is allocated on the basis of the fair market values of the individual assets acquired.

> **Example 11.** T purchases a building and land for $100,000. The fair market value of the building is $60,000, and the fair market value of the land is $40,000. Therefore, the basis of the building is $60,000, and the basis of the land is $40,000.

## GIFT BASIS

When a taxpayer receives property as a gift, there is, of course, no cost to the recipient. However, a basis is assigned to the property received depending on the date of the gift, the basis of the property to the donor, and the fair market value of the property.[16]

*Gifts Prior to 1921.* If the gift property was acquired prior to 1921, its basis for income tax purposes is its fair market value on the date of the gift.[17]

*Present Gift Basis Rules If No Gift Tax is Paid.* The present basis rules for gifts of property may be described as follows:

—If the donee subsequently disposes of gift property in a transaction which results in a gain, the basis to the donee is the same as the donor's adjusted basis (i. e., gain basis).[18] Therefore, *a gain results* if the amount realized from the disposition exceeds the donor's adjusted basis.

> **Example 12.** T purchased stock in 19X2 for $10,000. He gave the stock to his son, S, in 19X3, when its fair market value was $15,000. Assuming no gift tax was paid on the transfer and the property is subsequently sold by S for $15,000, S's basis would be $10,000 and S would have a realized gain of $5,000.

    —If the donee subsequently disposes of gift property in a transaction which results in a loss, the basis to the donee is the

---

**16.** § 102(a). See the Glossary of Tax Terms (Appendix C) for a definition of the term "gift."

**17.** § 1015(c) and Reg. § 1.1015–3(a).

**18.** § 1015(a) and Reg. § 1.1015–1(a)(1).

lower of the donor's adjusted basis or fair market value on the date of the gift (i. e., loss basis).[19] Therefore, *a loss results if the amount realized* from the disposition is less than the lower of the donor's adjusted basis or fair market value at the date of the gift.

**Example 13.** T purchases stock in 19X2 for $10,000. T gives the stock to his son, S, in 19X3 when its fair market value is $7,000. S later sells the stock for $6,000. S's basis is $7,000 (fair market value is less than donor's adjusted basis of $10,000), and the loss from the sale is $1,000 ($7,000 basis less the $6,000 amount realized).

Note that the loss rule prevents the donee from receiving a tax benefit from the decline in value while the donor held the property. Therefore, in the prior example, S has a loss of $1,000 and not $4,000. The $3,000 difference represents the decline in value while T held the property. It is perhaps ironic, however, that the basis for gain rule may eventually result in the donee's being subject to income tax on the appreciation which occurs while the donor held the property.

If the amount of the sales proceeds is between the basis for loss and the basis for gain, no gain or loss is realized. See Example 16.

*Adjustment for Gift Tax.* If gift taxes are paid by the donor, the donee's gain basis may exceed the adjusted basis of the property to the donor. This will occur only if the fair market value of the property at the date of the gift is greater than the donor's adjusted basis (i. e., the property has appreciated in value). The portion of the gift tax paid that is associated with the appreciation is added to the donor's basis in calculating the donee's gain basis for the property. The formula, in this circumstance, for calculating the donee's gain basis is as follows:[20]

$$\text{Donee's gain basis} = \text{Donor's adjusted basis}$$
$$+ \frac{\text{Unrealized appreciation}}{\text{Fair market value}} \times \text{Gift tax paid}$$

**Example 14.** F made a gift of stock to S in 1983, when the fair market value of the stock was $40,000. F had purchased the stock in 1978 for $10,000. Since the donor's basis is $10,000 and the fair market value is $40,000, three-fourths ($30,000/$40,000) of the gift tax paid is added to the basis of the property. If the gift tax is $4,000, S's basis in the property is $13,000 [$10,000 + $3,000 (¾ of the $4,000 gift tax)].

**Example 15.** F made a gift of stock to S in 1983 when the fair market value of the stock was $40,000. F had purchased the stock

---

19. Ibid.
20. § 1015(d)(6).

in 1978 for $45,000. Since there is no unrealized appreciation at the date of the gift, none of the gift tax paid of $4,000 is added to the donor's basis in calculating the donee's gain basis. Therefore, the donee's gain basis is $45,000.

For gifts made prior to 1977, the full amount of the gift tax paid is added to the donor's basis, up to the fair market value of the property. Thus, in Example 14, if the gift was made prior to 1977, the basis of the property would be $14,000 ($10,000 + $4,000). In Example 15, the basis would still be $45,000 ($45,000 + $0).

*Holding Period.* Two additional rules relating to gift property follow:

—The holding period of property acquired by gift begins on the date the property was acquired by the donor if the donor's adjusted basis is the basis to the donee (i. e., gain basis rule).[21] The holding period starts on the date of the gift if fair market value is the basis to the donee (i. e., loss basis rule). The significance of the holding period for capital assets is discussed in Chapter 10.

—The basis for depreciation on depreciable gift property generally is the donor's adjusted basis.[22] Using the higher fair market value on the date of the gift would allow the donee to escape tax on the donor's appreciation through higher depreciation deductions.

The following example summarizes the basis and holding period rules for gift property:

**Example 16.** T acquires 100 shares of X Corporation stock on December 30, 1978, for $40,000. On January 3, 1983, when the stock has a fair market value of $38,000, T gives it to S. T pays a gift tax of $4,000. There is no increase in basis for a portion of the gift tax paid, since the property has not appreciated in value. S's basis for determining loss is $38,000 (fair market value), since the fair market value on the date of the gift is less than the donor's adjusted basis.

—If S sells the stock for $45,000, he has a recognized gain of $5,000. The holding period for determining whether the capital gain is short-term or long-term begins on December 30, 1978, the date the property was acquired by the donor.

—If S sells the stock for $36,000, he has a recognized loss of $2,000. The holding period for determining whether the capital loss is short-term or long-term begins on January 3, 1983, the date of the gift.

---

**21.** § 1223(2).
**22.** § § 1011 and 167(g).

—If S sells the property for $39,000, there is no gain or loss, since the amount realized is less than the gain basis of $40,000 and more than the loss basis of $38,000.

## PROPERTY ACQUIRED FROM A DECEDENT

*General Rule.*  The basis of property acquired from a decedent is generally its fair market value at the date of death.[23] The property's basis is its fair market value six months after the date of death if the executor or administrator of the estate elects the alternate valuation date for estate tax purposes.[24]

Thus, both unrealized appreciation and decline in value are taken into consideration in determining the basis of the property for income tax purposes.

**Example 17.**  D inherited property from her father who died in 1983. Her father's adjusted basis for the property at date of death was $35,000. The property's fair market value at date of death was $50,000. The alternate valuation date was not elected. D's basis for income tax purposes is $50,000. This is commonly referred to as the stepped-up basis rule.

**Example 18.**  Assume the same facts as in Example 17 except the property's fair market value at date of death was $20,000. D's basis for income tax purposes is $20,000.

*Survivor's Share of Property.*  Both the decedent's share and the survivor's share of community property have a basis equal to fair market value on the date of the decedent's death.[25] This result is produced for the decedent's share of the community property in that it flows to the surviving spouse from the estate (i. e., fair market value basis for inherited property). Likewise, the surviving spouse's share of the community property is deemed to be acquired by bequest, devise, or inheritance from the decedent. Therefore, it will also have a basis equal to fair market value.

**Example 19.**  H and W reside in a community property state. H and W own community property (200 shares of XYZ stock) which was acquired in 1973 for $100,000. Assume that H dies in 1983 when the securities are valued at $300,000. One-half of the XYZ stock is included in H's estate. If W inherits H's share of the community property, the basis for determining gain or loss is:

—$300,000 [$150,000 (W's share of one-half of the community property) plus $150,000 (one-half × $300,000, the value

---

**23.**  § 1014(a).
**24.**  If the alternate valuation date is elected and the property is distributed or otherwise disposed of within six months after the date of death, the basis of the property is its fair market value as of the date of disposition.
**25.**  § 1014(b)(6).

of XYZ stock at date of death)] for the 200 shares of XYZ stock.

In a common law state, only one-half of jointly held property of spouses (tenants by the entirety or joint tenants with rights of survivorship) is includible in the estate.[26] In such a case, no adjustment of the cost basis is permitted for the excluded property interest.

*Holding Period of Property Acquired from a Decedent.* Under § 1223, the holding period of property acquired from a decedent is deemed to be long-term (i. e., held for more than one year). Suppose, for example, D purchases property on December 6, 19X2, and dies on January 10, 19X3. Assume further that the executor of D's estate sells the property on October 20, 19X3, in order to raise cash to pay expenses of the estate. For purposes of determining whether or not any gain or loss recognized on the sale by the estate is long-term or short-term (see Chapter 10), the law treats the property as having been held by the estate for more than one year. Thus, any such gain or loss would be long-term gain or loss.

## WASH SALE

Section 1091 stipulates that in certain cases, a realized loss on the sale or exchange of stock or securities is not recognized. Specifically, if a taxpayer sells or exchanges stock or securities and within 30 days before or after the date of such sale or exchange acquires substantially identical stock or securities, any loss realized from the sale or exchange is not recognized.[27] The term "acquire" means acquire by purchase or in a taxable exchange and includes an option to purchase substantially identical securities. "Substantially identical," means the same in all important particulars. Corporate bonds and preferred stock are normally not considered substantially identical to the corporation's common stock; however, if the bonds and preferred stock are convertible into common stock, they may be considered substantially identical under certain circumstances. Attempts to avoid the application of § 1091 by having a related taxpayer repurchase the securities have been unsuccessful. These wash sale provisions do not apply to gains.

Recognition of the loss is disallowed because the taxpayer is considered to be in substantially the same economic position after the sale and repurchase as before the sale and repurchase. However, this rule does not apply to taxpayers engaged in the business of buying and selling securities. The average investor, however, is not allowed to create losses through wash sales to offset income for tax purposes.

*Basis Rule.* Realized loss not recognized is added to the basis of the substantially identical stock or securities whose acquisition re-

---

**26.** § 2040(a).

**27.** § 1091(a).

sulted in the nonrecognition of loss.[28] In other words, the basis of the replacement stock or securities is increased by the amount of the unrecognized loss. If the loss were not added to the basis of the newly acquired stock or securities, the taxpayer would never recover the entire basis of the old stock or securities. By adding the unrecognized loss to the basis of the newly acquired stock or securities, the taxpayer is able to recover the cost of the new stock or securities plus the unrecovered cost or other basis of the old stock or securities. That is, the taxpayer will have a greater loss or lesser gain from the subsequent disposition of the new stock or securities to the extent of the unrecognized loss from the wash sale.

Since the basis of the new stock or securities includes the unrecovered portion of the basis of the formerly held stock or securities, the holding period of the new stock or securities begins on the date the old stock or securities were acquired.[29] The following examples illustrate the application of the wash sale rules:

> **Example 20.** T owns 100 shares of A Corporation stock (adjusted basis of $20,000), 50 shares of which she sells for $8,000. Ten days later, T purchases 50 shares of the same stock for $7,000. T's realized loss of $2,000 ($8,000 less $10,000 adjusted basis of 50 shares) is not recognized because it resulted from a wash sale. Her basis in the newly acquired stock is $9,000 ($7,000 purchase price plus $2,000 unrecognized loss from the wash sale).

When the taxpayer acquires less than the number of shares sold in a wash sale, the loss from the sale is prorated between recognized and unrecognized loss on the basis of the ratio of the number of shares acquired to the number of shares sold.[30]

## CONVERSION OF PROPERTY FROM PERSONAL USE TO BUSINESS OR INCOME-PRODUCING USE

As discussed previously, losses from the sale of personal use assets are not recognized for tax purposes, but losses from the sale of business and income-producing assets are deductible. Can a taxpayer convert a personal use asset which has declined in value to business use and then sell the asset to recognize a business loss? The law prevents this by requiring that the original basis for loss on personal use assets converted to business or income-producing use is the lower of the property's adjusted basis or fair market value on the date of conversion. Thus, if a taxpayer whose personal residence had an adjusted basis of $100,000 converted it to rental use when it was worth $60,000, it would have a basis of $60,000 for purposes of determining

---

**28.**  § 1091(d).
**29.**  § 1223(4) and Reg. § 1.1223–1(d).
**30.**  § 1091(b) and Reg. § 1.1091–1(c).

the loss upon its subsequent sale. The $40,000 decline in value is a personal loss and can never be recognized for tax purposes. The gain basis for converted property is simply its adjusted basis on the date of conversion. The law is not concerned with gains on converted property, because gains are recognized regardless of whether property is business, income-producing, or personal use.

The basis for loss is also the basis for depreciating the converted property. This is an exception to the general rule which provides that the basis for depreciation is the gain basis (e. g., property received by gift). This exception prevents the taxpayer from recovering a personal loss indirectly through depreciation of the higher original basis.

**Example 21.** At a time when her personal residence (adjusted basis of $40,000) is worth $50,000, T converts one-half of it to rental use. (Assume the property is not ACRS recovery property.) At this point, the estimated useful life of the residence is 20 years and there is no estimated salvage value. After renting the converted portion for five years, T sells the property for $44,000. Assume all amounts relate only to the building; the land has been accounted for separately. T has a $2,000 realized gain from the sale of the personal use portion of the residence and a $7,000 realized gain from the sale of the rental portion. These gains are computed as follows:

|  | Personal Use | Rental |
| --- | --- | --- |
| Original basis for gain and loss— adjusted basis on date of conversion (Fair market value is greater than the adjusted basis) | $ 20,000 | $ 20,000 |
| Depreciation—five years | None | 5,000 |
| Adjusted basis—date of sale | $ 20,000 | $ 15,000 |
| Amount realized | 22,000 | 22,000 |
| Realized gain | $  2,000 | $  7,000 |

# NONTAXABLE EXCHANGES

In a nontaxable exchange, realized gains or losses are not recognized. However, the nonrecognition is usually temporary; the recognition of gain or loss is merely postponed (i. e., deferred) until the property received in the nontaxable exchange is subsequently disposed of in a taxable transaction. This is accomplished by assigning a carryover basis to the replacement property.

**Example 22.** T exchanges property with an adjusted basis of $10,000 and a fair market value of $12,000 for property with a fair market value of $12,000. The transaction qualifies for nontaxable exchange treatment. T has a realized gain of $2,000 ($12,000 − $10,000). His recognized gain is $0. His basis for the replacement property is a carryover basis of $10,000. Therefore, assuming the replacement property is nondepreciable, if T subsequently sells the replacement property for $12,000, his realized and recognized gain will be the $2,000 gain that was deferred (i. e., postponed) in the nontaxable transaction. If the replacement property is depreciable, the carryover basis of $10,000 is used in calculating depreciation.

The tax law recognizes that nontaxable exchanges result in a change in the form but not in the substance of the taxpayer's relative economic position. The replacement property received in the exchange is viewed as substantially a continuation of the old investment. In other words, the taxpayer has merely replaced existing property with new property and is in substantially the same relative economic position after the transaction as before the transaction. Furthermore, this type of transaction does not provide the taxpayer with the wherewithal to pay the tax on any realized gain. Certain exceptions should be noted. For example, the nonrecognition provisions do not apply to realized losses from the sale of personal use assets. Such losses are not recognized because they are personal in nature, not because of any nonrecognition provision.

In some nontaxable exchanges, only part of the property received in the transaction will qualify for nonrecognition treatment. If the taxpayer receives cash or other nonqualifying property, part or all of the realized gain from the exchange is recognized. In these instances, gain is recognized because the taxpayer has changed or improved his or her relative economic position and has the wherewithal to pay income tax to the extent of cash or other property received. The following sections of the chapter deal with situations in which realized gains or losses are not immediately recognized.

The major types of transactions which receive nontaxable exchange treatment are as follows:

—Like-kind exchanges.    (Trade in auto )

—Involuntary conversions.

—Sale of a residence.

—Exchange of stock for property by a corporation.

—Exchange of stock for stock of the same corporation by a shareholder.

—Certain exchanges of U. S. obligations.

—Certain reacquisitions of real property.

—Contribution of property by a partner to a partnership in exchange for a partnership interest.

—Contribution of property by a shareholder to a controlled corporation in exchange for stock.

With the exception of the last two types, which are covered in Chapter

20, each of these types of nontaxable exchanges is covered in this chapter.

# LIKE-KIND EXCHANGES

Section 1031 provides that "no gain or loss shall be recognized if property held for productive use in trade or business or for investment . . . is exchanged solely for property of a like-kind to be held either for productive use in trade or business or for investment."[31]

Like-kind exchanges include business for business, business for investment, investment for business, or investment for investment property.[32] Property held for personal use, inventory, and securities do not qualify under the like-kind exchange provisions.

## LIKE-KIND PROPERTY

"The words 'like-kind' have reference to the nature or character of the property and not to its grade or quality. One kind or class of property may not . . . be exchanged for property of a different kind or class."[33]

Under this broad definition of like-kind exchanges, real estate can be exchanged only for other real estate and personalty can be exchanged only for other personalty. For example, the exchange of a machine for an office building is not a like-kind exchange. Real estate includes principally rental buildings, office and store buildings, manufacturing plants, warehouses, and land. It is immaterial whether real estate is improved or unimproved. Thus, unimproved land can be exchanged for an apartment house. Personalty includes principally machines, equipment, trucks, and automobiles. Of course, if the property exchanged (real estate or personalty) is held for personal use, the exchange will not qualify as a like-kind exchange under § 1031.

> **Example 23.** T made the following exchanges during the taxable year:
>
> (a) Inventory for a machine used in business.
>
> (b) Land held for investment for a building used in business.
>
> (c) Stock held for investment for equipment used in business.
>
> (d) A business truck for a business machine.
>
> (e) An automobile used for personal transportation for a machine used in business.
>
> Exchanges (b), investment real property for business real property, and (d), business personalty for business personalty, qualify

---

**31.** § 1031(a).

**32.** § 1031(a) and Reg. § 1.1031(a)–1(a).

**33.** Reg. § 1.1031(a)–1(b).

under § 1031(a). Exchanges (a), inventory; (c), stock; and (e), the personal use automobile, do not qualify.

## MUST BE AN EXCHANGE

The transaction must actually involve a direct exchange of property to qualify as a like-kind exchange. Thus, the sale of old property and the purchase of new property, even though like-kind, is generally not an exchange. However, if the two transactions are mutually dependent, the IRS may treat the two interdependent transactions as a like-kind exchange. For example, if the taxpayer sells an old business machine to a dealer and purchases a new one from the same dealer, a like-kind exchange could result.

The taxpayer might want to avoid nontaxable exchange treatment. Recognition of gain gives the taxpayer a higher basis for depreciation. To the extent that such gains would, if recognized, receive favorable capital gain treatment, it may be preferable to avoid the nonrecognition provisions through an indirect exchange transaction (i. e., by the sale of property to one individual followed by a purchase of similar property from another individual). However, in many instances, it is not possible to recognize capital gain on the sale of depreciable property, since part or all of the gain is recaptured as ordinary income.[34] If gain recognition is postponed, the recapture potential carries over to the new property received in the like-kind exchange. The taxpayer may want to avoid nontaxable exchange treatment so that a realized loss can be recognized.

## BOOT

Realized losses are not recognized on like-kind exchanges even if boot is received.[35] However, realized gains are recognized to the extent of boot received.[36] Boot is cash or property, other than like-kind property. Cash given in a like-kind exchange has no effect on the recognition of realized gains or losses. If property other than cash is given and such property is not like-kind, realized gain or loss on such property will have to be recognized.

> **Example 24.** T and S exchange equipment, and such exchange qualifies as like-kind under § 1031. T receives from S like-kind equipment with a fair market value of $25,000 and property which is not like-kind with a fair market value of $6,000. T gives up like-kind equipment with an adjusted basis of $12,000 and property which is not like-kind with an adjusted basis of $8,000. Although T's realized gain appears to be $11,000 ($25,000 +

---

**34.** § § 1245 and 1250. See Chapter 10 for an explanation of these Code provisions.
**35.** § 1031(c) and Reg. § 1.1031(c)–1.
**36.** § 1031(b) and Reg. § 1.1031(b)–1(a).

$6,000 − $12,000 − $8,000), he must report the like-kind and nonlike-kind elements separately. T's realized gain on the like-kind exchange is $13,000 ($25,000 − $12,000). On the property which is not like-kind, T has a realized loss of $2,000 ($6,000 − $8,000). The $13,000 gain is not recognized, but the $2,000 loss is recognized.

To summarize, if the taxpayer has a realized gain from a like-kind exchange and receives boot, the realized gain is recognized to the extent of the boot received. The recognized gain cannot exceed the realized gain regardless of the amount of boot received.

> **Example 25.** T and S exchange machinery, and such exchange qualifies as like-kind under § 1031. Since T's machinery (basis of $20,000) is worth $24,000 while S's machine has a value of $19,000, S also gives T cash of $5,000. T's recognized gain is $4,000, the lesser of the realized gain (i. e., $24,000 − $20,000 = $4,000) or the value of the boot received (i. e., $5,000).

> **Example 26.** Assume the same facts as in Example 25 except that S's machine is worth $21,000 (not $19,000). Under these circumstances, S gives T cash of $3,000 to make up the difference. T's recognized gain is $3,000, the lesser of the realized gain (i. e., $4,000) or the value of the boot received (i. e., $3,000).

If a transferee either assumes a liability or takes property subject to a liability, the amount of the liability is received by the party making the transfer.

## BASIS OF PROPERTY RECEIVED

If an exchange does not qualify under § 1031, gain or loss is recognized, and the basis of property received in the exchange is its fair market value.[37] If the exchange qualifies for nonrecognition, the basis of property received must be adjusted to reflect any postponed gain or loss. The basis of like-kind property received in the exchange is its fair market value less postponed gain or plus postponed loss.

If there is a postponed loss, nonrecognition creates a situation in which the taxpayer has recovered less than the cost or other basis of the property exchanged in an amount equal to the unrecognized loss. If there is a postponed gain, the taxpayer has recovered more than the cost or other basis of the old property exchanged in an amount equal to the unrecognized gain.

> **Example 27.** T exchanges a building (used in his business) with an adjusted basis of $30,000 and fair market value of $38,000 for land with a fair market value of $38,000 which will be held as an investment. The exchange qualifies as like-kind (e. g., an ex-

---

37.   § 1031(d) and Reg. § 1.1031(d)–1(c).

change of business real property for investment real property). Thus, the basis of the land is its fair market value of $38,000 less the $8,000 postponed gain on the building. If the land is later sold for its fair market value of $38,000, the $8,000 postponed gain will be recognized.

**Example 28.** Assume the same facts as in Example 27 except that the building has an adjusted basis of $48,000 and fair market value of only $38,000. The basis in the newly acquired land is $48,000 (its fair market value of $38,000 plus the $10,000 unrecognized loss on the building). If the land is later sold for its fair market value of $38,000, the $10,000 postponed loss will be recognized.

The Code provides an alternative approach for determining the basis of like-kind property received:[38]

Adjusted basis of property surrendered
+ Boot given
+ Gain recognized
− Boot received
= Basis of like-kind property received

This approach is logical in terms of the recovery of cost doctrine. That is, the unrecovered cost or other basis is increased by additional cost (boot given) or decreased by cost recovered (boot received). Finally, any gain recognized is included in the basis of the new property, because the taxpayer has been taxed on that amount and is now entitled to recover it tax-free.

The holding period of the property surrendered in the exchange carries over and "tacks on" to the holding period of the like-kind property received.[39] The logic of this rule is derived from the basic concept of the new property as a continuation of the old investment.

The following comprehensive example illustrates the like-kind exchange rules:

**Example 29.** T exchanged the following old machines for new machines in five independent like-kind exchanges:

| Exchange | Adjusted Basis of Old Machine | Fair Market Value of New Machine | Boot Given | Boot Received |
|---|---|---|---|---|
| 1 | $ 4,000 | $ 9,000 | $ −0− | $ −0− |
| 2 | 4,000 | 9,000 | 3,000 | −0− |
| 3 | 4,000 | 9,000 | 6,000 | −0− |
| 4 | 4,000 | 9,000 | −0− | 3,000 |
| 5 | 4,000 | 3,500 | −0− | 300 |

---

**38.** § 1031(d) and Reg. § 1.1031(d)–1(a) and (b).
**39.** § 1223(1) and Reg. § 1.1223–1(a).

T's realized and recognized gains and losses and the basis of each of the like-kind properties received are:

| Exchange | Realized Gain (Loss) | Recognized Gain (Loss) | New Basis Calculation | | | | |
|---|---|---|---|---|---|---|---|
| | | | Old Adj. Basis + | Boot Given + | Gain Recognized – | Boot Received = | New Basis |
| 1 | $ 5,000 | $ –0– | $ 4,000 + | $ –0– + | $ –0– – | $ –0– = | $ 4,000* |
| 2 | 2,000 | –0– | 4,000 + | 3,000 + | –0– – | –0– = | 7,000 |
| 3 | (1,000) | –(0)– | 4,000 + | 6,000 + | –0– – | –0– = | 10,000** |
| 4 | 8,000 | 3,000 | 4,000 + | –0– + | 3,000 – | 3,000 = | 4,000 |
| 5 | ( 200) | –(0)– | 4,000 + | –0– + | –0– – | 300 = | 3,700 |

*Basis may be determined in gain situations under the alternative method by subtracting the gain not recognized from the fair market value of the new property, i. e.,
$9,000 – $5,000 = $4,000 for Exchange 1.
$9,000 – $2,000 = $7,000 for Exchange 2.
$9,000 – $5,000 = $4,000 for Exchange 4.
**In loss situations, basis may be determined by adding the loss not recognized to the fair market value of the new property, i. e.,
$9,000 + $1,000 = $10,000 for Exchange 3.
$3,500 + $200 = $3,700 for Exchange 5.

# INVOLUNTARY CONVERSIONS

## GENERAL SCHEME

Section 1033(a) provides that a taxpayer who suffers an involuntary conversion of property may postpone recognition of gain realized from the conversion. The objective of this provision is to provide relief to the taxpayer who has suffered hardship and who does not have the wherewithal to pay the tax on any gain realized from the conversion to the extent he or she reinvests the amount realized from the conversion in replacement property. The rules for nonrecognition of gain are:[40]

—If the amount realized exceeds the amount reinvested in replacement property, realized gain is recognized to the extent of the excess.

—If the amount reinvested in replacement property equals or exceeds the amount realized, realized gain is not recognized.

The following two examples illustrate the application of these rules:

**Example 30.** T's property with an adjusted basis of $20,000 is condemned by the state. T is awarded $50,000 as compensation for the involuntarily converted property. T elects to postpone gain under § 1033. T's realized gain is $30,000 ($50,000 amount realized less $20,000 adjusted basis). T reinvests $40,000 in replacement property. The recognized gain under § 1033 is $10,000 [excess of $50,000 (amount realized) over $40,000 (amount reinvested)]. The remaining $20,000 of realized gain is postponed.

---

**40.** § 1033(a).

**Example 31.** Assume the same facts as in Example 30 except that T reinvests $60,000 in replacement property. Since T reinvested an amount at least equal to the condemnation award, T's entire realized gain of $30,000 is not recognized and is postponed, if T so elects.

## INVOLUNTARY CONVERSION DEFINED

An involuntary conversion is the result of the destruction (complete or partial), theft, seizure, requisition or condemnation, or the sale or exchange under threat or imminence of requisition or condemnation of the taxpayer's property.[41] The threat or imminence of condemnation requires that the taxpayer has obtained confirmation that there has been a decision to acquire the property for public use and that the taxpayer has reasonable grounds to believe the property will be taken. The sale of property to a party other than the authority threatening to condemn it, by a taxpayer with reasonable grounds to believe that the necessary steps to condemn the property eventually will be instituted, qualifies as an involuntary conversion under § 1033. The sale of property to a condemning authority by a taxpayer who acquired the property from its former owner with the knowledge that the property was under threat of condemnation also qualifies as an involuntary conversion under § 1033.

Although most involuntary conversions are casualties or condemnations, there are some special situations included within the definition. Involuntary conversions, for example, include livestock destroyed by or on account of disease or exchanged or sold because of disease or solely on account of drought.

## COMPUTING THE AMOUNT REALIZED

The amount realized from the condemnation of property usually includes only the amount received as compensation for the property. Any amount received which is designated as severance damages by both the government and the taxpayer is not included in the amount realized. Severance awards usually occur when only a portion of the entire property is condemned (e. g., a strip of land is taken to build a highway). Severance damages are awarded because the value of the taxpayer's remaining property has declined as a result of the condemnation. Such damages reduce the basis of the property. However, (1) if severance damages are used to restore the usability of the remaining property or (2) if the usefulness of the remaining property is destroyed by the condemnation and it is sold and replaced at a cost exceeding the sum of the condemnation award, severance damages, and sales

---

**41.** § 1033(a) and Reg. § § 1.1033(a)–1(a) and –2(a).

proceeds, the nonrecognition provision of § 1033 applies to the severance damages.

## REPLACEMENT PROPERTY

The requirements for replacement property under § 1033 are generally more restrictive than those for like-kind property under § 1031. The basic requirement is that the replacement property be "similar or related in service or use" to the involuntarily converted property.[42]

Until 1964, the IRS held the position that "similar or related in service or use" meant that replacement property must be functionally the same as the involuntarily converted property (the functional use test). This test requires that the taxpayer's use of the replacement property and the involuntarily converted property must be the same. To illustrate, a rental residence replaced by a personal residence does not meet this test. A manufacturing plant replaced by a wholesale grocery warehouse does not meet this test either.

*Special Rules.* Under one set of circumstances, the broader replacement rules for like-kind exchanges are substituted for the narrow replacement rules normally used for involuntary conversion. This beneficial result occurs if business real property or investment real property is condemned. Therefore, the taxpayer has substantially more flexibility in terms of his or her selection of replacement property. For example, improved real property can be replaced with unimproved real property. Another special rule provides that proceeds from the involuntary conversion of livestock due to soil or other environmental contamination need be replaced only by any property to be used for farming, including real property.[43]

The rules concerning the nature of replacement property are illustrated in Example 32.

### Example 32.

| Type of Property and User | Like-kind Test | Functional Use Test |
|---|---|---|
| —Land used by a manufacturing company is condemned by a local government authority | x | |
| —Apartment and land held by an investor is sold due to the threat or imminence of condemnation | x | |
| —A manufacturing plant was destroyed by fire; therefore, replacement property must consist of another manufacturing plant which is functionally the same as the property converted | | x |

---

42. § 1033(a) and Reg. § 1.1033(a)–1.
43. § 1033(f) and (g)(1) and Reg. § 1.1033(f)–1(a).

## TIME LIMITATION ON REPLACEMENT

The taxpayer has a two-year period (three years for condemnations of real property used in a trade or business or held for investment) after the close of the taxable year in which any gain is realized from the involuntary conversion to replace the property.[44] This rule affords as much as three years from the date of realization of gain (or possibly as much as four years in the case of condemnation of business or investment real property) to replace if the realization of gain took place on the first day of the taxable year. The rule was changed from one year to two years, and the replacement period was extended to three years for real property condemnations to permit adequate time to acquire replacement property.

> **Example 33.** T's warehouse is destroyed by fire on December 16, 19X2. The adjusted basis is $325,000. Proceeds of $400,000 are received from the insurance company on January 10, 19X3. T is a calendar year taxpayer. The latest date for replacement is December 31, 19X5 (i. e., end of the taxable year in which realized gain occurred plus two years). The critical date is not the date the involuntary conversion occurred but rather the date of gain realization.

> **Example 34.** Assume the same facts as in Example 33 except T's warehouse is condemned. The latest date for replacement is December 31, 19X6 (i. e., end of taxable year in which realized gain occurred plus three years).

## NONRECOGNITION OF GAIN

Nonrecognition of gain can be either mandatory or elective depending upon whether the conversion is directly (into replacement property) or into money.

*Direct Conversion.* If the conversion is directly into replacement property rather than into money, nonrecognition of realized gain is mandatory and the basis of the replacement property is the same as the adjusted basis of the converted property.[45] Direct conversion is rare in practice and usually involves condemnation.

*Conversion into Money.* If the conversion is into money, "at the election of the taxpayer the gain shall be recognized only to the extent that the amount realized upon such conversion . . . exceeds the cost of such other property or such stock."[46] This is the usual case, and non-recognition (postponement) is elective.

A special rule allows the taxpayer to purchase 80 percent or more

---

**44.** § 1033(a)(2)(B) and Reg. § § 1.1033(a)–2(c)(3) and 1.1033(f)–1(b).

**45.** § 1033(a)(1) and (b) and Reg. § 1.1033(a)–2(b).

**46.** § 1033(a)(2)(A) and Reg. § 1.1033(a)–2(c)(1).

of the stock of a corporation owning property which qualifies as replacement property in lieu of purchasing the replacement property directly. This rule does not apply, however, to condemnations of real property held for business or investment use when the like-kind reinvestment rules are applicable.[47]

The basis of the replacement property is its cost less postponed gain.[48] The holding period of the replacement property, if the election to postpone gain is made, includes the holding period of the converted property.[49]

Section 1033 applies only to gains and not to losses. Losses from involuntary conversions are recognized if the property is held for business or income-producing purposes. Personal casualty losses are recognized, but condemnation losses related to personal use assets (e. g., a personal residence) are neither recognized nor postponed.

> **Example 35.** T's residence with an adjusted basis of $50,000 is condemned by the state. T receives $20,000 from the state. T's realized loss of $30,000 is neither recognized nor postponed regardless of how much T reinvests in replacement property, because losses from the condemnation of personal use property are never recognized. If the property were business or income-producing, the loss would be recognized. If the personal loss were a casualty loss (e. g., a loss from fire, storm, theft), it would be recognized subject to the limitations of § 165(c)(3) and Reg. § 1.165–7. Refer to Chapter 6 for a detailed discussion of the casualty loss provisions.

Examples 36 and 37 illustrate the application of the involuntary conversion rules:

> **Example 36.** T's building (used in his trade or business activity) with an adjusted basis of $50,000, is destroyed by fire in 19X2. In 19X2, T receives an insurance reimbursement for the loss in the amount of $100,000. T invests $75,000 in a new building.
>
> (a) T has until December 31, 19X4, to make the new investment and qualify for the nonrecognition election under § 1033(a)(3)(A).
>
> (b) T's realized gain is $50,000 ($100,000 insurance proceeds less $50,000 adjusted basis of old building).
>
> (c) Assuming the replacement property qualifies under § 1033(a)(3), T's recognized gain is $25,000. He reinvested $25,000 less than the insurance proceeds ($100,000 proceeds

---

**47.** § 1033(g)(2) and Reg. § 1.1033(g)–1(b).
**48.** § 1033(b).
**49.** § 1223(1)(A) and Reg. § 1.1223–1(a).

minus $75,000 reinvested), and therefore, his realized gain is recognized to that extent.

(d) T's basis in the new building is $50,000. This is its cost of $75,000 less the postponed gain of $25,000 (realized gain of $50,000 less recognized gain of $25,000).

(e) The computation of realization, recognition, and basis would apply even if T were a real estate dealer and the building destroyed by fire were part of his inventory. Section 1033 does not generally exclude inventory as does § 1031.

**Example 37.** Assume the same facts as in Example 36 except that T receives only $45,000 (instead of $100,000) of insurance proceeds. T would have a realized and recognized loss of $5,000, and the basis of the new building would be its cost of $75,000.

## INVOLUNTARY CONVERSION OF A PERSONAL RESIDENCE

The tax consequences of the involuntary conversion of a personal residence depend upon whether the conversion is a casualty or condemnation and whether a realized loss or gain results.

*Loss Situations.* If the conversion is a condemnation, the realized loss is not recognized. Loss from the condemnation of a personal use asset is never recognized. If the conversion is a casualty (e. g., a loss from fire or storm), the loss is recognized subject to the personal casualty loss limitations.

*Gain Situations.* If the conversion is a condemnation, the gain may be postponed under either § 1033 or § 1034. That is, the taxpayer may elect to treat the condemnation as a sale under the deferral of gain rules relating to the sale of a personal residence under § 1034 which are presented subsequently. If the conversion is a casualty, the gain can be postponed only under the involuntary conversion provisions of § 1033.

## REPORTING CONSIDERATIONS

If the taxpayer elects to postpone gain, because he or she either has replaced or intends to replace the converted property within the prescribed time period, supporting details should be included in a statement attached to the return for the taxable year in which gain is realized. If the property has not been replaced before filing the return for the taxable year in which gain is realized, the taxpayer should attach a supporting statement to the return for the taxable year in which the property is replaced.

If the property either is not replaced within the prescribed period or is replaced at a cost less than anticipated, an amended return must be filed for the taxable year in which the election was made. If no election is made in the return for the taxable year in which gain is realized, an election may still be made within the prescribed time period by filing a claim for credit or refund.

For individuals, a single casualty or theft loss (and if only one item is involved) to personal use property is reported directly on Schedule A of Form 1040. In all other cases, involuntary conversions from casualty and theft are reported first on Form 4684, Casualties and Thefts. From Form 4684, the amounts are reported generally on Form 4797, Supplemental Schedule of Gains and Losses, unless Form 4797 is not required. In the latter case, the amounts are reported directly on the tax return involved.

Except for personal use property, recognized gains and losses from involuntary conversions other than by casualty and theft are reported on Form 4797. As stated previously, if the property involved in the involuntary conversion (other than by casualty and theft) is personal use property, any loss is not recognized; any gain is treated as a voluntary sale.

## SALE OF A RESIDENCE—§ 1034

A realized loss from the sale of a personal residence is not recognized, because the residence is personal use property. A realized gain is, however, subject to taxation. There are two provisions in the tax law whereby all or part of a realized gain is either postponed or excluded from taxation. The first of these, § 1034, is discussed below. The second, § 121, is discussed later in the chapter.

Section 1034 provides for the mandatory nonrecognition of gain from the sale or exchange of a personal residence.[50] Both the old and new residences must qualify as the taxpayer's principal residence. A houseboat or house trailer qualifies if used by the taxpayer as his or her principal residence.

The reason for not recognizing gain from the sale or exchange of a residence which is replaced by a new residence within the prescribed time period (discussed below) is basically that the new residence is substantially a continuation of the investment. Also, if the proceeds from the sale are reinvested, the taxpayer does not have the wherewithal to pay tax on the gain. Beyond these fundamental concepts, Congress, in enacting § 1034, was concerned with the hardship of involuntary moves and the socially desirable objective of encouraging the mobility of labor.

### REPLACEMENT PERIOD

The Economic Recovery Tax Act of 1981 extended the period within which the old residence must be replaced. The period now begins two

---

**50.** § 1034(a) and Reg. § 1.1034–1(a) and (b)(1) and (2).

years before sale and ends two years after sale.[51] This two-year period applies whether the new residence is purchased or constructed. Also, the taxpayer must physically occupy and use the new residence as the principal residence within this same time period. The two-year period is effective for sales and exchanges after July 20, 1981, and for sales and exchanges on or before that date with respect to which the rollover period had not expired as of July 20, 1981. However, it does not apply to sales and exchanges with respect to which the 18-month period (prior replacement period for purchased residence) had expired before July 20, 1981. The occupancy requirement has been strictly construed by the IRS and the courts, and even circumstances beyond a taxpayer's control do not excuse noncompliance.

> **Example 38.** T sells her personal residence from which she realizes a gain of $50,000. Although the construction of a new residence begins immediately after the sale, unstable soil conditions and a trade union strike cause unforeseen delays in construction. The new residence ultimately is completed and occupied by T 25 months after the sale of the old residence. Since the occupancy requirement has not been satisfied, § 1034 is inapplicable and T must recognize a gain of $50,000 on the sale of the old residence.

Taxpayers might be inclined to make liberal use of § 1034 as a means of speculating when the price of residential housing is rising. Without any time restriction on its use, § 1034 would permit deferral of gain on multiple sales of principal residences, each one of which would result in an economic profit. The Code curbs this approach by precluding the application of § 1034 to any sales occurring within two years of its last use.[52]

The two-year rule precluding multiple use of § 1034 could work a hardship where a taxpayer has been transferred by his or her employer and therefore has little choice in the matter. For this reason, § 1034 was amended to provide an exception to the two-year rule when the sale results from a change in the location of employment.[53] To qualify for the exception, a taxpayer must meet the distance and length-of-employment requirements specified for the deduction of moving expenses under § 217.[54]

The running of the time periods specified above is suspended during any time the taxpayer or spouse is on extended active duty (over 90 days or for an indefinite period) with the Armed Forces of the United States after the date the old residence is sold.[55] This suspen-

---

**51.** § 1034(a).
**52.** § 1034(d)(1).
**53.** § 1034(d)(2).
**54.** Refer to Chapter 6 for the discussion of the rules governing the deduction for moving expenses.
**55.** § 1034(h) and Reg. § 1.1034–1(g)(1).

sion is limited to four years after the date the old residence is sold. A similar suspension is available to U. S. citizens who are employed outside the U. S. by nongovernmental employers (i. e., expatriates). In no event, however, may § 1034 apply unless the replacement occurs within four years of the date when the principal residence was sold.[56]

## PRINCIPAL RESIDENCE

As indicated above, both the old and new residences must be the taxpayer's principal residence. Whether property is the taxpayer's principal residence is dependent ". . . upon all the facts and circumstances in each case."[57]

> **Example 39.** T sells his principal residence and moves to Norfolk, Virginia, where he is employed. He decides to rent an apartment in Norfolk because of its proximity to his place of employment. He purchases a beach house at Virginia Beach which he occupies most weekends. T does not intend to live in the beach house other than on weekends. The apartment in Norfolk is his principal residence. Therefore, the purchase of the beach house does not qualify as an appropriate replacement.

If the old residence ceases to be the taxpayer's principal residence prior to its sale or the new residence ceases to be the principal residence before the taxpayer occupies it, the nonrecognition provision does not apply. For example, if the taxpayer abandons the old residence prior to its sale, it no longer qualifies as a principal residence. If the old residence is converted to other than personal use (e. g., rental) prior to its sale, the nonrecognition provision, of course, does not apply. If only partially converted to business use, gain from the sale of the personal use portion still qualifies for nonrecognition.

However, temporarily renting out the old residence prior to sale does not necessarily terminate its status as the taxpayer's principal residence, nor does temporarily renting out the new residence before it is occupied by the taxpayer.

## NONRECOGNITION OF GAIN REQUIREMENTS

Under § 1034(a), realized gain from the sale of the old residence is not recognized if the taxpayer reinvests an amount at least equal to the adjusted sales price of the old residence. Realized gain is recognized to the extent the taxpayer does not reinvest the adjusted sales price in a new residence. Therefore, the amount not reinvested is treated similarly to boot received in a like-kind exchange. Adjusted sales price is the amount realized from the sale of the old residence less fixing-up expenses.

---

**56.** § 1034(k).
**57.** Reg. § 1.1034–(c)(3).

Fixing-up expenses are expenses incurred by the taxpayer to assist in the sale of the old residence. They are personal in nature and not deductible by the taxpayer. Fixing-up expenses are distinguishable from selling expenses, which are deducted from the selling price to determine the amount realized. Selling expenses include items such as advertising the property for sale, real estate broker commissions, legal fees in connection with the sale, and loan placement fees paid by the taxpayer as a condition to the arrangement of financing for the buyer. To the extent that selling expenses are deducted as moving expenses, they are not allowed as deductions in the computation of the amount realized. Fixing-up expenses include items such as ordinary repairs, painting, and wallpapering.

Fixing-up expenses must (1) be incurred for work performed during the 90-day period ending on the date of the contract of sale, (2) be paid within 30 days after the date of sale, and (3) be noncapital expenditures.

Fixing-up expenses are subtracted from the amount realized in arriving at adjusted sales price. Realized gain is not recognized and is postponed to the extent the adjusted sales price is reinvested in a new residence. Therefore, the greater the fixing-up expenses, the less the adjusted sales price, and the less that needs to be reinvested in a new residence in order to postpone the realized gain from the sale of the old residence.

However, fixing-up expenses are not considered in determining realized gain. They are considered only in determining how much realized gain is to be postponed. In addition, fixing-up expenses have no direct effect on the basis of the new residence. Indirectly, through their effect on postponed gain, they can bring about a greater or lesser basis of the new residence. The effects of fixing-up expenses on the computation of gain realized and recognized and on the basis of the new residence are illustrated in Figure II and in Example 41.

## CAPITAL IMPROVEMENTS

Capital improvements are added to the cost basis of a personal residence for the purpose of computing gain or loss on a subsequent sale or other disposition of the property.[58] However, the cost of a replacement residence (for determining the nonrecognition of gain under § 1034) includes only capital improvements incurred during the period beginning two years before the date of sale of the old residence and ending two years after such date.

**Example 40.** T purchases a replacement residence on January 2, 19X2, and sells her former residence on January 16, 19X2. T makes capital improvements to the replacement residence over a

---

**58.** § 1034(c)(2).

three-year period beginning on January 4, 19X2. The improvements made prior to the date of sale (from January 4, 19X2, to January 16, 19X2) are added to the cost basis of the replacement residence for computing the nonrecognized gain on the sale of the former residence, because these costs were incurred during the two-year period prior to January 16, 19X2. The improvements incurred within two years following the date of the sale (January 16, 19X2) are also capitalized in determining the cost of the replacement residence under § 1034. Capital improvements made after the two-year period are added to the cost basis solely for determining gain or loss upon a subsequent sale of the replacement residence.

## BASIS OF THE NEW RESIDENCE

The basis of the new residence is its cost less unrecognized (postponed) gain.[59] If there is any postponed gain, the holding period of the new residence includes the holding period of the old residence.[60]

Figure II
OPERATION OF § 1034

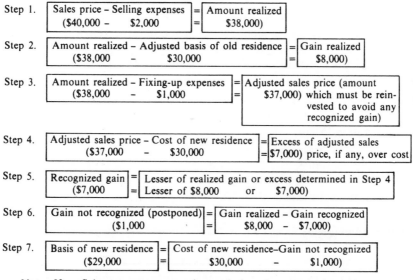

Note: If no fixing-up expenses were incurred, the gain recognized would have been $8,000 instead of $7,000 and the adjusted basis of the new residence would have been $30,000.

---

**59.** § 1034(e) and Reg. § § 1.1034–1(e) and 1.1016–5(d).
**60.** § 1223(7) and Reg. § 1.1223–1(g).

Figure II summarizes the sale of residence concepts. Example 41 illustrates these concepts and the application of the nonrecognition provision.

> **Example 41.** T sells her personal residence (adjusted basis of $36,000) for $44,000. She receives only $41,400 after payment of a brokerage fee of $2,600. Ten days before the sale, T incurred and paid for qualified fixing-up expenses of $1,400. Two months later, T acquires a new residence. Determine the gain, if any, T must recognize and the basis of the new residence under each of the following circumstances:
>
> —The residence acquired two months after the sale of the old residence cost $60,000. The cost of the new residence has no effect on determining the realized gain from the sale of the old residence. The realized gain is $5,400 ($41,400 amount realized less $36,000 adjusted basis of old residence). None of the gain is recognized, because T reinvested at least $40,000 (the adjusted sales price, which equals $41,400 − $1,400 fixing-up expenses) in the new residence. The $5,400 gain is postponed, and the basis of the new residence is $54,600 ($60,000 cost less $5,400 postponed gain).
>
> —The new residence cost $38,000. Of the realized gain of $5,400, $2,000 is recognized, because T reinvested $2,000 less than the adjusted sales price of $40,000. The remaining gain of $3,400 is not recognized and is postponed. The basis of the new residence is $34,600 ($38,000 cost less $3,400 postponed gain).
>
> —The new residence cost $32,000. All of the realized gain of $5,400 is recognized, because T reinvested $8,000 less than the adjusted sales price of $40,000. Since the amount not reinvested exceeds the realized gain, the entire gain is recognized and § 1034 does not apply. The basis of the new residence is simply its cost of $32,000, because there is no postponed gain.

## REPORTING PROCEDURES

The taxpayer is required to report the details of the sale of the residence in the tax return for the taxable year in which gain is realized even if all of the gain is postponed. If a new residence is acquired and occupied before filing, a statement should be attached to the return showing the purchase date, its cost, and date of occupancy. Form 2119, Sale or Exchange of Principal Residence, may be used to show the details of the sale and replacement, and a copy should be retained by the taxpayer as support for the basis of the new residence. If a replacement residence has not been purchased when the return is filed, the taxpayer should submit the details of the purchase in the return of the taxable year during which it occurs. If the old residence is not replaced within the prescribed time period or if some recognized gain results, the taxpayer must file an amended return for the year in which the sale took place.

# SALE OF A RESIDENCE—§ 121

Taxpayers age 55 or older who sell or exchange their principal residence after July 20, 1981, may elect to exclude up to $125,000 ($62,500 for married individuals filing separate returns) of realized gain from the sale or exchange.[61] The election can be made only once.[62] This provision is contrasted with § 1034 where nonrecognition is mandatory and may occur many times during a taxpayer's lifetime. Also, § 121 differs from § 1034 in that it does not require the taxpayer to purchase a new residence. The excluded gain is never recognized, whereas the unrecognized gain under § 1034 is postponed by subtracting it from the cost of a new residence in calculating the adjusted basis.

This provision is the only case in the tax law where a realized gain from the disposition of property is not recognized and not postponed. In other words, the provision allows the taxpayer a permanent recovery of more than the cost or other basis of the residence tax-free.

The reason for § 121 is simply the desire of the Congress to relieve older citizens of the large capital gains tax they might incur from the sale of a personal residence. The dollar and age limitations restrict the benefit of § 121 to taxpayers who presumably have a greater need for increased tax-free dollars.

## REQUIREMENTS

The taxpayer must be at least 55 before the date of the sale and have owned and used the residence as a principal residence for at least three years during the five-year period ending on the date of sale. If a former residence is involuntarily converted and any gain is postponed under § 1033, the holding period of the former residence is added to the holding period of the replacement residence in determining whether the above ownership and use period requirements are met. Short temporary absences (e. g., vacations) count as periods of use. If the residence is owned jointly by husband and wife, only one of the spouses is required to meet these requirements if a joint return is filed for the taxable year in which the sale took place.

---

**61.** § 121(a) and (b). The exclusion was limited to $100,000 for sales or exchanges prior to July 20, 1981.

**62.** § 121(b)(2) and Reg. § 1.121–2(b). Only one election may be made by married individuals.

Taxpayers age 65 or older who sold or exchanged their principal residence prior to July 26, 1981, may elect to substitute "five years during the eight-year period" for the "three years during the five-year period" test.

## RELATIONSHIP TO OTHER PROVISIONS

The taxpayer can treat an involuntary conversion of a principal residence as a sale for purposes of § 121(a). Any gain not excluded under § 121 is then subject to postponement under § 1033 or § 1034 (condemnation only) assuming the requirements of those provisions are met.

Any gain not excluded under § 121 from the sale of a residence is subject to postponement under § 1034, assuming the requirements of that provision are met. This relationship is illustrated in Examples 42 and 43.

## COMPUTATION PROCEDURE

The following example illustrates the application of this provision:

**Example 42.** Assume the same facts as in Example 41 except T does not acquire a new residence and meets the requirements of § 121. T may elect not to recognize all of the $5,400 realized gain, since the realized gain is not in excess of $125,000.

The following comprehensive example illustrates the application of both the § 121 and § 1034 provisions:

**Example 43.** T sells his personal residence (adjusted basis of $32,000) for $205,000, of which he receives only $195,400 after the payment of selling expenses. Ten days before the sale, T incurred and paid for qualified fixing-up expenses of $6,400.

(a) T's realized gain is $163,400 ($195,400 amount realized less $32,000 adjusted basis of residence). If he is under age 55 and does not acquire a new residence within the prescribed time period, T has a recognized gain of $163,400.

(b) Assume T is age 55, does not acquire a new residence, and elects to exclude a portion of the gain under § 121. T's recognized gain is $38,400. This is the difference between the realized gain of $163,400 and $125,000 not recognized under § 121.

(c) Assume T is age 55, acquires a new residence for $40,000 within the prescribed time period, *and* elects under § 121. T's recognized gain is $24,000, computed as follows:

| | |
|---|---|
| Adjusted sales price ($195,400 − $6,400) | $ 189,000 |
| Less tax-free gain | 125,000* |
| | $ 64,000 |
| Less cost of new residence | 40,000 |
| Recognized gain | $ 24,000 |

The basis of the new residence in this case is $25,600 ($40,000 cost of new residence less $14,400 postponed gain). The postponed gain is the difference between the realized gain of $163,400 and $149,000 (i. e., $125,000 tax-free gain plus $24,000 recognized gain).

*The taxpayer is not required to reinvest an amount equal to the tax-free gain ($125,000). If T were required to reinvest such amount, the requirement would negate the benefits of § 121.

# OTHER NONRECOGNITION PROVISIONS

Several additional nonrecognition provisions, which are not as common as those already discussed, are treated briefly in the remainder of this chapter.

## EXCHANGE OF STOCK FOR PROPERTY—§ 1032

Under this section, no gain or loss is recognized to a corporation on the receipt of money or other property in exchange for its stock (including treasury stock). In other words, no gain or loss is recognized by a corporation when it deals in its own stock. This provision is consistent with the accounting treatment of such transactions.

## EXCHANGE OF CERTAIN INSURANCE POLICIES—§ 1035

Under this provision, no gain or loss is recognized from the exchange of certain insurance contracts or policies. The rules relating to exchanges not solely in kind and the basis of the property acquired are the same as under § 1031. Exchanges qualifying for nonrecognition include (1) the exchange of life insurance contracts, (2) the exchange of a life insurance contract for an endowment or annuity contract, (3) the exchange of an endowment contract for another endowment contract which provides for regular payments beginning at a date not later than the date payments would have begun under the contract exchanged, (4) the exchange of an endowment contract for an annuity contract, or (5) the exchange of annuity contracts.

## EXCHANGE OF STOCK FOR STOCK OF THE SAME CORPORATION—§ 1036

No gain or loss is recognized from the exchange of common stock solely for common stock in the same corporation or from the exchange of preferred stock for preferred stock in the same corporation. Exchanges between individual stockholders as well as between a stockholder and the corporation are included. The rules relating to exchanges not solely in kind and the basis of the property acquired are the same as under § 1031. For example, a nonrecognition exchange occurs when common stock with different rights, such as voting for nonvoting, is exchanged. Gain or loss from the exchange of common for preferred or preferred for common usually is recognized even though the stock exchanged is in the same corporation.

### CERTAIN REACQUISITIONS OF REAL PROPERTY—§ 1038

Under this provision, no loss is recognized from the repossession of real property which is sold on an installment basis. Gain is recognized to a limited extent.

This chapter has covered certain situations in which realized gains or losses are not recognized (i. e., nontaxable exchanges). Chapter 10 is concerned with the nature of recognized gains and losses. That is, if a gain or loss is recognized, is it an ordinary or capital gain or loss? Chapter 10 discusses the tax consequences of capital gains and losses.

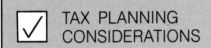

### SALE OF SECURITIES PRIOR TO YEAR-END

Taxpayers are frequently advised to sell depreciated securities prior to year-end to establish deductible capital losses for the current tax year. If a taxpayer has recognized short-term capital gains during the year, it may be desirable to offset such short-term gains with long- or short-term capital losses through the sale of depreciated securities at year-end. To accomplish this, an investor may sell a security and immediately replace it with a similar (although not substantially identical) security without violating the wash sale provisions (e. g., a sale of Bethlehem Steel common stock and a purchase of U. S. Steel common stock is not a wash sale). Also, a sale of one monthly issue of a municipal bond fund coupled with the purchase of another monthly issue is permitted.

### WASH SALES

Because the wash sale provisions do not apply to gains, it may be desirable to engage in a wash sale prior to the end of the year. This recognized capital gain may be used to offset capital losses or capital loss carryovers from prior years.

## COST IDENTIFICATION AND DOCUMENTATION CONSIDERATIONS

It is important for taxpayers to identify the cost of properties and securities for future documentation of a sale or other disposition. If multiple assets are acquired in a single transaction, the purchase agreement should specify the separate values of individual assets. If separate values are not provided in the purchase agreement, the taxpayer should obtain appraisals of the properties to establish their value.

## SELECTION OF PROPERTY FOR MAKING GIFTS

A donor should generally make gifts of appreciated property because income tax is avoided (by the donor) on the unrealized gain. Further, the basis of the property to the donee may be increased by a portion of the gift tax paid by the donor.

Taxpayers should generally not make gifts of depreciated property (i. e., property which would be sold at a loss), because the donor does not receive an income tax deduction for the unrealized loss element. In addition, the donee may not receive benefit from this unrealized loss upon the subsequent sale of the property. The unrealized loss may never be recognized, because the loss basis of the donee is the lower of the donor's cost or the fair market value on the date of the gift.

## SELECTION OF PROPERTY FOR MAKING BEQUESTS

A decedent should generally make bequests of appreciated property because income tax is avoided (by the decedent and the inheritor of the property) on the unrealized gain.

In a community property state, both the decedent's and the survivor's basis in community property is fair market value on the date of the decedent's death. Therefore, income tax is avoided on the unrealized gain attributable to both the decedent's and survivor's share of the community property.

> **Example 44.** H and W reside in a community property state. On the date of H's death, H and W own land held for investment purposes as community property, with an adjusted basis of $100,000 and a fair market value of $600,000. If they had sold the property prior to H's death, the recognized gain would have been $500,000. If W inherits H's share of the property and sells the property for $700,000, the recognized gain will be $100,000, the appreciation only since H's death.

Taxpayers generally should not make bequests of depreciated property (i. e., property which could be sold at a loss), because the decedent does not receive an income tax deduction for the unrealized loss element. In addition, the inheritor will not receive benefit from this unrealized loss upon the subsequent sale of the property.

## LIKE-KIND EXCHANGES

Since application of the like-kind provisions is not elective, in certain instances, it may be preferable to avoid falling under § 1031. If the like-kind provisions do not apply, the end result may be the recognition of long-term capital gain and a higher basis for the newly acquired asset. The immediate recognition of gain may be preferable in certain situations (e. g., if the taxpayer has unused net operating loss carryovers).

> **Example 45.** T sells a machine (used in his business) with an adjusted basis of $3,000 for $4,000. T also acquires a new business machine for $9,000. If § 1031 applies, the $1,000 gain is not recognized and the basis of the new machine is reduced by $1,000. If § 1031 does not apply, a $1,000 gain is recognized and may receive favorable long-term capital gain treatment to the extent that the gain is not recognized as ordinary income due to the depreciation recapture provisions (see Chapter 10). In addition, the basis for depreciation on the new machine is $9,000 rather than $8,000, since there is no unrecognized gain.

## INVOLUNTARY CONVERSIONS

In certain cases, a taxpayer may prefer to recognize gain from an involuntary conversion. Keep in mind that § 1033, unlike § 1031 (dealing with like-kind exchanges), is an elective provision.

> **Example 46.** T has a $40,000 realized gain from the involuntary conversion of an office building. The entire proceeds are reinvested in a new office building. T, however, does not elect to postpone gain under § 1033 because of an expiring net operating loss carryover which is offset against the gain. Furthermore, by not electing § 1033, T's basis in the replacement property will be its cost.

## SALE OF A PERSONAL RESIDENCE

*Principal Residence Requirement.* Section 1034 will not apply unless the property involved is the taxpayer's principal residence. In this connection, one potential hurdle can arise in cases where the residence has been rented and has not been occupied by the taxpayer for an extended period of time. Depending on the circumstances, the IRS might contend that the property has been abandoned by the taxpayer as his or her principal residence. The key to the abandonment issue is whether or not the taxpayer intended to reoccupy the property and use it as a principal residence upon his or her return to the locale. If the residence, in fact, is not reoccupied, the taxpayer should have a good reason to explain why this did not take place.

> **Example 47.** T is transferred by her employer to another office out of the state on a three-year assignment. It is the understanding of the parties that the assignment is temporary, and upon its completion, T will return to the original job site. During her absence, T rents her principal residence and lives in an apartment at the new location. Although T had every intention of reoccupying her residence, when she returns from the temporary assignment, she finds that it no longer suits her needs. Specifically, the public school located nearby where she had planned to send her children has been closed. As a consequence, T sells the residence and replaces it with one more conveniently located to a public school. Under these circumstances, it would appear that T is in an excellent position to show that the property never was abandoned as her principal residence. The reason it was not reoccupied prior to sale can be explained satisfactorily.

The principal residence requirement could cause difficulty where a taxpayer works in two places and maintains multiple households. In such cases, the principal residence will be the location where the taxpayer lives most of the time.

> **Example 48.** E is a vice-president of Z Corporation and in this capacity spends about an equal amount of time in the company's New York City and Miami offices. E owns a house in each location and expects to retire in about five years. At that point, he plans to sell his New York home and use some of the proceeds to make improvements on the Miami property. Both homes have appreciated in value since their acquisition, and such appreciation can be expected to continue.

From a tax planning standpoint, E should be looking toward the use of § § 121 and 1034 to shelter some or all of the gain he will realize on the future sale of the New York City home. To do this, he should arrange his affairs so as to spend more than six months each year at that location. Upon its sale, therefore, the New York home will be his principal residence.

*Section 121 Considerations.* Older individuals who may be contemplating a move from their home to an apartment should consider the following possibilities for minimizing or deferring taxes:

—Wait until age 55 to sell the residence and elect under § 121 to exclude up to $125,000 of the realized gain.

—Sell the personal residence under an installment contract to spread the gain over several years.

—Sell the personal residence and purchase a condominium instead of renting an apartment, thereby permitting further deferral of the cumulative unrecognized gain.

The use of § 121 should be carefully considered. Although such use avoids the immediate recognition of gain, the election utilizes the full $125,000 allowed.

**Example 49.** In 1983, T, age 55, sells his personal residence for an amount that yields a realized gain of $5,000. Presuming T does not plan to reinvest the sale proceeds in a new principal residence (i. e., take advantage of the deferral possibility of § 1034), should he avoid the recognition of this gain by utilizing § 121? Electing § 121 would mean that T would waste $120,000 of his lifetime exclusion.

In this connection, the use of § 121 by one spouse precludes the other spouse from later taking advantage of the exclusion.

**Example 50.** Assume the same facts as in Example 49 except that T was married to W at the time of the sale. Later, T and W are divorced and W marries R. If T used the § 121 exclusion, it is unavailable to W and R, even though either one of them may otherwise qualify.

Taxpayers should maintain records of both the purchase and sale of personal residences, since the sale of one residence results in an adjustment of the basis of the new residence if the deferral provisions of § 1034 apply. Form 2119 should be filed with the tax return and retained as support for the basis of the new residence. Detailed cost records should be retained for an indefinite period.

## PROBLEM MATERIALS

### Questions for Class Discussion

1. Upon the sale or other disposition of property, what three questions should be considered for income tax purposes?

2. When will a property transaction result in a realized gain? A realized loss?

3. What is included in the amount realized from a sale or other disposition of property?

4. What is the definition of fair market value?

5. Explain the relationship of depreciation (or the cost recovery allowance under ERTA) to adjusted basis and implementation of the recovery of cost doctrine.

6. Define recognized gain and recognized loss.

7. Why are gains from the sale or exchange of personal use assets recognized when such losses are never recognized?

8. Outline the general rules for determining the basis of stock which is sold if the owner holds more than one lot of the stock.

9. How is cost allocated for lump-sum purchases?

10. Why must gifts of property be given a basis to the donee?

11. What are the rules for determining the basis of property received as gifts after 1920?

12. Under what circumstances is it possible to recognize no gain or loss on the sale of an asset which was previously received as a gift?

13. How do gift taxes paid by the donor affect the income tax rules for gift property?

14. Discuss the differences in tax treatment between property sold prior to death and property which is inherited. Why is this important?

15. At the time of T's death, the value of his gross estate, much of which comprised marketable securities, was $300,000. Six months later, the fair market value had increased to $340,000.

    (a) Why might the executor of T's estate elect to use the alternate valuation date for estate tax purposes?

    (b) Suppose part of T's gross estate includes his share of community property. What effect, if any, would the election of the alternate valuation date have on his surviving spouse's share of the community property?

16. What is a wash sale? Why isn't a realized loss recognized on a wash sale? How is the recovery of cost doctrine maintained?

17. Give some examples of when tax planning can be implemented relative to property transactions.

18. In general, what is a nontaxable exchange? Are nontaxable exchanges ever taxed? If so, how?

19. Why would a taxpayer want to avoid like-kind exchange treatment?

20. What is boot and how does it affect a like-kind exchange when received by the taxpayer? When boot is given?

21. What adjustment is made to the basis of property received in a like-kind exchange when boot is received? When it is given?

22. Is a postponed gain from a like-kind exchange ever recognized?

23. How is the basis of property received in a like-kind exchange determined?

24. What is the holding period of property received in a like-kind exchange? Why?

25. What are the rules for determining nonrecognition of gain from an involuntary conversion?

26. What constitutes an involuntary conversion?

27. How long does a taxpayer have to replace involuntarily converted property and still qualify for nonrecognition of gain under § 1033?

28. When is nonrecognition of gain from an involuntary conversion elective?

29. Does § 1033 cover losses? Explain how the following losses are treated for income tax purposes:

    (a) Business property losses from involuntary conversion.

(b) Income-producing property losses from involuntary conversion.

(c) Personal casualty losses.

(d) Personal condemnation losses.

30. Why are personal condemnation losses neither recognized nor postponed?

31. What is the tax treatment in the following cases when a personal residence is involuntarily converted and a loss results:

(a) The conversion is a casualty.

(b) The conversion is a condemnation.

32. Discuss the justification for nonrecognition of gain on the sale or exchange of a principal residence.

33. What is the basis of the new residence if there is a realized loss?

34. What is meant by principal residence in the sale or exchange of a residence?

35. What is adjusted sales price? What are fixing-up expenses? Selling expenses?

36. Explain how the following are determined on the sale or exchange of a residence:

(a) Realized gain.

(b) Recognized gain.

(c) Postponed gain.

(d) Basis of new residence.

37. What does the § 121 exclusion cover? Is it elective?

38. How many times can § 121 exclusion treatment be elected by a taxpayer? If the taxpayer is filing a joint return with his or her spouse, do both taxpayers have to meet the age requirement?

39. How is the amount of gain not recognized under § 121 determined?

40. Can any other provision or provisions be applied to any remaining gain which is not excluded under § 121?

## Problems

41. R bought a rental house at the beginning of 19X2 for $80,000, of which $10,000 is allocated to the land and $70,000 to the building. Early in 19X4, he had a tennis court built in the backyard at a cost of $5,000. Depreciation is $2,000 a year on the house and $200 a year on the court. At the beginning of 19X7, R sells the house and tennis court for $125,000 cash.

(a) What is his realized gain (loss)?

(b) If an original mortgage of $20,000 is still outstanding and the buyer assumes the mortgage in addition to the cash payment, what is the realized gain (loss)?

(c) If the buyer takes the property subject to the mortgage, what is R's realized gain (loss)?

42. A machine was purchased January 1, 19X2, at a cost of $50,000. The

useful life of the asset is five years with no salvage value. Depreciation was deducted and allowed for 19X2 through 19X6 as follows:

| | |
|---|---|
| 19X2 | $ 1,000 |
| 19X3 | –0– |
| 19X4 | 10,000 |
| 19X5 | –0– |
| 19X6 | 10,000 |

What is the adjusted basis of the asset as of December 31, 19X6?

43. Four years ago B acquired an airplane for use in her business for $100,000. Since then, B has added equipment worth $20,000. Straight-line depreciation in the amount of $44,000 has been taken. B sold the airplane to P for $30,000 cash and property having a fair market value of $20,000. P also assumed a mortgage of $90,000 and accrued property taxes of $2,000. What is B's realized gain or loss? *C.P.A.*

44. T buys a watch from his employer for $2,500. The fair market value of the watch is $6,000. Assuming that the excess amount of $3,500 represents compensation for services rendered:

(a) What is T's basis in the watch?    6000

(b) Why?

45. R makes the following purchases and sales of stock:

| Transaction | Date | No. of Shares | Company | Price |
|---|---|---|---|---|
| Purchase | 1-1-X3 | 300 | MDG | $ 75 |
| Purchase | 6-1-X3 | 150 | RU | 300 |
| Purchase | 11-1-X3 | 60 | MDG | 60 |
| Sale | 12-3-X3 | 180 | MDG | 60 |
| Purchase | 3-1-X4 | 120 | RU | 375 |
| Sale | 8-1-X4 | 90 | RU | 330 |
| Sale | 1-1-X5 | 150 | MDG | 90 |
| Sale | 2-1-X5 | 75 | RU | 420 |

Assuming that R is unable to identify the particular lots which are sold with the original purchase, what is the realized gain (loss) on each type of stock as of:

(a) 7-1-X3

(b) 12-31-X3

(c) 12-31-X4

(d) 7-1-X5

46. T received various gifts over the years. He has decided to dispose of the following gifts:

(a) In 1923, he received land worth $20,000. The donor's adjusted basis was $24,000. He sells the land for $15,000 in 1983. Loss (9000)

(b) In 1935, he received stock in G Company. The donor's basis was $1,000. The fair market value on the date of the gift was $2,000. T sells the stock for $2,500 in 1983. 1500 g.

(c) In 1920, he received a Rolls Royce worth $22,000. The donor's basis for the auto was $16,000. He sells the auto for $35,000 in 1983.

(d) In 1951, he received land worth $12,000. The donor's adjusted basis was $9,000. He sells the land for $4,000 in 1983.

What is the realized gain (loss) from each of the above transactions? Assume that no gift tax was paid in any of the gift transactions.

47. L receives a gift of income-producing property which has an adjusted basis of $20,000 on the date of the gift. The fair market value of the property on the date of the gift is $18,000. Gift tax amounting to $400 was paid by the donor. L later sells the property for $19,000. Determine L's recognized gain or loss.

48. R receives a gift of property (after 1976) which has a fair market value of $100,000 on the date of gift. The donor's adjusted basis for the property was $40,000. Assume the donor paid gift tax of $16,000 on the gift. What is R's basis for gain or loss and for depreciation?

49. D bought a hotel for $720,000 on January 1, 1981. In January 1983, she died and left the hotel to E. D had deducted $42,000 depreciation on the hotel prior to her death. The fair market value in January 1983 was $780,000.

(a) What is the basis of the property to E?

(b) If the land is worth $240,000, what is E's basis for depreciation?

50. W purchased 50 shares of A Corporation common stock for $2,500 on May 12, 19X4. On August 12, 19X4, W purchased 25 additional shares for $1,375 and on August 27, 19X4, purchased 10 additional shares for $500. On September 3, 19X4, he sold the 50 shares purchased on May 12, 19X4, for $2,000.

(a) What is W's realized gain or loss on September 3, 19X4?

(b) What is his recognized gain or loss?

(c) What is the basis of W's remaining shares after the sale on September 3?

51. Which of the following qualify as like-kind exchanges under § 1031?

(a) Improved for unimproved real estate.

(b) Crane (used in business) for inventory.

(c) Rental house for truck (used in business).

(d) Business equipment for securities.

(e) Delicatessen for bakery (both used for business).

(f) Personal residence for apartment building (held for investment).

(g) Rental house for land (both held for investment).

52. What is the basis of the new property for each of the following?

(a) Lake-front property held for investment (fair market value $160,000) acquired in an exchange for an apartment building held for investment (adjusted basis $160,000).

(b) Barber shop (adjusted basis $30,000) for grocery store (fair market value $24,000), both held for business use.

(c) Drugstore (adjusted basis $30,000) for bulldozer (fair market value $20,000), both held for business use.

(d) IBM common stock (adjusted basis $2,500) for shoe shine stand used in business (fair market value $5,000).

(e) Rental house (adjusted basis $20,000) for land held for investment (fair market value $22,500).

53. F buys a warehouse with a 35-year life for $90,000 (ignore land) in January 19X2. The warehouse is not ACRS recovery property. Its estimated salvage value is zero, and F uses the straight-line method of depreciation. She exchanges the warehouse at the beginning of 19X6 for an office building to be used in a business which has a fair market value of $84,000. The newly acquired office building is depreciated at the rate of $3,000 a year. At the beginning of 19X8, F sells the office building for $75,000. What is the realized, recognized, and postponed gain (loss) and the new basis for each of these transactions?

54. Determine the realized, recognized, and postponed gain (loss) and the new basis for each of the following like-kind exchanges:      C. P. A

| | Adjusted Basis of Old Asset | Boot Given | Fair Market Value of New Asset | Boot Received |
|---|---|---|---|---|
| (a) | $ 7,000 | –0– | $ 4,000 | $ 4,000 |
| (b) | 4,000 | 2,000 | 5,000 | –0– |
| (c) | 2,000 | –0– | 1,000 | 1,200 |
| (d) | 3,000 | 7,000 | 8,000 | –0– |
| (e) | 2,500 | –0– | 2,000 | 1,500 |
| (f) | 8,000 | –0– | 10,000 | –0– |
| (g) | 10,000 | –0– | 11,000 | 1,000 |
| (h) | 6,000 | –0– | 7,500 | –0– |
| (i) | 10,000 | –0– | 9,000 | –0– |

55. Determine the realized, recognized and postponed gain (loss) for both A and B on the independent exchanges described below and calculate the new basis for each of the following transactions:

(a) A gives up a bus (used in business) with an adjusted basis of $3,000 and a fair market value of $2,500. B gives up office furniture with an adjusted basis of $1,000 and a fair market value of $1,500. B also gives A $1,000.

(b) A gives up office furniture with an adjusted basis of $8,000 and a fair market value of $6,000. He also gives B $1,000. B gives up business equipment with an adjusted basis of $4,500 and a fair market value of $7,000.

(c) A gives up an apartment building with an adjusted basis of $200,000 and a fair market value of $600,000. The apartment building carries a $250,000 mortgage which is assumed by B. B gives up a parking garage which was used in business with an adjusted basis of $250,000 and a fair market value of $350,000.

56. Do the following qualify for involuntary conversion treatment?

(a) Purchase of a sporting goods store as a replacement for a bookstore (used in business) which was destroyed by fire.

(b) Sale of a home because a neighbor converted his residence into a nightclub.

(c) Purchase of an airplane to replace a shrimp boat (used in business) which was wrecked by a hurricane.

(d) Destruction of taxpayer's residence by tornado.

(e) Purchase by an investor of an apartment building to replace a rental house destroyed by flood.

57. What is the *maximum* postponed gain (loss) for the following involuntary conversions:

| Property | Type of Conversion | Amount Realized | Adjusted Basis | Amount Reinvested |
|---|---|---|---|---|
| (a) Drugstore (business) | condemned | $ 160,000 | $ 120,000 | $ 100,000 |
| (b) Apartments (investment) | casualty | 100,000 | 120,000 | 200,000 |
| (c) Grocery store (business) | casualty | 400,000 | 300,000 | 350,000 |
| (d) Residence (personal) | casualty | 16,000 | 18,000 | 17,000 |
| (e) Vacant lot (investment) | condemned | 240,000 | 160,000 | 240,000 |
| (f) Residence (personal) | casualty | 20,000 | 18,000 | 19,000 |
| (g) Residence (personal) | condemned | 18,000 | 20,000 | 26,000 |
| (h) Apartments (investment) | condemned | 150,000 | 100,000 | 200,000 |

58. A taxpayer realizes $50,000 from the involuntary conversion of a factory. The adjusted basis of the factory was $25,000, and in the same year taxpayer spends $40,000 for a new factory.

(a) What is the realized gain or loss?

(b) What is the recognized gain or loss?

(c) What is the basis of the new factory?

(d) If taxpayer does not elect nonrecognition, what is the recognized gain and the basis of the new factory?

59. Which of the following are selling expenses, fixing-up expenses, or neither?

N (a) New swimming pool.

S (b) Legal fees to clear title to residence.

F (c) Painting outside of residence.

F (d) Repairing leaky plumbing.

N (e) New roof.

S (f) Advertising the residence for sale.

F (g) Painting living and dining rooms.

S (h) Broker commissions.

60. A taxpayer, age 47, decides to sell his residence, which has a basis of $22,500. In April 19X5, he spends $900 to paint the outside. In May 19X5, he sells the house for $27,000. Real estate brokerage commissions and other selling expenses are $1,000. In October 19X5, the taxpayer buys a new residence for $23,000.

(a) What is the taxpayer's realized gain or loss?

(b) The recognized gain or loss?

(c) The adjusted basis of the new residence?

What is the realized, recognized, and postponed gain (loss), the new basis, and the adjusted sales price for each of the following? Assume that none of the taxpayers are 55 years of age or older.

(a) R sells her residence for $90,000. The adjusted basis was $55,000. The selling expenses were $5,000. The fixing-up expenses were $3,000. She did not reinvest in a new residence.

(b) D sells his residence for $170,000. The adjusted basis was $120,000. The selling expenses were $4,000. The fixing-up expenses were $6,000. D reinvested $160,000 in a new personal residence.

(c) M sells her residence for $65,000. It had an adjusted basis of $35,000. The selling expenses were $1,000. The fixing-up expenses were $2,000. She reinvested $40,000.

(d) B sells his residence for $70,000. It has an adjusted basis of $65,000. The selling expenses were $6,000. He reinvested $80,000.

(e) D sells his residence for $100,000, and his mortgage was assumed by the buyer. The adjusted basis was $80,000; the mortgage, $50,000. The selling expenses were $4,000. The fixing-up expenses were $2,000. He reinvested $120,000.

## Cumulative Problems

62. R, age 67, is married and files a joint return with his wife, W, age 65. R and W are both retired. In 1983, they received Social Security benefits of $2,400.

R, who retired on January 1, 1981, receives benefits from a qualified pension plan of $600 a month for life. His total contributions to the plan were $18,000. He treated all retirement benefits received in 1981 and 1982 as a tax-free return on his investment.

W, who retired on December 31, 1982, received benefits of $800 a month beginning on January 1, 1983. Her life expectancy was 18 years from the annuity starting date, and her investment in the qualified pension plan was $57,600.

On September 27, 1982, R and W received a 10% stock dividend on 50 shares of stock they owned. They had paid $11 a share for the stock in 1976. On December 15, 1983, they sold the five shares received as a stock dividend for $30 a share.

Shortly after her retirement, W sold the car she had used in commuting to and from work. She paid $5,000 for the car in 1980 and sold it for $2,000. R and W received a gift of 100 shares of stock from their son, X, in 1976. X's basis in the stock was $30 a share, and the stock's fair market value at the date of gift was $25 a share. No gift tax was paid. R and W sold the stock in October 1983 for $15 a share.

R and W paid estimated Federal income tax of $200 and had itemized deductions of $3,800.

Compute their net tax payable (or refund due) for 1983. (Use the 1982 Tax Table for this computation. The 1983 Tax Table was not available at the date of publication of this text.)

63. G, age 41, is single and has no dependents. She is a self-employed

operator of a sole proprietorship. During 1983, gross income from her business was $120,000 and business expenses were $65,000. In addition, she had several property transactions related to her business. These transactions are not reflected in the above income and expense figures.

(a) Cash received on trade of a parcel of land on the outskirts of town (held for two years as a site for a new warehouse) for a lot near G's store. G intends to build a new warehouse on the lot. The old parcel has a fair market value of $28,000 and adjusted basis of $25,000. The fair market value of the new lot was $24,000.      $ 4,000

(b) Condemnation award from state for an acre of unimproved land (used for parking delivery vans) adjacent to the store (adjusted basis of the land was $12,000).      30,000

(c) Cost of an acre of unimproved land across the street from the store (the land is to be used for parking delivery vans).      25,000

G's personal transactions for 1983 are these:

(d) Cash received in exchange of 50 shares of X Corporation stock (adjusted basis of $20 a share, fair market value of $50 a share) for 50 shares of Y Corporation stock (fair market value of $40 a share). X Corporation and Y Corporation are not related, and G had held the X Corporation stock for two years.      500

(e) Amount realized on the sale of a condominium G used as her personal residence. The condominium was acquired in 1981 as a replacement for the house in which she formerly resided. She paid $60,000 for the condominium, and the amount realized for the house she sold was $80,000 (no fixing-up expenses and adjusted basis was $50,000). G is moving into an apartment and does not intend to replace the condominium.      65,000

(f) Cost of insulation installed in the condominium six months before it was sold. In 1980, G spent $1,300 to insulate the house she had owned prior to acquiring the condominium.      1,600

(g) Loss of amount G loaned to a friend in 1981 (the friend declared bankruptcy in 1983).      3,000

(h) G's interest income on personal savings accounts.      500

(i) Itemized deductions in 1983.      3,900

(j) Estimated Federal income tax payments.      21,000

Compute G's lowest net tax payable (or refund due) for 1983, assuming G makes any available election(s) which will reduce the tax. [Any gain recognized from items (a), (b), or (c) is § 1231 gain, which is discussed in Chapter 10, and this gain is to be treated as long-term capital gain.]

## Tax Form Problem

64. Ted Black, age 64, sold his personal residence on October 16, 1982, for $180,000. To make the house more attractive to buyers, he incurred fixing-up expenses of $1,000 on September 12, 1982. He paid a real estate broker's commission of $9,000 on the sale. Ted had paid $60,000 for his home and had lived in it for the past eight years. In December, he bought a much smaller home for $55,000. Ted elects to exclude gain under § 121. Compute the gain recognized (if any) on the sale of Ted's old residence, and determine the basis of his new residence. Use Form 2119 for your computations.

# Chapter 10

# Property Transactions: Capital Gains and Losses, Section 1231, and Recapture Provisions

## GENERAL CONSIDERATIONS

### RATIONALE FOR FAVORABLE CAPITAL GAIN TREATMENT

Given that a gain or loss is recognized, is it capital or ordinary? The capital gain provisions are intended to encourage the formation of private capital investment and to encourage risk taking by investors. In addition, preferential capital gain treatment is, in part, a recognition that appreciation in value over a long period should not be taxed in full in the year of realization. Favorable capital gain rates, in effect, offset the adverse "bunching effect" caused by recognition of all the gain in one year.[1]

This chapter is also concerned with § 1231, which applies to the sale or exchange of business properties and certain involuntary conversions, and with recapture provisions, which provide that certain gains which might otherwise qualify for long-term capital gain treatment or would not otherwise be recognized receive ordinary income treatment.

### GENERAL SCHEME OF TAXATION

Net capital gains (i. e., the excess of net long-term capital gain over net short-term capital loss) of noncorporate taxpayers are subject to a

---

1. Refer to the discussion under "Mitigating the Effect of the Annual Accounting Period Concept" in Chapter 1.

60 percent capital gain deduction for gains realized and installment payments received on or after November 1, 1978.[2] Ordinary gains (including short-term capital gains) are taxable in full and subject to the taxpayer's regular tax rates. The preferential treatment given long-term capital gains is discussed in detail later in the chapter.

Treatment as an ordinary loss generally is preferable to capital loss treatment, since ordinary losses are deductible in full, while the deductibility of capital losses is subject to certain limitations. The sum of an individual taxpayer's excess long-term and short-term capital losses for a taxable year is limited to a maximum $3,000 deduction.[3] However, both long-term and short-term capital losses are offset dollar for dollar against capital gains before this limitation comes into effect.

Short-term capital losses are preferable to long-term capital losses, because the latter are deductible only 50 cents on the dollar (after offsetting capital gains). The capital loss rules are discussed in detail later in the chapter.

A capital gain or loss arises from the recognition of gain or loss from the sale or exchange of a capital asset. In addition, a long-term capital gain or loss results only when a capital asset has been held for more than one year. If the capital asset has not been held for more than the required one-year period, the resulting capital gain or loss is short-term.

# WHAT IS A CAPITAL ASSET?

## DEFINITION OF A CAPITAL ASSET

Capital assets are not directly defined in the Code. § 1221 defines a capital asset as property held by the taxpayer (whether or not connected with his trade or business), but *not* including:

—Stock in trade, inventory, or property held primarily for sale to customers in the ordinary course of a trade or business. The Supreme Court, in *Malat v. Riddell,* defined primarily as meaning "of first importance" or "principally."[4]

—Depreciable property or real estate used in a trade or business.

—Certain copyrights, literary, musical, or artistic compositions, letters or memorandums, or similar property. (a) These assets are not capital assets if they are held by a taxpayer whose efforts created the property. (b) A letter, memorandum, or similar property is not a capital asset if it is held by a taxpayer for whom it was produced. In addition, the asset is not a capital

---

2.  § 1202(a) and Rev.Rul. 79–22, 1979–1 C.B. 275.
3.  § 1211(b).
4.  66–1 USTC ¶ 9317, 17 AFTR2d 604, 86 S.Ct. 1030 (USSC, 1966).

asset when the basis of such property is determined, for purposes of determining gain from a sale or exchange, in whole or part by reference to the basis of such property in the hands of a taxpayer described in (a) or (b).

—Accounts or notes receivable acquired in the ordinary course of a trade or business for services rendered or from the sale of inventory.

—Certain U. S. government publications. U.S. publications that are not capital assets are those (a) received by a taxpayer from the U.S. government other than by purchase at the price at which they are offered for sale to the public or (b) held by a taxpayer whose basis is determined by reference to a taxpayer described in (a).

Thus, the Code indirectly defines a capital asset by describing those items which are not capital assets. Therefore, by definition all other assets held by the taxpayer are capital assets. The principal assets excluded from the definition of a capital asset are inventory and business fixed assets (i. e., buildings, land, machinery, and equipment). Therefore, gains or losses from the disposition of these assets result in ordinary gain or loss instead of capital gain or loss. Business fixed assets may, however, qualify for long-term capital gains treatment under § 1231 (discussed later in the chapter).

The principal capital assets held by an individual taxpayer include personal use (as opposed to business) assets such as a personal residence or an automobile and assets held for investment purposes (e. g., land and corporate stock). Of course, losses from the sale or exchange of a taxpayer's personal use assets (as opposed to business or investment assets) are not recognized; therefore, their classification as capital assets is irrelevant for capital loss purposes.

## STATUTORY EXPANSIONS

In many cases, Congress has felt it necessary to expand the general definition of a capital asset as contained in § 1221.

*Dealers in Securities.* As a general rule, securities held by a dealer are considered to be inventory and are not, therefore, subject to capital gain or loss treatment. A dealer in securities is a merchant (e. g., a brokerage firm) that regularly engages in the purchase and resale of securities to customers. The dealer must identify any securities being held for investment. Prior to August 13, 1981, if a dealer clearly identified certain securities as held for investment purposes within 30 days after their acquisition, and they were not held at any time after such identification primarily for sale to customers in the ordinary course of business, gain from their sale was capital gain. Generally, since August 13, 1981, for tax years ending after August 12, 1981, if a dealer clearly identifies certain securities as held for investment purposes by the close of business on the date of their acquisition, gain from their sale will be capital gain. Losses are capital losses if at any time the securities have been clearly identified by the dealer as held for investment.[5]

*Real Property Subdivided for Sale.* Substantial development activities relative to real property may result in the owner's being considered a dealer for tax purposes. Thus, income from the sale of real estate property lots is treated as the sale of inventory (ordinary income) if the owner is considered to be a dealer. Section 1237 provides relief for investors in real estate who engage in limited development activities by allowing capital gain treatment if certain requirements are met. Section 1237 should be consulted for details relating to this special treatment.

*Lump-sum Distributions.* Section 402(a)(2) provides that lump-sum distributions from qualified pension and profit sharing plans are treated as long-term capital gain to the extent that the distribution exceeds the taxpayer's contributions to the plan. However, the amount treated as capital gain is limited to the portion of the excess which is attributable to participation in the plan prior to January 1, 1974. The amount attributable to participation after December 31, 1973, is ordinary income. A lump-sum distribution is defined generally as a distribution of the employee's entire balance within one taxable year following any of the following: death or disability of the employee, age 59½, or separation from service with the employer. The amount treated as ordinary income is subject to a special elective 10-year forward averaging procedure which can somewhat lighten the burden of this ordinary income treatment. An employee may now elect to treat all of the gain as ordinary income rather than a portion as long-term capital gain. In some instances, this election is preferable due to the imposition of the alternative minimum tax on the long-term capital gain portion and due to the favorable averaging treatment for the ordinary income amount.

*Nonbusiness Bad Debts.* As discussed in Chapter 6, nonbusiness bad debts are treated as short-term capital losses in the taxable year in which they become completely worthless, regardless of how long the debt has been outstanding. This is an excellent example of statutory expansion in the capital gain and loss area. Determining whether the property involved is a capital asset or not, whether a sale or exchange has taken place, and the holding period involved is not a problem, because the Code automatically provides that nonbusiness bad debts are, in all cases, short-term capital losses.

---

**5.** § 1236.

# SALE OR EXCHANGE

Recognition of capital gain or loss requires a sale or exchange of a capital asset. Section 1222 uses the term "sale or exchange" but does not define it. Generally, a sale involves the receipt of money or the assumption of liabilities for property, and an exchange involves the transfer of property for other property. Thus, an involuntary conversion (casualty, theft, or condemnation) is not a sale or exchange. In several areas, the determination of whether a sale or exchange has taken place has been clarified by the enactment of Code sections which specifically provide for sale or exchange treatment.

## WORTHLESS SECURITIES

Section 165(g)(1) provides that "if any security which is a capital asset becomes worthless during the taxable year, the loss resulting therefrom shall . . . be treated as a loss from the sale or exchange, on the last day of the taxable year, of a capital asset."

The reason for this provision is to solve the problems of determining (1) whether a sale or exchange has taken place and (2) when the loss occurs. The transaction is treated as being analogous to a sale or exchange of the security for no consideration. Therefore, an amount equal to the entire adjusted basis of the security is a capital loss. It should be noted that under certain circumstances, the worthless stock of a subsidiary corporation may be treated as an ordinary loss by the parent company.[6]

A loss from worthless securities, which would otherwise be short-term, may be converted to long-term, because the holding period is extended to the last day of the taxable year, regardless of when the security actually became worthless.

> **Example 1.** T purchases stock in P Corporation on December 1, 19X2, for $10,000. On August 1, 19X3, the corporation files a petition in a bankruptcy proceeding. In accordance with § 165(g)(1), T has a $10,000 long-term capital loss for taxable year 19X3. The stock is considered to be sold or exchanged on December 31, 19X3, which results in a holding period of more than one year.

This provision does not solve the problem of determining in what year the loss took place. A common identifiable event that often establishes the worthlessness of securities occurs when the corporation enters bankruptcy proceedings.

---

**6.** § 165(g)(3).

## SPECIAL RULE—RETIREMENT OF CORPORATE OBLIGATIONS

Under the general rule, the collection of a debt obligation does not constitute a sale or exchange. Therefore, any gain or loss on the collection of a note or other obligation cannot be capital gain or loss, since there is no sale or exchange. Section 1232 provides an exception for corporate and certain government obligations. The retirement of corporate and certain government obligations is considered to be an exchange and, therefore, usually is subject to capital gain or loss treatment.

> **Example 2.** T acquires XYZ Corporation bonds at $980 in the open market. If the bonds are held to maturity, the $20 difference between the maturity value of $1,000 and the taxpayer's cost of $980 is treated as a capital gain. If the obligation were issued by an individual instead of a corporation, the gain would be ordinary income rather than capital gain, since there was no sale or exchange.

Special rules apply to corporate and certain government obligations which were issued at a discount after May 27, 1969. Gain on the retirement or the sale of such discount obligations generally is treated as long-term capital gain if the obligation is a capital asset to the holder and has been held for the required long-term holding period (more than one year in 1978 and subsequent years).

## OPTIONS

As a general rule, the sale or exchange of an option to buy or sell property results in capital gain or loss if the property subject to the option is (or would be) a capital asset in the hands of the option holder.[7]

*Loss from Failure to Exercise Options.* If an option holder fails to exercise the option, the lapse of the option is considered a sale or exchange on the option expiration date. Thus, the loss is a capital loss if the property subject to the option is (or would be) a capital asset in the hands of the option holder.

The grantor of an option receives short-term capital gain or loss treatment upon the closing of the transaction for options granted after September 1, 1976. For example, an individual investor who owns certain stock may write a call option which entitles the purchaser of the option to acquire the stock at a certain price. The writer of the call receives a premium (e. g., 10 percent) for writing the option. If the price of the stock does not increase during the option period, the option will be allowed to expire unexercised. Upon the expiration of the option, the premium received is treated by the grantor as short-

---

**7.** § 1234.

term capital gain instead of ordinary income. The provisions of § 1234 do not apply to options held for sale to customers (i. e., inventory).

*Exercise of Options by Grantee.* If the option is exercised, the amount paid for the option is added to the selling price of the property subject to the option. This increases the gain to the grantor upon the sale of the property. The gain is capital or ordinary depending on the nature of the property sold. The grantee, of course, adds the cost of the option to the basis of the property. The grantor recognizes short-term capital gain or loss upon the closing of the transaction.

> **Example 3.** On September 15, 1976, X purchases 100 shares of Y Company stock for $5,000. On January 1, 1983, he writes a call option on the stock which gives the option holder the right to buy the stock for $6,000 during the following six-month period. X receives a call premium of $500 for writing the call.
>
> > —If the call is exercised by the option holder on August 1, 1983, X has $1,500 ($6,000 + $500 − $5,000) of long-term capital gain from the sale of the stock.
> >
> > —Assume that X decides to sell his stock prior to exercise for $6,000 and enters into a closing transaction by purchasing a call on 100 shares of Y Company stock for $5,000. Since the Y stock is selling for $6,000, X must pay a call premium of $1,000. He recognizes a $500 short-term capital loss [$1,000 (call premium paid) − $500 (call premium received)] on the closing transaction. On the actual sale of the Y Company stock, X has a long-term capital gain of $1,000 [$6,000 (selling price) − $5,000 (cost)].
> >
> > —Assume that the original option expired unexercised. X has a $500 short-term capital gain equal to the call premium received for writing the option. This gain is not recognized until the option expires.

## PATENTS

*Rationale for Capital Gain Treatment.* In certain circumstances, § 1235 may result in long-term capital gain treatment upon the sale of a patent. The justification for § 1235 (which results in preferential long-term capital gain) is primarily to encourage technological progress. This is perhaps ironic if the provision is contrasted with the treatment of authors, composers, and artists. The latter do not qualify for capital gain treatment in any case, because the results of their efforts are not capital assets and do not qualify under § 1231. Presumably, Congress did not choose to use the tax law to encourage cultural endeavors.[8] The following example illustrates the application of § 1235:

(your own Patent has zero basis).

---

8.   Refer to Chapter 1 for a discussion of how the tax law encourages certain economic activities.

(If you bought the patent it is a cap. asset.)

**Example 4.** T, a druggist, invents a pill-counting machine which he patents. In consideration of a lump-sum payment of $200,000 plus $10 per machine sold, T assigns the patent to Drug Products, Inc. Assuming T has transferred all substantial rights, the question of whether the transfer is a sale or exchange of a capital asset is not relevant. T automatically has a long-term capital gain from both the lump-sum payment and the $10 per machine royalty to the extent that these proceeds exceed his basis for the patent.

*Statutory Requirements.* The key issues relating to the transfer of patent rights are (1) whether the patent is a capital asset, (2) whether the transfer is a sale or exchange, and (3) whether all substantial rights to the patent (or an undivided interest therein) are transferred. Section 1235 was enacted primarily to resolve the issue of whether the transfer is a sale or exchange of a capital asset. This Section provides that:

> a transfer . . . of property consisting of all substantial rights to a patent, or an undivided interest therein which includes a part of all such rights, by any holder shall be considered the sale or exchange of a capital asset held for more than one year, regardless of whether or not payments in consideration of such transfer are (1) payable periodically over a period generally coterminous with the transferee's use of the patent, or (2) contingent on the productivity, use, or disposition of the property transferred.

If the transfer meets the requirements of § 1235, any gain or loss is automatically a long-term capital gain or loss regardless of whether the patent is a capital asset or not, whether the transfer is a sale or exchange, and how long the patent was held by the transferor.

## FRANCHISES

Prior to the enactment of § 1253 in 1969, there was a great deal of controversy in the courts with respect to the proper tax treatment relative to transfers of franchises. The key issue was whether the transfer was a sale or exchange as opposed to a license. Section 1253(a) generally solves this problem by providing that "a transfer of a franchise, trademark, or trade name shall not be treated as a sale or exchange of a capital asset if the transferor retains any significant power, right, or continuing interest with respect to the subject matter of the franchise, trademark, or trade name." Payments contingent on productivity, use, or disposition of the franchise, trademark, or trade name also are not treated as a sale or exchange of a capital asset.

A franchise is defined as an agreement which gives the transferee the right to distribute, sell, or provide goods, services, or facilities, within a specified area. A transfer includes the granting of a franchise, the transfer of a franchise by a grantee to a third party, or the renewal of a franchise.

> **Example 5.** T grants a franchise to U to sell fast foods. Payments to T are contingent on the profitability of the franchise outlet. The payments are ordinary income to T and deductible as a business expense by U.

> **Example 6.** T, a grantee of a franchise, sells the franchise to a third party. Payments to T are not contingent, and all significant powers, rights, and continuing interests are transferred. The payments are capital gain to T if the franchise is a capital asset.

*Sports Franchises.* Section 1253 does not apply to professional sports franchises.[9] However, the Tax Reform Act of 1976 imposed certain restrictions upon the allocation of the costs of acquiring a sports franchise to the cost basis of player contracts.[10] In addition, if a sports franchise is sold, gain from the sale of the player contracts is now subject to depreciation recapture as ordinary income under § 1245.[11]

## LEASE CANCELLATION PAYMENTS

The tax treatment of payments received in consideration of a lease cancellation depends on whether the recipient is the lessor or the lessee and whether the lease is a capital asset or not.[12]

*Lessee Treatment.* Payments received by a lessee in consideration of a lease cancellation are capital gains if the lease is a capital asset or § 1231 asset.[13] Generally, a lessee's lease would be a capital asset if the property is used for the lessee's personal use (e.g., his residence). A lessee's lease would be an ordinary asset if the property is used in the lessee's trade or business.

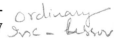
*Cap gain to the lessee.*

*Lessor Treatment.* Payments received by a lessor in consideration of a lease cancellation are always ordinary income, because they are considered to be in lieu of rental payments.

*Ordinary Inc — lessor.*

# HOLDING PERIOD

The required holding period for long-term capital gain or loss is "more than one year" for 1978 and subsequent years. (The holding period was "more than nine months" for 1977 and "more than six months"

---

**9.** § 1253(e).
**10.** § 1056.
**11.** § 1245(a)(4). See the discussion of the recapture provisions later in this chapter.
**12.** See the Glossary of Tax Terms (Appendix C) for definitions of the terms lessor and lessee.
**13.** § 1241 and Reg. § 1.1241–1(a).

for prior years.[14]) Conversely, gains or losses from the sale or exchange of capital assets not held for more than one year are short-term capital gains or losses.[15] In computing the holding period, start counting on the day after the property was acquired. In subsequent months, this same day is the start of a new month.[16] The following example illustrates the computation of the holding period:

> **Example 7.** T purchases a capital asset on March 15, 19X2, and sells it on March 16, 19X3. T's holding period is more than one year. If T had sold the asset on March 15, 19X3, the holding period would have been one year and the gain or loss would have been short-term.

A capital asset acquired on the last day of any month must not be disposed of until on or after the first day of the thirteenth succeeding month to be held for more than one year.[17]

> **Example 8.** T purchases a capital asset on January 31, 19X2, and sells it on February 1, 19X3. T's holding period is more than one year, and any gain or loss on the sale is long-term.

## REVIEW OF VARIOUS HOLDING PERIOD RULES

Section 1223 provides detailed rules for determining holding period. The application of these rules depends on the type of asset and how it was acquired.

*Tax-free Exchanges.* The holding period of property received in a nontaxable exchange includes the holding period of the former asset if the property which has been exchanged is a capital or § 1231 asset.[18] In certain nontaxable transactions involving a substituted basis, the holding period of the former property is "tacked on" to the holding period of the newly acquired property.

> **Example 9.** X exchanges a business truck for another truck in a like-kind exchange under § 1031. The holding period of the truck exchanged tacks on to the holding period of the new truck.

> **Example 10.** T sells his former personal residence and acquires a new residence. If the transaction qualifies under § 1034 for non-recognition of gain on the sale of a residence, the holding period of the new residence includes the holding period of the former residence.[19]

---

**14.** § 1223(3) and (4).
**15.** § 1222(1) and (2).
**16.** *Your Federal Income Tax.* IRS Publication 17 (Rev. Nov. 81), p. 111.
**17.** Rev.Rul. 66–7, 1966–1 C.B. 188.
**18.** § 1223(1).
**19.** § 1223(7).

*Certain Nontaxable Transactions Involving a Carryover of Basis.* The holding period of a former owner of property is tacked on to the present owner's holding period if the transaction is nontaxable and the basis of the property to the former owner carries over to the new owner.

**Example 11.** T transfers land to a controlled corporation in exchange for its common stock. If the transaction is nontaxable under § 351 (discussed more fully in Chapter 12), the corporation's holding period for the land includes the period the land was held by T.

**Example 12.** T acquires 100 shares of A Corporation stock for $1,000 on December 31, 19X2. The shares are transferred by gift to S on December 31, 19X3, when the stock is worth $2,000. S's holding period begins with the date the stock was acquired by T, since the donor's basis of $1,000 becomes the basis for determining gain or loss on a subsequent sale by S.

**Example 13.** Assume the same facts as in Example 12 except that the fair market value of the shares is only $800 on the date of the gift. The holding period begins on the date of the gift if S sells the stock for a loss, since the value of the shares at the date of the gift is used in the determination of basis.[20] If the shares are sold for $500 on April 1, 19X3, S has a $300 recognized capital loss and the holding period is from December 31, 19X2, to April 1, 19X3 (thus, the loss is short-term).

## SPECIAL RULES FOR SHORT SALES

The holding period of property sold short is determined under special rules provided in § 1233. A short sale occurs when a taxpayer sells borrowed property and repays the lender with substantially identical property either held on the date of the sale or purchased after the sale. Short sales usually involve corporate stock. The seller's objective is to make a profit in anticipation of a decline in the price of the stock. If the price declines, the seller in a short sale recognizes a profit equal to the difference between the sales price of the borrowed stock and the price paid for the replacement stock.

Section 1233(a) provides that "gain or loss from the short sale of property shall be considered as gain or loss from the sale or exchange of a capital asset to the extent that the property . . . used to close the short sale constitutes a capital asset in the hands of the taxpayer." No gain or loss is recognized until the short sale is closed.[21]

The general rule is that the holding period of the property sold

---

**20.** § 1223(2) and Reg. § 1.1223–1(b).
**21.** Reg. § 1.1233–1(a)(1).

short is determined by the length of time the seller held the property used to repay the lender when closing the short sale.

If substantially identical property has been held for less than the required long-term holding period (e. g., one year or less in 1978 and subsequent years) on the date of the short sale, the gain or loss is short-term.[22] If substantially identical property is acquired after the date of the short sale and on or before the closing date, the gain or loss is also short-term. If, however, substantially identical property has been held for the required long-term holding period on the date of the short sale, a gain on closing is long-term if the substantially identical property is used to close the sale but a loss on closing is long-term regardless of whether the substantially identical property is used to close the sale.[23]

The purpose of these special rules is to prevent the taxpayer from engaging in short sales in order to convert short-term capital gains to long-term capital gains or convert long-term capital losses to short-term capital losses. The discussion of capital gains and losses later in this chapter points out the advantage of long-term capital gains and short-term capital losses over short-term capital gains and long-term capital losses. The following examples illustrate the application of the special rules for short sales:

> **Example 14.** On January 2, 19X6, T purchases five shares of XYZ Corporation common stock for $100. On April 14, 19X6, she engages in a short sale of five shares of the same stock for $150. On August 15, T closes the short sale by repaying the borrowed stock with the five shares purchased on January 2. T has a $50 short-term capital gain from the short sale, because she held substantially identical shares for less than the required long-term holding period on the date of the short sale.

> **Example 15.** Assume the same facts as in Example 14 except that T closes the short sale on August 29 by repaying the borrowed stock with five shares purchased on August 29 for $200. Assume further that on August 30, T sells the five shares purchased on January 2 for $200. T has a $50 short-term capital loss from the short sale, because substantially identical shares were acquired after the short sale and on or before closing the sale. T has a $100 short-term capital gain from the sale on August 30, because she held substantially identical shares for less than the required long-term holding period when she sold short. The holding period for the shares sold on August 30 therefore begins on the closing date, August 29.[24]

---

**22.** § 1233(b) and Reg. § 1.1233–1(c)(1) and (2).

**23.** § 1233(d) and Reg. § 1.1233–1(c)(4).

**24.** § 1233(b)(2) and Reg. § 1.1233–1(c)(2).

**Example 16.**  On January 2, 19X2, T purchases five shares of X Corporation common stock for $100. She purchases five more shares of the same stock on April 14, 19X3, for $200. On August 15, 19X3, she sells short five shares of the same stock for $150. On September 30, she repays the borrowed stock with the five shares purchased on April 14 and sells the five shares purchased on January 2, 19X2, for $200. T has a $50 long-term capital loss from the short sale, because she held substantially identical shares for more than one year on the date of the short sale. T has a $100 long-term capital gain from the sale of the shares purchased on January 2, 19X2.

# TAX TREATMENT OF CAPITAL GAINS AND LOSSES OF NONCORPORATE TAXPAYERS

## TREATMENT OF CAPITAL GAINS

*Computation of Net Capital Gain.*  The first step in the computation is to net all long-term capital gains (LTCG) and losses (LTCL) and all short-term capital gains (STCG) and losses (STCL). The result is the taxpayer's net long-term capital gain (NLTCG) or loss (NLTCL) and net short-term capital gain (NSTCG) or loss (NSTCL).[25]

**Example 17.**  Some possible results of the first step in netting capital gains and losses are shown below. Assume that each case is independent (i. e., assume the taxpayer's only capital gains and losses are those shown in the given case).

| Case | STCG | STCL | LTCG | LTCL | Result of Netting | Description of Result |
|---|---|---|---|---|---|---|
| A | $ 8,000 | ($ 5,000) | | | $ 3,000 | NSTCG |
| B | $ 2,000 | ($ 7,000) | | | ($ 5,000) | NSTCL |
| C | | | $ 9,000 | ($ 1,000) | $ 8,000 | NLTCG |
| D | | | $ 8,800 | ($ 9,800) | ($ 1,000) | NLTCL |

The second step in netting capital gains and losses requires off-setting any positive and negative amounts which remain after the first netting step. This procedure is illustrated in the following examples.

**Example 18.**  Assume that T had all the capital gains and losses specified in Cases B and C in Example 17:

---

**25.**  § 1222(5), (6), (7) and (8).

| | | |
|---|---|---|
| Case C ($9,000 LTCG − $1,000 LTCL) | $ 8,000 | NLTCG |
| Case B ($2,000 STCG − $7,000 STCL) | ($ 5,000) | NSTCL |
| Excess of NLTCG over NSTCL | $ 3,000 | |

The $3,000 excess of NLTCG over NSTCL in Example 18 is defined as *net capital gain* (NCG).[26] Section 1202(a) provides favorable tax treatment for net capital gain. Noncorporate taxpayers are allowed to deduct 60 percent of net capital gain as a deduction for adjusted gross income. Thus, T may deduct $1,800 (60% of $3,000 NCG) in arriving at adjusted gross income, which means that only 40 percent of net capital gain is taxable.

**Example 19.** Assume that U had all the capital gains and losses specified in Cases A and D in Example 17:

| | | |
|---|---|---|
| Case A ($8,000 STCG − $5,000 STCL) | $ 3,000 | NSTCG |
| Case D ($8,800 LTCG − $9,800 LTCL) | ($ 1,000) | NLTCL |
| Excess of NSTCG over NLTCL | $ 2,000 | |

There is no special name for the excess of NSTCG over NLTCL, nor is there any special tax treatment. The nature of the gain is short-term, and the gain is included in U's gross income. The 60 percent capital gain deduction applies only to net capital gain (NCG). A review of Example 18 indicates that the nature of NCG is long-term while the nature of the gain in Example 19 is short-term.

Section 1222(9) defines the total excess of capital gains over capital losses as *capital gain net income*. However, the term has no special significance as far as tax treatment is concerned. If a taxpayer has both net capital gain and an excess of NSTCG over NLTCL (the total of the two being capital gain net income), this does not affect the treatment of either item. Net capital gain is reduced by the capital gain deduction (as shown in Example 18), and the excess of NSTCG over NLTCL is fully taxable (as shown in Example 19).

Capital gain planning is an important element in the development of an overall tax plan. Because of the 60 percent capital gain deduction, only 40 percent of net capital gain is taxable. This lowers the effective tax rate on net capital gain. To illustrate, assume a noncorporate taxpayer in the 50 percent bracket has $10,000 of ordinary income (e. g., interest). The effective rate on this ordinary income is 50 percent. On the other hand, assume the $10,000 is net capital gain. Only $4,000 of the net capital gain is taxable ($10,000 NCG − $6,000 capital gain deduction). The tax on net capital gain is only $2,000 ($4,000 × 50%), which results in an effective tax rate of 20 percent ($2,000 tax ÷ $10,000 NCG).

The effective rate on net capital gain for individuals can be com-

---

**26.** § 1222(11).

puted by multiplying the individual's marginal tax rate by 40 percent (since only 40 percent of NCG is taxable). Thus, in the previous illustration, the taxpayer's effective rate on net capital gain of 20 percent could have been computed by multiplying the marginal rate of 50 percent by 40 percent. A taxpayer in the 30 percent bracket, for example, would pay an effective rate on net capital gain of 12 percent (30% × 40%).

## TREATMENT OF CAPITAL LOSSES

*Computation of Net Capital Loss.*   The computation of a taxpayer's *net capital loss* involves the same netting process used for computing capital gain net income. A net capital loss results if the taxpayer's capital losses exceed the capital gains for the taxable year.[27] Again, it is necessary to differentiate between long-term and short-term capital losses. Both long-term and short-term capital losses offset either long-term or short-term capital gains. Losses remaining after such offset are treated differently depending on whether they are long-term or short-term.[28]

**Example 20.**   Three different individual taxpayers have the following capital gains and losses during the year:

| Taxpayer | LTCG | LTCL | STCG | STCL |
|---|---|---|---|---|
| R | $ 1,000 | ($ 2,800) | $ 1,000 | ($   500) |
| S | 1,000 | (   500) | 1,000 | (  2,800) |
| T | 400 | (  1,200) | 500 | (  1,200) |

R's net capital loss for the year is $1,300 (NLTCL of $1,800 less NSTCG of $500), all of which is long-term.

S's net capital loss is $1,300 (NSTCL of $1,800 less NLTCG of $500), all of which is short-term.

T's net capital loss is $1,500 (NLTCL of $800 plus NSTCL of $700), and it is part long-term ($800) and part short-term ($700).

*Treatment of Net Capital Loss.*   The general rule is that a net capital loss is deductible from gross income up to an amount equal to the lower of (1) the taxpayer's "taxable income, as adjusted" [taxable income figured without regard to gains or losses from sales or exchanges of capital assets and reduced (but not below zero) by the appropriate zero bracket amount] or (2) $3,000.[29] As a practical matter,

---

**27.**   § 1222(10) defines a net capital loss as the net loss after the deduction from ordinary taxable income (discussed later in this chapter). But this definition confuses the discussion of the treatment of capital losses, and therefore, capital loss is defined for practical purposes as the net loss before the deduction from ordinary taxable income.

**28.**   § 1211(b)(1) and Reg. § 1.1211–1(b)(1).

**29.**   § 1211(b) and Reg. § 1.1211–1(b)(2) and (6).

the taxpayer's "taxable income, as adjusted" usually will exceed these dollar limitations, and subsequent discussion assumes that it does. Married persons filing separate returns are each limited to one-half of the allowable amounts.[30]

*Special Limitation for Long-term Capital Loss After 1969.* Prior to 1970, both long-term and short-term capital losses offset ordinary taxable income dollar for dollar up to $1,000. Since net capital gains were previously subject to a 50 percent capital gain deduction, Congress changed the law effective January 1, 1970, to give a similar effect to long-term net capital losses. The change causes taxpayers to permanently lose a dollar of long-term net capital loss for every dollar of such loss deducted from ordinary taxable income.[31]

> **Example 21.** T has a net capital loss of $5,000 in 1983 of which $3,000 is long-term and $2,000 is short-term. Since short-term capital losses are always deducted first[32] and the total amount which is deductible is limited to $3,000, T deducts the $2,000 of net short-term loss and $1,000 of net long-term loss. The $1,000 deduction effectively uses up $2,000 of the net long-term loss. Therefore, only $1,000 of long-term net capital loss is carried over to 1984 as a long-term capital loss.

*Carryovers.* Taxpayers are allowed to carry over indefinitely unused capital losses, short-term or long-term (except for amounts of long-term capital loss permanently lost as a result of the 50 percent reduction).[33] Unused capital losses are carried over according to their original nature. That is, if a short-term capital loss is carried over to the following year, it is treated the same as a short-term capital loss occurring in that year. Accordingly, such a loss first would be used to offset short-term capital gains occurring in the following year.

> **Example 22.** In 19X2, T incurred LTCL of $11,000 and STCL of $1,000. In 19X3, T has no capital gains or losses.
>
> —T's capital loss for taxable year 19X2 is $12,000. T deducts $3,000 [$1,000 (short-term) and $2,000 (long-term) in 19X2]. The long-term portion ($2,000) of the loss deducted uses up $4,000 of the total long-term capital loss; thus, T has $7,000 (long-term) to carry over to 19X3.
>
> —T deducts $3,000 (long-term) in 19X3, using up $6,000 of the $7,000 long-term loss carried over from 19X2, and carries over $1,000 (long-term) to 19X4.

---

**30.** § 1211(b)(2) and Reg. § 1.1211–1(b)(7)(i).
**31.** § 1211(b)(1)(C)(ii) and Reg. § 1.1211–1(b)(2)(iii).
**32.** Reg. § 1.1211–1(b)(4)(i).
**33.** § 1212(b) and Reg. § 1.1212–1(b).

## REPORTING PROCEDURES

Capital gains and losses are reported on Schedule D of Form 1040. Part I of Schedule D provides for the reporting of short-term capital gains and losses, while Part II deals with long-term transactions (see below). On page 2 of Schedule D, Part III summarizes the results of Parts I and II and, as appropriate, allows for the 60 percent long-term capital gain deduction or applies the limitations on the deduction for capital losses. Part V concerns post-1969 capital loss carryovers, both short- and long-term. Schedule D is reproduced in Appendix B.

# TAX TREATMENT
# OF CAPITAL GAINS AND
# LOSSES OF CORPORATE TAXPAYERS

The treatment of a corporation's net capital gain or loss differs from the rules for individuals. Briefly, the differences are:

—There is no 60 percent capital gain deduction.[34]

—An alternative tax rate of 28 percent is allowed in computing the tax on net capital gain.[35]

—Capital losses offset only capital gains; no deduction is permitted against ordinary taxable income (whereas a $3,000 deduction is allowed to individuals).[36]

—There is a five-year carryover and a three-year carryback period for net capital losses.[37] Corporate carryovers and carrybacks are always treated as short-term, regardless of their original nature.

The rules applicable to corporations are discussed in greater detail in Chapter 12.

# SECTION 1231 ASSETS

## RELATIONSHIP TO § 1221

Section 1221(2) provides that depreciable or real property used in a trade or business is not a capital asset.[38] Thus, recognized gains from the disposition of such types of property (principally machinery and equipment, buildings, and land) would be ordinary income as opposed to capital gain. Section 1231, however, provides that in certain cases (i. e., when a holding period requirement is satisfied) long-term capi-

---

**34.** § 1202.
**35.** § 1201(a)(2).
**36.** § 1211(a).
**37.** § 1212(a)(1).
**38.** § 1221(2) and Reg. § 1.1221–1(b).

tal gain treatment may apply to sales, exchanges, and involuntary conversions of these business assets. Section 1231 also applies in certain cases to involuntary conversions of capital assets. The latter would not otherwise qualify for long-term capital gain treatment under § 1222, because an involuntary conversion is not a sale or exchange.

On the loss side, however, § 1231 may allow for ordinary (as opposed to capital) loss treatment. It seems, therefore, that § 1231 provides for the best of all possible worlds: capital gain treatment for gains and ordinary loss treatment for losses.

## JUSTIFICATION FOR FAVORABLE TAX TREATMENT

The highly favorable capital gain/ordinary loss treatment sanctioned by § 1231 can be explained by examining several historical developments. Prior to 1938, business property had been included in the definition of capital assets. Thus, if such property was sold for a loss (not an unlikely possibility during the years of the depression), a capital loss resulted. If, however, such property were depreciable and could be retained for its estimated useful life, much (if not all) of its cost could be recovered in the form of depreciation. Because the allowance for depreciation was fully deductible whereas capital losses were not, the tax law favored those who did not dispose of an asset. Congress recognized this inequity when it removed business property from the capital asset classification. During the period 1938–1942, therefore, all such gains and losses were ordinary gains and losses.

With the advent of World War II, however, several conditions forced Congress to reexamine the situation regarding business assets. First, the tax law did not encourage the sale of such assets if, as was usually the case, the result would be a large gain taxed as ordinary income. This was not a desirable result, since the premium should be on shifting business assets to those who could utilize them more effectively in the war production effort. Second, the government or its instrumentalities was acquiring, through the condemnation process, considerable business property for use by vital industries. Often the condemnation awards resulted in large gains to those taxpayers who were forced to part with their property and deprived them of the benefits of future depreciation deductions. Of course, the condemnations constituted involuntary conversions, the gain from which could be deferred through timely reinvestment in property that was "similar or related in service or use." But where was such property to be found in view of wartime restrictions and other governmental condemnations? The end product did not seem equitable: a large ordinary gain due to government action and no deferral possibility due to government restrictions.

In recognition of these two conditions, in 1942 Congress eased the tax bite on the disposition of some business property by allowing preferential capital gain treatment. Thus, the present scheme of § 1231 and the dichotomy of capital gain/ordinary loss treatment evolved due to a combination of economic considerations existing in 1938 and in 1942.

## PROPERTY INCLUDED

Section 1231 property includes:

—Depreciable or real property used in a trade or business (principally, machinery and equipment, buildings and land).[39] Inventory and property described in § 1221(3) (such as copyrights and literary compositions) and certain U. S. government publications described in § 1221(6) are not § 1231 property.[40]

—Timber, coal, or domestic iron ore to which § 631 applies.[41]

—Livestock (regardless of age) held for draft, breeding, dairy, or sporting purposes. Poultry is not included.[42]

—Unharvested crop on land used in a trade or business.[43]

—Certain capital assets.

*Certain Capital Assets.* The peculiar role that personal use capital assets can play in a § 1231 determination probably is the most confusing part of this whole area. Recall that involuntary conversions deal with two major categories: casualties (including thefts) and condemnations. The casualty gains and losses on involuntary conversions of assets (both business and personal) held for more than one year are combined (see Figure I). If the result is a gain, all of the casualty gains and losses are § 1231 transactions. If the result is a loss, § 1231 classification does not take place. Thus, a personal use capital asset that is subject to a casualty (e. g., a personal residence that is damaged by fire or a personal automobile that is stolen) may or may not be a § 1231 asset, depending on how the netting process works out.

Involuntary conversions due to condemnation are handled differently. If they involve *recognized* gains or losses of assets (both business and personal) held for more than one year, they are considered to be § 1231 assets. But since a loss from the condemnation of a personal use capital asset is not recognized, it cannot be classified as a § 1231 transaction. Consequently, only gains from the condemnation of personal use assets can be covered under § 1231.

When personal use assets are involved, why is it that a casualty loss *might* receive § 1231 treatment, whereas a condemnation loss

---

**39.** § 1231(b)(1) and Reg. § 1.1231–1(a).
**40.** § § 1231(b)(1)(A) through (D).
**41.** § 1231(b)(2).
**42.** § 1231(b)(3).
**43.** § 1231(b)(4).

cannot? The answer is quite simple. Section 165(c)(3) allows a deduction for personal casualty losses (refer to Chapter 6), while no provision in the Code accords similar treatment for condemnation losses. Recall that § 1033 (see Chapter 9) allows deferral of gains on involuntary conversions (including those resulting from condemnations) but does not apply to losses. This variation in treatment between casualty and condemnation losses sheds considerable light on what § 1231 is all about. Section 1231 has no effect on whether or not realized gain or loss is recognized. Instead, it merely dictates how such gain or loss might be classified (i. e., ordinary or capital) under certain conditions.

## EXCLUDED PROPERTY

Section 1231 property does not include:

—Property not held for more than one year.[44] Since the benefit of § 1231 is long-term capital gain treatment, the holding period must correspond with the same holding period which applies to capital assets. Livestock must be held either 12 or 24 months or more. Unharvested crops do not have to be held for the required long-term holding period, but the land must be held for more than one year.

—Property where casualty losses exceed casualty gains for the taxable year.[45] If a taxpayer has a net casualty loss, the individual casualty gains and losses are treated as ordinary gains and losses.[46]

—Inventory and property held primarily for sale to customers.[47]

—Section 1221(3) property (e. g., copyrights, literary compositions) and § 1221(6) property (i. e., certain U. S. government publications).[48]

## GENERAL PROCEDURE FOR § 1231 COMPUTATION

The tax treatment of § 1231 gains or losses depends on the results of a rather complex netting procedure. The steps in this netting procedure are described below.

*Step 1.* Net all gains and losses from casualties and thefts of property held for more than one year. The losses from personal casualties are determined after reduction by the $100 floor. Casualty gains result when insurance proceeds exceed the adjusted basis of the property.

---

**44.** § 1231(a) and Reg. § 1.1231–1(a).
**45.** § 1231(a) and Reg. § 1.1231–1(e)(3).
**46.** Reg. §§ 1.1231–1(e)(3) and –1(g) Example 2.
**47.** §§ 1231(b)(1)(A) and (B) and Reg. § 1.1231–1(a).
**48.** §§ 1231(b)(1)(C) and (D).

(a) If the casualty gains exceed the casualty losses, add the excess to the other § 1231 gains for the taxable year.[49]

(b) If the casualty losses exceed the casualty gains, exclude all losses and gains from further § 1231 computation.[50] If this is the case, all casualty gains are ordinary income. Business casualty losses are deductible *for* adjusted gross income. Personal casualty losses in excess of $100 per casualty are deductible *from* adjusted gross income (to the extent they exceed 10 percent of adjusted gross income).

*Step 2.* After adding any net casualty gain from Step 1(a) to the other § 1231 gains (including recognized gains and losses from condemnations), net all § 1231 gains and losses.

(a) If the gains exceed losses, the excess is a long-term capital gain.[51]

(b) If the losses exceed gains, all gains are ordinary income; business losses are deductible *for* adjusted gross income; and personal casualty losses in excess of $100 per casualty are deductible *from* adjusted gross income (to the extent they exceed 10 percent of adjusted gross income).[52]

If the taxpayer is in a position to recognize § 1231 gains in one year and § 1231 losses in another year, the losses will not have to be offset against the gains. The result is that all the gains in one year are long-term capital gains and all the losses in the other year are ordinary losses deductible in full against ordinary income. Figure I summarizes the § 1231 computational procedure.

The following examples illustrate the application of the § 1231 computation procedure.

**Example 23.** During 1983, T had $25,000 of adjusted gross income before considering the following recognized gains and losses:

| Capital gains and losses | |
|---|---|
| Long-term capital gain | $ 3,000 |
| Long-term capital loss | (400) |
| Short-term capital gain | 1,000 |
| Short-term capital loss | (200) |

| Casualties | |
|---|---|
| Theft of diamond ring (owned four months) | (800)* |
| Fire damage to personal residence (owned 10 years) | (400)* |
| Gain from insurance recovery on accidental destruction of business truck (owned two years) | 200 |

(*As adjusted for the $100 floor on personal casualty losses.)

---

**49.** § 1231(a) and Reg. § 1.1231–1(e)(1).
**50.** § 1231(a) and Reg. § 1.1231–1(e)(3).
**51.** § 1231(a). The gains and losses are reported individually on the tax return.
**52.** Ibid.

## Figure I

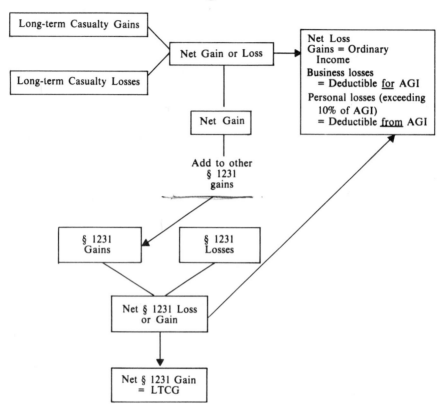

| § 1231 gains and losses from depreciable business assets held over one year | |
| --- | --- |
| Asset A | 300 |
| Asset B | 1,100 |
| Asset C | (500) |

| Gains and losses from depreciable business assets held one year or less | |
| --- | --- |
| Asset D | 200 |
| Asset E | (300) |

(* As adjusted for the $100 floor on personal casualty losses.)

Disregarding the recapture of depreciation possibility (discussed later in the chapter), the tax treatment of the above gains and losses is as follows:

—The theft of the diamond ring is not a § 1231 transaction, because it was not held for more than one year. The $800 loss is potentially deductible *from* AGI (if T's casualty losses exceed 10% of AGI).

—The casualty loss of $400 exceeds the casualty gain of $200. Therefore, both the loss and gain are excluded from § 1231 treatment. The $400 loss is potentially deductible *from* adjusted gross income (personal loss) and the $200 gain is ordinary income.

—The gains from § 1231 transactions (Assets A, B, and C) exceed the losses by $900 ($1,400 less $500). This excess is a long-term capital gain and is added to T's other long-term capital gains.

—T's net long-term capital gain is $3,500 ($3,000 plus $900 from § 1231 transactions less the long-term capital loss of $400). T's net short-term capital gain is $800 ($1,000 less $200). The result is capital gain net income of $4,300. The long-term portion ($3,500) is subject to the 60% capital gain deduction. The $800 short-term portion is ordinary income and subject to T's regular tax rates.

—The gain and loss from Assets D and E (depreciable business assets held for less than the required holding period) are treated as ordinary gain and loss by T.

Results of the gains and losses on<br>T's tax computation

| | |
|---|---:|
| Included portion of NLTCG [$3,500 − ($3,500 × 60%)] | $ 1,400 |
| STCG | 800 |
| Ordinary gain from truck casualty | 200 |
| Ordinary gain from sale of Asset D | 200 |
| Ordinary loss from sale of Asset E | (300) |
| AGI from other sources | 25,000 |
| AGI | $27,300 |

T would have casualty losses of $800 (diamong ring) + $400 (personal residence). The combined loss of $1,200 is deductible only to the extent it exceeds 10% of AGI. Thus, none of the $1,200 is deductible ($27,300 × 10% = $2,730).

**Example 24.** Assume the same facts as in Example 23 except the loss from Asset C was $1,500 instead of $500.

—The treatment of the casualty losses is the same as in Example 1.

—The losses from § 1231 transactions now exceed the gains by $100 ($1,500 less $1,400). The result is that the gains from Assets A and B are ordinary income and the loss from Asset C is a deduction *for* adjusted gross income (i. e., a business loss). The same result can be achieved by simply treating the $100 net loss as a deduction *for* adjusted gross income.

—Capital gain net income gain is $3,400 ($2,600 long-term plus $800 short-term). The $2,600 long-term portion is subject to the 60% capital gain deduction. The $800 short-term portion is ordinary income.

| Results of the gains and losses on T's tax computation | |
|---|---:|
| Included portion of NLTCG [$2,600 − ($2,600 × 60%)] | $ 1,040 |
| STCG | 800 |
| Net ordinary loss on Assets A, B, and C | ( 100) |
| Ordinary gain from truck casualty | 200 |
| Ordinary gain from sale of Asset D | 200 |
| Ordinary loss from sale of Asset E | ( 300) |
| AGI from other sources | 25,000 |
| AGI | $26,840 |

None of the personal casualty loss would be deductible, since $1,200 does not exceed 10% of $26,840.

**Example 25.** Assume the same facts as in Example 23 except that the casualty gain was $600 instead of $200.

—The casualty gain of $600 exceeds the casualty loss of $400; therefore, the $200 excess gain is added to the other § 1231 gains.

—The gains from § 1231 transactions (Assets A, B, and C and the net casualty gain) exceed the losses by $1,100 ($1,400 plus net casualty gain of $200 less $500). This excess is a long-term capital gain and is added to T's other long-term capital gains.

—T's net long-term capital gain is $3,700 ($3,000 plus $1,100 from § 1231 transactions less the long-term capital loss of $400). T's net short-term capital gain is $800. The result is capital gain net income of $4,500. The long-term portion ($3,700) is subject to the 60% capital gain deduction. The $800 short-term portion is ordinary income and subject to T's regular tax rates.

| Results of the gain and losses on T's tax computation | |
|---|---:|
| Included portion of NLTCG [$3,700 − ($3,700 × 60%)] | $ 1,480 |
| STCG | 800 |
| Ordinary gain from sale of Asset D | 200 |
| Ordinary loss from sale of Asset E | ( 300) |
| AGI from other sources | 25,000 |
| AGI | $27,180 |

The personal casualty loss is $800 (diamond ring). The $400 (personal residence) casualty loss has been absorbed against the $600 (truck) casualty gain. None of $800 is deductible, because it does not exceed 10% of $27,180.

# SECTION 1245 RECAPTURE

Section 1245 was enacted to prevent taxpayers from receiving the dual benefits of depreciation deductions which offset ordinary income plus long-term capital gain treatment under § 1231 on the disposition of the depreciated property.

> **Example 26.** T purchased a business machine for $100,000 and deducted $60,000 of depreciation on the machine before selling it for $80,000. If it were not for § 1245, only 40% of the $40,000 § 1231 gain ($80,000 less $40,000 of adjusted basis) would be subject to tax. The 60% capital gain deduction would result in only $16,000 of gain being taxed. If the depreciation recapture rules were not applicable, T would receive a net tax benefit by deducting depreciation as an ordinary deduction in the years prior to the sale. Section 1245 prevents this otherwise favorable result by recapturing as ordinary income (not § 1231 gain) any gain to the extent of depreciation taken since 1962. In this example, the entire $40,000 gain would be taxed as ordinary income, assuming the machine was acquired after 1961 or that depreciation taken since 1962 is at least $40,000.

Section 1245 provides, in general, that the portion of recognized gain from the sale or other disposition of § 1245 property which represents depreciation taken since January 1, 1962 (including additional first year depreciation under § 179 on assets acquired prior to 1981), is recaptured as ordinary income. Any gain in excess of the amount recaptured as ordinary income will be § 1231 gain.

This provision also applies to recognized gains from the sale or other disposition of § 1245 recovery property under the Economic Recovery Tax Act of 1981 (ERTA). Section 1245 recapture also applies to amounts expensed under § 179 as amended by ERTA of 1981 (refer to Chapter 6). In addition, § 1245 applies to the reduction of basis for one-half of the investment credit required by new § 48(q)(5), which was added by TEFRA (refer to the discussion in Chapter 6). This basis reduction rule applies to property placed in service after 1982. Finally, § 1245 provisions apply to 15-year nonresidential real property if its cost is recovered under the statutory percentage method of the accelerated cost recovery system.

## SECTION 1245 PROPERTY

Generally, § 1245 property includes all depreciable personalty (e. g., machinery and equipment), including livestock. Buildings and their structural components are not § 1245 property. The following property is also subject to § 1245 treatment:

—Amortizable personalty such as patents, copyrights and leaseholds of § 1245 property. Professional baseball and football player contracts are § 1245 property.

—Elevators and escalators. However, only depreciation taken after June 30, 1963, is recaptured.

—Certain depreciable tangible real property (other than buildings and their structural components) employed as an integral part of certain activities such as manufacturing and production.

—Pollution control facilities, railroad grading and tunnel bores, on-the-job training, and child care facilities on which amortization is taken.

—Single purpose agricultural and horticultural structures and petroleum storage facilities.

—As noted above, 15-year nonresidential real estate for which accelerated cost recovery is used is subject to the § 1245 recapture rules, although it is technically not § 1245 property.

## SECTION 1245 POTENTIAL

The following examples express the general application of § 1245.

**Example 27.**  Assume T owns § 1245 property with an estimated useful life of 12 years, acquisition cost on January 1, 1973, of $12,000, and no salvage value. The asset is sold on January 1, 1983, for $13,000. Depreciation amounting to $10,000 has been deducted under the straight-line method.

—The recognized gain from the sale is $11,000. This is the amount realized of $13,000 less the adjusted basis of $2,000 ($12,000 cost less $10,000 depreciation taken).

—Depreciation taken since January 1, 1962, is $10,000. Therefore, $10,000 of the $11,000 recognized gain is ordinary income and the remaining $1,000 gain is § 1231 gain.

**Example 28.**  Assume the same facts as in Example 27 except the asset is sold for $9,000 instead of $13,000.

—The recognized gain from the sale is $7,000. This is the amount realized of $9,000 less adjusted basis of $2,000.

—Depreciation taken since January 1, 1962, is $10,000. Therefore, since the $10,000 depreciation taken since January 1, 1962, exceeds the recognized gain of $7,000, the entire $7,000 recognized gain is ordinary income.

**Example 29.** Assume the same facts as in Example 27 except the asset is sold for $1,500 instead of $13,000.

— The recognized loss from the sale is $500. This is the amount realized of $1,500 less adjusted basis of $2,000.

— § 1245 does not apply, because the recapture rules do not apply to losses. The entire $500 recognized loss is § 1231 loss.

## OBSERVATIONS ON § 1245

— In most instances, the total depreciation taken since January 1, 1962, will exceed the recognized gain. Therefore, the disposition of § 1245 property usually results in ordinary income rather than gain under § 1231. Thus, generally, there will be no § 1231 gain unless the § 1245 property is disposed of for more than its original cost (refer to Example 27).

— Recapture applies to the total amount of depreciation allowed or allowable regardless of the depreciation method used.

— Recapture applies regardless of the holding period of the property. Of course, the entire recognized gain would be ordinary income if the property were held for one year or less, because § 1231 would not apply.

— Section 1245 does not apply to losses. Losses receive § 1231 treatment.

# SECTION 1250 RECAPTURE PRIOR TO ERTA OF 1981

Section 1250 was enacted in 1964 for depreciable real property. This provision prevents taxpayers from receiving both the benefits of accelerated depreciation deductions and subsequent long-term capital gain treatment upon the sale of real property. As was true in the case of § 1245, § 1250 does not apply to losses.

Section 1250 as originally enacted required recapture of a percentage of the *additional depreciation* deducted by the taxpayer. Additional depreciation is the excess of accelerated depreciation actually deducted over depreciation which would have been deductible if the straight-line method had been used. The percentage of additional depreciation subject to recapture was dependent on the period of time the property was held. Numerous modifications of § 1250 have added much complexity to these once simple provisions, as discussed below.

## SECTION 1250 POTENTIAL

For § 1250 property other than residential rental property, the potential recapture is equal to the amount of additional depreciation taken since December 31, 1969. (The rules for residential rental housing are discussed later in the chapter.) The lower of the potential § 1250 recapture amount or the gain is multiplied by a percentage to determine the amount of gain recaptured as ordinary income. The following general rules apply:

—Post-1969 additional depreciation is depreciation taken in excess of straight-line after December 31, 1969.

—The post-1969 percentage is 100 percent.

—If the property is held for one year or less (usually not the case) all depreciation taken, even under the straight-line method, is additional depreciation.

—Special rules apply to dispositions of substantially improved § 1250 property. These rules are rather technical, and the reader should consult the examples in the Regulations for illustrations of their application.

It should be observed that the recapture rules under § 1250 are substantially less punitive than § 1245 recapture rules, since only the amount of additional depreciation is subject to recapture. Straight-line depreciation (except for property held one year or less) is not recaptured.

## COMPUTING RECAPTURE

The following procedure is used to compute recapture on nonresidential real property under § 1250:

—Determine the gain from the sale or other disposition of the property.

—Determine post-1969 additional depreciation.

—The lower of the gain or the post-1969 additional depreciation is ordinary income.

—If any gain remains after the recapture of post-1969 additional depreciation, it is § 1231 gain.

The following example shows the application of the § 1250 computational procedure:

**Example 30.**  On January 3, 1971, T, an individual, acquired a new building at a cost of $200,000 for use in his business. The building had an estimated useful life of 50 years and no estimated salvage value. Depreciation has been taken under the double-declining method through December 31, 1982. Pertinent information with respect to depreciation taken follows:

| Year | Undepreciated Balance (Beginning of the Year) | Current Depreciation Provision | Straight-Line Depreciation | Additional Depreciation |
|------|------|------|------|------|
| 1971 | $ 200,000 | $ 8,000 | $ 4,000 | $ 4,000 |
| 1972 | 192,000 | 7,680 | 4,000 | 3,680 |
| 1973 | 184,320 | 7,373 | 4,000 | 3,373 |
| 1974 | 176,947 | 7,079 | 4,000 | 3,079 |
| 1975 | 169,868 | 6,795 | 4,000 | 2,795 |
| 1976 | 163,073 | 6,523 | 4,000 | 2,523 |
| 1977 | 156,550 | 6,262 | 4,000 | 2,262 |
| 1978 | 150,288 | 6,012 | 4,000 | 2,012 |
| 1979 | 144,276 | 5,771 | 4,000 | 1,771 |
| 1980 | 138,505 | 5,540 | 4,000 | 1,540 |
| 1981 | 132,965 | 5,319 | 4,000 | 1,319 |
| 1982 | 127,646 | 5,106 | 4,000 | 1,106 |
| 1983 | 122,540 | | | |
| Total 1971–1982 | | $ 77,460 | $ 48,000 | $ 29,460 |

On January 2, 1983, the building was sold for $147,638. Compute the amount of § 1250 ordinary income and § 1231 gain.

—The recognized gain from the sale is $25,098. This is the difference between the $147,638 realized and the $122,540 adjusted basis ($200,000 cost less $77,460 depreciation taken).

—Post-1969 additional depreciation is $29,460.

—The amount of post-1969 ordinary income is $25,098; the post-1969 additional depreciation of $29,460 is more than the recognized gain of $25,098.

—Since all of the $25,098 gain is recaptured as ordinary income under § 1250, there is no § 1231 gain to receive favorable long-term capital gain treatment.

# ACRS RULES FOR RECAPTURE— REAL PROPERTY

Under ACRS, the treatment of residential real property (e.g., apartment buildings) is unchanged; that is, gain is recaptured as ordinary income only to the extent of additional depreciation. In this case, additional depreciation is defined as the excess of the ACRS deduction using the statutory percentage method over the deduction which would be allowed using the straight-line method over 15 years.

**Example 31.** T acquired residential real property on January 1, 1982 at a cost of $100,000. He uses the statutory percentage method for computing the cost recovery allowance under ACRS. He sells the asset on January 1, 1985, for $120,000. The amount and nature of T's gain will be computed as follows:

| | | |
|---|---:|---:|
| Amount realized | | $ 120,000 |
| Adjusted basis: | | |
|   Cost | $ 100,000 | |
|   Minus cost recovery | | |
|     allowances: | | |

| | | | |
|---|---:|---:|---:|
|     1982 | $ 12,000 | | |
|     1983 | 10,000 | | |
|     1984 | 9,000 | 31,000 | 69,000 |
|   Gain realized | | | $ 51,000 |

If T had used the straight-line method, total cost recovery allowances would have been $20,000 [($100,000 ÷ 15) × 3 years]. Therefore, T must recapture the excess ACRS deduction of $11,000 ($31,000 − $20,000) as ordinary income. The remaining gain of $40,000 ($51,000 − $11,000) will be § 1231 gain.

Recapture on most nonresidential real property is no longer governed by § 1250. Instead, the § 1245 recapture provisions apply to real property other than (1) residential real property, (2) real property used predominantly outside the United States, (3) real property for which the optional straight-line election is made, and (4) certain government-financed or low-income housing (as described in § 1250(a)(1)(B)).[53] In other words, § 1245 recapture provisions apply to nonresidential real property located in the United States for which the ACRS statutory percentage method is used to compute the cost recovery allowance.

If the cost of nonresidential property subject to the § 1245 provisions is recovered under the statutory percentage method, gain is treated as ordinary income to the extent of *all* recovery allowances previously taken. On the other hand, if the optional straight-line method is elected, all gain will be § 1231 gain.

**Example 32.** Assume the same facts as in Example 31 except that the property is nonresidential real property. The gain of $51,000 will be treated as ordinary income to the extent of all cost recovery allowances previously taken. Thus, T will report ordinary income of $31,000 (total cost recovery allowances) and § 1231 gain of $20,000 ($51,000 gain − $31,000 recaptured as ordinary income).

**Example 33.** Assume the same facts as in Example 31 except that the property is nonresidential real property and that T elected the optional straight-line method over 15 years. T's entire gain of $40,000 [$120,000 amount realized − ($100,000 cost − $20,000 recovery allowances using straight-line method)] will be § 1231 gain. T will not be required to recognize any ordinary income on this transaction.

---

**53.**   § 1245(a)(1) and § 1245(a)(5).

# CONSIDERATIONS COMMON TO §§ 1245 AND 1250

## EXCEPTIONS

Recapture under §§ 1245 and 1250 does not apply to the following transactions:

1. *Gifts.*[54] However, the recapture potential carries over to the donee.[55]

**Example 34.** T gives his daughter, D, § 1245 property with an adjusted basis of $1,000. The amount of recapture potential (i. e., depreciation taken since January 1, 1962) is $700. D uses the property in her business and claims further depreciation of $100 before selling it for $1,900. D's recognized gain is $1,000 (amount realized of $1,900 less $900 adjusted basis), of which $800 is recaptured as ordinary income ($100 depreciation taken by D plus $700 recapture potential carried over from T). The remaining gain of $200 is § 1231 gain. Even if D used the property for personal purposes, the $700 recapture potential would still be carried over.

2. *Charitable Transfers.* The recapture potential reduces the amount of the charitable contribution deduction under § 170.[56]

**Example 35.** T donates to his church § 1245 property with a fair market value of $10,000 and an adjusted basis of $7,000. Assume that the amount of recapture potential is $2,000 (i. e., the amount of recapture that would occur if the property were sold). T's charitable contribution deduction (subject to the limitations discussed in Chapter 7) is $8,000 ($10,000 fair market value less $2,000 recapture potential).

3. *Like-kind Exchanges (§ 1031) and Involuntary Conversions (§ 1033).* Gain may be recognized to the extent of boot received under § 1031, and gain also may be recognized to the extent the proceeds from an involuntary conversion are not reinvested in similar property under § 1033. Such recognized gain is subject to recapture as ordinary income under §§ 1245 and 1250. In addition, gain may be recaptured to the extent of any non-Section 1245 like-kind property which is received in the exchange.[57]

---

54. §§ 1245(b)(1) and 1250(d)(1) and Reg. §§ 1.1245–4(a)(1) and 1.1250–3(a)(1).
55. Reg. §§ 1.1245–2(a)(4), 1.1250–2(d)(3) and 1.1250–3(a)(3).
56. § 170(e)(1)(A) and Reg. § 1.170–1(c)(3).
57. § 1245(b)(4) and Reg. § 1.1245–4(d). Also, see § 1250(d)(4) and Reg. § 1.1250–3(d)(1) for recapture rules applicable to real property.

**Example 36.** T exchanges § 1245 property with an adjusted basis of $300 for § 1245 property with a fair market value of $6,000. The exchange qualifies as a like-kind exchange under § 1031(a). T also gives $5,000 cash (boot). T's realized gain is $700 [amount realized of $6,000 less $5,300 (adjusted basis of property plus boot given)]. Assuming the recapture potential is $4,500, gain is not recognized, because no boot or non-Section 1245 like-kind property is received. The entire recapture potential of $4,500 carries over to the like-kind property received.

Recapture rules under §§ 1245 and 1250 override all other sections of the Code.

# SPECIAL
# RECAPTURE PROVISIONS

## RECAPTURE OF INVESTMENT CREDIT BASIS REDUCTION

The basis reduction under § 48(q) for investment tax credit was discussed in Chapter 6. This basis reduction amount is subject to § 1245 recapture. However, if there is an investment credit recapture upon disposition of the property, one-half of the investment credit recapture is added back to the property's basis before computing gain or loss.

**Example 37.** B purchased business machinery in January 1983 for $100,000. In 1983, B took $10,000 of investment credit ($100,000 × 10%) and $14,250 of cost recovery [$100,000 − ($10,000 × ½) = $95,000; $95,000 × 15% = $14,250)]. In February 1984, B found that the machine was ineffective and sold it for $84,750. B's gain or loss would be zero. B would have an investment credit recapture of $8,000. B's recomputed credit is $2,000 (2% of $100,000). The balance of the credit is recaptured. One-half of the $8,000 recaptured would be added back to the machine's basis. Thus, the basis at sale would be $84,750 ($100,000 − $5,000 − $14,250 + $4,000).

**Example 38.** Assume the same facts as in Example 37 except that B held the machine for six years and then sold it for $96,000. B would have no investment credit recapture, because he held the machine for the ACRS recovery period of at least five full years. His basis at sale would be zero. He would have taken $95,000 of cost recovery and $5,000 of basis reduction due to the investment credit. His gain is $96,000 ($96,000 sale price − zero basis), and it is all recaptured under § 1245 as ordinary income.

## GAIN FROM SALE OF DEPRECIABLE PROPERTY
## BETWEEN CERTAIN RELATED PARTIES

In general, § 1239 provides that in the case of a sale or exchange, directly or indirectly, of depreciable property (principally machinery, equipment, and buildings, but not land) between spouses or between an individual and his or her controlled corporation, any gain recognized is ordinary income. Depreciable means subject to depreciation in the hands of the transferee.

> **Example 39.** T sells a personal automobile to her controlled corporation. The automobile originally cost $5,000 and is sold for $7,000. The automobile is to be used in the corporation's business. If § 1239 did not exist, T would realize a long-term capital gain (assuming the asset is held more than one year) of $2,000. The income tax consequences would be favorable, because T's controlled corporation is entitled to depreciate the automobile (assuming business use) based upon the purchase price of $7,000. Under § 1239, the $2,000 gain is ordinary income.

Section 1239 was enacted to prevent certain related parties from enjoying the dual benefits of long-term capital gain treatment (transferor) and a stepped-up basis for depreciation (transferee). Recapture under § § 1245 and 1250 applies first before recapture under § 1239.

Control for purposes of § 1239 means ownership of 80 percent in value of the corporation's outstanding stock. In determining the percentage of stock owned, the taxpayer must include that owned by related taxpayers as determined under the constructive ownership rules of § 318.

It should be noted that § 267(a)(1) disallows a loss on the sale of property between related taxpayers. Therefore, a sale of property between related parties may result in ordinary income (if the property is depreciable) or a nondeductible loss.

Section 1239 applies regardless of whether the transfer is from a stockholder to the corporation or from the corporation to a stockholder. Ordinary income treatment also applies to transfers (after October 4, 1976) between two corporations controlled by the same stockholder. Prior to the change in the law, the courts held that § 1239 ordinary income treatment was not applicable to transfers between two controlled corporations.

> **Example 40.** T, the sole shareholder of X Corporation, sells a building (adjusted basis of $40,000) to the corporation for $100,000. Since the building was depreciated by T using the straight-line method, none of the depreciation will be recaptured under § 1250. Nevertheless, § 1239 applies to convert T's § 1231 gain of $60,000 to ordinary income. The basis of the building to X Corporation becomes $100,000 (its cost).

## RESIDENTIAL RENTAL HOUSING

Section 1250 recapture applies to the sale or other disposition of residential rental housing. The rules are the same as for other § 1250 property except that only the post-1975 excess depreciation is recaptured in full.[58] The post-1969 through 1975 recapture percentage is 100 percent less one percentage point for each full month the property is held over 100 months.[59] Therefore, the excess depreciation for periods after 1975 is initially applied against the recognized gain, and such amounts are recaptured in full as ordinary income. Any remaining gain is then tested under the percentage rules applicable to the post-1969 through 1975 period. If any of the recognized gain is not absorbed by the recapture rules pertaining to the post-1969 period, the remaining gain is § 1231 gain. Property qualifies as residential rental housing only if at least 80 percent of gross rental income is rental income from dwelling units.[60]

> **Example 41.** Assume the same facts as in Example 30 except the building is residential rental housing.
>
> —Post-1975 ordinary income is $12,533 (post-1975 additional depreciation of $12,533 is less than the recognized gain of $25,098).
>
> —Post-1969 through 1975 ordinary income is $5,520. The post-1969 through 1975 additional depreciation of $16,927 is more than the remaining gain of $12,565 ($25,098 less $12,533). The post-1969 through 1975 percentage is 44% [100% less (156% less 100%)]. The building was held for 156 months, or 56 months over 100 months. Thus, 44% of $12,565 is $5,529.
>
> —Since only $18,062 ($12,533 plus $5,529) is recaptured as ordinary income under § 1250, the remaining $7,036 ($25,098 − $18,062) of the $25,098 gain is § 1231 gain and may receive favorable long-term capital gain treatment.

## REHABILITATION EXPENDITURES FOR LOW-INCOME RENTAL HOUSING

Section 1250 recapture applies to the sale or other disposition of Federally assisted housing projects and low-income housing with respect to which rapid amortization of rehabilitation expenditures under § 167(k) has been taken. The rules are generally the same as for residential rental housing except that post-1975 excess depreciation is not recaptured in full (i. e., the post-1969 percentage rules continue to apply.)[61]

This preferential treatment afforded residential rental housing and low-income rental housing is the result of Congressional desire to

---

**58.**  § 1250(a)(1)(B)(v).
**59.**  § 1250(a)(1)(B)(iii) and Reg. § 1.1250–1(d)(1)(i)(c).
**60.**  § 167(j)(2)(B) and Reg. § 1.167(j)–3(b)(1)(i).
**61.**  § 1250(a)(1)(B)(iii). See the Glossary of Tax Terms (Appendix C) for a discussion of rehabilitation expenditures.

stimulate the construction and reconstruction of residential rental property. The special rules for depreciating or amortizing these properties are discussed in Chapter 6.

## FARM RECAPTURE PROVISIONS

The cash method of accounting can be and usually is used for farming operations. It should be noted, however, that certain large corporations and partnerships that are engaged in farming are required to use the accrual method of accounting and to capitalize preproductive period expenses.[62] Under the cash method, the taxpayer is allowed the dual benefits of current deductions for the costs of raising livestock and producing crops and long-term capital gain treatment under § 1231 on the sale or other disposition of farm property. Many higher income nonfarmer taxpayers have engaged in farming activities as a hobby. Such activities are particularly attractive if a nonfarmer is permitted a deduction for farm losses as an offset against income from nonfarming sources (e. g., salaries or professional fees). Therefore, Congress enacted two farm recapture provisions in 1969 with an eye toward minimizing the use of farming investments by higher income taxpayers as shelters for their income from other sources. The objective of these provisions was to limit long-term capital gain treatment for such taxpayers on the disposition of certain farm property. The farm recapture provisions are found in § § 1251 and 1252.

## INTANGIBLE DRILLING COSTS

Section 263(c) provides that taxpayers may elect to expense or capitalize intangible drilling and development costs. Intangible drilling and development costs (IDC) include all expenditures made by an operator (one who holds a working or operating interest in any tract or parcel of land) for wages, fuel, repairs, hauling, supplies, etc., incident to and necessary for the drilling of wells and preparation of wells for the production of oil or gas. In most instances, taxpayers have elected to expense IDC due to the opportunities for accelerating tax deductions.

Intangible drilling and development costs that are paid or incurred after December 31, 1975, are recaptured if such costs were expensed rather than capitalized. On the sale or other disposition of such oil or gas properties, the gain is treated as ordinary income to the extent of the lesser of the following.[63]

—IDC expensed after 1975 less amounts which would have been deductible as cost depletion if the IDC had been capitalized.

—The amount realized from the sale, exchange, or involuntary conversion of the property (or fair market value if the property

---

**62.** § § 447 and 464.
**63.** § 1254(a)(1).

is otherwise disposed of) in excess of the adjusted basis of the property.

Special rules are provided for determining recapture upon the sale or other disposition of a portion or an undivided interest in oil and gas property.[64]

> **Example 42.** X acquired a working interest in certain oil and gas properties for $50,000 during 1982. He incurred $10,000 of intangible development and drilling costs. X elected to expense these costs in 1982. In January 1983, the properties were sold for $60,000. Disregard any depreciation on tangible depreciable properties and assume that cost depletion would have amounted to $2,000. The gain realized and recognized is $10,000 ($60,000 − $50,000). The gain is recaptured as ordinary income to the extent of IDC less the amount which would have been deducted as cost depletion (e. g., $10,000 − $2,000) or $8,000, which is less than the amount realized ($10,000). Therefore, $8,000 is recaptured.

# REPORTING PROCEDURES

Noncapital gains and losses are reported on Form 4797, Supplemental Schedule of Gains and Losses. Before resorting to Form 4797, however, Form 4684, Casualties and Thefts, must be completed to determine whether or not such transactions will enter into the § 1231 computation procedure. Recall that this will occur only if a net gain results from casualties and thefts of property held for more than one year. Forms 4797 and 4684 are reproduced in Appendix B.

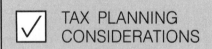

## TAX PLANNING CONSIDERATIONS

### MAXIMIZING BENEFITS

Due to the favorable tax rates applicable to long-term capital gains, consideration always should be given to the relative tax benefits which accrue from holding a capital asset for the required long-term holding period. Since net short-term capital gains are includible in income in full, consideration should be given prior to the end of the year to the sale of capital assets at a loss. This approach would help to offset any short-term gains which have been recognized during the year.

Ordinary losses generally are preferable to capital losses due to the limitations which are imposed on the deductibility of net capital

---

**64.** § 1254(a)(2).

losses and the requirement that capital losses be used to offset capital gains. The taxpayer may be able to convert what would otherwise have been capital loss to ordinary loss. For example, business (but not nonbusiness) bad debts, losses from the sale or exchange of small business investment company stock, and losses from the sale or exchange of small business company stock all result in ordinary losses.[65] Also, it should be noted that the acquisition of the stock of a supplier in order to assure a source of supply (with no substantial investment motive) should result in ordinary loss treatment if the stock is sold at a loss. Finally, if the taxpayer must generate a capital loss, it is preferable that it be a short-term capital loss.

Although capital losses can be carried over indefinitely, indefinite becomes definite when a taxpayer dies. Any loss carryovers not used by such taxpayer are permanently lost; that is, no tax benefit can be derived from the carryovers subsequent to death. Therefore, the potential benefit of carrying over capital losses diminishes when dealing with older taxpayers.

## SPREADING GAINS

It is usually beneficial to spread gains over more than one taxable year. In some cases, this can be accomplished through the installment sales method of accounting. The bunching of long-term capital gains in one taxable year can be detrimental if the alternative minimum tax applies. Since the alternative minimum tax is applicable only when it exceeds the regular Federal income tax liability for the year, it is possible to spread the long-term capital gains over several years and therefore avoid payment of any alternative minimum tax.

## YEAR-END PLANNING

Some general rules for timing the recognition of capital gains and losses near the end of a taxable year are these:

—If the taxpayer already has LTCL, recognize STCG.

**Example 43.** T has already incurred LTCL of $6,000 for the taxable year. Every dollar of STCG that T recognizes before the end of the year will result in offsetting income (i. e., STCG) which would be fully taxable against loss (i. e., LTCL) which would be deductible only 50 cents on the dollar. If T's only capital loss is the $6,000 capital loss, only $3,000 would be deductible in the taxable year. On the other hand, if T also recognized STCG of $6,000, the entire LTCL would be offset against the STCG.

—If the taxpayer already has STCG, recognize LTCL.
—If the taxpayer already has STCL, recognize STCG. Do not recognize LTCG, because then the 60 percent capital gains

---

**65.** §§ 166(d), 1242 and 1244. Refer to the discussion in Chapter 6.

deduction (for the noncorporate taxpayer) or alternative tax benefits (for corporate taxpayers) are eliminated on the gain, which is offset against the STCL.

**Example 44.** T, who is a 50% bracket taxpayer, has already incurred an STCL of $6,000. If T recognizes a $6,000 STCG before the end of the year, he will have used the STCL to offset $6,000 of income which would have been subject to a maximum tax rate of 50%. If T recognizes an LTCG, he will have used the STCL to offset $6,000 of income which would have been subject to a maximum tax rate of 20% (40% of the LTCG times the maximum tax rate of 50%). If T does not recognize any gain, he will be allowed to deduct $3,000 of the STCL this year and carry the remaining $3,000 over to next year.

## STOCK SALES

The following rules apply in determining the date of a stock sale:

—If the taxpayer is on the accrual basis, the date the sale is executed is the date of the sale. The execution date is the date the broker completes the transaction on the stock exchange.

—If the taxpayer is on the cash basis and the sale results in a gain, the date the sale is settled is the date of the sale. The settlement date is the date the cash or other property is paid for the stock.

—If the taxpayer is on the cash basis and the sale results in a loss, the date the sale is executed is the date of the sale.

Thus, year-end sales at a gain will not be recognized in the current year if the settlement date for the sale falls in the following year.

**Example 45.** T, a cash basis taxpayer, sells stock which results in a gain. The sale was executed on December 29, 19X2, and the settlement date is January 5, 19X3. The date of sale is January 5, 19X3 (the settlement date), because the sale resulted in a gain. If the sale resulted in a loss, the date of sale would be December 29, 19X2. For purposes of determining the holding period, however, the date of sale is December 29, 19X2 (the trade date).

Under the new installment sale provisions, recognition of the gain in Example 45 could be shifted to 19X2 by electing *not* to use the installment method when the taxable year 19X2 income tax return is filed. Installment treatment is automatic unless the taxpayer elects not to have installment treatment apply.

## PLANNING FOR CAPITAL ASSET STATUS

It is important to keep in mind that capital asset status often is a question of intent. Thus, property that is not a capital asset to one party may qualify as a capital asset to another party.

**Example 46.** T, a real estate dealer, transfers by gift a tract of land to S, her son. The land was part of T's inventory (i. e., it was held for resale) and was therefore not a capital asset to her. S, however, keeps the land as an investment. The land is a capital asset in S's hands, and any later taxable disposition by him of the property will yield a capital gain or loss.

If proper planning is carried out, even a dealer may obtain favorable long-term capital gain treatment on the sale of the type of property normally held for resale.

**Example 47.** T, a real estate dealer, segregates tract "A" from the real estate he regularly holds for resale and designates such property as being held for investment purposes. The property is not advertised for sale and is eventually disposed of several years later. The negotiations for the subsequent sale were initiated by the purchaser and not by T. Under these circumstances, it would appear that any gain or loss from the sale of tract "A" should be a capital gain or loss.

## EFFECT OF CAPITAL ASSET STATUS IN OTHER THAN SALE TRANSACTIONS

The nature of an asset (i. e., capital or ordinary) is important in determining the tax consequences that result when a sale or exchange occurs. It may, however, be just as significant absent a taxable sale or exchange. One such situation involves a donation of appreciated property to a qualified charity. Recall that the measure of the charitable contribution is fair market value when the property, if sold, would have yielded a long-term capital gain [refer to Chapter 7 and the discussion of § 170(e)].

**Example 48.** In 1983, T wants to donate a tract of unimproved land (basis of $40,000 and fair market value of $200,000 and held for more than one year) to Rutgers University (a qualified charitable organization). However, T currently is under audit by the IRS for capital gains she reported on certain real estate transactions during 1980–1982. Although T is not a licensed real estate broker, the IRS agent conducting the audit is contending that she has achieved dealer status by virtue of the number and frequency of the real estate transactions she has conducted. Under these circumstances, T would be well-advised to postpone the donation to Rutgers University until such time as her status is clarified. If she has achieved dealer status, the unimproved land may be inventory and T's charitable contribution deduction would be limited to $40,000. If not, and if the land is held as an investment, T's deduction becomes $200,000 (i. e., the fair market value of the property).

## TIMING OF § 1231 GAIN

Although §§ 1245 and 1250 recapture much of the gain from the disposition of business property, situations exist whereby § 1231 gain will be substantial. For instance, land held as a trade or business asset will generate either § 1231 gain or § 1231 loss. If the taxpayer already has a capital loss for the year, the sale of land at a gain should be postponed so that the net § 1231 gain is not netted against the capital loss. The capital loss deduction will, therefore, be maximized. If the taxpayer already has a § 1231 gain, § 1231 losses should be postponed to maximize the ordinary loss deduction. If the taxpayer already has a § 1231 loss, § 1231 gains should be postponed to maximize the ordinary loss deduction this year and the LTCG deduction next year.

> **Example 49.** T has a net short-term capital loss this year of $2,000. He could sell business land for a § 1231 gain of $3,000. He will have no other capital gains and losses or § 1231 gains and losses this year or next year. T is in the 30% tax bracket. He will have a $1,000 LTCG ($3,000 § 1231 gain − $2,000 STCL) for this year if he sells the land. He will pay a tax of 30% on $400 [$1,000 − ($1,000 × 60% LTCG deduction)], or $120. If T sells the land next year, he will have tax savings of $600 ($2,000 STCL × 30%) this year and pay a tax of 30% on $1,200 [$3,000 LTCG − ($3,000 × 60% LTCG deduction)], or $360, next year. The net tax savings from selling the land next year would be $240 ($600 tax savings this year − $360 tax payments next year). The difference between the two alternatives (sell land this year or sell land next year) is $360 ($120 tax payments from the first alternative plus $240 tax savings from the second alternative).

> **Example 50.** S has a § 1231 loss this year of $15,000. He could sell business equipment for a § 1231 gain of $20,000 and a § 1245 gain of $12,000. S's tax bracket is 50%. If he sells the equipment this year, he will pay a tax of $7,000. He would have a net LTCG of $5,000 ($20,000 § 1231 gain − $15,000 § 1231 loss). The tax on the taxable portion of the LTCG is $1,000 [$5,000 − ($5,000 × 60%) = $2,000; $2,000 × 50% = $1,000]. The tax on the § 1245 gain would be $6,000 ($12,000 × 50%). If S sold the equipment next year, the tax savings this year would be $7,500 ($15,000 × 50%). Next year, the tax would be $10,000 [$20,000 LTCG − ($20,000 × 60%) = $8,000; $8,000 × 50% = $4,000; $12,000 § 1245 gain × 50% = $6,000; $4,000 + $6,000 = $10,000]. For the two years, the combined tax would be $2,500. Under the first alternative (sell the equipment this year) the tax was $7,000. Postponing the equipment sale saves $4,500 in tax.

## TIMING OF RECAPTURE

Since recapture is usually not triggered until the property is sold or disposed of, it may be possible to plan for recapture in low bracket or loss years. If a taxpayer has net operating loss carryovers which are about to expire, the recognition of ordinary income from recapture may be advisable to absorb the loss carryovers.

**Example 51.** T has a $15,000 net operating loss carryover that will expire this year. He owns a machine which he plans to sell in the early part of next year. The expected gain of $17,000 from the sale of the machine will be recaptured as ordinary income under § 1245. T sells the machine prior to the end of this year and offsets $15,000 of the ordinary income against the net operating loss carryover.

## POSTPONING AND SHIFTING RECAPTURE

It is also possible to postpone recapture or to shift the burden of recapture to others. For example, recapture is avoided upon the disposition of a § 1231 asset if the taxpayer replaces the property by entering into a like-kind exchange. In this instance, recapture potential is merely carried over to the newly acquired property (refer to Example 36).

Recapture can be shifted to others through the gratuitous transfer of § 1245 or § 1250 property to family members. A subsequent sale of such property by the donee will trigger recapture to the donee rather than the donor (refer to Example 34). Such procedure would be advisable only if the donee is in a lower income tax bracket than the donor.

## AVOIDING RECAPTURE

Although not a very attractive tax planning approach, death eliminates all recapture potential.[66] In other words, any recapture potential does not carry over from a decedent to an estate or heir.

## ECONOMIC CONSIDERATIONS

The advisability of using accelerated depreciation methods should not be diminished by the fact that such depreciation amounts may subsequently be recaptured. Assuming no significant change in tax rates, the time value of money usually dictates deducting as much depreciation as possible (i. e., a dollar of depreciation deduction today usually is worth more than a dollar of ordinary income in the future).

## ACRS STRAIGHT-LINE ELECTION TO AVOID RECAPTURE

Since all cost recovery allowances must be recaptured on nonresidential property written off using the ACRS statutory percentage method (refer to Example 32), taxpayers should consider electing the optional straight-line method for cost recovery purposes. If the optional

---

**66.** § § 1245(b)(2) and 1250(d)(2).

straight-line method is elected, there is no recapture on disposition of the property (refer to Example 33).

---

## PROBLEM MATERIALS

---

### Questions for Discussion

*60% deduction*

1. What type of preferential treatment is afforded long-term capital gains? What is the justification for this treatment?

2. Is there any reason a taxpayer would prefer to recognize a loss as a capital loss rather than as an ordinary loss?

3. Define a long-term capital gain or loss.

4. What broad class of assets is not capital assets?

5. Can the sale of personal use assets result in capital losses? *no*

6. When is the worthlessness of a security which is a capital asset recognized? Does this always result in a capital loss? *sec 1244 stock — ordinary loss.*

7. What are the two requirements for the recognition of a capital gain or loss?

8. If an individual pays a $100 premium to acquire an option to buy stock, how does the call premium affect the basis of the stock if the option is exercised?

9. What is a franchise? In practice, does the transfer of a franchise usually result in capital gain (loss) treatment? Why or why not?

10. When are lease cancellation payments capital in nature?

11. How does one determine if a capital asset has been held for more than one year and is therefore eligible for long-term capital gain (or loss) treatment?

12. Define a short sale. Why does a seller enter into a short sale?

13. Differentiate between the capital loss carryover rules for unused capital losses of individuals and corporations.

14. What planning procedures are available to maximize the benefits of a long-term capital loss? Of a short-term capital loss? Why?

15. What type of transactions involving capital assets are included under § 1231? Why wouldn't they qualify for long-term capital gain treatment without § 1231?

16. Why was § 1231 originally enacted? Why is it still in the law today?

17. What is the effect of an asset's holding period on its ability to qualify for special treatment under § 1231? Why? *> 1 yr.*

18. Under what circumstances is a casualty gain not afforded long-term capital gain treatment? Why?

19. Describe the treatment that results if a taxpayer has net § 1231 losses.

20. What property is excluded from § 1231?

21. Why was § 1245 enacted? How does it achieve this objective?

22. Differentiate between the types of property covered by § § 1245 and 1250.

23. What are the two major differences in the computation of depreciation recapture under § § 1245 and 1250? Why do these differences exist?

24. List the tax-free transactions which do not cause recapture to be recognized immediately but require it to be carried over to the transferee.

25. What provisions do the recapture rules override?

26. Why was § 1239 enacted? How does it accomplish its goals?

27. Contrast the recapture treatment which is accorded to intangible drilling and development costs for 1976 and subsequent years with the treatment in prior years.

28. Comment on: Death eliminates all recapture potential. Why or why not?

## Problems

29. Dr. T purchased securities of D Corporation on November 1, 19X5, for $300. On July 1, 19X6, D Corporation filed bankruptcy proceedings.
    (a) What is the realized and recognized loss? *300*
    (b) Explain the nature of the loss. *— long term cap. loss.*
    (c) Would your answer change if Dr. T were a securities dealer and not a physician? Explain. *— ordinary business loss.*
    (d) If Dr. T dealt in securities but clearly identified these securities as held for investment on November 1, 19X5, would the answer to part (c) change? *yes .(*

30. T acquires an option on a new house at a fixed price. She is contemplating using the house as her personal residence. She decides to sell the option and not purchase the house.
    (a) Assume T sells the option for more than she paid for it. What is the nature of the gain?
    (b) Assume she sells the option at a loss. What is the nature of the loss?
    (c) Assume T is a real estate broker, intended to sell the house as a part of a new development project, and failed to exercise the option. What is the nature of the loss?

31. Roller Rink No. 3 wishes to sell the franchise it has from Roller Rink Corporation, to W, who is in the process of buying Roller Rink No. 3's equipment and location. Under the franchise terms, it can be sold only with the approval of Roller Rink Corporation. Roller Rink No. 3 purchased the five-year franchise three years ago for $20,000. Current basis is $10,000. They will sell it for $15,000. What kind of income is realized and recognized by Roller Rink No. 3?

32. F exchanges a business copying machine for another copier in a § 1031 like-kind exchange. F acquired the machine on March 12, 19X0, and the exchange occurred on July 3, 19X2.
    (a) When does the holding period of the new machine begin?
    (b) How would the answer to (a) change if the transaction were the replacement of a personal residence and the taxpayer qualified under § 1034? *— no change .*

33. T sells short 50 shares of ABC stock at $20 per share on January 1, 19X7. He buys 200 shares of ABC stock on April 1, 19X7, at $15 per share and

holds the latter until May 2, 19X8, at which time, 50 shares of the 200 share block are delivered to close the short sale made on January 1, 19X7.

(a) What is the amount and nature of T's gain or loss upon closing the short sale?

(b) When does the holding period for the remaining 150 shares begin?

34. U, an unmarried individual with no dependents, has the following transactions in 1983:

| | | |
|---|---|---|
| Taxable income (exclusive of capital gains and losses) | $ 15,000 | |
| Long-term capital gain | 4,000 | |
| Long-term capital loss | (900) | |
| Short-term capital gain | 1,000 | |
| Short-term capital loss | (1,600) | |

What is U's net capital gain or loss? What is U's adjusted gross income?

35. X, an unmarried individual with no dependents, has the following 1983 transactions:

| | |
|---|---|
| Taxable income (exclusive of capital gains and losses) | $ 15,000 |
| Long-term capital loss | (5,000) |
| Long-term capital gain | 2,000 |
| Short-term capital loss (carried to 1983 from 1982) | (2,000) |

What is X's net capital gain or loss? What is X's adjusted gross income?

36. B, an unmarried individual with no dependents, has the following transactions in 1983:

| | |
|---|---|
| Taxable income (exclusive of capital gain and losses) | $ 15,000 |
| Long-term capital loss | (3,000) |
| Long-term capital loss (carried to 1983 from 1982) | (1,000) |
| Short-term capital gain | 11,000 |
| Short-term capital loss (carried over to 1983 from 1982) | (6,000) |

What is B's net capital gain or loss? What is X's adjusted gross income?

37. S, a married individual filing a separate return, has the following capital gains and losses in 1983:

| | |
|---|---|
| Long-term capital loss | $ (3,000) |
| Short-term capital gain | 2,000 |
| Short-term capital loss (carryover from 1982) | (3,000) |

Explain the tax treatment of these items.

38. In 1983, K realized a short-term capital gain of $2,000, a long-term capital gain of $12,000 and a long-term capital loss of $2,000.

What is K's net capital gain or loss? How is it treated?

39. T's airplane, used for vacations and acquired for that purpose in 19X0 at a cost of $50,000, was requisitioned by the government in 19X6 for $10,000. What are T's tax consequences?

40. D is the sole proprietor of a trampoline shop. During 1983, the following transactions occurred:

(1) Unimproved land adjacent to the store was condemned by the city on February 1, 1983. The condemnation proceeds were $25,000. The land, acquired in 1957, had an allocable basis of $15,000. D has additional parking across the street and plans to use the condemnation proceeds to build his inventory.

(2) A truck used to deliver trampolines was sold on January 2, 1983, for $3,500. The truck was purchased on January 2, 1980, for $6,000. The vehicle was depreciated over a six-year life using the 200% declining-balance method. On the date of sale, the adjusted basis was $2,667.

(3) D sold an antique rowing machine at an auction. Net proceeds were $3,900. The rowing machine was purchased as used equipment 27 years ago for $5,200 and had been depreciated over a 20-year life using the straight-line method. Depreciation taken after December 31, 1961, was $2,700. The adjusted basis of the machine was $500 (salvage value) on the date of sale.

(4) D sold an apartment building for $200,000 on September 1, 1983. The rental property was purchased on September 1, 1980, for $150,000 and was being depreciated over a 30-year life using the straight-line method. At the date of sale, the adjusted basis was $135,000.

(5) D's personal yacht was stolen September 5, 1983. It had been purchased in August 1983 at a cost of $25,000. The fair market value immediately preceding the theft was $20,000. D was insured for 50% of the original cost, and he received $12,500 on December 1, 1983.

(6) A 1982 Buick was sold by D on May 1, 1983, for $9,600. The vehicle was used exclusively for personal purposes. It has been purchased on September 1, 1981, for $10,800.

(7) An adding machine used by D's bookkeeper was sold on June 1, 1983. Net proceeds of the sale were $135. The machine was purchased on June 2, 1979, for $350. It was being depreciated over a five-year life employing the straight-line method. The adjusted basis on the date of sale was $70.

(8) D's trampoline stretching machine (owned for two years) was stolen on May 5, 1983, but the business insurance company will not pay any of it's value because D failed to pay the premium.

    (a) For each transaction, what is the amount of recognized gain or loss and what is its nature?

    (b) For all transactions, what is the amount of net long-term capital gain?

41. V, an individual taxpayer, files her income tax return on the calendar year basis. Her recognized gains and losses for 19X8 of the kind described in § 1231 are as follows:

(a) $3,000 gain reported in 19X8 (under § 453) on installment sale in 19X7 of warehouse used in business (including land and building held for six years).
                               *1231 gain*

(b) $2,000 gain on sale of moving vehicles used in warehouse business and subject to depreciation allowance, held for three years. *— ordinary inc — dep recapt*

(c) $8,000 loss from theft of unregistered bearer bonds, held 18 months.
    *Personal Casualty loss*     *8000 —*
                                       *100*
                                    *7900*

*Personal Casualty loss 19ov .*

(d) $2,000 loss in storm of pleasure yacht, purchased in 19X1 for $2,900 and having a fair market value at the time of the storm of $2,000.

What are the tax consequences to V for each of these items? *ded . from A GJ .*

42. S Corporation owns two lathes. Lathe A was purchased on January 12, 19X6, for $15,000 and has an adjusted basis of $10,000, while lathe B was purchased for $8,000 on January 12, 19X9, and has an adjusted basis of $6,000. S Corporation sells the two assets on November 16, 19X9, for $11,000 and $7,000, respectively.

(a) What is the realized and recognized gain on each?

(b) Describe its nature.

(c) If S Corporation sold lathes as a business, how would the answers change?

43. On March 1, 19X1, N buys and places in service a new machine for $25,000. On April 1, 19X4, N sells the machine for $15,000. Cost recovery deductions to date have been $14,500.

(a) What is N's realized and recognized gain?

(b) What is its nature?

44. On January 1, 19X1, T acquired a building (not ACRS recovery property) used in its business for $600,000. Later, depreciation expense was $150,000. On January 1, 19X9, the building was sold for $800,000. At the time of the sale, additional depreciation taken attributable to periods after December 31, 1969, amounted to $35,000.

(a) What amount is § 1250 ordinary income?

(b) How would the answer change if rehabilitation expenditures were involved?

45. Residential real property purchased in 1980 with an adjusted basis of $60,000 is sold in 1983 for $78,000. Depreciation attributable to the property for tax years 1980 through 1983 is $20,000, of which $4,000 is additional depreciation.

(a) Identify the amount and nature of the gain?

(b) Would the answer change if the property were nonresidential real property? *NO.*

46. P donated equipment to a qualified charitable organization on January 3, 19X6. P purchased the equipment new on January 1, 19X3, for $100,000 and was taking depreciation under the accelerated cost recovery system (statutory percentage method) for five-year property. At the time of the gift, the property had a fair market value of $130,000. What are the tax consequences to P in the year of the gift?

47. T transferred forklifts used in his factory, with recapture potential of $6,500, to a dealer in exchange for new forklifts worth $8,000 and $1,500 of marketable securities. The transaction qualified as a § 1031 like-kind exchange. T had an adjusted basis in the equipment of $6,000.

(a) What is T's realized and recognized gain or loss?

(b) What is the nature of the gain or loss?

(c) How would the answer to (a) or (b) change if no marketable securities are involved?

48. In 19X3, C purchased new business equipment for $5,000. On his 19X3 return, C claimed depreciation of $750 using the accelerated cost recovery system (statutory percentage method). On January 1, 19X4, a tornado destroyed the equipment and C received $4,500 from his insurance company. The equipment was replaced for $3,800. What is C's recognized gain or loss and what is its nature?

49. M owns an apartment building that qualifies as residential rental housing. It was purchased new in January 1981, and M has taken depreciation under the statutory percentage method. The building cost $90,000 when purchased and was expected to have a 20-year life with no salvage value. The building was sold in January 1984 for $200,000.

   (a) What is the recognized gain?

   (b) Describe its composition?

   (c) How would the answers change if the sale is to M's spouse?

50. J acquired a working interest in certain oil and gas properties during 1982 for $125,000. In the same year, she also incurred intangible drilling costs of $60,000 which she elected to expense on her 1982 tax return. If the IDC had been capitalized, cost depletion of $6,000 would have been allowed. In January 1983, J sells her interest in the oil and gas properties for $140,000.

   (a) Calculate the amount of gain or loss realized and recognized in 1983. (Ignore any depreciation on tangible depreciable property.)

   (b) What amount, if any, is ordinary income?

## Cumulative Problems

51. T is an automobile mechanic. He is single, age 28, and has no dependents. In April 1983, while tinkering with his automobile, T devised a carburetor modification kit which increases gas mileage by 20 percent. He patented the invention and in June sold it to X Corporation for a lump-sum payment of $250,000 plus $5 per kit sold. Other information of potential tax consequence is given below.

   | | |
   |---|---:|
   | (a) Cash received from X Corporation, which sold 20,000 of the kits in 1983. | $ 100,000 |
   | (b) Wages earned as a mechanic from January 1 through June 17. | 4,300 |
   | (c) Points paid on a $200,000 mortgage T incurred to buy a luxurious new home (he had previously lived in an apartment). | 6,000 |
   | (d) State sales taxes paid on four new automobiles T acquired in 1983. | 2,200 |
   | (e) T has continued his experimental activities and is now working on several potentially patentable automotive devices (costs incurred include rent paid for a garage, materials, supplies, etc.). | 14,000 |
   | (f) Various itemized deductions (not including any potential deductions above). | 9,400 |
   | (g) Interest on savings account. | 6,200 |

   Compute taxable income for 1983.

52. J is a self-employed contractor (single, no dependents) who operates the X Company, a sole proprietorship. During 1983, X Company had gross sales of $635,000 and business expenses of $550,000, including the cost recovery allowance on the assets bought, sold, or exchanged during 1983. However, the above income and expense figures do not reflect gains or losses on the following property transactions.

    (a) X Company purchased a Model 1200 tractor in 1980 for $21,000. On July 1, 1983, when the adjusted basis of the Model 1200 was $14,000 ($21,000 cost − $7,000 accumulated depreciation), the tractor was traded for a Model 800. The fair market value of the Model 800 tractor was $12,000. X Company received $6,000 cash boot from the dealer.

    (b) X Company had a ditchdigging machine which was completely destroyed by fire in October. The machine, which X Company had owned for two years, had an adjusted basis of $6,400, but X Company received only $3,000 from the insurance company. The machine was replaced at a cost of $8,000.

    (c) In 1980, J converted his personal automobile to business use. J had paid $5,400 for the auto, which had a fair market value of $3,800 at the date of conversion. In 1983, X Company sold the automobile, on which depreciation of $2,200 had been taken, for $1,000.

    (d) X Company sold a vacant lot it had been holding for a new store location. Because of a change in plans, the property no longer was needed. The lot, which had an adjusted basis of $15,000, was sold for $17,000. X Company had owned the lot for 14 months.

    J had the following transaction involving a personal asset not related to his business.

    J's records reveal the following additional information.

    (e) Dividends received on stock in a domestic corporation amounted to $400, and itemized deductions were $6,900.

    Compute J's taxable income for 1983.

## Tax Form Problems

53. Linda Franklin is an attorney. During 1982, she had the following property transactions.

    (a) Sales of stock held for investment:

| Stock | Selling Price | Basis | Date Sold | Date Acquired |
|---|---|---|---|---|
| A Corporation | $ 2,000 | $ 1,400 | 6/30/82 | 8/4/81 |
| B Corporation | 8,000 | 10,500 | 12/31/82 | 7/15/82 |
| C, Inc. | 9,400 | 5,400 | 7/26/82 | 5/2/78 |
| D Corporation | 1,800 | 2,900 | 10/18/82 | 10/17/81 |

    (b) Complete destruction of travel trailer in a wreck on August 1 (basis, $6,500; market value, $5,000; reimbursement for loss by insurance company, $3,000). Linda had bought the trailer on June 12, 1980.

    (c) Sale of photocopying machine used in business for $2,800 on November 6. She had acquired the machine on April 29, 1980, for $4,000 and had taken $1,800 depreciation on it.

(d) Sale of typewriter, used in business, on January 15 for $500. The typewriter was acquired on May 8, 1980, at a cost of $1,000; depreciation (including additional first-year depreciation) of $440 had been deducted.

Compute Linda Franklin's gains and losses from these transactions using Schedule D, Form 4684 and Form 4797.

## Cumulative Tax Return Problem

54. T, age 40, operates a retail business as a sole proprietorship. He incurred the following transactions during the year (1982) regarding his business and personal activities:

(a) A delivery truck was sold for $4,000 on January 1, 1982. The truck was acquired on January 1, 1979, at a total cost of $6,000. The truck was depreciated over a three-year life using straight-line depreciation. The adjusted basis on the date of sale was $1,000.

(b) T traded an old office machine used in his business for a new one on December 1, 1982. The new machine cost $3,800. T was allowed $1,000 for the old machine, which had an adjusted basis of $1,500, and paid $2,800 in cash. The old machine was acquired on December 1, 1978, and straight-line depreciation was taken.

(c) In December 1982, T sold 100 shares of XYZ stock for $3,500, which had been purchased in August of the same year for $3,000.

(d) T sold his personal residence for $60,000 in December 1982, which had been acquired in 1978. Selling expenses amounted to $4,000, and the adjusted basis of the house was $46,000. T moved into a rental apartment and does not plan to reinvest the proceeds in a new residence.

Complete T's net gain or loss from the above transactions and describe the nature of the gain or loss. Preparation of Schedule D of Form 1040, Form 2119 (Sale or Exchange of Personal Residence), and Form 4797 (Supplemental Schedule of Gains and Losses) is necessary.

# Chapter 11

# Special Tax Computations

Once gross income has been determined (refer to Chapters 3 and 4) and various deductions accounted for (refer to Chapters 5–7), the income tax liability can be computed. Generally the computation procedure requires only familiarity with the Tax Table and Tax Rate Schedule methods (discussed in Chapter 2). Some taxpayers, however, may qualify for certain beneficial computation methods (e. g., income averaging) or may be subject to taxes in addition to the regular income tax (e. g., the alternative minimum tax, the self-employment tax). This chapter deals with the special methods available for determining the income tax and the various other taxes imposed.

An entire subchapter of the Code, Subchapter E, is devoted to accounting periods and accounting methods. Over the long run, the accounting period used by a taxpayer will not affect the aggregate amount of reported taxable income. However, taxable income for any particular year may vary significantly due to the use of a particular reporting period. In addition, because of the progressive nature of tax rates, advantages can be obtained from the use of a particular method of accounting. Through the choice of accounting methods or periods, it is possible to postpone the recognition of taxable income and to enjoy the benefits from such deferral of the related tax. The latter half of this chapter covers accounting periods and selected accounting methods.

# SPECIAL METHODS
# FOR COMPUTING THE TAX

## INCOME AVERAGING

The finality of the annual accounting period concept, when considered along with the progression of the income tax rates, could cause real hardship in a rags-to-riches type of situation.

> **Example 1.** Over a five-year period, R and T (each is a married individual filing a joint return) have the following income tax results:[1]

| | R | | T | |
|---|---|---|---|---|
| Year | Taxable Income | Tax Due | Taxable Income | Tax Due |
| 19X1 | $ 14,000 | $ 1,638 | $ 5,000 | $ 195 |
| 19X2 | 14,000 | 1,638 | 5,000 | 195 |
| 19X3 | 14,000 | 1,638 | 5,000 | 195 |
| 19X4 | 14,000 | 1,638 | 5,000 | 195 |
| 19X5 | 14,000 | 1,638 | 50,000 | 13,305 |
| Totals | $ 70,000 | $ 8,190 | $ 70,000 | $ 14,085 |

> Although both R and T have the same taxable income over a five-year period (i. e., $70,000), T pays additional income taxes of $5,895 ($14,085 − $8,190).

The purpose, then, of the income averaging provisions is to provide relief from the bunching effects of *unusual* amounts of income received in any one year. As noted below, the tax law quantifies what is *unusual* by applying a percentage (i. e., the 120 percent rule) to the average income of the past four years and requiring that the current income exceed this average by a specified amount (i. e., the $3,000 rule).

At the outset, it is important to recognize that the income averaging provisions do not violate the finality of the annual accounting period concept. Thus, income averaging does not call for the filing of amended tax returns for the base period (i. e., the past four years), but merely considers the base period average in arriving at how the income tax for the current year is to be computed. Nor does the income averaging procedure call for the use of special tax rates. It merely determines how the tax is to be computed in working with the regular Tax Rate Schedules. It is important to note that the Tax Rate Schedules must be used in computing the tax using the income averaging method. The Tax Table cannot be used if income averaging is elected.

---

1. The tax due amounts on taxable income up to $50,000 are based on the 1982 Tax Table. The tax on $50,000 taxable income is based on the 1982 Tax Rate Schedule.

In order to qualify for income averaging, the following two requirements must be met:[2]

—The taxpayer must be an eligible individual.

—Averageable income must be more than $3,000.

*Eligible Individual.* An eligible individual is one who meets the citizenship or residence test and the support test. The first test requires U. S. citizenship or resident status throughout the computation year (i. e., the year income averaging is elected) and the base period years (i. e., the four preceding years).

Under the support test, the taxpayer must have provided more than 50 percent of his or her own support in each of the base period years. If married in any base period year, both spouses must have provided at least 50 percent of their combined support.

The support test is waived in the following situations:

1.  If the taxpayer is at least 25 years old in the computation year and not a full-time student for any of the four years after reaching age 21.

2.  If more than one-half of taxable income for the computation year is attributable to work done largely during two or more of the taxpayer's base period years.

3.  If a joint return is filed in the computation year and the taxpayer who had been supported by another in any base period year does not provide more than 25 percent of the combined adjusted gross income of both spouses for such computation year.[3]

The support test and some of the exceptions thereto are illustrated below:

**Example 2.** While attending college on a full-time basis from 19X4–19X7, T (age 25) was supported by her parents. Based on these facts, T does not meet the support test and therefore cannot make use of income averaging for 19X8. She does not fit within exception 1, due to the full-time student restriction.

**Example 3.** In 19X8, P receives 90% of her taxable income from a novel written by her during 19X4–19X7. Even if P were the dependent of another during the base period, the support test is waived through the application of exception 2.

**Example 4.** H and W were married in 19X8. Although H supported himself during the base period of 19X4–19X7, W was a dependent of her parents. During 19X8, their combined adjusted gross income was earned 80% by H and 20% by W. If H and W file

---

**2.**  § 1301.
**3.**  § 1303.

a joint return for 19X8, the support test is waived for W under exception 3.

*Averageable Income.* Presuming an eligible individual is involved, income averaging is available only if the averageable income exceeds $3,000. Averageable income is defined by the Code as being the taxable income for the computation year less 120 percent of average base period income. In arriving at average base period income, add the taxable income for each of the prior four years and divide the result by four. Because the determination of taxable income was not necessary for taxpayers using the Tax Table for years 1977 through 1980, a special computation is required by such taxpayers to determine taxable income for those base period years that are applicable. This computation is illustrated in the following example.

**Example 5.** H and W, who are married and have no dependents, had Tax Table income as follows: $22,000 in 1979 and $24,800 in 1980. For 1981, they had taxable income of $24,000, and in 1982 they had taxable income of $26,000. Their base period income is computed as shown below.

| Year | Tax Table Income | Exemptions[4] | Taxable Income |
|------|------------------|---------------|----------------|
| 1979 | $ 22,000 | $ 2,000 | $ 20,000 |
| 1980 | 24,800 | 2,000 | 22,800 |
| 1981 | | | 24,000 |
| 1982 | | | 26,000 |
| | | Total | $ 92,800 |

**Example 6.** Assume the same facts as in Example 5 and that H and W had taxable income of $43,200 in 1983. Averageable income is computed as shown below:

| | |
|---|---|
| Taxable income for the computation year | $ 43,200 |
| Less: Nonaverageable income [$23,200 (average base period income) × 120%] | 27,840 |
| Averageable income | $ 15,360 |

Since averageable income exceeds $3,000, and assuming all other conditions are met, H and W may use income averaging for 1983.

In determining averageable income, Schedule G (Income Averaging) of Form 1040 deviates from the procedure followed above by introducing a shortcut approach.[5] Instead of dividing total base period

---

4. The amount allowed for an exemption was $750 in 1978. This amount was raised to the current level of $1,000 in 1979.

5. The procedure used in Example 6, however, follows that specified in the Internal Revenue Code [§ 1302(a)(1)].

income by four and multiplying the quotient by 120 percent, merely multiply the total base period income by 30 percent.

*Computation Procedure.* Once the key amounts have been determined (e. g., base period income, taxable income for the computation year, averageable income), income averaging proceeds as follows:[6]

*Step 1.* Determine the nonaverageable income. Using the Schedule G shortcut approach, this would be 30 percent of total base period income.

*Step 2.* Add 20 percent of averageable income.

*Step 3.* Using the appropriate Tax Rate Schedule (i. e., X, Y, or Z in Appendix A), compute the tax on the sum reached in Step 2.

*Step 4.* Compute the tax on the Step 1 amount.

*Step 5.* Subtract the tax computed in Step 4 from that computed in Step 3 and multiply the difference by four.

*Step 6.* Add the product determined in Step 5 to the tax determined in Step 3.

Step 6, then, yields the amount of tax due by using the income averaging procedure.

**Example 7.** Assume the same facts as in Example 5. Determine the income tax liability of H and W both without and with the use of income averaging.

Without income averaging:

The tax on $43,200 [see 1983 Schedule Y (Appendix A)] is $6,624 + $2,800 [35% × $8,000 (taxable income in excess of $35,200)]                    $ 9,424

With income averaging:

*Step 1.* $92,800 (base period income) × 30% (Schedule G shortcut approach) = $27,840 (nonaverageable income).

*Step 2.* $27,840 (nonaverageable income) + $3,072 [20% × $15,360 (averageable income)] = $30,912.

*Step 3.* Tax on Step 2 amount of $30,912 [see 1983 Schedule Y, first column (Appendix A)] is $5,034 + $304 [30% × $1,012 (the amount computed at Step 2 in excess of $29,900)], or $5,338.

*Step 4.* Tax on Step 1 amount of $27,840 [see Schedule Y, first column (Appendix A)] is $3,656 + $842 [26% × $3,240 (the amount of nonaverageable income in excess of $24,600)], or $4,498.

---

6. § 1301.

*Step 5.*   $5,338 (Step 3) − $4,498 (Step 4) = $840 × 4 = $3,360.

*Step 6.*   $3,360 (Step 5) + $5,338 (Step 3) = income tax liability with income averaging       <u>$ 8,698</u>

Thus, Mr. and Mrs. T would save $726 [$9,424 (tax without) − $8,698 (tax with) by using income averaging].

The tax computations in this example are rounded to the nearest dollar.

*Reporting Procedures.* Income averaging is elected by completing Schedule G of Form 1040. Schedule G is reproduced in Appendix B. For purposes of illustration, a filled-in Schedule G is shown on the following page. Assume that John and Betty Doe are a married couple, with no dependents, filing a joint return. Their Tax Table income (amount from Form 1040, line 34) was $17,500 in 1978, $20,000 in 1979, and $22,000 in 1980. Their taxable income was $26,000 for 1981 and $50,000 for 1982. Note that the computation procedures are slightly different from those in Example 7, which is based on 1983 as the computation year.

*Other Considerations.* Income averaging is an elective provision which generally must be elected by the taxpayer within the period of limitations applicable to claims for refunds.[7]

> **Example 8.** T, a calendar year taxpayer, files his return for 1980 on March 3, 1981. When preparing his return for 1981, T discovers that the use of income averaging would have reduced his income tax liability for 1980 by $920. On April 3, 1982, T files an amended return (Form 1040X) for 1980 electing the income averaging provisions. As T's amended return is timely (i. e., not barred by the statute of limitations), the utilization of income averaging is proper.

Income averaging cannot be elected, however, if the taxpayer claims an exclusion from earned income while employed outside the U. S.

The income averaging provisions can become very complex when the marital status of a taxpayer changes for any of the base period years or the computation year. Special allocation procedures may be necessary, but a discussion of these rules is beyond the scope of this text.

## ALTERNATIVE MINIMUM TAX

Unlike income averaging, the minimum tax is not beneficial to taxpayers. Instead of saving tax dollars through special computation procedures, it could result in additional income tax liability.

---

7. § 1304(a).

**Schedule G**
(Form 1040)
Department of the Treasury (0)
Internal Revenue Service

# Income Averaging

▶ See instructions on back.   ▶ Attach to Form 1040.

OMB No. 1545–0074

**1982**
20

Name(s) as shown on Form 1040
John and Betty Doe

Your social security number
123 : 45 : 6789

## Step 1      Figure your income for 1978-1981

| | | | | | |
|---|---|---|---|---|---|
| **1978** | 1 Fill in the amount from your 1978 Form 1040 (line 34) or Form 1040A (line 10) . . . . . . . . . . | **1** | 17,500 | | |
| | 2 Multiply your total exemptions in 1978 by $750. . . | **2** | 1,500 | | |
| | 3 Subtract line 2 from line 1. If less than zero, enter zero . . . . . . . . | | | **3** | 16,000 |
| **1979** | 4 Fill in the amount from your 1979 Form 1040 (line 34) or Form 1040A (line 11) . . . . . . . . . . | **4** | 20,000 | | |
| | 5 Multiply your total exemptions in 1979 by $1,000 . . . | **5** | 2,000 | | |
| | 6 Subtract line 5 from line 4. If less than zero, enter zero. . . . . . . . | | | **6** | 18,000 |
| **1980** | 7 Fill in the amount from your 1980 Form 1040 (line 34) or Form 1040A (line 11) . . . . . . . . . . | **7** | 22,000 | | |
| | 8 Multiply your total exemptions in 1980 by $1,000 . . . | **8** | 2,000 | | |
| | 9 Subtract line 8 from line 7. If less than zero, enter zero. . . . . . . . | | | **9** | 20,000 |
| **1981** | 10 Taxable income. Fill in the amount from your 1981 Form 1040 (line 34) or Form 1040A (line 12). If less than zero, enter zero . . . | | | **10** | 26,000 |
| **Total** | 11 Fill in all income earned outside of the United States or within U.S. possessions and excluded for 1978 through 1981 . . . . . . . . . . | | | **11** | |
| | 12 Add lines 3, 6, 9, 10 and 11 . . . . . . . . . . | | | **12** | 80,000 |

## Step 2      Figure your averageable income

|  | | | |
|---|---|---|---|
| Multiply the amount on line 12 by 30% (.30) . . . . . . . . . . | | | |
| 13 Write in the answer . . . . . . . . . . | **13** | 24,000 | |
| 14 Fill in your taxable income for 1982 from Form 1040, line 37 . . . . . . . | **14** | 50,000 | |
| 15 If you received a premature or excessive distribution subject to a penalty under section 72, see instructions . . . . . . . . | **15** | | |
| 16 Subtract line 15 from line 14 . . . . . . . . . . | **16** | 50,000 | |
| 17 If you live in a community property state and are filing a separate return, see instructions . . . . | **17** | | |
| 18 Subtract line 17 from line 16. If less than zero, enter zero . . . . . . . | **18** | 50,000 | |
| 19 Write in the amount from line 13 above . . . . . . . . . . | **19** | 24,000 | |
| 20 Subtract line 19 from line 18. This is your averageable income . . . . . . . | **20** | 26,000 | |

### If line 20 is $3,000 or less, do not complete the rest of this form. You do not qualify for income averaging.

## Step 3      Figure your tax

|  | | | | |
|---|---|---|---|---|
| Multiply the amount on line 20 by 20% (.20) . . . . . . . . . . | | | | |
| 21 Write in the answer . . . . . . . . . . | | | **21** | 5,200 |
| 22 Write in the amount from line 13 above . . . . . . . . . . | | | **22** | 24,000 |
| 23 Add lines 21 and 22 . . . . . . . . . . | | | **23** | 29,200 |
| 24 Write in the amount from line 17 above . . . . . . . . . . | | | **24** | |
| 25 Add lines 23 and 24 . . . . . . . . . . | | | **25** | 29,200 |
| 26 Tax on amount on line 25 (from Tax Rate Schedule X, Y, or Z) . . . | | | **26** | 5,371 |
| 27 Tax on amount on line 23 (from Tax Rate Schedule X, Y, or Z) . . . | **27** | 5,371 | | |
| 28 Tax on amount on line 22 (from Tax Rate Schedule X, Y, or Z) . . . | **28** | 3,887 | | |
| 29 Subtract line 28 from line 27 . . . . . . . . . | **29** | 1,484 | | |
| Multiply the amount on line 29 by 4 . . . . . . . | | | | |
| 30 Write in the answer . . . . . . . . . . | | | **30** | 5,936 |
| If you have no entry on line 15, skip lines 31 through 33 and go to line 34. | | | | |
| 31 Tax on amount on line 14 (from Tax Rate Schedule X, Y, or Z) . . . | **31** | | | |
| 32 Tax on amount on line 16 (from Tax Rate Schedule X, Y, or Z) . . . | **32** | | | |
| 33 Subtract line 32 from line 31 . . . . . . . . . | | | **33** | |
| 34 Add lines 26, 30, and 33. Write the result here and on Form 1040, line 38. Be sure to check the Schedule G box on that line . . . . . . . . . . | | | **34** | 11,307 |

**G**

For Paperwork Reduction Act Notice, see Form 1040 instructions.

In enacting the first minimum tax, Congress was concerned over statistical data compiled by the Department of the Treasury which revealed that some taxpayers with large economic incomes were able to avoid the usual tax associated with such amounts. This reduction in income taxes was being accomplished legally through various investments that resulted in preferential treatment for tax purposes (i. e., "items of tax preference"). That Congress was distressed with the inequity that resulted from such tax avoidance is a point clearly made by the following extract from the Report by the Ways and Means Committee of the House of Representatives on the Tax Reform Act of 1969:

> This is obviously an unfair situation. In view of the tax burden on our citizens, at this time, it is particularly essential that our taxes be distributed in a fair manner. Your committee believes that no one should be permitted to avoid his fair share of the tax burden—to shift his tax load to the backs of other taxpayers.[8]

Thus, the minimum tax on items of tax preference that came about was intended as a means of accomplishing more equitable distribution of the tax burden among taxpayers. Originally, it was a special tax of 10 percent levied against specified items of tax preference in excess of $30,000.

Prior to 1983, the tax law included two forms of the minimum tax: the regular minimum tax and the alternative minimum tax. The Tax Equity and Fiscal Responsibility Act of 1982 repealed the regular minimum tax, for tax years after 1982, while retaining and expanding the scope of the alternative minimum tax. The regular minimum tax was often referred to as the "add-on" minimum tax, since the effect of its application was to add the amount of the tax on to the income tax as usually determined. By way of contrast, the alternative minimum tax is a substitute for the income tax and must be used when it produces a greater tax liability.

## COMPUTATION OF THE ALTERNATIVE MINIMUM TAX

Congress has added a challenging new chapter to the history of the alternative minimum tax with the Tax Equity and Fiscal Responsibility Act of 1982 (TEFRA). For tax years beginning after 1982, the alternative minimum tax has been restructured and its scope has been expanded. Coping with the new alternative minimum tax for individuals is a difficult task, which requires an understanding of the new formula for computing the tax base (see Figure I). Also required is an understanding of several new terms (see Figure II) introduced by TEFRA.

---

8.  1969–3 C.B. 249.

**Figure I**

FORMULA FOR COMPUTING ALTERNATIVE
MINIMUM TAX BASE (§55)

Adjusted gross income (computed without regard to any net operating loss).
Minus:
> Alternative tax net operating loss deduction.
> Alternative tax itemized deductions.
> Amounts included in income under § 667
>> (i. e., income included due to a distribution of accumulated trust income).

Plus:
> Tax preferences items (§ 57).

Equals:
> Alternative minimum taxable income (AMTI).

Minus:
> Exemption amount.

Equals:
> Alternative minimum tax base.

Computation of the alternative minimum tax base requires an understanding of each component of the formula in Figure I. The more complex of these components are discussed in detail in the following sections.

*Alternative Tax Net Operating Loss Deduction.* In computing taxable income, taxpayers are allowed to deduct net operating loss (NOL) carryovers and carrybacks. The income tax NOL must be modified, however, in computing alternative minimum taxable income (AMTI)[9]. The starting point in computing the alternative tax NOL is the regular NOL computed for income tax purposes. The income tax NOL must be reduced for tax preference items deducted in the NOL year.

> **Example 9.** In 1983, T, who does not itemize, incurred a net operating loss of $10,000. T's deductions in 1983 included tax preference items of $1,800. His alternative tax NOL for 1984 will be $8,200 [$10,000 (NOL for 1983)—$1,800 (tax preferences deducted in computing the 1983 NOL)].

In Example 9, if the adjustment were not made to the income tax NOL, the $1,800 in tax preference items deducted in 1983 would have the effect of reducing AMTI in 1984. This would weaken the entire concept of the alternative minimum tax as a tax on preference items.

An additional limitation on the alternative tax NOL is that it must be computed taking into account only those itemized deductions allowed as alternative tax itemized deductions (see the following section) in the NOL year.

If a taxpayer has an alternative tax NOL that is carried back or over to another year, such alternative tax NOL must be used against

---

**9.** § 55(d).

AMTI in the carryback or carryover year, even if the regular tax rather than the alternative minimum tax applies.

**Example 10.** K's alternative tax NOL for 1984 (carried over from 1983) is $10,000. Her AMTI before considering the alternative tax NOL is $25,000. Because K's regular income tax exceeds the alternative minimum tax, the alternative minimum tax does not apply. Nevertheless, K's alternative tax NOL of $10,000 is "used up" in 1984 and is not available for carryover to a later year.

The above rules apply to post-1982 net operating losses. Special transitional rules apply to pre-1983 net operating losses.

*Alternative Tax Itemized Deductions.* Some itemized deductions that are allowed in computing taxable income are not allowed in computing AMTI. Allowable alternative tax itemized deductions are limited to casualty losses, gambling losses, charitable contributions, medical expenses in excess of 10 percent of adjusted gross income (although the floor is five percent for income tax purposes), qualified interest (see Figure II), and estate tax on income in respect of a decedent.

*Tax Preference Items.* An important step in computing the alternative minimum tax is to arrive at the sum of the items of tax preference.[10] Under TEFRA provisions, most of the preference items subject to the add-on minimum tax were retained. The most commonly encountered items of tax preference from pre-TEFRA law are summarized below.

—Accelerated depreciation on realty in excess of what would have been allowed under the straight-line method;

—The bargain element in certain stock options in the year the options are exercised;

—The excess of the depletion deduction over the adjusted basis of the property at the end of the year (figured before deducting the depletion for the year);

—Depreciation or amortization for leased personalty in excess of the amount that would have been allowed under the straight-line method;

—The excess of intangible drilling and development costs of oil, gas, and geothermal wells deducted during the year minus the sum of (1) the amount allowed if the costs had been capitalized and written-off under the straight-line method and (2) the net income for the year from oil, gas, and geothermal properties; and,

—For cost recovery property (i. e., property placed in service in 1981 and later) subject to a lease, the excess of the cost recovery

---

10. All tax preference items are specified in § 57.

allowance over the deduction which would have been allowable had the property been depreciated using the straight-line method and the half-year convention for a period of years specified in § 57(a)(12).

The 60 percent net capital gain deduction, which was subject to the alternative minimum tax under pre-TEFRA law, continues as a tax preference item under the TEFRA provisions.

New items of tax preference added by TEFRA are summarized below.

— Dividends excluded from gross income under § 116 ($100 on a single return, $200 on a joint return).

— Interest excluded from gross income under § 128 (i. e., All-Savers interest).

— Interest excluded from gross income under the 15 percent net interest exclusion rule (which takes effect after 1984).

— Excess deductions for mining exploration and development expenditures (i. e., deductions in excess of ratable amortization over 10 years).

— Bargain element at the date of exercise of incentive stock options (i. e., the excess of the fair market value of the stock over the option price at the date the option is exercised).

*Exemption Amount.* The exemption amount is $40,000 for married taxpayers filing joint returns, $30,000 for single taxpayers, and $20,000 for married taxpayers filing separate returns.[11]

*New Terms Introduced by TEFRA.* TEFRA added several new terms related to the new alternative tax itemized deduction for qualified interest. These terms are defined in Figure II.

## Figure II
### DEFINITIONS OF NEW TERMS[12]

**Qualified interest**—interest considered an alternative tax itemized deduction which includes (1) qualified housing interest plus (2) other interest to the extent it does not exceed net investment income.

**Qualified housing interest**—interest paid or accrued during the taxable year on indebtedness incurred in acquiring, constructing, or substantially rehabilitating any property used (1) as the principal residence of the taxpayer at the time the interest is paid or accrued or (2) as a qualified dwelling of the taxpayer or any member of his or her family [within the meaning of § 267(c)(4)].

**Qualified dwelling**—any house, apartment, condominium, or mobile home (not used on a transient basis) used by the taxpayer or any member of his or her family [within the meaning of § 267(c)(4)] during the taxable year.

---

11. § 55(f).
12. §§ 57(e) and 58(i)(5).

## Figure II *(continued)*

**Qualified net investment income**—the excess of qualified investment income over qualified investment expenses.

**Qualified investment income**—includes (1) gross income from interest, dividends, rents, and royalties; (2) amounts recaptured as ordinary income under §§ 1245, 1250, and 1254, but only to the extent such income is not derived from the conduct of a trade or business; (3) any net capital gain attributable to the disposition of property held for investment; and (4) any dividends excluded under § 116 (i. e., $100 on a single return, $200 on a joint return) or any interest excluded under the All-Savers provisions.

**Qualified investment expenses**—deductions directly connected with the production of qualified investment income to the extent that (1) such deductions are allowable in computing adjusted gross income and (2) such deductions are not items of tax preference.

**Qualified expenditures**—expenditures which, under an election provided in § 58(i), may be written off over a 10-year period to avoid creating a tax preference item; these expenditures, which qualify for immediate write-off unless such election is made, include (among others) circulation expenditures, research and experimental expenditures, and intangible drilling and development expenditures.

*Illustration of the Alternative Minimum Tax Computation.* The complex new provisions for computation of the alternative minimum tax are illustrated in the following example.

**Example 11.** T, who is single, has taxable income for 1983 as follows:

| | | |
|---|---:|---:|
| Salary | | $110,000 |
| Capital gain ($250,000 net capital gain from sale of stocks—$150,000 capital gain deduction) | | 100,000 |
| | | $210,000 |
| Less: Employee business expenses | | 10,000 |
| Adjusted gross income | | $200,000 |
| Less: Excess itemized deductions— medical expenses ($35,000—5% of $200,000 AGI) | $25,000** | |
| Taxes | 10,000 | |
| Interest: | | |
|     Home mortgage** | $30,000 | |
|     Other** | 5,300 | |
| Contributions** | 7,000 | |
| Casualty losses** | 4,000 | |
| | $81,300 | |
| Less: Zero bracket amount | 2,300 | $ 79,000 |
| | | $121,000 |
| Less: Exemption | | 1,000 |
| Taxable income | | $120,000 |

Deductions marked by a double asterisk are allowed as *alternative tax itemized deductions.* Alternative minimum taxable income is computed as follows:

| | | |
|---|---:|---:|
| Adjusted gross income | | $200,000 |
| Less: Alternative tax itemized deductions: | | |
|     Medical expenses | $15,000[1] | |
|     Home mortgage interest | 35,300[2] | |
|     Contributions | 7,000 | |
|     Casualty losses | 4,000 | 61,300 |
| | | $138,700 |
| Plus: Tax preference (capital gain deduction) | | 150,000 |
| Alternative minimum taxable income | | $288,700 |
| Less: Exemption | | 30,000 |
| Minimum tax base | | $258,700 |
| Rate | | .20[3] |
| | | $ 51,740 |
| Less: Regular tax on $120,000 taxable income | | 49,473 |
| Alternative minimum tax | | $ 2,267 |

[1] Total medical expenses were $35,000, reduced by 5% of AGI, resulting in an itemized deduction of $25,000. However, for alternative minimum tax purposes, the reduction is 10%, which leaves an alternative minimum tax itemized deduction of $15,000 ($35,000 − 10% of $200,000 AGI).

[2] In this illustration, all interest is deductible in computing alternative minimum taxable income. Home mortgage interest is always deductible. Other interest ($5,300) is deductible to the extent of net investment income included in the minimum tax base. For this purpose, net capital gain is treated as net investment income.

[3] The rate for the new alternative minimum tax is a flat 20%. It replaces the two-tier tax structure (10% and 20%) in effect under prior law.

Although there are many other detailed rules in the new TEFRA provisions, space limitations require that some be omitted in this discussion. However, there are two additional features which require comment.

First, nonrefundable credits other than the foreign tax credit are not allowed as offsets against the alternative minimum tax. The foreign tax credit may be utilized, but it is subject to a limitation based on income from sources outside the United States.[13]

Second, individuals may avoid having a tax preference item on certain *qualified expenditures* (see definition in Figure II). This is accomplished by an election to amortize ratably over a 10-year period in lieu of expensing such amounts in the year incurred.[14]

# ACCOUNTING PERIODS

## IN GENERAL

Our tax determination and collection system is founded on the concept of an annual reporting by the taxable entity of its income, deductions, and credits. Most individual taxpayers use a calendar year,

---

**13.** § 55(c)(2).
**14.** § 58(i).

since the Code and Regulations place restrictions upon the use of a fiscal year for taxpayers who do not keep books.[15] However, both corporate and noncorporate taxpayers may elect to use a fiscal year ending on the last day of any month (other than December), provided the books of the taxpayer are maintained on the basis of the same fiscal year. Generally, a taxable year may not exceed 12 calendar months. However, if certain requirements are met, a taxpayer may elect to use an annual period which varies from 52 to 53 weeks.[16] In such case, the year-end must be on the same day of the week (e. g., the Tuesday falling closest to October 31 or the last Tuesday in October).

> **Example 12.** T is in the business of selling farm supplies. His natural business year terminates at the end of October with the completion of harvesting. At the end of the fiscal year, it is necessary to take an inventory, and it is most easily accomplished on a Tuesday. Therefore, T could adopt a 52–53 week year ending on the Tuesday nearest October 31. If this method is selected, the year-end date may fall in the following month if closer to October 31. The year ending in 1984 will contain 52 weeks beginning on Wednesday, November 2, 1983, and ending on Tuesday, October 30, 1984. The year ending in 1984 will also have 52 weeks beginning on Wednesday, October 31, 1984, and ending on Tuesday, October 29, 1985.

Partnerships are subject to additional restrictions to prevent partners from deferring partnership income by selecting a different year-end for the partnership (e. g., if the year for the partnership ended on January 31 and the partners used a calendar year, partnership profits for the first 11 months would not be reported by the partners until the following year). In brief, the law provides that the partnership tax year must generally be the same as the year used by its principal partners.[17]

## MAKING THE ELECTION

A taxpayer elects to use a calendar or fiscal year by the timely filing of the initial tax return. For all subsequent years, this same period must be used unless prior approval for change is obtained from the IRS.

Newly formed corporations often fail to make a valid election to

---

**15.**  § 441(c) and Reg. § 1.441–1(b)(1)(ii).

**16.**  § 441(f).

**17.**  § 706(b)(2). However, the IRS is authorized to allow the partner's and partnership's tax year to differ if there is a good business purpose for the different years. See Rev.Proc. 72–51, 1972–2 C.B. 832 for the procedure for a change in the partnership year.

use a fiscal year, because the company has erroneously concluded that the due date of the election is based on the date the corporation began business rather than the date the corporation comes into existence. Under Reg. § 1.6012–2(a), the election must be keyed to the date the corporation comes into existence, which is usually the date it receives its charter from the state. Failure to make a valid election to use a fiscal year automatically places the corporation on the calendar year.

> **Example 13.** Y Corporation received its charter on June 15, 19X1, but did not begin business until October 2, 19X1. The corporation would like to be on a fiscal year ending September 30. Thus, a short period return should be filed by December 15, 19X1, for the period June 15, 19X1, through September 30, 19X1, even though no business activity was conducted during that time. If Y Corporation's initial return was filed erroneously (e. g., the return included only the period from October 2, 19X1, through September 30, 19X2), the election to use a fiscal year is not valid and the corporation must use a calendar year.

## CHANGES IN THE ACCOUNTING PERIOD

A taxpayer must obtain consent from the IRS before changing the tax year.[18] This power to approve or not to approve a change is significant in that it permits the IRS to issue authoritative administrative guidelines which must be met by taxpayers who wish to change their accounting period. An application for permission to change tax years must be made on Form 1128, Application for Change in Accounting Period, and must be filed on or before the fifteenth day of the second calendar month following the close of the short period.

> **Example 14.** Beginning in 19X2, T Corporation, a calendar year taxpayer, would like to switch to a fiscal year ending March 31. The corporation must file Form 1128 by May 15, 19X2.

*IRS Requirements.* The IRS will not grant permission for the change unless the taxpayer can establish a "substantial business purpose" for the change. One substantial business purpose is a request to change to a tax year that coincides with the natural business year. Generally, the natural business year will end at or soon after the peak period of business. Thus, a ski lodge may end its year on March 31; a Miami Beach hotel on May 31; a department store on January 31; a soft drink bottler on September 30; and a college textbook publisher on June 30. If a business does not have a peak income period, it may not be able to establish a natural business year and may therefore be prevented from changing its tax year.

---

**18.**  § 442.

## TAXABLE PERIODS OF LESS THAN ONE YEAR

A short year is a period of less than 12 calendar months. A taxpayer may have a short year for (1) the first tax reporting period, (2) the final income tax return, or (3) a change in the tax year. A taxpayer is not required to annualize the taxable income for the short period for computing the tax liability if the short period constitutes the first or final period (i. e., the computations are the same as for a return filed for a 12-month period).

## REQUIREMENT TO ANNUALIZE TAXABLE INCOME

If the short period results from a change in the taxpayer's annual accounting period, the taxable income for such period must be annualized. Due to the progressive tax rate structure, taxpayers could reap substantial tax benefits during the short period if such annualization of income were not required. Once the taxable income is annualized, the tax must first be computed on the amount of annualized income. The annualized tax is then converted to a short period tax. The latter conversion is accomplished as follows:

$$\text{Tax on annualized income} \times \frac{\text{Number of months in the short period}}{12}$$

For individuals, annualizing requires some special adjustments:[19]

—Deductions must be itemized for the short period (the zero bracket amount is not allowed), but itemized deductions are not reduced by the zero bracket amount.

—Personal and dependency exemptions must be prorated.

**Example 15.** Mr. and Mrs. B obtained permission to change from a calendar year to a fiscal year ending September 30. For the short period, January 1 through September 30, 1983, they had income and deductions as follows:

| | | |
|---|---:|---:|
| Gross income (all earned by Mr. B) | | $ 28,800 |
| Less: Deductions *for* adjusted gross income | | 3,000 |
| Adjusted gross income | | $ 25,800 |
| Minus: | | |
| Deductions *from* adjusted gross income (itemized deductions) | $ 5,000 | |
| Personal exemptions $\left[ 3 \times \$1,000 \times \frac{9}{12} \right]$ | 2,250 | 7,250 |
| Modified taxable income[a] | | $ 18,550 |

[a]Modified taxable income is defined at § 443(b)(3).

---

**19.** § 443(b)(1).

Annualized income—

$$\left(\$18{,}550 \times \frac{12}{9}\right) \qquad\qquad\qquad\qquad \$\ 24{,}733$$

    Add zero bracket amount                      3,400

                                               $\ 28,133$

Tax on annualized income                  $\ 4,575$[b]

Short period tax $\left(\$4{,}575 \times \dfrac{9}{12}\right)$         $\ 3,431$

[b]The Tax Rate Schedules (not the Tax Table) must be used. See § 3(b)(2). Tax on $28,133 was computed using the 1983 rate schedule for married taxpayers filing jointly.

# ACCOUNTING METHODS

## PERMISSIBLE METHODS

Section 446 requires that taxable income be computed under the method of accounting regularly employed by the taxpayer in keeping its books, provided the method clearly reflects income. The Code recognizes as generally permissible methods:

    —The cash receipts and disbursements method.

    —The accrual method.

    —A hybrid method (a combination of cash and accrual).

The Regulations refer to the above alternatives as "overall-methods" and add that the term "method of accounting" includes not only the overall method of accounting of the taxpayer but also the accounting treatment of any item.

Any of the three methods of accounting may be used if the method is consistently employed and clearly reflects income. However, the taxpayer is required to use the accrual method for sales and costs of goods sold if inventories are an income-producing factor to the business. Special methods are also permitted for installment sales, for long-term construction contracts, and for farmers.

A taxpayer who has more than one trade or business may use a different method of accounting for each trade or business activity. Furthermore, a different method of accounting may be used to determine income from a trade or business than is used to compute nonbusiness items of income and deductions. For example, an individual's income from an unincorporated business could be determined under the accrual method, whereas the cash method could be used for all other types of income (e. g., interest and dividends) and deductions (e. g., itemized deductions).

The Code grants the IRS broad powers to determine whether the taxpayer's accounting method clearly reflects income. Thus, if the method employed does not clearly reflect income, the IRS has the power to prescribe the method to be used by the taxpayer. This authority falls under § 446(b) which states:

> If no method of accounting has been regularly used by the taxpayer, or if the method used does not clearly reflect income, the computation of taxable income shall be made under such method as, in the opinion of the Secretary or his delegate, does clearly reflect income.

Under these broad powers, the IRS may require that a taxpayer involuntarily change to another method of accounting. For example, the Regulations now require taxpayers to adopt the full absorption inventory costing method if they are not presently using this method.

## CASH RECEIPTS AND DISBURSEMENTS METHOD— CASH BASIS

Most individuals and many businesses use the cash basis to report income and deductions. The popularity of this method can largely be attributed to its simplicity and flexibility. Under the cash method, income is not recognized until the taxpayer receives (actually or constructively) cash or its equivalent. Deductions are generally permitted in the year of payment. Thus, year-end accounts receivable, payables, and accrued items of income and deductions are not included in the determination of taxable income. The cash basis permits a taxpayer to postpone or accelerate the payment of expenses and in some cases to defer the collection of income.

*Constructive Receipt of Income.* An item of gross income must be recognized by the taxpayer in the year it is actually or constructively received in the form of cash or its equivalent. A "cash equivalent" is anything with a readily ascertainable market value. Income is constructively received when it is credited to the taxpayer's account, set apart for him or her, or otherwise made available so that he or she may draw upon it at any time or so that he or she could have drawn upon it during the taxable year if notice of intention to withdraw had been given. Chapter 3 includes a more comprehensive discussion of the doctrine of constructive receipt.

*Deductions.* Generally, the cash basis taxpayer is permitted a deduction only in the year of actual payment. The doctrine of constructive receipt has no corollary principle applicable to deductions (i. e., payment must actually be made before the deduction is allowed).

**Example 16.** T owns 100% of X Corporation's common stock and serves as its president. Both T and X Corporation are cash basis taxpayers. In December, T declared a $5,000 bonus payable to himself. T's total compensation, including the $5,000 bonus, was reasonable in amount. The corporation had sufficient cash to pay the bonus in December, and there were no substantial limitations or restrictions on the withdrawal of such funds. T was in constructive receipt of the income in December. The cash basis corporation, however, would not be entitled to a deduction in December, since the bonus was not actually paid in that month.

**Example 17.** Assume the same facts as in Example 16 except that X Corporation uses the accrual basis of accounting and T (the shareholder) is on the cash basis. The unpaid salary might possibly be disallowed under § 267 (see "Transactions Between Related Parties" in Chapter 5). However, if the shareholder is deemed to have constructively received the salary in December, it would follow that the corporation would be deemed to have made the payment in December. Thus, X Corporation should be entitled to the $5,000 deduction for the bonus in December and T should include the bonus in gross income in December, because he was in constructive receipt of such amount.

*Exceptions.* Not all cash payments are deductible in the period in which the payment is made. If an expenditure is for "an asset having a useful life which extends substantially beyond the close of the taxable year," the cash basis taxpayer must account for the item in the same manner as an accrual basis taxpayer. The cost of the asset must be capitalized and amortized or depreciated over its useful life. Also, if a taxpayer acquires an asset and part of the consideration paid is in the form of a note or mortgage, the total cost of the asset is used to compute the annual amortization or depreciation even though the taxpayer has not paid off the note or mortgage.

*Prepaid Expenses.* A cash basis taxpayer generally is required to capitalize payments that create an asset having a useful life which extends substantially beyond the end of the tax year.

Under the Tax Reform Act of 1976, prepaid interest must be capitalized and amortized over the life of the loan, except in the case of points paid in connection with the purchase or improvement of a personal residence.[20]

Taxpayers have also attempted to deduct prepaid cattle feed costs in the year paid as a form of tax shelter. This type of shelter results in a shifting of deductions into an earlier year, since the cattle investor's income is not recognized until the following year when the cattle are sold. The position of the IRS is that such costs should be capitalized if the full deduction in the year of payment "distorts" income or if the payment is, in fact, a deposit. Some courts have permitted a current deduction in the year of payment when the terms of the prepaid feed agreement required the taxpayer to accept a specific quantity at a fixed price or to substitute specific quantities at a maximum price. Limitations have recently been imposed on "farming syndicates"

---

**20.** § 461(g). Refer to the discussion in Chapter 7.

which require such taxpayers to use the accrual basis to account for feed, seed, and fertilizer.

One should recognize that there is a lack of consistency in the treatment of prepaid income and deductions. The recipient of prepaid income (as discussed in Chapter 3) generally must recognize income in the year of receipt, regardless of the taxpayer's method of accounting; but the taxpayer making a prepayment may be required to capitalize such amounts.

> **Example 18.** A, an accrual basis taxpayer, rented a restaurant building for a 24-month period for $5,000. This amount was prepaid on the date the lease was signed. C, the tenant, was a cash basis taxpayer. A must include the entire $5,000 as rental income in the year received, even though he is an accrual basis taxpayer and the $5,000 is not yet earned. C must capitalize the $5,000 of prepaid rent and amortize the cost over 24 months, even though he is a cash basis taxpayer.

## ACCRUAL METHOD

The Regulations provide that "under the accrual method of accounting, income is includible in gross income when (1) all the events have occurred which fix the right to receive such income and (2) the amount thereof can be determined with reasonable accuracy."

> **Example 19.** A, a calendar year taxpayer who uses the accrual basis of accounting, was to receive a bonus equal to 6% of B Corporation's net income for its fiscal year ending each June 30. For the fiscal year ending June 30, 19X1, B Corporation had net income of $240,000, and for the six months ending December 31, 19X1, the corporation's net income was $150,000. A will report $14,400 (.06 × $240,000) for 19X1, because her rights to the amount became fixed when B Corporation's year closed. However, A would not accrue income based on the corporation's profits for the last six months of 19X1, since her right to the income does not accrue until the close of the corporation's tax year.

*Reserves for Estimated Expenses.* In financial accounting, reserves or allowances for estimated expenses frequently are provided to attain a proper matching of costs and revenues for an accounting period. Allowances for estimated expenses often are accrued for bad debts, sales returns, warranty service costs, collection expenses, and maintenance expense. However, except in the case of bad debts, reserves for expenses are seldom permitted for tax purposes. Code § 166 specifically provides for the use of the reserve method in accounting for bad debts. However, the courts have not generally permitted the use of other types of reserves for estimated expenses, since the all events test (definite liability that can be reasonably estimated) cannot be satisfied at the time the addition is made to the reserve.

## HYBRID METHOD

A hybrid method of accounting involves the use of more than one method. For example, a taxpayer who uses the accrual basis to report sales and cost of goods sold but uses the cash basis to report other items of income and expense is employing a hybrid method. The Code permits the use of a hybrid method provided the taxpayer's income is clearly reflected.[21] A taxpayer who uses the accrual method for business expenses must also use the accrual method for business income (i. e., a cash method for income items may not be used if the taxpayer's expenses are accounted for under the accrual basis).

It may be preferable for a business which is required to report sales and cost of sales on the accrual method to report other items of income and expense under the cash method. The cash method permits greater flexibility in the timing of income and expense recognition.

## CHANGE OF METHOD

The taxpayer, in effect, makes an election to use a particular accounting method when an initial tax return is filed using a particular method. If a subsequent change in method is desired, the taxpayer must obtain the permission of the IRS.

As previously mentioned, the term "accounting method" encompasses not only the overall accounting method used by the taxpayer (i. e., the cash or accrual method), but also the treatment of any material item of income or deduction. Thus, a change in the method of deducting property taxes from a cash basis to an accrual basis which results in a deduction for taxes in a different year would constitute a change in an accounting method. Other examples of accounting method changes include changes involving the method or basis used in the valuation of inventories and a change from the direct charge-off method to the allowance method for deducting bad debts.

# SPECIAL ACCOUNTING METHODS

Generally, accrual basis taxpayers recognize income when goods are sold and shipped to the customer. Cash basis taxpayers generally recognize income from a sale on the collection of cash from the customer. The tax law provides special accounting methods, however, for unusual situations (e. g., long-term contracts when the contract requires more than 12 months to complete). In addition, the installment method (which is a variation of the cash method) is available to taxpayers if certain conditions are met. These special methods were en-

---

**21.** § 446(c).

acted, in part, to provide equity based on the wherewithal to pay concept (i. e., the taxpayer does not have the cash to pay the tax at the time of sale).

## LONG-TERM CONTRACTS

Regulation § 1.451–3(b) defines a "long-term contract" as follows: a building, installation, construction, or manufacturing contract which (1) is not completed within the taxable year entered into and (2) is either (a) a contract involving the manufacture of unique items not normally carried in finished goods inventory or (b) a contract which normally requires more than 12 months to complete.

> **Example 20.** T, a calendar year taxpayer, entered into two contracts during the year. One contract was to construct a special building foundation. Work was to begin in October 19X1 and was to be completed by June 19X2. The position of the IRS is that the contract is not long-term even though it straddles two years, because it takes less than 12 months to complete. It should be noted that these Regulations have been successfully challenged by taxpayers in a number of cases. The second contract was for architectural services to be performed on a new building over a two-year period. These services will not qualify for long-term contract treatment, because the taxpayer will not "build, install, or construct."

In the year the costs are incurred for such long-term contracts, the taxpayer may elect to use either (1) the completed contract, (2) percentage of completion, (3) cash, (4) accrual, or (5) a hybrid method. Once the election is made, the taxpayer must apply the same method to all subsequent long-term contracts unless permission is obtained for a change in accounting method.

*Completed Contract Method.* Under the completed contract method, no revenue from the contract is recognized until the contract is completed and accepted. However, a taxpayer may not delay completion of a contract for the principal purpose of deferring tax. Nevertheless, it may be possible for a taxpayer to select the year in which income is recognized by either accelerating or decelerating nearly completed projects prior to the end of the tax year. Some courts have, in effect, applied a *de minimus* rule holding that a contract is complete upon its substantial completion (i. e., minor amounts of work to be completed or defects to be corrected do not postpone the recognition of income if the contract has been accepted). Other courts have applied a literal interpretation to the Regulations and have required total completion and acceptance of the contract. In TEFRA, Congress directed IRS to issue new regulations clarifying when a contract is completed.

*Percentage of Completion Method.* Under the percentage of completion method, a portion of the gross contract price is included in income during each period. The accrued amount represents the percentage of the contract which is completed during the year multiplied by the gross contract price. All of the expenditures made on the contract during the year (after adjustment for variations between the beginning and ending inventories of materials and supplies) are deductible as an offset against the accrued revenue.

The Regulations provide that an estimate of the percentage of completion may be determined by either of the following methods:

—By comparing the costs incurred with the estimated total costs.

—By comparing the work performed with the estimated total work to be performed.

If the estimate is based upon a comparison of work performed, certificates of architects or engineers or other appropriate documentation must be available for inspection on audit by the IRS.

*Comparison of the Completed Contract and Percentage of Completion Methods.* To illustrate the two methods, assume a contractor agrees to construct a building for $125,000. In the initial year of construction, costs of $80,000 are incurred and the architect estimates the job is 80 percent complete. In the second year, the contract is completed at an additional cost of $25,000.

COMPLETED CONTRACT METHOD

|  | Year 1 | Year 2 |
|---|---|---|
| Revenue | –0– | $ 125,000 |
| Costs incurred on the contract | — | (105,000) |
| Gross profit | –0– | $  20,000 |

COMPLETED CONTRACT METHOD

|  | Year 1 | Year 2 |
|---|---|---|
| Revenue | –0– | $ 125,000 |
| Costs incurred on the contract | — | (105,000) |
| Gross profit | –0– | $  20,000 |

As illustrated above, an advantage of the completed contract method is the deferral of income. This means that the contractor has the use of funds which would otherwise be paid to the government as income taxes during periods prior to completion.

## INSTALLMENT METHOD

Under the general rule for computing the gain or loss from the sale of property, the entire amount of gain or loss is recognized upon the sale or other disposition of the property.

**Example 21.** A sold property to B for $20,000 cash plus B's note (fair market value and face amount of $80,000). A's basis in the property was $40,000. Gain or loss computed under the cash or accrual basis would be as follows:

|  |  |  |
|---|---|---|
| Amount realized: | | |
|    Cash down payment | $ | 20,000 |
|    Notes receivable | | 80,000 |
| | $ | 100,000 |
| Basis in the property | | (40,000) |
| Realized gain | $ | 60,000 |

In the prior example, the general rule for recognizing gain or loss requires A to pay a substantial amount of tax on the gain in the year of sale even though only $20,000 cash was received. Congress enacted the installment sale provisions to prevent this sort of hardship by allowing the taxpayer to spread the gain from installment sales over the collection period.

The installment sales method is a very important tax planning tool. In addition to its obvious tax deferral possibilities, the installment method can be used to avoid a bunching of income; and in the case of the sale of a capital asset, the installment method may sufficiently spread the capital gain to avoid or reduce any alternative minimum tax (discussed earlier in the chapter).

*Overview of the Installment Sales Provisions.* The enactment of the Installment Sales Revision Act of 1980 made significant changes in the treatment of sales where payments are received in other than the year of the sale. As presently structured, the relevant Code provisions are summarized below:

| Section | Subject |
|---|---|
| 453 | General rules governing the installment method (e. g., when applicable), related-party transfers, and special situations (e. g., certain corporate liquidations). |
| 453A | Use of the installment method by dealers in personal property (i. e., personalty). |
| 453B | Gain or loss recognition upon the disposition of installment obligations. |
| 1038 | Rules governing the repossession of real estate sold under the installment method. |

Since the rules governing dealers in personal property (i. e., § 453A) are unique, they are considered first.

## INSTALLMENT METHOD—DEALERS IN PERSONAL PROPERTY

In order to qualify as a dealer in personal property, the taxpayer must regularly sell personal property on the installment plan.[22] "Regularly" would seem to imply a high ratio of installment sales to total sales. However, the Tax Court has interpreted the "regularly sells" requirement to mean that the taxpayer holds himself or herself out to the public as selling on the installment plan.

The election may be used to report income both from revolving charge accounts (i. e., consumer charge accounts with extended payment privileges) and traditional installment contracts. At this point, it is not clear whether or not single payment accounts will qualify. Under prior law, more than one payment was necessary before the installment method could be used.

*Making the Election.* In the case of a new business, the election is made by reporting the income under the installment method. A statement should be attached to the return indicating that the election is being made. If a dealer in personal property has been using the accrual method in reporting gains, conversion to the installment method represents a change in an accounting method and requires the consent of the IRS. Under prior law, special adjustments for prior sales were required by the change, which led to a degree of double taxation. Commencing in 1981, no such adjustments are necessary.

> **Example 22.** In 1982, Z Corporation (a calendar year taxpayer) began its retail operations. In reporting gain on installment sales during 1982 and 1983, the accrual method was used. In March of 1984, Z Corporation decides to adopt the installment method. Pursuant to this decision, a Form 3115 is filed and approval of the change is obtained from the IRS. Z Corporation now will account for the 1984 sales using the installment method. Any further collections on its 1982 and 1983 sales will not result in income, since the gain element already has been recognized.

> **Example 23.** Assume the same facts as in Example 22 except that Z Corporation chose to use the installment method when it filed its first income tax return (i. e., for tax year 1982). Because no change in accounting method is involved, the use of the installment method is automatic and the consent of the IRS is not necessary.

*Computing the Realized Gross Profit.* The gross profit percentages may be computed for each sale, and the percentage can then be applied to each collection. In most instances, however, all of the in-

---

22.　§ 453A(a)(1).

stallment sales for a particular year are grouped and one gross-profit percentage for the year is computed.

> **Example 24.** X Company is a new business that sells wood stoves. X Company sells three models on the installment plan. Total sales and cost of goods sold for each model are presented below.

| Model | Sales | Cost of Goods Sold | Gross Profit | Gross Profit % | Collections |
|---|---|---|---|---|---|
| 1 | $ 60,000 | $ 24,000 | $ 36,000 | 60% | $ 20,000 |
| 2 | 90,000 | 45,000 | 45,000 | 50% | 60,000 |
| 3 | 50,000 | 40,000 | 10,000 | 20% | 20,000 |
| | $ 200,000 | $ 109,000 | $ 91,000 | 45.5% | $ 100,000 |

> X Company can elect to report its recognized gross profit for the year by relating collections to the particular model using the first method; gross profit is computed to be $46,000 [$20,000 × 60% + ($60,000 × 50%) + ($20,000 × 20%)]. The gross profit using the average method is $45,500 ($100,000 × 45.5%), computed by applying an average gross profit percentage to total collections.

The dealer may add carrying charges or interest (as determined at the time of the sale) to the cash selling price of the property.[23] Alternatively, the carrying charges may be reported separately (e. g., as interest income), in which case, payments received first are applied to the carrying charges (accrued interest).[24]

> **Example 25.** T, a home appliance dealer, had installment sales, cost of goods sold, and gross profit computed under the accrual method as follows:

| | Installment Sales (Including Carrying Charges and Interest) | Cost of Goods Sold | Gross Profit | Gross Profit % |
|---|---|---|---|---|
| 19X1 | $ 100,000 | $ 60,000 | $ 40,000 | 40% |
| 19X2 | 120,000 | 90,000 | 30,000 | 25% |
| 19X3 | 150,000 | 105,000 | 45,000 | 30% |

> In computing the gross profit under the installment method on the 19X3 return, the dealer must take into account collections on current and previous years' installment sales as follows:

---

**23.** § 453A(a)(2).
**24.** § 453A(b).

| Year of Sale | 19X3 Collections | | Gross Profit % | Gross Profit on Collections |
|---|---|---|---|---|
| 19X1 | $ 20,000 | × | 40% | $　8,000 |
| 19X2 | 50,000 | × | 25% | 12,500 |
| 19X3 | 60,000 | × | 30% | 18,000 |
| Total 19X3 realized gross profit | | | | $ 38,500 |

*Installment Sales—Property Other Than Inventory.* As discussed above, the Code contains special rules for installment reporting by dealers in personal property. Other taxpayers who desire to use the installment method must meet the requirements set forth in § 453.

　—There must be a sale of property (as contrasted to services).

　—The property must not be of a kind which "is required to be included in the inventory of the taxpayer if on hand at the close of the taxable year."[25]

If the property sold is of the right kind, the next issue is whether there was an installment sale. All that is required to meet the latter requirement is that at least one payment will be received in a tax year other than the year of sale.[26]

> **Example 26.** Z sold land on December 31, 19X1, and received the seller's note receivable. The note was paid in 19X2. Under the installment method, Z would report her entire gain in 19X2 rather than 19X1 (the years he would have reported the gain by the cash or accrual method).

*The Nonelective Aspect.* Regardless of the taxpayer's method of accounting, as a general rule installment sales must be reported by the installment method.[27] A special election is required to report the gain by any other method of accounting (see further discussion in a subsequent section of this chapter).

*Computing the Gain for the Period.* The gain reported on each sale is computed by the following formula:

$$\frac{\text{Total gain}}{\text{Contract price}} \times \text{Payments received} = \text{Recognized gain}$$

The computation of the total gain for a taxpayer who is not a dealer in real property is the selling price reduced by selling expenses and the adjusted basis of the property. For a dealer in real property,

---

**25.**　§ 453(b)(1)(B).

**26.**　§ § 453(b)(1), applicable to sales after October 19, 1980. Under pre-1980 law, the IRS took the position that the installment method could not be used if the entire selling price was received in one year.

**27.**　§ 453(a). Under pre-1980 law, the installment method had to be elected.

selling expenses are treated as a business expense and therefore are deducted in full in the year of the sale, rather than being used to offset the selling price.

The contract price generally is the amount (excluding interest) the seller will ultimately collect from the purchaser. Therefore, the contract price is the selling price less the seller's mortgage or notes which are assumed by the buyer. Payments received are the collections on the contract price received in the tax year and thus is generally the cash received (excluding interest income). If the buyer pays any of the seller's expenses, the amount paid is considered constructively received by the seller. Additional items that are considered payments are discussed after the basic calculations have been illustrated.

**Example 27.** The seller is not a dealer and the facts are as follows:

| | | |
|---|---:|---:|
| Sales price: | | |
|     Cash down payment | $ 1,000 | |
|     Seller's mortgage assumed | 3,000 | |
|     Notes payable to the seller | 13,000 | $ 17,000 |
| Selling expenses | | (500) |
| Seller's basis | | (10,000) |
| Total gain | | $ 6,500 |

The contract price is $14,000 ($17,000 − $3,000). Assuming the $1,000 is the only payment in the year of sale, the gain in that year is computed as follows:

$$\frac{\$6,500 \text{ (total gain)}}{\$14,000 \text{ (contract price)}} \times \$1,000 = \$464 \text{ (gain recognized in year of sale)}$$

If the sum of the nondealer's basis and selling expenses is less than the liabilities assumed by the buyer, the difference must be added to the contract price and to the payments received in the year of sale. This adjustment to the contract price is required so that the ratio of total gain divided by contract price will not be greater than one.

**Example 28.** Assume the same facts as in Example 27 except that the seller's basis in the property is only $2,000. The total gain, therefore, is $14,500. Payments in the year of sale are $1,500.

| | |
|---|---:|
| Down payment | $ 1,000 |
| Excess of mortgage assumed over seller's basis | |
|     and expenses ($3,000 − $2,000 − $500) | 500 |
| | $ 1,500 |

The contract price is $14,500 [$17,000 (selling price) − $3,000 (seller's mortgage assumed) + $500 (excess of seller's expenses and mortgage assumed over seller's basis)], and the gain in the year of sale is computed as follows:

$$\frac{\$14,500 \text{ (total gain)}}{\$14,500 \text{ (contract price)}} \times \$1,500 = \$1,500$$

In subsequent years, all amounts the seller collects on note principal ($13,000) will be recognized gain.

The character of the gain depends on the type of asset sold. When the gain includes some ordinary income under §§ 1245 and 1250, as well as § 1231 gain, the Regulations require that all ordinary income be recognized before the § 1231 gain is reported.

*Other Amounts Considered Payments Received.* Congress and the IRS have added the following items to be considered as payments received in the year of sale:

—Purchaser's evidence of indebtedness payable on demand and certain other readily tradable obligations (e. g., bonds traded on a stock exchange).

—Purchaser's evidence of indebtedness secured by cash or its equivalent.

In the absence of the first adjustments, the seller would have almost complete control over the year he or she reported the gain—whenever he or she demands payment or sells the tradable obligations. Also, the seller receiving the obligations secured by cash can often post them as collateral for a loan and have the cash from the sale; thus, there would be no justification for deferring the tax.

*Imputed Interest.* Section 483 provides that if a deferred payment contract for the sale of property with a selling price of at least $3,000 does not contain a reasonable interest rate, a reasonable rate is imputed. The imputing of interest effectively restates the selling price of the property to equal the sum of the payments in the year of sale and the discounted present value of the future payments. The difference between the present value of a future payment and its face amount is taxed as interest income when collections are received. Thus, § 483 prevents sellers of capital assets from increasing the selling price to reflect the equivalent of unstated interest on deferred payments and thereby converting ordinary (interest) income into long-term capital gains.

Currently under the Regulations, if a contract entered into on or after July 1, 1981, does not provide a simple interest rate of at least nine percent, a rate of 10 percent (compounded semiannually) is imputed. However, the maximum imputed interest rate is only seven percent in the case of sales of land to a family member (the seller's brothers, sisters, spouse, ancestors, or lineal descendants) after June 30, 1981. It seems Congress decided family members should be allowed some of a "good thing"—the ability to convert some interest income into capital gain.

> **Example 29.** S sold land to P for $15,000 cash and an installment note with $15,000 due each year for the following nine years. No interest is stated in the agreement, and S's basis in the land is $30,000. In the absence of the imputed interest rules, S's total capital gain would be $120,000 ($150,000 − $30,000).
>
> In the following schedule, the selling price, contract price, and capital gain are calculated with interest imputed at 10% (assuming P is not a family member) and at 7% (assuming P is a family member).

|  | 10% | 7% |
|---|---|---|
| Present value of $15,000/year for 9 years | $ 86,385 | $ 98,923 |
| Down payment | 15,000 | 15,000 |
| Selling price (also contract price) | $ 101,385 | $ 113,923 |
| Minus basis | 30,000 | 30,000 |
| Total capital gain | $ 71,385 | $ 83,923 |
| Total interest ($120,000 less capital gain) | $ 48,615 | $ 36,077 |

This example demonstrates that the family member has $12,538 more capital gain and $12,538 less interest income than does the nonfamily member under these conditions.

*Disposition of Installment Obligations.* Section 453B prevents taxpayers from avoiding the recognition of deferred gross profit on installment obligations through various means (e. g., the sale of installment notes or the distribution of such notes to shareholders). This provision of the Code requires the taxpayer to, in effect, pay the tax on the portion of gross profits which was previously deferred. Section 453B(a) provides as follows:

> If an installment is satisfied at other than its face value or distributed, transmitted, sold, or otherwise disposed of, gain or loss shall result to the extent of the difference between the basis of the obligation and either of the following:
>
> 1. The amount realized, in the case of satisfaction at other than face value or a sale or exchange.
>
> 2. The fair market value of the obligation at the time of distribution, transmission, or disposition, in the case of the distribution, transmission, or disposition other than by sale or exchange.

The gift of an installment note will be treated as a taxable disposition by the donor. One court, however, has held that no gain will be recognized when the donee also is the obligor. New § 453B(f)(1) clarifies this matter by making the cancellation a taxable disposition. Furthermore, § 453B(f)(2) holds that the amount realized from the cancellation will be the face amount of the note if the parties (i. e., obligor and obligee) are related to each other.

> **Example 30.** F cancels a note issued by D (F's daughter) that arose in connection with the sale of property. At the time of the cancellation, the note had a basis to F of $10,000, a face amount of $25,000, and a fair market value of $20,000. Presuming the sale fell under § 453, the cancellation now results in gain of $15,000 to F.

Certain exceptions to the recognition of gain provisions are provided for transfers of installment obligations pursuant to tax-free incorporations under § 351, contributions of capital to a partnership, certain corporate liquidations, and transfers due to the taxpayer's death.[28] In such instances, the deferred profit is merely shifted to the transferee who is responsible for the payment of tax on the subsequent collections of the installment obligations.

## ELECTING OUT OF THE INSTALLMENT METHOD

A taxpayer can elect not to use the installment method. The election is made by reporting on a timely filed return the gain computed by the taxpayer's usual method of accounting (cash or accrual). The Regulations contain rules which will usually result in a decision in favor of the installment method (as demonstrated below). However, in each case presented, the tax adviser should consider all alternatives.

> **Example 31.** S sold real property to P for $70,000 cash plus notes payable with a face amount of $30,000 and a fair market value of only $10,000. The difference between the face amount and value of the notes was due to their terms—interest only for 10 years (at 10%) and then principal payments spread over an additional 10 years. According to a reliable appraiser, the value of the property was $85,000. The seller's basis in the property was $75,000, and he had $5,000 selling expenses.

> Accrual Basis
>
> | | | |
> |---|---|---:|
> | Amount realized | | |
> | Cash down payment | $ | 70,000 |
> | Notes (face amount) | | 30,000 |
> | | $ | 100,000 |
> | Basis plus selling expenses | | 80,000 |
> | Recognized gain | $ | 20,000 |

---

28.  § § 453B(c) and (d). See Chapter 12 for a discussion of some of these subjects.

Installment Method

$$\frac{\text{Gain}}{\text{Contract price}} \times \text{payments received} =$$

$$\frac{\$20,000}{\$100,000} \times \$70,000 = \$14,000 \text{ gain in the year of sale}$$

If S is an accrual basis taxpayer, he should defer his gain through the use of the installment method (unless he has a capital loss carryover to offset the gain). As a cash basis taxpayer, however, he would report only $5,000 gain in the year of sale:

| | |
|---|---:|
| Fair market value of the property sold | $ 85,000 |
| Less: Basis and selling expenses | 80,000 |
| Recognized gain | $ 5,000 |

Although the numbers in Example 31 favored the cash basis, an additional consideration must be factored into the analysis. The $9,000 ($14,000 − $5,000) gain deferred until the note is collected will not be a capital gain, even though the property sold was a capital asset. This is true because a collection is not deemed to be a "sale or exchange" which is a requisite for a capital gain.

It should be noted that in Example 31, the cash basis taxpayer was required to treat the fair market value of the property sold as the amount realized. Under prior law, the amount realized was determined solely by reference to the cash received and the value of the installment obligations. Generally, the value of the cash and notes will equal the value of the property sold, but this is not always true. In some cases, the credit standing of the buyer will affect the value of the installment notes; also, the terms of the sale are often tailored to meet the seller's particular needs (cash flow and tax objectives). Regardless of a difference between the two values, the new Regulations clearly provide that the amount realized from a fixed obligation cannot be less than the value of the property sold reduced by the cash down payment.

*Revocation of the Election.* Permission of the IRS is required to revoke an election not to use the installment method. The stickiness of the election is an added peril.

# INVENTORIES

Generally, tax accounting and financial accounting for inventories are much the same:

—The use of inventories is necessary to clearly reflect the income of any business engaged in the production and sale or purchase and sale of goods.

—The inventories should include all finished goods, goods in process, and raw materials and supplies which will become part of the product (including containers).

—Inventory rules must give effect to the "best" accounting practice of a particular trade or business, and the taxpayer's method should be consistently followed from year to year.

—All items included in inventory should be valued at either (a) cost or (b) the lower of cost or market value.

The following are not acceptable methods or practices in valuing inventories:

—A deduction for a reserve for anticipated price changes.

—The use of a constant price or nominal value for a so-called normal quantity of materials or goods in stock (e. g., the base stock method).

—The inclusion of stock in transit in inventory to which title is not vested in the taxpayer.

—The direct costing approach (i. e., excluding fixed indirect production costs from inventory).

—The prime costing approach (i. e., excluding all indirect production costs from inventory).

The reason for the similarities between tax and financial accounting for inventories is that § 471 sets forth what appears to be a two-prong test. Under this provision "inventories shall be taken . . . on such basis . . . as conforming as nearly as may be to the *best accounting practice* in the trade or business and as most *clearly reflecting the income*." The best accounting practice is synonymous with generally accepted accounting principles (hereafter referred to as GAAP). However, the IRS determines whether an inventory method clearly reflects income.

In *Thor Power Tool Co. v. Comm.*, there was a conflict between the two tests.[29] The taxpayer's method of valuing obsolete parts was in conformity with GAAP. The IRS, however, successfully argued that the clear reflection of income test was not satisfied because the taxpayer's procedures for valuing its inventories were contrary to the Regulations. Under the taxpayer's method, inventories for parts in excess of estimated future sales were written off (i. e., expensed), although the parts were kept on hand and their asking prices were not reduced. Under Reg. § 1.471–4(b), inventories cannot be written down unless the selling prices also are reduced.

The taxpayer contended that conformity to GAAP creates a presumption that the method clearly reflects income. The Supreme Court disagreed, concluding that the clear reflection of income test was "paramount." Moreover, it is the opinion of the IRS which controls in de-

---

**29.** 79–1 USTC ¶ 9139, 43 AFTR2d 79–362, 99 S.Ct. 773 (USSC, 1979).

termining whether the method of inventory clearly reflects income. Thus, the best accounting practice test was rendered practically meaningless. It follows that the taxpayer's method of inventory must strictly conform to the Regulations, regardless of what GAAP might require.

## DETERMINING INVENTORY COST

For merchandise purchased, cost is the invoice price less trade discounts, plus freight and other handling charges. Cash discounts approximating a fair interest rate can be deducted or capitalized at the taxpayer's option providing the method used is consistently applied.

The cost of goods produced or manufactured by the taxpayer must be determined by using the full absorption method of inventory costing. Under this method, production costs (e. g., direct materials and labor) must be included in computing the cost of the inventory. In addition, all indirect production costs must be included in inventory except for the following:

(a) So-called Category 2 costs need not be included in inventory (e. g., advertising, selling, administrative, distribution, interest).

(b) So-called Category 3 costs may be either included or excluded depending on the taxpayer's treatment of such costs for financial reporting purposes (e. g., property and payroll taxes, depreciation, certain employee benefits).

Category 3 costs may be excluded from inventory only if the treatment of a particular item is consistent with generally accepted accounting principles. Furthermore, the IRS has ruled that the determination of whether the treatment of the item is consistent with generally accepted accounting principles should be decided without regard to the materiality of the item or the consistency of its treatment.

> **Example 32.** The taxpayer is in a manufacturing business and has consistently expensed, in the year of accrual, the real property tax on the factory. The company accountant recognizes that the property tax should be included in manufacturing overhead (thus, included in the cost of the inventory). However, because the item is not material, the accountant does not require that the financial statements be adjusted. To comply with the Regulations, the property tax must be added to the cost of goods sold and ending inventory rather than deducted currently.

A taxpayer may use the standard cost method to value inventory. However, if indirect production cost variances are significant, a pro rata portion of the variance must be reallocated to the ending inventories.

*Lower of Cost or Market.* Except for those taxpayers who use the LIFO method, inventories may be valued at the lower of cost or replacement cost (i. e., market). Those taxpayers using LIFO must value inventory at cost. However, the write-down of damaged or shop-worn merchandise and goods which are otherwise unsalable at normal prices is not considered to be an application of the lower of cost or market method. Such items should be valued at bona fide selling price less direct cost of disposal.

In the case of excess inventories (as in *Thor Power Tool Co.*, discussed above), the goods can be written down only to the taxpayer's offering price. If the offering price on the goods is not reduced, the goods must be valued at cost.

**Example 33.**  The Z Publishing Company invested $50,000 in printing 10,000 copies of a book. Although only 7,000 copies were sold in the first three years and none in the next five years, management is convinced that the book will become a classic in 20 years. Z Company leaves the price the same as it was when first distributed (i. e., $15 per copy). The remaining 3,000 books must be valued at cost (i. e., $15,000). It should be noted that the tax law provides an incentive for the taxpayer to destroy or abandon its excess inventory and obtain an immediate deduction rather than waiting for the event of future sales.

In applying this method, each item included in the inventory must be valued at the lower of its cost or market value.

**Example 34.**  The taxpayer's ending inventory is valued below:

| Item | Cost | Market | Lower of Cost or Market |
|------|------|--------|-------------------------|
| A | $ 5,000 | $  4,000 | $  4,000 |
| B | 3,000 | 2,000 | 2,000 |
| C | 1,500 | 6,000 | 1,500 |
|   | $ 9,500 | $ 12,000 | $ 7,500 |

Under the lower of cost or market method, the taxpayer's inventory would be valued at $7,500 rather than $9,500.

*Determining Cost—Specific Identification, FIFO, and LIFO.*  In some cases, it is feasible to determine the cost of the particular item sold. For example, an automobile dealer can easily determine the specific cost of each automobile which has been sold. However, in most businesses it is necessary to resort to a flow of goods assumption such as "first in, first out" (FIFO), "last in, first out" (LIFO), or an average cost method. A taxpayer may use any of these methods provided the method selected is consistently applied from year to year.

During a period of rising prices, LIFO will generally produce a lower ending inventory valuation and will result in a greater cost of goods sold than would be obtained under the FIFO method. The effects on computing costs of goods sold using LIFO and FIFO are illustrated in the following example:

**Example 35.** On January 1, 19X1, the taxpayer opened a retail store to sell refrigerators. At least 10 refrigerators must be carried in inventory to satisfy customer demands. The initial investment in the 10 refrigerators is $5,000. During the period, 10 refrigerators were sold at $750 each and were replaced at a cost of $6,000 ($600 each). Gross profit under the LIFO and FIFO methods is computed below:

|  |  | FIFO |  | LIFO |
|---|---|---|---|---|
| Sales (10 × $750) |  | $ 7,500 |  | $ 7,500 |
| Beginning inventory | $ 5,000 |  | $ 5,000 |  |
| Purchases | 6,000 |  | 6,000 |  |
|  | 11,000 |  | 11,000 |  |
| Ending inventory: |  |  |  |  |
| 10 × $600 | (6,000) |  |  |  |
| 10 × $500 |  |  | (5,000) |  |
| Cost of goods sold |  | (5,000) |  | (6,000) |
| Gross profit |  | $ 2,500 |  | $ 1,500 |

## THE LIFO ELECTION

A taxpayer may adopt LIFO by merely using the method in the tax return for the year of the change and by attaching Form 970 to the tax return. Thus, a taxpayer does not have to request approval for changes within the first 180 days of the tax year. Once the election is made, it cannot be revoked. However, a prospective change from LIFO to any other inventory method can be made if the consent of the IRS is obtained. Currently, the IRS will grant automatic approval if the request is timely filed and the taxpayer agrees to a 10-year spread of any positive adjustment.

The beginning inventory valuation for the first year LIFO is used is computed by the costing method employed in the preceding year. Thus, the beginning LIFO inventory is generally the same as the closing inventory for the preceding year. However, since lower of cost or market cannot be used in conjunction with LIFO, previous write-downs to market for items included in the beginning inventory must be restored to income. The amount the inventories are written up is an adjustment due to a change in accounting method. However, the usual rules for disposition of the adjustments under Rev.Proc. 80–51 are not applicable.[30] Section 472(d), effective for tax years beginning 1982 and thereafter, allows the taxpayer to spread the adjustment ratably over the year of the change and the two succeeding years.

**Example 36.** In 1982, T used the lower of cost or market FIFO inventory method. The FIFO cost of its ending inventory was

---

30. 1980–1 C.B. 582.

$30,000, and the inventory's market value was $24,000. Therefore, the ending inventory for 1982 was $24,000. T switched to LIFO in 1983 and was required to write up the beginning inventory to $30,000. T must add $2,000 ($6,000 ÷ 3) to his income for each of the years 1983, 1984, and 1985.

Congress added § 472(d) to the Code to overrule the previous IRS policy of requiring that the entire adjustment be included in income for the year preceding the change to LIFO.

Once the LIFO election is made for tax purposes, the taxpayer's financial reports to owners and creditors must also be prepared on the basis of LIFO.[31] The conformity of financial to tax reporting is specifically required by the Code and is strictly enforced by the IRS. However, under Regulations proposed in 1979, the taxpayer is allowed to make a footnote disclosure of the net income computed by another method of inventory valuation (e. g., FIFO).

*Simplified LIFO.* Although tax practitioners have long been aware of the tax deferrals available under LIFO, prior to 1982 very few companies used LIFO. In the eyes of Congress, LIFO was conspicuous by its absence from the returns of small businesses. For many taxpayers, a series of hurdles in the LIFO Regulations made the cost of compliance outweigh the benefits of LIFO.

As part of the Economic Recovery Tax Act of 1981, Congress ordered the IRS to lower the bars to the LIFO election. The IRS was directed to write regulations which would allow the taxpayer an election to calculate inventory at year-end prices (FIFO) and then convert this value to base period prices through the use of a government published index.[32] The advantage to using an index is that the taxpayer does not have to determine the actual base period cost of each item in his or her ending inventory, one of the high compliance costs of the formerly used LIFO valuation methods.

> **Example 37.** In 1984 L's Lawnmower Shop, Inc. adopted the LIFO inventory method. Its equipment inventories at year-end prices (FIFO) were as follows:
>
> | 1983 | $ 30,000 |
> |------|----------|
> | 1984 | 36,000 |
> | 1985 | 45,000 |
>
> The producer price index values for the classification "lawn equipment, power tools, and other hardware" for all relevant years were 1983, 120.2%; 1984, 129.2%; 1985, 132.7%.

---

31. § 472(c).
32. § 472(f).

The company would first convert its ending inventories to LIFO base period prices as follows:

$$1984 \qquad \frac{120.2}{129.2} \times \$36{,}000 = \underline{\underline{\$33{,}492}}$$

$$1985 \qquad \frac{120.2}{132.7} \times \$45{,}000 = \underline{\underline{\$40{,}761}}$$

Its ending inventory for 1985 is composed of three layers:

| | |
|---|---:|
| Base period | $ 30,000 |
| 1984 additions at base period prices ($33,492 − $30,000 = $3,492) converted to 1984 year-end | |
| prices $= \dfrac{129.2 \ (1984)}{120.2 \ (1983)} \times \$3{,}492$ | 3,753 |
| 1985 additions at base period prices ($40,761 − $33,492 = $7,269) converted to 1985 year-end prices | |
| $\dfrac{132.7 \ (1985)}{120.2 \ (1983)} \times \$7{,}269 =$ | 8,025 |
| 1985 LIFO inventory | $ 41,778 |

The forthcoming Regulations will provide detailed rules for selecting appropriate indexes.

*Single Pool LIFO.*  Taxpayers who elect to use LIFO must divide their inventories into pools. For example, an appliance store may have separate inventory classifications (or pools) for televisions, refrigerators and freezers, laundry equipment, and other appliances. Thus, if at the end of a particular year the television inventory is depleted, the taxpayer must recapture the taxes deferred from that inventory pool.

**Example 38.** At the beginning of 19X8, the taxpayer had an inventory of televisions with a LIFO cost of $50,000. The FIFO value of the goods would have been $90,000. The difference between the FIFO and LIFO values is income deferred from tax due to the use of LIFO ($90,000 − $50,000 = $40,000). If the company had been out of stock at year-end and purchases were $300,000, its cost of goods sold would have been $300,000 + $90,000 = $390,000 under FIFO but is only $350,000 under LIFO; thus, the deferred taxes on $40,000 ($390,000 − $350,000 = $40,000) would be recaptured.

In Example 38, if the company had only one inventory pool—appliances—there would be less risk of depleting its base stock (e. g., a decrease in televisions could be countered by an increase in refrigerators on hand). It should be apparent that the taxpayer prefers his or her LIFO pools to be as broad as possible. On the other hand, the IRS favors narrow pools.

What constitutes a pool has long been a source of controversy between the IRS and taxpayers. Undoubtedly, the potential entanglement with the IRS over the composition of pools has discouraged some taxpayers from using LIFO. In 1981, Congress legislated away these problems for some small businesses by directing the Commissioner to draft regulations which would allow these taxpayers to use a one-pool LIFO inventory method.

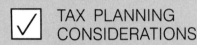

TAX PLANNING
CONSIDERATIONS

## INCOME AVERAGING

A taxpayer who anticipates that he or she may be able to income average in either the current year or the near future should have available the necessary information regarding the base period years.

> **Example 39.** Because T has received a substantial raise in her job, she believes that she will qualify for income averaging in 19X8. In checking her personal files, however, T is able to locate only the copies of the income tax returns for 19X5–19X7. Apparently, the tax return for 19X4 has been either misplaced or destroyed.

What should T do? In no event, should she proceed to income average without accurate information on *all* base period years. Thus, an estimate as to her taxable income for 19X4 would not be proper. It behooves her, therefore, to obtain a copy of her 19X4 return. She can do this by filing Form 4506, Request for Copy of Tax Form, with the IRS. Form 4506 should be sent to the *same* IRS office where the return was filed. The IRS charges $1 for one page and 10 cents for each additional page for this reproduction service and specifies that the taxpayer should allow 30 days for delivery.[33]

One should recognize that the income averaging procedure may not be confined to a single year but may benefit the taxpayer in several successive years.

> **Example 40.** Through 19X8, T had yearly taxable income as follows:

---

**33.** Payment for the copies should not be enclosed with Form 4506, since the IRS will send the taxpayer a statement for the charges.

| Year | Taxable Income |
|------|----------------|
| 19X3 | $ 10,000 |
| 19X4 | 10,000 |
| 19X5 | 10,000 |
| 19X6 | 10,000 |
| 19X7 | 50,000 |
| 19X8 | 50,000 |

Based on these facts, it is quite clear that T should qualify for income averaging for tax year 19X7.[34] But what about tax year 19X8? Although the tax savings will not be as large, income averaging should be available.[35] The reason the tax savings will not be as large is that 19X3 (taxable income of $10,000) is dropped and the 19X7 (taxable income of $50,000) is added as one of the base period years.

## MINIMUM TAX

For most taxpayers, the alternative minimum tax probably will not pose any threat for any of several reasons.

—Absent significant amounts of items of tax preference, the alternative minimum tax will not apply. Items of tax preference result from certain investments, and investments require capital. Many taxpayers either do not have this kind of capital available or choose more conventional investments that yield limited amounts of long-term capital gain (e. g., stocks and bonds).

—The amount of the exemption allowed will keep items of tax preference from being subject to the alternative minimum tax. Recall that the exemption is $40,000 for married taxpayers filing joint returns, $30,000 for single taxpayers, and $20,000 for married taxpayers filing separate returns. For example, a single taxpayer could absorb up to $30,000 in items of tax preference without having to worry about the alternative minimum tax.

The alternative minimum tax can prove troublesome when taxpayers have large amounts of long-term capital gains in any single year.

**Example 41.** During 1983, T sells real estate held as an investment (adjusted basis of $40,000) for $200,000 and thereby recognizes a long-term capital gain of $160,000.

---

**34.** Averageable income for 19X7 is $38,000 ($50,000–$12,000), and this is in excess of $3,000.
**35.** Averageable income for 19X8 is $26,000 ($50,000–$24,000), which is greater than $3,000.

**Example 42.**  Assume the same facts as in Example 41 except that the sale is structured as follows: $40,000 down payment with the balance payable in equal annual installments (at 12% interest) over the next four years. As a result of the sale, T recognizes a long-term capital gain of $32,000 in the year of the sale and in each of the next four years.

In order to circumvent or control the alternative minimum tax, the procedure followed in Example 42 usually is to be preferred. Unlike the result that took place in Example 41, the bunching of large amounts of long-term capital gain in a single year can be avoided.

## ACCOUNTING PERIODS

Practically all individuals adopt calendar year reporting with the filing of their initial returns. And there is no reason to change the year. However, there are often good business and tax reasons to place a corporation on a fiscal year. If a newly formed corporation is profitable in its first year of operation, by closing the tax year before the end of 12 months, the corporation can keep its income in the lower tax brackets.

## CHANGES IN ACCOUNTING METHODS

When a taxpayer elects a method of accounting for a particular item of income or deduction, he or she has not made a life-long commitment. Changes are easily made by filing an application with the IRS during the first 180 days of the tax year of the change. In the case of a change to LIFO, advance approval by the IRS is not required.

In the case of a new corporation experiencing losses or earning very little income, tax deferrals may not be in order. However, once the corporation's income begins moving up the rate schedule, accounting methods that defer income or accelerate deductions should be utilized (e. g., installment method, reserve method for bad debts, and LIFO).

Under Rev.Proc. 80–51, the newly profitable business will be allowed to spread its negative adjustments over no more years than the former method was used. Thus, if a business had little or no profits in the first five years but expects profits in the sixth and subsequent years, it could change, for example, to the reserve for bad debts method and spread the adjustment into five profitable years.

## INSTALLMENT METHOD

Dealers in personal property can enjoy deferrals of taxes that do not have to be paid until the final year of operations. At the end of each year, some income is always deferred (as compared to the income that would have been taxed under the accrual method).

Sale of noninventory property on the installment method allows the taxpayer to accomplish the following goals: (1) defer taxes, (2) avoid bunching of income and resulting application of high progressive rates, and (3) avoid the alternative minimum tax on capital gains.

In a few rare cases, the taxpayer may minimize the present value of his or her taxes by electing out of the installment method and using either the cash method or, in even rarer cases, the open transaction method. The cash method may be preferable where the seller receives the bulk of the selling price as cash in the year of sale. However, calculations should be made by both methods, and the ordinary income consequences of collections on notes with value less than their face amounts must be considered. The open transaction method can be used only where the properties exchanged cannot be valued because of contingencies. It should also be recognized that if the election out was improvidently made, IRS permission is required to amend the return and change to the installment method. Thus, electing out is a serious step.

A disposition of an installment obligation is also a serious matter. Gifts of the obligations will accelerate income to the seller. The list of taxable and nontaxable dispositions of installment obligations should not be trusted to memory. In each instance where transfers of installment obligations are contemplated, the practitioner should conduct research to be sure he or she knows the consequences.

## LIFO

Because inflation is expected for the foreseeable future, and as a result of the new simplified procedures, the use of LIFO will probably become more common. The recordkeeping requirements under the simplified procedures are minimal, and the tax savings are obvious. The only major disadvantage to LIFO is the financial-to-tax conformity requirement. However, this disadvantage can be overcome through footnote disclosure of earnings as computed under FIFO.

## PROBLEM MATERIALS

### Questions for Class Discussion

1. A taxpayer makes the following remark: "Although I was able to use income averaging last year, this year it appears to be out of the question since my income has not increased." Do you agree? Why or why not?

2. Could a taxpayer be eligible for income averaging in a year in which he or she was not gainfully employed? Explain.

3. "In most cases, a college graduate should be able to income average in the first year of full-time employment." Please comment.

4. While being supported by others during a six-year period, T created a musical composition which proved to be a large financial success. Could T qualify for income averaging? What further information, if any, would you want to know before resolving this question?

5. H and W are married and file a joint return in 1983. H was self-supporting during the base period years 1979–1982. W was a college student during the entire base period and was claimed as a dependent by her parents. Is there any possibility H and W can use the income averaging method for 1983?

6. In determining the alternative minimum tax, what is the relevance of items of tax preference?

7. Does the alternative minimum tax apply to long-term capital gains recognized by an individual taxpayer? Explain.

8. When would a fiscal year be preferable to a calendar year? How is a fiscal year elected?

9. In which of the following situations must a taxpayer annualize income?
   (a) The first tax year.  *no*
   (b) The year an individual marries.  *no*
   (c) The final return.  *yes*
   (d) A year of a change in the tax year.  *yes*

10. Compare the cash basis and accrual basis of accounting as applied to:
    (a) Fixed assets.  — *same for both.*
    (b) Prepaid rental income. —
    (c) Prepaid interest expense.
    (d) A note received for services performed if the market value and face amount of the note differ.
    (e) The deduction for a contested item.

11. What is the general rule as to when income is recognized under the accrual basis of accounting?

12. What is the general rule as to when a deduction will be recognized under the accrual basis of accounting?

13. For several years, a taxpayer has consistently used the accrual basis to report income and deductions. During the year, she bought some rental property and would like to report the income from the property on the cash method. Would the use of the cash basis to report the rental income constitute a change in accounting method?

14. The taxpayer began work on a contract in June 19X1 and completed the contract in April 19X2.

    (a) Can the percentage of completion method be used to report the income from the contract?  — *require > 12 months to complete or special order item.*

(b) If the taxpayer in (a) uses the accrual basis to report income, assuming no advance payments are received, when will the income be recognized? *when the contract is accepted by the contractor*

15. What are the tax advantages of the completed contract method? *deferred until contract is completed.*

16. T sold land and would like to report the gain under the installment method. How is the election made?

17. In 19X1, the taxpayer sold some real estate and received an installment note. The sale met all of the requirements for using the installment method, but the taxpayer did not know that the installment method could be used. Thus, the entire gain was reported in the year of sale. In 19X2, it is discovered that the taxpayer could have used the installment method. Is there anything that can be done? Explain.

18. How does the buyer's assumption of the seller's liabilities in an installment sale affect the following:

    (a) Selling price. *(included in the selling price)*

    (b) Contract price. *Amt seller collects from the buyer.*

    (c) Buyer's payments in the year of sale.

19. S advertises a tract of land (held as an investment) for sale at a cash price of $100,000. P desires to purchase the property but requires three years in order to obtain all of the funds. As a compromise, S accepts the three-year arrangement but only if the selling price is raised from $100,000 to $120,000. What is S trying to accomplish for tax purposes?

20. What is "cost"? How is "lower of cost or market" computed for purposes of valuing inventories?

## Problems

21. In which of the following independent situations are the individuals eligible to use income averaging:

    (a) H and W were married during the current year. H provided more than 50% of his own support during the previous four years. W, however, was supported by her parents prior to their marriage. W had adjusted gross income of $20,000 during the current year, and they plan to file a joint return. H's adjusted gross income is $40,000.

    (b) T, a single individual, is 27 years old. He was supported by his parents during college but has provided all of his own support during the past five years. T attended graduate school on a part-time basis during the past three years to earn an M.B.A.

    (c) H and W are 27 years old and were married when they were both 22. During the past four years, H has been attending graduate school on a full-time basis to earn a Ph.D. Both H and W were employed on a part-time basis during the base-year period and provided 60% of their own support. During the current year, H received his Ph.D. and was fully employed as a professor. H and W earned $40,000 during the current year and were self-supporting.

22. T is single and an eligible individual for income averaging. Her only income for the computation and the base period years was from wages. T's taxable income for the past six years is listed below:

| Year | Taxable Income |
|------|----------------|
| 1978 | $  7,200 |
| 1979 | 5,000 |
| 1980 | 11,950 |
| 1981 | 17,000 |
| 1982 | 25,200 |
| 1983 | 37,750 |

(a) Assume the computation year is 1982. Can T benefit from income averaging?

(b) Assume the computation year is 1983. Can T benefit from income averaging?

23. V is married, with no dependents, and expects to file a joint return. The relevant information for 1983 is summarized below:

| | |
|---|---|
| Net income from a consulting practice conducted on a part-time basis | $ 150,000 |
| Interest and dividends (after exclusion) | 40,000 |
| Salary from a full-time job | 60,000 |
| Items of tax preference which qualify as deductions *for* adjusted gross income | 15,000 |
| Unreimbursed employee travel expenses | 10,000 |
| Other deductions *for* adjusted gross income | 20,000 |

Taxable income for 1983 proves to be $190,000.

During the period 1979–1982, Mr. and Mrs. V had average taxable income of $100,000. Presuming Mr. and Mrs. V are eligible individuals, compute their tax liability under income averaging and under the regular method.

24. T, who is single, has the following items relative to her tax return for 1983:

| | |
|---|---|
| Bargain element from the exercise of an incentive stock option | $ 50,000 |
| Accelerated depreciation on real estate investments (straight-line depreciation would have yielded $60,000) | 80,000 |
| Net capital gain deduction (60% of $150,000) | 90,000 |
| Alternative tax itemized deductions | 20,000 |

For 1983, T's adjusted gross income is $150,000 and the Federal income tax liability (as usually determined) is $22,000.

(a) Determine the items of tax preference T has for 1983. 160,000

(b) Calculate the alternative minimum tax (if any) for 1983.

25. Q, Inc. received its charter on February 11, 19X1. However, the company decided to postpone the beginning of business operations until June 1, 19X1. Q Corporation would like to use a fiscal year ending on June 30. How and when should the election be made?

26. P Corporation is in the business of sales and home deliveries of fuel oil and currently uses a calendar year for reporting its taxable income. However, P's natural business year ends April 30. For the short period, January 1, 1982, through April 30, 1982, the corporation earned $16,000.

(a) What must P Corporation do to change its taxable year? 16, wX3 = 48000:

(b) Compute P Corporation's tax for the short period.

tax 8370.
3.90
= 2790.

27. A is an accrual basis taxpayer. Gross income for the year was $85,000, which included $5,000 for services provided a customer. The customer paid with a note. The market value of the note was only $4,000 due to the poor financial condition of the customer. A's accounts receivable of $40,000 include approximately $800 in discounts that will be given for early payments. A's total expenses per books were $50,000. This includes $3,500 of office supplies purchased from a supplier; they have not been paid for as of year-end. A discovered that the supplier had billed him twice for the same $500 order, but the supplier contends that A ordered, and received, two identical shipments. Also included in total expenses per books was $6,000 in addition to the reserve for service under product warranties. An analysis of that account is presented below:

Reserves

| | |
|---|---|
| Cost incurred $6,000 | $ 15,000 beginning balance |
| | $ 5,000 additions |

$ 14,000 balance

Compute A's correct taxable income under the accrual basis.

28. C, a cash basis taxpayer, has adjusted gross income of $40,000 before considering the effect of the following payments made on December 31, 19X1 (in connection with business activities):

(a) January 19X2 rent—$1,000

(b) January 19X2 through June 19X3 property insurance—$2,700

(c) A refundable deposit for telephone extensions—$300

(d) 19X2 professional dues and subscriptions—$480

(e) January through June 19X2 interest on a real estate mortgage—$3,200

(f) Payment on a lawyer's bill for services rendered in 19X0, net of a $500 refundable deposit made in 19X0—$1,500.

Compute C's adjusted gross income.

29. The R Construction Company reports its income by the completed contract method. At the end of 19X1, the company completed a contract to construct a building at a total cost of $980,000. The contract price was $1,200,000. However, the customer refused to accept the work and would not pay anything on the contract, because he claimed the roof did not meet specifications. R's engineers estimated it would cost $140,000 to bring the roof up to the customer's standards. In 19X2, the dispute was settled in the customer's favor; the roof was improved at a cost of $170,000, and the customer accepted the building and paid the $1,200,000.

(a) What would be the effects of the above on R's taxable income for 19X1 and 19X2?

(b) Same as above except R had $1,100,000 accumulated cost under the contract at the end of 19X1.

30. S, who is not a dealer, sold an apartment house to P during the current year (19X2). The closing statement for the sale is presented below:

| | | |
|---|---:|---:|
| Total selling price | | $ 200,000 |
| Add: P's share of taxes (six months) | | |
|   paid by S | | 5,000 |
| Less: S's mortgage assumed by P | $ 110,000 | |
| P's refundable binder ("earnest | | |
|   money") paid in 19X1 | 2,000 | |
| P's 9% installment note given to S | 60,000 | |
| S's real estate commissions and | | |
|   attorney's fees | 15,000 | (187,000) |
| Cash paid to S at closing | | $ 18,000 |
| | | |
| Cash due from P = $18,000 + $15,000 | | |
|   expenses | | $ 33,000 |

During 19X2, S collected $8,000 in principal on the installment note and $4,000 interest. S's basis in the property was $140,000 [$170,000 − $30,000 (depreciation)], and there was $6,000 in potential depreciation recapture under § 1250.

(a) Compute the following:

   (1) Total gain.

   (2) Contract price.

   (3) Payments received in the year of sale.

   (4) Recognized gain in the year of sale and the character of such gain.

(*Hint:* Think carefully about the manner in which the property taxes are handled before you begin your computations.)

(b) Same as (a)(2) and (3) except S's basis in the property was $90,000.

31. Z sold land in 19X1 with a cost of $60,000 for $100,000. The sales agreement called for a $25,000 down payment and a $25,000 payment on the first day of each year plus 10% interest. What would be the consequences of the following (treat each part independently and assume Z uses the installment method whenever possible):

(a) The purchaser prematurely mailed a check for the January 1, 19X2, payment, which was delivered to Z on December 31, 19X1.

(b) In 19X2, Z gave one of the $25,000 installment obligations to a close relative.

(c) In 19X2, Z transferred the installment obligations ($50,000) to his 100% owned corporation.

(d) Z died on January 1, 19X2, after collecting $25,000 of the principal.

32. T, a cash basis taxpayer, sold stock in 19X1 for $40,000 plus 9% notes with a face amount of $60,000 and a market value of only $40,000. T's basis in the stock was $25,000, and its fair market value was $85,000. In 19X2, she collected the face amounts of the notes. What is T's income in 19X1 and 19X2 from the sale and collections presuming she elects out of the installment method?

33. In 19X2, T changed from the use of the lower of cost or market FIFO method to the LIFO method. The ending inventory for 19X1 was computed as follows:

| Item | FIFO Cost | Replacement Cost | Lower of Cost or Market |
|------|-----------|------------------|-------------------------|
| A | $ 10,000 | $ 18,000 | $ 10,000 |
| B | 25,000 | 20,000 | 20,000 |
| | | | $ 30,000 |

(a) What is the correct beginning inventory in 19X2 under the LIFO method?

(b) What immediate tax consequences (if any) would result from the switch to LIFO?

## Cumulative Problems

34. X is single, age 46, and has no dependents. In 1983, he earned a salary of $150,000 as vice-president of ABC Manufacturing Corporation. Over the years, he has invested wisely and owns several thousand shares of stock, an apartment complex, and mineral property.

In January 1983, X sold 500 shares of stock for a gain of $50,000. He had owned the stock for 12 years. X received dividends of $15,100 on the stock he retained.

On May 20, 1983, X exercised his rights under ABC's incentive stock option plan. For an option price of $26,000, he acquired stock worth $53,000.

Gross rental income from the apartment complex was $140,000. Deductible expenses for the complex were $105,000, including depreciation of $55,000. If the straight-line method had been used, depreciation would have been $30,000.

X received income of $60,000 from an interest in a mineral property. X's depletion deduction was $40,000 (his basis in the property at the beginning of the year was $24,000).

X received $10,000 interest on corporate bonds in 1983. His itemized deductions were $51,300. X's average base period income for the years 1979, 1980, 1981, and 1982 was $160,000. X's alternative minimum tax itemized deductions were $40,000.

Compute X's lowest legal tax liability, before prepayments or credits, for 1983.

35. R, age 38, is single and has no dependents. He is independently wealthy as a result of having inherited sizable holdings in real estate and corporate stocks and bonds. R is a minister at First Methodist Church, but he accepts no salary from the church. However, he does reside in the church's parsonage free of charge. The rental value of the parsonage is $400 a month. The church also provides R a cash grocery allowance of $50 a week. Examination of R's financial records provides the following information for 1983.

(a) On January 16, 1983, R sold 2,000 shares of stock for a gain of $100,000. The stock was acquired four years ago.

(b) R received gross rental income of $160,000 from an apartment complex he owns.

(c) Expenses related to the apartment complex were $145,000, including declining-balance depreciation of $68,000 (straight-line depreciation would have been $41,000).

(d) R's dividend and interest income was $40,100.

(e) R had the following itemized deductions *from* adjusted gross income:

    (1) $70,000 contribution to Methodist church.

    (2) $21,000 interest.

    (3) $8,500 state and local taxes.

    (4) $3,000 medical expenses (in excess of 5% of adjusted gross income).

    (5) $1,000 casualty loss (in excess of the $100 and the 10% limitations).

Compute R's tax, including alternative minimum tax, if applicable, before prepayments or credits for 1983. Use the 1983 Tax Rate Schedule for your computation.

## Tax Form Problem

36. James Berry, who is eligible to use income averaging, has never been married. His taxable income in 1982 was $112,000. This was a considerable increase over his taxable income of the four previous years, as shown below:

| Year | Taxable Income |
|------|----------------|
| 1981 | $ 56,000 |
| 1980 | $ 53,000 |
| 1979 | $ 49,000 |
| 1978 | $ 42,000 |

Compute James Berry's income tax, before prepayments or credits for 1982 using Schedule G of Form 1040.

## Chapter 12

# Taxation of Corporations: Organization and Capital Structure

## THE TAX TREATMENT OF VARIOUS BUSINESS FORMS

Business operations can be conducted in a number of different forms. Among the various possibilities are:

—Sole proprietorships.

—Partnerships.

—Trusts and estates.

—Subchapter S corporations. (Also known as S corporations).

—Regular corporations. (Also known as Subchapter C corporations).

For Federal income tax purposes, the distinction between these forms of business organizations becomes very important. A brief summary of the tax treatment of each form will highlight these distinctions.

1. Sole proprietorships are not separate taxable entities from the individual who owns the proprietorship. The owner of the business will, therefore, report all business transactions on his or her individual income tax return.

2. Partnerships are not subject to the income tax. Under the conduit concept, the various tax attributes of the partnership's operations flow through to the individual partners to be reported on their personal income tax returns (see Example 1). Although a partnership is not a tax-paying entity, it is

a reporting entity. Form 1065 is used to aggregate partnership transactions for the tax year and to allocate their pass-through to the individual partners. The tax consequences of the partnership form of business organization are outlined in Subchapter K of the Internal Revenue Code and are the subject of Chapter 17.

3.  The income tax treatment of trusts and estates is in some respects similar and in others dissimilar to the partnership approach. In terms of similarity, income is taxed only once. However, tax may be imposed on the entity. Unlike a partnership, therefore, a trust or an estate may be subject to the Federal income tax. Whether the income will be taxed to a trust or an estate or to its beneficiaries generally depends on whether the income is retained by the entity or distributed to the beneficiaries. In the event of distribution, a modified form of the conduit principle is followed to preserve for the beneficiary the character of certain income (e. g., nontaxable interest on municipal bonds). The income taxation of trusts and estates is treated in Chapter 20.

4.  Subchapter S of the Code permits certain corporations to elect special tax treatment. Such special treatment generally means avoidance of any income tax at the corporate level. A corporate loss will pass through to the shareholders. S corporations are like partnerships in that the owners of the entity report all gains and losses on their individual returns. The conduit concept is applied as it is to trusts and estates that make current distributions. The tax treatment of S corporations and their shareholders is the subject of Chapter 16.

5.  The regular corporate form of doing business carries with it the imposition of the corporate income tax. For Federal income tax purposes, therefore, the corporation is recognized as a separate tax-paying entity. This produces what is known as a double tax effect: Income is taxed to the corporation as earned and taxed again to the shareholders as dividends when distributed. Also, the tax attributes of various types of income lose their identity as they pass through the corporate entity.

**Example 1.** During the current year, X Company recognizes a long-term capital gain and receives tax-exempt interest, both of which are distributed to its owners. If X Company is a regular corporation, the distribution to the shareholders constitutes a dividend. The fact that it originated from long-term capital gain and tax-exempt interest is of no consequence.[1] On the other hand,

---

1.  As noted in Chapter 13, such items will, however, affect the distributing corporation's earnings and profits.

if X Company is a partnership or an S corporation, the long-term capital gain and tax-exempt interest retain their identity as they pass through to the individual partners.

The tax consequences of operating a business in the regular corporate form fall within Subchapter C of the Code and are the subject of Chapters 12 through 14. Corporations that either unreasonably accumulate earnings or meet the definition of a personal holding company may be subject to further taxation. These so-called penalty taxes are imposed in addition to the corporation income tax and are discussed in Chapter 15.

Clearly, then, the form of organization chosen to carry on a trade or business has a significant effect on Federal income tax consequences. Though tax considerations may not control the choice, it could be unfortunate if they are not taken into account.

## WHAT IS A CORPORATION?

The first step in any discussion of the Federal income tax treatment of corporations must be definitional. More specifically, what is a corporation? At first glance, the answer to this question would appear to be quite simple. Merely look to the appropriate state law to determine whether the entity has satisfied the specified requirements for corporate status. Have articles of incorporation been drawn up and filed with the state regulatory agency? Has a charter been granted? Has stock been issued to shareholders? These are all points to consider.

Compliance with state law, although important, may not tell the full story as to whether or not an entity is to be recognized as a corporation for tax purposes. On the one hand, a corporation qualifying under state law may be disregarded as a taxable entity if it is a mere "sham." On the other hand, an organization not qualifying as a regular corporation under state law may be taxed as a corporation under the association approach. These two possibilities are discussed in the following sections.

*Disregard of Corporate Entity.*   In most cases, the IRS and the courts will recognize a corporation legally constituted under state law. In exceptional situations, however, the corporate entity may be disregarded because it lacks substance.[2] The key to such treatment rests with the degree of business activity conducted at the corporate level. Thus, the more the corporation does in connection with its trade

---

2.   The reader should bear in mind that the textual discussion relates to the classification of an entity for *Federal* income tax purposes. State corporate income taxes or other corporate taxes (e. g., franchise taxes) may still be imposed. An entity may quite possibly be treated as a corporation for state tax purposes and not for Federal or vice versa. This will become even more apparent when dealing with S corporations (Chapter 16), such status not being recognized by most states.

or business, the less the likelihood that it will be treated as a sham and disregarded as a separate entity.

> **Example 2.** C and D are joint owners of a tract of unimproved real estate that they wish to protect from future creditors. Consequently, C and D form R Corporation to which they transfer the land in return for all of the latter's stock. The corporation merely holds title to the land and conducts no other activities. In all respects, R Corporation meets the requirements of a corporation under applicable state law.

> **Example 3.** Assume the same facts as in Example 2. In addition to holding title to the land, R Corporation leases the property, collects rents, and pays the property taxes thereon.

R Corporation probably would not be recognized as a separate entity under the facts set forth in Example 2. In Example 3, however, the opposite should prove true. It appears that enough activity has taken place at the corporate level to warrant the conclusion that R Corporation should be treated as a real corporation for Federal income tax purposes.[3]

Whether the IRS or the taxpayers will attempt to disregard the corporate entity must, of course, depend on the circumstances of each particular situation. More often than not, the IRS may be trying to disregard (or "collapse") a corporation in order to make its income taxable directly to the shareholders.[4] In other situations, a corporation might be trying to avoid the corporate income tax or to permit its shareholders to take advantage of excess corporate deductions and losses.[5]

Theoretically speaking, the disregard of corporate entity approach should be equally available to both the IRS and the taxpayers. From a practical standpoint, however, taxpayers have enjoyed considerably less success than the IRS.[6] Courts generally conclude that since the taxpayers created the corporation in the first place, they later should not be permitted to disregard it in order to avoid taxes.

*Associations Taxed as Corporations.* Section 7701(a)(3) defines a corporation to include "associations, joint stock companies, and insurance companies." What Congress intended by the inclusion of "associ-

---

**3.** A classic case in this area is *Paymer v. Comm.*, 45–2 USTC ¶ 9353, 33 AFTR 1536, 150 F.2d 334 (CA–2, 1945). Here, two corporations were involved. The Court chose to disregard one corporate entity but to recognize the other.

**4.** See, for example, *Patterson v. Comm.*, 25 TCM 1230, T.C.Memo. 1966–239.

**5.** An election under Subchapter S would accomplish this if it was timely made and the parties qualified. See Chapter 16.

**6.** See, for example, *Rafferty Farms, Inc. v. U. S.*, 75–1 USTC ¶ 9271, 35 AFTR2d 75–811, 511 F.2d 1234 (CA–8, 1975) and *Collins v. U. S.*, 75–2 USTC ¶ 9553, 36 AFTR2d 75–5175, 514 F.2d 1282 (CA–5, 1975).

ations" in the definitions has never been entirely clear. Judicial decisions have clarified the status of associations and the relationship between associations and corporations.

The designation given to the entity under state law is not controlling. In one case, what was a business trust under state law was deemed to be an association (and therefore taxable as a corporation) for Federal income tax purposes.[7] In another case, a partnership of physicians was held to be an association even though state law prohibited the practice of medicine in the corporate form.[8]

Whether or not an entity will be considered an association for Federal income tax purposes depends upon the number of corporate characteristics it possesses. According to court decisions and Regulation § 301.7701–2(a), corporate characteristics include:

1. Associates.
2. An objective to carry on a business and divide the gains therefrom.
3. Continuity of life.
4. Centralized management.
5. Limited liability.
6. Free transferability of interests.

The Regulations state that an unincorporated organization shall not be classified as an association unless it possesses more corporate than noncorporate characteristics. In making the determination, the characteristics common to both corporate and noncorporate business organizations shall be disregarded.[9]

Both corporations and partnerships generally have associates (i. e., shareholders and partners) and an objective to carry on a business and divide the gains. In testing whether a particular partnership is an association, these criteria would be disregarded. It then becomes a matter of determining whether the partnership possesses a majority of the remaining corporate characteristics (refer to items 3 through 6). Does the partnership terminate upon the withdrawal or death of a partner (i. e., no continuity of life)? Is the management of the partnership centralized or do all partners participate therein? Are all partners individually liable for the debts of the partnership or is the liability of some limited to their actual investment in the partnership (i. e., limited partnership)? May a partner freely transfer his or her interest without the consent of the other partners? Courts have ruled that any partnership lacking two or more of these characteristics will

---

7. *Morrissey v. Comm.*, 36–1 USTC ¶ 9020, 16 AFTR 1274, 56 S.Ct. 289 (USSC, 1936).
8. *U. S. v. Kintner*, 54–2 USTC ¶ 9626, 47 AFTR 995, 216 F.2d 418 (CA–9, 1954).
9. Reg. § 301.7701–2(a)(3).

not be classified as an association. Conversely, any partnership having three or more of these characteristics will be classified as an association.[10]

In the case of trusts, the first two characteristics listed above would have to be considered in testing for association status. The conventional type of trust often does not have associates and usually restricts its activities to investments as opposed to carrying on a trade or business. These characteristics, however, are common to corporations. Consequently, whether a trust qualifies as an association depends upon the satisfaction of a *majority of all six* corporate characteristics.

From a taxpayer's standpoint, the desirability of association status turns on the tax implications involved. In some cases, the parties may find it advantageous to have the entity taxed as a corporation while in others they may not. These possibilities are explored at length in the TAX PLANNING CONSIDERATIONS portion of this chapter.

# AN INTRODUCTION TO THE INCOME TAXATION OF CORPORATIONS

## AN OVERVIEW OF CORPORATE VERSUS INDIVIDUAL INCOME TAX TREATMENT

In any discussion of how corporations are treated under the Federal income tax, the best approach is to compare such treatment with that applicable to individual taxpayers.

*Similarities.* The gross income of a corporation is determined in much the same manner as it is determined for individuals. Thus, gross income includes compensation for services rendered, income derived from a business, gains from dealings in property, interest, rents, royalties, dividends—to name only a few such items [§ 61(a)]. Both individuals and corporations are entitled to exclusions from gross income; however, fewer exclusions are allowed in the case of corporate taxpayers. Interest on municipal bonds would be excluded from gross income whether the bondholder is an individual or a corporate taxpayer [§ 103].

Gains and losses from property transactions are handled similarly. For example, whether a gain or loss is capital or ordinary depends upon the nature of the asset in the hands of the taxpayer making the taxable disposition. Code § 1221, in defining what is not a capital asset, makes no distinction between corporate and noncorporate taxpayers. In the area of nontaxable exchanges, corporations are

---

10. See *Zuckman v. U. S.*, 75-2 USTC ¶ 9778, 36 AFTR2d 6193, 524 F.2d 729 (Ct.Cls., 1975) and *P. G. Larson*, 66 T.C. 159 (1976).

like individuals in that no gain or loss is recognized by them on a like-kind exchange (§ 1031) and recognized gain may be deferred on an involuntary conversion of property (§ 1033). For obvious reasons, the nonrecognition of gain provisions dealing with the sale of a personal residence (§ § 121 and 1034) do not apply to corporations. But both corporations and individuals are vulnerable to the disallowance of losses on sales of property to related parties (§ 267(a)(1)) or on the wash sales of securities (§ 1091). However, the wash sale rules do not apply to individuals who are traders or dealers in securities or to corporations which are dealers if the sales of the securities are in the ordinary course of the corporation's business. Upon the sale or other taxable disposition of depreciable property, the recapture rules (e. g., § § 1245 and 1250) generally make no distinctions between corporate and noncorporate taxpayers.

The business deductions of corporations also parallel those available to individuals. Therefore, deductions will be allowed for all ordinary and necessary expenses paid or incurred in carrying on a trade or business under the general rule of § 162(a). Specific provision is made for the deductibility of interest (§ 163), certain taxes (§ 164), losses (§ 165), bad debts (§ 166), accelerated cost recovery (§ 168), charitable contributions (§ 170), net operating losses (§ 172), research and experimental expenditures (§ 174), and other less common deductions. No deduction will be permitted for interest paid or incurred on amounts borrowed to purchase or carry tax-exempt securities [§ 265(2)]. The same holds true for expenses contrary to public policy [e. g., § § 162(c) and (f)] and certain unpaid expenses and interest between related parties [§ 267(a)(2)].

Many of the tax credits available to individuals also can be claimed by corporations. This is certainly the case with two of the most important—the investment tax credit (§ 38) and the foreign tax credit (§ 33). Corporations are not, however, entitled to the credit for the elderly (§ 37) and the credit for certain earned income (§ 43).

Corporations generally have the same choices of accounting periods and methods as do individual taxpayers. Like an individual, a corporation may choose a calendar year or a fiscal year for reporting purposes (§ 441). Permissible accounting methods include the cash or accrual method (§ 446(c)), the installment method (§ 453), or, for use in conjunction with long-term contracts, the percentage of completion or the completed contract method (Reg. § 1.451–3).

*Dissimilarities.* There exist, however, significant variations in the income taxation of corporations and individuals. A major variation is that different tax rates apply to corporations (§ 11) and to individuals (§ 1). Corporate tax rates are discussed in a later section of this chapter.

All allowable corporate deductions are treated as business deductions. Thus, the determination of adjusted gross income (§ 62), so essential in the case of individual taxpayers, has no relevance to corporations. Taxable income simply is computed by subtracting from gross income all allowable deductions and losses. As such, corporations need not be concerned with itemized deductions (e. g., § § 211–220) or the zero bracket amount [§ 63(d)]. Likewise, the deduction for personal and dependency exemptions (§ § 151 through 154) is not available.

Because corporations can have only business deductions and losses, the $100 floor on the deductible portion of personal casualty and theft losses does not apply [§ 165(c)]. Also, expenses paid or incurred on property held for the production of income or in connection with the determination, collection, or refund of any tax would be deductible as a business expense [i. e., § 162(a) applies rather than § 212].

> **Example 4.** During 19X6, X (a calendar year taxpayer) pays $300 to a CPA for the preparation of a 19X5 Federal income tax return. If X is an individual, the $300 tax return preparation fee can only be claimed as an itemized deduction and would not be available if X chose not to itemize. On the other hand, if X is a corporation, the fee would be deductible in full as a business expense under § 162.

## SPECIFIC PROVISIONS COMPARED

—Although the capital gains and losses of individuals and corporations are computed in the same manner, their tax treatment is substantially different [e. g., § § 1201(a), 1211(a), and 1212(a)].

—The percentages used to determine the maximum charitable contribution allowance are not the same for corporate and noncorporate taxpayers [§ 170(b)(2)].

—Net operating losses of individuals and corporations require different adjustments for carryback and carryover purposes [§ 172(d)(4), (5), and (6)].

—Corporations are entitled to certain special deductions. The most important of these are the deduction for dividends received from other domestic corporations (§ 243) and the write-off of organizational expenditures (§ 248). Corporations are not allowed the $100 dividend exclusion available to individuals (§ 116).

These differences in the income tax treatment of corporate and individual taxpayers are discussed in depth in the sections to follow.

## CAPITAL GAINS AND LOSSES

Capital gains and losses result from the taxable sales or exchanges of capital assets. Whether such gains and losses would be long-term or short-term depends upon the holding period of the assets sold or exchanged. Each year a taxpayer's long-term capital gains and losses are combined and the result is either a *net* long-term capital gain or a *net* long-term capital loss. A similar aggregation is made with short-term capital gains and losses, the result being a *net* short-term capital gain or a *net* short-term capital loss (§ 1222). The following combinations and results are possible:

1. A net long-term capital gain and a net short-term capital loss. These are combined and the result is either a net capital gain or a net capital loss. Net long-term capital gains receive preferential tax treatment. Net capital losses of corporate and noncorporate taxpayers are treated differently (see below).

2. A net long-term capital gain and a net short-term capital gain. No further combination is made. Net long-term capital gains receive preferential tax treatment and net short-term capital gains are taxed as ordinary income.

3. A net long-term capital loss and a net short-term capital gain. These are combined and the result is either a net capital gain or a net capital loss. Net short-term capital gains are taxed as ordinary income.

4. A net long-term capital loss and a net short-term capital loss. No further combination is made.

*Capital Gains.*  In the case of an individual taxpayer, long-term capital gains (combinations 1 and 2) are included in gross income with an offsetting 60 percent long-term capital gain deduction. (§ 1202).

> **Example 5.**  T, an individual, has the following capital transactions during 19X3: a net long-term capital gain of $10,000 and a net short-term capital gain of $4,000. T may include the $10,000 long-term capital gain in gross income and claim a $6,000 capital gain deduction. The short-term capital gain of $4,000 must be included in gross income (combination 2).

The treatment of long-term capital gains in the hands of corporate taxpayers differs from the above example in two respects. First, the 60 percent long-term capital gain deduction is not available. Second, net long-term capital gains for corporations are taxed at an alternative tax rate of 28 percent [§ 1201(a)]. Consequently, a corporation can either include the full long-term capital gain in income (no capital gain deduction allowed) or add the alternative tax to the regular tax liability.

> **Example 6.**  Assume the same facts as in Example 5 except that T is a corporate taxpayer. T Corporation may include the $10,000 of long-term capital gain in gross income, but with no offsetting capital gain deduction. Under the alternative tax computation, $2,800 (i. e., 28% × $10,000) is added to T Corporation's regular

tax liability. In either case, the net short-term capital gain of $4,000 must be included in gross income.

Whether corporate taxpayers should use the alternative tax computation depends, of course, on the tax savings generated.

*Capital Losses.* Differences also exist between corporate and noncorporate taxpayers in the income tax treatment of net capital losses (combinations 1, 3, and 4, described previously). Generally, noncorporate taxpayers can deduct up to $3,000 of such net losses against other income [§ 1211(b)]. However, if the net loss is a long-term capital loss, it will require $2 of loss to generate $1 of deduction. Any remaining capital losses can be carried forward to future years until absorbed by capital gains or by the $3,000 (with exceptions noted above) deduction [§ 1212(b)]. Carryovers do not lose their identity but remain either long or short-term.

> **Example 7.** T, an individual, incurs a net long-term capital loss of $7,500 for calendar year 19X8. Assuming adequate taxable income, T may deduct $3,000 of this loss on his 19X8 return. The remaining $1,500 (i. e., $7,500 − $6,000) of the loss is carried to 19X9 and years thereafter until completely deducted. The $1,500 will be carried forward as a long-term capital loss.

Unlike individuals, corporate taxpayers are not permitted to claim any net capital losses as a deduction against ordinary income [§ 1211(a)]. Capital losses, therefore, can be used only as an offset against capital gains. Corporations may, however, carry back net capital losses to three preceding years, applying them first to the earliest year in point of time. Carryforwards are allowed for a period of five years from the year of the loss [§ 1212(a)]. When carried back or forward, a long-term capital loss becomes a short-term capital loss.

> **Example 8.** Assume the same facts as in Example 7 except that T is a corporation. None of the $7,500 long-term capital loss incurred in 19X8 can be deducted in that year. T Corporation may, however, carry the loss back to years 19X5, 19X6, and 19X7 (in this order) and apply it to any capital gains recognized in these years. If the carryback does not exhaust the loss, it may be carried forward to calendar years 19X9, 19X0, 19X1, 19X2, and 19X3 (in this order). Either a carryback or a carryforward of the long-term capital loss converts it to a short-term capital loss.

## CHARITABLE CONTRIBUTIONS

No deduction will be allowed to either corporate or noncorporate taxpayers for a charitable contribution unless the recipient is a qualified charitable organization within the meaning of § 170(c). Generally, a deduction will be allowed only for the year in which the payment is made. However, an important exception is made in the case of *accrual basis corporations.* Here the deduction may be claimed in the year preceding payment if the contribution has been authorized by the board of directors by the end of that year and is, in fact, paid on or before the fifteenth day of the third month of the next year [§ 170(a)(2)].

> **Example 9.** On December 28, 19X5, XYZ Company, a calendar year accrual basis taxpayer, authorizes a $5,000 donation to the Atlanta Symphony Association (a qualified charitable organization). The donation is made on March 14, 19X6. If XYZ Company is a partnership, the contribution can be deducted only in 19X6.[11]

> **Example 10.** Assume the same facts as in Example 9 except that the XYZ Company is a corporation. Presuming the December 28, 19X5, authorization was made by its board of directors, XYZ Company may claim the $5,000 donation as a deduction for calendar year 19X5. If it was not, the deduction may still be claimed for calendar year 19X6.

*Property Contributions.* Property contributions are governed by the following rules:

1. Generally, the measure of the deduction is the fair market value of the property on the date of its donation.

2. The deduction for "ordinary income property" that has appreciated in value is generally limited to the adjusted basis of the property. The Tax Reform Act of 1976 amended § 170(e) to permit a corporate taxpayer to deduct its basis plus one-half of the appreciated value of ordinary income property (not to exceed twice the basis of the property) if the property is used in a manner related to the exempt purpose of the donee and the donee uses the property solely for the care of the ill, needy, or infants. The Economic Recovery Tax Act of 1981 now permits a deduction for basis plus one-half of the appreciated value of ordinary income property for gifts of scientific property to colleges and universities for use in research activities, provided the following conditions are met: (a) the property was constructed by the taxpayer, (b) the gift was made within two years of the substantial completion of construction, (c) the donee is the original user of the property, (d) at least 80 percent of the property's use by the charitable organization will be for research or experimentation, and (e) the property was not transferred in exchange for money, other property, or services. The donor corporation must secure a written statement that requirements for the use of property

---

11. Each partner will pick up his or her allocable portion of the charitable contribution deduction as of December 31, 19X6 (the end of the partnership's tax year). See Chapter 17.

for the ill, needy, or infants or for research purposes have been met. "Ordinary income property" is defined as property which would not have yielded long-term capital gain if sold or otherwise disposed of in a taxable exchange [§ 170(e)(1)(A)].

3. Normally, appreciated property, which if sold would have resulted in a long-term capital gain to the donor, can be claimed at its fair market value on the date of contribution. This rule is, however, subject to two exceptions. The first exception involves the charitable contribution of tangible personal property, the use of which by the donee is unrelated to the purpose or function constituting the basis for its tax-exempt status.[12] The second exception relates to the donation of *any* long-term capital gain property to certain private foundations.[13] In either of these situations, the deduction is limited to the fair market value of the property less 40 percent ($^{28}/_{46}$ in the case of a corporation) of the long-term gain which would have been recognized if such property had been sold [§ 170(e)(1)(B)].

**Example 11.** X donates an art collection (basis of $40,000 and fair market value of $100,000) to the Atlanta Symphony Association (a qualified charitable organization) to help raise funds for a special summer concert program. The art collection is tangible personal property, and its use is not related to the purpose or function constituting the basis for the Atlanta Symphony Association's exempt status. If X is an individual, the measure of the charitable contribution is $76,000 [$100,000 (fair market value of the collection) − $24,000 (40% × $60,000 capital gain potential)]. If X is a corporation, the deduction is $63,478 [$100,000 − $36,522 ($^{28}/_{46}$ × $60,000)]. Both results are predicated on the assumption that the art collection is a capital asset held for more than one year. If not, the deduction for corporate and noncorporate taxpayers would be limited to $40,000 (i. e., the lower of the fair market value of the property or its adjusted basis on the date of its donation).

*Limitations Imposed on Charitable Contribution Deductions.* Like individuals, corporations are not permitted an unlimited charitable contribution deduction.[14] For any one year, a corporate taxpayer is limited to 10 percent (five percent prior to 1982) of taxable income, computed without regard to the charitable contribution deduction, any net operating loss carryback or capital loss carryback, and the

---

**12.** Tangible personalty excludes real estate and intangible property (e. g., stocks and bonds).

**13.** As defined in § 509(a).

**14.** The percentage limitations applicable to individuals are set forth in § 170(b)(1).

dividends received deduction [§ 170(b)(2)]. Any contributions in excess of the 10 percent limitation may be carried forward to the five succeeding tax years. Any carryforward must be added to subsequent contributions and will be subject to the 10 percent limitation. In applying this limitation, the current year's contributions must be deducted first, with excess deductions from previous years deducted in order of time [§ 170(d)(2) and Reg. § 1.170–2(g)].

> **Example 12.** During 19X4, T Corporation (a calendar year taxpayer) had the following income and expenses:
>
> | | |
> |---|---:|
> | Income from operations | $ 140,000 |
> | Expenses from operations | 110,000 |
> | Dividends received | 10,000 |
> | Charitable contributions made in May of 19X4 | 5,000 |

For purposes of the 10 percent limitation *only*, T Corporation's taxable income is $40,000 [$140,000 − $110,000 + $10,000]. Consequently, the allowable charitable deduction for 19X4 is $4,000 [10% × $40,000]. The $1,000 unused portion of the contribution can be carried forward to 19X5, 19X6, 19X7, 19X8, and 19X9 (in that order) until exhausted.

> **Example 13.** Assume the same facts as in Example 12. In 19X5, T Corporation has taxable income of $50,000 and makes a charitable contribution of $4,500. The maximum deduction allowed for 19X5 would be $5,000 [10% × $50,000]. The first $4,500 of the allowed deduction must be allocated to the contribution made in 19X5, and $500 of the balance is carried over from 19X4. The remaining $500 of the 19X4 contribution may be carried over to 19X6, etc.

## NET OPERATING LOSSES

The net operating loss of a corporation, which may be carried back three years and forward 15 (for losses arising after December 31, 1975) to offset taxable income for those years, is not subject to the adjustments required for individual taxpayers. A corporation does not adjust its tax loss for the year for capital gains and losses as do individual taxpayers. This is true because a corporation is not permitted a deduction for net capital losses, and the capital gain is not subject to a capital gain deduction. A corporation does not make adjustments for nonbusiness deductions as do individual taxpayers. Further, a corporation is allowed to include the dividends received deduction (see below) in computing its net operating loss [§ 172(d)].

> **Example 14.** In 19X5, X Corporation has gross income of $200,000 and deductions of $300,000, excluding the dividends received deduction. X Corporation had received taxable divi-

dends of $100,000 from A Corporation, a domestic corporation which is not a member of a controlled group with X. X Corporation has a net operating loss of $185,000, computed as follows:

| | | |
|---|---:|---:|
| Gross income (including dividends) | | $ 200,000 |
| Less: | | |
| Business deductions | $ 300,000 | |
| Dividends received deduction | | |
| (85% of $100,000) | 85,000 | 385,000 |
| Taxable income (or loss) | | $ (185,000) |

The net operating loss is carried back three years to 19X2. Assume X Corporation had taxable income of $40,000 in 19X2. The carryover to 19X3 is $145,000, computed as follows:

| | |
|---|---:|
| Taxable income for 19X2 | $    40,000 |
| Less net operating loss carryback | 185,000 |
| Taxable income for 19X2 after net operating loss carryback (carryover to 19X3) | $ (145,000) |

## DEDUCTIONS AVAILABLE ONLY TO CORPORATIONS

*Dividends Received Deduction.* A corporation is allowed a deduction equal to (a) 85 percent of the amount of dividends received from a domestic corporation or (b) 100 percent of the amount of dividends received from a corporation which is a member of a controlled group with the recipient corporation [§ 243(a)].

The purpose of the 85 percent dividends received deduction is to prevent triple taxation. Absent the deduction, income paid to a corporation in the form of a dividend would be subject to taxation for a second time (once to the distributing corporation) with no corresponding deduction to the distributing corporation. Later, when the recipient corporation paid the income to its individual shareholders, it would again be subject to taxation with no corresponding deduction to the corporation. The dividends received deduction alleviates some of this inequity by causing only a small amount of dividend income to be subject to taxation at the corporate level.

The dividends received deduction is limited to 85 percent of the taxable income of a corporation computed without regard to the net operating loss, the dividends received deduction, and any capital loss carryback to the current tax year. However, the taxable income limitation does not apply if the corporation has a net operating loss for the current taxable year [§ § 246(b)(1) and (2)].

**Example 15.** In the current year, T Corporation has the following income and expenses:

| | |
|---|---|
| Gross income from operations | $ 400,000 |
| Expenses from operations | $ 340,000 |
| Dividends received from domestic corporations | $ 200,000 |

The dividends received deduction is $170,000 (85% × $200,000) unless 85% of taxable income is less. Because taxable income (for this purpose) is $260,000 ($400,000 − $340,000 + $200,000), and 85% of $260,000 is $221,000, the full $170,000 will be allowed.

> **Example 16.** Assume the same facts as in Example 15 except that T Corporation's gross income from operations is $320,000 (instead of $400,000). The usual dividends received deduction of $170,000 (85% × $200,000) is now limited to 85% of the taxable income. Since 85% of $180,000 ($320,000 − $340,000 + $200,000) is $153,000, this amount is the dividends received deduction (i. e., $153,000 is less than $170,000). The full $170,000 cannot be claimed because it does not generate, or add to, a net operating loss. (Taxable income of $180,000 less $170,000 does not result in a net operating loss.)

> **Example 17.** Assume the same facts as in Example 15 except that T Corporation's gross income from operations is $300,000 (instead of $400,000). The usual dividends received deduction of $170,000 can now be claimed under the net operating loss exception. Taxable income of $160,000 ($300,000 − $340,000 + $200,000) less $170,000 generates a net operating loss of $10,000.

In summary, Example 15 reflects the general rule that the dividends received deduction is 85 percent of the qualifying dividends. Example 16 presents the exception whereby the deduction may be limited to 85 percent of taxable income. Example 17 indicates the situation in which the taxable income exception will not apply because allowance of the full deduction generates or adds to a net operating loss.

*Deduction of Organizational Expenditures.* Expenses incurred in connection with the organization of a corporation normally are chargeable to a capital account. That they benefit the corporation during its existence seems clear. But how can they be amortized when most corporations possess unlimited life? The lack of a determinable and limited estimated useful life would, therefore, preclude any tax write-off. Code § 248 was enacted to solve this problem.

Under § 248, a corporation may elect to amortize organizational expenditures over a period of 60 months or more. The period begins with the month in which the corporation begins business.[15] Organizational expenditures subject to the election include legal services

---

**15.** The month in which a corporation begins business may not be immediately apparent. See Reg. § 1.248–1(a)(3). For a similar problem in the Subchapter S area see Reg. § 1.1372–2(b)(1) and Chapter 16.

incident to organization (e. g., drafting the corporate charter, bylaws, minutes or organizational meetings, terms of original stock certificates), necessary accounting services, expenses of temporary directors and of organizational meetings of directors or stockholders, and fees paid to the state of incorporation.[16] Expenditures that do not qualify include those connected with issuing or selling shares of stock or other securities (e. g., commissions, professional fees, and printing costs) or with the transfer of assets to a corporation.

To qualify for the election, the expenditure must be *incurred* before the end of the taxable year in which the corporation begins business. In this regard, the corporation's method of accounting is of no consequence. Thus, an expense incurred by a cash basis corporation in its first tax year would qualify even though not paid until a subsequent year.

The election is made in a statement attached to the corporation's return for its first taxable year. The return and statement must be filed no later than the due date of the return (including any extensions). The statement must set forth the description and amount of the expenditure involved, the date such expenditures were incurred, the month in which the corporation began business, and the number of months (not less than 60) over which such expenditures are to be deducted ratably.

If the election is not made on a timely basis, organizational expenditures cannot be deducted until the corporation ceases to do business and liquidates. These expenditures will be deductible if the corporate charter limits the life of the corporation.

> **Example 18.** T Corporation, an accrual basis taxpayer, was formed and began operations on May 1, 19X5. The following expenses were incurred during its first year of operations (May 1–December 31, 19X5):

| | |
|---|---|
| Expenses of temporary directors and of organizational meetings | $ 500 |
| Fee paid to the state of incorporation | 100 |
| Accounting services incident to organization | 200 |
| Legal services for drafting the corporate charter and bylaws | 400 |
| Expenses incident to the printing and sale of stock certificates | 300 |

Assume T Corporation makes a timely election under § 248 to amortize qualifying organizational expenses over a period of 60 months. The monthly amortization would be $20 [($500 + $100 + $200 + $400) ÷ 60 months], and $160 ($20 × 8 months) would be

---

**16.** Reg. § 1.248–1(b).

deductible for tax year 19X5. Note that the $300 of expenses incident to the printing and sale of stock certificates does not qualify for the election.

Organizational expenditures are to be distinguished from "start-up" expenditures covered by § 195. Start-up expenditures refer to various investigation expenses involved in entering a new business, whether they be incurred by a corporate or a noncorporate taxpayer. Such expenditures (e. g., travel, market surveys, financial audits, legal fees), at the election of the taxpayer, can be amortized over a period of 60 months or longer rather than be capitalized as part of the cost of the business acquired.

# DETERMINING THE CORPORATE INCOME TAX LIABILITY

## CORPORATE INCOME TAX RATES

Unlike the income tax rates applicable to noncorporate taxpayers, the corporate rates are only mildly progressive. Past, present, and future rates are summarized below:[17]

|  | Tax Years Beginning in | | |
|---|---|---|---|
| Taxable Income | 1979, 1980, and 1981 | 1982 | 1983 and After |
| $      1–$   25,000 | 17% | 16% | 15% |
| 25,001–     50,000 | 20 | 19 | 18 |
| 50,001–     75,000 | 30 | 30 | 30 |
| 75,001–   100,000 | 40 | 40 | 40 |
| Over $100,000 | 46 | 46 | 46 |

**Example 19.** T Corporation, a calendar year taxpayer, has taxable income of $100,000 in 1982. Its income tax liability will be $26,250, computed as follows:

| 16% of $25,000 | $  4,000 |
|---|---|
| 19% of $25,000 | 4,750 |
| 30% of $25,000 | 7,500 |
| 40% of $25,000 | 10,000 |
| Total tax | $ 26,250 |

**Example 20.** T Corporation, a calendar year taxpayer has taxable income of $150,000 in 1983. Its income tax liability would be computed as follows:

---

17.   § 11(b).

| | |
|---|---:|
| 15% of $25,000 | $ 3,750 |
| 18% of $25,000 | 4,500 |
| 30% of $25,000 | 7,500 |
| 40% of $25,000 | 10,000 |
| 46% of $50,000 | 23,000 |
| Total tax | $ 48,750 |

A shortcut approach for determining the income tax liability of a corporation with taxable income *in excess of $100,000* would be to start with $26,250 for 1982 (or $25,750 for 1983 and thereafter) and add 46 percent of the amount beyond $100,000. Thus, in Example 20 the tax would be $25,750 plus $23,000 (i. e., 46% of $50,000) or $48,750. Taxable income will have to be prorated for fiscal year corporations whenever there is a change in tax rates from one calendar year to another.[18]

## CORPORATE TAX PREFERENCES AND THE MINIMUM TAX

Prior to the Tax Equity and Fiscal Responsibility Act of 1982 (TEFRA), a corporation was subject to the add-on (or regular) minimum tax of 15 percent on certain tax preference items. Unlike individuals, however, they were not subject to the alternative minimum tax. Since the tax preferences reduced a great deal of corporate income tax liability and the add-on (regular) minimum tax did not yield sufficient revenue, Congress in its TEFRA deliberations seriously considered extending the alternative minimum tax to corporations.

Apparently, Congress felt that such a course of action would be too drastic, since most of these so-called tax preference items served legitimate social needs (e. g., rapid amortization of pollution control facilities) or economic needs (e. g., percentage depletion on iron ore and coal, mineral exploration and development costs, write-off of intangible drilling costs, capital gain on the sale of real property). The alternative finally taken under TEFRA was to reduce the immediate benefits of such tax preferences and, with minor adjustments, to leave the existing minimum tax on corporations as it was.

*Changes in Corporate Tax Preferences.* One major modification concerns what happens when a taxpayer disposes of § 1250 property (i. e., depreciable real estate used in a trade or business). Usually, the resulting gain comprises two elements: the § 1250 portion (recaptured as ordinary income) and the § 1231 part (treated as long-term capital gain). Commencing with taxable dispositions after 1982, 15 percent of the § 1231 portion will be reclassified as ordinary income.

---

**18.** In this regard, use of the *Worksheet for Fiscal Year Corporations—Tax Computation Schedule* (available from the IRS) is recommended.

Other adjustments required for certain tax preference items include, but are not limited to, those summarized below:

—For integrated oil companies (i. e., those other than independent producers), the deduction for intangible drilling costs is reduced by 15 percent. The amount not allowed as a current deduction must be capitalized and amortized over a three-year period. No investment tax credit is allowed on the amount so capitalized.

—Any percentage depletion claimed on iron ore and coal in excess of the cost basis of the property will be reduced by 15 percent (effective for taxable years after 1983).

—Fifteen percent of otherwise deductible mineral exploration and development costs must be capitalized and amortized over a five-year period.

—Costs that qualify for rapid write-off of pollution control facilities must be reduced by 15 percent. This 15 percent cutback will be subject to the regular ACRS rules.

A portion of a corporation's excess of net long-term capital gain over short-term capital loss is a tax preference. For tax years beginning after December 31, 1978, this figure is multiplied by a fraction, the numerator of which is the highest tax rate of the corporation for the taxable year minus the alternative tax of 28 percent and the denominator of which is 46 percent. For corporations, tax preferences are reduced by the greater of $10,000 or the regular tax liability.

A corporation must file Form 4626 if it has tax preferences in excess of $10,000.

*Corporate Minimum Tax.* Although the add-on (or regular) minimum tax is retained for corporations and the rate continues to be 15 percent of the tax preferences in excess of $10,000, certain adjustments in determining the base for the application of the tax are necessary to preclude a double impact. For example, if a tax preference item has been reduced by the 15 percent adjustments noted above, such adjustments should be taken into account. This can be accomplished by multiplying the total amount of the tax preference item by 71.6 percent.

## PAYMENT AND FILING REQUIREMENTS FOR CORPORATIONS

*Quarterly Estimated Tax Payments.* Prior law permitted corporate taxpayers to avoid the penalty for underpayment of income tax if at least 80 percent was paid in by the fifteenth day of the last month of the tax year (e. g., for a calendar year taxpayer, this entailed a 20 percent payment on April 15, June 15, September 15, and December 15). For taxable years beginning after December 31, 1982, TEFRA substitutes a 90 percent rule. Thus, the quarterly payment threshold amount rises from 20 percent to 22.5 percent.

In connection with the possible application of the penalty for underpayment, the following points should be noted:

—The applicable rate will be that currently in effect for interest determination.

—Unlike the interest computation, however, daily compounding is not in order.

—If at least 80 percent is paid in, only 75 percent of the going rate is applied [e. g., if the interest rate is 20 percent, the penalty rate becomes 15 percent (75 percent of 20 percent)].

*Final Tax Payment.* Under past law, a corporation had the option of paying the remaining tax liability (i. e., 20 percent) one-half (i. e., 10 percent) on the due date of the return (March 15 for a calendar year taxpayer) and the remaining balance two and one-half months later. For taxable years beginning after 1982, this deferral option has been eliminated.

Assuming a calendar year taxpayer, these changes in corporate tax payments can be summarized as follows:

|  | Taxable Years Beginning | |
|---|---|---|
|  | Before 1983 | After 1982 |
| April 15 (first payment) | 20% | 22.5% |
| June 15 (second payment) | 20 | 22.5 |
| September 15 (third payment) | 20 | 22.5 |
| December 15 (fourth payment) | 20 | 22.5 |
| March 15 (½ of final payment) | 10 | 10.0 |
| June 15 (½ of final payment) | 10 | –0– |
|  | 100% | 100% |

*Filing Requirements.* A corporation must file a return regardless of whether or not it has taxable income [§ 6012(a)(2)]. If a corporation was not in existence throughout an entire annual accounting period, it is required to file a return for that fractional part of a year during which it was in existence. In addition, the corporation must file a return even though it has ceased to do business if it has valuable claims for which it will bring suit. It is relieved of filing returns once it ceases business and dissolves, retaining no assets, whether or not under state law it is treated as a corporation for certain limited purposes connected with the winding up of its affairs, such as for the purpose of suing and being sued.

The corporate return is filed on Form 1120. Corporations electing under Subchapter S (see Chapter 16) file on Form 1120S. Both Form 1120 and Form 1120S are reproduced in appendix B. The return must be filed on or before the fifteenth day of the third month following the close of a corporation's accounting year. Corporations can receive an automatic extension of three months for filing the corporate return by filing Form 7004 by the due date for the return [§ 6081]. However, the extension may be terminated by the IRS upon mailing to the taxpayer corporation a 10-day notice. An additional extension of time, not automatic, may be granted by filing Form 7005.

## RECONCILIATION OF TAXABLE INCOME AND FINANCIAL NET INCOME

Taxable income and financial net income for a corporation are seldom the same amount. For example, a difference may arise if the corporation uses accelerated cost recovery system (ACRS) for tax purposes and straight-line depreciation for financial purposes. Consequently, cost recovery allowable for tax purposes may differ from book depreciation.

Many items of income for accounting purposes, such as proceeds from a life insurance policy on the death of a corporate officer and interest on municipal bonds, may not be taxable income. Some expense items for financial purposes, such as expenses to produce tax-exempt income, estimated warranty reserves, a net capital loss, and Federal income taxes, may not be deductible for tax purposes.

Schedule M–1 on the last page of Form 1120 is used to reconcile financial net income (net income after Federal income taxes) with taxable income (as computed on the corporate tax return before the deduction for a net operating loss and for the dividends received deduction). In the left-hand column of Schedule M–1, net income per books is added to the Federal income tax liability for the year, the excess of capital losses over capital gains (which cannot be deducted in the current year), taxable income which is not income in the current year for financial purposes, and expenses recorded on the books which are not deductible on the tax return. In the right-hand column, income recorded on the books which is not currently taxable or is tax-exempt and deductions for tax purposes which are not expenses for financial purposes are deducted from the left-hand column total to arrive at taxable income (before the net operating loss or the dividends received deduction).

> **Example 21.** During 1984, T Corporation had the following transactions:
>
> | | |
> |---|---:|
> | Net income per books | $ 93,450 |
> | Taxable income | 40,000 |
> | Federal income tax liability [(15% × $25,000) + (18% × $15,000)] | 6,450 |
> | Interest income from tax-exempt bonds | 5,000 |
> | Interest paid on loan, the proceeds of which were used to purchase the tax-exempt bonds | 500 |
> | Life insurance proceeds received by reason of the death of a key employee | 50,000 |
> | Premiums paid on the keyman life insurance policy | 2,600 |
> | Excess of capital losses over capital gains | 2,000 |

For book purposes, T Corporation determines depreciation under the straight-line method. For tax purposes, however, ACRS is claimed and yields $10,000 more than the straight-line method. T Corporation's Schedule M–1 for the current year appears below.

**Schedule M–1** Reconciliation of Income Per Books With Income Per Return Do not complete this schedule if your total assets (line 14, column (D), above) are less than $25,000.

| | | | |
|---|---|---|---|
| 1 Net income per books . . . . . . . . . . | 93,450 | 7 Income recorded on books this year not included in this return (itemize) | |
| 2 Federal income tax . . . . . . . . . . | 6,450 | (a) Tax-exempt interest $ 5,000 | |
| 3 Excess of capital losses over capital gains . . . . | 2,000 | Life insurance proceeds on keyman, $50,000 | 55,000 |
| 4 Income subject to tax not recorded on books this year (itemize) _____ | | 8 Deductions in this tax return not charged against book income this year (itemize) | |
| 5 Expenses recorded on books this year not deducted in this return (itemize) | | (a) Depreciation . . . . $10,000 | |
| (a) Depreciation . . . . . $_____ | | (b) Contributions carryover . $_____ | |
| (b) Contributions carryover . . $_____ | | | |
| Interest on tax-exempt bonds | 500 | | 10,000 |
| Premiums on life insurance | 2,600 | 9    Total of lines 7 and 8 . . . . | 65,000 |
| 6    Total of lines 1 through 5 . . . . . | 105,000 | 10 Income (line 28, page 1)—line 6 less 9 . . | 40,000 |

Schedule M–2 reconciles unappropriated retained earnings at the beginning of the year with unappropriated retained earnings at year-end. The net income per books, as entered on the first line of Schedule M–1, less dividend distributions during the year equals ending retained earnings. Other sources of increases or decreases in retained earnings are also listed on Schedule M–2.

**Example 22.** Assume the same facts as in Example 21. T Corporation's beginning balance in unappropriated retained earnings is $125,000, and during the year it distributed a cash dividend of $30,000 to its shareholders. Based on these further assumptions, T Corporation's Schedule M–2 for the current year is reproduced below:

**Schedule M–2** Analysis of Unappropriated Retained Earnings Per Books (line 24 above) Do not complete this schedule if your total assets (line 14, column (D), above) are less than $25,000.

| | | | |
|---|---|---|---|
| 1 Balance at beginning of year . . . . . . | 125,000 | 5 Distributions: (a) Cash . . . . . . | 30,000 |
| 2 Net income per books . . . . . . . . | 93,450 | (b) Stock . . . . . . | |
| 3 Other increases (itemize) _____ | | (c) Property . . . . . | |
| _____ | | 6 Other decreases (itemize) _____ | |
| _____ | | _____ | |
| _____ | | 7    Total of lines 5 and 6 . . . . | 30,000 |
| 4    Total of lines 1, 2, and 3 . . . . . | 218,450 | 8 Balance at end of year (line 4 less 7) . . | 188,450 |

# ORGANIZATION OF AND TRANSFERS TO CONTROLLED CORPORATIONS

## IN GENERAL

Absent special provisions in the Code, a transfer of property to a corporation in exchange for stock would be a sale or exchange of property and would constitute a taxable transaction. Gain or loss would be measured by the difference between the tax basis of the property transferred and the value of the stock received. Section 351 provides for the nonrecognition of gain or loss upon the transfer of property to a corporation solely in exchange for stock or securities if the persons transferring such property are in control of the corporation immediately after the transfer. The nonrecognition of gain or loss reflects the principle of continuity of the taxpayer's investment. There is no real change in the taxpayer's economic status. The investment in certain properties carries over to the investment in corporate stock or securities. The same principle governs the nonrecognition of gain or loss on like-kind exchanges under § 1031.[19] Gain is postponed until a substantive change in the taxpayer's investment occurs (i. e., a sale to or a taxable exchange with outsiders). This approach can be justified under the wherewithal to pay concept discussed in Chapter 1.

Section 351(a) provides that gain or loss is not recognized upon the transfer by one or more persons of property to a corporation solely in exchange for stock or securities in that corporation if, immediately after the exchange, such person or persons are in control of the corporation to which the property was transferred. Section 351(b) provides that if property or money, other than stock or securities, is received by the transferors, gain will be recognized to the extent of the lesser of the gain realized or boot received (i. e., the amount of money and the fair market value of other property received). Loss is never recognized.

The nonrecognition of gain or loss is accompanied by a carryover of basis. Section 358(a) provides that the basis of stock or securities received in a § 351 transfer is the same as the basis the taxpayers had in the property transferred, increased by any gain recognized on the exchange and decreased by boot received. Section 362(a) provides that the basis of properties received by the corporation is the basis in the hands of the transferor increased by the amount of any gain recognized to the transferor shareholder.

> **Example 23.**  A and B, individuals, form X Corporation. A transfers property with an adjusted basis of $30,000, fair market value of $60,000, for 50% of the stock. B transfers property with an adjusted basis of $40,000, fair market value of $60,000, for the remaining 50% of the stock. Gain is not recognized on the transfer because it qualifies under § 351. The basis of the stock to A is $30,000, while the basis of the stock to B is $40,000. X Corporation has a basis of $30,000 in the property transferred by A and a basis of $40,000 in the property transferred by B.

> **Example 24.**  C and D form Y Corporation with the following investment: C transfers property (basis of $30,000 and fair mar-

---

**19.**  Section 1031(a) covers the exchange of property held for productive use in a trade or business or for investment, but it specifically excludes "stock, bonds . . . or other securities."

ket value of $70,000) while D transfers cash of $60,000. Each receives 50 shares of the Y Corporation stock but C also receives $10,000 in cash. Assume each share of the Y Corporation stock is worth $1,200. Although C's realized gain is $40,000 [i. e., $60,000 (the value of 50 shares of Y Corporation stock) + $10,000 (cash received) − $30,000 (basis of the property transferred)], only $10,000 (the amount of the boot) is recognized. C's basis in the Y Corporation stock becomes $30,000 [i. e., $30,000 (basis of the property transferred) + $10,000 (gain recognized by C) − $10,000 (cash received)]. Y Corporation's basis in the property transferred by C is $40,000 [$30,000 (basis of the property to C) + $10,000 (gain recognized to C)]. D neither realizes nor recognizes gain or loss and will have a basis in the Y Corporation stock of $60,000.

**Example 25.** Assume the same facts as in Example 24 except that C's basis in the property transferred is $68,000 (instead of $30,000). Because recognized gain cannot exceed realized gain, the transfer generates only $2,000 of gain to C. The basis of the Y Corporation stock to C becomes $60,000 [i. e., $68,000 (basis of property transferred) + $2,000 (gain recognized) − $10,000 (cash received)]. Y Corporation's basis in the property received from C is $70,000 [i. e., $68,000 (basis of the property to C) + $2,000 (gain recognized by C)].

There are three requirements for nonrecognition of gain or loss: (a) a transfer of property for (b) stock or securities if (c) the transferors are in control of the transferee corporation.

## TRANSFER OF PROPERTY

Questions concerning exactly what constitutes property for purposes of § 351 have arisen. Services rendered are specifically excluded by the Code from the definition of property. With this exception, the definition of property is comprehensive. Unrealized receivables for a cash basis taxpayer are considered property, for example.[20] Secret processes and formulas, as well as secret information in the general nature of a patentable inventory, also qualify as property under § 351.[21]

## STOCK AND SECURITIES

If property is transferred to a corporation in exchange for any property other than stock and securities, the property constitutes boot and is taxable to the transferor shareholder. The Regulations state

---

**20.** *Hempt Brothers, Inc. v. U. S.,* 74–1 USTC ¶ 9188, 33 AFTR2d 74–570, 490 F.2d 1172 (CA–3, 1974).
**21.** Rev.Rul. 64–56, 1964–1 C.B. 133.

that stock rights and stock warrants are not included in the term "stock or securities."[22] Generally, however, the term "stock" needs no clarification. On the other hand, the definition of a "security" can be a problem. A security is an obligation of the corporation; however, courts have required that the definition of "security" be limited to long-term obligations and exclude short-term notes. Courts have held short-term notes to be the equivalent of cash.[23]

There is no definite length of time to maturity established to draw a line between long-term and short-term securities. Some courts would draw the line at five years; others at 10 years. In *Camp Wolters Enterprises, Inc.,* the Court stated:

> The test as to whether notes are securities is not a mechanical determination of the time period of the note. Though time is an important factor, the controlling consideration is an overall evaluation of the nature of the debt, degree of participation and continuing interest in the business, the extent of proprietary interest compared with the similarity of the note to a cash payment, the purpose of the advances, etc.[24]

## CONTROL OF THE TRANSFEREE CORPORATION

To qualify as a nontaxable transaction under § 351, the transferor must be in control of the transferee corporation immediately after the exchange. "Control" for these purposes requires the person or persons transferring the property to own, immediately after the transfer, stock possessing at least 80 percent of the total combined voting power of all classes of stock entitled to vote and at least 80 percent of the total *number* of shares of all other classes of stock of the corporation [§ 368(c)]. Control may apply to a single person or to several individuals if they are all parties to an integrated transaction. If more than one person is involved, the Regulations affirm that the exchange does not necessarily require simultaneous exchanges by two or more persons, but it does comprehend situations in which the rights of the parties have been previously defined and the execution of the agreement proceeds ". . . with an expedition consistent with orderly procedure."[25]

> **Example 26.** A exchanges property which cost him $60,000, but which has a fair market value of $100,000, for 70% of the stock of X Corporation. The other 30% is owned by B, who ac-

22. Reg. § 1.351–1(a)(1)(ii).
23. *Turner v. Comm.,* 62–1 USTC ¶ 9488, 9 AFTR2d 1528, 303 F.2d 94 (CA–4, 1962). But compare *U. S. v. Mills, Jr.,* 68–2 USTC ¶ 9503, 22 AFTR2d 5302, 399 F.2d 944 (CA–5, 1968).
24. 22 T.C. 737 (1955).
25. Reg. § 1.351–1(a)(1).

quired it several years ago. The fair market value of the stock is $100,000. A realizes a taxable gain of $40,000 on the transfer. If A and B had transferred property to X Corporation in a simultaneous transaction or in separate transactions, both of which related to the execution of a previous agreement, with A receiving 70% of the stock and B receiving 30%, gain would not have been recognized to either party.

Section 351 treatment will be lost if stock is transferred to persons who did not contribute property, causing those who did to lack control immediately after the exchange. However, if a person performs services for the corporation in exchange for stock and also transfers some property, he is treated as a member of the transferring group although he is taxed on the value of the stock issued for services.

Control is not lost if stock received by shareholders in a § 351 exchange is sold to persons who are not parties to the exchange shortly after the transaction, unless the plan for ultimate sale of the stock existed before the exchange.[26]

Section 351 is mandatory and not elective. If a transaction falls within the provisions of § 351, neither gain nor loss is recognized on the transfer (except that gain is recognized to the extent of boot received), and there is a carryover of basis.

## ASSUMPTION OF LIABILITIES—§ 357

Absent § 357 of the Code, the transfer of mortgaged property to a controlled corporation would trigger gain to the extent of the mortgage, whether the controlled corporation assumed the mortgage or took property subject to it. This is the case in nontaxable like-kind exchanges under § 1031. Liabilities assumed by the other party are considered the equivalent of cash and treated as boot. Section 357(a) provides, however, that the assumption of a liability by the acquiring corporation, or the corporation taking property subject to a liability, will not produce boot to the transferor shareholder in a § 351 transaction. Nevertheless, liabilities assumed by the transferee corporation are treated as "other property or money" as far as basis of stock received in the transfer is concerned. The basis of the stock received must be reduced by the amount of the liabilities assumed by the corporation [§ 358(d)].

> **Example 27.** C transfers property with an adjusted basis of $60,000, fair market value of $100,000, to X Corporation for 100% of the stock in X. The property is subject to a liability of $25,000 which X Corporation assumes. The exchange is tax-free

---

**26.** *Wilgard Realty Co. v. Comm.*, 42–1 USTC ¶ 9452, 29 AFTR 325, 127 F.2d 514 (CA–2, 1942).

under § § 351 and 357. However, under § 358(d), the basis to C of the stock in X Corporation is only $35,000 (basis of property transferred, $60,000, less amount of mortgage assumed, $25,000). The basis of the property to X Corporation is $60,000.

There are two exceptions to the rule of § 357(a). Section 357(b) provides that if the principal purpose of the assumption of the liabilities is to avoid tax *or* if there is no bona fide business purpose behind the exchange, the liabilities, in total, will be treated as money received and taxed as boot. Further, § 357(c) provides that if the sum of the liabilities exceeds the adjusted basis of the properties transferred, the excess is taxable gain.

*Tax Avoidance or No Bona Fide Business Purpose Exception.* Section 357(b)(1)(A) generally poses few problems. A tax avoidance purpose for transferring liabilities to a controlled corporation would seem unlikely in view of the basis adjustment necessitated by § 358(d). Since the liabilities transferred reduce the basis of the stock or securities received for the property, any realized gain is merely deferred and not avoided. Such gain would materialize when and if the stock is disposed of in a taxable sale or exchange.

Satisfying the bona fide business purpose will not be difficult if the liabilities were incurred in connection with the transferor's normal course of conducting his or her trade or business. But the bona fide business purpose requirement will cause difficulty if the liability is taken out shortly before the property is transferred and the proceeds therefrom are utilized for personal purposes.[27] This type of situation seems akin to a distribution of cash by the corporation which would, of course, be taxed as boot.

**Example 28.** D transfers real estate (basis of $40,000 and fair market value of $90,000) to a controlled corporation in return for stock in such corporation. Shortly before the transfer, D mortgages the real estate and uses the $20,000 proceeds to meet personal obligations. Along with the real estate, the mortgage is transferred to the corporation. In this case, it would appear that the assumption of the mortgage lacks a bona fide business purpose within the meaning of § 357(b)(1)(B). Because the amount of the liability is considered boot, D has a taxable gain on the transfer of $20,000 [§ 351(b)].[28]

*Liabilities in Excess of Basis Exception.* Section 357(c) states that if the sum of liabilities assumed and the liabilities to which transferred property is subject exceeds the total of the adjusted bases

---

**27.** See, for example, *Campbell, Jr. v. Wheeler,* 65–1 USTC ¶ 9294, 15 AFTR2d 578, 342 F.2d 837 (CA–5, 1965).
**28.** The effect of the application of § 357(b) is to taint *all* liabilities transferred even though some may be supported by a bona fide business purpose.

of the properties transferred, the excess is taxable gain. Absent this provision, if liabilities exceed basis in property exchanged, a taxpayer would have a negative basis in the stock or securities received in the controlled corporation. Section 357(c) alleviates the negative basis problem; the excess over basis is gain to the transferor.

> **Example 29.**   A, an individual, transfers assets with an adjusted tax basis of $40,000 to a newly formed corporation in exchange for 100% of the stock. The corporation assumes liabilities on the transferred properties in the amount of $50,000. Absent § 357(c), A's basis in the stock of the new corporation would be a negative $10,000 (basis of property transferred, $40,000, plus gain recognized, $0, less boot received, $0, less liabilities assumed, $50,000). Section 357(c) causes A to recognize a gain of $10,000. The stock will have a zero basis in A's hands, and the negative basis problem is eliminated (basis of property transferred, $40,000, plus gain recognized, $10,000, less boot received, $0, less liabilities assumed, $50,000).

If both § 357(b) and (c) apply to the same transfer (i. e., the liability is not supported by a bona fide business purpose and also exceeds the basis of the properties transferred), § 357(b) predominates.[29] This could be of significance because § 357(b) does not create gain on the transfer, as does § 357(c), but merely converts the liability to boot. Thus, the realized gain limitation continues to apply to § 357(b) transactions.

## RECAPTURE CONSIDERATIONS

*Recapture of Accelerated Cost Recovery (Depreciation).*   In a pure § 351(a) nontaxable transfer (i. e., no boot involved) to a controlled corporation, the recapture of accelerated cost recovery rules do not apply.[30] Moreover, any recapture potential of the property carries over to the corporation as it steps into the shoes of the transferor-shareholder for purposes of basis determination.

> **Example 30.**   T transfers to a controlled corporation depreciable real estate (basis of $30,000 and a fair market value of $100,000) in return for additional stock. If sold by T, the property would have yielded a gain of $70,000, of which $20,000 would be recaptured as ordinary income under § 1250. If the transfer comes within § 351(a) because of the absence of boot, T has no recognized gain and no accelerated cost recovery to recapture. Should the corporation later dispose of the real estate in a taxable transaction, it will have to take into account the § 1250 recapture potential originating with T.

---

**29.**   § 357(c)(2)(A).
**30.**   §§ 1245(b)(3) and 1250(d)(3).

*Recapture of the Investment Tax Credit.* Two problems arise with the transfer of § 38 property (i. e., property which yielded an investment tax credit on its acquisition). First, does the transfer to a controlled corporation trigger a recapture of the credit to the transferor-shareholder? Second, will a subsequent and premature disposition of the property by the transferee-corporation cause recapture and from whom will the credit be recaptured?

In answer to the first question posed, § 47(b) precludes recapture with respect to a taxpayer who merely changes "the form of conducting the trade or business so long as the property is retained in such trade or business as § 38 property and the taxpayer retains a substantial interest in such trade or business." What is meant by the retention of a substantial interest in the business is not entirely clear. The Regulation in point does not offer much guidance when it suggests that the exchange of a five percent interest in a partnership for a five percent interest in a corporation constitutes the retention of a substantial interest.[31] But what about a 50 percent interest in a partnership for a 20 percent interest in a corporation? These are close judgment questions which eventually will have to be resolved by the courts.[32]

One should note that the recapture of the investment credit can operate independently of § 351. Thus, recapture of the credit can take place on a transfer of § 38 property to a controlled corporation even though no gain is recognized to the transferor under § 351(a). In this regard, the investment credit recapture rules differ from those applicable to depreciation and cost recovery. In the latter two cases, the recapture of depreciation and cost recovery comes into play only if the transfer results in recognized gain to the transferor.

Even if the recapture of the investment credit is avoided on the transfer of property to a controlled corporation, the transferor-shareholder does not cease to be vulnerable. Unlike the recapture of depreciation situation, the potential stays with the transferor-shareholder. Consequently, recapture can take place at the shareholder level if the corporation prematurely disposes of the property *or* if the shareholder terminates his or her substantial interest in the business through disposition of stock.[33]

> **Example 31.** In 1981, T (an individual) purchased § 38 property for $12,000. T claimed an investment credit of $1,200 based on a recovery period of five years [see § 46(c)(7)]. In 1982, T forms X Corporation through the incorporation of his sole proprietor-

---

**31.** Reg. § 1.47–3(f)(2)(ii).

**32.** In *James Soares,* 50 T.C. 909 (1968), the Court found that the exchange of a 48% interest in a partnership for a 7.22% interest in a corporation was not the retention of a substantial interest in the business. Thus, recapture of the investment credit took place on the transfer to the corporation.

**33.** Reg. § 1.47–3(f)(5) and *W. F. Blevins,* 61 T.C. 547 (1974).

ship. In return for all of the stock in the corporation, T transfers all of his assets (including the § 38 property). In 1985, four years after its purchase by T, X Corporation sells the § 38 property at a loss. Under these circumstances, T must recapture $240 of the credit previously claimed.[34] The fact that the property was sold at a loss by X Corporation makes no difference in the recapture of the investment credit. No recapture of the credit occurred upon the property's transfer to X Corporation because T retained a substantial interest in the business.

**Example 32.** Assume the same facts as in Example 31 except that X Corporation does not sell the § 38 property but continues to use it in its trade or business until the full five years has run. In 1985, however, T makes gifts to family members of 75% of the stock he holds in X Corporation. These gifts terminate T's substantial interest in the business, and T must recapture some of the investment credit previously claimed.

## TAX BENEFIT RULE

A taxpayer may have to take into income the recovery of an item previously expensed. Such income, however, will be limited to the amount of the deduction that actually produced a tax savings. The relevance of the tax benefit rule to transfers to controlled corporations under § 351 was first apparent in connection with accounts receivable and the reserve for bad debts.

**Example 33.** T, an accrual basis individual, incorporates her sole proprietorship. In return for all of the stock of the corporation, T transfers, among other assets, accounts receivable with a face amount of $100,000 and a reserve for bad debts of $10,000 (i. e., book value of $90,000). The addition to the reserve was previously deducted by T. The deduction resulted in a tax benefit to T of $10,000.

The IRS took the position that § 351 did not insulate the transfer from the tax benefit rule.[35] Since T had previously deducted the reserve for bad debts and such reserve was no longer necessary to her, the full $10,000 should be taken into income. In *Nash v. U. S.*, the Supreme Court disagreed.[36] Operating on the assumption that the stock T received must be worth only $90,000 (the book value of the

---

**34.** Since the § 38 property was acquired after 1980, the rules contained in the Economic Recovery Tax Act (ERTA) of 1981 govern. Under ERTA, recapture is reduced by 2% for each full year the property is held prior to disposition (2% × 4 years = 8%, in this case). Hence, only 2 percent (10% minus 8%) of the credit is subject to recapture. Keep in mind, however, that pre-ERTA recapture rules apply to the disposition of § 38 property acquired prior to 1981.

**35.** Rev.Rul. 62–128, 1962–2 C.B. 139.

**36.** 70–1 USTC ¶ 9405, 25 AFTR2d 1177, 90 S.Ct. 1550 (USSC, 1970).

receivables), the situation was compared to a sale. Because no gain would have resulted had the receivables been sold for $90,000, why should it matter that they were transferred to a controlled corporation under § 351?

The Supreme Court decision in *Nash*, however, does not imply that the tax benefit rule is inapplicable to transfers to controlled corporations when no gain is otherwise recognized under § 351(a). Returning to the facts in Example 33, suppose T was one of several transferors, and the value of the stock she received exceeded the book value of the receivables (i. e., $90,000). Could the excess be vulnerable to income recognition by virtue of the application of the tax benefit rule? The answer to this question has not been specifically passed upon by the courts.[37]

# CAPITAL STRUCTURE OF A CORPORATION

## CAPITAL CONTRIBUTIONS

The receipt of money or property in exchange for capital stock (including treasury stock) produces neither gain nor loss to the recipient corporation [§ 1032]. Gross income of a corporation also does not include shareholders' contributions of money or property to the capital of the corporation [§ 118]. Additional funds received from shareholders through voluntary pro rata payments are not income to the corporation even though there is no increase in the outstanding shares of stock of the corporation. Such payments represent an additional price paid for the shares held by the stockholders and are treated as additions to the operating capital of the corporation.[38]

Contributions by nonshareholders, such as land contributed to a corporation by a civic group or a governmental group to induce the corporation to locate in a particular community, are also excluded from the gross income of a corporation.

The basis of property received by a corporation from a shareholder as a contribution to capital is the basis of the property in the hands of the shareholder increased by any gain recognized to the shareholder [§ 362(a)]. For property transferred to a corporation by a nonshareholder as a contribution to capital, the basis of the property is zero. If money is received by a corporation as a contribution to capital from a nonshareholder, the basis of any property acquired with the money during a 12-month period beginning on the day the contribution was received is reduced by the amount of the contribution. The excess of money received over the cost of new property is used to reduce the basis of other property held by the corporation [§ 362(c)]. The excess is applied in reduction of basis in the following

---

**37.** As will be seen in Chapter 14, the tax benefit rule is receiving wide application in the area of corporate liquidations.
**38.** Reg. § 1.118–1.

order: (a) depreciable property, (b) property subject to amortization, (c) property subject to depletion, and (d) all other remaining properties. The reduction of the basis of property within each category is made in proportion to the relative bases of the properties.[39]

> **Example 34.** Assume a television company charges its customers an initial fee to hook up to a new television system installed in the area. These contributions will be used to finance the total cost of constructing the television facilities. The customers will then make monthly payments for the television service. Even though the initial payments were for capital expenditures, they still represent payments for services to be rendered by the television company, and as such, they are taxable income and not contributions to capital by nonshareholders.

> **Example 35.** A city donates land to X Corporation as an inducement for X to locate in the city. The receipt of the land does not represent taxable income. However, its basis to the corporation is zero. Assume the city also pays the corporation $10,000 in cash. The money is not taxable income to the corporation. However, when the corporation purchases property with the $10,000 (within the next 12 months), the basis of such property is reduced by $10,000.

## DEBT IN THE CAPITAL STRUCTURE

*Advantages of Debt.* In forming a corporation, shareholders should consider the relationship between debt and equity in the capital structure. Section 351 provides for nonrecognition of gain on a transfer for either stock or securities (i. e., long-term debt). Consequently, a shareholder can transfer property and receive both stock and long-term debt tax-free. The advantages of receiving long-term debt are numerous. Interest on debt is deductible by the corporation, whereas dividend payments are not. Further, the shareholders are not taxed on loan repayments unless they exceed basis. As long as a corporation has earnings and profits (see Chapter 13), an investment in stock cannot be withdrawn tax-free. Any withdrawals will be deemed to be taxable dividends to the extent of earnings and profits of the distributing corporation.

> **Example 36.** A, an individual, transfers assets with a tax basis of $100,000 to a newly formed corporation for 100% of the stock. The basis of the assets to the corporation is $100,000. In the first year of operations, the corporation has net income of $40,000. Such earnings are credited to the earnings and profits account of the corporation. If the corporation distributes $9,000 to A, it will be a taxable dividend with no corresponding deduction to the corporation. Assume A transferred the assets for stock and debt in

---

**39.** Reg. § 1.362–2(b).

the amount of $50,000, payable in equal annual installments of $5,000 and bearing interest at the rate of 8%. The transfer would still be tax-free because the securities, the long-term debt, have a maturity date of 10 years. At the end of the year, the corporation would pay A $4,000 interest which would be tax deductible to it. The $5,000 principal repayment on the loan would not be taxed to A.

*Reclassification of Debt as Equity.*　In certain instances, the IRS will contend that debt is really an equity interest and will deny the shareholders the tax advantages of debt financing. If the debt instrument has too many features of stock, it may be treated as a form of stock, and principal and interest payments will be considered dividends.

Though the form of the instrument will not assure debt treatment, the failure to observe certain formalities in the creation of the debt may lead to an assumption that the purported debt is, in fact, a form of stock. The debt should be in proper legal form, should bear a legitimate rate of interest, should have a definite maturity date, and should be repaid on a timely basis. Payments should not be contingent upon earnings. Further, the debt should not be subordinated to other liabilities, and proportionate holdings of stock and debt should be avoided.

Section 385 was added to the Internal Revenue Code in 1969. This section lists several factors which *may* be used to determine whether a debtor-creditor relationship or a shareholder-corporation relationship exists. The obvious thrust of § 385, however, is to turn the matter over to the U. S. Treasury Department to prescribe Regulations that would provide more definite guidelines as to when a corporation is or is not thinly capitalized. After a wondrous deliberation of more than a decade, such Regulations were proposed and, with significant modifications, scheduled to be completed in 1980.[40] However, the effective date of such Regulations has been postponed. Furthermore, because the Treasury Department has announced that they will be further revised, as of the time of this writing, their content is unknown.

 **TAX PLANNING CONSIDERATIONS**

## CORPORATE VERSUS NONCORPORATE FORMS OF BUSINESS ORGANIZATION

The decision to use the corporate form in conducting a trade or business must be weighed carefully. Besides the nontax considerations

---

**40.**　Reg. § § 1.385–1 to –10.

attendant to the corporate form (i. e., limited liability, continuity of life, free transferability of interest, centralized management), tax ramifications will play an important role in any such decision. Close attention should be paid to the following:

1.  The regular corporate form means the imposition of the corporate income tax. Corporate-source income will be taxed twice—once as earned by the corporation and again when distributed to the shareholders. Since dividends are not deductible, a strong incentive exists in a closely-held corporation to structure corporate distributions in a deductible form. Thus, profits may be bailed out by the shareholders in the form of salaries, interest, or rents. Such procedures lead to a multitude of problems, one of which, the reclassification of debt as equity, has been discussed. The problems of unreasonable salaries and rents are covered in Chapter 13 in the discussion of constructive dividends.

2.  Corporate source income loses its identity as it passes through the corporation to the shareholders. Thus, items possessing preferential tax treatment (e. g., interest on municipal bonds, long-term capital gains) are not taxed as such to the shareholders.

3.  As will be noted in Chapter 13, it may be difficult for shareholders to recover some or all of their investment in the corporation without an ordinary income result, since most corporate distributions are treated as dividends to the extent of the corporation's earnings and profits. Structuring the capital of the corporation to include debt is a partial solution to this problem. Thus, the shareholder-creditor could recoup part of his or her investment through the tax-free repayment of principal. Too much debt, however, may lead to such debt being reclassified as equity.

4.  Corporate losses cannot be passed through to the shareholders.

5.  Long-term capital gains and losses generally receive more favorable tax treatment in the hands of noncorporate taxpayers.[41]

6.  The liquidation of a corporation may well generate tax consequences to both the corporation and its shareholders (see Chapter 14).

7.  On the positive side, the corporate form may be advantageous for shareholders in high individual tax brackets. With a cur-

---

**41.** Points 1, 4, and 5 could be resolved through a Subchapter S election (see Chapter 16), assuming the corporation qualifies for such an election. The same can be said for point 2.

rent maximum corporate income tax rate of 46 percent, such shareholders would be motivated to avoid dividend distributions and retain profits within the corporation. An abuse of this approach, however, could lead to the imposition of the penalty tax on unreasonable accumulation of earnings or the special tax on personal holding companies (see Chapter 15).

8. The corporate form does provide the shareholders with the opportunity to be treated as employees for tax purposes if they, in fact, render services to the corporation. Such status makes a number of attractive tax-sheltered fringe benefits available. These include but are not limited to group-term life insurance (§ 79), the $5,000 death gratuity [§ 101(b)(1)], accident and health plans (§ § 105 and 106), meals and lodging (§ 119), and qualified pension and profit sharing plans (§ § 401–404). These benefits are not available to partners and sole proprietors.

## THE ASSOCIATION ROUTE

Consideration 8 led to the popularity of the professional association. The major tax incentive involved was to cover the shareholder-employees under a qualified pension plan. Professionals, particularly physicians, who were not permitted to form regular corporations, either because of state law prohibitions or ethical restrictions, created organizations with sufficient corporate attributes to be classified as associations. The position of the IRS on the status of these professional associations (whether or not they should be treated as corporations for tax purposes) vacillated over a period of years. After a series of judicial losses, however, the IRS has accepted their association status, assuming certain conditions are satisfied.[42]

The popularity of the professional association is declining in light of the changes made by the Employee Retirement Income Security Act of 1974, and the Tax Equity and Fiscal Responsibility Act of 1982 (TEFRA). Vesting and coverage requirements have made qualified plans more costly and less attractive taxwise. At the same time, improvements were made to the H.R. 10 (Keogh) type of plan available to self-employed taxpayers.[43] Consequently, the difference between employee and self-employed status (i. e., qualified plans *versus* H.R. 10) is fast disappearing.

---

**42.** T.I.R. 1019; Rev.Rul. 70–101, 1970–1 C.B. 278; Rev.Rul. 70–455, 1970–2 C.B. 297; Rev.Rul. 72–468, 1972–2 C.B. 647; Rev.Rul. 73–596, 1973–2 C.B. 424; and, Rev.Rul. 74–439, 1974–2 C.B. 405.

**43.** The contribution percentage was raised from 10% to 15% of net earnings from self-employment. Also, the maximum that can be deducted in any one year was increased from $2,500 to $7,500 and, starting in 1982, to $15,000. Further increases are scheduled under TEFRA.

## WORKING WITH § 351

Effective tax planning with transfers of property to corporations involves a clear understanding of § 351 and its related Code provisions. The most important question in planning is simply: Does compliance with the requirements of § 351 yield the desired tax result?

*Utilizing § 351.* In using § 351(a), one should insure that all parties transferring property (which includes cash) receive control of the corporation. Although simultaneous transfers are not necessary, a long period of time between transfers could be vulnerable if the transfers are not properly documented as part of a single plan.

> **Example 37.** C, D, and E decide to form the X Corporation with the following investment: cash of $100,000 from C, real estate worth $100,000 (basis of $20,000) from D, and a patent worth $100,000 (basis of zero) from E. In return for this investment, each party is to receive one-third of the corporation's authorized stock of 300 shares. On June 1, 19X4, after the corporate charter is granted, C transfers cash of $100,000 in return for 100 shares. Two months later, D transfers the real estate for another 100 shares. On December 3, 19X4, E transfers the patent for the remaining 100 shares.

Taken in isolation, the transfers by D and E would result in recognized gain to each. Section 351 would not be applicable because neither D nor E achieves the required 80 percent control. If, however, the parties are in a position to prove that all transfers were part of the same plan, C's transfer can be counted and the 80 percent requirement is satisfied. To do this, the parties should document and preserve evidence of their intentions. Also, it would be helpful to have some reasonable explanation for the delay in D's and E's transfer.

To meet the requirements of § 351, mere momentary control on the part of the transferor may not suffice if loss of control is compelled by a prearranged agreement.[44]

> **Example 38.** For many years, T operated a business as a sole proprietor employing R as manager. In order to dissuade R from quitting and going out on her own, T promised her a 30% interest in the business. To fulfill this promise, T transfers the business to newly formed X Corporation in return for all its stock. Immediately thereafter, T transfers 30% of the stock to R. Section 351 probably would not apply to the transfer by T to X Corporation; it appears that T was under an obligation to relinquish control. If this is not the case and such loss of control was by voluntary act on the part of T, momentary control would suffice.[45]

---

**44.** Rev.Rul. 54–96, 1954–1 C.B. 111.

**45.** Compare *Fahs v. Florida Machine and Foundry Co.,* 48–2 USTC ¶ 9329, 36 AFTR 1151, 168 F.2d 957 (CA–5, 1948) with *John C. O'Connor,* 16 TCM 213, T.C.Memo. 1957–50.

Be sure that later transfers of property to an existing corporation satisfy the control requirement if recognition of gain is to be avoided. In this connection, a transferor's interest cannot be counted if the stock or securities received are of relatively small value in comparison to the value of those already owned and the primary purpose of the transfer is to qualify other transferors for § 351 treatment.[46] For purposes of issuing advance rulings, the IRS follows a policy of treating the amount transferred as *not* being relatively small in value if it is equal to, or in excess of, 10 percent of the fair market value of the stock and securities already owned by such person.[47]

> **Example 39.** At a point when R Corporation has 800 shares outstanding (owned equally by T and her son) and worth $1,000 each, it issues an additional 200 shares to T in exchange for land (basis of $20,000 and fair market value of $200,000). Presuming the son makes no contribution, T's transfer does not meet the requirements of § 351. Since the son's ownership interest cannot be counted (he was not a transferor), T must satisfy the control requirement on her own. In this regard, she falls short, since she ended up with 600 shares [400 shares (originally owned) + 200 shares (newly received)] out of 1,000 shares now outstanding for only a 60% interest.[48] Thus, T must recognize a gain of $180,000 on the transfer.

> **Example 40.** To make the transfer in Example 39 fall under § 351, what needs to be done? One possibility would be to include the son as a transferor in order that his ownership interest can be counted in meeting the control requirement. In using the IRS guidelines to avoid the "relatively small in value" hurdle, this would entail an investment on the part of the son (for additional stock) of at least $40,000 in cash or property [10% × $400,000 (fair market value of the shares already owned)]. If this approach is taken, § 351 will apply to T and none of her realized gain of $180,000 will be recognized.

To keep the matter in perspective, be in a position to recognize when § 351 is not relevant.

> **Example 41.** Assume the same facts as in Example 39 except that T receives no additional shares in R Corporation in exchange for the transfer of the land. Because T has made a contribution to capital, compliance with § 351 is of no consequence. No gain will be recognized by T due to such contribution, although a basis

---

**46.**   Reg. § 1.351–1(a)(1)(ii).
**47.**   Rev.Proc. 76–22, 1976–1 C.B. 562.
**48.**   The stock attribution rules of § 318 (see Chapter 13) do not apply to § 351 transfers. Consequently, the shares held by the son are not treated as being constructively owned by the mother.

adjustment is in order as to her original 400 shares. Other tax consequences, however, may materialize.[49]

*Avoiding § 351.* Because § 351(a) provides for the nonrecognition of gain on transfers to controlled corporations, it is often regarded as a relief provision favoring taxpayers. There could be situations, however, where the avoidance of § 351(a) produces a more advantageous tax result. The transferors might prefer to recognize gain on the transfer of property if they cannot be particularly harmed by the gain, either because they are in low tax brackets or because the gain will receive preferential long-term capital gain treatment. Keep in mind that the basis of the property to the corporation will be affected by the applicability or inapplicability of § 351(a).

> **Example 42.** C and D form the X corporation with a $20,000 cash investment. Shortly thereafter, they "sell" to the corporation a patent they have developed (basis of zero) for $2,000,000, such sum payable in interest-bearing notes extending over an eight-year period. C and D elect to report the gain on the sale of the patent under the installment method [§ 453].

What have C and D tried to accomplish by structuring the transfeas a purported "sale"? First, the $2,000,000 gain recognized probably will be long-term capital gain.[50] Even better, the election of the installment method avoids the bunching of such gain and permits C and D to spread recognition thereof over the eight-year payout period. Second, X Corporation receives a basis in the patent of $2,000,000. Since a patent is an amortizable asset, the step-up in basis my be written off over its estimated useful life. Third, the interest element of the notes permits C and D to bail out corporate profits over the next eight years in a form deductible to the corporation. It is hoped that deductible interest would then become a substitute for nondeductible dividends.

What could go wrong with the intended tax consequences?

1. The IRS could attempt to collapse the "sale" by taking the approach that the transfer really falls under § 351(a).[51] As

---

**49.** Because the son has benefited from T's capital contribution (i. e., his shares are, as a result, worth more), a gift has taken place. It could be, therefore, that T's capital contribution could lead to the imposition of a gift tax liability. In this connection, see Chapter 19.

**50.** Long-term capital gain would materialize from the general tax concepts applicable to the sale or exchange of capital assets. This presumes the patent is a capital asset in the hands of C and D, held for the required holding period, and a sale or exchange has taken place. The special provision of § 1235, normally relied on in the disposition of patent transfers, need not be utilized. At any rate, its use in this case is precluded by the related-person provision of § 1235(d).

**51.** *U. S. v. Hertwig*, 68–2 USTC ¶ 9495, 22 AFTR2d 5249, 398 F.2d 452 (CA–5, 1968); *Robert W. Adams*, 58 T.C. 41 (1972); and, *D'Angelo Associates, Inc.*, 70 T.C. 121 (1978).

such, the shareholders recognize no gain and their zero basis in the patent carries over to the corporation [§ 362(b)].

2. The IRS could argue that the notes issued by X Corporation are really a form of stock and such debt should be reclassified as equity. If the argument succeeds, the corporation's interest payments on the notes become nondeductible dividends. Even worse, any principal payments on the notes also would be taxed to C and D as dividends to the extent of X Corporation's earnings and profits (see Chapter 13).

3. Since a patent is depreciable property, § 1239 might apply to convert long-term capital gain (or § 1231 gain) into ordinary income. For § 1239 to become operative, however, either C *or* D must own more than 80 percent in value of the outstanding stock in X Corporation. In meeting the more than 80 percent test, the stock ownership of C and D is subject to the constructive ownership rules of § 318.

In reaching the § 351(a) result (see point 1), it becomes necessary to conclude that C and D received *solely* stock or securities in X Corporation in return for the property transferred. But would the notes be classified as securities? The maturity period of the notes (i. e., eight years), although not controlling, is important. As noted previously, however, what is or is not a security is still unclear when maturity periods of five to 10 years are involved. If it can be assumed that the notes are not securities or stock (see point 2), then the taxpayers would accomplish essentially the same desired tax result through § 351(b). The notes now become other property (boot), and the shareholders recognize a capital gain to the extent of the fair market value of such notes. The basis of the patent to the corporation becomes its basis in the hands of the transferors (i. e., zero) *plus* the gain recognized by them.

In summary, the procedures followed in Example 42 appear highly susceptible to challenge by the IRS. Modifications that would be helpful in reducing the tax risk involved include:

—Disassociate the sale of the patent from the formation of the corporation. Certainly, some time span should separate the two events. Perhaps the patent could have been leased to the corporation for a period of time, with the later sale proving to be the solution to the initial unsatisfactory arrangement.

—Shorten the maturity period of the notes. Consequently, even if the sale is tied to the § 351 formation, the chance of boot treatment under § 351(b) is improved.

—Capitalize the corporation with more equity and less debt. Lessening the debt-to-equity ratio reduces the hazards of stock reclassification.

Another reason why a particular transferor may wish to avoid § 351 concerns possible loss recognition. Recall that § 351(a) refers to the nonrecognition of both gains and losses. In a boot situation, § 351(b)(2) specifically states: "No loss to such recipient shall be recognized." The course of action for a transferor who desires to recognize loss on the transfer of property with a basis in excess of fair market value could be any of several alternatives.

—Sell the property to the corporation for its stock. As noted above, this procedure may be collapsed by the IRS. If the sale is disregarded, the transferor ends up under § 351(a) with a realized, but unrecognized, loss.

—Sell the property to the corporation for "other property" or boot. Because the transferor receives no stock or securities, § 351 is inapplicable.

—Transfer the property to the corporation in return for securities. Surprisingly, the IRS has held that § 351 does not apply to a transferor who receives only securities and no stock.[52] In both this and the previous alternatives, one would have to watch for the possible disallowance of the loss under § 267.

---

## PROBLEM MATERIALS

### Discussion Questions

1. Briefly discuss the income tax consequences of the various forms of business organization in relation to the following:

   (a) The tax treatment of sole proprietorships.

   (b) Partnerships and the conduit concept.

   (c) Partnerships as reporting entities.

   (d) The similarities and dissimilarities between the tax treatment of partnerships, trusts, and estates.

   (e) The similarities between S corporations and partnerships.

   (f) The dissimilarities between S corporations and regular corporations.

2. What effect does state law have in determining whether an entity is to be treated as a corporation for Federal income tax purposes?

3. Under what circumstances may a corporation legally constituted under state law be disregarded for Federal income tax purposes?

4. Why might the IRS attempt to disregard a legally constituted corporate entity? Why might the shareholders attempt such?

5. Evaluate the disadvantages of using the corporate form in carrying on a trade or business in light of the following:

   (a) No deduction is permitted for dividend distributions.

   (b) The conduit concept does not apply.

---

**52.**  Rev.Rul. 73–472, 1973–2 C.B. 115. But compare Rev.Rul. 73–473, 1973–2 C.B. 115.

6. Evaluate the advantages of using the corporate form in carrying on a trade or business in light of the following:

   (a) Shareholders are in high individual income tax brackets.

   (b) Employee status for tax purposes. — *tax free fringe benefits*

7. What is an association? How is it taxed?

8. Under what circumstances might the owners of a business desire to have it classified as an association? Not to be so classified?

9. Compare the income tax treatment of corporations and individuals in the following respects:

   (a) Applicable tax rates.

   (b) Adjusted gross income determination.

   (c) The deduction for casualty losses.

   (d) Allowable tax credits.

   (e) Dividends received from domestic corporations.

   (f) Net operating losses.

   (g) The minimum tax.

10. Compare the tax treatment of corporate and noncorporate taxpayers' capital gains and losses with respect to:

    (a) The long-term capital gain deduction.

    (b) The alternative tax.

    (c) A net long-term capital loss.

    (d) A net short-term capital loss.

    (e) Capital loss carrybacks.

    (f) Capital loss carryovers.

11. What is the justification for the dividends received deduction?

12. Under what circumstances may the dividends received deduction exceed 85% of the corporation's taxable income?

13. Compare the tax treatment of corporate and noncorporate taxpayers' charitable contributions with respect to:

    (a) The year of the deduction for an accrual basis taxpayer.

    (b) The percentage limitations on the maximum deduction allowed for any one year.

    (c) The amount of the deduction allowed for the donations of property.

14. In connection with organizational expenditures, comment on the following:

    (a) Those which qualify for amortization.

    (b) Those which do not qualify for amortization.

    (c) The period over which amortization can take place.

    (d) Expenses incurred but not paid by a cash basis corporation.

    (e) Expenses incurred by a corporation in its second year of operations.

    (f) The alternative if no election to amortize is made.

    (g) The timing of the election to amortize.

15. What is the tax effect to a corporation of the receipt of money or property as a capital contribution?

   (a) What is the corporation's tax basis in the property received from a shareholder?

   (b) From a nonshareholder?

16. What purpose is served by Schedule M–1 of Form 1120? By Schedule M–2?

17. In terms of justification and effect, Code § 351 (i. e., transfer to corporation controlled by transferor) and Code § 1031 (i. e., like-kind exchanges) are much alike. Explain.

18. What does the term "property" include for purposes of § 351?

19. In arriving at the basis of stock received by a shareholder in a § 351 transfer, describe the effect of the following:

   (a) The shareholder receives other property (boot) in addition to stock.

   (b) Along with the property, the shareholder transfers a liability to the corporation.

   (c) The shareholder's basis in the property transferred to the corporation.

20. How does a corporation determine its basis in property received pursuant to a § 351 transfer?

21. What are "securities" for purposes of § 351? What difference does it make if debt instruments do or do not qualify as securities?

22. What is the control requirement of § 351? Describe the effect of the following in satisfying this requirement:

   (a) A shareholder renders services to the corporation for stock.

   (b) A shareholder both renders services and transfers property to the corporation for stock.

   (c) A shareholder has only momentary control after the transfer.

   (d) A long period of time elapses between the transfers of property by different shareholders.

23. What is the general rule of § 357(a) with regard to the transfer of liabilities?

   (a) The exception of § 357(b)?

   (b) The exception of § 357(c)?

24. Assuming a § 351(a) nontaxable transfer, explain the tax effect, if any, of the following transactions:

   (a) The transfer of depreciable property with recapture potential under § 1245 or § 1250.

   (b) The later sale of such property by the corporation.

   (c) The transfer of property upon which an investment tax credit has previously been claimed by the transferor.

   (d) The later sale of such property by the corporation.

25. Under what conditions may a transferor wish to avoid the application of § 351(a) upon the transfer of property to a controlled corporation?

26. Explain the tax benefit rule. Could it be applied to cause the recognition of gain in a § 351(a) transfer?

27. In structuring the capitalization of a corporation, what are the advantages of utilizing debt as opposed to equity?

28. What factors are taken into account in determining whether or not a corporation is thinly capitalized?

29. Describe the tax effect to the corporation and its shareholders when it is deemed to be thinly capitalized.

## Problems

30. Using the legend provided, classify each statement listed below.

### Legend

I = Applies only to individual taxpayers

C = Applies only to corporate taxpayers

B = Applies to both individual and corporate taxpayers

N = Applies to neither individual nor corporate taxpayers

(a) A net capital loss can be carried back.

(b) Net long-term capital losses are carried forward as short-term capital losses.

(c) The long-term capital gain deduction is available.

(d) A $1,000 net short-term capital loss in the current year can be deducted against ordinary income only to the extent of $500.

(e) The alternative tax is 28% of the net long-term capital gain.

(f) The carryforward period for net capital losses is five years.

(g) The applicable tax rates are progressive.

(h) The minimum tax does not apply.

(i) The investment tax credit applies.

(j) Net operating losses are not allowed to be carried back.

(k) The retirement income credit applies.

(l) The first $100 of qualified dividends received is excluded from gross income.

31. For taxable year 1982, a corporation has gross profits of $250,000 from its sales, dividends of $90,000 from qualifying domestic corporations, and interest on municipal bonds of $9,000. Its business deductions total $60,000. Compute its tax liability for 1982. Compute its tax liability if these transactions occurred in 1983.

32. A corporation donated the following properties to various qualified charities during the current taxable year: inventory with a tax basis of $45,000 (fair market value of $60,000) to a university, land held for investment with a tax basis of $150,000 (fair market value of $210,000) to a church which promptly sold the property, stock in another corporation with a tax basis of $18,000 (fair market value of $60,000) to a private foundation. What is the corporation's charitable contribution deduction before applying the 10% limitation?

33. During 19X2, T Corporation (a calendar year taxpayer) had the following income and expenses:

| | |
|---|---:|
| Income from operations | $180,000 |
| Expenses from operations | 100,000 |
| Qualifying dividends from domestic corporations | 10,000 |
| Net operating loss carryback from 19X3 | 2,000 |

On June 3, 19X2, T Corporation made a contribution to a qualified charitable organization of $10,500 in cash (not included in any of the items listed above).

(a) Determine T Corporation's charitable contribution deduction for 19X2.

(b) What happens to any excess charitable deduction not allowable for 19X2?

34. During 19X6, a corporation has $100,000 of gross income and $125,000 in allowable business deductions. Included in gross income is $30,000 in qualifying dividends from domestic corporations.

(a) Determine the corporation's net operating loss for 19X6.

(b) What happens to the loss if the corporation was newly created in 19X6?

(c) Newly created in 19X3?

35. A corporation has gross income from its business operations of $50,000. Its business deductions are $70,000. Dividends from domestic corporations total $10,000. What is the corporation's net operating loss?

36. In the current year, a corporation had the following income and expenses:

| | |
|---|---:|
| Gross income from operations | $60,000 |
| Expenses from operations | 68,000 |
| Qualifying dividends from domestic corporations | 40,000 |

(a) Determine the corporation's dividends received deduction.

(b) Compute the deduction assuming the expenses from operations were only $64,000 (instead of $68,000).

37. P Corporation was formed on December 1, 19X2. Qualifying organizational expenses were incurred and paid as follows:

| | |
|---|---:|
| Incurred and paid in December 19X2 | $ 10,000 |
| Incurred in December 19X2 but paid in January 19X3 | 5,000 |
| Incurred and paid in February 19X3 | 3,000 |

Assume P Corporation makes a timely election under § 248 to amortize organizational expenditures over a period of 60 months. What amount may be amortized in the corporation's first tax year under each of the assumptions appearing below:

(a) P Corporation adopts a calendar year and the cash basis of accounting for tax purposes.

(b) Same as (a) except that P Corporation does not adopt a calendar year but chooses, instead, a fiscal year of December 1–November 30.

(c) P Corporation adopts a calendar year and the accrual basis of accounting for tax purposes.

(d) Same as (c) except that P Corporation does not adopt a calendar year but chooses, instead, a fiscal year of December 1–November 30.

38. For 19X9, T Corporation, an accrual basis, calendar year taxpayer, had net income per books of $46,850 and the following special transactions:

*Schedule M-1*
*Page B-45*

| | |
|---|---:|
| Rent income received in 19X9 ($11,000 is prepaid and relates to 19X0). Note: Prepaid rent is taxed in the year it is received.) | $ 20,000 |
| Capital loss in excess of capital gains (no carryback to prior years) | 2,500 |
| Interest on loan to carry tax-exempt bonds | 1,500 |
| Interest income on tax-exempt bonds | 1,000 |
| Accelerated depreciation in excess of straight-line (straight-line was used for "book" purposes) | 2,000 |
| Federal income tax liability for 19X9 | 17,150 |

Using Schedule M–1 of Form 1120, compute T Corporation's taxable income for 19X9.

39. X Corporation receives 30 acres of land and $10,000 cash from Plainland City to locate its office and plant in this community. The 30 acres of land are worth $50,000. X Corporation uses the $10,000 in cash to purchase equipment. What are the tax consequences to X Corporation upon the receipt of the land and cash from Plainland City?

40. J and B form Y Corporation with the following investment:

| | Property Transferred | | Number of |
|---|---|---|---|
| | Basis to Transferor | Fair Market Value | Shares Issued |
| From J— | | | |
| Land & building | $ 60,000 | $ 480,000 | 100 |
| Mortgage on land & building | 180,000 | | |
| From B— | | | |
| Cash | 120,000 | 120,000 | 100 |
| Machinery | 120,000 | 180,000 | |

The mortgage is assumed by Y Corporation.

(a) How much gain, if any, must J recognize?

(b) What will be J's basis in the Y Corporation stock?

(c) What will be Y Corporation's basis in the land and building?

(d) How much gain, if any, must B recognize?

(e) What will be B's basis in the Y Corporation stock?

(f) What will be Y Corporation's basis in the machinery?

41. C, D, E, and F (all individuals) form the X Corporation with the following investment:

| | Property Transferred | | Number of |
| | Basis to Transferor | Fair Market Value | Shares Issued |
| --- | --- | --- | --- |
| From C— | | | |
| Cash | $ 60,000 | $ 60,000 ⎱ | 90 |
| Machinery | 40,000 | 30,000 ⎰ | |
| From D— | | | |
| Land & building | 20,000 | 75,000 ⎱ | |
| Mortgage on land | | ⎬ | 50 |
| & building | 25,000 | 25,000 ⎰ | |
| From E— | | | |
| Patent | 55,000 | 50,000 | 40* |
| From F— | | | |
| Personal services | | | |
| rendered to X | | | |
| Corporation | 0 | 10,000 | 10 |

In addition to the 40 shares (*), E receives $10,000 in cash.

The mortgage transferred by D is assumed by X Corporation. Assume the value of each share of X Corporation stock is $1,000.

(a) What, if any, is C's recognized gain or loss?

(b) What basis will C have in the X Corporation stock?

(c) What basis will X Corporation have in the machinery?

(d) How much gain or loss must D recognize?

(e) What basis will D have in the X Corporation stock?

(f) What basis will X Corporation have in the land and building?

(g) How much gain or loss must E recognize?

(h) What basis will E have in the X Corporation stock?

(i) What basis will X Corporation have in the patent?

(j) How much income, if any, must F recognize?

(k) What basis will F have in the X Corporation stock?

42. Indicate whether the following statements are true or false:

(a) If both § 357(b) and § 357 (c) apply, the latter will control.

(b) For § 357(b) to apply, the transfer of the liability must be for the purpose of tax avoidance *and* lack a bona fide business purpose.

(c) Section 357(c) will not apply if there is no realized gain on the transfer.

(d) The application of § 357(b) to a transfer to a controlled corporation would not affect the basis of the stock received by the transferor.

(e) T transfers property (upon which an investment tax credit has previously been claimed) to a controlled corporation. A later sale of the property by the corporation could trigger recapture of the credit to T.

(f) Same as (e). A later sale of the stock by T could trigger recapture of the credit to T.

(g) T transfers depreciable property to a controlled corporation. The property possesses a recapture potential under § 1245. A later sale of the property by the corporation could trigger recapture of depreciation to T.

(h) T transfers accounts receivable (face amount of $50,000) and a reserve for bad debts of $5,000 for stock in a controlled corporation worth $45,000. Under these circumstances, the tax benefit rule will not cause any recognition of gain to T.

43. X Corporation had the following income and expenses in taxable year 1983:

| | |
|---|---:|
| Gross income from operations | $ 900,000 |
| Dividends from domestic corporations | 60,000 |
| Interest income | 30,000 |
| Expenses | 600,000 |

Compute its tax liability (ignore minimum tax computations).

44. Assume the same facts as in 43 except that X Corporation also has a long-term capital loss of $30,000. Compute its tax liability.

# Chapter 13

# Corporate Distributions
# Not in Complete Liquidation

A working knowledge of the rules pertaining to corporate distributions is essential for anyone dealing with the tax problems of corporations and their shareholders. The form of such distributions is important because it can produce varying tax results to shareholders. Tax consequences to the distributing corporation may also differ. Dividends are taxed as ordinary income to the recipient shareholder (however, stock dividends may not be taxed at all), while stock redemptions (qualifying under § 302) generally receive capital gain or loss treatment. Concerning the distributing corporation, the rules differ with respect to the distribution of appreciated property pursuant to a stock redemption as compared to those governing other forms of corporate distributions.

## DIVIDEND DISTRIBUTIONS

### TAXABLE DIVIDENDS—IN GENERAL

Distributions by a corporation to its shareholders are presumed to be dividends unless the parties can prove otherwise. Section 316 makes such distributions, whether in the form of cash or other property, ordinary dividend income to a shareholder to the extent of the distribution's pro rata share of earnings and profits (E & P) of the distributing corporation accumulated since February 28, 1913, or to the extent of corporate earnings and profits (E & P) for the current year.

Under § 301(c), the portion of a corporate distribution which is not taxed as a dividend (because of insufficient E & P) will be nontaxable to the extent of the shareholder's basis in the stock and will reduce that basis accordingly. The excess of the distribution over the shareholder's basis is treated as a capital gain, if the stock is a capital asset.

> **Example 1.** As of January 1, 19X1, X Corporation (a calendar year taxpayer) has accumulated E & P of $30,000. In 19X1, the corporation distributes $40,000 to its *equal* shareholders, C and D. Only $30,000 of the $40,000 distribution is a taxable dividend. Suppose C's basis in his stock is $8,000, while D's basis is $4,000. Under these conditions, C must recognize a taxable dividend of $15,000 and reduce the basis of the stock from $8,000 to $3,000. The $20,000 D receives from X Corporation will be accounted for as follows: a taxable dividend of $15,000, a reduction in stock basis from $4,000 to zero, and a capital gain of $1,000.

Since it is the key to dividend treatment of corporate distributions, the importance of earnings and profits (E & P) cannot be emphasized enough.

## EARNINGS AND PROFITS (E & P)—§ 312

The term "earnings and profits" is not defined by the Code. Although § 312 lists certain transactions that affect E & P, it stops short of a complete definition. E & P does possess similarities to the accounting concept of retained earnings (i. e., earnings retained in the business); however, E & P and retained earnings are often not the same. For example, a stock dividend is treated for financial accounting purposes as a capitalization of retained earnings (i. e., it is debited to the retained earnings account and credited to a capital stock account), but it does not decrease E & P. Similarly, the elimination of a deficit in a "quasi-reorganization" increases retained earnings but does not increase E & P.

To fully understand the concept of E & P, it is helpful to keep several observations in mind. First, E & P might well be described as the factor which fixes the upper limit on the amount of dividend income shareholders would have to recognize as a result of a distribution by the corporation. In this sense, E & P represents the corporation's economic ability to pay a dividend without impairing its capital. Therefore, the effect of a specific transaction on the E & P account may be determined simply by considering whether or not the transaction increases or decreases the corporation's capacity to pay a dividend.

> **Example 2.** A corporation sells property (basis of $10,000) to its sole shareholder for $8,000. Due to § 267 (i. e., disallowance of

losses on sales between related parties), the $2,000 loss cannot be deducted in arriving at the corporation's taxable income for the year. But since the overall economic effect of the transaction is a decrease in the corporation's assets by $2,000, the loss will reduce the current E & P for the year of sale.

**Example 3.** A corporation pays a $10,000 premium on a keyman insurance policy (i. e., the corporation is the owner and beneficiary of the policy) covering the life of its president. As a result of the payment, the cash surrender value of the policy is increased by $7,000. None of the $10,000 premium would be deductible for tax purposes, but current E & P would be reduced by $3,000. Note that the $7,000 addition to the cash surrender value of the policy is a corporate economic gain available for distributions to shareholders.

**Example 4.** A corporation collects $100,000 on a keyman life insurance policy. At the time the policy matured on the death of the insured-employee, it possessed a cash surrender value of $30,000. None of the $100,000 will be included in the corporation's taxable income [see § 101(a)], but $70,000 would be added to the current E & P account.

**Example 5.** During 19X1, a corporation makes charitable contributions, $12,000 of which cannot be deducted in arriving at the taxable income for the year because of the 10% limitation of § 170(b)(2). However, pursuant to § 170(d)(2), the $12,000 is carried over to 19X2 and fully deducted in that year. The excess charitable contribution would reduce the corporation's current E & P for 19X1 by $12,000 and increase its current E & P for 19X2, when the deduction is allowed, by a like amount. The increase in E & P in 19X2 is necessitated by the fact that the charitable contribution carryover reduces the taxable income for that year (the starting point for computing E & P) and already has been taken into account in determining the E & P for 19X1.

*Computation of E & P.* E & P is increased by earnings for the taxable year computed in the same manner as is used in determining taxable income. If the corporation uses the cash method of accounting in computing taxable income, it must also use the cash method to determine the changes in E & P.[1]

E & P is increased for all items of income. Interest on municipal bonds, for example, though not taxed to the corporation, would increase its E & P.[2] Gains and losses from property transactions generally affect the determination of E & P only to the extent they are recognized for tax purposes. Thus, a gain on an involuntary conver-

---

1. Reg. § 1.312–6(a).
2. Reg. § 1.312–6(b).

sion not recognized by the corporation because the insurance proceeds are reinvested in property that is similar or related in service or use to the property converted (§ 1033) would not affect E & P. But the E & P account can be affected by both deductible and nondeductible items. Consequently, excess capital losses, expenses incurred to produce tax-exempt income, and Federal income taxes all reduce E & P, although such items do not enter into the calculation of taxable income.

The E & P account can be reduced only by cost depletion, even though the corporation may be using percentage (i. e., statutory) depletion for income tax purposes.[3] E & P cannot be reduced for accelerated depreciation for tax years beginning after June 30, 1972.[4] However, if a depreciation method such as units of production or machine hours is used, the adjustment to E & P can be determined on this basis.[5] If an accelerated method of computing depreciation, such as declining-balance or sum-of-years' digits, is used, the adjustment to E & P must be determined under the straight-line method. Later, when the asset is sold, the increase or decrease in E & P is computed by using the adjusted basis of the asset for E & P purposes.[6]

For cost recovery computed under ACRS pursuant to the Economic Recovery Tax Act of 1981, a corporation must compute earnings and profits using the straight-line recovery method over recovery periods that are longer than those used under ACRS. The extended recovery periods that must be used to compute earnings and profits are five years for three-year property, 12 years for five-year property, 25 years for 10-year property, and 35 years for 15-year property. These rules are applicable for assets placed in service after December 31, 1980.

> **Example 6.** On January 2, 1981, X Corporation purchased a machine for $30,000, which asset is then depreciated under ACRS. Assume the asset was sold on January 2, 1983, for $27,000. For purposes of determining taxable income, cost recovery claimed on the machine was $4,500 for 1981 and $6,600 for 1982. E & P, however, would have been reduced by only $3,750 (the straight-line method using a 12-year extended recovery period and a half-year convention). As of January 2, 1983, the machine has an adjusted basis of $18,900 [$30,000 − ($4,500 + $6,600)] for taxable income purposes. On this date the E & P basis would be $26,250 [$30,000 − ($1,250 + $2,500)]. Thus, the sale results in a taxable gain of $8,100 ($27,000 − $18,900) and an increase in E & P of $750 ($27,000 − $26,250).

3. Reg. § 1.312–6(c)(1),
4. § 312(k).
5. Reg. § 1.312–15(a)(2).
6. § 312(f)(1) and Reg. § 1.312–7(c)(2) (Ex. 3).

*The Source of the Distribution.* In determining the source of a dividend distribution, a dividend is deemed to have been made first from current E & P and then from E & P accumulated since February 28, 1913.[7]

> **Example 7.** As of January 1, 19X1, Y Corporation has a deficit in accumulated E & P of $30,000. For tax year 19X1, it has current E & P of $10,000. In 19X1, the corporation distributed $5,000 to its shareholders. The $5,000 distribution will be treated as a taxable dividend, since it is deemed to have been made from current E & P. This will be the case even though Y Corporation will still have a deficit in its accumulated E & P at the end of 19X1.

If a distribution exceeds the current year's E & P, the portion of each distribution deemed to have been made from current E & P is that percentage which the total E & P for the year bears to the total distributions for that year.[8] This can make a difference if any of the shareholders sell their stock during the year.

*Distinguishing Between Current and Accumulated E & P.* Accumulated E & P can be defined as the total of all previous years' current E & P as computed on the first day of each taxable year in accordance with the tax law in effect during that year. The factors which affect the computation of the current E & P for any one year have been discussed previously. Why must the distinction be drawn between current and accumulated E & P when it is clear that distributions are taxable if and to the extent that current *and* accumulated E & P exist?

1. When there exists a deficit in accumulated E & P and a positive current E & P, distributions will be regarded as dividends to the extent of the current E & P. Refer to Example 7.

2. Current E & P is allocated on a pro rata basis to the distributions made during the year; accumulated E & P is applied (to the extent necessary) in chronological order beginning with the earliest distributions.

3. Unless and until the parties can show otherwise, it is presumed that any distribution is covered by current E & P.

4. When there exists a deficit in current E & P (i. e., a current loss develops) and a positive balance in accumulated E & P, the accounts are netted at the date of distribution. If the resulting balance is zero or a deficit, the distribution is a return of capital. If a positive balance results, the distribution will represent a dividend to such extent. Any loss is allocated

---

7. Reg. § 1.316–2(a).
8. Reg. § 1.316–2(b).

ratably during the year unless the parties can show otherwise.[9]

Distinctions 3 and 4 are illustrated below:

**Example 8.**  Q Corporation uses a fiscal year of July 1 through
June 30 for tax purposes; Q Corporation's only shareholder, T,
uses a calendar year. As of July 1, 19X4, Q Corporation had a
zero balance in its accumulated E & P account. For fiscal year
19X4–19X5, the corporation suffered a $5,000 operating loss. On
August 1, 19X4, Q Corporation distributes $10,000 to T. The dis-
tribution represents dividend income to T and must be reported
as such when she files her income tax return for calendar year
19X4 on or before April 15, 19X5. Because T cannot prove until
June 30, 19X5, that the corporation had a deficit for fiscal 19X4–
19X5, she must assume the $10,000 distribution was fully cov-
ered by current E & P. When T learns of the deficit, she can, of
course, file an amended return for 19X4 showing the $10,000 as a
return of capital.

**Example 9.**  As of January 1, 19X5, R Corporation (a calendar
year taxpayer) has accumulated E & P of $10,000. During 19X5,
the corporation incurred a $15,000 net loss from operations which
accrued ratably throughout the year. On July 1, 19X5, R Corporation distributes $6,000 in cash to H, its sole shareholder. The
balance of both accumulated and current E & P as of July 1,
19X5, must be determined and netted because of the deficit in
current E & P. The balance at this date would be $2,500 [$10,000
(accumulated E & P) − $7,500 (one-half of the current deficit of
$15,000]. Of the $6,000 distribution, $2,500 would be taxed as a
dividend and $3,500 would represent a return of capital.

## PROPERTY DIVIDENDS

When a corporation distributes property, rather than cash, to a noncorporate shareholder, the amount distributed is measured by the fair
market value of the property on the date of distribution. Section
301(c) is applicable to such distributions. Thus, the portion of the distribution covered by existing E & P is a dividend, and any excess is
treated as a return of capital. If the fair market value of the property
distributed exceeded the corporation's E & P and the shareholder's
basis in the stock investment, a capital gain would result. If the
shareholder is another corporation, the amount distributed is the
*lesser* of (a) the fair market value of the property or (b) the adjusted
basis of the property in the hands of the distributing corporation immediately before the distribution, increased by the amount of gain

---

9.  Reg. § 1.316–2(b).

recognized to the distributing corporation.[10] For both noncorporate and corporate shareholders, the amount distributed is reduced by any liabilities to which the distributed property is subject immediately before and immediately after the distribution and by any liabilities of the corporation assumed by the shareholder in connection with the distribution.[11]

A shareholder's status—corporate or noncorporate—determines the basis assumed in property distributed. If the distribution is to a noncorporate shareholder, the basis is the fair market value of the property on the date of the distribution. In the case of a corporate shareholder, however, the basis of the property received is the lesser of (a) its fair market value or (b) the adjusted basis of such property in the hands of the distributing corporation, increased by any gain recognized by the distributing corporation.[12]

> **Example 10.** P Corporation has E & P of $60,000. It distributes land with a fair market value of $50,000 (adjusted basis of $30,000) to its sole shareholder, T (an individual). The land is subject to a liability of $10,000, which T assumes. T would have a taxable dividend of $40,000 [$50,000 (fair market value) − $10,000 (liability)]. The basis of the land to T is $50,000.

> **Example 11.** M Corporation is owned equally by two shareholders, T (an individual) and N Corporation. During the year, it distributes 100 shares of Zenith, Inc. stock to each of its two shareholders. Each share of the stock has a basis to M Corporation of $20 and a fair market value of $30. Assume the distribution is fully covered by M Corporation's E & P and is not pursuant to a corporate reorganization. Based on these circumstances, dividend income must be recognized by the shareholders as follows: $3,000 by T and $2,000 by N Corporation. The shareholders will take as their basis in the Zenith stock $3,000 and $2,000, respectively.

> **Example 12.** Ten percent of X Corporation is owned by Y Corporation. X Corporation has ample E & P to cover any distributions made during the year. One such distribution made to Y Corporation consists of a vacant lot with adjusted basis of $5,000 and a fair market value of $3,000. Y Corporation has a taxable dividend of $3,000, and its basis in the lot becomes $3,000.

The special rule governing property distributions received by corporate shareholders exists because of the 85 percent dividends received deduction allowed by § 243. Returning to Example 11, suppose N Corporation were treated the same as T. N Corporation would re-

---

10.   § 301(b).
11.   § 301(b)(2).
12.   § 301(d).

ceive a $3,000 basis in the stock, but only $450 [i. e., $3,000 − (85% × $3,000)] would be subject to tax. The rule, therefore, prevents a corporate shareholder from obtaining a step-up in basis in appreciated property at a cost of only a 15 percent inclusion in income.

Depreciated property is usually not a suitable subject for distribution as a property dividend. Note what has happened in Example 12. The loss of $2,000 (adjusted basis $5,000, fair market value $3,000), in effect, disappears. If, instead, the lot had first been sold and the $3,000 proceeds distributed, the loss would have been preserved for X Corporation.

## CONSTRUCTIVE DIVIDENDS

A distribution by a corporation to its shareholders can be treated as a dividend for Federal income tax purposes even though it is not formally declared or designated as a dividend or issued pro rata to all shareholders. Nor must the distribution satisfy the legal requirements of a dividend as set forth by applicable state law. The key factor determining dividend status is a measurable economic benefit conveyed to the shareholder. This benefit, often described as a constructive dividend, is distinguishable from actual corporate distributions of cash and property in form only.[13]

Constructive dividend situations usually arise in the context of the closely-held corporation. Here, the dealings between the parties are less structured, and frequently, formalities are not preserved. The constructive dividend serves as a substitute for actual distributions and is intended to accomplish some tax objective not available through the use of direct dividends. The shareholders may attempt to bail out corporate profits in a form deductible to the corporation (see, for example, items 6 through 8 following). Recall that dividend distributions do not provide the distributing corporation with an income tax deduction, although they do reduce E & P. Alternatively, the shareholders may be seeking benefits for themselves while avoiding the recognition of income (see, for example, items 1 through 5). Constructive dividends are, in reality, disguised dividends.

Do not conclude, however, that all constructive dividends are deliberate attempts to avoid actual and formal dividends. Often, constructive dividends are inadvertent, and consequently, a dividend result may come as a surprise to the parties (see, for example, item 1). For this reason, if none other, an awareness of the various constructive dividend situations is essential to protect the parties from unanticipated tax consequences. The types of constructive dividends most frequently encountered are summarized:

---

**13.** The term "constructive dividend" also was used in connection with corporations that have elected Subchapter S. Here a constructive dividend was the passthrough to the shareholders of the corporation's undistributed taxable income (UTI).

1. Personal use by a shareholder of corporate-owned property (e. g., company-owned automobiles, airplanes, yachts, fishing camps, hunting lodges). The measure of dividend income to the shareholder would be the fair rental value of the property for the period of its personal use.[14]

2. A bargain sale of corporate property to the shareholders. The measure of the constructive dividend is the difference between amounts paid for the property and its fair market value on the date of sale. Such questionable situations might be avoided by appraising the property on or about the date of sale. The appraised value becomes the price to be paid by the shareholders.

3. A bargain rental of corporate property to its shareholders. The measure of the constructive dividend would be the excess of the property's fair rental value over the rent actually paid. As in item 2, the importance of appraisal data to avoid any questionable situations should be readily apparent.

4. The satisfaction by the corporation of a shareholder's personal obligation to a third party. The obligation involved need not be legally binding on the shareholder but may, in fact, be a moral obligation. Forgiveness by the corporation of shareholder indebtedness can create an identical problem.

5. Advances by a corporation to a shareholder that are not bona fide (i. e., real) loans. Whether an advance qualifies as a bona fide loan is a question of fact to be determined in light of the particular circumstances. Factors to be considered include whether the advance is on open account or is evidenced by a written instrument; whether interest is provided for and the rate of such interest; whether the shareholder furnished collateral or other security for the advance; how long the advance has been outstanding; whether any payments have been made; excluding dividend sources, the shareholder's financial capability to repay the advance; the use made of the funds by the shareholder (e. g., to pay routine bills versus nonrecurring, extraordinary expenses); the regularity of such advances; and the dividend-paying history of the corporation.

6. Interest and principal payments made by a corporation where debt is reclassified as equity (refer to Chapter 12).

7. Excessive rentals paid by a corporation for the use of shareholder property.

---

14. This result presumes the ownership of the property to be in the corporation. If not, and the ownership can be attributed to the shareholder, the measure of the constructive dividend would be the cost of the property. In this regard, bare legal title at the corporate level may not suffice.

8.  Compensation paid to shareholder-employees that is deemed unreasonable.

As noted in item 8, excessive salary payments to shareholder-employees are usually termed "unreasonable compensation." The excess over reasonable compensation is frequently deemed a constructive dividend and, therefore, is not deductible by the corporation. In determining the reasonableness of salary payments, factors to be considered are the employee's qualifications; a comparison of salaries with dividend distributions; the prevailing rates of compensation for comparable positions in comparable business concerns; the nature and scope of the employee's work; the size and complexity of the business; a comparison of salaries paid to both gross and net income; the salary policy of the taxpayer with respect to all employees; and, in the case of a small corporation with a limited number of officers, the amount of compensation paid the particular employee in previous years.

Constructive distributions possess the same tax attributes as actual distributions. Thus, an individual shareholder would be entitled to the exclusion provided by § 116 and a corporate shareholder to the dividends received deduction of § 243. The constructive distribution would be a taxable dividend only to the extent of the corporation's current and accumulated E & P. As usual, the task of proving that the distribution constitutes a return of capital because of inadequate E & P rests with the taxpayer.

## CONSEQUENCES TO THE CORPORATION OF A PROPERTY DIVIDEND

A property distribution by a corporation to its shareholders poses two questions. Does the distribution result in recognized gain to the corporation making the distribution? What effect will the distribution have on the corporation's E & P? The answers to these questions are discussed below.

*Tax Effect on the Distributing Corporation.* As a general rule, no gain or loss is recognized to a corporation when it distributes appreciated or depreciated property as a dividend to its shareholders.[15] Sections 311(b) and (c), 453B, 1245(a), 1250(a), and 1252(a) provide exceptions to this general rule. A review of these exceptions follows.

1.  *LIFO Property.* Under § 311(b), a corporation distributing inventory determined under the LIFO method must recognize gain to the extent the cost of such goods arrived at under the FIFO method exceeds the cost of the goods using the LIFO method. Absent this provision, a corporation could avoid paying tax on low-basis inventory kept under the LIFO inventory method.

---

**15.**  § 311(a).

**Example 13.** Z Corporation distributes 100 units of product A to its shareholders. Product A is inventoried under the LIFO method and carries a cost basis of $1,300. Had the inventory been determined under the FIFO method, cost basis would have been $2,400. Z Corporation must recognize gain of $1,100 (i. e., $2,400 − $1,300) on the distribution.

**Example 14.** Suppose the inventory distributed in Example 13 possessed a fair market value of $4,000. Though Z Corporation still must recognize $1,100 as a gain, its E & P account is increased by $2,700 (i. e., $4,000 − $1,300) and decreased by $4,000 [see § 312(b)]. (Note: This assumes adequate E & P to cover the full reduction.)

2. *Property Subject to a Liability in Excess of Basis.* Section 311(c) requires the recognition of gain upon the distribution of property as a dividend if the property is subject to a liability which exceeds its adjusted basis. Gain is recognized to the extent of this excess. If the shareholder does not assume the liability, the gain recognized cannot be greater than the excess of the fair market value of the property over its adjusted basis.

**Example 15.** X Corporation distributes to its shareholders land with a basis of $10,000. The land has a fair market value of $30,000 and is subject to a liability of $15,000. X Corporation has a gain of $5,000 on the distribution. If the fair market value of the land is only $13,000, the gain recognized would be limited to $3,000.

3. *Installment Obligations.* When a corporation distributes an installment obligation to its shareholders, gain is recognized to the distributing corporation under § 453B in an amount equal to the difference between the basis of the obligation and its fair market value on the date of distribution. The basis of an installment obligation is its face amount less the portion of the obligation which would be income if satisfied in full.

**Example 16.** R Corporation has installment notes with a face amount of $20,000 from the sale of property on the installment method (gross profit percentage being 40%). The corporation distributes the notes as a dividend when their fair market value is $19,000. R Corporation must report gain in the amount of $7,000 computed as follows:

| | | |
|---|---:|---:|
| Fair market value of notes | | $ 19,000 |
| Face amount of notes | $ 20,000 | |
| Amount of income to be reported if the notes were satisfied in full (i.e., 40% × $20,000) | 8,000 | |
| Basis of notes | | 12,000 |
| Gain recognized on distribution | | $   7,000 |

4. *Depreciable Property.* If depreciable property is distributed by a corporation to its shareholders, the distributing corporation must recognize gain to the extent of depreciation recapture under § § 1245 and 1250. Further, the distribution of farm property may cause the distributing corporation to recognize gain pursuant to § 1252.

> **Example 17.** V Corporation distributes to its shareholders depreciable real estate with an adjusted basis of $60,000 and a fair market value of $80,000. If the property had been sold by the corporation, gain of $20,000 would have resulted, $15,000 of which would have been recaptured under § 1250 as ordinary income. V Corporation recognizes $15,000 of ordinary income on the distribution of the depreciable property.

There is recapture if property on which an investment credit has been taken is subsequently distributed as a dividend before the useful life chosen for investment tax credit purposes has expired.[16]

> **Example 18.** On January 10, 1985, W Corporation distributes to its sole shareholder machinery (basis of $6,000 and fair market value of $5,000). The property was acquired four years ago (i. e., in 1981) at a cost of $12,000. In the year of acquisition, the corporation claimed an investment tax credit of $1,200 (i. e., 10% × $12,000) based on a clear life of five years. Code § 47 will require W Corporation to recapture $240 of the credit previously taken as additional tax liability.[17] Section 1245 is not applicable in this case because recapture of depreciation occurs only if there is a realized *gain* on the disposition of the property.

*Effect of Corporate Distributions on E & P.* In the event of a corporate distribution, the E & P account is reduced by the amount of money distributed or by the adjusted basis of property distributed less the amount of any liability to which the property distributed was subject or which the shareholder assumed with respect to the property distribution.[18]

If appreciated inventory is distributed to a shareholder, the E & P account is increased by the excess of the fair market value of the inventory over its adjusted basis and is decreased by the lesser of (a) the fair market value of the inventory assets or (b) the E & P of the corporation. The term "inventory" includes unrealized receivables.

---

**16.** § 47(a)(1).

**17.** Property with a five-year recovery period under ACRS is allowed a 10% investment tax credit. However, the credit is recaptured in the amount of 20% for each year held less than the five years. Here, because the asset was held for four years, the recapture is only 20%, or $240. Each full year as asset is held before disposition reduces recapture by 2%. Consequently, for an asset held four years, the correct investment tax credit should have been only 8%.

**18.** § § 312(a) and (c).

**Example 19.** M Corporation distributes property (not inventory) to its sole shareholder, T (an individual). The property had a fair market value of $20,000 and an adjusted basis of $15,000. M Corporation's E & P ($50,000 prior to the distribution) is reduced by $15,000, even though T must report dividend income of $20,000 (as discussed above).

**Example 20.** Assume the same facts as in Example 19 with these exceptions: The fair market value of the property is $15,000 and its adjusted basis in the hands of M Corporation is $20,000. The E & P account will be reduced by $20,000, and T must report dividend income of $15,000.

**Example 21.** Assume the same facts as in Example 19 with this addition: The property is subject to a liability of $5,000. E & P would now be reduced by $10,000 [$15,000 (adjusted basis) − $5,000 (mortgage)].

**Example 22.** Assume that the property distributed by M Corporation to T, as in Example 19, is inventory with a fair market value of $20,000 and an adjusted basis of $15,000. Upon its distribution, the E & P of M Corporation would be decreased by $15,000 (increased $5,000 by the excess of fair market value over adjusted basis and decreased $20,000 by the lesser of fair market value or E & P).

Under no circumstances may a distribution, whether cash or property, either generate or add to a deficit in E & P. Deficits can arise only through corporate losses.

## STOCK DIVIDENDS AND STOCK RIGHTS    *Skip*

*Stock Dividends—§ 305.* Because there is no change in a shareholder's proportionate interest in a corporation upon receipt of a stock dividend, these distributions were initially accorded tax-free treatment.

The current provisions of § 305 are based on the proportionate interest concept. Holders of convertible securities are considered shareholders; consequently, payment of interest on convertible debentures will cause stock dividends paid on common stock to be taxable unless an adjustment is made on the conversion ratio or conversion price to reflect the stock dividend.[19]

Stock dividends are not taxable if they are pro rata distributions of stock, or stock rights, on common stock. Section 305(b) contains five exceptions to the general rule that stock dividends are nontaxable. These exceptions deal with various disproportionate distribution situ-

---

**19.** See Reg. § 1.305–3(d) for illustrations on how to compute required adjustments on conversion ratios or prices.

ations. If stock dividends are not taxable, there is no reduction in the corporation's E & P.[20] If the stock dividends are taxable, the distribution is treated by the distributing corporation in the same manner as any other taxable property dividend.

If stock dividends are taxable, basis to the shareholder-distributee is fair market value and the holding period starts on the date of receipt. If a stock dividend is not taxable, § 307 requires that the basis of the stock on which the dividend is distributed be reallocated. If the dividend shares are identical to these formerly held shares, basis in the old stock is reallocated by dividing the taxpayer's cost in the old stock by the total number of shares. If the dividend stock is not identical to the underlying shares (a stock dividend of preferred on common, for example), basis is determined by allocating cost of the formerly held shares between the old and new stock according to the fair market value of each. Holding period will include the holding period of the formerly held stock.[21]

> **Example 23.** A, an individual, bought 1,000 shares of stock two years ago for $10,000. In the current tax year, A received 10 shares of common stock as a nontaxable stock dividend. A's basis of $10,000 would be divided by 1,010; consequently, each share of stock would have a basis of $9.90 instead of the pre-dividend $10 basis.

> **Example 24.** Assume A received, instead, a nontaxable preferred stock dividend of 100 shares. The preferred stock has a fair market value of $1,000, and the common stock, on which the preferred is distributed, has a fair market value of $19,000. After the receipt of the stock dividend, the basis of the common stock is $9,500, and the basis of the preferred is $500, computed as follows:

| | | |
|---|---|---|
| Fair market value of common | | $19,000 |
| Fair market value of preferred | | 1,000 |
| | | $20,000 |
| Basis of common: 19/20 × $10,000 | = | $ 9,500 |
| Basis of preferred: 1/20 × $10,000 | = | $   500 |

*Stock Rights.*  The rules for determining taxability of stock rights are identical to those determining taxability of stock dividends. If the rights are taxable, the recipient has income to the extent of the fair market value of the rights. The fair market value then becomes the shareholder-distributee's basis in the rights.[22] If the rights are

---

**20.**  § 312(d)(1).
**21.**  § 1223(5).
**22.**  Reg. § 1.305–1(b).

exercised, the holding period for the new stock is the date the rights (whether taxable or nontaxable) are exercised. The basis of the new stock is the basis of the rights plus the amount of any other consideration given.

If stock rights are not taxable and the value of the rights is less than 15 percent of the value of the old stock, the basis of the rights is zero unless the shareholder elects to have some of the basis in the formerly held stock allocated to the rights.[23] If the fair market value of the rights is 15 percent of the value of the old stock and the rights are exercised or sold, the shareholder must allocate some of the basis in the formerly held stock to the rights. When the value is less than 15 percent of the value of the stock and the shareholder makes an election to allocate basis to the rights, such an election is made in the form of a statement attached to the shareholder's return for the year in which the rights are received.

> **Example 25.** A corporation with common stock outstanding declares a nontaxable dividend payable in rights to subscribe to common stock. Each right entitles the holder to purchase one share of stock for $90. One right is issued for every two shares of stock owned. T owns 400 shares of stock purchased two years ago for $15,000. At the time of the distribution of the rights, the market value of the common stock is $100 per share and the market value of the rights is $8 per right. T receives 200 rights. He exercises 100 rights and sells the remaining 100 rights three months later for $9 per right. T need not allocate the cost of the original stock to the rights, because the value of the rights is less than 15% of the value of the stock ($1,600 ÷ $40,000 = 4%).
>
> If T does not allocate his original stock basis to the rights, his basis in the new stock will be $9,000 ($90 × 100). Sale of the rights would produce long-term capital gain of $900 ($9 × 100). The holding period of the rights starts with the date the original 400 shares of stock were acquired. The holding period of the new stock begins on the date it was purchased.
>
> If T elects to allocate basis to the rights, his basis in the rights would be $577, computed as follows: $1,600 (value of rights) ÷ $41,600 (value of rights and stock) × $15,000 = $577. His basis in the stock would be $14,423 [(40,000 ÷ 41,600) × $15,000 = $14,423]. When he exercises the rights, his basis in the new stock would be $9,288.50 [$9,000 (cost) + $288.50 (basis in 100 rights)]. Sale of the rights would produce a long-term capital gain of $611.50 [$900 (selling price) − $288.50 (basis in the remaining 100 rights)].

---

**23.** § 307(b)(1).

*skip*                          STOCK REDEMPTIONS—
                                   EXCHANGE TREATMENT

To have a long-term capital gain, a capital asset held for more than 12 months must be sold or *exchanged* for consideration in excess of basis. Section 317 defines a stock redemption as an *exchange* between a corporation and its shareholder of that corporation's stock for property. Putting these two rules together, therefore, provides a shareholder with an opportunity to obtain favorable long-term capital gain treatment from a corporate distribution. The problem, however, comes with structuring the distribution so that it qualifies under one of the types of stock redemptions stipulated in the Code as being entitled to *exchange* treatment. Failure to qualify means the distribution will be treated as a dividend with ordinary income consequences. In this regard, it does not matter whether the parties intended a stock redemption to take place or whether the transfer is considered a stock redemption under applicable state law.

## HISTORICAL BACKGROUND AND OVERVIEW

Before the 1954 Code, stock redemptions which constituted ordinary taxable dividends were distinguished from those qualifying for capital gain treatment by the so-called dividend equivalency rule. When a redemption was essentially equivalent to a dividend, it would not qualify as a stock redemption; the entire amount received by the shareholder would be subject to taxation as ordinary income to the extent of the corporation's E & P.

> **Example 26.**  A, an individual, owns 100% of the stock of X Corporation. X Corporation has E & P of $50,000. A sells one-half of his shares to the corporation for $50,000. His basis in one-half of the stock is $10,000, and he has held the stock for five years. If the sale of the stock to X Corporation qualified as a stock redemption, A would have a long-term capital gain of $40,000. However, such a distribution is essentially equivalent to a dividend. A's percentage of ownership of the corporation has not changed. Consequently, he is deemed to have received a taxable dividend of $50,000.

Under the 1954 Code, the following major types of stock redemptions qualify for exchange treatment and will, as a result, avoid dividend income consequences:

—Distributions not essentially equivalent to a dividend [§ 302(b)(1)].

—Distributions substantially disproportionate in terms of shareholder effect [§ 302(b)(2)].

—Distributions in complete termination of a shareholder's interest [§ 302(b)(3)].

—Distributions to pay a shareholder's death taxes [§ 303].

## STOCK ATTRIBUTION RULES

In order to deter the use of certain qualifying stock redemptions as a means of achieving capital gains in related-party situations, § 318 imposes constructive ownership of stock (i. e., stock attribution) rules. In testing for a stock redemption, therefore, a shareholder may have to take into account the stock owned by others if they fall within the definition of related parties. Related parties include immediate family, specifically, spouses, children, grandchildren, and parents. Attribution also takes place *from* and *to* partnerships, estates, trusts, and corporations (50 percent or more ownership required in the case of corporations).

> **Example 27.**  T, an individual, owns 30% of the stock in X Corporation, the other 70% being held by her children. For purposes of § 318, T is treated as owning 100% of the stock in X Corporation. She owns 30% directly and, because of the family attribution rules, 70% indirectly.

> **Example 28.**  C, an individual, owns 50% of the stock in Y Corporation. The other 50% is owned by a partnership in which C has a 20% interest. C is deemed to own 60% of Y Corporation: 50% directly and, because of the partnership interest, 10% indirectly.

The stock attribution rules of § 318 do not apply to stock redemptions to pay death taxes [§ 303]. Under certain conditions, the *family* attribution rules (refer to Example 27) do not apply to stock redemptions in complete termination of a shareholder's interest [§ 302(b)(3)].

## NOT ESSENTIALLY EQUIVALENT TO A DIVIDEND STOCK REDEMPTIONS—§ 302(b)(1)

There are few objective tests to determine when a redemption is or is not essentially equivalent to a dividend. This provision was specifically added to provide for redemptions of preferred stock.[24] Often, such stock is called in by the corporation without the shareholder's exercising any control over the redemption. Some courts interpreted § 302(b)(1) to mean a redemption would be granted capital gain treatment if there was a business purpose for the redemption and there was no tax avoidance scheme to bail out dividends at favorable tax rates. The real question was whether the stock attribution rules of

---

**24.**  See S.Rept.No.1622, 83d Cong., 2d Sess., at 44.

§ 318(a) applied to this provision. However, some courts appeared to be less concerned with the application of § 318(a) and more concerned with the presence of a business purpose for the redemption.

The question of the applicability of § 318 was presumably settled by the Supreme Court in *U. S. v. Davis.*[25] In *Davis,* taxpayer and his wife owned one-half of the common stock of a corporation. Taxpayer made an additional contribution of $25,000 for 1,000 shares of preferred stock, purchasing the preferred stock to increase the company's working capital so that it might qualify for a government loan. It was understood that the corporation would redeem the preferred stock after the loan was repaid. In the interim, taxpayer acquired the remaining common stock in the corporation and transferred it to his son and daughter. After the loan was fully repaid, the corporation redeemed taxpayer's preferred stock for $25,000. Taxpayer did not report the $25,000 on his personal income tax return, concluding it was a stock redemption under § 302 and did not exceed his stock basis. The IRS contended that the redemption was essentially equivalent to a dividend and was taxable as ordinary income under § § 301 and 316. The Court of Appeals held that the redemption was not essentially equivalent to a dividend within the meaning of § 302(b)(1), because the redemption was a final step in a course of action that had a legitimate business purpose. The Supreme Court reversed the Court of Appeals, noting that under § 318(a), taxpayer constructively owned all the stock of the corporation. The Court further stated that § 318(a) applies to § 302(b)(1); consequently, taxpayer was deemed the owner of all the common stock either directly or indirectly. The Court concluded that a sole stockholder who causes part of his or her shares to be redeemed by the corporation can never qualify the redemption for capital gain treatment under § 302(b)(1). Such a redemption is always essentially equivalent to a dividend. The Court stated that to qualify for a stock redemption under § 302(b)(1), there must be ". . . a meaningful reduction of the shareholder's proportionate interest in the corporation." Two judges dissented, stating the majority opinion ". . . effectively cancels section 302(b)(1) from the Code."

If a redemption is treated as an ordinary dividend, the shareholder's basis in the stock redeemed attaches to the remaining stock. According to the Regulations, this basis would attach to other stock held by the taxpayer (or to stock he or she owns constructively).[26]

> **Example 29.** Husband and wife each own 50 shares in X Corporation, representing 100% of the stock of X. All the stock was purchased for $50,000. Husband transfers one-half of his stock to his wife. Later, the corporation redeems his remaining one-half. Assuming the rules governing the complete termination

**25.** 70–1 USTC ¶ 9289, 25 AFTR2d 70–827, 90 S.Ct. 1041 (USSC, 1970).

**26.** Reg. § 1.302–2(c).

of a shareholder's interest under § 302(b)(3) would not apply, such a redemption would be treated as a taxable dividend. His basis in the remaining stock, $12,500, would attach to his wife's stock so that she would have a basis of $50,000 in the 75 shares she currently owns in X Corporation.

## SUBSTANTIALLY DISPROPORTIONATE REDEMPTIONS—§ 302(b)(2)

A redemption of stock qualifies for capital gain treatment under § 302(b)(2) if two conditions are met.

1.  The distribution must be substantially disproportionate. To be substantially disproportionate, the shareholder must own, after the distribution, less than 80 percent of total interest in the corporation prior to his or her redemption. For example, if a shareholder has a 60 percent ownership in a corporation, which redeems part of the stock, the redemption is substantially disproportionate only if the percentage ownership after the redemption is less than 48 percent (80% of 60%).

2.  The shareholder must own, after the distribution, less than 50 percent of the total combined voting power of all classes of stock entitled to vote.

In determining the percentage ownership of the shareholder, it must be remembered that the constructive ownership rules of § 318(a) apply.

**Example 30.**  A, B, and C, unrelated individuals, own 30 shares, 30 shares, and 40 shares, respectively, in X Corporation. X Corporation has E & P of $200,000. The corporation redeems 20 shares of C's stock for $30,000. C paid $200 a share for the stock two years ago. After the redemption, C has a 25% interest in the corporation [20 shares of a total of 80 shares (100 − 20)]. This represents less than 80% of his original ownership (40% × 80% = 32%) and less than 50% of the total voting power; consequently, the distribution qualifies as a stock redemption. C has a long-term capital gain of $26,000 [$30,000 − $4,000 (20 shares × ($200)].

**Example 31.**  Given the situation in Example 30, assume, in addition, that B and C are father and son. The redemption described previously would not qualify for capital gain treatment. C is deemed to own the stock of B so that after the redemption, he would have 50 shares of a total of 80 shares, more than 50% ownership. He would also fail the 80% test. Before the redemption, C is deemed a 70% owner (40 shares owned by him and 30 shares owned by B, his son). After the redemption, he is deemed a 62.5% owner (20 shares owned directly by him and 30 shares owned by B from a total of 80 shares). C has a taxable dividend of $30,000.

## COMPLETE TERMINATION OF A SHAREHOLDER'S INTEREST REDEMPTIONS—§ 302(b)(3)

If a shareholder terminates his or her entire stock ownership in a corporation through a stock redemption, the redemption will qualify for capital gain treatment. Such a complete termination would obviously meet the substantially disproportionate rules of § 302(b)(2). The difference in the two provisions is that the constructive ownership rules of § 318(a)(1) do not apply to § 302(b)(3) if (1) the former shareholder has no interest, other than that of a creditor, in the corporation after the redemption (including an interest as an officer, director, or employee) for at least 10 years, and (2) the former shareholder files an agreement to notify the IRS of any acquisition within the 10-year period and to retain all necessary records pertaining to the redemption during this time period. A shareholder can reacquire an interest in the corporation by bequest or inheritance, but in no other manner.

The required agreement should be in the form of a separate statement signed by the shareholder and attached to the return for the year in which the redemption occurred. The agreement should recite that the shareholder agrees to notify the appropriate District Director within 30 days of a reacquisition of an interest in the corporation occurring within 10 years from the redemption.

## REDEMPTIONS TO PAY DEATH TAXES—§ 303

Section 303 provides an executor the opportunity to redeem stock in a closely-held corporation at capital gain rates when the stock represents a substantial amount of the gross estate of the shareholder-decedent. The redemption is effected to provide the estate with liquidity. Stock in a closely-held corporation is generally not readily marketable; however, it could be redeemed if § 302 would not cause ordinary dividend treatment. Section 303, to an extent, alleviates this problem.

Section 303 is, in effect, an exception to § 302(b). If a stock redemption qualifies under § 303, the rules of § 302(b) do not apply. The redemption will qualify for capital gain treatment regardless of whether it is substantially disproportionate or not essentially equivalent to a dividend. Section 303 applies when a distribution is made with respect to stock of a corporation, the value of which stock, in the gross estate of a decedent, is in excess of 35 percent of the value of the adjusted gross estate of the decedent. In determining the 35 percent requirement, stock of two or more corporations is treated as the stock of a single corporation if more than 20 percent in value of the outstanding stock of each corporation is included in the decedent's gross estate.

**Example 32.** The adjusted gross estate of a decedent is $300,000. The gross estate includes stock in X and Y Corporations valued at $100,000 and $80,000, respectively. Unless the two corporations can be treated as a single corporation, § 303 will not apply to a redemption of the stock. Assume the decedent owned all the stock of X Corporation and 80% of the stock of Y. Section 303 would then apply because more than 20% of the value of the outstanding stock of both corporations would be included in the decedent's estate. The 35% test would be met when the stock is treated as that of a single corporation.

Section 303 could provide a double benefit. If the stock has appreciated in value, such appreciation would not be taxed because the value of the stock on the date of death (or the alternate valuation date when elected) becomes the income tax basis to the estate or heirs.

Section 303 could apply to the heirs of the decedent as well as to the decedent's executor or administrator. For example, if stock is given by a decedent within three years of death and is included in the gross estate (see Chapter 18), § 303 might be applicable to a redemption of such stock if its percentage requirements are met.

Section 303 applies only to the extent of the sum of the estate, inheritance, legacy, and succession taxes imposed by reason of the decedent's death and to the extent of the amount of funeral and administration expenses allowable as deductions to the estate. Prior to the Tax Reform Act of 1976, there was no requirement that the estate have a liquidity problem or that the proceeds of the redemption be used specifically to pay these taxes and expenses. However, for persons dying after December 31, 1976, stock that can qualify for capital gain treatment must be redeemed from a shareholder whose interest in the estate is reduced by the payment of these taxes and expenses.

## EFFECT ON THE CORPORATION REDEEMING ITS STOCK

Having considered the different types of stock redemptions that will receive exchange treatment and result in capital gain or loss to the shareholder, what is the tax effect to the corporation redeeming its stock? If the corporation uses property to carry out the redemption, there exists the possibility that it might have to recognize gain on the distribution. Furthermore, one needs to determine what effect, if any, the redemption will have on the corporation's E & P. These matters are discussed below in the following paragraphs.

*Recognition of Gain to the Corporation.*   Generally, as noted above, no gain or loss is recognized to the corporation upon the distribution of property to its shareholders. Section 311 provides exceptions with respect to LIFO inventory property and property subject to a liability in excess of its basis. The recapture rules of §§ 1245, 1250, and 1252 and the assignment of income doctrine provide further exceptions. With respect to a stock redemption using appreciated property (other than a corporate obligation), § 311(d) provides that the distributing corporation recognize gain to the extent of the appreciation. This provision applies even if the distribution does not qualify a shareholder for capital gain treatment.

> **Example 33.**  R Corporation uses land (basis of $10,000 and fair market value of $30,000) to redeem some of the stock of a shareholder that is worth $30,000. R Corporation must recognize a gain of $20,000 as a result of the redemption. This is true even though the shareholder may have dividend income of $30,000 because the requirements of § 302 are not met.

There are exceptions to § 311(d). One notable exception is that § 311(d) does not apply to distributions in redemption of stock to pay death taxes [§ 303].

*Effect on Earnings and Profits.*  The E & P account of a corporation is reduced as a result of a stock redemption except for the part of the distribution chargeable to the capital account.[27] In an early case, *Helvering v. Jarvis,* the Fourth Court of Appeals established the rule that the amount chargeable to the capital account is figured by multiplying the balance in the capital account by the ratio between the redeemed shares and the total shares outstanding before redemption.[28]

> **Example 34.**  X Corporation has 100 shares of stock outstanding. It redeems 30 shares for $100,000 at a time when it has paid-in capital of $120,000 and E & P of $150,000. The charge to capital would be 30% of the amount in the paid-in capital account ($36,000), and the remainder of the redemption price ($64,000) would be a reduction of E & P.

## OTHER CORPORATE DISTRIBUTIONS

Partial liquidations of a corporation, if in compliance with the statutory requirements of § 302(e), will result in exchange treatment to the shareholders. Distributions of stock and securities of a controlled corporation to the shareholders of the parent corporation will be free of any ta . consequences if they fall under § 355. Both of these types of corporate distributions possess similarities to stock redemptions and dividend distributions but are not discussed because of their limited applicability.

## SUMMARY OF TAX CONSEQUENCES OF CORPORATE DISTRIBUTIONS

1.  Without a special provision, corporate distributions are taxed as dividend income to the recipient shareholder to the extent of his or her share of the distributing corporation's E & P accumulated since

---

27.  § 312(e) and Reg. § 1.312–5.
28.  41–2 USTC ¶ 9752, 28 AFTR 404, 123 F.2d 742 (CA–4, 1941).

February 28, 1913, or to the extent of a pro rata share of current E & P. Any excess is treated as a return of capital to the extent of the shareholder's basis in the stock and, therefore, as capital gain. (See § § 301 and 316.)

2.  With regard to noncorporate shareholders, property distributions are considered dividends (taxed as noted in item 1 above) in the amount of their fair market value. Corporate shareholders are taxed on the lesser of (a) the fair market value or (b) the adjusted basis of such property in the hands of the distributing corporation increased by the amount of any gain recognized to the distributing corporation. The amount deemed distributed is reduced by any liabilities to which the property distributed is subject immediately before and immediately after the distribution and any liability of the corporation assumed by the shareholder in connection with the distribution. The shareholder's basis in such property is, for noncorporate shareholders, the fair market value and, for corporate shareholders, the lesser of (a) the fair market value or (b) the adjusted basis of such property in the hands of the distributing corporation increased by any gain recognized to the distributing corporation.

3.  Earnings and profits of a corporation are increased by corporate earnings for the taxable year computed in the same manner as the corporation computes its taxable income. The account is increased for all items of income, whether taxed or not, and reduced by all items of expense, whether deductible or not. The E & P account is reduced by the amount of any money distributed or by the adjusted basis of property distributed less the amount of any liability to which property distributed was subject or which the shareholder assumed with respect to a property distribution. Earnings and profits can be reduced only by cost depletion and, for tax years beginning after June 30, 1972, by depreciation computed in no greater amount than that using the straight-line method (or a comparable method which charges depreciation proportionately over the life of the asset). Under the accelerated cost recovery system, special periods are provided for determining the effect on E & P. To preclude significant diminution of the E & P account (and thereby facilitate return of capital distributions), these periods are notably longer than the ACRS class life. If appreciated inventory is distributed to a shareholder, the E & P account is increased by the amount of the excess of the value of the inventory property over its adjusted basis and is decreased by the lesser of (a) the fair market value of the inventory assets or (b) the E & P. (See § 312.)

4.  A corporation is not taxed on corporate distributions unless (a) it distributes LIFO inventory which would have a higher cost if valued under the FIFO method, (b) property distributed is subject to a mortgage in excess of its tax basis to the distributing corporation, (c) an installment obligation is distributed, (d) depreciable property which is subject to depreciation recapture rules under § § 1245 and 1250 is distributed, or (e) farm property subject to recapture under

§1252 is distributed. (See § 311.) There is also a recapture of investment credit on property subject to such credit which is distributed before its useful life—determined for the purpose of claiming an investment credit—has expired.

5.   As a general rule, stock dividends or stock rights (representing stock in the distributing corporation) are not taxed. There are five exceptions: (a) distributions which are payable either in stock or property; (b) distributions which have the result of the receipt of property by some shareholders and an increase in the proportionate interest of other shareholders in the assets or E & P of the distributing corporation; (c) distributions which result in the receipt of preferred stock by some common shareholders and the receipt of common stock by other shareholders; (d) distributions on preferred stock other than an increase in the conversion ratio of convertible preferred stock made solely to take account of a stock dividend or stock split with respect to stock into which the preferred is convertible; and (e) distributions of convertible preferred stock, unless it can be shown that the distribution will not result in a disproportionate distribution. Changes in conversion ratios, changes in redemption prices, and differences between issue price and redemption price are taxable dividends. (See § 305.)

6.   Stock redemptions which qualify under § 302(b) are given capital gain treatment. Section 302(b) requires that such distributions either be substantially disproportionate or not be essentially equivalent to a dividend. In making such determination, the rules in § 318(a) determining the constructive ownership of stock apply, unless the shareholder redeems all his or her interest in the corporation and does not reacquire (other than by bequest or inheritance) any interest (except as a creditor) for 10 years after the redemption.

7.   If stock included in a decedent's estate represents at least 35 percent of the adjusted taxable estate, it may upon redemption qualify for capital gain treatment separate and apart from § 302(b). Section 303 provides automatic capital gain treatment on the redemption of such stock.

8.   A corporation is taxed on the appreciation of property distributed in *redemption* of its stock with certain limited exceptions noted in § 311(d).

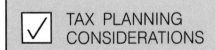

## CORPORATE DISTRIBUTIONS

In connection with the preceding discussion of corporate distributions, the following points might well need reinforcement:

—Because E & P is the measure of dividend income, its periodic determination is essential to corporate planning. Thus, an E & P account should be established and maintained, particularly if there exists the possibility that a corporate distribution might represent a return of capital.

—Accumulated E & P is the sum of all past years' current E & P. There exists no statute of limitations on the computation of E & P. The IRS could, for example, redetermine a corporation's current E & P for a tax year long since passed. Such a change would obviously affect accumulated E & P and would have a direct impact on the taxability of current distributions to shareholders.

—Taxpayers should be aware that manipulating distributions to avoid or minimize dividend exposure is possible.

> **Example 35.**  Q Corporation has accumulated E & P of $100,000 as of January 1, 19X5. During 19X5, it expects to have earnings from operations of $80,000 and to make a cash distribution of $60,000. Q Corporation also expects to sell a particular asset for a loss of $100,000. Thus, it anticipates incurring a deficit of $20,000 for the year. The best approach would be to recognize the loss as soon as possible and, immediately therefter, make the cash distribution to its shareholders. Suppose these two steps took place on January 1, 19X5. Because the current E & P for 19X5 will have a deficit, the accumulated E & P account must be brought up-to-date (refer to Example 9 in this chapter). Thus, at the time of the distribution, the combined E & P balance is zero [i. e., $100,000 (beginning balance in accumulated E & P) − $100,000 (existing deficit in current E & P)], and the $60,000 distribution to the shareholders constitutes a return of capital. (Note: Current deficits are allocated pro rata throughout the year unless the parties can prove otherwise. Here they can.)

> **Example 36.**  After several unprofitable years, Y Corporation has a deficit in accumulated E & P of $100,000 as of January 1, 19X5. Starting in 19X5, Y Corporation expects to generate annual E & P of $50,000 for the next four years and would like to distribute this amount to its shareholders. The corporation's cash position (for dividend purposes) will correspond to the current E & P generated. Compare the following possibilities:
>
> I.  On December 31 of 19X5, 19X6, 19X7, and 19X8, Y Corporation distributes a cash dividend of $50,000.
>
> II. On December 31 of 19X6 and 19X8, Y Corporation distributes a cash dividend of $100,000.

Alternative I leads to an overall result of $200,000 in dividend income, since each $50,000 distribution is fully covered by current E & P. Alternative II, however, results in only $100,000 of dividend income to the shareholders. The remaining $100,000 is a return of capital. Why? At the time Y Corporation made its first distribution of $100,000 on December 31, 19X6, it had a deficit of $50,000 in accumulated E & P (the original deficit of $100,000 is reduced by the $50,000 of current E & P from 19X5). Consequently, the $100,000 distribution yields a $50,000 dividend (the current E & P for 19X6) and $50,000 as a return of capital. As of January 1, 19X7, Y Corporation's accumulated E & P now has a deficit balance of $50,000 (a distribution cannot increase a deficit in E & P). Add in $50,000 of current E & P from 19X7, and the balance as of January 1, 19X8, is zero. Thus, the second distribution of $100,000 made on December 31, 19X8, also yields $50,000 of dividends (the current E & P for 19X8) and $50,000 as a return of capital.

## CONSTRUCTIVE DIVIDENDS

Tax planning can be particularly effective in avoiding constructive dividend situations.

—Shareholders should try to structure their dealings with the corporation on an arm's length basis. For example, reasonable rent should be paid for the use of corporate property or a fair price should be paid for its purchase. Needless to say, the parties should make every effort to support the amount involved with appraisal data or market information obtained from reliable sources at or close to the time of the transaction.

—Dealings between shareholders and a closely-held corporation should be formalized as much as possible. In the case of loans to shareholders, for example, the parties should provide for an adequate rate of interest, written evidence of the debt, and a realistic repayment schedule that is not only arranged but also followed.

—If corporate profits are to be bailed out by the shareholders in a form deductible to the corporation, a balanced mix of the different alternatives could lessen the risk of disallowance by the IRS. Rent for the use of shareholder property, interest on amounts borrowed from shareholders, or salaries for services rendered by shareholders are all feasible substitutes for dividend distributions. But overdoing any one approach may well attract the attention of the IRS. Too much interest, for example, might mean the corporation is thinly capitalized, and therefore, some of the debt really represents equity investment.

—Much can be done to protect against the disallowance of corporate deductions for compensation that is determined to be unreasonable in amount. Below is an illustration, all too common in a family corporation, of what *not* to do.

> **Example 37.** Z Corporation is wholly owned by T. Corporate employees and annual salaries include Mrs. T ($8,000), T, Jr. ($4,000), T ($50,000), and E ($20,000). The operation of Z Corporation is shared about equally between T and E (an unrelated party). Mrs. T (T's wife) performed significant services for the corporation during its formative years but now merely attends the annual meeting of the board of directors. T, Jr. (T's son) is a full-time student and occasionally signs papers for the corporation in his capacity as treasurer. Z Corporation has not distributed a dividend for 10 years, although it has accumulated substantial E & P. What is wrong with this situation?
>
> > —Mrs. T's salary seems vulnerable unless one can prove that some or all of the $8,000 annual salary is payment for services rendered to the corporation in prior years (i. e., she was underpaid for those years).[29]
> >
> > —T, Jr.'s salary is also vulnerable; he does not appear to earn the $4,000 paid to him by the corporation. True, neither T, Jr. nor Mrs. T is a shareholder, but each one's relationship to T is enough of a tie-in to raise the unreasonable compensation issue.
> >
> > —T's salary appears susceptible to challenge. Why, for instance, is he receiving $30,000 more than E when it appears each shares equally in the operation of the corporation?
> >
> > —No dividends have been distributed by Z Corporation for 10 years, although the corporation is capable of doing so.

## STOCK REDEMPTIONS

Several observations come to mind in connection with tax planning for stock redemptions.

> —The § 302(b)(1) variety (i. e., not essentially equivalent to a dividend) provides minimal utility and should be relied upon only as a last resort. Instead, the redemption should be structured to fit one of the safe harbors of either § 302(b)(2) (i. e., substantially disproportionate), § 302(b)(3) (i. e., complete termination), or § 303 (i. e., to pay death taxes).
>
> —In the case of a family corporation in which all of the share-

---

**29.** See, for example, *R. J. Nicoll Co.*, 59 T.C. 37 (1972).

holders are related to each other, the only hope of a successful redemption might lie in the use of § 302(b)(3) or § 303. But in using § 302(b)(3), be careful that the family stock attribution rules are avoided. Here, strict compliance with § 302(c)(2) (i.e., the withdrawing shareholder does not continue as an employee of the corporation, etc., and does not reacquire an interest in the corporation within 10 years) is crucial.

—The alternative to a successful stock redemption or partial liquidation is, of course, dividend treatment of the distribution under § 301. But do not conclude that a dividend is always undesirable from a tax standpoint. Suppose the distributing corporation has little, if any, E & P. Or the distributee-shareholder is another corporation. In the latter regard, dividend treatment might well be preferred due to the availability of the 85 percent dividends received deduction.

—When using the § 303 redemption, the amount to be sheltered from dividend treatment is the sum of death taxes and certain estate administration expenses. Nevertheless, a redemption in excess of the limitation will not destroy the applicability of § 303. Even better, any such excess (if properly structured) might qualify under § 302. Thus, § 302 can be used to pick up where § 303 left off.

—The timing and sequence of a redemption should be carefully handled.

> **Example 38.** P Corporation's stock is held as follows: R (60 shares), S (20 shares), and T (20 shares). R, S, and T are all individuals and are not related to each other. In early 19X1, the corporation redeems 21 of R's shares. Shortly thereafter, it redeems five of S's shares. Does R's redemption qualify as substantially disproportionate? Taken in isolation, it would appear to meet the requirements of § 302(b)(2)—the 80% and 50% tests have been satisfied. Yet, if the IRS takes into account the later redemption of S's shares, R has not satisfied the 50% test; he still owns $39/74$ of the corporation after both redemptions.[30] Some time lag between the two redemptions, therefore, would have placed R in a better position to argue against collapsing the series of redemptions into one.

## PROBLEM MATERIALS

### Discussion Questions

1. What is meant by the term "earnings and profits"?
2. Why is it important to distinguish between "current" and "accumulated" E & P?

---

30.  § 302(b)(2)(D).

3. Describe the effect of a distribution in a year when the distributing corporation has:

   (a) A deficit in accumulated E & P and a positive amount in current E & P.

   (b) A positive amount in accumulated E & P and a deficit in current E & P.

   (c) A deficit in both current and accumulated E & P.

   (d) A positive amount in both current and accumulated E & P.

4. In 19X0, a corporation determined its current E & P to be $100,000. In 19X5, it makes a distribution to its shareholders of $200,000. The IRS contends that the current E & P of the corporation for 19X0 really was $150,000. Can the IRS successfully make this contention? What difference would the additional $50,000 in E & P make? *after audit*

5. If a corporation is chartered in a state that prohibits the payment of dividends that impair "paid-in capital," is it possible for the corporation to pay a dividend that is a return of capital for tax purposes and yet comply with state law? Discuss.

6. Under what circumstances does the distributing corporation recognize income when it distributes appreciated property as a dividend to its shareholders? What if property is distributed as a stock redemption?

7. What are constructive dividends?

8. Why is it important that an advance from a corporation to a shareholder be categorized as a bona fide loan? With regard to the resolution of this issue, comment on the relevance of the following factors:

   (a) The corporation has never paid a dividend. — *it can't pay loan.*

   (b) The advance is on open account. — *If the money is paid back it is a loan*

   (c) The advance provides for 2% interest. — *bargain loan —*

   (d) No date is specified for the repayment of the advance. — *less than what is regd by a legal note*

   (e) The advance was used by the shareholder to pay personal bills. — *okay plain a bona fide loan*

   (f) The advance is repaid by the shareholder immediately after the transaction was questioned by the IRS on audit of the corporate income tax return. — *not a bona fide loan.*

9. How can shareholders bail out corporate profits in such a manner as to provide the corporation with a deduction? What are the risks involved?

10. Whether compensation paid to a corporate employee is reasonable is, of course, a question of fact to be determined from the surrounding circumstances. How would the resolution of this problem be affected by each factor set forth below?

   (a) The employee is not a shareholder but is related to the sole owner of the corporate-employer.

   (b) The employee-shareholder never completed high school.

   (c) The employee-shareholder is a full-time college student.

   (d) The employee-shareholder was underpaid for her services during the formative period of the corporate-employer.

   (e) The corporate-employer pays a nominal dividend each year.

   (f) Year-end bonuses are paid to all shareholder-employees.

11. How are nontaxable stock rights handled for tax purposes? Taxable stock rights?

12. Can a shareholder incur a loss on a stock redemption? Explain.

13. It has been said that a shareholder in a family corporation may have difficulty effectively utilizing § 302(b)(2) (i. e., substantially disproportionate) as a means of carrying out a stock redemption. Why? What other alternatives are available?

14. Under what circumstances does § 303 apply to a stock redemption? What is the tax effect of the application of § 303?

## Problems

15. M Corporation has beginning E & P of $40,000. Its current taxable income is $10,000. During the year, it distributed property worth $60,000, adjusted basis of $30,000, to one of its individual shareholders, T. T assumes a liability on the property in the amount of $10,000. The corporation had tax-exempt interest income of $2,000 and received $40,000 on a term life insurance policy on the death of a corporate officer. Premiums on the policy for the year were $1,000. What is the amount of taxable income to T? What is the amount of E & P for M Corporation after the property distribution? What is T's tax basis in the property he received? (Note: Disregard the effect of the corporate income tax.)

16. How would your answer to Problem 15 change if the property were distributed to a corporate shareholder?

17. X Corporation, with E & P of $300,000, distributes property worth $60,000, adjusted tax basis of $120,000, to Y, a corporate shareholder. The property is subject to a liability of $30,000, which Y assumes. What is the amount of dividend income to Y, and what is its basis in the property received? How does the distribution affect the X Corporation's E & P account?

18. The retained earnings account for Z Corporation on January 1, 19X5, was $60,000. In 19X4, the corporation distributed a cash dividend, charging the retained earnings account with $100,000. Assuming the E & P and retained earnings accounts for the corporation were the same figure prior to 19X4, what would E & P be on December 31, 19X5, given the following information: taxable income for 19X5 of $40,000 after deducting depreciation of $20,000 computed by using the declining-balance method (straight-line depreciation would have been $10,000), tax-exempt interest of $6,000, and dividends declared of $10,000. (Note: Ignore any income tax liability.)

19. A machine, useful life of five years under ACRS, was purchased on January 1, 19X3, for $160,000. The machine had an adjusted basis of $67,200 on January 1, 19X6, when it was sold for $140,000. What is the gain on the sale and what adjustment is made to the E & P account of the corporation?

20. W, Inc., a closely-held corporation, has lost money since its incorporation. Its E & P account shows a deficit. In 19X5, the corporation made advances in the amount of $50,000 to its principal shareholder. These advances were treated as loans on the corporate books; however, no notes were executed. Upon auditing the tax return of the shareholder, the IRS con-

tends the $50,000 is taxable income to the shareholder. Is the $50,000 taxable income?

21. B paid $60,000 three years ago for 45 shares of stock in U Corporation. In December 19X5, she received a nontaxable stock dividend of five additional shares in U Corporation. She sells the five shares in January of 19X6 for $8,000. What is her gain, and how is it taxed?

22. R Corporation declares a nontaxable dividend payable in rights to subscribe to common stock. Five rights entitles the holder to subscribe to one share of stock. One right is issued for each share of stock owned. For five rights and $50, a shareholder can purchase one share of stock. S, a shareholder, owns 600 shares of stock which she purchased two years ago for $33,000. At the date of distribution of the rights, the market value of the stock was $100, and the market value of the rights was $10 per right. S receives 600 rights. She exercises 400 of the rights and purchases 80 additional shares of stock. She sells the remaining 200 rights for $4,000. What are the tax consequences of these transactions to S?

23. V Corporation has 1,000 shares of common stock outstanding. The shares are owned as follows: H, 400 shares; I, 400 shares; and J, 200 shares. The corporation redeems 100 shares of the stock owned by J for $45,000. J paid $100 per share for her stock two years ago. The E & P of V Corporation was $100,000 on the date of redemption. What is the tax effect to J of the redemption?

24. In Problem 23, assume H is the father of J. How would this affect the tax status of the redemption? What if H were her brother instead of her father?

25. The R & D Corporation had E & P of $45,000 when it made a current distribution of inventories with a cost of $60,000 (FIFO method) and a fair market value of $105,000. Determine the shareholder's taxable income from the distribution.

26. Complete the schedule below for each case:

| | Accumulated E & P Beginning of Year | Current E & P | Cash Distributions (all on last day of year) | Amount Taxable | Return of Capital |
|---|---|---|---|---|---|
| (a) | $150,000 | $45,000 | $75,000 | $ _____ | $ _____ |
| (b) | 15,000 | 37,500 | 63,000 | _____ | _____ |
| (c) | (135,000) | 60,000 | 45,000 | _____ | _____ |
| (d) | 52,500 | (45,000) | 37,500 | _____ | _____ |

(e) Same as (d) except the distribution of $37,500 is made on June 30 and the corporation uses the calendar year for tax purposes.

    _____ _____

27. The stock of the BC Corporation is owned as follows:

| | |
|---|---|
| Mr. B, Sr. | 25% |
| Mr. C, Sr. (B's brother) | 25% |
| T Corporation (100% of the stock is owned by Mr. C, Sr.) | 10% |
| Mrs. B (B, Sr.'s wife) | 10% |
| Mr. B, Jr. | 10% |
| Mr. C, Jr. | 15% |
| Mrs. C (C, Sr.'s wife) | 5% |

What would be the effects of the following redemptions on the shareholders and the corporation? (Work each problem independently based on the above ownership.)

(a) One-half of Mrs. B's shares are redeemed for $60,000 in cash. Mrs. B's basis in the redeemed shares is $20,000.

(b) One-half of T Corporation's stock is redeemed by a distribution of land with a value of $60,000 and a basis to the corporation of $8,000. T Corporation's basis in the redeemed stock was $20,000.

(c) All of Mr. B, Sr.'s stock is redeemed for $200,000 cash. His basis in the stock was $100,000.

(d) Following Mr. C, Sr.'s death, one-half of his stock (held by his estate) was redeemed to pay death taxes. The redemption price was $180,000, his cost was $50,000, and the value of the stock on the date of his death was $140,000.

28.   On December 31, 19X5, prior to a stock redemption, the TB Corporation had accumulated E & P of $50,000 and paid-in capital from the 1,000 shares outstanding of $150,000. One-half of the stock was purchased by the corporation on that date for $75,000 cash in a redemption that was not equivalent to a dividend. In 19X6, the corporation had current E & P of $25,000 and distributed $50,000 in cash to the shareholders on December 31. How much taxable income did the shareholders realize from the $50,000 distribution?

29.   X Corporation sells property, basis of $200,000, fair market value of $180,000, to its sole shareholder for $160,000. How much loss can the corporation deduct as a result of this transaction? What is the effect on the corporation's E & P for the year of sale?

30.   X Corporation collects $150,000 on a keyman life insurance policy. The policy possessed a cash surrender value of $20,000 at date of death. What is the effect of this collection on the corporation's taxable income and on its E & P?

31.   A Corporation distributes LIFO inventory to its shareholders. Basis of the inventory is $16,000. Had the inventory cost been determined under FIFO, the basis would be $24,000. Market value of the inventory is $32,000. What is the effect of this distribution on the corporation's taxable income and on its E & P?

32.   AB Corporation distributes to its shareholders realty with a basis of $5,000 and fair market vaue of $10,000. The realty is subject to a liability of $7,500. What is the effect of this distribution on taxable income of the corporation?

33.   XY Corporation distributes, to its shareholder, equipment with a basis of $6,000 and fair market value of $7,000. The property was acquired two years ago at a cost of $8,000. In the year of acquisition, the corporation claimed an investment tax credit of $800 (10% of $8,000) based on class life of five years. What are the tax consequences to XY Corporation on this transaction?

*skip*

# Corporate Distributions in Complete Liquidation and an Overview of Corporate Reorganizations

*skip*

*Two types of liquidation*
*12 month —*
*30 days —*

When a stock redemption or a partial liquidation is transacted, the assumption usually is that the corporation will continue as a separate entity. With complete liquidations, however, corporate existence terminates. In view of the difference in the result, the tax rules governing these types of distributions are not the same. This chapter reviews the tax impact of complete liquidations on the corporation making the distributions and on the shareholders receiving such distributions.

## COMPLETE LIQUIDATIONS—AN OVERVIEW

Since the income tax provisions applicable to corporate liquidations are somewhat complex, an introductory summary will be helpful in sorting out the various applicable rules. Following the summary, distributions in liquidation are compared with those relating to stock redemptions and dividends (discussed in Chapter 13).

### SUMMARY OF THE TAX CONSEQUENCES APPLICABLE TO COMPLETE LIQUIDATIONS

*Effect on the Corporation.* Two major tax provisions govern the tax effect of a complete liquidation on the corporation being liquidated.

—Under § 336 no gain or loss is recognized to a corporation distributing assets directly to its shareholders in return for their stock. Referred to as the "in kind" type of distribution, it is distinguishable from the situation where the corporation first sells the assets, then distributes the sale proceeds to its shareholders (see below). The general rule providing for no gain or loss on in kind distributions is subject to numerous exceptions. The corporation may have to recognize gain (or make a direct addition to its tax liability) if the assets distributed consist of installment notes receivable, assets subject to the recapture of depreciation or the investment tax credit, or, as to plans of liquidation adopted after December 31, 1982, LIFO inventory. Further exceptions include the possible application of the tax benefit rule.

—Under § 337, no gain or loss is recognized to a corporation that sells property and, within a 12-month period, distributes all of its assets in complete liquidation. Known as the 12-month liquidation, it covers only the sale of property. As defined in § 337(b), "property" generally does not include installment notes receivable, accounts receivable, and inventory. The same exceptions relating to distributions in kind under § 336 (i. e.; recapture of depreciation, etc.), apply to the 12-month liquidation. In these cases, the sale of property is not protected from the recognition of gain (or a direct addition to tax liability).

Sections 336 and 337 can apply to the same liquidation. Consequently, distributions in kind would be covered by § 336, while sales by the corporation could fall under the 12-month liquidation of § 337. However, § 337 is not available for the liquidation of a collapsible corporation (see below), the one-month liquidation of § 333 (see below), and for most liquidations of a subsidiary corporation under § 332 (see below).

*Effect on the Shareholder.* The tax treatment of a shareholder receiving a distribution in complete liquidation is subject to a general rule and three exceptions.

—The *general rule* of § 331 applies exchange treatment to the shareholder. Gain or loss will be recognized measured by the difference between the fair market value of the assets received from the corporation and the adjusted basis of the stock surrendered. When the stock is a capital asset, any gain or loss will be capital. The shareholder's basis in the assets received from the corporation will be their fair market value on the date of distribution [§ 334(a)]. The general rule of § 331, therefore, follows the same approach taken with stock redemptions that qualify for exchange treatment (refer to Chapter 13).

—Section 341 converts any long-term capital gain the shareholder might otherwise have under the general rule into ordinary income if the corporation being liquidated is collapsible.

—Section 333 (known as the one-month liquidation) limits the shareholder's recognized gain to the greater of the proportionate share of the corporation's E & P or its cash *and* securities acquired since 1953. In no event, however, can more gain be recognized than is realized. A noncorporate shareholder must classify such gain as dividend income to the extent of a ratable share of E & P. Any excess recognized gain (where the corporation's cash plus post-1953 securities exceed its E & P) is capital gain. All of a corporate shareholder's gain will be capital. The basis of property received pursuant to a § 333 liquidation will be the basis of the stock given up less the cash received plus the gain recognized by the shareholder [§ 334(c)]. The one-month liquidation is optional with the shareholders. If elected, the tax consequences described replace those applicable under the general rule of § 331.

—Section 332, however, is not elective. When a parent corporation liquidates its subsidiary corporation, no gain or loss is recognized to the parent. This provision applies only where the parent owns 80 percent or more of the stock of the subsidiary. The basis to the parent of the assets received from the subsidiary depends on whether the general rule of § 334(b)(1) or the exception of § 338 applies. In the case of the general rule, the parent will take as its basis the same basis the assets had in the hands of the subsidiary. The exception (known as the *Kimbell-Diamond* rule, or the single transaction approach) treats the parent, in effect, as having purchased the assets when it purchased the subsidiary's stock. Therefore, the cost of the stock to the parent becomes its basis in the subsidiary's assets received in liquidation.

*Comparative Illustrations.* The examples appearing below compare the tax effect of the different types of liquidations.

**Example 1.** X Corporation has as its only asset unimproved land (adjusted basis of $100,000 and fair market value of $150,000). T, an individual, owns all of the outstanding stock in X Corporation, such stock having an adjusted basis of $80,000. X Corporation distributes the land to T in complete cancellation of all its outstanding stock. At the time of its liquidation, X Corporation's E & P is $30,000.

*Effect on the Corporation.* No gain is recognized by X Corporation, since the land is distributed in kind to T (§ 336). The same result materializes if the corporation sells the land and distributes the proceeds and the requirements of the 12-month liquidation (§ 337) are satisfied.

*Effect on the Shareholder.* Pursuant to the general rule of § 331, T must recognize a gain of $70,000 [$150,000 (fair market value of the land) − $80,000 (adjusted basis of the stock)]. If the stock is a capital asset, the gain would be capital. T's basis in the land becomes $150,000, its fair market value on the date of the distribution [§ 334(a)].

**Example 2.** Assume the same facts as in Example 1 except that T elects to have the one-month liquidation of § 333 apply.

*Effect on the Corporation.* No gain is recognized by X Corporation, since the land is distributed in kind to T (§ 336). Because the 12-month liquidation of § 337 is not available for the one-month liquidation of § 333, a sale of the land by the corporation would yield a recognizable gain of $50,000 [$150,000 (sale proceeds) − $100,000 (adjusted basis of the land).[1]

*Effect on the Shareholder.* Under § 333, T must recognize dividend income of $30,000, the greater of the corporation's E & P ($30,000) or its cash ($0) plus post-1953 securities ($0). By the application of § 334(c), T's basis in the land becomes $110,000 [$80,000 (adjusted basis in the stock) − $0 (cash received) + $30,000 (gain recognized)].

**Example 3.** Assume the same facts as in Example 1 except that T is a corporation rather than an individual. Since T Corporation now is a parent and X Corporation is a subsidiary, the liquidation of X Corporation must fall under § 332.

*Effect on the Corporation.* No gain is recognized by X Corporation, since the land is distributed in kind to T Corporation (§ 336). Because the 12-month liquidation of § 337 generally is not available for the parent-subsidiary type of liquidation of § 332, a sale of the land by X Corporation would yield a recognizable gain of $50,000.

*Effect on the Shareholder.* In the liquidation of a subsidiary by a parent, no gain or loss is recognized by the parent corporation (§ 332). T Corporation's basis in the land it receives depends on whether the general rule of § 334(b)(1) or the exception of § 338 applies. Under the general rule, T Corporation's basis becomes $100,000—the subsidiary's basis in the land carried over to the parent corporation. If the single transaction exception of § 338 applies, the basis becomes $80,000—the parent's basis in the subsidiary's stock carries over to the land.

---

**1.** The gain of $50,000 less the corporate income tax it generates would be added to X Corporation's E & P (refer to Chapter 13). Under § 333, this forces T to recognize additional dividend income on the liquidation.

## LIQUIDATIONS, STOCK REDEMPTIONS, AND DIVIDEND DISTRIBUTIONS—A COMPARISON OF THE EFFECTS UPON SHAREHOLDERS

Liquidations and stock redemptions parallel each other insofar as the E & P of the distributing corporation is concerned. Except for one type of liquidation (i. e., the one-month election of § 333), the E & P of the corporation undergoing liquidation has no tax impact on the gain or loss to be recognized by the shareholders. Such is the case because § 301 (governing dividend distributions) is specifically made inapplicable to complete liquidations.[2]

> **Example 4.** Z Corporation, with E & P of $40,000, makes a cash distribution of $50,000 to one of its shareholders. Assume the shareholder's basis in the Z Corporation stock is $20,000. If the distribution is not in complete liquidation or if it does not qualify as a stock redemption, the shareholder must recognize dividend income of $40,000 (i. e., the amount of Z Corporation's E & P) and must treat the remaining $10,000 of the distribution as a return of capital. On the other hand, if the distribution is pursuant to a complete liquidation or qualifies for exchange treatment as a stock redemption, the shareholder will have a recognized gain of $30,000 [$50,000 (the amount of the distribution) − $20,000 (the basis in the stock)]. In the latter case, note that Z Corporation's E & P is of no consequence to the tax result.

In the event the distribution results in a *loss* to the shareholder, there could be an important distinction between stock redemptions and complete liquidations. The distinction could arise because § 267 (i. e., disallowance of losses between related parties) is applicable to stock redemptions but not to complete liquidations.

> **Example 5.** The stock of P Corporation is owned equally by three brothers, R, S, and T. At a point when T's basis in his stock investment is $40,000, the corporation distributes $30,000 to him in cancellation of all his shares. If the distribution is a stock redemption, the $10,000 realized loss is not recognized due to the application of § 267(a).[3] T and P Corporation are related parties because T is deemed to own more than 50% in value of the corporation's outstanding stock [§ 267(b)(2)]. Although T's direct ownership is limited to 33⅓%, through his brothers he owns indirectly another 66⅔% for a total of 100% [§ § 267(c)(2) and (4)]. Had the distribution qualified as a complete liquidation, T's $10,000 realized loss would be recognizable.

---

2. § 331(b).

3. *McCarthy v. Conley, Jr.*, 65–1 USTC ¶ 9262, 15 AFTR2d 447, 341 F.2d 948 (CA–2, 1965).

With reference to the basis of noncash property received from the corporation, the rules governing liquidations and stock redemptions are identical.

Section 334(a) specifies that the basis of such property distributed pursuant to a complete liquidation under § 331 shall be its fair market value on the date of distribution.

# EFFECT ON THE DISTRIBUTING CORPORATION

The tax consequences to the corporation in the process of liquidation are governed by § § 336 and 337. Section 336 covers distributions of corporate property in kind (i. e., the property is distributed as is), while § 337 deals with sales of corporate property with the distribution of the proceeds thereof to the shareholders. These Code provisions are not mutually exclusive, and both can, and frequently will, apply to the same liquidation.

## DISTRIBUTIONS IN KIND UNDER § 336

Section 336 provides that no gain or loss will be recognized to the distributing corporation upon the distribution of its property in complete liquidation. As usual, the general rule is subject to exceptions.

— Gain results from the distribution of installment notes receivable. The measure of the gain will be the difference between the fair market value of the note on the date of distribution and its adjusted basis in the hands of the corporation [§ § 336 and 453B(a)].

— Gain results on the distribution of LIFO inventory as to plans of liquidation adopted after December 31, 1982. The measure of the gain is the excess of the cost of the inventory using the FIFO method over the cost using LIFO [§ 336(b)].

— To the extent of any depreciation that would have been recaptured had the property been sold by the corporation, ordinary income will result [§ § 1245(d) and 1250(i)].

— Since the distribution will be treated as a disposition, recapture of some or all of any investment credit previously claimed by the distributing corporation may be in order [§ 47(a)]. Unlike the recapture of depreciation which produces ordinary income, the recapture of the investment credit means a direct addition to the tax liability of the corporation.

— Under certain conditions (see the discussion of § 337 below) the *Court Holding Company*[4] concept could apply to attribute to

---

4. *Comm. v. Court Holding Co.*, 45–1 USTC ¶ 9215, 33 AFTR 593, 65 S.Ct. 707 (USSC, 1945).

the corporation the sale by the shareholders of property distributed to them. Thus, the sale could be attributed to the corporation if all or most of the negotiations were completed at the corporate level. As a result, the corporation would be forced to recognize as gain the difference between the selling price and its adjusted basis in the property.

—The corporation will have to take into income any assets distributed to the shareholders for which it has previously claimed a deduction. This matter, previously in doubt, has been resolved by the U. S. Supreme Court.[5]

—The distributing corporation may have to recognize income under any one of several nebulous concepts of tax law. One such concept, the anticipatory assignment of income doctrine, could be applied. The authority of the IRS to make adjustments to a taxpayer's method of accounting in order to clearly reflect income [§ 446(b)] might be exercised to generate income to the corporation.

> **Example 6.**  U Corporation is a construction company reporting its income from operations on the completed contract method of accounting (i. e., no income is recognized until the contract is completed). Prior to the completion of a particularly lucrative construction contract, U Corporation liquidates and distributes its assets (including its construction contracts) to its shareholders in complete liquidation. Such avoidance of income recognition on the uncompleted construction contracts clearly does not reflect U Corporation's earnings, and the IRS may try to place U Corporation on a percentage of completion method of accounting (i. e., recognition of income proportionate to the percentage of contract completed).[6]

---

5.  See Rev.Rul. 74–396, 1974–2 C.B. 106 and Rev.Rul. 78–278, 1978–2 C.B. 134 for the position of the IRS on this issue. In *Bliss Dairy, Inc. v. Comm.,* 81–1 USTC ¶ 9429, 47 AFTR2d 81–1547, 645 F.2d 19 (CA–9, 1981), the Ninth Court of Appeals refused to apply the tax benefit rule to a distribution of assets under § 336. Under a plan of liquidation, a dairy corporation distributed cattle feed to its shareholder in the fiscal year following the year the cost of the feed was deducted. The Court stated that because the feed was distributed to shareholders, there was no sale of assets by the liquidating corporation and, therefore, the corporation itself received no benefit. A contrary result, and one that is compatible with the position of the IRS, was reached in *Tennessee-Carolina Transportation, Inc. v. Comm.,* 78–2 USTC ¶ 9671, 42 AFTR2d 78–5716, 582 F.2d 378 (CA–6, 1978). This conflict in the Courts of Appeals was resolved when the U. S. Supreme Court reversed *Bliss Dairy, Inc.* in 83–1 USTC ¶ 9229, 51 AFTR2d 83–874, 103 S.Ct. 1134 (1983).

6.  The classic cases in this area are *Jud Plumbing & Heating Co. v. Comm.,* 46–1 USTC ¶ 9177, 34 AFTR 1025, 153 F.2d 681 (CA–5, 1946) and *Standard Paving Co. v. Comm.,* 51–2 USTC ¶ 9376, 40 AFTR 1022, 190 F.2d 330 (CA–10, 1951).

The preceding rules parallel those applicable to corporations using property to effect a *redemption* of stock (refer to Chapter 13). There are, however, several important differences. For example, § 311(d) applies to *most* stock redemptions but not to complete liquidations. Consequently, the use of appreciated property to carry out a stock redemption could trigger gain to the distributing corporation.

> **Example 7.** V Corporation distributes unimproved land (basis of $20,000 and fair market value of $60,000) to one of its shareholders. If the distribution is made pursuant to a stock redemption and the limited exceptions of § 311(d)(2) do not apply, V Corporation must recognize a gain of $40,000. The distribution would not result in any gain to V Corporation if it was made pursuant to a complete liquidation.

Another difference arises when the subject matter of the distribution is property with a liability in excess of basis. Here, stock redemptions are treated no differently than regular dividend distributions, and the distributing corporation is susceptible to the recognition of gain under § 311(c). Such is not the case, however, when the distribution is made pursuant to a complete liquidation.[7]

As to plans of liquidation adopted before 1983, gain was not recognized to the distributing corporation when LIFO inventory property was distributed in a partial or complete liquidation. However, as to distributions of LIFO inventory for plans of liquidation adopted after 1982, the same treatment applicable to dividend distributions and stock redemption occurs. The liquidating corporation is susceptible to the recognition of gain under § 311(b).

> **Example 8.** W Corporation distributes appreciated LIFO inventory (basis of $30,000) to one of its shareholders. The basis of the inventory under the FIFO method of inventory valuation would have been $50,000. If the distribution is a property dividend or pursuant to a stock redemption, W Corporation must recognize a gain of $20,000 (refer to Chapter 13). The distribution would not generate any gain to the corporation if it was made pursuant to complete liquidation occurring before 1983. As to plans of liquidations adopted after 1982, there would be a gain of $20,000.

## SALES BY THE LIQUIDATING CORPORATION— THE 12-MONTH LIQUIDATION OF § 337

As was true of § 336, § 337 deals with the effect on the corporation of a liquidation. Section 337 was added to the Code to provide a solution to the uncertainty created by two Supreme Court cases, *Commis-*

---

7. Reg. § 1.311–1(a).

*sioner v. Court Holding Company* and *U. S. v. Cumberland Public Service Company*.[8]

In *Commissioner v. Court Holding Company,* a corporation was organized solely to buy and hold an apartment building. While the corporation had title to the apartment building, negotiations for sale of the building took place. Because the corporation's attorney advised the parties that a large corporate tax would have to be paid on the sale, the corporation liquidated and transferred the building to its shareholders, a husband and wife. The shareholders then sold the building. Mr. Justice Black wrote the opinion of the Supreme Court which held that gain on the sale of the building must be attributed to the corporation. The executed sale was, in substance, a sale by the corporation. Five years later, in *U. S. v. Cumberland Public Service Company,* Mr. Justice Black again wrote the opinion of the Supreme Court, this time stating that gain would not be attributed to the corporation in a fact situation not substantially different from that in *Court Holding Company.*

In the *Cumberland Public Service* case, a closely-held corporation offered to sell all its stock to a cooperative. The cooperative refused to buy the stock, but countered with an offer to buy the assets of the corporation. In order to avoid paying a corporate tax on the sale, the corporation liquidated, and the shareholders sold the assets to the cooperative. Justice Black concluded that because the corporation did not make the sale, it owed no tax. Black distinguished the *Court Holding Company* decision on the ground that findings of fact by the Tax Court in that case established that the sale had been made by the corporation.

The *Court Holding Company* and the *Cumberland Public Service* cases presented different tax treatment for a corporation which sold its assets and then liquidated versus a corporation which liquidated first, with the shareholders then effecting the sale. Further, it created a tax trap for the unwary who might arrange for the sale of corporate assets prior to liquidation. The tax consequences of sales made in the course of liquidation depended primarily upon the formal manner in which the transaction was arranged. Section 337 was added to the Code in 1954 to provide a definitive rule which would eliminate these uncertainties.

Section 337 states that if a corporation distributes all its assets in complete liquidation within 12 months after the adoption of a plan of liquidation, no gain or loss will be recognized on the sale of property by the corporation during the 12-month period. As a result, the tax treatment for a corporation selling its assets and then liquidating is no different from that of the corporation which liquidates first, with the shareholders later selling the assets. The problem is that § 337

---

**8.**  *U. S. v. Cumberland Public Service Co.,* 50–1 USTC ¶ 9129, 38 AFTR 978, 70 S.Ct. 280 (USSC, 1950). Refer to Footnote 4 for the citation to *Comm. v. Court Holding Co.*

applies only to complete liquidations. Further, liquidations pursuant to the one-month type of § 333 and the liquidations of most subsidiary corporations pursuant to § 332 are not covered by § 337 [§ 337 (c)(1) and (2)]. The decisions in *Court Holding Company* and *Cumberland Public Service* would presumably still apply to these transactions.[9] There are other limitations in applying § 337. By its own terms, § 337 is not applicable to some sales.

*Definition of "Property" Under § 337.* Section 337 applies to the sale of property by the liquidating corporation. Section 337(b) excepts from the term (a) inventory or property held by the corporation primarily for sale to customers in the ordinary course of its trade or business, (b) installment obligations acquired upon the sale of inventory items, and (c) installment obligations acquired with respect to property sold or exchanged before the date of the adoption of a plan of liquidation. However, § 337(b)(2) does permit inventory to be included as property if substantially all of the inventory is sold in bulk to one person in one transaction. However, with respect to LIFO inventory, even though sold in bulk, § 337(f) requires that the LIFO recapture amount (i. e., the excess of inventory costed under FIFO over inventory costed under LIFO) be recognized as gain on disposition made pursuant to plans adopted after December 31, 1982.

*Tax Benefit Rule.* Income is recognized by a liquidating corporation, despite § 337, under the so-called tax benefit rule. If a corporation sells supplies it previously expensed, the corporation must recognize the proceeds from the sale of the supplies as income to the extent prior years' deductions produced a tax benefit to the corporation.[10]

> **Example 9.** Pursuant to a complete liquidation under § 337, P Corporation sells rental uniforms for $100,000. Such uniforms were expensed as acquired and, therefore, had a zero basis to the corporation at the time of the sale. To the extent P Corporation was able to obtain a tax benefit from the deduction for uniform purchases, it has income from the sale. The measure of the income is not the corporate income tax actually saved through the deduction but the amount deducted which reduced taxes. In no event, however, would P Corporation have to recognize income in excess of $100,000.[11]

---

9. In *Aaron Cohen,* 63 T.C. 527 (1975), the Court held *Court Holding Company* applicable to a § 333 liquidation. Because the contract of sale was entered into prior to the liquidation, gain on such sale was attributable to the corporation.
10. See *Comm. v. Anders,* 69–2 USTC ¶ 9478, 24 AFTR2d 69–5133, 414 F.2d 1283 (CA–10, 1969), and *Connery v. U. S.,* 72–1 USTC ¶ 9441, 29 AFTR2d 72–1188, 460 F.2d 1130 (CA–3, 1972).
11. *Estate of David B. Munter,* 63 T.C. 663 (1975).

The tax benefit rule has been applied to the allowance for bad debts. The IRS had taken the position that a corporation has income to the extent of the bad debt reserve account when it sells its accounts receivable regardless of the amount realized from the sale. The IRS now has modified its position in the light of the Supreme Court decision in *Nash v. U. S.* (refer to Chapter 12).[12] The IRS will attribute income to the corporation only if the receivables are sold for more than book value (i. e., face amount less the balance in the reserve).

**Example 10.** Q Corporation, an accrual basis taxpayer, adopts a plan of complete liquidation under § 337. Its accounts receivable (face amount of $100,000 with a reserve for bad debts of $10,000) are sold for $95,000. Subject to the tax benefit rule, the sale results in $5,000 of income to Q Corporation.

*Recapture Rules.* Sections 1245, 1250, and 1252 do not except the nonrecognition provisions of § 337 from their recapture rules; consequently, these sections override § 337. Income is recognized by a liquidating corporation to the extent there would be a recapture of depreciation should depreciable assets be sold at their fair market values. Further, those assets which would produce a loss upon a sale cannot be offset against those producing a gain.

Because § 337 is subordinate to § 47, there is also investment credit recapture should a liquidating corporation dispose of § 38 assets prematurely.

*Straddle Sales.* Although the avowed purpose of § 337 is to protect a corporation from recognizing a gain on the sale of property during the liquidation period, a price must be paid for such treatment. The price is found in the language of § 337(a), which also disallows the recognition of any loss from the sale of property covered therein. To circumvent this result (i. e., nonrecognition of both gains and losses), the straddle sale approach was devised. Quite simply, it involves selling the *loss* assets *before* the plan of liquidation is adopted (§ 337 would be inapplicable) and selling the *gain* assets *after* the plan is adopted (§ 337 would be applicable). Consequently, the corporation could recognize its losses and avoid recognition of its gains.

**Example 11.** R Corporation owns Asset A (basis of $30,000 and fair market value of $20,000) and Asset B (basis of $20,000 and fair market value of $30,000). Both assets qualify as property for the purposes of § 337. On June 1, 19X1, Asset A is sold for $20,000. On July 1, 19X1, R Corporation adopts a plan of complete liquidation. Shortly thereafter, Asset B is sold for $30,000. What has been accomplished taxwise? Presuming the straddle sale approach is effective (i. e., Asset A is sold prior to the adop-

---

12. The current position of the IRS is stated in Rev.Rul. 78–279, 1978–2 C.B. 135.

tion of a plan of liquidation), R Corporation may recognize a loss of $10,000. The realized gain of $10,000 on the sale of Asset B is not recognized because its sale is effected after § 337 becomes applicable.

**Example 12.** Assume the same facts as in Example 11 except that both Assets A and B are sold after July 1, 19X1. Since the sales occur after the plan of liquidation was adopted, neither gain nor loss will be recognized. This treatment results because of the applicability of § 337 to both sales.

The key to the success of the straddle sale approach (Example 11) is an exact determination of when the plan of liquidation was adopted. Ordinarily, the controlling date is the date of adoption by the shareholders of a resolution authorizing the distribution of all the assets of the corporation in complete liquidation.[13] But could the IRS successfully contend that the plan was really adopted when the corporation decided to first sell its loss assets? Such being the case, both losses and gains would go unrecognized if the liquidation took place within 12 months from the date of adoption of the "informal" plan.

Although courts have not been hesitant to find an informal plan of complete liquidation when no formal plan was adopted,[14] the presence of a formal plan appears to control.[15] Consequently, the straddle sale approach has been recognized when the parties have been careful to adopt a formal plan *after* the sale of the loss assets.[16]

*Expenses of Liquidation.* The expenses involved in liquidating a corporation fall into two major categories:

—General liquidation expenses. Examples include the legal and accounting cost of drafting a plan of liquidation or the cost of revocation of the corporate charter.

—Specific liquidation expenses relating to the disposition or sale of corporate assets. Examples include a brokerage commission for the sale of real estate or a legal fee to clear title and effect a transfer of property in kind to a shareholder.

General liquidation expenses are deductible to the corporation as business expenses under § 162. The tax treatment of specific liquidation expenses has not always been clear. When they relate to distributions in kind under § 336 or to the sale of assets outside the scope of

---

**13.** Reg. § 1.337–2(b) does provide for the recognition of *both* gains and losses when the corporation sells substantially all of its property *prior* to the adoption of a plan of complete liquidation. In other cases, however, the date of the adoption of the plan of liquidation shall be determined from all of the facts and circumstances.
**14.** *Alameda Realty Corporation,* 42 T.C. 273 (1964) and *Jessie B. Mitchell,* 31 TCM 1077, T.C.Memo. 1972–219.
**15.** But see *Harold O. Wales,* 50 T.C. 399 (1968) dealing with § 333 liquidations.
**16.** *Virginia Ice and Freezing Corp.,* 30 T.C. 1251 (1958) and *City Bank of Washington,* 38 T.C. 713 (1962).

§ 337, such expenses are deductible. If associated with the sale of assets under § 337, current law requires the expenses to be offset against the selling price. Such treatment, in effect, disallows any deduction. The offset decreases realized gain or increases realized loss, neither of which can be recognized.

> **Example 13.** During its liquidation, R Corporation incurs the following expenses:

| | |
|---|---:|
| General liquidation expenses | $ 12,000 |
| Legal expenses to effect a distribution (in kind under § 336) | 200 |
| Sales commissions to dispose of inventory (not covered under § 337) | 3,000 |
| Brokerage fee on sale of real estate (covered under § 337) | 8,000 |

R Corporation can deduct only $15,200 (i. e., $12,000 + $200 + $3,000). The $8,000 brokerage fee must be applied against the selling price of the real estate.

*Involuntary Conversions.* If a corporation has its major asset or assets destroyed in a casualty (e. g., fire, storm), the shareholders may want to discontinue the business and liquidate the corporation. But what if the anticipated insurance recovery from the destruction of the asset(s) will generate a large realized gain? Can the recognition of any such gain be avoided through the use of § 337? Absent the adoption of a plan of complete liquidation prior to the casualty (an unlikely or suspicious possibility), § 337 was held by the Supreme Court to be not applicable to the gain.[17]

Because the decision reached by the Supreme Court could lead to harsh results by making § 337 unavailable to many involuntary conversions, the Revenue Act of 1978 added subsection (e) to § 337. Under this provision, an involuntary conversion occurring within 60 days preceding the adoption of the plan will be deemed to fall within the 12-month period following such adoption. Thus, the shelter of § 337 can be obtained if the parties act within 60 days of the conversion.

*Assets Retained to Pay Claims.* Section 337 requires the distribution of all corporate assets within 12 months from the adoption of a

---

17. *Central Tablet Manufacturing Co. v. U. S.,* 74–2 USTC ¶ 9511, 34 AFTR2d 74–5200, 94 S.Ct. 2516 (USSC, 1974). The rationale behind the decision was based on when the gain from the involuntary conversion is realized. If the gain is realized when the casualty occurs, the result reached by the Court, then a subsequent adoption of a plan of complete liquidation cannot avoid its recognition. The taxpayers had argued that the gain is realized when the insurance recovery occurs and, therefore, followed in point of time the adoption of the plan.

plan of liquidation; however, assets may be retained to pay claims.[18] These assets must be reasonable in amount in relation to the specific liabilities involved and must be set apart for the purpose of paying such liabilities. Assets may be retained to pay contingent liabilities and expenses of liquidation.[19]

*Installment Sales.* As noted above, § 336 (dealing with distributions in kind in liquidation) excepts the disposition of installment obligations pursuant to § 453B from its nonrecognition provisions. Similarly, § 337(b) provides that installment obligations acquired from the sale or exchange of inventory and installment obligations acquired *before* the date of adoption of a plan of liquidation from the sale of property other than inventory are not included in the term "property" for the purposes of nonrecognition treatment. Section 453B(d)(2)(B) states that if an installment obligation, which would have produced no gain or loss to the corporation pursuant to § 337, is distributed by a corporation in the course of liquidation, gain or loss is not recognized. However, this rule does not apply to installment obligations arising from the sale of property subject to depreciation recapture.

Briefly, the provisions with respect to installment obligations are as follows: Installment obligations arising from (a) the sale of inventory property in bulk or (b) the sale of noninventory property (other than recapture property) *after* the date of adoption of a plan of liquidation are subject to the nonrecognition provisions.

> **Example 14.** On January 8, 19X1, V Corporation adopts a plan of complete liquidation. During the course of the liquidation (completed within 12 months), V Corporation distributes to its shareholders the following installment notes receivable:
>
> > Note #1 received from the sale of corporate property in 19X0.
> >
> > Note #2 received from the bulk sale of inventory on March 20, 19X1.
> >
> > Note #3 received from the sale of nondepreciable property on June 1, 19X1.
>
> Only the distribution of Note #1 will cause tax consequences to V Corporation. Since the bulk sale of the inventory and the sale of the nondepreciable property result in no recognized gain to the corporation (under § 337), the distribution of Note #2 and Note #3 is protected.

---

**18.** If shareholders cannot be located, a distribution to a trustee or other person authorized by law to receive distributions for the benefit of such shareholders is considered a liquidating distribution. See Reg. § 1.337–2(b).

**19.** Reg. § 1.337–1 and Rev.Rul. 80–150, 1980–1 C.B. 316.

# EFFECT ON THE SHAREHOLDER— THE GENERAL RULE

As noted at the beginning of this chapter, in terms of their effect on a shareholder, liquidations fall into one of three major classifications:

—The general rule of § 331 with basis determined under § 334(a).

—The liquidation of a subsidiary by a parent corporation. Here, § 332 applies and the basis is determined under either § 334(b)(1) or § 338.

—The one-month liquidation of § 333 with basis determined under § 334(c).

### THE GENERAL RULE—§ 331

In the case of a complete liquidation, the general rule under § 331(a)(1) provides for exchange treatment. Since § 1002 requires the recognition of gain or loss on the sale or exchange of property, the end result is to treat the shareholder as having sold his or her stock to the corporation being liquidated. Thus, the difference between the liquidation proceeds and the adjusted basis of the stock (i. e., realized gain or loss), becomes the amount that is recognized. If the stock is a capital asset in the hands of the shareholder, capital gain or loss results. As is usually true, the burden of proof is on the taxpayer to furnish evidence on the adjusted basis of the stock. In the absence of such evidence, therefore, the stock will be deemed to have a zero basis and the full amount of the liquidation proceeds represents the amount of the gain to be recognized.

Section 334(a) provides that under the general rule of § 331, the income tax basis to the shareholder of property received in a liquidation will be its fair market value on the date of distribution.

# EFFECT ON THE SHAREHOLDER— COMPLETE LIQUIDATION PURSUANT TO § 333

Section 333 is an exception to the general rule that a shareholder has a gain or loss upon a corporate liquidation.[20] If shareholders elect and the liquidation is completed within one calendar month, § 333 postpones the recognition of gain on assets with substantial appreciation unrealized by the corporation on the date of liquidation. However, the shareholder does have recognized gain in an amount equal to the

---

**20.** The predecessor to § 333 was enacted to permit and encourage the liquidation of personal holding companies in light of the imposition of the personal holding company tax (see Chapter 15). Intended as a temporary relief provision, it has, like many other Code sections, become a permanent fixture.

greater of (a) the stockholder's share of earnings and profits accumulated after February 28, 1913, or (b) amounts received by the shareholder consisting of money and stock and securities acquired by the corporation after 1953. In no event may recognized gain exceed realized gain. Only "qualifying electing" shareholders are entitled to the benefits of § 333.

### QUALIFYING ELECTING SHAREHOLDERS

A corporate shareholder owning 50 percent or more of the stock of a liquidating corporation cannot qualify under § 333. The remaining shareholders are divided into two groups: (a) noncorporate shareholders and (b) those corporate shareholders owning less than 50 percent of stock in the liquidating corporation. Owners of stock possessing at least 80 percent of the total combined voting power of all classes of stock owned by shareholders in one of the above-mentioned groups must elect the provisions of § 333. If the 80 percent requirement is not met, the one-month liquidation treatment is not available to any member of that group. If owners of 80 percent of the stock in a particular group have elected § 333, and if a particular shareholder involved has also elected, such party becomes a "qualifying electing shareholder."

Shareholders not qualifying for or electing § 333 would come under the general rule of § 331, and their gain or loss would be determined by the difference between the fair market value of the liquidating distribution and the adjusted basis of the stock investment.

### MAKING THE ELECTION AND THE ONE-MONTH REQUIREMENT

An election to have liquidation proceeds taxed under § 333 is made on Form 964. The original and one copy of the form must be filed by the shareholder within 30 days after the adoption of a plan of liquidation.[21] If form 964 is not filed within the 30-day period, the shareholder cannot utilize the provisions of § 333. Once an election of § 333 is made, it cannot later be revoked.

But even if the election is properly made and timely filed, § 333 will not apply unless the corporation is liquidated within one calendar month.[22] This requirement has led many to refer to the § 333 type of liquidation as the one-month liquidation. The one month chosen to carry out the liquidation need not be the same month in which the election was made. In this regard, it is easy to confuse the 30-day rule noted above with the one-month requirement.

---

**21.**  § 333(d) and Reg. § 1.333–3.
**22.**  § 333(a)(2).

**Example 15.** On June 1, 19X1, the shareholders of Y Corporation adopt a plan for its complete liquidation. By June 28, 19X1, each shareholder executes and files a Form 964 electing § 333. The liquidation of Y Corporation commences on August 3, 19X1, and is concluded before the end of the month. Section 333 is applicable: Both the 30-day and the one-month requirements have been satisfied.

## COMPUTATION OF GAIN UNDER § 333

As is the case under § 331, amounts received by shareholders electing under § 333 are treated as in full payment of their stock. Gain or loss is computed separately on each share of stock owned by a qualified electing shareholder.[23] The limited recognition of gain under § 333 applies only to *gain realized* on stock. Gain on some shares cannot be offset by losses on others.

Gain on each share of stock held by a qualified electing shareholder at the time of adoption of a plan of liquidation is recognized under § 333 only to the extent of the *greater* of (a) the shareholder's ratable portion of E & P of the corporation accumulated after February 28, 1913, computed as of the last day of the month of liquidation, without reduction for distributions made during that month and including all items of income and expense accrued to the date on which the transfer of all property under the liquidation is completed; or (b) the shareholder's ratable portion of the sum of cash and the fair market value of all stock or securities (acquired by the corporation after December 31, 1953) received by the shareholder. Dividend income to noncorporate shareholders is that portion of recognized gain not in excess of the shareholder's ratable share of E & P accumulated after February 28, 1913. The remainder of the gain is either short-term or long-term capital gain, depending on the length of time the stock has been held. A qualified electing corporate shareholder has no dividend income; all recognized gain is capital gain.[24]

**Example 16.** The *independent* cases appearing below illustrate the possible tax consequences to a shareholder under a § 333 liquidation:

---

**23.** Reg. § 1.333–4(a).
**24.** § 333(f) and Reg. § 1.333–4(b). The reason corporate shareholders are forced into capital gain treatment is easily explained. If this type of shareholder were permitted dividend treatment as to a pro rata share of the distributing corporation's E & P (as is the case with noncorporate shareholders), the tax impact would be mitigated through the application of the 85% dividends received deduction of § 243. Capital gain treatment therefore leads to a harsher tax effect on a corporate shareholder.

| Case | Type of Shareholder | Distributing Corporation* | | Shareholder's Realized Gain | Shareholder's Recognized Gain | |
|------|---------------------|------|------|------|------|------|
| | | E & P | Cash Plus Post-1953 Securities | | Capital | Dividend |
| A | Corporation | $ 10,000 | $ 10,000 | $ 5,000 | $ 5,000 | $ –0– |
| B | Corporation | 10,000 | 20,000 | 40,000 | 20,000 | –0– |
| C | Corporation | 20,000 | 10,000 | 30,000 | 20,000 | –0– |
| D | Individual | 10,000 | 10,000 | 5,000 | –0– | 5,000 |
| E | Individual | 10,000 | 20,000 | 40,000 | 10,000 | 10,000 |
| F | Individual | 20,000 | 10,000 | 30,000 | –0– | 20,000 |

* Represents the shareholder's pro rata portion of these items.

In Example 16, note that gain recognized for both corporate and noncorporate shareholders can never exceed realized gain (Cases A and D). Also, all recognized gain by a corporate shareholder must be capital gain (Cases A, B, and C). An individual has a capital gain only if his share of cash plus post-1953 securities exceeds his share of the corporation's E & P (contrast Cases E and F).

## BASIS OF PROPERTY RECEIVED PURSUANT TO § 333

Property received in a liquidation wherein there is limited recognized gain is the same as the basis of the shares redeemed decreased by the amount of any money received and increased by gain recognized and unsecured liabilities assumed by the shareholders. This amount is allocated to the various assets received on the basis of their net fair market values (net fair market value of an asset is fair market value less any specific mortgage or pledge to which it is subject). Basis of a particular asset, as determined in this manner, is increased for any liens on that asset.[25] If a lien applies to several properties, the amount of the lien is divided among the properties on the basis of the fair market value of each property.[26]

**Example 17.** At the time of its liquidation in the current year, Z Corporation has E & P of $40,000 and the following assets and liabilities:

| | Basis to Z Corporation | Fair Market Value |
|---|---|---|
| Cash | $ 30,000 | $ 30,000 |
| Gulf Oil Corporation stock (held as an investment since 1968) | 40,000 | 30,000 |
| Unimproved land | 10,000 | 20,000 |
| Notes payable to outsiders | 10,000 | 10,000 |

25. Reg. § 1.334–2.
26. For an excellent explanation of how basis is determined and allocated to property received in a § 333 liquidation, see *Ralph R. Garrow*, 43 T.C. 890 (1965).

All assets and liabilities are distributed to T, an individual and the sole shareholder. The notes payable do not relate to any specific asset but are secured by the general credit of the corporation. At the time of the liquidation, T's basis in the Z Corporation stock is $20,000. Assume the liquidation falls under § 333.

—T has a recognized gain of $50,000. Realized gain is computed as follows: $70,000 (fair market value of all the assets received *less* the notes payable) − $20,000 (T's basis in the Z Corporation stock). T's recognized gain is the greater of $40,000 (E & P) *or* $60,000 [$30,000 (cash) + $30,000 (post-1953 securities)] not to exceed his realized gain of $50,000.

—Of the $50,000 of recognized gain, $10,000 is capital gain and $40,000 is dividend income. Under § 333(e), capital gain is limited to the excess of $60,000 [$30,000 (cash) + $30,000 (post-1953 securities)] over $40,000 (E & P). But the total gain, both capital gain and dividend income, cannot exceed recognized gain of $50,000. Because $40,000 of the $50,000 recognized is dividend income (limited to E & P), only $10,000 is treated as a capital gain.

—Total basis to be allocated is $50,000 determined as follows: $20,000 (T's basis in the Z Corporation stock) + $50,000 (gain recognized by T) + $10,000 (liabilities assumed) − $30,000 (cash received). The amount allocated to the unimproved land is computed below:

$$\left[\frac{\$20,000\ (\text{FMV of the land})}{\substack{\$20,000\ (\text{FMV}\\ \text{of the land}) +\\ \$30,000\ (\text{FMV of}\\ \text{the Gulf stock})}}\right] \times \left[\substack{\$50,000\ (\text{total basis}\\ \text{to be allocated})}\right] = \substack{\$20,000\ (\text{basis}\\ \text{in the land})}$$

A similar computation, but with the numerator of the fraction changed from $20,000 to $30,000, allocates a basis of $30,000 to the Gulf Oil Corporation stock.

**Example 18.** Assume the same facts as in Example 17 except that notes payable constitute a specific lien against the unimproved land.

—T's recognized gain and the nature of such gain remains the same (see above).

—The basis to be allocated among all assets is $40,000 determined as follows: $20,000 (T's basis in the Z Corporation stock) + $50,000 (gain recognized by T) − $30,000 (cash received). The amount allocated to the Gulf stock becomes $30,000 [($30,000/$40,000) × $40,000]. In the case of the land, however, start with $10,000 [($10,000/$40,000) ×

$40,000] and add $10,000 (the specific lien) for a total of $20,000. Since the liability relates to the land, it affects only the basis of that asset. Also, note that the numerator of the second fraction (i. e., $10,000) and the denominator of both fractions (i. e., $40,000) consider the value of the land net of the liability.

## EFFECT ON THE DISTRIBUTING CORPORATION

Code § 333 provides for a specified tax result for an electing shareholder. As such, it does not carry any direct tax consequences to the corporation being liquidated. There is, however, one important indirect effect on the corporation. When § 333 is utilized by any shareholder, § 337 becomes unavailable to the corporation.[27] Thus, gains and losses from the sale of corporate assets during the liquidation period become fully recognizable. From a planning standpoint, therefore, corporations undergoing liquidation should avoid sales of gain property and distribute such assets in kind to the shareholders under § 336. The tax consequences to the corporation resulting from a distribution in kind under § 336 were reviewed earlier in this chapter.

Besides the possible recognition of gain at the corporate level, there exists another reason to avoid sales of property in connection with § 333 liquidations. Recall that one of the criteria determining the tax consequences to the electing shareholder is the E & P of the distributing corporation. Hence, sales by the corporation of gain property (through their effect on E & P) might well increase the dividend income to be recognized by a noncorporate shareholder or the capital gain by a corporate shareholder. In this connection, the *Court Holding Company* doctrine could pose a real danger. If, for example, later sales by the shareholders of distributed property are attributed to the corporation, a double tax impact could materialize–tax to the liquidating corporation on any gain recognized plus a tax to the shareholders on any E & P so generated.

## LIQUIDATION OF A SUBSIDIARY

Section 332, like the one-month liquidation of § 333, is an exception to the general rule that the shareholder recognizes gain or loss on a corporate liquidation. If a parent corporation liquidates a subsidiary corporation in which it owns at least 80 percent of the voting stock, no gain or loss is recognized under § 332. Section 333 differs from § 332 in that some gain may be recognized under § 333.

The requirements for application of § 332 are (a) the parent must own at least 80 percent of the voting stock of the subsidiary and at least 80 percent of all other classes of stock except nonvoting preferred, (b) the subsidiary must distribute all its property in complete

---

**27.**  § 337(c)(1)(B).

redemption of all its stock within the taxable year or within three years from the close of the tax year in which a plan was adopted and the first distribution occurred, and (c) the subsidiary must be solvent. If these requirements are met, § 332 becomes mandatory.

When a series of distributions occur in the liquidation of a subsidiary corporation, the parent corporation must own the required amount of stock (80 percent) on the date of adoption of a plan of liquidation and at all times until all property has been distributed.[28] If the parent fails to qualify at any time, the provisions for nonrecognition of gain or loss do not apply to any distribution. If a liquidation is not completed within one taxable year, then for each taxable year which falls wholly or partly within the period of liquidation, the parent corporation shall file with its income tax return a waiver of the statute of limitations on assessment. The parent corporation may be forced to file a bond with the District Director to insure prompt payment of taxes should § 332 not apply.

For the taxable year in which the plan of liquidation is adopted and for all taxable years within the period of liquidation, the parent corporation must file with its return a statement of all facts pertaining to the liquidation, including a copy of the plan, a list of all properties received showing cost and fair market value, a statement of indebtedness of the subsidiary corporation to the parent, and a statement of ownership of all classes of stock of the liquidating corporation.

## BASIS OF PROPERTY RECEIVED BY THE PARENT CORPORATION

*The General Rule of § 334(b)(1).* Unless a parent corporation elects under § 338, property received by the parent corporation in a complete liquidation of its subsidiary under § 332 has the same basis it had in the hands of the subsidiary.[29] The parent's basis in stock of the liquidated subsidiary disappears. This is true even though some of the property was transferred to the parent in satisfaction of debt owed the parent by the subsidiary.

> **Example 19.** P, the parent corporation, has a basis of $20,000 in stock in S Corporation, a subsidiary in which it owns 85% of all classes of stock. P Corporation purchased the stock of S Corporation 10 years ago. In the current year, P Corporation liquidates S Corporation and acquires assets worth $50,000 with a tax basis to S Corporation of $40,000. P Corporation would have a basis of $40,000 in the assets, with a potential gain upon sale of $10,000.

---

28. As is true with § 333 (i. e., the one-month liquidation) and § 337 (i. e., the 12-month liquidation), the date of the adoption of a plan of complete liquidation could be crucial in determining whether § 332 applies. See, for example, *George L. Riggs, Inc.*, 64 T.C. 474 (1975).
29. § 334(b)(1) and Reg. § 1.334–1(b).

P Corporation's original $20,000 basis in S Corporation stock disappears.

**Example 20.** P Corporation has a basis of $60,000 in stock in S Corporation, a subsidiary acquired 10 years ago. It liquidates S Corporation and receives assets worth $50,000 with a tax basis to S Corporation of $40,000. P Corporation again has a basis of $40,000 in the assets it acquired from S Corporation. If it sells the assets, it will have a gain of $10,000 in spite of the fact that its basis in S Corporation stock was $60,000. P Corporation's loss will never be recognized.

Because the parent corporation takes the subsidiary's basis in its assets, the carryover rules of § 381 apply. The parent would acquire a net operating loss of the subsidiary, any investment credit carryover, capital loss carryover, and a carryover of E & P of the subsidiary. Section 381 applies to most tax-free reorganizations and to a tax-free liquidation under § 332 if the subsidiary's bases in its assets carry over to the parent.

*Election of § 338.* Under the general rule of § 332(b)(1), several problems developed when a subsidiary was liquidated shortly after acquisition by a parent corporation.

1.  When the basis of the subsidiary's assets was in excess of the purchase price of the stock, the parent received a step-up in basis in such assets at no tax cost. If, for example, the parent paid $100,000 for the subsidiary's stock and the basis of the assets transferred to the parent was $150,000, the parent enjoys a $50,000 benefit without any gain recognition. The $50,000 increase in basis of the subsidiary's assets could lead to additional depreciation deductions and either more loss or less gain upon the later disposition of the assets by the parent.

2.  If the basis of the subsidiary's assets was below the purchase price of the stock, the parent suffered a step-down in basis in such assets with no attendant tax benefit. Return to Example 20. If the situation is changed slightly—the subsidiary's stock is not held for 10 years, but the subsidiary is liquidated shortly after acquisition—the basic inequity of the "no loss" situation is apparent.[30]

---

**30.**  There could be any number of reasons why one corporation would pay more for the stock in another corporation than the latter's basis in its assets. For one, the basis of assets has no necessary correlation to their fair market values. For another, the acquiring corporation may not have any choice in the matter if it really wants the assets. The shareholders in the acquired corporation may prefer to sell their stock rather than the assets of the corporation. Tax consequences, undoubtedly, would have some bearing on such a decision.

In the landmark decision of *Kimbell-Diamond Milling Co. v. Comm.*,[31] the courts finally resolved these problems. When a parent corporation liquidates a subsidiary shortly after the acquisition of its stock, the parent is really purchasing the assets of the subsidiary. Consequently, the bases of such assets should be the cost of the stock. Known as the "single transaction" approach, the basis determination is not made under the general rule of § 334(b)(1). Since the Court's decision left in doubt precisely when the single transaction approach should apply, Congress enacted the predecessor of § 338. The purpose of this provision is to give assets acquired by a parent corporation upon liquidation of its subsidiary the same basis which the parent held in the stock of the subsidiary.

*Operational Rules Under § 338.* The application of § 338 depends on the following conditions being satisfied:

—An election must be made by the parent (acquiring) corporation within 75 days of the acquisition date of the stock of the subsidiary (target) corporation, such election being irrevocable. Through the issuance of Regulations, the IRS is to determine how the election will be made [§ 338(g)]. In certain cases, the election can be imposed upon the taxpayer (i. e., treated as "deemed" made) [§ 338(e)].

—The acquisition date is the date on which the parent satisfies the 80 percent ownership requirement. The acquisition date must fall within the acquisition period. The acquisition period commences with the first purchase of stock and runs for 12 months. Stated differently, the parent (acquiring) corporation has 12 months in which to acquire control (i. e., 80 percent) of the target corporation.

—The stock has to satisfy the 80 percent control requirement. Basically, this entails acquiring the stock in a taxable transaction (e. g., § 351 and other nonrecognition provisions did not apply) [§ 338(h)(3)].

If the § 338 election is made (or deemed made), the following results transpire:

—The target corporation will be treated as if it had sold its assets to the parent corporation under § 337 (the 12-month liquidation provision) for the purchase price of the stock [§ 338(a)(1)]. This means no gain or loss treatment as to target's "§ 337 property" but will lead to tax consequences as to items not so included (e. g., recapture of depreciation and the investment tax

---

31. *Kimbell-Diamond Milling Co. v. Comm.*, 14 T.C. 74 (1950), *aff'd.* in 51–1 USTC ¶ 9201, 40 AFTR 328, 187 F.2d 718 (CA–5, 1951).

credit, LIFO inventory adjustments, application of the tax benefit rule).

—Target corporation will be treated as a *new* corporation as of the beginning of the day after the acquisition date [§ 338(a)(2)]. Therefore, target corporation's taxable year ends on the date of its acquisition. Although it does seem consistent with the hypothetical sale treatment under § 337, target corporation does not have to be liquidated by the parent corporation. This could be advantageous if, for example, target corporation held a nonassignable asset (e. g., franchise, license, contract).

—In determining the parent's basis in its qualified stock investment, a special "gross-up" procedure will be necessary when the percentage of ownership is less than 100 percent on the acquisition date [§ 338(b)(2)]. The grossed-up basis of the parent's stock investment will be allocated to target's assets in accordance with Regulations to be issued by the IRS [§ 338(b)(3)].

*A Comparison of* § § *334(b)(1) and 338.*   Under the general rule of § 334(b)(1), a subsidiary's basis in its assets carries over to the parent corporation upon liquidation. The recapture rules of §§ 1245, 1250, 1251, and 1252 do not apply to liquidations of subsidiary corporations when basis is determined under § 334(b)(1). Nor does § 47's provision for investment credit recapture apply. These sections except such liquidations from their provisions.[32] Consequently, a subsidiary liquidation pursuant to § § 332 and 334(b)(1) is completely tax-free.

On the other hand, a liquidation pursuant to § § 332 and 338, while tax-free to the parent, does produce taxable income to the subsidiary under the recapture rules of §§ 1245, 1250, and 1252. For plans of liquidation adopted after December 31, 1982, the subsidiary also must recognize the recapture amount on LIFO inventory. Section 47, dealing with the recapture of the investment tax credit, also applies. Whether or not the tax benefit rule and the assignment of income doctrine apply to the subsidiary is not clear. In Revenue Ruling 74–396, the IRS held that the unused portion of previously expensed supplies would be income to the liquidated subsidiary in a complete liquidation, excluding liquidations in which basis is carried over pursuant to § 334(b)(1).

If a liquidation under § 332 qualifies under § 338, the holding period of the property received by the parent corporation begins on the date the parent acquired the subsidiary's stock. In a liquidation under § 334(b)(1), the holding period of the subsidiary carries over to the parent.

---

**32.**   See, for example, § § 1245(b)(3), 1250(d)(3), and 47(b)(2).

# EFFECT ON THE SHAREHOLDER—
# COLLAPSIBLE CORPORATIONS UNDER § 341

## THE PROBLEM

The tax avoidance objective that § 341 seeks to preclude is easily demonstrated by the use of an illustration.

> **Example 21.** C (a motion picture producer), D (a leading actor), and E (a leading actress) organize the M Corporation to film a motion picture. Each invests $50,000 in return for all of the stock, and M Corporation borrows $300,000 to cover the estimated $450,000 cost of production. Since C, D, and E receive only modest compensation for their services, the estimated cost of production is considerably less than normal. After the film is completed, a preview is held. Based on reviews of the critics, the film is appraised at a value of $900,000. M Corporation is liquidated, and the film is distributed in kind to its shareholders. The film is subsequently released by the shareholders; over the next several years it earns $900,000 in royalty income. What have the parties expected to accomplish?
>
> —The corporation realizes none of the $900,000 in royalty income.
>
> —The corporation recognizes no gain on the liquidation because of § 336 (a distribution in kind in liquidation).
>
> —The shareholders recognize a capital gain of $450,000 on the liquidation of the corporation. The gain is determined under the general rule of § 331 and represents the difference between $900,000 (the fair market value of the film) and $450,000 [$150,000 (shareholders' basis in the stock) + $300,000 (corporate liabilities assumed)].
>
> —Under § 334(a), the shareholders receive a $900,000 basis in the film (its fair market value on the date of distribution).
>
> —None of the $900,000 of royalties received from the showing of the film will be recognized as income to the shareholders. Because the shareholders will use the cost recovery approach as to the royalty income, the $900,000 basis must first be absorbed. In the event more or less than $900,000 ultimately is recovered, gain or loss will be recognized accordingly.

The shareholders hope to obtain a step-up in basis at capital gain rates. More important, the corporation is "collapsed" before it realizes any income, thereby neutralizing the double tax attendant to conducting a business in the corporate form.

Although it started with the motion picture industry, the collapsible corporation approach worked equally well with construction projects. Once the project was completed and before any sales were made, the corporation was liquidated and its assets distributed in kind under § 336. The shareholders then proceeded to sell the units, offsetting the sale proceeds against their new basis.

## THE STATUTORY SOLUTION

Section 117(m) of the 1939 Code, the predecessor of the present § 341, converted long-term capital gain into ordinary income if the distributing corporation was collapsible. Returning to Example 21, C, D, and E would each recognize ordinary income of $150,000 (for a total of $450,000) on the liquidation of M Corporation. But § 341 goes beyond the classic liquidation situation and covers two additional possibilities. First, a corporate distribution not in liquidation could convert long-term capital gain into ordinary income. Second, similar conversion occurs upon the sale of stock by a shareholder to another party.

> **Example 22.** Assume the same facts as in Example 21, except that M Corporation is not liquidated. Prior to the release of the film, the corporation distributes to each of its shareholders excess borrowed funds of $60,000 (for a total of $180,000) not needed for production. Because the distribution occurs before M Corporation has generated any E & P, no dividend results. Under usual rules, each shareholder would report a $10,000 capital gain. The remaining $50,000 constitutes a return of capital [see § 301(c) and Chapter 13]. Section 341(a)(3) would transform the $10,000 of long-term capital gain into ordinary income if the distributing corporation is collapsible.

> **Example 23.** Assume the same facts as in Example 21 except that C sells his stock for $200,000 after the film is completed and prior to M Corporation's liquidation. Section 341(a)(1) would convert any long-term capital gain from the sale to ordinary income if M Corporation is collapsible.

Section 341 does not generate gain—it merely transforms long-term capital gain into ordinary income. Consequently, nontaxable exchanges involving collapsible corporation stock (e. g., transfers to controlled corporations under § 351—refer to Chapter 12) would not be affected. Section 341 is inapplicable to short-term capital gains and to losses.

# CORPORATE REORGANIZATIONS

A corporate combination, usually referred to as a "reorganization," can be either a taxable or a nontaxable transaction. Assuming a business combination is taxable, § 1001 of the Code provides that the seller's gain or loss is measured by the difference between the amount realized and the basis of property surrendered. The purchaser's basis for the property received is the amount paid for such property, and the holding period begins on the date of purchase.

There are certain exchanges specifically excepted from tax recognition by the Code. For example, § 1031 provides that no gain or loss shall be recognized if property held for productive use or for investment is exchanged solely for ". . . property of a like kind . . ." Section 1033, if elected by the taxpayer, provides for partial or complete nonrecognition of gain if property destroyed, seized, or stolen is compulsorily or involuntarily converted into similar property. Further, § 351 provides for nonrecognition of gain upon the transfer of property to a controlled corporation. Finally, § § 361 and 368 provide for nonrecognition of gain in certain corporate reorganizations. The Regulations state the underlying assumption behind such nonrecognition of gain or loss—

> . . . the new property is substantially a continuation of the old investment still unliquidated; and, in the case of reorganizations, that the new enterprise, the new corporate structure, and the new property are substantially continuations of the old still unliquidated.[33]

## SUMMARY OF THE DIFFERENT TYPES OF REORGANIZATIONS

Section 368(a) of the Code specifies seven reorganizations which will qualify as nontaxable exchanges. It is important that the planner of a nontaxable business combination determine well in advance that the proposed transaction falls specifically within one of these seven described types. If the transaction fails to qualify, it will not be granted special tax treatment.

Section 368(a)(1) states that the term "reorganization" means:

(A) A statutory merger or consolidation.

(B) The acquisition by one corporation, in exchange solely for all or a part of its voting stock (or in exchange solely for all or a part of the voting stock of a corporation which is in control of the acquiring corporation), of stock of another corporation if, immediately after the acquisition, the acquiring corporation has control of such other corporation (whether or not such acquiring corporation had control immediately before the acquisition).

(C) The acquisition by one corporation, in exchange solely for all or a part of its voting stock (or in exchange solely for all or a part of the voting stock of a corporation which is in control of

---

33. Reg. § 1.1011–2(c).

the acquiring corporation), of substantially all of the properties of another corporation, but in determining whether the exchange is solely for stock the assumption by the acquiring corporation of a liability of the other, or the fact that property acquired is subject to a liability, shall be disregarded.

(D) A transfer by a corporation of all or a part of its assets to another corporation if immediately after the transfer the transferor, or one or more of its shareholders (including persons who were shareholders immediately before the transfer), or any combination thereof, is in control of the corporation to which the assets are transferred, but only if, in pursuance of the plan, stock or securities of the corporation to which the assets are transferred are distributed in a transaction which qualifies under § § 354, 355, or 356.

(E) A recapitalization.

(F) A mere change in identity, form or place of organization, however effected.

(G) A transfer by a corporation of all or a part of its assets to another corporation in a bankruptcy or receivership proceeding but only if in pursuance of the plan, stock and securities of the transferee corporation are distributed in a transaction which qualifies under § § 354, 355, or 356.

These seven different types of tax-free reorganizations are designated by the letters identifying each: "Type A," "Type B," "Type C," "Type D," "Type E," "Type F," and "Type G," reorganizations. Basically, excepting the recapitalization (E), the change in form (F), and the insolvent corporation (G) provisions, a tax-free reorganization is (a) a statutory merger or consolidation, (b) an exchange of stock for voting stock, (c) an exchange of assets for voting stock, or (d) a divisive reorganization (the so-called spin-off, split-off, or split-up).

## GENERAL CONSEQUENCES OF TAX-FREE REORGANIZATIONS

Generally, no gain or loss is recognized to the security holders of the various corporations involved in a tax-free reorganization in the exchange of their stock and securities[34] except when they receive cash or other consideration in addition to stock and securities.[35] As far as securities (long-term debt) are concerned, however, gain is not recognized if securities are surrendered in the same principal amount (or a

---

**34.** The term "securities" includes bonds and long-term notes. Short-term notes are not considered to be securities. The problem of drawing a line between short-term and long-term notes was discussed in Chapter 12. Some courts include notes with a five-year maturity date as long-term; others, ten years.

**35.** § 358(a).

greater principal amount) as the principal amount of the securities received.

If additional consideration is received, gain is recognized but not in excess of the sum of money and the fair market value of other property received.[36] If the distribution has the effect of the distribution of a dividend, any recognized gain is a taxable dividend to the extent of the stockholder's share of the corporation's earnings and profits. The remainder is treated as an exchange of property.[37] Loss is never recognized. The tax basis of stock and securities received by a shareholder pursuant to a tax-free reorganization will be the same as the basis of those surrendered, decreased by the amount of boot received and increased by the amount of gain and dividend income, if any, recognized on the transaction.[38]

> **Example 24.**  A, an individual, exchanges stock he owns in X Corporation for stock in Y Corporation plus $2,000 cash. The exchange is pursuant to a tax-free reorganization of both corporations. A paid $10,000 for the stock in X two years ago. The stock in Y possesses a fair market value of $12,000. A has a realized gain of $4,000 ($12,000 + $2,000 − $10,000) which is recognized to the extent of the boot received, $2,000. Assume the distribution has the effect of a dividend. If A's share of earnings and profits in X is $1,000, that amount would be a taxable dividend. The remaining $1,000 would be treated as a gain from the exchange of property. A's basis in the Y stock would be $10,000 [$10,000 (basis in stock surrendered) − $2,000 (boot received) + $2,000 (gain and dividend income recognized)].

> **Example 25.**  Assume A's basis in the X stock was $15,000. A would have a realized loss of $1,000 on the exchange, none of which would be recognized. His basis in the Y stock would be $13,000 [$15,000 (basis in stock surrendered) − $2,000 (boot received)].

Because there is a substituted basis in tax-free reorganizations, the unrecognized gain or loss will be recognized when the new stock or securities are disposed of in a taxable transaction.

No gain or loss is recognized to the acquired corporation on the exchange of property pursuant to a tax-free reorganization.[39] If the acquired corporation receives cash or other property in the exchange, as well as stock or securities in the acquiring corporation, gain is recognized to the corporation on such other property only if the corporation fails to distribute the "other property" to its shareholders. If

---

**36.**　§ 356(a)(1).
**37.**　§ 356(a)(2).
**38.**　§ 358.
**39.**　§ 361(a).

the acquired corporation distributes boot received in a tax-free reorganization, the shareholders, and not the corporation, are taxed on any recognized gain occasioned by the receipt of boot.[40]

Gain or loss also is not recognized by the acquiring corporation.[41] Property received from the acquired corporation retains the basis it had in the hands of the acquired corporation, increased by the amount of gain recognized to the acquired corporation on the transfer.[42]

If a corporate exchange qualifies as a tax-free reorganization under one of the seven types mentioned, the tax consequences described are automatic regardless of the intent of the parties involved.

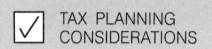

## TAX PLANNING CONSIDERATIONS

### EFFECT ON THE CORPORATION

The effect of a liquidation on the distributing corporation is governed by § 336 (i. e., distributions in kind) and § 337 (i. e., sales during the 12-month period). These two provisions may, however, be combined to achieve a minimum tax effect.

> **Example 26.** X Corporation is in the process of complete liquidation and has met all of the requirements of § 337. It possesses 2,000 units of appreciated inventory (non-LIFO), 500 of which the shareholders would like distributed to them. The other 1,500 units are to be sold to a third party. Can the distribution and sale be accomplished tax-free? Yes, if the proper order is observed. First, the corporation should distribute the 500 units to its shareholders. The in kind distribution would be nontaxable under § 336. Second, the remaining 1,500 units can be sold in one transaction and to one person. As such, this disposition of the remaining inventory qualifies as a "bulk sale," the gain from which is not recognized by virtue of § 337(b)(2).

Because the determination of whether a transfer of inventory qualifies as a bulk sale is made at the time of its sale and not tied to previous dispositions, the possibility of loss sales should not be overlooked.

> **Example 27.** Y Corporation is in the process of complete liquidation and has satisfied all the requirements of § 337. It owns

---

**40.** § 361(b). If the acquired corporation has sufficient earnings and profits and the shareholders receive pro rata distributions as boot, the boot is treated as a dividend and taxed as ordinary income and not as capital gain. See *Shimberg v. U. S.,* 78–2 USTC ¶ 9607, 42 AFTR2d 78–5575, 577 F.2d 283 (CA–5, 1978).
**41.** § 361(a).
**42.** § 362(b).

3,000 units of inventory (non-LIFO), half of which have appreciated in value over their basis. The other 1,500 units would yield a loss if sold. If all the inventory units are sold to one person in one transaction, neither gain nor loss is recognizable. Instead, why not sell the loss units first, followed by the sale of the gain units? The loss will be recognized because inventory (unless sold in bulk) does not qualify as property for purposes of the nonrecognition provisions of § 337. But since the gain sale is a bulk sale, § 337 applies to prevent the gain from being recognized. To insure against the possibility that the IRS might try to merge both sales as one transaction, each sale should be kept separate and distinct. Selling the inventory to different purchasers would help.

Another possibility exists in utilizing the bulk sale of inventory provisions of § 337. The Code directs nonrecognition of gain or loss treatment in the case of a bulk sale of inventory "attributable to a trade or business of the corporation." It is possible, therefore, to have a bulk sale of one type of inventory and not of another.

> **Example 28.** Z Corporation is engaged in the construction of homes for resale and also operates a retail outlet from which it sells home appliances to the general public. After the adoption of a plan of complete liquidation, the corporation sells its inventory of finished homes to various buyers. The inventory of home appliances, however, is sold to another corporation engaged in the same retailing business. The sale of the homes would result in recognized gain or loss to Z Corporation; however, the sale of the home appliances would not. In the latter case, it is assumed Z Corporation has met the requirements of § 337 and that the inventory is not determined under the LIFO method.

Other points to be considered in planning the desired tax result for a corporation in its liquidation are summarized below:

—A sale of accounts receivable for more than book value will trigger recapture of some or all of the reserve for bad debts due to the application of the tax benefit rule. Consequently, care should be taken in making an appropriate allocation to accounts receivable when these items are sold with other assets to the same purchaser. The same approach should be taken with property that possesses recapture of depreciation potential under §§ 1245 and 1250. Proper allocation of the purchase price can reduce the recognized gain from the sale of such assets and therefore limit the amount that has to be recaptured as ordinary income.[43]

—With respect to attorney's fees incurred during liquidation, a proper allocation of such fees to general liquidation expenses,

---

43. *Dorothy G. Armstrong,* 36 TCM 137, T.C.Memo. 1977–30.

to the sale of property outside the scope of § 337, or to a distribution of property in kind under § 336 will cause such fees to be deductible to the corporation as a business expense under § 162. If the fees are associated with the sale of assets under § 337, they will be required to be offset against the selling price and as a result will not be allowed as deductions.

—In making nontaxable distributions in kind under § 336, watch for the possible application of *Court Holding Company*. Particularly if the shareholders sell the property immediately after its receipt to the same parties who previously negotiated the sale with the corporation, the sale might be attributed to the corporation. In some cases, § 337 could neutralize the corporation's imputed gain if the distribution and sale occur within the 12-month liquidation period. It would not, however, if the asset distributed does not constitute property within the definition of § 337.

—Depending on the resolution of the issue by the Supreme Court, it may be that a § 336 distribution in kind will avoid the application of the tax benefit rule.

—For major asset corporations that suffer an involuntary conversion, the 60-day grace period of § 337(e) does not solve all timing problems. First of all, 60 days is not a long period of time. It is not inconceivable that 60 days may pass without the parties recognizing the need to adopt a plan of complete liquidation under § 337. Second, it is not always clear in this kind of situation what direction the parties ultimately will take. It may be, for example, that the use of § 1033 is preferable, since it avoids gain at both the corporation and shareholder levels. Nevertheless, compliance with the requirements of § 1033 can prove troublesome. Not only do all of the insurance (or condemnation) proceeds have to be reinvested within a specified period of time, but the replacement usually must be in property that is "similar or related in service or use." Such property may be difficult to find. Or if the insurance claim is contested, how much needs to be reinvested to avoid any recognition of gain? All of these variables could make the decision as to whether to liquidate (and make use of § 337) or continue in business (and make use of § 1033) a protracted one. The parties, however, can buy time by making use of the § 337(e) grace period and adopting a plan of complete liquidation. This keeps the § 337 option open. Bear in mind that the adoption of the plan does not require that the liquidation actually be carried out.

—In the case of straddle sales, be sure a *formal* plan of liquidation is adopted *after* the sale. The complete absence of a formal plan may enable the IRS to infer the adoption of an informal plan prior to the sale of the loss assets. This would disallow all gains and losses if the complete liquidation occurs within 12 months, or if not within 12 months, it could make all gains and losses taxable.

—Although the use of § 337 usually is advantageous to the taxpayer, in some situations it may prove to be an unwise choice. Suppose, for example, a plan is adopted and the amount of losses realized from the sales of corporate property exceeds the realized gains. Can anything be done to make § 337 inoperative so as to permit the recognition of both losses and gains? The obvious way to avoid § 337 would be to violate the 12-month rule by delaying the final liquidating distributions to the shareholders.[44]

## EFFECT ON THE SHAREHOLDER

Shareholders will, under the general rule of § 331, have recognized gain or loss measured by the difference between the liquidation proceeds and the basis of the stock given up. In cases of a large gain, a shareholder may wish to consider shifting it to others. One approach is to give the stock to family members or donate it to charity. Whether this procedure will be successful depends on the timing of the transfer. If the donee of the stock is not in a position to prevent the liquidation of the corporation, the donor will be deemed to have made an anticipatory assignment of income. As a result, the gain will still be taxed to the donor. Hence, advance planning becomes crucial in arriving at the desired tax result.

One important decision which must be made is the type of liquidation most favorable to the shareholders. Section 333 (i. e., the one-month type), an elective provision, should be weighed very carefully.

—Large amounts of E & P at the corporate level may generate dividend income to the individual shareholder or capital gain to the corporate shareholder. Remember that sales by the corporation of gain property during the liquidation process could aggravate the problem further because of their effect on E & P.

—Even if little or no gain is recognized by the shareholder on a § 333 liquidation, the key to the choice of this election may lie with what happens to the property after distribution and how the property is classified in the hands of the shareholder.

> **Example 29.** T, the sole shareholder of V Corporation, receives inventory (value of $80,000) and land (value of $20,000) in complete liquidation. T's basis in the V Corporation stock investment is $10,000. The inventory will be a noncapital asset to T because he is engaged in the same trade or business as the corporation.

---

44. Rev.Rul. 77–150, 1977–1 C.B. 88.

In all probability, T would be ill-advised to elect § 333, even if no gain resulted from the liquidation. Under § 334(c) his basis in the inventory would be $8,000 [($80,000/ $100,000) × $10,000 (the basis in the stock)]. A post-liquidation sale of the inventory for $80,000 would result in ordinary income of $72,000 [$80,000 (sales price) − $8,000 (allocated basis)]. If § 333 is not elected and the general rule of § 331 takes effect, T's basis in the inventory becomes $80,000 [§ 334(a)]. Thus, T substitutes $90,000 of capital gain [$100,000 (fair market value of all assets received) − $10,000 (the basis in the stock)] for $72,000 of ordinary income. Also, his basis in the land is $20,000 as opposed to the $2,000 [($20,000/$100,000) × $10,000] it would have if § 333 had been elected.

**Example 30.** Assume the same facts as in Example 29 except that V Corporation's only asset is land (value of $100,000) which T intends to hold as an investment. Presuming no gain results to T if § 333 is utilized, the election appears highly attractive. True, T's basis now becomes $10,000 (i. e., his basis in the stock). But because T does not intend to immediately dispose of the land, his low basis is of little consequence. Further, any gain on a later sale of the land investment would be capital. The alternative (use of the general rule of § 331) does provide a basis of $100,000 but would force T to recognize a gain of $90,000 [$100,000 (value of the land) − $10,000 (basis in the stock] upon liquidation. Utilizing § 333 carries the advantage of postponing the recognition of gain without changing its classification (i. e., capital *versus* ordinary).

In the event § 333 is to be used, close attention should be paid to the applicable procedural rules for making the election and carrying out the liquidation. Strict compliance with the 30-day and one-month requirements is essential.

Unlike § 333, the use of § 332 for the liquidation of a subsidiary is not elective. Nevertheless, some flexibility may be available.

—Whether § 332 applies depends on the 80 percent stock ownership test. Given some substance to the transaction, § 332 may well be avoided if a parent corporation reduces its stock ownership in the subsidiary below this percentage. On the other hand, the opposite approach may be desirable. A parent could make § 332 applicable by acquiring enough additional stock in the subsidiary to meet the 80 percent test.

—Once § 332 becomes operative, less latitude is present in determining the parent's basis in the subsidiary's assets. If § 334(b)(1) applies, the subsidiary's basis carries over to the parent. With § 338 controlling, the parent's basis becomes the cost of the stock.

# PROBLEM MATERIALS

## Discussion Questions

1. Compare stock redemptions and liquidations with other corporate distributions in terms of the following:

   (a) Recognition of gain to the shareholder.

   (b) Recognition of gain by the distributing corporation.

   (c) Effect on the distributing corporation's E & P.

2. Compare stock redemptions with liquidations in terms of the following:

   (a) Possible application of § 311 to the distributing corporation.

   (b) Possible disallowance of a loss (i. e., § 267) to a shareholder.

3. Presuming the general rule of § 331 applies, would it make any difference to the shareholder whether he or she receives cash or property distributions from the corporation being liquidated? Explain.

4. What problem led to the enactment of § 337 (the 12-month liquidation)?

5. Can the same liquidation involve the application of both § § 336 and 337? Explain.

6. Why is § 337 termed the 12-month liquidation?

7. How would the liquidating corporation be taxed on the sale of the following assets under § 337?

   (a) Inventory.

   (b) Depreciable property.

   (c) Property upon which an investment tax credit has previously been claimed.

   (d) Trade accounts receivable.

8. What is a straddle sale?

   (a) What are its advantages?

   (b) What danger, if any, exists that it might not be successful?

9. What constitutes a plan of liquidation for purposes of § 337?

10. Discuss the tax treatment of liquidation expenses in connection with the following:

    (a) General liquidation expenses.

    (b) Expenses relating to a distribution of assets in kind.

    (c) Expenses relating to a sale of property, the gain from which is not recognized under § 337.

    (d) Expenses relating to a sale of assets, the gain from which is recognized by the corporation.

11. Suppose a corporation has its major asset destroyed by fire. Under what circumstances may any gain resulting from the insurance proceeds be nonrecognizable under § 337?

12. Under what conditions, if any, may a corporation retain assets beyond a 12-month period from the adoption of a plan of complete liquidation without losing the benefits of § 337?

13. Why is a § 333 liquidation referred to as a one-month liquidation?

14. Under what conditions might a § 333 liquidation be advantageous? Disadvantageous?

15. Under what circumstances may an individual shareholder elect § 333? A corporate shareholder?

16. If some shareholders elect § 333, what tax consequences ensue to those who do not?

17. With regard to § 333, distinguish between the 30-day and the one-month requirements.

18. In determining the amount and classification of gain to the shareholders under § 333, comment on the effect of the following:

    (a) The E & P of the corporation being liquidated.

    (b) The type of shareholder involved (i. e., corporate or noncorporate).

    (c) The shareholder's *realized* gain.

    (d) The amount of the liquidating corporation's cash plus post-1953 securities.

19. In arriving at the basis of property received pursuant to a § 333 liquidation, what impact would the following have?

    (a) The shareholder's recognized gain.

    (b) The shareholder's basis in the stock investment.

    (c) The cash received by the shareholder.

    (d) The shareholder assumes a general liability of the corporation.

    (e) The shareholder assumes a liability of the corporation which relates to a specific asset received in the distribution.

20. In terms of the applicability of § 332, describe the effect of each of the factors appearing below:

    (a) The adoption of a plan of complete liquidation.

    (b) The period of time in which the corporation must liquidate.

    (c) The amount of stock held by the parent corporation.

21. Explain the problem that led to the *Kimbell-Diamond* decision.

22. What are the requirements for the application of § 338?

23. Under what circumstances could the application of § 338 be beneficial to the parent corporation? Detrimental?

24. Compare § § 334(b)(1) and 338 with respect to the following:

    (a) Carryover to the parent of the subsidiary's corporate attributes.

    (b) Recognition by the subsidiary of gain or loss on distributions to its parent.

25. Briefly describe the hoped-for tax results taxpayers were trying to achieve through the use of the collapsible corporation approach.

26. How can § 341 affect a sale by a shareholder of his or her stock to a third party? A distribution not in liquidation by the corporation to its shareholders?

## Problems

27. Indicate whether the following statements relating to § § 336 and 337 liquidations are true or false:

    (a) Liquidation expenses incurred in carrying out a nontaxable distribution of property in kind under § 336 would not be deductible to the corporation.

    (b) The distribution in kind in 1983 of LIFO inventory under § 336 results in recognizable gain to the distributing corporation because of § 336(b).

    (c) Under the Treasury Department Regulations, if a corporation sells substantially all of its assets prior to the adoption of a plan of complete liquidation under § 337, both gains and losses must be recognized on such sales.

    (d) Section 337 cannot be used in the case of a stock redemption.

    (e) Once adopted, a § 337 plan cannot later be rescinded.

    (f) The *Court Holding Company* concept could be applicable to trigger the recognition of gain at the corporate level of distribution of property in kind under § 336.

    (g) Section 337 cannot be used in connection with a § 333 liquidation.

    (h) Under § 337, assets of the liquidating corporation may be retained beyond the 12-month period to meet the claims of third-party creditors.

    (i) Section 337(a) protects the liquidating corporation from the recapture of depreciation on the sale of § 1250 property during the 12-month liquidation period.

    (j) A bulk sale of inventory at a loss under § 337 would generate a nonrecognizable loss.

28. Indicate whether the following statements relating to § § 336 and 337 liquidations are true or false:

    (a) Section 337 will be inapplicable unless a written plan of complete liquidation is adopted.

    (b) A distribution in kind of § 38 property under § 336 will avoid any recapture of the investment credit.

    (c) General liquidation expenses (i. e., not related to the sale of assets) are deductible by the liquidating corporation even though a plan under § 337 is in effect.

    (d) A liquidating corporation may have more than one bulk sale of inventory under § 337.

    (e) To carry out a successful straddle sale under § 337, the liquidating corporation should sell its loss assets after the 12-month liquidation period is concluded.

    (f) Prior to the enactment of § 337, a liquidating corporation always had to recognize gain on the disposition of its appreciated assets.

    (g) The application of the tax benefit rule to trigger the recognition of gain on the sale of assets under § 337 would not be a problem if the corporation being liquidated used the cash method of accounting for tax purposes.

    (h) The adoption of § 337 precludes the application of § 336.

29. On June 1, 19X2, T Corporation adopts a plan of complete liquidation under § 337. Assuming the liquidation is carried out within the 12-month period, determine the gain (or loss), income (or expense), that the corporation must recognize from each of the following transactions:

    (a) On January 15, 19X2, T Corporation sells some of its inventory (basis of $40,000, FMV of $32,000) to one of its customers.

    (b) On July 1, 19X2, T Corporation sells to outsiders some machinery acquired four years ago (adjusted basis of $10,000) for $30,000.

    (c) On August 3, 19X2, T Corporation distributes installment notes receivable (basis of $30,000) to its shareholders. The installment notes resulted from a sale in 19X1 of unimproved land and possess a present value of $54,000, face amount of $60,000.

    (d) On August 5, 19X2, T Corporation sells its remaining non-LIFO inventory (basis of $10,000) to one of its customers for $25,000.

    (e) On September 1, 19X2, T Corporation pays an attorney $600 to have its corporate charter revoked.

30. X Corporation distributes appreciated LIFO inventory (basis of $50,000) to A, its shareholder, as part of a complete liquidation (plan of liquidation was adopted January 2, 1983). The basis of the inventory under the FIFO method of inventory valuation would have been $80,000. What gain, if any, must X Corporation recognize on the distribution?

31. Z Corporation is liquidated in 19X2 by Z, its sole shareholder, at a time when its E & P is $40,000. Pursuant to the liquidation, Z an individual, receives the following items:

|  | Basis to Z Corporation | Fair Market Value |
|---|---|---|
| Cash | $ 40,000 | $ 40,000 |
| Accounts receivable | 20,000 | 20,000 |
| Land | 40,000 | 60,000 |
| Mortgage payable | (20,000) | N/A |
| Stock (acquired in 19X9) | 80,000 | 60,000 |

    On the date of liquidation, Z has a basis in his Z Corporation stock of $80,000. The land is transferred to Z subject to the mortgage. Assume the liquidation takes place under § 333.

    (a) What is Z's realized gain?

    (b) Recognized gain?

    (c) How much of the recognized gain is capital gain?

    (d) What will be Z Corporation's recognized gain?

    (e) What basis will Z have in the stock?

    (f) What basis will Z have in the land?

32. Indicate whether the following statements relating to § 333 liquidations are true or false:

    (a) If the E & P of the liquidating corporation is larger than the corporate-shareholder's realized gain, all of the recognized gain will be ordinary income.

(b) If the E & P of the liquidating corporation is less than the individual-shareholder's realized gain, some of the recognized gain may be capital gain.

(c) If the liquidating corporation has no E & P, no gain will be recognized by its shareholders.

(d) Unlike § 332, § 333 is an elective provision.

(e) Section 333 may be applicable to some shareholders and not applicable to other shareholders in the same corporation.

(f) Under § 333, the liquidation of the corporation must take place within one month from the date the plan of liquidation is adopted.

33. Z Corporation adopts a plan of liquidation in the current year. Its shares are owned as follows: J, 100 shares; K, 100 shares; and P Corporation, 100 shares. The financial statement of Z Corporation is as follows:

*Assets*

|  | Basis to Z Corporation | Fair Market Value |
|---|---|---|
| Cash | $ 60,000 | $ 60,000 |
| Inventory | 100,000 | 90,000 |
| Machinery (depreciation allowed of $40,000) | 160,000 | 210,000 |
| Land | 200,000 | 240,000 |
|  | $ 520,000 | $ 600,000 |

*Liabilities and Stockholders' Equity*

|  | Basis to Z Corporation | Fair Market Value |
|---|---|---|
| Accounts payable | $ 140,000 | $ 140,000 |
| Stockholders' equity— |  |  |
| Common stock | 300,000 | 460,000 |
| Retained earnings | 80,000 |  |
|  | $ 520,000 | $ 600,000 |

E & P equals retained earnings on the date of adoption of the plan of liquidation. There are no immediate plans for selling the machinery and land. What plan of liquidation should be followed, and what steps should be taken to perfect the liquidation for tax purposes?

34. The shareholders of B Corporation are R, S, and T, each owning 100 shares of stock. The financial statement of B Corporation is as follows:

*Assets*

|  | Basis to B Corporation | Fair Market Value |
|---|---|---|
| Cash | $ 40,000 | $ 40,000 |
| Land | 200,000 | 800,000 |
|  | $ 240,000 | $ 840,000 |

*Liabilities and Stockholders' Equity*

| | | |
|---|---|---|
| Accounts payable | $ 20,000 | $ 20,000 |
| Mortgages payable | 320,000 | 320,000 |
| Common stock | 60,000 | 500,000 |
| Deficit | (160,000) | |
| | $ 240,000 | $ 840,000 |

The corporation adopts a plan of liquidation. There are no present plans to sell the land. The shareholders plan to divide the land and farm it in their individual capacities. Compute the gain upon liquidation and the basis of the land to each individual shareholder (a) assuming the liquidation is pursuant to § 333 and (b) assuming the liquidation is pursuant to §§ 331 and 337. Assume the shareholders' basis in the stock is the same as the common stock account listed on the books of B Corporation.

35. At the time of its liquidation under § 332, S Corporation had the following assets and liabilities:

| | Basis to S Corporation | Fair Market Value |
|---|---|---|
| Cash | $ 240,000 | $ 240,000 |
| Marketable securities | 180,000 | 480,000 |
| Unimproved land | 300,000 | 600,000 |
| Unsecured bank loan | (60,000) | (60,000) |
| Mortgage on land | (180,000) | (180,000) |

P Corporation, the sole shareholder of S Corporation, has a basis in its stock investment of $720,000. At the time of its liquidation, S Corporation's E & P was $960,000.

(a) How much gain (or loss) will S Corporation recognize if it distributes all of its assets and liabilities to P Corporation?

(b) How much gain (or loss) will P Corporation recognize?

(c) If § 334(b)(1) applies, what will be P Corporation's basis in the marketable securities it receives from S Corporation?

(d) What will be its basis in the unimproved land?

36. S Corporation is owned by W, who is interested in selling either his stock in S Corporation or its assets. The financial statement of S Corporation as of December 31, 19X5, is as follows:

*Assets*

| | Basis to S Corporation | Fair Market Value |
|---|---|---|
| Cash | $ 7,500 | $ 7,500 |
| Accounts receivable | 5,000 | 5,000 |
| Inventory | 7,500 | 12,500 |
| Equipment (depreciation allowed of $20,000) | 25,000 | 50,000 |
| Land | 50,000 | 100,000 |
| | $ 95,000 | $ 175,000 |

*Liabilities and Stockholders' Equity*

| | | |
|---|---:|---:|
| Accounts payable | $ 20,000 | $ 20,000 |
| Mortgages payable | 25,000 | 25,000 |
| Common stock | 12,500 | 130,000 |
| Retained earnings | 37,500 | |
| | $ 95,000 | $ 175,000 |

P Corporation is interested in purchasing S Corporation. Should P Corporation purchase the stock for $130,000 or the assets for $175,000? If stock is purchased for $130,000, what steps should P Corporation take to secure maximum tax benefits?

# Chapter 15

# Corporate Accumulations

In Chapter 16, one major technique for minimization of the tax liability of closely-held corporations is discussed—the Subchapter S election. However, some of the corporations that fall into the "closely-held" category either may not qualify for the election or may find it unattractive. For these other taxpayers, how can corporate earnings be transmitted to the stockholders while at the same time insuring a deduction for the corporation? One method is to reduce the amount of equity capital invested in a controlled corporation by increasing the debt obligations. In other words, convert dividends into interest payments which are deductible by the corporation. There are limits to this method. The Internal Revenue Service may contend that the capital structure is unrealistic and the debt is not *bona fide*. For these reasons, the IRS will disallow the corporate deduction for interest expense (refer to Chapter 12).

An alternative possibility is to convert the earnings of the closely-held corporation into compensation to the officers, generally the major shareholders. The compensation is a deductible expense. If it were not for the reasonableness requirement, officers-stockholders could withdraw all corporate profits as salaries and thereby eliminate the corporate tax (refer to Chapter 13). However, the reasonableness requirement prevents a corporation from deducting as salaries what are, in fact, nondeductible dividends.

Another approach entails the lease of shareholder-owned property to the corporation. The corporation (the lessee) deducts the lease payment from gross income and saves taxes at the corporate level. Although the stockholders must recognize the rental payments as ordinary income, there is an overall tax savings because the corporation obtains deductions for what are essentially dividend payments. However, the IRS may classify such payments as "disguised dividends" and disallow the rental deductions (refer to Chapter 13).

A fourth method is simply to accumulate the earnings at the corporate level. Congress took steps to stem such accumulations as early as the first income tax law enacted under the Sixteenth Amendment. Today, in addition to the usual corporate income tax, an extra tax is imposed on earnings which are accumulated beyond the reasonable needs of the business. Also, a penalty tax may be imposed on undistributed personal holding company income.

This chapter demonstrates how the accumulation of earnings may be employed without leading to adverse tax consequences—the imposition of additional taxes.

# PENALTY TAX ON UNREASONABLE ACCUMULATIONS

One method of optimizing the distribution of earnings in a closely-held corporation is to accumulate the earnings until the most advantageous time to distribute them to shareholders is reached.[1] If the board of directors is aware of the tax problems of the shareholders, it can channel earnings into their pockets with a minimum of tax cost by using any of several mechanisms. The corporation can distribute dividends only in years when the major shareholders are in marginal tax brackets. Alternatively, dividend distributions might be curtailed causing the value of the stock to increase, in a manner similar to that of a savings account, as the retained earnings (and the earnings and profits account) increase. Later, the stockholders can sell their stock at an amount that reflects the increased retained earnings and incur tax at the favorable capital gain rates. Third, the corporation could be liquidated. In this case, the retained earnings would be transmitted to the stockholders tax-free or at the cost of only one capital gains tax. Or fourth, the stockholders may choose to retain their shares. Upon death, the estate or heirs would receive a step-up in basis equal to the fair market value of the stock on date of death or, if elected, on the alternate valuation date. As a result, the increment in value repre-

---

1.  Note that the penalty tax has also been imposed on publicly held corporations. See *Golconda Mining Corp.,* 58 T.C. 139 (1972) and 58 T.C. 736 (1972), *rev'd.* in 74–2 USTC ¶ 9845, 35 AFTR2d 75–336, 507 F.2d 594 (CA–9, 1974) and *Trico Products v. Comm.,* 43–2 USTC ¶ 9540, 31 AFTR 394, 137 F.2d 424 (CA–2, 1943). The IRS will impose the tax in whatever situations it deems appropriate; the Service asserts that there is no legal restriction which bars it from applying the tax to publicly held corporations. Rev.Rul. 75–305, 1975–2 C.B. 228.

sented by the step-up in basis would be largely attributable to the earnings retained by the corporation and would not be subject to income taxation.

However, there are problems involved in any situation in which corporate earnings are accumulated. Earnings retained in the business to avoid the imposition of the tax that would have been imposed on distributions to the shareholder could be subject to a penalty tax.

## THE ELEMENT OF INTENT

When a corporation is formed or availed of to shield its stockholders from individual taxes by accumulating rather than distributing earnings and profits, the "bad" purpose for accumulating earnings is considered to exist.[2] This subjective test, in effect, asks: "Did the corporation and shareholder(s) *intend* to retain the earnings in order to avoid the tax on dividends?" According to the Supreme Court, this tax avoidance motive need *not* be the dominant or controlling purpose for accumulating the earnings to trigger application of the penalty tax; it need only be a contributing factor to the retention of earnings.[3] If a corporation accumulates funds beyond its reasonable needs, such action is determinative of the existence of a "bad" purpose, unless the contrary may be proven by the preponderance of the evidence.[4] The fact that the business is a mere holding or investment company is *prima facie* evidence of this tax avoidance purpose.[5]

## IMPOSITION OF THE TAX
## AND THE ACCUMULATED EARNINGS CREDIT

The tax is imposed in addition to the regular corporate tax and the minimum tax. The rates are 27½ percent on the first $100,000 of accumulated taxable income and 38½ percent on all accumulated taxable income in excess of the first $100,000. Most corporations are allowed a minimum $250,000 credit against accumulated taxable income, even though it may be accumulating earnings beyond its reasonable business needs. However, personal service corporations in health, law, engineering, architecture, accounting, actuarial science, performing arts, and consulting are limited to a $150,000 accumulated earnings credit. Moreover, a nonservice corporation (other than a holding or investment company) can retain more than $250,000 of accumulated earnings if the company can justify that the accumulation is necessary to meet the reasonable needs of the business.[6]

---

**2.**  § 532(a).
**3.**  *U. S. v. The Donruss Co.,* 69–1 USTC ¶ 9167, 23 AFTR2d 69–418, 89 S.Ct. 501 (USSC, 1969).
**4.**  § 533(a).
**5.**  § 533(b). See, for example, *H. C. Cockrell Warehouse Corp.,* 71 T.C. 1036 (1979).
**6.**  §§ 535(c) and 537; see also Reg. § 1.537–1.

The accumulated earnings credit is the greater of the following:

1.  The current earnings and profits for the tax year which are needed to meet the reasonable needs of the business (see the discussion below) less the net long-term capital gain for the year (net of any tax thereon). In determining the reasonable needs for any one year, the accumulated earnings and profits of past years must be taken into account.

2.  The amount by which $250,000 exceeds the accumulated earnings and profits of the corporation at the close of the preceding tax year (designated as the "minimum credit").

**Example 1.** T Corporation, a calendar year manufacturing concern, has accumulated E & P of $120,000 as of December 31, 1983. For 1984, it has no capital gains and current E & P of $140,000. A realistic estimate places T Corporation's reasonable needs of the business for 1984 at $200,000. T Corporation's accumulated earnings credit based on the reasonable needs of the business would be $80,000 [$200,000 (reasonable needs of the business) − $120,000 (accumulated E & P)]. The minimum accumulated earnings credit would be $130,000 [$250,000 (minimum credit allowed for nonservice corporations) − $120,000 (accumulated E & P as of the close of the preceding tax year)]. Thus, the credit becomes $130,000 (i. e., the greater of $80,000 or $130,000).

Several observations should be made about the accumulated earnings credit. First, the minimum credit of $250,000 is of no consequence as long as the prior year's ending balance in accumulated E & P is $250,000 or more. Second, when the credit is based on reasonable needs, the credit is the amount which exceeds accumulated E & P. Third, a taxpayer must choose between the reasonable needs credit or the minimum credit. Combining the two in the same year is not permissible. Fourth, although the § 531 tax is not imposed on accumulated E & P, the amount of the credit depends upon the balance of this account as of the end of the preceding year.

## REASONABLE NEEDS OF THE BUSINESS

It has been firmly established that if a corporation's funds are invested in assets essential to the needs of the business, the IRS will have a difficult time imposing the accumulated earnings tax. "Thus, the size of the accumulated earnings and profits or surplus is not the crucial factor; rather it is the reasonableness and nature of the surplus."[7] What are the reasonable business needs of a corporation? This is precisely the point upon which difficulty arises and which creates controversy with the IRS.

---

7. *Smoot Sand & Gravel Corp. v. Comm.*, 60–1 USTC ¶ 9241, 5 AFTR2d 626, 274 F.2d 495 (CA–4, 1960).

*Justifiable Needs—In General.*  The reasonable needs of a business include its reasonably anticipated needs.[8] These anticipated needs must be specific, definite, and feasible. There have been a number of court cases which illustrate that indefinite plans referred to only briefly in corporate minutes merely provide a false feeling of security for the taxpayer.[9]

The Regulations list some legitimate reasons which may indicate that the earnings of a corporation are being accumulated to meet the reasonable needs of the business. Earnings may be allowed to accumulate to provide for *bona fide* expansion of the business enterprise or replacement of plant and facilities as well as to acquire a business enterprise through the purchase of stock or assets. Provision for the retirement of *bona fide* indebtedness created in connection with the trade or business (e. g., the establishment of a sinking fund for the retirement of bonds issued by the corporation) is a legitimate reason for accumulating earnings under ordinary circumstances. To provide necessary working capital for the business (e. g., to acquire inventories) and to provide for investment or loans to suppliers or customers, if necessary to maintain the business of the corporation, are valid grounds for accumulating earnings.[10] Funds may be retained for self-insurance[11] and realistic business contingencies (e. g., lawsuits, patent infringement).[12] Accumulations in order to avoid an unfavorable competitive position[13] and to carry keyman life insurance policies[14] are justifiable.

The reasonable business needs of a company also include the post-death § 303 redemption requirements of a corporation.[15] Accumulations for such purposes are limited to the amount needed (or reasonably anticipated to be needed) to effect a redemption of stock included in the gross estate of the decedent-shareholder.[16] This

---

**8.**  § 537(a)(1).

**9.**  *Fine Realty, Inc. v. U. S.*, 62–2 USTC ¶ 9758, 10 AFTR2d 5751, 209 F.Supp. 286 (D.Ct.Minn., 1962); *Young's Rubber Corp.*, 21 TCM 1593, T.C.Memo. 1962–300; *Motor Fuel Carriers, Inc. v. U. S.*, 65–2 USTC ¶ 9454, 15 AFTR2d 1153, 244 F.Supp. 380 (D.Ct.Fla., 1965).

**10.**  Reg. § 1.537–2(b).

**11.**  *Halby Chemicals Co., Inc. v. U. S.*, 67–2 USTC ¶ 9500, 19 AFTR2d 1589 (Ct.Cls., 1967).

**12.**  *Dielectric Materials Co.*, 57 T.C. 587 (1972).

**13.**  *North Valley Metabolic Laboratories*, 34 TCM 400, T.C.Memo. 1975–79.

**14.**  *Emeloid Co. v. Comm.*, 51–1 USTC ¶ 66,013, 40 AFTR 674, 189 F.2d 230 (CA–3, 1951). Keyman life insurance is a policy on the life of a key employee which is owned by and made payable to his or her employer. Such insurance would enable the employer to recoup some of the economic loss which might materialize upon the untimely death of the key employee.

**15.**  The § 303 redemption to pay death taxes and administration expenses of a deceased shareholder was discussed in Chapter 13.

**16.**  § 537(a)(2) and (b)(1).

amount may not exceed the sum of the death taxes and funeral and administrative expenses allowable under § § 2053 and 2106.[17]

The Revenue Act of 1978 amends § 537(b) to provide that reasonable accumulations to pay future product liability losses shall represent a reasonably anticipated need of the business. Guidelines for the application of this change are to be prescribed by the IRS in the form of Regulations. The amendment to § 537(b) is effective for tax years beginning after September 30, 1979.

*Justifiable Needs—Working Capital Requirements in Inventory Situations.* For many years the penalty tax on accumulated earnings was based upon the concept of retained earnings. The courts generally looked at retained earnings alone to determine whether there was an unreasonable accumulation. However, a corporation may have a large retained earnings balance and yet possess no liquid assets with which to pay dividends. Therefore, the emphasis should more appropriately be placed upon the liquidity of a corporation. Does the business have liquid assets *not* needed which could be used to pay dividends? However, it was not until 1960 that the courts began to use this liquidity approach.[18]

Gradually the courts began to develop a test based on the normal operating cycle of a business. Initially, a standard of one year's operating expenses was adopted as the appropriate benchmark.[19] Subsequently, the reasonable needs of the business were divided into two categories:

—Working capital needed for day-by-day operations.

—Expenditures of a noncurrent nature (extraordinary expenses).

The courts seized upon the operating cycle because it had the advantage of objectivity for purposes of determining working capital. There are two distinct cycles in a normal business:

1. Purchase of inventory ⟶ the production process ⟶ finished goods inventory
2. Sale of merchandise ⟶ accounts receivable ⟶ cash collection

A systematic operating cycle formula was developed in *Bardahl Manufacturing Co.* and *Bardahl International Corp.*[20] Thus, the technique became known as the *Bardahl* formula.

---

**17.** § 303(a).

**18.** See *Smoot Sand & Gravel Corp. v. Comm.,* cited in Footnote 7.

**19.** *Sterling Distributors, Inc. v. U. S.,* 63–1 USTC ¶ 9288, 11 AFTR2d 767, 313 F.2d 803 (CA–5, 1963).

**20.** *Bardahl Manufacturing Co.,* 24 TCM 1030, T.C.Memo. 1965–200; *Bardahl International Corp.,* 25 TCM 935, T.C.Memo. 1966–182. See also *Apollo Industries, Inc. v. Comm.,* 66–1 USTC ¶ 9294, 17 AFTR2d 518, 358 F.2d 867 (CA–1, 1966).

The standard method now used to determine the reasonable working capital needs for a corporation may be outlined as follows:[21]

$$\text{Inventory Cycle} = \frac{\text{Average[22] Inventory}}{\text{Cost of Goods Sold}}$$

*Plus*

$$\text{Accounts Receivable Cycle} = \frac{\text{Average Accounts Receivable}}{\text{Net Sales}}$$

*Minus*

$$\text{Accounts Payable Cycle} = \frac{\text{Average Accounts Payable[23]}}{\text{Purchases}}$$

*Equals*    A Decimal Percentage

The decimal percentage derived above, when multiplied by the cost of goods sold plus general, administrative, and selling expenses (not including Federal income taxes and depreciation),[24] equals the working capital needs of the business.

If the statistically computed working capital needs plus any extraordinary expenses are more than the current year's net working capital, there is no penalty tax.

However, if working capital needs plus any extraordinary expenses are less than the current year's net working capital, the possibility of the imposition of a penalty tax does exist.[25]

In *Bardahl Manufacturing Corp.*, the costs and expenses used in the formula were those of the following year, whereas in *Bardahl International Corp.*, costs and expenses of the current year were used. Use of the subsequent year's expected costs seems to be the more equitable position.

The IRS normally takes the position that the operating cycle should be reduced by the accounts payable cycle, since the payment of

---

**21.** These formulas assume that working capital needs are computed on a yearly basis; however, this may not provide the most favorable result. A business which experiences seasonally based high and low cycles illustrates this point. For example, a construction company can justify a greater working capital need if computations are based on a cycle which includes the winter months only and not an annual average.
**22.** Although the *Bardahl* formula requires the use of average turnover, the Tax Court has approved the use of peak amounts for those items which produce higher working capital needs. *Magic Mart, Inc.*, 51 T.C. 775 (1969). But see, *Bahan Textile Machinery Co. v. U. S.*, 72–1 USTC ¶ 9321, 29 AFTR2d 72–666, 341 F.Supp. 962 (D.Ct.S.C., 1970).
**23.** The accounts payable cycle was developed in *Kingsbury Investments, Inc.*, 28 TCM 1082, T.C.Memo. 1969–205. See also, *W. L. Mead, Inc.*, 34 TCM 924, T.C.Memo. 1975–215.
**24.** In *W. L. Mead, Inc.*, cited in Footnote 23, the Tax Court allowed depreciation to be included in the expenses of a service film with no inventory. Likewise, in *Doug-Long, Inc.*, 72 T.C. 158 (1979), the Tax Court allowed a truck stop to include quarterly estimated tax payments in operating expenses.
**25.** *Electric Regulator Corp. v. Comm.*, 64–2, USTC ¶ 9705, 14 AFTR2d 5447, 336 F.2d 339 (CA–2, 1964) used "quick assets."

such expenses may be postponed by various credit arrangements which will reduce the operating capital requirements. However, a number of court cases have omitted this reduction. In any case, a corporate tax planner should not have to rely on creditors to avoid the accumulated earnings penalty tax. The corporation with the most acute working capital problem will probably have a large accounts payable balance. If the previously outlined formula for determining reasonable working capital needs is used, a large accounts payable balance will result in a sizable reduction in the maximum working capital allowable before the tax is imposed. For tax planning purposes, a corporation should hold accounts payable at a reduced level.

*No Justifiable Needs.* Certain situations do *not* call for the accumulation of earnings. For example, accumulating earnings to make loans to shareholders[26] or brother-sister corporations is not considered within the reasonable needs of the business.[27] Accumulations to retire stock without curtailment of the business and for unrealistic business hazards (e. g., depression of the U. S. economy) are invalid reasons for accumulating funds,[28] as are accumulations made to carry out investments in properties or securities unrelated to the corporation's activity.[29]

> **Example 2.** M, Inc., a trucking company, has considered the purchase of various vehicles and other facilities directly related to its business for a period of years. It has, at the same time, invested in oil and gas drilling projects (mostly wildcats). Despite substantial accumulated earnings, the corporation made no distributions of dividends during the same period. The Claims Court imposed the penalty tax, because the plan to acquire vehicles and facilities was not supported by documents in existence or prepared during the taxable years at issue. Furthermore, accumulations to further the oil and gas investments were unjustified. (The company was not in the oil and gas business, and the corporation was only a minority investor.)[30]

*Measuring the Accumulation.* Should the cost or fair market value of assets be used to determine whether a corporation has accumulated earnings and profits beyond its reasonable needs? This issue remains unclear. The Supreme Court has indicated that fair market value is to be used when dealing with marketable securities.[31]

---

**26.** Reg. § 1.537–2(c)(1), (2), and (3).

**27.** See *Young's Rubber Corp.* cited in Footnote 9.

**28.** *Turnbull, Inc. v. Comm.,* 67–1 USTC ¶ 9221, 19 AFTR2d 609, 373 F.2d 91 (CA–5, 1967) and Reg. § 1.537–2(c)(5).

**29.** Reg. § 1.537–2(c)(4).

**30.** *Cataphote Corp. of Miss. v. U. S.,* 75–2 USTC ¶ 9753, 36 AFTR2d 75–5990 (Ct.Cls., 1975).

**31.** *Ivan Allen Co. v. U. S.,* 75–2 USTC ¶ 9557, 36 AFTR2d 75–5200, 95 S.Ct. 2501 (USSC, 1975).

Although the Court admitted that the concept of earnings and profits does not include unrealized appreciation, it asserted that to determine if accumulated earnings are reasonable the current asset ratio must be considered. Thus, the Court looked to the economic realities of the situation and held that fair market value is to be used with respect to readily marketable securities. The Court's opinion did not touch on the proper basis for valuation of assets other than marketable securities; however, the IRS may assert that this rule should be extended to include other assets. Therefore, tax advisers and corporate personnel should regularly check all security holdings to guard against accumulations caused by the appreciation of investments.

> **Example 3.** C Company had accumulated earnings and profits of approximately $2,000,000. Five years ago, the company invested $150,000 in various stocks and bonds. At the end of the current tax year, the fair market value of these securities approximated $2,500,000. Two of C Company's shareholders, father and son, owned 75% of the stock. If these securities are valued at cost, current assets minus current liabilities are deemed to be equal to the reasonable needs of the business. However, if the marketable securities are valued at their $2,500,000 fair market value, the value of the liquid assets would greatly exceed the corporation's reasonable needs. Under the Supreme Court's economic reality test the fair market value must be used; consequently, the corporation would be subject to the § 531 penalty tax.

## MECHANICS OF THE PENALTY TAX

The taxable base of the accumulated earnings tax is a company's accumulated taxable income (ATI). Taxable income of the corporation is modified as follows:[32]

$$\text{ATI} = \text{taxable income} \pm \text{certain adjustments} - \text{the dividends paid deduction} - \text{the accumulated earnings credit}$$

These "certain adjustments" include the following items:[33]
As deductions—

1. Corporate income tax (§ 11).
2. Charitable contributions in excess of 10 percent of adjusted taxable income.
3. Net capital losses disallowed by § 1211.
4. Excess of net long-term capital gain over net short-term capital loss (diminished by the capital gain tax).

---

**32.** § 535(a).
**33.** § 535(b).

And as additions—

1. Capital loss carryovers and carrybacks.
2. Net operating loss deduction.
3. The 85 percent dividends received deduction.

Payment of dividends reduces the amount of accumulated taxable income subject to the penalty tax. The dividends paid deduction includes those dividends paid during the tax year which the shareholders must report as ordinary income *and* any dividends paid within two and one-half months after the close of the tax year.[34] Further, a shareholder may file a consent statement to treat as a dividend the amount specified in such consent. A consent dividend is taxed to the stockholder even though it is not actually distributed. However, the consent dividend is treated as a contribution to the capital of the corporation (i. e., paid-in capital) by the stockholder.[35]

*Classify Corp*

**Example 4.** A nonservice closely-held corporation has the following financial transactions for calendar year 1984:

| | |
|---|---:|
| Taxable income | $ 300,000 |
| Tax liability | 117,750 |
| Excess charitable contributions | 22,000 |
| Long-term capital gain | 40,000 |
| Short-term capital loss | 80,000 |
| Dividends received | 100,000 |
| Research and development expenses | 46,000 |
| Dividends paid in 1984 | 40,000 |
| Accumulated earnings (1/1/84) | 220,000 |

Presuming the corporation is subject to the § 531 tax and has *no* reasonable business needs which would justify its accumulations, the accumulated taxable income is calculated as follows:

| | | |
|---|---:|---:|
| Taxable income | | $ 300,000 |
| Plus: 85% dividends received deduction | | 85,000 |
| | | $ 385,000 |
| Less: Tax liability | $ 117,750 | |
| Excess charitable contributions | 22,000 | |
| Net short-term capital loss | 40,000 | |
| Dividends paid | 40,000 | |
| Accumulated earnings credit | | |
| carryover ($250,000 − $220,000) | 30,000 | 249,750 |
| Accumulated taxable income | | $ 135,250 |

*several*

Thus, the accumulated earnings penalty tax for 1984 would be $40,571.25 [($100,000 × 27½%) + ($35,250 × 38½%)].

*extremely*

---

**34.** §§ 535(a), 561(a), and 563(a).

**35.** § 565(a) and (c)(2). The consent dividend procedure would be appropriate if the corporation is not in a position to make a cash or property distribution to its shareholders.

**Example 5.**  In Example 4, assume that the reasonable needs of the business of § 535(c) amount to $270,000 in 1984. The current year's accumulated earnings would be reduced by $50,000, rather than the $30,000, of accumulated earnings credit carryover. Thus, accumulated taxable income would be $115,250, and the penalty tax would be $32,775. Note that the first $220,000 of accumulated earnings *cannot* be omitted in determining whether taxable income for the current year is reasonably needed by the enterprise.

# PERSONAL HOLDING COMPANY PENALTY TAX

The personal holding company (PHC) tax was enacted to discourage the sheltering of certain types of passive income in corporations owned by high tax bracket individuals. These "incorporated pocketbooks" were frequently found in the entertainment and construction industries. For example, a taxpayer could shelter the income from securities in a corporation which would pay no dividends and allow the corporation's stock to increase in value. Thus, as with the accumulated earnings tax, the purpose of the PHC tax is to force the distribution of corporate earnings to the shareholders. However, in any one year, the IRS cannot impose both the PHC tax and the accumulated earnings tax.[36]

Whether a corporation may be included within the statutory definition of a personal holding company for any particular year depends upon the facts and circumstances in evidence during that year.[37] Therefore, personal holding company status may be conferred even in the absence of any such active intent on the part of the corporation. For example, in *Weiss v. U. S.,*[38] a manufacturing operation adopted a plan of complete liquidation under § 337, sold its business, and invested the proceeds of the sale in U.S. Treasury bills and certificates of deposits.[39] During the liquidating corporation's last tax year, 100 percent of its adjusted ordinary gross income was interest income. Since the corporation was owned by one stockholder, the corporation was a PHC, even though in the process of liquidation.

Certain types of corporations are expressly excluded from PHC status:

---

**36.**  § 532(b)(1) and Reg. § 1.541–1(a).

**37.**  *Affiliated Enterprises, Inc. v. Comm.,* 44–1 USTC ¶ 9178, 32 AFTR 153, 140 F.2d 647 (CA–10, 1944).

**38.**  75–2 USTC ¶ 9538, 36 AFTR2d 75–5186 (D.Ct.Ohio, 1975). See also, *O'Sullivan Rubber Co. v. Comm.,* 41–2 USTC ¶ 9521, 27 AFTR 529, 120 F.2d 845 (CA–2, 1941).

**39.**  Section 337 often permits a corporation to avoid the recognition of gain upon the sale of its assets if such sales are effected within a 12-month period and are pursuant to a plan of complete liquidation. Refer to Chapter 14.

—Tax-exempt organizations under § 501(a).

—Banks and domestic building and loan associations.

—Life insurance companies.

—Surety companies.

—Foreign personal holding companies.

—Lending or finance companies.

—Foreign corporations.

—Small business investment companies.[40]

## DEFINITION OF A PERSONAL HOLDING COMPANY

Two tests are incorporated within the PHC provisions:

—Was more than 50 percent of the *value* of the outstanding stock owned by five or fewer individuals at any time during the *last half* of the taxable year?

—Is a substantial portion (60 percent or more) of the corporate income (adjusted ordinary gross income) composed of passive types of income such as dividends, interest, rents, royalties, or certain personal service income?

If the answer to both of these questions is affirmative, then the corporation is classified as a PHC. Once classified as a PHC, the corporation is required to pay a 50 percent (70 percent prior to 1982) penalty tax in addition to the regular corporate income tax.

*Stock Ownership Test.* To meet the stock ownership test, more than 50 percent *in value* of the outstanding stock must be owned, directly or indirectly, by or for not more than five individuals sometime during the last half of the tax year. Thus, if the corporation has nine or fewer stockholders, it automatically meets this test. If 10 unrelated individuals own an *equal* portion of the value of the outstanding stock, the stock ownership requirement would not be met. However, if these 10 individuals do not hold equal value, the test would be met.

Notice that this ownership test is based on fair market value and is not based on the number of shares outstanding. Fair market value is determined in light of all the circumstances and is based on the company's net worth, earning and dividend paying capacity, appreciation of assets, and other relevant factors. If there are two or more classes of stock outstanding, the total value of all the stock should be allocated among the various classes according to the relative value of each class.[41]

In determining the stock ownership of an individual, very broad

---

**40.** § 542(c).
**41.** Reg. § 1.542–3(c).

constructive ownership rules are applicable. Under § 544, the following attribution rules determine indirect ownership:

1. Any stock owned by a corporation, partnership, trust, or estate is considered to be owned proportionately by its stockholders, partners, or beneficiaries.

2. The stock owned by the members of an individual's family (brothers, sisters, spouse, ancestors, and lineal descendants) or by his or her partner is considered to be owned by such individual.

3. If an individual has an option to purchase stock, such stock is regarded as owned by such person.[42]

4. Convertible securities are treated as outstanding stock.

Attribution rules 2, 3, and 4 are applicable only for the purpose of classifying a corporation as a personal holding company and cannot be used to avoid the application of the PHC provisions. Basically, these broad constructive ownership rules make it difficult for a closely-held corporation to avoid application of the stock ownership test.

*The Gross Income Test.* The gross income test is met if 60 percent or more of the corporation's *adjusted ordinary gross income* (AOGI) is composed of certain passive income items (i. e., PHC income). Adjusted ordinary gross income is calculated by subtracting from gross income (as defined by § 61):

—Gains from the sale or disposition of capital assets.

—Section 1231 gains.

—Expenditures attributable to income from rents and mineral royalties (such as depreciation, property taxes, interest expense, and rental payments).[43]

The deduction of the first two items from gross income results in the intermediate concept *ordinary gross income* (OGI), the use of which is noted subsequently. The starting point, gross income, is not necessarily synonymous with gross receipts. In fact, for transactions in stocks, securities, and commodities, the term "gross income" includes only the excess of gains over any losses.[44]

Personal holding company income includes income from dividends; interest; royalties; annuities; rents; mineral, oil, and gas royalties; copyright royalties; produced film rents; and amounts from certain personal service contracts. Any amount from personal service contracts is classified as PHC income only if (a) some person other than the corporation has the right to designate, by name or by de-

---

42. For examples of how these constructive ownership rules operate, see Reg. §§ 1.544–2, –3(a), and –4.
43. §§ 543(b)(1) and (2).
44. Reg. § 1.542–2.

scription, the individual who is to perform the services, and (b) the person so designated owns, directly or indirectly, 25 percent or more in value of the outstanding stock of the corporation at some time during the taxable year.[45]

> **Example 6.** M Corporation has four stockholders, and its adjusted ordinary gross income (AOGI) is $95,000, composed of gross income from a merchandising operation of $40,000, interest income of $15,000, dividend income of $25,000, and adjusted income from rents of $15,000. Total passive income is $55,000 ($15,000 + $25,000 + $15,000). Since 60% of AOGI (i. e., $57,000) is greater than the passive income ($55,000), this corporation is not a personal holding company.

> **Example 7.** Assume in Example 6 that the corporation received $21,000 in interest income rather than $15,000. Total passive income is now $61,000 ($21,000 + $25,000 + $15,000). Since 60% of AOGI (i. e., $60,600) is less than passive income of $61,000, this corporation is a personal holding company.

Rental income is normally classified as PHC income, but it can be excluded from that category if two tests are met. The first test is met if a corporation's adjusted income from rents is 50 percent or more of the corporation's AOGI. The second test is satisfied if the total dividends paid for the tax year are dividends considered as paid on the last day of the tax year and consent dividends equal to or greater than the amount by which the nonrent PHC income exceeds 10 percent of ordinary gross income.[46] Of course, the taxpayer wishes to meet both tests so that the rent income can be excluded from PHC income for purposes of the gross income test referred to above. (See Figure II later in the chapter.)

With respect to this 50 percent test, "adjusted income from rents" is defined as gross income from rents reduced by the deductions allowable under § 534(b)(2). These deductions are depreciation, property taxes, interest, and rent. Generally, compensation is not included in the term "rents" and is not an allowable deduction. The final amount included in AOGI as adjusted income from rents cannot be less than zero.

> **Example 8.** Assume that Z Corporation has rental income of $10,000 and the following business deductions:

| | |
|---|---:|
| Depreciation on rental property | $ 1,000 |
| Interest on mortgage | 2,500 |
| Real property taxes | 1,500 |
| Salaries and other business expenses (§ 162) | 3,000 |

---

**45.** § 543(a)(7). For an application of the "right to designate," see *Thomas P. Byrnes, Inc.,* 73 T.C. 416 (1979).
**46.** § 543(a)(2).

The adjusted income from rents included in AOGI is $5,000 (i. e., $10,000 − $1,000 − $2,500 − $1,500). Salaries and other § 162 expenses do not affect the calculation of AOGI.

A company deriving its income primarily from rental activities may avoid PHC status by merely distributing as dividends the amount of nonrental PHC income which exceeds 10 percent of its ordinary gross income.

**Example 9.**　　During the tax year, N Corporation receives $15,000 in rent income, $4,000 in dividends, and a $1,000 long-term capital gain. Corporate deductions for depreciation, interest, and real estate taxes allocable to the rental income amount to $10,000. The company paid a total of $2,500 in dividends to its eight shareholders. The company's OGI would be $19,000 [($15,000 + $4,000 + $1,000 = $20,000) − $1,000], and AOGI would be $9,000 ($19,000 − $10,000). Since adjusted rent income of $5,000 ($15,000 − $10,000) exceeds $4,500, 50% of AOGI ($9,000), this corporation meets the 50% test. Nonrental PHC income is $4,000, and 10% of OGI is only $1,900. Therefore, dividends of at least $2,100 ($4,000 − $1,900) must be paid to meet the 10% test. Since $2,500 in dividends are paid, N Corporation meets the 10% test; the rental income is not classified as PHC income.

Similar to rental income, adjusted income from mineral, oil, and gas royalties may be excluded from PHC income classification if three tests are met.[47] First, adjusted income from such royalties must constitute 50 percent or more of AOGI. Second, nonroyalty PHC income may not exceed 10 percent of OGI. Notice that this 10 percent test is not accompanied by the dividend "escape clause" described above in relation to rental income; therefore, corporations receiving income from mineral, oil, or gas royalties must be careful to minimize non-royalty PHC income. Furthermore, adjusted income from rents and copyright royalties is considered to be nonroyalty PHC income whether or not treated as such by § 543(a)(2) and (4).[48] Third, the company's business expenses under § 162 (other than compensation paid to stockholders) must be at least 15 percent of AOGI.

**Example 10.**　　P Corporation has gross income of $4,000 which consists of gross income from oil royalties in the amount of $2,500, $400 of dividends, and $1,100 from the sale of merchandise. The total amount of the deductions for depletion, interest, and property and severance taxes allocable to the gross income from oil royalties equals $1,000. Deductions allowable under § 162 amount to $450. P Corporation's AOGI equals $3,000

---

**47.**　§ 543(a)(3).
**48.**　Prop.Reg. § § 1.543–6(b)(2)(ii) and (iii).

($4,000 − $1,000), and its adjusted income from oil royalties is
$1,500 ($2,500 − $1,000). Since the adjusted income from oil roy-
alties constitutes 50% or more of the AOGI, test one is met. Non-
royalty PHC is $400 (composed solely of the $400 of dividends).
Such amount is not more than 10% of OGI; therefore, the second
test is satisfied. Since the $450 of § 162 expenses equals 15% of
AOGI ($3,000), the third requirement is satisfied. P Corpo-
ration's adjusted income from oil royalties does not constitute
PHC income.

## CALCULATION OF THE PHC TAX

To this point, the discussion has focused on the determination of personal holding company status. If an entity is classified as a PHC, a
new set of computations is relevant in determining the amount upon
which the 50 percent tax is imposed. This tax base is called undistributed PHC income (UPHC income). Basically, this amount is taxable
income, subject to certain adjustments, *minus* the dividends paid deduction.

The starting point is corporate taxable income determined as for
regular tax purposes. To this amount the following adjustments must
be made:

—The normal Federal income tax accrual (other than the PHC
tax and the accumulated earnings tax) for the tax year is deductible. The deduction is determined under the accrual
method even though the corporation may actually use the cash
receipts and disbursement method. Any contested, unpaid tax
is not considered accrued until the issue is resolved.[49]

—Excess charitable contributions beyond the corporate limitation of 10 percent of taxable income may be deducted up to the
20 percent, 30 percent, or 50 percent limitations imposed upon
individuals.[50]

—The excess of long-term capital gain over short-term capital
loss (net of tax) is deducted from taxable income.[51] Thus,
long-term capital gains may be accumulated in a corporation
and not be subject to the PHC tax.

—The dividends received deduction and other special deductions
allowed by § § 241 through 250 (other than the organizational
expense deduction) are not available. Such amounts must be
added back to taxable income to determine the penalty
tax base.[52]

**49.**  Reg. § 1.545–2(a)(1)(i).
**50.**  Reg. § 1.545–2(b)(2)(ii).
**51.**  § 545(b)(5) and *Litchfield Securities Corp. v. U. S.*, 64–1 USTC ¶ 9106, 12
AFTR2d 6042, 325 F.2d 667 (CA–2, 1963).
**52.**  § 545(b)(3).

—Any net operating loss, except for the preceding year, must be added back.[53]

—Under certain conditions, business expenses and depreciation attributable to nonbusiness property owned by the corporation that exceed the income derived from such property must be added back to taxable income to determine UPHC income.[54]

The above adjustments to taxable income result in a figure called *adjusted taxable income.*

*The Dividends Paid Deduction.* Since the purpose of the PHC penalty tax is to force a corporation to pay dividends, five types of dividends paid deductions reduce the amount subject to the 50 percent penalty tax. First, dividends actually paid during the tax year ordinarily reduce UPHC income.[55] However, such distributions must be pro rata. They must exhibit no preference to any shares of stock over shares of the same class or to any class of stock over other classes outstanding.[56] This prohibition is especially harsh when portions of an employee-stockholder's salary are declared unreasonable and classified as a disguised or constructive dividend.[57] In the case of a property dividend, the dividends paid deduction is limited to the adjusted basis of the property (not its fair market value) in the hands of the distributing corporation at the time of the distribution.[58]

> **Example 11.** Three individuals are equal stockholders in a personal holding company. A property dividend with an adjusted basis of $20,000 (FMV of $30,000) is paid to the three stockholders in the following proportion: 25%, 35%, and 40%. This is not a pro rata distribution; therefore, the dividends are not deductible from UPHC income.

A two and one-half month grace period following the close of the tax year exists. Dividends paid during this period may be treated as paid during the tax year just closed. However, the amount allowed as a deduction from UPHC income cannot exceed either (1) the UPHC income for the tax year or (2) 20 percent of the total dividends distributed during the tax year.[59] Reasonable cause may not be used to overcome the 20 percent limitation even if the taxpayer relied upon incorrect advice given by an accountant.[60]

---

**53.** § 545(b)(4).
**54.** § 545(b)(6).
**55.** § § 561(a)(1) and 562.
**56.** § 562(c).
**57.** See Chapter 13 and *Henry Schwartz Corp.*, 60 T.C. 728 (1973).
**58.** Reg. § 1.562–1(a). and *Fulman v. U. S.*, 78–1 USTC ¶ 9247, 41 AFTR2d 78–698, 98 S.Ct. 841 (USSC, 1978).
**59.** § § 563(b) and 543(a)(2)(B)(ii).
**60.** *Kenneth Farmer Darrow*, 64 T.C. 217 (1975).

The consent dividend procedure involves a hypothetical distribution of the corporate income which is taxed to the stockholders. Since the consent dividend is taxable, a dividends paid deduction is allowed. The stockholder's basis in his stock is increased by the consent dividend (i. e., a contribution to capital), and a subsequent actual distribution of the consent dividend should not be taxed. The consent election is filed by the stockholders at any time before the due date of the corporate tax return. The consent dividend is considered distributed by the corporation on the last day of the tax year and is included in the gross income of the shareholder in the tax year in which or with which the tax year of the corporation ends. The obvious disadvantage of this special election is that the stockholders must pay taxes on dividends which they do not actually receive. However, if cash is not available for dividend distributions, the consent dividend route is a logical alternative.

Even after a corporation has been classified as a PHC, a belated dividend distribution made in a subsequent tax year can avoid the PHC penalty tax. This deficiency dividend provision allows the payment of a dividend within 90 days after the determination of the PHC tax deficiency for a prior tax year. A determination occurs when a decision of a court is final, a closing agreement under § 7121 is signed, or a written agreement is signed between the taxpayer and a District Director. Note that the dividend distribution cannot be made before the determination or after the running of the 90-day time period.[61] Furthermore, the deficiency dividend procedure does not relieve the taxpayer of interest, additional amounts, or assessable penalties computed with respect to the PHC tax.[62]

There may be a dividend carryover from two prior years available to reduce the adjusted taxable income of a PHC. When the dividends paid by a company in its prior years exceed its adjusted taxable income for such years, the excess amount may be deducted in the current year. See § 564(b) for the manner of computing this dividend carryover.

*Personal Holding Company Planning Model.* Some of the complex personal holding company provisions may be developed into a flow chart format. Figure I and Figure II provide a personal holding company planning model and the rules for the rent exclusion test, respectively.

---

**61.** See *Leck Co., Inc. v. U. S.,* 73–2 USTC ¶ 9694, 32 AFTR2d 73–5891 (D.Ct.Minn., 1973) in which the taxpayer made distributions prior to the determination of the PHC tax liability and was denied deficiency dividend treatment. However, see *Hanco Distributing, Inc. v. U. S.,* 73–2 USTC ¶ 9632, 32 AFTR2d 73–5485 (D.Ct.Utah, 1973). In this case, the taxpayer was allowed deficiency treatment although the letter of the law was, by mistake, not followed.

**62.** § 547(a).

## Figure I*
### PERSONAL HOLDING COMPANY PLANNING MODEL

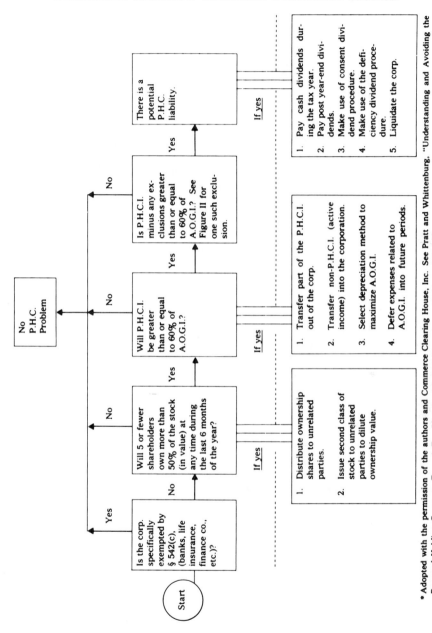

*Adopted with the permission of the authors and Commerce Clearing House, Inc. See Pratt and Whittenburg, "Understanding and Avoiding the Personal Holding Company Tax: A Tax Planning Model," Taxes (June 1975), pp. 366–367.

**Figure II***

RENT EXCLUSION TEST

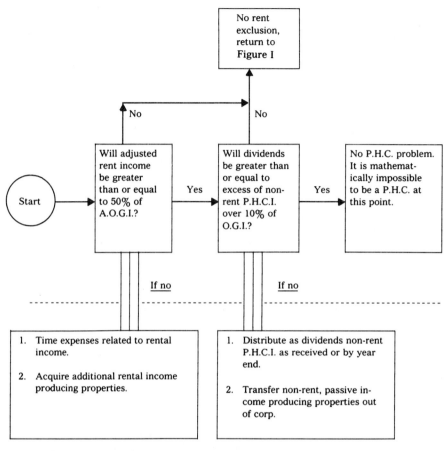

* Adopted with the permission of the authors and Commerce Clearing House, Inc. See Pratt and Whittenburg, "Understanding and Avoiding the Personal Holding Company Tax: A Tax Planning Model," *Taxes* (June 1975), pp. 366–367.

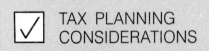 TAX PLANNING
CONSIDERATIONS

## THE § 531 TAX

*Justifying the Accumulations.* The key defense against imposition of the § 531 tax is a successful assertion that the accumulations are necessary to meet the reasonable needs of the business. Several points should be kept in mind:

—To the extent possible, the justification for the accumulation should be documented. If, for example, the corporation plans to acquire additional physical facilities for use in its trade or business, the minutes of the board of directors' meetings should reflect the decision. Furthermore, such documentation should take place during the period of accumulation. This may require some foresight on the part of the taxpayer, but meaningful planning to avoid a tax problem should not be based on what happens after the issue has been raised by an agent as the result of an audit. In the case of a profitable closely-held corporation that accumulates some or all of its profits, the parties might well operate under the assumption that § 531 is always a potential issue. Recognition of a tax problem at an early stage is the first step in its satisfactory resolution.

—Keep in mind that multiple reasons for making an accumulation are not only permissible but invariably advisable. Suppose, for example, a manufacturing corporation plans to expand its plant. It would not be wise to stop with the cost of such expansion as the only justification for all accumulations. What about further justification based on the corporation's working capital requirements as determined under the *Bardahl* formula or some variation thereof? Other reasons for making the accumulation may well be present and should be recognized.

—The reasons for the accumulation should be sincere and, once established, pursued to the extent feasible.

> **Example 12.** In 19X0, the board of directors of S Corporation decide to accumulate $1,000,000 to fund the replacement of its plant. Five years pass and no steps are taken to initiate construction.

> **Example 13.** In 19X0, the board of directors of Y Corporation decide to accumulate $1,000,000 to fund the replacement of its plant. In the ensuing five-year period, the following steps are taken: a site selection committee is appointed (19X1), a site is chosen (19X2), the site (i. e., land) is purchased (19X3), an architect is retained and plans are drawn up for the new plant (19X4), bids are requested and submitted for the construction of the new plant (19X5).

Compare Examples 12 and 13. Quite obviously, Y Corporation is in a much better position to justify the accumulation. Even though the plant has not yet been replaced some five years after the accumulations began, the progress toward its ultimate construction speaks for itself. On the other hand, S Corporation may be hard-pressed to prove the sincerity of its objective for the accumulations in light of its failure to follow through on the projected replacement.

—The amount of the accumulation should be realistic under the circumstances.

> **Example 14.**  W Corporation plans to replace certain machinery at an estimated cost of $500,000. The original machinery was purchased for $300,000 and, because of $250,000 in depreciation deducted for tax purposes, possesses a present book value of $50,000. How much of an accumulation can be justified for the replacement to avoid the § 531 tax? At first blush, one might consider $500,000 as the appropriate amount, since this represents the estimated replacement cost of the machinery. But what about the $250,000 in depreciation that W Corporation has already deducted? If it is counted again as part of a reasonable accumulation, a double tax benefit results. Only $250,000 [i. e., $50,000 (the unrecovered cost of the old machinery) + $200,000 (the additional outlay necessary)] can be justified as the appropriate amount for an accumulation.[63]

> **Example 15.**  During the current year, a competitor files a $2,000,000 patent infringement suit against Z Corporation. Competent legal counsel advises Z Corporation that the suit is groundless. Under such conditions, the corporation can hardly justify accumulating $2,000,000 because of the pending lawsuit.

—Since the § 531 tax is imposed on an annual basis, justification for accumulations may vary from year to year.[64]

> **Example 16.**  For calendar years 19X1 and 19X2, R Corporation was able to justify large accumulations due to a pending additional income tax assessment. In early 19X3, the assessment is settled and paid. After its settlement, R Corporation can no longer consider the assessment as a reasonably anticipated need of the business.

*Danger of Loans to Shareholders.*  The presence of loans made by a corporation to its shareholders often raises the § 531 issue. If this same corporation has a poor dividend-paying record, it becomes particularly vulnerable. When one recalls that the avowed goal of the

---

**63.**  *Battelstein Investment Co. v. U. S.,* 71–1 USTC ¶ 9227, 27 AFTR2d 71–713, 442 F.2d 87 (CA–5, 1971).
**64.**  Compare *Hardin's Bakeries, Inc. v. Martin, Jr.,* 67–1 USTC ¶ 9253, 19 AFTR2d 647, 293 F.Supp. 1129 (D.Ct.Miss., 1967) with *Hardin v. U. S.,* 70–2 USTC ¶ 9676, 26 AFTR2d 70–5852 (D.Ct.Miss., 1970).

§ 531 tax is to force certain corporations to distribute dividends, the focus becomes clear. If a corporation can spare funds for loans to shareholders, it certainly has the capacity to pay dividends. Unfortunately, the presence of such loans can cause other tax problems for the parties.

> **Example 17.** During the year in question, Q Corporation made advances of $120,000 to its sole shareholder, T. Although prosperous and maintaining substantial accumulations, Q Corporation has never paid a dividend. Under these circumstances, the IRS could move in either of two directions. The Service could assess the § 531 tax against Q Corporation for its unreasonable accumulation of earnings. Alternatively, the IRS could argue that the advances were not bona fide loans but, instead, taxable dividends.[65] Such a dual approach places the taxpayers in a somewhat difficult position. If, for example, they contend that the advance was a bona fide loan, T avoids dividend income but Q Corporation becomes vulnerable to the imposition of the § 531 tax.[66] On the other hand, a concession that the advance was not a loan hurts T but helps Q Corporation avoid the penalty tax.

*Role of Dividends.* The relationship between dividend distribution and the § 531 tax needs further clarification. It would be helpful to pose and answer several questions. First, can the payment of enough dividends completely avoid the § 531 tax? The answer must be in the affirmative because of the operation of § 535. Recall that this provision defines "accumulated taxable income" as *taxable income* [adjusted by § 535(b)] *minus the sum of the dividends paid deduction* [defined in § 561] *and the accumulated earnings credit* [defined in § 535(c)]. Since the § 531 tax is imposed on "accumulated taxable income," no tax would be due if the dividends paid and the accumulated earnings credit are large enough to offset taxable income. Enough dividends, therefore, will avoid the tax.[67] Second, can the payment of *some* dividends completely avoid the § 531 tax? As the question is worded, the answer must be *no*. Theoretically, even significant dividend distributions will not insulate a corporation from the tax.[68] From a practical standpoint, however, the payment of dividends indicates that the corporation is not being used exclusively to shield its shareholders from tax consequences. To the extent this reflects

---

**65.** Refer to the discussion of constructive dividends in Chapter 13.

**66.** *Ray v. U. S.,* 69–1 USTC ¶ 9334, 23 AFTR2d 69–1141, 409 F.2d 1322 (CA–6, 1969).

**67.** Such dividends must, however, be taxable to the shareholders. Nontaxable stock dividends issued under § 305(a) do not affect the dividends paid deduction.

**68.** In *Henry Van Hummell, Inc.* v. *Comm.,* 66–2 USTC ¶ 9610, 18 AFTR2d 5500, 364 F.2d 746 (CA–10, 1966), the § 531 tax was imposed even though the corporation paid out over 60% of its taxable income as dividends.

the good faith of the parties and the lack of tax avoidance motivation, it is a factor the IRS will consider with regard to the § 531 issue.

## THE § 541 TAX

*Sections 531 and 541 Compared.*  A review of several important distinctions between the penalty tax on the unreasonable accumulation of earnings (§ 531) and the tax on personal holding companies (§ 541) will set the stage for the presentation of tax planning considerations applicable to the § 541 tax.

—Unlike § 531, there is no element of intent necessary for the imposition of the § 541 tax.[69] This makes § 541 a real trap for the unwary.

—The imposition of the § 541 tax is not affected by the past history of the corporation. Thus, it could be just as applicable to a newly formed corporation as to one that has been in existence for many years. Obviously, such is not the case with the § 531 tax; past accumulations have a direct bearing on the determination of the accumulated earnings credit. In this sense, younger corporations are less vulnerable to the § 531 tax, since complete insulation generally is guaranteed until accumulations exceed $250,000.

—Although one could conclude that both taxes pose threats for closely-held corporations, the stock ownership test of § 542(a)(2) makes this very explicit with regard to the § 541 tax. The absence of specific statutory criteria in the § 531 area has led to considerable confusion concerning which corporations are and are not covered. It appears that publicly held corporations can be subject to the § 531 tax if corporate policy is dominated by certain shareholders who are using the corporate form to avoid income taxes on dividends through the accumulation of corporate profits.[70]

—Sufficient dividend distributions can negate both taxes. In the case of § 531, however, such dividends must be distributed on a timely basis. Both taxes allow a two and one-half month grace period and provide for the consent dividend procedure. Only the § 541 tax allows the deficiency dividend procedure.

—Differences in reporting procedures arise because the § 541 tax is a self-assessed tax; the § 531 tax is not. For example, if a

---

**69.**  In light of the Supreme Court decision in *Donruss* (refer to Footnote 3 and the text thereto), one wonders what role, if any, intent will play in the future in aiding taxpayers to avoid the § 531 tax. In this connection, see the dissenting opinion in this case issued by Justice Harlan.

**70.**  At the time of this writing, the issue has not been settled by the courts. Refer to the discussion in Footnote 1.

corporation is a personal holding company, it must file a Schedule PH along with its Form 1120 (the corporate income tax return) for the year involved. Failure to file the Schedule PH can result in the imposition of interest and penalties and also brings into play a special six-year statute of limitations for the assessment of the § 541 tax.[71] On the other hand, the § 531 tax is assessed by the IRS and consequently requires no reporting procedures on the part of the corporate taxpayer.

*Avoiding the § 541 Tax.* The classification of a corporation as a personal holding company requires the satisfaction of *both* the stock ownership and the gross income tests. Obviously, then, failure to meet either of these two tests will avoid PHC status and the § 541 tax.

—The stock ownership test of § 542(a)(2) can be handled through a dispersion of stock ownership. Success may not be achieved, however, unless the tax planner watches the application of the stock attribution rules of § 544.

—Remember the following relationship when working with the gross income test:

$$\frac{\text{PHC income}}{\text{AOGI}} = 60\% \text{ or more}$$

Decreasing the numerator (PHC income) or increasing the denominator (AOGI) of the fraction will reduce the resulting percentage. Keeping the resulting percentage below 60 percent precludes classification as a personal holding company. To control PHC income, investments in low-yield, high-growth securities are preferable to those that generate heavy interest or dividend income. Capital gains from the sale of such securities will not affect personal holding company status, since they are not included in either the numerator or the denominator of the fraction. Investments in tax-exempt securities are also attractive because the interest income therefrom, like capital gains, carries no effect in applying the gross income test.

—Income from personal service contracts may, under certain conditions, constitute PHC income.

**Example 18.** B, C, and D (all attorneys) are equal shareholders in X Company, a professional association engaged in the practice of law. E, a new client, retains the X Company to pursue a legal claim. Under the terms of the retainer agreement, B is designated as the attorney who will perform the legal services. The suit is successful, and 30% of the judgment E recovers is paid to X Company as a fee. Since the

---

**71.**  § 6501(f). Also, see Chapter 21.

parties have met all of the requirements of § 543(a)(7), the fee received by X Company is PHC income.[72]

The result reached in Example 18 could have been avoided had B not been specifically designated in the retainer agreement as the party to perform the services.

—Rent income may or may not be PHC income. The relative amount of rent income is the key consideration. If

$$\frac{\text{Adjusted income from rents}}{\text{AOGI}} = 50\% \text{ or more}$$

and nonrent PHC income less 10 percent of OGI is distributed as a dividend, rent income will not be PHC income. Maximizing adjusted income from rents clearly will improve the situation for taxpayers. Since adjusted income from rents represents gross rents less expenses attributable thereto, a conservative approach in determining such expenses would be helpful. The taxpayer should be encouraged to minimize depreciation (e. g., choose straight-line over accelerated cost recovery method) and to capitalize, rather than expense, certain repairs. This approach to the handling of expenses attributable to rental property has to be confusing for taxpayers because it contradicts what is normally done to reduce income tax consequences.

Personal holding company status need not carry tragic tax consequences if the parties are aware of the issue and take appropriate steps. Since the tax is imposed on undistributed personal holding company income, properly timed dividend distributions will neutralize the tax and avoid interest and penalties. Also, as long as a corporation holds PHC status, the § 531 tax cannot be imposed.

> **Example 19.** X Corporation is owned entirely by two sisters, R and S (ages 86 and 88, respectively). X Corporation's major assets comprise investments in low-yield and high-growth securities, unimproved real estate, and tax-exempt bonds, all of which have a realizable value of $500,000. The basis of the stock in X Corporation to each sister is $50,000.

The liquidation of X Corporation (a frequent solution to undesired PHC status) would be disastrous to the two sisters. As noted in the discussion of § 331 in Chapter 14, such liquidation would result in the recognition of a capital gain of $400,000.[73] In this case, therefore, it

---

**72.** The example presumes X Company will be treated as a corporation for Federal tax purposes. As noted in Chapter 12, this is the usual result of professional association status.

**73.** Although long-term capital gains are entitled to a 60% deduction, the bunching effect has to be taken into account.

would be preferable to live with personal holding company status. Considering the nature of the assets held by X Corporation, this may not be difficult to do. Keep in mind that the interest from the tax-exempt bonds is not PHC income. Should X Corporation desire to sell any of its investments, the long-term capital gain that would result also is not PHC income. The PHC tax on any other income (i. e., the dividends from the securities) can be controlled through enough dividend distributions to reduce undistributed PHCI to zero. Furthermore, as long as X Corporation remains a PHC, it is insulated from the § 531 tax (the imposition of which would be highly probable in this case).

The liquidation of X Corporation should await the deaths of R and S and consequently should be carried out by their estates or heirs.[74] By virtue of the application of § 1014 , the income tax basis in the stock would be stepped-up to its fair market value on the date of death and much, if not all, of the capital gain potential presently existing would be eliminated.

## PROBLEM MATERIALS

### Discussion Questions

1. List some valid business reasons for accumulating funds in a closely-held corporation.

2. Explain the purpose(s) underlying the creation of the accumulated earnings penalty tax and the personal holding company tax.

3. Explain the consent dividend procedure of § 565. *not actually paid out. Reclassified as Contributed capital.*

4. To determine whether earnings and profits are at a reasonable level, should assets be valued at cost or fair market value?

5. Explain the *Bardahl* formula. How could it be improved?

6. Why is it desirable for a closely-held corporation to maintain a good dividend record (i. e., pay some dividends each year)?

7. May a holding or investment company accumulate more than $250,000 of earnings if the company can justify that such excess is necessary to meet the reasonable needs of the business?

8. A holding company's only income item during 19X6 is a $300,000 long-term capital gain. Calculate any accumulated earnings penalty tax.

9. Can the IRS impose both the PHC tax and the accumulated earnings tax upon a construction company?

10. Explain the PHC stock ownership test. Why is the stock's value important?

11. Briefly outline the constructive ownership rules of § 544.

---

**74.** A redemption of stock to pay death taxes and administration expenses might well be a viable alternative to a liquidation of the corporation. Refer to the discussion of § 303 in Chapter 13.

12. How is AOGI calculated?

13. Diagram (or flow chart) the rent exclusion tests for purposes of the PHC tax.

14. Explain some ways of avoiding PHC status.

15. Explain the deficiency dividend election.

16. Relate the following points to the avoidance of the § 531 tax.

    (a) Documentation of justification for the accumulation.

    (b) Multiple justifications for the accumulation.

    (c) Follow-up on the established justification for the accumulation.

    (d) Loans by the corporation to its shareholders.

    (e) The corporation's record of substantial dividend payments.

17. Relate the following points to the avoidance of the § 541 tax.

    (a) Sale of stock to outsiders.

    (b) An increase in AOGI.

    (c) A decrease in PHC income.

    (d) Long-term capital gains recognized by the corporation.

    (e) Corporate investment in tax-exempt bonds.

    (f) Income from personal service contracts.

    (g) The choice of straight-line depreciation for rental property owned by the corporation.

18. Compare the § 531 tax to the § 541 tax on the basis of the items given below.

    (a) The element of intent.

    (b) Applicability of the tax to a newly created corporation.

    (c) Applicability of the tax to a publicly held corporation.

    (d) The two and one-half month rule with respect to the dividends paid deduction.

    (e) The availability of the deficiency dividend procedure.

    (f) Procedures for reporting and paying the tax.

## Problems

19. A nonservice corporation has $250,000 of accumulated earnings and profits at the beginning of the tax year 1984. During the year, the corporation accumulates an additional $80,000 of after-tax earnings. The corporation at the end of the year can justify the retention of $220,000 for its reasonable business needs. What is the maximum amount that may be subjected to the accumulated earnings tax in 1984?

20. A calendar year medical services corporation has accumulated earnings and profits of $90,000 on January 1, 1984. For the calendar year of 1984, the corporation has taxable income of $100,000 with an income tax liability of $25,750. This corporation has no reasonable needs which justify an accumulation of its earnings and profits. Calculate the amount vulnerable to the accumulated earnings penalty tax.

21. On May 15, 19X6, a corporation paid a $97,000 tax based upon the unreasonable accumulation of corporate earnings and profits for the year ended December 31, 19X5. What effect, if any, would the imposition of this tax have on the shareholders of the corporation?

22. A manufacturing corporation had accumulated earnings and profits on January 1, 1984, of $250,000. Its taxable income for the year 1984 was $75,000 on which it owed accrued income taxes of $15,750. The corporation paid no dividends during the year. There were no other adjustments to determine accumulated taxable income. Assume that the Claims Court determined that the corporation is subject to the accumulated earnings tax and that the reasonable needs of the business required retained earnings in the total amount of $256,500. Determine the amount subject to the accumulated earnings tax and explain why.

23. A construction corporation is accumulating a significant amount of earnings and profits. Although the corporation is closely-held, it is not a personal holding company. The following facts relate to the tax year 1984.

    —Taxable income, $450,000.

    —Dividend income from a qualified domestic corporation, $30,000.

    —Dividends paid in 1984, $70,000.

    —Consent dividends, $35,000.

    —Dividends paid on 2/1/85, 5,000.

    —Accumulated earnings credit, $10,000.

    —Excess charitable contributions of $9,000 (i.e., the portion in excess of the amount allowed as a deduction in computing the § 11 tax).

    —Net capital loss for 1984 of $3,000.

    Compute both the corporate income tax and any accumulated earnings tax.

24. The following facts relate to a closely-held legal services corporation's 1984 tax year:

    | | |
    |---|---:|
    | Net taxable income | $ 400,000 |
    | Federal income tax | 163,750 |
    | Excess charitable contributions | 20,000 |
    | Long-term capital gain | 20,000 |
    | Short-term capital loss | 40,000 |
    | Dividends received | 120,000 |
    | Dividends paid | 60,000 |
    | Accumulated earnings, 1/1/84 | 130,000 |

    (a) Assume that this is not a personal holding company. Calculate any accumulated earnings tax.

    (b) Can the deficiency dividend procedure be applicable to the accumulated earnings tax?

25. A wholly owned motor freight corporation has permitted its earnings to accumulate. The company has no inventory but wishes to use the *Bardahl* formula to determine the amount of operating capital required for a business cycle. The following facts are relevant.

| Yearly revenues | $ 3,300,000 |
| Average accounts receivable | 300,000 |
| Yearly expenses | 3,500,000 |
| Average accounts payable | 213,000 |

(a) Determine the turnover rate of average accounts receivable.

(b) Determine the number of days in the accounts receivable cycle.

(c) Determine the expenses for one accounts receivable cycle.

(d) Determine the number of days in the accounts payable cycle.

(e) Determine the nondeferred expenses for the accounts receivable cycle.

(f) Determine the operating capital needed for one business cycle.

(g) Why should the time allowed a taxpayer for the payment of accounts payable be taken into consideration in applying the *Bardahl* formula?

26. The financial adviser of a dental services corporation provides you with the following data for 1984:

| Accumulated earnings and profits, 1/1/84 | $ 275,000 |
| Taxable income, including a net long-term capital gain of $40,000 | 160,000 |
| Earnings and profits retained for the reasonable needs of the business for 1984 | 40,000 |
| Dividends paid, 6/15/84 | 51,000 |
| Consent dividends | 35,000 |

(a) Calculate any accumulated earnings penalty tax. Assume this corporation is not a personal holding company.

(b) Assume the accumulated taxable earnings (after payment of dividends) are $200,000 in 1985; calculate the accumulated earnings penalty tax, if any.

27. A corporation is having accumulated income problems but has no accounts receivable. T, the corporation's accountant, provides you with the following information. Calculate the working capital *required* for the corporation if purchases total $140,000.

Year-end balances:

| Current assets | |
| Cash | $ 25,000 |
| Inventory (average) | 72,000 |
| | $ 97,000 |
| Current liabilities | 17,000 |
| Working capital available | $ 80,000 |

Income statement:

| | | |
|---|---:|---:|
| Gross sales | | $ 330,000 |
| Less: Sales returns and allowances | | 30,000 |
| | | $ 300,000 |
| Less: Cost of goods sold | $ 170,000 | |
| Sales and administrative expenses | 45,000 | |
| Depreciation | 20,000 | |
| Income taxes | 15,000 | 250,000 |
| Net income | | $ 50,000 |

28. A corporation has gross income of $20,000 which consists of $11,000 of rental income and $9,000 of dividend income. The corporation has $3,000 of rental income adjustments and pays $8,000 of dividends to its nine shareholders.

(a) Calculate adjusted income from rents.

(b) Calculate adjusted ordinary gross income.

(c) Is the so-called 50 percent test met? Show calculations.

(d) Is the 10 percent rental income test met? Show calculations.

(e) Is the corporation a personal holding company?

29. Assume one change in the situation in Problem 28. Rental income adjustments are decreased from $3,000 to $2,000. Answer the same questions as in Problem 28.

30. A corporation has interest income of $20,000, rental income of $60,000, and income from an operating business (not PHC income) of $30,000. Expenses in the amount of $15,000 relate directly to the rental income. Assume there are nine stockholders and the 10 percent test is met. Is this corporation a PHC? Explain.

31. A corporation has $10,000 of dividend income, $40,000 of gross income from rents, and $30,000 of personal service income (not PHC income). Expenses in the amount of $30,000 relate directly to the rent income. Assume there are eight stockholders and the 10 percent test is met. Is this corporation a PHC? Explain.

32. A corporation has gross income of $20,000 which consists of gross income from rent of $15,000, dividends of $1,500, a capital gain from the sale of securities of $1,000, and $2,500 from the sale of merchandise. Deductions directly related to the rent income total $10,000.

(a) Calculate OGI.

(b) Calculate AOGI.

(c) Calculate adjusted income from rents.

(d) Does the rental income constitute PHC income? Explain.

(e) Is this corporation a PHC (assuming there are four shareholders)?

# Chapter 16

# Subchapter S Corporations

## GENERAL CONSIDERATIONS

A portion of the Internal Revenue Code of 1954, designated as Subchapter S,[1] contains § § 1361–1379. The provisions involved allow for the unique treatment of certain corporations for Federal income tax purposes. At the outset, it is important to stress that a Subchapter S corporation is, in terms of legal characteristics under state law, no different from any other corporation. The election of Subchapter S, therefore, merely makes the operational provisions of § § 1361–1379 applicable as to the Federal income tax.

### ADVANTAGES OF THE CORPORATE FORM

Operating a business in the corporate form entails numerous tax and nontax advantages. Among the more important nontax advantages are the attributes of continuity of existence, free transferability of ownership interests, and limited liability. The corporation, possessing continuity of existence, will survive the withdrawal or death of any of its owners (i. e., shareholders). Thus, the corporation normally will continue to exist until such time as the shareholders decide upon its liquidation. Free transferability of ownership interests permits shareholders to dispose of stock in whatever manner they see fit. This flexibility may be crucial in a family setting in which an individual

---

1. The Subchapter S Revision Act of 1982 labels a Subchapter S corporation as an "S corporation."

desires to shift some of the income from the business to related parties in lower income tax brackets. As noted in Chapter 17, this may be impossible to accomplish if the business is being operated in the partnership form. Often, the key nontax advantage the corporate form offers is the limited liability characteristic. If a corporation fails, a shareholder's loss is limited to the amount of the stock investment. When one contrasts this result with what could happen in a partnership setting, where all of a partner's personal assets may be at the mercy of the partnership's creditors, the disparity in treatment becomes quite clear.

## DISADVANTAGES OF THE CORPORATE FORM

Operating a business in the corporate form carries several distinct tax disadvantages. First, the system of double taxation materializes. Profits are taxed to the corporation as earned and to the shareholders when and if distributed as dividends. Second, losses suffered at the corporate level cannot be passed through to the shareholders. Such losses remain locked within the corporation and are unavailable to the shareholders.[2] This last disadvantage would be of considerable importance in the formation of a new business where losses in the early years are often anticipated. Obviously, the owners of a business would like to receive the immediate tax advantage of such losses.

## SUBCHAPTER S IN PERSPECTIVE

Because of the tax disadvantages just noted, there is considerable support for the proposition that many persons have been deterred from using the corporate form although they may have had good reasons (e. g., limited liability) for preferring it. In the interest of preventing tax considerations from interfering with the exercise of sound business judgment (i. e., whether to operate a business in the corporate form),[3] Congress in 1958 enacted Subchapter S of the Code.

Basically, Subchapter S (§ § 1361 through 1379) permits certain corporations to avoid the corporate income tax and enables them to pass through operating losses to their shareholders. It represents an attempt to achieve a measure of tax neutrality in resolving the difficult problem of whether a business should be conducted as a sole proprietorship, partnership, or corporation.

In dealing with the provisions of Subchapter S, certain observations should be kept clearly in mind.

---

2. The losses might eventually materialize upon the sale of the stock or during the liquidation of the corporation. Such losses would, however, probably be capital and not ordinary.

3. The same justification applies to § 351, which permits tax-free incorporation of a new or existing business. Refer to Chapter 12.

1.  Subchapter S is an elective provision. Failure to make the election will mean that the rules applicable to the taxation of corporations (i. e., Subchapter C status) and shareholders will apply (refer to Chapter 12).

2.  S corporations are true corporations in the legal sense. The Subchapter S election encompasses only the Federal income tax consequences of electing corporations. In fact, many states do not recognize the Subchapter S election, and in such cases, S corporations are subject to the state corporate income tax and whatever other state corporate taxes are imposed.

3.  S corporations are not treated by Federal income tax law as either partnerships or regular corporations. The tax treatment is almost like partnership taxation, but it involves a unique set of tax rules.

4.  Because Subchapter S is a relief provision, strict compliance with the application Code provisions generally has been required by both the IRS and the courts. Slight deviation from the various governing requirements may, therefore, lead to an undesirable and often unexpected tax result (e. g., the loss of the Subchapter S election).

5.  The Subchapter S election is not available to all corporations. It is available only to small business corporations as defined in § 1361.[4]

# QUALIFICATION

## DEFINITIONS OF A SMALL BUSINESS CORPORATION

A small business corporation:[5]

—Is a domestic corporation.

—Is not an "ineligible corporation."

—Has no more than 35 shareholders.

—Has as its shareholders only individuals, estates, and certain trusts.

---

**4.**  Somewhat confusing is the fact that the Code contains several definitions of small business corporation, each pertinent to a different tax consequence. For example, compare the definition in § 1361 with that contained in § 1244(c)(2), which relates to ordinary loss treatment for stock losses. These provisions are not, however, mutually exclusive. Thus, a corporation can be a small business corporation for both purposes as long as it satisfies each definition.

**5.**  § 1361(b)(1). Note that the definition of "small" for purposes of Subchapter S relates to the number of shareholders and not to the size of the corporation. This approach is to be sharply contrasted with § 1244, which looks to the capitalization of the corporation.

—Issues only one class of stock.

—Does not have a nonresident alien stockholder.

*Ineligible Corporation Limitation.* In addition to being a domestic corporation, a small business corporation cannot be a member of an affiliated group, as defined in § 1504 [without regard to the exceptions contained in subsection (b)]. Thus, an S corporation cannot own 80 percent or more of the stock of another corporation. Under certain conditions, however, a corporation may establish one or more inactive affiliates, looking to the possibility that such companies may be needed in the future. The "affiliated group" prohibition does not apply as long as the affiliated corporations do not engage in business or produce taxable income.[6]

> **Example 1.** T Corporation is formed in Texas to develop and promote a new fast-food franchise system designated "Texas Chicken Delight." If successful in Texas, the shareholders of T Corporation plan to expand the operation to New Mexico, Oklahoma, Arkansas, and Louisiana. With this in mind and with a view toward protecting the name and product identification of the parent corporation, T Corporation forms subsidiaries in each of these states. Although T Corporation, together with its subsidiaries, is now a member of an affiliated group, it can qualify as a small business corporation as long as the subsidiaries remain inactive and generate no taxable income. If any of the subsidiaries begin conducting business, T Corporation can no longer maintain its Subchapter S election.

*Number of Shareholders Limitation.* For taxable years beginning after 1982, an electing corporation is limited to 35 shareholders.[7] This number corresponds to the private placement exemption under Federal securities law. In testing for the 35 shareholders limitation, husband and wife are to be treated as one shareholder as long as they remain married. Further, the estate of a husband or wife along with the surviving spouse is treated as one shareholder.[8]

> **Example 2.** H and W (husband and wife) jointly own 10 shares in S Corporation, with the remaining 90 shares outstanding owned by 34 other persons. H and W are divorced, and pursuant to the property settlement approved by the court, the 10 shares held by H and W are divided between them (five to each). Before the divorce settlement, S Corporation had only 35 shareholders. After the settlement, it has 36 shareholders and can no longer qualify as a small business corporation.

---

**6.** § 1361(c)(6).

**7.** § 1361(b)(1)(A). For tax year 1982, an S corporation could have no more than 25 shareholders. For tax years 1977–1981, the maximum number was 15.

**8.** § 1361(c)(1).

*Type of Shareholder Limitation.* To be a small business corporation, all the corporation's shareholders must be either individuals, estates, or certain trusts.[9] Stated differently, none of the shareholders may be partnerships, corporations, or nonqualifying trusts. The justification for this limitation is related to the 35 shareholders restriction. If, for example, a partnership with 40 partners were qualified to be a shareholder, could it not be said that there would be at least 40 owners of the corporation? If this were permitted, the 35 shareholders restriction could be easily circumvented by indirect ownership. Keep in mind that an S corporation can be a partner in a partnership or can own stock of another corporation or all the stock of an inactive subsidiary corporation.

*Nonresident Alien Prohibition.* A corporation will not qualify as a small business corporation if it has, as one of its shareholders, a nonresident alien.[10] In a community property jurisdiction where one of the spouses is married to a nonresident alien, this rule could provide a real trap for the unwary.[11] A resident alien or a nonresident U. S. citizen would be permissible S shareholders.

*One Class of Stock Limitation.* There must be only one class of stock issued and outstanding.[12] Congress apparently felt that the capital structure of a small business corporation should be kept simple. Allowing more than one class of stock (e. g., common and preferred) would complicate the pass-through to the shareholders of various corporate tax attributes. Authorized and unissued stock or treasury stock of another class will not disqualify the corporation. Likewise, unexercised stock options, warrants, and convertible debentures do not constitute a second class of stock.

## MAKING THE ELECTION

Having determined what corporations qualify for the Subchapter S election (i. e., meet the definition of a small business corporation), it is now appropriate to consider the mechanics of the election. The key factors are who must make the election and when it must be made.

*Who Must Elect.* The election is made by filing Form 2553, and all shareholders must consent thereto.[13] For this purpose, both husband and wife must file consents if their stock is held as joint tenants,

---

9. § 1361(b)(1)(B).
10. § 1361(b)(1)(C).
11. See, for example, *Ward v. U. S.,* 81–2 USTC ¶ 9519, 48 AFTR2d 81–5337, 661 F.2d 226 (Ct. Cls., 1981), where the Court found that the stock was owned as community property. Since the taxpayer-shareholder (a U. S. citizen) was married to a citizen and resident of Mexico, the nonresident alien prohibition was violated. If the taxpayer-shareholder had held the stock as his separate property, the Subchapter S election would have been valid.
12. § 1361(b)(1)(D).
13. § 1362(a)(2).

tenants in common, tenants by the entirety, or community property. Since the husband and wife are generally considered as one shareholder for purposes of the 35 shareholders limitation (see above), this inconsistency in treatment has led to considerable taxpayer grief— particularly in community property states where the spouses may not realize that their stock is jointly owned as a community asset.

The consent of a minor shareholder can be made by the minor or legal or natural guardian (e. g., parent). If the stock is held under a state Uniform Gifts to Minors Act, the custodian of the stock may consent for the minor, but only if the custodian is also the minor's legal or natural guardian. The minor would not be required to issue a new consent when coming of age and the custodianship terminates.[14]

*When the Election Must Be Made.*   A corporation makes the election at any time during the entire taxable year preceding the election year or on or before the fifteenth day of the third month of the tax year of election.[15] There is no statutory authority for obtaining an extension of time for filing an election or a consent. An election cannot be made for an entity not yet in existence.[16] But when does a new corporation come into being and start the election period running? Reg. § 1.1372–(2)(b)(1) specifies that the first month begins at the earliest occurrence of any of the following events: (1) when the corporation has shareholders, (2) when it acquires assets, or (3) when it begins doing business.[17]

> **Example 3.**   Several individuals subscribe to shares of stock and file articles of incorporation for T Corporation on June 18, 1984. The corporation acquires assets and begins doing business on June 29, 1984. If, under applicable state law, the corporation has shareholders when its articles of incorporation are filed with the state, the election must be filed no later than 2½ months from June 18, 1984, to be effective for 1984.

If the election is not timely, it will be ineffective for that tax year. Under current rules, no new election is necessary, but Subchapter S status does not begin until the next taxable year.

> **Example 4.**   Assume the same facts as in Example 3 with the further stipulation that the filing of the election does not occur until November 3, 1984 (more than 2½ months from the beginning of the taxable year). If T Corporation uses the calendar year for tax purposes, it would commence in Subchapter S status on January 1, 1985.

---

**14.**   Rev.Rul. 66–116, 1966–1 C.B. 198, Rev.Rul. 68–227, 1968–1 C.B. 381, and Rev.Rul. 71–287, 1971–2 C.B. 317.

**15.**   § 1362(b)(1).

**16.**   See, for example, *T. H. Campbell & Bros., Inc.,* 34 TCM 695, T.C.Memo. 1975.

**17.**   For support of Reg. § 1.1372–(2)(b)(1) see, for example, *Thomas E. Bone,* 52 T.C. 913 (1969), and *Nick A. Artukovich,* 61 T.C. 101 (1973).

If the eligibility requirements are not met for the entire preelection portion of the year for which the election is made, or if consents of all shareholders who had disposed of their stock prior to the making of the election are not obtained, or if the election is made after 2½ months, the election does not become effective until the following tax year.[18] This rule prevents the allocation of income and losses to preelection shareholders who either were ineligible to hold S corporation stock or did not consent to the election. Once an election is made, it does not have to be renewed and remains in effect unless otherwise lost (see below).

## LOSS OF THE ELECTION

A Subchapter S election can be lost in any of the following ways:

—A new shareholder owning more than one-half of the voting stock affirmatively refuses to consent to the election.

—A majority of the shareholders voluntarily revoke the election.

—The number of shareholders exceeds the maximum allowable limitation.

—A class of stock other than voting or nonvoting common stock is created.

—There is an acquisition of a subsidiary other than certain non-operating subsidiaries.

—The corporation fails the passive investment income limitation.

—A nonresident alien becomes a shareholder.

Some of these possibilities are explored under a separate subheading in the pages to follow.

*Affirmative Refusal.* For tax years beginning after December 31, 1976, and before January 1, 1983, a new shareholder could affirmatively refuse to consent to a Subchapter S election on or before the sixtieth day after the day on which the stock was acquired and thereby terminate the election.[19] After 1982, a new shareholder of an S corporation after the initial election does not have the power to terminate the election by affirmatively refusing to consent to the election unless the new shareholder owns more than one-half the voting stock.[20] A new minority shareholder, therefore, is now bound by the initial election.

*Voluntary Revocation.* Section 1362(d)(1) permits a voluntary revocation of the election if a majority of the shareholders consent. A

---

**18.**   § 1362(b)(3).
**19.**   Prior § 1372(e)(1)(A). For years before 1977, § 1372(e)(1) required that a new shareholder affirmatively consent within 30 days from the acquisition of the stock.
**20.**   § 1362(d)(1)(B).

revocation filed up to and including the fifteenth day of the third month of the tax year is effective for the entire tax year, unless a prospective effective date is specified. A revocation made after the fifteenth day of the third month of the tax year is effective on the first day of the following tax year (unless a prospective date is specified, in which case the termination is effective as of the specified date).

**Example 5.** The shareholders of T Corporation, a calendar year S corporation, elect to revoke the election on January 5, 19X6. Assuming the election is duly executed and timely filed, T Corporation will become a regular corporation for calendar year 19X6. If, on the other hand, the election is not made until June 19X6, T Corporation will not become a regular corporation until calendar year 19X7.

A revocation that designates a prospective effective date results in the splitting of the year into a short Subchapter S tax year and a short Subchapter C tax year. The day *before* the day on which the revocation occurs is treated as the last day of a short Subchapter S tax year, and the day on which the revocation occurs is treated as the first day of the short regular corporate tax year (i. e., Subchapter C treatment). The corporation should allocate the income or loss for the entire year on a pro rata basis; there is no requirement that the books of the corporation be closed as of the revocation date.[21]

**Example 6.** Assume the same facts as in Example 5 except that the corporation elects the prospective date of July 1, 19X6, as the revocation date. June 30, 19X6, shall be treated as the last day of the short Subchapter S tax year. The short regular corporate tax year shall run from July 1, 19X6, to December 31, 19X6. Any income or loss for the entire year shall be allocated pro rata between the short years.

Rather than a pro rata allocation, the corporation can elect with the consent of all individuals who were shareholders at any time during the year to report the income or loss on each return (Form 1120S and Form 1120) on the basis of income, or loss shown on the corporate permanent records (including working papers). Under the alternative method, items are attributed to the short Subchapter S and Subchapter C years according to the time they were incurred (as reflected in the records).[22] That is, the items are assigned to each short tax year under the normal tax accounting rules.

*Cessation of Small Business Corporation Status.* A corporation not only must be a small business corporation to make the Subchapter S election but must continue to qualify as such to keep the election. In other words, meeting the definition of a small business corporation is

---

**21.** §§ 1362(e)(1) and (2).
**22.** § 1362(e)(3).

a continuing requirement for maintaining Subchapter S status. Disqualification is an involuntary termination, and the loss of the election applies as of the date on which the event occurs.[23]

> **Example 7.** T Corporation has been a calendar year S corporation for three years. In 19X2, one of its 35 shareholders sells *some* of his stock to an outsider on August 13. T Corporation now has 36 shareholders, and it ceases to be a small business corporation. For calendar year 19X2, T Corporation will be treated as an S corporation through August 12, 19X2, and as a regular corporation from August 13 through December 31, 19X2.

*Passive Investment Income Limitations.* Prior to 1982, the law provided for an involuntary termination of the election in the event the corporation had gross receipts consisting of more than 20 percent in passive investment income. After 1981, an S corporation that has no Subchapter C accumulated earnings and profits at the end of the tax year is no longer covered by a passive investment income limitation. Such a corporation can have any amount of passive investment income.

There is a passive investment income limitation for corporations with accumulated earnings and profits from years in which the corporation was a regular Subchapter C corporation. If such a corporation has passive income in excess of 25 percent of gross receipts for three consecutive tax years, the Subchapter S election is terminated as of the beginning of the following tax year.[24]

> **Example 8.** For 1982, 1983, and 1984, B Corporation, a calendar year Subchapter S corporation, has had passive income in excess of 25 percent of the gross receipts. If the B Corporation has accumulated earnings and profits from years in which it was a regular Subchapter C corporation, the election is terminated beginning January 1, 1985.

According to § 1362(d)(3)(B), the harmful earnings and profits are generated only in years in which a Subchapter S election was not in effect. Since everything is reflected in basis adjustment, an S corporation cannot generate earnings and profits. However, Subchapter C earnings and profits could be acquired by an S corporation from a regular corporation where earnings and profits carry over under § 381.

*Passive Investment Income Penalty Tax.* A tax is imposed on the excess passive income of S corporations with accumulated earnings and profits from Subchapter C years.[25] The tax rate is 46 percent (the

---

**23.** § 1362(d)(2)(B). For years before 1983, the loss of the election applied to the entire tax year in which the disqualification occurred.
**24.** § 1362(d)(3)(A)(ii).
**25.** § 1375(a).

highest corporate rate) on that portion of the corporation's net passive income that bears the same ratio to the total net passive income for the tax year as the excess gross passive income bears to the total gross passive income for the year. However, the amount subject to the tax may not exceed the taxable income of the corporation.[26]

Passive investment income means gross receipts derived from royalties, rents, dividends, interest, annuities, and sales and exchanges of stocks and securities.[27] To prevent the churning of assets, only the net gain from the disposition of capital assets (other than stocks and securities) is taken into account in computing gross receipts. Net passive income means passive income reduced by any deductions directly connected with the production of such income. Nonrefundable credits are not allowable against the § 1375 tax, and any gain subject to tax is exempt from the capital gain tax under § 1374. Any tax due to the application of § 1375 reduces the amount the shareholders must take into income.

An S corporation's excess net passive income (ENPI) may be calculated from the following formula:

$$\text{Excess net passive income} = \frac{\begin{array}{c}\text{Passive investment income}\\\text{in excess of 25\% of}\\\text{gross receipts for the year}\end{array}}{\begin{array}{c}\text{Passive investment}\\\text{income for the year}\end{array}} \times \begin{array}{c}\text{Net passive}\\\text{investment income}\\\text{for the year}\end{array}$$

The excess net passive income cannot exceed the corporate taxable income for the year without regard to any net operating loss deduction under § 172 or the special deductions allowed by § § 241–250 (except the organization expense deduction in § 248).

> **Example 9.** At the end of 1984, S Corporation, an electing corporation, has gross receipts totaling $264,000 (of which $110,000 is passive investment income). Expenditures directly connected to the production of the passive investment income total $30,000. Therefore, S Corporation has net passive investment income of $80,000 ($110,000 − $30,000), and the amount by which its passive investment income for tax year 1984 exceeds 25% of its gross receipts is $44,000 ($110,000 passive investment income less $66,000). Excess net passive income is $32,000, calculated as follows:
>
> $$\text{ENPI} = \frac{\$44,000}{\$110,000} \times \$80,000 = \$32,000$$
>
> S Corporation's passive investment income tax for 1984, therefore, is $14,720 ($32,000 × 46%).

---

**26.** § 1375(b).
**27.** § 1362(d)(3)(D)(i).

*Types of Passive Investment Income.* Although the definition of passive investment income appears to parallel that of personal holding company income (refer to Chapter 15), the two are not identical. For example, long-term capital gain from the sale of securities would be passive investment income but would not be personal holding company income. Also, there are no relief provisions for rent income similar to the personal holding company rules. Other differences exist.

The inclusion of gains from the sale of securities within the definition of passive investment income generally has made it difficult, if not impossible, for corporations dealing in security transactions to achieve Subchapter S status.[28] The same was true for finance companies before 1983, since interest was passive investment income and loan repayments are not (under the Regulations) includible in gross receipts.[29] However, for tax years after 1982, the law was amended to exclude from passive income any interest on deferred payment sales of property held for sale to customers (described in § 1221) as well as interest income from the conduct of a finance or lending business as defined in § 542(c)(6).[30]

Rents present a unique problem. Although classified by the Code as passive investment income, the Regulations state that rents will not fall into this category if the corporation (landlord) renders significant, not just regular, services to the occupant (tenant).

> **Example 10.** T Corporation owns and operates an apartment building. Although the corporation provides utilities for the building, maintains the lobby in the building, and furnishes trash collection for the tenants, this does not constitute the rendition of significant services for the occupants.[31] Thus, the rents paid by the tenants of the building represent passive investment income to T Corporation.

> **Example 11.** Assume the fact situation as in Example 10, with one addition—T Corporation also furnishes maid service to its tenants. Now the services rendered are significant, in that they go beyond what one might normally expect the landlord of an apartment building to provide.[32] Under these changed circumstances, the rental income is no longer passive investment income.

---

**28.** See for example, *Buhler Mortgage Co., Inc.,* 51 T.C. 971 (1969).

**29.** See, for example, *Marshall v. Comm.,* 75–1 USTC ¶ 9160, 35 AFTR2d 75–526, 510 F.2d 259 (CA–10, 1975).

**30.** § 1362(d)(3)(D).

**31.** *Bramlette Building Corp., Inc.,* 52 T.C. 200 (1969), *aff'd.* in 70–1 USTC ¶ 9361, 25 AFTR2d 70–1061, 424 F.2d 751 (CA–5, 1970) and *City Markets, Inc. v. Comm.,* 70–2 USTC ¶ 9691, 26 AFTR2d 70–5760, 433 F.2d 1240 (CA–6, 1970).

**32.** For various rulings clarifying the meaning of "significant" see, for example, Rev.Rul. 65–91, 1965–1 C.B. 431; Rev.Rul. 65–83, 1965–1 C.B. 430; Rev.Rul. 65–40, 1965–1 C.B. 429; Rev.Rul. 64–232, 1964–2 C.B. 334; and Rev.Rul. 61–112, 1961–1 C.B. 399.

*Reelection After Termination.* After the election has been terminated, § 1362(g) enforces a five-year waiting period before a new election can be made. The Code does, however, allow for the IRS to make exceptions to this rule and to permit an earlier reelection by the corporation. If the election is inadvertently terminated, the IRS can waive the effect of the terminating event for any period if the corporation timely corrects the event and if the corporation and shareholders agree to be treated as if the election had been in effect for such period.[33]

The Senate Finance Committee expects the IRS to be reasonable in granting waivers so that corporations (whose S eligibility requirements have been inadvertently lost) do not suffer the tax consequences of a termination if no tax avoidance would result from continued Subchapter S treatment. The Committee indicates that it would be appropriate to waive the terminating event when the one class of stock requirement is inadvertently breached but no tax avoidance has resulted. The waiver may be made retroactive for all years or retroactive for the period in which the entity again became eligible for Subchapter S treatment.[34]

# OPERATIONAL RULES

An S corporation is a tax-reporting rather than a taxpaying entity. In this respect, the entity is taxed much like a partnership. Under the conduit concept, the taxable income of an S corporation flows through to its shareholders whether or not it is distributed in the form of actual dividends. Likewise, losses of the entity are allocated to the shareholders and are reported by them on their individual tax returns. Other corporate transactions that flow through under the conduit concept include net long-term capital gains and losses, charitable contributions, tax-exempt interest, foreign tax credits, and investment tax credits. Parallel to the partnership rules under § 702, each shareholder of an S corporation takes into account separately his or her pro rata share of certain items of income, deductions, and credits.

## COMPUTATION OF TAXABLE INCOME

After 1982, Subchapter S taxable income or loss generally is determined according to the tax rules applicable to partnerships in § 703, except that the amortization of organization expenditures under § 248 is an allowable deduction.[35] Thus, Subchapter S taxable income or loss is arrived at according to the tax rules applicable to individuals.

---

**33.** § 1362(f).
**34.** Sen. Fin. Com. Rep. No. 97640 on H.R. 6055, "Subchapter S Revision Act of 1982," September 8, 1982.
**35.** § 1363(b).

Although an S corporation generally is not a taxable entity, § 703(a) requires that Subchapter S taxable income be separately computed.

Deductions usually allowable to individuals are allowable to S corporations, except that provisions of the Code governing the computation of taxable income applicable only to corporations, such as the dividends received deduction (i. e., § 243) or the special rules regarding corporate tax preferences (§ 291), do not apply. Further, no deduction is allowable for the zero bracket amount, personal exemptions, foreign taxes, net operating losses, medical and dental expenses, alimony, personal moving expenses, and expenses for care of certain dependents.[36]

In general, items are divided into (1) nonseparately computed income or losses and (2) separated income, losses, deductions, and credits that could affect the liability for tax of any shareholders. In essence, the residue of nonseparate items is lumped into an undifferentiated amount that constitutes Subchapter S § 702(a)(8) taxable income or loss. Each shareholder receives a pro rata portion of this amount. Under § 1366(a)(1), a shareholder who dies during the year must report the share of the pro rata items up to the date of death on his or her final individual income tax return. Elections generally are made at the corporate level, except for those elections which the partners of a partnership may make separately (e. g., foreign tax credit election).

The following items are separately stated, and each shareholder takes into account his or her pro rata share (i. e., it is passed through):[37]

1. Tax-exempt income.[38]
2. Long-term and short-term capital gains and losses.
3. Section 1231 gains and losses.
4. Charitable contributions.
5. Foreign tax credits.
6. Basis of § 38 new and used property, used for calculating the investment tax credit or immediate expensing under § 179.
7. Dividends.
8. Depletion.
9. Foreign income or losses.
10. Wagering gains or losses [§ 165(d)].
11. Nonbusiness income or loss (§ 212).
12. Recoveries of prior taxes, bad debts, and delinquency amounts (§ 111).

---

**36.** § 703(a)(2).
**37.** § § 1366(a) and (b).
**38.** Tax-exempt income passes through to the shareholders and increases their tax bases. A subsequent distribution does not result in taxation of the tax-exempt income.

13. Soil and water conservation expenditures [§ 263(c)].
14. Intangible drilling costs [§ 263(c)].
15. Mining exploration expenditures (§ 617).
16. Discharge of indebtedness (§ 108).
17. Amortization of reforestation expenditures (§ 194).
18. Investment interest, income, and expenses covered under § 163(d).

An S corporation is treated as an intermediary with respect to the withholding on payment of interest and dividends it receives (§ 3453). Carryovers from years in which the corporation was not an S corporation are not allowable while in Subchapter S status.[39]

**Example 12.** The following is the income statement for the B Company, an S corporation:

| | | |
|---|---:|---:|
| Sales | | $ 40,000 |
| Less cost of sales | | 23,000 |
| Gross profit on sales | | $ 17,000 |
| Less: | | |
|     Interest expense | $ 1,200 | |
|     Charitable contributions | 400 | |
|     Advertising expenses | 1,500 | |
|     Other operating expenses | 2,000 | 5,100 |
| | | $ 11,900 |
| Add:  Tax-exempt income | $ 300 | |
|     Dividend income | 200 | |
|     Long-term capital gain | 500 | |
| | $ 1,000 | |
| Less:  Short-term capital loss | (150) | 850 |
| Net income per books | | $ 12,750 |

Subchapter S taxable income for B Company is calculated as follows, using net income for book purposes as a point of departure:

| | | | |
|---|---:|---:|---:|
| Net income per books | | | $ 12,750 |
| Separated items: | | | |
| Deduct:  Tax-exempt interest | | $ 300 | |
|     Dividend income | | 200 | |
|     Long-term capital gain | | 500 | |
| | | (1,000) | |
| Add:  Charitable contributions | $ 400 | | |
|     Short-term capital loss | 150 | 550 | |
| Net | | | (450) |
| Subchapter S taxable income | | | $ 12,300 |

The $12,300 of Subchapter S taxable income as well as the separated items should be divided among the shareholders based upon their stock ownership.

---

**39.** § 1371(b).

## ORDER OF CASH AND PROPERTY DISTRIBUTIONS

The amount of any distribution to a shareholder is equal to the amount of the cash plus the fair market value of any property distributed. Either of two sets of distribution rules applies, depending upon whether the electing corporation has accumulated earnings and profits.

A distribution by an S corporation having no earnings and profits is not includible in gross income to the extent that it does not exceed the shareholder's adjusted basis in stock. When the amount of the distribution exceeds the adjusted basis of the stock, such excess is treated as a gain from the sale or exchange of property (i. e., capital gain in most cases.[40]

> **Example 13.** P, Inc., a calendar year S corporation has no accumulated earnings and profits at the end of 1982 or 1983. J, an individual shareholder, receives a cash dividend during 1984 of $12,200 from P, Inc. J's basis in his stock is $9,700. J shall recognize a capital gain from the cash distribution of $2,500, the excess of the distribution over the stock basis ($12,200 − $9,700). The remaining $9,700 is tax-free.

The treatment of a distribution by an S corporation with accumulated earnings and profits is summarized as follows:

1. Tax-free up to the amount in the accumulated adjustments account (AAA). This accumulated adjustments account is composed of post-1982 accumulated gross income less deductible expenses not previously distributed.[41] No adjustments are made in the accumulated adjustments account for tax-exempt income and for any expenses not deductible in computing taxable income and not chargeable to a capital account.

2. Any previously taxed income (PTI) in the corporation under the prior set of rules follows next on a tax-free basis. However, PTI probably cannot be distributed in property other than in cash [according to Reg. § 1.1375–4(b) under prior law].

3. A distribution in excess of the accumulated adjustments account is treated as a dividend to the extent of accumulated earnings and profits. Accordingly, such amount is subject to the § 116 dividend exclusion.

4. Any residual amount is applied against the shareholder's remaining basis in his or her stock. Such amount is considered to be a return of capital, which is not taxable and does not qualify for the dividend exclusion. To the extent a prop-

---

**40.** § 1368(b).
**41.** §§ 1368(c)(1) and (e)(1). Before 1983, a similar account was called previously taxed income (PTI).

erty distribution is treated as a return of basis, the basis is reduced by the fair market value of the asset.

5. Distributions that exceed the shareholder's tax basis for the stock are taxable as capital gains (with no dividend exclusion) unless the corporation is collapsible.

These rules apply to a shareholder regardless of the manner in which the stock is acquired.

Any distribution of cash by the corporation with respect to its stock during a post-termination transition period of one year is applied against and reduces the adjusted basis of the stock to the extent that the amount of the distribution does not exceed the accumulated adjustments account.[42] Thus, a terminated S corporation should make a cash distribution to the extent of all previously undistributed net income items for all Subchapter S tax years during the one-year period following termination.

If a corporation was an S corporation in a taxable year before January 1, 1983, both § § 1375(d) and (f) of the prior law are applicable with respect to undistributed taxable income (UTI) for any tax year beginning before January 1, 1983.[43] Thus, previously taxed income may be distributed tax-free to the shareholder who included it in income. Further, a distribution of UTI within the 2½-month grace period of the first tax year subject to the new law is considered a tax-free distribution of the UTI for the prior year.

> **Example 14.** In 1984, X Corporation, a calendar year S corporation, has a post-1982 accumulated adjustment account of $5,500. In addition, it has accumulated earnings and profits from pre-1983 years of $4,500. T, the sole shareholder, receives in 1984 a $19,000 cash distribution from X Corporation. If T's basis in his stock investment is $8,400, the distribution will be treated as follows:

| | |
|---|---:|
| Nontaxable accumulated adjustment account | $  5,500 |
| Taxable dividend | 4,500 |
| Nontaxable return of capital | 8,400 |
| Capital gain | 600 |
| Total amount of the distribution | $ 19,000 |

## CORPORATE TREATMENT OF CERTAIN PROPERTY DISTRIBUTIONS

After 1982, a gain is recognized by an S corporation on any distribution of appreciated property (other than in a complete liquidation) in the same manner as if the asset had been sold to the share-

---

**42.** § § 1371(e) and 1377(b).

**43.** § 1379(c).

holder at its fair market value.[44] Of course, the corporate gain is passed through to the shareholders. There is an important reason for this rule. Otherwise, property could be distributed tax-free (other than for certain recapture) and later sold without income recognition to the shareholder because of the stepped-up basis equal to fair market value. A loss will not be recognized on depreciated assets. The character of the gain—capital gain or ordinary income—will depend upon the type of asset being distributed.

> **Example 15.** S Corporation, an S corporation, distributes a tract of land held as an investment to T, a majority shareholder. The land was purchased for $22,000 many years ago, but is currently worth $82,000. Under § 1363(d), S Corporation must recognize a gain of $60,000.

## THE SHAREHOLDER'S TAX BASIS

The initial tax basis of stock in an S corporation is calculated similarly to the basis of stock in a regular corporation, depending upon the manner in which shares are acquired (e. g., gift, inheritance, purchase). Once the initial tax basis is determined, various transactions during the life of the corporation affect the shareholder's basis in the stock. Essentially, the basis rules for an S corporation are analogous to those provided for partnerships under § 705. (See Chapter 17.)

A shareholder's basis in the electing corporation is increased by further stock purchases, the sum of current and prior years' distributive share of Subchapter S income not distributed, any income retained by the electing corporation that was exempt from tax, and the excess of the deductions for depletion over the basis of the property, subject to depletion. The income and loss adjustments for any corporate year apply first to adjust the basis before the distribution rules come into play for such year. Further, a shareholder's basis in the electing corporation is decreased (but not below zero) by the amount of money and the fair market value of property distributed to the shareholder by the corporation, by the sum of current and prior years' distributive share of deductible Subchapter S losses, and by the shareholder's share of nondeductible corporate expenditures that are not capital expenditures.[45] A shareholder's stock basis can never be reduced below zero, and any excess decrease is applied to reduce (but not below zero) the shareholder's basis in any indebtedness of the electing corporation to the shareholder. Any pass-through of income for a particular year must first increase the shareholder's basis in loans to the corporation to the extent the basis was previously reduced by the pass-through of losses.[46]

---

44. § 1363(d).
45. § 1367(a).
46. § 1367(b)(2).

**Example 16.** T, a sole shareholder, has a $7,000 stock basis and a $2,000 loan basis in a calendar year S corporation at the beginning of 1984. Subchapter S net income during 1984 is $8,200. There is a short-term capital loss of $2,300 and $2,000 of tax-exempt interest income. A total of $15,000 is distributed to T on November 15, 1984. T's basis in his stock is zero, and his loan basis is $1,900 ($2,000 − $100) at the end of 1984:

| | |
|---|---:|
| Beginning basis in the stock | $ 7,000 |
| Income | 8,200 |
| Short-term capital loss | (2,300) |
| Tax-exempt interest income | 2,000 |
| | $ 14,900 |
| Less distribution | −14,900 |
| Final basis in the stock | $ —0— |

Because stock basis cannot be reduced below zero, the $100 excess distribution reduces the loan basis.

## NET OPERATING LOSS

One major advantage of a Subchapter S election is the ability to pass through any net operating loss (NOL) of the corporation directly to its shareholders. Under § 1366(a)(1)(A), such a loss is deductible by the shareholders for the year in which the corporation's tax year ends. The corporation is not entitled to the NOL. The loss is deducted from an individual's gross income in arriving at adjusted gross income, and the shareholder's stock basis is reduced to the extent of any pass-through of the net operating loss.

Net operating losses are allocated among shareholders in the same manner as is income. NOLs are allocated on a daily basis to all shareholders who owned stock during the tax year.[47] Presumably, transferred shares are considered to be held by the transferee (not the transferor) on the date of the transfer.

**Example 17.** An S corporation has a $20,000 NOL for the current year. The stock was at all times during the tax year owned by the same 10 shareholders, each of whom owned 10% of the stock. Each shareholder is entitled to deduct $2,000 from gross income for the tax year in which the corporate tax year ends.

An S corporation's NOL pass-through cannot exceed a shareholder's adjusted basis in the stock plus the basis of any loans made to the corporation. In both situations, the end-of-tax-year basis is specified. If a taxpayer is unable to prove the tax basis, the NOL pass-through can be denied.[48] In essence, a shareholder's stock basis cannot go

---

47. § 1377(a)(1).
48. See *Donald J. Sauvigne*, 30 TCM 123, T.C.Memo. 1971–30.

below zero. As noted previously, once a shareholder's adjusted stock basis has been eliminated by an NOL, any excess net operating loss is used to reduce the shareholder's basis for any loans made to the corporation (but never below zero). The basis for loans is established by the actual advances made to the corporation and not by indirect loans or guaranteed loans.

A shareholder's share of an NOL may be greater than both the stock basis and the basis of the indebtedness. In such case, a shareholder is entitled to carry forward a loss to the extent that the loss passed through for the year exceeds both the stock basis and the loan basis. Any loss carried forward may be deducted *only* by the same shareholder if and when the basis in the stock of and loans to the corporation is restored.[49] Further, any loss carryover at the end of a one-year post-termination transition period is lost forever.[50] The post-termination transition period is the later of (1) one year after the effective date of the termination of a Subchapter S election or the due date for the last Subchapter S return (whichever is later) or (2) 120 days after the determination that the corporation's Subchapter S election had terminated for a previous year. Thus, if a shareholder has a loss carryover, he or she should increase the stock/loan basis and flow through the loss before disposing of the stock.

Net operating losses from regular-corporation years cannot be utilized at the corporate level, nor can they be passed through to the shareholders. Further, the running of the carryforward period continues during Subchapter S status.[51] Thus, it may not be appropriate for a corporation that has unused net operating losses to make this election. Further, if a corporation is expecting losses in the future, an election should be made before the loss year.

The NOL provisions create a need for sound tax planning during the last election year and the post-termination transition period. If it appears that the S corporation is going to sustain a net operating loss or use up any loss carryover, each shareholder's basis should be analyzed to determine if it can absorb the share of the loss. If basis is insufficient to absorb the loss, further investments should be considered before the end of the post-termination transition year. Such investment can be accomplished through additional lending to the corporation, or more stock can be purchased from the corporation or from other shareholders to increase basis. This action will insure full benefit from the net operating loss or loss carryover.

> **Example 18.** A calendar year regular corporation has a net operating loss in 19X5 of $20,000. A valid Subchapter S election is made in 19X6, and there is another $20,000 NOL in that year.

---

49. § 1366(d).
50. § 1377(b).
51. § 1371(b).

The stock of the corporation was at all times during 19X6 owned by the same 10 shareholders, each of whom owned 10% of the stock. T, one of the 10 shareholders, has an adjusted basis at the beginning of 19X6 of $1,800. None of the 19X5 NOL may be carried forward into the Subchapter S year. Although T's share of the 19X6 NOL is $2,000, the deduction for the loss is limited to $1,800 in 19X6 with a $200 carryover.

If a loan basis has been reduced and is not restored by the end of the last electing year, income will result when the loan later is repaid in a Subchapter C year. If the corporation issued a note as evidence of the debt, repayment constitutes an amount received in exchange for a capital asset, and the amount that exceeds the shareholder's basis is entitled to capital gain treatment.[52] However, if the loan is made on open account, the repayment constitutes ordinary income to the extent that it exceeds the shareholder's basis for the loan.[53] Thus, a note should be given to obtain capital gain treatment for the income that results from a loan's repayment in a Subchapter C tax year. Better yet, repay the loan before the termination of the Subchapter S election.

## TAX TREATMENT OF LONG-TERM CAPITAL GAINS

Although an S corporation generally is a tax-reporting rather than a taxpaying entity, certain long-term capital gains may be taxed under § 1374(a). The effect of § 1374 is to hinder the use of Subchapter S on a "one-shot" basis to avoid the tax on corporate capital gains. Before passage of this corporate capital gain tax, a regular corporation could "save" its capital asset sales for several years, then elect Subchapter S, sell the capital assets, and pass such gains to the shareholders to avoid the capital gain tax at the corporate level.

> **Example 19.** Corporation S operates several years as a regular corporation but postpones most of its capital asset dispositions. During the current year, the corporation elects Subchapter S and disposes of all of its accumulated capital assets. Without § 1374, any capital gains would pass through to the shareholders, avoiding the corporate tax. Next year the Subchapter S election could be terminated and the corporation could begin accumulating its capital asset transactions until the next time it makes the one-shot election.

*Tax Consequences at the Corporation Level.* Under § 1374(a), an S corporation is taxed on capital gains if it meets all of the following requirements. First, the taxable income of the corporation must ex-

---

**52.** *Joe M. Smith,* 48 T.C. 872 (1967), *aff'd.* and *rev'd.* in 70–1 USTC ¶ 9327, 25 AFTR2d 70–936, 424 F.2d 219 (CA–9, 1970) and Rev.Rul. 64–162, 1964–1 C.B. 304.
**53.** Rev.Rul. 68–537, 1968–2 C.B. 372.

ceed $25,000. Second, the excess of the net long-term capital gain (LTCG) over the net short-term capital loss must exceed $25,000. Third, this amount must exceed 50 percent of the corporation's taxable income for the year.

However, the corporation may fall within the above requirements and still avoid the special tax at the corporate level because of certain exceptions to these rules. Under § 1374(c), the tax does not apply to those corporations that have had valid elections in effect for the three previous tax years. Moreover, a new corporation in existence for less than four tax years can avoid the tax if it has operated under Subchapter S since it was founded. Thus, the corporation that has elected Subchapter S for sound business reasons generally will find its pattern of taxation unaffected by the realization of capital gains.

Any capital gain subject to the passive investment income tax in § 1375 is not subject to the § 1374 penalty tax.[54] Code § 1231 gains are not aggregated with capital gains at the corporate level but pass through separately.

*Tax Consequences at the Shareholder Level.* A net long-term capital gain retains its character when passed through to the shareholders. After 1982, net capital gains are no longer offset by ordinary losses at the corporate level.

> **Example 20.** An S corporation has three equal shareholders and incurs a net long-term capital gain of $9,000 for the current tax year. In the same year, the corporation has taxable income and current earnings and profits in excess of $9,000. If no distributions are made, each shareholder must include $3,000 in gross income as a long-term capital gain.

> **Example 21.** During 19X5, S Corporation has a $20,000 ordinary loss and a net long-term capital gain of $30,000. T, the sole shareholder, must report a long-term capital gain of $30,000 and a $20,000 Subchapter S ordinary loss at the shareholder level.

The amount includible in the gross income of a shareholder as a dividend is treated as a long-term capital gain to the extent of the shareholder's pro rata share of the S corporation's net LTCG for the year of distribution. The corporate net LTCG is, of course, reduced by any capital gain special tax imposed by § 1374. Under § 1371(c), the earnings and profits of an S corporation are not reduced by any amount except for certain adjustments for redemptions, liquidations, reorganizations, and divisive transactions and the portion of a distribution treated as a dividend under § 1368(c)(2).

> **Example 22.** Z Corporation, an electing S corporation with one shareholder, T, has a net long-term capital gain of $48,000 and

---

54. § 1375(c)(2).

Subchapter S taxable income of $3,000. The corporation has no accumulated earnings and profits and has an accumulated adjustments account of $12,200. During 19X5, it made cash distributions of $56,000 to T. The corporation paid a $6,440 capital gain tax. T would treat $41,560 as an LTCG ($48,000 − $6,440), $3,000 as ordinary income, and $11,440 tax-free distribution from the accumulated adjustments account.

## PARTNERSHIP RULES APPLY TO FRINGE BENEFITS

After 1982, the treatment of fringe benefits to any shareholder owning more than two percent of the stock of the corporation is the same as that of a partner in a partnership. The constructive ownership rules of § 318 (refer to Chapter 13) are applicable in determining the two percent ownership test.[55] Thus, such a shareholder-employee is not regarded as an employee for purposes of the following benefits:

—Group-term life insurance (§ 79).

—The $5,000 death benefit exclusion [§ 101(b)].

—The exclusion from income of amounts paid for an accident and health plan (§ 105).

—The exclusion from income of amounts paid by an employer to an accident and health plan (§ 106).

—Exclusion from income of meals and lodging furnished for the convenience of the employer (§ 119).

—Workers' compensation payments on behalf of the shareholder-employee.

**Example 23.** P Corporation, an electing S corporation, pays for the medical care of two shareholder-employees during 19X4. T, an individual owning 2% of the stock, receives $1,700. S, an individual owning 20% of the stock, receives $3,100. The $1,700 would be deducted as a business expense by P Corporation. The $3,100 paid on behalf of S is not deductible by the corporation because of § 703(a)(2)(E) and § 1363(b)(2). S can deduct the $3,100 only to the extent personal medical expenses are allowable as an itemized deduction under § 213.

An S corporation in existence as of September 28, 1982, may continue any existing fringe benefits on such date until the first tax year after December 31, 1987. The Subchapter S election must continue in effect, and there must not be a 50 percent change of ownership.

For tax years after 1983, the regular corporate rules for retirement plans apply to an S corporation. Thus, contributions to a defined contribution plan are limited to the smaller of $30,000 or 25 percent of

---

**55.** §§ 1372(a) and (b).

compensation. The limitation on maximum accrued benefits of a defined benefit plan is the smaller of $90,000 or 100 percent of compensation. Although more restrictive "top-heavy" rules may apply to an S corporation, most of the structural differences favoring a regular corporate plan are eliminated.

## OTHER OPERATIONAL RULES

*Choice of Tax Year.* After October 20, 1982, a corporation that makes a Subchapter S election is required to use either a calendar year or some other accounting period for which the corporation establishes a business purpose to the satisfaction of the IRS. (A 52- to 53-week taxable year is an example of an acceptable accounting period to the IRS.) A corporation with a Subchapter S election in effect on October 20, 1982, may continue its current tax year so long as 50 percent or more of the outstanding stock in such corporation on that date continues to be owned by the same shareholders.[56] Transfers of stock as gifts to family members by reason of death or pursuant to certain existing buy-sell agreements are not considered changes in ownership with respect to this transitional rule.

*Investment Tax Credit.* A Subchapter S election is treated as a mere change in the form of conducting a trade or business for purposes of the investment credit recapture. However, the S corporation still continues to be liable for any investment credit recapture for Subchapter C taxable years.[57]

Any investment credit the S corporation is allowed from the purchase of § 38 property passes through to the shareholders on a pro rata basis.[58] There exist important, and somewhat subtle, rules regarding possible recapture of the credit.

Since the credit passes through to the shareholders, recapture falls upon them when the corporation disposes of the property (or ceases to use it as § 38 property) prematurely. Recapture may also be required of any shareholder who prematurely disposes (by sale or otherwise) of too much of the stock. According to Regulation § 1.47–4(a)(ii), which has been judicially tested, a disposition of more than one-third of a shareholder's stock interest existing at the time the credit was passed through will trigger recapture.[59]

*Miscellaneous Rules.* Other points that should be mentioned to complete the discussion of the possible effects of various Code provisions on S corporations can be summarized as follows:

---

**56.** § 1378(c).
**57.** § 1371(d).
**58.** § 1366(a)(1)(A).
**59.** *Charbonnet v. U. S.*, 72–1 USTC ¶ 9266, 29 AFTR2d 72–633, 455 F.2d 1195 (CA–5, 1972).

—Section § 1367(b)(3) indicates that net operating losses and any related basis adjustments shall apply before the application of § 165(g) where the stock becomes worthless.

—It is still beneficial for an S corporation to issue § 1244 stock.

—Excess investment interest of the corporation passes through to the shareholders. Like other items, such pass-through is allocated on a pro rata basis.[60]

—The hobby loss provisions of § 183 are applicable to S corporations.

—Foreign taxes paid by an electing corporation will pass through and shall be claimed either as a deduction or credit (subject to the applicable limitations).[61]

—Any family member who renders services or furnishes capital to an electing corporation must be paid a reasonable compensation or the IRS can make adjustments to reflect the value of such services or capital.[62] This rule may make it difficult for related parties to shift Subchapter S taxable income to children or other family members.

—The percentage or cost depletion allowance is computed separately by each shareholder. Each shareholder is treated as having produced his or her pro rata share of the production of the electing corporation and each is allocated a respective share of the adjusted basis of the electing corporation as to oil or gas property held by the corporation.[63]

—An S corporation is placed on the cash method of accounting for purposes of deducting business expenses and interest owed to a cash basis related party (including a shareholder who owns at least two percent of the stock in the corporation).[64] Thus, the timing of the shareholder's income and the corporate deduction must match.

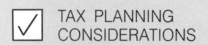

## TAX PLANNING CONSIDERATIONS

### DETERMINING WHEN THE ELECTION IS ADVISABLE

Effective tax planning with Subchapter S begins with determining whether the election is appropriate. In this context, one should consider the following factors:

---

**60.** § 163(d)(4)(C).
**61.** § 1373(a).
**62.** § 1366(e).
**63.** § 613A(c)(13).
**64.** §§ 267(b) and (f).

—Are losses from the business anticipated? If so, the election may be highly attractive because these losses pass through to the shareholders.

—What are the tax brackets of the shareholders? If the shareholders are in high individual income tax brackets, it may be desirable to avoid Subchapter S and have profits taxed to the corporation at lower rates (e. g., 15 percent or 18 percent). With the immediate pass-through of what would be Subchapter S taxable income avoided, profits of the corporation may later be bailed out by the shareholders at capital gain rates through stock redemptions, liquidating distributions, or sales of stock to others; received as dividend distributions in low tax bracket years; or negated by a partial or complete step-up in basis at the death of the shareholder.[65] On the other hand, if the shareholders are in low individual income tax brackets, the pass-through of corporate profits does not impact so forcefully, and avoidance of the corporate income tax becomes the paramount consideration. Under these circumstances, the Subchapter S election could be highly attractive. Bear in mind, however, that an S corporation escapes the Federal corporate income tax but may not be immune from state and local taxes imposed on corporations.

—Closely allied to the above is the possible pass-through to the shareholders of any investment credit the corporation may be allowed on the acquisition of § 38 property. Such pass-through would occur if the corporation has elected Subchapter S.

—Does a regular corporation anticipate significant long-term capital gains or § 1231 gains in the next taxable year? Assuming the corporation does, it might consider the one-shot election approach, whereby Subchapter S status would be in effect for only the year of recognition of these gains. After the year of recognition, the corporation could either voluntarily revoke the election or arrange to have the election terminate through involuntary means. Although some of these gains might be taxed to the corporation by virtue of § § 1374 and 1375, the overall tax consequence probably would be less severe than if the election had not been made.[66]

—Does a regular corporation have a net operating loss carryover from a prior year? Keep in mind that such loss cannot be used in a Subchapter S year. Even worse, Subchapter S years count

---

**65.** See the discussion of § 1014 in Chapter 9.

**66.** The loss of the election probably would bring into play the five-year waiting period of § 1362(g) before a new election can be made. Under such circumstances, it is doubtful that the IRS would be willing to waive this waiting period. There is, therefore, a definite constraint on how often the one-shot election can be utilized.

in the 15-year carryover limitation. But even if the Subchapter S election is made, one might consider losing the election before the carryover limitation expires. This would permit utilization of the loss by what is now a regular corporation.

Keep in mind that except for the operational rules contained in § § 1361–1377, an S corporation will fall within many of the other provisions contained in the Code and generally applicable to all corporations. In the case of a stock redemption, for example, one would look to the rules set forth in § § 302 and 303 (refer to Chapter 13). Likewise, the liquidation of an S corporation would involve § § 336 and 337 as to the effect on the corporation and § § 331, 332, and 333 as to the effect on the shareholder (refer to Chapter 14).

## MAKING A PROPER ELECTION

Once the parties have decided the election is appropriate, it becomes essential to insure that it is properly made.

—Make sure all shareholders consent thereto. If any doubt exists concerning the shareholder status of an individual, it would be wise to have such party issue a consent anyway. Not enough consents will be fatal; the same cannot be said for too many consents.

—Be sure that the election is timely and properly filed. Along this line, either hand carry the election to an IRS office or send it by certified or registered mail. Needless to say, a copy of the election should become part of the corporation's permanent files.

—Regarding the above, be careful to ascertain when the first 2½-month period begins to run for a newly formed corporation. Remember that an election made too soon (i. e., before the corporation is in existence) is just as ineffective as one made too late. If serious doubt exists concerning when this period begins, more than one election might be considered a practical means of guaranteeing the desired result.

## PRESERVING THE ELECTION

Recall, however, how an election can be lost. To preserve an election, the following points should be kept in mind:

—As a starting place, all parties concerned should be made aware of the various transactions that lead to the loss of an election.

—Watch for possible disqualification as a small business corporation. For example, the divorce of a shareholder, accompanied by a property settlement, could violate the 35 shareholders limitation. Or the death of a shareholder could result in a nonqualifying trust becoming a shareholder. The latter circumstance might well be avoided by utilizing a buy and sell agreement binding the deceased shareholder's estate to turn in the stock to the corporation for redemption or, as an alternative, to sell it to the surviving shareholders.

—Make sure a new majority shareholder (including the estate of a deceased shareholder) does not file a refusal to continue the election.

—Watch for the passive investment income limitation of § 1375(a). Avoid a consecutive third year with excess passive investment income if a corporation has accumulated earnings and profits. In this connection, assets that produce passive investment income (e. g., stocks and bonds, certain rent properties) might well be retained by the shareholders in their individual capacities and thereby kept out of the corporation.

—Do not transfer stock to a nonresident alien.

—Do not create an active affiliate.

## PLANNING THE OPERATION OF THE CORPORATION

Operating an S corporation to achieve optimum tax savings for all parties involved requires a great deal of care and, most important, an understanding of the applicable tax rules.

—Under the new rules, it is advisable to avoid accumulated earnings and profits. There is the ever present danger of terminating the election because of excess passive investment income in three consecutive years. Further, there is the § 1375 penalty tax on excess passive net income. Thus, try to eliminate such accumulated earnings and profits through a dividend distribution or liquidation of the corporation with a subsequent reincorporation. Especially if you are going to create a personal holding company, immediately elect Subchapter S treatment to avoid accumulated earnings and profits from a Subchapter C year.

—If excess passive income is a problem, try to put the passive income into the first two years and hold the passive income in the third year below the 25 percent mark. Or get rid of the earnings and profits before the end of the third year.

—Be careful of a 50 percent change in stock ownership. In such a case, a fiscal year corporation must change to a calendar year. Further, "grandfather" fringe benefits in existence on September 28, 1982, will fall under the new partnership treatment.

—Do not issue a fatal second class of stock. Issue straight debt to avoid creating a second class of stock. Establish an instrument with a written unconditional promise to pay on demand or on a specific date a sum certain in money with a fixed interest rate and payment date.

—Section 1368(e)(1)(A) indicates that a net loss allocated to a shareholder reduces the accumulated adjustments account (AAA). This required adjustment should encourage an electing corporation to make annual distributions of net income to avoid the reduction of an AAA by a future net loss.

—A net loss in excess of tax basis may be carried forward and deducted only by the same shareholder in succeeding years. Thus, before disposing of the stock, increase the basis of such stock/loan to flow through the loss. The next shareholder does not obtain the carryover loss.

—Any unused carryover loss in existence on termination of the Subchapter S election may be deducted only in the next tax year and is limited to the individual's *stock* basis (not loan basis) in the post-termination year.[67] The shareholder may wish to purchase more stock to increase the tax basis in order to absorb the loss.

—There are still some differences in cash and property distributions. Old previously taxed income in an electing corporation can be distributed only in cash. Also, a distribution of appreciated property by an S corporation results in a gain allocated to and reported by the shareholders.

—The amount of salary that a shareholder-employee of an S corporation is paid can have varying tax consequences and should be carefully considered. Larger amounts might be advantageous if the maximum contribution allowed under the retirement plan has not been reached. Smaller amounts may be beneficial if the parties are trying to shift taxable income to lower-bracket shareholders, to lessen payroll taxes, to curtail a reduction of Social Security benefits, or to reduce losses that do not pass through because of the basis limitation. Many of the problems that do arise in this area can be solved with advanced planning. Most often, this involves making before-the-fact projections of the tax positions of the parties involved.

—The IRS does have the power to require that reasonable compensation be paid to family members who render services or provide capital to the S corporation. Section § 1366(e) allows the IRS to make adjustments in the items taken into account by family-member shareholders to reflect the value of services (or capital) provided by such parties.

—Try, as best as possible, to time the acquisition by the corporation of § 38 property to provide maximum benefit to the shareholders on the pass-through of the investment credit. Also, be careful of recapture situations that might be triggered through

---

**67.** § 1366(d)(3).

a premature disposition of § 38 property or by a shareholder's disposition of the stock.

—An S corporation may use the installment tax method under § 453 and avoid tax on capital gains. If a corporation anticipates a capital gain in excess of $25,000, it may elect to spread the gain over a number of years or, at least, beyond the third electing year. This manner of circumventing the capital gain tax can be most fruitful when § § 1245 and 1250 assets are involved. Under both Reg. § § 1.1245–6(d) and 1.1250–1(c)(6), all ordinary income is recognized first; thus, the S corporation can recognize the ordinary income first and save the § 1231 gains for years after the third electing year.

—If the shareholders of an S corporation decide to terminate the election through involuntary means, make sure that the disqualifying act possesses substance. When the intent of the parties is obvious and the act represents a technical noncompliance rather than a real change, the IRS may be able to disregard it and keep the parties in Subchapter S status.[68]

---

## PROBLEM MATERIALS

---

### Discussion Questions

1. What are the major advantages and disadvantages of a Subchapter S election?

2. Which of the following items could be considered to be disadvantageous (or potential hazards) for Subchapter S elections?

   (a) The 85% dividends received deduction is lost.

   (b) Foreign tax credit is not available.— *advantage*

   (c) Net operating loss at the corporate level cannot be utilized.— *advantage*

   (d) Constructive dividends are not actually distributed.— *dis.*

   (e) Locked-in AAA occurs after termination. —

   (f) AAA is a personal right that cannot be transferred.— *dis.*

   (g) Basis in stock is increased by constructive dividends. -

   (h) Trust is treated as a shareholder.

   (i) Salaries of certain shareholders are not high enough.— *dis*

3. What happens to net operating losses incurred in preelection years when an S corporation terminates its election?

4. What is the tax effect on its shareholders who have AAAs when an S corporation terminates its election and makes subsequent distributions?

---

68. See *Clarence L. Hook,* 58 T.C. 267 (1972).

5. An S corporation has taxable income of $10,000 for its first electing tax year 19X9 and accumulated earnings and profits through 19X8 of $20,000 (prior to the election). During 19X9, the corporation pays a $16,000 cash dividend to its sole shareholder who has a basis in the stock of $6,500. What amount qualifies for the dividend exclusion?

6. X, Inc. (a calendar year corporation), has a $25,000 net operating loss for 19X5. On January 10, 19X6, the president contacts you for advice as to the practicality of an S election for 19X6. Apparently the president is expecting another $30,000 net operating loss this year. Discuss the possibility and effect of the election.

7. K is considering creating an S corporation for her interior decorating business. She has a friend who has an S corporation with a January 31 fiscal year. She wishes to set up a similar fiscal year. Please advise K.

8. Y's basis in his S corporation is $5,500, but he anticipates that his share of the net operating loss for this year will be $7,400. The tax year is not closed. Advise Y.

9. P, age 57, owns 25% of an S corporation in which her share of AAA is $77,500. After seeing a slide movie on estate planning, she suggests to you (her adviser) that she would like to place one-half of this stock in a trust for her 12-year-old grandson. Do you recommend this procedure? Why?

10. Q is the sole owner of a calendar year S corporation that manufactures solar water heaters. On March 9, Q realizes that the corporation is going to make a very large profit. Discuss how Q can terminate his corporation's Subchapter S election.

11. One of your friends who is married to a nonresident alien would like to incorporate his business and elect Subchapter S. Discuss any potential problems.

12. S Company, an S corporation, distributes land worth $88,000 to a 50% shareholder, T, in 1984. The land cost $22,000 three years ago. Discuss any tax impact on the corporation as well as on the shareholder from this distribution. The corporation has no accumulated earnings and profits, and the basis in the stock is $102,000.

13. For a calendar year corporation, a termination of a Subchapter S election is effective as of the first day of the following tax year in which of the following situations?

(a) A partnership becomes a shareholder on April 2.

(b) There is a failure of the passive investment income limitation.

(c) A new 45% shareholder affirmative refuses to consent to the Subchapter S election.

(d) Shareholders owning 57% of the outstanding stock file a formal revocation on February 23.

(e) A fatal second class of stock is issued on March 3.

(f) The electing corporation becomes a member of an affiliated group on March 10.

14. T, a shareholder-employee, owns 11% of an S corporation which was incorporated in 1983. Which of the following items are deductible by this corporation if paid on behalf of T in 1984?

(a) Salary of $22,000.

(b) $370 paid for an accident and health plan under §§ 105 and 106.

✓(c) Bonus of $9,050.

(d) Premiums of $625 on the cost of $45,000 of group-term life insurance.

(e) $2,075 of meals and lodging furnished to T for the convenience of the corporation.

(f) $5,000 of employee death benefits paid to T's beneficiary (wife) on his death in November.

15. Which of the following income items are considered generally to be passive investment income as defined in § 1362(d)(3)(D)?

(a) Royalties from a book.

(b) Mineral royalties.

(c) Long-term capital gain from the sale of land held as an investment.

(d) Annuity income.

(e) Section 1245 gain from the sale of an automobile.

(f) Section 1231 gain from the sale of real estate.

(g) Receipts received from the liquidation of a 60%-owned subsidiary.

(h) Dividend income from a domestic corporation.

(i) Dividend income from a foreign corporation.

(j) Rent income from an apartment unit.

(k) Interest income.

(l) Long-term capital gain from the sale of stock held as an investment.

16. Q, Inc., recently had its Subchapter S election involuntarily terminated. Does the corporation have to wait five years before making a new election?


## Problems

17. S Corporation, a calendar year electing S corporation, has no accumulated earnings and profits in 1983. The corporation makes a cash dividend of $90,000 to Q, an individual shareholder. Q's accumulated adjustment account is $40,000, and the adjusted basis in his stock is $70,000. Determine how this distribution shall be taxed.

18. In Problem 17, assume the same facts except that Q's share of earnings and profits is $10,000. Would your answer change?

19. At the end of 1984, D Corporation, an S corporation, has gross receipts of $190,000 and gross income of $170,000. The corporation has accumulated earnings and profits of $22,000 and taxable income of $35,000. It has passive investment income of $100,000, with $30,000 of expenses directly related to the production of passive investment income. Calculate this company's excess net passive income (ENPI) and any § 1375 penalty tax.

20. A corporation has a net operating loss in 19X4 of $20,000. A valid Subchapter S election is made in 19X5, and again there is a $20,000 NOL. The stock of the corporation was at all times during 19X5 owned by the same 10 shareholders, each of whom owned 10% of the stock. If R, one of the 10 shareholders, has an adjusted basis at the beginning of 19X5 of $1,600, what amount, if any, may she deduct on her individual tax return for 19X5? Assume the corporation uses a calendar year for tax purposes.

M owns stock in an S corporation. The corporation sustains a net operating loss during 19X9, and M's share of the loss is $45,000. Her adjusted basis in the stock is $24,000, but she has a loan outstanding to the corporation in the amount of $3,000. What amount, if any, is she entitled to deduct with respect to the NOL?

 S Corporation's profit and loss statement for 1984 shows a net profit of $75,000 (i. e., book income). The business is an S corporation, and there are three equal shareholders. From supplemental data, you obtain the following information about the corporation for 1984:

| | |
|---|---:|
| Advertising expense | $ 7,000 |
| Tax-exempt income | 1,500 |
| Dividends received | 9,000 |
| Section 1231 gain | 6,000 |
| Section 1245 gain | 20,000 |
| Recovery of bad debts | 3,500 |
| Capital losses | 6,000 |
| Salary to owners (each) | 8,000 |
| Cost of goods sold | 82,000 |

(a) Compute Subchapter S § 702(a)(8) taxable income or (loss). $61,000

(b) What would be a shareholder's allocated portion of § 702(a)(8) taxable income or (loss)? ⅓ × 61,000

(c) If one of the shareholders and his wife have $10,000 of personal dividends, what would be their taxable dividends if they file a joint return. $12,800

23. The tax return of S Corporation, an electing S corporation, shows a net loss of $8,700 [i.e., §702(a)(8) loss] for 1984. G, an individual, owns 30% of the stock during the entire year. While auditing the corporate books, you obtain the following information for 1984:

| | |
|---|---:|
| Salaries paid to the three owners | $42,000 |
| Charitable contributions | 6,000 |
| Tax-exempt interest | 1,500 |
| Dividends received ($4,000 was from | |
| a foreign company) | 9,000 |
| Section 1231 loss | 3,000 |
| Section 1245 gain | 15,000 |
| Recoveries of prior property taxes | 3,000 |
| Cost of goods sold | 64,000 |
| Capital losses | 4,500 |
| Selling expenses | 4,200 |
| Long-term capital gains | 15,000 |

(a) Compute book income or (loss).

(b) If G's tax basis in his stock is $2,200, what amount may he deduct in 1984 on his individual tax return?

24. B owns 50% of the stock in an S corporation. This corporation sustains a $12,000 net operating loss and a $2,000 capital loss during 19X9. B's adjusted basis in her stock is $2,000, but she has a loan outstanding to the corporation for $3,000. What amount, if any, is she entitled to deduct with respect to these losses on her Form 1040 for 19X9?

25. I Corporation, an electing S corporation, had a net operating loss of $36,500 in 19X8. E and B were the equal and only shareholders of the

corporation from January 1 to January 21, 19X8. On January 21,19X9, E sold his stock to B for $41,000. At the beginning of 19X8, both E and B had a basis of $40,000 in the stock of the corporation. (Note: On the date of the sale, stock is regarded as being held by the transferee.)

16 - 17 18
ex - 17.

(a) What amount, if any, of the NOL will flow through to E? —$ 1000

(b) What amount of the NOL will pass through to B? — 35,500

(c) What gain, if any, will be taxable to E on the sale of his stock? — 2,000

26. Z purchased all the stock of S Corporation on March 1, 19X8, for $200,000. Throughout 19X8 and 19X9, the corporation was an S corporation. During 19X8, the corporation did not make any distribution and reported a profit of $20,450, of which $5,000 was attributable to the period before Z acquired the stock. Because of illness, Z sold his stock in S Corporation on October 20, 19X9. The corporation operated at a loss of $13,860 during 19X9 but did make a $4,000 dividend distribution on July 1, 19X9. Four thousand dollars of the loss was sustained after Z sold his stock. (Assume no special election is made.)

(a) What amount, if any, of the corporation's income must Z include in his gross income for 19X8? Assume a non-leap year.

(b) Determine the amount, if any, of the corporation's net operating loss for 19X9 that Z may deduct.

(c) Calculate Z's gain (or loss) if he sells his entire interest in S Corporation for $225,000.

27. In the independent statements below, indicate whether the transaction will increase (+), decrease (−), or have no effect (NE) on the adjusted basis of a shareholder's stock.

(a) Tax-exempt income.

(b) Long-term capital gain.

(c) Net operating loss.

(d) Section 1231 gain.

(e) Excess of percentage depletion over the basis of the property.

(f) Section 702(a)(8) income.

(g) Nontaxable return-of-capital distribution by the corporation.

(h) Charitable contributions.

(i) Business gift in excess of $25.

(j) Section 1245 gain.

(k) Dividends received.

(l) Short-term capital loss.

(m) Recovery of a bad debt.

(n) Long-term capital loss.

28. Q, an S corporation, reports its income on a calendar year basis. On April 1, 19X3 (a non-leap year), the corporation issues a second class of stock, which terminates the election. Through March 31, the corporate records show that the corporation has $42,000 of income, $22,000 of deductions, and $18,000 of tax credits. On December 31, 19X3, the tax records

indicate that the corporation has earned $340,000 of income and has deductions of $180,000 and tax credits of $43,000. Assume no special elections are made.

(a) The sole shareholder would show what amounts on his individual return in 19X3?

(b) Compute the taxable income of the Subchapter C corporation

29. A calendar year S corporation purchases $200,000 of new § 38 property with a five-year cost recovery class. A owns 50% of the stock for the entire year. B sells his 50% stock interest to C on November 1, 1984 (a non-leap year). Calculate the division of the § 38 property among the shareholders.

# Chapter 17

# Partnerships

Before enactment of the Internal Revenue Code of 1954, taxpayers operating a business in partnership form were faced with a high degree of uncertainty as to the tax consequences of their activities. This uncertainty was attributable to the lack of statutory rules governing the tax effects of transactions between partners and their partnership. The absence of clarifying provisions in the 1939 Code[1] resulted in a reliance on case law in tax planning for partners and partnerships, and the paucity of relevant cases contributed to the need for specific legislation.

Subchapter K of the 1954 Code contains the basic statutory rules governing the tax consequences of transactions between partners and between partners and their partnerships. Passage of these provisions (§ § 701 through 761) has, for the most part, rendered much of the pre-1954 case law inapplicable. However, many of the statutory rules of Subchapter K and the general approach taken in drafting the partnership provisions can be traced to judicial decisions rendered before 1954. Unfortunately, the limited number of cases decided within the past two decades under the new law offers little guidance in the tax planning for many unsettled issues. As a consequence, taxpayers and

---

**1.** Although Supplement F of the 1939 Code contained nine sections dealing with the taxation of partners and partnerships, the lack of detail in these provisions and the increasing complexities of the business environment made these statutory guidelines inadequate for tax planning purposes.

their advisers must rely heavily upon the specific statutory language
of Subchapter K and related Treasury Regulations.

## NATURE OF PARTNERSHIP TAXATION

Unlike corporations, estates, and trusts, partnerships are not considered separate tax entities. Instead, partnership members are subject
to income tax on their distributive share of the partnership's income,
even if an actual distribution is not made.[2] Thus, the partnership tax
return (Form 1065) serves only as an information device to determine
the character and amount of each partner's distributive share of partnership income and expense.[3]

Although a partnership is not considered a separate taxable entity for purposes of determining and paying Federal income taxes, it
is treated as such for purposes of making various elections and selecting its taxable year, method of depreciation, and accounting methods.
Also, a partnership is treated as a separate legal entity under civil
law with the right to own property in its own name and to transact
business free from the personal debts of its partners.[4]

The unique treatment of partners and partnerships under the
current Federal income tax provisions can be traced to two general
concepts of a partnership which evolved long before enactment of the
1954 Code. These two concepts, the *entity concept* and the *aggregate or
conduit concept*, have been applied in both civil and common law, and
their influence can be seen in practically every statutory provision of
Subchapter K of the 1954 Code. The entity concept treats partners
and partnerships as distinctly separate units. This concept gives the
partnership its own tax "personality." As mentioned above, the partnership may select its own tax year (subject to limitations discussed
later), depreciation method, and accounting method. This is a direct
reflection of the entity concept. In contrast, from the perspective of the
aggregate or conduit concept, the partnership is merely a channel
through which flow income, credits, deductions, etc., to the partners.
The partners, not the partnership, are taxed on the partnership's
earnings.

Influence of the entity concept can be found in the statutory rules
requiring a partnership to file an information tax return, allowing it
to select its own tax year and method of accounting, and treating a
partner as a party separate and distinct from the partnership in certain transactions between partners and their partnerships. Under the

---

**2.** Section 701 contains the statutory rule that the partners are liable for income tax
in their separate or individual capacities. The partnership itself cannot be subject to
the income tax on its earnings.

**3.** § 6031.

**4.** See, for instance, the Uniform Partnership Act and the Uniform Limited Partnership Act, which have been adopted by most states and govern the legal conduct of
businesses operating in the partnership form.

aggregate or conduit concept, however, a partnership is considered as nothing more than a collection of taxpayers joined in an agency relationship with each other. The influence of this concept can be found in provisions imposing the income tax on the individual partners rather than on the partnership and in the disallowance of certain deductions and all tax credits to the partnership. These deductions and credits must flow through to the individual partners for an ultimate tax determination.

Many sections of the Code contain a blend of both the entity and aggregate concepts. For instance, the statutory provisions concerning the formation, operation, and liquidation of a partnership contain elements of both concepts. With some rules directed only toward the entity concept, others based solely on the conduit concept, and still more containing a mixture of both concepts, an individual studying the partnership provisions for the first time might find this area of the income tax law difficult to grasp. However, by concentrating on the basic purpose underlying each of the partnership rules, the rationale and general approach to partnership taxation can be better understood.

## WHAT IS A PARTNERSHIP?

The Uniform Partnership Act defines a partnership as "an association of two or more persons to carry on as co-owners a business for profit."[5] Similarly, a common law definition considers a partnership to be the contractual relationship existing between two or more persons who join together to carry on a trade or business, each contributing money, property, labor, or skill, and all with the expectation of sharing in the profits and losses of the business. The definition of a partnership for Federal income tax purposes, however, is much broader than under state law.

Sections 761(a) and 7701(a)(2) of the Code define a partnership as a syndicate, group, pool, joint venture, or other unincorporated organization through or by means of which any business, financial operation, or venture is carried on and which is not classified as a corporation, or a trust or estate. This definition of a partnership, carried over from the 1939 Code, provides adequate guidance in the classification of the many typical partnerships. However, as discussed in greater detail in Chapter 12, certain types of unincorporated businesses have been classified as corporations for Federal income tax purposes. If the organization exhibits the characteristics of an *association* developed by the Supreme Court[6] and contained in the Treasury Regulations,[7] it will be classified as a corporation regardless of the

---

5.  § 6(1), Uniform Partnership Act.
6.  *Morrissey v. Comm.*, 36–1 USTC ¶ 9020, 16 AFTR 1274, 56 S.Ct. 289 (USSC, 1935).
7.  Reg. § 301.7701–2(a).

intent of its owners. Thus, classification as a partnership for tax purposes can be much more complex than the basic definition might indicate.

Avoiding the corporate classification does not automatically qualify an organization for partnership status, however. For instance, a joint undertaking to share the expenses of constructing and maintaining a ditch to drain surface water from their properties does not qualify the owners as partners. Likewise, mere co-ownership of property which is maintained, kept in repair, and rented or leased does not constitute a partnership. For example, if tenants in common of farm property lease it to a farmer for a cash rental or a share of the crops, they do not necessarily create a partnership. The Regulations provide, however, that tenants in common may be partners if they actively carry on a trade, business, financial operation, or venture and divide the profits.[8] Thus, a partnership would exist if the co-owners of an apartment building leased space and, in addition, provided services to the occupants either directly or through an agent.

## EXCLUSION FROM PARTNERSHIP TAXATION

Under § 761(a) certain unincorporated organizations may be excluded, completely or partially, from treatment as partnerships for Federal income tax purposes. The exclusion applies only to organizations availed of (1) for investment purposes rather than the active conduct of a business or (2) for the joint production, extraction, or use of property, but not for the purpose of selling the services or products produced or extracted. All of the members of the organization must agree to the election and be able to compute their income without the necessity of computing partnership taxable income.

## WHO IS A PARTNER?

Section 761(b) defines a partner as one who is a member of a partnership. Unlike the Subchapter S corporate shareholder restrictions, there are no limitations on who may be an owner of a partnership interest. For instance, an individual, estate, trust, corporation, or another partnership can each be a partner in the same partnership. However, certain problems can arise when a minor child is a member of a family partnership or when a corporation is the general partner in a limited partnership.

## PARTNERSHIP FORMATION

The basic provisions applicable to the formation of a partnership are contained in §§ 721 through 723. Like their counterparts in the cor-

---

8. Reg. § 301.7701–3(a).

porate formation area, these statutes provide for the tax-free formation of a partnership, admission of new partners, and the determination of basis of a partnership interest and the basis of property transferred to the partnership. Standing alone, however, these rules do not, in all situations, assure the nonrecognition of gain or loss upon the formation of a partnership. Therefore, other sections of the Code contain provisions which supplement the basic rules of Subchapter K. For instance, the depreciation recapture provisions of §§ 1245 and 1250 are structured to provide for tax-free transfers of depreciable property to a partnership. Likewise, § 47(b) provides that no recapture of investment tax credit is required by the contributing partner if the contributed property continues to qualify as § 38 property and the partner retains a substantial interest in the partnership.

## CONTRIBUTIONS TO PARTNERSHIP

Section 721 contains the general rule that no gain or loss is recognized to a partnership or any of its partners upon the contribution of property in exchange for a capital interest in the partnership. In addition to providing for nonrecognition of gain or loss on the initial transfers in formation of the partnership, this general rule applies to all subsequent contributions of property. Thus, the partners of an existing partnership can be insulated from the recognition of gain or loss upon the admission of a new partner if the partnership interest is in exchange for a contribution of property which qualifies under the general rule. The insulation of the partners in this manner is a reflection of the entity concept; the partnership, once formed, is a separate entity capable of engaging in transactions.

The nonrecognition provision of § 721 does not apply to all transfers to a partnership, however. Although cash contributions and almost all other contributions of tangible or intangible properties are covered by the general rule, there are several circumstances to which § 721 is inapplicable. For instance, the Regulations provide that if the transfer of property by a partner to the partnership results in the receipt of money or other consideration by the partner, the transaction will be treated as a sale or exchange rather than as a contribution under § 721.[9] Thus, the contributor must receive an interest in the partnership if the transfer is to be tax-free.

Another situation to which the general rule of nonrecognition is inapplicable involves the receipt of a partnership interest in exchange for services rendered or to be rendered to the partnership. The partnership interest received in exchange for services can be either a *capi-*

---

**9.** Reg. § 1.721–1(a). But see *John H. Otey,* 70 T.C. 312 (1978) *aff'd.* in 80–2 USTC ¶ 9817, 47 AFTR2d 81–301, 634 F.2d 1046 (CA–6, 1980), where taxpayer was able to avoid this result.

*tal interest, a profits interest,* or both. The Regulations provide that the fair market value of any part of an interest in partnership capital transferred to a partner for services shall be considered as compensation for such services.[10] The recipient must recognize the amount so determined as ordinary income in the year actually or constructively received. If a profits interest in a partnership is received for *future services,* the Regulations[11] imply that the recipient will not be taxed immediately. Instead, the service partner will simply report his or her share of partnership profits annually as such profits are determined. However, if the profits interest is received for *past services* and the interest has a determinable fair market value, the recipient may be taxed immediately on the receipt of such interest.

> **Example 1.** In 19X8, C receives a 20% capital and profits interest in the AB Partnership for services previously rendered to the partnership. At the time of the transfer, the partnership had assets with a fair market value of $50,000 and no liabilities. Section 721 will not apply to this transaction. Thus, C must include $10,000 (the fair market value of the capital interest received) as ordinary income in his 19X8 tax year. Additionally, C must include his share of partnership profits in each of his future taxable years as these profits are reported by the partnership, unless the value of the profits interest can be determined immediately (which is not ordinarily the case).

Referring to Example 1, the AB Partnership is permitted to treat such a transaction as a guaranteed payment and may be entitled to a $10,000 deduction in determining its taxable income for 19X8. Furthermore, each of the partners who surrendered a portion of his or her capital interest to C will be treated as if part of his or her partnership interest was sold and be required to recognize gain or loss on the sale.

It should also be noted that although a partner may have different capital and profit interest percentages, it is more common to find that such interests are equal. Thus, one should assume that all future references to a percentage of capital interest in a partnership implies an equal percentage profits interest unless otherwise specified.

The nonrecognition provision of § 721 would not be applicable if the partnership is used solely to effect a tax-free exchange of properties. For example, assume that two partners in the same partnership have properties which they wish to exchange free of tax. Assume further that the properties involved cannot qualify under any other nonrecognition provision of the Code (e. g., a like-kind exchange under § 1031). Each partner contributes property to the partnership; shortly thereafter, each receives what is hoped to be a nontaxable distribution of the property contributed by the other. Under such circum-

---

10. Reg. § 1.721–1(b)(1).
11. See § 83 and the Regulations thereunder.

stances, the IRS will simply collapse the transactions into a single taxable exchange.

Section 721(b) was added to the Code by the Tax Reform Act of 1976 to provide another exception to the general rule of nonrecognition of gain on the contribution of property to a partnership. The contributing partner is required to recognize any gain realized on the transfer of property to a partnership which would be treated as an investment company (within the meaning of § 351) if the partnership were incorporated. A partnership will be considered an investment company if, after the transfer, more than 80 percent of the value of its assets (excluding cash and nonconvertible debt obligations) is held for investment and is readily marketable stocks or securities. The purpose of this provision is to prevent investors from using the partnership form to either diversify their investment portfolios or exchange stocks or securities on a tax-free basis. Similar action had been taken by Congress in 1967 to prevent the use of the nonrecognition provision of § 351 (involving tax-free transfers to controlled corporations) to accomplish the same result [see § 351(e)].

Finally, § 721 may effectively be inapplicable in the case of contributions of property subject to a liability in excess of basis. The interaction of § § 752(b) and 731 may require recognition of gain in this situation.

## BASIS OF PARTNERSHIP INTEREST

The basis of a partnership interest acquired in a nontaxable transfer of property to the partnership is determined under § 722. The contributing partner's basis in the partnership interest received is the sum of money contributed plus the adjusted basis of any other property transferred to the partnership. However, if gain or loss is recognized on the transfer or if ordinary income results, the basis must be adjusted accordingly.

> **Example 2.** In return for the rendition of services and the contribution of property (basis of $50,000, fair market value of $80,000) to the KLM Partnership, A receives a 25% capital interest valued at $100,000. The contribution of property is nontaxable under § 721. However, the receipt of a partnership interest for the rendition of services results in compensation to A of $20,000 (value of partnership interest of $100,000 less value of property contributed of $80,000). A's basis in the KLM Partnership interest is $70,000 (basis of the property contributed of $50,000 plus ordinary income recognized of $20,000).

It is quite common for the partner contributing property other than money to insist that his or her capital account on the books of the partnership reflect the agreed-upon fair market value of the property at the time of the contribution. Recording contributed property at fair market value on the partnership's books and records is in accord with generally accepted accounting principles. However, neither the contributing partner's tax basis in his or her partnership interest nor the partnership's tax basis in the contributed property will be affected by this financial accounting treatment.

> **Example 3.** U and V form an equal partnership with a cash contribution of $30,000 from U and a property contribution (adjusted basis of $18,000 and fair market value of $30,000) from V. Although the books of the UV Partnership may reflect a credit of $30,000 to each partner's capital account, only U will have a tax basis of $30,000 in his partnership interest. V's tax basis in his partnership interest will be $18,000, the amount of his tax basis in the property contributed to the partnership.

If the property contributed by partner V above is recorded at its agreed fair market value, the partnership's books and tax basis will differ as follows:

|  | Assets | |
| --- | --- | --- |
|  | Per Books | Tax Basis |
| Cash | $ 30,000 | $ 30,000 |
| Property | 30,000 | 18,000 |
| Total | $ 60,000 | $ 48,000 |

|  | Liabilities and Capital | |
| --- | --- | --- |
| Capital Accounts: | | |
| U | $ 30,000 | $ 30,000 |
| V | 30,000 | 18,000 |
| Total | $ 60,000 | $ 48,000 |

An unfortunate result of recording contributed assets at fair market value is that the partnership's financial records will not reflect the tax basis of its assets. Consequently, the contributing partner's capital account cannot be used as the starting point for determining his or her tax basis in the partnership interest without considering a per-books-to-tax-adjustment. More important, if the property contributed by partner V in Example 3 ever is sold, or if it is depreciable, recording only its fair market value on contribution to the partnership could lead to a series of subsequent errors in reporting taxable income or loss of the partnership.

When property subject to a liability is contributed to a partnership or if the partnership assumes any of the transferor partner's liabilities, the basis of the partnership interest must be reduced by the amount of the liabilities assumed by the other partners. Correspondingly, the noncontributing partners may increase their basis by that portion of the liabilities they assumed upon the transfer. Generally, each partner's loss-sharing ratio is used to determine the amount of any liabilities he or she is deemed to have assumed. Absent some specific reference to the contrary, it is assumed that the partners have agreed to share losses in the same ratio as they share profits. These adjustments to the basis of a partnership interest result from the application of § 752. Under § 752(a), an increase in a partner's share of partnership liabilities is treated as a contribution of money made by the partner to the partnership. Likewise, § 752(b) requires that a decrease in a partner's share of partnership liabilities is to be considered as a distribution of money by the partnership.

> **Example 4.** X, Y, and Z form the XYZ Partnership with the following contributions: cash of $50,000 from X for a 50% interest in capital and profits, cash of $25,000 from Y for a 25% interest, and property valued at $33,000 from Z for a 25% interest. The property contributed by Z has an adjusted basis of $15,000 and is subject to a mortgage of $8,000, which is assumed by the partnership. Z's basis in his interest in the XYZ Partnership is $9,000 determined as follows:

| | |
|---|---|
| Adjusted basis of Z's contributed property | $ 15,000 |
| Less portion of mortgage assumed by X and Y and treated as a distribution of money to Z (75% of $8,000) | 6,000 |
| Basis of Z's interest in XYZ Partnership | $ 9,000 |

> **Example 5.** Assuming the same facts as in Example 4, X and Y will have a basis in their partnership interest of $54,000 and $27,000, respectively.

| | X | Y |
|---|---|---|
| Cash contribution | $ 50,000 | $ 25,000 |
| Plus portion of mortgage assumed and treated as an additional cash contribution: | | |
| (50% of $8,000) | 4,000 | |
| (25% of $8,000) | | 2,000 |
| Basis of interest in XYZ Partnership | $ 54,000 | $ 27,000 |

The basis of a contributing partner's interest may be reduced to zero if the property transferred is subject to a liability in excess of the property's basis. It should be noted, however, that the basis of a partnership interest, like the basis of any other kind of property, never can be negative. Thus, if the portion of the liability assumed by the noncontributing partners exceeds the contributing partner's basis, *recognizable* gain will result. Further, § 731 provides that such a gain shall be considered as a gain from the sale of a partnership interest, and under § 741, the gain would be considered a capital gain. However, ordinary income may result if the transferred property was subject to depreciation recapture.

> **Example 6.** Assume the same facts as in Example 4 except that the property contributed by Z has a fair market value of $49,000 and is subject to a mortgage of $24,000 (instead of $8,000). Z's basis in his partnership interest would be reduced to zero, and he would have a *realized* gain of $3,000 determined as follows:

| | |
|---|---|
| Adjusted basis of the property to Z | $ 15,000 |
| Less portion of mortgage assumed by X and Y and treated as a distribution of money to Z (75% of $24,000) | 18,000 |
| Realized gain | ($ 3,000) |

> The $3,000 in excess of basis is treated as a capital gain from the sale or exchange of a partnership interest under § 731(a) unless the depreciation recapture provisions are applicable. Further, the holding period of the contributed property must be used to determine whether the gain is a long-term capital gain. [Note that the interaction of § § 752(b) and 731 negates the nonrecognition provision of § 721.]

Even though the partner who contributes property subject to a liability will personally assume a portion of that liability, this amount will not be added to the partnership interest's basis. This portion obviously does not represent an increase in the partner's liabilities. If the required recognition of $3,000 gain by partner Z in Example 6 appears to be a harsh tax consequence, consider what would have occurred if the property had been contributed to a corporation. Under § 357(c), the entire excess of the liability over Z's basis in the property (i. e., $9,000) would have resulted in a taxable gain to him. The use of the partnership form in this instance, therefore, results in a tax benefit to Z.

The basis of a partnership interest acquired other than by the contribution of property must be determined under provisions of the Code outside Subchapter K.[12] For instance, if the partnership interest is acquired by purchase, the basis will be determined under § 1012.

---

**12.** § 742.

Likewise, if the partnership interest is acquired by gift or inheritance, the basis will be determined under § 1015 and § 1014, respectively.

After its initial determination, the basis of a partnership interest is subject to continuous fluctuations. A partner's basis will be *increased* by additional contributions and the sum of his or her current and prior years' distributive share of:

—Taxable income of the partnership, including capital gains.

—Tax-exempt income of the partnership.

—The excess of the deductions for depletion over the basis of the partnership's property subject to depletion.[13]

Similarly, the basis of a partner's interest will be *decreased,* but not below zero, by distribution of partnership property, by the amount of the partner's deduction for depletion under § 611 with respect to oil and gas wells, and by the sum of the current and prior years' distributive share of:

—Partnership losses, including capital losses.

—Partnership expenditures which are not deductible in computing taxable income or loss and which are not capital expenditures.

Changes in the liabilities (including trade accounts payable, bank loans, etc.) of a partnership also will affect the basis of a partnership interest. For instance, a partner's basis is *increased* by the assumption of partnership liabilities and by the pro rata share of liabilities incurred by the partnership. Likewise, the partner's basis is *decreased* by the amount of any of the personal liabilities assumed by the partnership and by the pro rata share of any decreases in the liabilities of the partnership. The impact of changes in a partnership's liabilities on its partners' respective bases in their partnership interests reflects the aggregate concept of partnership taxation. If the partnership is viewed only as a common pool of assets to which each partner contributes, any changes in this pool will have a corresponding impact on the partners' interest in those assets. Thus, when the acquisition of partnership assets is financed by creditors, the partners are treated as if they each borrowed proportionate amounts of money and contributed them to the partnership, which then used the money to purchase the assets. Likewise, if partnership assets are used to satisfy obligations to creditors, the partners are treated as if they constructively received a distribution of money from the partnership and then satisfied the obligations. Consequently, as the partnership's pool of assets increases or decreases, the partners' bases in their partnership interest will increase or decrease simultaneously.

Finally, § 705(b) provides an *alternative rule* for determining the

---

13.   § 705(a) and Reg. § 1.705–1(a)(2).

basis of a partnership interest when a partner cannot practically apply the basis determination rules cited above or if, in the opinion of the IRS, it is reasonable to conclude from a consideration of all the facts that the result produced will not vary substantially from the regular approach. Under the alternative rule, the adjusted basis of a partnership interest may be determined by reference to a partner's share of the adjusted basis of property that would be distributable upon termination of the partnership. In using the alternative rule, however, certain adjustments would be required to reflect any significant discrepancies in the adjusted basis of partnership property arising as a result of contributed property, transfers of partnership interests, or distributions of property to the partners.

> **Example 7.** R, S, and T are equal partners in the RST Partnership, which owns various properties with an adjusted basis of $18,000. Including income earned and retained of $6,000, the partnership's total adjusted basis of its property is $24,000. Since each partner's share in the adjusted basis of the partnership property is one-third of this amount, under the alternative rule, each partner's adjusted basis for his or her partnership interest would be $8,000.

> **Example 8.** Assume the same facts in Example 7 except that partner R sells his partnership interest to U for $10,000 at a time when the partnership's property had appreciated in value to $30,000. The basis of U's one-third interest in the partnership will be his cost. However, reference to the partnership's total adjusted basis in its property would yield only $8,000 for a one-third interest. Therefore, U will be allowed an adjustment of $2,000 under the alternative rule to reflect his basis in the acquired partnership interest.

## PARTNERSHIP'S BASIS IN CONTRIBUTED PROPERTY

Section 723 states that the basis of property contributed to a partnership by a partner shall be the adjusted basis of such property to the contributing partner at the time of the contribution, increased by the amount of any gain recognized by the contributing partner as a result of the transfer. Additionally, the holding period of such property for the partnership includes the period during which it was held by the contributing partner, since the partnership's basis in the property is the same basis the property had in the hands of the partner.[14]

> **Example 9.** K and L form an equal partnership with a contribution of land valued at $100,000 from K and a contribution of equipment valued at $150,000 from L. K's basis in the land is

---

**14.** § 1223(2) and Reg. § 1.723–1.

$30,000. The equipment contributed by L has an adjusted basis of $20,000 and is subject to a mortgage of $50,000, which is assumed by the partnership. K's basis in her partnership interest will be $55,000 ($30,000 basis in the land contributed increased by 50% of the $50,000 mortgage on the equipment). L's basis in his partnership interest will be reduced to zero, and he will have a taxable gain of $5,000 as a result of the $25,000 portion of the mortgage K is treated as having assumed. The required gain recognition by L results in an increase in basis of the equipment to the partnership. Rather than having a carryover basis of $20,000, the partnership will have an adjusted basis of $25,000 for the equipment. Also note that L's gain will be considered as ordinary income to the extent of any § 1245 depreciation recapture potential associated with the transferred equipment.

Although the contributing partner's basis and holding period of property will carry over to the partnership, the transfer of certain depreciable property could result in unfavorable tax consequences. For instance, a partnership will not be allowed the option to expense any part of the cost of § 179 property whose basis is determined by reference to the transferor partner.[15] Although the Economic Recovery Tax Act of 1981 (ERTA) provides this particular limitation, a similar limitation was imposed under prior law for old § 179 additional first-year (bonus) depreciation. Additionally, ERTA added § 168(f)(10) to the Code in order to prevent a partnership from using any accelerated cost recovery method or recovery period which would differ from the transferor partner's method and remaining recovery period. Similar rules existed under prior law which prohibited a partnership from using accelerated depreciation methods if the contributing partner was considered the original user of the property. Thus, if the loss of any expense or cost recovery deductions would be detrimental to the contributing partner, consideration should be given to retaining ownership of the property and leasing it to the partnership until the beneficial deductions are exhausted.

# PARTNERSHIP OPERATION

The statutory provisions which govern the operation of a partnership are contained in Code § § 701 through 708. These rules govern who is taxed on the partnership's income, how such income is determined, and how and when it must be reported. Also included are the rules governing the determination of the basis of a partnership interest and the effect of transactions between a partner and his or her partnership.

---

15. § 179(d)(2)(C).

## MEASURING AND REPORTING PARTNERSHIP INCOME

Although a partnership is not subject to Federal income taxation,[16] it is required to determine its taxable income and file an income tax return for information purposes.[17] The tax return, Form 1065, is due on the fifteenth day of the fourth month following the close of the taxable year of the partnership. Concurrent with this filing, the partnership is required to provide each partner with a Schedule K–1 indicating his or her distributive share of all items of income, deductions, and credits. This enables each partner to timely file his or her own personal income tax return. To encourage compliance with this reporting requirement, § 6698 imposes a penalty on the partnership of $50 per month (or fraction thereof), but not to exceed five months, for failure to file a complete and timely information return without reasonable cause. The monthly penalty is assessed for each partner in the partnership during any part of the taxable year. Thus, if a partnership with 20 partners failed to file Form 1065 for its taxable year (without reasonable cause), the partnership would be liable for a penalty of $5,000 ($50 × 20 × 5). More important, every general partner of the partnership would be personally liable for the entire penalty. The key schedules of Form 1065 and their contents are examined in greater detail below.

The principal purpose of the partnership return is to provide information necessary for determining the character and amount of each partner's distributive share of the partnership's income, expenses, and credits (an application of the aggregate or conduit concept of partnerships). Form 1065 and its function are not only influenced by the aggregate concept; this form also is used to make various elections. With few exceptions, the partnership must make the elections affecting the computation of its taxable income. For instance, selection of the cash or accrual method of accounting, an election not to use the installment method of reporting sales, or the option to expense intangible drilling and development costs must be made by the partnership and will apply to all partners in all partnership transactions. The electing capacity of the partnership is an expression of the entity concept.

The measurement and reporting of partnership income requires a two-step approach. First, § 702(a) requires that certain transactions be segregated and reported separately on the partnership return (and on each partner's Schedule K–1):

---

**16.** Section 701 provides that a partnership shall not be subject to the income tax. Instead, the income tax is imposed on the partners in their separate or individual capacities. This is a reflection of the conduit concept discussed previously. It should be noted, however, that a partnership is subject to other Federal tax provisions. For instance, a partnership is required to pay the employer's share of Social Security taxes and unemployment taxes, and it must withhold income taxes on its employees' salaries or wages.

**17.** § 6031.

1.  Gains and losses from sales or exchanges of capital assets held for not more than one year (short-term capital gains and losses).

2.  Gains and losses from sales or exchange of capital assets held for more than one year (long-term capital gains and losses).

3.  Gains and losses from sales or involuntary conversions of real or depreciable property used in the business and held for more than one year (i. e., § 1231 gains or losses).

4.  Charitable contributions as defined in § 170(c).

5.  Dividends qualifying for the § 116 exclusion.

6.  Taxes paid or accrued to foreign countries and to possessions of the United States which may be claimed as a credit.

7.  Other items of income, gain, loss, deduction, or credit, to the extent provided by the Regulations.

8.  Taxable income or loss, exclusive of the items above.

The Regulations expand the list of those items to be segregated and reported separately as indicated in category 7:

—Recoveries of bad debts, prior taxes, and delinquency amounts (§ 111).

—Gains and losses from wagering transactions [§ 165(d)].

—Soil and water conservation expenditures (§ 175).

—Nonbusiness expenses (§ 212).

—Medical and dental expenses (§ 213).

—Alimony payments (§ 215).

—Amounts representing taxes and interest paid to cooperative housing corporations (§ 216).

—Intangible drilling and development costs [§ 263(c)].

—Exploration expenditures (§ § 615 and 617).

—Income, gain, or loss to the partnership arising from a distribution of unrealized receivables [§ 751(b)].

—Partially tax-exempt interest on obligations of the U. S. or its instrumentalities.

—Any items of income, gain, loss, deduction, or credit subject to a special allocation under the partnership agreement which differs from the allocation of partnership taxable income or loss generally.

In addition, the Regulations require that each partner take into account separately his or her distributive share of any partnership item if it would result in an income tax liability for the partner different from that which would result if he or she did not take the item into account separately.[18] Thus, each partner must take into account separately his or her share of all partnership items which would be considered tax preference items for purposes of the minimum tax and his or her share of the partnership's investment in (or premature disposition of) any property qualifying for the investment tax credit.

The reason for the required segregation and direct allocation to the individual partners of the foregoing items is rooted in the aggregate or conduit concept. This first stage of measuring and reporting partnership income is necessary because the items subject to this treatment affect the computation of various exclusions, deductions, and credits at the partner level. Thus, these items must pass through the partnership directly to the individual partners without loss of identity.

The second stage of the measurement and reporting process deals with all partnership items not segregated or directly allocated as described above.[19] All items not separately stated under § 702(a) are netted at the partnership level. In this process, the taxable income of a partnership is computed in the same manner as is the taxable income of an individual taxpayer, except that a partnership is not allowed the following deductions:[20]

—The zero bracket amount.

—The deduction for personal exemptions.

—The deduction for taxes paid to foreign countries or possessions of the United States.

—The deduction for charitable contributions.

—The deduction for net operating losses.

—The additional itemized deductions allowed individuals in § § 211 through 223.

—The deduction for depletion under § 611 with respect to oil and gas interests.

The result of this second stage is the partnership's ordinary income or loss and is reported on the first page (line 24) of Form 1065. This amount and each of the items requiring separate statement are reported on Schedule K of the partnership's information return. Each then is allocated and separately reported on a Schedule K–1 for each partner in accordance with his or her distributive share of each item. Each of the partners must then report on his or her own tax return the distributive share of both the segregated items and the partnership's ordinary income or loss, regardless of whether or not an actual distribution is made. Page 1 of Form 1065, a Schedule K, and page 1 of

**18.** Reg. § 1.702–1(a)(8)(ii).
**19.** § 702(a)(8).
**20.** § 703(a).

Schedule K–1 are reproduced on the following pages. In comparing Schedules K and K–1, notice that each line on Schedule K is also reflected on every Schedule K–1. Schedule K–1 also provides instructions for partners who are individual taxpayers as to where and on which tax return form to report their respective shares of all items.

It is important to note that actual withdrawals made by a partner during the year are treated as distributions made on the last day of the partnership's tax year. Furthermore, if a partner's withdrawals exceed the share of partnership income, the partner may be required to recognize the excess as income unless repayment is required. If repayment is required, the excess drawings would be treated as a loan rather than a current distribution. Partnership distributions are discussed in greater detail in a later section of the chapter.

## ALLOCATING PARTNERSHIP INCOME

Under § 704(a), a partner's distributive share of any partnership item is to be determined by the partnership agreement. Thus, the partnership agreement may provide different ratios for sharing various items of income, gain, loss, deductions, or credits among the individual partners. A partner's ability to specifically allocate such items is not without restrictions, however. Section 704(b) states that a partner's distributive share of income, gain, loss, deduction, or credit shall be determined in accordance with the partner's interest in the partnership (determined by taking into account all of the facts and circumstances) if:

—The partnership agreement does not provide as to the partner's distributive share of such items, *or*

—The allocation to a partner of such items under the agreement does not have *substantial economic effect.*

The Regulations provide that the manner in which profits or losses are actually recorded on the partnership books (i. e., their division between the partners' accounts) generally will determine the profit- and loss-sharing ratios in the absence of a partnership agreement.[21] Additionally, in determining whether an allocation has substantial economic effect, the Regulations[22] and case law[23] suggest that the allocation actually must affect the dollar amount of a partner's share of income or loss independent of the tax consequences.

---

**21.**　Reg. § 1.704–1(b)(1).

**22.**　Reg. § 1.704–1(b)(2).

**23.**　See *Stanley C. Orrisch,* 55 T.C. 395 (1971), *aff'd.* in 31 AFTR2d 73–1069 (CA–9, 1973); and, *Martin Magaziner,* 37 TCM 873, T.C.Memo. 1978–205.

Form **1065**

Department of the Treasury
Internal Revenue Service

# U.S. Partnership Return of Income

For calendar year 1982, or fiscal year
beginning .................................., 1982, and ending .................................., 19........

OMB No. 1545–0099

**1982**

| | |
|---|---|
| **A** Principal business activity (see page 12 of Instructions) | Use IRS label. Other- wise, please print or type. |
| **B** Principal product or service (see page 12 of Instructions) | |
| **C** Business code number (see page 12 of Instructions) | |

Name

Number and street

City or town, State, and ZIP code

**D** Employer identification no.

**E** Date business started

**F** Enter total assets from Schedule L, line 13, column (D).
$

**G** Check method of accounting: (1) ☐ Cash (2) ☐ Accrual (3) ☐ Other.

**H** Check applicable boxes: (1) ☐ Final return (2) ☐ Change in address (3) ☐ Amended return.

**I** Check if the partnership meets **ALL** the requirements shown on page 3 of the Instructions under "Filing a Complete Return." ▶ ☐

| | Yes | No | | Yes | No |
|---|---|---|---|---|---|
| **J** Is this partnership a limited partnership (see page 2 of Instructions)? . . . . . . . . . . | | | **O** At any time during the tax year, did the partnership have an interest in or a signature or other authority over a bank account, securities account, or other financial account in a foreign country (see page 3 of Instructions)? . . . . | | |
| **K** Number of partners in this partnership ................ | | | | | |
| **L** Is this partnership a partner in another partnership? . . . | | | | | |
| **M** Are any partners in this partnership also partnerships? . . | | | **P** Was the partnership the grantor of, or transferor to, a foreign trust which existed during the current tax year, whether or not the partnership or any partner has any beneficial interest in it? If "Yes," you may have to file Forms 3520, 3520–A, or 926. (See page 4 of Instructions.) . . . . | | |
| **N** (1) How many months in 1982 was this partnership actively operated? ................. | | | | | |
| (2) Was this partnership in operation at the end of 1982? . | | | | | |

## Income

| | | |
|---|---|---|
| **1a** Gross receipts or sales $...................... **1b** Minus returns and allowances $.......................... Balance ▶ | **1c** | |
| **2** Cost of goods sold and/or operations (Schedule A, line 8) . . . . . . . . . . . | **2** | |
| **3** Gross profit (subtract line 2 from line 1c) . . . . . . . . . . . . . | **3** | |
| **4** Ordinary income (loss) from other partnerships and fiduciaries . . . . . . . . | **4** | |
| **5** Nonqualifying interest and nonqualifying dividends . . . . . . . . . . . | **5** | |
| **6a** Gross rents $........................... **6b** Minus rental expenses (attach schedule) $......................... Balance net rental (loss) . . . . . . . . . . . . . . . ▶ | **6c** | |
| **7** Net income (loss) from royalties (attach schedule) . . . . . . . . . . . | **7** | |
| **8** Net farm profit (loss) (attach Schedule F (Form 1040)) . . . . . . . . . . | **8** | |
| **9** Net gain (loss) (Form 4797, line 11) . . . . . . . . . . . . . . | **9** | |
| **10** Other income (loss) . . . . . . . . . . . . . . . . . . . | **10** | |
| **11** **TOTAL** income (loss) (combine lines 3 through 10) . . . . . . . . . . | **11** | |

## Deductions

| | | |
|---|---|---|
| **12a** Salaries and wages (other than to partners) $..................... **12b** Minus jobs credit $...................... Balance ▶ | **12c** | |
| **13** Guaranteed payments to partners (see page 5 of Instructions) . . . . . . . . | **13** | |
| **14** Rent . . . . . . . . . . . . . . . . . . . . . . . | **14** | |
| **15a** Total deductible interest expense not claimed elsewhere on return (see page 5 of Instructions) . . . . . . . . . . . . . . **15a** | | |
| **b** Interest expense required to be passed through to partners on Schedules K and K–1, lines 13, 21a(2), and 21a(3) . . . . . . . . **15b** | | |
| **c** Subtract line 15b from line 15a . . . . . . . . . . . . . . | **15c** | |
| **16** Taxes . . . . . . . . . . . . . . . . . . . . . . . | **16** | |
| **17** Bad debts (see page 5 of Instructions) . . . . . . . . . . . . . | **17** | |
| **18** Repairs . . . . . . . . . . . . . . . . . . . . . . | **18** | |
| **19a** Depreciation from Form 4562 (attach Form 4562) $........................... **19b** Minus depreciation claimed in Schedule A and elsewhere on return $........................... Balance ▶ . . . . . | **19c** | |
| **20** Depletion (**DO NOT DEDUCT OIL AND GAS DEPLETION.** See page 5 of Instructions.) . . . | **20** | |
| **21a** Retirement plans, etc. (see page 5 of Instructions) . . . . . . . . . . . | **21a** | |
| **b** Employee benefit programs (see page 6 of Instructions) . . . . . . . . . . | **21b** | |
| **22** Other deductions (attach schedule) . . . . . . . . . . . . . . | **22** | |
| **23** **TOTAL** deductions (add amounts in column for lines 12c through 22) . . . . . . | **23** | |
| **24** Ordinary income (loss) (subtract line 23 from line 11) . . . . . . . . . . | **24** | |

**Please Sign Here**

Under penalties of perjury, I declare that I have examined this return, including accompanying schedules and statements, and to the best of my knowledge and belief it is true, correct, and complete. Declaration of preparer (other than taxpayer) is based on all information of which preparer has any knowledge.

▶ Signature of general partner ▶ Date

**Paid Preparer's Use Only**

| Preparer's signature ▶ | Date | Check if self-em- ployed ▶ ☐ | Preparer's social security no. |
|---|---|---|---|
| Firm's name (or yours, if self-employed) and address ▶ | | E.I. No. ▶ | |
| | | ZIP code ▶ | |

For Paperwork Reduction Act Notice, see page 1 of Form 1065 Instructions.

## Schedule K—PARTNERS' SHARES OF INCOME, CREDITS, DEDUCTIONS, ETC. (See Pages 7–11 of Instructions.)

| | a. Distributive share items | | b. Total amount |
|---|---|---|---|
| **Income (loss)** | 1 Ordinary income (loss) (page 1, line 24) . . . . . . . . . . . . . . . . | 1 | |
| | 2 Guaranteed payments . . . . . . . . . . . . . . . . . . . . | 2 | |
| | 3 Interest from All-Savers Certificates . . . . . . . . . . . . . . . | 3 | |
| | 4 Dividends qualifying for exclusion . . . . . . . . . . . . . . . | 4 | |
| | 5 Net short-term capital gain (loss) (Schedule D, line 4) . . . . . . . . . | 5 | |
| | 6 Net long-term capital gain (loss) (Schedule D, line 9) . . . . . . . . . | 6 | |
| | 7 Net gain (loss) from involuntary conversions due to casualty or theft (Form 4684) . | 7 | |
| | 8 Other net gain (loss) under section 1231 . . . . . . . . . . . . . | 8 | |
| | 9 Other (attach schedule) . . . . . . . . . . . . . . . . . . | 9 | |
| **Deductions** | 10 Charitable contributions (attach list): 50% ............., 30% ............., 20% ............. | 10 | |
| | 11 Expense deduction for recovery property (section 179 expense) from Part I, Section A, Form 4562 (must not be more than $5,000) . . . . . . . . . . . . | 11 | |
| | 12a Payments for partners to an IRA . . . . . . . . . . . . . | 12a | |
| | b Payments for partners to a Keogh Plan (Type of plan ▶....................) . . . . | 12b | |
| | c Payments for partners to Simplified Employee Pension (SEP) . . . . . . . | 12c | |
| | 13 Other (attach schedule) . . . . . . . . . . . . . . . . . . | 13 | |
| **Credits** | 14 Jobs credit . . . . . . . . . . . . . . . . . . . . | 14 | |
| | 15 Credit for alcohol used as fuel . . . . . . . . . . . . . . . | 15 | |
| | 16 Credit for income tax withheld on interest and dividend income (see instructions) . . . | 16 | |
| | 17 Other (attach schedule) . . . . . . . . . . . . . . . . . | 17 | |
| **Other** | 18a Gross farming or fishing income . . . . . . . . . . . . . . . | 18a | |
| | b Net earnings (loss) from self-employment . . . . . . . . . . . | 18b | |
| | c Other (attach schedule) . . . . . . . . . . . . . . . . . | | |
| **Specially Allocated Items** | 19a Short-term capital gain (loss) . . . . . . . . . . . . . . . | 19a | |
| | b Long-term capital gain (loss) . . . . . . . . . . . . . . . | 19b | |
| | c Ordinary gain (loss) (attach schedule) . . . . . . . . . . . . . | 19c | |
| | d Other (attach schedule) . . . . . . . . . . . . . . . . . | 19d | |
| **Tax Preference Items** | 20a Accelerated depreciation on real property: | | |
| |   (1) Low-income rental housing (167(k)) . . . . . . . . . . | 20a(1) | |
| |   (2) Other nonrecovery real property or 15-year real property . . . . . . . . | 20a(2) | |
| | b Accelerated depreciation on leased personal property or leased recovery property other than 15-year real property . . . . . . . . . . . . . . . . | 20b | |
| | c Amortization . . . . . . . . . . . . . . . . . . . | 20c | |
| | d Reserves for losses on bad debts of financial institutions . . . . . . . . . | 20d | |
| | e Depletion (other than oil and gas) . . . . . . . . . . . . . . | 20e | |
| | f (1) Excess intangible drilling costs from oil, gas, or geothermal wells . . . . . | 20f(1) | |
| |   (2) Net income from oil, gas, or geothermal wells . . . . . . . . | 20f(2) | |
| | g Other (attach schedule) . . . . . . . . . . . . . . . . . | | |
| **Investment Interest** | 21a Investment interest expense: | | |
| |   (1) Indebtedness incurred before 12/17/69 . . . . . . . . . . | 21a(1) | |
| |   (2) Indebtedness incurred before 9/11/75, but after 12/16/69 . . . . . . . | 21a(2) | |
| |   (3) Indebtedness incurred after 9/10/75 . . . . . . . . . . . | 21a(3) | |
| | b Net investment income (loss) . . . . . . . . . . . . . . . | 21b | |
| | c Excess expenses from "net lease property" . . . . . . . . . . . | 21c | |
| | d Excess of net long-term capital gain over net short-term capital loss from investment property . . . . | 21d | |
| **Foreign Taxes** | 22a Type of income.................................................. | | |
| | b Foreign country or U.S. possession ........................................ | | |
| | c Total gross income from sources outside the U.S. (attach schedule) . . . . . . . | 22c | |
| | d Total applicable deductions and losses (attach schedule) . . . . . . . . . | 22d | |
| | e Total foreign taxes (check one): ☐ Paid ☐ Accrued . . . . . . . . . . | 22e | |
| | f Reduction in taxes available for credit (attach schedule) . . . . . . . . . | 22f | |
| | g Other (attach schedule) . . . . . . . . . . . . . . . . . | 22g | |

**SCHEDULE K-1**
**(Form 1065)**

Department of the Treasury
Internal Revenue Service

**Partner's Share of Income, Credits, Deductions, etc.—1982**
For calendar year 1982 or fiscal year
beginning ........................................., 1982, and ending ........................................., 19.........
(Complete for and give to each partner. Instructions for partners attached to Copy C.)

OMB No. 1545–0099

**Copy A**
**(File with Form 1065)**

| Partner's identifying number ▶ | Partnership's identifying number ▶ |
|---|---|
| Partner's name, address, and ZIP code | Partnership's name, address, and ZIP code |

**A** Is partner a general partner (see page 2 of Instructions)? . . . . . . . . . . . . ☐ Yes ☐ No

**B** Partner's share of liabilities (see page 7 of Instructions):
Nonrecourse . . . . . . . . . . $................................
Other . . . . . . . . . . . . . $................................

**C** Enter partner's percentage of:

| | (i) Before decrease or termination | (ii) End of year |
|---|---|---|
| Profit sharing . . . . . . . | ...................% | ...................% |
| Loss sharing . . . . . . . | ...................% | ...................% |
| Ownership of capital . . . . . | ...................% | ...................% |

**D** What type of entity is this partner? ▶

**E** Reconciliation of partner's capital account:

| a. Capital account at beginning of year | b. Capital contributed during year | c. Ordinary income (loss) from line 1 | d. Income not included in column c, plus non-taxable income | e. Losses not included in column c, plus un-allowable deductions | f. Withdrawals and distributions | g. Capital account at end of year |
|---|---|---|---|---|---|---|
| | | | | | | |

| | | a. Distributive share item | b. Amount | c. 1040 filers enter the amount in column b on: |
|---|---|---|---|---|
| **Income (loss)** | 1 | Ordinary income (loss) . . . . . . . . . . . . . . | ........................ | Sch. E, Part II, col. (c) or (d) |
| | 2 | Guaranteed payments . . . . . . . . . . . . | ........................ | Sch. E, Part II, column (d) |
| | 3 | Interest from All-Savers Certificates . . . . . . . . | ........................ | Sch. B, Part I, line 4 |
| | 4 | Dividends qualifying for exclusion . . . . . . . . | ........................ | Sch. B, Part II, line 9 |
| | 5 | Net short-term capital gain (loss) . . . . . . . . | ........................ | Sch. D, line 3, col. f. or g. |
| | 6 | Net long-term capital gain (loss) . . . . . . . . . | ........................ | Sch. D, line 10, col. f. or g. |
| | 7 | Net gain (loss) from involuntary conversions due to casualty or theft . . . . | ........................ | Form 4684, line 20 |
| | 8 | Other net gain (loss) under section 1231 . . . . . . | ........................ | Form 4797, line 1 |
| | 9 | Other (attach schedule) | ........................ | (Enter on applicable lines of your return) |
| **Deductions** | 10 | Charitable contributions: 50%................, 30%................, 20%................ | ........................ | See Form 1040 instr. |
| | 11 | Expense deduction for recovery property (section 179 expense) . . | ........................ | Sch. E, Part II, line 28 |
| | 12a | Payments for partner to an IRA . . . . . . . . . | ........................ | Form 1040, line 25 |
| | b | Payments for partner to a Keogh Plan (Type of plan ▶................) . . | ........................ | Form 1040, line 26 |
| | c | Payments for partner to Simplified Employee Pension (SEP) . . . . . | ........................ | Form 1040, line 26 (Enter on applicable lines of your return) |
| | 13 | Other (attach schedule) . . . . . . . . . . . . | ........................ | |
| **Credits** | 14 | Jobs credit . . . . . . . . . . . . . . . | ........................ | Form 5884 |
| | 15 | Credit for alcohol used as fuel . . . . . . . . . . | ........................ | Form 6478 |
| | 16 | Credit for income tax withheld on interest and dividend income . . | ........................ | See Form 1040 instr. |
| | 17 | Other (attach schedule) . . . . . . . . . . . . | ........................ | (Enter on applicable lines of your return) |
| **Other** | 18a | Gross farming or fishing income . . . . . . . . . | ........................ | |
| | b | Net earnings (loss) from self-employment . . . . . . . | ........................ | Sch. SE, Part I (Enter on applicable lines of your return) |
| | c | Other (attach schedule) . . . . . . . . . . . . | ////////// | |
| **Specially Allocated Items** | 19a | Short-term capital gain (loss) . . . . . . . . . . | ........................ | Sch. D, line 3, col. f. or g. |
| | b | Long-term capital gain (loss) . . . . . . . . . . | ........................ | Sch. D, line 10, col. f. or g. |
| | c | Ordinary gain (loss) (attach schedule) . . . . . . . | ........................ | Form 4797, line 9 |
| | d | Other (attach schedule) . . . . . . . . . . . . | ////////// | Sch. E, Part II |
| **Tax Preference Items** | 20a | Accelerated depreciation on real property: | ////////// | |
| | | (1) Low-income rental housing (167(k)) . . . . . . . | ........................ | Form 4625, line 1(a)(1) |
| | | (2) Other nonrecovery real property or 15-year real property . . . | ........................ | Form 4625, line 1(a)(2) |
| | b | Accelerated depreciation on leased personal property or leased recovery property other than 15-year real property . . . . . . | ........................ | Form 4625, line 1(b) |
| | c | Amortization . . . . . . . . . . . . . . . | ........................ | Form 4625, line 1(c) |
| | d | Reserves for losses on bad debts of financial institutions . . . . | ........................ | Form 4625, line 1(d) |
| | e | Depletion (other than oil and gas) . . . . . . . . . | ........................ | Form 4625, line 1(e) |
| | f | (1) Excess intangible drilling costs from oil, gas, or geothermal wells . . . . | ........................ | See Form 4625 instr. |
| | | (2) Net income from oil, gas, or geothermal wells . . . . . . | ////////// | |
| | g | Other (attach schedule) . . . . . . . . . . . . | ////////// | |

**For Paperwork Reduction Act Notice, see page 1 of Form 1065 Instructions.**        363–098–1

A special allocation which results in the shifting of tax benefits benefits to those partners who could take full advantage of selected items of income, deductions, or credits certainly would be subject to close scrutiny from the IRS. However, Congress has provided for special allocations of depreciation, depletion, and gain or loss with respect to contributed property to mitigate the inequities which might arise due to the differing nature of property contributed to a partnership by individual partners.[24] For instance, if in forming a partnership one partner contributed cash and another partner contributed property which had a fair market value greater than its adjusted basis, it would be inequitable to prohibit an allocation of all the depreciation to the cash contributor. (Example 10 illustrates this situation.)

Section 704(c) states that if the partnership agreement so provides, depreciation, depletion, and gain or loss with respect to property contributed to a partnership can be shared among the partners in a manner that will take into account the discrepancy between the basis of the property to the partnership and its fair market value at the time of contribution. Such an allocation may apply to all property contributed or to specific items. In any case, the amount allocated to the partners in this manner cannot exceed the total of the amount properly allowable to the partnership.

> **Example 10.** In forming an equal partnership, A contributes cash of $100,000 and B contributes an office building with an adjusted basis of $40,000 and a fair market value of $100,000. A has, in effect, purchased a one-half interest in the property for $50,000. If the building is to be depreciated at the straight-line rate of 10% per year, it would appear that A should receive a depreciation deduction of $5,000. However, the total depreciation properly allowable to the partnership is only $4,000 (10% of the adjusted basis of $40,000), and no more than this amount can be allocated among the partners. In the absence of a special allocation agreement, A and B will share equally in the $4,000 of allowable depreciation. This would be inequitable to A. The inequity arises because A "purchased" one-half of the property for $50,000. Straight-line depreciation at a 10% rate would mean an annual depreciation deduction of $5,000 for A; however, the maximum allowable to the partnership is $4,000 per year. Instead of A and B sharing equally in the $4,000 maximum, it would be equitable to allocate the entire $4,000 deduction to A, assuming the partnership agreement provides for the allocation.

> **Example 11.** Assume the same facts as in Example 10 except that the building is sold for $110,000 shortly after it was contributed to the partnership. In the absence of a provision in the partnership agreement providing for a special allocation of the gain

---

24. § 704(c).

on the sale, the taxable gain of $70,000 ($110,000 sales price less the adjusted basis of $40,000) must be divided equally between A and B. This would be an inequitable result for A, since his real economic gain is only $5,000, one-half of the $10,000 of appreciation on the building after it was contributed to the partnership. Under § 704(c), the partnership agreement can provide that the $60,000 of precontribution gain ($100,000 fair market value less $40,000 adjusted basis) will be assigned to B and the remaining gain of $10,000 will be allocated to each partner on an equal basis.

## BASIS ADJUSTMENTS AND LIMITATIONS ON LOSSES

As stated earlier, once the basis of a contributing partner's interest in a partnership is determined, it is subject to continuous fluctuation. A partner's basis in the partnership interest is increased by further contributions, the sum of current and prior years' distributive share of partnership income not withdrawn, any income retained by the partnership which was exempt from tax, and the excess of the deductions for depletion over the basis of the property subject to depletion. Likewise, a partner's basis in the partnership interest is decreased by the amount of money and the adjusted basis of property distributed to the partner by the partnership, the sum of current and prior years' distributive share of deductible partnership losses, and by the partner's share of nondeductible partnership expenditures which are not capital expenditures (e. g., charitable contributions and investment interest expenses). Recall, however, that a partner's basis in the partnership interest can never be reduced below zero.[25]

The basis of a partnership interest also must be adjusted for changes in the liabilities of the partnership. Recall that any increase in a partner's share of liabilities of a partnership or any increase in a partner's individual liabilities by reason of the partner's assumption of partnership liabilities is treated as a contribution of money by that partner to the partnership and thus increases the basis of the partnership interest.[26] Similarly, any decrease in a partner's share of the liabilities of the partnership or any decrease in the partner's individual liabilities by reason of the assumption of such liabilities by the partnership is treated as a distribution of money to such partner by the partnership and decreases the basis of his or her partnership interest.[27] These adjustments are automatic and will occur regardless of the partnership's method of accounting.

**Example 12.** A and B are equal partners in the AB Partnership. In order to purchase a parcel of real estate to be used as a

---

**25.** § 705(a)(2).
**26.** § 752(a).
**27.** § 752(b).

potential office site, the partnership borrows $50,000 from a local savings and loan association. As a result of this increase in partnership liabilities, the basis of both A's and B's partnership interests is increased by $25,000.

**Example 13.**   Assume the same facts as in Example 12 except that the AB Partnership repays $20,000 of the loan. The resulting decrease in partnership liabilities requires a decrease of $10,000 each to A's and B's basis in their respective partnership interests.

**Example 14.**   Assume the same facts as in Example 12 except that the partnership decides not to use the real estate after all. Instead, the property is distributed by the partnership to A. At the time of the distribution, the property had an adjusted basis of $50,000 and a fair market value of the same amount and was subject to a mortgage of $30,000. As a result of the distribution, there is a net decrease of $35,000 in A's basis in his partnership interest computed as follows:

| | |
|---|---:|
| Decrease in an amount equal to the adjusted basis of property distributed | $ 50,000 |
| Decrease as a result of the reduction in A's share of partnership liabilities (½ of $30,000) | 15,000 |
| Increase as a result of the assumption of a partnership liability | (30,000) |
| Net decrease | $ 35,000 |

**Example 15.**   Assume the same facts as in Example 14. What effect will the distribution of the real estate to A have on B's basis in the partnership interest? B's basis will be decreased by $15,000, since the distribution resulted in a reduction of his share of the partnership's liabilities.

The basis adjustments illustrated above result from the application of § § 705, 733, and 752. In addition to these statutory provisions, § 704(d) provides the rule regarding the limitation of a partner's deduction of partnership losses. Specifically, a partner's deduction of the distributive share of partnership losses (including capital losses) is limited to the adjusted basis of the partnership interest at the end of the partnership year in which the losses were incurred. For this purpose, any distribution made to the partner during the year must be taken into account before losses are applied against basis.

The limitation of § 704(d) is similar to the limitation on losses provided by § 1366(d) in the case of S corporations. Partnership losses may be carried forward by the partner and utilized against future increases in the basis of the partnership interest. Such increases might result from additional capital contributions to the partnership, from additional partnership liabilities, or from future partnership income.

> **Example 16.** C and D do business as the CD Partnership, sharing profits and losses equally. All parties use the calendar year for tax purposes. As of January 1, 19X6, C's basis in his partnership interest is $25,000. The partnership sustained an operating loss of $80,000 in 19X6 and earned a profit of $70,000 in 19X7. For the calendar year 19X6, C may claim only $25,000 of his $40,000 distributive share of the partnership loss (one-half of $80,000 loss). As a result, the basis in his partnership interest will be reduced to zero as of January 1, 19X7, and he must carry forward the remaining $15,000 of partnership losses.

> **Example 17.** Assuming the same facts in Example 16, what will be the income tax consequences for C in 19X7? Since the partnership earned a profit of $70,000 for the calendar year 19X7, C will report income from his partnership of $20,000 ($35,000 distributive share of income for 19X7 less the $15,000 loss not allowed for 19X6). The adjusted basis of his partnership interest now becomes $20,000.

It should be noted that partner C could have claimed his entire $40,000 share of the 19X6 partnership loss if he had contributed an additional $15,000 or more in capital by December 31, 19X6. Likewise, if the partnership had incurred additional debt of $30,000 or more, by year end, C's basis would have been increased to permit the deductibility of his entire share of the distributive loss. Thus, if partnership losses are projected for a given year, careful tax planning can insure the deductibility of a partner's distributive share of such losses.

The Tax Reform Act of 1976 introduced a new statutory provision, § 465, and amended § 704(d) to limit losses that a partner may deduct to his or her adjusted basis in the partnership (which represents the amount the partner has *at risk* in the partnership activity at the end of its taxable year). The Revenue Act of 1978 made subsequent changes in both of these statutes in order to expand the application of the at-risk limitations.

## TAXABLE YEARS OF PARTNER AND PARTNERSHIP

In computing a partner's taxable income for a specific year, § 706(a) requires that each partner include in income his or her distributive share of partnership income and any guaranteed payments from a partnership whose tax year ends with or within the partner's taxable year. Thus, a partner would report his or her income for a partnership year ended January 31, 19X7, on his or her 19X7 income tax return.

Under this provision, there can be an effective deferral of a partner's share of partnership income of up to 11 months. This deferral is possible because any drawings against a partner's distributive share of partnership income are treated as made on the last day of the partnership's taxable year. In fact, distributions made after January 31, 19X6, will not be reported by the partners until they file their 19X7 tax returns. Because of this deferral possibility, § 706(b) and the Regulations generally provide that the IRS must consent to any adoption or change of a partnership taxable year.[28] There are, however, two principal exceptions to this rule:

1. A partnership may adopt the same taxable year as all of its principal partners (partners with a five percent or greater interest in capital and profits) without consent. Additionally, an existing partnership may change to the same taxable year as all of its principal partners or to the same taxable year that all of its principal partners are concurrently adopting.

2. If not all of the principal partners are on the same taxable year, a partnership may initially adopt a calendar year. In both this situation and the exception cited above, a principal partner is any partner having an interest of five percent or more in partnership profits or capital.

When consent is required, it will be conditional upon a finding of a business purpose for the adoption or change. However, the IRS normally will give consent if the effective deferral of income does not exceed three months.[29] The tax effect of the deferral, however, will be spread over 10 years. The excess of income over expense for the first three months following the change of taxable years is added to income of the preceding partnership taxable year. One-tenth of the excess may then be deducted, beginning in this preceding tax year, over a 10-year period.

Under § 443, a partnership that changes its tax year should file its return for a short period but should not annualize the partnership taxable income. The partnership must attach to the return either a copy of the letter from the IRS granting permission to change or a statement indicating that the partnership is changing its tax year to the tax year of all its principal partners or to the tax year to which all its principal partners are concurrently changing. However, a principal partner may not change to a taxable year other than that of the partnership unless it is established to the satisfaction of the IRS that there is a valid business purpose for such change.[30]

Once established, when does a partnership's tax year close? The taxable year of a partnership closes upon termination of the partner-

---

28. Reg. § 1.706–1(b).
29. Rev.Proc. 72–51, 1972–2 C.B. 832.
30. § 706(b)(2).

ship; however, its tax year generally does not close upon the death of a partner, the entry of a new partner, or the liquidation, sale, or exchange of an existing partnership interest. In the case of the sale or liquidation of an entire interest, the partnership's tax year will close as to that partner disposing of the partnership interest. However, this rule does not apply in the event the disposition involves less than an entire partnership interest. Additionally, the taxable year of the partnership will close as to a deceased partner if the partnership agreement so provides. However, close of the partnership's taxable year with respect to a deceased partner usually should be avoided because of the bunching of income (partnership income from more than 12 months included in one taxable year of a partner) which will result on the decedent's final income tax return.

The termination of a partnership will, of course, close its tax year. In addition to the clear-cut situation involving outright liquidation or other dissolution of the partnership, § 708(b)(1) states that an existing partnership will be considered as terminated if either of the following occurs:

1. No part of any business, financial operation, or venture of the partnership continues to be carried on by any of its partners in a partnership.

2. Within a 12-month period there is a sale or exchange of 50 percent or more of the total interest in partnership capital and profits.[31]

The consequences of some of the rules discussed above are illustrated by the following examples:

**Example 18.** At the time of her death on November 20, 19X6, R owned a one-third interest in the RST Partnership. The partnership uses a fiscal year of October 1 to September 30 for tax purposes, while R used a calendar year. Further assume that the partnership agreement does not contain a provision for termination or a special accounting upon the death of a partner. Under these circumstances, the partnership's tax year does not close as to R upon her death. Instead, income from the fiscal year October 1, 19X6, through September 30, 19X7, will be taxed to R's estate or other successor in interest as of September 30, 19X7. Income from the fiscal year ending September 30, 19X6, must, however, be reported on R's final income tax return covering the period from January 1, 19X6, to November 20, 19X6.

**Example 19.** Assume the same facts as in Example 18 except that the partnership agreement provides for the termination of a partner's interest as of the date of death with a special accounting to be rendered at that time. Although R's death will not affect her

---

**31.** § 708(b)(1)(A) and (B).

surviving partners, it will close the partnership's tax year as to R. Thus, R's final income tax return for the 19X6 calendar year must include both her share of the partnership income for fiscal year ending September 30, 19X6, and for the period from October 1, 19X6, to the date of her death, November 20, 19X6.

**Example 20.** Assume the same facts as in Example 18 except that R does not die on November 20, 19X6, but instead, sells her entire partnership interest to a third party. Again, the partnership's tax year will not close with respect to the remaining partners. However, R must include her share of the partnership income for the fiscal year ending September 30, 19X6, and for the short period ending on the date she disposed of her entire partnership interest, November 20, 19X6, on her 19X6 return.

**Example 21.** Assume the same facts as in Example 20 except that R's entire interest represents 60% of the partnership rather than a one-third interest. The result of the disposition of this 60% interest does not change as to R, but the same is not true for the remaining partners. Since an interest of 50% or more in the partnership has changed hands, § 708(b)(1)(B) requires that the partnership's tax year be closed as of November 20, 19X6, for all partners; the RST Partnership is considered to be terminated on that date.

## TRANSACTIONS BETWEEN PARTNER AND PARTNERSHIP

The entity theory of a partnership has been adopted in the general rule governing transactions between a partner and the partnership. Thus, under § 707(a), a partner engaging in a transaction with the partnership can be regarded as a nonpartner or outsider. Applications of this rule include:

—Loans of money or property by the partnership to the partner or by the partner to the partnership.

—The sale of property by a partner to the partnership or the purchase of property by the partner from the partnership.

—The rendition of services by the partnership to the partner or by the partner to the partnership.

Transactions between a partner and the partnership are subject to close scrutiny, however. Furthermore, § 707(b) disallows losses and requires ordinary rather than capital gain treatment for certain transactions between partners and a partnership. For instance, under § 707(b)(1), losses from the sale or exchange of property will be disallowed if they arise in either of the following cases:

1. Between a partnership and a partner whose direct or indirect interest in the capital or profits of the partnership is more than 50 percent.

    2.   Between two partnerships in which the same persons own more than 50 percent interest in the capital or profits.

If one of the purchasers later sells the property, any gain realized will be recognized only to the extent that it exceeds the loss previously disallowed. This is, of course, the same approach taken in § 267(d) with respect to disallowed losses between related parties.[32]

> **Example 22.** R owns a 35% interest in the capital and profits of the RST Partnership. On September 1, 19X6, R sells property with an adjusted basis of $50,000 to the partnership for its fair market value of $35,000. Assuming R is not related to any of her partners [within the meaning of § 267(c)], she has a recognized loss of $15,000.

> **Example 23.** Assume the same facts as in Example 22 except that one of R's partners, T, is her brother who owns a 40% interest in the capital and profits of the partnership. Section 707(b)(3) provides that the constructive ownership of a partnership interest is to be determined by § 267(c). Under § 267(c)(4), there is constructive ownership between brothers and sisters; thus, R is deemed to own a 75% interest in the partnership (35% direct ownership plus the 40% interest owned by T). Consequently, § 707(b)(1)(A) is applicable and R's $15,000 loss is disallowed.

> **Example 24.** Assume the same facts as in Example 23. If the RST Partnership later sells the property for $40,000, none of the $5,000 (sale price of $40,000 less adjusted basis to partnership of $35,000) gain will be recognizable. Section 267(d) permits the partnership to offset any subsequent gain by the loss previously disallowed. The unused $10,000 of R's disallowed loss disappears.

Under § 707(b)(2), gains are treated as ordinary income in a sale or exchange of property directly or indirectly between a partner and partnership, or between two partnerships, if more than 80 percent of the capital or profits interest in the partnership or partnerships is owned directly or indirectly by the same person or persons. This rule does not apply, however, if the property in the hands of the transferee (purchaser) immediately after the transfer is a capital asset.[33]

    In evaluating the 50 percent test for losses or the 80 percent test for gains, the following rules are applicable:

    1.   Any interest owned, directly or indirectly, by or for a corporation, partnership, estate, or trust is considered to be owned

---

**32.**   Actually, the need for § 707(b)(1) can be seen by examining the description of related parties under § 267. There is no mention of a partner and his or her partnership as related parties for purposes of § 267(a). Thus, without § 707(b)(1), losses arising from transactions between a controlling partner and his or her partnership would be allowed.

**33.**   § 707(b)(2).

proportionately by or for its shareholders, partners, or beneficiaries.

2.　An individual is considered as owning the interest owned, directly or indirectly, by or for his or her family members.

3.　The family of an individual includes only brothers and sisters (whether by the whole or half-blood), spouse, ancestors, and lineal descendants.

4.　An interest constructively owned by a person under rule 1 is treated, for applying rules 1 and 2, as actually owned by that person. However, an interest constructively owned by an individual under rule 2 is not treated as owned by him or her for the purpose of again applying rule 2 to make another the constructive owner of the interest.

Payments made by a partnership to one of its partners for services rendered or for the use of capital to the extent they are determined without regard to the income of the partnership are treated by the partnership in the same manner as payments made to a person who is not a partner. Referred to as *guaranteed payments* under § 707(c), such payments generally are deductible by the partnership as a business expense and must be reported as ordinary income by the receiving partner. Their deductibility distinguishes guaranteed payments from a partner's distributive share of income which is not deductible by the partnership. The Tax Reform Act of 1976 amended § 707(c) to clarify an earlier misconception that guaranteed payments made by a partnership automatically were deductible by the partnership. Specifically, the revised § 707(c) states that a guaranteed payment is deductible by a partnership if it is not a capital expenditure under § 263 and if it meets the tests of § 162(a) as an ordinary and necessary business expense.

> **Example 25.**　Under the terms of the LMN Partnership agreement, N is entitled to a fixed annual salary of $18,000, without regard to the income of the partnership. He also is to share in the profits and losses of the partnership as an equal partner. After deducting the guaranteed payment, the partnership has $36,000 of ordinary income. N must include $30,000 as ordinary income in his income tax return for his tax year with or within which the partnership tax year ends ($18,000 guaranteed payment plus his one-third distributive share of partnership income of $12,000).

If a partner is to receive a percentage of the partnership income with a stipulated minimum payment, the guaranteed payment is the amount by which the minimum guarantee exceeds the partner's share of the partnership income before taking into account the minimum guaranteed amount.

**Example 26.** Under the partnership agreement, M is to receive 40% of the partnership income but in no event less than $10,000. In the current year, the partnership has income of $15,000. M's share, without regard to the minimum guarantee, is $6,000 (40% of $15,000). Thus, the amount of the guaranteed payment that may be deducted by the partnership is $4,000 (excess of $10,000 minimum guarantee over $6,000 share of partnership income before deducting the guaranteed payment). M's income from the partnership is $10,000, and the remaining $5,000 will be reported by the other partners in proportion to their shares under the partnership agreement.

When the partnership agreement provides for a guaranteed payment and such payment results in a partnership loss, the partner must report the full amount of the guaranteed payment and separately take into account the distributive share of the loss. This assumes, however, that the partnership agreement provides for the partner receiving the guaranteed payment to share in the partnership losses resulting from such payments.

**Example 27.** Partner T in the STP Partnership is to receive a payment of $20,000 for services plus 20% of the partnership income or loss. After deducting the $20,000 payment to T, the partnership has a loss of $10,000. Of this amount, $2,000 (20% of $10,000) is T's distributive share of the partnership loss and, subject to the limitation imposed by § 704(d), is to be taken into account by him on his return. In addition, T must report the guaranteed payment of $20,000 as ordinary income.

**Example 28.** Assume the same facts as in Example 27 except that instead of a $10,000 loss, the partnership has $40,000 of capital gains and no deductions or items of income other than the $20,000 paid to T as a guaranteed payment. Since the items of partnership income or loss must be segregated under § 702(a), the partnership has a $20,000 ordinary loss and $40,000 in capital gains. Thus, T's 20% distributive share of these items is $4,000 ordinary loss and $8,000 capital gain. Additionally, T must report the $20,000 guaranteed payment as ordinary income.

Finally, it should be noted that a partner generally may not qualify as a partnership employee for tax purposes. For example, a partner receiving guaranteed payments will not be regarded as an employee of the partnership for the purposes of withholding of tax at the source or for qualified pension and profit sharing plans.

# PARTNERSHIP DISTRIBUTIONS

There are three basic types of distributions from a partnership, and a different set of rules governs the income tax consequences of each. The first category of partnership distributions includes distributions of cash and other property which will not result in the liquidation of the distributee partner's interest. A second type of partnership distribution involves liquidating distributions of money and other property. Distributions which affect the partner's proportionate interests in § 751 property of the partnership (disproportionate distributions) fall into the third category.

## NONLIQUIDATING DISTRIBUTIONS

The statutory provisions which govern the treatment of nonliquidating distributions of cash and other partnership property are contained in § § 731 through 733 of the Code. Section 731 controls the extent of recognition of gain or loss on partnership distributions. Sections 732 and 733 provide the rules for determining basis of property received in a distribution and the effect of distributions upon the distributee partner's basis in his or her partnership interest.

Section 731(b) states that no gain or loss shall be recognized by a partnership on the distribution of money or other property to a partner. Similarly, § 731(a) provides that as a general rule, no gain or loss is recognized by a partner receiving such distributions. More specifically, loss is never recognized by a partner and gain is recognized only if *money* received in a distribution exceeds the basis of the partner's interest immediately preceding the distribution. Thus, distributions of property other than money will never result in the recognition of gain or loss to the partner unless they involve disproportionate distributions of § 751 property. Any gain recognized is treated as gain from the *sale* or *exchange* of a partnership interest. The character of such gain would be determined under § 741, governing a sale of a partnership interest.

Section 733 provides that nonliquidating distributions from a partnership will reduce the distributee partner's basis in the partnership interest (but not below zero) by (1) the sum of money distributed and (2) the basis to such partner of distributed property other than money. Additionally, § 732 provides that the basis of property (other than money) distributed to a partner in a nonliquidating distribution is its adjusted basis to the partnership immediately before the distribution. However, the basis of the property may not exceed the adjusted basis of the partner's interest in the partnership reduced by any money received in the same transaction.

When the bases of distributed properties are limited by the partner's basis of the partner's partnership interest, an allocation of basis must be made under § 732(c). However, when there is no § 751 property involved, the "remaining" basis of the partner's interest will be allocated to the properties in the ratio of their adjusted bases to the partnership. Section 735(b) states that the holding period of the property received as a distribution includes that of the partnership.

**Example 29.**  D, a partner in the DEF Partnership, receives a nonliquidating distribution of $3,000 in cash and property, which has a basis to the partnership of $5,000. If D's adjusted basis in his partnership interest before the distribution is $7,000, no gain is recognized. However, the property will take a basis of $4,000 in the hands of D, and the basis of his partnership interest will be reduced to zero. Note that the cash received reduces the partner's basis in his partnership interest first. The $4,000 remaining basis in his partnership interest is then allocated to the property.

**Example 30.**  Assume the same facts as in Example 29 except that the cash distribution amounts to $9,000. Under these circumstances, D must recognize a gain of $2,000. Under § 731(a), the gain is considered to be recognized from the sale or exchange of a partnership interest. Additionally, the basis of the property in D's hands would be zero, and the basis of the partnership interest would be reduced to zero.

**Example 31.**  At the time R receives a nonliquidating distribution from the RST Partnership, the basis of her partnership interest is $30,000. The distribution consists of $5,000 of cash and property with an adjusted basis to the partnership of $15,000 and a fair market value of $20,000. R's basis in the property will be $15,000, and her basis in the partnership interest will be reduced to $10,000.

**Example 32.**  Assume the same facts as in Example 31 except that the cash distribution is $18,000 (instead of $5,000). R's basis in the property is now limited to $12,000, since $18,000 of the $30,000 basis in the partnership interest must first be allocated to the cash. Also, the basis of the partnership interest would be reduced to zero.

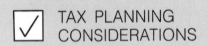

## TAX PLANNING CONSIDERATIONS

The principal factors contributing to the popularity of the partnership form of conducting a business are the ease with which a partnership can be formed and the flexibility allowed under the Federal income tax law for allocating items of partnership income, loss, deductions, or credits among the partners. The partnership form is not free of uncertain tax consequences, however. Conflicting concepts of partnership taxation and the lack of judicial interpretations of the partnership provisions of the Code require careful and continuous planning to insure the expected income tax results.

### SELECTING THE PARTNERSHIP FORM

The decision to use the partnership form in conducting a trade or business should be made only after a careful consideration of both tax and nontax differences among alternative forms of business organization. Nontax considerations such as the need to raise more capital or the desire to share the burden of any losses generally eliminate sole proprietorships as alternatives. Thus, when two or more persons are faced with the decision of selecting a form of doing business together, the comparison will be between a partnership and a corporation. The major differences between these alternative forms of business organizations are listed below.

—Unlike corporations, partnerships generally involve unlimited liability, lack continuity of life, and have restrictions on transferability of ownership interests. When such nontax considerations are extremely important, the corporate form may be preferable.

—Unlike partnerships, corporations are taxable entities separate and apart from their owners. Thus, unless S corporation status is elected (refer to Chapter 16), any corporate-source income will be taxed twice.

—Corporate income loses its identity as it passes through the corporation to its shareholders. Consequently, the income items eligible for preferential tax treatment (e. g., tax-exempt interest) are not taxed as such to the shareholders.

—Corporate losses cannot be passed through to the shareholders unless Subchapter S status is elected. More important, the basis of a shareholder's stock does not include corporate liabilities. Therefore, if the business is highly leveraged (i. e., financed by debt as opposed to equity capital) and losses are expected in the early years, the partnership form may be preferable.

—The sale of corporate stock usually results in capital gain or loss. The sale of a partnership interest can result in both ordinary income and capital gain or loss.

—As a separate entity, a corporation is free to select any fiscal year for tax purposes. Consequently, there is a possibility of up to 11 months of income tax deferral by establishing a February 1 to January 31 fiscal tax year. Recall that partnerships can, at best, offer a three-month deferral but only if permission is obtained from the IRS.

—Corporate ownership allows more flexibility for income splitting among family members through gifts of ownership interests. Family partnerships are carefully scrutinized by the IRS to prevent the assignment of income among family members.

—Partners must include their distributive share of partnership income in their tax year in which or within which the partnership's tax year closes. The method of accounting used by the partnership for measuring its income (i. e., cash or accrual method) will control. Cash basis shareholders generally are required to include salaries, interest, rents, or dividends from the corporation only when received. Thus, any income accumulated by the corporation will not be taxed to its shareholders until it is distributed. Partners are taxed on their respective share of partnership income whether or not it is distributed.

—As discussed in Chapter 15, the corporate form may be advantageous for shareholders in high individual tax brackets. With a maximum corporate income tax rate of 46 percent, such shareholders would be motivated to avoid dividend distributions and retain profits within the corporation. Recall, however, that an abuse of this approach could lead to the imposition of the penalty tax on unreasonable accumulation of earnings or the penalty tax on personal holding companies.

—Perhaps the most significant tax differences between partnerships and corporations are in the area of tax-sheltered fringe benefits. Recall that the corporate form provides shareholders with the opportunity to be treated as *employees* for tax purposes if they actually render services to the corporation. Such status makes a number of attractive tax-sheltered fringe benefits available. These include, but are not limited to, the following: group-term life insurance (§ 79), the $5,000 death gratuity [§ 101(b)(1)], accident and health plans (§ § 105 and 106), meals and lodging (§ 119), and qualified pension and profit sharing plans (§ § 401–404). These benefits can be substantial and are not available to the partners of a partnership.

## FORMATION AND OPERATION

In connection with the formation and operation of a partnership, the following points merit close attention:

—If a joint venture is formed solely for investment purposes or for the joint production, extraction, or use of property, consideration should be given to electing to be excluded from the partnership provisions of Subchapter K. In many situations, taxpayers may be uncertain as to whether they have formed a partnership and will be treated as such for income tax purposes. If the partnership form is undesirable and there is still the possibility that the organization may be a partnership for tax purposes, the election procedures under § 761 should be followed.

—If any part of an interest in partnership capital is transferred to a partner for services, the recipient must treat the fair market value of such interest as compensation for income tax purposes. Each of the partners surrendering a portion of his or her respective capital interest must report this transfer as a sale of a partnership interest and recognize gain or loss accordingly. If these results are not desirable, the service partner can be given a higher future profits interest in lieu of an immediate capital interest in the partnership.

—Recall that the contribution to a partnership of property subject to a liability in excess of its basis may result in gain recognition to the contributing partner. If the property contributed were subject to depreciation recapture, ordinary income would result. Also note that unless the partnership is considered the original user of depreciable property, it will not be allowed to deviate from the contributing partner's recovery period or method elected for such property. In situations such as these, thought should be given to retaining ownership of the property and leasing it to the partnership.

—Although the Code does not require a written partnership agreeement, many of the statutory provisions governing the tax consequences to partners and their partnerships refer to such an agreement. Remember, for instance, that § 704(a) provides for the determination of a partner's distributive share of income, gain, loss, deduction, or credit in accordance with the partnership agreement. Consequently, if taxpayers operating a business in the partnership form desire a measure of certainty as to the tax consequences of their activities, a carefully drafted partnership agreement is crucial. If such an agreement contains the obligations, rights, and powers of the partners, it should prove invaluable in settling controversies among partners and providing some degree of certainty as to the tax consequences of their actions.

—Taxpayers also should be alert to the potential advantages and pitfalls of special allocation agreements. If one partner assumes all of the economic risks associated with the formative years of the partnership, should not this partner be entitled to the tax benefits? A special allocation agreement can be used to assign all losses to this partner until such time as he or she has recouped his or her investment. Recall, however, that such arrangements are subject to the careful scrutiny of the IRS and must have substantial economic effect. As a result, great care should be exercised in drafting such agreements and adequate documentation should be drawn up and preserved to insure the desired tax results.

—Caution should be exercised when sales or exchanges are contemplated between a partnership and one of its partners if that partner will be considered a related party under § 707(b). Losses from such transactions will be disallowed, and certain gains may be treated as ordinary income (rather than as capital gain).

## PROBLEM MATERIALS

### Discussion Questions

1. Distinguish between the entity concept and the aggregate or conduit concept of a partnership.

2. What is a partnership for Federal income tax purposes?

3. Under what circumstances can organizations elect to be excluded from the partnership tax provisions? Why would an organization wish to be excluded?

4. Compare the nonrecognition of gain or loss on contributions to a partnership with the similar provision found in corporate formation (§ 351). What is (are) the major difference(s)? Similarities?

5. Under what circumstance does the receipt of a partnership interest result in ordinary income recognition? What is the effect of such an event on the partnership and the other partners?

6. How is a contributing partner's basis in a partnership interest determined?

7. If appreciated property is contributed to a partnership in exchange for a partnership interest, what basis does the partnership take in such property?

8. How is the holding period of a partnership interest determined? The partnership's holding period in contributed property?

9. What effect does the contribution of property subject to a liability have on the contributing partner's basis in his partnership interest? What is the effect on the bases of the other partners' interests?

10. What is the effect to the partner of a contribution of property subject to a liability in excess of the partner's basis in the property? To the partnership?

11. What transactions or events will cause a partner's basis in his or her partnership interest to continuously fluctuate?

12. Why is a partnership required to file an information return (Form 1065)?

13. Describe the two-step approach used in determining partnership income. Why is this computation necessary?

14. Under what circumstance can an allocation of income or expense to a partner differ from the general profit- and loss-sharing ratios? Under what circumstance would such an allocation be justified? What could go wrong?

15. To what extent can a partner deduct his or her distributive share of partnership losses? What happens to any unused losses?

16. When can a partnership have a taxable year different from its principal partners? When must a partner include his or her share of partnership income on his or her tax return?

17. Under what circumstances will a partnership's tax year close?

18. When may a partner engage in a transaction with the partnership without tax difficulties? What could go wrong?

19. What are guaranteed payments? When might such payments be used?

20. When will a nonliquidating distribution result in a gain to the recipient partner? How must the partner determine his or her basis in any property received? The basis in his or her partnership interest after the distribution?

## Problems

21.  R and S form an equal partnership with a cash contribution of $50,000 from R and a property contribution (adjusted basis of $30,000 and a fair market value of $50,000) from S.

   (a) How much gain, if any, must S recognize on the transfer? Must R recognize any gain?

   (b) What is R's basis in the partnership interest?

   (c) What is S's basis in the partnership interest?

   (d) What basis will the partnership have in the property transferred by S?

22. In return for the rendition of services and the contribution of property (basis of $5,000 and fair market value of $20,000) to the VW Partnership, U receives a 30% capital interest valued at $35,000.

   (a) How much income must U recognize?

   (b) What is U's basis in the partnership interest?

   (c) What are the potential tax consequences to the other partners and the VW Partnership?

23. The partnership agreement of the new UVW Partnership described in Problem 22 provides that any gain from the subsequent sale of the property contributed by U shall be allocated to him to the extent of any pre-contribution appreciation. Any excess gain is to be shared equally.

   (a) If the property is later sold for $18,000, how much of the gain must be recognized by U?

   (b) If the property is sold for $30,000, how much of the gain will be allocated to U?

24.  A, B, and C form the ABC Partnership on January 1, 19X7. In return for a 30% capital interest, A transfers property (basis of $16,000, fair market value of $25,000) subject to a liability of $10,000. The liability is assumed by the partnership. B transfers property (basis of $25,000, fair market value of $15,000) for a 30% capital interest, and C transfers cash of $20,000 for the remaining 40% interest.

   (a) How much gain must A recognize on the transfer?

   (b) What is A's basis in his partnership interest?

   (c) How much loss may B recognize on the transfer?

   (d) What is B's basis in his partnership interest?

   (e) C's basis in his partnership interest?

   (f) What basis will the ABC Partnership have in the property transferred by A?

   (g) The property transferred by B?

25. Assume the same facts as in Problem 24 except that the property contributed by A has a fair market value of $45,000 and is subject to a mortgage of $30,000.

    (a) How much gain must A recognize on the transfer?

    (b) What is A's basis in his partnership interest?

    (c) B's basis in his partnership interest?

    (d) C's basis in his partnership interest?

    (e) What basis will the ABC Partnership have in the property transferred by A?

26. If the ABC Partnership described in Problem 24 borrows $200,000 to purchase an office building, what effect, if any, will this have on each partner's basis in his partnership interest? What effect will the loan *repayment* have on each partner's basis?

27. As of January 1, 19X6, D had a basis of $24,000 in his 25% capital interest in the DEF Partnership. He and the partnership use the calendar year for tax purposes. The partnership incurred an operating loss of $100,000 for 19X6 and a profit of $8,000 for 19X7.

    (a) How much, if any, loss may D recognize for 19X6?

    (b) How much income must D recognize for 19X7?

    (c) What basis will D have in his partnership interest as of January 1, 19X7?

    (d) What basis will D have in his partnership interest as of January 1, 19X8?

    (e) What year-end tax planning would you suggest to insure that a partner could deduct all of his or her share of any partnership losses?

28. The ABCD Partnership is owned by four brothers (25% interest each). C sells investment property to the partnership for its fair market value of $30,000 (basis to C of $40,000).

    (a) How much loss, if any, may C recognize?

    (b) If the partnership later sells the property for $45,000, how much gain must it recognize?

    (c) If C's basis in the investment property was $20,000, instead of $40,000, how much capital gain, if any, would he recognize on the sale?

29. Under a partnership agreement, R, the owner of a 40% interest in the RST partnership, is entitled to a 40% interest in partnership profits. In no event will R receive less than $40,000. In 19X7, the partnership had taxable income of $90,000 before any adjustment for the minimum payment to R. As of January 1, 19X7, R's basis in his partnership interest was $30,000. On December 31, 19X7, the partnership distributed the $40,000 promised to R. All parties use the calendar year for tax purposes.

    (a) How much income must R recognize for 19X7?

    (b) What will be R's basis in his partnership interest as of January 1, 19X8?

    (c) Assuming that partners S and T each own a 30% interest in capital and profits of the partnership, how much income must each of them report for the year 19X7?

30. N, an equal partner in the MN Partnership, is to receive a payment of $20,000 for services plus 50% of the partnership's profits or losses. After deducting the $20,000 payment to N, the partnership has a loss of $12,000.

(a) How much, if any, of the $12,000 partnership loss will be allocated to N?

(b) What is the total income from the partnership that N must report on his personal income tax return?

31. At the time H receives a nonliquidating distribution, her basis in the partnership interest is $17,000. The distribution consists of cash of $3,000 and land with an adjusted basis of $12,000 and a fair market value of $15,000.

(a) How much gain, if any, must H recognize on the distribution? *0*

(b) What basis will H have in the distributed land? — *12,000*

(c) What is H's basis in her partnership interest after the distribution? *2000*

32. Assume the same facts as in Problem 31 except that the cash distribution amounts to $13,000 instead of $3,000.

(a) How much gain, if any, must H recognize on the distribution? *- 0*

(b) What basis will H have in the land? — *4000*

(c) What is H's basis in her partnership interest after the distribution? *- 0*

33. For each of the independent statements appearing below indicate whether the tax attribute is applicable only to partnerships (P), only to S corporations (S), to both forms of business (B), or to neither (N). (*Hint:* Refer to Chapter 16 regarding S corporations.)

(a) Flow-through to owners of net operating losses.

(b) Flow-through to owners of capital losses.

(c) Unrestricted selection of taxable year.

(d) An increase in the organization's trade accounts payable will increase the tax basis of the owner's interests.

(e) An owner's share of losses in excess of his or her tax basis can be carried forward indefinitely.

(f) A nonliquidating distribution of money or other property is generally not taxable to the owners.

(g) Income retained in the business will not be taxed to its owners until distributed to them.

34. For each of the independent statements appearing below indicate whether the tax attribute is applicable only to nonelecting (regular) corporations (C), only to partnerships (P), to both forms of business (B), or to neither (N).

(a) There are restrictions on the type and number of owners.

(b) The business income will be taxable to the owners rather than to the entity.

(c) Distributions of earnings to its owners will result in a tax deduction to the entity.

(d) The source characteristics of an entity's income flows through to its owners.

(e) Capital gains are subject to tax at the entity level.

(f) The costs of fringe benefits provided to its owners are deductible by the entity.

(g) Investment tax credits are passed through to the owners.

# Chapter 18

# The Federal Estate Tax

Prior to the enactment of the Tax Reform Act of 1976, Federal law imposed a tax on the gratuitous transfer of property in one of two ways. If the transfer was during the owner's life, it was subject to the Federal gift tax. If, however, the property passed by virtue of the death of the owner, the Federal estate tax applied. Both taxes were governed by different rules including a separate set of tax rates.

The Tax Reform Act of 1976 made significant changes to the approach taken by the Federal estate and gift taxes. Basically, it eliminated much of the distinction between life and death transfers. Instead of separate taxes, it substituted a unified transfer tax to cover all gratuitous transfers. In addition, current law eliminates the exemptions allowed under each tax and replaces them with a unified tax credit.

## NATURE OF THE DEATH TAX

The Federal estate tax dates from 1916 and, as is true with the origin of many taxes, was enacted to generate additional revenue in anticipation of this country's entry into World War I.[1]

The tax is designed to tax transfers at death, although it may have some application to lifetime transfers that become complete only

---

1. The constitutionality of the Federal estate tax was upheld in *New York Trust Co. v. Eisner,* 1 USTC ¶ 49, 3 AFTR 3110, 41 S.Ct. 506 (USSC, 1921).

upon the death of the donor or to certain gifts when made within three years of death. The tax is, in several respects, unlike the typical inheritance tax imposed by most states and some local jurisdictions. First, the Federal death tax is imposed on the decedent's entire estate. It is a tax on the right to pass property at death. Inheritance taxes are taxes on the right to receive property at death and are therefore levied on the beneficiaries.[2] Second, the relationship of the beneficiaries to the decedent usually has a direct bearing on the inheritance tax determination. In general, the more closely related the parties, the larger the exemption and the lower the applicable rates.[3] Except for one instance, the Federal death tax accords no difference in treatment based on the relationship of a decedent to his or her beneficiaries.[4]

*Estates Subject to Tax.* The Federal death tax is applied to the entire estate of a decedent, who, at the time of his or her death, was a resident or citizen of the United States.[5] If the decedent was a United States citizen, the residence at death makes no difference for this purpose.

If the decedent was neither a resident nor a citizen of the United States at the time of death, the Federal death tax will, nevertheless, be imposed on the value of any property situated within the United States. In such case, the tax determination is controlled by a separate Subchapter of the Internal Revenue Code.[6] In certain instances, these tax consequences outlined in the Internal Revenue Code may have been modified by death tax conventions (i. e., treaties) between the United States and various foreign countries.[7] Further coverage of this area is beyond the scope of this text; the discussion to follow is limited

---

**2.** As a practical matter, the inheritance tax will usually be paid by the executor or administrator of the estate. The executor has the legal responsibility under state law of collecting and paying over the tax. The amount involved, however, will have been deducted from the shares paid or to be paid each beneficiary.

**3.** For example, the Maine inheritance tax provides an exemption of $50,000 for surviving spouses with rates ranging from 5%–10% on the taxable portion. This is to be contrasted with an exemption of only $1,000 for strangers (unrelated to the deceased) with rates ranging from 14%–18% on the taxable portion. Other exemptions and rates fall in between these extremes to cover beneficiaries variously related to the decedent.

**4.** The one exception would be the marital deduction for qualifying transfers of property from the decedent to the surviving spouse.

**5.** § 2001. The term "United States" includes only the 50 states and the District of Columbia; it does not include U. S. possessions or territories. § 7701(a)(9).

**6.** Subchapter B (§ § 2101 through 2108) covers the estate tax treatment of decedents who are neither residents nor citizens. Subchapter A (§ § 2001 through 2056) covers the estate tax treatment of those who are either residents or citizens.

**7.** At present, the United States has death tax conventions with the following countries: Australia, Finland, France, Greece, Ireland, Italy, Japan, Netherlands, Norway, Republic of South Africa, Switzerland, and the United Kingdom. At the time of this writing, a death tax treaty with West Germany was pending ratification by the U. S. Senate.

to the tax treatment of decedents who were residents or citizens of the United States at the time of death.[8]

*Formula for the Federal Estate Tax.* The Federal unified transfer tax at death, commonly referred to as the Federal estate tax, is summarized below. [Note: Section (§) references are to the portion of the Internal Revenue Code involved.]

| | | |
|---|---:|---:|
| Gross estate (§ § 2031–2046) | | $  xxx,xxx |
| Less— | | |
|    Expenses, indebtedness, and | | |
|      taxes (§ 2053) | $  xx | |
|    Losses (§ 2054) | xx | |
|    Charitable bequests (§ 2055) | xx | |
|    Marital deduction (§ 2056) | xx | x,xxx |
| Taxable estate (§ 2051) | | $  xx,xxx |
| Add post-1976 taxable gifts | | |
|    [§ 2001(b)][9] | | x,xxx |
| Tax base | | $  xxx,xxx |
| Tentative tax on total transfers | | |
|    [§ 2001(c)][10] | | $  xx,xxx |
| Less— | | |
|    Unified transfer tax on post-1976 | | |
|      taxable gifts (i. e., gift taxes | | |
|      paid) | $  xx | |
|    Other tax credits (including the | | |
|      unified transfer tax credit) | | |
|      [§ § 2010–2016] | xx | x,xxx |
| Estate tax due | | $     xxx |

In lieu of the $30,000 lifetime or specific exemption for gift tax purposes (see Chapter 19) and the $60,000 exemption for estate tax purposes allowed prior to 1977, the current rules contain a unified transfer tax credit which applies both to life and death transfers. How this credit works and the actual computation of the unified transfer tax at death are covered later in this chapter and in Chapter 19.

The discussion of the Federal estate tax that follows will be developed to coincide with the pattern of the formula given above. Specifically, the treatment falls within the following major headings:

—Determining the gross estate.

—Fixing the amount of the estate subject to the tax.

—Computing and paying the tax (including a consideration of tax credits available).

---

8. Further information concerning Subchapter B (§ § 2101 through 2108) can be obtained by reading the Code Sections involved (and the Treasury Regulations thereunder). See also the Instructions to Form 706NA (U. S. Estate Tax Return for Estate of Nonresident not a Citizen of the U. S.)

9. Taxable gifts are explained in Chapter 19. For now, it is the amount of the gift reduced by various deductions and exclusions allowed.

10. See Appendix A–2 of the text for the unified transfer tax rates.

# GROSS ESTATE

Simply stated, the gross estate comprises all property which is subject to the Federal estate tax. This in turn depends on the provisions of the Internal Revenue Code as supplemented by IRS pronouncements and the judicial interpretations of Federal courts.

To be contrasted with the gross estate is the concept of the probate estate. Controlled by state (rather than Federal) law, the probate estate consists of all of a decedent's property subject to administration by the executor or administrator of the estate operating under the supervision of a local court of appropriate jurisdiction (usually designated as a probate court).[11] The probate estate is frequently smaller than the gross estate because it contains only property owned by the decedent at the time of death and passing to heirs under a will or under the law of intestacy (i. e., the order of distribution for those dying without a will).[12] As noted later, such items or the proceeds of many life insurance policies become part of the gross estate but are not included in the probate estate.

## PROPERTY OWNED BY THE DECEDENT—§ 2033

Property owned by the decedent at the time of death will be includible in the gross estate. The nature of the property or the use to which it was put during the decedent-owner's lifetime has no significance as far as the death tax is concerned. Thus, personal effects (clothing, etc.), stocks, bonds, furniture, jewelry, works of art, bank accounts, and interests in businesses conducted as sole proprietorships and partnerships are all included in the deceased owner's gross estate. In other words, no distinction is made between tangible or intangible, depreciable or nondepreciable, business or personal assets.

The application of § 2033 can be illustrated as follows:

**Example 1.** D dies owning some City of Denver bonds. The fair market value of the bonds plus any interest accrued to the date of D's death is includible in his gross estate. Although interest on municipals is normally not taxable under the Federal income tax, it is, nevertheless, property owned by D at the time of his death.

---

**11.** An executor (or executrix, in the case of a female) is the decedent's personal representative as appointed under the decedent's will. An administrator (or administratrix, in the case of a female) is appointed by the local probate court of appropriate jurisdiction, usually because the decedent failed to appoint an executor in his or her will (or such designated person refused to serve) or the decedent died without a will. **12.** All states provide for an order of distribution in the event someone dies without a will. Aside from the surviving spouse who receives some or all of the estate, the preference is usually in the following order: down to lineal descendants (e. g., children, grandchildren), up to lineal ascendants (e. g., parents, grandparents), and then out to collateral relations (e. g., brothers, sisters, aunts, and uncles).

**Example 2.** D dies on April 8, 19X4, at a time when she owns stock in X Corporation and in Y Corporation. On March 1, 19X4, both corporations authorized a cash dividend payable on May 1, 19X4. In the case of X Corporation, the dividend was payable to shareholders of record as of April 1, 19X4; while Y Corporation's date of record is April 10, 19X4. D's gross estate includes the following: the stock in X Corporation, the stock in Y Corporation, and the dividend on the X Corporation stock. It does not include the dividend on the Y Corporation stock.

**Example 3.** D dies holding some promissory notes issued to him by his son. In his will, D forgives these notes, relieving the son of any obligation to make payments thereon. The fair market value of these notes will be included in D's gross estate.

**Example 4.** D died while employed by Z Corporation. Pursuant to an informal but nonbinding company policy, Z Corporation awards one-half of D's annual salary to his widow as a death benefit. Presuming that D had no vested interest in and that the widow had no enforceable right to the payment, none of it will be includible in his gross estate.[13]

## DOWER AND CURTESY INTERESTS—§ 2034

In its common law (nonstatutory) form, dower generally gave a surviving widow a life estate in a portion of her deceased husband's estate (usually the real estate he owned) with the remainder passing to their children.[14] Most states have modified and codified these common law rules, and variations between jurisdictions are not unusual. In some states, for example, a widow's statutory share of her deceased husband's property may mean outright ownership in a percentage of both his real estate and personal property. Curtesy is a similar right held by the husband in his wife's property taking effect in the event he survives her. Most states have abolished the common law curtesy concept and have, in some cases, substituted a modified statutory version.

Dower and curtesy rights are incomplete interests and may never materialize. Thus, if a wife predeceases her husband, her dower interest in her husband's property is lost. This result is to be contrasted with the situation existing in community property jurisdictions.[15] A deceased spouse's interest in the community is considered complete

---

13. *Barr's Estate*, 40 T.C. 164 (1963).
14. The holder of a life estate, called a life tenant, has the right to the use of the property (including the right to the income therefrom) for his or her life. On the death of the life tenant, the property (called the remainder interest) passes to the designated remainderman.
15. Recall that the following states have the community property system in effect: Louisiana, Texas, New Mexico, Arizona, California, Washington, Idaho, and Nevada.

and is not lost by death. Thus, if a wife predeceases her husband, one-half of their community property passes to her heirs (or as she otherwise designates in her will).[16]

The distinction between dower (and curtesy) and community property becomes very important for Federal estate tax purposes. Code § 2034 makes it quite clear that anything passing from the deceased spouse to the surviving spouse in the form of dower (or curtesy) shall be included in the gross estate of the deceased spouse. On the other hand, neither § 2033 nor § 2034 forces the surviving spouse's share of the community into the gross estate of the deceased spouse; that interest is not incomplete but was his or hers before death.

These rules are illustrated in the following examples:

**Example 5.** D dies without a will leaving an estate of $600,000. Under state law, W (D's widow) is entitled to one-third of D's property. The $200,000 W receives will be included in D's gross estate.[17] (Note: If W predeceased D, her dower interest would be defeated, and neither her probate nor gross estate would include any of D's property.)

**Example 6.** D and W are husband and wife, have always lived in Texas (a community property state), and at the time of D's death held community property of $1,000,000. Only $500,000 of this property (D's share of the community) will be included in D's gross estate.[18] [Note: If W predeceased D, $500,000 of the community property (her share) would be included in her gross estate.]

## ADJUSTMENTS FOR GIFTS MADE WITHIN THREE YEARS OF DEATH—§ 2035

*Background.* For many years the tax law provided that the value of property given by a decedent within three years of death should be included in his or her gross estate. The rule, moreover, made sense under a system where the gift and estate taxes were separate from each other and one (the gift tax) provided for a lower set of rates. Under this type of structure, a provision was needed to preclude the obvious tax avoidance that would result from a deathbed transfer. Otherwise a decedent could enjoy the ownership of property almost up to the point of death and, by making the last-minute gift, bypass the higher estate tax rates. Congress arbitrarily settled on a three-year

---

**16.** Community property is that property acquired after marriage except through acquisition by gift, bequest, or devise (i. e., inheritance).

**17.** Depending on the nature of the interest W receives in the $200,000, this amount could qualify D's estate for a marital deduction under § 2056. This possibility is discussed at greater length in a subsequent section of this chapter. For the time being, however, the focus is on what is or is not included as part of the decedent's gross estate.

**18.** The inclusion comes under § 2033 (property owned by the decedent).

period during which such gifts would be vulnerable to inclusion in the donor's gross estate at their fair market value on date of death (or alternate valuation date if elected).

A further possibility for avoidance was the estate tax savings that could be accomplished on any gift tax that was paid as a result of the transfer. Because such funds were no longer held at death, they would not be included in the gross estate. Congress precluded this approach in the Tax Reform Act of 1976 by requiring the "gross-up" procedure. Under this approach, any gifts brought back into the gross estate must include the gift tax paid thereon. Any such gift tax, however, would be allowed as a credit against the estate tax of the donor-decedent.

If one operates on the assumption that no difference exists between the rates applicable to lifetime and death transfers (i. e., the same rate schedule applies), as is presently the case with the unified transfer tax scheme, why force inclusion in the gross estate of gifts made within a three-year period prior to the donor's death? Such inclusion only compelled the parties to revalue the property, since it was the fair market value of the property on the date of the donor's death (or alternate valuation date if elected) and not the value of the property on the date of the gift that measured what was added to the gross estate. Congress recognized these problems and in the Economic Recovery Tax Act of 1981 significantly revamped the approach of § 2035.

*Current Rules.* For donors dying after 1981, the following modifications of § 2035 were made:

—Except as noted below, gifts made within three years of death are treated the same as any other post-1976 taxable gifts. Consequently, they are added to the *taxable estate* in arriving at the tax base for applying the unified transfer tax at death (see the formula for the Federal estate tax discussed earlier in the chapter). This means the property will not have to be revalued because it is the fair market value on the date of the gift (not on the date of death) which will control.

—The gross-up approach, however, is retained. Thus, any gift tax paid on gifts made within three years of death must be added to the *gross estate.*

A series of illustrations should clarify how the Economic Recovery Tax Act (ERTA) changed § 2035.

**Example 7.** In 1980, D makes a taxable gift of property in the amount of $50,000 upon which he pays a gift tax of $6,000. At the time of his death in 1982, the property is worth $75,000. As to the transfer, D's gross estate must include $6,000 (the gross-up of the gift tax) and $50,000 must be added to his taxable estate in arriving at the tax base.

**Example 8.**  Assume the same facts as in Example 7 except that D died in 1981. Presuming the value of the property on the date of his death to be $75,000 with no election of the alternate valuation date, D's gross estate must include $81,000 [$75,000 (fair market value of the property on the date of the donor's death) + $6,000 (the gross-up for gift taxes paid)] as to the property.

The pre-ERTA three-year rule has been retained for transfers of property interests that would have been included in the gross estate by virtue of the application of § 2036 (transfers with a retained life estate), § 2037 (transfers taking effect at death), § 2038 (revocable transfers), § 2041 (powers of appointment), and § 2042 (proceeds of life insurance).

**Example 9.**  In 1982, D transferred an insurance policy on her life (worth $9,000 with a maturity value of $40,000) to S, the designated beneficiary. Due to the $10,000 annual exclusion (see Chapter 19), D incurred no gift tax on the transfer. Upon D's death in 1983, S receives the $40,000 in insurance proceeds. D's gross estate must include $40,000 concerning the policy.

*Observation.*  At this point, one might realistically pose the following question: What difference does it make whether a post-1976 taxable gift within three years of death is included in the gross estate or is added to the taxable estate in arriving at the tax base for Federal estate tax purposes? A quick reference to the estate tax formula (see earlier in this chapter) and the marital deduction (see later in this chapter) reveals that the size of the gross estate could have an impact on the amount of a marital deduction allowed to the estate of a deceased spouse. Probably more important is the fact that the treatment of a gift as an addition to the taxable estate freezes the value used in determining the tax base for the application of the unified transfer tax. By comparing the results reached in Examples 7 and 8, it should be apparent that inclusion in the gross estate resulted in the appreciation of $25,000 [$75,000 (fair market value on date of death) − $50,000 (fair market value on date of gift)] being subject to a transfer tax (Example 8). Although the numbers used reflect that the new rules are favorable to the taxpayer (Example 7), a negative impact would come about if the property has declined in value from the point of gift to the date of the donor's death.

## TRANSFERS WITH A RETAINED LIFE ESTATE—§ 2036

Code § § 2036 and 2038 were enacted on the premise that the estate tax can be avoided on lifetime transfers only if the decedent does not retain control over the property. The logic of this approach is somewhat difficult to dispute—one should not be able to escape the tax consequences of property transfers at death while at the same time remaining in a position during life to enjoy some or all of the fruits of ownership.

Code § 2036 requires inclusion of the value of any property transferred by the deceased during lifetime for less than adequate consideration (in money or money's worth) if there was retained:

1. The possession or enjoyment of, or the right to the income from, the property, *or*

2. The right, either alone or in conjunction with any person, to designate the persons who shall possess or enjoy the property or the income therefrom.

"The possession or enjoyment of, or the right to the income from, the property," as it appears in § 2036(a)(1), is considered to have been retained by or reserved to the decedent to the extent that such income, etc., is to be applied toward the discharge of a legal obligation of the decedent. The term "legal obligation" includes a legal obligation of the decedent to support a dependent during the decedent's lifetime.

The practical application of § 2036 can best be explained by turning to a series of illustrations.

> **Example 10.** F's will passes all of his property to a trust, income to D for his life (i. e., D is given a life estate), and upon D's death, the corpus (i. e., principal) goes to R (i. e., R is granted a remainder interest). On D's death, none of the trust property will be included in his gross estate. Although D held a life estate, § 2036 is inapplicable because he was not the transferor (F was) of the property.[19]

> **Example 11.** By deed, D transfers the remainder interest in her ranch to S, retaining for herself the right to continue occupying the property until death. Upon D's death the fair market value of the ranch will be included in her gross estate under § 2036(a)(1).

## REVOCABLE TRANSFERS—§ 2038

Another type of lifetime transfer that is drawn into a decedent's gross estate is covered by § 2038. Under this Section, the gross estate includes the value of property interests transferred by the decedent (except to the extent that the transfer was made for adequate and full consideration in money or money's worth) if the enjoyment of the property transferred was subject, at the date of his death, to any power of the decedent to alter, amend, revoke, or terminate the transfer. This includes the power to change the beneficiaries or the power to accelerate or increase any beneficiary's enjoyment of the property.

---

**19.** Section 2033 (property owned by the decedent) would compel inclusion in D's gross estate of any income distributions he was entitled to receive at the time of his death.

The capacity in which the decedent could exercise the power is immaterial. If the decedent gave property in trust, making himself or herself the trustee with the power to revoke the trust, the property would be included in his or her gross estate. If the decedent named another person as trustee with the power to revoke, but reserved the power to later appoint himself or herself trustee, the property would also be included in his or her gross estate. If, however, the power to alter, amend, revoke, or terminate was held at all times solely by a person other than the decedent and the decedent reserved no right to assume these powers, the property is not included in the decedent's gross estate under § 2038.

The Code and the Regulations make it quite clear that inclusion in the gross estate under § 2038 is not avoided by relinquishing a power within three years of death.[20]

These rules can be illustrated as follows:

**Example 12.** D transfers securities to S under the state's Uniform Gifts to Minors Act designating himself as the custodian. Under the Act, the custodian has the authority to terminate the custodianship at any time and distribute the proceeds to the minor. D dies four years later and before the custodianship is terminated.[21]

Although the transfer is effective for income tax purposes, it runs afoul of § 2038. Under this Section, the fair market value of the securities on the date of D's death will be included in his gross estate for Federal estate tax purposes.[22]

**Example 13.** Assume the same facts as in Example 12 except that D dissolves the custodianship (thereby turning the securities over to S) within three years of death. The fair market value of the securities on the date of D's death will be includible in his gross estate.[23]

**Example 14.** Assume the same facts as in Example 12 except that S becomes of age and the custodianship terminates prior to D's death. Presuming that the original transfer was not within three years of death, nothing will be included in D's gross estate upon his death.

---

**20.** § 2038(a)(1) and Reg. § 20.2038–1(e)(1).

**21.** The Uniform Gifts to Minors Act permits the ownership of securities to be transferred to a minor with someone designated as the custodian. The custodian has the right to sell the securities, collect any income therefrom, and otherwise act on behalf of the minor without court supervision. The custodianship arrangement is convenient and inexpensive. Under many state laws the custodianship now terminates when the minor reaches age 18. Some such statutes, however, allow the custodian the discretion of continuing the custodianship until age 21 (the old rule) if it was created prior to a certain date.

**22.** Rev.Rul. 57–366, 1957–2 C.B. 618. See also *Stuit v. Comm.*, 54 T.C. 580 (1970).

**23.** § 2035(d)(2).

**Example 15.** G transfers securities to S under the state's Uniform Gifts to Minors Act, designating D as the custodian. Nothing relating to these securities will be included in D's gross estate upon his death during the term of the custodianship. Code § 2038 is not applicable because D was not the transferor. G's death during the custodianship should cause no estate tax consequences; he has retained no interest or control over the property transferred.

In the area of incomplete transfers (i. e., § § 2036 and 2038), there is much overlap in terms of application. It is not unusual, therefore, to find that one or more of these Sections apply to a particular transfer.

## ANNUITIES—§ 2039

Annuities can be divided by their origin into commercial and noncommercial contracts. The noncommercial variety are those issued by private parties and, in some case, charitable organizations which do not regularly engage in such activities. Although both varieties have much in common, noncommercial annuities present special income tax problems and are not treated further in this discussion.

Reg. § 20.2039–1(b)(1) defines an annuity as representing "one or more payments extending over any period of time." According to this Regulation, the payments may be equal or unequal, conditional or unconditional, periodic or sporadic. Most commercial contracts fall into one of four general patterns:

1. *Straight-life annuity.* The insurance company promises to make periodic payments to X, the annuitant, during his or her life. Upon X's death, the company has no further obligation under the contract.

2. *Joint and survivor annuity.* The insurance company promises to make periodic payments to X and Y during their lives with the payments to continue, usually in a diminished amount, for the life of the survivor.

3. *Self and survivor annuity.* The company agrees to make periodic payments to X during his or her life and, upon X's death, to continue these payments for the life of a designated beneficiary. This and the preceding type of annuity are most frequently used by married couples.

4. *Refund feature.* The company agrees to return to the annuitant's estate or other designated beneficiary a portion of the investment in the contract in the event of his or her premature death.

*Nonemployment Arrangements.* In the case of a straight-life annuity contract, nothing will be included in the gross estate of the annuitant at death. Code § 2033 (i. e., property in which the decedent had an interest) does not apply because the annuitant's interest in the contract is terminated by death. Code § 2036 (i. e., transfers with a retained life estate) does not cover the situation; a transfer which is a "bona fide sale, for an adequate and full consideration in money or money's worth" is specifically excluded from § 2036 treatment. The purchase of a commercial annuity is presumed to entail adequate and full consideration unless some evidence exists to indicate that the parties were not acting at arm's length.

> **Example 16.** D purchases a straight-life annuity which will pay him $1,000 a month when he reaches age 65. D dies at age 70. Except for the payments he received prior to his death, nothing relating to this annuity will affect D's gross estate.[24]

In the case of a survivorship annuity [see classifications 2 and 3], the estate tax consequences under § 2039(a) are usually triggered by the death of the first annuitant. The amount included in the gross estate is the cost from the same company of a comparable annuity covering the survivor at his or her attained age on the date of the deceased annuitant's death.

> **Example 17.** Assume the same facts as in Example 16 except that the annuity contract provides for W to be paid $500 a month for life as a survivorship feature. W is 62 years of age when D dies. Under these circumstances, D's gross estate will include the cost of a comparable contract that would provide an annuity of $500 per month for the life of a person (male or female, as the case may be) age 62.

Full inclusion in the gross estate of the survivorship element is subject to the important exception of § 2039(b). Under this provision, the amount includible is to be based on the proportion of the deceased annuitant's contribution to the total cost of the contract. This can be expressed by the following formula:

$$\frac{\text{Decedent's contribution to purchase price}}{\text{Total purchase price of the annuity}} \times \text{Value of the annuity (or refund)}$$

at decedent's death = Amount includible in the deceased annuitant's gross estate

> **Example 18.** Assume the same facts as in Example 17 except that D and W are husband and wife and have always lived in a community property state. The premiums on the contract were paid with community funds. Because W contributed one-half of

---

24. D's income tax consequences prior to death would be governed by § 72. Based on the exclusion ratio under § 72(b) a portion of each payment would be non-taxable.

the cost of the contract, only one-half of the amount determined under Example 17 would be included in D's gross estate.[25]

*Employment Arrangements.* Two possibilities exist in the case of annuities arising out of an employment relationship. If pursuant to a nonqualified plan, any contribution by the employer toward the cost of the contract is treated as having been made by the deceased employee.[26] Therefore, it is fully included in the gross estate of the employee.

**Example 19.** While employed by X Corporation, D, a key employee, entered into a deferred pay contract with his employer. Under the contract, a portion of D's future annual salary increment was to be deferred until the earlier of his death, disability, or retirement.[27] Upon D's death prior to retirement, $180,000 (the amount accrued under the contract) is paid to S, D's designated beneficiary.[28] The $180,000 is included in D's gross estate, since the payment arises from a nonqualified plan.[29]

If the distribution is pursuant to a qualified plan[30] to which an employee has not contributed (i. e., a noncontributory plan), the inclusion or exclusion from the gross estate depends on the following circumstances:[31]

—No exclusion is in order if the distribution is to the estate of the employee.

—An exclusion will be allowed if the payment is not in a lump-sum form.[32] For estates of decedents dying after 1982, the exclusion is limited to $100,000.

—An exclusion will be allowed even when the distribution is in lump-sum form if the beneficiary elects to forego the advantages of the 10-year averaging provisions of § 402(a).[33]

---

**25.** The result reached in Example 18 is not unique to community property jurisdictions. For example, the outcome would have been the same in a noncommunity property state if W had furnished one-half of the consideration from her own funds.

**26.** § 2039(b).

**27.** Known as the "deferred pay contract," the procedure will be effective to defer the recognition of income to the employee until the payout period commences. The employee must, however, remain as a general creditor of the corporation and the deferral concerns amounts not yet earned. See Rev.Rul. 60–31 (1960–1 C.B. 174).

**28.** The $180,000 must be included in S's gross income and will be taxed in full.

**29.** *Goodman v. Granger,* 57–1 USTC ¶ 11,687, 51 AFTR 67, 243 F.2d 264 (CA–3, 1957).

**30.** A qualified plan is one that meets the requirements of § 401(a).

**31.** § 2039(c).

**32.** As defined in § 402(e)(4)(A). For Individual Retirement Accounts (IRAs), a lump-sum distribution is one that is received over a period of less than 36 months.

**33.** § 2039(f)(2). Keep in mind that distributions from noncontributory qualified plans will be subject to the Federal income tax. Section 402(a) mitigates the bunching effect of a lump-sum distribution by providing a special averaging procedure.

**Example 20.** D, an employee of Y Corporation, is covered under its noncontributory qualified pension plan. D dies prior to retirement, and under a settlement option provided for in the plan, D's vested interest of $210,000 is paid to his estate. The $210,000 distribution is part of D's gross estate.

**Example 21.** Assume the same facts as in Example 20 except that the settlement option chosen by D provides that the $210,000 (with appropriate interest) be paid to S over a five-year period. None of the distribution is included in D's gross estate if D died before 1983. If D died after 1982, only $100,000 may be excluded.

**Example 22.** Assume the same facts as in Example 20 except that the settlement option requires that the $210,000 be paid to S within six months of D's death. If D died before 1983, the full $210,000 will be excluded from the gross estate if S chooses to forego the 10-year averaging provisions of § 402(a) for income tax purposes. If D died after 1982, such a course of action will exclude only $100,000 of the proceeds. Presumably, the balance of the distribution (i.e., $110,000) would not be eligible for the § 402(a) income averaging procedure even though it will be included as part of the gross estate.

Similar rules apply to distributions under Individual Retirement Accounts (IRAs), Keogh (H.R. 10), and tax-sheltered annuity plans.

In the event the plan is contributory in nature (i. e., both employer and employee make contributions to the plan), the portion attributable to the employee's contribution generally will be included in the gross estate. This is determined by comparing the employee's contribution with the total contributions to the plan.

**Example 23.** D, an employee of Z Corporation, participates in its contributory qualified retirement plan. At the point of her death prior to her retirement, contributions to the plan were as follows: $80,000 by D and $160,000 by Z Corporation. Commencing in the year of her death, D's vested portion in the plan of $330,000 is paid to M (the designated beneficiary) in six annual installments (with interest provided for).[34] In resolving the exclusion and inclusion problem, determine how much of the distribution is attributable to the employee and how much to the employer.

---

**34.** Although the total contributions made to the plan were $240,000 [$80,000 (by D) + $160,000 (by Z Corporation)], the distribution on D's behalf is $330,000. Why? The obvious answer is that the $90,000 difference ($330,000 − $240,000) represents income generated by the plan assets.

Amount attributable to the employee's contribution—

$$\frac{\$80,000 \text{ (employee's contribution)}}{\$240,000 \text{ (total contribution by both parties)}} \times \$330,000$$

$$\text{(total amount of distribution)} = \$110,000$$

Amount attributable to the employer's contribution—

$$\frac{\$160,000 \text{ (employer's contribution)}}{\$240,000 \text{ (total contribution by both parties)}} \times \$330,000$$

$$\text{(total amount of distribution)} = \$220,000$$

If D died before 1983, the amount excluded from the gross estate therefore becomes $220,000. Thus, $110,000 must be included as part of the gross estate. If, however, D died after 1982, recall that the exclusion portion is limited to $100,000. Consequently, $100,000 is excluded and $230,000 [$330,000 (amount of distribution) − $100,000 (maximum exclusion allowed)] is included in the gross estate. Some of the distribution, of course, will be included in M's gross income.[35]

## JOINT INTERESTS—§ 2040

Assume that D and Y own an undivided, but equal, interest in a piece of property. Such joint ownership could fall into any one of four categories: joint tenancy, tenancy by the entirety, tenancy in common, or community property.

If D and Y hold ownership as joint tenants, the right of survivorship exists. If D predeceases Y, D's rights terminate and Y becomes the sole owner of the property. During his or her lifetime, a joint tenant usually possesses the right of severance—the right to have the property partitioned or to sell his or her interest to another. In the event of severance (either partition or sale), the right of survivorship ceases. If, for example, D sells his interest in a joint tenancy to Z, the joint tenancy terminates and Y and Z now hold the property as tenants in common.

A tenancy by the entirety is, basically, a joint tenancy between husband and wife. One important difference, however, is the absence of the right of severance, except by divorce. D, for example, may transfer his interest to Y, but he cannot sell to another or secure a partition of the property.

Acting together, husband and wife can terminate the tenancy by transferring their interest to a third party. Thus, D and Y may join together to sell their interest to Z.

---

**35.** Aside from any interest element, M must include $250,000 [$330,000 (the total distribution received) − $80,000 (D's contribution from after-tax dollars)] in gross income.

Under the tenancy in common and community property arrangements, the rights of each owner extend beyond his or her death. Thus, if D predeceases Y, one-half, or whatever interest he holds in the property, is included in his *probate* estate and passes to his heirs or other appointees. At least in the case of a tenancy in common, a tenant possesses the right to secure a partition of the property or to otherwise dispose of the interest. As to community property, however, partitions or other dispostions are not so easily accomplished and state law should be checked carefully in this regard.

The Federal estate tax treatment of tenancies in common or of community property follows the logical approach of taxing only that portion of the property included in the deceased owner's probate estate. Thus, if D, X, and Z are tenants in common in a tract of land, each owning an equal interest, and D dies, only one-third of the value of the property is included in the gross estate. This one-third interest is also the same amount which will pass to D's heirs or appointees.

> **Example 24.** D, X, and Z acquire a tract of land, ownership listed as tenants in common, each party furnishing $20,000 of the $60,000 purchase price. At a point when the property is worth $90,000, D dies. If D's undivided interest in the property is 33⅓%, the gross estate *and* probate estate includes $30,000.

*Joint Tenancies Between Persons Other Than Spouses.* In the case of certain joint tenancies, the tax consequences are different. All of the property is included in the deceased co-owner's gross estate unless it can be proved that the surviving co-owners contributed to the cost of the property.[36] If a contribution can be shown, the amount to be excluded is calculated by the following formula:

$$\frac{\text{Surviving co-owner's contribution}}{\text{Total cost of the property}} \times \text{Fair market value of the property}$$

In computing a survivor's contribution, any funds received as a gift *from the deceased co-owner* and applied to the cost of the property cannot be counted. However, it has been held that income or gain from gift assets can be so counted.

If the co-owners receive the property as a gift *from another,* each co-owner will be deemed to have contributed to the cost of his or her own interest.

*Joint Tenancies and Tenancies by the Entirety Between Spouses.* Prior to the Economic Recovery Tax Act of 1981, married persons who held property in joint tenancy or tenancy by the entirety were subject

---

**36.** § 2040.

to a myriad of rules, some being similar to those already discussed in connection with joint ownership between nonspouses. Several reasons convinced Congress to modify these rules for situations where the property is held jointly (with the right of survivorship) between husband and wife. These are summarized below.

— Simplification of the tax law was important in that most joint ownership arrangements involve husband and wife.

— Prior law placed an undue burden on the surviving spouse to prove his or her contribution to the cost of the property.

— In view of the unlimited marital deduction, both for estate (see later in this chapter) and gift (see Chapter 19) tax purposes, the old rules possessed little continuing validity.

Code § 2040(b), as amended, provides for an automatic-inclusion rule upon the death of the first joint-owner spouse to die after 1981. Regardless of the amount of the contribution furnished by each spouse, one-half of the value of the property will be included in the gross estate of the spouse that predeceases.

**Example 25.** In 1980, H purchases real estate for $100,000 using his separate funds and listing title as "H and W, joint tenants with the right of survivorship." H predeceases W four years later when the property is worth $300,000. If H and W are husband and wife, H's gross estate must include $150,000 (½ of $300,000) as to the property.

**Example 26.** Assume the same facts as in Example 25 except that it is W (instead of H) who dies first. Presuming the date of death value to be $300,000, W's gross estate must include $150,000 as to the property.[37] In this regard, it is of no consequence that W did not contribute to the cost of the real estate.

## PROCEEDS OF LIFE INSURANCE—§ 2042

Under § 2042, the gross estate includes the proceeds of life insurance on the decedent's life if (1) they are receivable by the estate, (2) they are receivable by another for the benefit of the estate, or (3) the decedent possessed an incident of ownership in the policy.

Life insurance on the life of another owned by a decedent at the time of his death would be included in his gross estate under § 2033 (i. e., property in which the decedent had an interest) and not under

---

**37.** In both Examples 25 and 26, inclusion in the gross estate of the first spouse to die will be neutralized by the new unlimited marital deduction allowed for estate tax purposes (see the discussion of § 2056 later in this chapter). Recall that under the right of survivorship feature, the surviving joint tenant obtains full ownership of the property. The marital deduction generally is allowed for property passing from one spouse to another.

§ 2042. The amount includible is the replacement value of the policy. Under these circumstances, inclusion of the face amount of the policy would be inappropriate; the policy has not yet matured.

> **Example 27.** At the time of his death, D owned a life insurance policy on the life of S, face amount of $100,000 and replacement value of $25,000, with W as the designated beneficiary. Since the policy has not matured at D's death, § 2042 is inapplicable. However, § 2033 (i. e., property in which the decedent had an interest) would compel the inclusion of $25,000 (the replacement value) in D's gross estate.[38]

The term "life insurance" includes whole life policies, term insurance, group life insurance, travel and accident insurance, endowment contracts (before being paid up), and death benefits paid by fraternal societies operating under the lodge system.

*Proceeds Payable to the Estate.* As noted above, proceeds of insurance on the life of the decedent receivable by the executor or administrator or payable to the decedent's estate are included in the gross estate. It is not necessary that the estate be specifically named as the beneficiary. For example, if the proceeds of the policy are receivable by an individual beneficiary and are subject to an obligation, legally binding upon the beneficiary, to pay taxes, debts, and other charges enforceable against the estate, the proceeds will be included in the decedent's gross estate to the extent of the beneficiary's obligation. If the proceeds of an insurance policy made payable to a decedent's estate are community assets and, under state law, one-half belongs to the surviving spouse, then only one-half of the proceeds will be considered as receivable by or for the benefit of the decedent's estate.

*The Incidents of Ownership Test.* Proceeds of insurance on the life of the decedent not receivable by or for the benefit of the estate are includible if the decedent possessed at his or her death any of the incidents of ownership in the policy, exercisable either alone or in conjunction with any other person, even if acting as trustee. In this connection, the term "incidents of ownership" does not mean only the ownership of the policy in a technical legal sense. Generally speaking, the term has reference to the right of the insured or his or her estate to the economic benefits of the policy. Thus, it includes the power to change beneficiaries, to revoke an assignment, to pledge the policy for a loan, or to surrender or cancel the policy.

> **Example 28.** At the time of death, D was the insured under a policy (face amount of $100,000) owned by S with W as the designated beneficiary. The policy originally was taken out by D five

---

**38.** If the policy were owned by D and W as community property, only $12,500 would be included in D's gross estate.

years ago and immediately transferred as a gift to S. Under the assignment, D transferred all rights in the policy except the right to change beneficiaries. D died without having exercised this right, and the policy proceeds are paid to W. Under § 2042(2), the retention of an incident of ownership in the policy (e. g., the right to change beneficiaries) by D forces $100,000 to be included in the gross estate.

A group life insurance policy taken out by the decedent's employer on the life of the decedent is included in the employee's gross estate if the decedent had the right to change beneficiaries, to cancel the policy, or exercise similar control over the policy. On the other hand, an irrevocable assignment by the employee-insured of all rights under the policy will be recognized for tax purposes under certain conditions. First, such assignment must be permitted under state law and under the terms of the insurance contract. Second, the employee must have possessed the right to convert the group policy into an individual insurance policy upon the termination of his employment (and such right was transferable and was in fact transferred).

# TAXABLE ESTATE

After the gross estate has been determined, the next step is to arrive at the taxable estate. By virtue of § 2051, the taxable estate is the gross estate less the following: expenses, indebtedness, and taxes (§ 2053); losses (§ 2054); charitable transfers (§ 2055) and the marital deduction (§ 2056).

## EXPENSES, INDEBTEDNESS, AND TAXES—§ 2053

A deduction is allowed for funeral expenses; expenses incurred in administering property; claims against the estate; and unpaid mortgages and other charges against property, the value of which is included in the gross estate without reduction for the mortgage or other indebtedness.[39]

Expenses incurred in administering community property are deductible only in proportion to the deceased spouse's interest in the community.[40]

*What Is Included?*  Administration expenses include commissions of the executor or administrator, attorney's fees of the estate, accountant's fees, court costs, and certain selling expenses for disposition of estate property.

Claims against the estate include property taxes accrued prior to the decedent's death, unpaid income taxes on income received by the

---

39.  § 2053(a).
40.  *U. S. v. Stapf,* 63–2 USTC ¶ 12,192, 12 AFTR2d 6326, 84 S.Ct. 248 (USSC, 1963).

decedent in his lifetime, and unpaid gift taxes on gifts made by the decedent in his lifetime.

Amounts that may be deducted as claims against the estate are only for enforceable personal obligations of the decedent at the time of his or her death. Deductions for claims founded on promises or agreements are limited to the extent that the liabilities were contracted in good faith and for adequate and full consideration in money or money's worth. However, a pledge or subscription in favor of a public, charitable, religious, or educational organization is deductible to the extent that it would have constituted an allowable deduction had it been a bequest.[41]

Deductible funeral expenses include the cost of interment, the burial plot or vault, a gravestone, perpetual care of the grave site, and the transportation expense of the person bringing the body to the place of burial. If the decedent had, prior to death, acquired cemetery lots for himself and his family, no deduction will be allowed, but such lots will not be included in his gross estate under § 2033 (i. e., property in which the decedent had an interest).

If, at the time of filing the death tax return (i. e., Form 706), the exact amount of an item deductible under § 2053 or § 2054 is not known, that item may nevertheless be entered on the return in an estimated amount provided the estimated amount is ascertainable with reasonable certainty and it can be shown that the item will be paid.

*Mortgages.* Unpaid mortgages and other indebtedness with respect to estate property will be allowed as a deduction under § 2053(a)(4) if the full value of the property is includible in the gross estate. This would be the case if the decedent was personally liable on the obligation. If the decedent was not personally liable on the obligation, the property should be included in the gross estate at its "net" value. In the latter situation, any excess of the obligation over the value of the property to which it relates would not be allowed as an estate tax deduction.

**Example 29.** At the time of her death, D owned a parcel of real estate with a fair market value of $100,000. She was personally liable on a purchase money mortgage of $30,000 on the real estate. The property must be included in D's gross estate at $100,000, and a deduction of $30,000 would be allowed for the liability.

**Example 30.** Assume the same facts as in Example 29 except that D was not personally liable on the mortgage. In this event, the property would be included in D's gross estate at its net value of $70,000, and the liability would not be separately deducted.

---

**41.** § 2053(c)(1)(A) and Reg. § 20.2053–5.

## LOSSES—§ 2054

Section 2054 permits an estate tax deduction for losses from casualty or theft incurred during the period of settlement of the estate. As is true with casualty or theft losses for income tax purposes, any anticipated insurance recovery must be taken into account in arriving at the amount of the deductible loss. If the casualty occurs to property after it has been distributed to an heir, the loss belongs to the heir and not to the estate. If the casualty occurs prior to the decedent's death, it should be claimed on his or her appropriate Form 1040. The fair market value of the property (if any) on the date of death plus any insurance recovery would, of course, be included in the gross estate.

As is true of certain administration expenses, a casualty or theft loss of estate property can be claimed as an income tax deduction on the fiduciary return of the estate (Form 1041). But the double deduction prohibition of § 642(g) applies; claiming the income tax deduction requires a waiver of the death tax deduction.

## TRANSFERS TO CHARITY—§ 2055

*Qualifying Transfers.* A deduction is allowed for the value of property in the decedent's gross estate that was transferred by him through testamentary disposition to (or for the use of):

1. The United States or any political subdivision therein, *or*

2. Any corporation or association organized and operated exclusively for religious, charitable, scientific, literary, or educational purposes, as long as no benefit inures to any private individual and no substantial activity is undertaken to carry on propaganda or otherwise attempt to influence legislation or participate in any political campaign on behalf of any candidate for public office, *or*

3. A trustee or trustees of a fraternal society, order, or association operating under the lodge system, if the transferred property is to be used exclusively for religious, charitable, scientific, literary or educational purposes, and no substantial activity is undertaken to carry on propaganda or otherwise attempt to influence legislation or participate in any political campaign on behalf of any candidate for public office, *or*

4. Any veteran's organization incorporated by an Act of Congress (or any of its subdivisions) as long as no benefit inures to any private individual.[42]

The organizations described above are identical to the ones that qualify for the Federal gift tax deduction under § 2522. With two

---

**42.** § 2055(a)(1), (2), (3), and (4).

exceptions, these are also the same organizations that will qualify a donee for an income tax deduction under § 170. These exceptions are:

—Certain nonprofit cemetery associations qualify for income tax but not death and gift tax purposes.[43]

—Foreign charities may qualify under the estate and gift tax but not under the income tax.[44]

No deduction will be allowed unless the charitable bequest is specified by a provision in the decedent's will or the transfer was made before death and the property is subsequently included in the gross estate. Generally speaking, a deduction does not materialize when an individual dies intestate (i. e., without a will). The bequest to charity must be mandatory as to the amount involved and cannot be based on the discretion of another. It is, however, permissible to allow another, such as the executor of the estate, the choice of which charity will receive the specified donation.

*Reduction for Certain Charges.* The deduction is limited to the amount actually available for charitable uses. Thus, if under the terms of the will or the provisions of local law,[45] or for any other reason, the Federal death tax or any other death tax is payable in whole or in part out of property the transfer of which would otherwise be allowable as a deduction, the sum deductible is the fair market value of the property on the applicable valuation date less the taxes chargeable thereto.[46] A reduction may also be made for any administration expenses payable out of the transferred property.

**Example 31.** In her will, D leaves real estate valued at $100,000 to an out-of-state but qualified charitable organization. Under applicable state law, the real estate so passing is chargeable with $5,000 of the death taxes and $2,000 of the administration expenses of the estate. The estate will be allowed a charitable deduction of only $93,000, the net amount passing to charity.

## MARITAL DEDUCTION—§ 2056

The marital deduction originated with the Revenue Act of 1948 as part of the same legislation which permitted married persons to secure the income-splitting advantages of filing joint income tax returns. The purpose of these statutory changes was to eliminate the major tax variations that could develop between taxpayers residing

---

**43.** Section 170(c)(5) does not have a counterpart in either § 2055 (i. e., death tax charitable contributions) or § 2522 (i. e., gift tax charitable contribution).

**44.** Compare the wording of § 170(c)(2)(A) with that of § 2055(a)(2) and § 2522(a)(2).

**45.** A portion of death taxes may be chargeable to a charitable bequest under a state apportionment statute.

**46.** § 2055(c).

in community property and in common law states. The marital deduction was designed to provide equity in the estate and gift tax areas.

In a community property state, for example, no marital deduction generally was allowed, since the surviving spouse already owned one-half of the community and such portion was not included in the deceased spouse's gross estate. In a common law state, however, most if not all of the assets often belonged to the breadwinner of the family. Upon such person predeceasing, all of these assets were included in his or her gross estate. [Recall that a dower or curtesy interest (regarding a surviving spouse's right to some of the deceased spouse's property) does not reduce the gross estate.] To equalize the situation, therefore, a marital deduction, usually equal to one-half of all separate assets, was allowed upon the death of the first spouse.

In the Economic Recovery Tax Act of 1981, Congress decided to dispense with these historical justifications and to recognize husband and wife as a single economic unit. Consistent with the approach taken under the income tax, spouses are to be considered as one for transfer tax purposes. By making the marital deduction unlimited in amount, neither the gift tax nor the estate tax will be imposed on outright interspousal transfers of property. Unlike prior law, the new unlimited marital deduction even includes one spouse's share of the community property transferred to the other spouse.

*Passing Concept.* The marital deduction is allowed only for property which is included in the deceased spouse's gross estate and which passes or has passed to the surviving spouse.[47] Property that passes from the decedent to the surviving spouse includes any interest received as (1) the decedent's legatee, devisee, heir, or donee, (2) the decedent's surviving tenant by the entirety or joint tenant, (3) the beneficiary of insurance on the life of the decedent.[48]

> **Example 32.** At the time of his death in 1983, D owned an insurance policy on his own life (face amount of $100,000) with W (his wife) as the designated beneficiary. D and W also owned real estate (worth $250,000) as tenants by the entirety (D having furnished all of the purchase price). As to these transfers, $225,000 ($100,000 + $125,000) would be included in D's gross estate and this amount represents the property which passes to W for purposes of the marital deduction.[49]

---

**47.** § 2056(a).

**48.** § 2056(d).

**49.** Inclusion in the gross estate would fall under § 2042 (i. e., proceeds of life insurance) and § 2040 (i. e., joint interests). Although D provided the full purchase price for the real estate, § 2040(b) requires inclusion of only one-half of the value of the property when one spouse predeceases the other.

Under certain conditions, disclaimers of property by the surviving spouse in favor of some other heir will affect the amount that passes and therefore qualifies for the marital deduction. Thus, if W is entitled to $400,000 of H's property but disclaims (i.e., refuses) $100,000 in favor of S, the residuary legatee under the will, the $100,000 will pass from H to S and not from H to W. Disclaimers by some other heir in favor of the surviving spouse may have a similar effect. Suppose W, as residuary legatee, will receive $300,000 under H's will, but the will also provides that S is to receive a specific bequest of $100,000. If S issues a timely disclaimer in favor of W, the amount passing from H to W for purposes of the marital deduction will be increased from $300,000 to $400,000.

When a property interest passes to the surviving spouse, subject to a mortgage or other encumbrance, or when an obligation is imposed upon the surviving spouse in connection with the passing of a property interest, only the net value of the interest after reduction by the amount of the mortgage or other encumbrance qualifies for the marital deduction. However, if the executor is required, under the terms of the decedent's will or under local law, to discharge the mortgage or other encumbrance out of other assets of the estate or to reimburse the surviving spouse, the payment or reimbursement constitutes an additional interest passing to the surviving spouse.

Federal death taxes or other death taxes that are paid out of the surviving spouse's share of the gross estate are not included in the value of property passing to the surviving spouse. Therefore, it is usually preferable for the deceased spouse's will to provide that death taxes be paid out of the portion of the estate that does not qualify for the marital deduction.

## COMPUTING AND PAYING THE TAX

### IN GENERAL

The gross death tax is computed by applying the rate of tax from § 2001 to the value of the taxable estate. Which rate schedule is used depends on when death occurred. If before 1977, the estate tax rates apply. If death occurred after 1976, the unified transfer tax rates apply. (See Appendix A for rate tables.)

**Example 33.** D dies in 1983 leaving a taxable estate of $400,000. The unified transfer tax on a transfer of more than $250,000 but not over $500,000 is $70,800 plus 34% of the excess over $250,000. Thus, $70,800 + (34% × $150,000) yields a tentative tax of $121,800.

In arriving at the tentative tax under the unified transfer tax rates, any taxable gifts made after 1976 must be added to the taxable estate. This adjustment is explained in Chapter 19. For now, it must be assumed that no such gifts occurred in arriving at the result reached in Example 33.

The net estate tax or the death transfer tax payable is determined by deducting from the tentative estate tax the allowable credits for:

—The unified transfer tax.

—State death taxes.

—Federal gift taxes.

—Federal estate taxes on prior transfers.

—Foreign death taxes.

Each of these five death tax credits is considered separately.

## THE UNIFIED TRANSFER TAX CREDIT—§ 2010

In lieu of the previous $60,000 estate tax exemption, the Tax Reform Act of 1976 provides the estate of each person dying after 1976 with a transfer tax credit.[50] The amount of the credit starts with $30,000 and increases to $192,800 over a transitional period as set forth below:

| Year of Death | Amount of Credit | Amount of Exemption Equivalent |
|---|---|---|
| 1977 | $ 30,000 | $ 120,667 |
| 1978 | 34,000 | 134,000 |
| 1979 | 38,000 | 147,333 |
| 1980 | 42,500 | 161,563 |
| 1981 | 47,000 | 175,625 |
| 1982 | 62,800 | 225,000 |
| 1983 | 79,300 | 275,000 |
| 1984 | 96,300 | 325,000 |
| 1985 | 121,800 | 400,000 |
| 1986 | 155,800 | 500,000 |
| 1987 & thereafter | 192,800 | 600,000 |

The amount of the exemption equivalent is the taxable estate plus post-1976 taxable gifts (i. e., the tax base) that will pass free of the estate tax by virtue of the unified transfer tax credit. Other estate tax credits (see below), of course, could add to this amount.

**Example 34.** The $79,300 credit for 1983 is the equivalent of exempting $275,000 from the tax base. The estate tax on

---

**50.** The avowed purpose of substituting a credit for the $60,000 exemption was to reduce the number of estates that would be subject to the Federal estate tax. The original phase-in (Tax Reform Act of 1976) was scheduled to level off at $47,000 in 1981. Due to the continuing inflationary trend in the economy, the phase-in with a stairstep increase in the amount of the credit was extended to 1987 (Economic Recovery Tax Act of 1981).

$275,000 (see Appendix A) would be $70,800 plus 34% of the excess over $250,000. Thus, $70,800 + $8,500 equals $79,300.

Under § 2505(b), a similar credit is allowed for taxable gifts made after 1976 (see Chapter 19).

## CREDIT FOR STATE DEATH TAXES—§ 2011

Section 2011 allows a limited credit for the amount of any death, inheritance, legacy, or succession tax actually paid to any state (or to the District of Columbia) attributable to any property included in the gross estate. Like the credit for foreign death taxes paid, the purpose of this provision is to mitigate the harshness of subjecting the same property to multiple death taxes.

The credit allowed is limited to the lesser of the amount of tax actually paid or the amount provided for in a table contained in § 2011(b). (See Appendix A.) No credit is available if the adjusted taxable estate is $40,000 or less.

> **Example 35.** D's adjusted taxable estate is $38,000, and the state of appropriate jurisdiction imposes a death tax of $1,500 on this amount. None of the $1,500 paid qualifies for the death tax credit.

> **Example 36.** D's adjusted taxable estate is $140,000 and the state of appropriate jurisdiction imposes a death tax of $3,000 on this amount. Of the $3,000 paid in state death taxes, only $1,200 would be deductible in view of the table contained in § 2011(b).

As noted in Examples 35 and 36, it may be entirely possible that the credit allowed by § 2011 proves to be less than the amount of state death taxes paid. The reverse is, of course, possible but usually not the case. Most states insure that the minimum tax payable to the jurisdiction is at least equal to the credit allowed by the table contained in § 2011(b). Sometimes this result is accomplished by a "sponge" tax superimposed on the regular inheritance tax. Thus, if the regular inheritance tax yielded $2,500, but the maximum credit allowed by the table is $3,200, a sponge tax would impose an additional $700 in state death taxes. In other states, the whole state death tax liability depends entirely upon the amount allowed for Federal death tax purposes as the credit under § 2011(b). Thus, in the previous illustration, the state inheritance tax would be an automatic $3,200.

In arriving at the credit allowed for persons dying after 1976, the taxable estate is reduced by the $60,000 exemption previously allowed for Federal estate tax purposes. This adjustment (to arrive at the adjusted taxable estate) is required even though the $60,000 exemption no longer is allowed in computing the unified transfer tax at death.

## CREDIT FOR GIFT TAXES—§ 2012

A credit is allowed under § 2012 against the estate tax for any Federal gift tax paid on a gift of property subsequently included in the donor-decedent's gross estate.

> **Example 37.** In 1965, D transfers a remainder interest in a farm to her children, retaining for herself a life estate. As a result of the transfer, D incurred and paid a Federal gift tax of $45,000. D dies in 1983 when the property is worth $400,000. Since the application of § 2036 (retention of a life estate) forces the inclusion of the farm in D's gross estate, a double-tax situation results. To mitigate this effect, § 2012 allows D's estate a credit for some or all of the $45,000 in gift taxes previously paid.

The adjustments that might be necessary in working out the amount of the credit could become somewhat complicated and are discussed further.[51]

Under the Tax Reform Act of 1976, only taxable gifts made after 1976 will be added to the donor's taxable estate in arriving at the base for the application of the unified transfer tax at death. To the extent these gifts have exceeded the unified transfer tax credit and have generated a tax, such tax should be credited against the transfer tax due at death.

## CREDIT FOR TAX ON PRIOR TRANSFERS—§ 2013

Suppose, for example, D owns some property which he passes at death to S. Shortly thereafter, S dies and passes the property to R. Assuming both estates are subject to the Federal death tax, one can easily imagine the multiple effect involved in successive death situations. In order to mitigate the possible multiple taxation which might result, § 2013 provides relief in the form of a credit for a death tax on prior transfers.[52] Thus, to return to the hypothetical case stated previously, S's estate may be able to claim as a death tax credit some of the taxes paid by D's estate.

The credit is limited to the lesser of the following amounts:

1. The amount of the Federal death tax attributable to the transferred property in the transferor's estate.

2. The amount of the Federal death tax attributable to the transferred property in the decedent's estate.

---

**51.** These are illustrated and explained in the Instructions to Form 706 and in Reg. § 20.2012–1.

**52.** The double death tax effect might not be complete if S were D's spouse and some or all of the property passing from D to S qualified D's estate for a marital deduction. For this reason, § 2013(d)(3) requires an adjustment to determine the credit for tax on prior transfers in the event the marital deduction is a factor.

To apply the foregoing limitations, certain adjustments must be made which will not be covered in this text.[53] One must note, however, that it is not necessary for the transferred property to be identified in the present decedent's estate or for it to be in existence at the time of his or her death. It is sufficient that the transfer of property was subjected to the Federal death tax in the estate of the transferor and that the transferor died within the prescribed period of time.

If the transferor died within two years before or two years after the present decedent's death, the credit is allowed in full (subject to the limitations noted above). If the transferor died more than two years before the decedent, the credit is a certain percentage: 80 percent if the transferor died within the third or fourth year preceding the decedent's death, 60 percent if within the fifth or sixth year, 40 percent if within the seventh or eighth year, and 20 percent if within the ninth or tenth year.

> **Example 38.** Pursuant to D's will, S inherits property. One year later S dies. Assume the estate tax attributable to the inclusion of the property in D's gross estate is $15,000 and that attributable to the inclusion of the property in S's gross estate is $12,000. Under these circumstances, S's estate may claim a credit against its death tax of $12,000 [see limitation (b) above].

> **Example 39.** Assume the same facts as in Example 38 except that S dies three years after D's death. The applicable credit is now 80% of $12,000, or $9,600.

## CREDIT FOR FOREIGN DEATH TAXES—§ 2014

Under § 2014, a credit is allowed against the death tax for any estate, inheritance, legacy, or succession tax actually paid to any foreign country. For purposes of this provision, the term "foreign country" not only means states in the international sense but also refers to possessions or political subdivisions of foreign states and to possessions of the United States.

The credit is allowed for death taxes paid (1) with respect to property situated within the foreign country to which the tax is paid, (2) with respect to property included in the decedent's gross estate, and (3) with respect to the decedent's estate. No credit is allowed for interest or penalties paid in connection with foreign death taxes.

The credit is limited to the lesser of the following amounts:

1. The amount of the foreign death tax attributable to the property situated in the country imposing the tax and included in the decedent's gross estate for Federal death tax purposes.

2. The amount of the Federal death tax attributable to particular property situated in a foreign country, subject to death tax

---

**53.** See the Instructions to Form 706 and Reg. § 20.2013–2 and 20.2013–3.

in that country, and included in the decedent's gross estate for Federal death tax purposes.

Both of these limitations may require certain adjustments to arrive at the amount of the allowable credit. Such adjustments are illustrated in the Regulations and are not discussed in this text. In addition to the credit for foreign death taxes under the provisions of Federal estate tax law, similar credits are allowable under death tax conventions with a number of foreign countries.[54] If a credit is allowed either under the provisions of law or under the provisions of a convention, there is allowed that credit which is most beneficial to the estate.

## THE FEDERAL ESTATE TAX RETURN

A Federal estate tax return, if required, is due nine months after the date of the decedent's death.[55] This time limit applies to all estates regardless of the nationality or residence of the decedent.

In the case of the estate of a citizen or resident of the United States dying after 1976, a Form 706 (Estate Tax Return) must be filed by the executor or administrator under the following conditions:[56]

| Year of Death | Gross Estate in Excess of |
|---|---|
| 1977 | $ 120,000 |
| 1978 | 134,000 |
| 1979 | 147,000 |
| 1980 | 161,000 |
| 1981 | 175,000 |
| 1982 | 225,000 |
| 1983 | 275,000 |
| 1984 | 325,000 |
| 1985 | 400,000 |
| 1986 | 500,000 |
| 1987 & thereafter | 600,000 |

For purposes of meeting the filing requirements, the gross estate is reduced by the sum of:

—Taxable gifts made after 1976 (other than those included in the gross estate), *and*

—The amount of the $30,000 specific gift tax exemption allowed the decedent on gifts made after September 8, 1976, and before January 1, 1977 (see Chapter 19).

---

54. For the list of countries with which the United States has death tax conventions, refer to Footnote 7.
55. § 6075(a).
56. § 6018(a)(1).

**Example 40.** D dies in 1983 leaving a gross estate of $275,000. In the past, D had made taxable gifts as follows: $40,000 in 1975 and $10,000 in 1978. Under these circumstances, D's estate must file a Form 706. Although the taxable gift made in 1975 is disregarded, the $10,000 taxable gift made in 1978 reduces the filing requirement to $265,000 ($275,000 − $10,000).

Form 706 must be filed with the IRS Service Center serving the district in which the decedent was domiciled at the time of his or her death.

The return must be accompanied by various documents relevant to the determination of tax liability. Among items which must be included are statements on Form 712 to be obtained from the insurance companies involved for each insurance policy listed in the return.

Penalties are provided for willful failure to make and file a timely return and for willful attempts to evade or defeat payment of tax.[57]

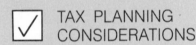

TAX PLANNING CONSIDERATIONS

## PROPER HANDLING OF ESTATE TAX DEDUCTIONS

*The Marital Deduction in Perspective.* When planning for the estate tax marital deduction, both tax and nontax factors have to be taken into account. In the tax area, there exist two major goals which guide planning. These are the equalization and the deferral approaches described below:

— Attempt to equalize the estates of both spouses. Clearly, for example, the estate tax on $1,000,000 is more than double the estate tax on $500,000 [compare $345,800 with $311,600 ($155,800 × 2)].[58]

— Try to postpone estate taxation as long as possible. On a $1,000,000 estate, for example, what is the time value of $345,800 in estate taxes deferred for a period of, say, 10 years?

Planning prior to the Economic Recovery Tax Act of 1981 generally represented a compromise between the equalization and the deferral approaches. In part, the equalization route was motivated by several provisions in the tax law. First, the maximum marital deduction was limited to 50 percent of the adjusted gross estate. Consequently, any amount in excess of the 50 percent limit passing to the

---

57. See, for example, § § 6651, 6653, 6672, and 7203.
58. § 2001(c) and Appendix A.

surviving spouse did not qualify for the marital deduction. Second, the unified transfer tax credit for 1981 and thereafter was scheduled to level off at $47,000. As a result, a surviving spouse that died after 1981 was supposed to have only a $47,000 credit available. Third, and for larger estates, the maximum marginal estate tax bracket could reach as high as 70 percent.

The changes made by the Economic Recovery Tax Act of 1981 will have a noticeable impact on the stress previously placed on the equalization approach. To begin with, the new unlimited marital deduction enables the planner to avoid entirely the estate tax upon the death of first spouse to die. Although too much property to the surviving spouse violates the equalization goal, if the surviving spouse lives long enough, the unified transfer tax credit reaches the maximum phase-in amount of $192,800 (for 1987 and thereafter).[59] Also, for persons dying after 1984, the top bracket of the unified transfer tax is due to be lowered to 50 percent.[60] All of these scheduled changes, therefore, add impetus to the deferral approach. This means, of course, making optimum use of the marital deduction by passing enough property to the surviving spouse to eliminate the estate tax of the first spouse to die.

But tax planning must remain flexible and be tailored to the individual circumstances of the parties involved. Before the equalization approach is cast aside, therefore, consider the following variables:

—Both spouses are of advanced age and/or in poor health and neither is expected to survive the other for a prolonged period of time. For example, one cannot plan on a $192,800 unified transfer tax credit if the surviving spouse is not expected to live until 1987.

—The spouse that is expected to survive has considerable assets of his or her own. To illustrate, a spouse that passes a $250,000 estate to the survivor who already has assets of $1,000,000 is trading a 32 percent bracket for a later 43 percent bracket.

—Because of inflation, real estate worth $250,000 today when it passes to the surviving spouse may be worth $1,000,000 five years later when the survivor dies.

—There always is the possibility that the phase-in of the increase in the unified transfer tax credit and/or the lowering of the marginal top bracket rate to 50 percent may not take place. Predicting what Congress will or will not do is, to say the least, dangerous. In the estate and gift tax area, moreover, the Tax Reform Act of 1976 and the Economic Recovery Tax Act of 1981 provide a track record of radical changes. It would be ludicrous to say that further changes could not occur.

---

**59.** § 2010.
**60.** § 2001(c)(2).

*The Marital Deduction—Sophistication of the Deferral Approach.* When the saving of estate taxes for the family unit is the sole consideration, the equalization and deferral approaches can be combined with maximum effect.

> **Example 41.** At the time of his death in 1983, H had never made any post-1976 taxable gifts or used his specific exemption on any pre-1977 gifts. Under H's will, his disposable estate of $1,000,000 passes to W, his surviving spouse.[61]

> **Example 42.** Assume the same facts as in Example 41 except that H's will provides as follows: $275,000 to the children and the remainder (i. e., $725,000) to W.

From a tax standpoint, which is the better plan? Although no estate tax results from either arrangement, Example 41 represents overkill in terms of the marital deduction. Why place an additional $275,000 in W's potential estate when it can pass free of tax to the children through the application of the $79,300 unified transfer tax credit available for 1983?[62] Clearly, then, the arrangement in Example 42 is to be preferred, as it avoids unnecessary concentration of wealth in W's estate.

## PROBLEM MATERIALS

### Discussion Questions

1. What are the major differences between the Federal estate tax and the typical inheritance tax levied by most states?

2. Distinguish between:

    (a) The gross estate and the taxable estate.

    (b) The gross estate and the probate estate.

3. Distinguish between:

    (a) Dower and curtesy and a surviving spouse's statutory share of the deceased spouse's property.

    (b) Dower and curtesy (or its statutory version) and a surviving spouse's share of his or her community property.

    What difference do these distinctions carry for Federal estate tax purposes?

4. After 1982, any taxable gift made within three years of the donor's death will be treated the same for estate tax purposes as any post-1976 taxable gift. Do you agree or disagree with this statement? Why?

---

**61.** For this purpose, disposable estate means the gross estate less administration and other expenses and debts.

**62.** The exemption equivalent of a credit of $79,300 is $275,000.

5. After 1982, no taxable gifts made within three years of death will be included in the gross estate of the donor. Evaluate the soundness of this statement.

6. What difference, if any, does it make whether a gift made within three years of death is or is not included in the donor's gross estate?

7. What objective did Congress hope to accomplish by enacting §§ 2036 and 2038?

8. Comment on the following in connection with §§ 2036 and 2038:

   (a) The decedent was not the grantor of the property interest.

   (b) The decedent's interest was received in exchange for full and adequate consideration.

9. Using community property, H creates a trust, life estate to W (H's wife), remainder to their children upon her death.

   (a) Any estate tax effect upon H's death four years later?

   (b) Any estate tax effect upon W's death five years later?

10. Under what circumstances could a distribution from a qualified pension plan be included in a deceased employee's gross estate?

11. Why will a straight-life annuity not be included in the gross estate of the annuitant on his or her death? Consider §§ 2033, 2036, and 2039.

12. From the standpoint of death tax consequences, summarize the differences between a tenancy in common, joint tenancy, tenancy by the entirety, and community property.

13. H and W (husband and wife) hold considerable property as tenants by the entirety with the right of survivorship. Assuming that the purchase price for the properties was furnished by H, comment on the estate tax ramifications under each of the following assumptions:
    (a) H dies first.

    (b) W dies first.

    (c) H dies first and W dies two years after H.

14. Under what conditions will the proceeds of life insurance be includible in the gross estate of the insured?

15. For purposes of § 2042, what is included in the term "life insurance"?

16. What constitutes an "incident of ownership" in a life insurance policy?

17. What is necessary to keep group life insurance out of the gross estate of the insured-employee?

18. Under what Code provision would an insurance policy on another's life be included in the gross estate of the owner? Why?

19. What expenses are deductible under § 2053?

20. How are casualty losses incurred during the administration of an estate handled for Federal death tax purposes?

21. What was the Congressional purpose surrounding the enactment of § 2056 which created the marital deduction?

22. In connection with the credit for state death taxes (§ 2011) comment on the following:

(a) The Congressional purpose underlying § 2011.

(b) The amount of the state death taxes exceeds the maximum allowed.

(c) The taxable estate is under $40,000.

(d) The possibility of a state-imposed "sponge" tax.

23. Regarding the credit for tax on prior transfers (§ 2013), comment on the following:

(a) The justification for the credit.

(b) The necessity to trace property from one estate to another.

(c) The marital deduction was allowed the first estate.

(d) The time interval between deaths.

24. In connection with the Federal death tax return, comment on the following:

(a) When is it required?

(b) When must it be filed?

(c) What supporting documents must be filed with the return?

## Problems

25. Two years prior to her death in 1983, D (a widow) made the following gifts: cash of $10,000 and a paid-up insurance policy on her life (value of $20,000 and a face amount of $50,000). How much, if any, of this property should be included in her gross estate?

26. Indicate in each of the situations appearing below whether the death of D would bring into play (as to D's gross estate) the application of § 2036 or § 2038 (or both). Unless otherwise stated, assume that all situations are independent of each other and that § 2035 (transfers within three years of death) does not apply.

(a) In 1978, D transferred property to a newly created trust retaining for himself the income therefrom for his life (i. e., a life estate), remainder to his children upon D's death. In the current year, D dies and the trust principal is paid to the children.

(b) Pursuant to F's will, D is granted a life estate in property placed in trust, remainder upon D's death to D's children. In the current year, D dies and the corpus of the trust is paid to D's children.

(c) In 1977, D and W (husband and wife) transfer community property in trust, income to them for life, remainder to pass to their children upon the death of the last survivor (either D or W). In the current year, D predeceases W.

(d) In 1978, D transfers stock to G (age 6) under the state's Uniform Gifts to Minors Act, designating himself as the custodian. Under applicable state law, the custodian has the right to accumulate income on behalf of the minor and, at any time, to terminate the custodianship and distribute all of the stock and accumulated income to the minor. D dies in the current year while the custodianship is still in effect.

(e) Assume the same facts as in (d) except that G dies several months prior to D.

(f) In 1974, F creates a trust, life estate to B, remainder to D or his estate. In the current year, D predeceases B.

27. At the time of his death in 1983, D was employed by M Corporation and was a participant in the company's pension plan. By reason of his death, $180,000 is distributed from the plan on D's behalf. Of the total payments made to the plan during his employment and credited to his account, D contributed one-third. Two-thirds of the amount was contributed by M Corporation. Discuss the death tax consequences of the distribution based on the following assumptions:

    (a) The plan was qualified and the $180,000 was paid over a four-year period to W, D's designated beneficiary.

    (b) The plan was qualified and the $180,000 was paid to D's estate.

    (c) Same as (a) except that the plan was not qualified.

    (d) Same as (b) except that the plan was not qualified.

28. Using separate property, D purchases an annuity (total premiums of $40,000) from an insurance company. Under the terms of the annuity contract, D is to receive $6,000 per year for life upon reaching a specified age. In the event D does not recover his investment in the contract prior to death, the balance of such investment is to be paid to W, D's wife. Discuss the estate tax ramifications of the following possibilities:

    (a) D dies after having received $30,000 under the contract. The insurance company pays the $10,000 balance to W.

    (b) D dies after having received $55,000 under the contract.

    (c) W predeceases D after he has received $45,000 under the contract.

    (d) Assume the same facts as in (a) except that the premiums on the policy were paid from community funds (rather than from D's separate property).

29. In 1978, H and W (husband and wife) acquire real estate at a cost of $100,000. H predeceases W in 1983 when the property is worth $500,000. Discuss the estate tax consequences upon H's death based on the following independent assumptions:

    (a) H and W were equal tenants in common.

    (b) H and W held the land as community property.

    (c) H and W held the land as joint tenants with the right of survivorship. H furnished all of the purchase price.

    (d) H and W held the land as tenants by the entirety. W furnished all of the purchase price.

30. Comment on how each of the following independent situations should be handled for estate tax purposes:

    (a) Prior to her death in 1983, D issued a note payable to her daughter in the amount of $100,000 for which no consideration was ever received by D. After D's death, the daughter files a claim against the estate and collects $100,000 on the note.

    (b) At the time of her death, D (a widow) owned 10 cemetery lots (each worth $5,000) which she had purchased many years ago for herself and her family.

    (c) At the time of his death, D owned some real estate valued at $200,000 with a mortgage thereon of $80,000. D was personally liable on the mortgage.

(d) At the time of his death, D was delinquent in the payment of back Federal income taxes. Such taxes are paid by D's executor from assets of the estate.

31. On September 20, 1983, D incurs a casualty loss of property worth $12,000 (the reasonably anticipated insurance recovery is $2,000). Shortly thereafter, D dies. D's estate, however, pursues the claim against the insurance company and collects $2,000 for the estate nine months after D's death. Discuss the tax ramifications of these transactions.

32. Four different persons (D, E, F, and G) die in 1983, each leaving a taxable estate of $1,000,000 and none having made any post-1976 taxable gifts. Each decedent leaves a surviving spouse and a will dictating the disposition of their property.

   (a) Under D's will, the full taxable estate passes to a qualified charity.

   (b) Under E's will, the full taxable estate passes to the surviving spouse.

   (c) Under F's will, the taxable estate is to be divided between the surviving spouse and a qualified charitable organization.

   (d) Under G's will, $275,000 passes to the children and the balance (i. e., $725,000) goes to the surviving spouse.

   From a tax standpoint, evaluate the various testamentary schemes.

33. Determine the tentative tax in each of the independent situations appearing below (assume death occurs in 1983 and no prior taxable gifts have been made):

| | Case A | Case B |
|---|---|---|
| Gross estate | $ 1,000,000 | $ 500,000 |
| §§ 2053 and 2054 expenses and losses | 50,000 | 30,000 |
| Charitable bequest (§ 2055) | 100,000 | — |
| Marital deduction (§ 2056) | — | 200,000 |

34. D dies in 1983 leaving all of his property to W, his wife. Information concerning D's estate appears below:

| | |
|---|---|
| Gross estate | $ 1,000,000 |
| §§ 2053 and 2054 expenses and losses | 80,000 |

   The only taxable gift made by D during his life was $100,000 to S in 1975. Determine D's unified transfer tax at death.

35. Presuming no post-1976, taxable gifts have been made and disregarding all credits except the unified transfer tax credit of § 2010, determine the estate tax in each of the following independent situations:

| | Case A | Case B | Case C |
|---|---|---|---|
| | (Death in 1982) | (Death in 1983) | (Death in 1984) |
| Gross estate | $ 500,000 | $ 2,000,000 | $ 6,000,000 |
| §§ 2053 and 2054 expenses and losses | 50,000 | 150,000 | 400,000 |
| Charitable bequest | — | 200,000 | 500,000 |
| Marital deduction | — | 800,000 | — |

36. In each of the independent situations appearing below, determine whether or not a Form 706 needs to be filed by the estate:

|  | Case A | Case B | Case C |
|---|---|---|---|
|  | (Death in 1982) | (Death in 1983) | (Death in 1987) |
| Gross estate | $ 250,000 | $ 300,000 | $ 700,000 |
| Post-1976 taxable gifts | 30,000 | 25,000 | 110,000 |

# Chapter 19

# The Federal Gift Tax and Certain State Transfer Taxes

## THE FEDERAL GIFT TAX

Under the changes made by the Tax Reform Act of 1976, the Federal gift tax has been combined with the Federal estate tax and a new unified tax on both life and death transfers has been substituted. However, since the changes did not take effect until after 1976, the former gift tax rules apply to all lifetime transfers made prior to 1977.

### IN GENERAL

The Federal gift tax is imposed on the right to transfer property by one person (i. e., the donor) to another (i. e., the donee) for less than full and adequate consideration. The tax is payable by the donor.[1] If, however, the donor fails to pay the tax when due, the donee may be liable for the tax to the extent of the value of the property received.[2]

First enacted in 1926, the Federal gift tax was designed to improve upon the effectiveness of the income and estate tax. Apparently, Congress felt that one should not be able to give away property, thereby shifting the income tax consequences to others and further avoiding estate taxes on the death of the transferor, without incurring some tax liability. The answer, then, was the Federal gift tax which covered inter vivos (i. e., lifetime) transfers.

---

**1.** § 2502(d).
**2.** § 6324(b).

*Requirements for a Gift.* For a gift to be complete under state law, the following elements must be present:

1. A donor competent to make a gift.
2. A donee capable of receiving and possessing the property.
3. Donative intent on behalf of the donor.
4. Actual and constructive delivery of the property to the donee or the donee's representative.
5. Acceptance of the gift by the donee.

What transfers are or are not completed gifts under state law is, of course, important in applying the Federal gift tax. But state law does not always control in this matter. For example, with reference to the element of donative intent [see (3)], the Regulations make it quite clear that this is not an essential factor in the application of the Federal gift tax to the transfer.

> **Example 1.** B (age 24) consents to marry D (age 62) if D transfers $200,000 of his property to her. The arrangement is set forth in a prenuptial agreement, D makes the transfer, and B and D are married. Obviously, D lacked donative intent and in most states there is no gift from D to B. Nevertheless, the transfer would be subject to the Federal gift tax.

The key to the result reached in Example 1 and to the status of other types of transfers is whether full and adequate consideration in money or money's worth was given for the property transferred.[3] Although there is such consideration present in Example 1 (i. e., property for marriage) for purposes of state law, Reg. § 25.2512–8 states: "A consideration not reducible to a value in money or money's worth, as love and affection, promise of marriage, etc., is to be wholly disregarded, and the entire value of the property transferred constitutes the amount of the gift."

The Federal gift tax does not apply to transfers that are incomplete. Thus, if the transferor retains the right to reclaim the property or, for all intents and purposes, has not really parted with the possession of the property, then a taxable event has not taken place.

> **Example 2.** D creates a trust, income payable to S, remainder to R. Under the terms of the trust instrument, D can revoke the trust at any time and repossess trust corpus and income therefrom. No gift takes place on the creation of the trusts; D has not ceased to have dominion and control over the property.

> **Example 3.** Assume the same facts as in Example 2 except that one year after the transfer, D relinquishes his right to terminate

---

3. § 2512(b).

the trust. At this point, the transfer becomes complete and the Federal gift tax applies.

*Persons Subject to the Tax.* To determine whether a transfer is subject to the Federal gift tax, one must first ascertain if the donor is a citizen or resident of the United States. If not a citizen or a resident, then it becomes important to determine whether the property involved in the gift was situated within the United States.

The Federal gift tax is applied to all transfers by gift of property wherever situated by individuals who, at the time of the gift, were citizens or residents of the United States. The term "United States" includes only the 50 states and the District of Columbia; it does not include United States possessions or territories. For a United States citizen, the place of residence at the time of the gift is immaterial.

For individuals who are neither citizens nor residents of the United States, the Federal gift tax is applied only to gifts of property situated within the United States.[4] A gift of intangible personal property (e. g., stocks and bonds) usually is not subject to the Federal gift tax when made by nonresident alien individuals.[5]

A gift by a corporation is considered a gift by its individual stockholders. A gift to a corporation is generally considered as a gift to its individual stockholders except that in certain cases, a gift to a charitable, public, political, or similar organization may be regarded as a gift to the organization as a single entity.

*The Scheme of the Gift Tax—Transfers After 1976.* Assuming the gift tax applies to the donor, proceed as follows:

| | | |
|---|---:|---:|
| Determine whether the transfers are or are not covered by referring to §§ 2511 through 2519; list the fair market value of only the covered transfers | | $ xxx,xxx |
| Determine the deductions allowed by § 2522 (charitable), § 2523 (marital) | $ xx,xxx | |
| Claim the annual exclusion (per donee) under § 2503(b), if available | 10,000[6] | xx,xxx |
| Taxable gifts [as defined by § 2503(a)] for the current period | | $ xx,xxx |
| Add: Taxable gifts from prior years | | xx,xxx |
| Total of current and past taxable gifts | | $ xx,xxx |

---

**4.** § 2511(a).

**5.** § 2501(a)(2) and (3).

**6.** The annual exclusion prior to 1982 was $3,000. The change to $10,000 was made by the Economic Recovery Tax Act of 1981 to allow larger gifts to be exempt from the Federal gift tax. Such change has to be commended in light of the inflationary trend in the economy. In the case of gifts of jointly owned property (e. g., joint tenancies, tenancies by the entirety, tenancies in common, community property) or in the case of gifts by one spouse when the election to split gifts under § 2513 is made, the maximum annual exclusion would be $20,000 per donee.

| | |
|---|---|
| Compute the gift tax on the total of current and past taxable gifts by using the rates found in Appendix A | $    x,xxx |
| Subtract: The gift tax paid or deemed paid on past taxable gifts | $     xxx |
| Gift tax due on transfers during the current period | $     xxx |

Note that the Federal gift tax, unlike the Federal income tax, is cumulative in effect. Thus, the donor's tax liability will depend on the amount of current taxable gifts *plus* past taxable gifts. From the tax liability so derived can be subtracted the amount of gift tax previously paid or deemed paid on past taxable gifts.

> **Example 4.**  During 1983, D made taxable gifts of $100,000. Her only prior taxable gift was in 1977 and involved property worth $150,000. As a result of the 1977 transfer, D paid a gift tax of $38,800. D's gift tax liability for 1983 would be $32,000 computed as follows:

| | |
|---|---|
| Current gift | $  100,000 |
| Add: All past taxable gifts | 150,000 |
| Tax base | $  250,000 |
| Gift tax on $250,000 as derived from § 2001(c) (see Appendix A) | $   70,800 |
| Less: Gift tax paid on past taxable gifts | 38,800 |
| Gift tax on the 1983 transfer | $   32,000[7] |

Example 4 reflects how the cumulative aspects of the Federal gift tax work out in actual dollars. Had D been able to disregard the past taxable gifts made, she could have based the tax on only the $100,000 of taxable gifts transferred during 1983. Turning to the rates contained in § 2001(c), this would have generated a gift tax of $23,800 instead of the $32,000 actually incurred. Thus, the cumulative aspects of the Federal gift tax, when combined with the progressive nature of the rates, will force additional transfers into higher tax brackets.

Also note that Example 4 dealt with "taxable" gifts. By definition, therefore, the transfers D made (both past and present) have already been adjusted for the annual exclusion and whatever other deductions were allowable.

In arriving at the transfer tax on gifts made after 1976, it is necessary to include taxable gifts made prior to 1977. The effect of this adjustment is to tax the later gifts at a higher rate due to the progressive nature of the unified transfer tax. Since the result is to tax pre-

---

7.  The determination of the gift tax paid on the 1977 transfer and the gift tax due on the 1983 gift has disregarded the effect of the unified transfer tax credit. Such effect is discussed later in this chapter.

1977 gifts twice (i. e., once when made and once when added to post-1976 gifts), a credit is allowed for the tax on the pre-1977 gifts. The credit does not depend upon the amount of gift tax actually paid but is theoretically based on the gift tax that would have been paid had the unified transfer tax applied.[8]

> **Example 5.** Prior to 1977, T made taxable gifts of $500,000 upon which a Federal gift tax of $109,275 was paid (see Appendix A). Assume T makes further taxable gifts of $500,000 in 1983. *Disregarding the effect of the unified transfer tax credit* (see later in this chapter), the unified transfer tax on the 1983 gifts would be determined as follows:

| | |
|---|---:|
| Taxable gifts made in 1983 | $ 500,000 |
| Taxable gifts made prior to 1977 | 500,000 |
| Total taxable gifts | $ 1,000,000 |
| Unified transfer tax on total taxable gifts (see Appendix A) | $ 345,800 |
| Deemed paid tax on taxable gifts made prior to 1977 (see Appendix A) | 155,800 |
| Unified transfer tax on taxable gifts made in 1983 | $ 190,000 |

*The Scheme of the Gift Tax—Transfers Prior to 1977.* Taxable gifts made prior to 1977 were determined in the same manner as those made after 1976 with one major exception: A $30,000 specific exemption was allowed. Such exemption could be used anytime a gift exceeded the annual exclusion and was not offset by either the charitable or marital deduction. A donor, however, had only one $30,000 specific exemption per lifetime.

Pre-1977 taxable gifts were subject to a separate set of rates, such rates being lower than the estate tax rates. The two sets of rates were replaced by the unified transfer tax, and the $30,000 specific exemption (allowed for gift tax purposes) and the $60,000 deduction (allowed for estate tax purposes) were replaced by the unified transfer tax credit.

*Effect of Pre-1977 Gifts on the Federal Estate Tax.* Persons dying prior to 1977 were subject to the Federal estate tax. Property transferred prior to death was subject to the Federal gift tax and, generally, was not subject to the estate tax upon the death of the donor. Exceptions where both the Federal gift tax and the Federal estate tax might apply to the same property were discussed in Chapter 18 and include certain incomplete transfers (§ § 2036 and 2038).

---

**8.** The reason for this "deemed paid" credit is attributable to the fact that the tax rates under the unified transfer tax are higher than those that existed under the separate gift tax. Allowing a credit for the gift tax actually paid on pre-1977 taxable gifts, therefore, would be unfair.

*Effect of Pre-1977 and Post-1976 Gifts on the Unified Transfer Tax at Death.*  Although pre-1977 taxable gifts must be taken into account in determining the tax on post-1976 gifts (refer to Example 5), they are not considered in determining the unified transfer tax at death for persons dying after 1976. Again, exceptions might be certain incomplete transfers under § § 2036 and 2038.

Post-1976 taxable gifts *are* added to the taxable estate in arriving at the unified transfer tax at death applicable to persons dying after 1976.[9] It is therefore extremely important to distinguish between pre-1977 and post-1976 taxable gifts, since one does not affect the unified transfer tax at death while the other does. To mitigate the effect of double taxation, however, the transfer tax paid on post-1976 gifts reduces the transfer tax imposed at death.

> **Example 6.**  Assume the same facts as in Example 5 with the further stipulation that T dies in 1986, leaving a taxable estate of $1,000,000. Again, *disregarding the effect of the unified tax credit,* T's transfer tax at death would be computed as follows:

| | |
|---|---:|
| Taxable estate | $ 1,000,000 |
| Taxable gifts made in 1983 | 500,000 |
| Total gift and death transfers | $ 1,500,000 |
| Unified transfer tax on all transfers (see Appendix A) | $   555,800 |
| Unified transfer tax on taxable gifts made in 1983 (refer to Example 5) | 190,000 |
| Unified transfer tax at death | $   365,800 |

Note that the pre-1977 gifts are not included in determining the transfer tax at death. Also, the unified transfer tax on the taxable gifts made in 1983 (i. e., $190,000) is allowed as a credit against the unified transfer tax on all transfers (i. e., $555,800) to yield a unified transfer tax at death of $365,800.

## TRANSFERS IN GENERAL

Whether or not a transfer will constitute one subject to the Federal gift tax (or the unified transfer tax, as the case may be) will depend upon the application of § § 2511 through 2519 and the Regulations thereunder. Recall, however, that one of the key elements of a gift is a transfer not supported by a full and adequate consideration in money or money's worth. Reg. § 25.2512–8 does provide that "a sale, exchange, or other transfer of property made in the ordinary course of business (a transaction which is bona fide, at arm's length, and free of any donative intent) will be considered as made for an adequate and full consideration in money or money's worth." Thus, whether a trans-

---

**9.**   § 2001(b)(2).

fer takes place in a business setting could make a great deal of difference for gift tax purposes.

**Example 7.** D loans money to S in connection with a business venture. About a year later, D forgives part of the loan. D probably has not made a gift to S if they are unrelated parties.[10]

**Example 8.** Assume the same facts as in Example 7 except that D and S are father and son and no business venture is involved. If the loan itself was not, in fact, a disguised gift, the later forgiveness will probably be treated as a gift.[11]

Do not conclude, however, that the presence of *some* consideration may be enough to preclude Federal gift tax consequences. Again, the answer may rest on whether the transfer occurred in a business setting.

**Example 9.** D sells S some real estate for $40,000. Unknown to D, the property contains valuable mineral deposits and is really worth $100,000. D may have made a bad business deal, but he has not made a gift to S of $60,000.

**Example 10.** Assume the same facts as in Example 9 except that D and S are father and son. In addition, D is very much aware of the fact that the property is really worth $100,000. D has made a gift to S of $60,000.

Transfers to political organizations [as defined in § 527(e)(1)] made after May 7, 1974, are exempt from the application of the Federal gift tax.[12] This change in the Code made unnecessary the previous practice whereby candidates for public office established multiple campaign committees in order to maximize the number of annual exclusions available to their contributors. As noted later, an annual exclusion of $10,000 (previously $3,000) for each donee passes free of the Federal gift tax.

Be careful to distinguish between lifetime (i. e., inter vivos) and death (i. e., testamentary) transfers.

**Example 11.** D buys a U. S. bond which he registers as follows: "D, payable to S upon D's death." There is no gift when D buys the bond; S has received only a mere expectancy (i. e., to obtain ownership of the bond at D's death). Anytime prior to his death, D may redeem or otherwise dispose of the bond and, thereby, cut off

---

**10.** The forgiveness could, however, result in taxable income to S under § 61(a)(12).
**11.** Loans between relatives are highly suspect and, on many occasions, have been treated as gifts. The issue usually arises when the creditor tries to claim a bad debt loss and the IRS contends that a bona fide debt never existed.
**12.** § 2501(a)(5).

S's interest. On D's death there is no gift because the bond passes to S by testamentary disposition.[13]

**Example 12.**  D purchases an insurance policy on his own life (face value of $100,000); he designates S as the beneficiary. Until his death, D remains the owner of the policy and pays all premiums thereon. In accordance with the reasoning set forth in Example 11, no gift to S has been made either when the policy was purchased or when D paid any of the premiums thereon. On D's death, the $100,000 proceeds pass to S as a testamentary and not an inter vivos transfer.[14]

## JOINT OWNERSHIP

*General Rule.*  Whether or not a gift results when property is transferred into some form of joint ownership will depend on the consideration furnished by each of the contributing parties for the ownership interest thereby acquired.[15]

**Example 13.**  D and S purchase real estate as tenants in common, each furnishing $20,000 of the $40,000 cost. If each is an equal owner in the property, no gift has occurred.

**Example 14.**  Assume the same facts as in Example 13 except that of the $40,000 purchase price, D furnishes $30,000 and S only $10,000. If each is an equal owner in the property, D has made a gift to S of $10,000.

**Example 15.**  M purchases real estate for $240,000, the title to the property being listed as follows: "M, D, and S as joint tenants with the right of survivorship." If under state law the mother (M), the daughter (D), and the son (S) are deemed to be equal owners in the property and each has the right of severance,[16] M will be treated as having made a gift of $80,000 to D and $80,000 to S.

*Exceptions.*  There exist several principal exceptions to the general rule that the creation of a joint ownership with disproportionate interests resulting from unequal consideration will trigger gift treatment. First, if the transfer involves a joint bank account, there is no gift at the time of the contribution. If a gift occurs, it will be when the noncontributing party withdraws the funds provided by the other

---

13.  It will be included in D's gross estate under § 2033 (property in which the decedent had an interest).
14.  The proceeds would be included in D's gross estate under § 2042(2). Refer to Chapter 18.
15.  For a description of the various forms of joint ownership, refer to Chapter 18.
16.  The right of severance allows a joint tenant to dispose of his or her interest and thereby destroy the joint tenancy. In a tenancy by the entirety (i. e., a joint tenancy between husband and wife) severance can be accomplished only by the consent of the parties.

joint tenant. Second, the same rule applies to the purchase of U. S. savings bonds. Again, any gift tax consequences will be postponed until such time as the noncontributing party appropriates some or all of the proceeds for his or her individual use.

> **Example 16.** D deposits $20,000 in a bank account under the names of D and S as joint tenants. Both D and S have the right to withdraw funds from the account without the other's consent or joinder. D has not made a gift to S when the account is established.

> **Example 17.** Assume the same facts as in Example 16. At some later date, S withdraws $5,000 from the account for her own use. At this point, D has made a gift to S of $5,000.

> **Example 18.** D purchases a U. S. savings bond which he registers in the names of D and S. After D dies, S redeems the bond. No gift takes place when D buys the bond. In addition, S's redemption is not treated as a gift because the bond passed to her by testamentary disposition (i. e., S acquired the bond by virtue of surviving D) and not through a lifetime transfer.[17]

*Husband and Wife Situations.* Prior to 1982, the creation of a joint tenancy or a tenancy by the entirety between husband and wife was governed by a labyrinth of intricate rules. In addition to the exceptions noted above (i. e., joint bank accounts and ownership of certain U. S. bonds), the important point was that a gift normally did not result if real estate was the subject of the tenancy. The parties, however, could make a special election to treat the creation of such a tenancy as a gift.[18] If the election was made, only one-half of the value of the realty would be included in the gross estate of the first spouse to die.

In an effort to simplify this area of the law and to further recognize husband and wife as a single economic unit, the Economic Recovery Tax Act of 1981 made substantial changes for joint tenancies between spouses and tenancies by the entirety created by gift after 1981. With the advent of the unlimited marital deduction, special rules no longer were considered to be necessary.[19]

> **Example 19.** H purchases real estate for $300,000 using his own funds. Title to the property is listed as "H and W as tenants by the entirety." If the purchase occurred after 1981 and H and W are husband and wife, no taxable gift results due to the operation of the marital deduction (see later in the chapter).

---

**17.** The fair market value of the bond would be includible in D's gross estate under § 2040.

**18.** § 2515(c) prior to revocation by the Economic Recovery Tax Act of 1981.

**19.** The Economic Recovery Tax Act of 1981 revoked § § 2515 and 2515A.

*Relationship to the Federal Estate Tax.*  Nonspousal joint tenancies continue to be governed by the general rule of § 2040(a).[20] Thus, the full value of the property will be included in the gross estate of the first joint tenant to die unless the survivor(s) can prove a contribution to the original purchase price. It could be, therefore, that a transfer that was subject to the gift tax upon the creation of the tenancy also will be subject to the estate tax upon the death of the tenant furnishing the original consideration. This seemingly harsh result is mitigated by allowing against the estate tax a credit for the gift tax previously paid.

Spousal joint tenancies and tenancies by the entirety (where death occurs after 1981) compel the inclusion of one-half of the value of the property in the gross estate of the first spouse to die.

## LIFE INSURANCE

The mere purchase of a life insurance contract with the designation of someone else as the beneficiary thereunder does not constitute a gift. As long as the purchaser still owns the policy, nothing has really passed to the beneficiary. Even on the death of the insured-owner, no gift takes place; the proceeds going to the beneficiary constitute a testamentary and not a lifetime transfer.[21] But consider the following possibility:

> **Example 20.**  D purchases an insurance policy on his own life which he transfers to S. D retains no interest in the policy (such as the power to change beneficiaries or to revest in himself or his estate the economic benefits of the policy). Under these circumstances, D has made a gift to S. Furthermore, if D continues to pay the premiums on the transferred policy, each payment will constitute a separate gift.

Under certain conditions, the death of the insured might represent a gift to the beneficiary of part or all of the proceeds. This may prove true when the owner of the policy is not the insured.

> **Example 21.**  D owns an insurance policy on the life of S with T as the designated beneficiary. Up until the time of S's death, D retained the right to change the beneficiary of the policy. The proceeds paid to T by the insurance company by reason of S's death constitute a gift from D to T.[22]

> **Example 22.**  H and W live in a community property state. With community funds H purchases an insurance policy on his own life

---

20.  Refer to Chapter 18.
21.  Such a transfer would be included in the insured-owner's gross estate under § 2042.
22.  *Goodman v. Comm.,* 46–1 USTC ¶ 10,275, 34 AFTR 1534, 156 F.2d 218 (CA–2, 1946).

with a face amount of $100,000 and designates S as the revocable beneficiary. On H's death, the proceeds of the policy are paid to S. If, under state law, H's death makes the transfer by W complete, W has made a gift to S of $50,000. Since the policy was held as community property, W was deemed to be the owner of one-half of the policy.[23]

## CERTAIN PROPERTY SETTLEMENTS—§ 2516

Normally, the settlement of certain marital rights is not regarded as being for consideration in money or money's worth and is therefore subject to the Federal gift tax.[24] As a special exception to this general approach, Congress saw fit to enact § 2516. Under this provision, transfers of property interests made under the terms of a written agreement between spouses in settlement of their marital or property rights are deemed to be for adequate consideration and are thereby exempt from the Federal gift tax if a final decree of divorce is obtained within two years after entering the agreement. Likewise, excluded are transfers to provide a reasonable allowance for the support of minor children (including legally adopted children) of a marriage. The agreement need not be approved by the divorce decree.

> **Example 23.** In settlement of her marital rights and pursuant to a written agreement, H transfers to W property worth $200,000. One month later, H and W are divorced. The requirements of § 2516 are satisfied; no gift results from the transfer.

Do not conclude, however, that certain property settlements incident to a divorce are tax-free. Although § 2516 may eliminate the application of the Federal gift tax, such settlements may carry severe income tax consequences.

## DEDUCTIONS AND EXCLUSIONS

As mentioned in an earlier section of this chapter, the deductions and exclusions for arriving at taxable gifts (as defined by § 2503) are as follows:

1. Charitable (§ 2522).
2. Marital (§ 2523).
3. Annual exclusion [§ 2503(b)].

In addition, the election to split gifts by husband and wife under § 2513 can lead to a doubling up of the annual exclusion (see item 3).

All of these items are discussed in the sections to follow.

---

**23.** Only one-half of the proceeds of the policy ($50,000) would be included in H's gross estate under § 2042.

**24.** See Reg. § 25.2512–8 and Example 1 in this chapter.

*Charitable Deduction.* There may be deducted from the total amount of gifts made during the year all gifts included and made to or for the use of:

1. The United States, any state, or any political subdivision thereof, or the District of Columbia, for exclusively public purposes.
2. Any corporation, trust, community chest (i. e., United Fund), fund or foundations, organized and operated exclusively for religious, charitable, scientific, literary, or educational purposes, if no part of the net earnings of the organization inures to the benefit of any private shareholder or individual, and no substantial part of its activities is carrying on propaganda, or otherwise attempting to influence legislation and which does not participate in or intervene in any political campaign on behalf of any candidate for public office.
3. A fraternal society, order, or association, operating under the lodge system, provided the gifts are to be used by the society, order, or association exclusively for one or more of the purposes set forth under item 2.
4. Any post or organization of war veterans or auxiliary unit or society thereof, if organized in the U.S. or any of its possessions, and if no part of its net earnings inures to the benefit of any private shareholder or individual.

As mentioned in Chapter 18, the above rules parallel those applicable to charitable transfers for death tax purposes under § 2055. Though similar to the rules governing charitable deductions for Federal income tax purposes, there exist two important exceptions. Donations to certain nonprofit cemetery associations qualify under the income tax but not under the death and gift tax.[25] Foreign charities may qualify under the death and gift tax but not under the income tax.[26]

*Marital Deduction—In General.* Like its counterpart in the estate tax area, the marital deduction for gift tax purposes was designed to place common law jurisdictions on a parity with what transpires under a community property system. Due to the progressive nature of the transfer tax rates, the estate tax, for example, on $1,000,000 is much more than twice the estate tax on $500,000. Meaningful estate planning, therefore, generally called for an equalization of the estates of married persons. In a community property state, this goal normally is achieved as a matter of course, since the earnings of one spouse belonged one-half to the other spouse. In a common law state, however, the earnings of the working spouse are his or her separate property. Thus, wealth tends to concentrate in the estate of the working

---

**25.** Compare § 170(c)(5) with § § 2055 and 2522.
**26.** Compare the wording of § 170(c)(2)(A) with that of § § 2055(a)(2) and 2522(a)(2).

spouse. The marital deduction, therefore, facilitated interspousal transfers as a means of equalizing the estates of married persons living in common law jurisdictions.

Until 1982, the § 2525 marital deduction generally was limited to 50 percent of the amount passing from one spouse to another. In 1981, Congress saw no need for continuing this artificial limitation, although it had historical justification for doing so (refer to the discussion above), and chose to look upon married persons as a single economic unit. Consistent with this new approach, a full marital deduction should be allowed for all qualifying interspousal transfers whether they be by inter vivos or testamentary means. Consequently, the Economic Recovery Tax Act of 1981 amends § 2525(a) so as to remove any percentage limitation on the amount of the marital deduction allowed for gift tax purposes.[27] Amazingly enough, the unlimited marital deduction also applies to community property that is converted to the separate property of one of the spouses.

> **Example 24.** H transfers to his wife (W) property worth $500,000. If the transfer occurred in 1981, H's marital deduction is $250,000. If the gift took place in 1982, the marital deduction becomes $500,000.

> **Example 25.** Assume the same facts as in Example 24 except that the $500,000 in property was part of their community. If the transfer occurred in 1981, H receives no marital deduction. If the gift took place in 1982, the marital deduction becomes $250,000 (the portion of H's share of the community which he converted to W's separate property).

*The Annual Exclusion—In General.* The first $10,000 of gifts made to any one person during any calendar year (except gifts of future interests in property) is excluded in determining the total amount of gifts for the year.[28] The annual exclusion is applied to all gifts of a present interest made during the calendar year in the order in which made until the $10,000 exclusion per donee is exhausted. For a gift in trust, each beneficiary of the trust is treated as a separate person for purposes of the exclusion.

A future interest may be defined as one which will come into being (as to use, possession, or enjoyment) at some future date. Examples of future interests would include such possessory rights, whether vested or contingent, as remainder and reversionary interests that are commonly encountered when property is transferred to a trust. On

---

**27.** For the changes made to § 2056 (i. e., the estate tax version of the marital deduction), refer to Chapter 18.

**28.** § 2503(b). Prior to 1982, the amount of the exclusion was $3,000. To eliminate many of the gifts that had to be reported, Congress in the Economic Recovery Tax Act of 1981 raised the exclusion to $10,000.

the other hand, a present interest is an unrestricted right to the immediate use, possession, or enjoyment of property or of the income therefrom.

> **Example 26.**  During the current year, D makes the following cash gifts: $8,000 to R and $12,000 to S. D may claim an annual exclusion of $8,000 with respect to R and 10,000 with respect to S.[29]

> **Example 27.**  By a lifetime gift D transfers property to a trust with a life estate (with income payable annually) to R and remainder upon R's death to S. D has made two gifts: one to R of a life estate and one to S of a remainder interest. The life estate is a present interest; therefore, it qualifies for the annual exclusion. The remainder interest granted to S is a future interest and does not qualify for the exclusion. Note that S's interest does not come into being until some future date (i. e., on the death of R).

Although Example 27 indicates that the gift of an income interest is a present interest, this may not always prove to be the case. If there is a possibility that the income beneficiary may not receive the immediate enjoyment of the property, then the transfer is one of a future interest.

> **Example 28.**  Assume the same facts as in Example 27 except that the income from the trust need not be payable annually to R but may, at the trustee's discretion, be accumulated and added to corpus. Since R's right to receive the income from the trust is conditioned on the trustee's discretion, it is not a present interest and no annual exclusion will be allowed. The mere possibility of diversion is enough; it would not matter if the trustee never exercised his or her discretion to accumulate and did, in fact, distribute the trust income to R annually.

*The Annual Exclusion—Trust for Minors.*  Code § 2503(c) offers an important exception to the future interest rules discussed above. Under this provision, a transfer for the benefit of a person who has not attained the age of 21 years on the date of the gift may be considered a gift of a present interest even though the minor is not given the unrestricted right to the immediate use, possession, or enjoyment of the property. In order for the § 2503(c) exception to apply, the following conditions must be satisfied:

—Both the property and its income may be expended by or for the benefit of the minor before he or she attains the age of 21.

---

**29.**  The $2,000 passing to S in excess of the $10,000 annual exclusion might not have generated any gift tax liability to D by virtue of the unified transfer tax credit under § 2505.

—Any portion of the property or its income not expended by the minor's attainment of age 21 shall pass to him or her at that time.

—If the minor dies before attaining the age of 21, the property and its income will be payable either to his or her estate or as he or she may appoint under a general power of appointment.

Thus, the § 2503(c) exception would allow a trustee to accumulate income on behalf of a minor beneficiary without converting the income interest to a future interest.

> **Example 29.** D places property in trust, income payable to S until he reaches 21, remainder to S or S's estate. Under the terms of the trust instrument, the trustee is empowered to accumulate the trust income or apply it towards S's benefit. In either event, the accumulated income and corpus must be paid to S whenever he reaches 21 years of age or to whomever he designates in his will if he dies before reaching such age. The conditions of § 2503(c) are satisfied; therefore, D's transfer qualifies for the annual exclusion. S's interest is a present interest.

*The Specific Exemption—Transfers by Gift Prior to 1977.* Code § 2521 allowed a lifetime exemption of $30,000 per donor. At the option of the donor, the exemption could be taken in the full amount in a single calendar quarter, or it could be spread over a period of quarters or years in such amounts as he or she saw fit.

The relationship between the annual exclusion and the specific exemption needs to be clarified. The annual exclusion is justified by the realization that gifts will occur on a periodic basis, particularly among family members. To impose a gift tax on smaller amounts not only would be unfair but would cause a severe problem of noncompliance by taxpayers. Apparently, Congress originally chose $3,000 as an arbitrary cutoff point. In addition, there is much to be said for the notion that a donor should be allowed a specific exemption (as was true of the Federal estate tax) for a certain amount of otherwise taxable gifts during his or her lifetime. Thus, it was determined that a donor could make gifts, in excess of the annual exclusion, of up to $30,000 per lifetime without incurring a gift tax liability.

*The Unified Tax Credit—Transfers by Gift After 1976.* Effective for transfers by gift after 1976, the Tax Reform Act of 1976 eliminated the $30,000 specific exemption and substituted a credit to be applied against the tax liability. The maximum credit is phased in as shown below:[30]

---

**30.** §§ 2505(a) and (b).

| Year or Period | Amount of Credit | Equivalent Taxable Gift |
|---|---|---|
| January 1, 1977, to<br>June 30, 1977 | $  6,000 | $  30,000 |
| July 1, 1977, to<br>December 31, 1977 | 30,000 | 120,667 |
| 1978 | 34,000 | 134,000 |
| 1979 | 38,000 | 147,333 |
| 1980 | 42,500 | 161,563 |
| 1981 | 47,000 | 175,625 |
| 1982 | 62,800 | 225,000 |
| 1983 | 79,300 | 275,000 |
| 1984 | 96,300 | 325,000 |
| 1985 | 121,800 | 400,000 |
| 1986 | 155,800 | 500,000 |
| 1987 and later | 192,800 | 600,000 |

With the exception of the period from January 1, 1977, to June 30, 1977, the credit allowed for the gift tax is the same as that available against the estate tax (refer to Chapter 18). Also note that the credit offsets the gift tax directly and, unlike the previous $30,000 specific exemption, is not considered in arriving at the amount of the taxable gift involved.

**Example 30.**  In 1982, M, a widow, makes a gift of $160,000 cash to her daughter. M's taxable gift on this transfer would be $150,000 [i. e., $160,000 (the amount of the gift) − $10,000 (the annual exclusion allowed)]. Turning to Appendix A and assuming M has never made any prior taxable gifts or utilized her $30,000 specific exemption, the transfer tax on the $150,000 taxable gift is $38,800. Since the tax does not exceed the $62,800 unified transfer tax credit applicable in 1982, M has no gift tax liability on the 1982 gift.

**Example 31.**  Assume the same facts as in Example 30 with the further condition that M makes another cash gift of $160,000 to her daughter in 1983. At this point M's gift tax liability would be determined as follows:

| | |
|---|---|
| Prior taxable gifts (see Example 30) | $ 150,000 |
| Taxable gift made in 1983 [i. e., $160,000<br>(the amount of the gift) − $10,000 (the<br>annual exclusion allowed)] | 150,000 |
| Total past and present taxable gifts | $ 300,000 |
| Unified transfer tax on past and present<br>taxable gifts as determined by the use of<br>Appendix A [$70,800 + (34% × $50,000)] | $  87,800 |
| Less:  Unified transfer tax credit appli-<br>cable to 1983 | 79,300 |
| Gift tax due on the 1983 transfer | $   8,500 |

To the extent that the $30,000 specific exemption has been claimed on gifts made prior to September 9, 1976, it will have no effect on the unified transfer tax credit available for transfers by gift or death after 1976. If, however, the $30,000 exemption was used on gifts made during the period September 9, 1976, through December 31, 1976, the unified transfer tax is reduced by 20 percent of the exemption so utilized.[31]

> **Example 32.** Net of the annual exclusion, D, a widower, made gifts of $10,000 in June of 1976 and $20,000 in December of 1976. Assume D has never used any of his specific exemption and chooses to use the full $30,000 to cover the 1976 gifts. Under these circumstances, the unified transfer tax credit will be reduced by $4,000 (i. e., 20% × $20,000).

*Gift Splitting.* In order to understand the reason for the gift-splitting election of § 2513, consider the following situations:

> **Example 33.** H and W are husband and wife and reside in Indiana, a common law state. H has been the only breadwinner in the family, and W has no significant amount of property of her own. Neither has made any prior taxable gifts or has used the $30,000 specific exemption previously available. In 1983, H makes a gift to S of $570,000. Presuming the election to split gifts did not exist, H's gift tax result is as follows:

| | |
|---|---:|
| Amount of gift | $ 570,000 |
| Less:   The annual exclusion allowed H | 10,000 |
| Taxable gift | $ 560,000 |
| Gift tax on $560,000 per Appendix A | |
|      [$155,800 + (37% × $60,000)] | $ 178,000 |
| Less:   Unified transfer tax credit | |
|          [§ 2505(b)] for 1983 | 79,300 |
| Gift tax liability | $ 98,700 |

> **Example 34.** Assume the same facts as in Example 33 except that H and W always have resided in California. Even though H is the sole breadwinner, the gift to S probably involves community property.[32] If this is the case, the gift tax result is worked out below:

---

31. § 2505(c).
32. Income from personal services generally is community income in a community property state.

|  | H | W |
|---|---|---|
| Amount of the gifts (50% of $570,000) | $ 285,000 | $ 285,000 |
| Less:  The annual exclusion allowed H and W | 10,000 | 10,000 |
| Taxable gifts | $ 275,000 | $ 275,000 |
| Gift tax on $275,000 as per Appendix A [$70,800 + (34% × $25,000)] | $ 79,300 | $ 79,300 |
| Less:  Unified transfer tax credit [§ 2505(b)] for 1983 | 79,300 | 79,300 |
| Gift tax liability | $ –0– | $ –0– |

By comparing the results of Examples 33 and 34, it should be quite apparent to the reader that married donors residing in community property jurisdictions possessed a significant gift tax advantage over those residing in common law states. To rectify this inequity, the Revenue Act of 1948[33] incorporated into the Code the predecessor to § 2513. Under this Section, a gift made by a person to someone other than his or her spouse may be considered for Federal gift tax purposes as having been made one-half by each spouse. Returning to Example 33, this means H and W could treat the gift passing to S as being made one-half by each of them, in spite of the fact that the cash may have belonged to H. Consequently, the parties were able to achieve the same tax result as that outlined in Example 34.

In order to split gifts, the spouses must be legally married to each other at the time of the gift. If they are divorced later in the calendar quarter, they may still split the gift if neither marries anyone else during that quarter. They both must signify on their separate gift tax returns their consent to have all gifts made in that calendar quarter split between them. In addition, both must be citizens or residents of the United States on the date of the gift. A gift from one spouse to the other spouse cannot be split. Such a gift might, however, be eligible for the marital deduction allowed by § 2523.

The § 2513 election to split gifts would not be necessary when husband and wife transfer community property to a third party. It would, however, be available if the subject of the gift consisted of the separate property of one of the spouses. The election, then, is not limited to residents of common law states.

## PROCEDURAL MATTERS

Having determined what transfers are subject to the Federal gift tax and the various deductions and exclusions available to the donor,

---

**33.** Recall that this Act was the same one that provided for the marital deduction and certain other adjustments of a similar nature (e. g., the income-splitting benefits of a joint return as reflected by the tax rates applicable to married persons filing jointly).

consideration should be accorded to the procedural aspects of the tax. The sections to follow discuss the return itself, the due dates for filing and paying the tax, and other related matters.

*The Federal Gift Tax Return.* For transfers by gift after 1981, a Form 709 (U. S. Gift Tax Return) must be filed whenever the gifts for any one calendar year exceed the annual exclusion or involve a gift of a future interest. Regardless of amount, however, transfers between spouses which are offset by the new unlimited marital deduction do not require the filing of a Form 709.[34]

> **Example 35.** In 1983, D makes five gifts, each in the amount of $10,000, to his five children. If the gifts do not involve future interests, a Form 709 need not be filed to report the transfers.

> **Example 36.** During 1983, M makes a gift of $20,000 cash of her separate property to her daughter. In order to double the amount of the annual exclusion allowed, F (M's husband) is willing to split the gift. Since the § 2513 election can be made only on a gift tax return, a Form 709 needs to be filed. This is the case in spite of the fact that no gift tax will be due as a result of the transfer.

> **Example 37.** In 1983, H makes a gift of $200,000 in securities to his wife. No Form 709 need be filed to report this transfer, as it will be offset by the § 2523 marital deduction.

Presuming a gift tax return is due, it must be filed on or before the fifteenth day of the April following the year of the gift.[35] As is the case with other Federal taxes, when the due date falls on Saturday, Sunday, or a legal holiday, the date for filing the return is the next business day. Note that the filing requirements for Form 709 have no correlation to the accounting year used by a donor for Federal income tax purposes. Thus, a fiscal year taxpayer would have to follow the April 15 rule as to any reportable gifts.

Gift tax returns should be filed with the District Director for the district in which the donor's legal residence or principal place of business is located. If the donor has no legal residence or principal place of business in an Internal Revenue District (i. e., a nonresident), the return must be filed with the Internal Revenue Service Center, Philadelphia, PA 19255.

The return must be accompanied by certain documents pertaining to the determination of tax liability. These include copies of instruments executed in connection with transfers of property, statements by insurance companies on Form 938 in connection with

---

**34.** § 6019(a)(2) as amended by the Economic Recovery Tax Act of 1981.
**35.** § 6075(b)(1).

every insurance policy listed on the return, copies of appraisals of real property, etc. If the return lists shares of stock in closely-held corporations, documents must be submitted pertinent to their valuation, such as balance sheets, profit and loss statements for each of the five years preceding the valuation date, and statements of dividends paid during that period.

*Extensions of Time and Payment of Tax.* If sufficient reason is shown, the Internal Revenue Service Centers are authorized to grant reasonable extensions of time for filing of the return.[36] Unless the donor is abroad, no extension in excess of six months may be granted. The application must be made before the due date of the return and must contain a full report of the causes for the delay. For a calendar year taxpayer, an extension of time for filing an income tax return also extends the time for filing the Form 709.[37] An extension of time to file the return does not extend the time for payment of the tax.

The tax shown on the gift tax return is to be paid by the donor at the time and place fixed for the filing of the return.[38] A reasonable extension of time, not to exceed six months (unless the donor is abroad), may be granted by the Service Center, at the request of the donor, for the payment of the tax shown on the return.[39] The extension will be granted only upon a satisfactory showing that payment on the due date will result in undue hardship. The term "undue hardship" means more than inconvenience to the taxpayer. It must appear that substantial financial loss (e. g., loss due to the sale of property at a sacrificial price) will result to the donor from making the gift tax payment on the due date. If a market exists, the sale of the property at the current market price is not ordinarily considered as resulting in an undue hardship.

Interest at the rate of 11 percent (for the period July 1, 1983–December 31, 1983) must be paid on any amount of tax that is not paid on or before the last date prescribed for the payment of the tax.[40] In addition, a penalty of one-half of one percent per month of the unpaid balance (up to a maximum of 25 percent) will be imposed unless the failure to pay was for reasonable cause.[41] A penalty is also imposed for failure to file a gift tax return.[42]

---

**36.** § 6081.
**37.** § 6057(b)(2).
**38.** § 6151.
**39.** § 6161(a)(1).
**40.** §§ 6621 and 6622. Interest accrues at 16% for tax liabilities arising and existing before July 1, 1983, and after December 31, 1982. Prior rates were as follows: 20% (February 1, 1982–December 31, 1982), 12% (February 1, 1980–January 31, 1982), 6% (February 1, 1978–January 31, 1980), 7% (February 1, 1976–January 31, 1978), 9% (July 1, 1975–January 31, 1976), and 6% before July 1975. The rate is now determined twice a year.
**41.** § 6651(a)(2).
**42.** § 6651(a)(1).

# CERTAIN STATE TRANSFER TAXES

## IN GENERAL

In addition to the transfer taxes levied by the Federal government (i. e., estate and gift taxes), some states impose comparable taxes. This may seem unfair because of the double tax result. But consider the area of income taxation; the same income may be subjected to tax at the Federal and state levels and even, in some cases, at the city or local government level.

The effect of multiple death taxes is somewhat mitigated by the credits allowed against the Federal estate tax under § 2011 (i. e., credit for state death taxes) and § 2014 (i. e., credit for foreign death taxes). However, there exists no like form of relief in the area of gift taxation. Thus, lifetime transfers could be subject to both Federal and state gift taxation with no credit or deduction available.[43]

## STATE DEATH TAXES

All states except Nevada levy some type of death tax. These laws follow one of two forms:

—An inheritance tax imposed on the right of the heirs to receive property from a decedent.

—An estate tax imposed on the decedent's right to pass property to his or her heirs.

*Inheritance Taxes.* Approximately one-half of the states levy an inheritance tax (see Figure I on page 19-24). Each law is, of course, different, but some of the following characteristics are common to most:

1. The heirs are divided into classes in accordance with their relationship to the decedent. Those most closely related, such as surviving spouses and lineal descendants, are granted larger exemptions than those more distantly related. Persons not related to the decedent, known as "strangers," receive little or no exemption from the tax.

2. In most cases the rates are progressive within a particular class. A minority of states impose a flat rate for each class.

---

**43.** The same absence of relief exists in the international area. Thus, a donor could be subject to a foreign and a U. S. gift tax on the same transfer. The one exception might be Japan and Australia, since the U. S. has gift tax conventions (i. e., treaties) with these countries. The effect of a gift tax convention, of course, would be to prevent such double taxation.

3. Life insurance proceeds payable by reason of the death of the insured are exempt, in whole or in part, if not received by the estate. In many states the exemption is limited to a maximum amount, such as the first $40,000.

4. The prior Federal exemption of $60,000 and the new unified transfer tax credit generally are not allowed. However, see the individual exemptions available to each heir as noted under item 1.

5. The usual Federal estate tax deductions are not allowed since the inheritance tax is not imposed upon the estate.

6. Many laws authorize exclusions for property passing from the decedent to his or her survivor because of the right of survivorship, as would be the case with joint tenancies and tenancies by the entirety.

7. The surviving spouse's share of community property is not taxed. This also is frequently true of the surviving spouse's statutory allowance.

8. Bequests to charitable organizations are not taxed. In some states, this exclusion does not cover foreign organizations (i. e., those located in other states and outside the United States).

9. A few states permit a small discount, perhaps five percent, for early payment of the tax. All provide for interest and penalties in the event of late filing and/or late payment.

10. The alternate valuation date election usually is not available. Thus, the date of death value controls for inheritance tax purposes. If the state imposes an income tax, the basis of property inherited from a decedent will be determined by the date of death value.

11. Although the inheritance tax is imposed on the heir, its collection and payment to the state or local authority usually is the responsibility of the executor or administrator of the estate. The executor may become personally liable for the tax if he or she fails to deduct it from the estate assets distributed to heirs.

Most of the states levying an inheritance tax also provide for a special tax to be absorbed by the estate in the event that the maximum Federal estate tax credit for state death taxes paid is not reached (see § 2011 and the discussion in Chapter 18). This special tax does not usually come into play, since the sum of all inheritance taxes paid almost always exceeds the credit allowed.

*State Estate Taxes.* About one-half of the states impose a death tax on the estate rather than on the heir (see Figure I on the following page). In several states, these statutes are quite simple and merely provide for the estate to pay whatever estate tax credit is allowed by § 2011. In other states, however, a separate set of rules has been set up, most of which are patterned after the Federal estate tax. Rates and exemptions are characteristically lower, and whatever deductions are allowed must be adjusted when the probate estate includes property located out of the state.

To a considerable extent, the similarity between the Federal estate tax and the state's version depends on when the latter was enacted or last revised. Differences have developed over the years because the state's estate tax has not been amended to keep pace with Federal changes.

*Jurisdiction.* In many cases, a decedent's property may be located in more than one state. The following guidelines are generally observed to determine which death tax applies:

—Real estate and tangible personal property, which includes currency, can be taxed only by the state in which they are located.

—Intangible property, such as stocks and bonds, can be taxed by the state in which it is located and by the state in which the owner was domiciled at the time of his or her death. Frequently, however, states have entered into interstate compacts with each other to prevent the imposition of double death taxes. Under such arrangements, the state in which the property is located will defer to the state of domicile if the latter extends the same privilege to its own citizens.

The domicile of a decedent is a matter to be decided under state law. Unfortunately, it is not impossible to encounter situations where a particular individual is deemed to be domiciled in more than one state at the time of his or her death.

## STATE GIFT TAXES

The 10 states imposing a gift tax are Colorado, Delaware, Louisiana, New York, North Carolina, Oregon, Rhode Island, South Carolina, Tennessee, and Wisconsin.

Most of these laws provide for lifetime exemptions, annual exclusions, and exempt charitable transfers. Like the Federal gift tax, the state taxes are cumulative in effect. But unlike the Federal statute, the amount of the tax depends on the relationship between donor and donee. Thus, larger exclusions and lower rates may apply when the donor and donee are more closely related to each other.

## Figure I
### STATE INHERITANCE, ESTATE, AND GIFT TAX LAWS

| STATE | Inheritance Tax | Additional Estate Tax for Federal Credit | Estate Tax | Estate Tax for Federal Credit Only | Gift Tax |
|---|---|---|---|---|---|
| Alabama | | | | x | |
| Alaska | | | | x | |
| Arizona | | | x | | |
| Arkansas | | | x | | |
| California | | | | x | |
| Colorado | | | | x | x |
| Connecticut | x | x | | | |
| Delaware | x | x | | | x |
| Florida | | | | x | |
| Georgia | | | x | | |
| Hawaii | x | x | | | |
| Idaho | x | x | | | |
| Illinois | | | | x | |
| Indiana | x | x | | | |
| Iowa | x | x | | | |
| Kansas | x | x | | | |
| Kentucky | x | x | | | |
| Louisiana | x | x | | | x |
| Maine | x | x | | | |
| Maryland | x | x | | | |
| Massachusetts | | | x | | |
| Michigan | x | x | | | |
| Minnesota | | x | x | | |
| Mississippi | | | x | | |
| Missouri | x | x | | | |
| Montana | x | x | | | |
| Nebraska | x | x | | | |
| Nevada | | | | | |
| New Hampshire | x | x | | | |
| New Jersey | x | x | | | |
| New Mexico | | | | x | |
| New York | | x | x | | x |
| North Carolina | x | x | | | x |
| North Dakota | | | | x | |
| Ohio | | x | x | | |
| Oklahoma | | x | x | | x |
| Oregon | x | x | | | x |
| Pennsylvania | x | x | | | |
| Rhode Island | x | x | x | | x |
| South Carolina | | x | x | | x |
| South Dakota | x | | | | |
| Tennessee | x | x | | | x |
| Texas | | | | x | |
| Utah | | | | x | |
| Vermont | | | | x | |
| Virginia | | | | x | |
| Washington | | | | x | |
| West Virginia | x | x | | | |
| Wisconsin | x | x | | | x |
| Wyoming | | | | x | |

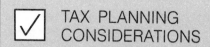

**TAX PLANNING CONSIDERATIONS**

Prior to 1977 there existed two sets of tax rates applicable to transfers for insufficient consideration. Since the gift tax rates were lower than the estate tax rates, this, by itself, placed a premium on lifetime giving as a means of reducing the overall tax burden. After 1976, however, the estate tax savings from a lifetime gift usually will be limited to the appreciation on the property that develops after the transfer is made. This result materializes because transfers by gift and by death are now subject to the same set of rates [i. e., the uniform transfer tax of § 2001(c)]. Also, taxable gifts made after 1976 must be added to the taxable estate in arriving at the amount of the estate tax.[44]

As to taxable gifts that generate a tax, consideration must be given to the time value to the donor of the gift taxes paid. Since the donor loses the use of these funds, the expected interval between a gift (the imposition of the gift tax) and death (the imposition of the death tax) might make the gift less attractive from an economic standpoint. On the plus side, however, is the estate tax savings that would result from any gift tax paid. Since these funds are no longer included in the gross estate of the donor (except as noted later for gifts within three years of death made after 1976), the estate tax thereon is avoided.

Gifts made after 1976 do, nevertheless, possess distinct advantages. First, and often most important, income from the property will generally be shifted to the donee. If the donee is in a lower bracket than the donor, the family unit will save on income taxes. Second, the proper spacing of gifts can further cut down the Federal gift tax by maximizing the number of annual exclusions available. Third, all states but one impose some type of death tax, but only a minority impose a gift tax. Thus, a gift might completely avoid a state transfer tax.

## SELECTING THE RIGHT PROPERTY FOR LIFETIME GIVING

*Income Tax Consequences to the Donor.* Presuming lifetime giving is desired, great care should be exercised in selecting the property to be given away. Of initial importance might be any income tax consequences to the donor generated by the gift.

**Example 38.** Last year, D sold real estate (basis of $40,000) to P (an unrelated party) for $100,000 receiving $20,000 in cash and P's note for $80,000. On a timely filed return, D did not elect out

---

44. Code § 2012 does, however, provide that any gift tax paid on such gift shall be credited against the transfer tax at death.

of the installment method of reporting the gain on the sale. This year, when the note has a fair market value of $76,000, D gives it to his son, S. In addition to last year's gain of $12,000 (60% × $20,000) on the down payment, D must now recognize $44,000 when he disposes of the note. This represents the difference between the fair market value of the note ($76,000) and D's unrecovered basis of $32,000 [$40,000 (original basis) − $8,000 (amount of basis applied against the down payment)]. The gift of an installment obligation is treated as a taxable disposition under § 453B(a).

If the obligor and obligee are related persons, the Installment Sales Revision Act of 1980 provides for a different result. In such cases, the entire unreported gain will be taxed on what, in effect, is a cancellation of the obligation. Referring to Example 38, assume the original sale was to S (a related party) and not to P (an unrelated party). Under § 453B(f)(2) when D (the obligee) gives (or otherwise cancels) the note to S (the obligor), D must recognize a gain of $48,000 [60% (gross profit percentage) × $80,000 (face amount of the note)]. In defining related person, § 453(f)(1) makes reference to the attribution rules of § 318(a) (refer to Chapter 13 and the discussion of certain stock redemptions.)

> **Example 39.** In 1981, D acquired some § 38 property for use in his trade or business, upon which was claimed an investment tax credit of $3,000 based on a cost of $30,000 and a recovery period of five years.[45] After using the property for one full year, D gives it to S. The premature disposition of the property will trigger recapture by D of $2,400 of the credit as additional tax liability in the year of the gift.[46]

Would there be any difference to D had the transfers outlined in the above examples been testamentary? In other words, suppose the property had passed to S by virtue of D's death rather than by gift. The disposition of an installment note receivable (Example 38) or § 38 property (Example 39) by death is not a taxable event under the income tax; therefore, the results would have been different.[47] But in Example 38 the unrealized gain, though not taxed to D, will not go

---

**45.** Under § 46(c)(7), the credit for § 38 property with a recovery period of five years is 10%.

**46.** §47(a)(5)(B) reduces the recapture amount by 2% for each full year the property is held. Expressed differently, D must recapture 80% of the $3,000 previously claimed as a credit.

**47.** § § 453B(c) and 47(b)(1). If the installment obligation passes to the obligor (or is otherwise cancelled by the obligee's will), this will be treated as a transfer by the obligee's estate and will trigger recognition of gain to the estate. If the parties are related persons [within the meaning of § 318(a)], the face amount of the obligation will be deemed to be its fair market value. See § 691(a)(5) added by the Installment Sales Revision Act of 1980.

unrecognized. As income in respect of a decedent it will be taxed to whoever collects the note. In Example 39, however, the investment credit recapture potential is removed by death. Thus, even if S sold the § 38 property right after D's death and before the five-year period had run, there would be no recapture of the credit.

*Income Tax Consequences to the Donee.* What about the income tax position of the donee? Certainly this must be an important factor in the donor's choice of property to transfer as a gift.

> **Example 40.** D makes a gift to S of depreciable tangible personalty (adjusted basis of $20,000 and a fair market value of $30,000) used in the trade or business. If D had sold the property for $30,000, a gain of $10,000 would have been recognized, all of which would have been ordinary income under the recapture of depreciation provisions of § 1245. The gift does not generate income to D; such transfers are excepted from the usual recapture of depreciation rules by § 1245(b)(1). The recapture potential of the property is, however, transferred to the donee. As a consequence, if S sold the property for $30,000 immediately after the gift, a gain of $10,000 must be recognized to S, all of which would be recaptured as ordinary income.

In Example 40, any gain, including the ordinary income element, would go unrecognized if the property was passed by death.[48]

Just because a testamentary transfer might produce a more favorable income tax result does not mean this type of property is always unsuitable for gifts. The owner of the property (i. e., D) may not be able to retain or be desirous of retaining it until death. If the property is to be disposed of before this time, shifting the income tax consequences to someone else (i. e., S) may be less costly taxwise to the family unit. Such might be the case if the donee (i. e., S) is in a lower tax bracket than the donor or has losses which will neutralize some or all of the gain on the later sale of the property.[49] On the other hand, the donee may not intend to sell the property. In this event, any built-in income tax potential should provide no real concern.

> **Example 41.** D owns a summer home in Arkansas which, because of its location and accessibility to recreational facilities, has been used for many years by the family for vacation purposes. The property has an adjusted basis of only $40,000 but has appreciated to a present value of $110,000. D would like to exclude the property from his gross estate but still keep it in the family. S,

---

**48.** § 1245(b)(2).
**49.** One must be wary of situations in which the sale by the donee is prearranged by the donor or the sale takes place shortly after the gift of the property. If this happens, the IRS may try to collapse the gift and argue that the sale really was made by the donor and not the donee. If its argument is successful, the income tax consequences will be attributed to the donor and not the donee.

D's son, plans to continue vacationing at the summer home and would make it available to the rest of the family in the event the property became his.

There is much to be said in favor of a gift of the summer home to S. Although S's basis for income tax purposes will be only $40,000, this creates no real problem because S does not plan to dispose of the property.

Example 41 raises another interesting point. Aside from the gift tax liability, what has D really lost by making the transfer? One would hope the donee-son will permit his father (D) to use the property for its intended recreational purpose. As long as such use is by invitation only and there exists no express or implied agreement requiring S to do so, the hoped-for estate tax result will be accomplished.[50]

*Use of Non-Income Producing Property.* Example 41 illustrates a possible characteristic of lifetime giving—the donor chooses property that is not income-producing. Therefore, the donor does not forego a source of income possibly needed to cover retirement years and, perhaps, extraordinary expenses (e. g., medical) that often materialize later in life. In this regard, the selection of life insurance policies is ideal for several reasons. First, aside from the cash surrender value, insurance carries little if any income-generating potential during the life of the insured. Second, the gift tax consequences are minimal when compared to the death tax result. Third, the income tax position of the donee is protected; § 101(a) excludes from taxation proceeds paid by reason of the death of the insured.

> **Example 42.** At a time when its value is $12,000, D transfers a policy (face amount of $100,000) on his life to S, the designated beneficiary. Five years later D dies and the insurance company pays S $100,000. D has made a gift to S of $12,000, and presuming D has not retained any incidents of ownership in the policy, none of the $100,000 proceeds will be included in the gross estate. By making the transfer, therefore, D has traded the death tax savings on $100,000 for whatever gift tax liability is generated by $12,000. Even better, the $100,000 S receives is not subject to the income tax.

The gift of group-term life insurance would be even more attractive taxwise. The value of such a policy would be negligible and probably would result in no gift tax consequences. In making such a transfer, however, one must be careful to observe the IRS guidelines

---

**50.** After the transfer, the parties must be careful to treat S as the true owner of the summer home. If not, the IRS may contend that D has retained "the possession or enjoyment" of the property. If this were the case, the property would be includible in D's gross estate upon his death by virtue of § 2036(a)(1).

in point. It is clear that accidental death policies (e. g., flight insurance) cannot be assigned and still avoid the gift-within-three-years-of-death problem.[51] If such a gift occurs, any hoped-for estate tax savings, of course, will be neutralized.

Before carrying out the transfer of non-income producing property, the economic situation of the donee must be assessed. To illustrate, what if the donee in Example 41 were financially unable to maintain the summer home? If, after the gift, the donor continued to provide the upkeep (e. g., pay for repairs, property taxes, casualty insurance), the IRS might disregard the gift and treat D as the true owner of the property with attendant adverse estate tax consequences upon his death. In Example 42, the donee may not be able to meet the premium payments to keep the policy in force. If the donor continues to pay the premiums on the policy, further gift tax consequences may result.[52] One effective solution to this problem might be to transfer income producing property (e. g., stocks, bonds) along with the non-income producing property. In this manner, the donee can use the income generated by the former to maintain and preserve the non-income producing property.

*Other Considerations in the Choice of Property.* In addition to the above, other considerations which might affect the type of property to be given include the following:

—Property which may be difficult to value for estate tax purposes. Though this substitutes one valuation problem for another, the gift tax valuation may be more easily resolved.

—Property located in other states and in foreign countries. Not only might this eliminate the possibility of multiple death taxes, but it could save on probate costs.[53]

—Property with a high income yield. Though this seems at odds with the discussion in connection with Example 41, it is predicated on the assumption that the donor can spare the income from the gift property and is in a high personal income tax bracket. In terms of the objective of family tax planning, it should follow that the donee is in a lower income tax bracket than is the donor.

—The liquidity of the property. Because many estates encounter a problem of liquidity, at least some cash or near-cash assets

**51.** *Berman v. U. S.,* 73–2 USTC ¶ 12,949, 33 AFTR2d 74–1366, 487 F.2d 70 (CA–5, 1973). Keep in mind that the three-year rule still covers gifts of life insurance. See § 2035(d)(2).

**52.** This would be the case only if the amount of the premium exceeded the annual exclusion of $10,000. If the donor was married and the election to split the gift is made, up to $20,000 of a premium payment could be sheltered from the gift tax.

**53.** Ancillary court proceedings may have to be instituted in the states or countries where the property is located to wind up the estate. Needless to mention, this means additional court costs, legal fees, etc.

(e. g., marketable securities) should be retained. Thus, an executor will not be forced to sell nonliquid assets at bargain prices in order to raise funds to meet pressing administration and other expenses.

## PROBLEM MATERIALS

### Discussion Questions

1. Upon whom is the Federal gift tax imposed? Suppose such party is unable to pay the tax?

2. What is the relationship between state law and the imposition of the Federal gift tax?

3. Under what circumstances could the Federal gift tax be imposed on a nonresident alien?

4. Explain what is meant by the statement that the Federal gift tax rates are cumulative in nature.

5. How would a gift to a corporation be treated for Federal gift tax purposes? A gift by a corporation?

6. Why is it significant to determine whether a transfer between parties takes place in a personal setting? A business setting?

7. Distinguish between a tenancy in common, a joint tenancy, and a tenancy by the entirety.

8. Under what circumstances will the creation of a joint tenancy not constitute a gift when one of the tenants furnishes more of the consideration than the other (or others)?

9. Using his funds, X purchases real estate and lists title as follows: "X and Y, joint tenants with the right of survivorship."

    (a) What gift tax result if X and Y are brothers?

    (b) Under (a) what estate tax result if X predeceases Y?

    (c) What gift tax result if X and Y are husband and wife?

    (d) Under (c) what estate tax result if X predeceases Y? If Y predeceases X?

10. Under what condition might the death of the insured represent a gift to the beneficiary of part or all of the proceeds of a life insurance policy?

11. In the absence of § 2516, why would certain property settlements incident to a divorce be subject to the Federal gift tax?

12. What are the requirements necessary for the application of § 2516?

13. In terms of qualified recipients, what is the difference between the charitable deduction for Federal income tax purposes and that allowed for Federal gift tax purposes?

14. How does the marital deduction for gift tax purposes differ from that allowed under the Federal estate tax?

15. Can a marital deduction materialize with respect to transfers between spouses residing in a community property state? Explain.

16. What is the justification for the annual exclusion?

17. What is a future interest? Why is it relevant to the Federal gift tax?

18. What is the purpose of § 2503(c)?

19. What is the reason for the gift-splitting provision of § 2513?

20. When is a Federal gift tax return due?

21. What is the difference between a state estate tax and a state inheritance tax?

22. Does the Code provide any form of relief for estates subject to both a state death tax and the Federal estate tax?

23. Does the Code provide any form of relief for lifetime transfers subject to both a state gift tax and the Federal gift tax?

## Problems

24. In each of the independent situations appearing below, indicate whether the transfer by D is, or could be, subject to the Federal gift tax.

    (a) D Corporation makes a contribution to an influential political figure.

    (b) D makes a contribution to B Corporation of which he is not a shareholder.

    (c) In consideration of his upcoming marriage to B, D establishes a savings account in her name.

    (d) Same as (c). After their marriage D establishes a joint checking account in the names of "D and B."

    (e) Same as (d). One year after the checking account was established, B withdraws all of the funds.

    (f) D enters into an agreement with B whereby he will transfer property to her in full satisfaction of her marital rights. One month after the agreement the transfer occurs. Later D and B are divorced.

    (g) D purchases U. S. savings bonds listing ownership as "D and B." Several years later, and after D's death, B redeems these bonds.

25. In each of the independent situations appearing below, indicate whether the transfer by D is, or could be, subject to the Federal gift tax.

    (a) D purchases real estate and lists title as "D and B as joint tenants." D and B are brothers.

    (b) Same as (a) except that D and B are husband and wife.

    (c) D creates a revocable trust with B as the designated beneficiary.

    (d) Same as (c). One year after creating the trust, D releases all power to revoke the trust.

    (e) D takes out an insurance policy on his life designating B as the beneficiary.

    (f) Same as (e). Two years later, D dies and the policy proceeds are paid to B.

    (g) D takes out an insurance policy on the life of W and designates B as the beneficiary. Shortly thereafter, W dies and the policy proceeds are paid to B.

26.  In 1976, R purchases real estate for $300,000 listing ownership as follows: "R and S, equal tenants in common." R predeceases S in 1983 when the property is worth $500,000. Prior to 1976, R had not made any taxable gifts or utilized the $30,000 specific exemption. Assume R and S are brothers.

   (a) Determine R's gift tax consequences, if any, in 1976.

   (b) How much, if any, of the property should be included in R's gross estate?

27.  In 1983, M makes a gift to her daughter of securities worth $300,000. M has never made any prior taxable gifts or utilized her $30,000 specific exemption. F (M's husband), however, made a taxable gift of $500,000 early in 1976 upon which he paid a gift tax of $109,275. At the time of F's gift he was not married to M.

   (a) Determine M's gift tax liability on the 1983 transfer assuming the parties choose not to make the election to split gifts under § 2513.

   (b) What would be the liability if the election to split the gift was made?

28.  In 1975, D makes a taxable gift of $100,000 upon which he pays a Federal gift tax of $15,525. D makes further taxable gifts as follows: $100,000 in 1980 and $100,000 in 1983. Compute D's gift tax liability for:

   (a) 1980

   (b) 1983

29.  D makes a gift of $33,000 on December 20, 1976, upon which no gift tax is paid because of the application of the annual exclusion and the specific exemption. If D dies in 1983 leaving a taxable estate of $400,000, determine the Federal estate tax liability.

30.  M makes a taxable gift of $100,000 in 1978 upon which she paid no gift tax because of the application of the unified transfer tax credit. If M dies in 1983 leaving a taxable estate of $500,000, compute the Federal estate tax liability.

31.  In each of the independent situations appearing below indicate whether the statement is true or false:

   (a) If an extension of time for filing the Federal gift tax return is obtained, no interest will accrue that might otherwise be due for failure to pay the tax on time.

   (b) If an extension of time for paying the Federal gift tax is obtained, no interest will accrue that might otherwise be due for failure to pay the tax on time.

   (c) The requirements for filing a Federal gift tax return are not affected by the availability of the marital deduction.

   (d) Inconvenience on the part of the donor qualifies as "undue hardship" for purposes of obtaining an extension of time for payment of the Federal gift tax.

   (e) Besides interest, a failure to pay a gift tax when due could result in the imposition of other penalties on the donor.

   (f) If a donor is using a fiscal year for Federal income tax purposes, the due date requirements for filing a Form 709 (U. S. Gift Tax Return) will be adjusted accordingly.

(g) During 1983, T makes gifts as follows: $12,000 to S (T's son) and $8,000 to D (T's daughter). Under these circumstances, no gift tax return (Form 709) need be filed, since the annual exclusion for two donees ($20,000) has not been exceeded.

(h) Prior to 1982, charitable gifts in excess of the annual exclusion had to be reported on Form 709 even though no gift tax was due as a result of the transfer.

(i) A calendar year taxpayer requests and obtains from the IRS an extension for filing her 1983 Federal income tax return. The extension also will apply to the filing of Form 709 as to any taxable gifts the taxpayer may have made in 1983.

(j) Interest on a gift tax deficiency always has accrued at the rate of 20%.

32. The following statements relate to state inheritance taxes and are either true or false.

(a) Every state allows a $60,000 exemption per estate.

(b) Life insurance proceeds, as with the Federal estate tax, are always subject to tax.

(c) An inheritance received by a cousin will generate the same tax liability as one of equal value passing to a son of the deceased.

(d) Inheritance tax rates generally are not graduated. Thus, a bequest of $500,000 would be taxed at the same rate as one valued at $50,000.

# Chapter 20

# Income Taxation
# of Trusts and Estates

## INTRODUCTION—AN OVERVIEW OF SUBCHAPTER J

Subchapter J ( § § 641 through 692) of the Internal Revenue Code of 1954 contains the statutory provisions governing the income taxation of estates, trusts, and beneficiaries. Sections 641 through 644 contain the rules for imposition of an income tax on estates and trusts; special rules for credits and deductions; definitions of income, distributable net income, and beneficiaries, and the special rule for the imposition of an additional tax upon trusts for gains recognized in certain sales or exchanges. The provisions which govern the amount of a distribution deduction allowed certain trusts and the amount to be included in gross income of the beneficiaries of such trusts are contained in § § 651 and 652, respectively. Similar statutory rules concerning distribution deductions for estates and complex trusts and inclusions in income of the beneficiaries of these entities are contained in § § 661 and 662. Sections 665 through 668 determine the tax treatment of excess distributions by trusts. Finally, § § 671 through 679 detail the tax treatment of trust income attributable to grantors or any others treated as substantial owners of any portion of a trust.

Most of the statutory provisions of Subchapter J are discussed below. As these income tax provisions are examined, the scheme of taxation of trusts and estates should become apparent. However, the reader should bear in mind throughout this discussion that for income tax purposes trusts and estates are divided into three categories:

1. Estates and ordinary trusts.
2. Grantor trusts.
3. Special trusts.

The primary concern of this chapter is the income taxation of estates and ordinary trusts. Grantor trusts and special trusts (such as alimony trusts and pension and profit sharing trusts) are beyond the scope of this text.

## WHAT IS A TRUST?

The Internal Revenue Code does not contain a definition of a trust. However, the Regulations explain that the term "trust" as used in the Code refers to an arrangement created by a will or by an inter vivos declaration through which trustees take title to property for the purpose of protecting or conserving it for the beneficiaries under the ordinary rules applied in chancery or probate courts.[1]

In the typical case, the creation of a trust involves three parties: the *grantor* (settlor), the *trustee* (either individual or corporate), and the *beneficiary*. Various other combinations are possible, however. For example, the grantor could also be a beneficiary of the trust (either directly or indirectly). Additionally, the grantor could be the trustee. However, a trust *will not be recognized* for tax purposes when *only one party* is involved. Such a situation occurs when the grantor places property in trust for himself or herself and designates himself or herself as the trustee. As discussed in more detail later, if the grantor remains a direct or indirect beneficiary of the trust, undesirable tax consequences could result. In such a case, the trust will be considered a *grantor trust* and some or all of its income will be taxable to the grantor.[2]

## TRUST BENEFICIARIES

Beneficiaries of a trust fall into two categories: those entitled to the income from the trust property and those entitled to the principal (or corpus) upon the expiration of the *income interest*. The latter interest is known as a *remainder interest* unless it is to pass to the grantor. If it passes to the grantor, it is termed a *reversionary interest*. The income interest may last for a term of years or until the happening of a certain event. For example, an income interest may be established for 10 years or until the beneficiary reaches a certain age (e. g., age 21 or age 35). If the income interest is based on the life of the beneficiary, such person is called a *life tenant*. The tax consequences to the beneficiary of a trust are discussed below in connection with the various types of trusts recognized for income tax purposes.

---

1. Reg. § 301.7701–4(a).
2. § 677.

## WHAT IS AN ESTATE?

An estate is created upon the death of an individual. During the period of administration of the estate, the decedent's legal representative (an executor or executrix if appointed under a will or an administrator or administratrix if appointed by a probate court) has the task of collecting and conserving all assets, satisfying liabilities (including state and Federal taxes), and distributing any remainder to the appointed heirs.

Since an estate is recognized as a separate taxable entity, it may be profitable, under certain circumstances, to prolong its administration. This situation is likely to arise when the heirs are already in a high income tax bracket and, therefore, would prefer to have the income generated by estate assets taxed to the estate. However, the tax authorities have recognized this possibility of shifting income to lower tax bracket taxpayers. The Regulations caution that if the administration of an estate is unreasonably prolonged, the estate *will be considered terminated* for Federal income tax purposes after the expiration of a reasonable period for the performance by the executor of all duties of administration.[3]

# NATURE OF TRUST AND ESTATE TAXATION

Unlike partnerships, estates and trusts are separate tax entities. In general, the income from estate and trust assets will be taxed to the entity or the beneficiary, but not to both. However, this rule is subject to several exceptions. For instance, some trusts may be treated as associations and, therefore, will be subject to the corporate income tax. Additionally, part or all of the income of certain trusts must be taxed to the grantor if too much dominion or control over the trust property or income is retained. For example, if the grantor retains the right to revoke the trust (known as a revocable trust), the trust will be disregarded for tax purposes and, as long as this right remains in effect, the trust income will be taxed to the grantor.

If an estate does not have title to the property, the income from the property will be taxed to whoever holds title. In most states, for example, the title to real estate does not pass through the estate but vests directly in the heir on the date of the owner's death. Income from such property would be taxed to the heir and not the estate. In the same manner, income from property transferred as a gift prior to death or income from the surviving spouse's share of community property would not be taxed to the estate.

In resolving the matter of ownership of a decedent's assets, applicable state law will control. However, do not conclude that property

---

3. Reg. § 1.641(b)–3(a).

which is subject to the Federal death tax (i. e., included in the decedent's gross estate) belongs to the estate, because there is no necessary correlation between the two. A gift within three years of death (under § 2035) could be subject to the death tax; but the property involved belongs to the donee, not the donor's estate, is not subject to estate administration, and is not available to the decedent's executor for the payment of debts and other estate expenses. The same holds true for the proceeds of most life insurance policies.

## FILING REQUIREMENTS

The fiduciary of an estate (administrator or executor) and of a trust (trustee) is required to file a Form 1041 (U. S. Fiduciary Income Tax Return) in the following situations:

—In the case of an estate if its gross income for the year is $600 or more.

—In the case of a trust if it has taxable income or, when no taxable income, if gross income is $600 or more.

—In the case of both an estate and a trust if it has a beneficiary that is a nonresident alien.[4]

Although the fiduciary is responsible for filing Form 1041 and paying any income tax due, such person is not personally liable for the tax. Except in certain cases, the IRS must look to the assets of the estate or the trust for the tax due. The fiduciary may become personally liable for such tax if he or she has made distributions of assets (e. g., payment of debts, satisfaction of bequests) and therefore renders the entity unable to pay the tax due. Section 6905 and the Regulations outline the procedure an executor or an administrator may use to obtain from the IRS a discharge from personal liability. Taking advantage of this procedure would be highly advisable before making any substantial distributions of estate assets.

The fiduciary return is due no later than the fifteenth day of the fourth month following the close of the entity's taxable year. The return should be filed with the Internal Revenue Service Center for the region in which the fiduciary resides or has his or her principal place of business. If it chooses to do so, an estate may pay its tax in quarterly payments (one-fourth each on or before the fifteenth day of the fourth, seventh, tenth, and thirteenth months).[5] A trust does not have this privilege, however, and the entire tax must be paid when its return is filed.

## ACCOUNTING PERIODS AND METHODS

An estate or trust may use any of the tax accounting methods available to individuals. The method of accounting used by the grantor of a

---

**4.** § 6012(a).
**5.** § 6152(a)(2).

trust or the decedent of an estate does not carry over. Once a method has been adopted, any change is subject to the same limitations applicable to other taxpayers.[6]

Since an estate or trust is a separate entity, it will have the same election available to any new taxpayer—the choice of a tax year. Thus, an estate of a calendar year decedent dying on March 3 could, if it chose to do so, select any fiscal year or report on a calendar year basis.[7] If the latter is elected, the estate's first taxable year would include the period from March 3 through December 31. More importantly, if the first or last tax years are short years (i. e., less than one year), income for such years need not be annualized. Finally, changes in accounting periods are subject to the same limitations applicable to other taxpayers.[8]

## TAX RATE AND PERSONAL EXEMPTION

The tax rates applicable to an estate or trust are the same as those for married persons filing separately. Note, however, that the $1,700 zero bracket amount applicable to married persons filing separately is not available to either an estate or a trust.[9] Estates and trusts also are precluded from using the Tax Table in determining the amount of income tax liability.[10]

In addition to the regular income tax, an estate or trust may be subject to the alternative minimum tax imposed on tax preference items.[11] Trusts also may be subject to a special tax imposed by § 644 on gains from the sale or exchange of certain appreciated property.

Both trusts and estates are allowed a personal exemption in computing the fiduciary tax liability. All estates are allowed a personal exemption of $600. The exemption available to a trust, however, is dependent upon the type of trust involved. A trust which is required to distribute all of its income currently (a simple trust) is allowed an exemption of $300. All other trusts (complex trusts) are allowed an exemption of only $100 per year.[12]

## THE CONDUIT CONCEPT

Recall that the general theory of income taxation of trusts and estates is to tax the income from such entities' assets to the entity itself or to the beneficiaries, but not both. Consistent with this approach, an estate or trust acts as a mere conduit for certain types of income, deduc-

---

**6.** See § 446 and the Regulations thereunder.

**7.** § 441.

**8.** See § 442 and the Regulations thereunder.

**9.** Compare the Tax Rate Schedules contained in § § 1(d) and 1(e). These are reproduced in Appendix A.

**10.** § 3(b)(3).

**11.** § 56.

**12.** § 642(b).

tions, and credits. This means that income which is allocable to a beneficiary, along with certain related deductions and credits, retains the same character as it had in the hands of the estate or trust. Thus, such items as interest on municipal bonds and long-term capital gains will retain their identity when passed on to the beneficiary. In this regard, the estate or trust is similar to the partnership form of business organization and unlike that of a regular corporation.

# TAXABLE INCOME
# OF TRUSTS AND ESTATES

Generally, the taxable income of an estate or trust is computed in the same manner as that of an individual. There are, however, several important exceptions and special provisions which distinguish the income taxation of trusts and estates from all other taxable entities. These exceptions are discussed below.

## GROSS INCOME

The gross income of an estate or trust is determined in the same manner as that of an individual. Section 641 provides that gross income includes:

1.  Income accumulated in trust for the benefit of unborn or unascertained persons or persons with contingent interests and income accumulated or held for future distributions under the terms of the will or trust.

2.  Income which is to be distributed currently by the fiduciary to the beneficiaries and income collected by a guardian of an infant which is to be held or distributed as the courts may direct.

3.  Income received by estates of deceased persons during the period of administration or settlement of the estate.

4.  Income which, in the discretion of the fiduciary, may be either distributed to the beneficiaries or accumulated.

Although all of the foregoing items may represent gross income to the estate or trust, keep in mind that an offsetting deduction may be allowed for item 2 and, to the extent paid or credited to the beneficiary, for items 3 and 4.

In determining the gain or loss to be recognized by an estate or trust upon the sale or other taxable disposition of assets, the rules for basis determination are similar to those applicable to other taxpayers. Thus, the basis of property to an estate received from a decedent would be determined under § 1014. Property received as a gift (the usual case in most trust arrangements) would be controlled by § 1015. Property acquired by a trust for valuable consideration will take on the grantor's basis increased by any gain (or decreased by any loss) recognized by the grantor on the transfer. These rules are illustrated by the examples that follow.

**Example 1.** In 19X4, G creates an irrevocable trust with a gift of 4,000 shares of X Corporation stock (basis to G of $160,000 and a fair market value of $152,000). A gift tax of $5,000 was paid on the transfer. In 19X7, the trust sells the stock for $140,000. The trust's basis for loss is $152,000 (the lower of the donor's basis of $160,000 or the fair market value on the date of the gift of $152,000); therefore, a long-term capital loss of $12,000 is recognized. The gift tax paid by G cannot be taken into account, because G's basis ($160,000) exceeds fair market value ($152,000). Recall that § 1015(d) permits the gift tax adjustment to basis only if the fair market value of the property exceeds the donor's basis at the time of the gift. Since the fair market value figure controls the determination of loss, the holding period of the trust starts with the date of the gift in accordance with § 1223(2).

**Example 2.** Assume the same facts as in Example 1 except that the stock is sold by the trust in 19X7 for $165,000. The sale results in a recognized long-term capital gain of $5,000 because the basis of the stock is G's basis of $160,000.

**Example 3.** In 19X5, M, the grantor of M Trust, sells to the trust 500 shares of Y Corporation stock (basis to M of $30,000) for its fair market value of $34,000. In 19X8, M Trust sells the stock for $36,000. The sale by the trust results in a recognized long-term capital gain of $2,000 because the basis of the property is $34,000 (M's basis of $30,000 plus $4,000 recognized gain).

Normally, no gain or loss is realized upon the distribution of property to a beneficiary pursuant to the provisions of a will or trust instrument. Suppose, however, that a will provides a cash bequest of $15,000 to an heir and the estate satisfies this obligation with property possessing a basis of $10,000 and a fair market value on the date of distribution of $15,000. The estate must recognize a gain of $5,000 on the distribution. This exception concerning the recognition of gain or loss on distributions also applies when a specific property bequest is satisfied with other property. Thus, suppose the will provides for 500 shares of R Corporation stock to pass to a beneficiary. If the beneficiary accepts an equal value in stock of T Corporation in satisfaction of the bequest, the estate must recognize a gain or loss measured by the difference between its basis in the T Corporation stock and the fair market value of the R Corporation stock on the date of the distribution. The satisfaction of a specific property bequest with cash, however, would not generate any tax consequences to the estate.

The exclusion for qualifying dividends received by an estate or trust provided by § 116 is allowed to the extent the dividends are not distributed or allocated to the beneficiaries. This procedure can be illustrated by the following simple example:

> **Example 4.**  A trust receives $2,000 in taxable dividends from qualifying domestic corporations, $1,400 of which are allocable to its beneficiaries. The trust may claim a dividend exclusion of $30 ($600/$2,000 × $100). The beneficiaries will be deemed to have received the dividends allocable to them on the *same date* as received by the estate or trust.

However, the amount claimed by an estate or trust will not diminish the exclusion to which each beneficiary is entitled. Thus, if a beneficiary receives dividends from an estate or trust and dividends from other sources which in total amount to $100 or more, he or she will be entitled to a $100 exclusion without regard to any exclusion claimed by the estate or trust.

## INCOME IN RESPECT OF A DECEDENT

The Regulations define income in respect of a decedent as follows:

> In general, the term "income in respect of a decedent" refers to those amounts to which a decedent was entitled as gross income but which were not properly includible in computing his taxable income for the taxable year ending with the date of his death or for a previous taxable year under the method of accounting employed by the decedent.[13]

It should be noted that the above definition stresses the condition that the income is earned at the time of death but is not includible in the decedent's final income tax return because of the method of accounting in use. In the case of a cash basis decedent, examples include accrued interest, rent, and other income items not constructively received prior to death. As to both cash and accrual basis decedents, examples include death benefits from qualified retirement plans and deferred pay contracts, income from a partnership whose tax year does not end with the death of the deceased partner, subsequent collection of installment notes receivable (being reported under § 453), and subsequent realization of contingent claims. Although income in respect of a decedent is of particular import to the decedent on the cash basis, one can see from the last set of examples that it also may affect many accrual basis taxpayers.

The tax consequences of income in respect of a decedent may be summarized as follows:

1.  The fair market value of the right on the appropriate valuation date (i. e., date of death or alternate valuation date) will

---

13.  Reg. § 1.691(a)–1(b).

be included in the decedent's gross estate and will be subject to the Federal death tax.[14]

2. The decedent's basis in the property carries over to the recipient (i. e., the estate or heirs). In other words, the basis remains unaffected by the amount included in the gross estate.

3. Gain or loss will be recognized to the recipient of the income (either the estate or heirs or both) measured by the difference between the amount realized and the adjusted basis of the right in the hands of the decedent. The classification of such gain or loss depends on the treatment it would have received if realized by the decedent prior to death. Thus, if the decedent would have realized capital gain, the recipient must do likewise.[15]

4. Expenses related to the income right (such as interest, taxes, and depletion) not properly reported on the final income tax return of the decedent can be claimed by the recipient if the obligation is associated with the income right.[16] Such expenses are known as *expenses in respect of a decedent* and are deductible *both for Federal death and income tax purposes.*

5. To mitigate the effect of double taxation (i. e., imposition of both the estate and income tax), § 691(c) allows the recipient an income tax deduction for the estate tax attributable to the income.[17]

## ORDINARY DEDUCTIONS

Recall that as a general rule, the taxable income of an estate or trust is computed in the same manner as that of an individual.[18] Thus, deductions would be allowed for ordinary and necessary expenses paid or incurred in carrying on a trade or business; for the production or collection of income; for the management, conservation, or maintenance of property; and in connection with the determination, collection, or refund of any tax. Also allowed are reasonable administration expenses, including fiduciary fees and litigation costs in connection with the duties of administration. Not allowed are expenses allocable to the production or collection of tax-exempt income or litigation costs resulting from a breach of fiduciary responsibility (i. e., mismanagement by an executor or trustee).

Under § 642(g), amounts deductible as administration expenses

---

**14.** § 2033.
**15.** § 691(a)(3) and Reg. § 1.691(a)–3.
**16.** § 691(b).
**17.** See Reg. § 1.691(c)–1 for further details concerning the computation of this deduction.
**18.** § 641(b).

or losses for estate tax purposes (under § § 2053 and 2054) cannot be claimed by the estate for income tax purposes unless the estate files a waiver of the estate tax deduction. Although these expenses cannot be deducted twice, they may be allocated as the fiduciary sees fit between Forms 706 and 1041 and need not be claimed in their entirety on either return.

The prohibition against double deductions does not extend to expenses in respect of a decedent which are deductible both for estate tax purposes and on the income tax return of the recipient of the income in respect of a decedent.[19] Trusts and estates also are allowed a deduction for depreciation and depletion. However, such deductions are required to be apportioned between all parties involved. For instance, the Regulations state that in the case of an estate, the allowable deduction for depreciation or depletion shall be apportioned between the estate and the heirs, legatees, and devisees on the basis of income of the estate which is allocable to each.[20]

Similarly, the allowable deduction for depreciation or depletion of property held in trust must be apportioned between the income beneficiaries and the trust on the basis of the trust income allocable to each.[21] If the trust instrument (or state law) requires or permits the trustee to maintain a reserve for depreciation, the deduction is first allocated to the trust to the extent that income is set aside for such reserve. Any part of the deduction in excess of this amount is apportioned between the income beneficiaries and the trust on the basis of the trust income allocable to each.[22]

> **Example 5.** G creates a trust, with S and D as income beneficiaries, by the transfer of income-producing depreciable property. Under the terms of the trust instrument, the income from the trust is to be distributed annually in equal shares and the trustee is authorized to set aside income as a depreciation reserve. For the current year, depreciation on the trust property amounts to $7,000, and the trustee allocates $5,000 of trust income as a depreciation reserve. The trust can claim $5,000 as a depreciation deduction, and S and D are entitled to $1,000 each.

> **Example 6.** Assume the same facts as in Example 5 except that under the trust instrument, the income of the trust is to be computed without regard to any depreciation deduction. Under these circumstances, the trust will obtain no deduction and the entire depreciation will be split between S and D.

The depreciation recapture provisions of the Code (§ § 1245 and 1250) would be applicable in the event property is sold or otherwise

---

19.  § 691(b).
20.  Reg. § 1.167(h)–1(c) and Reg. § 1.611–1(c)(5).
21.  § § 167(h) and 611(b)(3).
22.  Reg. § 1.167(h)–1(b) and Reg. § 1.611–1(c)(4).

disposed of in a taxable transfer. In determining the recapture potential of such property, it would be necessary to take into account any depreciation claimed by the original transferor when the entity assumes a substituted basis. Thus, on a sale by a trust of property received as a gift from the grantor, the amount of depreciation subject to recapture includes the depreciation claimed by the grantor prior to its transfer to the trust. Keep in mind that property passed by death does not carry the recapture potential of § § 1245 and 1250.

## DEDUCTION OF LOSSES

An estate or trust will be allowed a deduction for casualty or theft losses not compensated for by insurance or otherwise. Such losses also may be deductible by an estate for Federal estate tax purposes under § 2054. As a result, an income tax deduction will not be allowed an estate unless the estate tax deduction is waived in accordance with the procedure set forth in the Regulations.[23]

The net operating loss deduction allowed under § 172 also is available for estates and trusts. The carryback of a net operating loss may reduce the distributable net income of the trust or estate for the carryback year and therefore affect the amount that was taxed to the beneficiaries for that year. This permits the beneficiary to recompute his or her tax liability for such prior year and file a claim for a refund. The impact of such a carryback on the income taxation of the beneficiaries and the importance of the term "distributable net income" are discussed in a subsequent section of this chapter.

In computing a net operating loss, the estate or trust cannot take into account deductions for charitable contributions or for distributions to beneficiaries. Also, if any of a trust's income or deductions are assignable to the grantor, they cannot be considered. Whether depreciation will affect the loss computation depends upon its allowance to the trust as an income tax deduction. Thus, if the trust income is allocable entirely to the beneficiaries and the trust instrument makes no provision for a reserve for depreciation, it cannot be considered in determining the trust's net operating loss deduction.

In the event an estate or trust is terminated and the entity has an unabsorbed net operating loss carryover, such a loss may be passed on to the beneficiaries.[24] This matter is discussed at greater length in connection with the tax treatment of the beneficiaries of an estate or trust.

Certain losses realized by an estate or trust are also subject to disallowance. The rules disallowing losses are not unique; they are

---

**23.** See Reg. § 1.642(g)–1 for the required statement waiving the estate tax deduction. Also, see Reg. § § 1.165–7(c) and 1.165–8(b) requiring such a statement be filed in order to allow an income tax deduction for such losses.
**24.** § 642(h).

the same rules applicable to all taxpayers. Thus, the wash sale provision of § 1091 would disallow losses on the sale or other disposition of stock or securities when substantially identical stock or securities are acquired by the estate or trust within the prescribed 30-day period. Likewise, § 267 disallows certain losses, expenses, and interest with respect to transactions between related taxpayers. Under § 267(b), the term "related taxpayers" includes, in addition to other relationships, the following:

—A grantor and a fiduciary of any trust.

—A fiduciary of a trust and a fiduciary of another trust, if the same person is a grantor of both trusts.

—A fiduciary of a trust and a beneficiary of such trust.

—A fiduciary of a trust and a beneficiary of another trust, if the same person is a grantor of both trusts.

—A fiduciary of a trust and a corporation more than 50 percent in value of the outstanding stock of which is owned, directly or indirectly, by or for the trust or by or for a person who is a grantor of the trust.

Except for the possibility of unused losses in the year of termination, the capital losses of an estate or trust cannot be assigned to a beneficiary and are deductible only on the fiduciary return. The tax treatment of these losses is the same as for individual taxpayers. Recall, however, that in the case of property acquired from a decedent, any loss on its disposition will be deemed long-term under § 1223(11). For example, if an executor sells a capital asset five months after the decedent's death for less than its basis, a long-term capital loss results.

## CHARITABLE CONTRIBUTIONS

Section 642(c) provides that an estate or trust will be allowed a deduction for contributions to charitable organizations under the following conditions:

1. The contribution must be made pursuant to the will or trust instrument.

2. The recipient must be a qualified organization. For this purpose, qualified organizations include the same group of recipients that would qualify individual and corporate donors for the deduction except that estates and trusts are permitted the deduction for contributions to certain foreign charitable organizations.

3. Generally, the contribution must be paid in the tax year claimed, but a special rule permits a fiduciary to treat amounts paid in the following year as a deduction for the

preceding year.[25] This special rule treats estates and trusts more liberally than either individuals or corporations. In the case of individuals, the year of payment always controls. Under § 170(a)(2), accrual basis corporations may, under certain conditions, claim a deduction for the preceding year if paid within two and one-half months of the following tax year.

4. As a further exception to the year of payment rule, estates (and to a limited extent certain trusts) will be allowed a deduction for amounts permanently set aside for charitable purposes. The few trust situations which qualify under this exception are set forth in § 642(c)(2).

5. Unlike individuals and corporations, estates and trusts are not subject to any percentage limitations on the total amount that may be claimed as a charitable contribution deduction.

Although percentage limitations are inapplicable to an estate or trust, the full value of the amount contributed may not be deductible due to any of several special rules. First, the deduction is limited to amounts actually included in the gross income of the entity. Thus, a contribution of trust corpus would not be deductible unless the corpus had been included in the trust's gross income. In the event the entity has other nontaxable income (e. g., interest on municipal bonds), the contribution is deductible only in the proportion that the gross income bears to the total of the gross and nontaxable income. Second, § 642(c)(4) requires an adjustment when the estate or trust has a long-term capital gain in the tax year of the contribution. The deduction must be reduced by 60 percent of the long-term capital gain included in the total contribution. The amount of the capital gain included in the total contribution is determined as follows:

$$\frac{\text{Long-term capital gain}}{\text{Total gross income}} \times \text{Total contribution made}$$

Third, the deduction is not allowed to the extent that it is made possible through the receipt of unrelated business income under § 681.[26] These limitations are illustrated by the examples which follow.

**Example 7.** A trust has gross rents of $60,000, expenses attributable to the rents of $40,000, and nontaxable interest from state bonds of $20,000. Under the trust instrument, the trustee is directed to pay 30% of its net income to charity. Under this provision, the trustee does, in fact, pay $12,000 to charity

---

25. § 642(c)(1) and Reg. § 1.642(c)–1(b).
26. § 642(c)(4).

(30% × $40,000). The amount of the charitable deduction allowed is $9,000 ($60,000/$80,000) × $12,000.

**Example 8.** A trust has ordinary income of $90,000 and long-term capital gains of $60,000. Pursuant to the trust instrument, a charitable contribution of $30,000 is made. The amount of the capital gain included in the charitable contribution is $12,000 ($60,000/$150,000) × $30,000. Since $7,200 of this amount (60% × $12,000) will not be allowed, the charitable deduction is $22,800 ($30,000 − $7,200).

## DEDUCTION FOR DISTRIBUTIONS TO BENEFICIARIES

In the case of a simple trust, a deduction is allowed for the trust income which must be distributed currently; but in no event may this deduction exceed the trust's distributable net income.[27] Although the Internal Revenue Code does not use the term "simple trust," the Regulations state that a trust to which § 651 applies is referred to as a simple trust.[28] Under § 651(a), this is a trust which is required to distribute all of its income currently and which does not provide that any amounts may be paid, permanently set aside, or used for charitable purposes. The concept of distributable net income is explained later in connection with the tax treatment of beneficiaries.

An estate or a complex trust (i. e., a trust other than a simple trust) is allowed a deduction for amounts paid, credited, or required to be distributed to its beneficiaries. Section 661(a) provides that such deduction shall be the sum of the following:

1.  Any amount of income for such taxable year required to be distributed currently (including any amount required to be distributed which may be paid out of income or corpus to the extent such amount is paid out of income for such taxable year).

2.  Any other amounts properly paid or credited or required to be distributed for such taxable year.

The deduction for distributions to beneficiaries is limited in the same manner as it is for simple trusts. Thus, the deduction may not exceed the distributable net income of the estate or complex trust. Examples of complex trusts include trusts that accumulate income or distribute corpus, trusts in which the trustee has the power to accumulate or distribute (i. e., discretionary trusts), and trusts that make charitable contributions. It should be remembered that a trust may be a simple trust one year and a complex trust another year.

---

27. § 651(b).
28. Reg. § 1.651(a)–1.

## TAX CREDITS

An estate or trust will be allowed an investment credit to the extent not allocable to the beneficiaries. Similarly, any limitation on the credit for the purchase of qualifying used property is applied at both the entity level and the beneficiary level.[29] The recapture rules applicable to individuals also will apply to an estate or trust. An estate or trust also may claim the foreign tax credit allowed under § 901 to the extent not allocable to the beneficiaries.[30] Although neither estates nor trusts are allowed the tax credits for political campaign contributions, both are permitted to claim tax credits for wages paid to certain new employees. Like the investment tax credit, these tax credits must be apportioned between the estate or trust and the beneficiaries on the basis of the income allocable to each.

# TAXATION OF BENEFICIARIES

In considering the income tax treatment of beneficiaries of an estate or trust, certain basic concepts peculiar to this area of the Federal income tax should be recalled. First, the income of an estate or trust usually will be taxed to the entity or its beneficiaries but not to both. In certain cases, however, the income may be taxed to the grantor (or another person) of a trust if that party retains beneficial enjoyment or other control over trust income or corpus. Second, to the extent that the beneficiaries are taxed, the estate or trust serves as a mere conduit for the income involved. In other words, the income passed through from the entity does not lose its identity and will be classified by the beneficiaries in the same manner as if taxed to the estate or trust (e. g., a long-term capital gain realized by a trust remains a long-term capital gain to its beneficiaries). Third, the upper limit of a beneficiary's tax consequences will be set by the distributable net income of the entity.

The timing of any tax consequences to the beneficiary of a trust or an estate presents little problem except when the parties involved use different tax years. In such a situation involving a simple trust, § 652(c) provides that the amount which a beneficiary is required to include in gross income shall be based upon the amount of income of the trust for any taxable year or years of the trust ending within or with his or her taxable year. A similar rule regarding estates and complex trusts is specified in § 662(c).

**Example 9.** A trust uses a fiscal year of April 1 to March 31 for tax purposes. Its sole income beneficiary is a calendar year taxpayer. For the calendar year 19X6, the beneficiary would report

---

**29.** § 48(f).
**30.** § 642(a)(1).

whatever income was assignable to him or her for the trust's fiscal year April 1, 19X5, to March 31, 19X6. Note that if the trust was terminated as of December 31, 19X6, the beneficiary also would have to include any trust income assignable to him or her for the short year. This will result in a bunching of income.

## DISTRIBUTABLE NET INCOME

As noted earlier, the deduction for distributions to beneficiaries allowed an estate or trust always is limited to its *distributable net income*.[31] Likewise, the amount of income the beneficiaries must recognize cannot exceed distributable net income.[32] The importance of this concept, therefore, should be quite apparent. In essence, it is the tax expression of the trust accounting concept of income. Thus, it includes all distributable amounts, including tax-exempt income. However, it does not include capital gains allocable to corpus.

Distributable net income is computed by making the following adjustments specified by § 643 to the taxable income of the estate or trust:

1. Add back the deduction for distributions to beneficiaries.

2. Add back the personal exemption—$600 for estates, $300 for simple trusts, and $100 for complex trusts.

3. Add back the dividend or interest exclusion.

4. Add back *net* tax-exempt interest. In arriving at net tax-exempt interest, the total tax-exempt interest is reduced by any portion which is paid or set aside for charitable purposes and by related expenses nondeductible under § 265. The adjustment for nondeductible expenses is in the same proportion that total tax-exempt interest bears to total gross income (including tax-exempt interest).

5. Add back the long-term capital gain deduction.

6. Subtract any net capital gains taxable to the estate or trust (i. e., those allocable to corpus). In other words, the only net capital gains included in distributable net income are those attributable to beneficiaries or to charitable contributions.

7. Add back any *net* capital losses. In other words, capital losses are considered only to the extent that they affect the net capital gains included in distributable net income (refer to item 6).

8. In the case of simple trusts, subtract any extraordinary dividends and taxable stock dividends which the fiduciary, acting in good faith, allocates to corpus.

---

**31.**  § § 651(b) and 661(c).
**32.**  § § 652(a) and 662(a).

9.  Special treatment is required by § 643(a)(6) for the foreign income received from sources outside the United States by a foreign trust.

Because the computation of distributable net income requires starting with the taxable income of the estate or trust, and since taxable income is computed by deducting all of the expenses of the entity (whether or not they were allocated to corpus on the books of the estate or trust), note that distributable net income will be reduced by expenses chargeable to corpus. The effect of this procedure is to reduce the taxable income of the income beneficiaries, even though the actual distributions to them exceed distributable net income, because the distributions are not reduced by expenses allocated to corpus.

The computation procedure used to determine distributable net income and the deduction for distributions to beneficiaries allowed an estate or trust is illustrated in the following example.

**Example 10.** The trust instrument requires that all the income of a trust be distributed currently to D, the beneficiary. Capital gains are allocable to corpus, and all expenses are chargeable against corpus. During the taxable year, the trust has the following items of income deductions:

| | |
|---|---:|
| Dividends from domestic corporations | $ 25,000 |
| Extraordinary dividends allocated to corpus by the trustee in good faith | 10,000 |
| Taxable interest | 15,000 |
| Tax-exempt interest | 20,000 |
| Long-term capital gains | 10,000 |
| Trustee's commissions and miscellaneous expenses allocable to corpus | 6,000 |

The income of the trust determined under § 643(b) which is currently distributable to D is $60,000. This amount consists of dividends of $25,000, taxable interest of $15,000, and tax-exempt interest of $20,000. The trustee's commissions and miscellaneous expenses allocable to tax-exempt interest amount to $2,000 [($20,000/$60,000) × $6,000].

The distributable net income of the trust is $54,000, computed as follows:

| | | |
|---|---:|---:|
| Dividends | | $ 25,000 |
| Taxable interest | | 15,000 |
| Tax-exempt interest | $ 20,000 | |
| Less expenses allocable thereto | 2,000 | 18,000 |
| Total | | $ 58,000 |
| Less expenses [$6,000 − $2,000 (allocable to tax-exempt interest)] | | 4,000 |
| Distributable net income | | $ 54,000 |

In determining the distributable net income of $54,000 in Example 10, note that the taxable income of the trust was computed with the following modifications:

—No deduction was taken for the distributions to D.

—No deduction was taken for the $300 personal deduction of a simple trust (i. e., a trust required to distribute all income currently).

—The capital gains allocable to corpus were excluded, and the 60 percent long-term capital gain deduction was not taken.

—The extraordinary dividends allocated to corpus by the trustee in good faith were excluded.

—The dividend or interest exclusion was not taken.

—The tax-exempt interest (as adjusted for allocable expenses) was included.

## DISTRIBUTIONS BY SIMPLE TRUSTS

Section 651 deals with the deduction allowed a simple trust for distributions to its beneficiaries; § 652 concerns the tax treatment of the beneficiaries. Under the latter provision, the amount taxable to the beneficiaries is limited by the trust's distributable net income. Recall, however, that since distributable net income includes tax-exempt income, the amount taxable to beneficiaries could be less than such income. Also, in the case of more than one income beneficiary, distributable net income must be apportioned ratably according to the amount required to be distributed currently to each.

> **Example 11.** For calendar year 19X6, a simple trust has ordinary income of $40,000, a long-term capital gain of $15,000 (allocable to corpus), and a trustee commission expense of $4,000 (payable from corpus). Its two income beneficiaries, A and B, are entitled to the trust's annual income based on shares of 75% and 25%, respectively. Although A is entitled to receive $30,000 as his share (75% × $40,000), he will be taxed on only $27,000 (75% × distributable net income of $36,000). Likewise, B will be entitled to receive $10,000 (25% × $40,000) but will be taxed on only $9,000 (25% × distributable net income of $36,000). The $15,000 of capital gains will be taxed to the trust.

It is important to note that § 652 requires the foregoing treatment regardless of whether or not the income is actually distributed to the beneficiaries and without regard to their methods of accounting. Thus, in the preceding example, the tax consequences of A and B would be unaffected by the fact that they may have received none of the trust income during 19X6.

As noted earlier, a trust could be a simple trust one year and a complex trust in another. This is a very real likelihood with a discretionary trust; the trustee is given the power to distribute corpus to the income beneficiary. Thus, in those years when only income is distributed, the trust is a simple trust. However, in years when corpus also is distributed, it will be classified as a complex trust. Even a trust that always has been a simple trust because it cannot accumulate income or distribute corpus will be a complex trust in the year of its termination. This occurs because termination involves the distribution of corpus in satisfaction of the remainder or reversionary interests.

## DISTRIBUTIONS BY ESTATES AND COMPLEX TRUSTS

The distributions of an estate or complex trust must be categorized into a two-tier system which governs the priority of taxation of the distributions. Although the maximum amount of distributions which will be taxed to the beneficiaries is limited to distributable net income, this classification system determines which distributions will be taxed in full, which will be taxed only in part, and which will not be taxed.

Income required to be distributed currently, whether distributed or not, is categorized as a *first-tier distribution*. All other amounts properly paid, credited, or required to be distributed are considered to be *second-tier distributions*.[33] First-tier distributions are taxed in full to the beneficiaries if distributable net income is sufficient to cover these distributions. If the first-tier distributions exceed distributable net income, however, each beneficiary would be taxed only on a proportionate part of the distributable net income. Second-tier distributions are not taxed if the first-tier distributions exceed distributable net income. However, if both first and second-tier distributions are made and the first-tier distributions do not exceed distributable net income, the second-tier distributions will be taxed in part or in total if the combined distributions do not exceed distributable net income.

The tax effects of distributions from an estate or complex trust can be illustrated by considering each of the following four different situations:

1. Only first-tier distributions are made, but the sum of the distributions is less than distributable net income.

2. Only first-tier distributions are made, and the sum of the distributions exceeds distributable net income.

3. Both first- and second-tier distributions are made, but the first-tier distributions exceed distributable net income.

4. Both first- and second-tier distributions are made, and the first-tier distributions do not exceed distributable net income. However, the sum of both first- and second-tier distributions does exceed distributable net income.

---

33. § § 662(a)(1) and (2).

Distributions covered by the first situation can be illustrated by the following example:

> **Example 12.** The trust instrument provides that B, the sole income beneficiary, is to receive $20,000 annually. If the trust income is not sufficient to pay this amount, the trustee is empowered to invade corpus to the extent necessary. During the current year, the trust's distributable net income is $25,000, and pursuant to the trust instrument, $20,000 is paid to B. The measure of B's income is limited to $20,000. It should be noted, however, that trust income retains its character. Thus, if 20% of distributable net income were tax-exempt income, the beneficiary would be considered to have received $4,000 (20% × $20,000 distributed) of tax-exempt income. As a result, only $16,000 of the distributions would be taxable to B.

When only first-tier distributions are made and they exceed distributable net income (situation 2), the following formula must be used:

$$\frac{\text{First-tier distributions to the beneficiary}}{\text{First-tier distributions to all beneficiaries}} \times \begin{array}{c}\text{Distributable net}\\ \text{income (without}\\ \text{deduction for chari-}\\ \text{table contributions)}\end{array} = \begin{array}{c}\text{Amount bene-}\\ \text{ficiary must}\\ \text{include in}\\ \text{gross income}\end{array}$$

Note that in working with this formula, amounts passing to charitable organizations are not included.

> **Example 13.** A trust is required to distribute its current income as follows: 50% to A, 25% to B, and 25% to C (a qualifying charitable organization). During the current year, it has income of $40,000 and distributable net income of $27,000, without the deduction for charitable contributions. Pursuant to the trust instrument, the following amounts are paid out: $20,000 to A (50% × $40,000), $10,000 to B (25% × $40,000), and $10,000 to C (25% × $40,000). A must include $18,000 in gross income ($20,000/$30,000 × $27,000), and B must include $9,000 ($10,000/$30,000 × $27,000). Note that the distribution to the charitable organization was not considered in allocating distributable net income to the beneficiaries (the denominator of the fraction is only $30,000).

When both first- and second-tier distributions are made and the first-tier distributions exceed the distributable net income, the formula used in the preceding example would be applied to the first-tier distributions. Note, however, that none of the second-tier distributions would be taxed, because they are not considered to be from distributable net income.

If both first- and second-tier distributions are made and the first-tier distributions do not exceed distributable net income, but the total of both first- and second-tier distributions do exceed distributable net income (situation 4), the second-tier beneficiaries must recognize income as:

$$\frac{\text{Second-tier distributions to the beneficiary}}{\text{Second-tier distributions to all beneficiaries}} \times \begin{matrix}\text{Distributable net income}\\ \text{(less first-tier distri-}\\ \text{butions and charitable}\\ \text{contributions)}\end{matrix} = \begin{matrix}\text{The benefici-}\\ \text{ary's share of}\\ \text{distributable}\\ \text{net income}\end{matrix}$$

It should be noted that charitable contributions are taken into account at this point.

> **Example 14.**  The trust instrument requires that $20,000 of income be distributed annually to R. If any income remains, it may be accumulated or distributed to S, T, and U at the trustee's discretion. The trustee may also invade corpus for the benefit of R, S, T, or U. In the taxable year, the trust has distributable net income of $40,000 and the trustee distributes $20,000 of income to R. Of the remaining $20,000 of income, the trustee distributes $6,000 each to S, T, and U and an additional $6,000 to R. Since R is a first-tier beneficiary, she must include $20,000 as income. This leaves $20,000 in distributable net income which must be allocated over the $24,000 received by the second-tier beneficiaries (R, S, T, and U). R, S, T, and U each include $5,000 ($6,000/$24,000 × $20,000) in income. Thus, R, both a first- and second-tier beneficiary, is taxed on a total of $25,000 ($20,000 + $5,000).

## SEPARATE SHARE RULE

Section 663(c) states, in part, that for the sole purpose of determining the amount of distributable net income in the application of § § 661 and 662 in the case of a single trust with more than one beneficiary, substantially separate and independent shares of different beneficiaries in the trust shall be treated as *separate trusts*. The reason for this special rule can be illustrated as follows:

> **Example 15.**  Under the terms of the trust instrument, the trustee has discretion to distribute or accumulate income on behalf of G and H (in equal shares). The trustee also has the power to invade the corpus for the benefit of either beneficiary to the extent of his one-half interest in the trust. For the current year, the distributable net income of the trust is $10,000. Of this amount, $5,000 is distributed to G and $5,000 is accumulated on behalf of H. In addition, the trustee pays $20,000 from corpus to G. Without the separate share rule, G would be taxed on $10,000 (the amount of the distributable net income). With the separate share rule, G will be taxed on only $5,000, his share of the distributable net income, and will receive the $20,000 corpus distribu-

tion tax-free. The trust will be taxed on H's $5,000 share of distributable net income which is accumulated.

The separate share rule obviously is designed to prevent the inequity which would otherwise result if the corpus payment were treated under the regular rules applicable to second-tier beneficiaries. Referring to the preceding example, the effect of the separate share rule is to produce a two-trust result: one trust for G and one for H, each with distributable net income of $5,000.

# CHARACTER OF INCOME

Consistent with the conduit concept, various classes of income (e. g., dividends, long-term capital gains, tax-exempt interest) will have the same character in the hands of the beneficiaries that they had when received by the estate or trust.[34] However, if there are multiple beneficiaries *and* if all of the distributable net income is distributed, a problem arises with respect to the allocation of the various classes of income among the beneficiaries. Regulation § 1.662(b)–1 provides an answer to this problem; it requires the following treatment:

> The amounts are treated as consisting of the same proportion of each class of items entering into the computation of distributable net income as the total of each class bears to the total distributable net income of the estate or trust unless the terms of the governing instrument specifically allocate different classes of income to different beneficiaries or unless local law requires such an allocation.

Reduced to formula form this generally means:

$$\frac{\text{Beneficiary's total share of distributable net income}}{\text{Total distributable net income}} \times \begin{matrix}\text{Total of a particular}\\\text{class of distributable}\\\text{net income (e. g., tax-}\\\text{exempt interest)}\end{matrix} = \begin{matrix}\text{Beneficiary's share}\\\text{of the particular}\\\text{class of distribu-}\\\text{table net income}\end{matrix}$$

## ALLOCATION OF CLASSES OF INCOME

If the estate or trust distributes only part of its distributable net income, the total of a particular class of distributable net income deemed distributed must first be determined. This would be done as follows:

$$\frac{\text{Total distribution}}{\text{Total distributable net income}} \times \begin{matrix}\text{Total of a particular}\\\text{class of distributable}\\\text{net income}\end{matrix} = \begin{matrix}\text{Total of a particular}\\\text{class of distributable}\\\text{net income deemed dis-}\\\text{tributed}\end{matrix}$$

---

**34.**  § § 652(b) and 662(b).

**Example 16.** During the current year, a trust has distributable net income of $40,000 made up of the following: $10,000 of taxable interest, $10,000 of tax-exempt interest, and $20,000 of dividends. Of this income, $8,000 is distributed to M and $12,000 to N, both noncharitable beneficiaries. The amount of each particular class of distributable net income deemed distributed will be $5,000 of taxable interest ($20,000/$40,000) × $10,000, $5,000 of tax-exempt interest ($20,000/$40,000) × $10,000, and $10,000 of dividends ($20,000/$40,000) × $20,000. M's share of this income is $8,000, made up of $2,000 of taxable interest (40% × $5,000), $2,000 of tax-exempt interest (40% × $5,000), and $4,000 of dividends (40% × $10,000). The remaining amount of each income item deemed distributed would be N's share: $3,000 of taxable interest, $3,000 of tax-exempt interest, and $6,000 of dividends.

## SPECIAL ALLOCATIONS

Under certain circumstances, the parties involved may modify the method of allocation set forth above. The Regulations state that a modification will be permitted only to the extent that the allocation is required in the trust instrument and only to the extent that it has an economic effect independent of the income tax consequences of the allocation.[35] This requirement should sound familiar. Recall that substantial economic effect is required of any special allocations of various items of income, deductions, or credits in the partnership area [§ 704(b)].

**Example 17.** In the preceding example, suppose that the trustee has the discretion to allocate different classes of income to different beneficiaries and designates all of N's $12,000 distribution as being from the tax-exempt income. Such a designation *would not be recognized* for tax purposes, and the allocation result of Example 16 would be used.

**Example 18.** Suppose, however, that the trust instrument stipulated that N was to receive all of the income from tax-exempt securities, and pursuant to this provision, the $10,000 of the nontaxable interest is paid to him. Here, the allocation would be recognized, and $10,000 of N's $12,000 distribution would be tax-exempt.

## DEDUCTIONS RELATED TO CLASSES OF INCOME

To determine the amount of the various types of income, the gross amount of each item must be reduced by any related deductions.

---

**35.** Reg. § 1.652(b)–2(b).

When the related deductions exceed the income, however, the trustee may, within certain limits, apply the excess against whatever other class of income he or she chooses. In no event, however, may the excess deductions attributable to tax-exempt income be used to absorb other types of income. As noted earlier in Example 10, a pro rata share of *nonbusiness* deductions (e. g., trustee's commissions) must be assigned to nontaxable income.

*Charitable Contributions.*  The effect of a charitable contribution deduction on the amount taxable to beneficiaries was partially illustrated in Example 13. In general, the deduction will not affect the amounts taxable to first-tier beneficiaries, but it can reduce the tax consequences of second-tier beneficiaries if the deduction is paid out of current income.

*Capital Gains.*  Capital gains are taxable to the estate or trust unless paid, credited, or required to be distributed to the beneficiary under the governing instrument (i. e., decedent's will or trust agreement) or pursuant to local law. If capital gains are required to be distributed, they would be taxable to the beneficiary (to the extent of distributable net income) even if actually allocated to corpus.

*Losses.*  Losses of an estate or trust may not be passed through to the beneficiary except in the year of the estate or trust's termination. At that time, any unused losses (e. g., capital or net operating) or current deductions in excess of gross income can be deducted by the recipients of the estate or trust property (i. e., the residuary legatee under a will or the remainderman of a trust).[36]

# THE THROWBACK RULE

To understand the purpose and rationale of the throwback provision, the general nature of taxation of trusts and their beneficiaries must be reviewed. Recall that the general rule of taxation of trusts and beneficiaries is that the income from trust assets will be taxed to the trust itself or to the beneficiary, but not to both. Remember, also, that as a general rule a beneficiary is not taxed on any distributions in excess of the trust's distributable net income. Because of these general rules, trustees of complex trusts may be tempted to arrange distributions in such a manner that would result in a minimum of income tax consequences to all the parties involved. For instance, if the trust is in a lower tax bracket than its beneficiaries, income could be accumulated at the trust level for several years before being distributed to the beneficiaries. The tax consequences that would result to the beneficiaries in the year of distribution would be limited by the trust's distributable net income for that year. Even further tax savings could be achieved by the use of multiple trusts, because the in-

---

**36.**  § 642(h).

come during the accumulation period would be spread over more than one taxpaying entity, thereby avoiding the graduated tax rates.

In order to preclude the tax minimization schemes described above, the Code has for many years (since 1954) contained some type of *throwback rule*. Because of this type of rule, a beneficiary's tax on a distribution of income accumulated by a trust in a prior year will be equal to the increase in the beneficiary's tax for such prior year that would have resulted if the income had been distributed in the year it was earned by the trust. The tax as so computed, however, is levied for the actual year of the distribution. In essence, the purpose of the throwback rule is to place the beneficiaries of complex trusts in the same tax position they would have been in if they had received the distributions during the years in which the trust was accumulating the income.

A detailed description of the application of the throwback rule is beyond the scope of this text. Readers interested in a more in-depth coverage of the throwback rule should see the detailed examples of its operation contained in the Regulations and should also review tax Form 4970 (Tax on Accumulation Distribution of Trusts) and Schedule J—Form 1041 (Allocation of Accumulation Distribution) together with their respective instructions.

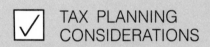

## TAX PLANNING CONSIDERATIONS

There are several specific tax planning possibilities which should prove helpful in minimizing the income tax effects on estates, trusts, and their beneficiaries. These items are discussed below in connection with post-mortem tax planning and the use of trusts as income tax savings devices.

### INCOME TAX PLANNING FOR ESTATES

Recall that as a separate entity, an estate can select its own tax year and accounting methods. The executor of an estate should consider selecting a fiscal year, because this will determine when beneficiaries must include income distributions from the estate in their own tax returns. Remember that beneficiaries must include the income for their tax year with or within which the estate's tax year ends. Proper selection could thus result in a smoothing out of income and reduce the income taxes for all parties involved. Caution also should be taken in determining when the estate is to be terminated. If a fiscal year had been selected for the estate, a bunching of income to the beneficiaries could occur in the year the estate is closed.

Although prolonging the termination of an estate can be effective for income tax planning, remember that the IRS carefully examines the purpose of keeping the estate open. Also, since unused losses of an estate will pass on to the beneficiaries, the estate should be closed at such a time that its beneficiaries can enjoy the maximum tax benefit of such losses.

Another very important tax planning opportunity involves the timing and amounts of income distributions to the beneficiaries. If the executor can make income distributions at his discretion, he should evaluate the relative income tax brackets of the estate and the beneficiaries. By properly timing such distributions, the overall income tax consequences can be minimized. Care should be taken, however, to time such distributions in light of the estate's distributable net income. Recall that the income distributions may be taxable to the extent of the estate's distributable net income.

Some of these tax planning opportunities for estates are illustrated in the following examples:

**Example 19.** B, the sole beneficiary of an estate is a calendar year cash basis taxpayer. If the estate elects a fiscal year of February 1 to January 31, all distributions during the period of February 1, 19X1, to December 31, 19X1, will be reported on B's tax return for calendar year 19X2 (due April 15, 19X3). Thus, any income taxes resulting from a $50,000 distribution made by the estate on March 1, 19X1, will be deferred until April 15, 19X3.

**Example 20.** For several years prior to his death on March 7, 19X1, D had entered into annual deferred compensation agreements with his employer. These agreements collectively called for the payment of $200,000 six months after D's retirement or death. To provide a maximum 12-month period within which to generate deductions to offset this large item of income in respect of a decedent, the executor or administrator of the estate should elect a fiscal year of September 1, 19X1, to August 31, 19X2. The election is made simply by filing the estate's first tax return for the short period of March 7, 19X1, to August 31, 19X1.

**Example 21.** Assume the same facts as in Example 19. If the estate is closed on December 15, 19X2, the distributable net income for both the fiscal year ending January 31, 19X2, and the final tax year ending December 15, 19X2, must be included in B's tax return for the calendar year 19X2. To avoid the effect of this bunching of income, the estate should not be closed until calendar year 19X3.

**Example 22.** Assume the same facts as in Example 21 except that the estate has substantial excess deductions for the period February 1, 19X2, to December 15, 19X2. If B is in a high marginal income tax bracket for calendar year 19X2, the estate should be closed so that the excess deductions will be passed through to its beneficiary. However, if B anticipates being in an even higher tax bracket in 19X3, termination of the estate should be postponed.

**Example 23.** An estate has an income beneficiary (B), a remainderperson (R), and distributable net income (DNI) of $40,000. If R has an expiring net operating loss, a distribution by the estate of $40,000 in property not specifically bequeathed will shift the tax consequences of DNI to R. Such a distribution will result in tax savings to B and the estate without any incremental tax consequences to R. Since distributions from an estate are not subject to the throwback rule, the estate might withhold distributions to B during tax years in which its marginal tax bracket is less than that of B.

One final note regarding income tax planning for an estate involves the dilemma of selecting a valuation for death tax purposes. Recall that the death tax valuation of an estate's assets could be a major factor in establishing the tax basis of each asset for subsequent depreciation or gain or loss determination when sold. Thus, the executor should consider the total tax consequences—both death tax and income tax—of selecting a valuation for estate tax purposes.

## INCOME TAX PLANNING WITH TRUSTS

The great variety of trusts provides the grantor, trustee, and beneficiaries with excellent opportunities for tax planning. One of the greatest advantages of trusts is the opportunity to shift income away from a higher tax bracket grantor to a lower tax bracket trust or its beneficiaries.

Like an estate, a trust is a separate taxable entity which can select its own tax year and accounting methods. The same tax planning available to the executor of an estate is available to the trustee in selecting a fiscal year for the trust. Also, the distributions from a trust are taxable to its beneficiaries to the extent of its distributable net income. Thus, if income distributions are discretionary, the trustee can time such distributions to minimize the income tax consequences to all parties. Remember, however, that the throwback rule applies to complex trusts, and consequently, the timing of distributions may prove to be of limited benefit and could result in a greater tax than if distributions had been made annually.

## PROBLEM MATERIALS

### Discussion Questions

1. When must an income tax return be filed for an estate? A trust? When could the fiduciary be held liable for the income tax due from an estate or trust?

2.  What is the general scheme of income taxation of trusts and estates? How does the conduit concept relate to this general approach?

3.  Under what circumstances could an estate be taxed on a distribution of property to a beneficiary? When could cash be used to avoid any tax consequences to the estate?

4.  What is income in respect of a decedent? What are the tax consequences to a recipient of income in respect of a decedent?

5.  How must an estate or trust treat its deductions for depreciation and depletion? How does this treatment differ from the deductibility of administrative expenses or losses for death tax purposes?

6.  What happens to net operating loss carryovers of an estate or trust if the entity is terminated before the deductions can be taken? How can this be a possible tax planning opportunity?

7.  Discuss the income tax treatment of charitable contributions made by an estate or trust. How does this treatment differ from the requirements for charitable contribution deductions of individual taxpayers? What effect does a long-term capital gain have on the charitable contribution deduction for an estate or trust?

8.  What is distributable net income? Why is this amount significant in the income taxation of estates, trusts, and their beneficiaries?

9.  Distinguish between first- and second-tier distributions from estates and complex trusts. Discuss the tax consequences to the beneficiaries receiving such distributions.

10.  What is the separate share rule? Why would this rule be of particular significance to a beneficiary who receives both first- and second-tier distributions?

11.  How must the various classes of income be allocated among multiple beneficiaries of an estate or trust?

12.  Under what circumstances would special allocations of particular classes of income to specific beneficiaries be recognized for income tax purposes?

13.  What is the throwback rule? When is it applicable? Why was such a rule adopted?

## Problems

14.  In 19X5, G created an irrevocable trust with a gift of 400 shares of Unimax stock, which had a basis to him of $20,000 and a fair market value of $18,000. G paid a gift tax of $1,000 on the transfer. In 19X8, the trust sells the stock for $16,000.

    (a) What is the trust's basis for determining the gain or loss?

    (b) What is the amount and character of the gain or loss?

15.  Assume the same facts as in the preceding problem except that the stock is sold by the trust in 19X8 for the following:

    (a) $21,000.

    (b) $19,000.

    Determine the amount and character of the gain or loss.

16. In accordance with instructions of the decedent's will, the estate distributes land having a fair market value of $30,000 and an adjusted basis to the estate of $25,000 as a specific gift of property.

    (a) What are the income tax consequences to the estate?

    (b) What are the income tax consequences to the beneficiary?

    (c) Would your answers to (a) and (b) be any different if the land were used to satisfy a specific cash bequest of $30,000?

17. A trust receives $1,200 in taxable dividends from a qualifying domestic corporation in 19X8. Of this amount, $300 is allocable to the beneficiaries of the trust.

    (a) Can the trust claim a dividend exclusion?

    (b) If so, how much?

18. F creates a trust, with S and D as income beneficiaries, by the transfer of a 10-unit apartment complex. Under the terms of the trust instrument, the income from the trust is to be distributed annually in equal shares, and the trustee is directed to set aside income as a depreciation reserve. Depreciation on the trust property for the current year amounts to $12,000, and the trustee allocates $9,000 of the trust income as a depreciation reserve.

    (a) How much of a depreciation deduction will be allowed to the trust?

    (b) Will the income beneficiaries be entitled to a depreciation deduction? If so, how much?

19. A trust has rental income of $40,000 (gross rents of $75,000 less expenses of $35,000) and nontaxable interest from state bonds of $25,000 for calendar year 19X8. In accordance with the trust instrument, the trustee pays $20,000 (40% of its net income) to a specified charity. How much of the charitable contribution may be deducted by the trust?

20. The X Trust had the following sources of income for the year 19X8:

    | | |
    |---|---:|
    | Dividends from a domestic corporation | $ 150,000 |
    | Taxable interest | 75,000 |
    | Long-term capital gains | 15,000 |
    | Tax-exempt interest | 60,000 |
    | Total | $ 300,000 |

    The trustee's commission for the year amounted to $20,000.

    (a) How much of the trustee's commission is allocable to tax-exempt income?

    (b) Can such amount be deducted by the trust?

    (c) Is there any possibility that your tax return preparation fee may not be deductible by the trust?

21. The Z Trust had taxable income of $4,000 for 19X8. In computing its taxable income, the following deductions and exclusions were used:

| | |
|---|---:|
| Deduction for distribution to Z | $ 30,000 |
| Long-term capital gain deduction | |
| (60% of 2,000) | 1,200 |
| Dividends received exclusion | 100 |
| Personal exemption of trust | 100 |
| Tax-exempt interest | 20,000 |
| Trustee's fee (total of $5,000, but only | |
| $3,000 deductible because $2,000 is allocated | |
| to tax-exempt income) | 3,000 |

(a) Is the trust required to distribute all of its income currently?

(b) What is the trust's distributable net income?

(c) If the trust distributed $65,000 to Z during the year, how much must Z recognize as trust income?

22. The LMN Trust is a simple trust which uses the calendar year for tax purposes. Its three income beneficiaries (L, M, and N) are entitled to the trust's annual income based on shares of one-third each. For the calendar year 19X8 the trust has ordinary income of $60,000, a long-term capital gain of $18,000 (allocable to corpus), and a trustee commission expense of $6,000, which is payable from corpus.

(a) What is the trust's distributable net income for 19X8?

(b) How much income is each beneficiary entitled to receive?

(c) How much of the trust's income will be taxed to each of the beneficiaries?

(d) Who will be taxed on the long-term capital gains?

23. The SP Trust uses a fiscal year of February 1 to January 31 for income tax purposes. A, the trust's sole income beneficiary, is a calendar year taxpayer. The trust is required to currently distribute all of its income to A. For its fiscal year ending January 31, 19X8, the trust has distributable net income of $30,000.

(a) How much of the trust's income will be taxed to A for the calendar year 19X8?

(b) If the SP Trust were terminated on December 21, 19X8, what effect would this have on your answer to (a)?

24. A trust is required to distribute $20,000 annually to its two income beneficiaries, A and B, in shares of 75% and 25%, respectively. If the trust income is not sufficient to pay these amounts, the trustee is empowered to invade corpus to the extent necessary. During the current year, the trust has distributable net income of $12,000 and the trustee distributed $15,000 to A and $5,000 to B.

(a) How much of the $15,000 distributed to A must be included in his gross income?

(b) How much of the $5,000 distributed to B must be included in his gross income?

(c) Are these distributions considered to be first-tier or second-tier distributions? What difference would it make to B if the trust instrument required that A was to receive $15,000 annually and any income remainder was to be paid to B, but in no event was B to receive less than $5,000?

25. A complex trust is required to distribute its current income as follows: $20,000 annually to A, and if any income remains, it may be distributed to B and C at the trustee's discretion. The trustee is also empowered to invade corpus for the benefit of A, B, and C. During the current year, the trust has distributable net income of $50,000. The trustee distributes $20,000 to A as required, $18,000 to both B and C, and an additional $18,000 to A.

    (a) What is the maximum amount of the $74,000 distributed which must be taxed to the beneficiaries?

    (b) How much will be taxed to A?

    (c) To B?

    (d) To C?

26. Under the terms of the trust instrument, the trustee has discretion to distribute or accumulate income on behalf of W, S, and D in equal shares. The trustee is also empowered to invade corpus for the benefit of any of the beneficiaries to the extent of their respective one-third interest in the trust. In 19X8, the trust has distributable net income of $48,000. Of this amount, $16,000 is distributed to W and $10,000 is distributed to S. The remaining $6,000 of S's share of trust income and D's entire $16,000 share are accumulated by the trust. Additionally, the trustee distributes $20,000 from corpus to W.

    (a) How much income is taxed to W? (Suggestion: Use the separate share rule.)

    (b) To S?

    (c) To D?

    (d) To the trust?

27. During the current year, a trust has $60,000 of distributable net income comprising $30,000 of dividends, $20,000 of taxable interest, and $10,000 of tax-exempt interest. The trust's two noncharitable income beneficiaries, S and T, receive $20,000 each.

    (a) How much of each class of income will be deemed to have been distributed?

    (b) How much of each class of income is deemed to have been distributed to S? To T?

28. For each of the independent statements appearing below, indicate whether the tax attribute is applicable only to estates (E), only to complex trusts (T), to both estates and complex trusts (B), or to neither (N).

    (a) Unrestricted selection of taxable year.

    (b) The entity's income tax liability may be paid in quarterly installments.

    (c) The entity must file an income tax return if its gross income for the year is $600 or more.

    (d) The entity must use the cash method of reporting its income and deductions.

    (e) The entity is entitled to a personal exemption of $600.

(f) In the year of its termination, the entity's net operating loss carryovers will be passed on to its beneficiaries.

(g) The entity's fiduciary is generally free to select the date of its termination.

(h) The entity's deduction for charitable contributions is not subject to a percentage limitation.

(i) Distributions from the entity may be subject to the throwback rule.

# Chapter 21

# Tax Administration
# and Practice

## TAX ADMINISTRATION

To provide quality tax consulting services, it is necessary to understand how the IRS is organized and how its various administrative groups function. For example, the taxpayer may object to a proposed deficiency assessment resulting from an IRS audit. The tax specialist must be familiar with IRS administrative appeal procedures to make a fully informed decision concerning appeal of the deficiency.

### IRS PROCEDURE—INDIVIDUAL RULINGS

Rulings which are issued by the National Office represent a written statement of the position of the IRS concerning the tax consequences of a course of action contemplated by the taxpayer. Individual rulings do not have the force and effect of law, but they do provide guidance and support for taxpayers in similar transactions. The IRS will issue rulings only on uncompleted, actual (rather than hypothetical) transactions or on transactions which have been completed prior to the filing of the tax return for the year in question.

The IRS will not, in certain circumstances, issue a ruling. It will not rule in cases which essentially involve a question of fact.[1] For example, no ruling will be issued to determine whether compensation paid to employees is reasonable in amount and therefore allowable as a deduction.[2]

---

1. Rev.Proc. 79–45, 1979–2 C.B. 508.
2. Rev.Proc. 82–22, 1982–1 C.B. 469.

A ruling simply represents the current opinion of the IRS on the tax consequences of a particular transaction with a given set of facts. IRS rulings are not immutable. They are frequently declared obsolete or superseded by new revenue rulings in response to tax law changes. However, revocation or modification of a ruling is usually not applied retroactively to the taxpayer who received the ruling if he or she acted in good faith in reliance upon the ruling and if the facts in the ruling request were in agreement with the completed transaction. The IRS may revoke any ruling if, upon subsequent audit, the agent finds a misstatement or omission of facts or substantial discrepancies between the facts in the ruling request and the actual situation. It should be noted that a ruling may be relied upon only by the taxpayer who requested and received it.

Issuance of rulings benefits both the IRS and the taxpayer. The IRS ruling policy is an attempt to promote a uniform application of the tax laws. In addition, other benefits may accrue to the government through the issuance of rulings. Rulings may reduce the volume of litigation or number of disputes with revenue agents which would otherwise result, and they give the IRS an awareness of the significant transactions being consummated by taxpayers. From the taxpayer's point of view, an advance ruling reduces the uncertainty of potential tax consequences resulting from a proposed course of action. Taxpayers frequently request a ruling prior to the consummation of a tax-free corporate reorganization because of the severe tax consequences which would result if the reorganization is subsequently deemed to be taxable. Liquidations, stock redemptions, and transfers to controlled corporations under § 351 are other sensitive areas in which taxpayers desire confirmation.

Individual rulings which are of both sufficient importance and general interest may be published as Revenue Rulings (in anonymous form) and thus made available to all taxpayers. Prior to 1976, the position of the IRS was that unpublished (letter) rulings were confidential information and should not be made available to other taxpayers. This position was successfully challenged by taxpayers as being in violation of the Freedom of Information Act.[3] Due to this litigation, the Tax Reform Act of 1976 inserted new provisions regarding public disclosure of IRS written determinations.[4] In general, all unpublished letter rulings, determination letters, and technical advice memoranda are now open to public inspection once identifying details and certain confidential information have been deleted. Letter rulings and technical advice memoranda now are reprinted and published by Prentice-Hall and Commerce Clearing House. The general availability of such materials should assist in the conduct of tax research and planning.

---

**3.** *Tax Analysts and Advocates v. Comm.*, 74–2 USTC ¶ 9635, 34 AFTR2d 74–5731, 505 F.2d 352 (CA–DC, 1974).

**4.** § 6110.

*Ruling Requests.*  To insure a relevant and informed response from the IRS, it is important to include a comprehensive statement of the facts in a ruling request. The request should detail the points of law to be covered in the ruling. In addition, documentation of the request with relevant authority (e. g., court cases and related Sections of the Internal Revenue Code and Regulations) is necessary. For example, the taxpayer should not merely request that a reorganization be treated as nontaxable. The request should include specific details:

—The exchange qualifies for nonrecognition of gain or loss under § 361(a).

—The exchange of stock or securities qualifies under § § 354 and 368(a)(1)(C), etc.

—The basis of stock received by the shareholders of both the acquired and the acquiring corporations is determined under § § 358 and 362, respectively.

## IRS PROCEDURE—ADDITIONAL ISSUANCES

In addition to unpublished letter rulings and published rulings, the IRS also issues:

—Revenue procedures.

—Determination letters.

—Technical advices.

The IRS has published a Statement of Procedural Rules, which is an expression of internal practices and policies.[5] For example, the IRS states the purposes of both revenue rulings and revenue procedures, defines them, and lists publication standards for both. This is an expression of policy the IRS will follow when issuing and publishing revenue rulings and revenue procedures.

Determination letters are issued by the District Director for completed transactions when the issues involved are covered by judicial or statutory authority, regulations, or rulings. Determination letters are issued for various death, gift, income, excise, and employment tax matters.

**Example 1.**  T Corporation recently opened a car clinic and, in connection, has employed numerous mechanics. The corporation is not certain if the mechanics are to be treated as employees or as independent contractors for withholding and payroll tax purposes. T Corporation may request a determination letter from the appropriate District Director.

**Example 2.**  Assume the same facts as in Example 1. T Corporation would like to establish a pension plan that qualifies for the

---

5.   Statement of Procedural Rules, 26 C.F.R. 601.201.

tax advantages of § § 401 through 404. To determine whether the plan qualifies, a determination letter can be requested and obtained from the IRS.

**Example 3.** A group of doctors plans to form an association to construct and operate a hospital. The determination letter procedure is appropriate to ascertain their status—either subject to the Federal income tax or tax-exempt.

Technical advice is rendered by the National Office to the District Director and/or Regional Commissioner in response to the specific request of an agent, Appellate Conferee, or District Director. The taxpayer may ask that a request for technical advice be made if an issue in dispute is not treated by the law or precedent and/or published rulings or regulations. Technical advice also is appropriate when there exists reason to believe that the tax law is not being administered consistently by the IRS. For example, a taxpayer may inquire why an agent proposes to disallow a certain expenditure when agents in other districts permit the deduction.

## THE AUDIT PROCESS

*Selection of Returns for Audit.* The IRS uses the Discriminant Function System (DIF) as a starting point in the selection of tax returns for audit. This selection procedure utilizes mathematical formulae to select tax returns which are most likely to contain errors and yield substantial amounts of additional tax revenues upon audit. Despite the use of computer selection processes, the ultimate selection of returns for audit is still conducted by the classification staff within the Audit Division of the IRS.

The IRS does not openly disclose all of its audit selection techniques;[6] however, the following observations may be made regarding the probability of a return's selection for audit:

—Certain groups of taxpayers are subject to audit more frequently than others. These groups include individuals with gross income in excess of $50,000, self-employed individuals with substantial business income and deductions, and cash businesses where the potential for tax avoidance is high.

**Example 4.** T owns and operates a liquor store on a cash-and-carry basis. As all of T's sales are for cash, T might well be a

---

**6.** Under the Freedom of Information Act, taxpayers have sued the IRS to disclose the criteria which are used to develop standards for auditing tax returns. The status of these cases is still not clear. However, the Economic Recovery Tax Act of 1981 amended § 6103(b)(2) to provide that nothing in any Federal law shall be interpreted to require disclosure of standards used for the selection of returns for examination. This new change is applicable to disclosures after July 19, 1981.

prime candidate for an audit by the IRS. Obviously, cash transactions are easier to conceal than those made on credit.

—If a taxpayer has been audited in a past year and such audit led to the assessment of a substantial deficiency, a return visit by the IRS is to be expected.

—An audit might materialize if information returns (e. g., Form W–2, Form 1099) are not in substantial agreement with the income reported on taxpayer's return.[7]

—If an individual's itemized deductions are in excess of norms established for various income levels, the probability of an audit is increased. Also, certain types of deductions (e. g., casualty and theft losses, office in the home, tax-sheltered investments) are sensitive areas, since the IRS realizes that many taxpayers will determine the amount of the deduction incorrectly or may not be entitled to the deduction at all.

—The filing of a refund claim by the taxpayer may prompt an audit of the return.

—Certain returns are selected on a random sample basis [known as the Taxpayer Compliance Measurement Program (TCMP)] to develop, update, and improve the DIF formulas (see above). TCMP is the long-range research effort of the IRS designed to measure and evaluate taxpayer compliance characteristics. TCMP audits are tedious and time-consuming, since the taxpayer generally is asked to verify most or all items on the tax return.

—Information obtained from other sources (e. g., other government agencies, news items, informants).

**Example 5.** T reports to the police that while he was out-of-town his home was burglarized and one of the items taken was a shoe box containing cash of $25,000. A representative of the IRS reading the newspaper account of the burglary might well wonder why someone would keep such a large amount of cash in a shoe box at home.

**Example 6.** After 15 years, B is discharged by her employer, Dr. F. Shortly thereafter, the IRS receives a letter from B informing them that Dr. F keeps two sets of books, one of which substantially understates his cash receipts.[8]

---

**7.** The IRS is able to correlate only some of the number of information returns with the returns filed by taxpayers.

**8.** Section 7623 and Reg. § 301.7623–1 enable the IRS to pay rewards to persons who provide information that leads to the detection and punishment of those who violate the tax laws. Such rewards may not exceed 10% of the taxes, fines, and penalties recovered as a result of such information.

Many individual taxpayers mistakenly assume that if they do not hear from the IRS within a few weeks following the filing of the return or if they have received a refund check, no audit will be forthcoming. As a practical matter, most individual returns are examined within two years from the date of filing. If not, they generally remain unaudited. All large corporations are subject to annual audits; and in many instances, tax years will remain open for extended periods, since the taxpayer may agree to waive the statute of limitations pending settlement of unresolved issues.

*Verification and Audit Procedures.* The tax return is initially checked for mathematical accuracy. A check is also made for deductions, exclusions, etc., which are clearly erroneous. An obvious error would be the failure to comply with the percentage limitation on the deduction for medical expenses. In such cases, the Service Center merely sends the taxpayer revised computations and a bill for the corrected amount of tax if the error results in additional tax liability. Taxpayers usually are able to settle such matters through direct correspondence with the IRS without the necessity of a formal audit.

Office audits are conducted by a representative of the District Director's office either in the office of the IRS or through correspondence. Individual returns with few or no items of business income are usually handled through the office audit procedure. In most instances, the taxpayer will merely be required to substantiate a deduction, credit, or item of income which appears on the return.

> **Example 7.** An individual may have claimed medical expenses which are in excess of a normal amount for taxpayers on a comparable income level. The taxpayer will be asked to present documentation in the form of cancelled checks, invoices, etc., for the item in question. Note the substantiation procedure here which is absent from the mathematical check and simple error discovery process mentioned above.

The field audit procedure is commonly used for corporate returns and for those of individuals engaged in business or professional activities. This type of audit generally entails a more complete examination of a taxpayer's transactions. By way of contrast, an office audit usually is directed towards fewer items and is therefore narrower in scope.

A field audit is conducted by IRS agents at the office or home of the taxpayer or at the office of the taxpayer's representative. It is common practice for tax firms to hold conferences with IRS agents in the firm's office during the field audit of a corporate client. The agent's work may be facilitated by a review of certain tax workpapers and discussions with the taxpayer's representative relative to items appearing on the tax return.

Upon a showing of good cause, a taxpayer may request and obtain a reassignment of his or her case from an office to a field audit. The inconvenience and expense involved in transporting records and other supporting data to the agent's office may constitute good cause for reassignment.

*Settlement with the Revenue Agent.* Following the audit, the IRS agent may either accept the return as filed or recommend certain adjustments. The Revenue Agent's Report (RAR) is reviewed by the agent's group supervisor and the Review Staff within the IRS. In many instances, the agent's proposed adjustments are approved. However, it is not uncommon for the Review Staff or group supervisor to request additional information or to raise new issues.

Agents must adhere strictly to IRS policy as reflected in published rulings, Regulations, and other releases. The agent cannot settle an unresolved issue based upon the probability of winning the case in court. In most instances, issues involving factual questions can be settled at the agent level, and it may be advantageous for both the taxpayer and the IRS to reach agreement at the earliest point in the settlement process. For example, it may be to the taxpayer's advantage to reach agreement at the agent level and avoid any further opportunity for the IRS to raise new issues.

Questions involving the percentage use of one's automobile in business or the useful life of a depreciable asset are inherently factual and easily may be settled at the agent level.

A deficiency (an amount in excess of tax shown on the return or tax previously assessed) may be proposed at the agent level. The taxpayer might wish to pursue to a higher level the disputed issues upon which this deficiency is based. The taxpayer's progress through the appeal process is discussed in subsequent sections of this chapter.

If agreement is reached upon the proposed deficiency, Form 870 (Waiver of Restrictions on Assessment and Collection of Deficiency in Tax) is signed by the taxpayer. One advantage to the taxpayer of signing Form 870 at this point is that interest stops accumulating on the deficiency 30 days after the form is filed.[9] When this form is signed, the taxpayer effectively waives his or her right to the receipt of a statutory notice of deficiency (i. e., the 90-day letter) and to subsequent petition to the Tax Court. In addition, it is no longer possible for the taxpayer to go to the Appeals Division. The signing of Form 870 at the agent level generally closes the case. However, since Form 870 does not have the effect of a closing agreement, even after the taxpayer pays the deficiency, he or she may subsequently sue for refund of the tax in a Federal District Court or in the Claims Court. Further, the IRS is not restricted by Form 870 and may assess additional deficiencies if deemed necessary.

See Figure I, which contains a graphic representation of the audit process from selection of return for audit to settlement at, or appeal from, the agent level.

---

**9.** § 6601(c).

## Figure I
### INCOME TAX APPEAL PROCEDURE OF THE
### INTERNAL REVENUE SERVICE

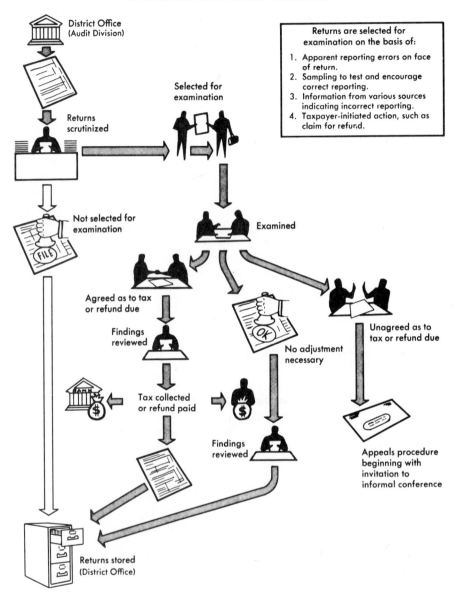

## THE TAXPAYER APPEAL PROCESS

If agreement cannot be reached at the agent level, the taxpayer receives a copy of the Revenue Agent's Report and a transmittal letter which is commonly referred to as the 30-day letter. The taxpayer is granted 30 days to request an administrative appeal. If an appeal is not requested, a statutory notice of deficiency will be issued (i. e., the 90-day letter).

If an appeal is desired, an appropriate request must be made to the Appeals Division.[10] Such request must be accompanied by a written protest except in the following cases:

—The proposed tax deficiency does not exceed $2,500 for any of the tax periods involved in the audit.

—The deficiency resulted from a correspondence or office type of audit (i. e., not as a result of a field audit).

When a protest is required, it should contain the following:

—A statement that the taxpayer wants to appeal the finding of the examining officer (i. e., agent) to the Regional Director of Appeals.

—The taxpayer's name and address.

—The date and symbols from the letter transmitting the proposed adjustments and findings that are being protested.

—The tax periods or tax years involved.

—An itemized schedule of the adjustments with which the taxpayer does not agree.

—A statement of the facts supporting the taxpayer's position on any contested factual issue.

—A statement outlining the law or other authority on which the taxpayer is relying.

The Appeals Division is authorized to settle all tax disputes based on the hazards of litigation. Since the Appeals Division has final settlement authority until a statutory notice of deficiency (i. e., the 90-day letter) has been issued, the taxpayer may be able to obtain a percentage settlement. In addition, an overall favorable settlement may be reached through a "trading" of disputed issues. The Appeals Division occasionally may raise new issues, although the Regulations prohibit such practice unless the grounds are substantial and of significant tax impact.[11] Trading new issues is officially prohibited by IRS policy.[12]

Both the Appeals Division and the taxpayer have the right to request technical advice from the National Office of the IRS.[13] When technical advice is favorable to the taxpayer, the Appeals Division is

---

10. Prior to October 1, 1978, the appeal from the agent level was either to a District Conference or the Appellate Division or to both. In an effort to simplify the procedures involved and to make the administrative appeals procedure more effective, the District Conference was eliminated and the Appellate Division was designated Appeals Division. Internal Revenue Release IR–2032, dated August 25, 1978.

11. Reg. § 601.106(d)(1).

12. Rev.Proc. 64–22, 1964–1 C.B. 689.

13. Reg. § 601.106(f)(10).

bound by such advice. If the technical advice, however, is favorable to the IRS, the Appeals Division may nevertheless settle the case based on the hazards of litigation.

If agreement cannot be reached with the Appeals Division, the IRS issues a statutory notice of deficiency (90-day letter) which gives the taxpayer 90 days to file a petition with the Tax Court. (See Figure II for a review of the income tax appeal procedures, including the consideration of claims for refund.) After the case has been docketed in the Tax Court, the taxpayer has the opportunity to arrange for possible pretrial settlement with the Regional Counsel of the IRS. The Appeals Division settlement power is transferred to the Regional Counsel when the case is docketed for a Tax Court trial after the issuance of the statutory notice of deficiency.[14]

The economic costs of a settlement offer from the Appeals Division should be weighed against the costs of litigation and the probability of winning the case. Consideration should be given to the impact of such settlement upon the tax liability for future periods in addition to the years under audit.

If a settlement is reached with the Appeals Division, the taxpayer is required to sign Form 870AD. The IRS considers this settlement to be binding upon both parties, absent fraud, malfeasance, concealment, or misrepresentation of material fact.

## INTEREST

An important consideration for the taxpayer during negotiations with the IRS is the interest which accrues upon overpayments, deficiency assessments, and unpaid taxes. A taxpayer may effectively stop the accrual of interest upon a deficiency assessment by signing Form 870 and paying the tax. This action may then be followed by a suit in a Federal District Court or the Claims Court for recovery of the amount of the tax payment. If the Tax Court is selected as a forum, the tax usually is not paid and interest continues to accrue.

*Determination of the Interest Rate.* In 1975, Congress began to recognize that the interest rate applicable to Federal tax underpayments and overpayments should be made more realistic in terms of what occurs in the business world. Accordingly, the Code was changed to authorize the IRS to adjust the percentage every two years to conform with commercial rates. A further amendment in 1981 changed the guidelines to provide for annual adjustments (as of each January 1) based on the average prime rate for the preceding September.

The Tax Equity and Fiscal Responsibility Act of 1982 (TEFRA) goes one step further by amending § 6621(b) to sanction semiannual adjustments as of January 1 and July 1 of each year. The adjustments

---

14.   Rev.Proc. 78–9, 1978–1 C.B. 563.

# Figure II
## INCOME TAX APPEAL PROCEDURE

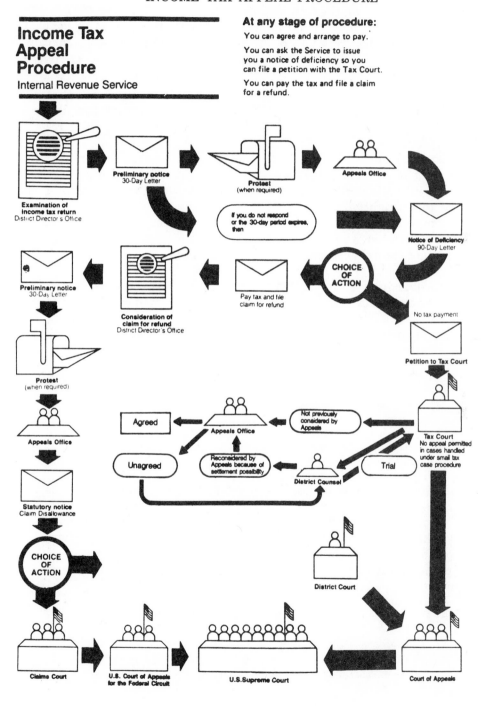

are to be based on the average prime rate for the six months ending on the last day of the previous September or March, whichever the case may be. For example, the first change took place on January 1, 1983, and established a new interest percentage predicated on the average prime rate for the period from April 1, 1982, through September 30, 1982. Effective January 1, 1983, the new rate is set at 16 percent; on July 1, 1983, the rate changes to 11 percent.[15]

*Computation of the Amount of Interest.* Prior law required that any interest on a deficiency or a refund be determined using the simple interest method. For interest accruing after 1982, new § 6622 requires that the amount be compounded daily. Depending on the interest rate applicable, the daily compounding approach conceivably could double the principal amount over a period of five years or so. Consequently, this change in the method of computing interest should not be taken lightly.

Congress has directed the IRS to prepare and make available tables through which the daily compounded amount can be determined. Such tables should ease the burden of those who prepare late returns where additional taxes are due.

The old rule (i. e., the simple interest method) continues to apply to the penalty on underpayments of estimated tax by individuals and corporations. However, the semiannual interest rate adjustments (discussed above) will have to be used in arriving at the amount of the underpayment-of-estimated-tax penalty.

*IRS Deficiency Assessments.* Under § 6601(c), interest usually accrues from the unextended due date of the return until 30 days after the taxpayer agrees to the deficiency by signing Form 870. If the taxpayer does not pay the amount shown on the IRS's "notice and demand" (tax bill) within 10 days, interest again accrues on the deficiency. However, no interest is imposed upon the portion of the tax bill which represents interest on the previous deficiency.[16]

*Refund of Taxpayer's Overpayments.* If the overpayment is refunded to the taxpayer within 45 days after the date the return is filed or is due, no interest is allowed.[17] Interest is authorized, however, when the taxpayer files an amended return or makes a claim for refund of prior year's tax (e. g., when net operating loss or investment credit carrybacks result in refunds of prior year's tax payments).

In the past and in light of high interest rates of up to 20 percent, it has proven advantageous for many taxpayers to delay filing various

---

**15.** The interest rate in the past was 20% from February 1, 1982, through December 31, 1982; 12% from February 1, 1980, through January 31, 1982; 6% from February 1, 1978, through January 31, 1980; 7% from February 1, 1976, through January 31, 1978; 9% from July 1, 1975, through January 31, 1976; and 6% prior to July 1975.
**16.** § § 6601(e)(2) and (4).
**17.** § 6611(e).

tax returns that lead to refunds. Thus, the IRS was placed in the unfortunate role of providing taxpayers with a high-yield savings account. The Tax Equity and Fiscal Responsibility Act of 1982 (TEFRA) purports to end this practice through amendment to § § 6601 and 6611. The gist of the amendments is to preclude any interest accruing on a refund until such time as the IRS is properly notified of the refund.

Specifically the new law (applicable to returns filed 30 days after September 3, 1982) places taxpayers applying for refunds in the following described positions:

—When a return is filed after the due date, interest on any overpayment accrues from the date of filing. However, no interest will be due if the IRS makes the refund within 45 days of the date of filing.

> **Example 8.** T, a calendar year taxpayer, files her return for 1982 on December 1, 1983, such return reflecting an overwithholding of $2,500. On June 10, 1984, T receives a refund of her 1982 overpayment. Under these circumstances, the interest on T's refund begins to accrue on December 1, 1983. [Note: Without the TEFRA change, the interest would have begun to accrue on the due date of the return (i. e., April 15, 1983).]

> **Example 9.** Assume the same facts as in Example 8 except that the refund is paid to T on January 10, 1984 (rather than June 10, 1984). No interest would be due on the refund as it has been made within 45 days of the filing of the return. (Note: Under prior law the result would have been the same because the 45-day period began to run on the later of the due date of the return or the day it was filed.)

—In no event will interest accrue on an overpayment unless the return that is filed is in "processible form." Generally, this means that the return must contain enough information to enable the IRS to identify the taxpayer and to determine the tax (and overpayment) involved.

—In the case of a carryback (e. g., net operating loss, capital loss, certain tax credits), interest on any refund will commence accruing on the due date of the return (disregarding extensions) for the year in which such carryback arises. Even then, however, no interest will accrue until a return is filed, or if filed, the IRS pays the refund within 45 days.

> **Example 10.** X Corporation, a calendar year taxpayer, incurs a net operating loss during 1982 which it can carry back to tax year 1979 for a refund. On December 27, 1983, it files a Form 1139 (Corporate Application for Tentative Refund) claiming the refund. The earliest that interest can commence accruing in this situation is March 15, 1983, but since the

return was not filed until December 27, 1983, the later date controls. If, however, the IRS pays the refund within 45 days of December 27, 1983, no interest is due. (Note: Under prior law, interest would have accrued as of January 1, 1983, and this was so regardless of when the return was filed.)

## PENALTIES

A penalty is treated as an addition to the tax liability rather than a deductible interest expense.[18] Some taxpayers mistakenly believe that penalties are deductible and do not fully appreciate the consequences of actions which trigger the imposition of such penalties.

*Failure to File and Failure to Pay.* For a failure to file a tax return by the due date (including extensions), a penalty of five percent per month (up to a maximum of 25 percent) is imposed on the amount of tax shown as due on the return.[19]

For a failure to pay the tax due as shown on the return, a penalty of one-half of one percent per month (up to a maximum of 25 percent) is imposed on the amount of the tax.[20] A comparable penalty is assessed if the taxpayer fails to pay a deficiency assessment within 10 days.[21]

In all of these cases, a fraction of a month counts as a full month. Also, note that these penalties relate to the net amount of the tax due.[22]

> **Example 11.** T, a calendar year taxpayer, has $18,000 withheld for income taxes by her employer during 1982. Her total tax liability for 1982 proves to be $20,000. Without obtaining an extension from the IRS, she files her Form 1040 in early August of 1983 and encloses a check for the balance due of $2,000. The failure to file and the failure to pay penalties apply to the $2,000.

During any month in which both the failure to file penalty and the failure to pay penalty apply, the failure to file penalty is reduced by the amount of the failure to pay penalty.[23]

> **Example 12.** R files his tax return 10 days after the due date. Along with the return he remits a check for $3,000 which is the balance of the tax owed by R. Disregarding the interest element, R's total penalties are as follows:

---

18. § 6659.
19. § 6651(a)(1).
20. § 6651(a)(2).
21. § 6651(a)(3).
22. § 6651(b).
23. § 6651(c)(1).

| | | |
|---|---:|---:|
| Failure to pay penalty (½ of 1% × $3,000) | | $ 15 |
| Plus: | | |
| Failure to file penalty (5% × $3,000) | $ 150 | |
| Less failure to pay penalty for the same period | 15 | |
| Failure to file penalty | | 135 |
| Total penalties | | $ 150 |

In Example 12, note that the penalties for one full month are imposed even though R was delinquent by only 10 days. Unlike the method used to compute interest, any part of a month is treated as a whole month.

Because the existing penalty for failure to file may not serve as a significant enough deterrent when the tax due is small or the delay in filing is short, TEFRA amends § 6651(c)(1) to provide for a minimum penalty. The minimum penalty is the *lesser* of $100 or the amount of tax still due.

The minimum penalty will apply only if the return is not filed within 60 days (with allowed extensions) of its due date. A showing of reasonable cause will excuse its imposition.

Please observe that the new minimum penalty is not in addition to the regular failure-to-file penalty. It merely is in lieu of such penalty in the event a higher amount is the result.

The amendment to § 6651 is effective for tax returns due after 1982.

As noted above, an extension of time granted by the IRS will avoid the failure to file penalty. It will not, however, exonerate the taxpayer from the failure to pay penalty. But if a taxpayer, for whatever reason, is not in a position to complete the return, how is he or she able to determine the tax liability? The Regulations mercifully provide some latitude in resolving this quandary. If the extension is of the automatic four-month variety sanctioned by Reg. § 1.6081–4, the penalty for failure to pay will not be imposed if the additional tax liability due is no greater than 10 percent of the tax shown on the return.[24]

**Example 13.** S, a calendar year taxpayer, is self-employed and during 1982 makes quarterly payments of estimated taxes of $40,000. In early April of 1983, she applies for and obtains a four-month extension for filing her 1982 income tax return. In late May of 1983, S completes her 1982 return and delivers it to the IRS along with a check covering the additional tax that is due of $3,900. Under these circumstances, S has circumvented both the failure to file and the failure to pay penalties. She will, however, owe interest on the $3,900 that was paid late.

---

24.  Reg. § 301.6651(c)(3)(i).

When the 10 percent rule is not satisfied, the failure to pay penalty will be imposed on the *full* amount due.

**Example 14.** Assume the same facts as in Example 13 except that S's additional tax liability proved to be $4,100 (rather than $3,900). In this event, a failure to pay penalty will be imposed on the full $4,100 that was paid late.

*Negligence Penalty.* A penalty for underpayment of a tax liability is imposed if the underpayment is attributable to negligence or intentional disregard of rules and regulations (but without intent to defraud).[25] The amount of the penalty is five percent of the underpayment.

The negligence penalty has been assessed when a taxpayer knowingly deducts personal expenditures as business expenses[26] or claims excessive business deductions that are not supported by adequate records or other substantiation.[27] The penalty will not be imposed, however, where an error is due to an honest misunderstanding of the facts or law which might occur with an average or reasonable person.

Part of the Economic Recovery Tax Act of 1981 reflects concern on the part of Congress over continued and, perhaps, increasing noncompliance by some taxpayers. Pursuant to this concern, § 6653 was amended (effective for taxes due after 1981) to provide a nondeductible addition to tax equal to 50 percent of the interest attributable to that portion of an underpayment resulting from the imposition of the negligence penalty.[28]

**Example 15.** T underpaid his taxes for 1983 in the amount of $20,000, such underpayment being attributable to negligence. If the interest on the underpayment was $4,000, T's total negligence penalty is determined as follows:

| | |
|---|---:|
| Regular negligence penalty (5% × $20,000) | $ 1,000 |
| Penalty imposed on the interest due as a result of the negligence (50% × $4,000) | 2,000 |
| Total negligence penalty | $ 3,000 |

*Fraud.* A 50 percent penalty is imposed on any underpayment resulting from fraud on the part of the taxpayer. Known as the "civil fraud" penalty, it attaches to the deficiency assessed by the IRS and not just to the items pertaining to the fraud. When applicable, however, the penalties for failure to file and for failure to pay do not come

---

**25.** § 6653(a)(1).
**26.** *James J. Arditto,* 30 TCM 866, T.C.Memo. 1971–210.
**27.** *David Axelrod,* 56 T.C. 248 (1971). Often, such situations involve taxpayers who fail to meet the substantiation requirements of § 274 (dealing with travel and entertainment deductions).
**28.** § 6653(a)(2).

into play. Likewise, the negligence penalty of five percent cannot be imposed.[29]

In a fraud type of situation, the burden of proof is on the IRS to show by a "preponderance of the evidence" that the taxpayer had a specific intent to evade a tax.[30] Although the Code and the Regulations do not provide any assistance in ascertaining what constitutes civil fraud, it seems clear that mere negligence on the part of the taxpayer (however great) will not suffice. In this regard, consideration has to be given to the particular facts involved. Thus, a taxpayer with limited education and business experience may be treated as only grossly negligent and, therefore, not be guilty of fraud. In a like situation, but one where the taxpayer is a knowledgeable person, the required intent to evade may be present so as to represent fraud and not negligence.

In addition to civil fraud penalties, the Code contains numerous criminal sanctions which carry varying monetary fines and/or imprisonment. The difference between civil and criminal fraud is one of degree. A characteristic of criminal fraud is the presence of willfulness on the part of the taxpayer. Thus, § 7201 dealing with attempts to evade or defeat a tax contains the following language:

> Any person who *willfully* attempts in any manner to evade or defeat any tax imposed by this title or the payment thereof shall, in addition to other penalties provided by law, be guilty of a felony and, upon conviction thereof, shall be fined not more than $100,000, ($500,000 in the case of a corporation) or imprisoned not more than five years, or both, together with the costs of prosecution. [Emphasis added.]

As to the burden of proof, the IRS must show that the taxpayer was guilty of willful evasion "beyond the shadow of any reasonable doubt." Recall that in the civil fraud area, the standard applied to measure culpability was "by a preponderance of the evidence."

*Failure to Pay Estimated Income Taxes.* A penalty is imposed for the failure to make adequate and timely estimated income tax payments. The penalty applies both to corporations and to individuals and is based on the rate of interest in effect (e. g., 16 percent from January 1–June 30, 1983) during the period.[31] The underpayment is computed on a quarterly basis and is an amount equal to 80 percent of

---

**29.** Note the precise wording of § 6653(a) [i. e., "(but without intent to defraud)"].

**30.** § 7454(a).

**31.** §§ 6654 and 6655. Section 6654(a) and § 6655(a) refer to the penalty as "an addition to the tax" (i. e., the income tax, self-employment tax). Since these so-called additions to the tax have the characteristics of penalties, they have been classified as such in the text. Unlike interest on an underpayment or a tax deficiency, additions to the tax and penalties are not deductible for income tax purposes.

the installment which would have been due if the estimated tax were based on the amount of the tax actually payable. The penalty is levied on the amount of the underpayment of the tax for the period of underpayment.

A series of exceptions are provided in the Code which may circumvent imposition of a penalty on the underpayment of estimated taxes.[32] For example, the penalty is not imposed if the installment payments equal or exceed the tax shown on the previous year's tax return. This permits those taxpayers who base their estimated tax payments on the prior year's tax liability to avoid any inadvertent imposition of the underpayment penalty.

*False Information with Respect to Withholding.*  Prior to the Economic Recovery Tax Act of 1981, a civil penalty of $50 could be imposed when the taxpayer claimed withholding allowances based on false information. The criminal penalty for willfully failing to supply information or for willfully supplying false or fraudulent information in connection with wage withholding was a fine of up to $500 and/or up to one year of imprisonment.

Since the Federal income tax is predicated on a pay-as-you-go approach, taxpayers who do not comply with the withholding procedures could well place themselves in a position where they would be unable to pay the taxes due for a particular year. Faced with what appeared to be increasing noncompliance with these reporting requirements, Congress amended the Code to provide stiffer monetary penalties. Effective for acts and failure to act after 1981, the civil penalty is raised to $500, while the criminal penalty becomes $1,000.[33] Consistent with the approach taken by Congress, the IRS amended its Regulations so as to require employers who receive from an employee a Form W–4 (Employee Withholding Allowance Certificate) that claims more than 14 exemptions to submit such Form to the IRS.[34]

> **Example 16.**  When first employed by X Corporation, T (a single person) completes a Form W–4 listing 19 exemptions. If the completion of this form occurred in 1982, T may be subject to a civil penalty of $500 or, if the act is willful, a criminal penalty of up to $1,000 and/or imprisonment of up to one year. In any event, X Corporation must apprise the IRS of the Form W–4 filed by T since more than 14 exemptions have been claimed.

*Failure to File and Deliver Information Returns.*  Under the tax law, certain payors are required to file a variety of information re-

---

32.  § § 6654(d) and 6655(d). These exceptions are explained in Form 2210 (Underpayment of Estimated Tax by Individuals). In the case of corporations, see Form 2220 (Underpayment of Estimated Income Tax by Corporations).
33.  § § 6682 and 7205 as amended by the Economic Recovery Tax Act of 1981.
34.  Reg. § 37.3402–1(e)(4) as modified by T.D. 7803 (1982–1 C.B. 155).

turns with the IRS.[35] Prior to the Economic Recovery Tax Act of 1981, the penalty for failing to file such returns was $1 per return, subject to a maximum of $1,000 for any one year. Effective for returns required to be filed after December 31, 1981, the penalty was increased to $10 for each return, subject to a maximum of $25,000 for any calendar year.[36] A like penalty was imposed on the payor for failure to provide a copy of any such return to the payee.[37]

Generally, TEFRA increases the penalties for failure to file and provide information returns from $10 per occurrence ($25,000 maximum) to $50 per occurrence ($50,000 maximum). With increased reporting requirements imposed (e. g., payors of interest and dividends, certain tip income), the activities subject to these penalties are correspondingly increased.

When the failure to comply is due to intentional disregard of the rules, the penalty cannot be less than 10 percent of the amount not properly reported. Furthermore, there exists no overall limitation of $50,000.

The vulnerability under these penalties extends beyond mere compliance with the rules requiring reporting to the IRS. It also encompasses the failure of payors, when required by law, to furnish information returns to payee-taxpayers.

The new TEFRA changes apply to returns or statements due after 1982. In this regard, the due date is determined without regard to extensions.

Both penalties (i. e., failure to file with the IRS and failure to furnish a copy to the payee) can be avoided if the taxpayer can show that the failure is due to reasonable cause and not to willful neglect.[38] In the past, the tax law contained penalties for failing to furnish a payor with a Taxpayer Identification Number (TIN) or to furnish the IRS with a payee's TIN when such procedure was required. Under § 6676, the penalty amount was $5 for each such failure. TEFRA amends § 6676 to increase this penalty to $50 per failure (but not to exceed a total of $50,000).

TEFRA does not change the $5 penalty presently in effect when a taxpayer omits the TIN from his or her own return. For many individuals, of course, the TIN is the person's Social Security number. All of these provisions carry the reasonable-cause exception. The changes to § 6676 are applicable to returns due (without regard to extensions) after 1982.

---

**35.** See, for example, § 6041 dealing with payments to independent contractors of $600 or more and § 6042 concerning dividends distributed by corporations aggregating $10 or more.
**36.** § 6652(a).
**37.** § 6678.
**38.** For the criminal versions of the civil penalties imposed by § § 6652 and 6678, see § § 7203 and 7204.

*Failure to Make Deposits of Taxes and Overstatements of Deposits.* When the business is not doing well or cash flow problems develop, there is a great temptation on the part of employers to "borrow" from Uncle Sam. One way this can be done is to fail to pay over to the IRS the amounts that have been withheld from the wages of employees for FICA and income tax purposes. Needless to say, the IRS does not appreciate being denied the use of such funds and has a number of weapons at its disposal to discourage the practice. Some of these penalties are summarized below:

—A penalty of five percent of any underdeposited amount not paid on or before the prescribed due date, unless it can be shown that the failure is due to reasonable cause and not due to willful neglect.[39]

—A penalty of 25 percent of any overstated deposit claim unless such overstatement is due to reasonable cause and not due to willful neglect.[40]

—Various criminal penalties.[41]

—A 100 percent penalty if the employer's actions are willful.[42] The penalty is based on the amount of the tax evaded, not collected, or not accounted for or paid over. Since the penalty is assessable against the "responsible person" of the business, it could be that more than one party may be vulnerable (e. g., the president and treasurer of a corporation).[43]

In addition to these penalties, of course, the actual tax due must be remitted. An employer remains liable for the amount that should have been paid over even though the withholdings have not been taken out of the wages of its employees.[44]

## ADMINISTRATIVE POWERS OF THE IRS

*Examination of Records.* For the purpose of determining the correct amount of tax due, the Code authorizes the IRS to examine the taxpayer's books and records and to summon those persons responsible to appear before the IRS and, when they appear, to produce the necessary books and records.[45] Taxpayers are required to maintain certain recordkeeping procedures and retain those records which are necessary to facilitate the audit.[46] It should be noted that the files,

---

**39.** § § 6656(a).
**40.** § 6656(b). This penalty, enacted as part of the Economic Recovery Tax Act of 1981, applies only to returns filed after August 31, 1981.
**41.** See, for example, § 7202 (willful failure to collect or pay over a tax).
**42.** § 6672.
**43.** Although the IRS might assess the penalty against more than one person, it cannot collect more than the 100 percent due.
**44.** § 3403.
**45.** § 7602.
**46.** § 6001.

workpapers, and other memoranda of a tax practitioner may be subpoenaed, since the courts have not extended to CPAs the privileged communication doctors and lawyers sometime possess with respect to their clients. In addition, the IRS has prescribed guidelines for retention of computer-based records including punched cards, magnetic tapes, discs, and other machine data.[47]

*Assessment and Demand.*  The Code permits the IRS to assess a deficiency and to demand payment for the tax.[48] However, no assessment or effort to collect the tax may be made until 90 days following the issuance of a statutory notice of a deficiency (i. e., the 90-day letter). The taxpayer is, therefore, given 90 days to file a petition to the U. S. Tax Court which effectively prevents the deficiency from being assessed or collected pending the outcome of the case.[49]

Certain exceptions to this assessment procedure should be noted:

—The IRS may issue a deficiency assessment without waiting 90 days if mathematical errors in the return incorrectly state the tax at less than the true liability.

—If the IRS believes the assessment or collection of a deficiency is in jeopardy, it may assess the deficiency and demand immediate payment.[50] The taxpayer is able to stay the collection of the jeopardy assessment by filing a bond for the amount of the tax and interest.[51] This action will prevent the sale of any property which has been seized by the IRS.

Following assessment of the tax, the IRS will issue a notice and demand for payment.[52] The taxpayer is usually given 10 days following the notice and demand for payment to pay the tax. If the tax is not paid, the IRS may place a tax lien upon the taxpayer's property.[53] In addition, the taxpayer's property may be seized and sold in order to satisfy the claim.[54] However, in certain cases, the Code provides for an extension in the payment of a deficiency to prevent "undue hardship."[55]

If property is transferred and the tax is not paid, the subsequent owners of the property may be liable for the tax. This pursuit of the tax liability against succeeding owners is referred to as transferee liability. For example, if an estate is insolvent and unable to pay the estate tax, the executor or the beneficiaries or both may be liable for its payment.[56]

---

**47.**  Rev.Proc. 73–13, 1973–1 C.B. 776, amplified by Rev.Proc. 74–46, 1974–2 C.B. 502.
**48.**  § 6212.
**49.**  § 6213.
**50.**  § 6861.
**51.**  § 6863(a).
**52.**  § 6303(a).
**53.**  § 6321.
**54.**  § 6331(b).
**55.**  § 6161(b).
**56.**  § 6901.

*Offers in Compromise and Closing Agreements.* The Code provides specific authority for the IRS to negotiate a compromise if there is doubt either in determining the amount of the actual liability or in the taxpayer's ability to pay the tax.[57] In Rev.Proc. 68–16, the IRS has enumerated situations in which closing agreements will be issued:[58]

1. An executor or administrator requires a determination of the tax liability either to facilitate the distribution of estate assets or to relieve himself or herself of fiduciary responsibility.

2. A liquidating corporation needs a determination of tax liability to proceed with the process of dissolution.

3. A taxpayer desires to close returns on an annual basis.

4. Creditors demand evidence of the tax liability.

If the taxpayer is financially unable to pay the total amount of the tax, a Form 656 (Offer in Compromise) must be filed with the District Director or the IRS Service Center. The IRS investigates the claim by evaluating the taxpayer's financial ability to pay the tax. In some instances, the compromise settlement will include an agreement for final settlement of the tax through payments of a specified percentage of the taxpayer's future earnings. The District Director must obtain approval from the IRS Regional Counsel if the amount involved exceeds $500. This settlement procedure usually entails lengthy periods of negotiation with the IRS and is generally used only in extreme cases.

A closing agreement is binding on both the Government and the IRS, except upon a subsequent showing of fraud, malfeasance, or misrepresentation of a material fact.[59] The closing agreement may be added to Form 870 in reaching agreement upon the entire amount of tax due for a year under audit, used when disputed issues carry over to future years, and employed to dispose of a dispute involving a specific issue for a prior year or a proposed transaction involving future years. If, for example, the IRS is willing to make substantial concessions in the valuation of assets for death tax purposes, it may require a closing agreement from the recipient of the property to establish the tax basis of the assets for income tax purposes.

## THE STATUTE OF LIMITATIONS

A statute of limitations defines the period of time during which one party may pursue against another party a cause of action or other suit allowed under the governing law. Failure to satisfy any requirement provides the other party with an absolute defense should he or she see fit to invoke the statute. Inequity would result if there were no statute

---

**57.** § 7122 and Reg. § 301.7122–1(a).

**58.** 1968–1 C.B. 770, § 4.01.

**59.** § 7121(b).

limiting action. Permitting the lapse of an extended period of time between the initiation of a claim and its pursuit could place the defense of such claim in jeopardy. Witnesses may have died or disappeared; records or other evidence may have been discarded or destroyed.

In terms of Federal tax consequences, it is important to distinguish between the statute of limitations on assessments by the IRS and the statute applicable to refund claims by a taxpayer.

*Assessment and the Statute of Limitations.* In general, any tax which is imposed must be assessed within three years of the filing of the return (or, if later, the due date of the return).[60] Some exceptions to this three-year limitation follow:

—If no return is filed or a fraudulent return is filed, assessments can be made at any time. There is, in effect, no statute of limitations.

—If a taxpayer omits an amount of gross income which is in excess of 25 percent of the gross income stated on the return, the statute of limitations is increased to six years. The courts have interpreted this extended period of limitations rule to include only those items affecting income and not the omission of items affecting cost of goods sold.[61] In addition, gross income includes capital gains in the *gross* amount (i. e., not reduced by capital losses).

**Example 17.** During 19X1, T (an individual taxpayer) had the following income transactions (all of which were duly reported on his timely filed return):

| | | |
|---|---:|---:|
| Gross receipts | | $ 480,000 |
| Less cost of goods sold | | $ (400,000) |
| Net business income | | $ 80,000 |
| Capital gains and losses— | | |
| Capital gain | $ 36,000 | |
| Capital loss | 12,000 | 24,000 |
| Total income | | $ 104,000 |

T retains your services in 19X5 as a tax consultant. It seems that he inadvertently omitted some income on his 19X1 return and he wishes to know if he is "safe" under the statute of limitations. The six-year statute of limitations would apply, putting T in a vulnerable position only if he omitted more than $129,000 on his 19X1 return [($480,000 + $36,000) × 25%].

---

60. §§ 6501(a) and (b)(1).
61. *The Colony, Inc. v. Comm.,* 58–2 USTC ¶ 9593, 1 AFTR2d 1894, 78 S.Ct. 1033 (USSC, 1958).

—Under § 6501, the statute of limitations may be extended by mutual consent of the District Director and the taxpayer. This extension covers a definite period and is made by signing Form 872. The extension is frequently requested by the IRS when the lapse of the statutory period is imminent and the audit has not been completed. In some situations, the extensions may apply only to unresolved issues. This practice is frequently applied to audits of corporate taxpayers and explains why many corporations have "open years." It is necessary for a tax specialist to understand prior tax law as it applies to these "open years."

Special rules relating to assessment are applicable in the following situations:

—Taxpayers (corporations, estates, etc.) may request a prompt assessment of the tax.

—The period for assessment of the personal holding company tax is extended to six years after the return is filed only if certain filing requirements are met.

—If a partnership or trust files a tax return (a partnership or trust return) in good faith and a later determination renders it taxable as a corporation, such return is deemed to be the corporate return for purposes of the statute of limitations.

—The assessment period for capital loss, net operating loss, and investment credit carrybacks is generally related to the determination of tax in the year of the loss or unused credit rather than in the carryback years.

If the tax is assessed within the period of limitations, the IRS has six years from the date of assessment to collect the tax.[62] However, if the IRS issues a statutory notice of deficiency to the taxpayer, who then files a Tax Court petition, the statute is suspended on both the deficiency assessment and the period of collection until 60 days after the decision in the Tax Court becomes final.[63]

*Refund Claims and the Statute of Limitations.* In order to receive a tax refund, the taxpayer is required to file a valid refund claim. The official form for filing a claim is Form 1040X for individuals and Form 1120X for corporations (Form 843 became obsolete for income tax refund claims after June 30, 1976). Also, prior to July 1, 1976, income tax refunds could be claimed by filing an amended tax return.[64] A refund claim must follow certain procedural requirements. If it does not, the claim may be rejected with no consideration of its merit. These procedural requirements include the following:

—A separate claim must be filed for each taxable period.

---

**62.** § 6502(a).
**63.** § 6503(a)(1).
**64.** Reg. § 301.6402–3.

—The grounds for the claim must be stated in sufficient detail.

—The statement of facts must be sufficient to permit IRS appraisal of the merits of the claim.

The refund claim must be filed within three years of the filing of the tax return or within two years following the payment of the tax if this period expires on a later date.[65] In most instances, the three-year period is relevant for determining running of the statute of limitations. To be allowed, a claim must be filed during this period.

Certain exceptions are incorporated in the Code which may inadvertently reduce the benefits of the refund claim.[66]

**Example 18.** On March 10, 19X2, T filed his 19X1 income tax return reflecting a tax of $10,500. On July 11, 19X3, he filed an amended 19X1 return showing an additional $3,000 of tax which was then paid. On May 20, 19X5, he filed a claim for refund of $4,500. Assuming T is correct concerning the claim for refund, how much tax can he recover? The answer is only $3,000. Because the claim was not filed within the three-year period, T is limited to the amount he actually paid during the past two years.

**Example 19.** D had $10,000 withheld in 19X1. Because of heavy itemized deductions, D assumed she had no further tax to pay for the year. For this reason, and because of the exigencies of business, and without securing an extension, she did not file her 19X1 return until June 9, 19X2. Actually, the return showed a refund of $600, which D ultimately received. On May 3, 19X5, D filed a $4,000 claim for refund of her 19X1 taxes. How much, if any, of the $4,000 may D recover? None. Although the time limitation was met (i. e., the claim was filed within three years of the filing of the return), the amount limitation was not. A refund cannot exceed the amount paid within three years preceding the filing of the claim, and for this purpose, D's withholdings were deemed paid as of April 15, 19X2. Had D requested and obtained an extension covering the filing of her 19X1 return, the claim for refund would have been timely and taxes paid would have exceeded the refund claimed.

Section 6511(d)(1) sets forth special rules for claims relating to bad debts and worthless securities. A seven-year period of limitations applies in lieu of the normal three-year rule. The extended period is provided in recognition of the inherent difficulty associated with identification of the exact year a bad debt or security becomes worthless.

Refund claims relative to capital or net operating loss carrybacks may be filed within three years after the time for filing the tax return

---

65. §§ 6511(a) and 6513(a).
66. § 6511(b).

(including extensions) for the year of the loss.[67] The IRS will acceler-ate the processing of a refund from a net operating loss carryback if Form 1045 (applicable to individuals) or Form 1139 (applicable to corporations) is utilized. But this special procedure is available only if the form is filed within the year following the year of the loss. In other cases, a Form 1040X or Form 1120X should be used.

If the taxpayer's refund claim is rejected by the IRS, a suit for refund generally may be filed six months after the filing of the claim.[68] This suit is filed in a Federal District Court or in the U.S. Claims Court.

# TAX PRACTICE

## THE TAX PRACTITIONER

*Definition.*   What is a tax practitioner? What service does the practitioner perform? To begin defining the term "tax practitioner," one should consider whether the individual is qualified to practice before the IRS. Generally, practice before the IRS is limited to CPAs, attorneys, and persons who have been enrolled to practice before the IRS (termed "enrollees"). In most cases, enrollees are admitted to practice only if they take and successfully pass a special examination administered by the IRS. CPAs and attorneys are not required to take this examination and are automatically admitted to practice if they are in good standing with the appropriate licensing board regulating their profession.

Persons other than CPAs, attorneys, and enrollees may, however, be allowed to practice before the IRS in limited situations. Circular 230 (issued by the Treasury Department and entitled "Rules Govern-ing the Practice of Attorneys and Agents Before the Internal Revenue Service") permits the following notable exceptions:

—A taxpayer may always represent himself or herself. A person also may represent a member of his or her immediate family if no compensation is received for such services.

—Regular full-time employees may represent their employers.

—Corporations may be represented by any of their bona fide offi-cers.

—Partnerships may be represented by any of the partners.

—Trusts, receiverships, guardianships, or estates may be repre-sented by their trustees, receivers, guardians, administrators, or executors.

—A taxpayer may be represented by whoever prepared the re-turn for the year in question. However, such representation cannot proceed beyond the agent level.

---

**67.**  § 6511(d)(2).
**68.**  § 6532(a)(1).

**Example 20.** T, an individual, is currently undergoing audit by the IRS for tax years 19X1 and 19X2. She prepared the 19X1 return herself but paid Z Company, a bookkeeping service, to prepare the 19X2 return. Z Company may represent T in matters concerning only 19X2. However, even with respect to 19X2, Z Company would be unable to represent T at an Appeals Division proceeding. T could, of course, represent herself, or she could retain a CPA, attorney, or enrollee to represent her in matters concerning both years under examination.

*Rules Governing Tax Practice.* Anyone can prepare a tax return or render tax advice, regardless of his or her educational background or level of competence. Nevertheless, there do exist some restraints which govern all parties engaged in rendering tax advice or preparing tax returns for the general public.

—If the party holds himself or herself out to the general public as possessing tax expertise, he or she could be liable to the client if services are performed in a negligent manner. At a minimum, the measure of such damage would be any interest and penalties the client incurs because of the practitioner's failure to exercise due care.

—If someone agrees to perform a service (e. g., preparation of a tax return) and, subsequently, fails to do so, the aggrieved party may be in a position to obtain damages for breach of contract.

—The IRS requires all persons who prepare tax returns for a fee to sign as preparer of the return.[69] Failure to comply with this requirement could result in penalty assessment against the preparer.

—The Code prescribes various penalties for the deliberate filing of false or fraudulent returns. Such penalties are applicable to a tax practitioner who either was aware of the situation or who actually perpetrated the false information or the fraud.[70]

—Code § 7216 prescribes penalties for tax practitioners who disclose to third parties information they have received from clients in connection with the preparation of tax returns or the rendering of tax advice.

**Example 21.** T operates a tax return preparation service. His brother-in-law, B, has just taken a job as a life insurance salesman. In order to help B find contacts, T furnishes B with a list of the names and addresses of all of his clients who report adjusted gross income of $10,000 or more. T is in violation of § 7216 and is subject to penalties.

---

**69.** Reg. § 1.6065–1(b)(1).

**70.** § 7206.

—All non-attorney tax practitioners should avoid becoming engaged in activities which constitute the unauthorized practice of law. If they engage in this practice, action could be instituted against them in the appropriate state court by the local or state bar association. What actions constitute the unauthorized practice of law are undefined, and the issue remains an open question upon which reasonable minds can easily differ.

*Other Legislative Penalties.*    Due to widespread abuse in the commercial tax return preparation field, the Tax Reform Act of 1976 included provisions to regulate the conduct of parties who prepare tax returns and claims for refund for compensation. The rules provide for disclosure requirements and ethical standards for income tax return preparers. Severe penalties are provided for noncompliance, and the IRS has the power to seek injunctive relief through court action to prohibit a preparer from engaging in certain unauthorized practices.

The following penalties were provided under the Tax Reform Act of 1976:

1.   A $100 penalty with respect to each return or claim for refund if the tax return preparer understates the taxpayer's liability and such understatement is due to the negligent or intentional disregard of rules and regulations. The term "rules and regulations" includes the Code, Regulations, and published rulings.[71]

     It should be noted that a preparer has not negligently or intentionally disregarded the rules and regulations if he or she in good faith and with a reasonable basis takes the position that a rule or regulation does not accurately reflect the Code.[72]

2.   A $500 per return penalty will be assessed on the preparer if the understatement of tax is due to a willful understatement of the taxpayer's tax liability.[73] For example, a willful understatement occurs where a preparer disregards information furnished by the taxpayer in an attempt to wrongfully reduce the tax liability.[74]

3.   A $25 penalty is assessed against the preparer for failure to sign a return or furnish the preparer's identifying number, and a $50 penalty is assessed for failure to retain a copy or list of taxpayers for whom returns or claims for refund have been prepared.[75]

---

**71.**   Reg. § 1.6694–3.
**72.**   Reg. § 1.6694–4.
**73.**   § 6694(b).
**74.**   Reg. § 1.6694–1(b)(2)(i).
**75.**   § § 6695(b), (c), and (d).

4. A $25 penalty is assessed if the preparer fails to furnish a copy of the return or claim for refund to the taxpayer unless the failure is due to reasonable cause and not due to willful neglect.[76]

5. A $500 penalty may be assessed if a preparer endorses or otherwise negotiates a check for refund of tax which is issued to the taxpayer.[77]

*Guidelines for the Imposition of the Negligence Penalty.* In connection with preparer penalties under § 6694(a) (refer to item 1), Rev.Proc. 80–40 provides guidelines as to what constitutes the negligent disregard of rules and regulations.[78] These guidelines are illustrated in a series of revenue rulings.[79]

## ETHICAL CONSIDERATIONS—"STATEMENTS ON RESPONSIBILITIES IN TAX PRACTICE"

In the belief that CPAs engaged in tax practice required further guidance in the resolution of ethical problems, the Tax Committee of the AICPA began issuing periodic statements on selected topics. The first of these "Statements on Responsibilities in Tax Practice" was released in 1964. The 10 that have been issued to date are summarized below.

1. A CPA should sign as preparer any Federal tax return which requires a preparer's signature if he or she completes it for and transmits it to the taxpayer or another, whether or not the work was done for compensation.

   **Example 22.** T, a CPA, prepares his neighbor's income tax return as a favor (i. e., no fee was charged). T should sign the return as preparer, even though Treasury Regulations indicate he need not sign if no fee is involved.

2. If the CPA is not the preparer of a Federal tax return but instead serves in the capacity of a reviewer, he or she is not required to sign as the preparer. At his or her discretion, the CPA may sign as preparer on a return prepared by the taxpayer or another if he or she reviews the return and, in the course of the review, acquires knowledge with respect to the return substantially equivalent to that which would have been acquired had he or she prepared the return.

3. A CPA should sign as the preparer of a Federal tax return only if he or she is satisfied that reasonable effort has been

---

**76.** § 6695(a).

**77.** § 6695(b).

**78.** 1980–2 C.B. 774.

**79.** Rev.Rul. 80–262 (1980–2 C.B. 375), Rev.Rul. 80–263 (1980–2 C.B. 376), Rev.Rul. 80–264 (1980–2 C.B. 377), Rev.Rul. 80–265 (1980–2 C.B. 377), and Rev.Rul. 80–266 (1980–2 C.B. 378).

made to provide appropriate answers to the questions on the return which are applicable to the taxpayer. When such questions are left unanswered, the reason for such omissions should be stated. The possibility that an answer to a question might prove disadvantageous to the taxpayer does not justify its omission or a statement of the reason for such omission.

**Example 23.** T, a CPA, is in the process of completing the 19X8 tax return for a client, X Corporation. During the year, X Corporation made a $20,000 cash distribution to its shareholders. T knows that the distribution is not covered by current earnings and profits but is not sure of the corporation's accumulated earnings and profits. Corporate management has decided to treat the distribution as a return of capital but is unwilling at this time to incur the expense and inconvenience of asking T to determine the balance of the accumulated earnings account. While completing Form 1120, T encounters the following question: "During this taxable year, did you pay dividends (other than stock dividends and distributions in exchange for stock) in excess of your current and accumulated earnings and profits?" Under these circumstances, T cannot answer *yes* or *no* to the question. The reason for his failure to do so should be explained in a note attached to the return. It does not matter that such a note may trigger an audit of the transaction by the IRS.

4.  A CPA may sign a return containing a departure from the treatment of an item on a prior year's tax return which was made pursuant to an administrative proceeding with the IRS. The departure need not be disclosed on the return.

**Example 24.** Upon audit of T Corporation's income tax return for 19X4, the IRS disallowed $10,000 of the $50,000 salary paid to its president and sole shareholder on the grounds of unreasonable compensation [§ 162(a)(1)]. You are the CPA who has been engaged to prepare T Corporation's income tax return for 19X5. Again, the corporation paid its president a salary of $50,000 and chose to deduct this amount. Because you are not bound in 19X5 by what the IRS deemed reasonable for 19X4, the full $50,000 can be claimed as a salary deduction.

5.  A CPA may prepare tax returns involving the use of estimates if such use is generally acceptable or if, under the circumstances, it is impractical to obtain exact data. When estimates are used, they should be presented in such a manner as to avoid the implication of greater accuracy than exists. The CPA should be satisfied that estimated amounts are not unreasonable under the circumstances.

**Example 25.** In connection with the preparation of his return for the past year, your client informs you that he estimates he gave $1,000 in cash to his church, none of which is supported by receipts or other substantiation. Considering the nature of the client's charitable inclinations, you feel the $1,000 amount is reasonable. Under these conditions, the deduction can be claimed. You should, however, advise the client of the lack of documentation and that as a result, some or all of these expenses could be disallowed by the IRS upon audit of the return. It would be improper, for example, to deduct only $999, as this implies greater accuracy than, in fact, exists.

6. A CPA should promptly advise a client upon learning of an error in a previously filed return or upon learning of a client's failure to file a required return. The advice can be oral or in writing and should include a recommendation of the corrective measures, if any, to be taken. The error or other omission should not be disclosed to the IRS without the client's consent. If the past error is material and is not corrected by the client, the CPA may be unable to prepare the current year's tax return. Such might be true if the error has a carryover effect that precludes the correct determination of the tax liability for the current year.

**Example 26.** In connection with the preparation of a client's 19X5 income tax return, you discover the final inventory for 19X4 was materially understated. First, you should advise the client to file an amended return for 19X4 reflecting the correct amount in final inventory. Second, if the client refuses to make this adjustment, you should consider whether the error will preclude you from preparing a substantially correct return for 19X5. Because this will probably be the case (the final inventory for 19X4 becomes the beginning inventory for 19X5), you should withdraw from the engagement. If the error is corrected by the client, you may proceed with the preparation of the tax return for 19X5. You should, however, assure yourself that the error is not repeated.

7. When the CPA is representing a client in an administrative proceeding with respect to a return in which there is an error known to the CPA that has resulted or may result in a material understatement of tax liability, he or she should request the client's agreement to disclose the error to the IRS. Lacking such agreement, the CPA may be compelled to withdraw from the engagement.

**Example 27.** While representing a client on an audit of her 19X5 income tax return, you discover that she inadvertently omitted a material amount of taxable income. First, you should advise the client that the omission be disclosed to the IRS. Second, if the client refuses to make the disclosure, you should consider withdrawing from the engagement. Whether you should or should not withdraw can generally be resolved by determining which alternative will least compromise the client's position. Withdrawal during the audit might trigger increased IRS scrutiny that would disclose the omission.

8.  In providing tax advice to a client, the CPA must use judgment to assure that the advice reflects professional competence and appropriately serves the client's needs. No standard format or guidelines can be established to cover all situations and circumstances involving written or oral advice by the CPA. The CPA may communicate with the client when subsequent developments affect advice previously provided with respect to significant matters. However, he or she cannot be expected to assume responsibility for initiating such communication, except while assisting a client in implementing procedures or plans associated with the advice provided. Of course, the CPA may undertake this obligation by specific agreement with his or her client.

    **Example 28.** In 19X4, your client requests advice concerning the tax implications of a proposed transaction. You prepare a written summary concerning this matter, and the client follows this advice in consummating the transaction. The client carries out the same transaction in 19X5, again relying on your advice but without checking with you concerning the continuing soundness of the original advice. It turns out that the law has been changed, and the tax advice is no longer correct. Unless you originally agreed to inform the client of any tax law changes affecting this matter, you should not be held responsible for his continued reliance. However, it is obvious that to fully serve your client you should follow up in such situations.

9.  In preparing a return, the CPA ordinarily may rely on information furnished by the client. The CPA is not required to examine or review documents or other evidence supporting the client's information in order to sign the return as preparer. Although the examination of supporting data is not required, the CPA should encourage clients to provide such supporting data when appropriate. The CPA should make use of the client's returns for prior years whenever feasible. The implications of information known to the CPA cannot be ignored, and accordingly, the CPA is required to make reasonable inquiries when the information as presented appears to be incorrect or incomplete. If a CPA prepares a

Federal tax return, it should be signed by the CPA with no modification of the preparer's declaration.

**Example 29.** A CPA can normally take a client's word concerning the validity of dependency exemptions. But suppose your client, a divorcee, wants to claim her three children (of whom she has custody) as dependents. If you know the dependency exemptions were awarded to her ex-husband by the divorce decree, then you must act in accordance with § 152(e)(2)(A)(i) in preparing the return. You should not claim the dependency exemptions on your client's tax return.

**Example 30.** While preparing a client's income tax return for 19X4, you review his income tax return for 19X3. In comparing the dividend income reported on the 19X3 Schedule B with that received in 19X4, you note a significant decrease. Further investigation reveals the variation is due to a stock sale in 19X4 which, until now, was unknown to you. Thus, the review of the 19X3 return has unearthed a transaction that should be reported on the 19X4 return.

10. In preparing a tax return, a CPA may take a position contrary to Treasury Department or IRS interpretations of the Code without disclosure, if there is reasonable support for the position. A CPA also may take a position contrary to a specific provision of the Code when there is reasonable support for the position. In such cases, however, the CPA should disclose the treatment on the tax return involved. In no event may a CPA take a position that lacks reasonable support, even when this position is disclosed on the return. Examples of reasonable support for taking a position contrary to the Code include (1) legal opinion or published writing of tax specialists regarding the constitutionality of a specific provision or (2) possible conflicts between two provisions of the Code.

Some of the recent provisions relative to the regulation of income tax preparers appear to be in conflict with positions of the AICPA's "Statements on Responsibilities in Tax Practice." For example, Statement No. 1 gives several illustrations of when a CPA is not considered to be a preparer, some of which may conflict with the Regulations issued by the IRS. Also, Statement No. 9 permits a CPA to rely on information furnished by a client without examination of the supporting evidence, whereas the Regulations require that a preparer must make further inquiry when a Code provision requires specific documentation.

A CPA accomplishes nothing by signing a return as the preparer with the following qualification: "Prepared without audit of the taxpayer's financial records." Keep in mind, these statements merely represent guides to action and are not part of the AICPA's Code of Professional Ethics. But because the statements are representative of standards followed by members of the profession, a violation thereof might indicate a deviation from the standard of due care exercised by most CPAs. The standard of due care is, of course, at the heart of any suit charging negligence that is brought against a CPA.

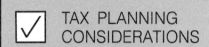

## TAX PLANNING CONSIDERATIONS

In this section, the potential advantages and disadvantages inherent in requesting a revenue ruling and selecting the court in which to pursue resolution of a tax case are explored.

### STRATEGY IN SEEKING AN ADMINISTRATIVE RULING

*Determination Letters.* In many instances, the request for an advance ruling or a determination letter from the IRS is a necessary or desirable planning strategy. The receipt of a favorable ruling or determination reduces the risk associated with a transaction when the tax results are in doubt. For example, the initiation or amendment of a pension or profit sharing plan should be accompanied by a determination letter from the District Director. Otherwise, on subsequent IRS review, the plan may not qualify and the tax deductibility of contributions to the plan will be disallowed. In some instances, the potential tax effects of a transaction are so numerous and of such consequence that to proceed without a ruling is unwise.

*Individual Rulings.* It may, in some cases, not be necessary or desirable to request an advance ruling. For example, it is generally not desirable to request a ruling if the tax results are doubtful, but the company is committed to completion of the transaction in any event. If a ruling is requested and negotiations with the IRS indicate that an adverse determination will be forthcoming, it is usually possible to have the ruling request withdrawn. However, the National Office of the IRS may forward its findings, along with a copy of the ruling request, to the District Director. In determining the advisability of a ruling request, consideration should be given to the potential exposure of other items in the tax returns of all "open years."

A ruling request may delay the consummation of a transaction if the issues are novel or complex. Frequently, a ruling can be processed within three months, although in some instances a delay of a year or more may be encountered.

*Technical Advice.* In the process of contesting a proposed deficiency with the Appeals Division, consideration should be given to a request for technical advice from the National Office of the IRS. If such advice is favorable to the taxpayer, it is binding on the Appeals Division. The request may be particularly appropriate when the practitioner feels that the agent or Appeals Division has been too literal in the interpretation of an IRS ruling.

## CONSIDERATIONS IN HANDLING AN IRS AUDIT

As a general rule, attempts should be made to settle disputes at the earliest possible stage of the administrative appeal process. New issues may be raised by IRS personnel if the case goes beyond the agent level. It is usually possible to limit the scope of the examination by furnishing pertinent information which is requested by the agent. Extraneous information or fortuitous comments may result in the opening of new issues and should therefore be avoided. Agents usually appreciate prompt and efficient response to inquiries, since their performance may in part be judged by their ability to close or settle assigned cases.

To the extent possible, it is advisable to conduct the investigation of field audits in the practitioner's office rather than in the client's office. This procedure permits greater control over the audit investigation and may facilitate the agent's review and prompt closure of the case.

Many practitioners feel that it is generally not advisable to have clients present at the scheduled conferences with the agent, since the client may give emotional or gratuitous comments which impair prompt settlement. If the client is not present, however, he or she should be advised of the status of negotiations. It should be clear that the client is the final authority with regard to any proposed settlement.

The tax practitioner's workpapers should include all research memoranda, and a list of resolved and unresolved issues should be continually updated during the course of the IRS audit. Occasionally, agents will request access to excessive amounts of accounting data for the purpose of engaging in a so called fishing expedition. Providing blanket access to working papers should be avoided. Workpapers should be carefully reviewed to minimize opportunities for the agent to raise new issues not otherwise apparent. It is generally advisable to provide the agent with copies of specific workpapers upon request. It should be noted that accountant's workpapers are not privileged and may therefore be subpoenaed by the IRS.

In unusual situations, a Special Agent may appear to gather evidence in the investigation of a possible fraud. When this occurs, the taxpayer should be advised to seek legal counsel to determine the extent of his or her cooperation in providing information to the agent. Also, frequently it is desirable for the tax adviser to consult personal legal counsel in such situations. If the taxpayer receives a revenue agent's report (RAR), this generally indicates that the IRS has decided not to initiate criminal prosecution proceedings. The IRS does not usually take any action upon a tax deficiency until the criminal matter has been resolved.

## PENALTIES

As previously discussed, penalties are imposed upon a taxpayer's failure to file a return or to pay a tax or both when due. These penalties can be avoided if the failure is due to reasonable cause and not due to willful neglect.[80] Reasonable cause, however, has not been liberally interpreted by the courts and should not be relied upon in the routine type of situation.[81] A safer way to avoid the failure to file penalty would be to obtain from the IRS an extension of time for filing the return. Although an extension of time for filing does not normally excuse the failure to pay penalty, it will do so in the case of the automatic four-month variety if the 90 percent rule has been satisfied (refer to Example 13).

In light of the current interest rates applicable, the penalty for failure to pay estimated taxes can become severe.[82] Often trapped by this provision are employed taxpayers with outside income. Such persons may forget about such outside income and place undue reliance on the amount withheld from wages and salaries as being adequate to cover their liability. For such persons, not only does April 15 provide a real shock (i. e., in terms of the additional tax owed) but a penalty situation may have evolved. One possible way for an employee to mitigate this problem (presuming the employer is willing to cooperate) is described below.

> **Example 31.** T, a calendar year taxpayer, is employed by X Corporation and earns (after withholdings) a monthly salary check of $3,000 payable at the end of each month. T also receives income from outside sources (e. g., interest, dividends, consulting fees). After some quick calculations in early October of 1983, T determines that he has underestimated his tax liability for 1983 by $6,000 and will be subject to the penalty for the first two quarters of 1983 and part of the third quarter. T, therefore, completes a new Form W–4 in which he arbitrarily raises his income tax withholding by $2,000 a month. X Corporation accepts the Form W–4, and as a result, an extra $6,000 is paid to the IRS on T's account for the payroll period from October through December 1983.

---

80. *Nicodemus v. U. S.,* 55–1 USTC ¶ 9126, 48 AFTR 1449, 132 F.Supp. 608 (D.Ct.Ida., 1954).
81. *Dustin v. Comm.,* 72–2 USTC ¶ 9610, 30 AFTR2d 72–5313, 467 F.2d 47 (CA–9, 1972), *aff'g.* 53 T.C. 491 (1969).
82. Keep in mind that this penalty is not deductible for income tax purposes.

The reason T avoids any penalties for the underpayment in Example 31 for the first three quarters is that withholding of taxes are allocated over the year involved. Thus, a portion of the additional $6,000 withheld in October–December is assigned to the January 1–April 15 period, the April 16–June 15 period, etc.[83] Had T merely paid the IRS an additional $6,000 in October, this would not have affected the penalty for the earlier quarters.

## PROBLEM MATERIALS

### Discussion Questions

1. Why is it necessary for a tax practitioner to be familiar with the IRS organization and its administrative appeal procedures?

2. Why does the IRS issue rulings solely on uncompleted actual transactions or upon transactions which have been completed prior to the filing of the tax return?

3. Under what circumstances will a ruling be revoked by the IRS and applied retroactively to the detriment of the taxpayer?

4. During the course of your research of a tax problem, you find that another company has received a favorable unpublished (letter) ruling approximately two years ago based on facts similar to your situation. What degree of reliance may be placed upon this ruling?

5. Under what circumstances might the request for an advance ruling be considered a necessity? Are there situations in which a ruling should not be requested? Why?

6. In what situations might a taxpayer seek a determination letter?

7. What purpose is served by a request for technical advice?

8. What, if any, is the relationship between DIF and TCMP?

9. A taxpayer is fearful of filing a claim for refund for a prior year because he is convinced that the claim will cause an audit by the IRS of that year's return. Please comment.

10. In March of 1983, T receives a refund check from the IRS for the amount of overpayment she claimed when she filed her 1982 return in January. Does this mean that her 1982 return will not be audited? Explain.

11. Comment on the following:

    (a) An RAR.

    (b) Form 870.

    (c) The 30-day letter.

    (d) The 90-day letter.

12. If a taxpayer wishes to go to the Appeals Division of the IRS, when is a written protest required?

---

**83.** § 6654(e)(2).

13. How may the running of interest on a deficiency assessment be stopped?

14. V, a calendar year taxpayer, files her 1982 income tax return on February 9, 1983, on which she claims a $1,200 refund. If V receives her refund check on May 2, 1983, will it include any interest? Explain.

15. In 1983, S's 1980 income tax return is audited by the IRS, and as a result, a deficiency is assessed. S is appalled by this development, since this means he will have to pay nondeductible interest at the rate of 20% from 1980 to the point of assessment. Is S under a misunderstanding on the tax rules concerning this matter? Explain.

16. Why may it be desirable to settle with the agent rather than to continue by appealing to a higher level within the IRS?

17. T, a self-employed, calendar year taxpayer, does not plan to prepay any of his taxes for 1983. Although he appreciates that there exists a 16% addition to tax for underpayments, since he is in the 50% bracket, this means an after-tax outlay of only 8%. Do you have any difficulty with T's assumptions?

18. What bearing should the interest rate currently in effect have on each of the following situations:

    (a) Whether a taxpayer litigates in the U. S. Tax Court or the Claims Court.

    (b) The penalty for underpayment of estimated taxes.

    (c) The negligence penalty.

19. Describe each of the following items:

    (a) A closing agreement.

    (b) An offer in compromise.

20. What is the applicable statute of limitations in each of the independent situations appearing below?

    (a) No return was ever filed by the taxpayer.

    (b) A corporation is determined to have been a personal holding company for the year in question.

    (c) For 19X0, the XYZ Associates filed a Form 1065 (i. e., a partnership return). In 19X5, the IRS determines that the organization was not a partnership in 19X0 but was, in fact, a corporation.

    (d) In 19X0, T incurred a bad debt loss which she failed to claim.

    (e) On his 19X0 return, a taxpayer inadvertently omitted a large amount of gross income.

    (f) Same as part (e), except that the omission was deliberate.

    (g) For 19X0, a taxpayer innocently overstated her deductions by a large amount.

21. Frequently, tax litigation involves unresolved questions relating to several years prior to the current year. How is it possible for the IRS to assess a deficiency for these years, since the statute of limitations expires three years from the date of filing of the tax return?

22. Are tax practitioners subject to a body of professional ethics? Describe them briefly.

23. Certain individuals have stated that the preparation of a tax return by a qualified professional lends credibility to the return. Therefore, CPAs and attorneys should act in an impartial manner in the preparation of tax returns and should serve the overall enforcement needs of society for the administration of tax justice. Should a tax professional be an "umpire" or an "advocate"? Explain.

24. The president of a corporation (your client) insists that certain corporate deductions for entertainment are proper. On the disallowance of these deductions, amounting to $5,000 per year for each of the three years under audit, you are unable to reach a settlement under the administrative appeal procedures of the IRS. The president of this company insists upon litigating the issue based on general principles. What is your advice?

## Problems

25. T, a calendar year taxpayer, does not file her 1982 return until June 3, 1983. At this point, she pays the $3,000 balance due on her 1982 tax liability of $30,000. T did not apply for and obtain any extension of time for filing the 1982 return. When questioned by the IRS on her delinquency, T asserts: "If I was too busy to file my regular tax return, I was too busy to request an extension."

    (a) Is T liable for any penalties for failure to file and for failure to pay?

    (b) If so, compute such penalties.

26. R, a calendar year taxpayer, was unable to file his 1982 income tax return on or before April 15, 1983. He does, however, apply for and obtain an automatic extension from the IRS. On May 10, 1983, R delivers his completed return to the IRS and remits the $4,000 balance due of his 1982 tax liability of $41,000.

    (a) Determine R's penalty for failure to file.

    (b) For failure to pay.

    (c) Would it make any difference as to your answers to parts (a) and (b) if R's tax liability for 1982 were $39,000 (instead of $41,000)? Explain.

27. During 19X2, T (an individual, calendar year taxpayer) had the following transactions, all of which were properly reported on a timely filed return:

| | | |
|---|---:|---:|
| Gross receipts | | $ 960,000 |
| Cost of goods sold | | 800,000 |
| Gross profit | | $ 160,000 |
| Capital gains and losses | | |
|   Capital gain | $ 72,000 | |
|   Capital loss | 24,000 | 48,000 |
| Total income | | $ 208,000 |

    (a) Presuming the absence of fraud on T's part, how much of an omission from gross income would be required to make the six-year statute of limitations apply?

    (b) Would it matter in your answer to part (a) if cost of goods sold had been inadvertently overstated by $100,000?

28. On April 3, 19X2, T filed his 19X1 income tax return reflecting a tax of $40,000. On June 30, 19X3, he filed an amended 19X1 return showing an additional $12,000 tax which was then paid. On May 20, 19X5, he filed a claim for refund of $18,000.

    (a) Assuming T is correct concerning the claim for refund, how much tax can he recover?

    (b) For what period is the interest payable on T's refund?

29. Ms. T had $40,000 withheld in 19X1. Because of heavy itemized deductions, she figured that she had no further tax to pay for the year. For this reason, and because of personal problems, and without securing an extension, she did not file her 19X1 return until July 1, 19X2. Actually, the return showed a refund of $2,400 which Ms. T ultimately received. On May 10, 19X5, Ms. T filed a $16,000 claim for refund of her 19X1 taxes.

    (a) How much, if any, of the $16,000 may Ms. T recover?

    (b) Would it have made any difference if Ms. T had requested and secured from the IRS an extension of time for filing her 19X1 tax return?

30. Indicate whether the following statements are true or false. (Note: SRTP = Statements on Responsibilities in Tax Practice):

    (a) In requiring a CPA to sign a tax return he or she has prepared for no compensation (e. g., as a favor to a neighbor or a relative), the SRTP go beyond what is required by the Treasury Regulations.

    (b) If a CPA does not prepare a return, then under no circumstances should he sign it as the preparer.

    (c) When a CPA has reasonable grounds for not answering an applicable question on a client's return, a brief explanation of the reason for the omission should not be provided because it would "flag" the return for audit by the IRS.

    (d) In preparing a taxpayer's return for 19X4, a CPA finds out that the client had 50% of his travel and entertainment deduction claimed for 19X2 disallowed on audit by the IRS. The CPA should feel bound by the prior administrative proceeding in determining his client's travel and entertainment expense deduction for 19X4.

    (e) If the client tells you that she had contributions of $500 for unsubstantiated cash donations to her church, you should deduct an odd amount on her return (e. g., $499), because an even amount (i. e., $500) would indicate to the IRS that her deduction was based on an estimate.

    (f) Basing an expense deduction on the client's estimates is not acceptable under the SRTP.

    (g) If a CPA knows that his client has a material error in a prior year's return, he should not, without the client's consent, disclose the error to the IRS.

    (h) If a CPA's client will not correct a material error in a prior year's return, he should not prepare the current year's return for the client.

    (i) If a CPA discovers, during an IRS audit, that his client has a material error in the return under examination, he should immediately withdraw from the engagement.

(j) If a CPA renders tax advice to the client in early 19X3, the client should be able to rely on such advice until April 15, 19X4. (The client prepared her own tax return.)

(k) The SRTP have the same force and effect as the AICPA's Code of Professional Ethics.

(l) In preparing a taxpayer's return, a CPA finds that he has taken a position which is contrary to the Treasury Regulations and that there is reasonable support for this position. The CPA is, therefore, obligated to disclose the difference on the taxpayer's return.

# Chapter 22

# Working with
# the Tax Law

## TAX SOURCES

Learning to work with the tax law involves the following three basic steps:

—Familiarity with the sources of the law.

—Application of research techniques.

—Effective use of planning procedures.

Statutory, administrative, and judicial sources of the tax law are considered first.

## STATUTORY SOURCES OF THE TAX LAW

*Origin of the Internal Revenue Code.* Prior to 1939, the statutory provisions relating to tax were contained in the individual revenue acts enacted by Congress. Because of the inconvenience and confusion that resulted from dealing with many separate acts, in 1939 Congress codified all of the Federal tax laws. Known as the Internal Revenue Code of 1939, the codification arranged all Federal tax provisions in a logical sequence and placed them in a separate part of the Federal statutes. A further rearrangement took place in 1954 and resulted in the Internal Revenue Code of 1954 which continues in effect to the present day.

The following observations will help clarify the significance of the codification procedure:

—With some exceptions, neither the 1939 nor the 1954 Codes substantially changed the tax law existing on the date of their enactment. Much of the 1939 Code, for example, was incorporated into the 1954 Code; the major change was the reorganization and renumbering of the tax provisions.[1]

—Statutory amendments to the tax law are integrated into the Code. The Tax Equity and Fiscal Responsibility Act of 1982, for example, became part of the Internal Revenue Code of 1954.

*The Legislative Process.*   Federal tax legislation generally originates in the House of Representatives where it is first considered by the House Ways and Means Committee.[2] If acceptable to the Committee, the proposed bill is referred to the whole House of Representatives for approval or disapproval. Approved bills are sent to the Senate where they are referred to the Senate Finance Committee for further consideration.[3] The next step involves referral from the Senate Finance Committee to the whole Senate. Assuming no disagreement between the House and Senate, passage by the Senate means referral to the President for approval or veto. If the bill is approved or if the President's veto is overridden, the bill becomes law and part of the Internal Revenue Code.

When the Senate version of the bill differs from that passed by the House,[4] the Joint Conference Committee, including members of both the House Ways and Means Committee and the Senate Finance Committee, is called upon to resolve these differences. The result, usually a compromise of the two versions, is then voted on by both the House and Senate. Acceptance by both bodies precedes referral to the President for approval or veto.

The typical legislative process dealing with tax bills is summarized as follows:

---

1.  This point is important in assessing judicial decisions interpreting provisions of the Internal Revenue Code of 1939. If the same provision was included in the Internal Revenue Code of 1954, the decision has continuing validity.

2.  Tax bills do originate in the Senate when they are attached as riders to other legislative proposals.

3.  Some tax provisions are commonly referred to by the number of the bill designated in the House when first proposed or by the name of the member of Congress sponsoring the legislation. For example, the Self-Employed Individuals Tax Retirement Act of 1962 is popularly known as H.R. 10 (i. e., House of Representatives Bill No. 10) or as the Keogh Act (i. e., Keogh being one of the members of Congress sponsoring the bill).

4.  This is frequently the case with major tax bills. One factor contributing to a different Senate version is the latitude each individual senator has to make amendments to a bill when the Senate as a whole is voting on a bill referred to it by the Senate Finance Committee. Less latitude is allowed in the House of Representatives. Thus, the whole House either accepts or rejects what is proposed by the House Ways and Means Committee, and changes from the floor are not commonplace.

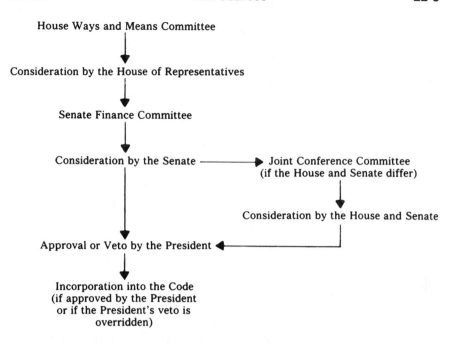

Referrals from the House Ways and Means Committee, the Senate Finance Committee, and the Joint Conference Committee are usually accompanied by committee reports. Because these committee reports often explain the provisions of the proposed legislation, they are a valuable source in ascertaining the intent of Congress. What Congress had in mind when it considers and enacts tax legislation is, of course, the key to interpreting such legislation.

The role of the Joint Conference Committee indicates the importance of compromise to the legislative process. The practical effect of the compromise process is illustrated by reviewing what happened in the Economic Recovery Tax Act of 1981 concerning change in the carryover of unused investment credits.

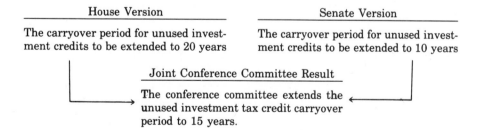

| House Version | Senate Version |
|---|---|
| The carryover period for unused investment credits to be extended to 20 years | The carryover period for unused investment credits to be extended to 10 years |

Joint Conference Committee Result

The conference committee extends the unused investment tax credit carryover period to 15 years.

*Arrangement of the Code.* In working with the Code it helps to understand the format followed. Note, for example, the following partial table of contents:

Subtitle A.  Income Taxes
     Chapter 1.  Normal Taxes and Surtaxes
          Subchapter A.  Determination of Tax Liability
               Part I.  Tax on Individuals
                    Sections 1–5
               Part II.  Tax on Corporations
                    Sections 11–12

* * *

In referring to a provision of the Code, the key is usually the section number involved. In designating Section 2(a) (dealing with the status of a surviving spouse), for example, it would be unnecessary to include Subtitle A, Chapter 1, Subchapter A, Part I. Merely mentioning Section 2(a) will suffice, since the section numbers run consecutively and do not begin again with each new subtitle, chapter, subchapter, or part. However, not all Code section numbers are used. Note that Part I ends with Section 5 and Part II starts with Section 11 (i. e., at present there are no Sections 6, 7, 8, 9, and 10).[5]

Among tax practitioners, a common way of referring to some specific area of income taxation is by subchapter designation. More common subchapter designations include Subchapter C ("Corporate Distributions and Adjustments"), Subchapter K ("Partners and Partnerships"), and Subchapter S ("Election of Certain Small Business Corporations as to Taxable Status"). Particularly in the last situation, it is much more convenient to describe the effect of the applicable Code provisions involved (Sections 1361–1379) as "Subchapter S status" rather than as the "Election of Certain Small Business Corporations as to Taxable Status."

*Citing the Code.*  Code sections often are broken down into subparts.[6] Section 2(a)(1)(A) serves as an example.[7]

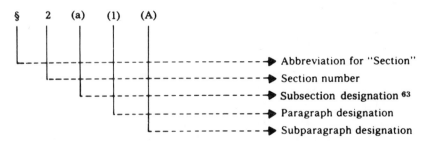

<hr />

**5.** When the 1954 Code was drafted, the omission of section numbers was intentional. This provided flexibility to incorporate later changes into the Code without disrupting its organization.
**6.** Some Code sections do not necessitate subparts. See, for example, § § 211 and 262.
**7.** Some Code sections omit the subsection designation and use, instead, the paragraph designation as the first subpart. See, for example, § 212(1) and § 1221(1).

Broken down as to content, § 2(a)(1)(A) becomes:

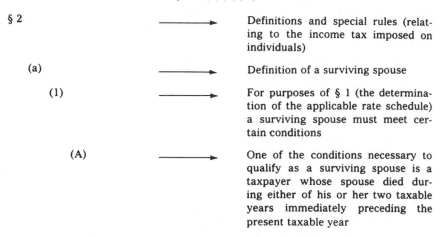

§ 2         ⟶    Definitions and special rules (relating to the income tax imposed on individuals)

   (a)       ⟶    Definition of a surviving spouse

     (1)     ⟶    For purposes of § 1 (the determination of the applicable rate schedule) a surviving spouse must meet certain conditions

       (A)   ⟶    One of the conditions necessary to qualify as a surviving spouse is a taxpayer whose spouse died during either of his or her two taxable years immediately preceding the present taxable year

Throughout the text, references to the Code sections are in the form given above. The symbols "§" and "§ §" are used in place of "Section" and "Sections." Unless otherwise stated, all Code references are to the Internal Revenue Code of 1954. The format followed in the text is summarized below.

| Complete Reference | Text Reference |
| --- | --- |
| Section 2(a)(1)(A) of the Internal Revenue Code of 1954 | § 2(a)(1)(A) |
| Sections 1 and 2 of the Internal Revenue Code of 1954 | § § 1 and 2 |
| Section 12(d) of the Internal Revenue Code of 1939[8] | § 12(d) of the Internal Revenue Code of 1939 |

## ADMINISTRATIVE SOURCES OF THE TAX LAW

The administrative sources of the Federal tax law can be grouped as follows: Treasury Department Regulations, Revenue Rulings and Procedures, and other administrative pronouncements. All are issued by either the U. S. Treasury Department or one of its instrumentalities [e. g., the Internal Revenue Service (IRS), or a District Director].

*Treasury Department Regulations.* Regulations are issued by the U. S. Treasury Department under authority granted by Congress.[9] Interpretative by nature, they provide taxpayers with considerable guidance on the meaning and application of the Code. Although not issued by Congress, Regulations do carry considerable weight and are an important factor to consider in complying with the tax law.

---

**8.** § 12(d) of the Internal Revenue Code of 1939 is the predecessor to § 2 of the Internal Revenue Code of 1954. Keep in mind that the 1954 Code has superseded the 1939 Code. The reason why a provision of the 1939 Code may be referred to is set forth in Footnote 1 of this chapter.

**9.** § 7805.

Since Regulations interpret the Code, they are arranged in the same sequence. Regulations are, however, prefixed by a number which designates the type of tax or administrative, procedural, or definitional matter to which they relate. For example, the prefix 1 designates the Regulations under the income tax law. Thus, the Regulations under Code § 2 would be cited as Reg. § 1.2 with subparts added for further identification. These subparts often have no correlation in numbering pattern with the Code subsections. The prefix 20 designates estate tax Regulations; 25 covers gift tax Regulations; 31 relates to employment taxes; and 301 refers to procedure and administration. This listing is not all-inclusive.

New Regulations and changes to existing Regulations are usually issued in proposed form before they are completed. The time interval between the proposal of a Regulation and its completion permits taxpayers and other interested parties to comment on the propriety of the proposal. Proposed Regulations under Code § 2, for example, would be cited as Prop.Reg. § 1.2.

Proposed and permanent Regulations are published in the *Federal Register* and are reproduced in major tax services. Final regulations are issued as Treasury Decisions (T.D.).

*Revenue Rulings and Revenue Procedures.* Revenue Rulings are official pronouncements of the National Office of the IRS and, like Regulations, are designed to provide interpretation of the tax law. However, they do not carry the same legal force and effect of Regulations and usually deal with more restricted problems. Both Revenue Rulings and Revenue Procedures serve an important function in that they afford guidance to both IRS personnel and taxpayers in handling routine tax matters.

Revenue Procedures are issued in the same manner as are Revenue Rulings, but they deal with the internal management practices and procedures of the IRS. Familiarity with these procedures can increase taxpayer compliance and assist the efficient administration of the tax laws by the IRS.

Revenue Rulings and Revenue Procedures are published weekly by the U. S. Government in the *Internal Revenue Bulletin* (I.R.B.). Semiannually, the bulletins for a six-month period are gathered together, reorganized by Code Section classification, and published in a bound volume designated *Cumulative Bulletin* (C.B.).[10] The proper

---

**10.** Usually only two volumes of the *Cumulative Bulletin* are published each year. However, when major tax legislation has been enacted by Congress, a third volume may be published containing the Congressional Committee Reports supporting the Revenue Act. See, for example, the third volume for 1974 dealing with the Employee Retirement Income Security Act of 1974 (ERISA). The 1974–3 *Cumulative Bulletin* contains the text of the Act itself and two House Reports plus the Conference Committee Report; 1974–3 Supp. contains additional Committee Reports and Congressional Record Excerpts relating to ERISA. This makes a total of four volumes of the *Cumulative Bulletin* for 1974: 1974–1, 1974–2, 1974–3, and 1974–3 Supp.

form for citing Rulings and Procedures depends on whether the item has been published in the *Cumulative Bulletins* or is available in I.R.B. form. Consider, for example, the following transition:

| | |
|---|---|
| Temporary Citation | Rev.Rul. 81–202, I.R.B. No. 34, 5.<br>*Explanation:* Revenue Ruling Number 202, appearing on page 5 of the 34th weekly issue of the *Internal Revenue Bulletin* for 1981. |
| Permanent Citation | Rev.Rul. 81–202, 1981–2 C.B. 93.<br>*Explanation:* Revenue Ruling Number 202, appearing on page 93 of Volume 2 of the *Cumulative Bulletin* for 1981. |

Since the second volume of the 1981 *Cumulative Bulletin* was not published until 1982, the I.R.B. citation must be used until that time. After the publication of the *Cumulative Bulletin*, the C.B. citation is proper. The basic portion of both citations (i. e., Rev.Rul. 81–202) indicates that this was the 202nd Revenue Ruling issued by the IRS during 1981.

Revenue Procedures are cited in the same manner, except that "Rev.Proc." is substituted for "Rev.Rul." Procedures, like Rulings, are published in the *Internal Revenue Bulletins* (the temporary source) and later transferred to the *Cumulative Bulletins* (the permanent source).

## JUDICIAL SOURCES OF THE TAX LAW

*The Judicial Process in General.* After a taxpayer has exhausted some or all of the remedies available within the IRS (i. e., no satisfactory settlement has been reached at the agent or at the Appeals Division level), the dispute can be taken to the Federal courts. The dispute is first considered by a court of original jurisdiction (known as a trial court) with any appeal (either by the taxpayer or the IRS) taken to the appropriate appellate court. In most situations, the taxpayer has a choice of any of four trial courts: a Federal District Court, the U. S. Claims Court, the U. S. Tax Court, or the Small Claims Division of the U. S. Tax Court. The trial and appellate court scheme for Federal tax litigation is illustrated in Figure I.

The broken line between the U. S. Tax Court and the Small Claims Division indicates that there is no appeal from the Small Claims Division. The jurisdiction of the Small Claims Division is limited to cases involving amounts of $5,000 or less.

Pursuant to the Federal Courts Improvement Act of 1982 (P.L. 97-164), on October 1, 1982, the U. S. Court of Claims, as previously constituted, ceased to exist. In its place is substituted the U. S. Claims Court. Decisions from this new trial court will be appealable to a new Court of Appeals for the Federal Circuit (designated as CA-FC).

**Figure I**

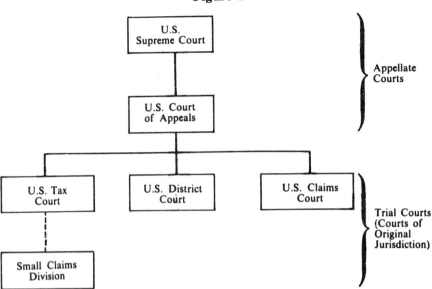

*Trial Courts.* Differences between the various trial courts (courts of original jurisdiction) are summarized below:

—There is only one Claims Court and only one Tax Court, but there are many Federal District Courts. The taxpayer does not select the District Court which will hear the dispute but must sue in that one which has jurisdiction.

—Each District Court has only one judge, the Claims Court has 16 judges, and the Tax Court has 19. In the case of the Tax Court, however, the whole court will decide a case (i. e., the court sits *en banc*) only when more important or novel tax issues are involved. Most cases will be heard and decided by one of the 19 judges.

—The Claims Court meets most often in Washington, D.C., while a District Court meets at a prescribed seat for the particular district. Since each state has at least one District Court and many of the more populous states have more, the problem of travel inconvenience and expense for the taxpayer and his or her counsel (present with many suits in the Claims Court) is largely eliminated. Although the Tax Court is officially based in Washington, D.C., the various judges travel to different parts of the country and hear cases at predetermined locations and dates. While this procedure eases the distance problem for the taxpayer, it could mean a delay before the case comes to trial and is decided.

—The Tax Court hears only tax cases; the Claims Court and District Courts hear nontax litigation as well. This difference, plus the fact that many Tax Court justices have been appointed from IRS or Treasury Department positions, has led some to conclude that the Tax Court has more expertise in tax matters.

—The only court in which a taxpayer can obtain a jury trial is a District Court. But since juries can decide only questions of fact and not questions of law, even those taxpayers who choose the District Court route often do not request a jury trial. In such event, the judge will decide all issues. Note that a District Court decision is controlling only in the district in which the court has jurisdiction.

—In order for the Claims Court or a District Court to have jurisdiction, the taxpayer must pay the tax deficiency assessed by the IRS and sue for a refund. If the taxpayer wins (assuming no successful appeal by the Government), the tax paid plus appropriate interest thereon will be recovered. In the case of the Tax Court, however jurisdiction is usually obtained without first paying the assessed tax deficiency. In the event the taxpayer loses in the Tax Court (and no appeal is taken or any such appeal is unsuccessful), the deficiency must be paid with appropriate interest.

—Appeals from a District Court or a Tax Court decision are to the appropriate U. S. Court of Appeals. Appeals from the Claims Court go to the Court of Appeals for the Federal Circuit.

*Appellate Courts.* Regarding appeals from a trial court, the following listing below indicates the Court of Appeals of appropriate jurisdiction:

| First | Fourth |
|---|---|
| Maine | Maryland |
| Massachusetts | North Carolina |
| New Hampshire | South Carolina |
| Rhode Island | Virginia |
| Puerto Rico | West Virginia |
| **Second** | **Fifth** |
| Connecticut | Canal Zone |
| New York | Louisiana |
| Vermont | Mississippi |
| | Texas |
| **Third** | |
| Delaware | **Sixth** |
| New Jersey | Kentucky |
| Pennsylvania | Michigan |
| Virgin Islands | Ohio |
| | Tennessee |
| **District of Columbia** | |
| Washington, D.C. | |

| Seventh | Tenth |
|---|---|
| Illinois | Colorado |
| Indiana | Kansas |
| Wisconsin | New Mexico |
|  | Oklahoma |
| **Eighth** | Utah |
| Arkansas | Wyoming |
| Iowa |  |
| Minnesota | **Eleventh**[11] |
| Missouri | Alabama |
| Nebraska | Florida |
| North Dakota | Georgia |
| South Dakota |  |
|  | **Federal Circuit** |
| **Ninth** | All of the jurisdictions |
| Alaska | (where the case originates |
| Arizona | in the Claims Court) |
| California |  |
| Hawaii |  |
| Idaho |  |
| Montana |  |
| Nevada |  |
| Oregon |  |
| Washington |  |
| Guam |  |

If the Government loses at the trial court level (i. e., District Court, Tax Court, or Claims Court), it need not (and frequently does not) appeal. The fact that an appeal is not made, however, does not indicate that the IRS agrees with the result and will not litigate similar issues in the future. There could be a number of reasons for the Service's failure to appeal. First, the current litigation load may be heavy, and as a consequence, the IRS may decide that available personnel resources should be assigned to other, more important, cases. Second, the IRS may determine that this is not a good case to appeal. Such might be true if the taxpayer is in a sympathetic position or the facts are particularly strong in his or her favor. In such event, the IRS may wait to test the legal issues involved with a taxpayer who has a much weaker case. Third, if the appeal is from a District Court or the Tax Court, the Court of Appeals of jurisdiction could have some bearing on whether or not the decision is made to go forward with an appeal. Based on past experience and precedent, the IRS may conclude that the chance for success on a particular issue might be more promising in another Court of Appeals. The IRS will wait for a similar case to arise in a different appellate court.

District Courts, the Tax Court, and the Claims Court must abide

---

**11.** The Eleventh Court of Appeals was created, effective October 1, 1981, by P.L. 96–452 (enacted in 1980). The states included therein were previously in the Fifth Court of Appeals. The reason for the division was due to the increase in population in the Sun Belt states and the enormity of the geographical area previously covered.

by the precedents set by the Court of Appeals of jurisdiction. A particular Court of Appeals need not follow the decisions of another Court of Appeals. All courts, however, must follow the decisions of the U. S. Supreme Court.

Appeal to the U. S. Supreme Court is by Writ of Certiorari. If the Court accepts jurisdiction, it will grant the Writ (i. e., *Cert. Granted*). Most often, it will deny jurisdiction (i. e., *Cert. Denied*). For whatever reason or reasons, the Supreme Court rarely hears tax cases. The Court usually grants certiorari to resolve a conflict among the Courts of Appeals (e. g., two or more appellate courts have assumed opposing positions on a particular issue). The granting of a Writ of Certiorari indicates that at least four members of the Supreme Court believe that the issue is of sufficient importance to be heard by the full court.

The role of appellate courts is limited to a review of the record of trial compiled by the trial courts. Thus, the appellate process usually involves a determination of whether or not the trial court applied the proper law in arriving at its decision. Rarely will an appellate court disturb a lower court's fact-finding determination.

The result of an appeal could be any of a number of possibilities. The appellate court could approve (affirm) or disapprove (reverse) the lower court's finding, and it could also send the case back for further consideration (remand). When many issues are involved, it is not unusual to encounter a mixed result. Thus, the lower court could be affirmed (i. e., *aff'd*.) on Issue A and reversed (i. e., *rev'd*.) on Issue B, and Issue C could be remanded (i. e., *rem'd*.) for additional fact finding.

When more than one judge is involved in the decision-making process, it is not uncommon for them to disagree with one another. In addition to the majority view, there could be one or more judges who "concur" (i. e., agree with the result reached but not with some or all of the reasoning) or "dissent" (i. e., disagree with the result). In any one case it is, of course, the majority view that controls. But concurring and dissenting views may have influence on other courts or, at some subsequent date when the composition of the court has changed, even on the same court.

Having concluded a brief description of the judicial process, it is appropriate to consider the more practical problem of the relationship of case law to tax research. As previously noted, court decisions are an important source of tax law. The ability to cite a case and to locate it is, therefore, a must in working with the tax law.

*Judicial Citations—The U. S. Tax Court.* A good starting point is with the U. S. Tax Court (formerly the Board of Tax Appeals). The Court issues two types of decisions: Regular and Memorandum. The distinction between the two involves both substance and form. In terms of substance, Memorandum decisions deal with situations necessitating only the application of already established principles of law; however, Regular decisions involve novel issues not previously resolved by the Court. In actual practice, however, this distinction is not always preserved. Not infrequently, Memorandum decisions will be encountered that appear to warrant Regular status and vice versa. At any rate, do not conclude that Memorandum decisions possess no value as precedents. Both represent the position of the Tax Court and, as such, can be relied upon.

Another important distinction between the Regular and Memorandum decisions issued by the Tax Court arises in connection with form. The Memorandum decisions officially are published in mimeograph form only, but Regular decisions are published by the U. S. Government in a series designated *Tax Court of the United States Reports*. Each volume of these *Reports* covers a six-month period (April 1 through September 30 and October 1 through March 31) and is given a succeeding volume number. But, as was true of the *Cumulative Bulletins,* there is usually a time lag between the date a decision is rendered and the date it appears in bound form. A temporary citation may be necessary to aid the researcher in locating a recent Regular decision. Consider, for example, the temporary and permanent citations for *John W. Green,* a decision filed on March 17, 1982:

| Temporary Citation | *John W. Green,* 78 T.C. __, No. 30 (1982) *Explanation:* Page number left blank because not yet known |
|---|---|
| Permanent Citation | *John W. Green,* 78 T.C. 428 (1982) *Explanation:* Page number now available |

Both citations tell us that the case will ultimately appear in Volume 78 of the *Tax Court of the United States Reports*. But until this volume is bound and made available to the general public, the page number must be left blank. Instead, the temporary citation identifies the case as being the 30th Regular decision issued by the Tax Court since Volume 77 ended. With this information, the decision can be easily located in either of the special Tax Court services published by Commerce Clearing House or Prentice-Hall. Once Volume 78 is released, the permanent citation can be substituted and the number of the case dropped.

Before 1943, the Tax Court was called the Board of Tax Appeals, and its decisions were published as the *United States Board of Tax Appeals Reports* (B.T.A.). These 47 volumes cover the period from 1924 to 1942. For example, the citation *Karl Pauli,* 11 B.T.A. 784 (1928) refers to the eleventh volume of the *Board of Tax Appeals Reports,* page 784, issued in 1928.

One further distinction between Regular and Memorandum decisions of the Tax Court involves the IRS procedure of acquiescence (i. e., "A" or "Acq.") or nonacquiescence (i. e., "NA" or "Nonacq."). If the IRS loses in a Regular decision, it will usually indicate whether it agrees or disagrees with the result reached by the Court. The acquiescence or nonacquiescence will be published in the *Internal Revenue Bulletin* and the *Cumulative Bulletin.* The procedure is not followed for Memorandum decisions or for the decisions of other courts. The IRS can retroactively revoke an acquiescence. The IRS sometimes issues an announcement that it will *or* will not follow a decision of another Federal court on similar facts.

Although Memorandum decisions are not published by the U. S. Government, they are published by Commerce Clearing House (CCH) and Prentice-Hall (P–H). Consider, for example, the three different ways that *Walter H. Johnson* may be cited:

*Walter H. Johnson,* T.C. Memo. 1975–245
> The 245th Memorandum Decision issued by the Tax Court in 1975.

*Walter H. Johnson,* 34 TCM 1056
> Page 1056 of Vol. 34 of the *CCH Tax Court Memorandum Decisions.*

*Walter H. Johnson,* P–H T.C. Mem.Dec. ¶ 75,245
> Paragraph 75,245 of the *P–H T.C. Memorandum Decisions.*

Note that the third citation contains the same information as the first. Thus, ¶ 75,245 indicates the following information about the case: year 1975, 245th T.C. Memo. Decision.[12]

*Judicial Citations—The U. S. District Court, Claims Court, and Court of Appeals.* District Court, Claims Court, Court of Appeals, and Supreme Court decisions dealing with Federal tax matters are reported in both the CCH, *U. S. Tax Cases* (USTC), and the P–H, *American Federal Tax Reports* (AFTR) series.

Federal District Court decisions, dealing with *both* tax and nontax issues, also are published by West Publishing Company in its Federal Supplement Series. Examples of how a District Court case can be cited in three different forms appear below:

*Simons-Eastern Co. v. U. S.,* 73–1 USTC ¶ 9279 (D.Ct.Ga., 1972).

*Explanation:* Reported in the first volume of the *U. S. Tax Cases* (i. e., USTC) published by Commerce Clearing House for calendar year 1973 (i. e., 73–1) and located at paragraph 9279 (i. e., ¶ 9279).

*Simons-Eastern Co. v. U. S.,* 31 AFTR2d 73–640(D.Ct.Ga., 1972).

*Explanation:* Reported in the 31st volume of the second series of the *American Federal Tax Reports* (i. e., AFTR2d) published by Prentice-Hall and commencing on page 640. The "73" preceding the page number indicates the year the case was published but is a designation used only in recent decisions.

---

12. In this text the Prentice-Hall citation for Memorandum decisions of the U. S. Tax Court is omitted. Thus, *Walter H. Johnson* is cited as 34 TCM 1056, T.C. Memo. 1975–245.

*Simons-Eastern Co. v. U. S.*, 354 F.Supp. 1003 (D.Ct.Ga., 1972).

*Explanation:* Reported in the 354th volume of the *Federal Supplement Series* (i. e., F.Supp.) published by West Publishing Co. and commencing on page 1003.

In all of the above citations note that the name of the case is the same (Simons-Eastern Co. being the taxpayer) as is the reference to the Federal District Court of Georgia (i. e., D.Ct.Ga.) and the year the decision was rendered (i. e., 1972).[13]

Decisions of the Claims Court (previously called the Court of Claims) and the Courts of Appeals are published in the USTCs, AFTRs, and a West Publishing Company reporter designated as the Federal Second Series (F.2d). Illustrations of the different forms follow:

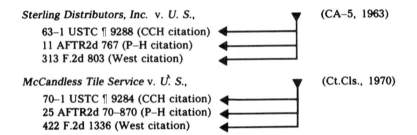

Note that *Sterling Distributors, Inc.* is a decision rendered by the Fifth Court of Appeals in 1963 (i. e., CA–5, 1963), while *McCandless Tile Service* is one rendered by the Court of Claims in 1970 (i. e., Ct.Cls., 1970), the predecessor of the Claims Court.

*Judicial Citations—The U. S. Supreme Court.* Like all other federal tax cases (except those rendered by the U. S. Tax Court), Supreme Court decisions are published by Commerce Clearing House in the USTCs and by Prentice-Hall in the AFTRs. The U. S. Government Printing Office also publishes these decisions in the *United States Supreme Court Reports* (i. e., U. S.) as does West Publishing Company in its *Supreme Court Reporter* (i. e., S.Ct.) and the Lawyer's Co-Operative Publishing Company in its *United States Reports, Lawyer's Edition* (i. e., L.Ed.). An illustration of the different ways the same case can be cited appears below:

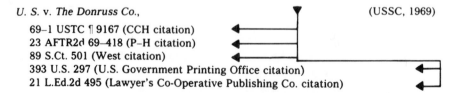

---

13. In the text the case is cited in the following form: *Simons-Eastern Co. v. U. S.*, 73–1 USTC ¶ 9279, 31 AFTR2d 73–640, 354 F.Supp. 1003 (D.Ct.Ga., 1972).

The parenthetical reference (USSC, 1969) identifies the decision as having been rendered by the U. S. Supreme Court in 1969. The citations given in this text for Supreme Court decisions are limited to the CCH (i. e., USTC), P–H (i. e., AFTR), and the West (i. e., S.Ct.) versions.

## WORKING WITH THE TAX LAW—TAX RESEARCH

Tax research is the method whereby one determines the best available solution to a situation that possesses tax consequences. In other words, it is the process of finding a competent and professional conclusion to a tax problem. The problem might originate either from completed or proposed transactions. In the case of a completed transaction, the objective of the research would be to determine the tax result of what has already taken place. For example, was the expenditure incurred by the taxpayer deductible or not deductible for tax purposes? When dealing with proposed transactions, however, the tax research process is directed toward the determination of possible tax consequences. To the extent that tax research leads to a choice of alternatives or otherwise influences the future actions of the taxpayer, it becomes the key to effective tax planning.

Tax research involves the following procedures:

—Identifying and refining the problem.

—Locating the appropriate tax law sources.

—Assessing the validity of the tax law sources.

—Arriving at the solution or at alternative solutions with due consideration given to nontax factors.

—Effectively communicating the solution to the taxpayer or the taxpayer's representative.

—Following up on the solution (where appropriate) in light of new developments.

These procedures are diagrammed in Figure II. The broken lines reflect those steps of particular interest when tax research is directed towards proposed, rather than completed, transactions.

### IDENTIFYING THE PROBLEM

Problem identification must start with a compilation of the relevant facts involved.[14] In this regard, *all* of the facts that may have a bear-

---

14. For an excellent discussion of the critical role of facts in carrying out tax research, see Ray M. Sommerfeld and G. Fred Streuling, *Tax Research Techniques,* Tax Study No. 5 (New York: The American Institute of Certified Public Accountants, 1976), Chapter 2.

**Figure II**

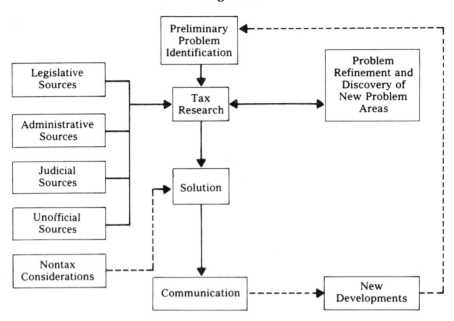

ing on the problem must be gathered because any omission could modify the solution to be reached. To illustrate, consider what appears to be a very simple problem.

> **Example 1.** On December 30, 19X0, X Corporation (a calendar year and accrual basis taxpayer) declares a $20,000 bonus payable to R, one of its employees. The stock of X Corporation is held by R, S, and T, all individuals. The problem: Is the bonus deductible by X Corporation?

*Refining the Problem.* Initial reaction would be to sanction the deduction in Example 1, since it has long been accepted that salaries or other compensation represent an ordinary and necessary expense in carrying on a trade or business [see § 162(a)]. Further investigation into this area reveals, however, that the accrual of year-end employee bonuses is subject to specific restrictions in § 404. Payments that are not made within a reasonable time period (i. e., by the due date of the tax return including extensions) are deductible only in the year of payment rather than in the year of accrual. Assume, however, further fact gathering reveals the following additional information:

—The bonus was accrued on December 30, 19X0, but not actually paid until July 1, 19X1.

—R uses the cash method of accounting for income tax purposes.

—The stock in X Corporation is owned in equal proportion by R, S, and T (i. e., each owns one-third of the stock).

—R, S, and T are brothers and sisters.

With these new facts, additional research leads to a consideration of § 267(a)(2) which overrides the general rules for deductibility under § 404. Under this Code provision, X Corporation would lose the deduction if all of the following three conditions are met:

1. X Corporation uses the accrual method of accounting while R uses the cash method.

2. The bonus is not paid within 2½ months from the end of the tax year in which accrued (in this case no later than March 15, 19X1).

3. R owns, directly or *indirectly,* more than 50% in the value of X Corporation's outstanding stock.

Has condition 3 been satisfied since R owns only 33⅓ percent of the stock in X Corporation? Further research reveals that an individual is deemed, for this purpose at least, to own all of the stock owned by members of his or her family [§ 267(c)(2)]. Because members of the family include brothers and sisters [§ 267(c)(4)], R owns 100 percent of the stock of X Corporation (i. e., 33⅓ percent directly and 66⅔ percent indirectly).[15] All three conditions having been met, it therefore appears that X Corporation will be denied a deduction for the accrued bonus.

*Further Refinement of the Problem.* One of the conditions necessary for the disallowance of X Corporation's deduction under § 267 was the failure to pay the bonus to R within 2½ months from the close of the tax year in which it was accrued. Suppose, however, further investigation reveals the following:

—R had the right to receive the bonus once it was authorized (or no later than March 15, 19X1).

—X Corporation had the duty and the financial capacity to pay the bonus when it was authorized.

In light of this new information, X Corporation's deduction might not be lost. Further research indicates that if R (the payee) is in constructive receipt of the income, X Corporation (the payor) will be considered to have made a constructive payment. Thus, the date of constructive payment, as opposed to the date of actual payment, will control for purposes of applying § 267. If constructive payment occurs no later than March 15, 19X1, the $20,000 bonus will be deductible to X Corporation for tax year 19X0 (the year of the accrual). Additional research would provide judicial authority setting forth guidelines on what does and does not constitute a constructive payment.

Even if the deduction of the bonus is not prevented by § 267, a further refinement of the problem should take into account the possible effect of § 162(a)(1). Under this provision, salaries and other com-

---

**15.** By virtue of the family attribution rules of § 267(c)(2), R has constructive ownership of the stock owned by his brothers and sisters. Thus, "indirect" ownership means "constructive" ownership.

pensation can be deducted only if "reasonable" in amount. To properly resolve the question of reasonableness, the researcher would need to gather such facts as the nature and extent of the services performed, the amount of other compensation paid to R in the same year as the bonus, the salaries paid by similar firms for similar services, and the dividend payment record of X Corporation. These facts, when tested by the Regulations under § 162 and court decisions on the subject, would provide the basis for assessing the reasonableness of the bonus and, consequently, its deductibility by X Corporation.

## LOCATING THE APPROPRIATE TAX LAW SOURCES

Once the problem is clearly defined, what is the next step? Although this is a matter of individual judgment, most involved tax research begins with the index volume number of the tax service. If the problem is not that complex, the researcher may bypass the tax service and turn directly to the Internal Revenue Code and the Treasury Regulations. For the beginner, this procedure saves time and will solve many of the more basic problems. If the researcher does not have a personal copy of the Code or Regulations, resorting to the appropriate volume(s) of a tax service will be necessary.

The major tax services available are listed below:

*Standard Federal Tax Reporter,* Commerce Clearing House.

*Federal Taxes,* Prentice-Hall.

Mertens, *Law of Federal Income Taxation,* Callaghan and Co.

*Tax Coordinator,* Research Institute of America.

*Tax Management Portfolios,* Bureau of National Affairs.

Rabkin and Johnson, *Federal Income, Gift and Estate Taxation,* Matthew Bender, Inc.

*Working With the Tax Services.* In this text it is not feasible to teach the use of any particular tax service—this can better be learned by practice.

There are, however, several important observations about the use of tax services that cannot be overemphasized. First, never forget to check for current developments. The main text of any service is not revised frequently enough to permit reliance on that portion as the *latest* word on any subject. Where such current developments can be found depends, of course, on which service is being used. Both the Commerce Clearing House and Prentice-Hall services contain a special volume devoted to current matters. Second, when dealing with a tax service synopsis of a Treasury Department pronouncement or a judicial decision, remember there is no substitute for the original source.

To illustrate, do not base a conclusion solely on a tax service's commentary on *Simons-Eastern Co. v. U. S.* If the case is vital to the research, look it up. It is possible that the facts of the case are distinguishable from those involved in the problem being researched. This is not to say that the case synopsis contained in the tax service is wrong—it might just be misleading or incomplete.

## ASSESSING THE VALIDITY OF THE TAX LAW SOURCE

Once a source has been located, the next procedure is to assess such source in light of the problem at hand. Proper assessment involves careful interpretation of the tax law with consideration as to its relevance and validity. In connection with validity, an important step is to check for recent changes in the tax law.

*Interpreting the Internal Revenue Code.* The language of the Code can be extremely difficult to comprehend fully. For example, a subsection [§ 341(e)] relating to collapsible corporations contains *one* sentence of more than 450 words. Within this same subsection are two other sentences of 300 and 340 words. One author has noted 10 common pitfalls in interpreting the Code:[16]

1. Determine the limitations and exceptions to a provision. Do not permit the language of the Code Section to carry greater or lesser weight than was intended.

2. Just because a Section fails to mention an item does not necessarily mean that the item is excluded.

3. Read definitional clauses carefully.

4. Do not overlook small words such as "and" and "or." There is a world of difference between these two words.

5. Read the Code Section completely; do not jump to conclusions. Return to Example 1 and the bonus X Corporation accrued on behalf of R. If the analysis of § 267 stopped with subsection (b)(1), it would appear that the bonus is deductible, since R owns only one-third of the stock in X Corporation and not "more than 50 percent." A further reading of § 267, however, reveals that R constructively owns all of the stock of his brothers and sisters (i. e., S and T). Because R is deemed to own "more than 50%" of X Corporation, the conclusion reached after only a partial examination is invalidated.

6. Watch out for cross-referenced and related provisions, since many Sections of the Code are interrelated.

7. Congress is at times not careful when reconciling new Code provisions with existing Sections. Conflicts among Sections, therefore, do arise.

---

16. H. G. Wong, "Ten Common Pitfalls in Reading the Internal Revenue Code," *The Practical Accountant* (July–August, 1972), pp. 30–33.

8. Be alert for hidden definitions; terms in a particular Code Section may be defined in the same Section *or in a separate Section.*

9. Some answers may not be found in the Code; therefore, a researcher may have to consult the Regulations and/or judicial decisions.[17]

10. Take careful note of measuring words such as "less than 50 percent"; "exceeds 35 percent"; "at least 80 percent"; and, "more than 80 percent."

*Assessing the Validity of a Treasury Regulation.* It is often stated that Treasury Regulations have the force and effect of law. This is certainly true for most Regulations, but there have been judicial decisions which have held a Regulation or a portion thereof invalid, usually on the grounds that the Regulation is contrary to the intent of Congress upon the enactment of a particular Code Section.

Keep in mind the following observations when assessing the validity of a Regulation:

—In a challenge, the burden of proof is on the taxpayer to show that the Regulation is wrong.

—If the taxpayer loses the challenge, the imposition of a penalty under § 6653(a) may result. This provision deals with the "intentional disregard of rules and regulations" on the part of the taxpayer.

—Some Regulations merely reprint or rephrase what Congress has stated in its Committee Reports issued in connection with the enactment of tax legislation. Such Regulations are "hard and solid" and almost impossible to overturn because they clearly reflect the intent of Congress.

—In some Code Sections, Congress has given to the "Secretary or his delegate" the authority to prescribe Regulations to carry out the details of administration or to otherwise complete the operating rules. Under such circumstances, it could almost be said that Congress is delegating its legislative powers to the Treasury Department. Regulations issued pursuant to this type of authority truly possess the force and effect of law and are often called "legislative regulations."

*Assessing the Validity of Other Administrative Sources of the Tax Law.* Revenue Rulings issued by the IRS carry less weight than Treasury Department Regulations. Rulings are important, however,

---

17. The Code is silent concerning the deductibility of education expenses. Such deductibility, however, falls under the general provision of § 162(a) (the allowance for "all the ordinary and necessary expenses paid or incurred during the taxable year in carrying on any trade or business . . ."). Guidelines for deductibility of education expenses can be found in Reg. § 1.162–5.

in that they reflect the position of the IRS on tax matters. In any dispute with the IRS on the interpretation of tax law, therefore, taxpayers should expect agents to follow the results reached in any applicable Rulings.

Revenue Rulings further tell the taxpayer the IRS's reaction to certain court decisions. Recall that the IRS follows a practice of either acquiescing (i. e., agreeing) or not acquiescing (i. e., not agreeing) with the *Regular* decisions of the U. S. Tax Court. This does not mean that a particular decision of the Tax Court is of no value if, for example, the IRS has nonacquiesced in the result. It does, however, indicate that the IRS will continue to litigate the issue involved.

*Assessing the Validity of Judicial Sources of the Tax Law.* The judicial process as it relates to the formulation of tax law has already been described. How much reliance can be placed on a particular decision depends upon the following variables:

—The level of the court. A decision rendered by a trial court (e. g., a Federal District Court) carries less weight than one issued by an appellate court (e. g., the Fifth Court of Appeals). Unless Congress changes the Code, decisions by the U. S. Supreme Court represent the last word on any tax issue.

—The legal residence of the taxpayer. If, for example, a taxpayer lives in Texas, a decision of the Fifth Court of Appeals means more than one rendered by the Second Court of Appeals. This is the case, since any appeal from a U. S. District Court or the U. S. Tax Court would be to the Fifth Court of Appeals and not to the Second Court of Appeals.

—Whether the decision represents the weight of authority on the issue. In other words, is it supported by the results reached by other courts?

—The outcome or status of the decision on appeal. For example, was the decision appealed and, if so, with what result?

## ARRIVING AT THE SOLUTION OR AT ALTERNATIVE SOLUTIONS

In Example 1 the problem was whether or not X Corporation could deduct a bonus of $20,000, declared on December 30, 19X0, and payable to R, one of its employees. A refinement of the problem added the additional information that the bonus was not paid until July 1, 19X1, and all of the stock of X Corporation was owned by R and his brother and sister. The end result was a disallowance of the deduction unless it could be shown that the bonus was constructively paid to R no later than March 15, 19X1. The solution, therefore, turned on whether the conditions for application of § 267 (i. e., disallowance of expenses involving related parties) were satisfied. But even if § 267 could be avoided, the bonus would have to pass the test of reasonableness set forth in § 162(a)(1). If, when added to the other compensation R received in 19X0 from X Corporation, some or all of the bonus is unreasonable, such amount will be disallowed as a deduction.

In summary, the solution to the problem depends upon the resolution of two questions of fact. First, has a constructive payment occurred? Second, is the compensation R received reasonable in amount? Under such circumstances, a clear-cut answer may not be possible. This, does not, however, detract from the value of the research. Often, a guarded judgment is the best possible solution that can be given to a tax problem.

# WORKING WITH THE TAX LAW— TAX PLANNING

Tax research and tax planning are inseparable. The primary purpose of effective tax planning is to reduce the taxpayer's total tax bill. This does not mean that the course of action selected must produce the lowest possible tax under the circumstances; the minimization must be considered in context with the legitimate business goals of the taxpayer.

A secondary objective of effective tax planning works toward a deferment or postponement of the tax. Specifically, this objective aims to accomplish any one or more of the following procedures: eradicating the tax entirely; eliminating the tax in the current year; deferring the receipt of income; converting ordinary income into capital gains; proliferating taxpayers (i. e., forming partnerships and corporations or making lifetime gifts to family members); eluding double taxation; avoiding ordinary income; or creating, increasing, or accelerating deductions. However, this second objective should be accepted with considerable reservation. Although the maxim "A bird in the hand is worth two in the bush" has general validity, there are frequent cases in which the rule breaks down. For example, a tax election in one year, although it accomplishes a current reduction in taxes, could saddle future years with a disadvantageous tax position.

## NONTAX CONSIDERATIONS

There is an honest danger that tax motivations may take on a significance that does not conform with the true values involved. In other words, tax considerations may operate to impair the exercise of sound business judgment by the taxpayer. Thus, the tax planning process may become a medium through which to accomplish ends that are socially and economically objectionable. Ostensibly, there exists a pronounced tendency for planning to go toward the opposing extremes of either not enough or too much emphasis on tax considerations. The happy medium—one that recognizes the significance of taxes, but not beyond the point at which planning serves to detract from the exercise of good business judgment—turns out to be the promised land that is seldom reached.

The remark is often made that a good rule to follow is to refrain from pursuing any course of action which would not be followed were it not for certain tax considerations. This statement is not entirely correct, but it does illustrate the desirability of preventing business logic from being "sacrificed at the altar of tax planning."

## TAX EVASION AND TAX AVOIDANCE

There is a fine line between legal tax planning and illegal tax planning—tax avoidance versus tax evasion. Tax avoidance is merely tax minimization through legal techniques. In this sense, tax avoidance becomes the proper objective of all tax planning. Evasion, while also aimed at the elimination or reduction of taxes, connotes the use of subterfuge and fraud as a means to an end. Popular usage—probably because of the common goals that are involved—has linked these two concepts to the extent that any true distinctions have been obliterated in the minds of many. Consequently, the taint created by the association of tax avoidance and tax evasion has deterred some taxpayers from properly taking advantage of the planning possibilities. The now-classic verbiage of Judge Learned Hand in *Commissioner v. Newman* reflects the true values the individual should have. In this opinion Judge Hand declared:

> Over and over again courts have said that there is nothing sinister in so arranging one's affairs as to keep taxes as low as possible. Everybody does so, rich or poor; and all do right, for nobody owes any public duty to pay more than the law demands: taxes are enforced extractions, not voluntary contributions. To demand more in the name of morals is mere cant.[18]

## FOLLOW-UP PROCEDURES

Because tax planning usually involves a proposed (as opposed to a completed) transaction, it is predicated upon the continuing validity of the advice based upon the tax research. A change in the tax law (either legislative, administrative, or judicial) could alter the original conclusion. Additional research may be necessary to test the solution in light of current developments (refer to one set of broken lines depicted in Figure II).

---

18. *Comm. v. Newman*, 47–1 USTC ¶ 9175, 35 AFTR 857, 159 F.2d 848 (CA–2, 1947).

## TAX PLANNING—A PRACTICAL APPLICATION

Returning to the facts of Example 1, what could have been done to protect X Corporation's deduction for the $20,000 bonus to R had the transaction not been completed? Concerning the § 267 issue (i. e., disallowance of accrued but unpaid expenses among certain related parties), the following steps should be taken:

—Pay the bonus to R by December 31, 19X0.

—If the payment is to be postponed, it should take place no later than March 15, 19X1. In this event, the parties should firmly establish X Corporation's liability to make the payment before the close of its tax year (i. e., December 31, 19X0).

What about any potential unreasonable compensation issue under § 162(a)(1)? One tax planning aid would be to make the amount of the bonus contingent on a predetermined formula. Bonuses arbitrarily determined at year-end are particularly suspect when paid to an employee-shareholder of a closely-held corporation. Regulation § 1.162–7(b)(2) states in part:

> Generally speaking, if contingent compensation is paid pursuant to a free bargain between the employer and the individual *made before the services are rendered,* not influenced by any consideration on the part of the employer other than that of securing on fair and advantageous terms the services of the individual, it should be allowed as a deduction *even though in the actual working out of the contract it may prove to be greater than the amount which would ordinarily be paid.* [Emphasis added.]

Thus, a contract entered into by R and X Corporation before the services are rendered (in early 19X0) establishing R's bonus as contingent on profits or some other measure of productivity would help justify a larger amount as reasonable than would otherwise be the case.

## PROBLEM MATERIALS

### Discussion Questions

1. Trace through Congress the path usually followed by a tax bill.

2. What is the function of the Joint Conference Committee of the House Ways and Means Committee and the Senate Finance Committee?

3. Why are committee reports of Congress important as a source of tax law?

4. The Tax Equity and Fiscal Responsibility Act of 1982 became part of the Internal Revenue Code of 1954. Explain the meaning of this statement.

5. Judicial decisions interpreting a provision of the Internal Revenue Code of 1939 are no longer of any value in view of the enactment of the Internal Revenue Code of 1954. Assess the validity of this statement.

6. Explain the reference to "Subchapter S."

7. What is a Proposed Regulation? How would a Proposed Regulation under § 541 be cited?

8. What is the difference, if any, between the *Internal Revenue Bulletin* (I.R.B.) and the *Cumulative Bulletin* (C.B.)?

9. Interpret each of the following citations:

    (a) Rev.Rul. 80–325, 1980–2 C.B. 5.

    (b) Rev.Proc. 80–32, 1980–2 C.B. 767.

10. Summarize the trial and appellate court system for Federal tax litigation.

11. List an advantage and a disadvantage of using the U. S. Tax Court as the trial court for Federal tax litigation.

12. List an advantage and a disadvantage of using a U. S. District Court as the trial court for Federal tax litigation.

13. Taxpayer lives in Michigan. In a controversy with the IRS, taxpayer loses at the trial court level. Describe the appeal procedure under the following different assumptions:

    (a) The trial court was the Small Claims Division of the U. S. Tax Court.

    (b) The trial court was the U. S. Tax Court.

    (c) The trial court was a U. S. District Court.

14. Suppose the U. S. Government loses a tax case in the U. S. District Court of Idaho but does not appeal the result. What does the failure to appeal signify?

15. Interpret each of the citations appearing below:

    (a) 54 T.C. 1514 (1970).

    (b) 408 F.2d 117 (CA–2, 1969).

    (c) 69–1 USTC ¶ 9319 (CA–2, 1969).

    (d) 23 AFTR2d 69–1090 (CA–2, 1969).

    (e) 293 F.Supp. 1129 (D.Ct., Miss., 1967).

    (f) 67–1 USTC ¶ 9253 (D.Ct., Miss., 1967).

    (g) 19 AFTR2d 647 (D.Ct., Miss., 1967).

    (h) 56 S.Ct. 289 (USSC, 1935).

    (i) 36–1 USTC ¶ 9020 (USSC, 1935).

    (j) 16 AFTR 1274 (USSC, 1935).

    (k) 422 F.2d 1336 (Ct.Cls., 1970).

16. Explain the following abbreviations:

    (a) CA–2

    (b) Cls.Ct.

    (c) *aff'd.*

    (d) *rev'd.*

(e) *rem'd.*

(f) *cert. denied*

(g) *acq.*

(h) B.T.A.

(i) USTC

(j) AFTR

(k) F.2d

(l) F.Supp.

(m) USSC

(n) S.Ct.

(o) D.Ct.

17. What is the difference between a Regular and a Memorandum decision of the U. S. Tax Court?

18. What is a "legislative" Regulation?

19. T, a college professor, teaches courses in the tax area. T feels comfortable with Subchapter C matters but has difficulty dealing with Subchapter K. Interpret this statement.

20. A student/friend majoring in sociology indicates that tax advisers are immoral since they merely help people cheat the government. Defend tax planning by tax advisers.

21. While researching a tax problem, why may the answer not be found in the Internal Revenue Code?

22. Once a tax problem is clearly defined, what is the next step?

## Problems

23. T, an individual taxpayer, has just been audited by the IRS and, as a result, has been assessed a substantial deficiency (which has not yet been paid) in additional income taxes. In preparing his defense, T advances the following possibilities:

    (a) Although a resident of Kentucky, T plans to sue in a U. S. District Court in Oregon which appears to be more favorably inclined towards taxpayers.

    (b) If (a) is not possible, T plans to take his case to a Kentucky state court where an uncle is the presiding judge.

    (c) Since T has found a B.T.A. decision that seems to help his case, he plans to rely on it under alternative (a) or (b).

    (d) If he loses at the trial court level, T plans to appeal either to the U. S. Claims Court or to the U. S. Second Court of Appeals. The reason for this choice is the presence of relatives in both Washington, D.C., and Chicago. Staying with these relatives could save T lodging expense while his appeal is being heard by the court selected.

    (e) Whether or not T wins at the trial court or appeals court level, he feels certain of success on an appeal to the U. S. Supreme Court.

    Evaluate T's notions concerning the judicial process as it applies to Federal income tax controversies.

24. Using the legend provided, classify each of the statements appearing below: (Note: More than one answer per statement may be appropriate.)

### Legend

D = Applies to the U. S. District Court

T = Applies to the U. S. Tax Court

C = Applies to the U. S. Claims Court

A = Applies to the U. S. Court of Appeals

U = Applies to the U. S. Supreme Court

N = Applies to none of the above

(a) Decides only Federal tax matters.

(b) Decisions are reported in the F.2d Series.

(c) Decisions are reported in the USTCs.

(d) Decisions are reported in the AFTRs.

(e) Appeal is by Writ of Certiorari.

(f) Court meets generally in Washington, D. C.

(g) A jury trial is available.

(h) Trial courts.

(i) Appellate courts.

(j) Has a Small Claims Division.

(k) The only trial court where the taxpayer does not have to first pay the tax assessed by the IRS.

## Research Problems

## CHAPTER 2

25. R was divorced during 19X6. She has custody of two minor children and contributed more than one-half of their support during 19X7. The divorce decree provides that her former husband J is required to pay $400 per month child support and is entitled to the dependency exemptions for income tax purposes. J paid the child support payments for the first six months of 19X7. However, J was unable to make the child support payments during the last six months of 19X7. R has little hope of receiving any future payments or a recovery of the unpaid amounts.

   (a) Is R entitled to claim the children as dependents in 19X7?

   (b) Is R entitled to claim the children in 19X8 and future years if the divorce decree is not modified and J does not make any child support payments?

   *Partial list of research aids:*

   *R. A. Gordon,* 33 TCM 732, T.C. Memo. 1974–169.

26. W was the owner-operator of several mobile home parks. He employed his three young children to assume certain duties, such as maintenance of the swimming pool, landscaping, office duties and other odd jobs. In 19X1, the youngest child (then age 7) was paid $1,600 and in 19X3 was paid $2,100.

The IRS disallowed W a deduction for 90% of the wages paid to the youngest child. Would you advise W to contest the ruling? If so, what arguments should W make in support of the deduction?

## CHAPTER 3

27. The taxpayer won $160,000 in the Irish Sweepstakes. However, because he is a minor (14 years old) local law requires that the winnings be placed in escrow and not be withdrawn until he is 18 years of age. When is the income subject to tax?

28. Mr. A is a commissioned agent for a large insurance company. During the year, he purchased a policy on his life and the lives of his children and received a commission. Mr. A treated the commission on these policies as a reduction in cost rather than as income. However, during an audit, the revenue agent indicates that Mr. A must include the commission in his gross income. The taxpayer seeks your assistance in resolving the matter with the agent.

    *Partial list of research aids:*

    *Ostheimer v. U. S.,* 59–1 USTC ¶ 9300, 3 AFTR2d 886, 264 F.2d 789 (CA–3, 1959).

    Rev.Rul. 55–273, 1955–1 C.B. 221.

## CHAPTER 4

29. S was asked by the Montgomery County School Board to resign her position as superintendent of public schools. She refused and submitted to the board a list of grievances. She also alleged that the board had damaged her professional reputation. S was later fired, but after threatening suit she was paid $20,000 by the board.

    S has supplied a doctor's testimony clearly showing that the dispute with the board caused her to become physically and mentally ill.

    Is the $20,000 taxable?

30. Mr. and Mrs. B are in the process of reaching a divorce settlement. Mr. B has agreed to pay Mrs. B $1,000 per month for the remainder of her life or until her remarriage. However, Mrs. B is concerned about the possibility of Mr. B's predeceasing her, and in that event, the assets in his estate might not be sufficient to continue payment of alimony. For this reason, she has requested that Mr. B continue to pay the premiums on an insurance policy on his life which designates Mrs. B as the beneficiary. Would Mrs. B be required to include the insurance premiums in her income as alimony?

    *Partial list of research aids:*

    *Blumenthal v. Comm.,* 50–2 USTC ¶ 9763, 39 AFTR 628, 183 F.2d 15 (CA–3, 1950).

    *Stevens v. Comm.,* 71–1 USTC ¶ 9242, 27 AFTR2d 71–747, 439 F.2d 69 (CA–2, 1971).

## CHAPTER 5

31. Taxpayer is in the wholesale liquor business in California where a posting of prices is required and no kickbacks or discounts are allowed. The taxpayer devised a system whereby he would issue "credits" to certain cus-

tomers when they purchased liquor. These credits could be used to buy more liquor (i. e., an additional bottle with each case of liquor purchased.) When customers cashed in their credits for additional liquor, the liquor was removed from inventory and became a part of cost of goods sold. Is the taxpayer entitled to the deduction for cost of goods sold?

*Partial list of research aids:*

§ 162(c)(2).

*James Alex,* 70 T.C. 322 (1978).

32. In 1980, T became interested in raising and showing dogs. After discussing the costs of producing and marketing the dogs with professional dog breeders, T made some calculations and determined that he could make a profit on a dog breeding operation within a few years. T named the operation T Kennels and had stationery, business cards, and pedigree forms made up using that name. T advertised and also hired a professional trainer. T maintained a separate checking account for the kennels. The cancelled checks served as the primary records of the enterprise.

The calculations from 1980 did not materialize. Some of the dogs suffered from unexpected injuries and illnesses. On two occasions, an entire litter of pups died because of the mother's "bad milk." T sold a few dogs without replacing them and retained others that were clearly not championship material. Despite T's degree in animal breeding and the two to three hours per day spent with the dogs, the operation sustained a loss for the next eight years. Gross income over the period totaled $4,000 while deductions claimed amounted to $52,000. Fortunately T had a full-time job in another field during this period, and his job earnings increased annually. Can T deduct the losses incurred in the dog breeding operation?

## CHAPTER 6

33. The City Light & Power Company constructed some new equipment for its own use. In addition to costs incurred for labor, materials, and overhead, it used some of its own existing equipment to construct these new assets. They were depreciated on the straight-line basis.

    (a) How should this depreciation be treated?

    (b) Assume the same facts except that the company used the double-declining balance method of depreciation and wanted to deduct currently the excess depreciation over straight-line. Is this treatment correct?

    *Partial list of research aids:*

    *Idaho Power Co. v. U. S.,* 74–2 USTC ¶ 9521, 34 AFTR2d 74–5244, 94 S.Ct. 2757 (USSC, 1974).

34. T was an executive for a savings and loan association. His job entailed obtaining new business and placing new loans. In an attempt to generate new business, T and his wife took vacation trips that were group tours for builders and contractors. Although there were few business meetings, T spent his time during sightseeing trips and entertainment functions becoming acquainted with builders and contractors and renewing old acquaintances. He discussed what services his company had to offer and did, in fact, increase business through these contacts, although no direct

relationship could be established. T and his wife did not particularly enjoy these tours but were encouraged to attend by T's employer. In fact, T's employer gave him time off in addition to his regular vacations to go on these tours. T incurred the expenses for the actual tours. Because of the increase in business, T received a promotion and increase in salary. Is T allowed a deduction under §§ 162 and 274 for these expenditures?

## CHAPTER 7

35. T suffers from a degenerative spinal disorder. Her physician, therefore, recommended the installation of a swimming pool at her residence for her use to prevent the onset of permanent paralysis. T's residence had a market value of approximately $500,000 before the swimming pool was installed. The swimming pool was built and an appraiser estimated that the value of T's home increased by $98,000 due to the addition.

    The pool cost $194,000, and T claimed a medical deduction on her tax return of $96,000. Upon audit of the return, the IRS determined that an adequate pool should have cost $70,000 and would increase the property value by only $39,000. Thus, the IRS claims that T should be entitled to a deduction of only $31,000.

    (a) Is there any ceiling limitation on the amount deductible as a medical expense?

    (b) Can capital expenses be deducted as medical expenses?

    (c) What is the significance of a "minimum adequate facility"? Should aesthetic or architectural qualities be considered in this determination?

    *Partial list of research aids:*

    Reg. § 1.213–1(e)(1)(iii).

    *Ferris v. Comm.,* 36 TCM 765, T.C.Memo. 1977–186.

36. Taxpayers acquired a residence in January 1979 and lived there until April 5, 1981, when a flood occurred. The flood caused major damage to the foundation, furniture, and clothing of the taxpayers. Immediately after the flood, the taxpayers moved into a trailer and commenced repair work on the house, which was not completed until May of 1982.

    On their tax return for 1982, taxpayers claimed a deduction for state and local general sales tax of $446 based on sales tax tables published by the IRS. In addition, they claimed a deduction for taxes of $247 which represented major purchases to replace items lost in the flood. Also, sales taxes which were the result of repairs to the house were deducted. Are these additional sales tax expenditures allowable as a deduction under § 164?

## CHAPTER 8

37. T acquired an automobile for $10,000 on January 1, 1979. During 1979, she used the automobile 50% for business and claimed investment credit of $167 ($5,000 × ⅓ × 10%) based on a three-year life. In 1980 and 1981, T used the automobile only 20% for business.

    (a) Is any amount of the original investment credit recaptured? If so, in what year?

    (b) Would your answer be different if T continued to use the automobile for business purposes and increased its business use to 60% during 1982?

*Partial list of research aids:*

Reg. § 1.47–2(e).

*J. Wade Harris,* 34 TCM 1192, T.C.Memo. 1975–276.

38. XYZ Company, a retailer, is planning to acquire a department store from its current owners for $1,200,000. The purchase price is allocated to the following items:

| | |
|---|---:|
| Land | $ 200,000 |
| Building | 400,000 |
| Components: | |
|     Central air-conditioning | 100,000 |
|     Wiring | 60,000 |
|     Elevators | 120,000 |
|     Fixtures, lighting, etc. | 80,000 |
|     Movable partitions | 40,000 |
|     Carpeting | 40,000 |
| Office furniture | 60,000 |
| Storage sheds for inventory | 100,000 |
| | $ 1,200,000 |

What items, if any, will qualify for the investment credit?

*Partial list of research aids:*

*Minot Federal Savings and Loan v. U. S.,* 71–1 USTC ¶ 9131, 27 AFTR2d 71–335, 435 F.2d 1368 (CA–8, 1971).

Rev.Rul. 75–178, 1975–1 C.B. 9.

# CHAPTER 9

39. On January 1, 19X5, X, a major shareholder in H Corporation, purchased land from the company for $300,000. The fair market value of the land is $1,200,000, and its basis in the hands of the corporation is $400,000.

    (a) What are the possible tax consequences to X?

    (b) What is the basis of the land to X?

    (c) What is the tax consequence to H Corporation?

40. Ms. G owned and used her house as her principal residence since 1946. However, 20% of the house was used for business purposes as an office. On January 1, 1981, when Ms. G was over 55, she retired and moved to North Carolina. Ms. G rented her former residence for six months before its sale, since no qualified buyer could be found. She purchased a new residence in North Carolina at a price which exceeded the adjusted sales price of the former residence.

    (a) What treatment should be given to the portion of the former residence used for business? Rental property?

    (b) May Ms. G make an election under § 121(a)?

    (c) Are the nonrecognition of gain provisions of § 1034 available to Ms. G?

*Partial list of research aids:*

*Robert G. Clapham,* 63 T.C. 505 (1975).

## CHAPTER 10

41. P has orally agreed to buy a business conducted by S (as a sole proprietorship) for $500,000. In completing the purchase agreement, S wants $50,000 of the $500,000 allocated to the goodwill of the business. P disagrees and maintains instead that the $50,000 should be allocated to S's promise not to compete with P in the same community for a specified period of time.

    (a) Why would P not want the $50,000 allocated to the goodwill of the business?

    (b) Why would S not want the $50,000 allocated to a covenant not to compete?

    *Partial list of research aids:*

    Reg. § 1.167(a)–(3).

    *Gary C. Halbert,* 37 TCM 408, T.C.Memo. 1978–88.

    *General Television, Inc. v. U. S.,* 79–2 USTC ¶ 9411, 44 AFTR2d 79–5115, 598 F.2d 1148 (CA–8, 1979).

42. In 1978, D (a real estate dealer) acquired a tract of unimproved land in the normal course of his business. Until June of 1979, D attempted to resell the property but without any success. Prospective purchasers that D contacted generally were not interested at all due to the remote location of the property. From June of 1979 on, therefore, D ceased to advertise the real estate for resale, nor was it listed with any other broker or dealer. Being busy with other business ventures, D literally forgot about the property. In 1983, and after the county had announced that it would build an access road to the area where the property was located, P contacted D concerning the availability of the real estate. After brief negotiations, the property was sold to P at a price that yielded a considerable gain to D. How might this gain be classified to D?

## CHAPTER 11

43. In 19X5, T signed a contract to play professional football with the Cincinnati Bengals. He received a lucrative contract which included a salary in excess of $100,000 a year plus a large bonus for signing. As a result of the significant increase in income over his earnings on summer jobs during his college years (19X1–19X4), T filed his 19X5 tax return using income averaging. IRS declared T ineligible for income averaging, asserting that he had not been self-supporting during the base period years. T argued (1) that an athletic scholarship received during his college years constituted support furnished by him during the base period and (2) that the bonus he received was income attributable to work performed by him in substantial part during the base period years, 19X1–19X4. Will T be allowed to use income averaging in 19X5?

44. H and W realized a large gain on the sale of business machinery and equipment in 19X7. In filing their tax return for 19X7, they did not report the capital gain deduction related to this gain as a tax preference item. The IRS contested this treatment and assessed H and W for minimum tax based on the argument that gain on business assets which is treated as capital gain gives rise to a tax preference item. H and W argued that the

gain was § 1231 gain rather than capital gain, and that no tax preference existed. Will H and W be successful in contesting the IRS assessment?

## CHAPTER 12

45. Dr. T, a radiologist, incorporates his private practice by forming a professional association (i. e., P.A.), in compliance with the requirements of applicable state law. To the newly formed P.A., Dr. T transfers all of his medical equipment (e. g., X-ray machines) in return for all of its stock. Not transferred, however, is the building in which Dr. T conducts his practice. Such building later is leased to the P.A. and continues to be used by Dr. T in his practice. Much of the equipment transferred to the P.A. was § 38 property acquired by Dr. T less than five years ago.

   Discuss any possible recapture problems under § 47 Dr. T might have in connection with these transactions.

   *Partial list of research aids:*

   Reg. § 1.47–3(f)(1).

   Rev.Rul. 76–514, 1976–2 C.B. 11.

46. A, a wealthy farmer, wants to take advantage of gift tax exclusions and give some of his property to his children. He decides to incorporate his farm operation in order to donate the property to his children more easily in the form of shares of stock. He transfers his property to a newly formed corporation for 100% of the stock. He gives 30% of the stock to his children immediately upon receipt. The IRS asserts, upon audit, that A is taxed on the initial transfer of property to the corporation because he failed to gain control of 80% of the stock. What result?

## CHAPTER 13

47. The stock of X Corporation is held 10% by Y and 90% by Z. W would like to purchase all of this stock but has the cash to pay for only 60%. X Corporation has enough cash on hand to redeem 40% of its shares. Consider and evaluate, in terms of X Corporation, Y, Z, and W, the following alternatives:

   (a) X Corporation redeems from Z 40% of the shares. W purchases the remaining 50% held by Z and the 10% owned by Y.

   (b) W borrows enough money from a bank to purchase all of Y's and Z's shares. Later, W has X Corporation redeem 40% of the shares purchased in order to pay off the bank loan.

   (c) X Corporation redeems all of Y's shares. W purchases 60% of the shares held by Z. X Corporation then redeems the remainder of Z's 30% interest.

   (d) X Corporation distributes 90% of its cash to Z and 10% to Y. This reduces the value of the stock to a level where W's cash is adequate to purchase all of Z's and Y's shares.

   *Partial list of research aids:*

   *Television Industries, Inc. v. Comm.,* 60–2 USTC ¶ 9795, 6 AFTR2d 5864, 284 F.2d 322 (CA–2, 1960).

   *Zenz v. Quinlivan,* 54–2 USTC ¶ 9445, 45 AFTR 1672, 213 F.2d 914 (CA–6, 1954).

   *U.S. v. Carey,* 61–1 USTC ¶ 9428, 7 AFTR2d 1301, 289 F.2d 531 (CA–8, 1961).

48. A owns 40% of X Corporation; his father owns the remaining 60%. A also owns 70% of Y Corporation with the remaining 30% being owned by his wife. A terminates his entire interest in X Corporation through a stock redemption which he reports as a long-term capital gain pursuant to § 302(b)(3). Three years later, Y Corporation enters into a contract with X Corporation whereby Y Corporation is given exclusive management authority over X Corporation's operations. Upon audit, the IRS disallows long-term capital gain treatment on the stock redemption in X Corporation contending that A acquired an interest in X within 10 years from the date of the redemption because of Y's management contract with X. What result?

## CHAPTER 14

49. During a period of two weeks, P Corporation acquires all of the stock of S Corporation at a cost of $1,200,000. Shortly thereafter, S Corporation is liquidated and its assets (adjusted basis of $500,000) are distributed in kind to P Corporation. After the liquidation, P Corporation assigns most of the $1,200,000 cost of the stock to the tangible assets it receives from S Corporation. Upon later audit, however, the IRS maintains that goodwill was one of the assets P Corporation acquired.

    (a) Why is the IRS taking this position?

    (b) What factors should be considered in resolving this issue (i. e., the presence or absence of goodwill)?

    *Partial list of research aids:*

    § 334(b)(2).

    Reg. § 1.167(a)–3.

    *Stevens Pass, Inc.,* 48 T.C. 532 (1967).

    *Smith, Inc., v. Comm.,* 79–1 USTC ¶ 9179, 43 AFTR2d 79–526, 591 F.2d 248 (CA–3, 1979).

50. After adopting a plan of complete liquidation, X Corporation makes a bulk sale of its inventory, the gain from which is not recognized under § 337. On its final income tax return (i. e., form 1120) for the year of liquidation, X Corporation reports a final inventory of zero but does not adjust the purchase account for the cost of the inventory sold in bulk. What is X Corporation trying to accomplish? What defense, if any, might the IRS raise?

    *Partial list of research aids:*

    *Winer v. Comm.,* 67–1 USTC ¶ 9169, 19 AFTR2d 423, 371 F.2d 684 (CA–1, 1967).

## CHAPTER 15

51. P Corporation, a closely-held corporation, owns all of the stock of S Corporation, with which it does not file a consolidated return. As of January 1, 19X0, P Corporation has a deficit in accumulated earnings and profits and anticipates no current earnings and profits for tax year 19X0. On the other hand, S Corporation has $700,000 in accumulated earnings and profits and expects current earnings and profits of at least $200,000. On July 1, 19X0, P Corporation borrows $200,000, from a local bank, using the stock in S Corporation as collateral for the loan. Shortly thereafter, P Corporation distributes the loan proceeds to its shareholders. S Corporation, although profitable in its past and current activities, has never paid a dividend.

(a) What are the hoped-for tax consequences of the loan and the distribution of the proceeds?

(b) What could go wrong in terms of what the taxpayers were trying to accomplish?

52. R Corporation and T Corporation are each wholly owned by the same individual. R's principal business is leasing trucks and realty to T Corporation. While auditing R in 1982, the IRS agent indicates that the rental income was personal holding company income. The agent asserts that the lease agreement constitutes "other arrangements" in Prop. Reg. § 1.543–9 whereby the stockholder obtains the use of corporate property. Research this conflict.

## CHAPTER 16

53. During 19X9, T's share of his S corporation's net operating loss is $7,000. At the end of the year, the adjusted basis of his stock in the corporation is $2,500. In addition, he has loaned $2,000 to the corporation. During the next year, his share of the income is $5,000, and the corporation repays T the $2,000 loan. Discuss all tax considerations.

54. Taxpayer P owns and operates an apartment unit. He is considering incorporating this project and electing S treatment. The apartment project furnishes the following services and facilities for the tenants:

—A swimming pool including patio, outdoor furniture, restrooms, and large beach umbrellas.

—A laundry room.

—A recreational room equipped with kitchen appliances and furniture that is available for parties and meetings.

—Individual storage compartments separate from the apartments.

—Apartments with full electric kitchen, dishwasher, carpeting, and draperies.

—Redecoration of each apartment every three years.

—Message service.

—Individual parking spaces.

—Optional cable television service.

—A full-time maintenance person for any kind of day-to-day repairs and odd jobs.

—Normal services such as utility hookups.

—Maintenance of a qualification fee at a nearby golf course to provide future tenants with the option to join the club.

    Advise this taxpayer about incorporating this apartment unit with respect to the passive investment income requirements in both § 1362(d)(3)(D) and § 543(a)(2).

## CHAPTER 17

55. In late December 19X6, the MAR Partnership admits T as a new partner with a 25% interest in capital and profits upon his investment of $100,000. Consider and evaluate the tax consequences to all parties of the following sequence of events:

(a) At the end of its calendar year 19X6, the partnership reports profits of $60,000, of which $15,000 is allocated to T even though he has been a partner for only two days of the year.

(b) As an inducement to T, the remaining partners agree that T will be allocated all of the projected losses for the year 19X7, $75,000. The loss is incurred as projected and is allocated in total to T.

(c) All partners have agreed that for years beginning after 19X7, losses will be allocated to those partners in the highest income brackets.

*Partial list of research aids:*

§§ 704(b) and 706(c)(2)(B).

*Stanley C. Orrisch,* 55 T.C. 395 (1970).

*Norman Rodman,* 32 TCM 1307, T.C.Memo, 1973–277.

*Jean P. Kresser,* 54 T.C. 1621 (1970).

Rev.Rul. 68–139, 1968–1 C.B. 311.

56. Under the terms of the STP Partnership agreement, T is to manage the day-to-day operations of the business and maintain all necessary books and records. In return for these services, T is to receive a fixed monthly salary of $3,000 without regard to the income of the partnership. She also is entitled to a one-third share of partnership profits determined after deducting her guaranteed salary. The partnership agreement further provides that T is not entitled to share in any partnership losses other than those resulting from the sale of capital assets. Both T and the partnership use the calendar year for tax purposes.

At the beginning of the current year, T's basis in her partnership interest was $40,000. During the year, T recorded each of her $3,000 monthly salary checks as withdrawals from the partnership. While preparing the partnership's Form 1065 for the current year, T notes that the partnership will report an operating loss of $15,000 without deducting her guaranteed salary. Estimating a personal income tax savings of $9,000, T plans to treat the entire $36,000 as tax-free withdrawals from the partnership. Will this be allowed for Federal income tax purposes?

*Partial list of research aids:*

Reg. §§ 1.707–1(c) and 1.731–(a).

*John W. Mangham,* 40 TCM 788, T.C.Memo. 1980–280.

*Jack C. Smith,* 40 TCM 1025, T.C.Memo. 1980–326.

## CHAPTER 18

57. Prior to her death in 1983, D entered into the following transactions:

(a) In 1982, she borrowed $35,000 from a bank, which sum she promptly loaned to her controlled corporation. The executor of D's estate repaid the bank loan but never attempted to collect the amount due D from the corporation.

(b) In 1978, D promised her sister, S, a bequest of $200,000 if S would move in with her and care for her during an illness (which eventually proved to be terminal). D never kept her promise, as her will was silent on any bequest to S. After D's death, S sued the estate and eventually recovered $120,000 for breach of contract.

(c) One of the assets in D's estate was a palatial residence which passed to R under a specific provision of the will. R did not want the residence, preferring, instead, cash. Per R's instructions, the residence was sold. Expenses incurred in connection with the sale were claimed as § 2053 expenses on the Form 706 filed by D's estate.

(d) Prior to her death, D incurred and paid certain medical expenses but did not have the opportunity to file a claim for partial reimbursement from her insurance company. After her death, the claim was filed by D's executor and the reimbursement was paid to the estate.

Discuss the estate tax and income tax ramifications of each of these transactions.

*Partial list of research aids:*

Code § § 61(a)(1) and (12), 111, 213, 691, 2033, and 2053.

*Estate of Allie W. Pittard,* 69 T.C. 391 (1977).

*Estate of Myron M. Miller,* 37 TCM 1547, T.C.Memo. 1978–374.

*Joseph F. Kenefic,* 36 TCM 1226, T.C.Memo. 1977–310.

*Hibernia Bank v. U. S.,* 78–2 USTC ¶ 13,261, 42 AFTR2d 78–6510, 581 F.2d 741 (CA–9, 1978).

Rev.Rul 78–292, 1978–2 C.B. 233.

58. D is a person of considerable means. One of his assets is a personal residence (worth $150,000) where he currently resides. In order to reduce his potential death tax liability, he suggests to you (his tax adviser) the possibility of transferring the residence to S. However, D would like to continue occupying the property until his death.

You are to advise D as to whether such a transfer would be effective for death tax purposes and, if so, under what circumstances. In this connection, consider the following assumptions:

(a) D and S are father and son.

(b) D and S are husband and wife.

*Partial list of research aids:*

Code § § 2035 and 2036.

Rev.Rul 70–155, 1970–1 C.B. 189.

*Tubbs v. U. S.,* 73–1 USTC ¶ 12,901 31 AFTR2d 1373, 472 F.2d 166 (CA–5, 1973).

*Estate of Roy D. Barlow,* 55 T.C. 666 (1971).

## CHAPTER 19

59. On June 16, 1982, H and W execute a trust instrument under the terms of which the income from specified ranch properties is to be paid to their children until July 1, 1992, when the property is to return to them or their estates. M, a friend of the family and a local banker, is appointed as the trustee of the trust. Due to unforeseen difficulties, the ranch properties are not transferred into the trust until July 2, 1982. H and W reside in a community property state, and the ranch properties are community assets.

Discuss the gift and income tax ramifications of this arrangement.

*Partial list of research aids:*

Code §§ 673 and 2503.

Reg. § 25.2512–9(f).

*C. O. Bibby,* 44 T.C. 638 (1965).

60. In 1971, M advanced funds to her son, S, for use in his business. In the note issued for the advance, no interest was provided for and S agreed to make repayment one year later. M died in 1982 without collecting on the advance and provided in her will that all debts due her from blood relations were forgiven. Under the applicable state statute of limitations, a debtor can bar action on a written obligation if suit or other collection procedure is not instituted by the creditor within five years of the due date of the note.
     Discuss the gift tax aspects of this factual situation.

*Partial list of research aids:*

Reg. § 25.2511–1(c).

*Estate of Grace Lang,* 64 T.C. 404 (1975).

Rev.Rul. 73–61, 1973–1 C.B. 408.

*Lester Crown,* 67 T.C. 1060 (1977).

## CHAPTER 20

61. In May 19X9, F creates a trust with income payable to his daughter (D), reversion to F or his estate upon the earlier of D's death or 10 years and one month from the date of creation of the trust. The trust is funded with 1,000 shares of X Corporation common stock valued at $100,000 and having a basis to F of $20,000. Discuss the potential tax consequences to F of each of the independent situations below.

    (a) F designates himself trustee in an effort to minimize expenses of the trust.

    (b) On April 15, 19X9, dividends were declared on the X Corporation stock, payable to stockholders of record on June 1, 19X9.

    (c) As a result of a broad decline in stock market prices during the summer months of 19X9, the independent trustee sells 500 shares of X Corporation stock for $45,000 and reinvests the proceeds in U. S. Treasury bills yielding 12% interest and maturing in one year.

    (d) Two years after creation of the trust, and at the insistence of his daughter, F transfers 200 shares of Y Corporation common stock to the trust. The stock is worth $50,000 and has a dividend-paying record of at least 10% annually.

*Partial list of research aids:*

Code §§ 644, 673, 674, and 677.

Reg. §§ 1.676(b)–1 and 1.677(a)–1(f).

*M. G. Anton,* 34 T.C. 842 (1960).

*C. O. Bibby,* 44 T.C. 638 (1965).

62. Two doctors, P and M, practice in a partnership known as the P-M Clinic. They own the clinic as tenants in common. In November 19X6, they approach you with a plan to create reversionary trusts for their children. Each trust would have slightly more than a 10-year life, and each doctor would transfer his undivided one-half interest in the clinic property into his trust

for his children. A bank will serve as an independent trustee for each doctor's grantor trust. On the day following the creation of the trusts, the P-M partnership is to enter into a lease agreement with the bank trustee for a period of 10 years. Their questions for your review and comments are as follows:

(a) Is this plan a viable income tax planning effort to get deductible contributions in the form of rent payments into a trust for their children?

(b) What could go wrong?

(c) Can you recommend a better plan?

*Partial list of research aids:*

*Perry v. U. S.,* 75–2 USTC ¶ 9629, 36 AFTR2d 75–5500, 520 F.2d 235 (CA–4, 1975).

*Mathews v. Comm.,* 75–2 USTC ¶ 9734, 36 AFTR2d 75–5965, 520 F.2d 323 (CA–5, 1975).

*Hudspeth v. Comm.,* 75–1 USTC ¶ 9224, 35 AFTR2d 75–676, 509 F.2d 1224 (CA–9, 1975).

## CHAPTER 21

63. In 19X1, Mr. and Mrs. T file a joint income tax return for tax year 19X0 reporting gross income of $50,000. The return was prepared by Mr. T and signed by both spouses. Unknown to Mrs. T, the return did not include $30,000 of income from wagering activities that Mr. T had earned during 19X0.

On audit of the return in 19X5, the $30,000 omission is discovered by the IRS. Since Mr. T has left for parts unknown, an income tax deficiency is assessed against Mrs. T.

Does Mrs. T have any defenses? In this connection, consider the following points:

(a) More than three years have elapsed since the due date of the return.

(b) The omission was of Mr. T's income and not of Mrs. T's income.

(c) Mr. T, not Mrs. T, prepared the return.

(d) Mr. T had an aggressive personality and on several occasions during their marriage had physically abused Mrs. T.

*Partial list of research aids:*

§ § 6013 and 6501.

64. Shortly before the statute of limitations was about to expire on a net operating loss carryback, T conferred with a nearby IRS office to obtain taxpayer assistance. The agent gave T several copies of Form 1045 (Application for Tentative Refund from Carryback of Net Operating Loss, Unused Investment Credit). One of these was properly completed by T and duly mailed to and received by the District Director two days prior to the expiration of the statute of limitations. Five days later, T received a form letter from the District Director's office informing him that he had used the wrong form and should, instead, file Form 1040X. The letter enclosed T's completed Form 1045. On the same day, T completed Form 1040X and sent it by registered mail to the District Director. One month thereafter, T received notice that his claim was barred by the statute of limitations. What are T's rights under the circumstances?

# APPENDIX A
# TAX RATE SCHEDULES AND TABLES

Page

A–1  1982, 1983, and After 1983 Income Tax
      Rate Schedules.................................. A-2

A–2  1982 Income Tax Tables ........................... A-6

A–3  Unified Transfer Tax Rate Schedule ................. A-12

A–4  1982 Optional State Sales Tax Tables................ A-17

A–5  Table for Computation of Maximum Credit
      for State Death Taxes ........................... A-21

A-1

## A–1 1982, 1983, AND AFTER 1983 INCOME TAX RATE SCHEDULES

# 1982 Tax Rate Schedules

Your zero bracket amount has been built into these Tax Rate Schedules.

**Caution:** You must use the Tax Table instead of these Tax Rate Schedules if your taxable income is less than $50,000 unless you use Schedule G (income averaging), to figure your tax. In that case, even if your taxable income is less than $50,000, use the rate schedules on this page to figure your tax.

### Schedule X

**Single Taxpayers**

Use this Schedule if you checked **Filing Status Box 1** on Form 1040—

| If the amount on Form 1040, line 37 is: Over— | But not Over— | Enter on Form 1040, line 38 | of the amount over— |
|---|---|---|---|
| $0 | $2,300 | —0— | |
| 2,300 | 3,400 | ............12% | $2,300 |
| 3,400 | 4,400 | $132+14% | 3,400 |
| 4,400 | 6,500 | 272+16% | 4,400 |
| 6,500 | 8,500 | 608+17% | 6,500 |
| 8,500 | 10,800 | 948+19% | 8,500 |
| 10,800 | 12,900 | 1,385+22% | 10,800 |
| 12,900 | 15,000 | 1,847+23% | 12,900 |
| 15,000 | 18,200 | 2,330+27% | 15,000 |
| 18,200 | 23,500 | 3,194+31% | 18,200 |
| 23,500 | 28,800 | 4,837+35% | 23,500 |
| 28,800 | 34,100 | 6,692+40% | 28,800 |
| 34,100 | 41,500 | 8,812+44% | 34,100 |
| 41,500 | .......... | 12,068+50% | 41,500 |

### Schedule Z

**Unmarried Heads of Household**

(including certain married persons who live apart (and abandoned spouses)—see page 6 of the instructions)

Use this schedule if you checked **Filing Status Box 4** on Form 1040—

| If the amount on Form 1040, line 37 is: Over— | But not Over— | Enter on Form 1040, line 38 | of the amount over— |
|---|---|---|---|
| $0 | $2,300 | —0— | |
| 2,300 | 4,400 | ............12% | $2,300 |
| 4,400 | 6,500 | $252+14% | 4,400 |
| 6,500 | 8,700 | 546+16% | 6,500 |
| 8,700 | 11,800 | 898+20% | 8,700 |
| 11,800 | 15,000 | 1,518+22% | 11,800 |
| 15,000 | 18,200 | 2,222+23% | 15,000 |
| 18,200 | 23,500 | 2,958+28% | 18,200 |
| 23,500 | 28,800 | 4,442+32% | 23,500 |
| 28,800 | 34,100 | 6,138+38% | 28,800 |
| 34,100 | 44,700 | 8,152+41% | 34,100 |
| 44,700 | 60,600 | 12,498+49% | 44,700 |
| 60,600 | .......... | 20,289+50% | 60,600 |

### Schedule Y

**Married Taxpayers and Qualifying Widows and Widowers**

**Married Filing Joint Returns and Qualifying Widows and Widowers**

Use this schedule if you checked **Filing Status Box 2 or 5** on Form 1040—

| If the amount on Form 1040, line 37 is: Over— | But not Over— | Enter on Form 1040, line 38 | of the amount over— |
|---|---|---|---|
| $0 | $3,400 | —0— | |
| 3,400 | 5,500 | ............12% | $3,400 |
| 5,500 | 7,600 | $252+14% | 5,500 |
| 7,600 | 11,900 | 546+16% | 7,600 |
| 11,900 | 16,000 | 1,234+19% | 11,900 |
| 16,000 | 20,200 | 2,013+22% | 16,000 |
| 20,200 | 24,600 | 2,937+25% | 20,200 |
| 24,600 | 29,900 | 4,037+29% | 24,600 |
| 29,900 | 35,200 | 5,574+33% | 29,900 |
| 35,200 | 45,800 | 7,323+39% | 35,200 |
| 45,800 | 60,000 | 11,457+44% | 45,800 |
| 60,000 | 85,600 | 17,705+49% | 60,000 |
| 85,600 | .......... | 30,249+50% | 85,600 |

**Married Filing Separate Returns**

Use this schedule if you checked **Filing Status Box 3** on Form 1040—

| If the amount on Form 1040, line 37 is: Over— | But not Over— | Enter on Form 1040, line 38 | of the amount over— |
|---|---|---|---|
| $0 | $1,700 | —0— | |
| 1,700 | 2,750 | ............12% | $1,700 |
| 2,750 | 3,800 | $126.00+14% | 2,750 |
| 3,800 | 5,950 | 273.00+16% | 3,800 |
| 5,950 | 8,000 | 617.00+19% | 5,950 |
| 8,000 | 10,100 | 1,006.50+22% | 8,000 |
| 10,100 | 12,300 | 1,468.50+25% | 10,100 |
| 12,300 | 14,950 | 2,018.50+29% | 12,300 |
| 14,950 | 17,600 | 2,787.00+33% | 14,950 |
| 17,600 | 22,900 | 3,661.50+39% | 17,600 |
| 22,900 | 30,000 | 5,728.50+44% | 22,900 |
| 30,000 | 42,800 | 8,852.50+49% | 30,000 |
| 42,800 | .......... | 15,124.50+50% | 42,800 |

**1983 Tax Rate Schedules**

### SCHEDULE X—Single Taxpayers

| If taxable income is: Over— | But not Over— | The tax is: | Of the amount Over— |
|---|---|---|---|
| $0 | $2,300 | —0— | |
| 2,300 | 3,400 | .......... 11% | $2,300 |
| 3,400 | 4,400 | $121+13% | 3,400 |
| 4,400 | 8,500 | 251+15% | 4,400 |
| 8,500 | 10,800 | 866+17% | 8,500 |
| 10,800 | 12,900 | 1,257+19% | 10,800 |
| 12,900 | 15,000 | 1,656+21% | 12,900 |
| 15,000 | 18,200 | 2,097+24% | 15,000 |
| 18,200 | 23,500 | 2,865+28% | 18,200 |
| 23,500 | 28,800 | 4,349+32% | 23,500 |
| 28,800 | 34,100 | 6,045+36% | 28,800 |
| 34,100 | 41,500 | 7,953+40% | 34,100 |
| 41,500 | 55,300 | 10,913+45% | 41,500 |
| 55,300 | .......... | 17,123+50% | 55,300 |

### SCHEDULE Z—Heads of Household

| If taxable income is: Over— | But not Over— | The tax is: | Of the amount Over— |
|---|---|---|---|
| $0 | $2,300 | —0— | |
| 2,300 | 4,400 | .......... 11% | $2,300 |
| 4,400 | 6,500 | $231+13% | 4,400 |
| 6,500 | 8,700 | 504+15% | 6,500 |
| 8,700 | 11,800 | 834+18% | 8,700 |
| 11,800 | 15,000 | 1,392+19% | 11,800 |
| 15,000 | 18,200 | 2,000+21% | 15,000 |
| 18,200 | 23,500 | 2,672+25% | 18,200 |
| 23,500 | 28,800 | 3,997+29% | 23,500 |
| 28,800 | 34,100 | 5,534+34% | 28,800 |
| 34,100 | 44,700 | 7,336+37% | 34,100 |
| 44,700 | 60,600 | 11,258+44% | 44,700 |
| 60,600 | 81,800 | 18,254+48% | 60,600 |
| 81,800 | .......... | 28,430+50% | 81,800 |

### SCHEDULE Y—Married Taxpayers and Qualifying Widows and Widowers

**Married Filing Joint Returns and Qualifying Widows and Widowers**

| If taxable income is: Over— | But not Over— | The tax is: | Of the amount Over— |
|---|---|---|---|
| $0 | $3,400 | —0— | |
| 3,400 | 5,500 | .......... 11% | $3,400 |
| 5,500 | 7,600 | $231+13% | 5,500 |
| 7,600 | 11,900 | 504+15% | 7,600 |
| 11,900 | 16,000 | 1,149+17% | 11,900 |
| 16,000 | 20,200 | 1,846+19% | 16,000 |
| 20,200 | 24,600 | 2,644+23% | 20,200 |
| 24,600 | 29,900 | 3,656+26% | 24,600 |
| 29,900 | 35,200 | 5,034+30% | 29,900 |
| 35,200 | 45,800 | 6,624+35% | 35,200 |
| 45,800 | 60,000 | 10,334+40% | 45,800 |
| 60,000 | 85,600 | 16,014+44% | 60,000 |
| 85,600 | 109,400 | 27,278+48% | 85,600 |
| 109,400 | .......... | 38,702+50% | 109,400 |

**Married Filing Separate Returns**

| If taxable income is: Over— | But not Over— | The tax is: | Of the amount Over— |
|---|---|---|---|
| $0 | $1,700 | —0— | |
| 1,700 | 2,750 | .......... 11% | $1,700 |
| 2,750 | 3,800 | $115.50+13% | 2,750 |
| 3,800 | 5,950 | 252.00+15% | 3,800 |
| 5,950 | 8,000 | 574.50+17% | 5,950 |
| 8,000 | 10,100 | 923.00+19% | 8,000 |
| 10,100 | 12,300 | 1,322.00+23% | 10,100 |
| 12,300 | 14,950 | 1,828.00+26% | 12,300 |
| 14,950 | 17,600 | 2,517.00+30% | 14,950 |
| 17,600 | 22,900 | 3,312.00+35% | 17,600 |
| 22,900 | 30,000 | 5,167.00+40% | 22,900 |
| 30,000 | 42,800 | 8,007.00+44% | 30,000 |
| 42,800 | 54,700 | 13,639.00+48% | 42,800 |
| 54,700 | .......... | 19,351.00+50% | 54,700 |

FOR TAXABLE YEARS BEGINNING AFTER 1983.—

## Single Taxpayers [Unmarried Individuals (Other Than Surviving Spouses and Heads of Households)].

| If taxable income is: | The tax is: |
|---|---|
| Not over $2,300 | No tax. |
| Over $2,300 but not over $3,400 | 11% of the excess over $2,300. |
| Over $3,400 but not over $4,400 | $121, plus 12% of the excess over $3,400. |
| Over $4,400 but not over $6,500 | $241, plus 14% of the excess over $4,400. |
| Over $6,500 but not over $8,500 | $535, plus 15% of the excess over $6,500. |
| Over $8,500 but not over $10,800 | $835, plus 16% of the excess over $8,500. |
| Over $10,800 but not over $12,900 | $1,203, plus 18% of the excess over $10,800. |
| Over $12,900 but not over $15,000 | $1,581, plus 20% of the excess over $12,900. |
| Over $15,000 but not over $18,200 | $2,001, plus 23% of the excess over $15,000. |
| Over $18,200 but not over $23,500 | $2,737, plus 26% of the excess over $18,200. |
| Over $23,500 but not over $28,800 | $4,115, plus 30% of the excess over $23,500. |
| Over $28,800 but not over $34,100 | $5,705, plus 34% of the excess over $28,800. |
| Over $34,100 but not over $41,500 | $7,507, plus 38% of the excess over $34,100. |
| Over $41,500 but not over $55,300 | $10,319, plus 42% of the excess over $41,500. |
| Over $55,300 but not over $81,800 | $16,115, plus 48% of the excess over $55,300. |
| Over $81,800 | $28,835, plus 50% of the excess over $81,800. |

## Unmarried Heads of Household

| If taxable income is: | The tax is: |
|---|---|
| Not over $2,300 | No tax. |
| Over $2,300 but not over $4,400 | 11% of the excess over $2,300. |
| Over $4,400 but not over $6,500 | $231, plus 12% of the excess over $4,400. |
| Over $6,500 but not over $8,700 | $483, plus 14% of the excess over $6,500. |
| Over $8,700 but not over $11,800 | $791, plus 17% of the excess over $8,700. |
| Over $11,800 but not over $15,000 | $1,318, plus 18% of the excess over $11,800. |
| Over $15,000 but not over $18,200 | $1,894, plus 20% of the excess over $15,000. |
| Over $18,200 but not over $23,500 | $2,534, plus 24% of the excess over $18,200. |
| Over $23,500 but not over $28,800 | $3,806, plus 28% of the excess over $23,500. |
| Over $28,800 but not over $34,100 | $5,290, plus 32% of the excess over $28,800. |
| Over $34,100 but not over $44,700 | $6,986, plus 35% of the excess over $34,100. |
| Over $44,700 but not over $60,600 | $10,696, plus 42% of the excess over $44,700. |
| Over $60,600 but not over $81,800 | $17,374, plus 45% of the excess over $60,600. |
| Over $81,800 but not over $108,300 | $26,914, plus 48% of the excess over $81,800. |
| Over $108,300 | $39,634, plus 50% of the excess over $108,300. |

FOR TAXABLE YEARS BEGINNING AFTER 1983.—

## Married Individuals Filing Joint Returns and Surviving Spouses

| If taxable income is: | The tax is: |
|---|---|
| Not over $3,400 | No tax. |
| Over $3,400 but not over $5,500 | 11% of the excess over $3,400. |
| Over $5,500 but not over $7,600 | $231, plus 12% of the excess over $5,500. |
| Over $7,600 but not over $11,900 | $483, plus 14% of the excess over $7,600. |
| Over $11,900 but not over $16,000 | $1,085, plus 16% of the excess over $11,900. |
| Over $16,000 but not over $20,200 | $1,741, plus 18% of the excess over $16,000. |
| Over $20,200 but not over $24,600 | $2,497, plus 22% of the excess over $20,200. |
| Over $24,600 but not over $29,900 | $3,465, plus 25% of the excess over $24,600. |
| Over $29,900 but not over $35,200 | $4,790, plus 28% of the excess over $29,900. |
| Over $35,200 but not over $45,800 | $6,274, plus 33% of the excess over $35,200. |
| Over $45,800 but not over $60,000 | $9,772, plus 38% of the excess over $45,800. |
| Over $60,000 but not over $85,600 | $15,168, plus 42% of the excess over $60,000. |
| Over $85,600 but not over $109,400 | $25,920, plus 45% of the excess over $85,600. |
| Over $109,400 but not over $162,400 | $36,630, plus 49% of the excess over $109,400. |
| Over $162,400 | $62,600, plus 50% of the excess over $162,400. |

. . . . .

## Married Individuals Filing Separate Returns

| If taxable income is: | The tax is: |
|---|---|
| Not over $1,700 | No tax. |
| Over $1,700 but not over $2,750 | 11% of the excess over $1,700. |
| Over $2,750 but not over $3,800 | $115.50, plus 12% of the excess over $2,750. |
| Over $3,800 but not over $5,950 | $241.50, plus 14% of the excess over $3,800. |
| Over $5,950 but not over $8,000 | $542.50, plus 16% of the excess over $5,950. |
| Over $8,000 but not over $10,100 | $870.50, plus 18% of the excess over $8,000. |
| Over $10,100 but not over $12,300 | $1248.50, plus 22% of the excess over $10,100. |
| Over $12,300 but not over $14,950 | $1732.50, plus 25% of the excess over $12,300. |
| Over $14,950 but not over $17,600 | $2,395, plus 28% of the excess over $14,950. |
| Over $17,600 but not over $22,900 | $3,137, plus 33% of the excess over $17,600. |
| Over $22,900 but not over $30,000 | $4,886, plus 38% of the excess over $22,900. |
| Over $30,000 but not over $42,800 | $7,584, plus 42% of the excess over $30,000. |
| Over $42,800 but not over $54,700 | $12,960, plus 45% of the excess over $42,800. |
| Over $54,700 but not over $81,200 | $18,315, plus 49% of the excess over $54,700. |
| Over $81,200 | $31,300, plus 50% of the excess over $81,200. |

## A–2 1982 INCOME TAX TABLES

# 1982 Tax Table

**Based on Taxable Income**
For persons with taxable incomes of less than $50,000.

**Example:** Mr. and Mrs. Brown are filing a joint return. Their taxable income on line 37 of Form 1040 is $25,325. First, they find the $25,300–25,350 income line. Next, they find the column for married filing jointly and read down the column. The amount shown where the income line and filing status column meet is $4,247. This is the tax amount they must write on line 38 of their return.

| At least | But less than | Single | Married filing jointly * | Married filing sepa- rately | Head of a house- hold |
|---|---|---|---|---|---|
| | | | Your tax is— | | |
| 25,250 | 25,300 | 5,458 | 4,233 | 6,774 | 5,010 |
| → 25,300 | 25,350 | 5,476 | (4,247) | 6,796 | 5,026 |
| 25,350 | 25,400 | 5,493 | 4,262 | 6,818 | 5,042 |

| If line 37 (taxable income) is— At least | But less than | Single | Married filing jointly * | Married filing sepa- rately | Head of a house- hold |
|---|---|---|---|---|---|
| | | | Your tax is— | | |
| 0 | 1,700 | 0 | 0 | 0 | 0 |
| 1,700 | 1,725 | 0 | 0 | a2 | 0 |
| 1,725 | 1,750 | 0 | 0 | 5 | 0 |
| 1,750 | 1,775 | 0 | 0 | 8 | 0 |
| 1,775 | 1,800 | 0 | 0 | 11 | 0 |
| 1,800 | 1,825 | 0 | 0 | 14 | 0 |
| 1,825 | 1,850 | 0 | 0 | 17 | 0 |
| 1,850 | 1,875 | 0 | 0 | 20 | 0 |
| 1,875 | 1,900 | 0 | 0 | 23 | 0 |
| 1,900 | 1,925 | 0 | 0 | 26 | 0 |
| 1,925 | 1,950 | 0 | 0 | 29 | 0 |
| 1,950 | 1,975 | 0 | 0 | 32 | 0 |
| 1,975 | 2,000 | 0 | 0 | 35 | 0 |
| **2,000** | | | | | |
| 2,000 | 2,025 | 0 | 0 | 38 | 0 |
| 2,025 | 2,050 | 0 | 0 | 41 | 0 |
| 2,050 | 2,075 | 0 | 0 | 44 | 0 |
| 2,075 | 2,100 | 0 | 0 | 47 | 0 |
| 2,100 | 2,125 | 0 | 0 | 50 | 0 |
| 2,125 | 2,150 | 0 | 0 | 53 | 0 |
| 2,150 | 2,175 | 0 | 0 | 56 | 0 |
| 2,175 | 2,200 | 0 | 0 | 59 | 0 |
| 2,200 | 2,225 | 0 | 0 | 62 | 0 |
| 2,225 | 2,250 | 0 | 0 | 65 | 0 |
| 2,250 | 2,275 | 0 | 0 | 68 | 0 |
| 2,275 | 2,300 | 0 | 0 | 71 | 0 |
| 2,300 | 2,325 | b2 | 0 | 74 | b2 |
| 2,325 | 2,350 | 5 | 0 | 77 | 5 |
| 2,350 | 2,375 | 8 | 0 | 80 | 8 |
| 2,375 | 2,400 | 11 | 0 | 83 | 11 |
| 2,400 | 2,425 | 14 | 0 | 86 | 14 |
| 2,425 | 2,450 | 17 | 0 | 89 | 17 |
| 2,450 | 2,475 | 20 | 0 | 92 | 20 |
| 2,475 | 2,500 | 23 | 0 | 95 | 23 |
| 2,500 | 2,525 | 26 | 0 | 98 | 26 |
| 2,525 | 2,550 | 29 | 0 | 101 | 29 |
| 2,550 | 2,575 | 32 | 0 | 104 | 32 |
| 2,575 | 2,600 | 35 | 0 | 107 | 35 |
| 2,600 | 2,625 | 38 | 0 | 110 | 38 |
| 2,625 | 2,650 | 41 | 0 | 113 | 41 |
| 2,650 | 2,675 | 44 | 0 | 116 | 44 |
| 2,675 | 2,700 | 47 | 0 | 119 | 47 |
| 2,700 | 2,725 | 50 | 0 | 122 | 50 |
| 2,725 | 2,750 | 53 | 0 | 125 | 53 |
| 2,750 | 2,775 | 56 | 0 | 128 | 56 |
| 2,775 | 2,800 | 59 | 0 | 131 | 59 |
| 2,800 | 2,825 | 62 | 0 | 135 | 62 |
| 2,825 | 2,850 | 65 | 0 | 138 | 65 |
| 2,850 | 2,875 | 68 | 0 | 142 | 68 |
| 2,875 | 2,900 | 71 | 0 | 145 | 71 |
| 2,900 | 2,925 | 74 | 0 | 149 | 74 |
| 2,925 | 2,950 | 77 | 0 | 152 | 77 |
| 2,950 | 2,975 | 80 | 0 | 156 | 80 |
| 2,975 | 3,000 | 83 | 0 | 159 | 83 |

| If line 37 (taxable income) is— At least | But less than | Single | Married filing jointly * | Married filing sepa- rately | Head of a house- hold |
|---|---|---|---|---|---|
| | | | Your tax is— | | |
| **3,000** | | | | | |
| 3,000 | 3,050 | 87 | 0 | 165 | 87 |
| 3,050 | 3,100 | 93 | 0 | 172 | 93 |
| 3,100 | 3,150 | 99 | 0 | 179 | 99 |
| 3,150 | 3,200 | 105 | 0 | 186 | 105 |
| 3,200 | 3,250 | 111 | 0 | 193 | 111 |
| 3,250 | 3,300 | 117 | 0 | 200 | 117 |
| 3,300 | 3,350 | 123 | 0 | 207 | 123 |
| 3,350 | 3,400 | 129 | 0 | 214 | 129 |
| 3,400 | 3,450 | 136 | c3 | 221 | 135 |
| 3,450 | 3,500 | 143 | 9 | 228 | 141 |
| 3,500 | 3,550 | 150 | 15 | 235 | 147 |
| 3,550 | 3,600 | 157 | 21 | 242 | 153 |
| 3,600 | 3,650 | 164 | 27 | 249 | 159 |
| 3,650 | 3,700 | 171 | 33 | 256 | 165 |
| 3,700 | 3,750 | 178 | 39 | 263 | 171 |
| 3,750 | 3,800 | 185 | 45 | 270 | 177 |
| 3,800 | 3,850 | 192 | 51 | 277 | 183 |
| 3,850 | 3,900 | 199 | 57 | 285 | 189 |
| 3,900 | 3,950 | 206 | 63 | 293 | 195 |
| 3,950 | 4,000 | 213 | 69 | 301 | 201 |
| **4,000** | | | | | |
| 4,000 | 4,050 | 220 | 75 | 309 | 207 |
| 4,050 | 4,100 | 227 | 81 | 317 | 213 |
| 4,100 | 4,150 | 234 | 87 | 325 | 219 |
| 4,150 | 4,200 | 241 | 93 | 333 | 225 |
| 4,200 | 4,250 | 248 | 99 | 341 | 231 |
| 4,250 | 4,300 | 255 | 105 | 349 | 237 |
| 4,300 | 4,350 | 262 | 111 | 357 | 243 |
| 4,350 | 4,400 | 269 | 117 | 365 | 249 |
| 4,400 | 4,450 | 276 | 123 | 373 | 256 |
| 4,450 | 4,500 | 284 | 129 | 381 | 263 |
| 4,500 | 4,550 | 292 | 135 | 389 | 270 |
| 4,550 | 4,600 | 300 | 141 | 397 | 277 |
| 4,600 | 4,650 | 308 | 147 | 405 | 284 |
| 4,650 | 4,700 | 316 | 153 | 413 | 291 |
| 4,700 | 4,750 | 324 | 159 | 421 | 298 |
| 4,750 | 4,800 | 332 | 165 | 429 | 305 |
| 4,800 | 4,850 | 340 | 171 | 437 | 312 |
| 4,850 | 4,900 | 348 | 177 | 445 | 319 |
| 4,900 | 4,950 | 356 | 183 | 453 | 326 |
| 4,950 | 5,000 | 364 | 189 | 461 | 333 |
| **5,000** | | | | | |
| 5,000 | 5,050 | 372 | 195 | 469 | 340 |
| 5,050 | 5,100 | 380 | 201 | 477 | 347 |
| 5,100 | 5,150 | 388 | 207 | 485 | 354 |
| 5,150 | 5,200 | 396 | 213 | 493 | 361 |
| 5,200 | 5,250 | 404 | 219 | 501 | 368 |
| 5,250 | 5,300 | 412 | 225 | 509 | 375 |
| 5,300 | 5,350 | 420 | 231 | 517 | 382 |
| 5,350 | 5,400 | 428 | 237 | 525 | 389 |
| 5,400 | 5,450 | 436 | 243 | 533 | 396 |
| 5,450 | 5,500 | 444 | 249 | 541 | 403 |

| If line 37 (taxable income) is— At least | But less than | Single | Married filing jointly * | Married filing sepa- rately | Head of a house- hold |
|---|---|---|---|---|---|
| | | | Your tax is— | | |
| 5,500 | 5,550 | 452 | 256 | 549 | 410 |
| 5,550 | 5,600 | 460 | 263 | 557 | 417 |
| 5,600 | 5,650 | 468 | 270 | 565 | 424 |
| 5,650 | 5,700 | 476 | 277 | 573 | 431 |
| 5,700 | 5,750 | 484 | 284 | 581 | 438 |
| 5,750 | 5,800 | 492 | 291 | 589 | 445 |
| 5,800 | 5,850 | 500 | 298 | 597 | 452 |
| 5,850 | 5,900 | 508 | 305 | 605 | 459 |
| 5,900 | 5,950 | 516 | 312 | 613 | 466 |
| 5,950 | 6,000 | 524 | 319 | 622 | 473 |
| **6,000** | | | | | |
| 6,000 | 6,050 | 532 | 326 | 631 | 480 |
| 6,050 | 6,100 | 540 | 333 | 641 | 487 |
| 6,100 | 6,150 | 548 | 340 | 650 | 494 |
| 6,150 | 6,200 | 556 | 347 | 660 | 501 |
| 6,200 | 6,250 | 564 | 354 | 669 | 508 |
| 6,250 | 6,300 | 572 | 361 | 679 | 515 |
| 6,300 | 6,350 | 580 | 368 | 688 | 522 |
| 6,350 | 6,400 | 588 | 375 | 698 | 529 |
| 6,400 | 6,450 | 596 | 382 | 707 | 536 |
| 6,450 | 6,500 | 604 | 389 | 717 | 543 |
| 6,500 | 6,550 | 612 | 396 | 726 | 550 |
| 6,550 | 6,600 | 621 | 403 | 736 | 558 |
| 6,600 | 6,650 | 629 | 410 | 745 | 566 |
| 6,650 | 6,700 | 638 | 417 | 755 | 574 |
| 6,700 | 6,750 | 646 | 424 | 764 | 582 |
| 6,750 | 6,800 | 655 | 431 | 774 | 590 |
| 6,800 | 6,850 | 663 | 438 | 783 | 598 |
| 6,850 | 6,900 | 672 | 445 | 793 | 606 |
| 6,900 | 6,950 | 680 | 452 | 802 | 614 |
| 6,950 | 7,000 | 689 | 459 | 812 | 622 |
| **7,000** | | | | | |
| 7,000 | 7,050 | 697 | 466 | 821 | 630 |
| 7,050 | 7,100 | 706 | 473 | 831 | 638 |
| 7,100 | 7,150 | 714 | 480 | 840 | 646 |
| 7,150 | 7,200 | 723 | 487 | 850 | 654 |
| 7,200 | 7,250 | 731 | 494 | 859 | 662 |
| 7,250 | 7,300 | 740 | 501 | 869 | 670 |
| 7,300 | 7,350 | 748 | 508 | 878 | 678 |
| 7,350 | 7,400 | 757 | 515 | 888 | 686 |
| 7,400 | 7,450 | 765 | 522 | 897 | 694 |
| 7,450 | 7,500 | 774 | 529 | 907 | 702 |
| 7,500 | 7,550 | 782 | 536 | 916 | 710 |
| 7,550 | 7,600 | 791 | 543 | 926 | 718 |
| 7,600 | 7,650 | 799 | 550 | 935 | 726 |
| 7,650 | 7,700 | 808 | 558 | 945 | 734 |
| 7,700 | 7,750 | 816 | 566 | 954 | 742 |
| 7,750 | 7,800 | 825 | 574 | 964 | 750 |
| 7,800 | 7,850 | 833 | 582 | 973 | 758 |
| 7,850 | 7,900 | 842 | 590 | 983 | 766 |
| 7,900 | 7,950 | 850 | 598 | 992 | 774 |
| 7,950 | 8,000 | 859 | 606 | 1,002 | 782 |

Continued on next page

*This column must also be used by a qualifying widow(er).

a If your taxable income is exactly $1,700, your tax is zero.
b If your taxable income is exactly $2,300, your tax is zero.
c If your taxable income is exactly $3,400, your tax is zero.

**1982 Tax Table (Continued)**

| If line 37 (taxable income) is— At least | But less than | Single | Married filing jointly* | Married filing separately | Head of a household |
|---|---|---|---|---|---|
| **8,000** | | | | | |
| 8,000 | 8,050 | 867 | 614 | 1,012 | 790 |
| 8,050 | 8,100 | 876 | 622 | 1,023 | 798 |
| 8,100 | 8,150 | 884 | 630 | 1,034 | 806 |
| 8,150 | 8,200 | 893 | 638 | 1,045 | 814 |
| 8,200 | 8,250 | 901 | 646 | 1,056 | 822 |
| 8,250 | 8,300 | 910 | 654 | 1,067 | 830 |
| 8,300 | 8,350 | 918 | 662 | 1,078 | 838 |
| 8,350 | 8,400 | 927 | 670 | 1,089 | 846 |
| 8,400 | 8,450 | 935 | 678 | 1,100 | 854 |
| 8,450 | 8,500 | 944 | 686 | 1,111 | 862 |
| 8,500 | 8,550 | 953 | 694 | 1,122 | 870 |
| 8,550 | 8,600 | 962 | 702 | 1,133 | 878 |
| 8,600 | 8,650 | 972 | 710 | 1,144 | 886 |
| 8,650 | 8,700 | 981 | 718 | 1,155 | 894 |
| 8,700 | 8,750 | 991 | 726 | 1,166 | 903 |
| 8,750 | 8,800 | 1,000 | 734 | 1,177 | 913 |
| 8,800 | 8,850 | 1,010 | 742 | 1,188 | 923 |
| 8,850 | 8,900 | 1,019 | 750 | 1,199 | 933 |
| 8,900 | 8,950 | 1,029 | 758 | 1,210 | 943 |
| 8,950 | 9,000 | 1,038 | 766 | 1,221 | 953 |
| **9,000** | | | | | |
| 9,000 | 9,050 | 1,048 | 774 | 1,232 | 963 |
| 9,050 | 9,100 | 1,057 | 782 | 1,243 | 973 |
| 9,100 | 9,150 | 1,067 | 790 | 1,254 | 983 |
| 9,150 | 9,200 | 1,076 | 798 | 1,265 | 993 |
| 9,200 | 9,250 | 1,086 | 806 | 1,276 | 1,003 |
| 9,250 | 9,300 | 1,095 | 814 | 1,287 | 1,013 |
| 9,300 | 9,350 | 1,105 | 822 | 1,298 | 1,023 |
| 9,350 | 9,400 | 1,114 | 830 | 1,309 | 1,033 |
| 9,400 | 9,450 | 1,124 | 838 | 1,320 | 1,043 |
| 9,450 | 9,500 | 1,133 | 846 | 1,331 | 1,053 |
| 9,500 | 9,550 | 1,143 | 854 | 1,342 | 1,063 |
| 9,550 | 9,600 | 1,152 | 862 | 1,353 | 1,073 |
| 9,600 | 9,650 | 1,162 | 870 | 1,364 | 1,083 |
| 9,650 | 9,700 | 1,171 | 878 | 1,375 | 1,093 |
| 9,700 | 9,750 | 1,181 | 886 | 1,386 | 1,103 |
| 9,750 | 9,800 | 1,190 | 894 | 1,397 | 1,113 |
| 9,800 | 9,850 | 1,200 | 902 | 1,408 | 1,123 |
| 9,850 | 9,900 | 1,209 | 910 | 1,419 | 1,133 |
| 9,900 | 9,950 | 1,219 | 918 | 1,430 | 1,143 |
| 9,950 | 10,000 | 1,228 | 926 | 1,441 | 1,153 |
| **10,000** | | | | | |
| 10,000 | 10,050 | 1,238 | 934 | 1,452 | 1,163 |
| 10,050 | 10,100 | 1,247 | 942 | 1,463 | 1,173 |
| 10,100 | 10,150 | 1,257 | 950 | 1,475 | 1,183 |
| 10,150 | 10,200 | 1,266 | 958 | 1,487 | 1,193 |
| 10,200 | 10,250 | 1,276 | 966 | 1,500 | 1,203 |
| 10,250 | 10,300 | 1,285 | 974 | 1,512 | 1,213 |
| 10,300 | 10,350 | 1,295 | 982 | 1,525 | 1,223 |
| 10,350 | 10,400 | 1,304 | 990 | 1,537 | 1,233 |
| 10,400 | 10,450 | 1,314 | 998 | 1,550 | 1,243 |
| 10,450 | 10,500 | 1,323 | 1,006 | 1,562 | 1,253 |
| 10,500 | 10,550 | 1,333 | 1,014 | 1,575 | 1,263 |
| 10,550 | 10,600 | 1,342 | 1,022 | 1,587 | 1,273 |
| 10,600 | 10,650 | 1,352 | 1,030 | 1,600 | 1,283 |
| 10,650 | 10,700 | 1,361 | 1,038 | 1,612 | 1,293 |
| 10,700 | 10,750 | 1,371 | 1,046 | 1,625 | 1,303 |

| If line 37 (taxable income) is— At least | But less than | Single | Married filing jointly* | Married filing separately | Head of a household |
|---|---|---|---|---|---|
| 10,750 | 10,800 | 1,380 | 1,054 | 1,637 | 1,313 |
| 10,800 | 10,850 | 1,391 | 1,062 | 1,650 | 1,323 |
| 10,850 | 10,900 | 1,402 | 1,070 | 1,662 | 1,333 |
| 10,900 | 10,950 | 1,413 | 1,078 | 1,675 | 1,343 |
| 10,950 | 11,000 | 1,424 | 1,086 | 1,687 | 1,353 |
| **11,000** | | | | | |
| 11,000 | 11,050 | 1,435 | 1,094 | 1,700 | 1,363 |
| 11,050 | 11,100 | 1,446 | 1,102 | 1,712 | 1,373 |
| 11,100 | 11,150 | 1,457 | 1,110 | 1,725 | 1,383 |
| 11,150 | 11,200 | 1,468 | 1,118 | 1,737 | 1,393 |
| 11,200 | 11,250 | 1,479 | 1,126 | 1,750 | 1,403 |
| 11,250 | 11,300 | 1,490 | 1,134 | 1,762 | 1,413 |
| 11,300 | 11,350 | 1,501 | 1,142 | 1,775 | 1,423 |
| 11,350 | 11,400 | 1,512 | 1,150 | 1,787 | 1,433 |
| 11,400 | 11,450 | 1,523 | 1,158 | 1,800 | 1,443 |
| 11,450 | 11,500 | 1,534 | 1,166 | 1,812 | 1,453 |
| 11,500 | 11,550 | 1,545 | 1,174 | 1,825 | 1,463 |
| 11,550 | 11,600 | 1,556 | 1,182 | 1,837 | 1,473 |
| 11,600 | 11,650 | 1,567 | 1,190 | 1,850 | 1,483 |
| 11,650 | 11,700 | 1,578 | 1,198 | 1,862 | 1,493 |
| 11,700 | 11,750 | 1,589 | 1,206 | 1,875 | 1,503 |
| 11,750 | 11,800 | 1,600 | 1,214 | 1,887 | 1,513 |
| 11,800 | 11,850 | 1,611 | 1,222 | 1,900 | 1,524 |
| 11,850 | 11,900 | 1,622 | 1,230 | 1,912 | 1,535 |
| 11,900 | 11,950 | 1,633 | 1,239 | 1,925 | 1,546 |
| 11,950 | 12,000 | 1,644 | 1,248 | 1,937 | 1,557 |
| **12,000** | | | | | |
| 12,000 | 12,050 | 1,655 | 1,258 | 1,950 | 1,568 |
| 12,050 | 12,100 | 1,666 | 1,267 | 1,962 | 1,579 |
| 12,100 | 12,150 | 1,677 | 1,277 | 1,975 | 1,590 |
| 12,150 | 12,200 | 1,688 | 1,286 | 1,987 | 1,601 |
| 12,200 | 12,250 | 1,699 | 1,296 | 2,000 | 1,612 |
| 12,250 | 12,300 | 1,710 | 1,305 | 2,012 | 1,623 |
| 12,300 | 12,350 | 1,721 | 1,315 | 2,026 | 1,634 |
| 12,350 | 12,400 | 1,732 | 1,324 | 2,040 | 1,645 |
| 12,400 | 12,450 | 1,743 | 1,334 | 2,055 | 1,656 |
| 12,450 | 12,500 | 1,754 | 1,343 | 2,069 | 1,667 |
| 12,500 | 12,550 | 1,765 | 1,353 | 2,084 | 1,678 |
| 12,550 | 12,600 | 1,776 | 1,362 | 2,098 | 1,689 |
| 12,600 | 12,650 | 1,787 | 1,372 | 2,113 | 1,700 |
| 12,650 | 12,700 | 1,798 | 1,381 | 2,127 | 1,711 |
| 12,700 | 12,750 | 1,809 | 1,391 | 2,142 | 1,722 |
| 12,750 | 12,800 | 1,820 | 1,400 | 2,156 | 1,733 |
| 12,800 | 12,850 | 1,831 | 1,410 | 2,171 | 1,744 |
| 12,850 | 12,900 | 1,842 | 1,419 | 2,185 | 1,755 |
| 12,900 | 12,950 | 1,853 | 1,429 | 2,200 | 1,766 |
| 12,950 | 13,000 | 1,864 | 1,438 | 2,214 | 1,777 |
| **13,000** | | | | | |
| 13,000 | 13,050 | 1,876 | 1,448 | 2,229 | 1,788 |
| 13,050 | 13,100 | 1,887 | 1,457 | 2,243 | 1,799 |
| 13,100 | 13,150 | 1,899 | 1,467 | 2,258 | 1,810 |
| 13,150 | 13,200 | 1,910 | 1,476 | 2,272 | 1,821 |
| 13,200 | 13,250 | 1,922 | 1,486 | 2,287 | 1,832 |
| 13,250 | 13,300 | 1,933 | 1,495 | 2,301 | 1,843 |
| 13,300 | 13,350 | 1,945 | 1,505 | 2,316 | 1,854 |
| 13,350 | 13,400 | 1,956 | 1,514 | 2,330 | 1,865 |
| 13,400 | 13,450 | 1,968 | 1,524 | 2,345 | 1,876 |
| 13,450 | 13,500 | 1,979 | 1,533 | 2,359 | 1,887 |

| If line 37 (taxable income) is— At least | But less than | Single | Married filing jointly* | Married filing separately | Head of a household |
|---|---|---|---|---|---|
| 13,500 | 13,550 | 1,991 | 1,543 | 2,374 | 1,898 |
| 13,550 | 13,600 | 2,002 | 1,552 | 2,388 | 1,909 |
| 13,600 | 13,650 | 2,014 | 1,562 | 2,403 | 1,920 |
| 13,650 | 13,700 | 2,025 | 1,571 | 2,417 | 1,931 |
| 13,700 | 13,750 | 2,037 | 1,581 | 2,432 | 1,942 |
| 13,750 | 13,800 | 2,048 | 1,590 | 2,446 | 1,953 |
| 13,800 | 13,850 | 2,060 | 1,600 | 2,461 | 1,964 |
| 13,850 | 13,900 | 2,071 | 1,609 | 2,475 | 1,975 |
| 13,900 | 13,950 | 2,083 | 1,619 | 2,490 | 1,986 |
| 13,950 | 14,000 | 2,094 | 1,628 | 2,504 | 1,997 |
| **14,000** | | | | | |
| 14,000 | 14,050 | 2,106 | 1,638 | 2,519 | 2,008 |
| 14,050 | 14,100 | 2,117 | 1,647 | 2,533 | 2,019 |
| 14,100 | 14,150 | 2,129 | 1,657 | 2,548 | 2,030 |
| 14,150 | 14,200 | 2,140 | 1,666 | 2,562 | 2,041 |
| 14,200 | 14,250 | 2,152 | 1,676 | 2,577 | 2,052 |
| 14,250 | 14,300 | 2,163 | 1,685 | 2,591 | 2,063 |
| 14,300 | 14,350 | 2,175 | 1,695 | 2,606 | 2,074 |
| 14,350 | 14,400 | 2,186 | 1,704 | 2,620 | 2,085 |
| 14,400 | 14,450 | 2,198 | 1,714 | 2,635 | 2,096 |
| 14,450 | 14,500 | 2,209 | 1,723 | 2,649 | 2,107 |
| 14,500 | 14,550 | 2,221 | 1,733 | 2,664 | 2,118 |
| 14,550 | 14,600 | 2,232 | 1,742 | 2,678 | 2,129 |
| 14,600 | 14,650 | 2,244 | 1,752 | 2,693 | 2,140 |
| 14,650 | 14,700 | 2,255 | 1,761 | 2,707 | 2,151 |
| 14,700 | 14,750 | 2,267 | 1,771 | 2,722 | 2,162 |
| 14,750 | 14,800 | 2,278 | 1,780 | 2,736 | 2,173 |
| 14,800 | 14,850 | 2,290 | 1,790 | 2,751 | 2,184 |
| 14,850 | 14,900 | 2,301 | 1,799 | 2,765 | 2,195 |
| 14,900 | 14,950 | 2,313 | 1,809 | 2,780 | 2,206 |
| 14,950 | 15,000 | 2,324 | 1,818 | 2,795 | 2,217 |
| **15,000** | | | | | |
| 15,000 | 15,050 | 2,337 | 1,828 | 2,812 | 2,228 |
| 15,050 | 15,100 | 2,350 | 1,837 | 2,828 | 2,239 |
| 15,100 | 15,150 | 2,364 | 1,847 | 2,845 | 2,251 |
| 15,150 | 15,200 | 2,377 | 1,856 | 2,861 | 2,262 |
| 15,200 | 15,250 | 2,391 | 1,866 | 2,878 | 2,274 |
| 15,250 | 15,300 | 2,404 | 1,875 | 2,894 | 2,285 |
| 15,300 | 15,350 | 2,418 | 1,885 | 2,911 | 2,297 |
| 15,350 | 15,400 | 2,431 | 1,894 | 2,927 | 2,308 |
| 15,400 | 15,450 | 2,445 | 1,904 | 2,944 | 2,320 |
| 15,450 | 15,500 | 2,458 | 1,913 | 2,960 | 2,331 |
| 15,500 | 15,550 | 2,472 | 1,923 | 2,977 | 2,343 |
| 15,550 | 15,600 | 2,485 | 1,932 | 2,993 | 2,354 |
| 15,600 | 15,650 | 2,499 | 1,942 | 3,010 | 2,366 |
| 15,650 | 15,700 | 2,512 | 1,951 | 3,026 | 2,377 |
| 15,700 | 15,750 | 2,526 | 1,961 | 3,043 | 2,389 |
| 15,750 | 15,800 | 2,539 | 1,970 | 3,059 | 2,400 |
| 15,800 | 15,850 | 2,553 | 1,980 | 3,076 | 2,412 |
| 15,850 | 15,900 | 2,566 | 1,989 | 3,092 | 2,423 |
| 15,900 | 15,950 | 2,580 | 1,999 | 3,109 | 2,435 |
| 15,950 | 16,000 | 2,593 | 2,008 | 3,125 | 2,446 |
| **16,000** | | | | | |
| 16,000 | 16,050 | 2,607 | 2,019 | 3,142 | 2,458 |
| 16,050 | 16,100 | 2,620 | 2,030 | 3,158 | 2,469 |
| 16,100 | 16,150 | 2,634 | 2,041 | 3,175 | 2,481 |
| 16,150 | 16,200 | 2,647 | 2,052 | 3,191 | 2,492 |
| 16,200 | 16,250 | 2,661 | 2,063 | 3,208 | 2,504 |

*This column must also be used by a qualifying widow(er).

Continued on next page

## 1982 Tax Table (Continued)

| If line 37 (taxable income) is— | | And you are— | | | |
|---|---|---|---|---|---|
| At least | But less than | Single | Married filing jointly * | Married filing separately | Head of a household |
| | | Your tax is— | | | |
| 16,250 | 16,300 | 2,674 | 2,074 | 3,224 | 2,515 |
| 16,300 | 16,350 | 2,688 | 2,085 | 3,241 | 2,527 |
| 16,350 | 16,400 | 2,701 | 2,096 | 3,257 | 2,538 |
| 16,400 | 16,450 | 2,715 | 2,107 | 3,274 | 2,550 |
| 16,450 | 16,500 | 2,728 | 2,118 | 3,290 | 2,561 |
| 16,500 | 16,550 | 2,742 | 2,129 | 3,307 | 2,573 |
| 16,550 | 16,600 | 2,755 | 2,140 | 3,323 | 2,584 |
| 16,600 | 16,650 | 2,769 | 2,151 | 3,340 | 2,596 |
| 16,650 | 16,700 | 2,782 | 2,162 | 3,356 | 2,607 |
| 16,700 | 16,750 | 2,796 | 2,173 | 3,373 | 2,619 |
| 16,750 | 16,800 | 2,809 | 2,184 | 3,389 | 2,630 |
| 16,800 | 16,850 | 2,823 | 2,195 | 3,406 | 2,642 |
| 16,850 | 16,900 | 2,836 | 2,206 | 3,422 | 2,653 |
| 16,900 | 16,950 | 2,850 | 2,217 | 3,439 | 2,665 |
| 16,950 | 17,000 | 2,863 | 2,228 | 3,455 | 2,676 |
| **17,000** | | | | | |
| 17,000 | 17,050 | 2,877 | 2,239 | 3,472 | 2,688 |
| 17,050 | 17,100 | 2,890 | 2,250 | 3,488 | 2,699 |
| 17,100 | 17,150 | 2,904 | 2,261 | 3,505 | 2,711 |
| 17,150 | 17,200 | 2,917 | 2,272 | 3,521 | 2,722 |
| 17,200 | 17,250 | 2,931 | 2,283 | 3,538 | 2,734 |
| 17,250 | 17,300 | 2,944 | 2,294 | 3,554 | 2,745 |
| 17,300 | 17,350 | 2,958 | 2,305 | 3,571 | 2,757 |
| 17,350 | 17,400 | 2,971 | 2,316 | 3,587 | 2,768 |
| 17,400 | 17,450 | 2,985 | 2,327 | 3,604 | 2,780 |
| 17,450 | 17,500 | 2,998 | 2,338 | 3,620 | 2,791 |
| 17,500 | 17,550 | 3,012 | 2,349 | 3,637 | 2,803 |
| 17,550 | 17,600 | 3,025 | 2,360 | 3,653 | 2,814 |
| 17,600 | 17,650 | 3,039 | 2,371 | 3,671 | 2,826 |
| 17,650 | 17,700 | 3,052 | 2,382 | 3,691 | 2,837 |
| 17,700 | 17,750 | 3,066 | 2,393 | 3,710 | 2,849 |
| 17,750 | 17,800 | 3,079 | 2,404 | 3,730 | 2,860 |
| 17,800 | 17,850 | 3,093 | 2,415 | 3,749 | 2,872 |
| 17,850 | 17,900 | 3,106 | 2,426 | 3,769 | 2,883 |
| 17,900 | 17,950 | 3,120 | 2,437 | 3,788 | 2,895 |
| 17,950 | 18,000 | 3,133 | 2,448 | 3,808 | 2,906 |
| **18,000** | | | | | |
| 18,000 | 18,050 | 3,147 | 2,459 | 3,827 | 2,918 |
| 18,050 | 18,100 | 3,160 | 2,470 | 3,847 | 2,929 |
| 18,100 | 18,150 | 3,174 | 2,481 | 3,866 | 2,941 |
| 18,150 | 18,200 | 3,187 | 2,492 | 3,886 | 2,952 |
| 18,200 | 18,250 | 3,202 | 2,503 | 3,905 | 2,965 |
| 18,250 | 18,300 | 3,217 | 2,514 | 3,925 | 2,979 |
| 18,300 | 18,350 | 3,233 | 2,525 | 3,944 | 2,993 |
| 18,350 | 18,400 | 3,248 | 2,536 | 3,964 | 3,007 |
| 18,400 | 18,450 | 3,264 | 2,547 | 3,983 | 3,021 |
| 18,450 | 18,500 | 3,279 | 2,558 | 4,003 | 3,035 |
| 18,500 | 18,550 | 3,295 | 2,569 | 4,022 | 3,049 |
| 18,550 | 18,600 | 3,310 | 2,580 | 4,042 | 3,063 |
| 18,600 | 18,650 | 3,326 | 2,591 | 4,061 | 3,077 |
| 18,650 | 18,700 | 3,341 | 2,602 | 4,081 | 3,091 |
| 18,700 | 18,750 | 3,357 | 2,613 | 4,100 | 3,105 |
| 18,750 | 18,800 | 3,372 | 2,624 | 4,120 | 3,119 |
| 18,800 | 18,850 | 3,388 | 2,635 | 4,139 | 3,133 |
| 18,850 | 18,900 | 3,403 | 2,646 | 4,159 | 3,147 |
| 18,900 | 18,950 | 3,419 | 2,657 | 4,178 | 3,161 |
| 18,950 | 19,000 | 3,434 | 2,668 | 4,198 | 3,175 |

| If line 37 (taxable income) is— | | And you are— | | | |
|---|---|---|---|---|---|
| At least | But less than | Single | Married filing jointly * | Married filing separately | Head of a household |
| | | Your tax is— | | | |
| **19,000** | | | | | |
| 19,000 | 19,050 | 3,450 | 2,679 | 4,217 | 3,189 |
| 19,050 | 19,100 | 3,465 | 2,690 | 4,237 | 3,203 |
| 19,100 | 19,150 | 3,481 | 2,701 | 4,256 | 3,217 |
| 19,150 | 19,200 | 3,496 | 2,712 | 4,276 | 3,231 |
| 19,200 | 19,250 | 3,512 | 2,723 | 4,295 | 3,245 |
| 19,250 | 19,300 | 3,527 | 2,734 | 4,315 | 3,259 |
| 19,300 | 19,350 | 3,543 | 2,745 | 4,334 | 3,273 |
| 19,350 | 19,400 | 3,558 | 2,756 | 4,354 | 3,287 |
| 19,400 | 19,450 | 3,574 | 2,767 | 4,373 | 3,301 |
| 19,450 | 19,500 | 3,589 | 2,778 | 4,393 | 3,315 |
| 19,500 | 19,550 | 3,605 | 2,789 | 4,412 | 3,329 |
| 19,550 | 19,600 | 3,620 | 2,800 | 4,432 | 3,343 |
| 19,600 | 19,650 | 3,636 | 2,811 | 4,451 | 3,357 |
| 19,650 | 19,700 | 3,651 | 2,822 | 4,471 | 3,371 |
| 19,700 | 19,750 | 3,667 | 2,833 | 4,490 | 3,385 |
| 19,750 | 19,800 | 3,682 | 2,844 | 4,510 | 3,399 |
| 19,800 | 19,850 | 3,698 | 2,855 | 4,529 | 3,413 |
| 19,850 | 19,900 | 3,713 | 2,866 | 4,549 | 3,427 |
| 19,900 | 19,950 | 3,729 | 2,877 | 4,568 | 3,441 |
| 19,950 | 20,000 | 3,744 | 2,888 | 4,588 | 3,455 |
| **20,000** | | | | | |
| 20,000 | 20,050 | 3,760 | 2,899 | 4,607 | 3,469 |
| 20,050 | 20,100 | 3,775 | 2,910 | 4,627 | 3,483 |
| 20,100 | 20,150 | 3,791 | 2,921 | 4,646 | 3,497 |
| 20,150 | 20,200 | 3,806 | 2,932 | 4,666 | 3,511 |
| 20,200 | 20,250 | 3,822 | 2,943 | 4,685 | 3,525 |
| 20,250 | 20,300 | 3,837 | 2,956 | 4,705 | 3,539 |
| 20,300 | 20,350 | 3,853 | 2,968 | 4,724 | 3,553 |
| 20,350 | 20,400 | 3,868 | 2,981 | 4,744 | 3,567 |
| 20,400 | 20,450 | 3,884 | 2,993 | 4,763 | 3,581 |
| 20,450 | 20,500 | 3,899 | 3,006 | 4,783 | 3,595 |
| 20,500 | 20,550 | 3,915 | 3,018 | 4,802 | 3,609 |
| 20,550 | 20,600 | 3,930 | 3,031 | 4,822 | 3,623 |
| 20,600 | 20,650 | 3,946 | 3,043 | 4,841 | 3,637 |
| 20,650 | 20,700 | 3,961 | 3,056 | 4,861 | 3,651 |
| 20,700 | 20,750 | 3,977 | 3,068 | 4,880 | 3,665 |
| 20,750 | 20,800 | 3,992 | 3,081 | 4,900 | 3,679 |
| 20,800 | 20,850 | 4,008 | 3,093 | 4,919 | 3,693 |
| 20,850 | 20,900 | 4,023 | 3,106 | 4,939 | 3,707 |
| 20,900 | 20,950 | 4,039 | 3,118 | 4,958 | 3,721 |
| 20,950 | 21,000 | 4,054 | 3,131 | 4,978 | 3,735 |
| **21,000** | | | | | |
| 21,000 | 21,050 | 4,070 | 3,143 | 4,997 | 3,749 |
| 21,050 | 21,100 | 4,085 | 3,156 | 5,017 | 3,763 |
| 21,100 | 21,150 | 4,101 | 3,168 | 5,036 | 3,777 |
| 21,150 | 21,200 | 4,116 | 3,181 | 5,056 | 3,791 |
| 21,200 | 21,250 | 4,132 | 3,193 | 5,075 | 3,805 |
| 21,250 | 21,300 | 4,147 | 3,206 | 5,095 | 3,819 |
| 21,300 | 21,350 | 4,163 | 3,218 | 5,114 | 3,833 |
| 21,350 | 21,400 | 4,178 | 3,231 | 5,134 | 3,847 |
| 21,400 | 21,450 | 4,194 | 3,243 | 5,153 | 3,861 |
| 21,450 | 21,500 | 4,209 | 3,256 | 5,173 | 3,875 |
| 21,500 | 21,550 | 4,225 | 3,268 | 5,192 | 3,889 |
| 21,550 | 21,600 | 4,240 | 3,281 | 5,212 | 3,903 |
| 21,600 | 21,650 | 4,256 | 3,293 | 5,231 | 3,917 |
| 21,650 | 21,700 | 4,271 | 3,306 | 5,251 | 3,931 |
| 21,700 | 21,750 | 4,287 | 3,318 | 5,270 | 3,945 |

| If line 37 (taxable income) is— | | And you are— | | | |
|---|---|---|---|---|---|
| At least | But less than | Single | Married filing jointly * | Married filing separately | Head of a household |
| | | Your tax is— | | | |
| 21,750 | 21,800 | 4,302 | 3,331 | 5,290 | 3,959 |
| 21,800 | 21,850 | 4,318 | 3,343 | 5,309 | 3,973 |
| 21,850 | 21,900 | 4,333 | 3,356 | 5,329 | 3,987 |
| 21,900 | 21,950 | 4,349 | 3,368 | 5,348 | 4,001 |
| 21,950 | 22,000 | 4,364 | 3,381 | 5,368 | 4,015 |
| **22,000** | | | | | |
| 22,000 | 22,050 | 4,380 | 3,393 | 5,387 | 4,029 |
| 22,050 | 22,100 | 4,395 | 3,406 | 5,407 | 4,043 |
| 22,100 | 22,150 | 4,411 | 3,418 | 5,426 | 4,057 |
| 22,150 | 22,200 | 4,426 | 3,431 | 5,446 | 4,071 |
| 22,200 | 22,250 | 4,442 | 3,443 | 5,465 | 4,085 |
| 22,250 | 22,300 | 4,457 | 3,456 | 5,485 | 4,099 |
| 22,300 | 22,350 | 4,473 | 3,468 | 5,504 | 4,113 |
| 22,350 | 22,400 | 4,488 | 3,481 | 5,524 | 4,127 |
| 22,400 | 22,450 | 4,504 | 3,493 | 5,543 | 4,141 |
| 22,450 | 22,500 | 4,519 | 3,506 | 5,563 | 4,155 |
| 22,500 | 22,550 | 4,535 | 3,518 | 5,582 | 4,169 |
| 22,550 | 22,600 | 4,550 | 3,531 | 5,602 | 4,183 |
| 22,600 | 22,650 | 4,566 | 3,543 | 5,621 | 4,197 |
| 22,650 | 22,700 | 4,581 | 3,556 | 5,641 | 4,211 |
| 22,700 | 22,750 | 4,597 | 3,568 | 5,660 | 4,225 |
| 22,750 | 22,800 | 4,612 | 3,581 | 5,680 | 4,239 |
| 22,800 | 22,850 | 4,628 | 3,593 | 5,699 | 4,253 |
| 22,850 | 22,900 | 4,643 | 3,606 | 5,719 | 4,267 |
| 22,900 | 22,950 | 4,659 | 3,618 | 5,740 | 4,281 |
| 22,950 | 23,000 | 4,674 | 3,631 | 5,762 | 4,295 |
| **23,000** | | | | | |
| 23,000 | 23,050 | 4,690 | 3,643 | 5,784 | 4,309 |
| 23,050 | 23,100 | 4,705 | 3,656 | 5,806 | 4,323 |
| 23,100 | 23,150 | 4,721 | 3,668 | 5,828 | 4,337 |
| 23,150 | 23,200 | 4,736 | 3,681 | 5,850 | 4,351 |
| 23,200 | 23,250 | 4,752 | 3,693 | 5,872 | 4,365 |
| 23,250 | 23,300 | 4,767 | 3,706 | 5,894 | 4,379 |
| 23,300 | 23,350 | 4,783 | 3,718 | 5,916 | 4,393 |
| 23,350 | 23,400 | 4,798 | 3,731 | 5,938 | 4,407 |
| 23,400 | 23,450 | 4,814 | 3,743 | 5,960 | 4,421 |
| 23,450 | 23,500 | 4,829 | 3,756 | 5,982 | 4,435 |
| 23,500 | 23,550 | 4,846 | 3,768 | 6,004 | 4,450 |
| 23,550 | 23,600 | 4,863 | 3,781 | 6,026 | 4,466 |
| 23,600 | 23,650 | 4,881 | 3,793 | 6,048 | 4,482 |
| 23,650 | 23,700 | 4,898 | 3,806 | 6,070 | 4,498 |
| 23,700 | 23,750 | 4,916 | 3,818 | 6,092 | 4,514 |
| 23,750 | 23,800 | 4,933 | 3,831 | 6,114 | 4,530 |
| 23,800 | 23,850 | 4,951 | 3,843 | 6,136 | 4,546 |
| 23,850 | 23,900 | 4,968 | 3,856 | 6,158 | 4,562 |
| 23,900 | 23,950 | 4,986 | 3,868 | 6,180 | 4,578 |
| 23,950 | 24,000 | 5,003 | 3,881 | 6,202 | 4,594 |
| **24,000** | | | | | |
| 24,000 | 24,050 | 5,021 | 3,893 | 6,224 | 4,610 |
| 24,050 | 24,100 | 5,038 | 3,906 | 6,246 | 4,626 |
| 24,100 | 24,150 | 5,056 | 3,918 | 6,268 | 4,642 |
| 24,150 | 24,200 | 5,073 | 3,931 | 6,290 | 4,658 |
| 24,200 | 24,250 | 5,091 | 3,943 | 6,312 | 4,674 |
| 24,250 | 24,300 | 5,108 | 3,956 | 6,334 | 4,690 |
| 24,300 | 24,350 | 5,126 | 3,968 | 6,356 | 4,706 |
| 24,350 | 24,400 | 5,143 | 3,981 | 6,378 | 4,722 |
| 24,400 | 24,450 | 5,161 | 3,993 | 6,400 | 4,738 |
| 24,450 | 24,500 | 5,178 | 4,006 | 6,422 | 4,754 |

*This column must also be used by a qualifying widow(er).

Continued on next page

**1982 Tax Table (Continued)**

| If line 37 (taxable income) is— | | And you are— | | | |
|---|---|---|---|---|---|
| At least | But less than | Single | Married filing jointly * | Married filing separately | Head of a household |
| | | Your tax is— | | | |
| 24,500 | 24,550 | 5,196 | 4,018 | 6,444 | 4,770 |
| 24,550 | 24,600 | 5,213 | 4,031 | 6,466 | 4,786 |
| 24,600 | 24,650 | 5,231 | 4,044 | 6,488 | 4,802 |
| 24,650 | 24,700 | 5,248 | 4,059 | 6,510 | 4,818 |
| 24,700 | 24,750 | 5,266 | 4,073 | 6,532 | 4,834 |
| 24,750 | 24,800 | 5,283 | 4,088 | 6,554 | 4,850 |
| 24,800 | 24,850 | 5,301 | 4,102 | 6,576 | 4,866 |
| 24,850 | 24,900 | 5,318 | 4,117 | 6,598 | 4,882 |
| 24,900 | 24,950 | 5,336 | 4,131 | 6,620 | 4,898 |
| 24,950 | 25,000 | 5,353 | 4,146 | 6,642 | 4,914 |
| **25,000** | | | | | |
| 25,000 | 25,050 | 5,371 | 4,160 | 6,664 | 4,930 |
| 25,050 | 25,100 | 5,388 | 4,175 | 6,686 | 4,946 |
| 25,100 | 25,150 | 5,406 | 4,189 | 6,708 | 4,962 |
| 25,150 | 25,200 | 5,423 | 4,204 | 6,730 | 4,978 |
| 25,200 | 25,250 | 5,441 | 4,218 | 6,752 | 4,994 |
| 25,250 | 25,300 | 5,458 | 4,233 | 6,774 | 5,010 |
| 25,300 | 25,350 | 5,476 | 4,247 | 6,796 | 5,026 |
| 25,350 | 25,400 | 5,493 | 4,262 | 6,818 | 5,042 |
| 25,400 | 25,450 | 5,511 | 4,276 | 6,840 | 5,058 |
| 25,450 | 25,500 | 5,528 | 4,291 | 6,862 | 5,074 |
| 25,500 | 25,550 | 5,546 | 4,305 | 6,884 | 5,090 |
| 25,550 | 25,600 | 5,563 | 4,320 | 6,906 | 5,106 |
| 25,600 | 25,650 | 5,581 | 4,334 | 6,928 | 5,122 |
| 25,650 | 25,700 | 5,598 | 4,349 | 6,950 | 5,138 |
| 25,700 | 25,750 | 5,616 | 4,363 | 6,972 | 5,154 |
| 25,750 | 25,800 | 5,633 | 4,378 | 6,994 | 5,170 |
| 25,800 | 25,850 | 5,651 | 4,392 | 7,016 | 5,186 |
| 25,850 | 25,900 | 5,668 | 4,407 | 7,038 | 5,202 |
| 25,900 | 25,950 | 5,686 | 4,421 | 7,060 | 5,218 |
| 25,950 | 26,000 | 5,703 | 4,436 | 7,082 | 5,234 |
| **26,000** | | | | | |
| 26,000 | 26,050 | 5,721 | 4,450 | 7,104 | 5,250 |
| 26,050 | 26,100 | 5,738 | 4,465 | 7,126 | 5,266 |
| 26,100 | 26,150 | 5,756 | 4,479 | 7,148 | 5,282 |
| 26,150 | 26,200 | 5,773 | 4,494 | 7,170 | 5,298 |
| 26,200 | 26,250 | 5,791 | 4,508 | 7,192 | 5,314 |
| 26,250 | 26,300 | 5,808 | 4,523 | 7,214 | 5,330 |
| 26,300 | 26,350 | 5,826 | 4,537 | 7,236 | 5,346 |
| 26,350 | 26,400 | 5,843 | 4,552 | 7,258 | 5,362 |
| 26,400 | 26,450 | 5,861 | 4,566 | 7,280 | 5,378 |
| 26,450 | 26,500 | 5,878 | 4,581 | 7,302 | 5,394 |
| 26,500 | 26,550 | 5,896 | 4,595 | 7,324 | 5,410 |
| 26,550 | 26,600 | 5,913 | 4,610 | 7,346 | 5,426 |
| 26,600 | 26,650 | 5,931 | 4,624 | 7,368 | 5,442 |
| 26,650 | 26,700 | 5,948 | 4,639 | 7,390 | 5,458 |
| 26,700 | 26,750 | 5,966 | 4,653 | 7,412 | 5,474 |
| 26,750 | 26,800 | 5,983 | 4,668 | 7,434 | 5,490 |
| 26,800 | 26,850 | 6,001 | 4,682 | 7,456 | 5,506 |
| 26,850 | 26,900 | 6,018 | 4,697 | 7,478 | 5,522 |
| 26,900 | 26,950 | 6,036 | 4,711 | 7,500 | 5,538 |
| 26,950 | 27,000 | 6,053 | 4,726 | 7,522 | 5,554 |
| **27,000** | | | | | |
| 27,000 | 27,050 | 6,071 | 4,740 | 7,544 | 5,570 |
| 27,050 | 27,100 | 6,088 | 4,755 | 7,566 | 5,586 |
| 27,100 | 27,150 | 6,106 | 4,769 | 7,588 | 5,602 |
| 27,150 | 27,200 | 6,123 | 4,784 | 7,610 | 5,618 |
| 27,200 | 27,250 | 6,141 | 4,798 | 7,632 | 5,634 |

| If line 37 (taxable income) is— | | And you are— | | | |
|---|---|---|---|---|---|
| At least | But less than | Single | Married filing jointly * | Married filing separately | Head of a household |
| | | Your tax is— | | | |
| 27,250 | 27,300 | 6,158 | 4,813 | 7,654 | 5,650 |
| 27,300 | 27,350 | 6,176 | 4,827 | 7,676 | 5,666 |
| 27,350 | 27,400 | 6,193 | 4,842 | 7,698 | 5,682 |
| 27,400 | 27,450 | 6,211 | 4,856 | 7,720 | 5,698 |
| 27,450 | 27,500 | 6,228 | 4,871 | 7,742 | 5,714 |
| 27,500 | 27,550 | 6,246 | 4,885 | 7,764 | 5,730 |
| 27,550 | 27,600 | 6,263 | 4,900 | 7,786 | 5,746 |
| 27,600 | 27,650 | 6,281 | 4,914 | 7,808 | 5,762 |
| 27,650 | 27,700 | 6,298 | 4,929 | 7,830 | 5,778 |
| 27,700 | 27,750 | 6,316 | 4,943 | 7,852 | 5,794 |
| 27,750 | 27,800 | 6,333 | 4,958 | 7,874 | 5,810 |
| 27,800 | 27,850 | 6,351 | 4,972 | 7,896 | 5,826 |
| 27,850 | 27,900 | 6,368 | 4,987 | 7,918 | 5,842 |
| 27,900 | 27,950 | 6,386 | 5,001 | 7,940 | 5,858 |
| 27,950 | 28,000 | 6,403 | 5,016 | 7,962 | 5,874 |
| **28,000** | | | | | |
| 28,000 | 28,050 | 6,421 | 5,030 | 7,984 | 5,890 |
| 28,050 | 28,100 | 6,438 | 5,045 | 8,006 | 5,906 |
| 28,100 | 28,150 | 6,456 | 5,059 | 8,028 | 5,922 |
| 28,150 | 28,200 | 6,473 | 5,074 | 8,050 | 5,938 |
| 28,200 | 28,250 | 6,491 | 5,088 | 8,072 | 5,954 |
| 28,250 | 28,300 | 6,508 | 5,103 | 8,094 | 5,970 |
| 28,300 | 28,350 | 6,526 | 5,117 | 8,116 | 5,986 |
| 28,350 | 28,400 | 6,543 | 5,132 | 8,138 | 6,002 |
| 28,400 | 28,450 | 6,561 | 5,146 | 8,160 | 6,018 |
| 28,450 | 28,500 | 6,578 | 5,161 | 8,182 | 6,034 |
| 28,500 | 28,550 | 6,596 | 5,175 | 8,204 | 6,050 |
| 28,550 | 28,600 | 6,613 | 5,190 | 8,226 | 6,066 |
| 28,600 | 28,650 | 6,631 | 5,204 | 8,248 | 6,082 |
| 28,650 | 28,700 | 6,648 | 5,219 | 8,270 | 6,098 |
| 28,700 | 28,750 | 6,666 | 5,233 | 8,292 | 6,114 |
| 28,750 | 28,800 | 6,683 | 5,248 | 8,314 | 6,130 |
| 28,800 | 28,850 | 6,702 | 5,262 | 8,336 | 6,148 |
| 28,850 | 28,900 | 6,722 | 5,277 | 8,358 | 6,167 |
| 28,900 | 28,950 | 6,742 | 5,291 | 8,380 | 6,186 |
| 28,950 | 29,000 | 6,762 | 5,306 | 8,402 | 6,205 |
| **29,000** | | | | | |
| 29,000 | 29,050 | 6,782 | 5,320 | 8,424 | 6,224 |
| 29,050 | 29,100 | 6,802 | 5,335 | 8,446 | 6,243 |
| 29,100 | 29,150 | 6,822 | 5,349 | 8,468 | 6,262 |
| 29,150 | 29,200 | 6,842 | 5,364 | 8,490 | 6,281 |
| 29,200 | 29,250 | 6,862 | 5,378 | 8,512 | 6,300 |
| 29,250 | 29,300 | 6,882 | 5,393 | 8,534 | 6,319 |
| 29,300 | 29,350 | 6,902 | 5,407 | 8,556 | 6,338 |
| 29,350 | 29,400 | 6,922 | 5,422 | 8,578 | 6,357 |
| 29,400 | 29,450 | 6,942 | 5,436 | 8,600 | 6,376 |
| 29,450 | 29,500 | 6,962 | 5,451 | 8,622 | 6,395 |
| 29,500 | 29,550 | 6,982 | 5,465 | 8,644 | 6,414 |
| 29,550 | 29,600 | 7,002 | 5,480 | 8,666 | 6,433 |
| 29,600 | 29,650 | 7,022 | 5,494 | 8,688 | 6,452 |
| 29,650 | 29,700 | 7,042 | 5,509 | 8,710 | 6,471 |
| 29,700 | 29,750 | 7,062 | 5,523 | 8,732 | 6,490 |
| 29,750 | 29,800 | 7,082 | 5,538 | 8,754 | 6,509 |
| 29,800 | 29,850 | 7,102 | 5,552 | 8,776 | 6,528 |
| 29,850 | 29,900 | 7,122 | 5,567 | 8,798 | 6,547 |
| 29,900 | 29,950 | 7,142 | 5,582 | 8,820 | 6,566 |
| 29,950 | 30,000 | 7,162 | 5,599 | 8,842 | 6,585 |

| If line 37 (taxable income) is— | | And you are— | | | |
|---|---|---|---|---|---|
| At least | But less than | Single | Married filing jointly * | Married filing separately | Head of a household |
| | | Your tax is— | | | |
| **30,000** | | | | | |
| 30,000 | 30,050 | 7,182 | 5,615 | 8,865 | 6,604 |
| 30,050 | 30,100 | 7,202 | 5,632 | 8,889 | 6,623 |
| 30,100 | 30,150 | 7,222 | 5,648 | 8,914 | 6,642 |
| 30,150 | 30,200 | 7,242 | 5,665 | 8,938 | 6,661 |
| 30,200 | 30,250 | 7,262 | 5,681 | 8,963 | 6,680 |
| 30,250 | 30,300 | 7,282 | 5,698 | 8,987 | 6,699 |
| 30,300 | 30,350 | 7,302 | 5,714 | 9,012 | 6,718 |
| 30,350 | 30,400 | 7,322 | 5,731 | 9,036 | 6,737 |
| 30,400 | 30,450 | 7,342 | 5,747 | 9,061 | 6,756 |
| 30,450 | 30,500 | 7,362 | 5,764 | 9,085 | 6,775 |
| 30,500 | 30,550 | 7,382 | 5,780 | 9,110 | 6,794 |
| 30,550 | 30,600 | 7,402 | 5,797 | 9,134 | 6,813 |
| 30,600 | 30,650 | 7,422 | 5,813 | 9,159 | 6,832 |
| 30,650 | 30,700 | 7,442 | 5,830 | 9,183 | 6,851 |
| 30,700 | 30,750 | 7,462 | 5,846 | 9,208 | 6,870 |
| 30,750 | 30,800 | 7,482 | 5,863 | 9,232 | 6,889 |
| 30,800 | 30,850 | 7,502 | 5,879 | 9,257 | 6,908 |
| 30,850 | 30,900 | 7,522 | 5,896 | 9,281 | 6,927 |
| 30,900 | 30,950 | 7,542 | 5,912 | 9,306 | 6,946 |
| 30,950 | 31,000 | 7,562 | 5,929 | 9,330 | 6,965 |
| **31,000** | | | | | |
| 31,000 | 31,050 | 7,582 | 5,945 | 9,355 | 6,984 |
| 31,050 | 31,100 | 7,602 | 5,962 | 9,379 | 7,003 |
| 31,100 | 31,150 | 7,622 | 5,978 | 9,404 | 7,022 |
| 31,150 | 31,200 | 7,642 | 5,995 | 9,428 | 7,041 |
| 31,200 | 31,250 | 7,662 | 6,011 | 9,453 | 7,060 |
| 31,250 | 31,300 | 7,682 | 6,028 | 9,477 | 7,079 |
| 31,300 | 31,350 | 7,702 | 6,044 | 9,502 | 7,098 |
| 31,350 | 31,400 | 7,722 | 6,061 | 9,526 | 7,117 |
| 31,400 | 31,450 | 7,742 | 6,077 | 9,551 | 7,136 |
| 31,450 | 31,500 | 7,762 | 6,094 | 9,575 | 7,155 |
| 31,500 | 31,550 | 7,782 | 6,110 | 9,600 | 7,174 |
| 31,550 | 31,600 | 7,802 | 6,127 | 9,624 | 7,193 |
| 31,600 | 31,650 | 7,822 | 6,143 | 9,649 | 7,212 |
| 31,650 | 31,700 | 7,842 | 6,160 | 9,673 | 7,231 |
| 31,700 | 31,750 | 7,862 | 6,176 | 9,698 | 7,250 |
| 31,750 | 31,800 | 7,882 | 6,193 | 9,722 | 7,269 |
| 31,800 | 31,850 | 7,902 | 6,209 | 9,747 | 7,288 |
| 31,850 | 31,900 | 7,922 | 6,226 | 9,771 | 7,307 |
| 31,900 | 31,950 | 7,942 | 6,242 | 9,796 | 7,326 |
| 31,950 | 32,000 | 7,962 | 6,259 | 9,820 | 7,345 |
| **32,000** | | | | | |
| 32,000 | 32,050 | 7,982 | 6,275 | 9,845 | 7,364 |
| 32,050 | 32,100 | 8,002 | 6,292 | 9,869 | 7,383 |
| 32,100 | 32,150 | 8,022 | 6,308 | 9,894 | 7,402 |
| 32,150 | 32,200 | 8,042 | 6,325 | 9,918 | 7,421 |
| 32,200 | 32,250 | 8,062 | 6,341 | 9,943 | 7,440 |
| 32,250 | 32,300 | 8,082 | 6,358 | 9,967 | 7,459 |
| 32,300 | 32,350 | 8,102 | 6,374 | 9,992 | 7,478 |
| 32,350 | 32,400 | 8,122 | 6,391 | 10,016 | 7,497 |
| 32,400 | 32,450 | 8,142 | 6,407 | 10,041 | 7,516 |
| 32,450 | 32,500 | 8,162 | 6,424 | 10,065 | 7,535 |
| 32,500 | 32,550 | 8,182 | 6,440 | 10,090 | 7,554 |
| 32,550 | 32,600 | 8,202 | 6,457 | 10,114 | 7,573 |
| 32,600 | 32,650 | 8,222 | 6,473 | 10,139 | 7,592 |
| 32,650 | 32,700 | 8,242 | 6,490 | 10,163 | 7,611 |
| 32,700 | 32,750 | 8,262 | 6,506 | 10,188 | 7,630 |

*This column must also be used by a qualifying widow(er).

Continued on next page

## 1982 Tax Table (Continued)

| If line 37 (taxable income) is— At least | But less than | And you are— Single | Married filing jointly * | Married filing separately | Head of a household |
|---|---|---|---|---|---|
| 32,750 | 32,800 | 8,282 | 6,523 | 10,212 | 7,649 |
| 32,800 | 32,850 | 8,302 | 6,539 | 10,237 | 7,668 |
| 32,850 | 32,900 | 8,322 | 6,556 | 10,261 | 7,687 |
| 32,900 | 32,950 | 8,342 | 6,572 | 10,286 | 7,706 |
| 32,950 | 33,000 | 8,362 | 6,589 | 10,310 | 7,725 |
| **33,000** | | | | | |
| 33,000 | 33,050 | 8,382 | 6,605 | 10,335 | 7,744 |
| 33,050 | 33,100 | 8,402 | 6,622 | 10,359 | 7,763 |
| 33,100 | 33,150 | 8,422 | 6,638 | 10,384 | 7,782 |
| 33,150 | 33,200 | 8,442 | 6,655 | 10,408 | 7,801 |
| 33,200 | 33,250 | 8,462 | 6,671 | 10,433 | 7,820 |
| 33,250 | 33,300 | 8,482 | 6,688 | 10,457 | 7,839 |
| 33,300 | 33,350 | 8,502 | 6,704 | 10,482 | 7,858 |
| 33,350 | 33,400 | 8,522 | 6,721 | 10,506 | 7,877 |
| 33,400 | 33,450 | 8,542 | 6,737 | 10,531 | 7,896 |
| 33,450 | 33,500 | 8,562 | 6,754 | 10,555 | 7,915 |
| 33,500 | 33,550 | 8,582 | 6,770 | 10,580 | 7,934 |
| 33,550 | 33,600 | 8,602 | 6,787 | 10,604 | 7,953 |
| 33,600 | 33,650 | 8,622 | 6,803 | 10,629 | 7,972 |
| 33,650 | 33,700 | 8,642 | 6,820 | 10,653 | 7,991 |
| 33,700 | 33,750 | 8,662 | 6,836 | 10,678 | 8,010 |
| 33,750 | 33,800 | 8,682 | 6,853 | 10,702 | 8,029 |
| 33,800 | 33,850 | 8,702 | 6,869 | 10,727 | 8,048 |
| 33,850 | 33,900 | 8,722 | 6,886 | 10,751 | 8,067 |
| 33,900 | 33,950 | 8,742 | 6,902 | 10,776 | 8,086 |
| 33,950 | 34,000 | 8,762 | 6,919 | 10,800 | 8,105 |
| **34,000** | | | | | |
| 34,000 | 34,050 | 8,782 | 6,935 | 10,825 | 8,124 |
| 34,050 | 34,100 | 8,802 | 6,952 | 10,849 | 8,143 |
| 34,100 | 34,150 | 8,823 | 6,968 | 10,874 | 8,162 |
| 34,150 | 34,200 | 8,845 | 6,985 | 10,898 | 8,183 |
| 34,200 | 34,250 | 8,867 | 7,001 | 10,923 | 8,203 |
| 34,250 | 34,300 | 8,889 | 7,018 | 10,947 | 8,224 |
| 34,300 | 34,350 | 8,911 | 7,034 | 10,972 | 8,244 |
| 34,350 | 34,400 | 8,933 | 7,051 | 10,996 | 8,265 |
| 34,400 | 34,450 | 8,955 | 7,067 | 11,021 | 8,285 |
| 34,450 | 34,500 | 8,977 | 7,084 | 11,045 | 8,306 |
| 34,500 | 34,550 | 8,999 | 7,100 | 11,070 | 8,326 |
| 34,550 | 34,600 | 9,021 | 7,117 | 11,094 | 8,347 |
| 34,600 | 34,650 | 9,043 | 7,133 | 11,119 | 8,367 |
| 34,650 | 34,700 | 9,065 | 7,150 | 11,143 | 8,388 |
| 34,700 | 34,750 | 9,087 | 7,166 | 11,168 | 8,408 |
| 34,750 | 34,800 | 9,109 | 7,183 | 11,192 | 8,429 |
| 34,800 | 34,850 | 9,131 | 7,199 | 11,217 | 8,449 |
| 34,850 | 34,900 | 9,153 | 7,216 | 11,241 | 8,470 |
| 34,900 | 34,950 | 9,175 | 7,232 | 11,266 | 8,490 |
| 34,950 | 35,000 | 9,197 | 7,249 | 11,290 | 8,511 |
| **35,000** | | | | | |
| 35,000 | 35,050 | 9,219 | 7,265 | 11,315 | 8,531 |
| 35,050 | 35,100 | 9,241 | 7,282 | 11,339 | 8,552 |
| 35,100 | 35,150 | 9,263 | 7,298 | 11,364 | 8,572 |
| 35,150 | 35,200 | 9,285 | 7,315 | 11,388 | 8,593 |
| 35,200 | 35,250 | 9,307 | 7,333 | 11,413 | 8,613 |
| 35,250 | 35,300 | 9,329 | 7,352 | 11,437 | 8,634 |
| 35,300 | 35,350 | 9,351 | 7,372 | 11,462 | 8,654 |
| 35,350 | 35,400 | 9,373 | 7,391 | 11,486 | 8,675 |
| 35,400 | 35,450 | 9,395 | 7,411 | 11,511 | 8,695 |
| 35,450 | 35,500 | 9,417 | 7,430 | 11,535 | 8,716 |
| 35,500 | 35,550 | 9,439 | 7,450 | 11,560 | 8,736 |
| 35,550 | 35,600 | 9,461 | 7,469 | 11,584 | 8,757 |
| 35,600 | 35,650 | 9,483 | 7,489 | 11,609 | 8,777 |
| 35,650 | 35,700 | 9,505 | 7,508 | 11,633 | 8,798 |
| 35,700 | 35,750 | 9,527 | 7,528 | 11,658 | 8,818 |
| 35,750 | 35,800 | 9,549 | 7,547 | 11,682 | 8,839 |
| 35,800 | 35,850 | 9,571 | 7,567 | 11,707 | 8,859 |
| 35,850 | 35,900 | 9,593 | 7,586 | 11,731 | 8,880 |
| 35,900 | 35,950 | 9,615 | 7,606 | 11,756 | 8,900 |
| 35,950 | 36,000 | 9,637 | 7,625 | 11,780 | 8,921 |
| **36,000** | | | | | |
| 36,000 | 36,050 | 9,659 | 7,645 | 11,805 | 8,941 |
| 36,050 | 36,100 | 9,681 | 7,664 | 11,829 | 8,962 |
| 36,100 | 36,150 | 9,703 | 7,684 | 11,854 | 8,982 |
| 36,150 | 36,200 | 9,725 | 7,703 | 11,878 | 9,003 |
| 36,200 | 36,250 | 9,747 | 7,723 | 11,903 | 9,023 |
| 36,250 | 36,300 | 9,769 | 7,742 | 11,927 | 9,044 |
| 36,300 | 36,350 | 9,791 | 7,762 | 11,952 | 9,064 |
| 36,350 | 36,400 | 9,813 | 7,781 | 11,976 | 9,085 |
| 36,400 | 36,450 | 9,835 | 7,801 | 12,001 | 9,105 |
| 36,450 | 36,500 | 9,857 | 7,820 | 12,025 | 9,126 |
| 36,500 | 36,550 | 9,879 | 7,840 | 12,050 | 9,146 |
| 36,550 | 36,600 | 9,901 | 7,859 | 12,074 | 9,167 |
| 36,600 | 36,650 | 9,923 | 7,879 | 12,099 | 9,187 |
| 36,650 | 36,700 | 9,945 | 7,898 | 12,123 | 9,208 |
| 36,700 | 36,750 | 9,967 | 7,918 | 12,148 | 9,228 |
| 36,750 | 36,800 | 9,989 | 7,937 | 12,172 | 9,249 |
| 36,800 | 36,850 | 10,011 | 7,957 | 12,197 | 9,269 |
| 36,850 | 36,900 | 10,033 | 7,976 | 12,221 | 9,290 |
| 36,900 | 36,950 | 10,055 | 7,996 | 12,246 | 9,310 |
| 36,950 | 37,000 | 10,077 | 8,015 | 12,270 | 9,331 |
| **37,000** | | | | | |
| 37,000 | 37,050 | 10,099 | 8,035 | 12,295 | 9,351 |
| 37,050 | 37,100 | 10,121 | 8,054 | 12,319 | 9,372 |
| 37,100 | 37,150 | 10,143 | 8,074 | 12,344 | 9,392 |
| 37,150 | 37,200 | 10,165 | 8,093 | 12,368 | 9,413 |
| 37,200 | 37,250 | 10,187 | 8,113 | 12,393 | 9,433 |
| 37,250 | 37,300 | 10,209 | 8,132 | 12,417 | 9,454 |
| 37,300 | 37,350 | 10,231 | 8,152 | 12,442 | 9,474 |
| 37,350 | 37,400 | 10,253 | 8,171 | 12,466 | 9,495 |
| 37,400 | 37,450 | 10,275 | 8,191 | 12,491 | 9,515 |
| 37,450 | 37,500 | 10,297 | 8,210 | 12,515 | 9,536 |
| 37,500 | 37,550 | 10,319 | 8,230 | 12,540 | 9,556 |
| 37,550 | 37,600 | 10,341 | 8,249 | 12,564 | 9,577 |
| 37,600 | 37,650 | 10,363 | 8,269 | 12,589 | 9,597 |
| 37,650 | 37,700 | 10,385 | 8,288 | 12,613 | 9,618 |
| 37,700 | 37,750 | 10,407 | 8,308 | 12,638 | 9,638 |
| 37,750 | 37,800 | 10,429 | 8,327 | 12,662 | 9,659 |
| 37,800 | 37,850 | 10,451 | 8,347 | 12,687 | 9,679 |
| 37,850 | 37,900 | 10,473 | 8,366 | 12,711 | 9,700 |
| 37,900 | 37,950 | 10,495 | 8,386 | 12,736 | 9,720 |
| 37,950 | 38,000 | 10,517 | 8,405 | 12,760 | 9,741 |
| **38,000** | | | | | |
| 38,000 | 38,050 | 10,539 | 8,425 | 12,785 | 9,761 |
| 38,050 | 38,100 | 10,561 | 8,444 | 12,809 | 9,782 |
| 38,100 | 38,150 | 10,583 | 8,464 | 12,834 | 9,802 |
| 38,150 | 38,200 | 10,605 | 8,483 | 12,858 | 9,823 |
| 38,200 | 38,250 | 10,627 | 8,503 | 12,883 | 9,843 |
| 38,250 | 38,300 | 10,649 | 8,522 | 12,907 | 9,864 |
| 38,300 | 38,350 | 10,671 | 8,542 | 12,932 | 9,884 |
| 38,350 | 38,400 | 10,693 | 8,561 | 12,956 | 9,905 |
| 38,400 | 38,450 | 10,715 | 8,581 | 12,981 | 9,925 |
| 38,450 | 38,500 | 10,737 | 8,600 | 13,005 | 9,946 |
| 38,500 | 38,550 | 10,759 | 8,620 | 13,030 | 9,966 |
| 38,550 | 38,600 | 10,781 | 8,639 | 13,054 | 9,987 |
| 38,600 | 38,650 | 10,803 | 8,659 | 13,079 | 10,007 |
| 38,650 | 38,700 | 10,825 | 8,678 | 13,103 | 10,028 |
| 38,700 | 38,750 | 10,847 | 8,698 | 13,128 | 10,048 |
| 38,750 | 38,800 | 10,869 | 8,717 | 13,152 | 10,069 |
| 38,800 | 38,850 | 10,891 | 8,737 | 13,177 | 10,089 |
| 38,850 | 38,900 | 10,913 | 8,756 | 13,201 | 10,110 |
| 38,900 | 38,950 | 10,935 | 8,776 | 13,226 | 10,130 |
| 38,950 | 39,000 | 10,957 | 8,795 | 13,250 | 10,151 |
| **39,000** | | | | | |
| 39,000 | 39,050 | 10,979 | 8,815 | 13,275 | 10,171 |
| 39,050 | 39,100 | 11,001 | 8,834 | 13,299 | 10,192 |
| 39,100 | 39,150 | 11,023 | 8,854 | 13,324 | 10,212 |
| 39,150 | 39,200 | 11,045 | 8,873 | 13,348 | 10,233 |
| 39,200 | 39,250 | 11,067 | 8,893 | 13,373 | 10,253 |
| 39,250 | 39,300 | 11,089 | 8,912 | 13,397 | 10,274 |
| 39,300 | 39,350 | 11,111 | 8,932 | 13,422 | 10,294 |
| 39,350 | 39,400 | 11,133 | 8,951 | 13,446 | 10,315 |
| 39,400 | 39,450 | 11,155 | 8,971 | 13,471 | 10,335 |
| 39,450 | 39,500 | 11,177 | 8,990 | 13,495 | 10,356 |
| 39,500 | 39,550 | 11,199 | 9,010 | 13,520 | 10,376 |
| 39,550 | 39,600 | 11,221 | 9,029 | 13,544 | 10,397 |
| 39,600 | 39,650 | 11,243 | 9,049 | 13,569 | 10,417 |
| 39,650 | 39,700 | 11,265 | 9,068 | 13,593 | 10,438 |
| 39,700 | 39,750 | 11,287 | 9,088 | 13,618 | 10,458 |
| 39,750 | 39,800 | 11,309 | 9,107 | 13,642 | 10,479 |
| 39,800 | 39,850 | 11,331 | 9,127 | 13,667 | 10,499 |
| 39,850 | 39,900 | 11,353 | 9,146 | 13,691 | 10,520 |
| 39,900 | 39,950 | 11,375 | 9,166 | 13,716 | 10,540 |
| 39,950 | 40,000 | 11,397 | 9,185 | 13,740 | 10,561 |
| **40,000** | | | | | |
| 40,000 | 40,050 | 11,419 | 9,205 | 13,765 | 10,581 |
| 40,050 | 40,100 | 11,441 | 9,224 | 13,789 | 10,602 |
| 40,100 | 40,150 | 11,463 | 9,244 | 13,814 | 10,622 |
| 40,150 | 40,200 | 11,485 | 9,263 | 13,838 | 10,643 |
| 40,200 | 40,250 | 11,507 | 9,283 | 13,863 | 10,663 |
| 40,250 | 40,300 | 11,529 | 9,302 | 13,887 | 10,684 |
| 40,300 | 40,350 | 11,551 | 9,322 | 13,912 | 10,704 |
| 40,350 | 40,400 | 11,573 | 9,341 | 13,936 | 10,725 |
| 40,400 | 40,450 | 11,595 | 9,361 | 13,961 | 10,745 |
| 40,450 | 40,500 | 11,617 | 9,380 | 13,985 | 10,766 |
| 40,500 | 40,550 | 11,639 | 9,400 | 14,010 | 10,786 |
| 40,550 | 40,600 | 11,661 | 9,419 | 14,034 | 10,807 |
| 40,600 | 40,650 | 11,683 | 9,439 | 14,059 | 10,827 |
| 40,650 | 40,700 | 11,705 | 9,458 | 14,083 | 10,848 |
| 40,700 | 40,750 | 11,727 | 9,478 | 14,108 | 10,868 |
| 40,750 | 40,800 | 11,749 | 9,497 | 14,132 | 10,889 |
| 40,800 | 40,850 | 11,771 | 9,517 | 14,157 | 10,909 |
| 40,850 | 40,900 | 11,793 | 9,536 | 14,181 | 10,930 |
| 40,900 | 40,950 | 11,815 | 9,556 | 14,206 | 10,950 |
| 40,950 | 41,000 | 11,837 | 9,575 | 14,230 | 10,971 |

*This column must also be used by a qualifying widow(er).

Continued on next page

**1982 Tax Table (Continued)**

| If line 37 (taxable income) is— At least | But less than | And you are— Single | Married filing jointly * | Married filing separately | Head of a house-hold |
|---|---|---|---|---|---|
| **41,000** | | | | | |
| 41,000 | 41,050 | 11,859 | 9,595 | 14,255 | 10,991 |
| 41,050 | 41,100 | 11,881 | 9,614 | 14,279 | 11,012 |
| 41,100 | 41,150 | 11,903 | 9,634 | 14,304 | 11,032 |
| 41,150 | 41,200 | 11,925 | 9,653 | 14,328 | 11,053 |
| 41,200 | 41,250 | 11,947 | 9,673 | 14,353 | 11,073 |
| 41,250 | 41,300 | 11,969 | 9,692 | 14,377 | 11,094 |
| 41,300 | 41,350 | 11,991 | 9,712 | 14,402 | 11,114 |
| 41,350 | 41,400 | 12,013 | 9,731 | 14,426 | 11,135 |
| 41,400 | 41,450 | 12,035 | 9,751 | 14,451 | 11,155 |
| 41,450 | 41,500 | 12,057 | 9,770 | 14,475 | 11,176 |
| 41,500 | 41,550 | 12,081 | 9,790 | 14,500 | 11,196 |
| 41,550 | 41,600 | 12,106 | 9,809 | 14,524 | 11,217 |
| 41,600 | 41,650 | 12,131 | 9,829 | 14,549 | 11,237 |
| 41,650 | 41,700 | 12,156 | 9,848 | 14,573 | 11,258 |
| 41,700 | 41,750 | 12,181 | 9,868 | 14,598 | 11,278 |
| 41,750 | 41,800 | 12,206 | 9,887 | 14,622 | 11,299 |
| 41,800 | 41,850 | 12,231 | 9,907 | 14,647 | 11,319 |
| 41,850 | 41,900 | 12,256 | 9,926 | 14,671 | 11,340 |
| 41,900 | 41,950 | 12,281 | 9,946 | 14,696 | 11,360 |
| 41,950 | 42,000 | 12,306 | 9,965 | 14,720 | 11,381 |
| **42,000** | | | | | |
| 42,000 | 42,050 | 12,331 | 9,985 | 14,745 | 11,401 |
| 42,050 | 42,100 | 12,356 | 10,004 | 14,769 | 11,422 |
| 42,100 | 42,150 | 12,381 | 10,024 | 14,794 | 11,442 |
| 42,150 | 42,200 | 12,406 | 10,043 | 14,818 | 11,463 |
| 42,200 | 42,250 | 12,431 | 10,063 | 14,843 | 11,483 |
| 42,250 | 42,300 | 12,456 | 10,082 | 14,867 | 11,504 |
| 42,300 | 42,350 | 12,481 | 10,102 | 14,892 | 11,524 |
| 42,350 | 42,400 | 12,506 | 10,121 | 14,916 | 11,545 |
| 42,400 | 42,450 | 12,531 | 10,141 | 14,941 | 11,565 |
| 42,450 | 42,500 | 12,556 | 10,160 | 14,965 | 11,586 |
| 42,500 | 42,550 | 12,581 | 10,180 | 14,990 | 11,606 |
| 42,550 | 42,600 | 12,606 | 10,199 | 15,014 | 11,627 |
| 42,600 | 42,650 | 12,631 | 10,219 | 15,039 | 11,647 |
| 42,650 | 42,700 | 12,656 | 10,238 | 15,063 | 11,668 |
| 42,700 | 42,750 | 12,681 | 10,258 | 15,088 | 11,688 |
| 42,750 | 42,800 | 12,706 | 10,277 | 15,112 | 11,709 |
| 42,800 | 42,850 | 12,731 | 10,297 | 15,137 | 11,729 |
| 42,850 | 42,900 | 12,756 | 10,316 | 15,162 | 11,750 |
| 42,900 | 42,950 | 12,781 | 10,336 | 15,187 | 11,770 |
| 42,950 | 43,000 | 12,806 | 10,355 | 15,212 | 11,791 |
| **43,000** | | | | | |
| 43,000 | 43,050 | 12,831 | 10,375 | 15,237 | 11,811 |
| 43,050 | 43,100 | 12,856 | 10,394 | 15,262 | 11,832 |
| 43,100 | 43,150 | 12,881 | 10,414 | 15,287 | 11,852 |
| 43,150 | 43,200 | 12,906 | 10,433 | 15,312 | 11,873 |
| 43,200 | 43,250 | 12,931 | 10,453 | 15,337 | 11,893 |
| 43,250 | 43,300 | 12,956 | 10,472 | 15,362 | 11,914 |
| 43,300 | 43,350 | 12,981 | 10,492 | 15,387 | 11,934 |
| 43,350 | 43,400 | 13,006 | 10,511 | 15,412 | 11,955 |
| 43,400 | 43,450 | 13,031 | 10,531 | 15,437 | 11,975 |
| 43,450 | 43,500 | 13,056 | 10,550 | 15,462 | 11,996 |
| 43,500 | 43,550 | 13,081 | 10,570 | 15,487 | 12,016 |
| 43,550 | 43,600 | 13,106 | 10,589 | 15,512 | 12,037 |
| 43,600 | 43,650 | 13,131 | 10,609 | 15,537 | 12,057 |
| 43,650 | 43,700 | 13,156 | 10,628 | 15,562 | 12,078 |
| 43,700 | 43,750 | 13,181 | 10,648 | 15,587 | 12,098 |
| 43,750 | 43,800 | 13,206 | 10,667 | 15,612 | 12,119 |
| 43,800 | 43,850 | 13,231 | 10,687 | 15,637 | 12,139 |
| 43,850 | 43,900 | 13,256 | 10,706 | 15,662 | 12,160 |
| 43,900 | 43,950 | 13,281 | 10,726 | 15,687 | 12,180 |
| 43,950 | 44,000 | 13,306 | 10,745 | 15,712 | 12,201 |

| If line 37 (taxable income) is— At least | But less than | And you are— Single | Married filing jointly * | Married filing separately | Head of a house-hold |
|---|---|---|---|---|---|
| **44,000** | | | | | |
| 44,000 | 44,050 | 13,331 | 10,765 | 15,737 | 12,221 |
| 44,050 | 44,100 | 13,356 | 10,784 | 15,762 | 12,242 |
| 44,100 | 44,150 | 13,381 | 10,804 | 15,787 | 12,262 |
| 44,150 | 44,200 | 13,406 | 10,823 | 15,812 | 12,283 |
| 44,200 | 44,250 | 13,431 | 10,843 | 15,837 | 12,303 |
| 44,250 | 44,300 | 13,456 | 10,862 | 15,862 | 12,324 |
| 44,300 | 44,350 | 13,481 | 10,882 | 15,887 | 12,344 |
| 44,350 | 44,400 | 13,506 | 10,901 | 15,912 | 12,365 |
| 44,400 | 44,450 | 13,531 | 10,921 | 15,937 | 12,385 |
| 44,450 | 44,500 | 13,556 | 10,940 | 15,962 | 12,406 |
| 44,500 | 44,550 | 13,581 | 10,960 | 15,987 | 12,426 |
| 44,550 | 44,600 | 13,606 | 10,979 | 16,012 | 12,447 |
| 44,600 | 44,650 | 13,631 | 10,999 | 16,037 | 12,467 |
| 44,650 | 44,700 | 13,656 | 11,018 | 16,062 | 12,488 |
| 44,700 | 44,750 | 13,681 | 11,038 | 16,087 | 12,510 |
| 44,750 | 44,800 | 13,706 | 11,057 | 16,112 | 12,535 |
| 44,800 | 44,850 | 13,731 | 11,077 | 16,137 | 12,559 |
| 44,850 | 44,900 | 13,756 | 11,096 | 16,162 | 12,584 |
| 44,900 | 44,950 | 13,781 | 11,116 | 16,187 | 12,608 |
| 44,950 | 45,000 | 13,806 | 11,135 | 16,212 | 12,633 |
| **45,000** | | | | | |
| 45,000 | 45,050 | 13,831 | 11,155 | 16,237 | 12,657 |
| 45,050 | 45,100 | 13,856 | 11,174 | 16,262 | 12,682 |
| 45,100 | 45,150 | 13,881 | 11,194 | 16,287 | 12,706 |
| 45,150 | 45,200 | 13,906 | 11,213 | 16,312 | 12,731 |
| 45,200 | 45,250 | 13,931 | 11,233 | 16,337 | 12,755 |
| 45,250 | 45,300 | 13,956 | 11,252 | 16,362 | 12,780 |
| 45,300 | 45,350 | 13,981 | 11,272 | 16,387 | 12,804 |
| 45,350 | 45,400 | 14,006 | 11,291 | 16,412 | 12,829 |
| 45,400 | 45,450 | 14,031 | 11,311 | 16,437 | 12,853 |
| 45,450 | 45,500 | 14,056 | 11,330 | 16,462 | 12,878 |
| 45,500 | 45,550 | 14,081 | 11,350 | 16,487 | 12,902 |
| 45,550 | 45,600 | 14,106 | 11,369 | 16,512 | 12,927 |
| 45,600 | 45,650 | 14,131 | 11,389 | 16,537 | 12,951 |
| 45,650 | 45,700 | 14,156 | 11,408 | 16,562 | 12,976 |
| 45,700 | 45,750 | 14,181 | 11,428 | 16,587 | 13,000 |
| 45,750 | 45,800 | 14,206 | 11,447 | 16,612 | 13,025 |
| 45,800 | 45,850 | 14,231 | 11,468 | 16,637 | 13,049 |
| 45,850 | 45,900 | 14,256 | 11,490 | 16,662 | 13,074 |
| 45,900 | 45,950 | 14,281 | 11,512 | 16,687 | 13,098 |
| 45,950 | 46,000 | 14,306 | 11,534 | 16,712 | 13,123 |
| **46,000** | | | | | |
| 46,000 | 46,050 | 14,331 | 11,556 | 16,737 | 13,147 |
| 46,050 | 46,100 | 14,356 | 11,578 | 16,762 | 13,172 |
| 46,100 | 46,150 | 14,381 | 11,600 | 16,787 | 13,196 |
| 46,150 | 46,200 | 14,406 | 11,622 | 16,812 | 13,221 |
| 46,200 | 46,250 | 14,431 | 11,644 | 16,837 | 13,245 |
| 46,250 | 46,300 | 14,456 | 11,666 | 16,862 | 13,270 |
| 46,300 | 46,350 | 14,481 | 11,688 | 16,887 | 13,294 |
| 46,350 | 46,400 | 14,506 | 11,710 | 16,912 | 13,319 |
| 46,400 | 46,450 | 14,531 | 11,732 | 16,937 | 13,343 |
| 46,450 | 46,500 | 14,556 | 11,754 | 16,962 | 13,368 |
| 46,500 | 46,550 | 14,581 | 11,776 | 16,987 | 13,392 |
| 46,550 | 46,600 | 14,606 | 11,798 | 17,012 | 13,417 |
| 46,600 | 46,650 | 14,631 | 11,820 | 17,037 | 13,441 |
| 46,650 | 46,700 | 14,656 | 11,842 | 17,062 | 13,466 |
| 46,700 | 46,750 | 14,681 | 11,864 | 17,087 | 13,490 |
| 46,750 | 46,800 | 14,706 | 11,886 | 17,112 | 13,515 |
| 46,800 | 46,850 | 14,731 | 11,908 | 17,137 | 13,539 |
| 46,850 | 46,900 | 14,756 | 11,930 | 17,162 | 13,564 |
| 46,900 | 46,950 | 14,781 | 11,952 | 17,187 | 13,588 |
| 46,950 | 47,000 | 14,806 | 11,974 | 17,212 | 13,613 |

| If line 37 (taxable income) is— At least | But less than | And you are— Single | Married filing jointly * | Married filing separately | Head of a house-hold |
|---|---|---|---|---|---|
| **47,000** | | | | | |
| 47,000 | 47,050 | 14,831 | 11,996 | 17,237 | 13,637 |
| 47,050 | 47,100 | 14,856 | 12,018 | 17,262 | 13,662 |
| 47,100 | 47,150 | 14,881 | 12,040 | 17,287 | 13,686 |
| 47,150 | 47,200 | 14,906 | 12,062 | 17,312 | 13,711 |
| 47,200 | 47,250 | 14,931 | 12,084 | 17,337 | 13,735 |
| 47,250 | 47,300 | 14,956 | 12,106 | 17,362 | 13,760 |
| 47,300 | 47,350 | 14,981 | 12,128 | 17,387 | 13,784 |
| 47,350 | 47,400 | 15,006 | 12,150 | 17,412 | 13,809 |
| 47,400 | 47,450 | 15,031 | 12,172 | 17,437 | 13,833 |
| 47,450 | 47,500 | 15,056 | 12,194 | 17,462 | 13,858 |
| 47,500 | 47,550 | 15,081 | 12,216 | 17,487 | 13,882 |
| 47,550 | 47,600 | 15,106 | 12,238 | 17,512 | 13,907 |
| 47,600 | 47,650 | 15,131 | 12,260 | 17,537 | 13,931 |
| 47,650 | 47,700 | 15,156 | 12,282 | 17,562 | 13,956 |
| 47,700 | 47,750 | 15,181 | 12,304 | 17,587 | 13,980 |
| 47,750 | 47,800 | 15,206 | 12,326 | 17,612 | 14,005 |
| 47,800 | 47,850 | 15,231 | 12,348 | 17,637 | 14,029 |
| 47,850 | 47,900 | 15,256 | 12,370 | 17,662 | 14,054 |
| 47,900 | 47,950 | 15,281 | 12,392 | 17,687 | 14,078 |
| 47,950 | 48,000 | 15,306 | 12,414 | 17,712 | 14,103 |
| **48,000** | | | | | |
| 48,000 | 48,050 | 15,331 | 12,436 | 17,737 | 14,127 |
| 48,050 | 48,100 | 15,356 | 12,458 | 17,762 | 14,152 |
| 48,100 | 48,150 | 15,381 | 12,480 | 17,787 | 14,176 |
| 48,150 | 48,200 | 15,406 | 12,502 | 17,812 | 14,201 |
| 48,200 | 48,250 | 15,431 | 12,524 | 17,837 | 14,225 |
| 48,250 | 48,300 | 15,456 | 12,546 | 17,862 | 14,250 |
| 48,300 | 48,350 | 15,481 | 12,568 | 17,887 | 14,274 |
| 48,350 | 48,400 | 15,506 | 12,590 | 17,912 | 14,299 |
| 48,400 | 48,450 | 15,531 | 12,612 | 17,937 | 14,323 |
| 48,450 | 48,500 | 15,556 | 12,634 | 17,962 | 14,348 |
| 48,500 | 48,550 | 15,581 | 12,656 | 17,987 | 14,372 |
| 48,550 | 48,600 | 15,606 | 12,678 | 18,012 | 14,397 |
| 48,600 | 48,650 | 15,631 | 12,700 | 18,037 | 14,421 |
| 48,650 | 48,700 | 15,656 | 12,722 | 18,062 | 14,446 |
| 48,700 | 48,750 | 15,681 | 12,744 | 18,087 | 14,470 |
| 48,750 | 48,800 | 15,706 | 12,766 | 18,112 | 14,495 |
| 48,800 | 48,850 | 15,731 | 12,788 | 18,137 | 14,519 |
| 48,850 | 48,900 | 15,756 | 12,810 | 18,162 | 14,544 |
| 48,900 | 48,950 | 15,781 | 12,832 | 18,187 | 14,568 |
| 48,950 | 49,000 | 15,806 | 12,854 | 18,212 | 14,593 |
| **49,000** | | | | | |
| 49,000 | 49,050 | 15,831 | 12,876 | 18,237 | 14,617 |
| 49,050 | 49,100 | 15,856 | 12,898 | 18,262 | 14,642 |
| 49,100 | 49,150 | 15,881 | 12,920 | 18,287 | 14,666 |
| 49,150 | 49,200 | 15,906 | 12,942 | 18,312 | 14,691 |
| 49,200 | 49,250 | 15,931 | 12,964 | 18,337 | 14,715 |
| 49,250 | 49,300 | 15,956 | 12,986 | 18,362 | 14,740 |
| 49,300 | 49,350 | 15,981 | 13,008 | 18,387 | 14,764 |
| 49,350 | 49,400 | 16,006 | 13,030 | 18,412 | 14,789 |
| 49,400 | 49,450 | 16,031 | 13,052 | 18,437 | 14,813 |
| 49,450 | 49,500 | 16,056 | 13,074 | 18,462 | 14,838 |
| 49,500 | 49,550 | 16,081 | 13,096 | 18,487 | 14,862 |
| 49,550 | 49,600 | 16,106 | 13,118 | 18,512 | 14,887 |
| 49,600 | 49,650 | 16,131 | 13,140 | 18,537 | 14,911 |
| 49,650 | 49,700 | 16,156 | 13,162 | 18,562 | 14,936 |
| 49,700 | 49,750 | 16,181 | 13,184 | 18,587 | 14,960 |
| 49,750 | 49,800 | 16,206 | 13,206 | 18,612 | 14,985 |
| 49,800 | 49,850 | 16,231 | 13,228 | 18,637 | 15,009 |
| 49,850 | 49,900 | 16,256 | 13,250 | 18,662 | 15,034 |
| 49,900 | 49,950 | 16,281 | 13,272 | 18,687 | 15,058 |
| 49,950 | 50,000 | 16,306 | 13,294 | 18,712 | 15,083 |

*This column must also be used by a qualifying widow(er).

**50,000 or over**—use tax rate schedules

# A–3 UNIFIED TRANSFER TAX RATE SCHEDULE

## For Gifts Made and For Deaths After 1976 and Before 1982

| If the amount with respect to which the tentative tax to be computed is: | The tentative tax is: |
|---|---|
| Not over $10,000 | 18 percent of such amount. |
| Over $10,000 but not over $20,000 | $1,800, plus 20 percent of the excess of such amount over $10,000. |
| Over $20,000 but not over $40,000 | $3,800, plus 22 percent of the excess of such amount over $20,000. |
| Over $40,000 but not over $60,000 | $8,200, plus 24 percent of the excess of such amount over $40,000. |
| Over $60,000 but not over $80,000 | $13,000, plus 26 percent of the excess of such amount over $60,000. |
| Over $80,000 but not over $100,000 | $18,200, plus 28 percent of the excess of such amount over $80,000. |
| Over $100,000 but not over $150,000 | $23,800, plus 30 percent of the excess of such amount over $100,000. |
| Over $150,000 but not over $250,000 | $38,800, plus 32 percent of the excess of such amount over $150,000. |
| Over $250,000 but not over $500,000 | $70,800, plus 34 percent of the excess of such amount over $250,000. |
| Over $500,000 but not over $750,000 | $155,800, plus 37 percent of the excess of such amount over $500,000. |
| Over $750,000 but not over $1,000,000 | $248,300, plus 39 percent of the excess of such amount over $750,000. |
| Over $1,000,000 but not over $1,250,000 | $345,800, plus 41 percent of the excess of such amount over $1,000,000. |
| Over $1,250,000 but not over $1,500,000 | $448,300, plus 43 percent of the excess of such amount over $1,250,000. |
| Over $1,500,000 but not over $2,000,000 | $555,800, plus 45 percent of the excess of such amount over $1,500,000. |
| Over $2,000,000 but not over $2,500,000 | $780,800, plus 49 percent of the excess of such amount over $2,000,000. |
| Over $2,500,000 but not over $3,000,000 | $1,025,800, plus 53 percent of the excess of such amount over $2,500,000. |
| Over $3,000,000 but not over $3,500,000 | $1,290,800, plus 57 percent of the excess of such amount over $3,000,000. |
| Over $3,500,000 but not over $4,000,000 | $1,575,800, plus 61 percent of the excess of such amount over $3,500,000. |
| Over $4,000,000 but not over $4,500,000 | $1,880,800, plus 65 percent over the excess of such amount over $4,000,000. |
| Over $4,500,000 but not over $5,000,000 | $2,205,800, plus 69 percent of the excess of such amount over $4,500,000. |
| Over $5,000,000 | $2,550,800, plus 70 percent of the excess of such amount over $5,000,000. |

# UNIFIED TRANSFER TAX RATE SCHEDULE

## For Gifts Made and For Deaths in 1982

| If the amount with respect to which the tentative tax to be computed is: | The tentative tax is: |
|---|---|
| Not over $10,000 | 18 percent of such amount. |
| Over $10,000 but not over $20,000 | $1,800, plus 20 percent of the excess of such amount over $10,000. |
| Over $20,000 but not over $40,000 | $3,800, plus 22 percent of the excess of such amount over $20,000. |
| Over $40,000 but not over $60,000 | $8,200, plus 24 percent of the excess of such amount over $40,000. |
| Over $60,000 but not over $80,000 | $13,000, plus 26 percent of the excess of such amount over $60,000. |
| Over $80,000 but not over $100,000 | $18,200, plus 28 percent of the excess of such amount over $80,000. |
| Over $100,000 but not over $150,000 | $23,800, plus 30 percent of the excess of such amount over $100,000. |
| Over $150,000 but not over $250,000 | $38,800, plus 32 percent of the excess of such amount over $150,000. |
| Over $250,000 but not over $500,000 | $70,800, plus 34 percent of the excess of such amount over $250,000. |
| Over $500,000 but not over $750,000 | $155,800, plus 37 percent of the excess of such amount over $500,000. |
| Over $750,000 but not over $1,000,000 | $248,300, plus 39 percent of the excess of such amount over $750,000. |
| Over $1,000,000 but not over $1,250,000 | $345,800, plus 41 percent of the excess of such amount over $1,000,000. |
| Over $1,250,000 but not over $1,500,000 | $448,300, plus 43 percent of the excess of such amount over $1,250,000. |
| Over $1,500,000 but not over $2,000,000 | $555,800, plus 45 percent of the excess of such amount over $1,500,000. |
| Over $2,000,000 but not over $2,500,000 | $780,800, plus 49 percent of the excess of such amount over $2,000,000. |
| Over $2,500,000 but not over $3,000,000 | $1,025,800, plus 53 percent of the excess of such amount over $2,500,000. |
| Over $3,000,000 but not over $3,500,000 | $1,290,800, plus 57 percent of the excess of such amount over $3,000,000. |
| Over $3,500,000 but not over $4,000,000 | $1,575,800, plus 61 percent of the excess of such amount over $3,500,000. |
| Over $4,000,000 | $1,880,800, plus 65 percent of the excess of such amount over $4,000,000. |

# UNIFIED TRANSFER TAX RATE SCHEDULE

## For Gifts Made and For Deaths in 1983

| If the amount with respect to which the tentative tax to be computed is: | The tentative tax is: |
| --- | --- |
| Not over $10,000 | 18 percent of such amount. |
| Over $10,000 but not over $20,000 | $1,800, plus 20 percent of the excess of such amount over $10,000. |
| Over $20,000 but not over $40,000 | $3,800, plus 22 percent of the excess of such amount over $20,000. |
| Over $40,000 but not over $60,000 | $8,200, plus 24 percent of the excess of such amount over $40,000. |
| Over $60,000 but not over $80,000 | $13,000, plus 26 percent of the excess of such amount over $60,000. |
| Over $80,000 but not over $100,000 | $18,200, plus 28 percent of the excess of such amount over $80,000. |
| Over $100,000 but not over $150,000 | $23,800, plus 30 percent of the excess of such amount over $100,000. |
| Over $150,000 but not over $250,000 | $38,800, plus 32 percent of the excess of such amount over $150,000. |
| Over $250,000 but not over $500,000 | $70,800, plus 34 percent of the excess of such amount over $250,000. |
| Over $500,000 but not over $750,000 | $155,800, plus 37 percent of the excess of such amount over $500,000. |
| Over $750,000 but not over $1,000,000 | $248,300, plus 39 percent of the excess of such amount over $750,000. |
| Over $1,000,000 but not over $1,250,000 | $345,800, plus 41 percent of the excess of such amount over $1,000,000. |
| Over $1,250,000 but not over $1,500,000 | $448,300, plus 43 percent of the excess of such amount over $1,250,000. |
| Over $1,500,000 but not over $2,000,000 | $555,800, plus 45 percent of the excess of such amount over $1,500,000. |
| Over $2,000,000 but not over $2,500,000 | $780,800, plus 49 percent of the excess of such amount over $2,000,000. |
| Over $2,500,000 but not over $3,000,000 | $1,025,800, plus 53 percent of the excess of such amount over $2,500,000. |
| Over $3,000,000 but not over $3,500,000 | $1,290,800, plus 57 percent of the excess of such amount over $3,000,000. |
| Over $3,500,000 | $1,575,800, plus 60 percent of the excess of such amount over $3,500,000. |

# UNIFIED TRANSFER TAX RATE SCHEDULE

## For Gifts Made and For Deaths in 1984

| If the amount with respect to which the tentative tax to be computed is: | The tentative tax is: |
|---|---|
| Not over $10,000 | 18 percent of such amount. |
| Over $10,000 but not over $20,000 | $1,800, plus 20 percent of the excess of such amount over $10,000. |
| Over $20,000 but not over $40,000 | $3,800, plus 22 percent of the excess of such amount over $20,000. |
| Over $40,000 but not over $60,000 | $8,200, plus 24 percent of the excess of such amount over $40,000. |
| Over $60,000 but not over $80,000 | $13,000, plus 26 percent of the excess of such amount over $60,000. |
| Over $80,000 but not over $100,000 | $18,200, plus 28 percent of the excess of such amount over $80,000. |
| Over $100,000 but not over $150,000 | $23,800, plus 30 percent of the excess of such amount over $100,000. |
| Over $150,000 but not over $250,000 | $38,800, plus 32 percent of the excess of such amount over $150,000. |
| Over $250,000 but not over $500,000 | $70,800, plus 34 percent of the excess of such amount over $250,000. |
| Over $500,000 but not over $750,000 | $155,800, plus 37 percent of the excess of such amount over $500,000. |
| Over $750,000 but not over $1,000,000 | $248,300, plus 39 percent of the excess of such amount over $750,000. |
| Over $1,000,000 but not over $1,250,000 | $345,800, plus 41 percent of the excess of such amount over $1,000,000. |
| Over $1,250,000 but not over $1,500,000 | $448,300, plus 43 percent of the excess of such amount over $1,250,000. |
| Over $1,500,000 but not over $2,000,000 | $555,800, plus 45 percent of the excess of such amount over $1,500,000. |
| Over $2,000,000 but not over $2,500,000 | $780,800, plus 49 percent of the excess of such amount over $2,000,000. |
| Over $2,500,000 but not over $3,000,000 | $1,025,800, plus 53 percent of the excess of such amount over $2,500,000. |
| Over $3,000,000 | $1,290,800, plus 55 percent of the excess of such amount over $3,000,000. |

# UNIFIED TRANSFER TAX RATE SCHEDULE

## For Gifts Made and For Deaths After 1984

| If the amount with respect to which the tentative tax to be computed is: | The tentative tax is: |
|---|---|
| Not over $10,000 | 18 percent of such amount. |
| Over $10,000 but not over $20,000 | $1,800, plus 20 percent of the excess of such amount over $10,000. |
| Over $20,000 but not over $40,000 | $3,800, plus 22 percent of the excess of such amount over $20,000. |
| Over $40,000 but not over $60,000 | $8,200, plus 24 percent of the excess of such amount over $40,000. |
| Over $60,000 but not over $80,000 | $13,000, plus 26 percent of the excess of such amount over $60,000. |
| Over $80,000 but not over $100,000 | $18,200, plus 28 percent of the excess of such amount over $80,000. |
| Over $100,000 but not over $150,000 | $23,800, plus 30 percent of the excess of such amount over $100,000. |
| Over $150,000 but not over $250,000 | $38,800, plus 32 percent of the excess of such amount over $150,000. |
| Over $250,000 but not over $500,000 | $70,800, plus 34 percent of the excess of such amount over $250,000. |
| Over $500,000 but not over $750,000 | $155,800, plus 37 percent of the excess of such amount over $500,000. |
| Over $750,000 but not over $1,000,000 | $248,300, plus 39 percent of the excess of such amount over $750,000. |
| Over $1,000,000 but not over $1,250,000 | $345,800, plus 41 percent of the excess of such amount over $1,000,000. |
| Over $1,250,000 but not over $1,500,000 | $448,300, plus 43 percent of the excess of such amount over $1,250,000. |
| Over $1,500,000 but not over $2,000,000 | $555,800, plus 45 percent of the excess of such amount over $1,500,000. |
| Over $2,000,000 but not over $2,500,000 | $780,800, plus 49 percent of the excess of such amount over $2,000,000. |
| Over $2,500,000 | $1,025,800, plus 50 percent of the excess of such amount over $2,500,000. |

# A–4 1982 OPTIONAL STATE SALES TAX TABLES

## 1982 Optional State Sales Tax Tables

Your itemized deduction for general sales tax paid can be estimated from these tables plus any qualifying sales taxes paid on the items listed on page 18.
To use the tables:

**Step 1**—Figure your total available income. (See note to the right).

**Step 2**—Count the number of exemptions for you and your family. Do not count exemptions claimed for being 65 or over or blind as part of your family size.

**Step 3 A**—If your total available income is not over $40,000, find the income line for your State on the tables and read across to find the amount of sales tax for your family size.

**Step 3 B**—If your income is over $40,000 but not over $100,000, find the deduction listed on the income line "$38,001–$40,000" for your family size and State. For each $5,000 (or part of $5,000) of income over $40,000, increase the deduction by the amount listed for the line "$40,001–$100,000."

**Step 3 C**—If your income is over $100,000, your sales tax deduction is limited to the deduction for income of $100,000. To figure your

(If you kept records that show you paid more sales tax than the table for your State indicates, you may claim the higher amount on Schedule A, line 13a.)

sales tax deduction, use Step 3 B but don't go over $100,000.

**Note:** Use the total of the amount on Form 1040, line 33, and nontaxable receipts such as social security, veterans', and railroad retirement benefits, workmen's compensation, untaxed portion of long-term capital gains or unemployment compensation, All-Savers interest exclusion, dividends exclusion, disability income exclusion, deduction for a married couple when both work, and public assistance payments.

### Alabama [1]

| Income | 1 | 2 | 3 | 4 | 5 | Over 5 |
|---|---|---|---|---|---|---|
| $1-$8,000 | 93 | 115 | 122 | 131 | 142 | 160 |
| $8,001-$10,000 | 109 | 132 | 142 | 153 | 165 | 185 |
| $10,001-$12,000 | 124 | 147 | 161 | 173 | 187 | 208 |
| $12,001-$14,000 | 138 | 161 | 178 | 191 | 206 | 228 |
| $14,001-$16,000 | 152 | 174 | 194 | 209 | 225 | 248 |
| $16,001-$18,000 | 164 | 186 | 210 | 226 | 242 | 266 |
| $18,001-$20,000 | 176 | 197 | 225 | 242 | 259 | 284 |
| $20,001-$22,000 | 188 | 208 | 239 | 257 | 275 | 301 |
| $22,001-$24,000 | 199 | 218 | 253 | 271 | 290 | 317 |
| $24,001-$26,000 | 210 | 228 | 266 | 285 | 305 | 332 |
| $26,001-$28,000 | 221 | 238 | 279 | 299 | 320 | 347 |
| $28,001-$30,000 | 231 | 247 | 291 | 313 | 334 | 362 |
| $30,001-$32,000 | 241 | 256 | 303 | 326 | 347 | 376 |
| $32,001-$34,000 | 251 | 265 | 315 | 338 | 360 | 390 |
| $34,001-$36,000 | 261 | 274 | 327 | 350 | 373 | 403 |
| $36,001-$38,000 | 271 | 282 | 338 | 362 | 386 | 416 |
| $38,001-$40,000 | 280 | 290 | 349 | 374 | 399 | 429 |
| $40,001-$100,000 (See Step 3B) | 14 | 15 | 17 | 19 | 20 | 21 |

### Arizona [2]

| Income | 1&2 | 3 | 4 | 5 | Over 5 |
|---|---|---|---|---|---|
| $1-$8,000 | 90 | 104 | 104 | 109 | 114 |
| $8,001-$10,000 | 105 | 122 | 122 | 129 | 134 |
| $10,001-$12,000 | 120 | 139 | 140 | 147 | 153 |
| $12,001-$14,000 | 133 | 155 | 157 | 165 | 170 |
| $14,001-$16,000 | 146 | 170 | 174 | 181 | 187 |
| $16,001-$18,000 | 158 | 184 | 190 | 197 | 203 |
| $18,001-$20,000 | 170 | 198 | 206 | 212 | 218 |
| $20,001-$22,000 | 181 | 211 | 221 | 226 | 233 |
| $22,001-$24,000 | 192 | 224 | 235 | 240 | 247 |
| $24,001-$26,000 | 203 | 236 | 249 | 254 | 261 |
| $26,001-$28,000 | 213 | 248 | 263 | 267 | 275 |
| $28,001-$30,000 | 223 | 260 | 277 | 280 | 288 |
| $30,001-$32,000 | 233 | 271 | 290 | 293 | 301 |
| $32,001-$34,000 | 242 | 282 | 303 | 305 | 313 |
| $34,001-$36,000 | 251 | 293 | 316 | 317 | 325 |
| $36,001-$38,000 | 260 | 304 | 329 | 329 | 337 |
| $38,001-$40,000 | 269 | 315 | 341 | 341 | 349 |
| $40,001-$100,000 (See Step 3B) | 13 | 16 | 17 | 17 | 17 |

### Arkansas [1]

| Income | 1 | 2 | 3 | 4 | 5 | Over 5 |
|---|---|---|---|---|---|---|
| $1-$8,000 | 78 | 97 | 102 | 109 | 116 | 132 |
| $8,001-$10,000 | 91 | 111 | 118 | 127 | 135 | 152 |
| $10,001-$12,000 | 103 | 123 | 134 | 143 | 153 | 170 |
| $12,001-$14,000 | 115 | 134 | 148 | 158 | 169 | 187 |
| $14,001-$16,000 | 125 | 145 | 161 | 173 | 184 | 202 |
| $16,001-$18,000 | 135 | 154 | 174 | 186 | 198 | 217 |
| $18,001-$20,000 | 145 | 163 | 186 | 199 | 212 | 231 |
| $20,001-$22,000 | 154 | 172 | 198 | 212 | 225 | 245 |
| $22,001-$24,000 | 163 | 181 | 209 | 224 | 238 | 258 |
| $24,001-$26,000 | 172 | 189 | 220 | 235 | 250 | 270 |
| $26,001-$28,000 | 180 | 197 | 230 | 246 | 262 | 282 |
| $28,001-$30,000 | 188 | 204 | 240 | 257 | 273 | 294 |
| $30,001-$32,000 | 196 | 211 | 250 | 268 | 284 | 305 |
| $32,001-$34,000 | 204 | 218 | 260 | 278 | 295 | 316 |
| $34,001-$36,000 | 211 | 225 | 270 | 288 | 306 | 326 |
| $36,001-$38,000 | 218 | 232 | 279 | 298 | 316 | 336 |
| $38,001-$40,000 | 225 | 239 | 288 | 308 | 326 | 346 |
| $40,001-$100,000 (See Step 3B) | 11 | 12 | 14 | 15 | 16 | 17 |

### California [3]

| Income | 1&2 | 3&4 | 5 | Over 5 |
|---|---|---|---|---|
| $1-$8,000 | 125 | 147 | 155 | 164 |
| $8,001-$10,000 | 147 | 173 | 183 | 193 |
| $10,001-$12,000 | 167 | 198 | 208 | 219 |
| $12,001-$14,000 | 186 | 220 | 232 | 243 |
| $14,001-$16,000 | 204 | 242 | 255 | 266 |
| $16,001-$18,000 | 222 | 263 | 276 | 288 |
| $18,001-$20,000 | 238 | 282 | 297 | 309 |
| $20,001-$22,000 | 254 | 301 | 317 | 330 |
| $22,001-$24,000 | 270 | 320 | 336 | 349 |
| $24,001-$26,000 | 285 | 338 | 355 | 368 |
| $26,001-$28,000 | 299 | 355 | 373 | 386 |
| $28,001-$30,000 | 313 | 372 | 391 | 404 |
| $30,001-$32,000 | 327 | 389 | 408 | 422 |
| $32,001-$34,000 | 341 | 405 | 425 | 439 |
| $34,001-$36,000 | 354 | 421 | 441 | 455 |
| $36,001-$38,000 | 367 | 436 | 457 | 471 |
| $38,001-$40,000 | 380 | 451 | 473 | 487 |
| $40,001-$100,000 (See Step 3B) | 19 | 23 | 24 | 24 |

### Colorado [2]

| Income | 1&2 | 3,4&5 | Over 5 |
|---|---|---|---|
| $1-$8,000 | 53 | 59 | 63 |
| $8,001-$10,000 | 63 | 71 | 75 |
| $10,001-$12,000 | 73 | 82 | 87 |
| $12,001-$14,000 | 82 | 93 | 98 |
| $14,001-$16,000 | 91 | 104 | 109 |
| $16,001-$18,000 | 99 | 114 | 120 |
| $18,001-$20,000 | 107 | 124 | 130 |
| $20,001-$22,000 | 115 | 134 | 140 |
| $22,001-$24,000 | 122 | 143 | 150 |
| $24,001-$26,000 | 129 | 152 | 159 |
| $26,001-$28,000 | 136 | 161 | 168 |
| $28,001-$30,000 | 143 | 169 | 177 |
| $30,001-$32,000 | 150 | 178 | 186 |
| $32,001-$34,000 | 157 | 187 | 195 |
| $34,001-$36,000 | 164 | 195 | 203 |
| $36,001-$38,000 | 170 | 203 | 211 |
| $38,001-$40,000 | 176 | 211 | 219 |
| $40,001-$100,000 (See Step 3B) | 9 | 11 | 11 |

### Connecticut

| Income | 1&2 | 3,4&5 | Over 5 |
|---|---|---|---|
| $1-$8,000 | 126 | 139 | 146 |
| $8,001-$10,000 | 150 | 167 | 175 |
| $10,001-$12,000 | 172 | 194 | 203 |
| $12,001-$14,000 | 194 | 220 | 229 |
| $14,001-$16,000 | 214 | 244 | 254 |
| $16,001-$18,000 | 234 | 268 | 279 |
| $18,001-$20,000 | 253 | 291 | 302 |
| $20,001-$22,000 | 271 | 313 | 325 |
| $22,001-$24,000 | 289 | 335 | 347 |
| $24,001-$26,000 | 306 | 357 | 369 |
| $26,001-$28,000 | 323 | 378 | 390 |
| $28,001-$30,000 | 340 | 398 | 411 |
| $30,001-$32,000 | 356 | 418 | 432 |
| $32,001-$34,000 | 372 | 438 | 452 |
| $34,001-$36,000 | 388 | 458 | 472 |
| $36,001-$38,000 | 403 | 477 | 491 |
| $38,001-$40,000 | 418 | 496 | 510 |
| $40,001-$100,000 (See Step 3B) | 21 | 25 | 26 |

### Dist. of Columbia

| Income | 1 | 2 | 3 | 4 | 5 | Over 5 |
|---|---|---|---|---|---|---|
| $1-$8,000 | 94 | 112 | 125 | 125 | 132 | 140 |
| $8,001-$10,000 | 110 | 129 | 145 | 146 | 155 | 164 |
| $10,001-$12,000 | 125 | 145 | 164 | 166 | 177 | 186 |
| $12,001-$14,000 | 139 | 159 | 182 | 186 | 197 | 206 |
| $14,001-$16,000 | 152 | 173 | 198 | 205 | 216 | 225 |
| $16,001-$18,000 | 165 | 186 | 213 | 223 | 234 | 244 |
| $18,001-$20,000 | 177 | 198 | 228 | 240 | 252 | 261 |
| $20,001-$22,000 | 189 | 210 | 242 | 256 | 268 | 278 |
| $22,001-$24,000 | 200 | 221 | 256 | 272 | 284 | 294 |
| $24,001-$26,000 | 211 | 232 | 269 | 287 | 300 | 310 |
| $26,001-$28,000 | 222 | 242 | 282 | 302 | 315 | 325 |
| $28,001-$30,000 | 232 | 252 | 295 | 317 | 330 | 340 |
| $30,001-$32,000 | 242 | 262 | 307 | 332 | 345 | 354 |
| $32,001-$34,000 | 252 | 272 | 319 | 346 | 359 | 368 |
| $34,001-$36,000 | 262 | 281 | 330 | 360 | 373 | 382 |
| $36,001-$38,000 | 271 | 290 | 341 | 373 | 387 | 396 |
| $38,001-$40,000 | 280 | 299 | 352 | 386 | 400 | 409 |
| $40,001-$100,000 (See Step 3B) | 14 | 15 | 18 | 19 | 20 | 20 |

| Income | Florida Family size 1&2 | 3 | 4 | 5 | Over 5 | Georgia[1] Family size 1 | 2 | 3 | 4 | 5 | Over 5 |
|---|---|---|---|---|---|---|---|---|---|---|---|
| $1-$8,000 | 86 | 99 | 99 | 105 | 111 | 82 | 103 | 110 | 116 | 125 | 141 |
| $8,001-$10,000 | 103 | 118 | 118 | 125 | 132 | 95 | 117 | 127 | 135 | 145 | 161 |
| $10,001-$12,000 | 119 | 136 | 137 | 145 | 152 | 107 | 130 | 143 | 152 | 163 | 180 |
| $12,001-$14,000 | 134 | 152 | 155 | 163 | 171 | 118 | 141 | 157 | 167 | 179 | 198 |
| $14,001-$16,000 | 148 | 168 | 173 | 181 | 189 | 129 | 152 | 171 | 182 | 195 | 214 |
| $16,001-$18,000 | 162 | 184 | 190 | 198 | 206 | 139 | 162 | 184 | 196 | 210 | 229 |
| $18,001-$20,000 | 175 | 199 | 206 | 215 | 223 | 149 | 171 | 196 | 209 | 224 | 244 |
| $20,001-$22,000 | 188 | 213 | 222 | 231 | 239 | 158 | 180 | 208 | 222 | 237 | 258 |
| $22,001-$24,000 | 201 | 227 | 238 | 247 | 255 | 167 | 189 | 219 | 234 | 250 | 271 |
| $24,001-$26,000 | 213 | 241 | 254 | 262 | 270 | 176 | 198 | 230 | 246 | 262 | 283 |
| $26,001-$28,000 | 225 | 254 | 269 | 277 | 285 | 184 | 206 | 240 | 258 | 274 | 295 |
| $28,001-$30,000 | 237 | 267 | 284 | 291 | 299 | 192 | 213 | 250 | 269 | 286 | 307 |
| $30,001-$32,000 | 248 | 280 | 299 | 305 | 313 | 200 | 220 | 260 | 280 | 297 | 319 |
| $32,001-$34,000 | 259 | 293 | 313 | 319 | 327 | 208 | 227 | 270 | 290 | 308 | 330 |
| $34,001-$36,000 | 270 | 305 | 327 | 333 | 341 | 215 | 234 | 279 | 300 | 319 | 341 |
| $36,001-$38,000 | 281 | 317 | 341 | 347 | 354 | 222 | 241 | 288 | 310 | 330 | 352 |
| $38,001-$40,000 | 292 | 329 | 354 | 360 | 367 | 229 | 247 | 297 | 320 | 340 | 362 |
| $40,001-$100,000 (See Step 3B) | 15 | 16 | 18 | 18 | 18 | 11 | 12 | 15 | 16 | 17 | 18 |

| Income | Hawaii Family size 1&2 | 3 | 4 | 5 | Over 5 | Idaho Family size 1 | 2 | 3 | 4 | 5 | Over 5 |
|---|---|---|---|---|---|---|---|---|---|---|---|
| $1-$8,000 | 158 | 180 | 183 | 190 | 204 | 68 | 84 | 90 | 97 | 106 | 121 |
| $8,001-$10,000 | 181 | 206 | 209 | 219 | 235 | 80 | 96 | 105 | 114 | 123 | 139 |
| $10,001-$12,000 | 201 | 228 | 234 | 245 | 263 | 91 | 106 | 118 | 128 | 139 | 155 |
| $12,001-$14,000 | 220 | 249 | 256 | 269 | 288 | 101 | 116 | 131 | 142 | 153 | 171 |
| $14,001-$16,000 | 238 | 268 | 277 | 292 | 312 | 110 | 126 | 143 | 155 | 167 | 185 |
| $16,001-$18,000 | 254 | 286 | 297 | 313 | 335 | 119 | 135 | 155 | 167 | 180 | 198 |
| $18,001-$20,000 | 270 | 303 | 315 | 333 | 356 | 128 | 143 | 166 | 179 | 192 | 211 |
| $20,001-$22,000 | 285 | 319 | 333 | 352 | 377 | 136 | 151 | 176 | 191 | 204 | 223 |
| $22,001-$24,000 | 299 | 335 | 350 | 371 | 397 | 144 | 158 | 186 | 202 | 215 | 235 |
| $24,001-$26,000 | 313 | 350 | 366 | 389 | 416 | 152 | 165 | 196 | 212 | 226 | 247 |
| $26,001-$28,000 | 326 | 364 | 382 | 406 | 434 | 160 | 172 | 205 | 222 | 237 | 258 |
| $28,001-$30,000 | 339 | 378 | 397 | 423 | 451 | 167 | 179 | 214 | 232 | 247 | 268 |
| $30,001-$32,000 | 351 | 391 | 412 | 439 | 468 | 174 | 186 | 223 | 242 | 257 | 278 |
| $32,001-$34,000 | 363 | 404 | 426 | 454 | 485 | 181 | 192 | 232 | 251 | 267 | 288 |
| $34,001-$36,000 | 375 | 416 | 440 | 469 | 501 | 188 | 198 | 241 | 260 | 277 | 298 |
| $36,001-$38,000 | 386 | 428 | 454 | 484 | 517 | 195 | 204 | 249 | 269 | 286 | 308 |
| $38,001-$40,000 | 397 | 440 | 467 | 499 | 533 | 201 | 209 | 257 | 278 | 295 | 317 |
| $40,001-$100,000 (See Step 3B) | 20 | 22 | 23 | 25 | 27 | 10 | 10 | 13 | 14 | 15 | 16 |

| Income | Illinois[4] Family size 1 | 2 | 3 | 4 | 5 | Over 5 | Indiana Family size 1&2 | 3&4 | 5 | Over 5 |
|---|---|---|---|---|---|---|---|---|---|---|
| $1-$8,000 | 109 | 132 | 142 | 148 | 160 | 176 | 93 | 110 | 118 | 124 |
| $8,001-$10,000 | 128 | 151 | 166 | 173 | 186 | 204 | 109 | 130 | 138 | 145 |
| $10,001-$12,000 | 145 | 168 | 188 | 196 | 210 | 229 | 124 | 148 | 157 | 165 |
| $12,001-$14,000 | 162 | 184 | 208 | 218 | 232 | 253 | 138 | 165 | 175 | 183 |
| $14,001-$16,000 | 177 | 199 | 227 | 238 | 253 | 274 | 151 | 181 | 191 | 200 |
| $16,001-$18,000 | 192 | 213 | 245 | 258 | 273 | 295 | 164 | 196 | 207 | 216 |
| $18,001-$20,000 | 206 | 226 | 262 | 276 | 293 | 315 | 176 | 211 | 222 | 232 |
| $20,001-$22,000 | 220 | 239 | 278 | 294 | 311 | 334 | 187 | 225 | 237 | 247 |
| $22,001-$24,000 | 233 | 251 | 294 | 312 | 329 | 352 | 198 | 238 | 251 | 261 |
| $24,001-$26,000 | 246 | 263 | 310 | 328 | 346 | 369 | 209 | 251 | 265 | 275 |
| $26,001-$28,000 | 258 | 274 | 325 | 344 | 362 | 386 | 220 | 264 | 278 | 289 |
| $28,001-$30,000 | 270 | 285 | 339 | 360 | 378 | 403 | 230 | 277 | 291 | 302 |
| $30,001-$32,000 | 282 | 295 | 353 | 376 | 394 | 419 | 240 | 289 | 304 | 315 |
| $32,001-$34,000 | 293 | 305 | 367 | 391 | 409 | 434 | 250 | 301 | 316 | 327 |
| $34,001-$36,000 | 304 | 315 | 380 | 406 | 424 | 449 | 259 | 313 | 328 | 339 |
| $36,001-$38,000 | 315 | 325 | 393 | 420 | 439 | 464 | 268 | 324 | 340 | 351 |
| $38,001-$40,000 | 326 | 334 | 406 | 434 | 453 | 478 | 277 | 335 | 352 | 363 |
| $40,001-$100,000 (See Step 3B) | 16 | 17 | 20 | 22 | 23 | 24 | 14 | 17 | 18 | 18 |

| Income | Iowa Family size 1&2 | 3,4&5 | Over 5 | Kansas[1] Family size 1 | 2 | 3 | 4 | 5 | Over 5 |
|---|---|---|---|---|---|---|---|---|---|
| $1-$8,000 | 71 | 79 | 85 | 72 | 90 | 95 | 102 | 108 | 122 |
| $8,001-$10,000 | 83 | 93 | 100 | 85 | 104 | 112 | 120 | 127 | 142 |
| $10,001-$12,000 | 95 | 107 | 114 | 96 | 116 | 127 | 136 | 144 | 160 |
| $12,001-$14,000 | 106 | 120 | 127 | 107 | 128 | 141 | 151 | 160 | 177 |
| $14,001-$16,000 | 116 | 132 | 139 | 117 | 138 | 155 | 165 | 176 | 193 |
| $16,001-$18,000 | 126 | 143 | 151 | 126 | 148 | 168 | 179 | 191 | 208 |
| $18,001-$20,000 | 135 | 154 | 162 | 135 | 158 | 180 | 192 | 205 | 222 |
| $20,001-$22,000 | 144 | 165 | 173 | 144 | 167 | 192 | 205 | 219 | 236 |
| $22,001-$24,000 | 153 | 176 | 183 | 153 | 176 | 203 | 217 | 232 | 249 |
| $24,001-$26,000 | 162 | 186 | 193 | 161 | 184 | 214 | 229 | 245 | 262 |
| $26,001-$28,000 | 170 | 196 | 203 | 169 | 192 | 225 | 240 | 257 | 274 |
| $28,001-$30,000 | 178 | 206 | 213 | 177 | 200 | 235 | 251 | 269 | 286 |
| $30,001-$32,000 | 186 | 215 | 222 | 185 | 208 | 245 | 262 | 281 | 298 |
| $32,001-$34,000 | 194 | 224 | 231 | 192 | 215 | 255 | 273 | 293 | 309 |
| $34,001-$36,000 | 201 | 233 | 240 | 199 | 222 | 265 | 284 | 304 | 320 |
| $36,001-$38,000 | 208 | 242 | 249 | 206 | 229 | 275 | 294 | 315 | 330 |
| $38,001-$40,000 | 215 | 251 | 258 | 212 | 236 | 284 | 304 | 325 | 340 |
| $40,001-$100,000 (See Step 3B) | 11 | 13 | 13 | 11 | 12 | 14 | 15 | 16 | 17 |

| Income | Kentucky Family size 1&2 | 3&4 | 5 | Over 5 | Louisiana[5] Family size 1&2 | 3&4 | 5 | Over 5 |
|---|---|---|---|---|---|---|---|---|
| $1-$8,000 | 94 | 105 | 111 | 117 | 60 | 67 | 70 | 73 |
| $8,001-$10,000 | 111 | 126 | 132 | 138 | 71 | 80 | 84 | 88 |
| $10,001-$12,000 | 127 | 145 | 152 | 158 | 82 | 92 | 97 | 101 |
| $12,001-$14,000 | 142 | 163 | 170 | 177 | 92 | 104 | 109 | 113 |
| $14,001-$16,000 | 156 | 181 | 188 | 195 | 101 | 115 | 121 | 125 |
| $16,001-$18,000 | 170 | 198 | 205 | 212 | 110 | 126 | 132 | 137 |
| $18,001-$20,000 | 183 | 214 | 222 | 229 | 119 | 136 | 143 | 148 |
| $20,001-$22,000 | 196 | 230 | 238 | 245 | 128 | 146 | 153 | 159 |
| $22,001-$24,000 | 208 | 245 | 254 | 260 | 136 | 156 | 163 | 169 |
| $24,001-$26,000 | 220 | 260 | 269 | 275 | 144 | 166 | 173 | 179 |
| $26,001-$28,000 | 232 | 274 | 284 | 290 | 152 | 175 | 183 | 189 |
| $28,001-$30,000 | 243 | 288 | 298 | 304 | 160 | 184 | 193 | 199 |
| $30,001-$32,000 | 254 | 302 | 312 | 318 | 168 | 193 | 202 | 209 |
| $32,001-$34,000 | 265 | 316 | 326 | 332 | 175 | 202 | 211 | 218 |
| $34,001-$36,000 | 276 | 330 | 340 | 345 | 182 | 211 | 220 | 227 |
| $36,001-$38,000 | 286 | 343 | 353 | 358 | 189 | 219 | 229 | 236 |
| $38,001-$40,000 | 296 | 356 | 366 | 371 | 196 | 227 | 238 | 245 |
| $40,001-$100,000 (See Step 3B) | 15 | 18 | 18 | 19 | 10 | 11 | 12 | 12 |

| Income | Maine[6] Family size 1&2 | 3&4 | 5 | Over 5 | Maryland Family size 1&2 | 3 | 4 | 5 | Over 5 | Massachusetts[7] Family size 1 & 2 | Over 2 |
|---|---|---|---|---|---|---|---|---|---|---|---|
| $1-$8,000 | 89 | 100 | 103 | 109 | 80 | 90 | 90 | 94 | 98 | 58 | 63 |
| $8,001-$10,000 | 106 | 120 | 124 | 130 | 95 | 108 | 108 | 113 | 118 | 69 | 76 |
| $10,001-$12,000 | 121 | 139 | 144 | 150 | 110 | 125 | 125 | 131 | 136 | 79 | 89 |
| $12,001-$14,000 | 135 | 157 | 163 | 169 | 124 | 141 | 143 | 149 | 154 | 89 | 101 |
| $14,001-$16,000 | 149 | 175 | 181 | 188 | 137 | 157 | 160 | 166 | 171 | 98 | 113 |
| $16,001-$18,000 | 162 | 192 | 198 | 205 | 150 | 172 | 177 | 182 | 188 | 107 | 124 |
| $18,001-$20,000 | 175 | 208 | 215 | 222 | 163 | 186 | 193 | 198 | 203 | 116 | 135 |
| $20,001-$22,000 | 187 | 224 | 231 | 239 | 175 | 200 | 209 | 213 | 219 | 124 | 146 |
| $22,001-$24,000 | 199 | 239 | 247 | 255 | 187 | 214 | 225 | 228 | 234 | 132 | 157 |
| $24,001-$26,000 | 211 | 254 | 263 | 271 | 198 | 227 | 240 | 243 | 249 | 140 | 168 |
| $26,001-$28,000 | 222 | 269 | 278 | 286 | 209 | 240 | 255 | 257 | 263 | 148 | 178 |
| $28,001-$30,000 | 233 | 283 | 293 | 301 | 220 | 253 | 270 | 271 | 278 | 155 | 188 |
| $30,001-$32,000 | 244 | 297 | 308 | 316 | 231 | 265 | 285 | 285 | 292 | 162 | 198 |
| $32,001-$34,000 | 255 | 311 | 322 | 330 | 242 | 277 | 299 | 299 | 305 | 169 | 208 |
| $34,001-$36,000 | 265 | 325 | 336 | 344 | 253 | 289 | 313 | 313 | 319 | 176 | 217 |
| $36,001-$38,000 | 275 | 338 | 350 | 358 | 263 | 301 | 327 | 327 | 332 | 183 | 227 |
| $38,001-$40,000 | 285 | 351 | 364 | 371 | 273 | 313 | 341 | 341 | 345 | 190 | 236 |
| $40,001-$100,000 (See Step 3B) | 14 | 18 | 18 | 19 | 14 | 16 | 17 | 17 | 17 | 10 | 12 |

[1] Local sales taxes are not included. Add an amount based on the ratio between the local and State sales tax rates considering the number of months the taxes have been in effect.

[2] Local sales taxes are not included. Add the amount paid.

[3] The 1¼ percent local sales tax is included. If the ½ of 1 percent sales tax is paid all year (Alameda, Contra Costa, San Francisco, Santa Clara, and Santa Cruz counties), add 8 percent to the table amount. Los Angeles and San Mateo counties for the ½ of 1 percent sales tax paid after June 30, 1982, add 4 percent to the table amount. Otherwise add a proportionate amount (see footnote 1).

[4] Local 1 percent sales taxes are included. If public transportation sales taxes are paid, compute the allowable deduction by the method in footnote 1.

[5] If your local sales tax applies to food for home consumption check your local newspaper during mid-January for the correct deduction. Otherwise see footnote 1.

[6] Sales tax paid on purchase of electricity of 750 KWH or more per month, can be added to the table amounts.

[7] Sales tax paid on the purchase of any single item of clothing for $175 or more can be added to the table amounts.

[8] Sales tax paid on purchases of natural gas or electricity can be added to the table amounts. For local sales tax see footnote 1.

[9] Local sales taxes are included.

[10] Local sales taxes are not included. If paid all year add 26 percent of the table amount for each 1 percent of local sales tax rate. Otherwise use a proportionate amount. For N.Y. City add 107 percent of the table amount.

(Footnotes continued on next page)

363-063-1

## 1982 Optional State Sales Tax Tables—Continued

| Income | Michigan | | | | Minnesota [8] | | Mississippi | | | | | | Missouri [1] | | | | | | Nebraska [1] | | | | | | Nevada [9] | | | | New Jersey | |
|---|---|---|---|---|---|---|---|---|---|---|---|---|---|---|---|---|---|---|---|---|---|---|---|---|---|---|---|---|---|---|
| | Family size 1&2 | 3&4 | 5 | Over 5 | Family size 1&2 | Over 2 | Family size 1 | 2 | 3 | 4 | 5 | Over 5 | Family size 1 | 2 | 3 | 4 | 5 | Over 5 | Family size 1 | 2 | 3 | 4 | 5 | Over 5 | Family size 1&2 | 3&4 | 5 | Over 5 | Family size 1&2 | Over 2 |
| $1-$8,000 | 88 | 102 | 108 | 113 | 74 | 83 | 137 | 168 | 179 | 189 | 203 | 226 | 76 | 91 | 96 | 103 | 111 | 125 | 86 | 107 | 114 | 123 | 132 | 149 | 94 | 106 | 111 | 115 | 68 | 76 |
| $8,001-$10,000 | 103 | 121 | 127 | 133 | 88 | 99 | 160 | 193 | 209 | 221 | 236 | 261 | 89 | 105 | 113 | 121 | 129 | 144 | 101 | 122 | 132 | 142 | 152 | 171 | 112 | 128 | 134 | 138 | 81 | 92 |
| $10,001-$12,000 | 118 | 138 | 145 | 151 | 101 | 114 | 180 | 215 | 236 | 250 | 267 | 293 | 101 | 117 | 128 | 137 | 146 | 162 | 113 | 135 | 149 | 159 | 171 | 190 | 129 | 148 | 154 | 159 | 93 | 107 |
| $12,001-$14,000 | 131 | 154 | 161 | 168 | 113 | 129 | 200 | 235 | 261 | 276 | 295 | 323 | 112 | 128 | 142 | 152 | 162 | 178 | 125 | 147 | 164 | 176 | 188 | 208 | 145 | 167 | 174 | 179 | 104 | 121 |
| $14,001-$16,000 | 144 | 169 | 177 | 184 | 124 | 143 | 218 | 254 | 285 | 301 | 322 | 350 | 123 | 139 | 155 | 166 | 176 | 193 | 136 | 158 | 178 | 191 | 204 | 225 | 160 | 186 | 193 | 199 | 115 | 135 |
| $16,001-$18,000 | 156 | 184 | 192 | 199 | 135 | 156 | 236 | 272 | 307 | 325 | 348 | 377 | 134 | 149 | 167 | 179 | 190 | 208 | 147 | 168 | 192 | 206 | 219 | 241 | 174 | 204 | 211 | 217 | 125 | 149 |
| $18,001-$20,000 | 168 | 198 | 207 | 214 | 146 | 169 | 252 | 289 | 329 | 348 | 372 | 402 | 144 | 158 | 179 | 192 | 204 | 222 | 157 | 178 | 205 | 219 | 234 | 256 | 188 | 221 | 229 | 235 | 135 | 162 |
| $20,001-$22,000 | 180 | 211 | 221 | 228 | 156 | 181 | 268 | 305 | 349 | 370 | 395 | 426 | 153 | 167 | 191 | 204 | 217 | 235 | 167 | 187 | 217 | 232 | 248 | 270 | 202 | 238 | 246 | 253 | 145 | 175 |
| $22,001-$24,000 | 191 | 224 | 234 | 241 | 166 | 193 | 283 | 320 | 369 | 391 | 418 | 449 | 162 | 176 | 202 | 216 | 229 | 247 | 176 | 196 | 229 | 245 | 261 | 284 | 215 | 254 | 263 | 270 | 155 | 188 |
| $24,001-$26,000 | 202 | 237 | 247 | 254 | 176 | 205 | 298 | 335 | 389 | 411 | 440 | 471 | 171 | 184 | 213 | 227 | 241 | 259 | 185 | 204 | 240 | 257 | 274 | 297 | 228 | 270 | 279 | 287 | 164 | 200 |
| $26,001-$28,000 | 212 | 249 | 260 | 267 | 185 | 217 | 313 | 349 | 407 | 431 | 461 | 492 | 180 | 192 | 223 | 238 | 252 | 271 | 194 | 212 | 251 | 269 | 286 | 309 | 241 | 286 | 295 | 303 | 173 | 212 |
| $28,001-$30,000 | 222 | 261 | 272 | 280 | 194 | 228 | 327 | 363 | 425 | 450 | 481 | 513 | 188 | 200 | 233 | 249 | 263 | 282 | 203 | 220 | 262 | 281 | 298 | 321 | 253 | 301 | 311 | 319 | 182 | 224 |
| $30,001-$32,000 | 232 | 273 | 284 | 292 | 203 | 239 | 341 | 376 | 443 | 469 | 501 | 533 | 196 | 207 | 243 | 260 | 274 | 293 | 211 | 228 | 272 | 292 | 310 | 333 | 265 | 316 | 326 | 335 | 190 | 236 |
| $32,001-$34,000 | 242 | 284 | 296 | 304 | 212 | 250 | 354 | 389 | 460 | 487 | 521 | 553 | 204 | 214 | 253 | 270 | 285 | 304 | 219 | 235 | 282 | 303 | 322 | 345 | 277 | 331 | 341 | 350 | 198 | 247 |
| $34,001-$36,000 | 252 | 295 | 308 | 316 | 221 | 261 | 367 | 402 | 477 | 505 | 540 | 572 | 212 | 221 | 262 | 280 | 295 | 315 | 227 | 242 | 292 | 313 | 333 | 356 | 288 | 346 | 356 | 365 | 206 | 258 |
| $36,001-$38,000 | 261 | 306 | 319 | 327 | 229 | 271 | 380 | 414 | 493 | 522 | 558 | 591 | 220 | 228 | 271 | 290 | 305 | 325 | 235 | 249 | 302 | 323 | 344 | 367 | 299 | 360 | 371 | 380 | 214 | 269 |
| $38,001-$40,000 | 270 | 317 | 330 | 338 | 237 | 281 | 392 | 426 | 509 | 539 | 576 | 609 | 227 | 234 | 280 | 299 | 315 | 335 | 242 | 255 | 311 | 333 | 354 | 377 | 310 | 374 | 385 | 394 | 222 | 280 |
| $40,001-$100,000 (See Step 3B) | 14 | 16 | 17 | 17 | 12 | 14 | 20 | 21 | 25 | 27 | 29 | 30 | 11 | 12 | 14 | 15 | 16 | 17 | 12 | 13 | 16 | 17 | 18 | 19 | 16 | 19 | 19 | 20 | 11 | 14 |

| Income | New Mexico [1] | | | | | | New York [10] | | | | North Carolina [11] | | | | | | North Dakota | | | Ohio [1] | | | | Oklahoma [1] | | | | | | Pennsylvania | |
|---|---|---|---|---|---|---|---|---|---|---|---|---|---|---|---|---|---|---|---|---|---|---|---|---|---|---|---|---|---|---|---|
| | Family size 1 | 2 | 3 | 4 | 5 | Over 5 | Family size 1&2 | 3&4 | 5 | Over 5 | Family size 1 | 2 | 3 | 4 | 5 | Over 5 | Family size 1&2 | 3,4&5 | Over 5 | Family size 1&2 | 3&4 | 5 | Over 5 | Family size 1 | 2 | 3 | 4 | 5 | Over 5 | Family size 1&2 | Over 2 |
| $1-$8,000 | 110 | 135 | 143 | 148 | 157 | 173 | 86 | 99 | 103 | 108 | 92 | 114 | 121 | 130 | 139 | 159 | 57 | 65 | 69 | 91 | 103 | 108 | 113 | 49 | 58 | 62 | 65 | 70 | 79 | 73 | 78 |
| $8,001-$10,000 | 127 | 155 | 166 | 173 | 183 | 200 | 103 | 118 | 123 | 128 | 108 | 131 | 141 | 151 | 162 | 183 | 68 | 77 | 82 | 109 | 124 | 129 | 135 | 58 | 67 | 73 | 77 | 82 | 91 | 88 | 95 |
| $10,001-$12,000 | 143 | 172 | 187 | 195 | 207 | 226 | 118 | 136 | 141 | 147 | 123 | 146 | 159 | 171 | 182 | 204 | 78 | 89 | 94 | 125 | 143 | 149 | 155 | 66 | 75 | 82 | 87 | 93 | 103 | 102 | 111 |
| $12,001-$14,000 | 158 | 188 | 206 | 217 | 229 | 249 | 132 | 152 | 159 | 165 | 137 | 159 | 176 | 189 | 202 | 224 | 87 | 100 | 106 | 140 | 161 | 158 | 174 | 73 | 82 | 91 | 97 | 103 | 114 | 115 | 126 |
| $14,001-$16,000 | 172 | 203 | 224 | 236 | 250 | 271 | 146 | 168 | 176 | 182 | 150 | 172 | 192 | 206 | 220 | 243 | 96 | 111 | 117 | 155 | 179 | 186 | 193 | 80 | 89 | 100 | 106 | 113 | 124 | 128 | 141 |
| $16,001-$18,000 | 185 | 217 | 241 | 255 | 270 | 292 | 159 | 183 | 192 | 198 | 162 | 184 | 207 | 222 | 237 | 261 | 105 | 121 | 127 | 169 | 196 | 203 | 210 | 87 | 96 | 108 | 115 | 122 | 133 | 141 | 156 |
| $18,001-$20,000 | 198 | 230 | 258 | 273 | 289 | 312 | 172 | 198 | 208 | 214 | 174 | 195 | 222 | 237 | 253 | 277 | 113 | 131 | 137 | 183 | 212 | 220 | 227 | 93 | 102 | 116 | 123 | 131 | 142 | 153 | 170 |
| $20,001-$22,000 | 210 | 243 | 274 | 291 | 307 | 331 | 184 | 212 | 223 | 229 | 185 | 206 | 236 | 252 | 268 | 293 | 121 | 141 | 147 | 196 | 228 | 236 | 244 | 99 | 108 | 123 | 131 | 139 | 151 | 164 | 183 |
| $22,001-$24,000 | 221 | 255 | 289 | 307 | 325 | 349 | 196 | 226 | 238 | 244 | 196 | 216 | 249 | 266 | 283 | 308 | 129 | 150 | 157 | 209 | 243 | 252 | 260 | 105 | 114 | 130 | 139 | 147 | 159 | 175 | 196 |
| $24,001-$26,000 | 232 | 266 | 303 | 323 | 342 | 367 | 208 | 240 | 252 | 258 | 207 | 226 | 262 | 280 | 298 | 323 | 136 | 159 | 166 | 221 | 258 | 267 | 276 | 111 | 119 | 137 | 147 | 155 | 167 | 186 | 209 |
| $26,001-$28,000 | 243 | 277 | 317 | 339 | 358 | 384 | 219 | 253 | 266 | 272 | 217 | 236 | 275 | 293 | 312 | 337 | 143 | 168 | 175 | 233 | 273 | 282 | 291 | 116 | 124 | 144 | 155 | 163 | 175 | 197 | 222 |
| $28,001-$30,000 | 254 | 288 | 331 | 354 | 374 | 401 | 230 | 266 | 280 | 286 | 227 | 245 | 287 | 306 | 325 | 351 | 150 | 177 | 184 | 245 | 287 | 297 | 306 | 121 | 129 | 151 | 162 | 170 | 183 | 208 | 235 |
| $30,001-$32,000 | 264 | 298 | 344 | 369 | 390 | 417 | 241 | 278 | 293 | 299 | 237 | 254 | 299 | 319 | 338 | 364 | 157 | 186 | 193 | 257 | 301 | 311 | 320 | 126 | 134 | 157 | 169 | 177 | 191 | 219 | 248 |
| $32,001-$34,000 | 274 | 308 | 357 | 384 | 405 | 433 | 252 | 290 | 306 | 312 | 247 | 263 | 310 | 331 | 351 | 377 | 164 | 194 | 201 | 268 | 315 | 325 | 334 | 131 | 139 | 163 | 176 | 184 | 198 | 230 | 261 |
| $34,001-$36,000 | 284 | 318 | 370 | 398 | 420 | 448 | 262 | 302 | 319 | 325 | 257 | 271 | 321 | 343 | 364 | 390 | 171 | 202 | 209 | 279 | 329 | 339 | 348 | 136 | 144 | 169 | 183 | 191 | 205 | 240 | 273 |
| $36,001-$38,000 | 293 | 328 | 382 | 412 | 435 | 463 | 272 | 314 | 332 | 337 | 266 | 279 | 332 | 355 | 376 | 402 | 177 | 210 | 217 | 290 | 342 | 353 | 362 | 141 | 148 | 175 | 189 | 198 | 212 | 250 | 285 |
| $38,001-$40,000 | 302 | 337 | 394 | 425 | 449 | 477 | 282 | 326 | 345 | 349 | 275 | 287 | 343 | 366 | 388 | 414 | 184 | 218 | 225 | 301 | 355 | 366 | 376 | 146 | 152 | 181 | 195 | 205 | 218 | 260 | 297 |
| $40,001-$100,000 (See Step 3B) | 15 | 17 | 20 | 21 | 22 | 24 | 14 | 16 | 17 | 17 | 14 | 14 | 17 | 18 | 19 | 21 | 9 | 11 | 11 | 15 | 18 | 18 | 19 | 7 | 8 | 9 | 10 | 10 | 11 | 13 | 15 |

## Top band

| Income | Rhode Island 1&2 | Rhode Island Over 2 | South Carolina 1 | SC 2 | SC 3 | SC 4 | SC 5 | SC Over 5 | South Dakota[12] 1 | SD 2 | SD 3 | SD 4 | SD 5 | SD Over 5 | Tennessee[1] 1 | TN 2 | TN 3 | TN 4 | TN 5 | TN Over 5 | Texas[1] 1&2 | TX 3&4 | TX 5 | TX Over 5 | Utah[12] 1 | UT 2 | UT 3 | UT 4 | UT 5 | UT Over 5 |
|---|---|---|---|---|---|---|---|---|---|---|---|---|---|---|---|---|---|---|---|---|---|---|---|---|---|---|---|---|---|---|
| $1-$8,000 | 88 | 94 | 101 | 120 | 127 | 135 | 146 | 164 | 108 | 133 | 138 | 147 | 158 | 178 | 114 | 137 | 147 | 155 | 167 | 192 | 67 | 77 | 82 | 87 | 120 | 143 | 152 | 161 | 172 | 195 |
| $8,001-$10,000 | 104 | 113 | 118 | 138 | 148 | 158 | 169 | 189 | 127 | 152 | 161 | 171 | 184 | 205 | 133 | 157 | 171 | 181 | 194 | 220 | 79 | 92 | 98 | 104 | 140 | 164 | 177 | 188 | 200 | 225 |
| $10,001-$12,000 | 120 | 131 | 134 | 154 | 168 | 178 | 191 | 211 | 145 | 170 | 183 | 194 | 208 | 230 | 151 | 175 | 191 | 204 | 219 | 245 | 91 | 106 | 113 | 119 | 159 | 183 | 200 | 213 | 226 | 252 |
| $12,001-$14,000 | 134 | 148 | 149 | 169 | 186 | 198 | 211 | 232 | 161 | 186 | 203 | 215 | 230 | 253 | 167 | 191 | 212 | 225 | 241 | 269 | 102 | 120 | 127 | 134 | 176 | 201 | 222 | 236 | 251 | 277 |
| $14,001-$16,000 | 148 | 164 | 163 | 182 | 203 | 216 | 230 | 252 | 176 | 202 | 221 | 235 | 251 | 275 | 183 | 207 | 231 | 246 | 263 | 291 | 113 | 133 | 141 | 148 | 193 | 217 | 242 | 258 | 274 | 300 |
| $16,001-$18,000 | 161 | 180 | 176 | 195 | 219 | 233 | 248 | 271 | 191 | 216 | 239 | 254 | 271 | 295 | 198 | 221 | 249 | 265 | 283 | 311 | 123 | 146 | 154 | 162 | 209 | 232 | 261 | 278 | 295 | 323 |
| $18,001-$20,000 | 174 | 196 | 189 | 208 | 235 | 250 | 265 | 288 | 205 | 230 | 256 | 272 | 290 | 315 | 212 | 235 | 266 | 283 | 302 | 331 | 133 | 158 | 167 | 175 | 224 | 247 | 279 | 298 | 316 | 344 |
| $20,001-$22,000 | 187 | 211 | 201 | 219 | 250 | 266 | 281 | 305 | 219 | 243 | 273 | 289 | 308 | 333 | 226 | 248 | 283 | 301 | 321 | 349 | 142 | 170 | 179 | 188 | 238 | 261 | 297 | 317 | 336 | 364 |
| $22,001-$24,000 | 199 | 225 | 213 | 230 | 264 | 281 | 297 | 321 | 232 | 255 | 289 | 306 | 326 | 351 | 239 | 260 | 299 | 318 | 339 | 367 | 151 | 181 | 191 | 200 | 252 | 274 | 314 | 335 | 355 | 383 |
| $24,001-$26,000 | 210 | 239 | 224 | 241 | 278 | 296 | 312 | 337 | 245 | 267 | 304 | 323 | 343 | 368 | 252 | 272 | 314 | 334 | 356 | 384 | 160 | 192 | 203 | 212 | 266 | 287 | 330 | 353 | 374 | 402 |
| $26,001-$28,000 | 221 | 253 | 235 | 251 | 291 | 310 | 327 | 352 | 258 | 279 | 319 | 339 | 359 | 385 | 264 | 284 | 329 | 350 | 372 | 401 | 169 | 203 | 214 | 224 | 279 | 299 | 346 | 370 | 392 | 420 |
| $28,001-$30,000 | 232 | 267 | 246 | 261 | 304 | 324 | 341 | 367 | 270 | 290 | 333 | 354 | 375 | 401 | 276 | 296 | 344 | 365 | 388 | 417 | 177 | 214 | 225 | 235 | 292 | 311 | 362 | 387 | 409 | 437 |
| $30,001-$32,000 | 243 | 281 | 256 | 271 | 317 | 337 | 355 | 381 | 282 | 301 | 347 | 369 | 391 | 417 | 288 | 307 | 358 | 380 | 404 | 432 | 185 | 225 | 236 | 247 | 304 | 322 | 377 | 403 | 426 | 454 |
| $32,001-$34,000 | 254 | 294 | 266 | 280 | 329 | 350 | 369 | 395 | 293 | 311 | 361 | 383 | 406 | 432 | 300 | 317 | 372 | 395 | 419 | 447 | 193 | 235 | 247 | 257 | 316 | 333 | 392 | 419 | 443 | 470 |
| $34,001-$36,000 | 265 | 307 | 276 | 289 | 341 | 363 | 382 | 408 | 304 | 321 | 375 | 397 | 421 | 447 | 311 | 327 | 385 | 409 | 434 | 462 | 201 | 245 | 257 | 268 | 328 | 344 | 406 | 434 | 459 | 486 |
| $36,001-$38,000 | 276 | 320 | 286 | 298 | 353 | 376 | 395 | 421 | 315 | 331 | 388 | 411 | 435 | 461 | 322 | 337 | 398 | 423 | 449 | 476 | 209 | 255 | 267 | 279 | 340 | 355 | 420 | 449 | 475 | 502 |
| $38,001-$40,000 | 286 | 333 | 296 | 307 | 365 | 388 | 407 | 434 | 326 | 341 | 400 | 425 | 449 | 475 | 333 | 347 | 411 | 436 | 463 | 490 | 217 | 265 | 277 | 289 | 351 | 365 | 434 | 464 | 490 | 517 |
| $40,001-$100,000 (See Step 3B) | 14 | 17 | 15 | 15 | 18 | 19 | 20 | 22 | 16 | 17 | 20 | 20 | 22 | 24 | 17 | 17 | 23 | 23 | 23 | 25 | 11 | 13 | 14 | 14 | 18 | 18 | 22 | 23 | 25 | 26 |

## Bottom band

| Income | Vermont 1 | VT 2 | VT 3 | VT 4 | VT 5 | VT Over 5 | Virginia[9] 1 | VA 2 | VA 3 | VA 4 | VA 5 | VA Over 5 | Washington[13] 1 | WA 2 | WA 3 | WA 4 | WA 5 | WA Over 5 | West Virginia 1&2 | WV 3&4 | WV 5 | WV Over 5 | Wisconsin[14] 1&2 | WI 3&4 | WI 5 | WI Over 5 | Wyoming[1] 1 | WY 2 | WY 3 | WY 4 | WY 5 | WY Over 5 |
|---|---|---|---|---|---|---|---|---|---|---|---|---|---|---|---|---|---|---|---|---|---|---|---|---|---|---|---|---|---|---|---|---|
| $1-$8,000 | 39 | 44 | 51 | 51 | 53 | 57 | 88 | 111 | 117 | 127 | 137 | 156 | 131 | 159 | 168 | 174 | 184 | 205 | 95 | 105 | 107 | 112 | 96 | 107 | 111 | 116 | 81 | 98 | 104 | 109 | 117 | 132 |
| $8,001-$10,000 | 47 | 53 | 61 | 61 | 64 | 68 | 104 | 127 | 137 | 148 | 159 | 179 | 155 | 184 | 198 | 206 | 218 | 240 | 114 | 126 | 130 | 135 | 115 | 128 | 133 | 139 | 95 | 112 | 121 | 127 | 136 | 152 |
| $10,001-$12,000 | 54 | 61 | 70 | 71 | 74 | 78 | 118 | 141 | 155 | 166 | 179 | 200 | 177 | 207 | 225 | 235 | 248 | 272 | 131 | 146 | 151 | 156 | 131 | 147 | 153 | 159 | 107 | 125 | 136 | 144 | 153 | 170 |
| $12,001-$14,000 | 61 | 68 | 79 | 81 | 84 | 88 | 131 | 154 | 171 | 184 | 197 | 220 | 197 | 228 | 251 | 262 | 277 | 302 | 148 | 166 | 171 | 177 | 147 | 166 | 172 | 179 | 119 | 136 | 151 | 159 | 169 | 187 |
| $14,001-$16,000 | 68 | 75 | 87 | 90 | 94 | 97 | 143 | 167 | 187 | 201 | 215 | 238 | 217 | 248 | 276 | 288 | 305 | 330 | 164 | 184 | 190 | 196 | 163 | 184 | 191 | 197 | 130 | 147 | 164 | 173 | 184 | 202 |
| $16,001-$18,000 | 74 | 82 | 95 | 99 | 103 | 106 | 155 | 178 | 202 | 216 | 231 | 255 | 235 | 266 | 299 | 313 | 331 | 357 | 179 | 202 | 209 | 215 | 177 | 201 | 209 | 215 | 140 | 157 | 176 | 187 | 198 | 217 |
| $18,001-$20,000 | 80 | 89 | 103 | 108 | 112 | 115 | 166 | 189 | 216 | 231 | 247 | 271 | 253 | 284 | 322 | 337 | 356 | 383 | 194 | 219 | 227 | 233 | 191 | 217 | 226 | 232 | 150 | 167 | 188 | 200 | 212 | 231 |
| $20,001-$22,000 | 86 | 95 | 110 | 117 | 121 | 123 | 177 | 199 | 230 | 245 | 262 | 286 | 270 | 301 | 343 | 360 | 381 | 408 | 209 | 236 | 245 | 251 | 205 | 233 | 242 | 249 | 159 | 176 | 200 | 213 | 225 | 244 |
| $22,001-$24,000 | 92 | 101 | 117 | 126 | 129 | 131 | 188 | 209 | 243 | 259 | 276 | 301 | 287 | 318 | 364 | 382 | 404 | 432 | 223 | 253 | 262 | 268 | 218 | 249 | 258 | 265 | 168 | 185 | 211 | 225 | 237 | 257 |
| $24,001-$26,000 | 98 | 107 | 124 | 134 | 137 | 139 | 198 | 219 | 256 | 273 | 290 | 315 | 303 | 334 | 385 | 403 | 427 | 455 | 236 | 269 | 279 | 285 | 231 | 264 | 274 | 281 | 177 | 193 | 222 | 236 | 249 | 269 |
| $26,001-$28,000 | 104 | 113 | 131 | 142 | 145 | 147 | 208 | 228 | 268 | 286 | 304 | 329 | 319 | 349 | 405 | 424 | 450 | 477 | 249 | 285 | 296 | 302 | 243 | 279 | 290 | 296 | 186 | 201 | 232 | 247 | 261 | 281 |
| $28,001-$30,000 | 110 | 119 | 138 | 150 | 153 | 155 | 218 | 237 | 280 | 298 | 317 | 342 | 334 | 364 | 424 | 445 | 471 | 499 | 262 | 300 | 312 | 318 | 255 | 294 | 305 | 311 | 194 | 209 | 242 | 258 | 273 | 293 |
| $30,001-$32,000 | 115 | 125 | 144 | 158 | 161 | 163 | 227 | 246 | 292 | 310 | 330 | 355 | 349 | 378 | 443 | 465 | 492 | 520 | 275 | 315 | 328 | 334 | 267 | 308 | 320 | 326 | 202 | 216 | 252 | 269 | 284 | 304 |
| $32,001-$34,000 | 120 | 130 | 150 | 166 | 169 | 170 | 236 | 254 | 303 | 322 | 342 | 368 | 364 | 392 | 461 | 485 | 513 | 541 | 288 | 330 | 344 | 350 | 279 | 322 | 334 | 341 | 210 | 223 | 261 | 280 | 294 | 315 |
| $34,001-$36,000 | 125 | 135 | 156 | 174 | 177 | 177 | 245 | 262 | 314 | 334 | 354 | 380 | 378 | 406 | 479 | 504 | 534 | 561 | 300 | 345 | 360 | 365 | 291 | 336 | 348 | 355 | 218 | 230 | 270 | 290 | 304 | 326 |
| $36,001-$38,000 | 130 | 140 | 162 | 182 | 184 | 184 | 254 | 270 | 325 | 345 | 366 | 391 | 392 | 419 | 497 | 523 | 554 | 581 | 312 | 359 | 375 | 380 | 302 | 350 | 362 | 369 | 226 | 237 | 279 | 300 | 314 | 336 |
| $38,001-$40,000 | 135 | 145 | 168 | 189 | 191 | 191 | 263 | 277 | 336 | 356 | 378 | 402 | 406 | 432 | 514 | 541 | 573 | 600 | 324 | 373 | 390 | 395 | 313 | 363 | 376 | 382 | 233 | 244 | 288 | 310 | 324 | 346 |
| $40,001-$100,000 (See Step 3B) | 7 | 7 | 8 | 9 | 10 | 10 | 13 | 14 | 17 | 18 | 19 | 20 | 20 | 22 | 26 | 27 | 29 | 30 | 16 | 19 | 20 | 20 | 16 | 18 | 19 | 19 | 12 | 12 | 14 | 16 | 16 | 17 |

11 Local sales taxes are included. Taxpayers not paying local sales taxes (Burke County) should use 75 percent of the table amount allowed.

12 Local ¾ percent sales taxes are included. Add 5 percent of table amount if the ¼ percent county sales tax for transportation is paid all year. Otherwise add a proportionate amount (see footnote 1).

13 Local ½ percent sales taxes are included. If the $\frac{3}{10}$'s of 1 percent sales tax for public transportation is paid all year add 5 percent to the table amount. Otherwise add a proportionate amount (see footnote 1).

14 Sales tax paid on purchases of natural gas or electricity (May through October) can be added to the table amounts.

363-063-1

## A–5 TABLE FOR COMPUTATION OF MAXIMUM CREDIT FOR STATE DEATH TAXES

### Table for Computation of Maximum Credit for State Death Taxes

| (A)<br><br>Taxable estate equal to or more than— | (B)<br><br>Taxable estate less than— | (C)<br><br>Credit on amount in column (A) | (D)<br>Rates of credit on excess over amount in column (A) |
|---|---|---|---|
| | | | Percent |
| 0 | $40,000 | 0 | None |
| $40,000 | 90,000 | 0 | 0.8 |
| 90,000 | 140,000 | $400 | 1.6 |
| 140,000 | 240,000 | 1,200 | 2.4 |
| 240,000 | 440,000 | 3,600 | 3.2 |
| 440,000 | 640,000 | 10,000 | 4.0 |
| 640,000 | 840,000 | 18,000 | 4.8 |
| 840,000 | 1,040,000 | 27,600 | 5.6 |
| 1,040,000 | 1,540,000 | 38,800 | 6.4 |
| 1,540,000 | 2,040,000 | 70,800 | 7.2 |
| 2,040,000 | 2,540,000 | 106,800 | 8.0 |
| 2,540,000 | 3,040,000 | 146,800 | 8.8 |
| 3,040,000 | 3,540,000 | 190,800 | 9.6 |
| 3,540,000 | 4,040,000 | 238,800 | 10.4 |
| 4,040,000 | 5,040,000 | 290,800 | 11.2 |
| 5,040,000 | 6,040,000 | 402,800 | 12.0 |
| 6,040,000 | 7,040,000 | 522,800 | 12.8 |
| 7,040,000 | 8,040,000 | 650,800 | 13.6 |
| 8,040,000 | 9,040,000 | 786,800 | 14.4 |
| 9,040,000 | 10,040,000 | 930,800 | 15.2 |
| 10,040,000 | ......... | 1,082,800 | 16.0 |

# APPENDIX B
# TAX FORMS

|   |   | Page |
|---|---|---|
| B–1 | Short Form 1040A U. S. Individual Income Tax Return.......................... | B-3 |
| B–2 | Form 1040EZ Income Tax Return for Single Filers with No Dependents........................ | B-5 |
| B–3 | Form 1040 U. S. Individual Income Tax Return ...... | B-7 |
|   | Schedules A & B—Itemized Deductions AND Interest and Dividend Income ..................... | B-9 |
|   | Schedule C Profit or (Loss) From Business or Profession......................................... | B-11 |
|   | Schedule D Capital Gains and Losses................ | B-13 |
|   | Schedule E Supplemental Income Schedule........... | B-15 |
|   | Schedule F Farm Income and Expenses.............. | B-17 |
|   | Schedule G Income Averaging........................ | B-19 |
|   | Schedules R & RP—Credit for the Elderly .......... | B-21 |
|   | Schedule SE Computation of Social Security Self-Employment Tax............................. | B-23 |
|   | Schedule W Deduction for a Married Couple When Both Work................................. | B-24 |
| B–4 | Form 1040–ES Declaration of Estimated Tax and Declaration-Voucher for Individuals .............. | B-25 |
|   | Form W–2 Wage and Tax Statement ............... | B-30 |
|   | Form W–4 Employee's Withholding Allowance Certificate ........................................ | B-31 |
|   | Form 1041 U. S. Fiduciary Income Tax Return....... | B-33 |
|   | Form 1045 Application for Tentative Refund ........ | B-38 |
| B–5 | Form 1120 U. S. Corporation Income Tax Return..... | B-42 |
| B–6 | Form 1120S U. S. Small Business Corporation Income Tax Return ............................... | B-46 |
|   | Schedule K–1 Shareholder's Share of Undistributed Taxable Income, etc................. | B-50 |
| B–7 | Form 1065 U. S. Partnership Return ............... | B-53 |
|   | Schedule K–1 Partner's Share of Income, Credits, Deductions, etc. .................................... | B-57 |
| B–8 | Form 2106 Employee Business Expenses............. | B-61 |
| B–9 | Form 2119 Sale or Exchange of Principal Residence......................................... | B-63 |

B–10  Form 2210 Underpayment of Estimated Tax by
      Individuals. . . . . . . . . . . . . . . . . . . . . . . . . . . . . . . . . . B-65

B–11  Form 2441 Credit for Child and Dependent Care
      Expenses . . . . . . . . . . . . . . . . . . . . . . . . . . . . . . . . . . . B-67

B–12  Form 3115 Application for Change in Accounting
      Method . . . . . . . . . . . . . . . . . . . . . . . . . . . . . . . . . . . . B-69

B–13  Form 3468 Computation of Investment Credit. . . . . . . B-73

B–14  Form 3903 Moving Expense Adjustment . . . . . . . . . . . B-75

B–15  Form 4255 Recapture of Investment Credit . . . . . . . . . B-77

B–16  Form 4684 Casualties and Thefts. . . . . . . . . . . . . . . . . B-79

B–17  Form 4797 Supplemental Schedule of Gains and
      Losses . . . . . . . . . . . . . . . . . . . . . . . . . . . . . . . . . . . . B-81

B–18  Form 4868 Application for Automatic Extension
      of Time to File U. S. Individual Income Tax
      Return. . . . . . . . . . . . . . . . . . . . . . . . . . . . . . . . . . . . . B-83

B–19  Form 5695 Residential Energy Credit. . . . . . . . . . . . . . B-85

B–20  Form 6251 Alternative Minimum Tax Computation . . B-87

## B–1 SHORT FORM 1040A U.S. INDIVIDUAL INCOME TAX RETURN

**1982**

Department of the Treasury — Internal Revenue Service

**Form 1040A US Individual Income Tax Return**

OMB No. 1545-0085

**Step 1**
**Name and address**
Use the IRS mailing label. Otherwise, print or type.

Your first name and initial (if joint return, also give spouse's name and initial)     Last name     Your social security no.

Present home address     Spouse's social security no.

City, town or post office, State, and ZIP code     Your occupation

Spouse's occupation

**Presidential Election Campaign Fund**

Do you want $1 to go to this fund? . . . . . . . . . . . . . . . . . ☐ Yes    ☐ No

If joint return, does your spouse want $1 to go to this fund? ☐ Yes    ☐ No

**Step 2**
**Filing status**
(Check only one)
**and Exemptions**

**1** ☐ Single (See if you can use Form 1040EZ.)

**2** ☐ Married filing joint return (even if only one had income)

**3** ☐ Married filing separate return. Enter spouse's social security no. above and full name here.

**4** ☐ Head of household (with qualifying person). If the qualifying person is your unmarried child but not your dependent, write this child's name here.

Always check the exemption box labeled Yourself. Check other boxes if they apply.

**5a** ☐ Yourself     ☐ 65 or over     ☐ Blind     Write number of boxes checked on 5a and b ☐

**b** ☐ Spouse     ☐ 65 or over     ☐ Blind

**c** First names of your dependent children who lived with you     Write number of children listed on 5c ☐

Attach Copy B of Forms W-2 here

**d** Other dependents:

| (1) Name | (2) Relationship | (3) Number of months lived in your home. | (4) Did dependent have income of $1,000 or more? | (5) Did you provide more than one-half of dependent's support? |
|---|---|---|---|---|
| | | | | |

Write number of other dependents listed on 5d ☐

**e** Total number of exemptions claimed . . . . . . . . . . . . . . . . . . . . . . . . . Add numbers entered in boxes above ☐

**Step 3**
**Adjusted gross income**

**6** Wages, salaries, tips, etc. *(Attach Forms W-2)*. . . . . . . . . . . . . . . . . . . . . . . . . . 6

**7** Interest income *(Complete page 2 if over $400 or you have any All-Savers interest)*. . . . . . . 7

**8a** Dividends _____ (Complete page 2 if over $400)    **8b** Exclusion _____    Subtract line 8b from 8a . . . 8c

**9a** Unemployment compensation (insurance). Total from Form(s) 1099-UC

**b** Taxable amount, if any, from worksheet on page 16 of Instructions . . . . . . . . . . . . . . . 9b

**10** Add lines 6, 7, 8c, and 9b. This is your total income. . . . . . . . . . . . . . . . . . . . 10

**11** Deduction for a married couple when both work. Complete the worksheet on page 17. . . . . . 11

**12** Subtract line 11 from line 10. This is your adjusted gross income. . . . . . . . . . . . . . 12

**Step 4**
**Taxable income**

**13** Allowable part of your charitable contributions. Complete the worksheet on page 18. . . . . . 13

**14** Subtract line 13 from line 12. . . . . . . . . . . . . . . . . . . . . . . . . . . . . . . . 14

**15** Multiply $1,000 by the total number of exemptions claimed in box 5e . . . . . . . . . . . . 15

**16** Subtract line 15 from line 14. This is your taxable income. . . . . . . . . . . . . . . . . 16

**Step 5**
**Tax, credits, and payments**

Attach check or money order here

**17a** Partial credit for political contributions. See page 19. . . . . . . ■ 17a

**b** Total Federal income tax withheld, from W-2 form(s). *(If line 6 is more than $32,400, see page 19.)*. . . . . . . . . . . . . . . . . . . . . . . . 17b

**Stop Here and Sign Below if You Want IRS to Figure Your Tax**

**c** Earned income credit, from worksheet on page 21 . . . . . . . 17c

**18** Add lines 17a, b, and c. These are your total credits and payments. . . . . . . . . . . . . . 18

**19a** Find tax on amount on line 16. Use tax table, pages 26-31. . . . . . 19a

**b** Advance EIC payment *(from W-2 form(s))*. . . . . . . . . . . . . 19b

**20** Add lines 19a and 19b. This is your total tax. . . . . . . . . . . . . . . . . . . . . . . . 20

**Step 6**
**Refund or amount you owe**

**21** If line 18 is larger than line 20, subtract line 20 from line 18. Enter the amount to be **refunded to you** . . . . . . . . . . . . . . . . . . . . . . . . . . . . . . . . . . . . . . . 21

**22** If line 20 is larger than line 18, subtract line 18 from line 20. Enter the **amount you owe.** Attach payment for full amount payable to "Internal Revenue Service." . . . . . . . . . . . . . 22

**Step 7**
**Sign your return**

I have read this return and any attachments filed with it. Under penalties of perjury, I declare that to the best of my knowledge and belief, the return and attachments are correct and complete.

▶ _____     ▶ _____

Your signature     Date     Spouse's signature (If filing jointly, BOTH must sign)

Paid preparer's signature     Date     Check if self-employed ☐     Preparer's social security no.

Firm's name (or yours, if self-employed)     E.I. no.

Address and Zip code

For **Privacy Act and Paperwork Reduction Act Notice,** see page 34.

## 1982 Form 1040A                                                                    Page 2

**Caution:** You may **NOT** file Form 1040A (you must file Form 1040 instead) if any of the following apply to you:

- You could be claimed as a dependent on your parent's return AND had interest, dividends, or other unearned income of $1,000 or more.
- You had a foreign financial account or were a grantor of, or transferor to, a foreign trust.
- You received interest or dividends as a nominee (in your name) for someone else.
- You received or paid accrued interest on securities transferred between interest payment dates.
- You received capital gain distributions or nontaxable distributions.
- You are choosing to exclude qualified reinvested dividends from a qualified public utility.
  **Note:** You may also be required to file Form 1040 for other reasons. See pages 4 through 6 of instructions.

**Part I** | **Interest income**

You must complete this part if you received over $400 in interest income, OR you received any interest from an All-Savers Certificate (ASC). Use lines 1 and 2 to report interest income other than ASC interest. Use lines 3 through 6 to report ASC interest. Use line 7 to add the totals from lines 2 and 6.

**Interest income from sources other than All-Savers Certificates. (See page 14)**

**1** List names of payers                     Amount

$
$
$
$
$
$
$
$

**2** Add amounts on line 1. This is your total interest from other than ASCs.                          2

**Interest income from All-Savers Certificates. (See page 14)**

**3** List names of payers                     Amount

$
$
$

**4** Add amounts on line 3.                                              4

**5** Write the amount of your ASC exclusion from the worksheet on page 14 of the instructions.                                                      5

**6** Subtract line 5 from line 4. This is your taxable ASC interest.                          6

**7** Add lines 2 and 6 and write your answer here. This is your total taxable interest. Also write this amount on line 7 of Form 1040A.                                             7

**Part II** | **Dividend income**

You must complete this part if you received over $400 in ordinary dividends. See page 15 for information on the dividend exclusion.

**8** List names of payers                     Amount

$
$
$
$
$
$

**9** Add amounts on line 8. Write your answer here and on line 8a of Form 1040A.                          9

## B–2 FORM 1040EZ INCOME TAX RETURN
## FOR SINGLE FILERS WITH NO DEPENDENTS

Department of the Treasury — Internal Revenue Service

**1982**   **Form 1040EZ Income Tax Return for
Single filers with no dependents**                      OMB No. 1545-0675

Instructions are on the back of this form.
Tax Table is in the 1040EZ and 1040A Tax Package.

---

**Name and address**

Use the IRS mailing label. If you don't have a label, print or type:

| Name (first, initial, last) | Social security number |

Present home address

City, town or post office, State, and ZIP code

---

**Presidential Election Campaign Fund**
Check this box ☐ if you want $1 of your tax to go to this fund.

---

**Figure your tax**

Attach Copy B of Forms W-2 here

**1** Wages, salaries, and tips. Attach your W-2 form(s).                1       .

**2** Interest income of $400 or less. If more than $400, you cannot use Form 1040EZ.  2      .

**3** Add line 1 and line 2. This is your **adjusted gross income**.     3       .

**4** Allowable part of your charitable contributions. Complete the worksheet on page 18. Do not write more than $25.     4       .

**5** Subtract line 4 from line 3.                                       5       .

**6** Amount of your personal exemption.                                 6    1,000.00

**7** Subtract line 6 from line 5. This is your **taxable income**.       7       .

**8** Enter your Federal income tax withheld. This is shown on your W-2 form(s).  8       .

**9** Use the tax table on pages 26-31 to find the **tax** on your taxable income on line 7.                            9       .

**Refund or amount you owe**

Attach tax payment here

**10** If line 8 is larger than line 9, subtract line 9 from line 8. Enter the amount of your **refund**.            10      .

**11** If line 9 is larger than line 8, subtract line 8 from line 9. Enter the **amount you owe**. Attach check or money order for the full amount payable to "Internal Revenue Service."     11      .

**Sign your return**

I have read this return. Under penalties of perjury, I declare that to the best of my knowledge and belief, the return is correct and complete.

Your signature                                   Date

**X**

For **Privacy Act and Paperwork Reduction Act Notice**, see page 34.

| You can use this form if: | You cannot use this form if: |
|---|---|
| • Your filing status is single | • Your filing status is other than single |
| • You do not claim exemptions for being 65 or over, **OR** for being blind | • You claim exemptions for being 65 or over, **OR** for being blind |
| • You do not claim any dependents | • You claim any dependents |
| • Your taxable income is less than $50,000 | • Your taxable income is $50,000 or more |
| • You had only wages, salaries, and tips and you had interest income of $400 or less | • You had income other than wages and interest income, **OR** you had interest of over $400 or any interest from an All-Savers Certificate |
| • You had no dividend income | • You had dividend income |

If you can't use this form, you must use Form 1040A or 1040 instead. See pages 4 through 6.
If you are uncertain about your filing status, dependents, or exemptions, read the step-by-step instructions for Form 1040A that begin on page 6.

## Completing your return

### Name and address
Use the mailing label from the back cover of the instruction booklet. Correct any errors right on the label. But don't place the label on your return until you have completed it. If you don't have a label, print or type the information in the spaces provided. If you don't have a social security number, see page 7.

### Presidential election campaign fund
This fund was established by Congress to help pay campaign costs of candidates running for President. You may have one of your tax dollars go to this fund by checking the box.

### Figure your tax
**Line 1.** Write on line 1 the total amount you received in wages, salaries, and tips from all employers.

Your employer should have reported your income on a 1982 wage statement, Form W-2. If you don't receive your W-2 form by February 15, contact your local IRS office. Attach W-2 form(s) to your return.

**Line 2.** Write on line 2 the total interest income you received from all sources, such as banks, savings and loans, credit unions, and other institutions with which you deposit money. You should receive an interest statement (usually Form 1099-INT) from each institution that paid you interest.

You cannot use Form 1040EZ if your total interest income is over $400 **or** you received interest income from an All-Savers Certificate.

**Line 4.** You can deduct 25% of what you gave to qualified charitable organizations in 1982. But if you gave $100 or more, you can't deduct more than $25. Complete the worksheet on page 18 to figure your deduction, and write the amount on line 4.

**Line 6.** Every taxpayer is entitled to one $1,000 personal exemption. If you are also entitled to additional exemptions for being 65 or over, for blindness, for your spouse, or for your dependent children or other dependents, you cannot use this form. You must use Form 1040A or Form 1040.

**Line 8.** Write the amount of Federal income tax withheld, as shown on your 1982 W-2 form(s). If you had two or more employers and had total wages of over $32,400, see page 19. If you want IRS to figure your tax for you, complete lines 1 through 8, sign, and date your return. If you want to figure your own tax, continue with these instructions.

**Line 9.** Use the amount on line 7 to find your tax in the tax table on pages 26-31. Be sure to use the column in the tax table for **single** taxpayers. Write the amount of tax on line 9.

### Refund or amount you owe
**Line 10.** Compare line 8 with line 9. If line 8 is larger than line 9, you are entitled to a refund. Subtract line 9 from line 8, and write the result on line 10.

**Line 11.** If line 9 is larger than line 8, you owe more tax. Subtract line 8 from line 9, and write the result on line 11. Attach your check or money order for the full amount. Write your social security number and "1982 Form 1040EZ" on your payment.

### Sign your return
You must sign and date your return. If you pay someone to prepare your return, that person must also sign it below the space for your signature and supply the other information required by IRS. See page 22.

## Mailing your return
Your return is due by **April 15, 1983.** Use the addressed envelope that came with the instruction booklet. If you don't have an addressed envelope, see page 25 for the correct address.

## B-3 FORM 1040 U.S. INDIVIDUAL INCOME TAX RETURN

Form **1040**

Department of the Treasury—Internal Revenue Service

**U.S. Individual Income Tax Return** 1982

For the year January 1–December 31, 1982, or other tax year beginning   , 1982, ending   , 19   .   OMB No. 1545-0074

| | |
|---|---|
| Use IRS label. Other-wise, please print or type. | Your first name and initial (if joint return, also give spouse's name and initial)    Last name    **Your social security number** |
| | Present home address (Number and street, including apartment number, or rural route)    **Spouse's social security no.** |
| | City, town or post office, State and ZIP code    Your occupation ▶    Spouse's occupation ▶ |

**Presidential Election Campaign** ▶ Do you want $1 to go to this fund? . . . . . . . . . . . . . . . . Yes ☐ No ☐
If joint return, does your spouse want $1 to go to this fund? . . . Yes ☐ No ☐

Note: Checking "Yes" will not increase your tax or re-duce your refund.

**Filing Status**

Check only one box.

1 ☐ Single

For Privacy Act and Paperwork Reduction Act Notice, see Instructions.

2 ☐ Married filing joint return (even if only one had income)

3 ☐ Married filing separate return. Enter spouse's social security no. above and full name here ▶ .............

4 ☐ Head of household (with qualifying person). (See page 6 of Instructions.) If the qualifying person is your un-married child but not your dependent, enter child's name ▶ .............

5 ☐ Qualifying widow(er) with dependent child (Year spouse died ▶ 19   ). (See page 6 of Instructions.)

**Exemptions**

Always check the box labeled Yourself. Check other boxes if they apply.

6a ☐ Yourself    ☐ 65 or over    ☐ Blind
b ☐ Spouse    ☐ 65 or over    ☐ Blind

} Enter number of boxes checked on 6a and b ▶ ☐

c First names of your dependent children who lived with you ▶ .............

} Enter number of children listed on 6c ▶ ☐

| d Other dependents: (1) Name | (2) Relationship | (3) Number of months lived in your home | (4) Did dependent have income of $1,000 or more? | (5) Did you provide more than one-half of dependent's support? |
|---|---|---|---|---|
| | | | | |
| | | | | |
| | | | | |
| | | | | |

Enter number of other dependents ▶ ☐

e Total number of exemptions claimed . . . . . . . . . . . . . . . . .

Add numbers entered in boxes above ▶ ☐

**Income**

Please attach Copy B of your Forms W–2 here.

If you do not have a W–2, see page 5 of Instructions.

Please attach check or money order here.

7 Wages, salaries, tips, etc. . . . . . . . . . . . . . . . . . .   **7**

8 Interest income (attach Schedule B if over $400 or you have any All-Savers interest) . . . .   **8**

9a Dividends (attach Schedule B if over $400) ............., 9b Exclusion............

c Subtract line 9b from line 9a . . . . . . . . . . . . . .   **9c**

10 Refunds of State and local income taxes (do not enter an amount unless you de-ducted those taxes in an earlier year—see page 9 of Instructions) . . . . . . . .   **10**

11 Alimony received . . . . . . . . . . . . . . . . . . . .   **11**

12 Business income or (loss) (attach Schedule C) . . . . . . . . . . . . ▶   **12**

13 Capital gain or (loss) (attach Schedule D) . . . . . . . . . . . . .   **13**

14 40% capital gain distributions not reported on line 13 (See page 9 of Instructions)   **14**

15 Supplemental gains or (losses) (attach Form 4797) . . . . . . . . . . .   **15**

16 Fully taxable pensions, IRA distributions, and annuities not reported on line 17 . .   **16**

17a Other pensions and annuities. Total received . . . . **17a**

b Taxable amount, if any, from worksheet on page 10 of Instructions . . . . . . .   **17b**

18 Rents, royalties, partnerships, estates, trusts, etc. (attach Schedule E) . . . . . .   **18**

19 Farm income or (loss) (attach Schedule F) . . . . . . . . . . . . . ▶   **19**

20a Unemployment compensation (insurance). Total received **20a**

b Taxable amount, if any, from worksheet on page 10 of Instructions . . . . . . . .   **20b**

21 Other income (state nature and source—see page 10 of Instructions) ▶ .............   **21**

22 **Total income.** Add amounts in column for lines 7 through 21 . . . . . . . . . . ▶   **22**

**Adjustments to Income**

(See Instruc-tions on page 11)

23 Moving expense (attach Form 3903 or 3903F) . . .   **23**

24 Employee business expenses (attach Form 2106) . .   **24**

25 Payments to an IRA. You **must** enter code from page 11 (........) . . . . . . . . . . . . . . .   **25**

26 Payments to a Keogh (H.R. 10) retirement plan . . .   **26**

27 Penalty on early withdrawal of savings . . . . . . .   **27**

28 Alimony paid . . . . . . . . . . . . . . . . . . .   **28**

29 Deduction for a married couple when both work (at-tach Schedule W) . . . . . . . . . . . . . . .   **29**

30 Disability income exclusion (attach Form 2440) . . .   **30**

31 Total adjustments. Add lines 23 through 30. . . . . . . . . . . ▶   **31**

**Adjusted Gross Income**

32 **Adjusted gross income.** Subtract line 31 from line 22. If this line is less than $10,000, see "Earned Income Credit" (line 62) on page 15 of Instructions. If you want IRS to figure your tax, see page 3 of Instructions . . . . . . . . ▶   **32**

363–062–2

Form 1040 (1982)                                                                                                    Page **2**

| | | | | |
|---|---|---|---|---|
| **Tax Compu-tation** (See Instruc-tions on page 12) | 33 | Amount from line 32 *(adjusted gross income)* . . . . . . . . . . . . . . . . . | 33 | |
| | 34a | If you itemize, complete Schedule A (Form 1040) and enter the amount from Schedule A, line 30 . . . . | 34a | |
| | | **Caution:** If you have unearned income and can be claimed as a dependent on your parent's return, check here ▶ ☐ and see page 12 of the Instructions. Also see page 12 of the Instructions if: <br> ● You are married filing a separate return and your spouse itemizes deductions, OR <br> ● You file Form 4563, OR    ● You are a dual-status alien. | | |
| | 34b | If you do not itemize, complete the worksheet on page 13. Then enter the allowable part of your charitable contributions here . . . . . . . . . . . . . . . . | 34b | |
| | 35 | Subtract line 34a or 34b, whichever applies, from line 33 . . . . . . . . . . | 35 | |
| | 36 | Multiply $1,000 by the total number of exemptions claimed on Form 1040, line 6e . . | 36 | |
| | 37 | Taxable Income. Subtract line 36 from line 35 . . . . . . . . . . . . . . . | 37 | |
| | 38 | Tax. Enter tax here and check if from ☐ Tax Table, ☐ Tax Rate Schedule X, Y, or Z, or ☐ Schedule G . . . . . . . . . . . . . . . . . . . . . . . . . . . | 38 | |
| | 39 | Additional Taxes. (See page 13 of Instructions.) Enter here and check if from ☐ Form 4970, ☐ Form 4972, ☐ Form 5544, or ☐ section 72 penalty taxes . . . . . . . . . . . | 39 | |
| | 40 | **Total.** Add lines 38 and 39 . . . . . . . . . . . . . . . . . . . . ▶ | 40 | |
| **Credits** (See Instruc-tions on page 13) | 41 | Credit for the elderly *(attach Schedules R&RP)* . . . . . | 41 | |
| | 42 | Foreign tax credit *(attach Form 1116)* . . . . . . . . | 42 | |
| | 43 | Investment credit *(attach Form 3468)* . . . . . . . . | 43 | |
| | 44 | Partial credit for political contributions . . . . . . . . | 44 | |
| | 45 | Credit for child and dependent care expenses (*attach* Form 2441) . | 45 | |
| | 46 | Jobs credit *(attach Form 5884)* . . . . . . . . . | 46 | |
| | 47 | Residential energy credit *(attach Form 5695)* . . . . . | 47 | |
| | 48 | Other credits—see page 14 ▶ | 48 | |
| | 49 | **Total credits.** Add lines 41 through 48 . . . . . . . . . . . . . . . . | 49 | |
| | 50 | **Balance.** Subtract line 49 from line 40 and enter difference (but not less than zero) . ▶ | 50 | |
| **Other Taxes** (Including Advance EIC Payments) | 51 | Self-employment tax *(attach Schedule SE)* . . . . . . . . . . . . . . . . | 51 | |
| | 52 | Minimum tax *(attach Form 4625)* . . . . . . . . . . . . . . . . . . . | 52 | |
| | 53 | Alternative minimum tax *(attach Form 6251)* . . . . . . . . . . . . . . . | 53 | |
| | 54 | Tax from recapture of investment credit *(attach Form 4255)* . . . . . . . . . | 54 | |
| | 55 | Social security (FICA) tax on tip income not reported to employer *(attach Form 4137)* . | 55 | |
| | 56 | Uncollected employee FICA and RRTA tax on tips *(from Form W–2)* . . . . . . . | 56 | |
| | 57 | Tax on an IRA *(attach Form 5329)* . . . . . . . . . . . . . . . . . . . | 57 | |
| | 58 | Advance earned income credit (EIC) payments received *(from Form W–2)* . . . . . | 58 | |
| 06 | 59 | **Total tax.** Add lines 50 through 58 . . . . . . . . . . . . . . ■ | 59 | |
| **Payments** Attach Forms W–2, W–2G, and W–2P to front. | 60 | Total Federal income tax withheld . . . . . . . . . . | 60 | |
| | 61 | 1982 estimated tax payments and amount applied from 1981 return . | 61 | |
| | 62 | Earned income credit. If line 33 is under $10,000, see page 15 of Instructions . . . . . . . . . . . . . . . | 62 | |
| | 63 | Amount paid with Form 4868 . . . . . . . . . . . | 63 | |
| | 64 | Excess FICA and RRTA tax withheld (two or more employers) . | 64 | |
| | 65 | Credit for Federal tax on special fuels and oils *(attach Form 4136)* . . . . . . . . . . . . . . . . . | 65 | |
| | 66 | Regulated Investment Company credit *(attach Form 2439)* | 66 | |
| | 67 | **Total.** Add lines 60 through 66 . . . . . . . . . . . . . . . . . ▶ | 67 | |
| **Refund or Amount You Owe** | 68 | If line 67 is larger than line 59, enter amount **OVERPAID** . . . . . . . . . . . ▶ | 68 | |
| | 69 | Amount of line 68 to be **REFUNDED TO YOU** . . . . . . . . . . . . . . ▶ | 69 | |
| | 70 | Amount of line 68 to be applied to your 1983 estimated tax . . . ▶ | 70 | |
| | 71 | If line 59 is larger than line 67, enter **AMOUNT YOU OWE.** Attach check or money order for full amount payable to Internal Revenue Service. Write your social security number and "1982 Form 1040" on it. ▶ (Check ▶ ☐ if Form 2210 (2210F) is attached. See page 16 of Instructions.) ▶ $ | 71 | |

| | |
|---|---|
| **Please Sign Here** | Under penalties of perjury, I declare that I have examined this return, including accompanying schedules and statements, and to the best of my knowledge and belief, it is true, correct, and complete. Declaration of preparer (other than taxpayer) is based on all information of which preparer has any knowledge. <br><br> ▶ _____  \| _____   ▶ _____ <br> Your signature                        Date                    Spouse's signature (if filing jointly, BOTH must sign) |
| **Paid Preparer's Use Only** | Preparer's signature ▶ _____ \| Date _____ \| Check if self-em-ployed ▶ ☐ \| Preparer's social security no. _____ <br> Firm's name (or yours, if self-employed) ▶ _____ and address \| E.I. No. ▶ _____ \| ZIP code ▶ _____ |

**Schedules A&B (Form 1040)**
Department of the Treasury
Internal Revenue Service

## Schedule A—Itemized Deductions
(Schedule B is on back)
▶ Attach to Form 1040.  ▶ See Instructions for Schedules A and B (Form 1040).

OMB No. 1545-0074

**1982**
07

Name(s) as shown on Form 1040

Your social security number

| | | | | |
|---|---|---|---|---|
| **Medical and Dental Expenses** (Do not include expenses reimbursed or paid by others.) (See page 17 of Instructions.) | 1 Medicines and drugs | 1 | | |
| | 2 Write 1% of Form 1040, line 33 | 2 | | |
| | 3 Subtract line 2 from line 1. If line 2 is more than line 1, write zero | 3 | | |
| | 4 Total insurance premiums you paid for medical and dental care | 4 | | |
| | 5 Other medical and dental expenses: | | | |
| | a Doctors, dentists, nurses, hospitals, etc. | 5a | | |
| | b Transportation | 5b | | |
| | c Other (list—include hearing aids, dentures, eyeglasses, etc.) ▶ | | | |
| | | 5c | | |
| | 6 Add lines 3 through 5c | 6 | | |
| | 7 Multiply amount on Form 1040, line 33, by 3% (.03) | 7 | | |
| | 8 Subtract line 7 from line 6. If line 7 is more than line 6, write zero | 8 | | |
| | 9 Write one-half of amount on line 4, but not more than $150 | 9 | | |
| | 10 COMPARE amounts on line 8 and line 9, and write the LARGER amount here ▶ | 10 | | |
| **Taxes** (See page 18 of Instructions.) | 11 State and local income | 11 | | |
| | 12 Real estate | 12 | | |
| | 13 a General sales (see sales tax tables) | 13a | | |
| | b General sales on motor vehicles | 13b | | |
| | 14 Other (list—include personal property) ▶ | 14 | | |
| | 15 Add lines 11 through 14. Write your answer here ▶ | 15 | | |
| **Interest Expense** (See page 19 of Instructions.) | 16 a Home mortgage interest paid to financial institutions | 16a | | |
| | b Home mortgage interest paid to individuals (show that person's name and address) ▶ | | | |
| | | 16b | | |
| | 17 Credit cards and charge accounts | 17 | | |
| | 18 Other (list) ▶ | | | |
| | | 18 | | |
| | 19 Add lines 16a through 18. Write your answer here ▶ | 19 | | |
| **Contributions** (See page 19 of Instructions.) | 20 a Cash contributions. (If you gave $3,000 or more to any one organization, report those contributions on line 20b.) | 20a | | |
| | b Cash contributions totaling $3,000 or more to any one organization. (Show to whom you gave and how much you gave.) ▶ | | | |
| | | 20b | | |
| | 21 Other than cash (see page 19 of Instructions for required statement) | 21 | | |
| | 22 Carryover from prior years | 22 | | |
| | 23 Add lines 20a through 22. Write your answer here ▶ | 23 | | |
| **Casualty and Theft Losses and Miscellaneous Deductions** (See page 20 of Instructions.) | 24 Total casualty or theft loss(es) (attach Form 4684) | 24 | | |
| | 25 a Union and professional dues | 25a | | |
| | b Tax return preparation fee | 25b | | |
| | 26 Other (list) ▶ | | | |
| | | 26 | | |
| | 27 Add lines 24 through 26. Write your answer here ▶ | 27 | | |
| **Summary of Itemized Deductions** (See page 20 of Instructions.) | 28 Add lines 10, 15, 19, 23, and 27 | 28 | 6200 | |
| | 29 If you checked Form 1040, Filing Status box { 2 or 5, write $3,400. 1 or 4, write $2,300. 3, write $1,700. } | 29 | 3400 | |
| | 30 Subtract line 29 from line 28. Write your answer here and on Form 1040, line 34a. (If line 29 is more than line 28, see the Instructions for line 30 on page 20.) ▶ | 30 | 2800 | |

**A**

For Paperwork Reduction Act Notice, see Form 1040 Instructions.

363-064 2

Schedules A&B (Form 1040) 1982     **Schedule B—Interest and Dividend Income**     OMB No. 1545-0074     Page **2**

Name(s) as shown on Form 1040 (Do not enter name and social security number if shown on other side) | Your social security number

| **Part I** **Interest Income** *(See pages 8 and 20 of Instructions.)* Also complete Part III if you received more than $400 in interest. | If you received more than **$400 in interest** or you received any interest from an All-Savers Certificate, you must complete Part I and list ALL interest received. If you received interest as a nominee for another, or you received or paid accrued interest on securities transferred between interest payment dates, please see page 20. |
|---|---|

| Interest income other than interest from All-Savers Certificates | | Amount |
|---|---|---|
| **1** Interest income from seller-financed mortgages. (See Instructions and show name of payer.) | **1** | |
| **2** Other interest income (list name of payer) _____ | | |
| | | |
| | | |
| | | |
| | | |
| | | |
| | | |
| | | |
| | | |
| | | |
| | | |
| | | |
| **3** Add lines 1 and 2 . . . . . . . . . . . . . . . . . | **3** | |

| Interest from All-Savers Certificates (ASCs). (See page 21.) | | Amount |
|---|---|---|
| **4** | | |
| | | |
| | | |
| **5** Add amounts on line 4 . . . . . . . . . . . . . . | **5** | |
| **6** Write the amount of your ASC exclusion from the worksheet on page 21 of Instructions . . . | **6** | |
| **7** Subtract line 6 from line 5 . . . . . . . . . . . . . . | **7** | |
| **8** Add lines 3 and 7. Write your answer here and on Form 1040, line 8 . . . ▶ | **8** | |

| **Part II** **Dividend Income** *(See pages 9 and 21 of Instructions.)* Also complete Part III if you received more than $400 in dividends. | If you received more than **$400 in gross dividends** (including capital gain distributions) and other distributions on stock, or you are electing to exclude qualified reinvested dividends from a public utility, complete Part II. If you received dividends as a nominee for another, see page 21. |
|---|---|

| Name of payer | | | Amount |
|---|---|---|---|
| **9** | | | |
| | | | |
| | | | |
| | | | |
| | | | |
| | | | |
| | | | |
| | | | |
| **10** Add amounts on line 9 . . . . . . . . . . . . . . . | | **10** | |
| **11** Capital gain distributions. Enter here and on line 13, Schedule D.* . . . . . . . . . . | **11** | | |
| **12** Nontaxable distributions. (See Instructions for adjustment to basis.) . | **12** | | |
| **13** Exclusion of qualified reinvested dividends from a public utility. (See Instructions.) . . . . . . . . . | **13** | | |
| **14** Add lines 11, 12, and 13 . . . . . . . . . . . . . . | | **14** | |
| **15** Subtract line 14 from line 10. Write your answer here and on Form 1040, line 9a . . ▶ | | **15** | |

**B**

*If you received capital gain distributions for the year and you do not need Schedule D to report any other gains or losses, do not file that schedule. Instead, enter 40% of your capital gain distributions on Form 1040, line 14.

| **Part III** **Foreign Accounts and Foreign Trusts** *(See page 21 of Instructions.)* | If you received more than **$400 of interest or dividends**, OR if you had a foreign account or were a grantor of, or a transferor to, a foreign trust, you must answer both questions in Part III. | Yes | No |
|---|---|---|---|
| | **16** At any time during the tax year, did you have an interest in or a signature or other authority over a bank account, securities account, or other financial account in a foreign country? . . . . . . . . | | |
| | **17** Were you the grantor of, or transferor to, a foreign trust which existed during the current tax year, whether or not you have any beneficial interest in it? If "Yes," you may have to file Forms 3520, 3520-A, or 926 . . . . . . . . . . . . . . . . . . . . . | | |

**For Paperwork Reduction Act Notice, see Form 1040 Instructions.**

**SCHEDULE C**
**(Form 1040)**
Department of the Treasury
Internal Revenue Service

# Profit or (Loss) From Business or Profession
(Sole Proprietorship)
Partnerships, Joint Ventures, etc., Must File Form 1065.
▶ Attach to Form 1040 or Form 1041.   ▶ See Instructions for Schedule C (Form 1040).

OMB. No. 1545-0074

**1982**
**08**

Name of proprietor

Social security number of proprietor

**A** Main business activity (see Instructions) ▶ _____ ; product ▶ _____

**B** Business name ▶ _____

**C** Employer identification number

**D** Business address (number and street) ▶ _____
City, State and ZIP Code ▶ _____

**E** Accounting method: **(1)** ☐ Cash   **(2)** ☐ Accrual   **(3)** ☐ Other (specify) ▶ _____

**C**

**F** Method(s) used to value closing inventory:
**(1)** ☐ Cost   **(2)** ☐ Lower of cost or market   **(3)** ☐ Other (if other, attach explanation)

| | Yes | No |
|---|---|---|

**G** Was there any major change in determining quantities, costs, or valuations between opening and closing inventory? . .
If "Yes," attach explanation.

**H** Did you deduct expenses for an office in your home? . . . . . . . . . . . .

**I** Did you operate this business at the end of 1982? . . . . . . . . . . . .

**J** How many months in 1982 did you actively operate this business? ▶ _____

## Part I   Income

| | | | | |
|---|---|---|---|---|
| **1 a** Gross receipts or sales . . . . . . . . . . | **1a** | | | |
| **b** Returns and allowances . . . . . . . . . | **1b** | | | |
| **c** Balance (subtract line 1b from line 1a) . . . . . . . . . . . . . . | **1c** | | | |
| **2** Cost of goods sold and/or operations (Schedule C–1, line 8) . . . . . . . . . . | **2** | | | |
| **3** Gross profit (subtract line 2 from line 1c) . . . . . . . . . . . . . . | **3** | | | |
| **4 a** Windfall Profit Tax Credit or Refund received in 1982 (see Instructions) . . . . . . | **4a** | | | |
| **b** Other income . . . . . . . . . . . . . . . . | **4b** | | | |
| **5** Total income (add lines 3, 4a, and 4b) . . . . . . . . . . . . . . . . ▶ | **5** | | | |

## Part II   Deductions

| | | | | | | |
|---|---|---|---|---|---|---|
| **6** Advertising . . . . . . . . | | | **25** Taxes (Do not include Windfall Profit Tax here. See line 29.) . . | | | |
| **7** Bad debts from sales or services (Cash method taxpayers, see Instructions) . . . . . . . . | | | **26** Travel and entertainment . . | | | |
| | | | **27** Utilities and telephone . . . | | | |
| **8** Bank service charges . . . . . | | | **28 a** Wages . . | | | |
| **9** Car and truck expenses . . . . | | | **b** Jobs credit | | | |
| **10** Commissions . . . . . . . | | | **c** Subtract line 28b from 28a . | | | |
| **11** Depletion . . . . . . . . | | | **29** Windfall Profit Tax withheld in 1982 . . . . . . . . . | | | |
| **12** Depreciation, including Section 179 expense deduction (from Form 4562) . . . . . . . | | | **30** Other expenses (specify): | | | |
| | | | **a** | | | |
| **13** Dues and publications . . . . | | | **b** | | | |
| **14** Employee benefit programs . . | | | **c** | | | |
| **15** Freight (not included on Schedule C–1) . | | | **d** | | | |
| **16** Insurance . . . . . . . . | | | **e** | | | |
| **17** Interest on business indebtedness | | | **f** | | | |
| **18** Laundry and cleaning . . . . | | | **g** | | | |
| **19** Legal and professional services . | | | **h** | | | |
| **20** Office supplies and postage . . . | | | **i** | | | |
| **21** Pension and profit-sharing plans . | | | **j** | | | |
| **22** Rent on business property . . . | | | **k** | | | |
| **23** Repairs . . . . . . . . . | | | **l** | | | |
| **24** Supplies (not included on Schedule C–1) . | | | **m** | | | |

| | | |
|---|---|---|
| **31** Total deductions (add amounts in columns for lines 6 through 30m) . . . . . . . ▶ | **31** | |

**32** Net profit or (loss) (subtract line 31 from line 5). If a profit, enter on Form 1040, line 12, and on Schedule SE, Part I, line 2 (or Form 1041, line 6). If a loss, go on to line 33 . . . . . . | **32** |

**33** If you have a loss, do you have amounts for which you are not "at risk" in this business (see Instructions)? . . ☐ Yes  ☐ No
If you checked "No," enter the loss on Form 1040, line 12, and on Schedule SE, Part I, line 2 (or Form 1041, line 6).

For Paperwork Reduction Act Notice, see Form 1040 Instructions.

363-065-2

**SCHEDULE C–1.—Cost of Goods Sold and/or Operations** (See Schedule C Instructions for Part I, line 2)

| | | | |
|---|---|---|---|
| 1 Inventory at beginning of year (if different from last year's closing inventory, attach explanation) . | **1** | | |
| 2 Purchases (less cost of items withdrawn for personal use) . . . . . . . . . . . . . | **2** | | |
| 3 Cost of labor (do not include salary paid to yourself) . . . . . . . . . . . . . | **3** | | |
| 4 Materials and supplies . . . . . . . . . . . . . . . . . . . . . | **4** | | |
| 5 Other costs . . . . . . . . . . . . . . . . . . . . . . | **5** | | |
| 6 Add lines 1 through 5 . . . . . . . . . . . . . . . . . . . | **6** | | |
| 7 Inventory at end of year . . . . . . . . . . . . . . . . . . | **7** | | |
| 8 Cost of goods sold and/or operations (subtract line 7 from line 6). Enter here and on Part I, line 2 . ▶ | **8** | | |

☆ U.S. GOVERNMENT PRINTING OFFICE : 1982—O-363-065

363-065-1

| SCHEDULE D (FORM 1040) | **Capital Gains and Losses** (Examples of property to be reported on this Schedule are gains and losses on stocks, bonds, and similar investments, and gains (but not losses) on personal assets such as a home or jewelry.) | OMB No. 1545-0074 |
|---|---|---|
| Department of the Treasury Internal Revenue Service | ▶ Attach to Form 1040.     ▶ See Instructions for Schedule D (Form 1040). | **1982** 14 |

| Name(s) as shown on Form 1040 | Your social security number |
|---|---|

**Part I    Short-term Capital Gains and Losses—Assets Held One Year or Less**     **D**

| a. Kind of property and description (Example, 100 shares 7% preferred of ''Z'' Co.) | b. Date acquired (Mo., day, yr.) | c. Date sold (Mo., day, yr.) | d. Gross sales price less expense of sale | e. Cost or other basis, as adjusted (see instructions page 23) | f. LOSS If column (e) is more than (d) subtract (d) from (e) | g. GAIN If column (d) is more than (e) subtract (e) from (d) |
|---|---|---|---|---|---|---|
| 1 | | | | | | |
| | | | | | | |
| | | | | | | |
| | | | | | | |
| | | | | | | |
| | | | | | | |
| | | | | | | |

2a  Gain from sale or exchange of a principal residence held one year or less, from Form 2119, lines 7 or 11 . . . . . . . . . . . . . .  **2a**

  b  Short-term capital gain from installment sales from Form 6252, line 21 or 29 .  **2b**

3  Net short-term gain or (loss) from partnerships and fiduciaries . . . . .  **3**

4  Add lines 1 through 3 in column f and column g . . . . . . . . .  **4** ( )

5  Combine line 4, column f and line 4, column g and enter the net gain or (loss) . . . . . . . .  **5**

6  Short-term capital loss carryover from years beginning after 1969 . . . . . . . . . . . .  **6** ( )

7  Net short-term gain or (loss), combine lines 5 and 6 . . . . . . . .  **7** *(600 00)*

**Part II    Long-term Capital Gains and Losses—Assets Held More Than One Year**

| 8 | | | | | | |
|---|---|---|---|---|---|---|
| | | | | | | |
| | | | | | | |
| | | | | | | |
| | | | | | | |
| | | | | | | |
| | | | | | | |
| | | | | | | |

9a  Gain from sale or exchange of a principal residence held more than one year, from Form 2119, lines 7, 11, 16 or 18 . . . . . . . . . . . . .  **9a**

  b  Long-term capital gain from installment sales from Form 6252, line 21 or 29 .  **9b**

10  Net long-term gain or (loss) from partnerships and fiduciaries . . . . .  **10**

11  Add lines 8 through 10 in column f and column g . . . . . . . . .  **11** ( )

12  Combine line 11, column f and line 11, column g and enter the net gain or (loss) . . . . . .  **12**

13  Capital gain distributions . . . . . . . . . . . . . . . . .  **13**

14  Enter gain from Form 4797, line 5(a)(1) . . . . . . . . . . . .  **14**

15  Enter your share of net long-term gain from small business corporations (Subchapter S) . . . .  **15**

16  Combine lines 12 through 15 . . . . . . . . . . . . . . . .  **16**

17  Long-term capital loss carryover from years beginning after 1969 . . . . . . .  **17** ( )

18  Net long-term gain or (loss), combine lines 16 and 17 . . . . . . . . . . . . . .  **18** *3100 00*

**Note:** Complete this form on reverse. However, if you have capital loss carryovers from years beginning before 1970, do not complete Parts III or V. See Form 4798 instead.

**For Paperwork Reduction Act Notice, see Form 1040 instructions**                                    363-066-1

Schedule D (Form 1040) 1982                                                                          Page **2**

**Part III**  Summary of Parts I and II

| | | | |
|---|---|---|---|
| **19** Combine lines 7 and 18, and enter the net gain or (loss) here . . . . . . . . . | | **19** | 2500 00 |

**Note:** *If line 19 is a loss, skip lines 20 through 22 and complete lines 23 and 24. If line 19 is a gain complete lines 20 through 22 and skip lines 23 and 24.* . . . . . . . . .

**20** If line 19 shows a gain, enter the smaller of line 18 or line 19. Enter zero if there is a loss or no entry on line 18 . . . . . . . . . . . . . . . . .    **20** | 2500

| | | |
|---|---|---|
| **21** Enter 60% of line 20 . . . . . . . . . . | **21** | 1500 00 |
| *If line 21 is more than zero, you may be liable for the alternative minimum tax. See Form 6251.* | | |
| **22** Subtract line 21 from line 19. Enter here and on Form 1040, line 13 . . . . . . . . . . | **22** | 1000 00 |

**23** If line 19 shows a loss, enter one of the following amounts:
(i)   If line 7 is zero or a net gain, enter 50% of line 19;
(ii)  If line 18 is zero or a net gain, enter line 19; or
(iii) If line 7 and line 18 are net losses, enter amount on line 7 added to 50% of the amount on line 18     **23**

**24** Enter here and as a loss on Form 1040, line 13, the smallest of:
(i)   The amount on line 23;
(ii)  $3,000 ($1,500 if married and filing a separate return); or
(iii) Taxable income, as adjusted . . . . . . . . . . . . . . . . . .     **24**

**Part IV**  Complete this Part Only if You Elect Out of the Installment Method And Report a Note or Other Obligation at Less Than Full Face Value

☐ Check here if you elect out of the installment method.

Enter the face amount of the note or other obligation ▶ .............................................................................
Enter the percentage of valuation of the note or other obligation ▶

**Part V**  Computation of Post-1969 Capital Loss Carryovers from 1982 to 1983
*(Complete this part if the loss on line 23 is more than the loss on line 24)*
**Note:** You do not have to complete Part V on the copy you file with IRS.

### Section A.—Short-term Capital Loss Carryover

| | | | |
|---|---|---|---|
| **25** Enter loss shown on line 7; if none, enter zero and skip lines 26 through 30—then go to line 31 . . | **25** | | |
| **26** Enter gain shown on line 18. If that line is blank or shows a loss, enter zero . . . . . . . . | **26** | | |
| **27** Reduce any loss on line 25 to the extent of any gain on line 26 . . . . . . . . . . . | **27** | | |
| **28** Enter amount shown on line 24 . . . . . . . . . . . . . . . . . | **28** | | |
| **29** Enter smaller of line 27 or 28 . . . . . . . . . . . . . . . . | **29** | | |
| **30** Subtract line 29 from line 27. This is your short-term capital loss carryover from 1982 to 1983 . . . | **30** | | |

### Section B.—Long-term Capital Loss Carryover

| | | | |
|---|---|---|---|
| **31** Subtract line 29 from line 28 (**Note:** *If you skipped lines 26 through 30, enter amount from line 24*) . | **31** | | |
| **32** Enter loss from line 18; if none, enter zero and skip lines 33 through 36 . . . . . . . . . | **32** | | |
| **33** Enter gain shown on line 7. If that line is blank or shows a loss, enter zero . . . . . . . . | **33** | | |
| **34** Reduce any loss on line 32 to the extent of any gain on line 33 . . . . . . . . . . . | **34** | | |
| **35** Multiply amount on line 31 by 2 . . . . . . . . . . . . . . . . . | **35** | | |
| **36** Subtract line 35 from line 34. This is your long-term capital loss carryover from 1982 to 1983 . . . | **36** | | |

☆ U.S GOVERNMENT PRINTING OFFICE : 1982—O-363-066                                      363—066-1

| | |
|---|---|
| **SCHEDULE E**<br>**(Form 1040)**<br>Department of the Treasury<br>Internal Revenue Service | **Supplemental Income Schedule**<br>(From rents and royalties, partnerships, estates and trusts, etc.)<br>▶ Attach to Form 1040. ▶ See Instructions for Schedule E (Form 1040). |

OMB No. 1545-0074

**1982**
15

Name(s) as shown on Form 1040 — Your social security number

**Part I   Rent and Royalty Income or Loss**

1 Are any of the expenses listed below for a vacation home or other recreational unit (see Instructions)? . . . . . ☐ Yes ☐ No

2 If you checked "Yes" to question 1, did you or a member of your family occupy the vacation home or other recreational unit for more than the greater of 14 days or 10% of the total days rented at fair rental value during the tax year? . ☐ Yes ☐ No

**Description of Properties**

Property A (Show kind and location)_____

Property B (Show kind and location)_____

Property C (Show kind and location)

| Rental and Royalty Income | | Properties | | | Totals<br>(Add columns<br>A, B, and C) |
|---|---|---|---|---|---|
| | | A | B | C | |
| 3 a Rents received . . . . . . . . . | | | | | 3 |
| b Royalties received . . . . . . . | | | | | |

| Rental and Royalty Expenses | | | | | | |
|---|---|---|---|---|---|---|
| 4 Advertising . . . . . . . . . | 4 | | | | | |
| 5 Auto and travel . . . . . . . | 5 | | | | | |
| 6 Cleaning and maintenance . . . . | 6 | | | | | |
| 7 Commissions . . . . . . . . | 7 | | | | | |
| 8 Insurance . . . . . . . . | 8 | | | | | |
| 9 Interest . . . . . . . . . | 9 | | | | | |
| 10 Legal and other professional fees . . | 10 | | | | | |
| 11 Repairs . . . . . . . . | 11 | | | | | |
| 12 Supplies . . . . . . . . . | 12 | | | | | |
| 13 Taxes (Do NOT include Windfall Profit Tax here. See Part III, line 35.) . . . | 13 | | | | | |
| 14 Utilities . . . . . . . . . . | 14 | | | | | |
| 15 Wages and salaries . . . . . . | 15 | | | | | |
| 16 Other (list) ▶ _____ | | | | | | |

| | | | | | | |
|---|---|---|---|---|---|---|
| 17 Total expenses other than depreciation and depletion. Add lines 4 through 16 | 17 | | | | | 17 |
| 18 Depreciation expense (see Instructions), or Depletion . . . . . . | 18 | | | | | 18 |
| 19 Total. Add lines 17 and 18 . . . . | 19 | | | | | |
| 20 Income or (loss) from rental or royalty properties. Subtract line 19 from line 3a (rents) or 3b (royalties) . . . . | 20 | | | | | |

**E**

21 Add properties with profits on line 20, and write the total profits here . . . . . . . . . . . | 21 |

22 Add properties with losses on line 20, and write the total (losses) here . . . . . . . . . . | 22 ( )

23 Combine amounts on lines 21 and 22, and write the net profit or (loss) here . . . . . . . . . . | 23 |

24 Net farm rental profit or (loss) from Form 4835, line 50 . . . . . . . . . . . . . | 24 |

25 Total rental or royalty income or (loss). Combine amounts on lines 23 and 24, and write the total here. If Parts II, III, and IV on page 2 do not apply to you, write the amount from line 25 on Form 1040, line 18. Otherwise, include the amount in line 37 of Schedule E . . . . . . . . . . . . . . . . . | 25 |

**For Paperwork Reduction Act Notice, see Form 1040 Instructions.**

363-067-1

Schedule E (Form 1040) 1982        Page **2**

**Part II**   **Income or Losses from Partnerships, Estates or Trusts, or Small Business Corporations**

If you report a loss below, do you have amounts invested in that activity for which you are not "at risk" (see Instructions)? ☐ Yes ☐ No

If "Yes," and your loss exceeded your amount "at risk," did you limit your loss to your amount "at risk?" . . . . . ☐ Yes ☐ No

| (a) Name | (b) Employer identification number | (c) Net loss (see instructions for "at risk" limitations) | (d) Net income |
|---|---|---|---|
| | | | |
| | | | |
| | | | |

**Partnerships**

26 Add amounts in columns (c) and (d) and write here . . . . . . . **26** (     )

27 Combine amounts in columns (c) and (d), line 26, and write net income or (loss) . . . . . **27**

28 Expense deduction for section 179 property, (Form 1065, Schedule K–1, line 11). Do not enter more than $5,000 ($2,500 if married filing separately) . . . . . . . . . . . . . **28** (    )

29 Total partnership income or (loss). Combine amounts on lines 27 and 28. Write here and include in line 37 below . . . . . . . . . . . . . . . . . . . . . . . **29**

**Estates or Trusts**

| | | | |
|---|---|---|---|
| | | | |
| | | | |

30 Add amounts in columns (c) and (d) and write here . . . . . . . . **30** (    )

31 Total estate or trust income or (loss). Combine amounts in columns (c) and (d), line 30. Write here and include in line 37 below . . . . . . . . . . . . . . . . **31**

**Small Business Corporations**

| | | | |
|---|---|---|---|
| | | | |
| | | | |

32 Add amounts in columns (c) and (d) and write here . . . . . . . . **32** (    )

33 Total small business corporation income or (loss). Combine amounts in columns (c) and (d), line 32. Write here and include in line 37 below . . . . . . . . . . . . . . . . **33**

**Part III**   **Windfall Profit Tax Summary**

34 Windfall profit tax credit or refund received in 1982 (see Instructions) . . . . . . . . . **34**

35 Windfall profit tax withheld in 1982 (see Instructions) . . . . . . . . . . . . **35** (    )

36 Combine amounts on lines 34 and 35. Write here and include in line 37 below . . . . . . . **36**

**Part IV**   **Summary**

37 TOTAL income or (loss). Combine lines 25, 29, 31, 33, and 36. Write here and on Form 1040, line 18 . ▶ **37**

38 Farmers and fishermen: Write your share of GROSS FARMING AND FISHING INCOME applicable to Parts I and II . . . . . . . . . . . . . . . . . . **38**

**Part V**   **Depreciation Claimed in Part I.**—Complete only if property was placed in service before January 1, 1981. For more space, use Form 4562. If you placed any property in service after December 31, 1980, use Form 4562 for all property; do NOT complete Part V.

| (a) Description of property | (b) Date acquired | (c) Cost or other basis | (d) Depreciation allowed or allowable in prior years | (e) Depreciation method | (f) Life or rate | (g) Depreciation for this year |
|---|---|---|---|---|---|---|
| **Property A** | | | | | | |
| | | | | | | |
| | | | | | | |
| | | | | | | |
| Totals (Property A) . . . . . . . . . | | | | | | |
| **Property B** | | | | | | |
| | | | | | | |
| | | | | | | |
| | | | | | | |
| Totals (Property B) . . . . . . . . . | | | | | | |
| **Property C** | | | | | | |
| | | | | | | |
| | | | | | | |
| | | | | | | |
| Totals (Property C) . . . . . . . . . | | | | | | |

**SCHEDULE F**
**(Form 1040)**

Department of the Treasury
Internal Revenue Service

# Farm Income and Expenses

▶ Attach to Form 1040, Form 1041, or Form 1065.
▶ See Instructions for Schedule F (Form 1040).

OMB No. 1545-0074

**19 82**

16

Name of proprietor(s)

Social security number

Farm name and address ▶

Employer identification number

## Part I   Farm Income—Cash Method

Do not include sales of livestock held for draft, breeding, sport, or dairy purposes; report these sales on Form 4797.

### Sales of Livestock and Other Items You Bought for Resale

| | a. Description | b. Amount | c. Cost or other basis |
|---|---|---|---|
| 1 | Livestock ▶ | | |
| 2 | Other items ▶ | | |
| 3 | Totals . . . . . | | |
| 4 | Profit or (loss), subtract line 3, column c, from line 3, column b . . . . . . . . . ▶ | | |

### Sales of Livestock and Produce You Raised and Other Farm Income

| | Kind | Amount |
|---|---|---|
| 5 | Cattle and calves . . . . . . . . . . | |
| 6 | Sheep . . . . . . . . . . . . | |
| 7 | Swine . . . . . . . . . . . . | |
| 8 | Poultry . . . . . . . . . . . | |
| 9 | Dairy products . . . . . . . . . | |
| 10 | Eggs . . . . . . . . . . . . | |
| 11 | Wool . . . . . . . . . . . . | |
| 12 | Cotton . . . . . . . . . . . | |
| 13 | Tobacco . . . . . . . . . . . | |
| 14 | Vegetables . . . . . . . . . . | |
| 15 | Soybeans . . . . . . . . . . | |
| 16 | Corn . . . . . . . . . . . . | |
| 17 | Other grains . . . . . . . . . . | |
| 18 | Hay and straw . . . . . . . . . | |
| 19 | Fruits and nuts . . . . . . . . . | |
| 20 | Machine work . . . . . . . . . | |
| 21 a | Patronage dividends . | |
| b | Less: Nonincome items . | |
| c | Net patronage dividends . . . . . . | |
| 22 | Per-unit retains . . . . . . . . . | |
| 23 | Nonpatronage distributions from exempt cooperatives . | |
| 24 | Agricultural program payments: a Cash . . . | |
| b | Materials and services . . . . . | |
| 25 | Commodity credit loans under election (or forfeited) . . | |
| 26 | Federal gasoline tax credit . . . . . . | |
| 27 | State gasoline tax refund . . . . . . | |
| 28 | Crop insurance proceeds . . . . . . | |
| 29 | Other (specify) ▶ | |
| 30 | Add amounts in column for lines 5 through 29 . | |
| 31 | **Gross profits*** (add lines 4 and 30) . . . . ▶ | |

## Part II   Farm Deductions—Cash and Accrual Method   **F**

Do not include personal or living expenses (such as taxes, insurance, repairs, etc., on your home), which do not produce farm income. Reduce the amount of your farm deductions by any reimbursement before entering the deduction below.

| | Items | Amount |
|---|---|---|
| 32 a | Labor hired . . . . . | |
| b | Jobs credit . . . . . | |
| c | Balance (subtract line 32b from line 32a) . . | |
| 33 | Repairs, maintenance . . | |
| 34 | Interest . . . . . . | |
| 35 | Rent of farm, pasture . . | |
| 36 | Feed purchased . . . . | |
| 37 | Seeds, plants purchased . | |
| 38 | Fertilizers, lime, chemicals . | |
| 39 | Machine hire . . . . . | |
| 40 | Supplies purchased . . . | |
| 41 | Breeding fees . . . . . | |
| 42 | Veterinary fees, medicine . | |
| 43 | Gasoline, fuel, oil . . . . | |
| 44 | Storage, warehousing . . | |
| 45 | Taxes . . . . . . . | |
| 46 | Insurance . . . . . . | |
| 47 | Utilities . . . . . . . | |
| 48 | Freight, trucking . . . . | |
| 49 | Conservation expenses . . | |
| 50 | Land clearing expenses . . | |
| 51 | Pension and profit-sharing plans . . . . . . | |
| 52 | Employee benefit programs other than line 51 . . . | |
| 53 | Other (specify) ▶ | |
| 54 | Total (add lines 32c through 53) . . . . | |
| 55 | Depreciation, including Section 179 expense deduction (from Form 4562) . . . | |
| 56 | Total deductions (add lines 54 and 55) . . . . | |

**57** Net farm profit or (loss) (subtract line 56 from line 31). If a profit, enter on Form 1040, line 19, and on Schedule SE, Part I, line 1. If a loss, go on to line 58. (Fiduciaries and partnerships, see the Instructions.) . . . . . . . . | **57** |

**58** If you have a loss, do you have amounts for which you are not "at risk" in this farm (see instructions)? . . . . ☐ **Yes** ☐ **No**
If you checked "No," enter the loss on Form 1040, line 19, and on Schedule SE, Part I, line 1.

*Use amount on line 31 for optional method of computing net earnings from self-employment. (See Schedule SE, Part II, line 4.)

**For Paperwork Reduction Act Notice, see Form 1040 Instructions.**

363-068-1

Schedule F (Form 1040) 1982     **17**                                          Page **2**

**Part III**   **Farm Income—Accrual Method** (Do not include sales of livestock held for draft, breeding, sport, or dairy purposes; report these sales on Form 4797 and omit them from "Inventory at beginning of year" column.)

| a. Kind | b. Inventory at beginning of year | c. Cost of items purchased during year | d. Sales during year | e. Inventory at end of year |
|---|---|---|---|---|
| 59 Cattle and calves | | | | |
| 60 Sheep | | | | |
| 61 Swine | | | | |
| 62 Poultry | | | | |
| 63 Dairy products | | | | |
| 64 Eggs | | | | |
| 65 Wool | | | | |
| 66 Cotton | | | | |
| 67 Tobacco | | | | |
| 68 Vegetables | | | | |
| 69 Soybeans | | | | |
| 70 Corn | | | | |
| 71 Other grains | | | | |
| 72 Hay and straw | | | | |
| 73 Fruits and nuts | | | | |
| 74 Machine Work | | | | |
| 75 Other (specify) ▶ | | | | |
| 76 Totals (enter here and in Part IV below) | (Enter on line 85) | (Enter on line 86) | (Enter on line 78) | (Enter on line 77) |

**Part IV**   **Summary of Income and Deductions—Accrual Method**

77 Inventory of livestock, crops, and products at end of year (line 76, column e) . . . . . . . .

78 Sales of livestock, crops, and products during year (line 76, column d) . . . . . . . . . .

79 Agricultural program payments: **a** Cash . . . . . . . . . . . . . . . . . .

                        **b** Materials and services . . . . . . . . . . . . . .

80 Commodity credit loans under election (or forfeited) . . . . . . . . . . . . . . .

81 Federal gasoline tax credit . . . . . . . . . . . . . . . . . . . . . .

82 State gasoline tax refund . . . . . . . . . . . . . . . . . . . . . . .

83 Other farm income (specify) ▶

84 Add lines 77 through 83 . . . . . . . . . . . . . . . . . . . . . . .

85 Inventory of livestock, crops, and products at beginning of year (line 76, column b) . . .

86 Cost of livestock and products purchased during year (line 76, column c) . . .

87 Total (add lines 85 and 86) . . . . . . . . . . . . . . . . . . . . .

88 **Gross profits*** (subtract line 87 from line 84) . . . . . . . . . . . . . . . ▶

89 Total deductions from Part II, line 56 . . . . . . . . . . . . . . . . . . .

90 Net farm profit or (loss) (subtract line 89 from line 88). If a profit, individuals enter on Form 1040, line 19, and on Schedule SE, Part I, line 1. If a loss, go to line 91. (Fiduciaries and partnerships, see the Instructions.) . . . . . . . . . . . . . . . . . . . . . . . **90**

91 If you have a loss, do you have amounts for which you are not "at risk" in this farm (see Instructions)? . .   ☐ **Yes**   ☐ **No**

     If you checked "No," enter the loss on Form 1040, line 19, and on Schedule SE, Part I, line 1.

*Use amount on line 88 for optional method of computing net earnings from self-employment. (See Schedule SE, Part II, line 4.)

☆ U.S. GOVERNMENT PRINTING OFFICE : 1982—O—363-068          363-068-1

**Schedule G**
(Form 1040)
Department of the Treasury
Internal Revenue Service

# Income Averaging

▶ See instructions on back.  ▶ Attach to Form 1040.

OMB No. 1545-0074
**1982**
20

Name(s) as shown on Form 1040 | Your social security number

## Step 1    Figure your income for 1978-1981

| 1978 | 1 | Fill in the amount from your 1978 Form 1040 (line 34) or Form 1040A (line 10) . . . . . . . . | 1 | | | |
| | 2 | Multiply your total exemptions in 1978 by $750 . . | 2 | | | |
| | 3 | Subtract line 2 from line 1. If less than zero, enter zero . . . . . . . . | | | 3 | |
| 1979 | 4 | Fill in the amount from your 1979 Form 1040 (line 34) or Form 1040A (line 11) . . . . . . . . | 4 | | | |
| | 5 | Multiply your total exemptions in 1979 by $1,000 . . . | 5 | | | |
| | 6 | Subtract line 5 from line 4. If less than zero, enter zero . . . . . . . . | | | 6 | |
| 1980 | 7 | Fill in the amount from your 1980 Form 1040 (line 34) or Form 1040A (line 11) . . . . . . . . | 7 | | | |
| | 8 | Multiply your total exemptions in 1980 by $1,000 . . . | 8 | | | |
| | 9 | Subtract line 8 from line 7. If less than zero, enter zero . . . . . . . . | | | 9 | |
| 1981 | 10 | Taxable income. Fill in the amount from your 1981 Form 1040 (line 34) or Form 1040A (line 12). If less than zero, enter zero . . . . . . . . | | | 10 | |
| Total | 11 | Fill in all income earned outside of the United States or within U.S. possessions and excluded for 1978 through 1981 . . . . . . . . | | 11 | | |
| | 12 | Add lines 3, 6, 9, 10 and 11 . . . . . . . . | | | 12 | |

## Step 2    Figure your averageable income

Multiply the amount on line 12 by 30% (.30) . . . . . . . . .
13 Write in the answer . . . . . . . . | 13 |
14 Fill in your taxable income for 1982 from Form 1040, line 37 . | 14 |
15 If you received a premature or excessive distribution subject to a penalty under section 72, see instructions . . . . . | 15 |
16 Subtract line 15 from line 14 . . . . . . . . | 16 |
17 If you live in a community property state and are filing a separate return, see instructions . . . | 17 |
18 Subtract line 17 from line 16. If less than zero, enter zero . . . . . . . . | 18 |
19 Write in the amount from line 13 above . . . . . . . . | 19 |
20 Subtract line 19 from line 18. This is your averageable income . . . . . . . . | 20 |

### If line 20 is $3,000 or less, do not complete the rest of this form. You do not qualify for income averaging.

## Step 3    Figure your tax

Multiply the amount on line 20 by 20% (.20) . . . . . . . . .
21 Write in the answer . . . . . . . . | 21 |
22 Write in the amount from line 13 above . . . . . . . . | 22 |
23 Add lines 21 and 22 . . . . . . . . | 23 |
24 Write in the amount from line 17 above . . . . . . . . | 24 |
25 Add lines 23 and 24 . . . . . . . . | 25 |
26 Tax on amount on line 25 (from Tax Rate Schedule X, Y, or Z) . . . | 26 |
27 Tax on amount on line 23 (from Tax Rate Schedule X, Y, or Z) . . | 27 |
28 Tax on amount on line 22 (from Tax Rate Schedule X, Y, or Z) . . | 28 |
29 Subtract line 28 from line 27 . . . . . | 29 |
Multiply the amount on line 29 by 4 . . . . . . .
30 Write in the answer . . . . . . . . | 30 |
If you have no entry on line 15, skip lines 31 through 33 and go to line 34.
31 Tax on amount on line 14 (from Tax Rate Schedule X, Y, or Z) . . | 31 |
32 Tax on amount on line 16 (from Tax Rate Schedule X, Y, or Z) . . | 32 |
33 Subtract line 32 from line 31 . . . . . . . . | 33 |
34 Add lines 26, 30, and 33. Write the result here and on Form 1040, line 38. Be sure to check the Schedule G box on that line . . . . . . . . | 34 |

**G**

For Paperwork Reduction Act Notice, see Form 1040 instructions.

363-259-1

## Instructions

If your income this year is much greater than the average of your income for the past 4 base period years (1978–1981), you may be able to pay less tax by income averaging. To see if you qualify, complete lines 1–20 of this schedule. If line 20 is more than $3,000, fill in the rest of this schedule to see if you will save by income averaging.

If you are eligible, and line 34 of this schedule is less than your tax using other methods, you may choose the income averaging method. You must attach this schedule to your Form 1040 to choose the benefits of income averaging. Generally, you may make or change this choice anytime within 3 years from the date you filed your return.

For more information and a filled-in sample Schedule G, please get **Publication 506**, Income Averaging.

### Who Can Income Average?

To be eligible to file Schedule G with Form 1040, you (and your spouse, if you are filing a joint return) must meet the following requirements:

**(1) Citizenship or residence.**—You must have been a U.S. citizen or resident for all of 1982. You are not eligible if you were a nonresident alien at any time during the 5 tax years ending with 1982.

**(2) Support.**—You must have furnished at least 50% of your own support for each of the years 1978 through 1981. In a year in which you were married, you and your spouse must have provided at least 50% of the support of both of you. For the definition of support, see Form 1040 Instructions, page 7.

*Exceptions:* Disregard the support requirement if any one of the three following situations applies to you:

(1) You were 25 or older before the end of 1982 and were not a full-time student during 4 or more of your tax years which began after you reached 21; or

(2) More than 50% of your 1982 taxable income (line 14) is from work you performed in substantial part during 2 or more of the 4 tax years before 1982; or

(3) You file a joint return for 1982 and your income for 1982 is not more than 25% of the total combined adjusted gross income (line 33, Form 1040).

For the definition of full-time student, see Form 1040 Instructions, page 7.

**Caution:** In the same year you file Schedule G you may not claim the benefits of sections 911 or 931 through 934 (I.R. Code).

### Figure Your Income for 1978–1981.

**(1)** Use your separate income and deductions for all years if you were unmarried in 1978 through 1982.

**(2)** Use the combined income and deductions of you and your spouse for a base period year:

- If you are married in 1982, and
- If you file a joint return with your spouse or are a qualifying widow(er) in 1982, and
- If you were not married to any other spouse in that base period year.

**(3)** If (1) and (2) do not apply, your separate base period income is the largest of the following amounts:

(a) Your separate income and deductions for the base period year;

(b) Half of the base period income from adding your separate income and deductions to the separate income and deductions of your spouse for that base period year; or

(c) Half of the base period income from adding your separate income and deductions to your 1982 spouse's separate income and deductions for that base period year.

**Note:** *If you were married to one spouse in a base period year and are married and file a joint return with a different spouse in 1982, your separate base period income is the larger of (3)(a) or (b) above. Combine that amount with your 1982 spouse's separate base period income for that base period year.*

### Figuring Your Separate Income and Deductions.

The amount of your separate income and deductions for a base period year is your gross income for that year minus your allowable deductions.

If you filed a joint return for a base period year, your separate deductions are:

**(1)** For deductions allowable in figuring your adjusted gross income, the sum of those deductions attributable to your gross income; and

**(2)** For deductions allowable in figuring taxable income (exemptions and itemized deductions), the amount from multiplying the deductions allowable on the joint return by a fraction whose numerator is your adjusted gross income and whose denominator is the combined adjusted gross income on the joint return. However, if 85% or more of the combined adjusted gross income of you and your spouse is attributable to one spouse, all deductions allowable in figuring taxable income are allowable to that spouse.

**Community property laws.**—In figuring your separate taxable income when community property laws apply, you must take into account:

- all of your earned income without regard to the community property laws, or
- your share of the community earned income under community property laws, whichever is more.

If you must figure your separate taxable income for any of the base period years, attach a statement showing the computation and the names under which the returns were filed.

## Line-by-Line Instructions

**Lines 1–10.**—If you did not file a return for any year from 1978 through 1981, enter the amounts that would otherwise be reportable on the appropriate lines. If the amount reported on your return for any of the years was changed by an amended return or by the Internal Revenue Service, enter the corrected amount.

**Line 11.**—If you excluded any income in any year from 1978 through 1981 because the income was earned from sources outside the United States or within U.S. possessions, fill in the total amount of income (less deductions) that you excluded during that period. Otherwise, leave line 11 blank.

**Line 15.**—If you are or were an owner-employee, and you received income in 1982 from a premature or excessive distribution from a Keogh (H.R. 10) plan or trust that was subject to a penalty under section 72(m)(5), fill in the amount of that income on this line. Or, if you were an employee in a qualified plan and made deductible voluntary contributions, and received a premature distribution of those contributions subject to a penalty under section 72(o), include that amount on line 15. If you received a premature distribution under an annuity contract subject to a penalty under section 72(q), that amount must also be included on line 15. Otherwise, leave line 15 blank.

**Line 17.**—You must make this adjustment if you are married, a resident of a community property State, and file a separate return for 1982. Enter the community earned income you reported minus that part of the income which is attributable to your services. Skip this line if the earned income attributable to your services is more than 50% of your combined community earned income.

**Example:**

| Community Earned Income | Attributable to Service of | | |
|---|---|---|---|
| | John | Carol | Both |
| . | $40,000 | $20,000 | $60,000 |

- **John,** filing a separate return, has no adjustment since the amount of earned income attributable to the services of John ($40,000) is more than 50% of the combined community earned income ($30,000).

- **Carol,** filing a separate return, must include $10,000 in the total for line 17. This is the excess of the 50% of the community earned income reportable by Carol ($30,000) over the amount of community earned income attributable to Carol's services ($20,000).

**Lines 26, 27, 28, 31 and 32.**—Figure the tax using Tax Rate Schedule X, Y, or Z from the 1040 instructions.

**Line 34.**—If the tax on this line is less than the tax figured in any other way, enter the amount from this line on Form 1040, line 38, and check the Schedule G box on that line.

| Schedules R & RP | **Credit for the Elderly** | OMB No. 1545-0074 |
|---|---|---|

Schedules R & RP
(Form 1040)
Department of the Treasury
Internal Revenue Service

**Credit for the Elderly**
▶ See Instructions for Schedules R and RP.
▶ Attach to Form 1040. ▶ Schedule RP is on back.

OMB No. 1545-0074
19**82**
21

Name(s) as shown on Form 1040 | Your social security number

**Please Note:** *IRS will figure your Credit for the Elderly and compute your tax. Please see "IRS Will Figure Your Tax and Some of Your Credits" on page 3 of the Form 1040 instructions and complete the applicable lines on Form 1040 and Schedule R or RP.*

## Should You Use Schedule R or RP?

| If you are: | And were: | Use Schedule: |
|---|---|---|
| Single | ▶ 65 or over . . . . . . . . . . . . . . . . . . . . . | R |
| | ▶ under 65 and had income from a public retirement system . . . . . . . | RP |
| Married, filing separate return [1] | ▶ 65 or over (unless joining in the election to use Schedule RP with your spouse who is under 65 and had income from a public retirement system) . . . . . . | R |
| | ▶ under 65 and had income from a public retirement system (unless your spouse is 65 or over and does not join in the election to use Schedule RP) . . . . . . | RP |
| Married, filing joint return | ▶ both 65 or over . . . . . . . . . . . . . . . . . | R |
| | ▶ one 65 or over, and one under 65 with no income or income other than from a public retirement system . . . . . . . . . . . . . . . . | R |
| | ▶ both under 65 and one or both had income from a public retirement system . . | RP |
| | ▶ one 65 or over, and one under 65 with income from a public retirement system . | R or RP [2] |

[1] You can take the credit on a separate return ONLY if you and your spouse lived apart for the whole year. See "Purpose" in Schedules R&RP instructions for limitation.
[2] Figure your credit on both schedules to see which gives you more credit.

**Schedule R** **Credit for the Elderly—For People 65 or Over**
If you received nontaxable pensions (social security, etc.) of $3,750 or more, or your adjusted gross income (Form 1040, line 33) was $17,500 or more, or your tax (Form 1040, line 40) is zero, you cannot take the Credit for the Elderly. Do not file this schedule.

**Filing Status and Age** (check only one box)
A ☐ Single, 65 or over
B ☐ Married filing joint return, only one spouse 65 or over
C ☐ Married filing joint return, both 65 or over
D ☐ Married filing separate return, 65 or over, and did not live with spouse at any time in 1982

**R**

1 Enter: { $2,500 if you checked box A or B . . . . . . . . . . .
$3,750 if you checked box C . . . . . . . . . . . .
$1,875 if you checked box D . . . . . . . . . . . . } . . . . . . . . . . | 1 |

2 a Enter amounts you received as pensions or annuities under the Social Security Act or under the Railroad Retirement Act (but not supplemental annuities), and certain other exclusions from gross income (see instructions). If none, you must enter zero . . . . . . . | 2a |

b Enter amount from Form 1040, line 33 . . . | 2b |

c Enter: { $7,500 if you checked box A . . .
$10,000 if you checked box B or C .
$5,000 if you checked box D . . } . | 2c |

d Subtract line 2c from 2b. If line 2c is more than line 2b, enter zero . . . . . . . | 2d |

e Enter one-half (½) of line 2d . . . . . . . . | 2e |

3 Add lines 2a and 2e. (If line 3 is the same or more than line 1, you cannot take the credit; do not file this schedule. If line 3 is less than line 1, go on to line 4.) . . . . . . . . . . . | 3 |
4 Subtract line 3 from line 1 . . . . . . . . . . . . . . . . . . | 4 |
5 Multiply line 4 by 15% (.15) . . . . . . . . . . . . . . . . . | 5 |
6 Enter amount of tax from Form 1040, line 40 . . . . . . . . . . . . | 6 |
7 Enter the amount from line 5 or line 6, above, whichever is less. This is your **Credit for the Elderly.** Enter the same amount on Form 1040, line 41 . . . . . . . . . . . . . . ▶ | 7 |

**For Paperwork Reduction Act Notice, see page 1 of separate instructions.**

363–070–1

Schedules R&RP (Form 1040) 1982

OMB No. 1545-0074

| Name(s) as shown on Form 1040 | Your social security number |
|---|---|

**Schedule RP** **Credit for the Elderly—For People Under 65 Who Had Pension or Annuity Income from a Public Retirement System** 21

If you are under 72 and received nontaxable pensions (social security etc.) of $2,500 or more, or your earned income (salaries, wages, etc.) was $3,950 or more, or your tax (Form 1040, line 40) is zero, you cannot take the Credit for the Elderly. Do not file this schedule.

Name(s) of public retirement system(s)

**Filing Status and Age (check only one box)**

A ☐ Single, under 65

B ☐ Married filing joint return, one spouse is under 65, and that person had income from a public retirement system. (If you checked this box and had community property income, see Community Property Income in the instructions.)

C ☐ Married filing joint return, both under 65. (If you checked this box and had community property income, see Community Property Income in the instructions.)

D ☐ Married filing separate return, under 65, and did not live with your spouse at any time in 1982.

E ☐ Married filing separate return, 65 or over, did not live with your spouse at any time in 1982, and you are joining with your spouse in electing to use Schedule RP.

**RP**

**Column (b)**—Fill out column (b) whether you file a separate or joint return.
**Column (a)**—Fill out column (a) only if you file a joint return and your spouse has retirement income as set forth in line 5. Use it to show amounts for:
- The wife, if both of you were under 65, or
- The spouse who was 65 or over.

|  | (a) | (b) |
|---|---|---|
| **1** Enter: { $2,500 if you checked box A . . . . . . . . . $2,500 if you checked box B or C, and are using only column (b). If you are using both columns (a) and (b) because both you and your spouse have retirement income as set forth in line 5, allocate $3,750 between you and your spouse, but do not enter more than $2,500 for either of you. It will generally be to your benefit to allocate the greater amount to the spouse with more retirement income . . . . . . . . . $1,875 if you checked box D or box E . . . . . . . } **1** | | |
| **2** Enter: | | |
| **a** Amounts you received as pensions or annuities under the Social Security Act or under the Railroad Retirement Act (but not supplemental annuities), and certain other exclusions from gross income (see instructions). **If none, you must enter zero** . . . . . . . . . . . . . . . **2a** | | |
| **b** Earned income such as wages, salaries, fees, etc. you received (does not apply to people 72 or over). (See instructions for definition of earned income.): | | |
| (i) If you are under 62, enter earned income that is over $900 . . . **2b(i)** | | |
| (ii) If you are 62 or over but under 72, enter an amount that you will figure as follows: If earned income is $1,200 or less, enter zero . . . . If earned income is over $1,200 but not over $1,700, enter one-half of the amount over $1,200. . . . . If earned income is over $1,700, enter the amount over $1,450 . . . . . . . . . . . . . . } . . . **2b(ii)** | | |
| **3** Add lines 2a and 2b . . . . . . . . . . . . . . . . **3** | | |
| **4** Subtract line 3 from line 1. (If the result for either column is more than zero, go on. If the result for either column is zero or less, do not complete the rest of the lines in that column. If the result for both columns is zero or less, you cannot take the credit; do not file this schedule.) . . . . . . . . . **4** | | |
| **5** Retirement income: | | |
| **a** If under 65— Enter only income from pensions and annuities under public retirement systems (e.g. Federal, State Governments, etc.) that you received as a result of your services or services of your spouse that you reported as income. Do not enter social security, railroad retirement or certain other payments reported on line 2a . . . . . . . . . **5a** | | |
| **b** If 65 or over— Enter total of pensions and annuities, interest, dividends, proceeds of retirement bonds, and amounts you received from individual retirement arrangements and individual retirement annuities that you reported as income, and gross rents from: Schedule E, Part I, columns A–C, line 3a and Form 4835, line 24. Also include your share of gross rents from partnerships and your share of taxable rents from estates and trusts . . . . . **5b** | | |
| **6** Enter amount from line 4 or line 5, whichever is less . . . . . . . . . **6** | | |
| **7** Add amounts in columns (a) and (b) of line 6. Enter total here . . . . . . . . . . . . ▶ **7** | | |
| **8** Multiply line 7 by 15% (.15) . . . . . . . . . . . . . . . . . . . . **8** | | |
| **9** Enter amount of tax from Form 1040, line 40 . . . . . . . . . . . . . . . . **9** | | |
| **10** Enter the amount from line 8 or line 9, above, whichever is less. This is your **Credit for the Elderly.** Enter the same amount on Form 1040, line 41 . . . . . . . . . . . . . . . . . . ▶ **10** | | |

SCHEDULE SE
(Form 1040)

Department of the Treasury
Internal Revenue Service

## Computation of Social Security Self-Employment Tax

▶ See Instructions for Schedule SE (Form 1040).
▶ Attach to Form 1040.

OMB No. 1545-0074

1982

22

| Name of self-employed person (as shown on social security card) | Social security number of self-employed person ▶ | | |
|---|---|---|---|

**Part I** Regular Computation of Net Earnings from Self-Employment

1 Net profit or (loss) from Schedule F (Form 1040), line 57 or line 90, and farm partnerships, Schedule K–1 (Form 1065), line 18b . . . . . . . . . . . . . . . **1**

2 Net profit or (loss) from Schedule C (Form 1040), line 32, and Schedule K–1 (Form 1065), line 18b (other than farming). See instructions for kinds of income to report.
**Note:** If you are exempt from self-employment tax on your earnings as a minister, member of a religious order, or Christian Science practitioner because you filed Form 4361, check here ▶ ☐.
If you have other earnings of $400 or more that are subject to self-employment tax, include those earnings on this line . . . . . . . . . . . . . . . . . . . **2**

**Part II** Optional Computation of Net Earnings from Self-Employment

Generally, this part may be used only if:
- Your gross farm profits were not more than $2,400, or
- Your gross farm profits were more than $2,400 and your net farm profits were less than $1,600, or
- Your net nonfarm profits were less than $1,600 and less than two-thirds ($2/3$) of your gross nonfarm income.
See instructions for other limitations.

3 Maximum income for optional methods . . . . . . . . . . . . . . . **3** | $1,600 | 00

4 Farm Optional Method—Enter two-thirds ($2/3$) of gross profits from Schedule F (Form 1040), line 31 or line 88, and farm partnerships, Schedule K–1 (Form 1065), line 18a, or $1,600, whichever is smaller . . . . . . . . . . . . . . . . . . **4**

5 Subtract line 4 from line 3 . . . . . . . . . . . . . . . **5**

6 Nonfarm Optional Method—Enter the smaller of two-thirds ($2/3$) of gross profits from Schedule C (Form 1040), line 3, and Schedule K–1 (Form 1065), line 18c (other than farming), $1,600, or, if you elected the farm optional method, the amount on line 5 . . . . . . . . . . . . **6**

**Part III** Computation of Social Security Self-Employment Tax    **SE**

7 Enter the amount from Part I, line 1, or, if you elected the farm optional method, Part II, line 4 . . **7**

8 Enter the amount from Part I, line 2, or, if you elected the nonfarm optional method, Part II, line 6 . **8**

9 Add lines 7 and 8. If less than $400, you are not subject to self-employment tax. Do not fill in the rest of the schedule . . . . . . . . . . . . . . . . . . . . . **9**

10 The largest amount of combined wages and self-employment earnings subject to social security or railroad retirement tax for 1982 is . . . . . . . . . . . . . . . . . **10** | $32,400 | 00

11 a Total FICA wages from Forms W–2 and RRTA compensation . . | **11a** |
   b Unreported tips subject to FICA tax from Form 4137, line 9, or to RRTA tax . . . . . . . . . . . . . . . . | **11b** |

   c Add lines 11a and 11b . . . . . . . . . . . . . . . . **11c**

12 Subtract line 11c from line 10 . . . . . . . . . . . . . . . **12**

13 Enter the smaller of line 9 or line 12 . . . . . . . . . . . . . . . **13**
   If line 13 is $32,400, fill in $3,029.40 on line 14. Otherwise, multiply line 13 by .0935 and enter the result on line 14 . . . . . . . . . . . . . . . . . . . . | .0935 |

14 Self-employment tax. Enter this amount on Form 1040, line 51 . . . . . . . . . . **14**

For Paperwork Reduction Act Notice, see Form 1040 Instructions.

363-071-1

☆ U.S. GOVERNMENT PRINTING OFFICE: 1982—O-363-071

## Schedule W
(Form 1040)
Department of the Treasury
Internal Revenue Service

### Deduction for a Married Couple When Both Work

▶ Attach to Form 1040. ▶ For Paperwork Reduction Act Notice, see Form 1040 Instructions.

OMB No. 1545-0074

**1982**

37

Names as shown on Form 1040 | Your social security number

**Purpose.**—Use this schedule to claim a deduction if:
- you are married filing a joint return,
- both you and your spouse have Qualified Earned Income, and
- you do not exclude income earned abroad or in U.S. possessions or claim the foreign housing deduction.

Generally, earned income is income you receive for services you provide such as wages, salaries, tips, and commissions. It also includes income earned from self-

employment. It does not include items such as interest, dividends, pensions, annuities, non-taxable income, distributions from an IRA, or deferred compensation.

**Caution:** *Do not consider community property laws in figuring your earned income.*

**Adjustments.**—Your earned income must be reduced by certain deductions that apply to it to figure Qualified Earned Income. Enter in the proper column of line 4 below, the amounts from Form 1040:
- line 24—Employee Business Expenses,
- line 25—Payments to an IRA,

- line 26—Payments to a Keogh plan, &
- line 31—Repayment of supplemental unemployment benefits (Sub-pay).

**Example.**—You earn a salary of $20,000 and have $6,000 of employee business expenses on line 24 of Form 1040. Your spouse earns $17,000 and puts $2,000 into an IRA (line 25 of Form 1040). Your Qualified Earned Income is $14,000 and your spouse's is $15,000. Therefore, on your joint return you can take a deduction of $700 (.05 × $14,000).

| | | (a) You | (b) Your spouse |
|---|---|---|---|
| 1 Wages, salaries, tips, etc., from line 7 of Form 1040. (Do not include any amount your spouse pays you.) . . . . . . . . . . . . . | 1 | | |
| 2 Net profit or (loss) from self-employment (from Schedule C or F (Form 1040), Form 1065 (Schedule K–1), and any other taxable self-employment income) . | 2 | | |
| 3 Combine lines 1 and 2. This is your total earned income . . . . . . . | 3 | | |
| 4 Adjustments from Form 1040, lines 24, 25, 26, and any repayment of Sub-pay written in on line 31 (see instructions above) . | 4 | | |
| 5 Subtract line 4 from line 3. This is your Qualified Earned Income . . . . . | 5 | | |
| 6 Write in the amount from line 5(a) or 5(b), whichever is smaller, BUT DO NOT WRITE MORE THAN $30,000 . . . . . . . . . . . . . . . . . . . . . | 6 | | |
| 7 Multiply line 6 by 5% (.05) . . . . . . . . . . . . . . . . . . . | 7 | × .05 | |
| 8 Write in the answer here and on Form 1040, line 29 . . . . . . . . . . . . | 8 | | |

# B-4 FORM 1040-ES DECLARATION OF ESTIMATED TAX AND DECLARATION-VOUCHER FOR INDIVIDUALS

**Form 1040-ES**

Department of the Treasury
Internal Revenue Service

## Estimated Tax for Individuals

▶ This form is primarily for first time filers.

OMB No. 1545-0087

**1983**

## Instructions

**Paperwork Reduction Act Notice.**—We ask for the information to carry out the Internal Revenue laws of the United States. We need it to ensure that you are complying with these laws and to allow us to figure and collect the right amount of tax. You are required to give us this information.

This form is primarily for first-time filers. After your first payment-voucher is received in the Internal Revenue Service Center, IRS will mail you a 1040-ES package. Your name, address, and social security number will be preprinted on the vouchers. You should use these vouchers in making the remaining payments of estimated tax for the year. Using the preprinted vouchers will speed processing, reduce the chance of error, and help save your government processing costs.

This form can also be used if you did not receive a 1040-ES package, or if you lost it. Complete the appropriate payment-voucher and mail it with your payment to your Internal Revenue Service Center (see page 2 for address).

**"Estimated tax"** is the amount of tax you expect to owe for the year after subtracting the amount of tax you expect to have withheld and the amount of any credits you plan to take.

You do not have to pay estimated tax if your 1983 income tax return will show (1) a tax refund or (2) a tax balance due of less than $300.

**A. Who Must Make Estimated Tax Payments.**—The rules below are for U.S. citizens or residents and for residents of Puerto Rico, Virgin Islands, Guam, or American Samoa. (If you are a nonresident alien, use **Form 1040-ES (NR).**) You must make estimated tax payments if your estimated tax balance due is $300 or more **AND** if either item (1) or (2) below applies to you.

You expect your 1983 gross income:

(1) To include more than $500 from sources other than wages subject to withholding.

(2) Or to be more than:

● $20,000 if you are single, a head of household, or a qualifying widow or widower;

● $20,000 if you are married, can make joint estimated tax payments, and your spouse has not received wages for 1983;

● $10,000 if you are married, can make joint estimated tax payments, and both of you have received wages for 1983;

● $5,000 if you are married and cannot make joint estimated tax payments. (No joint estimated tax payments may be made if: (1) either you or your spouse is a nonresident alien, (2) you are separated under a decree of divorce or separate maintenance, or (3) you have different tax years.)

**Note:** *If you must make estimated tax payments and receive salaries and wages,*

you may not be having enough tax withheld during the year. To avoid making estimated tax payments, consider asking your employer to take more tax out of your earnings. To do this, file a new **Form W-4,** Employee's Withholding Allowance Certificate, with your employer and make sure you will not owe $300 or more in tax.

**B. How to Figure Your Estimated Tax.**—Use the Estimated Tax Worksheet on page 3, the 1983 Tax Rate Schedules in these instructions, and your 1982 tax return as a guide for figuring your estimated tax.

Most of the items on the worksheet are self-explanatory. However, the instructions below provide additional information for filling out certain lines.

**Caution: Generally, you are required to itemize your deductions if:**

● you have unearned income of $1,000 or more and can be claimed as a dependent on your parent's return;

● you are married filing a separate return and your spouse itemizes deductions;

● you file **Form 4563,** Exclusion of Income From Sources in United States Possessions; **OR**

● you are a dual-status alien.

For more information, see the 1982 Instructions for **Form 1040.** If you must itemize and line 2b of the Estimated Tax Worksheet is more than line 2a, subtract 2a from 2b. Add this amount to line 1 of the worksheet and enter the total on line 3. Disregard the instructions for lines 2c, 2d, and 3 on the worksheet.

The following tax law changes for 1983 may affect your 1983 estimated tax.

1. A 10% tax withholding on interest and dividend income beginning July 1, 1983.

2. Withholding of income tax from pensions, annuities, and certain deferred income.

3. Adjusted gross income limitation on medical and dental expenses is increased from 3% to 5%. Also the separate deduction (not to exceed $150) for medical insurance has been eliminated.

4. Nonbusiness casualty losses are allowed only to the extent they exceed 10% of adjusted gross income.

To figure the "Deduction for a married couple when both work," use **Schedule W (Form 1040).** You should substitute 10% for 5% on line 7 of Schedule W.

For more details, see **Publication 505,** Tax Withholding and Estimated Tax.

**Line 7—Additional taxes.**—Enter on line 7 any additional taxes from:

● **Form 4970,** Tax on Accumulation Distribution of Trusts;

● **Form 4972,** Special 10-Year Averaging Method;

● **Form 5544,** Multiple Recipient Special 10-Year Averaging Method; **OR**

● Section 72 penalty taxes.

**Line 12—Self-employment tax.**—If you and your spouse make joint estimated tax payments and both have self-employment income, figure the estimated self-employ-

ment tax separately. Enter the total amount on line 12.

**C. How to Use the Payment-Voucher.**—Each payment-voucher has the date when the voucher is due for calendar year taxpayers. Please use the correct voucher.

(1) Enter your name, address, and social security number in the space provided on the payment-voucher. If you are filing a joint payment-voucher, your spouse's name and social security number should be included on the voucher. If you file a joint payment-voucher and have different last names, please separate them with an "and." For example: "John Brown and Mary Smith."

(2) Enter the amount of your payment on line 1 of the voucher.

(3) If you paid too much tax on your 1982 Form 1040, you may have chosen to apply the overpayment to your estimated tax for 1983. If so, you may apply all or part of the overpayment to this voucher.

(4) Tear off the voucher at the perforation.

(5) Attach, but do not staple, your check or money order to the payment-voucher. Make check or money order payable to Internal Revenue Service. Please write your social security number and "1983 Form 1040-ES" on your check or money order. Please fill in the Record of Estimated Tax Payments on page 2 so you will have a record of your past payments.

(6) Mail your payment-voucher to the Internal Revenue Service Center for the place where you live. Use the address for your State shown on page 2.

**D. When to Pay Your Estimated Tax.**—The general rule is that you must make your first estimated tax payment by April 15, 1983. You may either pay all of your estimated tax at that time or pay in four equal amounts that are due by April 15, 1983; June 15, 1983; September 15, 1983; and January 17, 1984. Exceptions to the general rule are listed below.

**(1) Other payment dates.**—In some cases, such as a change in income, you may have to make your first estimated tax payment after April 15, 1983. The payment dates are as follows:

If the requirement is met after:  /  Payment date is:

● April 1 and before June 2  —  June 15, 1983
● June 1 and before Sept. 2  —  Sept. 15, 1983
● Sept. 1  —  Jan. 17, 1984

**Note:** *You may use the "Amended Estimated Tax Schedule" on page 2 to figure your amended estimated tax.*

You may pay your estimated tax in equal amounts. If the first payment you are required to make is due:

● June 15, 1983, enter ⅓;
● September 15, 1983, enter ½;
● January 17, 1984, enter all;
of line 17 on line 18 of the worksheet and on line 1 of the payment-voucher.

If you file your 1983 Form 1040 by January 31, 1984, and pay the entire balance due, then you do not have to—

(Continued on page 2)

363-282-1

- make your first payment which would be due on January 17, 1984; **OR**
- make your last payment.

**(2) Farmers and fishermen.**—If at least two-thirds of your gross income for 1982 or 1983 is from farming or fishing, you may do one of the following:

- Pay all your estimated tax by January 17, 1984; **OR**
- File Form 1040 for 1983 by March 1, 1984, and pay the total tax due. In this case, you do not need to make estimated tax payments for 1983.

**(3) Fiscal year.**—If your return is on a fiscal year basis, your due dates are the 15th day of the 4th, 6th, and 9th months of your fiscal year and the 1st month of the following fiscal year. If any date falls on a Saturday, Sunday, or legal holiday, use the next regular workday.

**E. Penalty for Not Paying Enough Estimated Tax.**—You may be charged a penalty for not paying enough estimated tax, or for not making the payments on time. The penalty does not apply if each payment is timely and:

- Is at least 80% (66⅔% for farmers and fishermen) of the amount of income and self-employment taxes due (figured using the taxes and credits specified in **Publication 505**) as shown on your return for 1983; **OR**
- Is based on one of the exceptions shown on **Form 2210,** Underpayment of Estimated Tax by Individuals (**Form 2210F,** Underpayment of Estimated Tax by Farmers and Fishermen).

Also the penalty does not apply if you are a U.S. citizen or resident and you had no tax liability for a full 12-month preceding tax year. This applies to tax years beginning after December 31, 1982.

**Note:** You may be required to make payments of past due amounts to avoid further penalty. You may have to make these payments if you do not make your estimated tax payments on time, or if you did not pay the correct amount for a previous payment date.

**Example:** On June 1, 1983, you find out that you should have made an estimated tax payment for April 15. You should immediately fill out the payment-voucher due April 15, 1983, and send in the required amount (¼ × 1983 estimated tax).

**If you changed your name** because of marriage, divorce, etc. and you made estimated tax payments using your old name, you should attach a brief statement to the front of your 1983 income tax return. In it explain all the estimated tax payments you and your spouse made during the tax year, give the name of the Service Center where you made the payments, and give the name(s) and social security number(s) under which you made payments.

**F. Where to File Your Payment-Voucher.**—Mail your payment-voucher to the Internal Revenue Service Center for the place where you live.

**If you are located in:**    **Use this address:**

| If you are located in: | Use this address: |
|---|---|
| New Jersey, New York City, and counties of Nassau, Rockland, Suffolk, and Westchester | Holtsville, NY 00501 |
| New York (all other Counties), Connecticut, Maine, Massachusetts, New Hampshire, Rhode Island, Vermont | Andover, MA 05501 |
| District of Columbia, Delaware, Maryland, Pennsylvania | Philadelphia, PA 19255 |
| Alabama, Florida, Georgia, Mississippi, South Carolina | Atlanta, GA 31101 |
| Michigan, Ohio | Cincinnati, OH 45999 |
| Arkansas, Kansas, Louisiana, New Mexico, Oklahoma, Texas | Austin, TX 73301 |
| Alaska, Arizona, Colorado, Idaho, Minnesota, Montana, Nebraska, Nevada, North Dakota, Oregon, South Dakota, Utah, Washington, Wyoming | Ogden, UT 84201 |
| Illinois, Iowa, Missouri, Wisconsin | Kansas City, MO 64999 |
| California, Hawaii | Fresno, CA 93888 |
| Indiana, Kentucky, North Carolina, Tennessee, Virginia, West Virginia | Memphis, TN 37501 |
| American Samoa | Philadelphia, PA 19255 |
| Guam | Commissioner of Revenue and Taxation Agana, GU 96910 |
| Puerto Rico (or if excluding income under section 933) | Philadelphia, PA 19255 |
| Virgin Islands: Non-permanent residents | |
| Virgin Islands: Permanent residents | Department of Finance Tax Division Charlotte Amalie St. Thomas, VI 00801 |
| A.P.O. or F.P.O. address of: | Miami—Atlanta, GA 31101 New York—Holtsville, NY 00501 San Francisco—Fresno, CA 93883 Seattle—Ogden, UT 84201 |
| Foreign country, U.S. citizens and those excluding income under section 911 or 931, or claiming the housing deduction under section 911 | Philadelphia, PA 19255 |

---

**Record of Estimated Tax Payments**

| Payment number | (a) Date | (b) Amount | (c) 1982 overpayment credit applied | (d) Total amount paid and credited (add (b) and (c)) |
|---|---|---|---|---|
| 1 | | | | |
| 2 | | | | |
| 3 | | | | |
| 4 | | | | |
| Total . . . ▶ | | | | |

**Note:** If you are not required to make the estimated tax payment due April 15, 1983, at this time, you may have to make a payment by a later date. See Instruction D(1).

---

**Amended Estimated Tax Schedule** (Use if your estimated tax changes during the year)

| | | |
|---|---|---|
| 1 Amended estimated tax . . . . . . . . . . . . . . . . . | | 1 |
| 2 Less: a Amount of 1982 overpayment chosen for credit to 1983 estimated tax and applied to date . . . . . . . . . . . . . | 2a | |
| b Estimated tax payments to date . . . . . . . . . . | 2b | |
| c Total of lines 2a and b . . . . . . . . . . . . . . | | 2c |
| 3 Unpaid balance (subtract line 2c from line 1) . . . . . . . . . | | 3 |
| 4 Amount to be paid (line 3 divided by number of remaining payment dates) . . . . . . . . . . | | 4 |

---

**1983 Estimated Tax Worksheet (Keep for your records—Do Not Send to Internal Revenue Service)**

| | | |
|---|---|---|
| **1** Enter amount of Adjusted Gross Income you expect in 1983 . . . . . . . . . . . . . . . . . | **1** | |
| **2 a** If you plan to itemize deductions, enter the estimated total of your deductions. If you do not plan to itemize deductions, skip to line 2c and enter zero . . **2a** | | |
| **b** Enter } $3,400 if married filing a joint return (or qualifying widow(er)) . . <br> $2,300 if single (or head of household) . . . . . . . . . . <br> $1,700 if married filing a separate return . . . . . . . **2b** | | |
| **c** Subtract line 2b from line 2a (if zero or less, enter zero) . . . . . . . . . . . | **2c** | |
| **d** If you do not itemize deductions, enter your allowable deduction, if any, for charitable contributions (see page 13 of the 1982 Instructions for Form 1040) . . . . . . . . . . . **2d** | | |
| **3** Subtract line 2c or 2d, whichever applies, from line 1 . . . . . . . . . . **3** | | |
| **4** Exemptions (multiply $1,000 times number of personal exemptions) . . . . . . . . **4** | | |
| **5** Subtract line 4 from line 3 . . . . . . . . . . . . . . . . . . . **5** | | |
| **6 Tax.** (Figure your tax on line 5 by using Tax Rate Schedule X, Y, or Z in these instructions. DO NOT use the Tax Table or Tax Rate Schedule X, Y, or Z in the 1982 Form 1040 Instructions.) . . . . . . **6** | | |
| **7** Enter any additional taxes (see line 7 Instruction) . . . . . . . . . . **7** | | |
| **8** Add lines 6 and 7 . . . . . . . . . . . . . . . . . . **8** | | |
| **9** Credits (credit for the elderly, credit for child and dependent care expenses, investment credit, residential energy credit, etc.) . . . . . . . . . . . . . . . . **9** | | |
| **10** Subtract line 9 from line 8 . . . . . . . . . . . . . . . . **10** | | |
| **11** Tax from recapture of investment credit . . . . . . . . . . . . . **11** | | |
| **12** Estimate of 1983 self-employment income $................................; if $35,700 or more, enter $3,337.95; if less, multiply the amount by .0935 (see line 12 Instruction for additional information) . . . . . . **12** | | |
| **13** Tax on premature distributions from an IRA . . . . . . . . . . . . . **13** | | |
| **14** Add lines 10 through 13 . . . . . . . . . . . . . . . . **14** | | |
| **15 a** Earned income credit . . . . . . . . . . . . . . **15a** | | |
| **b** Estimated income tax withheld and to be withheld (including income tax withholding on interest and dividends) during 1983 . . . . . . . **15b** | | |
| **c** Credit for Federal tax on special fuels and oils (see Form 4136) . . . . . **15c** | | |
| **16** Total (add lines 15a, b, and c) . . . . . . . . . . . . . . . . . **16** | | |
| **17** Estimated tax (subtract line 16 from line 14). If $300 or more, fill out and file the payment-voucher along with your payment; if less, no payment is required at this time . . . . . . . . **17** | | |

**Caution:** You are required to prepay at least 80% of your tax liability each year. If you prepay less than 80% of your actual tax liability you will be subject to a penalty (see Instruction E). To avoid this, make sure your estimate is as accurate as possible. If you are unsure of your estimate, you may want to pay more than 80% of the amount you have estimated. In determining the amount of your estimated tax, you may take into account any of the four exceptions to the underpayment penalty. For more information on these exceptions, please get **Publication 505.**

| | | |
|---|---|---|
| **18** If the first payment you are required to make is due April 15, 1983, enter ¼ of line 17 here and on line 1 of your payment-voucher. You may round off cents to the nearest whole dollar. If you wish to pay more estimated tax than is shown on line 17, you may do so . . . . . . . . . . . . . **18** | | |

**Tear off here**

------------------------------------------------------------------------

**Form 1040-ES** | **1983**
Department of the Treasury
Internal Revenue Service | Payment-
Voucher

OMB No. 1545-0087

**Return this voucher with check or money order payable to the Internal Revenue Service.
Please do not send cash or staple your payment to this voucher.**

(Calendar year—Due Jan. 17, 1984)

| | Your social security number | Spouse's number, if joint payment |
|---|---|---|
| **1** Amount of payment $................................ | | |
| | First name and middle initial (of both spouses if joint payment) | Last name |
| **2** Fiscal year filers enter year ending | | |
| ------------------------------------ <br> (month and year) | Address (Number and street) | |
| | City, State, and ZIP code | |

*(Please type or print)*

**For Paperwork Reduction Act Notice, see instructions on page 1.**
363–282–2

**Page 3**

**1983 Tax Rate Schedules**
Caution: Do not use these Tax Rate Schedules to figure your 1982 taxes. Use only to figure your 1983 estimated taxes.

**SCHEDULE X—Single Taxpayers**

| If line 5 is: Over— | But not Over— | The tax is: | Of the amount Over— |
|---|---|---|---|
| $0 | $2,300 | —0— | |
| 2,300 | 3,400 | .......... 11% | $2,300 |
| 3,400 | 4,400 | $121+13% | 3,400 |
| 4,400 | 8,500 | 251+15% | 4,400 |
| 8,500 | 10,800 | 866+17% | 8,500 |
| 10,800 | 12,900 | 1,257+19% | 10,800 |
| 12,900 | 15,000 | 1,656+21% | 12,900 |
| 15,000 | 18,200 | 2,097+24% | 15,000 |
| 18,200 | 23,500 | 2,865+28% | 18,200 |
| 23,500 | 28,800 | 4,349+32% | 23,500 |
| 28,800 | 34,100 | 6,045+36% | 28,800 |
| 34,100 | 41,500 | 7,953+40% | 34,100 |
| 41,500 | 55,300 | 10,913+45% | 41,500 |
| 55,300 | .......... | 17,123+50% | 55,300 |

**SCHEDULE Z—Heads of Household**

| If line 5 is: Over— | But not Over— | The tax is: | Of the amount Over— |
|---|---|---|---|
| $0 | $2,300 | —0— | |
| 2,300 | 4,400 | .......... 11% | $2,300 |
| 4,400 | 6,500 | $231+13% | 4,400 |
| 6,500 | 8,700 | 504+15% | 6,500 |
| 8,700 | 11,800 | 834+18% | 8,700 |
| 11,800 | 15,000 | 1,392+19% | 11,800 |
| 15,000 | 18,200 | 2,000+21% | 15,000 |
| 18,200 | 23,500 | 2,672+25% | 18,200 |
| 23,500 | 28,800 | 3,997+29% | 23,500 |
| 28,800 | 34,100 | 5,534+34% | 28,800 |
| 34,100 | 44,700 | 7,336+37% | 34,100 |
| 44,700 | 60,600 | 11,258+44% | 44,700 |
| 60,600 | 81,800 | 18,254+48% | 60,600 |
| 81,800 | .......... | 28,430+50% | 81,800 |

**SCHEDULE Y—Married Taxpayers and Qualifying Widows and Widowers**

**Married Filing Joint Returns and Qualifying Widows and Widowers**

| If line 5 is: Over— | But not Over— | The tax is: | Of the amount Over— |
|---|---|---|---|
| $0 | $3,400 | —0— | |
| 3,400 | 5,500 | .......... 11% | $3,400 |
| 5,500 | 7,600 | $231+13% | 5,500 |
| 7,600 | 11,900 | 504+15% | 7,600 |
| 11,900 | 16,000 | 1,149+17% | 11,900 |
| 16,000 | 20,200 | 1,846+19% | 16,000 |
| 20,200 | 24,600 | 2,644+23% | 20,200 |
| 24,600 | 29,900 | 3,656+26% | 24,600 |
| 29,900 | 35,200 | 5,034+30% | 29,900 |
| 35,200 | 45,800 | 6,624+35% | 35,200 |
| 45,800 | 60,000 | 10,334+40% | 45,800 |
| 60,000 | 85,600 | 16,014+44% | 60,000 |
| 85,600 | 109,400 | 27,278+48% | 85,600 |
| 109,400 | .......... | 38,702+50% | 109,400 |

**Married Filing Separate Returns**

| If line 5 is: Over— | But not Over— | The tax is: | Of the amount Over— |
|---|---|---|---|
| $0 | $1,700 | —0— | |
| 1,700 | 2,750 | .......... 11% | $1,700 |
| 2,750 | 3,800 | $115.50+13% | 2,750 |
| 3,800 | 5,950 | 252.00+15% | 3,800 |
| 5,950 | 8,000 | 574.50+17% | 5,950 |
| 8,000 | 10,100 | 923.00+19% | 8,000 |
| 10,100 | 12,300 | 1,322.00+23% | 10,100 |
| 12,300 | 14,950 | 1,828.00+26% | 12,300 |
| 14,950 | 17,600 | 2,517.00+30% | 14,950 |
| 17,600 | 22,900 | 3,312.00+35% | 17,600 |
| 22,900 | 30,000 | 5,167.00+40% | 22,900 |
| 30,000 | 42,800 | 8,007.00+44% | 30,000 |
| 42,800 | 54,700 | 13,639.00+48% | 42,800 |
| 54,700 | .......... | 19,351.00+50% | 54,700 |

Form **1040-ES** | **1983**
Department of the Treasury
Internal Revenue Service | Payment-Voucher

Return this voucher with check or money order payable to the Internal Revenue Service.
Please do not send cash or staple your payment to this voucher.

OMB No. 1545–0087

(Calendar year—Due Sept. 15, 1983)

1 Amount of payment $ ............................

2 Fiscal year filers enter year ending

------------------------------------------
(month and year)

Please type or print

Your social security number | Spouse's number, if joint payment

First name and middle initial (of both spouses if joint payment) | Last name

Address (Number and street)

City, State, and ZIP code

**For Paperwork Reduction Act Notice, see instructions on page 1.**

**Tear off here**

Form **1040-ES** | **1983**
Department of the Treasury
Internal Revenue Service | Payment-Voucher

Return this voucher with check or money order payable to the Internal Revenue Service.
Please do not send cash or staple your payment to this voucher.

OMB No. 1545–0087

(Calendar year—Due June 15, 1983)

1 Amount of payment $ ............................

2 Fiscal year filers enter year ending

------------------------------------------
(month and year)

Please type or print

Your social security number | Spouse's number, if joint payment

First name and middle initial (of both spouses if joint payment) | Last name

Address (Number and street)

City, State, and ZIP code

**For Paperwork Reduction Act Notice, see instructions on page 1.**

**Tear off here**

Form **1040-ES** | **1983**
Department of the Treasury
Internal Revenue Service | Payment-Voucher

Return this voucher with check or money order payable to the Internal Revenue Service.
Please do not send cash or staple your payment to this voucher.

OMB No. 1545–0087

(Calendar year—Due April 15, 1983)

1 Amount of payment $ ............................

2 Fiscal year filers enter year ending

------------------------------------------
(month and year)

Please type or print

Your social security number | Spouse's number, if joint payment

First name and middle initial (of both spouses if joint payment) | Last name

Address (Number and street)

City, State, and ZIP code

**For Paperwork Reduction Act Notice, see instructions on page 1.**

363–282–1          ☆ U.S. GOVERNMENT PRINTING OFFICE : 1982—O–363–282          **Page 5**

| 1 Control number | 22222 | OMB No. 1545-0008 | | | |
|---|---|---|---|---|---|

**2 Employer's name, address, and ZIP code**

**3 Employer's identification number** | **4 Employer's State number**

| 5 Stat. em-ployee | De-ceased | Pension plan | Legal rep. | 942 emp. | Sub-total | Cor-rection | Void |
|---|---|---|---|---|---|---|---|
| ☐ | ☐ | ☐ | ☐ | ☐ | ☐ | ☐ | ☐ |

**6** | **7 Advance EIC payment**

**8 Employee's social security number** | **9 Federal income tax withheld** | **10 Wages, tips, other compensation** | **11 FICA tax withheld**

**12 Employee's name, address, and ZIP code** | **13 FICA wages** | **14 FICA tips**

**16 Employer's use**

| 17 State income tax | 18 State wages, tips, etc. | 19 Name of State |
|---|---|---|
| 20 Local income tax | 21 Local wages, tips, etc. | 22 Name of locality |

Form **W-2 Wage and Tax Statement 1982**  **Copy B To be filed with employee's FEDERAL tax return**  Department of the Treasury
This information is being furnished to the Internal Revenue Service.  Internal Revenue Service

## Notice to Employee:

You must file a tax return regardless of your income if any amount is shown in box 7, Advance EIC (earned income credit) payment.

File Copy B of this form with your 1982 Federal income tax return. Attach Copy 2 to your 1982 State or local income tax return. Please keep Copy C for your records. You can use it to prove your right to social security benefits. If your name, social security number, or address is incorrect, please correct Copies B, C, and 2 and tell your employer.

If you have already filed your tax return, or this W-2 corrects the one you included with your return, please amend your Form 1040 or 1040A by filing Form 1040X.

If you have nonwage income of more than $500 and will owe tax of $200 or more, ($300 for 1983) you should file Form 1040-ES, Declaration of Estimated Tax for Individuals, and pay the tax in installments during the year. If you retired during 1982 or plan to retire soon, you may have to pay tax on your income either by filing Form 1040-ES or by having tax withheld from your pension or annuity. See **Publication 505**, Tax Withholding and Estimated Tax, for details.

**Credit for Social Security (FICA) Tax.**—If more than one employer paid you wages during 1982 and more than the maximum FICA employee tax, railroad retirement (RRTA) tax, or combined FICA and RRTA tax was withheld, you can claim the excess as a credit against your Federal income tax. (Please see your Federal income tax return instructions.) The FICA rate of 6.70%, under Public Law 95–216, includes 1.30% for hospital insurance benefits and 5.40% for retirement, survivors, and disability insurance.

**Box 5. Pension plan.**—If you were covered by a government employee plan, a qualified pension or profit-sharing retirement plan, or a tax sheltered annuity plan, the Pension plan box may be marked. Armed Forces reservists, National Guard members, or volunteer firefighters, who have a retirement savings arrangement, should see **Publication 590**, Tax Information on Individual Retirement Arrangements.

## Instructions for Preparing Form W–2

The 6-part wage and tax statement is acceptable in most States. If you are in doubt, ask your appropriate State or local official.

Prepare Form W–2 for each of your employees to whom any of the following items applied during 1982.

(a) You withheld income tax or FICA (social security) tax.
(b) You would have withheld income tax if the employee had not claimed more than one withholding allowance.
(c) You paid $600 or more.
(d) You paid any amount for services, if you are in a trade or business. Include the cash value of any payment you made that was not in cash.

By January 31, 1983, give Copies B, C, and 2 to each person who was your employee during 1982. For anyone who stopped working for you before the end of 1982, you may give copies any time after employment ends. If the employee asks for Form W–2, give him or her the completed copies within 30 days of the request or the final wage payment, whichever is later. Send Copy A to the Social Security Administration by February 28, 1983. (For more information, please see Forms 941, 942, W–3, or Circular E. Farmers, see Circular A.)

See separate **Instructions for Forms W–2 and W–2P** for more information on how to complete Form W–2.

**Paperwork Reduction Act Notice.**—The Paperwork Reduction Act of 1980 says we must tell you why we are collecting this information, how we will use it, and whether you have to give it to us. We ask for the information to carry out the Internal Revenue laws of the United States. We need it to ensure that you are complying with these laws and to allow us to figure and collect the right amount of tax. You are required to give us this information.

☆ U.S. GOVERNMENT PRINTING OFFICE: 1982—O-343-030 EI-36-2441915

| Form **W-4** (Rev. January 1983) | Department of the Treasury—Internal Revenue Service **Employee's Withholding Allowance Certificate** | OMB No. 1545–0010 Expires 8–31–85 |

**1** Type or print your full name

**2** Your social security number

Home address (number and street or rural route)

City or town, State, and ZIP code

**3** Marital Status

☐ Single    ☐ Married

☐ Married, but withhold at higher Single rate

**Note:** If married, but legally separated, or spouse is a nonresident alien, check the Single box.

**4** Total number of allowances you are claiming (from line F of the worksheet on page 2) . . . . . . . . . . .

**5** Additional amount, if any, you want deducted from each pay . . . . . . . . . . . . . . . .   $

**6** I claim exemption from withholding because (see instructions and check boxes below that apply):

  **a** ☐ Last year I did not owe any Federal income tax and had a right to a full refund of **ALL** income tax withheld, **AND**

  **b** ☐ This year I do not expect to owe any Federal income tax and expect to have a right to a full refund of   | Year

    **ALL** income tax withheld. If both a and b apply, enter the year effective and "EXEMPT" here . . ▶

  **c** If you entered "EXEMPT" on line 6b, are you a full-time student? . . . . . . . . . . . . . . . ☐ Yes   ☐ No

Under the penalties of perjury, I certify that I am entitled to the number of withholding allowances claimed on this certificate, or if claiming exemption from withholding, that I am entitled to claim the exempt status.

Employee's signature ▶     Date ▶         , 19

**7** Employer's name and address (Employer: Complete 7, 8, and 9 only if sending to IRS)    | **8** Office code | **9** Employer identification number

-------------------------------------- ▶ Detach along this line. Give the top part of this form to employer; keep the lower part for your records. --------------------------------------

**Privacy Act and Paperwork Reduction Act Notice.**—If you do not give your employer a certificate, you will be treated as a single person with no withholding allowances as required by IRC sections 3402(l) and 3401(e). We ask for this information to carry out the Internal Revenue laws of the United States. We may give the information to the Dept. of Justice for civil or criminal litigation and to the States and the District of Columbia for use in administering their tax laws.

**Purpose.**—The law requires that you complete Form W–4 so that your employer can withhold Federal income tax from your pay. Your Form W–4 remains in effect until you change it or, if you entered "EXEMPT" on line 6b above, until February 15 of next year. By correctly completing this form, you can fit the amount of tax withheld from your wages to your tax liability.

If you got a large refund last year, you may be having too much tax withheld. If so, you may want to increase the number of your allowances on line 4 by claiming any other allowances you are entitled to. The kinds of allowances, and how to figure them, are explained in detail below.

If you owed a large amount of tax last year, you may not be having enough tax withheld. If so, you can claim fewer allowances on line 4, or ask that an additional amount be withheld on line 5, or both.

If the number of withholding allowances you are entitled to claim decreases to less than you are now claiming, you must file a new W–4 with your employer within 10 days.

The instructions below explain how to fill in Form W–4. Publication 505 contains more information on withholding. You can get it from most IRS offices.

For more information about who qualifies as your dependent, what deductions you can take, and what tax credits you qualify for, see the Form 1040 Instructions.

**Line-By-Line Instructions**

Fill in the identifying information in boxes 1 and 2. If you are married and want tax withheld at the regular rate for married persons, check "Married" in box 3. If you are married and want tax withheld at the higher Single rate (because both you and your spouse work, for example), check the box "Married, but withhold at higher Single rate" in box 3.

**Line 4 of Form W–4**

**Total number of allowances.**—Use the worksheet on page 2 to figure your allowances. Add the number of allowances for

each category explained below. Enter the total on line 4.

If you are single and hold more than one job, you may not claim the same allowances with more than one employer at the same time. If you are married and both you and your spouse are employed, you may not both claim the same allowances with both of your employers at the same time. To have the highest amount of tax withheld, claim "0" allowances on line 4.

**A. Personal allowances.**—You can claim the following personal allowances:

1 for yourself, 1 if you are 65 or older, and 1 if you are blind.

If you are married and your spouse either does not work or is not claiming his or her allowances on a separate W–4, you may also claim the following allowances: 1 for your spouse, 1 if your spouse is 65 or older, and 1 if your spouse is blind.

**B. Special withholding allowance.**—Claim the special withholding allowance if you are single and have one job **or** you are married, have one job, and your spouse does not work. You may still claim this allowance so long as the total wages earned on other jobs by you or your spouse (or both) is 10% or less of the combined total wages. Use this special withholding allowance only to figure your withholding. Do not claim it when you file your return.

**C. Allowances for dependents.**—You may claim one allowance for each dependent you will be able to claim on your Federal income tax return.

**Note:** If you are not claiming any deductions or credits, skip D and E, add lines A, B, and C, enter the total on line F and carry the total over to line 4 of W–4.

Before you claim allowances under D and E, total your non-wage taxable income (interest, dividends, self-employment income, etc.) and subtract this amount from estimated deductions you would otherwise enter in D1. If your non-wage income is greater than the amount of estimated deductions, you cannot claim any allowances under D. Moreover, you should take one-third of the excess (non-wage income over estimated deductions) and add this to the appropriate "A" value in Table 1 if determining allowances under E.

**D. Allowances for estimated deductions.**—If you expect to itemize deductions, you can claim additional withholding allowances. See Schedule A (Form 1040) for deductions you can itemize.

You can also count deductible amounts you pay for (1) alimony (2) qualified retirement contributions including Keogh (H.R. 10) plans (3) moving expenses (4) employee business expenses (Part I of Form 2106) (5) the deduction for two-earner married couples, (6) net losses shown on Schedules C, D, E, and F (Form 1040), the last line of Part II of Form 4797, the net operating loss carryover, (7) penalty on early withdrawal of savings, and (8) direct charitable contributions. **Note:** Check with your employer to see if any tax is being withheld on moving expenses or IRA contributions. Do not include these amounts if tax is not being withheld; otherwise, you may be underwithheld. For details see Publication 505.

The deduction allowed two-earner married couples is 10% of the lesser of $30,-000 or the qualified earned income of the spouse with the lower income. Once you have determined these deductions, enter the total on line D1 of the worksheet on page 2 and figure the number of withholding allowances for them.

**E. Allowances for estimated tax credits.**—If you expect to take credits like those shown on lines 41 through 48 on the 1982 Form 1040 (child care, residential energy, etc.), use the table on the top of page 2 to figure the number of additional allowances you can claim. Include the earned income credit if you are not receiving advance payment of it, and any excess FICA tax withheld. Also, if you expect to income average, include the amount of the reduction in tax because of averaging when using the table.

**Line 5 of Form W–4**

**Additional amount, if any, you want deducted from each pay.**—If you are not having enough tax withheld from your pay, you may ask your employer to withhold more by filling in an additional amount on line 5. Often married couples, both of whom are working, and persons with two

363–044–2          Form **W–4** (Rev. 1–83)

or more jobs need to have additional tax withheld. You may also need to have additional tax withheld because you have income other than wages, such as interest and dividends, capital gains, rents, alimony received, etc. Estimate the amount you will be underwithheld and divide that amount by the number of pay periods in the year. Enter the additional amount you want withheld each pay period on line 5.

### Line 6 of Form W–4

**Exemption from withholding.**—You can claim exemption from withholding only if last year you did not owe any Federal income tax and had a right to a refund of all income tax withheld, and this year you do not expect to owe any Federal income tax and expect to have a right to a refund of all income tax withheld. If you qualify, check boxes 6a and b, write the year exempt status is effective and "EXEMPT" on line 6b, and answer Yes or No to the question on line 6c.

If you want to claim exemption from withholding next year, you must file a new W–4 with your employer on or before February 15 of next year. If you are not having Federal income tax withheld this year, but expect to have a tax liability next year, the law requires you to give your employer a new W–4 by December 1 of this year. If you are covered by FICA, your employer must withhold social security tax.

You may be fined $500 if you file, with no reasonable basis, a W–4 that results in less tax being withheld than is properly allowable. In addition, criminal penalties apply for willfully supplying false or fraudulent information or failing to supply information requiring an increase in withholding.

Your employer must send to IRS any W–4 claiming more than 14 withholding allowances **or** claiming exemption from withholding if the wages are expected to usually exceed $200 a week. The employer is to complete boxes 7, 8, and 9 only on copies of the W–4 sent to IRS.

---

### Table 1—For Figuring Your Withholding Allowances For Estimated Tax Credits and Income Averaging (Line E)

| Estimated Salaries and Wages from all Sources | Single Employees (A) | Single Employees (B) | Head of Household Employees (A) | Head of Household Employees (B) | Married Employees (When Spouse not Employed) (A) | Married Employees (When Spouse not Employed) (B) | Married Employees (When Both Spouses are Employed) (A) | Married Employees (When Both Spouses are Employed) (B) |
|---|---|---|---|---|---|---|---|---|
| Under $15,000 | $ 100 | $160 | $ 50 | $160 | $ 80 | $120 | $ 0 | $120 |
| 15,000–25,000 | 150 | 250 | 0 | 250 | 90 | 180 | 360 | 180 |
| 25,001–35,000 | 200 | 320 | 0 | 320 | 130 | 260 | 840 | 230 |
| 35,001–45,000 | 390 | 370 | 0 | 370 | 180 | 340 | 1,590 | 260 |
| 45,001–55,000 | 1,120 | 370 | 0 | 370 | 250 | 360 | 2,300 | 350 |
| 55,001–65,000 | 2,150 | 370 | 670 | 370 | 560 | 370 | 3,130 | 350 |
| Over 65,000 | 3,320 | 370 | 1,640 | 370 | 1,110 | 370 | 4,000 | 370 |

---

### Worksheet to Figure Your Withholding Allowances to be Entered on Line 4 of Form W–4

**A** Personal allowances . . . . . . . . . . . . . . . . . . . . . . . . . . . ▶ | **A**

**B** Special withholding allowance (not to exceed 1 allowance—see instructions on page 1) . . . . . . ▶ | **B**

**C** Allowances for dependents . . . . . . . . . . . . . . . . . . . . . . . ▶ | **C**

If you are not claiming any deductions or credits, skip lines D and E.

**D** Allowances for estimated deductions:

  **1** Enter the total amount of your estimated itemized deductions, alimony payments, qualified retirement contributions including Keogh (H.R. 10) plans, deduction for two-earner married couples, business losses including net operating loss carryovers, moving expenses, employee business expenses, penalty on early withdrawal of savings, and direct charitable contributions for the year . . . . . . . . . . . . . . . . . . **1** $

  **2** If you do not plan to itemize deductions, enter $500 on line D2. If you plan to itemize, find your total estimated salaries and wages amount in the left column of the table below. (Include salaries and wages of both spouses.) Read across to the right and enter the amount from the column that applies to you. Enter that amount on line D2 . . . ▶ **2** $

| Estimated salaries and wages from all sources: | Single and Head of Household Employees (only one job) | Married Employees (one spouse working and one job only) | Employees with more than one job or Married Employees with both spouses working [1] |
|---|---|---|---|
| Under $15,000 | . . $2,800 | . . . . $3,900 | . . . . . 40% |
| 15,000–35,000 | . . 2,800 | . . . . 3,900 | . . . . . 23% of estimated salaries and wages |
| 35,001–50,000 | . . 9% of estimated salaries and wages | . . 3,900 | . . . . . 20% of estimated salaries and wages |
| Over $50,000 | . . 11% of estimated salaries and wages | . . 8% of estimated salaries and wages | . . . . . 18% |

  **3** Subtract line D2 from line D1 (But not less than zero) . . . . . . . . . . . ▶ **3** $

  **4** Divide the amount on line D3 by $1,000 (increase any fraction to the next whole number). Enter here . . ▶ **D**

**E** Allowances for estimated tax credits and income averaging: use Table 1 above for figuring withholding allowances

  **1** Enter estimated tax credits, excess FICA tax withheld, and tax reduction from income averaging and tax withheld on interest and dividends . . . . . . . . . . . . . . . . . . . . $

  **2** Enter the column (A) amount for your salary range and filing status (single, etc.) However, enter 0 if you claim 1 or more allowances on line D4. . . . . . . . . . . . . . . . . . $

  **3** Subtract line 2 from line 1 (If zero or less, do not complete lines 4 and 5) . . . $

  **4** Find the column (B) amount for your salary range and filing status . . . . . . . $

  **5** Divide line 3 by line 4. Increase any fraction to the next whole number. This is the maximum number of withholding allowances for estimated tax credits and income averaging. Enter here . . . . . . . . . ▶ **E**

  **Example:** A taxpayer who expects to file a Federal income tax return as a single person estimates annual wages of $12,000 and tax credits of $650. The $12,000 falls in the wage bracket of under $15,000. The value in column (A) is 100. Subtracting this from the estimated credits of 650 leaves 550. The value in column (B) is 160. Dividing 550 by 160 gives 3.4. Since any fraction is increased to the next whole number, show 4 on line E.

**F** Total (add lines A through E). Enter total here and on line 4 of Form W–4 . . . . . . . . . . . ▶ **F**

[1] If you earn 10% or less of your total wages from other jobs or one spouse earns 10% or less of the couple's combined total wages, you can use the "Single and Head of Household Employees (only one job)" or "Married Employees (one spouse working and one job only)" table, whichever is appropriate.

**Form 1041**
Department of the Treasury
Internal Revenue Service

## U.S. Fiduciary Income Tax Return
For the calendar year 1982 or fiscal year

beginning ..................................., 1982, and ending ..................................., 19 ......

OMB No. 1545–0092

**1982**

**Check applicable boxes:**
- ☐ Decedent's estate
- ☐ Bankruptcy estate
- ☐ Testamentary trust
- ☐ Generation-skipping trust
- ☐ Simple trust ($300)
- ☐ Complex trust ($100)
- ☐ Complex trust ($300)
- ☐ Grantor type trust
- ☐ Family estate trust
- ☐ Pooled income fund

Name of estate or trust (Grantor type trust, see instructions)

Name and title of fiduciary

Address of fiduciary (number and street)

City, State, and ZIP code

**Employer identification number**

Nonexempt charitable and split-interest trusts check applicable boxes (See instructions):
- ☐ Described in section 4947(a)(1)
- ☐ Not treated as a private foundation
- ☐ Described in section 4947(a)(2)

**Check applicable boxes:** ☐ First return  ☐ Final return  ☐ Ancillary return  ☐ Amended return
Change in fiduciary's  ☐ Name or  ☐ Address

### Income

| | | |
|---|---|---|
| 1 | Dividends (Enter full amount before exclusion) | 1 |
| 2 | Interest income (Enter full amount before exclusion) | 2 |
| 3 | Partnership income or (loss) | 3 |
| 4 | Income from another estate or trust | 4 |
| 5 | Net rent and royalty income or (loss) from line 44 | 5 |
| 6 | Net business and farm income or (loss) (Attach Schedules C and F (Form 1040)) | 6 |
| 7 | Capital gain or (loss) (Attach Schedule D (Form 1041)) | 7 |
| 8 | Ordinary gain or (loss) (Attach Form 4797) | 8 |
| 9 | Other income (State nature of income) | 9 |
| 10 | Total income (Add lines 1 through 9) ▶ | 10 |

### Deductions

| | | |
|---|---|---|
| 11 | Interest | 11 |
| 12 | Taxes | 12 |
| 13 | Charitable deduction (from line 53) | 13 |
| 14 | Fiduciary fees | 14 |
| 15 | Attorney, accountant, and return preparer fees | 15 |
| 16 | Other deductions (Attach a separate sheet listing deductions) | 16 |
| 17 | Total (Add lines 11 through 16) ▶ | 17 |
| 18 | Subtract line 17 from line 10 | 18 |
| 19 | Income distribution deduction (from line 68) (See specific instructions) (Attach Schedule K-1 (Form 1041)) | 19 |
| 20 | Dividend and interest exclusion (See instructions) | 20 |
| 21 | Estate tax deduction (Attach computation) | 21 |
| 22 | Long-term capital gain deduction from Schedule D (Form 1041) (Charity ☐—See instructions) | 22 |
| 23 | Exemption | 23 |
| 24 | Total (Add lines 19 through 23) ▶ | 24 |
| 25 | Taxable income of fiduciary (Subtract line 24 from line 18) ▶ | 25 |

### Computation of Tax

| | | |
|---|---|---|
| 26 | Tax: **a** Tax rate schedule ..................; **b** Other tax ..................; Total ▶ | 26c |
| 27 | Credits: **a** Foreign tax ..................; **b** Investment ..................; **c** Jobs ..................; Total ▶ | 27d |
| 28 | Credits: **a** Alcohol fuel ..................; **b** Nonconventional fuel ..................; **c** Research ..................; Total ▶ | 28d |
| 29 | Total (Add lines 27d and 28d) ▶ | 29 |
| 30 | Balance (Subtract line 29 from line 26c) | 30 |
| 31 | Tax from: **a** Form 4255 ..................; **b** Form 4626 ..................; Total ▶ | 31c |
| 32 | Alternative minimum tax (Attach Form 6251) | 32 |
| 33 | Total (Add lines 30 through 32) ▶ | 33 |
| 34 | Other credits (See instruction for line 34) | 34 |
| 35 | Federal income tax: **a** Previously paid ▶..................; **b** Withheld ▶..................; Total ▶ | 35c |
| 36 | Total (Add lines 34 and 35c) ▶ | 36 |
| 37 | Balance of tax due (Subtract line 36 from line 33) (See instruction K) | 37 |
| 38 | Overpayment (Subtract line 33 from line 36) | 38 |

**Please Sign Here**

Under penalties of perjury, I declare that I have examined this return, including accompanying schedules and statements, and to the best of my knowledge and belief, it is true, correct, and complete. Declaration of preparer (other than fiduciary) is based on all information of which preparer has any knowledge.

▶ Signature of fiduciary or officer representing fiduciary

▶ Date

**Paid Preparer's Use Only**

| Preparer's signature ▶ | Date | Check if self-employed ☐ | Preparer's social security no. |
|---|---|---|---|
| Firm's name (or yours, if self-employed) and address ▶ | | E.I. No. ▶ | |
| | | ZIP code ▶ | |

**For Privacy Act and Paperwork Reduction Act Notice, see page 1 of the instructions.**

363–085–1

Form **1041** (1982)

Form 1041 (1982)          **Page 2**

### Schedule A.—NET RENT AND ROYALTY INCOME (If more space is needed, attach additional sheets of same size.)

| (a) Kind and location of property | (b) Total amount of rents | (c) Total amount of royalties | (d) Fiduciary's share of depreciation (explain on Form 4562) or depletion (attach computation) | (e) Other expenses (Repairs, etc.) attach statement) |
|---|---|---|---|---|
| 39 | | | | |
| 40 | | | | |
| 41 | | | | |
| 42 | | | | |
| 43 Totals | | | | |
| 44 Net income or (loss) (column (b) plus column (c) less columns (d) and (e)). Enter here and on line 5 . . | 44 | | | |

### Do not complete Schedules B and C for a simple trust

### Schedule B.—CHARITABLE DEDUCTION (Write the name and address of the charitable organization on an attached sheet.)

| | | |
|---|---|---|
| 45 Amounts paid or permanently set aside for charitable purposes from current year's income . . . . . | 45 | |
| 46 Tax-exempt interest allocable to charitable distribution (See instructions) . . . . . . . . . | 46 | |
| **(Complete lines 47 and 48 below only if gain on Schedule D (Form 1041), line 17, column (b), exceeds loss on Schedule D (Form 1041), line 16, column (b).)** | | |
| 47 a Long-term capital gain included on line 45 (See instructions) . . . . . . . . . . . | 47a | |
|     b Enter gain on Schedule D (Form 1041), line 17, column (b), minus loss on Schedule D (Form 1041), line 16, column (b) . | 47b | |
|     c Enter gain on Schedule D (Form 1041), line 17, column (c), minus loss on Schedule D (Form 1041), line 16, column (c) . | 47c | |
| 48 Enter 60% of the amount on line 47a, 47b, or 47c, whichever is the smallest . . . . . . . . | 48 | |
| 49 Add line 46 and line 48 . . . . . . . . . . . . . . . . . . . . . . . . . | 49 | |
| 50 Balance (Subtract line 49 from line 45) . . . . . . . . . . . . . . . . . . . . | 50 | |
| 51 Enter the short-term capital gain and 40% of the net long-term capital gain of the current tax year allocable to corpus, paid or permanently set aside for charitable purposes . . . . . . . . . . . . . | 51 | |
| 52 Amounts paid or permanently set aside for charitable purposes other than from income of the current year (See instructions) . | 52 | |
| 53 Total (Add lines 50, 51, and 52). Enter here and on line 13 . . . . . . . . . . . . . | 53 | |

### Schedule C.—INCOME DISTRIBUTION DEDUCTION

| | | |
|---|---|---|
| 54 Enter amount from line 18 if the amount on line 10 exceeds the amount on line 17 . . . . . . | 54 | |
| 55 a Tax-exempt interest, as adjusted (See instructions) . . . . . . . . . . . . . . . | 55a | |
|     b Net gain shown on Schedule D (Form 1041), line 18, column (a). If net loss, enter zero . . . . . | 55b | |
|     c Add line 51 and 40% of the amount on line 47a, 47b, or 47c, whichever is the smallest . . . . . | 55c | |
|     d Short-term capital gain included on line 45 . . . . . . . . . . . . . . . . . | 55d | |
|     e If amount on line 7 is a loss, enter amount here as a positive figure . . . . . . . . . . . | 55e | |
| 56 Total (Add lines 54 through 55e) . . . . . . . . . . . . . . . . . . . . . . | 56 | |
| 57 If amount on line 7 is a gain, enter amount here . . . . . . . . . . . . . . . . . | 57 | |
| 58 Distributable net income (Subtract line 57 from line 56) . . . . . . . . . . . . . . . | 58 | |
| 59 If a complex trust, amount of income for the tax year determined under the governing instrument (accounting income) . . . . . . . . . 59 | | |
| 60 Amount of income required to be distributed currently (See instructions) . . . . . . . . . | 60 | |
| 61 Other amounts paid, credited, or otherwise required to be distributed (See instructions) . . . . . | 61 | |
| 62 Total (Add lines 60 and 61) (If greater than line 59, see instructions) . . . . . . . . . . | 62 | |
| 63 Enter the total of tax-exempt income included on lines 60 and 61, as adjusted (See instructions) . . . | 63 | |
| 64 Balance (Subtract line 63 from line 62) . . . . . . . . . . . . . . . . . . . . | 64 | |
| 65 Enter distributable net income from line 58 . . . . . . . . . . . . . . . . . . | 65 | |
| 66 Enter the amount from line 55a . . . . . . . . . . . . . . . . . . . . . . | 66 | |
| 67 Balance (Subtract line 66 from line 65) . . . . . . . . . . . . . . . . . . . . | 67 | |
| 68 Income distribution deduction. Enter here and on line 19 the amount on line 64 or line 67, whichever is less . | 68 | |

| | Yes | No | | | Yes | No |
|---|---|---|---|---|---|---|
| 69 Date trust was created or, if an estate, date of decedent's death. | | | 73 At any time during the tax year did the estate or trust have an interest in or a signature or other authority over a bank account, securities account, or other financial account in a foreign country? (See the instructions for question 73) . . . | | |
| 70 Did the estate or trust receive tax-exempt income? . . . . If "Yes," attach a computation of the allocation of expenses. | | | | | |
| 71 If a complex trust making the section 663(b) election, check the "Yes" box . . . . . . . . . . . . . . | | | 74 Was the estate or trust the grantor of, or transferor to, a foreign trust which existed during the current tax year, whether or not the estate or trust has any beneficial interest in it? If "Yes," you may have to file Form 3520, 3520-A, or 926 . . . . | | |
| 72 Did the estate or trust receive all or any part of the earnings (salary, wages, and other compensation) of any individual by reason of a contract assignment or similar arrangement? . . . | | | | | |

     363-085-1

| SCHEDULE K-1 (Form 1041) Department of the Treasury Internal Revenue Service | **Beneficiary's Share of Income, Deductions, Credits, etc.—1982** for the calendar year 1982, or fiscal year beginning ............................, 1982, ending ............................, 19 ......... (Complete for each beneficiary) | OMB No. 1545-0092 **Copy A** File with Form 1041 |

Name of estate or trust ▶

| Beneficiary's identifying number ▶ | Estate or trust's employer identification number ▶ |
| Beneficiary's name, address, and ZIP code | Fiduciary's name, address, and ZIP code |

| **a.** Allocable share item | **b.** Amount | **c.** Form 1040 filers enter column b amounts as indicated below |
|---|---|---|
| Your income from a fiscal year estate or trust must be included in your tax year during which the fiscal year of the estate or trust ends. | | |
| 1 Dividends (amount before exclusion) . . . . . . . . . . | | Schedule B, Part II, line 9 |
| 2 Interest from All-Savers Certificates . . . . . . . . . | | Schedule B, Part I, line 4 |
| 3 (a) Net short-term capital gain or (loss) . . . . . . . . | | Schedule D, line 3, column f or g |
| (b) Net long-term capital gain or (loss) . . . . . . . . | | Schedule D, line 10, column f or g |
| 4 Other taxable income (itemize): | | |
| (a) (1) .......................................................... | | |
| (2) .......................................................... | | |
| (b) Total of lines 4(a)(1) and (2) . . . . . . . . . . | | |
| (c) Depreciation (including cost recovery) and depletion . . . | | |
| (d) Amortization deductions (itemize): | | |
| (1) .......................................................... | | |
| (2) .......................................................... | | |
| (e) Total of lines 4(c), 4(d)(1), and 4(d)(2) . . . . . . . | | |
| (f) Line 4(b) minus line 4(e) . . . . . . . . . . . . | | Schedule E, Part II |
| 5 Estate tax deduction (Attach computation) . . . . . . . | | Schedule A, line 26 |
| 6 Excess deductions on termination (Attach computation) . . . | | Schedule A, line 26 |
| 7 Tax preference items: | | |
| (a) Accelerated depreciation on: | | |
| (1) Low-income rental housing (167(k)) . . . . . . . | | Form 4625, line 1(a)(1)* |
| (2) Other real property (See instructions) . . . . . . | | Form 4625, line 1(a)(2)* |
| (3) Personal property subject to a lease (See instructions) . | | Form 4625, line 1(b)* |
| (b) Depletion . . . . . . . . . . . . . . . . | | Form 4625, line 1(e)* |
| (c) Other (itemize): | | |
| (1) .......................................................... | | Enter on applicable line of Form 4625* |
| (2) .......................................................... | | Enter on applicable line of Form 4625* |
| 8 Income tax withheld on interest and dividend income (See instructions) . . . . . . . . . . . . . . . . | | |
| 9 Foreign taxes (List on a separate sheet) . . . . . . . . | | Form 1116 or Schedule A (Form 1040), line 14 |
| 10 Property eligible for investment credit: | | |
| Unadjusted basis of new recovery property | (a) 3-Year . . . . . . . . | | Form 3468, line 1(a) |
| | (b) Other . . . . . . . . . | | Form 3468, line 1(b) |
| Unadjusted basis of used recovery property | (c) 3-Year . . . . . . . . | | Form 3468, line 1(c) |
| | (d) Other . . . . . . . . . | | Form 3468, line 1(d) |
| Nonrecovery property (see instruction 10) (Attach schedule) . | | |
| 11 Other (itemize): | | |
| (a) .......................................................... | | |
| (b) .......................................................... | | (Enter on applicable line of appropriate tax form) |
| (c) .......................................................... | | |
| (d) .......................................................... | | |

*See instructions

For **Privacy Act and Paperwork Reduction Act Notice**, see page 1 of the Instructions for Form 1041.

363-091-1

# Instructions

*References are to the Internal Revenue Code, unless otherwise noted.*

Schedule K–1 (Form 1041) is used by the fiduciary to report the beneficiary's income from the estate or trust. Fiduciary means trustee, executor, executrix, administrator, administratrix, or persons in possession of property of a decedent's estate.

You may find additional helpful information in **Publication 559**, Tax Information for Survivors, Executors, and Administrators. This publication is available from the Internal Revenue Service.

## General Instructions

**A. Who must file.**—The fiduciary (or one of the joint fiduciaries) must file Schedule K–1 (or an approved substitute) with Form 1041. If there is more than one beneficiary, file a separate Schedule K–1 for each beneficiary. File Copy A with Form 1041. You may use Copy B for the section 6041(d) notice to the beneficiary if one is required. You may keep Copy C.

A section 6041(d) notice is required by January 31 following the calendar year during which you make payments of $600 or more in the course of your trade or business. An example is a bank conducting a trust business and making payments of trust income of $600 or more during a calendar year to a trust beneficiary. See section 6041 and related regulations for more information.

**B. Beneficiary's identifying number.**—As a payer of income, you are required under section 6109 to request and provide a proper identifying number for each recipient of income. Enter this number on all Schedules K–1 or approved substitutes when you file your return. Individuals and business recipients are responsible for giving you their taxpayer identification numbers upon request.

Under section 6676 the payer is charged a $50 penalty for each failure to provide a required taxpayer identification number (not to exceed $50,000 for any calendar year), unless reasonable cause is established for not providing it. If reasonable cause exists, please explain in an attached signed affidavit.

**C. Substitute forms.**—You do not need prior IRS approval for substitute Schedules K–1 that include the OMB number and that (a) show only the line items that a taxpayer needs if those line items have the same numbers and titles and are in the same order as on the comparable IRS Schedule K–1; or (b) are an exact copy of an IRS Schedule K–1. You must have prior approval for other substitute Schedules K–1. You may apply for it by writing to: Internal Revenue Service, 1111 Constitution Avenue, NW, Washington, DC 20224, Attention: D:R:R:IM.

**D. Beneficiary's income.**—If no special computations are required, use the following instructions to compute the beneficiary's income from the estate or trust. In other cases, see **Publication 559** and sections 652, 662, and 663 and related regulations. For example, different computations are required if capital gains and losses or a charitable deduction are involved. In addition, the terms of the governing instrument or local law may require different computations.

**Income.**—The beneficiary must include in gross income the smaller of (1) the amounts paid, credited, or required to be distributed, or (2) the proportionate share of distributable net income, reduced in either case by the share of distributable tax-exempt income minus the allowable expense not allowable as a deduction on Form 1041.

**Character of income.**—The beneficiary's income is considered to have the same proportion of each class of items entering into the computation of distributable net income

that the total of each class has to the distributable net income.

**Allocation of deductions.**—Use the following method to allocate the items of deduction that enter into the computation of distributable net income among the items of distributable net income. Subtract the deductions attributable to one class of income from that income. Subtract those deductions not attributable to one class of income from any class, but be sure a reasonable proportion is subtracted from tax-exempt income. Except for deductions allocable to tax-exempt income, you may allocate excess deductions attributable to one class of income to other classes. You may not allocate any of the deductions in the computation of distributable net income to items attributable to corpus or to income not included in distributable net income. Except for the final year and for depreciation or depletion allocations in excess of income (see Rev. Rul. 74–530, 1974–2 C.B. 188), you may not show any negative amounts for any class of income because the beneficiary generally may not claim losses or deductions of the estate or trust.

**Allocation of credits.**—In general, the estate or trust or the beneficiaries may claim applicable tax credits according to how the income is divided. For more information, see the appropriate Code sections for the tax credits.

**Gifts and bequests.**—Do not include in the beneficiary's income any gifts or bequests of a specific sum of money or of specific property under the terms of the governing instrument that are paid or credited in three installments or less. Amounts that can be paid or credited only from income of the estate or trust do not qualify as a gift or bequest of a specific sum of money.

**Past years.**—Do not include in the beneficiary's income amounts deducted on Form 1041 for an earlier year that were credited or required to be distributed in that earlier year.

**E. Beneficiary's tax year.**—The beneficiary's income from the estate or trust must be included in the beneficiary's tax year during which the tax year of the estate or trust ends. See **Publication 559** for more information including the effect of the death of a beneficiary during the tax year of the estate or trust.

## Instructions for Line Items

The instructions below are numbered to correspond to the applicable line items on Schedule K–1 (Form 1041).

**1. Dividends.**—Enter the beneficiary's share of the dividend income that qualifies for exclusion.

**2. Interest from All-Savers Certificates.**—Enter the beneficiary's share of the interest income from All-Savers Certificates as defined in the Instructions for Form 1041, instruction for line 20. Do not include interest from a certificate that is redeemed before maturity or used as collateral or security for a loan. Although an estate or trust may not exclude the interest on an All-Savers Certificate that it purchases, the interest retains its character when distributed to a beneficiary so that the beneficiary may be entitled to exclude it from gross income as All-Savers Certificate interest.

**3(a). Net short-term capital gain or (loss).**—Enter the beneficiary's share of the net short-term capital gain. Do not enter a loss for any year before the final year of the estate or trust. If for the final year there is a capital loss carryover, enter the beneficiary's share of the short-term capital loss carryover as a loss in parentheses. However, if the beneficiary is a corporation, enter the beneficiary's share of all carryover capital losses as a loss in parentheses. See **Publication 559** and section 642(h) and related regulations for more information.

*(Instructions continued on back of Copy C)*

*(Instructions continued from back of Copy A)*

**3(b). Net long-term capital gain or (loss).**—Enter the beneficiary's share of the net long-term capital gain. Do not enter a loss for any year before the final year of the estate or trust. If for the final year there is a capital loss carryover, enter the beneficiary's share of the long-term capital loss carryover as a loss in parentheses. (If the beneficiary is a corporation, see instruction 3(a).) See **Publication 559** and section 642(h) and related regulations for more information.

**4(a). Other taxable income.**—Itemize by type of income the beneficiary's share of the other taxable income not reportable on line 1, 2, 3(a), or 3(b). This includes dividends that do not qualify for exclusion and interest on an All-Savers Certificate not reportable on line 2.

**4(c). Depreciation (including cost recovery) and depletion.**—Enter the beneficiary's share of the depreciation and depletion deductions. For a trust, divide the deductions for depreciation and depletion between the fiduciary and the beneficiaries as specified in the trust instrument. If the trust instrument does not specify, divide the deductions in the same way that the trust instrument provides for dividing the income between the fiduciary and the beneficiaries. For an estate, divide the deductions for depreciation and depletion between the estate and the beneficiaries in the same way the estate income is allocated to each. See **Publication 559** and regulations sections 1.642(e)–1, 1.167(h)–1, and 1.611–1(c) for more information about the division of these deductions.

**4(d). Amortization deductions.**—Itemize the beneficiary's share of the amortization deductions. Divide the amortization deductions between the fiduciary and the beneficiaries in the same way that the depreciation and depletion deductions are divided.

**5. Estate tax deduction.**—See **Publication 559** and section 691(c) and related regulations for information on how to figure the estate tax deduction. Figure the deduction on a separate sheet. Attach the sheet to this return. Enter the beneficiary's deduction.

**6. Excess deductions on termination.**—If this is the final return and there are excess deductions on termination or a net operating loss carryover, see **Publication 559** and section 642(h) and related regulations. Figure the deductions on an attached sheet. Enter the beneficiary's share of the excess deductions on line 6. The appropriate line for reporting the beneficiary's share of the net operating loss carryover depends on whether the deduction will be allowable in computing adjusted gross income or only in computing taxable income on the beneficiary's income tax return. Thus, the beneficiary's share of a net operating loss carryover would generally be entered on line 4(d)(2). In this case, write "N.O.L. carryover" to the left of the figure. However, if the last tax year of the estate or trust is the last year in which a net operating loss may be taken, the deduction, to the extent it is not absorbed in that year by the estate or trust, is treated as an excess deduction. Enter on line 6 the beneficiary's share of this portion of the net operating loss, which is treated as an excess deduction, and the beneficiary's share of other excess deductions.

**7. Tax preference items.**—Tax preference items under section 57 include the following:

● Accelerated depreciation on real property that is nonrecovery property or 15-year real property.

● Accelerated depreciation on leased property that is personal property or recovery property other than 15-year real property.

  ● Amortization of certified pollution control facilities.
  ● Depletion.
  ● Amortization of child care facilities.
  ● Intangible drilling costs.

New tax preference rules apply for tax years beginning after December 31, 1982. For beneficiary reporting purposes, fiscal year estates and trusts must report tax preference items under the new rules for beneficiaries' tax years beginning after 1982. For example, a trust with a tax year ending July 31, 1983, reports tax preference items under the new rules to its calendar year 1983 beneficiaries.

The new rules add the following tax preference items:

● Excess mining exploration and development costs.

● Excess circulation and research and experimental expenditures.

● Incentive stock options to the extent the fair market value of the stock exceeds the option price.

The new rules delete the following tax preference item:

● Amortization of child care facilities.

In general, tax preference items are divided between the estate or trust and the beneficiaries in the same way the income is divided. See regulations section 1.58–3 and **Publication 909**, Minimum Tax and Alternative Minimum Tax, for more information about tax preference items. Enter the beneficiary's tax preference items on the applicable lines. Attach a separate sheet if needed.

**8. Income tax withheld.**—If the estate or trust has a fiscal year ending after June 30, 1983, enter on line 8 the income tax withheld on interest, dividend, and patronage dividend income paid after June 30, 1983, and before the end of the fiscal year that is allocated to the beneficiary. (Do not reduce the amount of the interest, dividend, or patronage dividend income reported on lines 1, 2, and 4(a) by the amount of the income tax withheld.) The income tax withheld is allocated between the estate or trust and the beneficiaries on the basis of their respective share of the interest, dividend, and patronage dividend income.

**9. Foreign taxes.**—See **Publication 559**, **Publication 514**, Foreign Tax Credit for U.S. Citizens and Resident Aliens, and section 642(a) and related regulations for information about foreign taxes. List on an attached sheet the beneficiary's share of the applicable foreign taxes paid or accrued and the various foreign source figures needed for the beneficiary's foreign tax credit.

**10. Property eligible for investment credit.**—If a part of the investment (other than for section 48(q) election property, commuter highway vehicles, business energy and qualified rehabilitation expenditures) is apportioned to the beneficiary, enter the recovery property information allocable to the beneficiary on the appropriate lines in item 10. For nonrecovery property attach to each Schedule K–1 a separate schedule which shows each beneficiary's share of nonrecovery property eligible for the credit. This schedule should use the format of the worksheet in the Form 3468 instructions for nonrecovery property. See **Publication 572**, Investment Credit, and **Form 3468**, Computation of Investment Credit, for more information.

**11. Other.**—Itemize on line 11 or on an attached sheet the beneficiary's tax information for which there is no other line on Schedule K–1. This includes the allocable share, if any, of investment income (section 163(d)), section 48(q) election property, the business energy, qualified rehabilitation expenditure, and commuter highway vehicle investment credit, the portion of the investment credit from a cooperative organization specially allocated under section 46(h), the jobs credit, the alcohol fuel credit, the nonconventional source fuel credit, the increased research credit, the information a beneficiary will need to refigure an earlier year investment credit and WIN wages from a 1981–1982 fiscal year estate or trust. See the instructions for Form 1041 for more information about these credits.

# Application for Tentative Refund

Form **1045**
(Rev. November 1982)
Department of the Treasury
Internal Revenue Service

(See instruction C for when to file)
Do Not Attach to Your Income Tax Return—File Separately to Expedite Processing
▶ For use by taxpayers other than corporations.

OMB No. 1545-0098
Expires 9-30-85

**Please type or print**

| Name | Employer identification number |
|---|---|
| Number and street | Your social security number |
| City or town, State, and ZIP code | Spouse's social security number |

**1** This application is filed to carryback: ▶
(If no entry in 1(a) skip lines 6 to 12)

| (a) Net operating loss (from page 2, line 10) | (b) Unused invest-ment credit | (c) Unused WIN credit | (d) Unused jobs credit | (e) Unused research credit |
|---|---|---|---|---|
| $ | $ | $ | $ | $ |

**2** Return for year of carryback or overpayment under section 1341(b)(1) . . ▶

| (a) Tax year ended | (b) Date filed | (c) Service center where filed |
|---|---|---|
| | | |

**3** (a) Preceding tax year(s) affected by carryback

| | (b) Did spouse file a separate return? | (c) Service center where return(s) were filed (City and State) |
|---|---|---|
| 3rd | ☐ Yes ☐ No | |
| 2nd | ☐ Yes ☐ No | |
| 1st | ☐ Yes ☐ No | |

**4** If you changed your accounting period, give date permission to change was granted ▶

**5** Have you filed a petition in Tax Court for the year or years to which the carryback is to be applied? . . . . ☐ Yes ☐ No

| Computation of Decrease in Tax | 3rd preceding tax year ended ▶ | | 2nd preceding tax year ended ▶ | | 1st preceding tax year ended ▶ | |
|---|---|---|---|---|---|---|
| | (a) Before carryback | (b) After carryback | (c) Before carryback | (d) After carryback | (e) Before carryback | (f) After carryback |
| **6** Adjusted gross income from tax return . . | | | | | | |
| **7** Net operating loss deduction after carryback (See Instructions—Attach computation) . . . . . . . . | | | | | | |
| **8** Subtract line 7 from line 6 . . . . . | | | | | | |
| **9** Deductions (see instructions) . . . . | | | | | | |
| **10** Subtract line 9 from line 8 . . . . . | | | | | | |
| **11** Exemptions . . . . . . . . . | | | | | | |
| **12** Taxable income (subtract line 11 from 10) . | | | | | | |
| **13** Income tax . . . . . . . . . | | | | | | |
| **14** Foreign tax credit . . . . . . . | | | | | | |
| **15** Investment credit . . . . . . . | | | | | | |
| **16** WIN credit . . . . . . . . . | | | | | | |
| **17** Jobs credit . . . . . . . . . | | | | | | |
| **18** Research credit . . . . . . . . | | | | | | |
| **19** Other credits (identify) . . . . . . | | | | | | |
| **20** Total credits (add lines 14 through 19) . . | | | | | | |
| **21** Subtract line 20 from line 13 . . . . | | | | | | |
| **22** Recapture of investment credit . . . . | | | | | | |
| **23** Minimum tax . . . . . . . . | | | | | | |
| **24** Alternative minimum tax . . . . . . | | | | | | |
| **25** Self-employment tax . . . . . . | | | | | | |
| **26** Other taxes . . . . . . . . . | | | | | | |
| **27** Total tax liability (add lines 21 through 26) . | | | | | | |
| **28** Enter amount from line 27, cols. (b), (d) and (f) . . . . . . . . . | | | | | | |
| **29** Decrease in tax (subtract line 28 from 27) . | | | | | | |

**30** Overpayment of tax due to a claim of right adjustment under section 1341(b)(1)—attach computation . . .

Under penalties of perjury, I declare that I have examined this application (including any accompanying schedules and statements), and to the best of my knowledge and belief, it is true, correct, and complete.

_____                    _____
(Your signature and date)     (If application is filed jointly, both you and your spouse must sign)     (Spouse's signature and date)

For Paperwork Reduction Act Notice, see page 3.                                  Form **1045** (Rev. 11-82)

## Schedule A (Form 1045)—Computation of Net Operating Loss

1 Adjusted gross income from 1982 Form 1040, line 33 (estates and trusts—see instructions) . . . | **1** |

2 Deductions (applies to individuals only):

  a Enter amount from 1982 Form 1040, line 34a or 34b . . . . . | **2a** |

  b On your 1982 Form 1040, if you checked Filing Status box . { 2 or 5, enter $3,400 / 1 or 4, enter $2,300 / 3, enter $1,700 . . } | **2b** |

  c Multiply $1,000 by the total number of exemptions on 1982 Form 1040, line 6e . | **2c** |

  d Add lines 2a through 2c (estates and trusts, enter zero) . . . . . . . . . . . | **2d** | ( )

3 Combine lines 1 and 2d . . . . . . . . . . . | **3** |

**Note:** *If result is zero or more, do not complete rest of schedule. You do not have a net operating loss.*

Adjustments:

4 Exemptions from line 2c above, or from your tax return . . . . . | **4** |

5 Enter your 60% capital gain deduction from your 1982 Schedule D, Form 4798, or that was excluded from Form 1040, line 14 . . . . . . . | **5** |

6 a Enter the excess of your nonbusiness capital losses over your nonbusiness capital gains . . | **6a** |

  b Enter the excess of your business capital losses over your business capital gains plus nonbusiness capital gains not used in figuring line 8(c) . . . . . . . . . . | **6b** |

  c Enter total of lines 6(a) and 6(b) but not more than your capital loss limitation . . . . | **6c** |

7 Net operating loss deduction from other years . . . . . . . . | **7** |

8 a Nonbusiness deductions . . . . . . . | **8a** |

  b Nonbusiness income plus the excess of your nonbusiness capital gains over your nonbusiness capital losses . . . . . . . . | **8b** |

  c Subtract line 8b from line 8a. If 8b is more than 8a, enter zero . . . | **8c** |

9 Add lines 4, 5, 6c, 7, and 8c . . . . . . . . . . . . . | **9** |

10 Combine lines 3 and 9. This is your net operating loss. Enter here and on page 1, line 1a . . . | **10** |

  **Caution:** *If the amount to be entered on line 10 is zero or more, you do not have a net operating loss.*

### Instructions for Schedule A (Form 1045)—Computation of Net Operating Loss

Use this schedule to figure your net operating loss that is available for carryback or carryover.

**Line 1.**—Estates and trusts, enter your taxable income from your appropriate tax return.

**Line 6.**—If your business capital gains plus your nonbusiness capital gains not used in figuring line 8(c) are more than your business capital losses, enter zero on line 6(b). If you have a net capital loss for the year, do not include in line 6(c), your net capital loss not allowed this year because of the capital loss limitation. For more information, see regulations section 1.172-3 and Publication 536, Net Operating Losses and the At-Risk Limits.

**Line 8(a) and 8(b).**—Nonbusiness income and deductions are those not connected with a trade or business.

Your **zero bracket amount** from line 2(b), above, is allowed as a nonbusiness deduction if you do not itemize deductions. Itemized deductions are usually nonbusiness also except for casualty loss deductions and any employee business expenses such as union dues, uniforms, tools, and educational expenses.

**Salaries and wages** you received are trade or business income.

**Gain or loss on sale** or other disposition of real or depreciable property used in your trade or business is business income or loss.

**Loss from the sale of accounts receivable,** if such accounts arose under the accrual method of accounting in your business, is a business deduction.

**Casualty losses and theft losses** are considered attributable to a trade or business. This is true even if they involve nonbusiness property.

**Your proportionate share** of a partnership's income or loss is business income or loss.

**Losses on stock** in small business corporations that qualify as ordinary losses are business losses.

**Your pro rata share** of a net operating loss from an electing small business corporation (Subchapter S) is a business loss. Any share of the income or gain, other than salaries, from a subchapter S corporation is nonbusiness income or gain.

**Loss resulting from the sale** or exchange of small business investment company stock that qualifies as an ordinary loss, is a loss attributable to your trade or business.

**The deduction allowed for payments** made by a self-employed person to a retirement plan is a nonbusiness deduction.

Page 2

## General Instructions For Form 1045

*(Section references are to the Internal
Revenue Code unless otherwise specified)*

**Paperwork Reduction Act Notice.**—The Paperwork Reduction Act of 1980 says we must tell you why we are collecting this information, how we will use it, and whether you have to give it to us. We ask for the information to carry out the Internal Revenue laws of the United States. We need it to ensure that you are complying with these laws and to allow us to figure and collect the right amount of tax. You are required to give us this information.

**A. Purpose.**—An individual, estate, or trust must use this form to apply for:

• A quick refund of taxes from carryback of a net operating loss, unused investment credit, unused WIN credit, unused jobs credit, or unused research credit.

• A quick refund of taxes from an overpayment of tax due to a claim of right adjustment under section 1341(b)(1).

**Note.** You may elect to carryover a net operating loss instead of first carrying it back, by attaching a statement to that effect on a return filed on time (including any extensions) for the year of the loss. Once you make such an election, it is irrevocable for that tax year. The carryover is limited to 15 years, whether or not you first use a carryback.

**B. Where to File.**—File this form with the Internal Revenue Service Center where you are required to file your income tax return.

*Do not attach Form 1045 to your income tax return.*

**C. When to File.**—File within 1 year after the end of the year in which the net operating loss, unused credit, or claim of right adjustment arose, but only after you have filed the return for that year.

If an unused credit arises, you may carry it back 3 more years when:

• A net operating loss carryback eliminates or reduces an investment credit, WIN credit, jobs credit, or research credit in an earlier year.

• An investment credit carryback reduces a WIN credit, jobs credit, or research credit in an earlier year.

• A WIN credit carryback reduces a jobs credit, or research credit in an earlier year.

• A jobs credit carryback reduces a research credit in an earlier year.

Since the unused credit created affects the taxes of a year or years before the 3 years preceding the loss year or unused credit year, you must use a second Form 1045 for the earlier year(s). You must also file the second application within 1 year after the year of the net operating loss or unused credit. To expedite processing, file the two Forms 1045 together.

**D. Allowance of Adjustment.**—The IRS will act on this application within 90 days from the later of:

• The date you file the application; or

• The last day of the month in which the due date falls (including any extension of time granted) for filing the return for the tax year of the net operating loss or unused credit. (For an overpayment of tax under section 1341(b)(1), 90 days from the date of the overpayment.)

*Additional Information.*—We may need to contact you (or your authorized representative if you have one) for more information so we can act on your application. If you want to designate a representative for us to contact (for example your accountant or tax return preparer), please attach a copy of your authorization to Form 1045. You may use for this purpose Form 2848, Power of Attorney and Declaration of Representative, or Form 2848–D, Tax Information Authorization and Declaration of Representative.

**E. Disallowance of Application.**—Any application may be disallowed if it has material omissions or math errors that the IRS believes it cannot correct within the 90-day period. This application for a tentative carryback adjustment is not a claim for credit or refund. If it is disallowed in whole or in part, no suit may be brought in any court for the recovery of that tax. But you may file a regular claim for credit or refund before the limitation period expires, as explained in instruction G.

**F. Excess Allowances.**—Any amount applied, credited, or refunded based on this application that the IRS later determines to be excessive may be billed as if it were due to a math or clerical error on the return.

**G. Form 1040X (or other Amended Return).**—If you are an individual, you can get a refund by filing Form 1040X instead of Form 1045. An estate, trust, or fiduciary may file an amended return. Generally, you must file Form 1040X (or amended return) within 3 years after the due date of the return for the tax year of the net operating loss or unused credit.

If you use Form 1040X or an amended return, attach a computation of your net operating loss. You may use Schedule A (Form 1045). Complete a separate Form 1040X or amended return for each year for which you request an adjustment.

## Line-By-Line Instructions For Form 1045

*Enter in columns (a), (c) and (e) your tax for the applicable carryback year as shown on your original or amended return. If the return was examined, enter the amounts determined as a result of the examination.*

**Line 1(a)—Net operating loss carryback.**—Figure your net operating loss carryback on Schedule A (Form 1045).

Generally, you must first carry a net operating loss back to the 3rd tax year before the loss. Carry to the 2nd preceding year any amount of the loss not used to offset taxable income (adjusted, as explained below) for the 3rd preceding year. Carry to the 1st preceding year any amount of the loss not used to offset such income for the 3rd and 2nd preceding years. When the loss is not all used to offset taxable income (adjusted) in the 3 preceding years, you may carry the balance over to the 15 succeeding years (after the net operating loss year) in the order they occur. You cannot carry to any later tax years the balance of the loss (if any) not applied in the 3 carryback and 15 carryover years.

For election in regard to the part of a net operating loss from a foreign expropriation loss, product liability loss, and other exceptions to the general rule, see section 172(b) and the regulations.

If you filed a joint return for some, but not all, of the years involved in the carryback, see section 1.172–7 of the regulations before applying the carryback.

**Lines 1(b), (c), (d), and (e)—Carryback of unused investment credit, unused WIN credit, unused jobs credit, or unused research credit.**—If you claim a tentative adjustment based on the carryback of any of these credits, attach:

• A detailed computation showing how you figured the credit carryback, and

• A recomputation of the credit after you apply the carryback. Make the recomputation on the appropriate credit form, or on an attachment that follows the format of the form, for the tax year of the tentative allowance.

**Line 7—Computation of net operating loss when it is not fully absorbed in preceding tax years.**—The amount of a net operating loss you may carry to the next year, after applying it to an earlier year or years, is the excess, if any, of the net operating loss carryback over the taxable income of those earlier years, figured with the following modifications:

(1) Your deduction for capital losses must not be more than the capital gains included in gross income.

(2) You are not permitted any deduction for the excess of a net long-term capital gain over a net short-term capital loss.

(3) Determine your taxable income for the earlier tax year(s) without taking into account the net operating loss carryback from the loss year or any later tax year. Net operating losses, otherwise allowable as carrybacks or carryovers, occurring in tax years before the loss year, are taken into account in figuring the taxable income for the earlier tax year.

(4) You may not claim any personal exemptions.

(5) Any deductions claimed, except charitable contributions, that are based on or limited to a percentage of adjusted gross income (such as medical expenses) must be refigured on the basis of the adjusted gross income after you apply adjustments

(1), (2), and (3) above. Determine the deduction for charitable contributions using the same adjustments except that you do not take into account any net operating losses you carry back.

(6) Your zero bracket amount is allowed as a deduction. This amount is $3,400 if married filing joint return or qualifying widow(er) with dependent child; $2,300 if single or head of household; or $1,700 if married filing separately.

The taxable income as modified is to be considered not less than zero.

**Example.**—*You, as a single individual had a net operating loss for the calendar year 1982 of $8,000 that you have carried back to 1979. Your taxable income for 1979 was $6,260, consisting of your salary of $15,000 less the following: $3,000 deduction for capital losses, excess itemized deductions of $4,740, and personal exemptions of $1,000. Your excess itemized deductions consisted of charitable contributions of $6,000 ($8,000 actually given but deduction limited to 50% of $12,000 adjusted gross income); medical expenses of $140 ($500 actually paid but deductions limited to expenses of more than 3% of $12,000 adjusted gross income); other itemized deductions of $900; less your zero bracket amount of $2,300.*

| | |
|---|---:|
| Net operating loss for 1982 . . . . . . . . . | $8,000 |
| Less taxable income for 1979 figured with required modifications: | |
| Salary . . . . . . . . . . . . $15,000 | |
| Less allowable deduction for capital losses . –0– | |
| Adjusted gross income . . . . . . $15,000 | |
| Less excess itemized deductions: | |
|   Charitable contributions (adjusted to limit deduction to 50% of $15,000 adjusted gross income) . . . $7,500 | |
|   Medical expenses (adjusted to limit deduction to amount that is more than 3% of $15,000 adjusted gross income) . . . . . 50 | |
|   Other itemized deductions . . . . . 900 | |
|     8,450 | |
|   Zero bracket amount . (2,300) | |
| Excess deductions . . . . . . . $6,150 | |
| Less personal exemptions allowed . 0 | |
| Less zero bracket amount . . . 2,300 | |
| Total deductions . . . . . . . | $8,450 |
| Taxable income for 1979 as modified . . . . . | $6,550 |
| Amount of 1982 net operating loss (unused) to be carried to 1980 . . . . . . . . . . . . | $1,450 |

### Line 9—Deductions.

*Individuals.*—Enter the amount shown on your Form 1040, line 33 (line 32b in 1981). If you used Form 1040A, enter zero. If you made an entry on Schedule TC (Form 1040), Part II, line 4 (worksheet in 1981), enter that amount on this line. Then add lines 8 and 9, instead of subtracting, and enter the result on line 10.

### Line 10.—If you are an individual and you use the Tax Tables in 1979 or 1980, make no entry on lines 11 and 12. Enter on line 13 the tax on the income reported on line 10.

### Line 13—Income tax.—For columns (b), (d), and (f), refigure your tax after taking the carryback into account. Attach a detailed computation. The tax form and instructions for the applicable year will help you make this computation. Include on this line any tax from Form 4970, Form 4972, Form 5544, Form 5405, and any section 72(m)(5) penalty tax.

If you qualified for income averaging for a particular year, you may later become disqualified or have a reduced benefit because of a net operating loss carryback. A net operating loss carryback may also make you eligible for income averaging for a year when you previously did not qualify.

**Computation of tax when the net operating loss is fully absorbed in the earliest preceding tax year.**—In refiguring your tax for the year to which the net operating loss is carried and fully absorbed, determine the deduction for charitable contributions without regard to any net operating loss carryback. Any other deductions claimed, based on or limited to a percentage of your adjusted gross income (such as medical expenses) must be refigured on the basis of your adjusted gross income, determined after you apply the net operating loss carryback. Also, any credits based on or limited by the tax must be refigured on the tax as determined after you apply the net operating loss carryback.

**Example.**—*You, as a single individual, have a net operating loss for 1982 of $8,000. You can carryback the loss and apply it against your income for 1979. Since there are no other carrybacks or carryovers to 1979, the $8,000 will be your net operating loss deduction. How to figure your tax for 1979, both before and after the carryback of the 1982 net operating loss, is shown below.*

| 1979 | Before Carryback | After Carryback |
|---|---:|---:|
| Adjusted Gross Income (AGI) as last determined . . . . | $17,000 | $17,000 |
| Less: Net operating loss deduction (fully absorbed) . . . | — | 8,000 |
| Adjusted Gross Income (AGI) as adjusted by carryback . . . | $17,000 | $ 9,000 |
| Less excess itemized deductions: | | |
| Contributions to United Way. (Although this is more than 50% of your AGI after the carryback, no adjustment is made because of the carryback) . . . . . . . $5,000 | | $5,000 |
| Medical expenses paid to physicians (actual payments of $970 limited to amounts in excess of 3% of your AGI, both before and after the carryback) . . . . . 460 | | 700 |
| Misc. itemized deductions . 900 | | 900 |
| Total itemized deductions . $6,360 | | $6,600 |
| Zero bracket amount . . . 2,300 | | 2,300 |
| Excess itemized deductions . . | $ 4,060 | $ 4,300 |
| Tax table income . . . . . | $12,940 | $ 4,700 |
| Tax on above . . . . . . | $ 1,825 | $ 198 |
| Less tax after carryback . . . | 198 | |
| Decrease in tax for 1979 (amount to be refunded) . . . . . | $ 1,627 | |

### Line 19—Other credits.—See your tax return for the carryback year for any additional credits (such as credit for the elderly, credit for contributions to candidates for public office, residential energy credits, etc.) that will apply in that year. If there is an entry on this line, identify the credit(s) claimed.

### Line 23—Minimum tax.—Refigure your minimum tax for an earlier year in which you had items of tax preference, if you carried a net operating loss or unused credit back to that year. Attach a recomputation of the minimum tax for the earlier year using Form 4625 or Form 4626, if an estate or trust.

### Line 24—Alternative minimum tax.—A carryback of an unused credit may increase your alternative minimum tax or first cause you to be liable for it. A carryback of a net operating loss may reduce your alternative minimum tax. Use Form 6251 to figure this tax, and attach a copy if there is any change to your alternative minimum tax liability.

### Line 25—Self-employment tax.—Do not adjust the self-employment tax because of any net operating loss carryback.

### Line 26—Other taxes.—See your tax return for the carryback year for any add on taxes not previously listed, such as tax from recomputing prior year WIN credit, that will apply in that year. If there is an entry on this line, identify the tax(es) that apply.

### Line 30—Overpayment of tax under section 1341(b)(1).—If you apply for a tentative refund based on an overpayment of tax under section 1341(b)(1), enter it on this line. Also attach a computation that shows the information required in regulation section 5.6411–1(d).

☆ U.S. GOVERNMENT PRINTING OFFICE: 1983–381–108:50

23-188-5979

## B-5 FORM 1120 U.S. CORPORATION INCOME TAX RETURN

### U.S. Corporation Income Tax Return

Form **1120**
Department of the Treasury
Internal Revenue Service

For calendar year 1982 or other tax year beginning .................., 1982, ending .................., 19.........
▶ For Paperwork Reduction Act Notice, see page 1 of the instructions

OMB No. 1545-0123

**1982**

| Check if a— | Use IRS label. Other-wise please print or type. | Name | D. Employer Identification number |
|---|---|---|---|
| A. Consolidated return ☐ | | | |
| B. Personal Holding Co. ☐ | | Number and street | E. Date incorporated |
| C. Business Code No. (See page 9 of Instructions) | | City or town, State, and ZIP code | F. Total assets (see Specific Instructions) $ |

**Gross Income**

| | | |
|---|---|---|
| 1 (a) Gross receipts or sales $ .............. (b) Less returns and allowances $ .............. Balance ▶ | 1(c) | |
| 2 Cost of goods sold (Schedule A) and/or operations (attach schedule) | 2 | |
| 3 Gross profit (subtract line 2 from line 1(c)) | 3 | |
| 4 Dividends (Schedule C) | 4 | |
| 5 Interest | 5 | |
| 6 Gross rents | 6 | |
| 7 Gross royalties | 7 | |
| 8 Capital gain net income (attach separate Schedule D) | 8 | |
| 9 Net gain or (loss) from Form 4797, line 11(a), Part II (attach Form 4797) | 9 | |
| 10 Other income (see instructions—attach schedule) | 10 | |
| 11      TOTAL income—Add lines 3 through 10 | 11 | |

**Deductions**

| | | |
|---|---|---|
| 12 Compensation of officers (Schedule E) | 12 | |
| 13 (a) Salaries and wages ............... 13(b) Less jobs credit ............... Balance ▶ | 13(c) | |
| 14 Repairs (see instructions) | 14 | |
| 15 Bad debts (Schedule F if reserve method is used) | 15 | |
| 16 Rents | 16 | |
| 17 Taxes | 17 | |
| 18 Interest | 18 | |
| 19 Contributions (not over 10% of line 30 adjusted per instructions) | 19 | |
| 20 Depreciation (attach Form 4562) . . . . 20 | | |
| 21 Less depreciation claimed in Schedule A and elsewhere on return . 21(a) (     ) | 21(b) | |
| 22 Depletion | 22 | |
| 23 Advertising | 23 | |
| 24 Pension, profit-sharing, etc. plans (see instructions) | 24 | |
| 25 Employee benefit programs (see instructions) | 25 | |
| 26 Other deductions (attach schedule) | 26 | |
| 27      TOTAL deductions—Add lines 12 through 26 | 27 | |
| 28 Taxable income before net operating loss deduction and special deductions (subtract line 27 from line 11) . | 28 | |
| 29 Less: (a) Net operating loss deduction (see instructions—attach schedule) . 29(a) | | |
|      (b) Special deductions (Schedule C) . . . . . 29(b) | 29 | |
| 30 Taxable income (subtract line 29 from line 28) | 30 | |

**Tax**

| | | |
|---|---|---|
| 31      TOTAL TAX (Schedule J) | 31 | |
| 32 Credits: (a) Overpayment from 1981 allowed as a credit . . | | |
|      (b) 1982 estimated tax payments | | |
|      (c) Less refund of 1982 estimated tax applied for on Form 4466 . (     ) | | |
|      (d) Tax deposited: Form 7004 ............... Form 7005 (attach) ............... Total ▶ | | |
|      (e) Credit from regulated investment companies (attach Form 2439) . . . . . | | |
|      (f) Federal tax on special fuels and oils (attach Form 4136) . . . . . | 32 | |
| 33 TAX DUE (subtract line 32 from line 31—If line 32 is greater than line 31, skip line 33 and go to line 34). See instruction C3 for depositary method of payment . . . . . . . . . (Check ▶ ☐ if Form 2220 is attached. See instruction D.) ▶ $ ............... | 33 | |
| 34 OVERPAYMENT (subtract line 31 from line 32) . . . . . . . . . | 34 | |
| 35 Enter amount of line 34 you want: **Credited to 1983 estimated tax** ............... Refunded ▶ | 35 | |

**Please Sign Here**

Under penalties of perjury, I declare that I have examined this return, including accompanying schedules and statements, and to the best of my knowledge and belief, it is true, correct, and complete. Declaration of preparer (other than taxpayer) is based on all information of which preparer has any knowledge.

| ▶ Signature of officer | Date | ▶ Title |
|---|---|---|

**Paid Preparer's Use Only**

| Preparer's signature ▶ | Date | Check if self-employed ▶ ☐ | Preparer's social security no. |
|---|---|---|---|
| Firm's name (or yours, if self-employed) and address ▶ | | E.I. No. ▶ | |
| | | ZIP code ▶ | |

363-121-1

**Form 1120 (1982)** | **Schedule A** Cost of Goods Sold (See instructions for Schedule A) | Page **2**

1 Inventory at beginning of year . . . . . . . . . . . . . . . . . . . . . . . . . . . . . . . .
2 Merchandise bought for manufacture or sale . . . . . . . . . . . . . . . . . . . . . . . . .
3 Salaries and wages . . . . . . . . . . . . . . . . . . . . . . . . . . . . . . . . . . . . .
4 Other costs (attach schedule) . . . . . . . . . . . . . . . . . . . . . . . . . . . . . . .
5 Total—Add lines 1 through 4 . . . . . . . . . . . . . . . . . . . . . . . . . . . . . . . .
6 Inventory at end of year . . . . . . . . . . . . . . . . . . . . . . . . . . . . . . . . . .
7 Cost of goods sold—Subtract line 6 from line 5. Enter here and on line 2, page 1 . . . . . . . .
8 (a) Check all methods used for valuing closing inventory:

  (i) ☐ Cost
  (ii) ☐ Lower of cost or market as described in Regulations section 1.471–4 (see instructions)
  (iii) ☐ Writedown of "subnormal" goods as described in Regulations section 1.471–2(c) (see instructions)
  (iv) ☐ Other (Specify method used and attach explanation) ▶ -----------------------------------------

  (b) Check if the LIFO inventory method was adopted this tax year for any goods (If checked, attach Form 970.) . . . . . ☐
  (c) If the LIFO inventory method was used for this tax year, enter percentage (or amounts) of closing inventory computed under LIFO. . . . . . . . . . . . . . . . . . . . . . . . . . . .
  (d) If you are engaged in manufacturing, did you value your inventory using the full absorption method (Regulations section 1.471–11)? . . . . . . . . . . . . . . . . . . . . . . . . . . . . ☐ Yes ☐ No
  (e) Was there any substantial change in determining quantities, cost, or valuations between opening and closing inventory? . . . ☐ Yes ☐ No
  If "Yes," attach explanation.

**Schedule C** Dividends and Special Deductions (See instructions for Schedule C)

| | (A) Dividends received | (B) % | (C) Special deductions: multiply (A) × (B) |
|---|---|---|---|
| 1 Domestic corporations subject to 85% deduction . . . . . . . . . . . | | 85 | |
| 2 Certain preferred stock of public utilities . . . . . . . . . . | | 59.13 | |
| 3 Foreign corporations subject to 85% deduction . . . . . . . . . . | | 85 | |
| 4 Wholly-owned foreign subsidiaries subject to 100% deduction (section 245(b)) . | | 100 | |
| 5 Total—Add lines 1 through 4. See instructions for limitation . . . . . . . . | | | |
| 6 Affiliated groups subject to the 100% deduction (section 243(a)(3)) . . . . | | 100 | |
| 7 Other dividends from foreign corporations not included in lines 3 and 4 . . . | | | |
| 8 Income from controlled foreign corporations under subpart F (attach Forms 5471) . | | | |
| 9 Foreign dividend gross-up (section 78) . . . . . . . . . . . . . . | | | |
| 10 DISC or former DISC dividends not included in line 1 (section 246(d)) . . . | | | |
| 11 Other dividends . . . . . . . . . . . . . . . . . . . . | | | |
| 12 Deduction for dividends paid on certain preferred stock of public utilities (see instructions) . . . . . . . . . . . . . . . . . . . . . . . . | | | |
| 13 Total dividends—Add lines 1 through 11. Enter here and on line 4, page 1 ▶ | | | |
| 14 Total deductions—Add lines 5, 6 and 12. Enter here and on line 29(b), page 1 ─────────▶ | | | |

**Schedule E** Compensation of Officers (See instruction for line 12) Complete Schedule E only if your total receipts (line 1(a), plus lines 4 through 10, of page 1, Form 1120) are $150,000 or more.

| 1. Name of officer | 2. Social security number | 3. Time devoted to business | Percent of corporation stock owned | | 6. Amount of compensation | 7. Expense account allowances |
|---|---|---|---|---|---|---|
| | | | 4. Common | 5. Preferred | | |
| | | | | | | |
| | | | | | | |
| | | | | | | |
| | | | | | | |
| | | | | | | |
| | | | | | | |
| Total compensation of officers—Enter here and on line 12, page 1 . . . . . . . . | | | | | | |

**Schedule F** Bad Debts—Reserve Method (See instruction for line 15)

| 1. Year | 2. Trade notes and accounts receivable outstanding at end of year | 3. Sales on account | Amount added to reserve | | 6. Amount charged against reserve | 7. Reserve for bad debts at end of year |
|---|---|---|---|---|---|---|
| | | | 4. Current year's provision | 5. Recoveries | | |
| 1977 | | | | | | |
| 1978 | | | | | | |
| 1979 | | | | | | |
| 1980 | | | | | | |
| 1981 | | | | | | |
| 1982 | | | | | | |

363–121–1

Form 1120 (1982)                                                                Page **3**

**Schedule J** **Tax Computation** (See instructions for Schedule J on page 7)

**Note:** *Fiscal year corporations, see instructions on page 10. If you are not a member of a controlled group of corporations (sections 1561 and 1563), omit lines 1 and 2, and enter on line 3, the amount from line 44, Part III, of the fiscal year worksheet provided on page 11 of the instructions.*

*Calendar year corporations, see instructions for Schedule J on page 7. If you are not a member of a controlled group of corporations (sections 1561 and 1563), omit lines 1 and 2, and start with line 3.*

1 Check if you are a member of a controlled group (see sections 1561 and 1563) . . . . . . ▶ ☐

2 If line 1 is checked, see instructions and enter your portion of the $25,000 amount in each taxable income bracket:
   (i) $................ (ii) $.............. (iii) $.............. (iv) $..............

3 Income tax (see instructions to figure the tax; enter this tax or alternative tax from Schedule D, whichever is less). Check if from Schedule D ▶ ☐ . . . . . . . . .

4 (a) Foreign tax credit (attach Form 1118) . . . . . . . . .

   (b) Investment credit (attach Form 3468) . . . . . . . .

   (c) Jobs credit (attach Form 5884) . . . . . . . . . .

   (d) Employee stock ownership credit (applies only to fiscal year 1982–83 corporations—see instructions) . . . . . . . . . .

   (e) Research credit (attach Form 6765) . . . . . . . . .

   (f) Possessions tax credit (attach Form 5735) . . . . . . .

   (g) Alcohol fuel credit (attach Form 6478) . . . . . . . .

   (h) Credit for fuel produced from a nonconventional source (see instructions) . . .

5 Total—Add lines 4(a) through 4(h) . . . . . . . . . .

6 Subtract line 5 from line 3 . . . . . . . . . .

7 Personal holding company tax (attach Schedule PH (Form 1120)) . . . . . . . .

8 Tax from recomputing prior-year investment credit (attach Form 4255) . . . . . .

9 Minimum tax on tax preference items (see instructions—attach Form 4626) . . . . .

10 Total tax—Add lines 6 through 9. Enter here and on line 31, page 1 . . . . . . . .

**Additional Information** (See page 8 of instructions)      | Yes | No |

G Did you claim a deduction for expenses connected with:

(1) Entertainment facility (boat, resort, ranch, etc.)?

(2) Living accommodations (except employees on business)? . .

(3) Employees attending conventions or meetings outside the North American area? (See section 274(h)) . . . . .

(4) Employees' families at conventions or meetings? . . . .

If "Yes," were any of these conventions or meetings outside the North American area? (See section 274(h)) . . . . .

(5) Employee or family vacations not reported on Form W–2? . .

H (1) Did you at the end of the tax year own, directly or indirectly, 50% or more of the voting stock of a domestic corporation? (For rules of attribution, see section 267(c).) . . . . .

If "Yes," attach a schedule showing: (a) name, address, and identifying number; (b) percentage owned; (c) taxable income or (loss) (e.g., if a Form 1120: from Form 1120, line 28, page 1) of such corporation for the tax year ending with or within your tax year; (d) highest amount owed by you to such corporation during the year; and (e) highest amount owed to you by such corporation during the year.

(2) Did any individual, partnership, corporation, estate or trust at the end of the tax year own, directly or indirectly, 50% or more of your voting stock? (For rules of attribution, see section 267(c).) If "Yes," complete (a) through (e) . . . . . .

(a) Attach a schedule showing name, address, and identifying number.

(b) Enter percentage owned ▶.......................

(c) Was the owner of such voting stock a person other than a U.S. person? (See instructions) . . . . . . . .

If "Yes," enter owner's country ▶.......................

(d) Enter highest amount owed by you to such owner during the year ▶.......................

(e) Enter highest amount owed to you by such owner during the year ▶.......................

(Note: For purposes of H(1) and H(2), "highest amount owed" includes loans and accounts receivable/payable.)

I Refer to page 9 of instructions and state the principal:
Business activity ...........................
Product or service ...........................

J Were you a U.S. shareholder of any controlled foreign corporation? (See sections 951 and 957.) If "Yes," attach Form 5471 for each such corporation

K At any time during the tax year, did you have an interest in or a signature or other authority over a bank account, securities account, or other financial account in a foreign country (see instructions)? . . . . . . . . . . . .

L Were you the grantor of, or transferor to, a foreign trust which existed during the current tax year, whether or not you have any beneficial interest in it? . . . . . . . . . .

If "Yes," you may have to file Forms 3520, 3520–A or 926.

M During this tax year, did you pay dividends (other than stock dividends and distributions in exchange for stock) in excess of your current and accumulated earnings and profits? (See sections 301 and 316) . . . . . . . . . .

If "Yes," file Form 5452. If this is a consolidated return, answer here for parent corporation and on Form 851, Affiliations Schedule, for each subsidiary.

N During this tax year was any part of your tax accounting records maintained on a computerized system? . . . . . . .

363–121–1

Form 1120 (1982)                                                                 Page 4

**Schedule L  Balance Sheets**

| ASSETS | Beginning of tax year | | End of tax year | |
|---|---|---|---|---|
| | (A) | (B) | (C) | (D) |
| 1 Cash . . . . . . . | | | | |
| 2 Trade notes and accounts receivable . . . . | | | | |
| (a) Less allowance for bad debts . . . . . | | | | |
| 3 Inventories . . . . . . . . . . . | | | | |
| 4 Federal and State government obligations . . . | | | | |
| 5 Other current assets (attach schedule) . . . . | | | | |
| 6 Loans to stockholders . . . . . . . . | | | | |
| 7 Mortgage and real estate loans . . . . . | | | | |
| 8 Other investments (attach schedule) . . . . | | | | |
| 9 Buildings and other depreciable assets . . . . | | | | |
| (a) Less accumulated depreciation . . . . . | | | | |
| 10 Depletable assets . . . . . . . . . | | | | |
| (a) Less accumulated depletion . . . . . | | | | |
| 11 Land (net of any amortization) . . . . . | | | | |
| 12 Intangible assets (amortizable only) . . . . | | | | |
| (a) Less accumulated amortization . . . . | | | | |
| 13 Other assets (attach schedule) . . . . . | | | | |
| 14 Total assets . . . . . . . . . . | | | | |
| **LIABILITIES AND STOCKHOLDERS' EQUITY** | | | | |
| 15 Accounts payable . . . . . . . . . | | | | |
| 16 Mtges, notes, bonds payable in less than 1 year . . | | | | |
| 17 Other current liabilities (attach schedule) . . . | | | | |
| 18 Loans from stockholders . . . . . . . | | | | |
| 19 Mtges, notes, bonds payable in 1 year or more . . | | | | |
| 20 Other liabilities (attach schedule) . . . . | | | | |
| 21 Capital stock: (a) Preferred stock . . . . | | | | |
| (b) Common stock . . . . . | | | | |
| 22 Paid-in or capital surplus . . . . . . | | | | |
| 23 Retained earnings—Appropriated (attach sch.) . | | | | |
| 24 Retained earnings—Unappropriated . . . . | | | | |
| 25 Less cost of treasury stock . . . . . . | ( ) | | ( ) | |
| 26 Total liabilities and stockholders' equity . . . . | | | | |

**Schedule M-1  Reconciliation of Income Per Books With Income Per Return** Do not complete this schedule if your total assets (line 14, column (D), above) are less than $25,000.

| | | | | |
|---|---|---|---|---|
| 1 Net income per books . . . . . . . . | 46,850 | | 7 Income recorded on books this year not included in this return (itemize) | |
| 2 Federal income tax . . . . . . . . | 17,150 | | (a) Tax-exempt interest $ 1000 | |
| 3 Excess of capital losses over capital gains . . . | 2,500 | | | |
| 4 Income subject to tax not recorded on books this year (itemize) Prepaid Rent | 11,000 | | | 1000 |
| | | | 8 Deductions in this tax return not charged against book income this year (itemize) | |
| 5 Expenses recorded on books this year not deducted in this return (itemize) | | | (a) Depreciation . . . $ 2000 | |
| (a) Depreciation . . . . . $ | | | (b) Contributions carryover . $ | |
| (b) Contributions carryover . . $ | | | | 2000 |
| Non-ded int exp | 1,500 | | 9 Total of lines 7 and 8 . . . . | 3000 |
| 6 Total of lines 1 through 5 . . . . | 79,000 | | 10 Income (line 28, page 1)—line 6 less 9 . . | 76,000 |

**Schedule M-2  Analysis of Unappropriated Retained Earnings Per Books (line 24 above)** Do not complete this schedule if your total assets (line 14, column (D), above) are less than $25,000.

| | | | | |
|---|---|---|---|---|
| 1 Balance at beginning of year . . . . . . | | | 5 Distributions: (a) Cash . . . . . | |
| 2 Net income per books . . . . . . . | | | (b) Stock . . . . . . | |
| 3 Other increases (itemize) | | | (c) Property . . . . . | |
| | | | 6 Other decreases (itemize) | |
| | | | | |
| | | | | |
| | | | 7 Total of lines 5 and 6 . . . . | |
| 4 Total of lines 1, 2, and 3 . . . . | | | 8 Balance at end of year (line 4 less 7) . . . | |

363-121-1                    ✯ U.S. GOVERNMENT PRINTING OFFICE: 1982—O-363-121

*(handwritten in left margin: ch-12 P-38)*

## B–6 FORM 1120S U.S. SMALL BUSINESS CORPORATION INCOME TAX RETURN

**Form 1120S**
Department of the Treasury
Internal Revenue Service

**U.S. Small Business Corporation Income Tax Return** for calendar year 1982 or

other tax year beginning ........................., 1982, ending ........................, 19.......

▶ **For Paperwork Reduction Act Notice, see page 1 of the instructions.**

OMB No. 1545–0130

**1982**

**A** Date of election as small business corporation

**B** Business code no. (see page 9 of Instructions)

Use IRS label. Otherwise, please print or type.

Name

Number and street

City or town, State, and ZIP code

**C** Employer identification no.

**D** Date incorporated

**E** Enter total assets from Schedule L, line 14, column D (see instructions)

$

**IMPORTANT**—All applicable lines and schedules must be filled in. *If section 465 (deductions limited to amount at risk) applies, see instruction for line 28.*

### Gross Income

| | | |
|---|---|---|
| 1 a Gross receipts or sales ..................... **1b** Less returns and allowances ................... Balance ▶ | 1c | |
| 2 Cost of goods sold (Schedule A) or operations (attach schedule) . . . . . . . . | 2 | |
| 3 Gross profit (subtract line 2 from line 1c) . . . . . . . . . . . . . . . | 3 | |
| 4 a Domestic dividends . . . . . . . . . . . . . . . . . . . . . | 4a | |
| b Foreign dividends . . . . . . . . . . . . . . . . . . . . . | 4b | |
| 5 Interest . . . . . . . . . . . . . . . . . . . . . . . . | 5 | |
| 6 Gross rents . . . . . . . . . . . . . . . . . . . . . . . | 6 | |
| 7 Gross royalties . . . . . . . . . . . . . . . . . . . . . . | 7 | |
| 8 Gains and losses (attach separate Schedule D (Form 1120S)): | | |
| a Net short-term capital gain reduced by any net long-term capital loss . . . . . | 8a | |
| b Net capital gain (if more than $25,000, see instructions for Part IV of Schedule D (Form 1120S)) . | 8b | |
| 9 Ordinary gain or (loss) from Form 4797, Part II, line 11(a) (attach Form 4797) . . . | 9 | |
| 10 Other income (see instructions—attach schedule) . . . . . . . . . . . . | 10 | |
| 11 **TOTAL** income—Add lines 3 through 10 . . . . . . . . . . . . . . | 11 | |

### Deductions

| | | |
|---|---|---|
| 12 Compensation of officers (Schedule E) . . . . . . . . . . . . . . . | 12 | |
| 13 a Salaries and wages ........................... **13b** Less jobs credit ................. Balance ▶ | 13c | |
| 14 Repairs (see instructions) . . . . . . . . . . . . . . . . . . . | 14 | |
| 15 Bad debts (Schedule F if reserve method is used) . . . . . . . . . . . . | 15 | |
| 16 Rents . . . . . . . . . . . . . . . . . . . . . . . . . | 16 | |
| 17 Taxes . . . . . . . . . . . . . . . . . . . . . . . . . | 17 | |
| 18 Interest . . . . . . . . . . . . . . . . . . . . . . . . | 18 | |
| 19 Contributions (not over 10% of line 28 adjusted per instructions) . . . . . . | 19 | |
| 20 Depreciation (attach Form 4562) . . . . . . . . . . . . . **20** | | |
| 21 Less depreciation claimed in Schedule A and elsewhere on return . . **21a** ( ) | 21b | |
| 22 Depletion . . . . . . . . . . . . . . . . . . . . . . . . | 22 | |
| 23 Advertising . . . . . . . . . . . . . . . . . . . . . . . . | 23 | |
| 24 Pension, profit-sharing, etc. plans (see instructions) . . . . . . . . . . | 24 | |
| 25 Employee benefit programs (see instructions) . . . . . . . . . . . . . | 25 | |
| 26 Other deductions (attach schedule) . . . . . . . . . . . . . . . . | 26 | |
| 27 **TOTAL** deductions—Add lines 12 through 26 . . . . . . . . . . . . | 27 | |
| 28 Taxable income (loss) (subtract line 27 from line 11) (see instructions) . . . . . . . | 28 | |

### Tax

| | | | |
|---|---|---|---|
| 29 a Excess net passive income tax (see instructions—attach schedule) . . | 29a | | |
| b Tax from Schedule D (Form 1120S), Part IV . . . . . . . | 29b | | 29 |
| 30 Payments: a Tax deposited with Form 7004 . . . . . . . | 30a | | |
| b Tax deposited with Form 7005 (attach copy) . . . . . | 30b | | |
| c Federal tax on special fuels and oils (attach Form 4136) . . . | 30c | | 30 |
| 31 TAX DUE (subtract line 30 from line 29). See instructions for paying the tax . . . . . ▶ | | | 31 |
| 32 OVERPAYMENT (subtract line 29 from line 30) . . . . . . . . . . . ▶ | | | 32 |

**Please Sign Here**

Under penalties of perjury, I declare that I have examined this return, including accompanying schedules and statements, and to the best of my knowledge and belief, it is true, correct, and complete. Declaration of preparer (other than taxpayer) is based on all information of which preparer has any knowledge.

▶ Signature of officer
Date
▶ Title

**Paid Preparer's Use Only**

| Preparer's signature ▶ | Date | Check if self-employed ▶ ☐ | Preparer's social security no. |
| Firm's name (or yours, if self-employed) and address ▶ | | E.I. No. ▶ | |
| | | ZIP code ▶ | |

363–140–1

**Schedule A** Cost of Goods Sold (See instructions for Schedule A)

1 Inventory at beginning of year . . . . . . . . . . . . .
2 Merchandise bought for manufacture or sale . . . . . . . .
3 Salaries and wages . . . . . . . . . . . . . . . .
4 Other costs (attach schedule) . . . . . . . . . . . . .
5 Total—Add lines 1 through 4 . . . . . . . . . . . . .
6 Inventory at end of year . . . . . . . . . . . . . . .
7 Cost of goods sold—Subtract line 6 from line 5. Enter here and on line 2, page 1 . . . . . . . .

8 a Check all methods used for valuing closing inventory:
    *(i)* ☐ Cost
    *(ii)* ☐ Lower of cost or market as described in regulations section 1.471–4 (see instructions)
    *(iii)* ☐ Writedown of "subnormal" goods as described in regulations section 1.471–2(c) (see instructions)
    *(iv)* ☐ Other (Specify method used and attach explanation) ▶ ----------------------------------------
  b Check if the LIFO inventory method was adopted this tax year for any goods (if checked, attach Form 970) · · · ☐
  c If the LIFO inventory method was used for this tax year, enter percentage (or amounts) of closing inventory computed under LIFO . . . . . . . . . . . . . . . . . .
  d If you are engaged in manufacturing, did you value your inventory using the full absorption method (regulations section 1.471–11)? . . . . . . . . . . . . . . . . . . . ☐ Yes ☐ No
  e Was there any substantial change in determining quantities, cost, or valuations between opening and closing inventory? . . . . . . . . . . . . . . . . . . . . . ☐ Yes ☐ No
    If "Yes," attach explanation.

## Additional Information Required

|  | | Yes | No |
|---|---|---|---|
| **F** Did you at the end of the tax year own, directly or indirectly, 50% or more of the voting stock of a domestic corporation? (For rules of attribution, see section 267(c).) . . . . . . . . . . . . | | | |
| If "Yes," attach a schedule showing: (1) name, address, and employer identification number; | | | |
| (2) percentage owned; | | | |
| (3) highest amount owed by you to such corporation during the year; and | | | |
| (4) highest amount owed to you by such corporation during the year. | | | |
| (Note: *For purposes of F(3) and F(4), "highest amount owed" includes loans and accounts receivable/payable.*) | | | |
| **G** Refer to page 9 of instructions and state the principal: | | | |
| Business activity ▶ ........................................; Product or service ▶ ........................... | | | |
| **H** Were you a member of a controlled group subject to the provisions of section 1561? . . . . . . . . . | | | |
| **I** If the corporation has a loss in an activity for the year, does the corporation have amounts for which it is not "at risk" in the activity (see instruction for line 28 of page 1)? . . . . . . . . . . . . . . . | | | |
| **J** Answer only if (1) this is the first Form 1120S return filed since your election to be treated as a small business corporation and (2) the corporation was in existence for the tax year prior to the election and had investment credit property: Was an agreement filed under regulations section 1.47–4(b)? . . . . . . . . . . . . . | | | |
| **K** Did you claim a deduction for expenses connected with: | | | |
| 1 Entertainment facilities (boat, resort, ranch, etc.)? . . . . . . . . . . . . . . . | | | |
| 2 Living accommodations (except for employees on business)? . . . . . . . . . . . . . | | | |
| 3 Employees attending conventions or meetings outside the North American area? (See section 274(h).) . . . . | | | |
| 4 Employees' families at conventions or meetings? . . . . . . . . . . . . . . . | | | |
| If "Yes," were any of these conventions or meetings outside the North American area? (See section 274(h).) . . | | | |
| 5 Employee or family vacations not reported on Form W–2? . . . . . . . . . . . . . . | | | |
| **L** At any time during the tax year, did you have an interest in or a signature or other authority over a bank account, securities account, or other financial account in a foreign country (see instructions)? . . . . . . . . . . | | | |
| **M** Were you the grantor of, or transferor to, a foreign trust which existed during the current tax year, whether or not you have any beneficial interest in it? If "Yes," you may have to file Forms 3520, 3520–A or 926 . . . . . . . | | | |
| **N** During this tax year was any part of your tax accounting records maintained on a computerized system? . . . . | | | |
| **O** Number of shareholders in the corporation at the end of the tax year ▶ ...................... | | | |
| **P** Was this firm in business at the end of 1982? . . . . . . . . . . . . . . . . . . . | | | |
| **Q** How many months in 1982 was this firm in business? . . . . . . . . . . . . . . . . . | | | |

363–140–1

Form 1120S (1982) Page **3**

| Schedule E | Compensation of Officers (Complete Schedule E only if your total receipts (line 1a, plus lines 4 through 10, of page 1, Form 1120S) are $150,000 or more.) (See instructions for line 12 of page 1) |
|---|---|

| 1. Name of officer | 2. Social security number | 3. Time devoted to business | 4. Percentage of corporation stock owned | 5. Amount of compensation | 6. Expense account allowances |
|---|---|---|---|---|---|
| | | | | | |
| | | | | | |
| | | | | | |
| | | | | | |
| | | | | | |
| Total compensation of officers—Enter here and on line 12, page 1 . . . . . . . | | | | | |

| Schedule F | Bad Debts—Reserve Method (See instructions for line 15 of page 1) |
|---|---|

| 1. Year | 2. Trade notes and accounts receivable outstanding at end of year | 3. Sales on account | Amount added to reserve | | 6. Amount charged against reserve | 7. Reserve for bad debts at end of year |
|---|---|---|---|---|---|---|
| | | | 4. Current year's provision | 5. Recoveries | | |
| 1977 | | | | | | |
| 1978 | | | | | | |
| 1979 | | | | | | |
| 1980 | | | | | | |
| 1981 | | | | | | |
| 1982 | | | | | | |

| Schedule K | Computation of Undistributed Taxable Income and Summary of Distributions and Other Items |
|---|---|

1 Taxable income (line 28, page 1) . . . . . . . . . .
2 Less: a Money distributed as dividends out of earnings and profits for the tax year . . .
    b Tax imposed on certain capital gains (line 29b, page 1) . . . . .
3 Corporation's undistributed taxable income (subtract line 2 from line 1) . . . . . . . .
4 Actual dividend distributions taxable as ordinary income. (Do not include amounts shown on line 6.) . .
5 Actual dividend distributions taxable as long-term capital gains (after tax) . . . . . . .
6 Actual dividend distributions taxable as ordinary income and qualifying for dividend exclusion
7 Nondividend distributions . . . . . . . .
8 Undistributed taxable income—taxable as ordinary income or (loss) (see instructions) . . . .
9 Undistributed taxable income—taxable as long-term capital gain (after tax) (see instructions) . . .
10 Investment credit property—Attach Form 3468 (See Instructions)
11 Interest on investment indebtedness
    a 1 Interest on investment indebtedness incurred before 12–17–69 . . . . . . . . .
      2 Interest on investment indebtedness incurred before 9–11–75, but after 12–16–69 . . . .
      3 Interest on investment indebtedness incurred after 9–10–75 . . . . . . . . . .
    b Net investment income or (loss) . . . . . . . . .
    c Excess expenses from "net lease property" . . . . . . . . . . . . .
    d Net capital gain attributable to investment property . . . . . . . . . . . . .
12 Items of tax preference (see instructions):
    a Accelerated depreciation on real property:
      1 Low-income rental housing (section 167(k)) . . . . . . . . .
      2 Other real property that is nonrecovery property or 15-year real property . . . . . . . .
    b Accelerated depreciation on leased property that is personal property or recovery property other than 15-year real property . . . . . . . . .
    c Amortization . . . . . . . . .
    d Reserve for losses on bad debts of financial institutions . . . . . . . .
    e Depletion . . . . . . . . .
    f Intangible drilling costs . . . . . . . .
    g Other (attach schedule) (see instructions) . . . . . . . . . . . . . .
    h Net capital gain (after tax) . . . . . . . . . .
13 a Jobs credit . . . . . . . . . . .
    b Credit for alcohol used as fuel . . . . . . . . .
    c Other (see instructions) . . . . . . . . . . . . . .

363–140–1

Form 1120S (1982)     Page **4**

| **Schedule L** Balance Sheets | | | | |
|---|---|---|---|---|
| **Assets** | Beginning of tax year | | End of tax year | |
| | A | B | C | D |
| 1 Cash . . . . . . . . . . . | | | | |
| 2 Trade notes and accounts receivable . . . . . | | | | |
|   a Less allowances for bad debts . . . . . | | | | |
| 3 Inventories . . . . . . . . | | | | |
| 4 Federal and State government obligations . . . . | | | | |
| 5 Other current assets (attach schedule) . . . . | | | | |
| 6 Loans to shareholders . . . . . . . | | | | |
| 7 Mortgage and real estate loans . . . . | | | | |
| 8 Other investments (attach schedule) . . . . . | | | | |
| 9 Buildings and other depreciable assets . . . | | | | |
|   a Less accumulated depreciation . . . . . | | | | |
| 10 Depletable assets . . . . . . . | | | | |
|   a Less accumulated depletion . . . . . . | | | | |
| 11 Land (net of any amortization) . . . . . | | | | |
| 12 Intangible assets (amortizable only) . . . | | | | |
|   a Less accumulated amortization . . . . | | | | |
| 13 Other assets (attach schedule) . . . . . | | | | |
| 14     Total assets . . . . . . . | | | | |
| **Liabilities and Shareholders' Equity** | | | | |
| 15 Accounts payable . . . . . . . . | | | | |
| 16 Mtges., notes, bonds payable in less than 1 year . . | | | | |
| 17 Other current liabilities (attach schedule) . . | | | | |
| 18 Loans from shareholders . . . . . . . | | | | |
| 19 Mtges., notes, bonds payable in 1 year or more . . | | | | |
| 20 Other liabilities (attach schedule) . . . . . | | | | |
| 21 Capital stock . . . . . . . . | | | | |
| 22 Paid-in or capital surplus . . . . . . | | | | |
| 23 Retained earnings—appropriated (attach schedule) . . | | | | |
| 24 Retained earnings—unappropriated . . . . | | | | |
| 25 Shareholders' undistributed taxable income previously taxed . | | | | |
| 26 Less cost of treasury stock . . . . . . | | (       ) | | (       ) |
| 27     Total liabilities and shareholders' equity . . | | | | |

**Schedule M-1** Reconciliation of Income on Books With Income on Return (line 28, page 1). Do not complete this schedule if your total assets (line 14, column D, above) are less than $25,000.

| | | | |
|---|---|---|---|
| 1 Net income on books . . . . . . . . | | 7 Income recorded on books this year not included in this return (itemize) | |
| 2 Federal income tax . . . . . . . | |   a Tax-exempt interest $............................. | |
| 3 Excess of capital losses over capital gains . . | | | |
| 4 Income subject to tax not recorded on books this year (itemize) $............................ | | 8 Deductions in this tax return not charged against book income this year (itemize) | |
| 5 Expenses recorded on books this year not deducted in this return (itemize) | |   a Depreciation . . . . $........................... | |
|   a Depreciation . . . . $........................... | |   b Contributions carryover . $........................ | |
|   b Contributions carryover . $........................ | | 9     Total of lines 7 and 8 . . . . . | |
| 6     Total of lines 1 through 5 . . . . . | | 10 Income—line 6 less line 9 . . . . . . | |

**Schedule M-2** Analysis of Unappropriated Retained Earnings on Books (line 24 above). Do not complete this schedule if your total assets (line 14, column D, above) are less than $25,000.

| | | | |
|---|---|---|---|
| 1 Balance at beginning of year . . . . . . | | 5 Distributions out of current or accumulated earnings and profits: a Cash . . . . . | |
| 2 Net income on books . . . . . . . | |               b Stock . . . . . | |
| 3 Other increases (itemize) ............................. | |               c Property . . . . . | |
| ..................................................... | | 6 Current year's undistributed taxable income or net operating loss (total of lines 8 and 9, Schedule K) . . . . . . . . . . . | |
| ..................................................... | | 7 Other decreases (itemize) ........................... | |
| ..................................................... | | | |
| ..................................................... | | 8     Total of lines 5, 6, and 7 . . . . | |
| 4     Total of lines 1, 2, and 3 . . . . . | | 9 Balance at end of year (line 4 less line 8) . . | |

**SCHEDULE K–1**
**(Form 1120S)**

Department of the Treasury
Internal Revenue Service

# Shareholder's Share of Undistributed Taxable Income, etc.—1982
For calendar year 1982 or other tax year

beginning ................................................, 1982, ending ................................................, 19........

(Do Not File—Keep For Your Records)

OMB No. 1545–0130

**Copy B**
**For Shareholder**

Shareholder's identifying number ▶

Shareholder's name, address, and ZIP code

Corporation's identifying number ▶

Corporation's name, address, and ZIP code

| Other Shareholder Information: | A. Stock ownership | | | B. Compensation | C. Percentage of time devoted to business |
|---|---|---|---|---|---|
| | Number of shares | Period held | | | |
| | | Date acquired | Date of disposition | | |

| **Part I** Income | (a) Amount | (b) Form 1040 references; for Form 1041, see Instruction A. |
|---|---|---|
| 1 Undistributed taxable income—ordinary income or (loss) . . . . . . . . ▪ | | Schedule E, Part II |
| (If line 1 is a loss, see instruction C for deductible amount.) | | |
| 2 Undistributed taxable income—net long-term capital gain (after tax) . . . . ▪ | | Schedule D, Part II |
| 3 Shareholder's share of losses from section 465 activities (see instruction D) . . ▪ | | |
| 4 Amount of loan repayments for "Loans from Shareholders" (see instruction E) . ▪ | | |

| **Part II** Interest on Investment Indebtedness (See Instruction A) | | Form 4952 references |
|---|---|---|
| 1 (a) Interest on investment indebtedness incurred before 12–17–69 . . . . . ▪ | | line 1 |
| (b) Interest on investment indebtedness incurred before 9–11–75 but after 12–16–69 . . . . | | line 15 |
| (c) Interest on investment indebtedness incurred after 9–10–75 . . . . . . ▪ | | line 5 |
| 2 Net investment income or (loss) . . . . . . . . . . . . . . ▪ | | line 2 or 10 |
| 3 Excess expenses from "net lease property" . . . . . . . . . . . ▪ | | lines 11 and 19 |
| 4 Net capital gain attributable to investment property . . . . . . . . . ▪ | | line 20 |

| **Part III** Items of Tax Preference | | Form 4625 references |
|---|---|---|
| 1 Accelerated depreciation on real property: | | |
| (a) Low-income rental housing (section 167(k)) . . . . . . . . . ▪ | | line 1(a)(1) |
| (b) Other real property that is nonrecovery property or 15-year real property . . | | line 1(a)(2) |
| 2 Accelerated depreciation on leased property that is personal property or recovery property other than 15-year real property . . . . . . . . . . . . . ▪ | | line 1(b) |
| 3 Amortization . . . . . . . . . . . . . . . . . . . . ▪ | | line 1(c) |
| 4 Reserves for losses on bad debts of financial institutions . . . . . . . ▪ | | line 1(d) |
| 5 Depletion . . . . . . . . . . . . . . . . . . . . . ▪ | | line 1(e) |
| 6 Intangible drilling costs . . . . . . . . . . . . . . . . ▪ | | line 1(f) |
| 7 Other (see instructions) (attach schedule) . . . . . . . . . . . ▪ | | |
| 8 Net capital gain (after tax) (see instructions) . . . . . . . . . . ▪ | | |

| **Part IV** Property Eligible for Investment Credit | | Form 3468 references |
|---|---|---|
| Unadjusted basis of new recovery property | (a) 3-Year . . . . . . . . . . ▪ | line 1(a) |
| | (b) Other . . . . . . . . . . ▪ | line 1(b) |
| Unadjusted basis of used recovery property | (c) 3-Year . . . . . . . . . . ▪ | line 1(c) |
| | (d) Other . . . . . . . . . . ▪ | line 1(d) |
| Nonrecovery property (see instructions) (attach schedule) . . . . . . . . ▪ | | |
| New commuter highway vehicle . . . . . . . . . . . . . . ▪ | | line 3 |
| Used commuter highway vehicle . . . . . . . . . . . . . . ▪ | | line 4 |
| Qualified rehabilitation expenditures (see instructions) . . . . . . . . ▪ | | |

| **Part V** Credits | | |
|---|---|---|
| 1 Jobs credit . . . . . . . . . . . . . . . . . . . . ▪ | | Form 5884 |
| 2 Credit for alcohol used as fuel . . . . . . . . . . . . . . ▪ | | Form 6478 |
| 3 Other (see instructions) . . . . . . . . . . . . . . . . ▪ | | |

For Paperwork Reduction Act Notice, see page 1 of Instructions for Form 1120S.

363–143–1

## Instructions for Shareholder

*(References are to the Internal Revenue Code.)*

**A. General Instructions.**—Schedule K–1 (Form 1120S) will help you when you prepare your income tax return. It shows your share of: undistributed taxable income or (loss) and other items that you must take into account when you file your tax return.

The line references in column (b) are to tax forms in use for the 1982 tax year. If you are using the Schedule K–1 information to file for a tax year beginning in 1983, enter the amounts on the corresponding line of the 1983 tax forms.

Report the income (or loss) in Part I on your tax return as follows: Report line 1, Part I, income (or loss) on Schedule E (Form 1040). Report line 2 income on the appropriate line of Schedule D (Form 1040). Form 1041 filers are to report the income (or loss) in Part I in corresponding lines of Form 1041 and Schedule D (Form 1041). See Instructions C and D for limits on losses reported on lines 1 and 3.

This schedule does not show the amount of actual dividend distributions the corporation paid you. The corporation must report such amounts totaling $10 or more during the calendar year to you on Form 1099–DIV. If any tax was withheld from dividend payments made after June 30, 1983, the 1983 Form 1099–DIV will also show the amount withheld. Report actual dividend distributions on Schedule B (Form 1040) and claim a credit for the amount withheld on Form 1040.

Use the items listed in Part II, combined with similar items from other sources, to complete Form 4952, Investment Interest Expense Deduction. Do **not** deduct this interest expense on your tax return (Form 1040 or Form 1041). These amounts have already been deducted in figuring your share of the taxable income (or loss) of the corporation. You may be required to adjust your share of undistributed taxable income (or loss) that the corporation reported on line 1, Part I. See the specific instructions for Form 4952 for details.

If your tax year begins in 1982, use items 1 through 6 listed in Part III, combined with similar items from other sources, to complete Form 4625, Computation of Minimum Tax—Individuals (Estates and trusts use Form 4626). Use item 8 of Part III, combined with capital gains and losses from other sources, to complete your 1982 Form 6251, Alternative Minimum Tax Computation, if applicable. If your tax year begins in 1983, use items 1 through 8 (including items from the attached schedule for line 7) to figure your alternative minimum tax for 1983. If the corporation attached a schedule showing that line 3 includes amortization for on-the-job training facilities and amortization for child-care facilities, exclude these amounts from the amortization entered on line 3 and use this reduced amount in figuring your alternative minimum tax for 1983.

Use the investment credit property items listed in Part IV, combined with investment credit property from other sources, to complete Form 3468, Computation of Investment Credit. (Your share of nonrecovery property of the corporation is listed in a separate statement. See the Instructions for Form 3468 on how to figure the credit for this property.) (Qualified rehabilitation expenditures will be listed on a separate statement if the corporation made separate expenditures for improvements to more than one building, etc., that qualify

for different credit rates (10%, 15%, 20%, or 25%).)

Part V—Line 1 shows your share of the jobs credit figured by the corporation. Enter this amount on Form 5884, Jobs Credit (and WIN Credit Carryover), and complete the form to figure the credit you are allowed on your tax return.

Line 2 shows your share of the corporation's credit for alcohol used as fuel. Enter this amount on Form 6478, Credit for Alcohol Used As Fuel, and complete the form to figure the credit you are allowed on your tax return.

Line 3 contains your share of other corporate credits not reported on lines 1 and 2 of Part V. These credits are: (1) nonconventional source fuel credit (enter this credit on a schedule you prepare yourself to determine the allowed credit to take on your tax return—see section 44D for computation provisions and other special rules for figuring the credit); (2) credit for increasing research activities (enter this credit on Form 6765, Credit for Increasing Research Activities, to figure the allowed credit to claim on your tax return); (3) unused regular or energy investment credit from a cooperative (enter these credits on the appropriate line of Form 3468, Computation of Investment Credit, to determine the allowed credit to take on your tax return); and (4) tax withheld on dividends, interest, or patronage dividends paid to the corporation (you claim a credit for this amount on Form 1040 (Form 1041 for estates and trusts) in the same manner as you claim a credit for amounts withheld by the corporation on payments of dividends and interest to you). The corporation has listed and identified each of these credits at the bottom of Schedule K–1.

**Separate Schedules.**—Schedules may be attached to Schedule K–1 that show your share of:

(1) Part III, line 7, tax preference items.—Use these items with items from other sources to figure your alternative minimum tax for 1983.

(2) Nonrecovery and energy investment credit property.—Use this property, with properties from other sources, to complete Form 3468.

(3) Information on investment credit property that was disposed of before the recovery period or life years originally assigned the property.—Use the information on the statement to complete Form 4255, Recapture of Investment Credit.

**B. When to report income, etc.**—Include your share of undistributed taxable income, etc., on your tax return for the year in which the tax year of the corporation ends. For example, if you are on the calendar year, and the corporation's tax year ends on January 31, 1983, you must take the above items into account on your return for calendar year 1983.

**C. If Part I, line 1, is a loss.**—The income or loss on line 1, Part I, is your full distributive share of the corporation's undistributed taxable income or loss for the year. It does not take into account the adjusted basis of your stock in the corporation and the adjusted basis of any indebtedness to you.

Section 1374(c)(2) limits the amount of loss you can deduct on your return to the sum of:

*(1)* the adjusted basis of your stock in the corporation, and

*(2)* the adjusted basis of any indebtedness of the corporation to you.

If your share of a loss is more than the

section 1374(c)(2) limitation, you may not deduct the excess in any tax year.

**D. Part I, losses from section 465 activities.**—Section 465 losses are entered on line 3 for information purposes only. These losses are also included in line 1, Part I. Section 465 losses are stated separately to help you determine the amount of each activity loss you may deduct on your return.

Section 465 rules limit the losses of a small business corporation engaged in any activity (except holding of real property other than mineral property) as a trade or business or for the production of income.

Your share of a section 465(d) loss from each activity for the tax year is allowed up to the amount you are "at risk" for the activity at the end of the corporation's tax year.

In general, you are "at risk" for an activity for the cash and adjusted basis of property you contributed to the activity and any amount borrowed for use in the activity for which you are personally liable.

Your proportionate share in the corporation is treated as a single activity to the extent the corporation is engaged in separate but similar activities. However, if the corporation is engaged in two different types of activities, you are considered to be engaged in two separate activities. You must make a separate determination of the amount you are "at risk" for each separate activity. See section 465 for details.

If a section 465 activity loss is in excess of the amount you are "at risk" for the activity, you must adjust the gain or loss on line 1, Part I, for the excess. A gain in line 1, Part I, would be increased by the excess and a loss would be decreased by the excess.

Any loss from an activity not allowed for the tax year because of section 465 is treated as a deduction allocable to the activity in the next tax year.

**E. Repayment of indebtedness with a reduced basis.**—If Part I, line 1, losses in earlier years were more than the adjusted basis of your stock in the corporation and have been applied to decrease the adjusted basis of your loans to the corporation in earlier years, any repayments of the loans in this year will result in taxable income to you to the extent that the repayments are more than the adjusted basis of the loan. The nature of the indebtedness determines whether you report the income as capital gain or ordinary income.

Part I, line 4, shows total loan repayments the corporation made to you during its tax year. If these payments result in income as explained above, report the income in the tax year you receive the payments. If your tax year is different than that of the corporation, and you cannot determine the amount of or year in which the loan repayments were received, ask the corporation to give you this information.

If the loan is repaid in installments, make a breakdown of each payment to show the computation of (1) return of capital and (2) income. (See section 1376 and the related regulations.)

363–143–2

# Instructions for Corporation

Copy A—Attach to Form 1120S.

Copy B—Give to each shareholder.

Copy C—Retain for your records.

*Substitute forms.*—Prior IRS approval is not required for (a) a substitute Schedule K–1 that shows the OMB control number and only the line items required for use by a taxpayer if those line items have the same numbers and titles and are in the same order as on the comparable IRS Schedule K–1; or (b) a substitute Schedule K–1 that is an exact facsimile of an IRS Schedule K–1 (including the OMB control number). Other substitute Schedules K–1 require prior approval. You may apply for approval of a substitute form by writing to: Internal Revenue Service, Attention D:R:R, 1111 Constitution Avenue, NW, Washington, DC 20224.

Complete a separate Schedule K–1 (Form 1120S) for each person who was a shareholder during the tax year. Additional instructions for completing Schedule K–1 are on pages 7 and 8 of the instructions for Form 1120S.

Schedule K–1 (Form 1120S) must show complete information for all persons who were shareholders of the corporation during any part of the tax year.

Please make sure the shareholder's name, identifying number, and other shareholder information are complete and legible.

The corporation may be subject to a penalty for each omission of a shareholder's identifying number unless the corporation establishes a reasonable cause for not providing it.

Under the tax treatment provided by Subchapter S, shareholders generally are taxed on their shares of the current taxable income of the corporation, whether or not actually distributed. In addition to undistributed taxable income, Schedule K–1 also includes each shareholder's share of:

- Section 465 activity losses,
- Loan repayment for loans from shareholders,
- Items of tax preference,
- Items used to figure the limitation on the deduction for investment interest expense,
- Property eligible for regular investment credit,
- Jobs credit,
- Alcohol fuel credit,
- Nonconventional source fuel credit,
- Credit for increasing research activities,
- Unused regular or energy investment credit from a cooperative, and
- Credit for income tax withheld on interest, dividends, and patronage dividends paid to the corporation (withholdings on dividends and interest paid to shareholders are reported separately on Forms 1099–DIV and Forms 1099–INT).

Separate statements are attached to Schedule K–1 to show each shareholder's share of:

- Certain tax preference items,
- Nonrecovery investment credit property,
- Property eligible for energy investment credit, and
- Property used in refiguring an earlier year investment credit.

On Form 1099–DIV, report actual dividend distributions totaling $10 or more to a shareholder during the calendar year and withholding on dividend distributions made after June 30, 1983.

If an earlier actual distribution reported to shareholders as ordinary income on Form 1099–DIV is determined to be capital gain at the close of the corporation's tax year, the corporation must issue corrected Forms 1099–DIV to the shareholders.

## B-7 FORM 1065 U.S. PARTNERSHIP RETURN

| Form **1065** | **U.S. Partnership Return of Income** | OMB No. 1545-0099 |
|---|---|---|
| Department of the Treasury Internal Revenue Service | For calendar year 1982, or fiscal year beginning ................., 1982, and ending ..................., 19........ | **1982** |

| | | | |
|---|---|---|---|
| **A** Principal business activity (see page 12 of Instructions) | Use IRS label. Other-wise, please print or type. | Name | **D** Employer identification no. |
| **B** Principal product or service (see page 12 of Instructions) | | Number and street | **E** Date business started |
| **C** Business code number (see page 12 of Instructions) | | City or town, State, and ZIP code | **F** Enter total assets from Sched-ule L, line 13, column (D). $ |

**G** Check method of accounting: (1) ☐ Cash (2) ☐ Accrual (3) ☐ Other.

**H** Check applicable boxes: (1) ☐ Final return (2) ☐ Change in address (3) ☐ Amended return.

**I** Check if the partnership meets ALL the requirements shown on page 3 of the Instructions under "Filing a Complete Return." ▶ ☐

| | Yes | No | | | Yes | No |
|---|---|---|---|---|---|---|
| **J** Is this partnership a limited partnership (see page 2 of Instructions)? . . . . . . . . . . . . | | | **O** At any time during the tax year, did the partnership have an interest in or a signature or other authority over a bank ac-count, securities account, or other financial account in a foreign country (see page 3 of Instructions)? . . . . | | | |
| **K** Number of partners in this partnership ................ | | | | | | |
| **L** Is this partnership a partner in another partnership? . . . | | | **P** Was the partnership the grantor of, or transferor to, a foreign trust which existed during the current tax year, whether or not the partnership or any partner has any beneficial in-terest in it? If "Yes," you may have to file Forms 3520, 3520-A, or 926. (See page 4 of Instructions.) . . . . | | | |
| **M** Are any partners in this partnership also partnerships? . . | | | | | | |
| **N (1)** How many months in 1982 was this partnership actively operated? ................. | | | | | | |
| **(2)** Was this partnership in operation at the end of 1982? . | | | | | | |

### Income

| | | |
|---|---|---|
| **1a** Gross receipts or sales $................. **1b** Minus returns and allowances $................. Balance ▶ | **1c** | |
| **2** Cost of goods sold and/or operations (Schedule A, line 8) . . . . . . . . . . . . . . | **2** | |
| **3** Gross profit (subtract line 2 from line 1c) . . . . . . . . . . . . . . . . | **3** | |
| **4** Ordinary income (loss) from other partnerships and fiduciaries . . . . . . . . . . | **4** | |
| **5** Nonqualifying interest and nonqualifying dividends . . . . . . . . . . . . . | **5** | |
| **6a** Gross rents $................. **6b** Minus rental expenses (attach schedule) $................. | | |
|     Balance net rental (loss) . . . . . . . . . . . . . . . . . . ▶ | **6c** | |
| **7** Net income (loss) from royalties (attach schedule) . . . . . . . . . . . . | **7** | |
| **8** Net farm profit (loss) (attach Schedule F (Form 1040)) . . . . . . . . . . . | **8** | |
| **9** Net gain (loss) (Form 4797, line 11) . . . . . . . . . . . . . . . . | **9** | |
| **10** Other income (loss) . . . . . . . . . . . . . . . . . . . . . | **10** | |
| **11**     **TOTAL** income (loss) (combine lines 3 through 10) . . . . . . . . . . . . | **11** | |

### Deductions

| | | |
|---|---|---|
| **12a** Salaries and wages (other than to partners) $................. **12b** Minus jobs credit $................. Balance ▶ | **12c** | |
| **13** Guaranteed payments to partners (see page 5 of Instructions) . . . . . . . . . | **13** | |
| **14** Rent . . . . . . . . . . . . . . . . . . . . . . . . . . | **14** | |
| **15a** Total deductible interest expense not claimed elsewhere on return (see page 5 of Instructions) . . . . . . . . . . | **15a** | |
|     **b** Interest expense required to be passed through to partners on Schedules K and K-1, lines 13, 21a(2), and 21a(3) . . . . . . . . . | **15b** | |
|     **c** Subtract line 15b from line 15a . . . . . . . . . . . . . . . . | **15c** | |
| **16** Taxes . . . . . . . . . . . . . . . . . . . . . . . . . | **16** | |
| **17** Bad debts (see page 5 of Instructions) . . . . . . . . . . . . . . . | **17** | |
| **18** Repairs . . . . . . . . . . . . . . . . . . . . . . . . | **18** | |
| **19a** Depreciation from Form 4562 (attach Form 4562) $................. **19b** Minus depreciation claimed in Schedule A and elsewhere on return $................. Balance ▶ . . . . | **19c** | |
| **20** Depletion (**DO NOT DEDUCT OIL AND GAS DEPLETION.** See page 5 of Instructions.) . . | **20** | |
| **21a** Retirement plans, etc. (see page 5 of Instructions) . . . . . . . . . . . | **21a** | |
|     **b** Employee benefit programs (see page 6 of Instructions) . . . . . . . . . . | **21b** | |
| **22** Other deductions (attach schedule) . . . . . . . . . . . . . . . . | **22** | |
| **23**     **TOTAL** deductions (add amounts in column for lines 12c through 22) . . . . . . . | **23** | |
| **24** Ordinary income (loss) (subtract line 23 from line 11) . . . . . . . . . . | **24** | |

**Please Sign Here**

Under penalties of perjury, I declare that I have examined this return, including accompanying schedules and statements, and to the best of my knowledge and belief it is true, correct, and complete. Declaration of preparer (other than taxpayer) is based on all information of which preparer has any knowledge.

▶ Signature of general partner        ▶ Date

| **Paid Preparer's Use Only** | Preparer's signature ▶ | Date | Check if self-em-ployed ▶ ☐ | Preparer's social security no. |
|---|---|---|---|---|
| | Firm's name (or yours, if self-employed) and address ▶ | | E.I. No. ▶ | |
| | | | ZIP code ▶ | |

For Paperwork Reduction Act Notice, see page 1 of Form 1065 Instructions.         363-096-2

## Schedule A—COST OF GOODS SOLD AND/OR OPERATIONS (See Page 6 of Instructions.)

| | | |
|---|---|---|
| 1 | Inventory at beginning of year . . . . . . . . . . . . . . . | **1** |
| 2 | Purchases minus cost of items withdrawn for personal use . . . . . . . . . . | **2** |
| 3 | Cost of labor . . . . . . . . . . . . . . . . . | **3** |
| 4 | Materials and supplies . . . . . . . . . . . . . . . | **4** |
| 5 | Other costs (attach schedule) . . . . . . . . . . . . . | **5** |
| 6 | Total (add lines 1 through 5) . . . . . . . . . . . . . | **6** |
| 7 | Inventory at end of year . . . . . . . . . . . . . . | **7** |
| 8 | Cost of goods sold (subtract line 7 from line 6). Enter here and on page 1, line 2 . . . . . . | **8** |

**9a** Check all methods used for valuing closing inventory:
(i) ☐ Cost; (ii) ☐ Lower of cost or market as described in regulations section 1.471–4 (see page 6 of Instructions); (iii) ☐ Writedown of "subnormal" goods as described in regulations section 1.471–2(c) (see page 6 of Instructions).

**b** Did you use any other method of inventory valuation not described in line 9a? . . . . . . . If "Yes," specify methods used and attach explanation.

|  | Yes | No |
|---|---|---|
| **c** Check if the LIFO method was adopted this tax year for any goods. (If checked, attach Form 970.) . . . . . . . . . . . . . ☐ | | |
| **d** If you are engaged in manufacturing, did you value your inventory using the full absorption method (regulations section 1.471–11)? . . . | | |
| **e** Was there any substantial change in determining quantities, cost, or valuations between opening and closing inventory? . . . . . . . If "Yes," attach explanation. | | |

## Schedule D—CAPITAL GAINS AND LOSSES (See Page 6 of Instructions.)

**Part I** Short-Term Capital Gains and Losses—Assets Held One Year or Less

| | a. Kind of property and description (Example, 100 shares of "Z" Co.) | b. Date acquired (mo., day, yr.) | c. Date sold (mo., day, yr.) | d. Gross sales price minus expenses of sale | e. Cost or other basis | f. Gain (loss) (d minus e) |
|---|---|---|---|---|---|---|
| 1 | | | | | | |
| | | | | | | |
| | | | | | | |
| | | | | | | |
| | | | | | | |

| | | |
|---|---|---|
| 2 | Short-term capital gain from installment sales from Form 6252, line 21 or 29 . . . . . . . | |
| 3 | Partnership's share of net short-term gain (loss), including specially allocated items, from other partnerships and from fiduciaries . . . . | |
| 4 | Net short-term gain (loss) from lines 1, 2, and 3. Enter here and on Schedule K (Form 1065), line 5 . . . . | |

**Part II** Long-Term Capital Gains and Losses—Assets Held More Than One Year

| | | | | | | |
|---|---|---|---|---|---|---|
| 5 | | | | | | |
| | | | | | | |
| | | | | | | |
| | | | | | | |
| | | | | | | |

| | | |
|---|---|---|
| 6 | Long-term capital gain from installment sales from Form 6252, line 21 or 29 . . . . . . . | |
| 7 | Partnership's share of net long-term gain (loss), including specially allocated items, from other partnerships and from fiduciaries . . . . . . . . . . . . . | |
| 8 | Capital gain distributions . . . . . . . . . . . . . . . . | |
| 9 | Net long-term gain (loss) from lines 5, 6, 7, and 8. Enter here and on Schedule K (Form 1065), line 6 . . . | |

## Schedule I—BAD DEBTS (See Page 5 of Instructions.)

| a. Year | b. Trade notes and accounts receivable outstanding at end of year | c. Sales on account | Amount added to reserve | | f. Amount charged against reserve | g. Reserve for bad debts at end of year |
|---|---|---|---|---|---|---|
| | | | d. Current year's provision | e. Recoveries | | |
| 1982 | | | | | | |

363–096–1

## Schedule K—PARTNERS' SHARES OF INCOME, CREDITS, DEDUCTIONS, ETC. (See Pages 7–11 of Instructions.)

| | | a. Distributive share items | | b. Total amount | |
|---|---|---|---|---|---|
| **Income (loss)** | 1 | Ordinary income (loss) (page 1, line 24) . . . . . . . . . . . | **1** | | |
| | 2 | Guaranteed payments . . . . . . . . . . . . . | **2** | | |
| | 3 | Interest from All-Savers Certificates . . . . . . . . . . . | **3** | | |
| | 4 | Dividends qualifying for exclusion . . . . . . . . . . . | **4** | | |
| | 5 | Net short-term capital gain (loss) (Schedule D, line 4) . . . . . | **5** | | |
| | 6 | Net long-term capital gain (loss) (Schedule D, line 9) . . . . . . | **6** | | |
| | 7 | Net gain (loss) from involuntary conversions due to casualty or theft (Form 4684) . . | **7** | | |
| | 8 | Other net gain (loss) under section 1231 . . . . . . . . . | **8** | | |
| | 9 | Other (attach schedule) . . . . . . . . . | **9** | | |
| **Deductions** | 10 | Charitable contributions (attach list): 50% .............. , 30% .............. , 20% .............. | **10** | | |
| | 11 | Expense deduction for recovery property (section 179 expense) from Part I, Section A, Form 4562 (must not be more than $5,000) . . . . . . . . . | **11** | | |
| | 12a | Payments for partners to an IRA . . . . . . . . . . | **12a** | | |
| | b | Payments for partners to a Keogh Plan (Type of plan ▶.............................) . . . . | **12b** | | |
| | c | Payments for partners to Simplified Employee Pension (SEP) . . . . . . . | **12c** | | |
| | 13 | Other (attach schedule) . . . . . . . . . . | **13** | | |
| **Credits** | 14 | Jobs credit . . . . . . . . . . . . . . . . | **14** | | |
| | 15 | Credit for alcohol used as fuel . . . . . . . . . . . . . | **15** | | |
| | 16 | Credit for income tax withheld on interest and dividend income (see instructions) . . . | **16** | | |
| | 17 | Other (attach schedule) . . . . . . . . . . | **17** | | |
| **Other** | 18a | Gross farming or fishing income . . . . . . . . . . . | **18a** | | |
| | b | Net earnings (loss) from self-employment . . . . . . . . . | **18b** | | |
| | c | Other (attach schedule) . . . . . . . . . . | | | |
| **Specially Allocated Items** | 19a | Short-term capital gain (loss) . . . . . . . . . . . | **19a** | | |
| | b | Long-term capital gain (loss) . . . . . . . . . . . . | **19b** | | |
| | c | Ordinary gain (loss) (attach schedule) . . . . . . . . . . | **19c** | | |
| | d | Other (attach schedule) . . . . . . . . . . . | **19d** | | |
| **Tax Preference Items** | 20a | Accelerated depreciation on real property: | | | |
| | | (1) Low-income rental housing (167(k)) . . . . . . . . . | **20a(1)** | | |
| | | (2) Other nonrecovery real property or 15-year real property . . . . . . . . | **20a(2)** | | |
| | b | Accelerated depreciation on leased personal property or leased recovery property other than 15-year real property . . . . . . . . . . | **20b** | | |
| | c | Amortization . . . . . . . . . . . . . . . | **20c** | | |
| | d | Reserves for losses on bad debts of financial institutions . . . . . . . . | **20d** | | |
| | e | Depletion (other than oil and gas) . . . . . . . . . . . . | **20e** | | |
| | f | (1) Excess intangible drilling costs from oil, gas, or geothermal wells . . . . . | **20f(1)** | | |
| | | (2) Net income from oil, gas, or geothermal wells . . . . . . . . . | **20f(2)** | | |
| | g | Other (attach schedule) . . . . . . . . . . . . | | | |
| **Investment Interest** | 21a | Investment interest expense: | | | |
| | | (1) Indebtedness incurred before 12/17/69 . . . . . . . . . | **21a(1)** | | |
| | | (2) Indebtedness incurred before 9/11/75, but after 12/16/69 . . . . . . | **21a(2)** | | |
| | | (3) Indebtedness incurred after 9/10/75 . . . . . . . . . . | **21a(3)** | | |
| | b | Net investment income (loss) . . . . . . . . . . . . | **21b** | | |
| | c | Excess expenses from "net lease property" . . . . . . . . . . | **21c** | | |
| | d | Excess of net long-term capital gain over net short-term capital loss from investment property . . . . | **21d** | | |
| **Foreign Taxes** | 22a | Type of income ......................................................... | | | |
| | b | Foreign country or U.S. possession ......................................... | | | |
| | c | Total gross income from sources outside the U.S. (attach schedule) . . . . . . | **22c** | | |
| | d | Total applicable deductions and losses (attach schedule) . . . . . . . . | **22d** | | |
| | e | Total foreign taxes (check one): ☐ Paid ☐ Accrued . . . . . . . . | **22e** | | |
| | f | Reduction in taxes available for credit (attach schedule) . . . . . . . . | **22f** | | |
| | g | Other (attach schedule) . . . . . . . . . . . . . . | **22g** | | |

Form 1065 (1982)                                                                Page **4**

### Schedule L—BALANCE SHEETS (See Page 11 of Instructions.)

| ASSETS | Beginning of tax year | | End of tax year | |
|---|---|---|---|---|
| | (A) | (B) | (C) | (D) |
| 1 Cash | | | | |
| 2 Trade notes and accounts receivable | | | | |
|   a. Minus allowance for bad debts | | | | |
| 3 Inventories | | | | |
| 4 Federal and State government obligations | | | | |
| 5 Other current assets (attach schedule) | | | | |
| 6 Mortgage and real estate loans | | | | |
| 7 Other investments (attach schedule) | | | | |
| 8 Buildings and other depreciable assets | | | | |
|   a Minus accumulated depreciation | | | | |
| 9 Depletable assets | | | | |
|   a Minus accumulated depletion | | | | |
| 10 Land (net of any amortization) | | | | |
| 11 Intangible assets (amortizable only) | | | | |
|   a Minus accumulated amortization | | | | |
| 12 Other assets (attach schedule) | | | | |
| 13     Total assets | | | | |
| **LIABILITIES AND CAPITAL** | | | | |
| 14 Accounts payable | | | | |
| 15 Mortgages, notes, and bonds payable in less than 1 year | | | | |
| 16 Other current liabilities (attach schedule) | | | | |
| 17 All nonrecourse loans | | | | |
| 18 Mortgages, notes, and bonds payable in 1 year or more | | | | |
| 19 Other liabilities (attach schedule) | | | | |
| 20 Partners' capital accounts | | | | |
| 21     Total liabilities and capital | | | | |

### Schedule M—RECONCILIATION OF PARTNERS' CAPITAL ACCOUNTS (See Page 11 of Instructions.)
(Show reconciliation of each partner's capital account on Schedule K–1, item E.)

| a. Capital account at beginning of year | b. Capital contributed during year | c. Ordinary income (loss) from page 1, line 24 | d. Income not included in column c, plus non-taxable income | e. Losses not included in column c, plus unallowable deductions | f. Withdrawals and distributions | g. Capital account at end of year |
|---|---|---|---|---|---|---|
| | | | | | | |

☆ U.S. GOVERNMENT PRINTING OFFICE : 1982—O-363-096

**SCHEDULE K–1
(Form 1065)**
Department of the Treasury
Internal Revenue Service

**Partner's Share of Income, Credits, Deductions, etc.—1982**
For calendar year 1982 or fiscal year
beginning ..................................., 1982, and ending ..................................., 19..........

OMB No. 1545–0099

**Copy C
(For partner)**
(Page 1 of 4 pages)

Partner's identifying number ▶

Partner's name, address, and ZIP code

Partnership's identifying number ▶

Partnership's name, address, and ZIP code

**A** Is partner a general partner (see attached instructions)? . .
. . . . . . . . . . . . . . . . . ☐ Yes ☐ No

**B** Partner's share of liabilities:
Nonrecourse . . . . . . . . . . $....................................
Other . . . . . . . . . . . . . $....................................

**C** Enter partner's percentage of:

| | (i) Before decrease or termination | (ii) End of year |
|---|---|---|
| Profit sharing . . . . . . | ...............% | ...............% |
| Loss sharing . . . . . . . | ...............% | ...............% |
| Ownership of capital . . . . | ...............% | ...............% |

**D** What type of entity is this partner? ▶

**E** Reconciliation of partner's capital account:

| a. Capital account at beginning of year | b. Capital contributed during year | c. Ordinary income (loss) from line 1 | d. Income not included in column c, plus non-taxable income | e. Losses not included in column c, plus un-allowable deductions | f. Withdrawals and distributions | g. Capital account at end of year |
|---|---|---|---|---|---|---|
| | | | | | | |

| | a. Distributive share item | b. Amount | c. 1040 filers enter the amount in column b on: |
|---|---|---|---|
| **Income (loss)** | **1** Ordinary income (loss) (see instructions for your tax return for loss limitations) . | .................. | Sch. E, Part II, col. (c) or (d) |
| | **2** Guaranteed payments . . . . . . . . . . . . . . . . . . | .................. | Sch. E, Part II, column (d) |
| | **3** Interest from All-Savers Certificates . . . . . . . . . . . | .................. | Sch. B, Part I, line 4 |
| | **4** Dividends qualifying for exclusion . . . . . . . . . . . | .................. | Sch. B, Part II, line 9 |
| | **5** Net short-term capital gain (loss) . . . . . . . . . . . | .................. | Sch. D, line 3, col. f. or g. |
| | **6** Net long-term capital gain (loss) . . . . . . . . . . . | .................. | Sch. D, line 10, col. f. or g. |
| | **7** Net gain (loss) from involuntary conversions due to casualty or theft . . . . | .................. | Form 4684, line 20 |
| | **8** Other net gain (loss) under section 1231 . . . . . . . . . | .................. | Form 4797, line 1 (Enter on applicable lines of your return) |
| | **9** Other (see attached schedule) . . . . . . . . . . . . . | .................. | |
| **Deductions** | **10** Charitable contributions: 50%.................., 30%.................., 20%.................. | .................. | See Form 1040 instr. |
| | **11** Expense deduction for recovery property (section 179 expense) . . | .................. | Sch. E, Part II, line 28 |
| | **12a** Payments for partner to an IRA . . . . . . . . . . . . | .................. | Form 1040, line 25 |
| | **b** Payments for partner to a Keogh Plan (Type of plan ▶.............) . . | .................. | Form 1040, line 26 |
| | **c** Payments for partner to Simplified Employee Pension (SEP) . . . . | .................. | Form 1040, line 26 (Enter on applicable lines of your return) |
| | **13** Other (see attached schedule) . . . . . . . . . . . . . | .................. | |
| **Credits** | **14** Jobs credit . . . . . . . . . . . . . . . | .................. | Form 5884 |
| | **15** Credit for alcohol used as fuel . . . . . . . . . . . | .................. | Form 6478 |
| | **16** Credit for income tax withheld on interest and dividend income . . | .................. | See Form 1040 instr. (Enter on applicable lines of your return) |
| | **17** Other (see attached schedule) . . . . . . . . . . . . | .................. | |
| **Other** | **18a** Gross farming or fishing income . . . . . . . . . . | .................. | See attached instructions |
| | **b** Net earnings (loss) from self-employment . . . . . . . . | ////////// | Sch. SE, Part I |
| | **c** Other (see attached schedule) . . . . . . . . . . . . | .................. | (Enter on applicable lines of your return) |
| **Specially allocated Items** | **19a** Short-term capital gain (loss) . . . . . . . . . . . | .................. | Sch. D, line 3, col. f. or g. |
| | **b** Long-term capital gain (loss) . . . . . . . . . . . | .................. | Sch. D, line 10, col. f. or g. |
| | **c** Ordinary gain (loss) (see attached schedule) . . . . . . . | .................. | Form 4797, line 9 |
| | **d** Other (see attached schedule) . . . . . . . . . . . | .................. | Sch. E, Part II |
| **Tax Preference Items** | **20a** Accelerated depreciation on real property: | ////////// | |
| | (1) Low-income rental housing (167(k)) . . . . . . . . | .................. | Form 4625, line 1(a)(1) |
| | (2) Other nonrecovery real property or 15-year real property . . . | .................. | Form 4625, line 1(a)(2) |
| | **b** Accelerated depreciation on leased personal property or leased recovery property other than 15-year real property . . . . . . | .................. | Form 4625, line 1(b) |
| | **c** Amortization . . . . . . . . . . . . . . . . | .................. | Form 4625, line 1(c) |
| | **d** Reserves for losses on bad debts of financial institutions . . . | .................. | Form 4625, line 1(d) |
| | **e** Depletion (other than oil and gas) . . . . . . . . . . | .................. | Form 4625, line 1(e) |
| | **f** (1) Excess intangible drilling costs from oil, gas, or geothermal wells . . . . | .................. | See Form 4625 instr. |
| | (2) Net income from oil, gas, or geothermal wells . . . . . . | ////////// | |
| | **g** Other (see attached schedule) . . . . . . . . . . . | ////////// | See attached instructions |

363–098–1

| | a. Distributive share item | b. Amount | c. 1040 filers enter the amount in column b on: |
|---|---|---|---|
| **Investment Interest** | **21a** Investment interest expense: | | |
| | (1) Indebtedness incurred before 12/17/69 . . . . . . . . | | Form 4952, line 1 |
| | (2) Indebtedness incurred before 9/11/75, but after 12/16/69 . . | | Form 4952, line 15 |
| | (3) Indebtedness incurred after 9/10/75 . . . . . . . . . | | Form 4952, line 5 |
| | **b** Net investment income (loss) . . . . . . . . . . . | | Form 4952, line 2 or 10a |
| | **c** Excess expenses from "net lease property" . . . . . . . | | Form 4952, lines 11 and 19 |
| | **d** Excess of net long-term capital gain over net short-term capital loss from investment property . . . . . . . . . . . . . . | | Form 4952, line 20 |
| **Foreign Taxes** | **22a** Type of income _____ | | Form 1116, Checkboxes |
| | **b** Name of foreign country or U.S. possession _____ | | Form 1116, Part I |
| | **c** Total gross income from sources outside the U.S. (see attached schedule) . . | | Form 1116, Part I |
| | **d** Total applicable deductions and losses (see attached schedule) . . | | Form 1116, Part I |
| | **e** Total foreign taxes (check one): ☐ Paid ☐ Accrued . . . . . | | Form 1116, Part II |
| | **f** Reduction in taxes available for credit (see attached schedule) . . | | Form 1116, Part III |
| | **g** Other (see attached schedule) . . . . . . . . . . . . | | Form 1116 instr. |
| **Property Eligible for Investment Credit** | **23** Unadjusted basis of new recovery property — **(a)** 3-Year . . . . . . . . . . | | Form 3468, line 1(a) or (e) |
| | **(b)** Other . . . . . . . . . . . | | Form 3468, line 1(b) or (f) |
| | Unadjusted basis of used recovery property — **(c)** 3-Year . . . . . . . . . . | | Form 3468, line 1(c) or (g) |
| | **(d)** Other . . . . . . . . . . . | | Form 3468, line 1(d) or (h) |
| | **(e)** Nonrecovery property (see attached schedule) . . . . . . . | | Form 3468 instr., line 2 |
| | **(f)** New commuter highway vehicle . . . . . . . . . . . | | Form 3468, line 3 |
| | **(g)** Used commuter highway vehicle . . . . . . . . . . | | Form 3468, line 4 |
| | **(h)** Qualified rehabilitation expenditures (Enter on Form 3468, line .) . . . . | | |

| | **24** Properties: | A | B | C | |
|---|---|---|---|---|---|
| **Property Subject to Recapture of Investment Credit** | **a** Description of property (state whether recovery or nonrecovery property) . | | | | Form 4255, top |
| | **b** Original rate . . . | | | | Form 4255, line 1 |
| | **c** Date placed in service | | | | Form 4255, line 2 |
| | **d** Cost or other basis . | | | | Form 4255, line 3 |
| | **e** Class of recovery property or original estimated useful life . . . . . | | | | Form 4255, line 4 |
| | **f** Applicable percentage . | | | | Form 4255, line 5 |
| | **g** Date item ceased to be investment credit property . | | | | Form 4255, line 8 |
| | **h** Period actually used . . | | | | Form 4255, line 9 |

## Schedule K–1, Copy C
## Instructions for the Partner

*(References are to the Internal Revenue Code.)*

### Purpose

The partnership uses Copy C of Schedule K–1 to report to you your share of the partnership's income, credits, and deductions. Please keep it for your records. Do not file it with your income tax return. Copy A has been filed with the IRS.

Although the partnership is not subject to income tax, you, the partner, are liable for income tax and self-employment tax on your share of the partnership income, whether or not distributed, and you must include your share on your tax return. Your share of any partnership income, gain, loss, deduction, or credit must also be reported on your return. Please read the **Limitation on Losses** under line 1 to figure how much of your share of any partnership loss is deductible.

### General Information

**Caution:** *If your partnership's tax year began after September 3, 1982, you must*
treat partnership items on your return consistent with the way the partnership treated the items on its filed return. This rule does not apply if your partnership is within the "small partnership" exception and does not elect to have the new procedures apply. See sections 6222 and 6231(a)(1) for more information.

If your treatment on your original or amended return is (or may be) inconsistent with the partnership's treatment, or if the partnership has not filed a return, you must file a statement with your original or amended return identifying and explaining the inconsistency (or noting that a partnership return has not been filed).

If you are required to file a statement but fail to do so, you may be subject to a penalty, and any deficiency that results from making the treatment of the inconsistent partnership item consistent with the partnership's treatment, may be assessed immediately.

The Service will issue details on what this statement must show.

In addition, if the items on this Schedule K–1 are from a foreign partnership, you may be required to report certain changes in your partnership interest. See section 6046A for more information.

**Regulated Futures Contracts and Straddle Positions.**—For information on how to report gains and losses from regulated futures contracts and straddles, see **Form 6781,** Gains and Losses From Commodity Futures Contracts and Straddle Positions.

**Windfall Profit Tax.**—If you are a producer of domestic crude oil, your partnership will inform you of your income tax deduction for the windfall profit tax.

**Errors.**—If you believe the partnership has made an error on your Schedule K–1, notify the partnership and ask for a corrected Schedule K–1. Do not change any items on your copy. See **Caution** above.

**International Boycotts.**—Every partnership that had operations in or related to a boycotting country, company, or national, must file Form 5713. If that partnership did not cooperate with an international boycott and notifies you of that fact, you do not have to file Form 5713, unless you had other boycotting operations.

If the partnership cooperated with an international boycott, it must give you a copy of the Form 5713 that it filed. You also must file Form 5713 to report the activities of the partnership and any other boycott operations of your own. You may lose certain tax benefits if the partnership participated in or cooperated with an international boycott. Please see Form 5713 and the instructions for details.

**Definitions.—**

**a. General Partner.** A general partner is a member of the organization who is personally liable for the obligations of the partnership.

**b. Limited Partner.** A limited partner is one whose potential personal liability for partnership debts is limited to the amount of money or other property that the partner contributed or is required to contribute to the partnership.

**c. Limited Partnership.** A limited partnership is a partnership composed of at least one general partner and one or more limited partners.

**d. Nonrecourse Loans.** Nonrecourse loans are those liabilities of the partnership for which none of the partners have any personal liability.

**Elections.—**Generally, the partnership decides how to figure taxable income from its operations. For example, it chooses the accounting method and depreciation methods it will use.

However, certain elections are made by you separately on your income tax return and not by the partnership. These elections are made under section 901 (foreign tax credit), section 617 (deduction and recapture of certain mining exploration expenditures, paid or incurred), section 57(c) (definition of net lease), section 163(d)(6) (limitation on interest on investment indebtedness), and sections 108(b)(5) or 108(d)(4) (income from discharge of indebtedness).

**Publications.—**For more information on the treatment of partnership income, deductions, and credits, see **Publication 541,** Tax Information on Partnerships, **Publication 535,** Business Expenses, **Publication 536,** Net Operating Losses and the At-Risk Limits, and **Publication 550,** Investment Income and Expenses.

## Specific Instructions

**Name, Address, and Identifying Number.** Your name, address, and identifying number, as well as the partnership's name, address, and identifying number, should be entered.

**Question B.** Question (B) should show your share of the partnership's nonrecourse liabilities and other liabilities as of the end of the year. If you terminated your interest in the partnership during the year, question (B) should show the share that existed immediately before the total disposition. (A partner's "other liability" is any partnership liability for which a partner is personally liable.)

Use the total of the two amounts for computing the adjusted basis of your partnership interest. Use the amount shown in "Other" to compute your amount at risk if the partnership was engaged in any activity other than real estate (other than mineral property). Do not include any amounts that are not at risk that may be included in "Other."

If your partnership is engaged in two or more different types of at risk activities, or a combination of at risk activities and any other activity, the partnership should give you a statement showing your share of nonrecourse liabilities and other liabilities for each activity.

See **Limitation on Losses** under line 1 for more information.

**Lines 1–24**

If you are an individual partner, take the amounts shown in column b and enter them on the lines on your tax return as indicated in column c. If you are not an individual partner, report the amounts in column b as instructed on your tax return.

**Note:** *The line numbers are references to forms in use for calendar year 1982. If you are a calendar year partner in a fiscal year 1982/1983 partnership, enter these amounts on the corresponding lines of the tax form in use for 1983.*

**Line 1.** The amount shown should reflect your share of ordinary income (loss) from all partnership business operations including at risk activities without reference to the adjusted basis of your partnership interest or your amount at risk.

**Limitation on Losses.—**Generally, you may not claim your share of a partnership loss (including capital loss) that is greater than the adjusted basis of your partnership interest at the end of the partnership's tax year.

However, special at risk rules, under section 465, apply if there is a loss from any activity (except the holding of real property, other than mineral property) carried on as a trade or business or for the production of income by the partnership. Generally, your deductible loss from each activity for the tax year is limited to the amount you are at risk for the activity at the end of the partnership's tax year, or the amount of the loss, whichever is less.

Generally, you are at risk for an activity for the cash and adjusted basis of other property you contributed to the activity and any amounts borrowed for use in the activity for which you are personally liable.

Your at risk amount does not include the proceeds from your share of any nonrecourse loan used to finance the activity or the acquisition of property used in the activity. However, you are at risk to the extent of the net fair market value of your own property (not used in the activity) which secures borrowed amounts for which you are not liable.

You are not at risk for cash, property, or borrowed amounts protected against loss by a guarantee, stop loss agreement, or other similar arrangement.

If your partnership is engaged in an activity described below in a. through e. (but not f.), you are not at risk with respect to that activity for amounts borrowed from a person who is related to you under section 267(b), or who has an interest (other than as a creditor) in the activity.

If you have amounts not at risk for an activity and share in the loss for that activity, you must figure the allowable loss to report on your tax return.

If the amount you have at risk is less than zero, you may be subject to the recapture provisions.

Any loss from a section 465 activity not allowed for this tax year will be treated as a deduction allocable to the activity in the next tax year.

Your interest in the partnership is treated as a single activity if the partnership is engaged in only one activity. If the partnership is engaged in two or more activities, you may be able to treat them as one activity if the activities are one of the following:

**a.** Films or video tapes

**b.** Section 1245 property which is leased or held for leasing

**c.** Farms

**d.** Oil and gas properties as defined under section 614

**e.** Geothermal properties as defined under section 614

**f.** Any other activities except real estate (other than mineral property) which constitute a trade or business carried on by the partnership if 65% or more of the losses for the tax year are allocable to partners who actively participate in the management of the trade or business. (You should get a separate statement of income, expenses, deductions, and credits for each activity from the partnership.)

If the partnership sells or otherwise disposes of (1) an asset used in the activity to which the at risk rules apply or (2) any part of its interest in such an activity (or if you sell or dispose of your interest), you should combine the gain or loss on the sale or disposition with the profit or loss from the activity to determine the net profit or loss from the activity. If this is a net loss, it may be limited because of the at risk rules.

Special transitional rules for movies, video tapes, and leasing activities can be found in section 204(c)(2) and (3) of the Tax Reform Act of 1976 and **Publication 536.**

If your partnership is engaged in an activity which is subject to the limitations of section 465(c)(1), you need to determine the amount you are at risk. To help you do this, the partnership should give you your share of the total pre-1976 loss(es) from a section 465(c)(1) activity (i.e., film or video tapes, section 1245 property leasing, farm, or oil and gas property) for which there existed a corresponding amount of nonrecourse liability at the end of the year in which this loss(es) occurred.

**Line 4.** For 1982, if you are an individual partner, you can subtract up to $100 ($200 on a joint return) of qualifying dividend income.

**Line 7.** The partnership will give you a schedule that separately shows your share of the amount to enter on Form 4684, line 20, column (B)(i) and column (B)(ii). On line 20, column (A), enter the words "From (name of partnership)."

**Line 9.** Amounts on this line are other items of income, gain, or loss not included on lines 1–8 such as: (1) interest from an All-Savers Certificate (ASC) (if in a prior year you excluded interest income from a partnership ASC and the partnership redeemed the ASC in the next year before its maturity, you must include in income any interest you excluded in a prior year from this ASC); (2) partnership gains from disposition of farm recapture property (see Form 4797) and other items to which sections 1251 and 1252 apply; (3) recoveries of bad debts, prior taxes, and delinquency amounts (section 111); (4) gains and losses from wagers (section 165(d)); (5) and any income, gain, or loss to the partnership under section 751(b). The partnership should give you a description and the amount of your share for each of these items.

**Line 11.** The **TOTAL** amount of section 179 expense you claim from **ALL** sources cannot be more than $5,000 ($2,500 if you are married filing a separate return). See **Form 4562,** Depreciation and Amortization for more information.

**Line 12b.** If there is a defined benefit plan, the partnership should give you a statement showing the amount of benefit accrued for the tax year.

363–098–1

**Line 13.** Amounts on this line are other deductions not included on lines 10–12c such as: other itemized deductions (1040 filers enter on Schedule A); any penalty on early withdrawal of savings; soil and water conservation expenditures (section 175); deduction and recapture of certain mining exploration expenditures paid or incurred (section 617); expenditures for the removal of architectural and transportation barriers to the elderly and handicapped which the partnership has elected to treat as a current expense (section 190); and intangible drilling costs (see **Publication 535** for more information). The partnership should give you a description and the amount of your share for each of these items.

**Line 14.** The amount shown is your share of the jobs credit. See Form 5884 for definitions, special rules, and limitations.

**Line 15.** Complete Form 6478 and attach it to your return.

**Line 17.** Amounts on this line are other credits (other than investment credit which is reported on line 23) not included in lines 14, 15, and 16, such as: nonconventional source fuel credit; unused credits from cooperatives; and the credit for increasing research activities (enter this credit on **Form 6765,** Credit for Increasing Research Activities). The partnership should give you a description and the amount of your share for each of these items.

**Line 18a.** If you are an individual partner, enter the amount from this line on Schedule E, Part IV, line 38. You may also use this amount to figure self-employment income under the optional method (Schedule SE (Form 1040), Part II).

**Line 18b.** Net earnings from self-employment must be adjusted by the section 179 expense claimed, unreimbursed partnership expenses claimed, and depletion claimed on oil and gas properties.

If the amount on this line is a loss, enter only the deductible amount on Schedule SE. See **Limitation on Losses** under line 1.

**Line 18c.** The partnership should give you a description and amount of your share for each of the following:

**a.** Taxes paid on undistributed capital gains by a regulated investment company. (Form 1040 filers enter on line 66, and add the words "from 1065.")

**b.** Number of gallons of the fuels used during the tax year for each type of use

identified on Form 4136 and in the related instructions.

**c.** Gross non-farm income which is used by an individual partner to figure self-employment income under the optional method (Schedule SE (Form 1040), Part II).

**d.** Your share of gross income from the property, share of production for the tax year, etc., needed to figure your depletion deduction for oil and gas wells. The partnership should also allocate to you a proportionate share of the adjusted basis of each partnership oil or gas property. The allocation of the basis of each property is made as specified in section 613A(c)(7)(D). See **Publication 535,** for how to figure your depletion deduction.

**e.** If you are a corporation, (1) any income allocable to you that is "timber preference income" under section 57(e), and (2) your share of construction period interest and taxes, if any. You must add your share of the amortization deduction for these items to your share of partnership income (loss) shown on Schedule K–1, line 1.

**Line 19.** Any items of income, gain, loss, deduction, or credit, subject to a special allocation under the partnership agreement that are different from the allocation of partnership income or loss, should be entered here and not on any other line on this form.

Income or gain will be shown as a positive number; losses will be shown with the number in parentheses; a credit will be labeled as "CR."

You must include specially allocated items in determining the limitations on losses discussed under line 1.

**Lines 20c and 20g.** If (1) your partnership is a fiscal year partnership whose tax year began in 1982 and ended in 1983; and (2) your tax year in which you are required to include the items shown on this Schedule K–1 began after 12/31/82:

**a.** Do not include on your return any amount on line 20c that is for amortization of on-the-job training facilities or amortization of child care facilities.

**b.** Enter the information on the schedule attached for line 20g on your tax return as instructed.

**Line 21.** If the partnership paid or accrued interest on debts it incurred to buy or hold investment property, the amount of in-

terest you can deduct may be limited. The partnership should have entered the interest on investment indebtedness and items of investment income and expenses, and gains and losses from the sale or exchange of investment property.

For more information and the special provisions that apply to "out of pocket" expenses and rental income from property subject to a net lease, see section 163(d) and **Publication 550,** Investment Income and Expenses. (Individuals, estates, and trusts, also see **Form 4952.**)

**Note:** Generally, if your **TOTAL** investment interest including investment interest **FROM ALL OTHER SOURCES** (including carryovers, etc.) is less than $10,000 ($5,000 if married filing separately), you do not need to get Form 4952. Instead, you may enter the amounts of investment interest directly on Schedule A (Form 1040) and/or Schedule E (Form 1040), whichever is applicable.

**Lines 22a–22g.** Use the information on lines 22a through 22g to figure your foreign tax credit. For more information, see:

- **Form 1116,** Computation of Foreign Tax Credit—Individual, Fiduciary, or Nonresident Alien, and the related instructions, or

- **Form 1118,** Computation of Foreign Tax Credit—Corporations, and the related instructions.

**Line 23.** Your share of the partnership's investment in qualifying property that is eligible for the investment credit should be entered. You are allowed a tax credit based on your pro rata share of this investment by filing **Form 3468,** Computation of Investment Credit. (For other information, see Form 3468 and related instructions.)

In addition to the qualifying property reported on line 23, the partnership will give you a separate schedule that shows your share of the partnership's investment in qualified energy property that is eligible for the credit, if any, and where to report it.

**Line 24.** When investment credit property is disposed of or ceases to qualify before the "life-years category" or "recovery period" assigned, you will be notified. You may have to recapture (pay back) the investment credit taken in prior years. Use the information on line 24 to figure your recapture tax on Form 4255.

You may also need Form 4255, if you disposed of more than one-third of your interest in a partnership. See **Publication 572,** Investment Credit, for more information.

## B–8 FORM 2106 EMPLOYEE BUSINESS EXPENSES

| Form **2106**<br>Department of the Treasury<br>Internal Revenue Service | **Employee Business Expenses**<br>(Please use Form 3903 to figure moving expense deduction.)<br>▶ Attach to Form 1040. | OMB No. 1545–0139<br>19**82**<br>54 |
|---|---|---|

| Your name | Social security number | Occupation in which expenses were incurred |
|---|---|---|
| Employer's name | Employer's address | |

**Part I**    **Employee Business Expenses Deductible in Figuring Adjusted Gross Income on Form 1040, Line 32**

| | |
|---|---|
| 1 Reimbursed and unreimbursed fares for airplane, boat, bus, taxicab, train, etc. . . . . . . . | **1** |
| 2 Reimbursed and unreimbursed expenses for meals and lodging while away from your main place of work . . . . | **2** |
| 3 Reimbursed and unreimbursed car expenses from Part II . . . . . . . . . . . . . . | **3** |
| 4 Reimbursed and unreimbursed outside salesperson's expenses other than those shown on lines 1, 2, and 3 ▶ | |
| | **4** |
| 5 Reimbursed expenses other than those shown on lines 1 through 4 . . . . . . . . . | **5** |
| 6 Add lines 1 through 5 . . . . . . . . . . . . . . . . . . . . . . . | **6** |
| 7 Employer's payments for these expenses only if not included on Form W–2 . . . . . . . | **7** |
| 8 If line 6 is more than line 7, subtract line 7 from line 6. Enter here and on Form 1040, line 24 . . | **8** |
| 9 If line 7 is more than line 6, subtract line 6 from line 7. Enter here and on Form 1040, line 7 . . | **9** |

**Part II**    **Car Expenses (Use either your actual expenses or the mileage rate.)**

| | Car 1 | Car 2 | Car 3 |
|---|---|---|---|
| A. Number of months you used car for business during 1982 | _____ months | _____ months | _____ months |
| B. Total mileage for months in line A . . . . . . . . . | _____ miles | _____ miles | _____ miles |
| C. Business part of line B mileage . . . . . . . . . . | _____ miles | _____ miles | _____ miles |

**Actual Expenses**   (Include expenses on lines 1 and 2 only for the months shown in line A, above.)

| | | Car 1 | Car 2 | Car 3 |
|---|---|---|---|---|
| 1 Gasoline, oil, lubrication, etc. . . . . . . . . . | **1** | | | |
| 2 Other . . . . . . . . . . . . . . . . | **2** | | | |
| 3 Total (add lines 1 and 2) . . . . . . . . . . . | **3** | | | |
| 4 Divide line C by line B, above . . . . . . . . . | **4** | % | % | % |
| 5 Multiply line 3 by line 4 . . . . . . . . . . . | **5** | | | |
| 6 Depreciation (based on percentage shown on line 4) . | **6** | | | |
| **Note:** Do not complete line 7 if you use ACRS or 12 months is entered on line A above. Go to line 8. | | | | |
| 7 Divide line 6 by 12 months . . . . . . . . . | **7** | | | |
| 8 Multiply line 7 by line A, or enter the amount from line 6 if line 7 was not completed . . . . . . . . . | **8** | | | |
| 9 Section 179 expense deduction (see instructions) . . | **9** | | | |
| 10 Business parking fees and tolls . . . . . . . . | **10** | | | |
| 11 Total (add lines 5, 8, 9, and 10). Enter here and in Part I, line 3 . . | **11** | | | |

**Mileage Rate**

| | | |
|---|---|---|
| 12 Enter the smaller of (a) 15,000 miles or (b) the total mileage (Car 1 + Car 2 + Car 3) from line C, above . . . . | **12** | miles |
| 13 Multiply line 12 by 20¢ (11¢ if applicable, see instructions) . . . . . . . . . . . . . . | **13** | |
| 14 Enter the total mileage, if any (Car 1 + Car 2 + Car 3) from line C that is over 15,000 miles . . . . . . | **14** | miles |
| 15 Multiply line 14 by 11¢ and enter here . . . . . . . . . . . . . . . . . . . | **15** | |
| 16 Business part of car interest, parking fees, tolls, and State and local taxes (except gasoline tax) . | **16** | |
| 17 Total (add lines 13, 15, and 16). Enter here and in Part I, line 3 . . . . . . . . | **17** | |

**Part III**    **Information About Educational Expenses Shown in Part I or on Schedule A (Form 1040)**

| | |
|---|---|
| 1 Did you need this education to meet the basic requirements for your business or profession? . . . . . . . | ☐ Yes ☐ No |
| 2 Will this study program qualify you for a new business or profession? . . . . . . . . . . . . . | ☐ Yes ☐ No |

**Note:** If your answer to question 1 or 2 is "Yes," stop here. You cannot deduct these expenses, even if you do not intend to change your business or profession.

3 If "No," list the courses you took and their relationship to your business or profession. ▶ _____

---

**For Paperwork Reduction Act Notice, see instructions on back.**      363–147–1      Form **2106** (1982)

## General Instructions

**Paperwork Reduction Act Notice.**—We ask for the information to carry out the Internal Revenue laws of the United States. We need it to ensure that you are complying with these laws and to allow us to figure and collect the right amount of tax. You are required to give us this information.

**Purpose.**—Use this form **or** a similar statement to show employee business expenses if:

● You were not required to account to your employer for your expenses; or

● You were required to account to your employer for your expenses but did not do so; or

● You were required to account to your employer and you did so, but your expenses were more than your reimbursement and you wish to deduct the excess expenses. For other situations, see **Publication 463.**

Complete and file Form 2106 if you have deductible educational expenses. See the instructions for Part III.

**Amounts to Include on Form 2106.**—Include the following kinds of expenses, provided you paid or incurred them in 1982 in connection with services you performed as an employee during 1982:

**a. Reimbursed expenses.** These are expenses you paid or incurred under a reimbursement or other expense allowance arrangement with your employer.

A reimbursement or other expense allowance arrangement exists if you receive a separate payment for expenses from your employer or, if both wages and the reimbursement or allowance are combined in one single payment, the reimbursement or allowance is specifically identified. If you are required to pay your own expenses, you do not have a reimbursement or expense allowance arrangement.

**b. Expenses for travel while away from home.** These are expenses you paid or incurred for travel, meals, and lodging while you were away from home or your main place of work overnight.

**c. Transportation expenses.** These are expenses you paid or incurred for transportation (cab fares, bus fares, etc. and a pro rata share of the expenses of operating your car) **other than for** (1) travel expenses as described in **b.** above; or (2) expenses paid or incurred for commuting to and from work.

**d. Outside salesperson's expenses.** These are any expenses you paid or incurred in soliciting business for your employer away from your employer's place of business. You are not an outside salesperson if your duties consist of service and delivery or if you do any selling at your employer's place of business.

Also include on Form 2106, line 7, Part I, payments you received as reimbursement for expenses you paid or incurred if these payments are not shown on your Form W–2 and you are otherwise required to file Form 2106.

**Amounts Not to Include on Form 2106.**—If you paid or incurred any employee business expenses other than those listed in **a.** through **d.**, report them on **Schedule A** (Form 1040), line 25 or 26, whichever applies.

**Attachments.**—If you need more space, attach additional sheets. Show on each sheet to which part of Form 2106 the separate sheet relates.

**Publications.**—See the following publications for more information about employee business expenses and the records you must keep:

● **Publication 463,** Travel, Entertainment, and Gift Expenses.

● **Publication 508,** Educational Expenses.

● **Publication 529,** Miscellaneous Deductions.

● **Publication 534,** Depreciation.

● **Publication 587,** Business Use of Your Home.

## Specific Instructions

### Part I

**Line 2.**—Do not deduct the cost of your meals or lodging on one-day trips when you did not need sleep or rest. However, you can deduct on line 1 or line 3, whichever applies, the transportation expenses you incurred on these one-day trips.

**Line 5.**—Complete this line if ALL of the following apply:

● You were not an outside salesperson; and

● You paid or incurred business expenses other than those described on lines 1 through 4; and

● You were partially or fully reimbursed for these expenses. (If you did not receive any reimbursement, report the expenses on Schedule A (Form 1040), line 25 or 26, whichever applies.); and

● Any reimbursement is shown either on your Form W–2 or on line 7, Part I, Form 2106.

Enter the following amount on line 5:

● If you were reimbursed in full, enter the total expenses.

● If you were partially reimbursed, enter the expenses to the extent of the reimbursement. Enter any excess expenses on Schedule A (Form 1040), line 25 or 26, whichever applies. Example: You paid $600 for educational expenses. Your employer reimbursed you $200. You would enter $200 on line 5 and $400 on Schedule A (Form 1040).

● If you received a partial reimbursement that was intended to cover all expenses described on lines 1, 2, 3, and 5, use the formula in **Publication 463** to figure the amount to enter.

## Part II

Generally, you may use either of two methods to determine your deductible car expenses for business purposes. These two methods are:

**a.** The **actual cost** of your car expenses (such as gas, oil, repairs, depreciation, section 179 expense, etc.). **OR**

**b.** The **standard mileage rate** which gives you a fixed deduction per business mile. **DO NOT** use this method if **any** of the following apply.

● The car is leased or used for hire; or

● More than one car is used in your business at a time; or

● You elect to expense deductions for recovery property under section 179; or

● Your car was placed in service before 1/1/81, and you used a method of depreciation other than straight-line in earlier years; or

● Your car was placed in service during 1981 and you used ACRS (Accelerated Cost Recovery System) on this car last year. In this case, you must use actual expenses for as long as you use this car for business purposes.

If you are eligible to use the standard mileage rate, you may want to figure your deduction under both methods and use whichever one gives you the larger deduction.

**Note:** *If you use the mileage rate, you are considered to have made an election to exclude this car from ACRS.*

### Actual Expenses

**Line 2.**—Include on this line your actual expenses for repairs, tires, supplies, insurance, taxes, tags, licenses, interest, etc.

**Line 6.**—Do not deduct depreciation in excess of your basis or if your car is fully depreciated. For more information, see **Publication 463.**

The method of depreciation you may use depends on when you started using your car for business purposes (placed the car in service).

**Cars placed in service before 1/1/81.**—If you used either straight-line depreciation or the standard mileage rate in earlier years, you may use either straight-line depreciation or the standard mileage rate this year. If you used a method of depreciation other than straight-line, continue to use that method. If you want to change to straight-line depreciation or to an-other method of depreciation, see **Publication 534.** You cannot change to the Accelerated Cost Recovery System (ACRS).

**Cars placed in service after 12/31/80.**—If you placed a car in service after 1980 and you do not use the standard mileage rate, you must use one of two methods for figuring depreciation under ACRS:

● One ACRS method lets you deduct the following percentages of the business cost or other basis of your car regardless of what month you placed the car in service—

1st year—25%
2nd year—38%
3rd year—37%

**Example:** You bought a new car, without a trade-in, for $10,000 in September 1982, and used it 60% for business. You did not make the section 179 election. Your basis for depreciation is $6,000 ($10,000 × 60%). For 1982, your depreciation deduction is $1,500 ($6,000 × 25%). If your percentage of business use changes in 1983, you must refigure your basis for depreciation.

● The other ACRS method allows you to use a straight-line method over a recovery period of 3, 5, or 12 years with the half-year convention.

Do not consider salvage value in either of the ACRS methods.

See **Publication 463** for details on how to figure the deduction under either method and on how to figure your basis for depreciation if you traded in your car during 1982 for another car.

**Investment Credit.**—If you placed a car in service during 1982, see **Form 3468,** Computation of Investment Credit, to determine the amount of investment credit you can take.

**Line 9.**—You may elect to expense the cost related to the percentage of business use of your car in an amount up to $5,000 ($2,500 if you are married filing a separate return). However, the total amount of section 179 expense you claim from all sources cannot be more than $5,000 ($2,500 if you are married filing a separate return). Reduce your basis for figuring depreciation on line 6 by any amount you elect to expense on line 9. See **Publication 463** for more information.

### Mileage Rate

Use 20¢ a mile for the first 15,000 miles of business use a year.

Use 11¢ a mile for each mile over 15,000 business miles a year. You must also use 11¢ a mile if your car is fully depreciated.

If you use the standard mileage rate to figure the cost of business use, the car is considered to have a useful life of 60,000 miles of business use at the maximum standard mileage rate. After 60,000 miles of business use at the maximum rate, the car is considered to be fully depreciated. (For details, see **Publication 463.**)

**Line 16.**—Enter the business part of what you spent for parking, tolls, interest, and State and local taxes (except gasoline tax). The business part of parking and tolls is the amount you paid or incurred for business purposes. The business part of interest and State and local taxes is the total amount for these items multiplied by the percentage you get when you divide line C by line B.

## Part III

If you show educational expenses in Part I or on Schedule A (Form 1040), complete Part III.

You can deduct the cost of education that helps you keep or improve your skills in the business or profession you are in now. This includes education that your employer, the law, or regulations require you to get in order to keep your job or your salary in this business or profession. Do not deduct the cost of study that helps you meet the basic requirements for your business or profession or qualifies you for a new business or profession even if you don't intend to change to a new business or profession. See **Publication 508** for more information on educational expenses.

## B-9 FORM 2119 SALE OR EXCHANGE OF PRINCIPAL RESIDENCE

| Form **2119** | **Sale or Exchange of Principal Residence** | OMB No. 1545-0072 |
|---|---|---|
| Department of the Treasury Internal Revenue Service | ▶ See instructions on back. ▶ Attach to Form 1040 for year of sale (see instruction C). | **1982** 24 |

*Do not include expenses that you deduct as moving expenses.*

| Name(s) as shown on Form 1040 | Your social security number |
|---|---|

| | | Yes | No |
|---|---|---|---|
| 1 (a) | Date former residence sold ▶ | | |
| (b) | Enter the face amount of any mortgage, note (for example second trust), or other financial instrument on which you will receive periodic payments of principal or interest from this sale ▶ | | |
| (c) | Have you ever postponed any gain on the sale or exchange of a principal residence? . . . . . . . . . | | |
| (d) | If you were on active duty in the U.S. Armed Forces or outside the U.S. after the date of sale of former residence, enter dates. From _____ to _____ | | |
| 2 (a) | If you bought or built a new residence, enter date you occupied it; Otherwise enter "none". ▶ | | |
| (b) | Did you use both the old and new properties as your principal residence? . . . . . . . . . . | | |
| (c) | Are any rooms in either residence rented out or used for business for which a deduction is allowed? . . . . (If "Yes" do not include gain in line 7 from the rented or business part; instead include in income on Form 4797.) | | |

### Part I  Gain and Adjusted Sales Price

| | | | |
|---|---|---|---|
| 3 | Selling price of residence. (Do not include selling price of personal property items.) . . . . . . . | 3 | 60 000 |
| 4 | Commissions and other expenses of sale not deducted as moving expenses . . . . . . . . . | 4 | 6000 |
| 5 | Amount realized (subtract line 4 from line 3) . . . . . . . . . . . . . . . | 5 | 54 000 |
| 6 | Basis of residence sold . . . . . . . . . . . . . . . . | 6  40 000 | | |
| 7 | Gain on sale (subtract line 6 from line 5). (If line 6 is more than line 5, enter zero and do not complete the rest of form.) If you bought another principal residence during the replacement period or if you elect the one time exclusion in Part III, continue with this form. Otherwise, enter the gain on Schedule D (Form 1040), line 2a or 9a* . . . . . . . . | 7  14 000 | 00 | |

*Realized 67*

If you haven't replaced your residence, do you plan to do so within the replacement period? ☐ Yes ☐ No

(If "Yes" see instruction C.)

| | | | |
|---|---|---|---|
| 8 | Fixing-up expenses (see instructions for time limits.) . . . . . . . . . . . . | 8 | 1000 |
| 9 | Adjusted sales price (subtract line 8 from line 5) . . . . . . . . . . . . . . | 9 | 53000 |

### Part II  Gain to be Postponed and Adjusted Basis of New Residence

| | | | |
|---|---|---|---|
| 10 | Cost of new residence . . . . . . . . . . . . . . . . . . . . | 10 | 75 000 |
| 11 | Gain taxable this year (Subtract line 10 from line 9. Do not enter more than line 7.) If line 10 is more than line 9, enter zero. Enter any taxable gain on Schedule D (Form 1040), line 2a or 9a. *If you were 55 or over on the date of sale, see Part III . . . . . . . . . . . . . . . | 11 | — 0 — |
| 12 | Gain to be postponed (subtract line 11 from line 7) . . . . . . . . . . . . | 12 | 14000 |
| 13 | Adjusted basis of new residence (subtract line 12 from line 10) . . . . . . . . | 13 | 61 000 |

### Part III  55 or over Exclusion, Gain to be Reported, and Adjusted Basis of New Residence

| | | Yes | No |
|---|---|---|---|
| 14 (a) | Were you 55 or over on date of sale? . . . . . . . . . . . . . . . | | |
| (b) | Was your spouse 55 or over on date of sale? . . . . . . . . . . . . (If you answered "No" to 14(a) and 14(b), do not complete the rest of form.) | | |
| (c) | If you answered "Yes" to 14(a) or 14(b) did you or your spouse own and use the property sold as your principal residence for a total of at least 3 years (except for short temporary absences) of the 5-year period before the sale? | | |
| (d) | If you answered "Yes" to 14(c), do you elect to take the once in a lifetime exclusion of the gain on the sale? . . (If "Yes," complete the rest of Part III. If "No," return to Part II, line 12.) | | |
| (e) | At time of sale, was the residence owned by: ☐ you, ☐ your spouse, ☐ both of you? | | |
| (f) | Social security number of spouse, at time of sale, if different from number on Form 1040 ▶................... (Enter "none" if you were not married at time of sale.) | | |

| | | | |
|---|---|---|---|
| 15 | Enter the smaller of line 7 or $125,000 ($62,500, if married filing separate return) . . . . | 15 | |
| 16 | Part of gain included (subtract line 15 from line 7) . . . . . . . . . . . . | 16 | |
| 17 | Cost of new residence. If you did not buy a new principal residence, enter "None." Then enter the gain from line 16 on Schedule D (Form 1040), line 9a,* and do not complete the rest of Form 2119 . . . . | 17 | |
| 18 | Gain taxable this year. (Subtract the sum of lines 15 and 17 from line 9. The result cannot be more than line 16.) If line 17 plus line 15 is more than line 9, enter zero. Enter any taxable gain on Schedule D (Form 1040), line 9a* . . . . | 18 | |
| 19 | Gain to be postponed (subtract line 18 from line 16) . . . . . . . . . . . | 19 | |
| 20 | Adjusted basis of new residence (subtract line 19 from line 17) . . . . . . . . . | 20 | |

*Caution: If you completed Form 6252 for the residence in 1(a), do not enter your taxable gain from Form 2119 on Schedule D.

**For Paperwork Reduction Act Notice, see back of form.**　　　　　　　　　363-148-1  Form **2119** (1982)

## Instructions

**Paperwork Reduction Act Notice.**—We ask for the information to carry out the Internal Revenue laws of the United States. We need it to ensure that you are complying with these laws and to allow us to figure and collect the right amount of tax. You are required to give us this information.

**A. Purpose.**—Use Form 2119 to report gain from selling your principal residence, whether or not you buy another. A loss is not deductible. Use this form to postpone gain or make the one-time election to exclude it from your income.

Report any taxable gain on Schedule D (Form 1040). However, if you sold your residence on the installment method, complete Form 6252, Computation of Installment Sale Income, in addition to Form 2119.

For more information, see **Publication 523**, Tax Information on Selling Your Home.

*Principal Residence.*—Postponement or Exclusion of gain applies only to the sale of your principal residence. Usually, the home where you live is your principal residence. It can be for example, a house, houseboat, housetrailer, cooperative apartment, or condominium. If you have more than one residence, your principal residence is the one you physically occupy most of the time.

**B. Postponing Gain on Sale of Principal Residence.**—Unless you elect to exclude gain from selling your principal residence, as described in instruction D, you may have to postpone the gain if you buy or build, and occupy another principal residence within 2 years before or after the sale. If, after you sell your old residence, you are on active duty in the U.S. Armed Forces for more than 90 days or you live and work outside the U.S., that time is not counted in figuring your replacement period. However, *this replacement period is never permitted to extend beyond 4 years after the date of sale.*

Any gain that you postpone in the year you sell your old residence is subtracted from the cost of your new residence and lowers its basis. If you sell the new residence in a later year and do not replace it, the postponed gain will be taxed then. However, see instruction D. If you do replace it, you may continue to postpone the gain. If you change your principal residence more than once during the replacement period, only the last residence you bought qualifies as your new residence for postponing gain, unless you sold the residence because of a job relocation and are allowed a moving expense deduction.

**C. When to File.**—File Form 2119 for the year of sale whether or not you have replaced your principal residence.

If you plan to replace your residence but have not done so by the time you file your return, and the replacement period has not expired, attach Form 2119 to Form 1040 for the year of sale, but complete lines 1(a), 2(a), and 3 through 7 only. In that case, do not include the gain on Schedule D. If you replace it after you file your return, within the replacement period, and it costs as much as the adjusted sales price of your old residence, write to notify the Director of the Internal Revenue Service

Center where you filed your return. Attach a new completed Form 2119 for the year of sale.

If you replace your residence after you file your return, within the replacement period, and it costs less than the adjusted sales price of the old one, or you do not replace it within the replacement period, file Form 1040X with a Schedule D and a new Form 2119 for the year of sale. Show the gain then. Interest will be charged on the additional tax due.

If you paid tax on the gain from selling your old residence and buy a new one within the replacement period, file Form 1040X with Form 2119 to claim any refund due you.

**D. Excluding Gain from Income.**—You can elect to exclude from your income part or all of the gain from the sale of your principal residence if you meet the following tests:

1. You were 55 or over on the date of the sale.
2. Neither you nor your spouse has already elected this exclusion after July 26, 1978.
3. You owned and occupied your residence for periods totaling at least 3 years within the 5 years ending on the date of sale.

The exclusion election is a once-in-a-lifetime election, so you may choose not to make it now.

The gain excluded from your income is never taxed. The rest of your gain is taxed in the year of sale, unless you replace the residence and postpone that part of the gain. Generally, you can make or revoke the exclusion election within 3 years from the date the return was due, including extensions, for the year you sold the residence. Use Form 1040X to amend your return.

*Married Taxpayers.*—If you and your spouse own the property jointly and file a joint return, only one of you must meet the age, ownership, and use tests for electing the exclusion. If you do not own the property jointly, only the owner must meet these tests, regardless of your filing status on Form 1040.

If you are married at the time of sale, both you and your spouse must make the election to exclude the gain. If you do not file a joint return with that spouse, that spouse must consent to the election by writing in the bottom margin of Form 2119 or on an attached statement, "I consent to Part III election," and signing.

The election does not apply separately to you and your spouse. If you and your spouse make an election during marriage and later divorce, no further elections are available to either of you or to your new spouse if you remarry.

**E. Applying Separate Gain to Basis of New Residence.**—Sometimes one spouse owns the old residence separately but both spouses own the new one jointly (or vice versa). In those cases the postponed gain from the old residence and the adjusted basis of the new one may be divided between the husband and wife.

You and your spouse may divide the gain and the adjusted basis if both of you:

1. use the old and new residences as your principal residence; and
2. sign a consent that says, "We con-

sent to reduce the basis of the new residence by the gain from selling the old residence." Write this statement in the bottom margin of Form 2119 or on an attached sheet, and sign it. If you both do not sign the consent, determine the recognition of gain in the regular way with no division.

## Line-By-Line Instructions

*Use Parts I and II to figure the gain that must be postponed. Complete Part III if you elect the one-time exclusion.*

**Line 3. Selling Price of Residence.**—Enter the amount of money you received, the amount of all notes, mortgages, or other liabilities to which the property was subject, and the fair market value of any other property you received.

**Note:** *Report interest from a note as income when received.*

**Line 4. Commissions and Other Expenses of Sale.**—This includes sales commissions, advertising expenses, attorney and legal fees, etc., incurred in order to sell the old residence. Loan charges, such as "loan placement fees" or "points" charged the seller, generally are selling expenses. Do not include amounts deducted as moving expenses.

**Line 6. Basis of Residence Sold.**—Include the original cost of the property, commissions, and other expenses incurred in buying it, plus the cost of improvements. Subtract any depreciation allowed or allowable, any casualty loss or energy credit you took on the residence, and the postponed gain on the sale or exchange of a previous principal residence. For more information, see **Publication 551**, Basis of Assets.

**Line 8. Fixing-up Expenses.**—These are decorating and repair expenses incurred only to help sell the old property. You must have incurred them for work performed within 90 days before the contract to sell was signed, and paid for within 30 days after the sale. Do not include capital expenditures for permanent improvements or replacements that are added to the basis of the property sold.

Use fixing-up expenses to figure the adjusted sales price only when you determine the gain on which tax is postponed. Do not deduct these expenses when you determine your actual profit from selling your old residence.

**Lines 10 and 17. Cost of New Residence.**—The cost of your new residence includes one or more of the following:

(a) cash payments;
(b) the amount of any mortgage or other debt on the new residence;
(c) commissions and other purchase expenses you paid that were not deducted as moving expenses;
(d) construction costs (when you build your own residence) made within 2 years before and 2 years after the sale of the old residence;
(e) if you buy rather than build your new residence, all capital expenditures made within 2 years before and 2 years after the sale of the old residence.

## B-10 FORM 2210 UNDERPAYMENT OF ESTIMATED TAX BY INDIVIDUALS

| Form **2210**<br>Department of the Treasury<br>Internal Revenue Service | **Underpayment of<br>Estimated Tax by Individuals**<br>▶ See instructions on back<br>▶ Attach to Form 1040 | OMB No. 1545-0140<br>19**82**<br>56 |
|---|---|---|

| Name(s) as shown on Form 1040 | Social security number |
|---|---|

### Part I — Figuring Your Underpayment

If you qualify to refigure the taxable amount of your unemployment compensation (line 20b, Form 1040, or line 9b, Form 1040A), check this box ▶ ☐. (See instructions under Taxable Unemployment Compensation.)

| | | |
|---|---|---|
| **1** 1982 tax (from Form 1040, line 59) . . . . . . . . . . . . . . | **1** | |
| **2** Add the amounts on lines 52, 53, 55, 56, 62, and 65, Form 1040. Also add tax on an IRA from Part I or III, Form 5329, reported on line 57, Form 1040. Write total here . . . . . . . . . . . . . | **2** | |
| **3** Subtract line 2 from line 1 . . . . . . . . . . . . . . . . . . | **3** | |
| **4** Add the amounts on lines 60 and 64, Form 1040, and write the total here . . . . | **4** | |
| **5** Subtract line 4 from line 3. (If less than $200, stop here; do not complete the rest of this form.) . . . | **5** | |
| **6** Multiply the amount on line 3 by .80 and enter result here . . . . . . . . . . . . | **6** | |

| | | Payment Due Dates | | | |
|---|---|---|---|---|---|
| | | **(a)**<br>Apr. 15, 1982 | **(b)**<br>June 15, 1982 | **(c)**<br>Sept. 15, 1982 | **(d)**<br>Jan. 17, 1983 |
| **7** Divide amount on line 6 by the number of payments required for the year (usually four). Enter the result in appropriate columns . . . . . . . . . | **7** | | | | |
| **8** Estimated tax paid and tax withheld (see instructions) | **8** | | | | |
| **9** Overpayment (on line 11) from previous period (see instructions) . . . . . . . . . . . . . | **9** | ▨ | | | |
| **10** Add lines 8 and 9 . . . . . . . . . . | **10** | | | | |
| **11** Underpayment. (Subtract line 10 from line 7.) **OR** Overpayment. (Subtract line 7 from line 10.) . . | **11** | | | | |

### Part II — Exceptions to the Penalty (Farmers and fishermen, see instructions for special exception.)

| | | | | | |
|---|---|---|---|---|---|
| **12** Total amount paid and withheld from January 1 to and including the payment due date shown . . | **12** | | | | |
| | | 25% of 1981 tax: | 50% of 1981 tax: | 75% of 1981 tax: | 100% of 1981 tax: |
| **13** Exception 1.—(See instructions.) Enter 1981 tax . . ▶ | **13** | $ | | | |
| | | Enter 25% of tax: | Enter 50% of tax: | Enter 75% of tax: | Enter 100% of tax: |
| **14** Exception 2.—Tax on 1981 income using 1982 rates and exemptions. (See instructions and attach computation.) | **14** | | | | |
| | | Enter 20% of tax: | Enter 40% of tax: | Enter 60% of tax: | |
| **15** Exception 3.—Tax on annualized 1982 income. (See instructions and attach computation.) . . . . | **15** | | | | Exceptions<br>Do Not<br>Apply ▨ |
| | | Enter 90% of tax: | Enter 90% of tax: | Enter 90% of tax: | |
| **16** Exception 4.—Tax on 1982 income over 3-, 5-, and 8-month periods. (See worksheet on back.) . . . | **16** | | | | |

### Part III — Figuring the Penalty (Complete lines 17a through 19, if none of the exceptions in Part II applies.)

| | | | | | |
|---|---|---|---|---|---|
| **17 a** Number of days after due date of payment to and including date of payment or December 31, 1982, whichever is earlier. If December 31 is earlier, enter 260, 199, and 107 respectively . . . . | **17a** | ▨ | | | ▨ |
| **b** Number of days after due date of payment to and including date of payment or April 15, 1983, whichever is earlier. If April 15 is earlier, enter 88 | **17b** | ▨ | | | ▨ |
| **c** Number of days after December 31, 1982, to and including date of payment or April 15, 1983, whichever is earlier. If April 15 is earlier, enter 105 in each column . . . . . . . . . . | **17c** | | | | ▨ |
| **18 a** $\frac{\text{Number of days on line 17a}}{365} \times 20\% \times \frac{\text{underpayment on}}{\text{line 11}}$ . . . . . | **18a** | ▨ | | | ▨ |
| **b** $\frac{\text{Number of days on line 17b}}{365} \times 16\% \times \frac{\text{underpayment on}}{\text{line 11}}$ . . . . . | **18b** | | | | ▨ |
| **c** $\frac{\text{Number of days on line 17c}}{365} \times 16\% \times \frac{\text{underpayment on}}{\text{line 11}}$ . . . . . | **18c** | | | | ▨ |
| **19** Penalty (add amounts on lines 18a, b, and c). Check the box below line 71 on Form 1040 and show this amount in the space provided. If you owe tax, add penalty to tax and show total on line 71. If you are due a refund, subtract penalty from overpayment on line 68 . . . . . . . . . . . . . . . . | **19** | | | | |

| For Paperwork Reduction Act Notice, see back of form. | 363-150-2 | Form **2210** (1982) |
|---|---|---|

## General Instructions

**Paperwork Reduction Act Notice.**—We ask for this information to carry out the Internal Revenue laws of the United States. We need it to ensure that you are complying with these laws and to allow us to figure and collect the right amount of tax. You are required to give us this information.

**Purpose.**—Everyone must prepay each year's tax, either by having tax withheld or by paying estimated tax. If you are not a qualified farmer or fisherman, use this form: (1) to see if you paid enough estimated tax in each of the four payment periods (Part I); (2) if you did not, to see if any of the exceptions apply (Part II); and (3) if none applies, to figure the penalty (Part III).

For more information about the penalty and the exceptions, see **Publication 505**, Tax Withholding and Estimated Tax. You can get publications from the IRS Forms Distribution Center for your State.

**Taxable Unemployment Compensation.**—If you received taxable unemployment compensation during 1982, you may be able to reduce the taxable amount for purposes of figuring any underpayment penalty. Please get **Publication 905**, Tax Information on Unemployment Compensation, to see if you qualify to use a reduced amount and, if so, how to figure the amount. If you qualify, check the box in Part I.

**Farmers and Fishermen.**—If you meet both the following tests, you do not owe a penalty for underpaying estimated tax. Do not file this form.

    (1) Your gross income from farming and fishing is at least two-thirds of your annual gross income for 1981 or 1982, and

    (2) You filed Form 1040 and paid the tax by March 1, 1983.

If you meet test (1) but not test (2), use **Form 2210F**, Underpayment of Estimated Tax by Farmers and Fishermen, to see if you owe a penalty.

For a definition of gross income: farmers, see **Publication 225**; fishermen, see **Publication 595**.

## Specific Instructions

**Part I.**—If line 5 is $200 or more, complete lines 6 through 11. Follow the instructions for lines 8 and 9. If you have an underpayment in any column on line 11, go to Part II.

**Line 8.**—You are considered to have paid any withheld Federal income tax or excess FICA/RRTA tax evenly over the whole year unless you can show otherwise. To figure even payments, divide the total amount withheld by 4, and enter the result in each column.

**Caution:** Complete lines 9 through 11 for one payment period before you go to the next period.

**Line 9.**—If you have an overpayment on line 11 in the column for the preceding period, subtract from that overpayment all earlier underpayments on line 11. Enter the result on line 9, in the column you are completing.

If you made more than one payment during a period, attach your computations. If you file your return and pay the tax due by January 31, 1983, you do not have to make the 4th installment (due January 17, 1983).

**Part II.**—You will not have to pay a penalty if: (1) you paid your 1982 tax payments (line 12) on time; and (2) the amount on line 12 is equal to or more than the tax figured under any of the four exceptions (explained later) for the same payment period. **No other exceptions apply.**

Since taxpayers most often meet exceptions 1 and 4 (explained later), you may want to try those exceptions first. Generally, if you receive income in a lump sum, such as a bonus, capital gains, or lottery winnings, you should consider exception 4 first.

If you cannot meet exception 1 or 4, read the explanations for exceptions 2 and 3 below. If you think exception 2 or 3 applies, please get **Publication 505**, which contains worksheets to help you figure these exceptions. (**Note:** *If you did not file a 1981 return, you may not use exception 1 or 2.*)

**Line 13.**—For exception 1, your 1981 return must cover 12 months and show a tax liability. Add the amounts on lines 47, 48, 50, and 53, Form 1040. Then add the tax from Part II, Form 5329, reported on line 52, Form 1040. Subtract the credits on lines 57 and 60, Form 1040. Also, if applicable, subtract the amount on line 3, Form 6249 (Rev. Jan. 1982) or 6249-A (1981). This is your 1981 tax. Write it in the space provided on line 13.

**Line 14.**—Exception 2 applies if your 1982 tax payments at least equal the tax (figured using the taxes and credits specified in **Publication 505**) that would have been due on your 1981 income (including self-employment income), if you had figured it using 1982 rates. Use the personal exemptions you are allowed for 1982, but use the other facts and law that apply to your 1981 return. Your 1981 return does not have to show a tax liability.

**Line 15.**—Exception 3 applies if your 1982 tax payments equal at least 80% of the tax (figured using the taxes and credits specified in **Publication 505**) on your annualized taxable income and self-employment income for periods from January 1, 1982, to March 31, May 31, or August 31, 1982.

**Line 16.**—Exception 4 applies if your 1982 tax payments equal at least 90% of the tax on your actual taxable income and self-employment income for the periods from January 1, 1982, to March 31, May 31, or August 31, 1982. Use the worksheet below to figure this exception.

| Exception 4 Worksheet | | 1/1/82 to 3/31/82 | 1/1/82 to 5/31/82 | 1/1/82 to 8/31/82 |
|---|---|---|---|---|
| 1 Enter your actual taxable income for the period . . . . . . . . . . . . | 1 | | | |
| 2 Enter tax on amount on line 1 from Tax Table, Tax Rate Schedule, or Schedule G . . . . | 2 | | | |
| 3 Enter the additional taxes from Form 1040, line 39, that apply for the period . . . . . | 3 | | | |
| 4 Enter self-employment tax from line 6 of the worksheet below . . . . . . . . . | 4 | | | |
| 5 Enter the total amounts on lines 54 and 58, Form 1040, that apply for the period . . . | 5 | | | |
| 6 Enter tax from Form 5329, Part II, reported on Form 1040, line 57, that applies for the period | 6 | | | |
| 7 Add lines 2 through 6 . . . . . . . . . . . . . . . . . . . . . . . . | 7 | | | |
| 8 Enter total credits from Form 1040, lines 41–48, 62, and 65, that apply for the period . | 8 | | | |
| 9 Subtract line 8 from line 7. Enter 90% of this amount on line 16, Part II, of this form . | 9 | | | |

| Self-Employment Tax Worksheet | | 1/1/82 to 3/31/82 | 1/1/82 to 5/31/82 | 1/1/82 to 8/31/82 |
|---|---|---|---|---|
| 1 Enter your actual self-employment income for the period . . . . . . . . . . . | 1 | | | |
| 2 Limit . . . . . . . . . . . . . . . . . . . . . . . . . . . . . . | 2 | $32,400 | $32,400 | $32,400 |
| 3 Enter your actual wages subject to FICA tax . . . . . . . . . . . . . . . . | 3 | | | |
| 4 Subtract line 3 from line 2 . . . . . . . . . . . . . . . . . . . . . . | 4 | | | |
| 5 Enter the amount on line 1 or 4, whichever is less . . . . . . . . . . . . . | 5 | | | |
| 6 Multiply the amount on line 5 by .0935 . . . . . . . . . . . . . . . . . . | 6 | | | |

# B–11 FORM 2441 CREDIT FOR CHILD AND DEPENDENT CARE EXPENSES

| Form **2441**<br>Department of the Treasury<br>Internal Revenue Service | **Credit for Child and Dependent Care Expenses**<br>▶ Attach to Form 1040.<br>▶ See Instructions below. | OMB No. 1545–0068<br>**1982**<br>26 |
|---|---|---|

| Name(s) as shown on Form 1040 | Your social security number |
|---|---|

**1** See the definition for "qualifying person" in the instructions. Then read the instructions for line 1.

| (a) Name of qualifying person | (b) Date of birth | (c) Relationship | (d) During 1982, the person lived with you for: | |
|---|---|---|---|---|
| | | | Months | Days |
| | | | | |
| | | | | |

**2** Persons or organizations who cared for those listed on line 1. See the instructions for line 2.

| (a) Name and address (If more space is needed, attach schedule) | (b) Social security number, if applicable | (c) Relationship, if any | (d) Period of care | | (e) Amount of 1982 expenses (include those not paid during the year) |
|---|---|---|---|---|---|
| | | | From Month—Day | To Month—Day | |
| | | | | | |

### To Figure Your Credit, You MUST Complete ALL Lines That Apply

**3** Add the amounts in column 2(e) . . . . . . . . . . . . . . .  **3**

**4** Enter $2,400 ($4,800 if you listed two or more names in line 1) or amount on line 3, whichever is less . . . . .  **4**

**5** Earned income (wages, salaries, tips, etc.). See the instructions for line 5. An entry MUST be made on this line.

   **(a)** If unmarried at end of 1982, enter your earned income . . . . . . . . . .  ▶  **5**

   **(b)** If married at end of 1982, enter:

      **(1)** Your earned income . . . $ _____ Enter the lesser

      **(2)** Your spouse's earned income $ _____ of b(1) or b(2) . .

**6** Enter the amount on line 4 or line 5, whichever is less . . . . . . . . .  **6**

**7** Amount on line 6 paid during 1982. An entry MUST be made on this line . . . . . ▶  **7**

**8** Multiply line 7 by percentage listed for your adjusted gross income in instructions for line 8 . . .  **8**

**9** Multiply child and dependent care expenses for 1981 paid in 1982 by 20 percent (.20) and enter the result here. See instructions for line 9 . . . . . . . . . . . . . . . .  **9**

**10** Add amounts on lines 8 and 9 . . . . . . . . . . . . . . . .  **10**

**11** Limitation:

   **a** Enter tax from Form 1040, line 40 . . . . . . . . . .  **11a**

   **b** Enter total of lines 41 through 44 of Form 1040. See instructions for line 11 . . . . . . . . . . . . . . . .  **11b**

   **c** Subtract line 11b from line 11a (if line 11b is more than line 11a, enter zero) . . . . . . .  **11c**

**12** Credit for child and dependent care expenses. Enter the smaller of line 10 or line 11c here and on Form 1040, line 45 .  **12**

| | Yes | No |
|---|---|---|
| **13** If payments listed on line 2 were made to an individual, complete the following: | | |
|   **(a)** If you paid $50 or more in a calendar quarter to an individual, were the services performed in your home? . . . . . . . . | | |
|   **(b)** If "Yes," have you filed appropriate wage tax returns on wages for services in your home (see instructions for line 13)? . . . . . | | |
|   **(c)** If answer to (b) is "Yes," enter your employer identification number . . . . . . ▶ | | |

## General Instructions

If you or your spouse worked or looked for work, and you spent money to care for a qualifying person, this form might save you tax.

**What is the Child and Dependent Care Expenses Credit?**—This is a credit you can take against your tax if you paid someone to care for your child or dependent so that you could work or look for work. You can also take the credit if you paid someone to care for your spouse. The instructions that follow list tests that must be met to take the credit. If you need more information, please get **Publication 503,** Child and Disabled Dependent Care.

For purposes of this credit, we have defined some of the terms used here. Refer to these when you read the instructions.

## Definitions

**A qualifying person can be:**

● Any person under age 15 whom you list as a dependent. (If you are divorced, legally separated, or separated under a written agreement, please see the Child Custody Test in the instructions.)

● Your spouse who is mentally or physically not able to care for himself or herself.

● Any person not able to care for himself or herself whom you can list as a dependent, or could list as a dependent except that he or she had income of $1,000 or more.

A **full-time student** is one who was enrolled in a school for the number of hours or classes that is considered full time. The student must have been enrolled at least 5 months during 1982.

## What Are Child and Dependent Care Expenses?

These expenses are the amounts you paid for household services and care of the qualifying person.

**Household Services.**—These are services performed by a cook, housekeeper, governess, maid, cleaning person, babysitter, etc. The services must have been needed to care for the qualifying person as well as run the home. For example, if you paid for the services of a maid or a cook, the services must have also been for the benefit of the qualifying person.

**Care of the Qualifying Person.**—Care includes cost of services for the well-being and protection of the qualifying person.

Care does not include expenses for food and clothes. If you paid for care that included these items and you cannot separate their cost, take the total payment.

**Example:** You paid a nursery school to care for your child and the school gave the child lunch. Since you cannot separate the cost of the lunch from the cost of the care, you can take all of the amount that you paid to the school.

This example would not apply if you had school costs for a child in the first grade or above because these costs cannot be counted in figuring the credit.

You can count care provided outside your home if the care was for your depend-

*(Continued on back)*

363–160–1

ent under age 15 or for any other qualifying person who regularly spends at least 8 hours each day in your household. Care that is provided outside your home by a dependent care center can be counted provided the center complies with all applicable State and local regulations. A dependent care center is a place that provides care for more than six persons (other than persons who live there) and receives a fee, payment, or grant for providing services for any of those persons, regardless of whether or not the center is run for profit.

You can claim medical expenses you paid for the qualifying person if you paid them so you could work or look for work. If you itemized deductions, you may want to take all or part of these expenses on Schedule A. For example, if you can't take all of the medical expenses on Form 2441 because your costs for care have reached the limit ($2,400 or $4,800), you can take the rest of the medical expenses on Schedule A. If you show all of the medical expenses on Schedule A, you cannot take on Form 2441 that part you could not deduct on Schedule A because of the 3-percent limit.

**To Take This Credit.**—You must file Form 1040, not Form 1040A, and you must meet all of the tests listed below.

*(1)* You paid for child and dependent care so you (and your spouse if you were married) could work or look for work. If you work and your spouse does not, you may still qualify to take this credit. See the instructions for line 5.

*(2)* One or more qualifying persons lived in your home.

*(3)* You (and your spouse if you were married) paid more than half the cost of keeping up your home. This cost includes rent; mortgage interest; utility charges; maintenance and repairs; property taxes and property insurance; and food costs (but not dining out).

*(4)* You must file a joint return if you were married. There are two exceptions to this rule. You can file a separate return if:

*(a)* You were legally separated; or

*(b)* You were living apart and:

• The qualifying person lived in your home for more than 6 months; and

• You paid more than half the cost of keeping up your home; and

• Your spouse did not live in your home during the last 6 months of your tax year.

*(5)* You paid someone, other than your spouse or a person for whom you could claim a dependency exemption, to care for the qualifying person.

You are allowed to pay a relative, including a grandparent, who was not your dependent. If the relative is your child, he or she must also have been 19 or over by the end of the year.

**Child Custody Test.**—If you were divorced, legally separated, or separated under a written agreement, your child is a qualifying person if you had custody for the longer period during 1982. The child must also have:

• Received over half of his or her support from the parents, and

• Been in the custody of one or both parents for more than half of 1982, and

• Been under 15, or physically or mentally unable to care for himself or herself.

**Credit Limit.**—The credit is a percentage of the amount you paid someone to care for the qualifying person. The most you can figure the credit on is $2,400 a year for one qualifying person ($4,800 for two or more).

## Specific Instructions

We have provided specific instructions for most of the lines on the form. Those lines that do not appear in the instructions are self-explanatory.

**Line 1.**—In column (d) show the number of months and days each person lived in your home during 1982. Count only the times when the person was qualified.

**Line 2.**—*In column (a)* show the name and address of the person or organization who cared for each qualifying person. If you listed a person who was your employee and who provided the care in your home, then in column (b) enter that person's social security number. Leave column (b) blank if the person: was not your employee; was self-employed; was an employee of an organization or a partnership; or did not provide the care in your home.

*In column (c)* write none if the person who provided the care was not related to you. If the care was provided by a relative, show the relationship to you.

**Line 5.**—This line is used to figure your *earned income.* Generally, you can figure earned income using steps (a) through (c) below. If you are unmarried, enter your amounts from Form 1040 when they are needed for the steps below. If you are married, each spouse's earned income will have to be figured separately and without regard to community property laws.

**If your spouse was a full-time student or not able to care for himself or herself,** use the greater of your spouse's monthly earned income or $200 a month ($400 if you listed two qualifying persons on line 1(a)) to determine his or her total income for the year.

If, in the same month, both you and your spouse were full-time students and did not work, you cannot use any amount paid that month to figure the credit. The same applies to a couple who did not work because neither was capable of self-care.

Reduce earned income by any net loss from self-employment. If your net earnings from self-employment are less than $1,600, you may be able to use the optional method to figure your self-employment income. Under this method, you may be able to increase your net earnings to $1,600. See **Publication 533,** Self-Employment Tax, for information. If you only have a loss from self-employment or your loss is more than your other earned income, and you do not use the optional method, you cannot take the credit.

(a) Enter one spouse's income from Form 1040, line 7 . . . _____

(b) Enter the same spouse's net profit or (loss) from Schedule C or Schedule F (Form 1040) if applicable _____

(c) Combine amounts on lines (a) and (b). (If the result is zero or less, enter zero.) . . . _____

If you are unmarried, enter the amount from (c) on line 5. If you are married, enter the amount from (c) on line 5(b)(1) and go back and figure your spouse's earned income using steps (a) through (c). Enter your spouse's earned income from (c) on line 5(b)(2). Enter the lesser of line 5(b) (1) or line 5(b)(2) on line 5.

**Line 7.**—How much of the amount on line 6 did you pay in 1982? Enter this amount on line 7. Do not list any amounts for 1982 that you did not pay until 1983.

**Line 8.**—Multiply the amount on line 7 by the percentage listed below for your adjusted gross income (AGI), Form 1040, line 33.

| AGI | Percentage | AGI | Percentage |
|---|---|---|---|
| Over— But not over— | | Over— But not over— | |
| 0 –$10,000 | 30% | $20,000 – 22,000 | 24% |
| $10,000 – 12,000 | 29% | 22,000 – 24,000 | 23% |
| 12,000 – 14,000 | 28% | 24,000 – 26,000 | 22% |
| 14,000 – 16,000 | 27% | 26,000 – 28,000 | 21% |
| 16,000 – 18,000 | 26% | 28,000 | 20% |
| 18,000 – 20,000 | 25% | | |

**Line 9.**—If you had child and dependent care expenses for 1981 that you did not pay until 1982, you may be able to increase the amount of credit you can take in 1982. To figure the increase in the amount of credit, multiply your 1981 child and dependent care expenses paid in 1982 by 20 percent. Your 1981 child and dependent care expenses must be within the 1981 limits. Attach a sheet similar to the example below, showing how you figured the increase.

**Example:** In 1981 you had child care expenses of $2,100 for your 12-year-old son. For one child, you were limited to $2,000. Of the $2,100, you paid $1,800 in 1981 and $300 in 1982. Your spouse's earned income of $5,000 was less than your earned income. You would be allowed to figure an increased credit of $40 in 1982, as follows:

(1) 1981 child care expenses paid in 1981 . $1,800

(2) 1981 child care expenses paid in 1982 . 300

(3) Total . . . . . . . . . . $2,100

(4) Limit for one qualifying person . . . $2,000

(5) Earned income reported in 1981 . . . $5,000

(6) Smaller of line 3, 4, or 5 . . . . . $2,000

(7) Subtract child care expenses on which credit was figured in 1981 . . . . 1,800

(8) 1981 child care expenses available for credit this year (1982) . . . . . $ 200

(9) Increase in 1982 credit. Multiply line 8 by 20% . . . . . . . . . . . $ 40

**Line 11.**—Your credit for child and dependent care expenses cannot be more than your tax after subtracting certain credits. To figure the allowable credit, enter your tax from Form 1040, line 40, on line 11a. Add the amounts, if any, you entered on Form 1040, lines 41 through 44. Also, add any WIN credit carryover you entered on Form 1040, line 46. Enter the total of these lines on line 11b. Subtract line 11b from 11a and enter the difference on line 11c. If line 11b is more than line 11a, enter zero on line 11c.

**Line 12.**—Enter the smaller of line 10 or 11c on this line and Form 1040, line 45. This is your credit for child and dependent care expenses.

**Line 13.**—In general, if you paid cash wages of $50 or more in a calendar quarter for household services to a person such as a cook, housekeeper, governess, maid, cleaning person, babysitter, etc., you must file an employment tax return. If you are not sure whether you should file an employment tax return, get Form 942, Employer's Quarterly Tax Return for Household Employees. **Note:** *You should file a Form 940, Employer's Annual Federal Unemployment Tax Return, for 1982 by January 31, 1983, if you paid cash wages of $1,000 or more for household services in any calendar quarter in 1981 or 1982.*

## B–12 FORM 3115 APPLICATION FOR CHANGE IN ACCOUNTING METHOD

| | | |
|---|---|---|
| Form **3115**<br>(Rev. Dec. 1981)<br>Department of the Treasury<br>Internal Revenue Service | **Application for Change in Accounting Method**<br>▶ For Paperwork Reduction Act Notice, see instructions on page 4.<br>Note: If you are applying for a change in accounting period, use Form 1128. | OMB No. 1545–0152<br>Expires 11–30–84<br>**CHECK ONE**<br>☐ Individual<br>☐ Partnership<br>☐ Corporation<br>☐ Cooperative (Sec. 1381(a))<br>☐ Insurance co. (Secs. 801, 821, or 831)<br>☐ Other (Specify) |

Name of applicant (if joint return is filed, show names of you and your spouse) | Identifying Number (See Instructions)

Address (Number and street)

City or town, State, and ZIP code

### Section A. Applicable To All Filers

**NOTE:** *Are you making an election under section 458 or 466?* . . . . . . . . . . . ☐ Yes ☐ No

*If "Yes," see Instructions for Section J on page 4. Do not fill in Section A.*

**1** The following change in accounting method is requested (check and complete appropriate spaces):

  **(a)** ☐ Overall method of accounting: from _____ to _____

  **(b)** ☐ The accounting treatment of (identify item) ▶ _____

    from (present method) ▶ _____ to (new method) ▶ _____

  **(c)** If Partnership, show number of partners ▶ _____ If Subchapter S corporation, show number of shareholders ▶ _____

  **(d)** Number of tax years present method has been used . . . . . . . . . . . ▶ _____

  **(e)** If change is granted, will this method be used for financial reporting purposes? . . . . ☐ Yes ☐ No

    If "No," please explain ▶ _____

**2 (a)** If a change is requested under 1(b) above, check the present overall method of accounting:

    ☐ Accrual    ☐ Cash    ☐ Hybrid (if a hybrid method is used, explain treatment of material items in detail)

  **(b)** If a change to the **Reserve Method** is requested, is it being made under Rev. Proc. 64–51? . . . . ☐ Yes ☐ No

  **(c)** If a change in depreciation method is requested, is it being made under Rev. Proc. 74–11? . . . . ☐ Yes ☐ No

  **(d)** Are you a manufacturer to whom Regulation section 1.471–11 applies? . . . . . . . ☐ Yes ☐ No

  **(e)** If "Yes," block is checked for line 2(d), are the items involved in this request properly inventoriable in accordance with Regulation section 1.471–11? . . . . . . . . . . . ☐ Yes ☐ No

    If "Yes," report the items and amounts on a separate page.

**3** Tax year of change begins (mo., day, year) ▶ _____ and ends (mo., day, year) ▶ _____

**4 (a)** Nature of business and principal source of income ▶ _____

  **(b)** Applicant's area code and telephone number ▶ _____ **(c)** District Director's office having jurisdiction ▶ _____

**5** If engaged in a business or profession: **(a)** Enter your taxable income or (loss)* from operations for tax purposes for the five (5) tax years preceding the year of change:

| 1st preceding year ended 19 | 2d preceding year ended 19 | 3d preceding year ended 19 | 4th preceding year ended 19 | 5th preceding year ended 19 |
|---|---|---|---|---|
| $ | $ | $ | $ | $ |

  **(b)** Enter the amount of net operating loss to be carried over to the year of change, if any . . . . $ _____

  **(c)** Amount of investment credit carryover to year of change, if any . . . . $ _____

  **(d)** Other credit carryover, if any. (Identify) ▶ _____ $ _____

  *Individuals enter net profit or (loss) from business; partnerships enter ordinary income or (loss).

**6** In the last 10 years, have you changed, or requested permission to change, your accounting period, your overall method of accounting, or the accounting treatment of any item? . . . . . . . . . . ☐ Yes ☐ No

  If "Yes," attach copy of ruling letter(s), if available. If copy of ruling letter(s) is not available, explain and give date permission was granted.

**7** Is applicant a member of an affiliated group filing a consolidated return for the tax year of change? . . . . ☐ Yes ☐ No

  **(a)** If "Yes," state parent corporation's name, identifying number, address, tax year, and Service Center where return is filed ▶ _____

  **(b)** If "Yes," provide the information requested in 5(a) above for each member of the affiliated group (attach schedule).

  **(c)** If "Yes," do all other members of the affiliated group employ the method of accounting for which the change is requested? ☐ Yes ☐ No. If "No," explain ▶ _____

**8** Is there an issue involving an overall change in accounting method or a change in the treatment of a material item pending before a field office of the IRS or any Federal court? . . . . . . . . . ☐ Yes ☐ No

  If "Yes," explain ▶ _____

**9** Does the adjustment under section 481(a) include a pre-1954 amount? . . . . . . . . . . ☐ Yes ☐ No

**10** Enter section 481(a) adjustments that would have been required if the requested change had been made for each tax year of the 3-year period preceding the year of change (see instructions for Section A on page 4) . . . . .

| 1st preceding year ended 19 | 2d preceding year ended 19 | 3d preceding year ended 19 |
|---|---|---|
| $ | $ | $ |

Under penalties of perjury, I declare that I have examined this application, including accompanying schedules and statements, and to the best of my knowledge and belief it is true, correct, and complete. Declaration of preparer (other than applicant) is based on all information of which preparer has any knowledge.

_____    _____    _____
Applicant's name      Signature and title      Date

_____    _____
Signature of individual or firm preparing the application (see General Instructions on page 4)      Date

## Section B. Change in Overall Method of Accounting

**1** If change is from the cash to the accrual method, check method to be employed for treating bad debts: ☐ Specific charge-off ☐ Reserve

If reserve method is to be adopted, complete item 2 under Section D below.

**2** The following amounts should be stated as of the end of the tax year **preceding** the year of change. If none, state "None." (Although some of the items listed below may not have been required in the computation of your taxable income due to your present method of accounting, it is necessary that they be entered here for this form to be complete. Show amounts attributable to long-term contracts on page 3, Section F.)

| | Amount | Show by (√) how treated on last year's return | |
|---|---|---|---|
| | | Included in income or deducted as expense | Excluded from income or not deducted as expense |
| **(a)** Income accrued but not received . . . . . | $ | | |
| **(b)** Income received before the date on which it was earned. | | | |
| State nature of income. If discount on installment loans, see Section C below _____ | | | |
| _____ | | | |
| _____ | | | |
| **(c)** Expenses accrued but not paid . . . . . | | | |
| **(d)** Other (specify) _____ | | | |
| **(e)** Prepaid expense previously deducted . . . | | | |
| **(f)** Supplies on hand previously deducted . . . | | | |
| **(g)** Inventory . . . . . . . . . Enter the amount of ending inventory **reported on your return** for the tax year preceding the year of change. $_____ | | | |
| **(h)** Reserve for bad debts . . . . . . . | | | |
| Net adjustment . . . . . . . . . | | $ | |

**3** Nature of inventory ▶ _____ **4** Method used for valuing inventories ▶ _____

**5** If the change is from the accrual to the cash method, have any receivables been sold in the past three years? ☐ Yes ☐ No

If "Yes," enter the amounts sold for each of the three years on a separate page.

**6** Attach copies of **Profit And Loss Statement** (Schedule F (Form 1040) in the case of Farmers) and **Balance Sheet,** if applicable, as of the close of the tax year preceding the year of change. State accounting method used when preparing balance sheet. If books of account are not kept, attach copy of the business schedule provided with your Federal income tax return or return of income for that period. **If amounts in 2 above do not agree with those shown on profit and loss statement and balance sheet, explain on separate page.**

## Section C. Change in Method of Reporting Interest (Discount) on Installment and Other Loans

**1** Change with respect to interest on ☐ Installment loans, ☐ Commercial loans, and ☐ Other loans (explain) ▶ _____

_____

**2** Amount of earned or realized interest that has not been reported on your return as of the end of the tax year preceding the year of change . . . . . . . . . . . . . . . . . . . . . . . . $_____

**3** Amount of unearned or unrealized interest that has been reported on your return as of the end of the tax year preceding the year of change . . . . . . . . . . . . . . . . . . . . . . . $_____

**4** Method of rebating in event of prepayment of loans ▶ _____

## Section D. Change in Method of Reporting Bad Debts

**1** If a change to the **Reserve Method** is requested and applicant has installment sales, are such sales reported on the installment method? ☐ Yes ☐ No

If "Yes," show whether change relates to: ☐ Installment sales, ☐ Sales other than installment sales, or ☐ Both.

**2** If a change to the **Reserve Method** is requested, provide the following information for the five tax years preceding the year of change:

| | 1st preceding year | 2d preceding year | 3d preceding year | 4th preceding year | 5th preceding year |
|---|---|---|---|---|---|
| Total sales . . . . . . . . | | | | | |
| Deductions for specific bad debts charged off [1] | | | | | |
| Recoveries of bad debts deducted in prior years . . . . . . . . . . . | | | | | |
| Year-end balances: | | | | | |
| Trade accounts receivable . . . | | | | | |
| Trade notes receivable [2] . . . . | | | | | |
| Installment accounts receivable [3] . | | | | | |
| Other receivables (explain in detail) | | | | | |

**3** If a change to the method of deducting specific bad debt items is requested, enter the amount in reserve for bad debts at end of the year preceding the year of change . . . . . . . . . . . . . . . . . . $_____

[1] If your return was examined, enter amount allowed as a result of the examination.
[2] If loan company, enter only capital portion.
[3] Applicable only to receivables attributable to sales reported on installment method. Enter only the capital portion of these receivables.

Form 3115 (Rev. 12–81)    **If no entries are made below, tear off this page and file only pages 1 and 2**    Page **3**

### Section E. Change in Method of Valuing Inventories. *See instruction for Section E on page 4.*

1 Nature of all inventories ▶ ................................................................................

2 Method of identifying goods in inventory . . . . . . . . . ☐ Specific identification    ☐ FIFO    ☐ LIFO.

If "LIFO," attach copy of Form 970 adopting that method and copies of any Forms 970 filed to extend the use of the method.

3 Show method and value of all inventories at the end of the tax year preceding the year of change under:

(a) Present method ▶ ....................................................................... $...............

(b) New method ▶ .......................................................................... $...............

(c) If pre-1954 adjustment is involved, provide only those amounts that can be substantiated . . . . . $...............

### Section F. Change in Method of Reporting Income from Contracts

1 Are your contracts long-term contracts as defined in Regulation section 1.451–3? . . . . . . . . . ☐ Yes    ☐ No

2 Method used for reporting long-term contracts . ☐ Completed  ☐ Percentage of completion  ☐ Accrual  ☐ Other (explain)

3 Method used for reporting short-term contracts . . . . . . . . . . . . . . . . . ☐ Accrual  ☐ Other (explain)

4 Adjustment required under section 481(a) . . . . . . . . . . . . . . . . . . . . . $...............

### Section G. Change in Method of Treating Vacation Pay

1 Is the plan(s) fully vested as of the end of the tax year preceding the year of the change? . . . . . . ☐ Yes    ☐ No

2 If "Yes," enter the amount of accrued vacation pay as of the end of the tax year preceding the year of change . . . $...............

3 Number of tax years plan(s) has been vested . . . . . . . . . . . . . . . . ▶ ...............

### Section H. Change in Overall Method of Reporting Income of Farmers to Cash Receipts and Disbursements Method

| **Note:** *Also complete Section B.* | 1st preceding yr. | 2d preceding yr. | 3d preceding yr. | 4th preceding yr. | 5th preceding yr. |
|---|---|---|---|---|---|
| 1 Total income from all sources . . | | | | | |
| 2 Net farm profit or (loss) . . . | | | | | |
| 3 Inventory: Crops, etc. . . . . . | | | | | |
| Livestock held for sale: | | | | | |
| Purchased . . . . . . | | | | | |
| Raised . . . . . . . | | | | | |
| Livestock held for draft, breeding, sport, or dairy purposes: | | | | | |
| Purchased . . . . . . | | | | | |
| Raised . . . . . . . | | | | | |
| Total inventory . . . . | | | | | |

Method used to value inventory (check appropriate block):
☐ Cost    ☐ Cost or market, whichever is lower    ☐ Farm price    ☐ Unit livestock price    ☐ Other (explain on separate page)

### Section I. Change in Method of Accounting for Depreciation

Applicants desiring to change their method of accounting for depreciation must complete this section. This information must be supplied for each account for which a change is requested. **Note:** *Certain changes in methods of accounting for depreciation may be filed with the Service Center where your return will be filed. See Rev. Proc. 74–11 for the methods covered.*

1 Date of acquisition ▶ ..................................................................................

2 Are you the original owner or the first user of the property? . . . . . . . . . . . . . . ☐ Yes    ☐ No

3 Is depreciation claimed under Regulation section 1.167(a)–11 (CLADR)? . . . . . . . . . . . . ☐ Yes    ☐ No

If "Yes," the only changes permitted are under Regulation section 1.167(a)–11(c)(1)(iii). Identify these changes on the tax return for the year of change.

4 Is the property public utility property? . . . . . . . . . . . . . . . . . . . . . . ☐ Yes    ☐ No

5 Location of the property (city and State) ▶ ......................................................

6 Type or character of the property ▶ ............................................................

7 Cost or other basis of the property and adjustments thereto (exclude land) . . . . . . . . . . $...............

8 Depreciation claimed in prior tax years (depreciation reserve) . . . . . . . . . . . . . $...............

9 Estimated salvage value . . . . . . . . . . . . . . . . . . . . . . . . . $...............

10 Estimated remaining useful life of the property ▶ ..............................................

11 If the declining balance method is requested, show percentage of straight line rate ▶ ...........

12 Other information, if any ▶ .....................................................................

### Section J. Change in Method of Accounting Not Listed Above (See instructions)

........................................................................................................

........................................................................................................

........................................................................................................

........................................................................................................

## General Instructions

**Note:** *If you are applying for a change in accounting period, use Form 1128.*

### Paperwork Reduction Act Notice

The Paperwork Reduction Act of 1980 says we must tell you why we are collecting this information, how we will use it, and whether you have to give it to us. We ask for the information to carry out the Internal Revenue laws of the United States. We need it to ensure that you are complying with these laws and to allow us to figure and collect the right amount of tax. You are required to give us this information.

### Purpose of Form

File this form to request a change in your accounting method, including the accounting treatment of any item.

**Generally, applicants must complete Section A.** In addition, complete the appropriate section (B through J) for which a change is desired.

**You must give all relevant facts, including a detailed description of your present and proposed methods. You must also state the reason(s) you believe approval to make the requested change should be granted.** Attach additional pages if more space is needed for explanations. Each page should show your name, address, and identifying number.

State whether you desire a conference in the National Office if the Service proposes to disapprove your application.

### Time and Place for Filing

Generally, applicants must file this form with the Commissioner of Internal Revenue, Washington, DC 20224, within the first 180 days of the tax year in which it is desired to make the change.

**Note:** *If this form is being filed in accordance with Rev. Proc. 74–11, see Section I below.*

### Identifying Number

**Individuals.**—Individuals should enter their social security number in this block. If the application is made on behalf of a husband and wife who file their income tax return jointly, enter the social security numbers of both. However, if an individual is engaged in a trade or business, enter the employer identification number instead of the social security number.

**Other.**—Applicants other than an individual should enter their employer identification number in this block.

### Signature

**Individuals.**—An individual desiring the change should sign the application. If the application pertains to a husband and wife, the names of both should appear in the heading and both should sign.

**Partnerships.**—The form should be signed with the partnership name followed by the signature of one of the partners and the words "Member of Partnership."

**Corporations, Cooperatives, and Insurance Companies.**—The form should show the name of the corporation, cooperative, or insurance company and the signature of the president, vice president, treasurer, assistant treasurer, or chief accounting officer (such as tax officer) authorized to sign, and their official title. Receivers, trustees, or assignees must sign any application they are required to file. For a subsidiary corporation filing a consolidated return with its parent, the form should be signed by an officer of the parent corporation.

**Fiduciaries.**—The form should show the name of the estate or trust and be signed by the fiduciary, executor, executrix, administrator, administratrix, etc. having legal authority to sign, and his or her title.

**Preparer other than partner, officer, etc.**—The signature of the individual or firm preparing the form should appear in the space provided on page 1. An application made by an agent on behalf of an applicant must be accompanied by a power of attorney authorizing the agent to sign for the applicant. If the agent is also authorized to represent the applicant before the IRS, receive a copy of the requested ruling, or perform any other act(s), the power of attorney must reflect such authorization(s).

## Specific Instructions

**Section A.**—(Item 10, page 1)—If providing the requested information causes you financial hardship or other serious inconvenience, you may do the following:

(1) Enter your best estimate of the percent of the section 481(a) adjustment that belongs to each year; and

(2) Explain in detail why you cannot provide the requested information.

If we later examine your return for the year of the change or for later years, we have the right to verify your statement at that time.

**Section B.**—(Item 2(b), page 2)—Include any amounts reported as income in a prior year although the income had not been accrued (earned) or received in the prior year; for example, discount on installment loans reported as income for the year in which the loans were made instead of for the year or years in which the income was received or earned.

**Section D.**—(Item 2, page 2)—A special procedure is available to change your method of accounting for bad debts from the specific charge-off method to the reserve method. Generally, if you comply with Rev. Proc. 64–51, as modified, you may assume the change has been approved.

Rev. Proc. 64–51, modified by Rev. Proc. 77–39, does not apply to your trade receivables that include items of unrealized income for Federal income tax purposes.

The Bad Debt Reserve must be determined as follows:

(1) Add together the net losses on bad debts for 5 years preceding the tax year of change.

(2) Divide this total by the sum of the amounts of outstanding trade receivables at the close of each of the 5 years.

(3) Multiply the amount of outstanding trade receivables at the close of the tax year of change by the resulting decimal in (2). This amount is the Bad Debt Reserve, the deduction for which is to be prorated over 10 years.

**Section E.**—Applicants must give complete details about the old method of valuing inventory and the proposed method. State whether all or part of your inventory is involved in the change.

*Inventories of retail merchants.*—The retail method of pricing inventories does not contemplate valuation of goods at the retail selling price. The retail selling prices of goods on hand must be reduced to approximate cost or cost or market, whichever is lower, by the adjustments required in Regulation section 1.471–8.

*Inventories of manufacturers and processors.*—Applicants requesting to change to the full absorption method of inventory costing must attach a schedule showing the treatment, under both their present and proposed methods, of all costs listed in Regulation sections 1.471–11(b)(2), (c)(2)(i) and (c)(2)(ii) for Federal income tax purposes, and all costs listed in or subject to Regulation section 1.471–11(c)(2)(iii) for tax and financial report purposes. If you plan to leave out one or more costs listed in Regulation section 1.471–11(c)(2)(iii) from the computation of the amount of inventoriable costs under the full absorption method, you must also attach the data required by either section 5.02 or 5.03 (whichever is appropriate) of Rev. Proc. 75–40.

*LIFO inventory changes.*—Attach a schedule with all the required computations when changing the method of figuring LIFO inventories. If you are changing from the LIFO to a non-LIFO method, attach a schedule with the following additional information:

(1) The specific types and classes of goods in the LIFO inventories involved in the proposed change and the comparative values of such inventories as of the end of the tax year preceding the year of change determined by (a) the LIFO method and (b) the proposed method and basis (such as cost or lower of cost or market).

(2) State whether the proposed method and basis conforms to the inventory method currently used with respect to non-LIFO inventories, if any, or that such method is otherwise consistent with Regulation section 1.472–6.

**Section F.**—Regulation section 1.451–3(b)(1) provides that, except as provided in Regulation section 1.451–3(b)(1)(ii), the term "long-term contract" means a building, installation, construction, or manufacturing contract that is not completed within the tax year in which it is entered into.

**Section I.**—Rev. Proc. 74–11 provides a procedure whereby applicants are considered to have obtained the consent of the Commissioner to change their method of accounting for depreciation. You must file 3115 with the Service Center where your return will be filed within the first 180 days of the tax year in which it is desired to make the change. Attach a copy of the form to the income tax return for the tax year of the change.

**Section J.**—Generally, this section should be used for requesting changes in a method of accounting for which provision has not been made elsewhere on this form.

If you are making an election under Code section 458 or 466, or section 373(c)(2) of the Revenue Act of 1978, show the applicable information required under Regulation section 1.458–10, or Temporary Regulation section 5.466–1 or 5.466–2.

## B-13 FORM 3468 COMPUTATION OF INVESTMENT CREDIT

| Form **3468** | **Computation of Investment Credit** | OMB No. 1545-0155 |
|---|---|---|
| Department of the Treasury Internal Revenue Service | ▶ Attach to your tax return. ▶ Schedule B (Business Energy Investment Credit) on back. | 19**82** 27 |

| Name(s) as shown on return | Identifying number |
|---|---|

**PART I.— Elections**

**A** The corporation elects the basic or basic and matching employee plan percentage under section 48(n)(1) . . . . . ☐

**B** I elect to increase my qualified investment to 100% for certain commuter highway vehicles under section 46(c)(6) . . ☐

**C** I elect to increase my qualified investment by all qualified progress expenditures made this and all later tax years . . . ☐

Enter total qualified progress expenditures included in column (4), Part II ▶ ------------------------

**D** I claim full credit on certain ships under section 46(g)(3) (See **Instruction B** for details.) . . . . . . . . . . ☐

**PART II.—Qualified Investment**

| 1 Recovery Property | | Line | (1) Class of Property | (2) Unadjusted Basis | (3) Applicable Percentage | (4) Qualified Investment (Column 2 × column 3) |
|---|---|---|---|---|---|---|
| Regular Percentage *b 125,000 limit* | New Property | (a) | 3-year | 6000 000 | 60 | 3600 |
| | | (b) | Other | | 100 | |
| | Used Property | (c) | 3-year | | 60 | |
| | | (d) | Other | | 100 | |
| §48(q) Election to Reduce Credit (instead of adjusting basis) FY 1982–83 filers only (see instr.) | New Property | (e) | 3-year | | 40 | |
| | | (f) | Other | | 80 | |
| | Used Property | (g) | 3-year | | 40 | |
| | | (h) | Other | | 80 | |

2 Nonrecovery property—Enter total qualified investment (See instructions for line 2) . . | **2** |

3 New commuter highway vehicle—Enter total qualified investment (See **Instruction D(2)**) . | **3** |

4 Used commuter highway vehicle—Enter total qualified investment (See **Instruction D(2)**) . | **4** | 3,600

5 **Total qualified investment in 10% property**—Add lines 1(a) through 1(h), 2, 3, and 4 (See instructions for special limits) . . . . . . . . . . . . . . | **5** |

6 Qualified rehabilitation expenditures—Enter total qualified investment for:

  **a** 30-year-old buildings . . . . . . . . . . . | **6a** |

  **b** 40-year-old buildings . . . . . . . . . . . | **6b** |

  **c** Certified historic structures (Enter the Dept. of Interior assigned project number --------------- ) | **6c** |

7 Corporations checking election box A above—add lines 5, 6a, 6b, and 6c . . | **7** |

**PART III.—Tentative Regular Investment Credit**

8 10% of line 5 . . . . . . . . . . . . . . . . | **8** | 360

9 15% of line 6a . . . . . . . . . . . . . . . . | **9** |

10 20% of line 6b . . . . . . . . . . . . . . . . | **10** |

11 25% of line 6c . . . . . . . . . . . . . . . . | **11** |

12 Corporations checking election box A (See **Instruction D(1)**)—

  **a** Basic 1% credit—Enter 1% of line 7 (1982–83 fiscal-year filers, see instructions for line 12) . | **12a** |

  **b** Matching credit (not more than 0.5%)—Allowable percentage times adjusted line 7 (attach schedule) . | **12b** |

13 Credit from cooperative—Enter regular investment credit from cooperatives . . . . | **13** |

14 Current year regular investment credit—Add lines 8 through 13 . . . . . . . . | **14** | 360

15 Carryover of unused credits . . . . . . . . . . . | **15** |

16 Carryback of unused credits . . . . . . . . . . . | **16** |

17 Tentative regular investment credit—Add lines 14, 15, and 16 . . . . . | **17** | $360

*— limited to $25,000 or our tax liability*

**PART IV.—Tax Liability Limitations**

18 **a** Individuals—From Form 1040, enter tax from line 38, page 2, plus any additional taxes from Form 4970

  **b** Estates and trusts—From Form 1041, enter tax from line 26a, plus any section 644 tax on trusts .

  **c** Corporations (1120 filers)—From Form 1120, Schedule J, enter tax from line 3 .

  **d** Other organizations—Enter tax before credits from return . | **18** |

19 **a** Individuals—From Form 1040, enter credits from lines 41 and 42 of page 2 .

  **b** Estates and trusts—From Form 1041, enter any foreign tax credit from line 27a .

  **c** Corporations (1120 filers)—From Form 1120, Schedule J, enter any foreign tax credit from line 4(a), plus any possessions tax credit from line 4(f) .

  **d** Other organizations—Enter any foreign or possessions tax credit . . . . . | **19** |

20 Income tax liability as adjusted (subtract line 19 from line 18) . . . . . | **20** |

21 **a** Enter smaller of line 20 or $25,000. See instruction for line 21 . . . . . . | **21a** |

  **b** If line 20 is more than $25,000—Enter 90% of the excess . . . . . . | **21b** |

22 Regular investment credit limitation—Add lines 21a and 21b . . . . . | **22** |

23 Allowed regular investment credit—Enter the smaller of line 17 or line 22 . . . . | **23** |

24 Business energy investment credit limitation—Subtract line 23 from line 20 . . . . | **24** |

25 Business energy investment credit—From line 14 of Schedule B (Form 3468) . . . | **25** |

26 Allowed business energy investment credit—Enter smaller of line 24 or line 25 . . . | **26** |

27 Total allowed regular and business energy investment credit—Add lines 23 and 26. Enter here and on Form 1040, line 43; Schedule J (Form 1120), line 4(b), page 3; or the proper line on other returns . | **27** |

**For Paperwork Reduction Act Notice, see separate instructions.**        363–167–2      Form **3468** (1982)

Form 3468 (1982)

## Schedule B  Business Energy Investment Credit

**1** Enter on lines 1(a) through 1(e) your qualified investment in business energy property that is the kind listed in the instructions for line 1, column (3).

| (1) Type of Property | Line | (2) Class of property or life years | (3) Code | (4) Unadjusted basis/Basis | (5) Applicable Percentage | (6) Qualified investment (Column 4 × column 5) |
|---|---|---|---|---|---|---|
| Recovery | (a) | 3-year | | | 60 | |
| | (b) | Other | | | 100 | |
| Nonrecovery | (c) | 3 or more but less than 5 | | | 33⅓ | |
| | (d) | 5 or more but less than 7 | | | 66⅔ | |
| | (e) | 7 or more | | | 100 | |

**2** Total 10% energy investment property—Add lines 1(a) through 1(e), column (6) . . **2**

**3** Enter on lines 3(a) through 3(e) the basis in qualified hydroelectric generating property. Enter nameplate capacity of the property (see instructions for line 3) ▶

| Recovery | (a) | 3-year | | | 60 | |
|---|---|---|---|---|---|---|
| | (b) | Other | | | 100 | |
| Nonrecovery | (c) | 3 or more but less than 5 | | | 33⅓ | |
| | (d) | 5 or more but less than 7 | | | 66⅔ | |
| | (e) | 7 or more | | | 100 | |

**4** Total 11% energy investment property—Add lines 3(a) through 3(e), column (6) . . **4**

**5** Enter on lines 5(a) through 5(e) the basis in energy property that is solar equipment, wind equipment, ocean thermal equipment, or geothermal equipment. (See instructions for line 5, column (3).)

| Recovery | (a) | 3-year | | | 60 | |
|---|---|---|---|---|---|---|
| | (b) | Other | | | 100 | |
| Nonrecovery | (c) | 3 or more but less than 5 | | | 33⅓ | |
| | (d) | 5 or more but less than 7 | | | 66⅔ | |
| | (e) | 7 or more | | | 100 | |

**6** Total 15% energy investment property—Add lines 5(a) through 5(e), column (6) . . **6**

**7** Enter 10% of line 2 . . . . . . . . . . . **7**

**8** Enter 11% of line 4 . . . . . . . . . . . **8**

**9** Enter 15% of line 6 . . . . . . . . . . . **9**

**10** Cooperative credit—Enter business energy investment credit from cooperatives . . **10**

**11** Current year business energy investment credit—Add lines 7 through 10 . . . . . **11**

**12** Carryover of unused credit(s) . . . . . . . . **12**

**13** Carryback of unused credit(s) . . . . . . . . **13**

**14** Tentative business energy investment credit—Add lines 11 through 13. Enter here and on line 25 of Form 3468 . . . . . . . . . **14**

## Instructions for Schedule B (Form 3468)

Energy property must meet the same requirements as regular investment credit property, except that the provisions of sections 48(a)(1) and 48(a)(3) do not apply. See Instructions for Form 3468 for definitions and rules regarding regular investment credit property.

Energy property must be acquired new. See sections 46(a)(2)(C) and 48(l)(1) through (17) for details.

See section 48(l)(17) for special rules on public utility property, and section 48(l)(11) (as amended by the Crude Oil Windfall Profit Tax Act of 1980) for special rules on property financed by Industrial Development Bonds.

### Specific Instructions

**One Credit Only.**—If property qualifies as more than one kind of energy property, you may take only one credit for the property.

**Lines 1, 3, and 5—Type of Property.**—For definition of recovery and nonrecovery

property, see the separate Instructions for Form 3468.

**Line 1—Column (3).**—Use the code letters from the following list to indicate the kind of property for which you are claiming a credit. If you enter more than one kind of property on a line, enter the code letter for each kind of property in column (3) and the code letter and dollar amount of each kind of property in the right hand margin.

The code letters are:

a. Alternative energy property, including biomass property
b. Specially defined energy property that reduces the energy consumed in an existing process, installed in connection with an existing industrial or commercial facility (see regulations section 1.48-9(f)).
c. Recycling equipment
d. Shale oil equipment
e. Equipment to produce natural gas from geopressured brine
f. Cogeneration equipment installed in an existing facility, but only if the cogeneration energy capacity of the facility is expanded. See section 48(l)(14).

g. Qualified intercity buses (see section 48(l)(16)(C) for the limitation on qualified investment for intercity buses based on the increase in operating seating capacity).

**Line 3.**—Figure your qualified investment in hydroelectric generating property. If the installed capacity is more than 25 megawatts, the 11% energy credit is allowed for only part of the qualified investment. See section 48(l)(13)(C).

In the space provided in line 3, enter the megawatts capacity of the generator as shown on the nameplate of the generator.

**Line 5—Column (3).**—Use the code letters from the following list to indicate the kind of property for which you are claiming a credit. Be sure to put the code or codes on the line for the correct recovery period or life years as explained in the instruction for line 1, column (3).

h. Solar equipment (but not passive solar equipment)
i. Wind equipment
j. Ocean thermal equipment
k. Geothermal equipment
See sections 48(l)(4) and 48(l)(3)(A)(viii) and (ix) for definitions and special rules that apply to these kinds of property.

## B-14 FORM 3903 MOVING EXPENSE ADJUSTMENT

| Form **3903**<br>Department of the Treasury<br>Internal Revenue Service | **Moving Expense Adjustment**<br>▶ Attach to Form 1040. | OMB No. 1545-0062<br>19**82**<br>62 |
|---|---|---|

| Name(s) as shown on Form 1040 | Your social security number |
|---|---|

**a** What is the distance from your **old** residence to your **new** work place? .............. miles  **b** What is the distance from your **old** residence to your **old** work place? .............. miles

**c** If the distance in **a** above is 35 or more miles farther than the the distance in **b** above, complete the rest of this form. If the distance is less than 35 miles, you cannot take a deduction for moving expenses. This rule does not apply to members of the armed forces.

| | | |
|---|---|---|
| 1 Transportation expenses in moving household goods and personal effects . . . . . . . . | **1** | |
| 2 Travel, meals, and lodging expenses in moving from old to new residence . . . . . . . . | **2** | |
| 3 Pre-move travel, meals, and lodging expenses in looking for a new residence after getting your job . . . . . | **3** | |
| 4 Temporary living expenses in new location or area during any 30 days in a row after getting your job . . . . . | **4** | |
| 5 Total. (Add lines 3 and 4.) . . . . . . . . | **5** | |
| 6 Enter the smaller of line 5 or $1,500 ($750 if married, filing a separate return, and you lived with your spouse who also started work during the tax year) . . | **6** | |
| 7 Expenses of: (Check one.)<br> **a** ☐ selling or exchanging your old residence; or<br> **b** ☐ if renting, settling an unexpired lease on your old residence . . . . | **7** | |
| 8 Expenses of: (Check one.)<br> **a** ☐ buying a new residence; or<br> **b** ☐ if renting, getting a lease on a new residence . . . . . . . | **8** | |
| 9 Total. (Add lines 6, 7, and 8.) . . . . . . . . . . . | **9** | |
| 10 Enter the smaller of line 9 or $3,000 ($1,500 if married, filing a separate return, and you lived with your spouse who also started work during the tax year) . . . . . . . . . . | **10** | |

**Note:** Use any amount on line 7a not deducted because of the $3,000 (or $1,500) limit to decrease the gain on the sale of your residence. Use any amount on line 8a not deducted because of the limit to increase the basis of your new residence. See "No Double Benefit" in instructions.

| | | |
|---|---|---|
| 11 Total moving expenses. (Add lines 1, 2, and 10.) . . . . . . . . . . | **11** | |
| 12 Reimbursements and allowances received for this move. (Do not enter reimbursements and allowances included on your Form W-2.) . . . . . . . . . . | **12** | |
| 13 Excess moving expenses. If line 12 is less than line 11, enter the difference here and on Form 1040, line 23 . . . . . . . . . | **13** | |
| 14 Excess moving reimbursement. If line 12 is more than line 11, enter the difference here and on Form 1040, line 21. Next to the amount write "Excess moving reimbursement." . . . . . . . . | **14** | |

## General Instructions

**Paperwork Reduction Act Notice.**—The Paperwork Reduction Act of 1980 says we must tell you why we are collecting this information, how we will use it, and whether you have to give it to us. We ask for the information to carry out the Internal Revenue laws of the United States. We need it to ensure that you are complying with these laws and to allow us to figure and collect the right amount of tax. You are required to give us this information.

**Who May Deduct Moving Expenses.**— If you moved your residence because of a change in the location of your job, you may be able to deduct your moving expenses. You may qualify for a deduction whether you are self-employed or an employee. But you must meet certain tests of distance and time, explained below. If you need more information, please get Publication 521, Moving Expenses.

**Note:** If you are a U.S. citizen or resident who moved to a new principal work place **outside** the United States or its possessions, get Form 3903F, Foreign Moving Expense Adjustment.

**Distance Test.**—Your new work place must be at least 35 miles farther from your old residence than your old work place was. For example, if your old work place was 3 miles from your old residence, your new work place must be at least 38 miles from that residence. If you did not have an old work place, your new work place must be at least 35 miles from your old residence. (The distance between two points is the shortest of the more commonly traveled routes between the points.)

**Time Test.**—If you are an employee, you must work full time for at least 39 weeks during the 12 months right after you move. If you are self-employed, you

must work for at least 39 weeks during the first 12 months and a total of 78 weeks during the 24 months right after you move.

You may deduct your moving expenses for 1982 even if you have not met the "time" test before your 1982 return is due. You may do this if you expect to meet the 39-week test by the end of 1983 or the 78-week test by the end of 1984. If you have not met the test by then, you will have to do one of the following:

● Amend your 1982 tax return on which you deducted moving expenses. To do this, use Form 1040X, Amended U.S. Individual Income Tax Return.

● Report as income on your tax return for the year you cannot meet the test the amount you deducted on your 1982 return.

*(Continued on back)*

If you do not deduct your moving expenses on your 1982 return, and you later meet the "time" test, you may file an amended return for 1982, taking the deduction. To do this, use Form 1040X.

**Exceptions to the Distance and Time Tests.**—You do not have to meet the "time" test in case of death or if your job ends because of disability, transfer for your employer's benefit, or layoff or other discharge besides willful misconduct.

You do not have to meet the "time" test if you meet the requirements, explained below, for retired people or survivors living outside the United States.

If you are in the armed forces, you do not have to meet the "distance and time" tests if the move is due to a permanent change of station. A permanent change of station includes a move in connection with and within 1 year of retirement or other termination of active duty. In figuring your moving expenses, do not deduct any moving expenses for moving services that were provided by the military or that were reimbursed to you and that you did not include in income. However, you may deduct your unreimbursed moving expenses, subject to the dollar limits. If you and your spouse or dependents are moved to or from different locations, treat the moves as a single move.

**Qualified Retired People or Survivors Living Outside the United States.**—If the requirements below are met, retired people or survivors who move to a U.S. residence are treated as if they moved to a new work place located in the United States. You are subject to the dollar limits and "distance" test explained on this form. Use this form instead of Form 3903F to claim your moving expenses.

**Retired People.**—You may deduct moving expenses for a move to a new residence in the United States when you actually retire, if both your old principal work place and your old residence were outside the United States.

**Survivors.**—You may deduct moving expenses for a move to a residence in the United States if you are the spouse or dependent of a person whose principal work place at the time of death was outside the United States. In addition, the expenses must be: (1) for a move that begins within 6 months after the decedent's death; and (2) must be from a former residence outside the United States that you lived in with the decedent at the time of death.

**Moving Expenses in General.**—You may deduct most, but not all, of the reasonable expenses you incur in moving your family and dependent household members. You may not include moving expenses for employees such as a servant, governess, or nurse.

Examples of expenses you CAN deduct are:

- Travel, meal, and lodging expenses during the move to the new residence.
- Temporary living expenses in the new location.
- Pre-move travel expenses.

Examples of expenses you CANNOT deduct are:

- Loss on the sale of your residence.
- Mortgage penalties.
- Cost of refitting carpets and draperies.
- Losses on quitting club memberships.

The line-by-line instructions below explain how to figure your moving expense deduction.

## Line-by-Line Instructions

To see whether you meet the "distance" test, fill in the number of miles for questions **a** and **b** at the top of the form. If you meet the test in **c**, continue with the items that follow.

We have provided specific instructions for most of the lines on the form. Those lines that do not appear in these instructions are self-explanatory.

**Line 1.**—Enter the actual cost of packing, crating, moving, storing in transit, and insuring your household goods and personal effects.

**Line 2.**—Enter the costs of travel from your old residence to your new residence. These include transportation, meals, and lodging on the way, including costs for the day you arrive. You may only include expenses for one trip. However, all the members of your household do not have to travel together or at the same time. If you use your own car, you may figure the expenses in either of two ways:

- Actual out-of-pocket expenses for gas and oil (keep records to verify the amounts); or
- At the rate of 9 cents a mile (keep records to verify your mileage).

You may add parking fees and tolls to the amount claimed under either method.

**Line 3.**—Include the costs of travel before you move in order to look for a new residence. You may deduct the costs only if:

- You began the housemunting trip after you got the job; and
- You returned to your old residence after looking for a new one; and
- You traveled to the general location of the new work place primarily to look for a new residence.

There is no limit on the number of housemunting trips made by you and members of your household that may be included on this line. Your househunting does not have to be successful to qualify for this deduction. If you used your own car, figure transportation costs the same way as in the instructions for line 2. If you are self-employed, you can deduct these househunting costs only if you had already made substantial arrangements to begin work in the new location.

**Line 4.**—Include the costs of meals and lodging while occupying temporary quarters in the area of your new work place. You may include these costs for any period of 30 days in a row after you get the job. If you are self-employed, you can count these temporary living expenses only if you had already made substantial arrangements to begin work in the new location.

**Lines 7 and 8.**—You may include most

of the costs to sell or buy a residence or to settle or get a lease. Examples of expenses you CAN include are:

- Sales commissions.
- Advertising costs.
- Attorney's fees.
- Title and escrow fees.
- State transfer taxes.
- Costs to settle an unexpired lease or to get a new lease.

Examples of expenses you CANNOT include are:

- Costs to improve the residence to help it sell.
- Charges for payment or prepayment of interest.
- Payments or prepayments of rent.

Check the appropriate box, **(a)** or **(b)**, for line 7 and for line 8 when you enter the amounts for these two lines.

**Line 12.**—Include all reimbursements and allowances for moving expenses in income. In general, Form W-2 includes such reimbursements and allowances. However, check with your employer if you are in doubt. Your employer must give you a statement showing a detailed breakdown of reimbursements or payments of moving expenses. **Form 4782,** Employee Moving Expense Information, may be used for this purpose. Use line 12 to report reimbursements and allowances that are not included elsewhere on Form 1040 or related schedules.

**No Double Benefit.**—You cannot take double benefits. For example, you cannot use the moving expense on line 7 that is part of your moving expense deduction to lower the amount of gain on the sale of your old residence. You also cannot use the moving expense on line 8 that is part of your moving expense deduction to add to the cost of your new residence. (Use **Form 2119,** Sale or Exchange of Principal Residence, to figure the gain, if any, you must report on the old residence and the adjusted cost of the new one.)

**Dollar Limits.**—Lines 1 and 2 (costs of moving household goods and travel expenses to your new residence) are not limited to any amount. All the other expenses (lines 3, 4, 7, and 8) together cannot be more than $3,000. In addition, line 3 (housemunting trip expenses) and line 4 (temporary living expenses) together cannot be more than $1,500. These are overall per-move limits.

There are some special cases:

- If both you and your spouse began work at new work places and shared the same new residence at the end of 1982, you must treat this as one move rather than two. If you file separate returns, each of you is limited to $1,500 for lines 3, 4, 7, and 8. Housemunting trip expenses and temporary living expenses (lines 3 and 4) are limited to $750 for each of you.

- If both you and your spouse began work at new work places but you moved to separate new residences, this is treated as two separate moves. If you file a joint return, lines 3, 4, 7, and 8 are limited to $6,000; and lines 3 and 4 are limited to $3,000. If you file separate returns, each of you is limited to $3,000 for lines 3, 4, 7, and 8; and to $1,500 for lines 3 and 4.

## B–15 FORM 4255 RECAPTURE OF INVESTMENT CREDIT

| Form **4255**<br>(Rev. Nov. 1982)<br>Department of the Treasury<br>Internal Revenue Service | **Recapture of Investment Credit**<br>(Including Energy Investment Credit)<br>▶ Attach to your income tax return | OMB No. 1545-0166<br>Expires 11-30-85<br><br>65 |
|---|---|---|

| Name(s) as shown on return | | Identifying number |
|---|---|---|

| Properties | Kind of property—State whether recovery or nonrecovery (see Form 3468 instructions for definitions). If energy property, show type. Also indicate if rehabilitation expenditure property. |
|---|---|
| **A** | |
| **B** | |
| **C** | |
| **D** | |
| **E** | |

**Original Investment Credit**

| Computation Steps:<br>(see Specific Instructions) | A | B | C | D | E |
|---|---|---|---|---|---|
| **1** Original rate of credit . . . . | | | | | |
| **2** Date property was placed in service . . . . . . . . . | | | | | |
| **3** Cost or other basis . . . . . | | | | | |
| **4** Original estimated useful life or class of property . . . . . | | | | | |
| **5** Applicable percentage . . . . | | | | | |
| **6** Original qualified investment (line 3 times line 5) . . . . . | | | | | |
| **7** Original credit (line 1 times line 6) . . . . . . . . | | | | | |
| **8** Date property ceased to be qualified investment credit property . | | | | | |
| **9** Number of full years between the date on line 2 and the date on line 8 . . . . . . . . . | | | | | |

**Computation of Recapture Tax**

| | A | B | C | D | E |
|---|---|---|---|---|---|
| **10** Recapture percentage . . . . | | | | | |
| **11** Tentative recapture tax—Line 7 times line 10 . . . . . . . | | | | | |

**12** Add line 11, columns A through E . . . . . . . . . . . . . . . . . . . . . .

**13 a** Enter tax from disposed qualified progress expenditure property (attach separate computation) . . . .

**b** Enter tax from any part of property ceasing to be at risk (attach separate computation) . . . . . . .

**14** Total—Add lines 12, 13a and 13b . . . . . . . . . . . . . . . . . .

**15** Portion of original credit (line 7) not used to offset tax in any year (Do not enter more than line 14—see instructions) . . . . . . . . . . . . . . . . . . . . . . . .

**16** Total increase in tax—Subtract line 15 from line 14. Enter here and on the proper line of your tax return. Do not use this amount to reduce current year's investment credit figured on Form 3468, Computation of Investment Credit. Any unused credit on line 15 cannot be used in any year as a carryback or carryover . . .

For Paperwork Reduction Act Notice, see instructions on back.     363-490-1     Form **4255** (Rev. 11-82)

## General Instructions

*References are to the Internal Revenue Code.*

**Paperwork Reduction Act Notice.—**We ask for this information to carry out the Internal Revenue laws of the United States. We need it to ensure that you are complying with these laws and to allow us to figure and collect the right amount of tax. You are required to give us this information.

**Purpose.—**Use Form 4255 to figure the increase in tax for the recapture of investment credit for regular and energy property. You must refigure the credit if you took it in an earlier year, but disposed of the property before the end of the recapture period, or the useful life you used to figure the original credit. You must also refigure the credit if you changed the use of the property so that it no longer qualifies as regular or energy investment credit property. Also, see instructions for line 13b regarding recapture if property ceases to be at risk.

For tax years beginning after December 31, 1982, election of subchapter S status does not automatically trigger recapture of investment credit taken before the election was effective. However, on disposition of the assets, the subchapter S corporation continues to be liable for any recapture of investment credit taken before the election.

If property on which you took both the regular and energy investment credit ceases to be energy credit property, but still qualifies as regular investment credit property, you need only refigure the energy investment credit. However, if you took both credits, and you dispose of the property, or the property ceases to be both energy and regular investment credit property, you must refigure both credits.

If you are a subchapter S corporation, a partnership, or an estate or trust that allocated any or all of the investment credit to the beneficiaries, you must give your shareholders, partners, or beneficiaries the information they need to refigure the credit. See regulations sections 1.47–4, 1.47–5 and 1.47–6.

**Special rules.—**If you took the credit on the following kinds of property, see the sections listed below before you complete Form 4255:

| Property | IRC section |
|---|---|
| Motion picture films and video tape | 47(a)(8) |
| Ships | 46(g)(4) |
| Commuter highway vehicles | 47(a)(4) |

If you dispose of property and you had elected the basic or basic and matching employee plan percentage for contributions to tax credit employee stock option plans, see section 48(n)(4).

If you took any credit for production of fuel from nonconventional sources, see section 44D(b)(4).

If, before the end of the recapture period, you dispose of recovery property placed in service after 1982, you must increase the basis of this property by 50% of the recapture amount before computing gain or loss on disposition. See section 48(q)(2) and (3). (This does not apply if you originally made the section 48(q)(4) election to take a reduced credit instead of reducing the basis of the property.)

For more information, see **Publication 572**, Investment Credit.

## Specific Instructions

**Note:** *Do not figure the recapture tax for qualified progress expenditure property or for property ceasing to be at risk on lines 1 through 12. Figure the recapture tax for these properties on separate schedules and enter the recapture tax on lines 13a and 13b. Include any unused credit for these properties on line 15.*

**Lines A through E.—**Describe the property for which you must refigure the regular or energy investment credit.

Fill in lines 1 through 11 for each property on which you are refiguring the credit. Use a separate column for each item. If you must recapture both the energy investment credit and the regular investment credit for the same item, use a separate column for each credit. If you need more columns, use additional Forms 4255, or other schedules with all the information shown on Form 4255. Enter the total from the separate sheets on line 12.

**Line 1.—**Enter the rate you used to figure the original credit as determined from the tables below:

**Regular Investment Property:**

Property (including public utility property) acquired or constructed and placed in service after January 21, 1975 . . . . . . 10%

*For property acquired or constructed before January 22, 1975, enter the rate used on your original Form 3468 (7% or 4%).*

Be sure to include any basic and matching ESOP or other credits listed under the special rules above.

See section 46(a)(2)(F) for the rates for qualified rehabilitation expenditures made after December 31, 1981.

**Energy Investment Property:**

Alternative energy property, specially defined energy property, recycling equipment, shale oil equipment, equipment for producing natural gas from geopressured brine, cogeneration equipment, and intercity buses . . . 10%

Qualified hydroelectric generating equipment . 11%

Solar and wind equipment acquired or constructed before 1/1/80 . . . . . . 10%

Solar and wind equipment, ocean thermal equipment, and geothermal equipment acquired or constructed after 12/31/79 . . . 15%

**Line 2.—**For both recovery and nonrecovery property, enter the first day of the first month, and the year, that the property was available for service.

**Line 3.—**Enter the cost or other basis of nonrecovery property (unadjusted basis of recovery property) that you used to figure the original credit.

**Line 4.—**Enter the estimated useful life that you used to figure the original credit for nonrecovery property. Enter the class of property for recovery property.

**Line 5.—**Enter the applicable percentage that you used to figure the original qualified investment from the tables below:

**Nonrecovery Property**

| Original estimated useful life: | Applicable percentage |
|---|---|
| 3 or more but less than 5 years | 33⅓% |
| 5 or more but less than 7 years | 66⅔% |
| 7 or more years | 100% |

**Recovery Property**

| Class of property | Applicable percentage |
|---|---|
| 3-year | 60% |
| Other | 100% |

**Section 48(q) Election Recovery Property**
(Placed in service after 12/31/82)

| Class of property | Applicable percentage |
|---|---|
| 3-year | 40% |
| Other | 80% |

**Line 8.—**See regulations section 1.47–1(c) for more information.

**Line 9.—**Do not enter partial years. If property was held less than 12 months, enter zero.

**Line 10.—**Enter the recapture percentage from the following tables:

**Nonrecovery Property**

| If number of full years on line 9 of Form 4255 is: | The recapture percentage for property with an original useful life of: | | |
|---|---|---|---|
| | 3 or more but less than 5 years is | 5 or more but less than 7 years is | 7 or more years is |
| 0 | 100 | 100 | 100 |
| 1 | 100 | 100 | 100 |
| 2 | 100 | 100 | 100 |
| 3 | 0 | 50 | 66.6 |
| 4 | 0 | 50 | 66.6 |
| 5 | 0 | 0 | 33.3 |
| 6 | 0 | 0 | 33.3 |

**Recovery Property**

| If number of full years on line 9 of Form 4255 is: | The recapture percentage for: | |
|---|---|---|
| | 3-year property is | 15-year, 10-year, and 5-year property is |
| 0 | 100 | 100 |
| 1 | 66 | 80 |
| 2 | 33 | 60 |
| 3 | 0 | 40 |
| 4 | 0 | 20 |

**Line 12.—**If you have used more than one Form 4255, or separate sheets to list additional items on which you figured an increase in tax, write on the dotted line "Tax from attached, $................." Include the amount in the total for line 12.

**Line 13a.—**See section 47(a)(3) for information on recapturing investment credit on the disposal of qualified progress expenditure property. Attach a separate computation schedule and enter the recapture tax on line 13a.

**Line 13b.—**For certain taxpayers, the basis or cost of property placed in service after February 18, 1981, is limited to the amount the taxpayer is at risk at year end. If property ceases to be at risk in a later year, recapture may be required. See section 47(d) for details. Attach a separate computation schedule to figure the recapture tax and enter the total tax on line 13b.

**Line 15.—**If you did not use all the credit you originally figured, either in the year you figured the credit or in a carryback or carryover year, you do not have to recapture the amount of the credit you did not use. You must also take into account the current year's unused credit in figuring the increase in tax. See regulations section 1.47–1(d), Revenue Ruling 72–221, and **Publication 572** for more information.

Figure the unused portion on a separate sheet and enter it on this line. Do not enter more than the recapture tax on line 14.

**Line 16.—**This is the total increase in tax. Enter it on the proper line of your tax return. Do not use this amount to reduce your current year's investment credit from Form 3468.

## B–16 FORM 4684 CASUALTIES AND THEFTS

Form **4684**
Department of the Treasury
Internal Revenue Service

### Casualties and Thefts
▶ See instructions on back.
▶ To be filed with Form 1040, 1041, 1065, 1120, etc.

OMB No. 1545–0177

**1982**
69

Name(s) as shown on tax return

Identifying Number

**Part I**    Casualty or Theft Gain or Loss (Use a separate Part I for each different casualty or theft.)

| | Item or article | Item or article | Item or article | Item or article |
|---|---|---|---|---|
| 1 (a) Kind of property and description . . . . | | | | |
|   (b) Date of purchase or acquisition . . . . . | | | | |
| 2 Cost or other basis of each item . . . . . . | | | | |
| 3 Insurance or other reimbursement you received or expect to receive . . . . . . . . . . | | | | |
| 4 Gain from casualty or theft. If line 3 is more than line 2, enter difference here and on line 15 or 20, column C. However, see instructions for line 19. Also, skip lines 5 through 14 . . . . . . . *If line 2 is more than line 3, skip line 4 and complete lines 5 through 14.* | | | | |
| 5 Fair market value before casualty or theft . . . | | | | |
| 6 Fair market value after casualty or theft . . . | | | | |
| 7 Subtract line 6 from line 5 . . . . . . . . | | | | |
| 8 Enter smaller of line 2 or line 7 . . . . . . *Note: If the loss was to property used in a trade or business or for income-producing purposes, and totally destroyed by a casualty or lost from theft, enter on line 8, in each column, the amount from line 2.* | | | | |
| 9 Subtract line 3 from line 8 . . . . . . . . | | | | |
| 10 Casualty or theft loss. Add amounts on line 9. See instructions for **How Many Forms To Complete** . . . . | | | | |
| 11 Enter the part of line 9 that is from trade, business, or income-producing property here and on line 15 or 20, column B(i) . . . | | | | |
| 12 Subtract line 11 from line 10 . . . . . . . | | | | |
| 13 Enter the amount from line 12 or $100, whichever is smaller . . . . . . . . . . | | | | |
| 14 Subtract line 13 from line 12. See instructions for **How Many Forms To Complete** before completing this line and the rest of this form. Enter here and on line 15 or 20, column B(ii) . . . . . . . . . . . . | | | | |

**Part II**    Summary of Gains and Losses (From separate Parts I)

| (A) Identify casualty or theft | (B) Losses from casualties or thefts | | (C) Gains from casualties or thefts includible in income |
|---|---|---|---|
| | (i) Trade, business, rental or royalty property | (ii) Other property | |
| **Casualty or Theft of Property Held One Year or Less** | | | |
| 15 | | | |
| 16 Totals. Add amounts on line 15 for each column . . . . . . . | | | |
| 17 Combine line 16, columns (B)(i) and (C). Enter the net gain or (loss) here and on Form 4797, Part II, line 8(a) . (If Form 4797 is not otherwise required, see instructions.) . . | | | |
| 18 Enter the amount from line 16, column (B)(ii) here and on line 24 of Schedule A (Form 1040)—Identify as "4684." See instructions before completing this line . . . . . . . . . . . . | | | |
| **Casualty or Theft of Property Held More Than One Year** | | | |
| 19 Any casualty or theft gains from Form 4797, Part III, line 26 . . . . . . . . | | | |
| 20 | | | |
| 21 Total losses. Add amounts on line 20, columns (B)(i) and (B)(ii) . . | | | //////// |
| 22 Total gains. Add lines 19 and 20, column (C) . . . . . . . . | | | |
| 23 Add line 21, columns (B)(i) and (B)(ii) . . . . . . . . . . | | | |

*If this form is filed by a partnership, enter amount from line 24a, 24b, or 25 on Schedule K (Form 1065), line 7.*

24 If the loss on line 23 is more than the gain on line 22:
  (a) Combine line 21, column (B)(i) and line 22. Enter the net gain or (loss) here and on Form 4797, Part II, line 8(a). (If Form 4797 is not otherwise required, see instructions.) . . . . . . . . . . . .
  (b) Enter the amount from line 21, column (B)(ii) here and on line 24 of Schedule A (Form 1040)—Identify as "4684." See instructions before completing this line . . . . . . . . . . .
25 If the loss on line 23 is equal to or smaller than the gain on line 22, enter the net gain here and on Form 4797, Part I, line 2(a). (If Form 4797 is not otherwise required, see instructions.) . . . . . . . . . . . .

For **Paperwork Reduction Act Notice, see back of form.**      363–184–1      Form **4684** (1982)

## General Instructions

*(Section references are to the Internal Revenue Code)*

**Paperwork Reduction Act Notice.**—We ask for this information to carry out the Internal Revenue laws of the United States. We need it to ensure that you are complying with these laws and to allow us to figure and collect the right amount of tax. You are required to give us this information.

**Purpose of Form.**—Use Form 4684 to figure your gain or loss from casualty or theft.

**How Many Forms To Complete**

- If you had only **one casualty or theft** during the year and only **four or fewer items** were lost or damaged in that one casualty or theft, complete only one Form 4684. Use a separate column of Part I for each item lost or damaged. Complete Part II only if you had a gain from the casualty or theft on any item or if the property lost or damaged was used in a trade or business or for income-producing purposes.

- If you had only **one casualty or theft** during the year, but **more than four items** were lost or damaged, you will need to complete additional Forms 4684 or additional sheets to list all of the items. Use a separate column in each Part I for each item lost or damaged. However, you need only complete Part I (and not Part II) of the forms provided that:
  - You are an individual (file Form 1040);
  - The casualty or theft was to property that was **not** used in a trade or business or for income-producing purposes; **and**
  - The loss of, or damage to, each item resulted in a loss (rather than a gain).

  Complete all of the forms through line 9. On one of the forms, enter on line 10 the total of the line 9 amounts from all of the forms and complete lines 11 through 14. Enter the amount from line 14 on line 24 of Schedule A (Form 1040). Do not complete Part II of Form 4684.

- If you had **more than one casualty or theft** during the year, or you had a gain on any item from one casualty or theft, or the property lost or damaged in the casualty or theft was used in a trade or business or for income-producing purposes, you must complete:
  - A separate Part I for each casualty or theft using a separate column in Part I for each item lost or damaged; and
  - One Part II of Form 4684 to summarize your gains and losses from casualties and thefts.

**Casualty or Theft Losses You May Deduct**

You may deduct losses arising from fire, storm, shipwreck, other casualty, theft (for example, larceny, embezzlement, and robbery), or damage to your car that is not the result of a willful act or willful negligence of the driver.

**When To Deduct a Loss**

**Casualty Loss.**—Deduct the part of your casualty loss that will not be reimbursed, in the tax year the casualty occurred. However, a disaster loss may be treated differently. See the section on Special Rule for Disaster Losses.

**Theft Loss.**—Deduct the part of your theft loss that will not be reimbursed, in the tax year you discover the theft.

If you are not sure whether part of your casualty or theft loss will be reimbursed, do not deduct that part until the tax year when you are reasonably certain that it will not be reimbursed.

If you are reimbursed for a loss you deducted in an earlier year, include the reimbursement in your income for the tax year in which you received it. Include it to the extent the deduction reduced your tax in the earlier year.

**Casualty or Theft Gains That You Must Report**

If the amount you received in insurance or other compensation is more than the cost or other basis of the property, you have a casualty or theft gain.

If you had a casualty or theft gain from trade, business, or income-producing property held more than one year, part or all of the gain may be ordinary income. See the instructions for line 19.

If property is destroyed or lost by casualty or theft and replaced with similar property, the gain may be partially or wholly nontaxable. Report on this form only the part of the gain that is taxable.

**How To Figure a Casualty Loss**

**Trade, Business, or Income-Producing Property.**—To figure a casualty loss from a trade or business or from income-producing property, measure the decrease in value by taking the building and other items into account separately. For example, if you had a rental property that was damaged by a storm, figure the loss on the building separately from any trees or shrubs that were damaged.

**Other Property.**—To figure a casualty loss involving real property and real property improvements not used in a trade or business, or for income-producing purposes, measure the decrease in value of the property as a whole.

**Special Rule for Disaster Losses**

A disaster loss is a loss which occurred in an area determined by the President of the United States to warrant Federal disaster assistance. You may elect to deduct the loss in the prior tax year as long as the loss would otherwise be allowed as a deduction in the year it occurred.

This election must be made by filing your return or amended return by the later of the following two dates:

(1) The due date for filing your original return (without extensions) for the tax year in which the disaster actually occurred.

(2) The due date for filing your original return (including any extension) for the tax year immediately before the tax year in which the disaster actually occurred.

The return claiming the disaster loss should specify the date or dates of the disaster and the city, town, county, and State in which the damaged or destroyed property was located.

You may revoke your election within 90 days after making it by returning to IRS any refund or credit you received from the election. If you revoke your election before receiving a refund, you must repay the refund within 30 days after receiving it.

**Note: To determine the amount to deduct for a disaster loss you must take into account any benefits you received from Federal or State programs to restore your property.**

**Publications.**—See the following publications for more information: **Publication 547,** Tax Information on Disasters, Casualties, and Thefts; **Publication 551,** Basis of Assets; and **Publication 584,** Disaster and Casualty Loss Workbook.

## Line-by-Line Instructions

**Line 2.**—Cost or other basis usually means original cost plus improvements, minus depreciation allowed or allowable, amortization, depletion, etc. Special rules apply to property received as a gift or inheritance.

**Lines 5, 6, and 7.**—Fair market value is the price at which the property would change hands between a willing buyer and a willing seller. Replacement cost is not fair market value. The fair market value of property after a theft is zero. Fair market value is generally determined by competent appraisal. This appraisal must take into account the effects of any general market decline that may occur at the same time as the casualty or theft. You may be able to use the cost of repairs to the damaged property as evidence of the loss of value. However, you must show the following:

(a) The repairs are necessary to restore the property to the condition it was in immediately before the casualty.

(b) The amount you spent for these repairs is not excessive.

(c) The repairs only correct the damage.

(d) The value of the property after the repairs is not, as a result of the repairs, more than the value of the property immediately before the casualty.

**Line 11.**—If the loss is from property partly used for personal purposes, such as a personal home with a rental unit, enter only the part used for trade, business, or income-producing purposes.

**Line 14.**—If you are an individual and meet the requirements for completing only Part I, enter the amount from line 14 on Schedule A (Form 1040), line 24.

**Caution:** If (1) for your tax year that begins in 1983 you had a **disaster loss** from property **not** used in a trade or business or for income-producing purposes, and (2) you choose to deduct the loss on your tax return that began in 1982, and (3) you are not required to complete Part II of Form 4684, subtract line 13 from line 12. Enter on line 14 the part of the remainder that is more than 10% of line 33, 1982 Form 1040. Attach a schedule showing this computation.

**Lines 15 and 20.**—Enter on line 15, all gains and losses to property held one year or less. Enter on line 20, all gains and losses to property held more than one year. However, see the instructions for line 19. If part of one casualty or theft is to property held one year or less, and part to property held more than one year, separate it according to how long the property was held. It may be necessary to allocate line 14.

**Column A.**—Use a separate line for each different casualty or theft.

**Column B(i).**—Enter the part of line 11 from trade, business, rental, or royalty property.

**Column B(ii).**—Enter the loss from line 14 and the part of line 11 not included in column B(i).

**Lines 17 and 24(a).**—If Form 4797 is not otherwise required, enter this amount on the applicable form as follows and identify as "4684":

Form 1040, line 15
Form 1120, page 1, line 9
Form 1065, page 1, line 9 (Form 4684, line 17 only)
Form 1041, page 1, line 8
Form 1120S, page 1, line 9

**Lines 18 and 24(b).**—Estates and trusts, enter amount from this line on Form 1041, line 16. Partnerships enter the amount from line 18 on Schedule K (Form 1065), line 13. Identify as "4684."

**Caution:** If (1) for your tax year that begins in 1983 you had a **disaster loss** from property **not** used in a trade or business or for income-producing purposes, and (2) you choose to deduct the loss on your tax return for your tax year that began in 1982—

- **Line 18.** Enter the part of line 16, column (B)(ii) that is more than 10% of line 33, 1982 Form 1040.
- **Line 24(b).** Enter the part of line 21, column (B)(ii) that is more than 10% of line 33, 1982 Form 1040.

**Note:** If both lines 16(B)(ii) and 21(B)(ii) show a loss, allocate one 10% amount between lines 16(B)(ii) and 21(B)(ii).

Attach a schedule showing this computation.

**Line 19.**—If you had a casualty or theft gain from trade, business, or income-producing property held more than one year, you may have to recapture part or all of the gain as ordinary income. If so, complete Form 4797, Part III and this line instead of completing line 18. See Form 4797.

**Line 25.**—If Form 4797 is not otherwise required, enter this amount on your appropriate Schedule D as follows and identify as "4684":

Schedule D (Form 1040), line 14
Schedule D (Form 1120), line 5
Schedule D (Form 1041), line 11
Schedule D (Form 1120S), line 5.

☆ U.S. GOVERNMENT PRINTING OFFICE : 1982—O-363-184

## B-17 FORM 4797 SUPPLEMENTAL SCHEDULE OF GAINS AND LOSSES

| Form **4797** | **Supplemental Schedule of Gains and Losses** | OMB No. 1545-0184 |
|---|---|---|
| Department of the Treasury Internal Revenue Service | (Includes Gains and Losses From Sales or Exchanges of Assets Used in a Trade or Business and Involuntary Conversions) To be filed with Form 1040, 1041, 1065, 1120, etc.—See Separate Instructions | **1982** 31 |

| Name(s) as shown on return | Identifying number |
|---|---|

**Part I** Sales or Exchanges of Property Used in a Trade or Business, and Involuntary Conversions From Other Than Casualty and Theft—Property Held More Than 1 Year (Except for Certain Livestock)

Note: Use Form 4684 to report involuntary conversions from casualty and theft.
Caution: If you sold property on which you claimed the investment credit, you may be liable for recapture of that credit. See Form 4255 for additional information.

| a. Kind of property and description | b. Date acquired (mo., day, yr.) | c. Date sold (mo., day, yr.) | d. Gross sales price minus expense of sale | e. Depreciation allowed (or allowable) since acquisition | f. Cost or other basis, plus improvements | g. LOSS (f minus the sum of d and e) | h. GAIN (d plus e minus f) |
|---|---|---|---|---|---|---|---|
| 1 | | | | | | | |
| | | | | | | | |
| | | | | | | | |
| | | | | | | | |
| | | | | | | | |

2 (a) Gain, if any, from Form 4684, line 25 . . . . . . . . .

(b) Section 1231 gain from installment sales from Form 6252, line 21 or 29 . . . . . .

3 Gain, if any, from line 26, Part III, on back of this form from other than casualty and theft . .

4 Add lines 1 through 3 in column g and column h . . . . . . . . . . . ( )

5 Combine line 4, column g and line 4, column h. Enter gain or (loss) here, and on the appropriate line as follows:
(a) For all except partnership returns:
(1) If line 5 is a gain, enter the gain as a long-term capital gain on Schedule D. See instruction E.
(2) If line 5 is zero or a loss, enter that amount on line 6.
(b) For partnership returns: Enter the amount from line 5 above, on Schedule K (Form 1065), line 8.

**Part II** Ordinary Gains and Losses

| a. Kind of property and description | b. Date acquired (mo., day, yr.) | c. Date sold (mo., day, yr.) | d. Gross sales price minus expense of sale | e. Depreciation allowed (or allowable) since acquisition | f. Cost or other basis, plus improvements | g. LOSS (f minus the sum of d and e) | h. GAIN (d plus e minus f) |
|---|---|---|---|---|---|---|---|
| 6 Loss, if any, from line 5(a)(2) . . . . . . . . | | | | | | | |
| 7 Gain, if any, from line 25, Part III on back of this form . . . . . | | | | | | | |
| 8 (a) Net gain or (loss) from Form 4684, lines 17 and 24a . . . . . | | | | | | | |
| (b) Ordinary gain from installment sales from Form 6252, line 20 or 28 . . . | | | | | | | |
| 9 Other ordinary gains and losses (include property held 1 year or less): | | | | | | | |
| | | | | | | | |
| | | | | | | | |
| | | | | | | | |
| | | | | | | | |

10 Add lines 6 through 9 in column g and column h . . . . . . . . . ( )

11 Combine line 10, column g and line 10, column h. Enter gain or (loss) here, and on the appropriate line as follows:
(a) For all except individual returns: Enter the gain or (loss) from line 11, on the return being filed. See instruction F for specific line reference.
(b) For individual returns:
(1) If the loss on line 6 includes a loss from Form 4684, Part II, column B(ii), enter that part of the loss here and on line 24 of Schedule A (Form 1040). Identify as from "Form 4797, line 11(b)(1)" . . . . .
(2) Redetermine the gain or (loss) on line 11, excluding the loss (if any) on line 11(b)(1). Enter here and on Form 1040, line 15 . . . . . . . . . .

**For Paperwork Reduction Act Notice, see page 1 of separate instructions.**  363-189-1  Form **4797** (1982)

Form 4797 (1982)      Page **2**

**Part III**   Gain From Disposition of Property Under Sections 1245, 1250, 1251, 1252, 1254, 1255

Skip lines 20 and 21 if you did not dispose of farm property or farmland, or if a partnership files this form.

**12** Description of sections 1245, 1250, 1251, 1252, 1254, and 1255 property:     Date acquired (mo., day, yr.)     Date sold (mo., day, yr.)

(A)
(B)
(C)
(D)

| Relate lines 12(A) through 12(D) to these columns ▶ ▶ ▶ | Property (A) | Property (B) | Property (C) | Property (D) |
|---|---|---|---|---|
| **13** Gross sales price minus expense of sale | | | | |
| **14** Cost or other basis | | | | |
| **15** Depreciation (or depletion) allowed (or allowable) | | | | |
| **16** Adjusted basis, subtract line 15 from line 14 | | | | |
| **17** Total gain, subtract line 16 from line 13 | | | | |
| **18** If section 1245 property: | | | | |
|   (a) Depreciation allowed (or allowable) after applicable date (see instructions) | | | | |
|   (b) Enter smaller of line 17 or 18(a) | | | | |
| **19** If section 1250 property: (If straight line depreciation used, enter zero on line 19(f).) | | | | |
|   (a) Additional depreciation after 12/31/75 | | | | |
|   (b) Applicable percentage times the smaller of line 17 or line 19(a) (see instruction G.4) | | | | |
|   (c) Subtract line 19(a) from line 17. If line 17 is not more than line 19(a), skip lines 19(d) and 19(e) | | | | |
|   (d) Additional depreciation after 12/31/69 and before 1/1/76 | | | | |
|   (e) Applicable percentage times the smaller of line 19(c) or 19(d) (see instruction G.4) | | | | |
|   (f) Add lines 19(b), and 19(e) | | | | |
| **20** If section 1251 property: | | | | |
|   (a) If farmland, enter soil, water, and land clearing expenses for current year and the four preceding years | | | | |
|   (b) If farm property other than land, subtract line 18(b) from line 17; if farmland, enter smaller of line 17 or 20(a) | | | | |
|   (c) Excess deductions account (see instruction G.5) | | | | |
|   (d) Enter smaller of line 20(b) or 20(c) | | | | |
| **21** If section 1252 property: | | | | |
|   (a) Soil, water, and land clearing expenses | | | | |
|   (b) Amount from line 20(d), if none enter zero | | | | |
|   (c) Subtract line 21(b) from line 21(a). If line 21(b) is more than line 21(a), enter zero | | | | |
|   (d) Line 21(c) times applicable percentage (see instruction G.5) | | | | |
|   (e) Subtract line 21(b) from line 17 | | | | |
|   (f) Enter smaller of line 21(d) or 21(e) | | | | |
| **22** If section 1254 property: | | | | |
|   (a) Intangible drilling and development costs deducted after 12/31/75 (see instruction G.6) | | | | |
|   (b) Enter smaller of line 17 or 22(a) | | | | |
| **23** If section 1255 property: | | | | |
|   (a) Applicable percentage of payments excluded from income under section 126 (see instruction G.7) | | | | |
|   (b) Enter the smaller of line 17 or 23(a) | | | | |

**Summary of Part III Gains (Complete Property columns (A) through (D) through line 23(b) before going to line 24)**

**24** Total gains for all properties (add columns (A) through (D), line 17) . . . . . . . . . . . . . .

**25** Add columns (A) through (D), lines 18(b), 19(f), 20(d), 21(f), 22(b) and 23(b). Enter here and on Part II, line 7 .

**26** Subtract line 25 from line 24. Enter the portion from casualty and theft on Form 4684, line 19; enter the portion from other than casualty and theft on Form 4797, Part I, line 3 . . . . . . . . . . . . . . . .

**Part IV**   Complete this Part Only if You Elect Out of the Installment Method And Report a Note or Other Obligation at Less Than Full Face Value

☐ Check here if you elect out of the installment method.

     Enter the face amount of the note or other obligation ▶ .......................................

     Enter the percentage of valuation of the note or other obligation ▶

## B–18 FORM 4868 APPLICATION FOR AUTOMATIC EXTENSION OF TIME TO FILE U.S. INDIVIDUAL INCOME TAX RETURN

| Form **4868**<br>Department of the Treasury<br>Internal Revenue Service | **Application for Automatic Extension of Time<br>to File U.S. Individual Income Tax Return** | OMB No. 1545-0188<br>**1982**<br>72 |
|---|---|---|

| Please<br>Print<br>or<br>Type | Your first name and initial (if joint return, also give spouse's name and initial)　　　Last name | Your social security number |
|---|---|---|
| | Present home address (Number and street, including apartment number, or rural route) | Spouse's social security no. |
| | City, town or post office, State, and ZIP code | |

**Note:** *File this form with the Internal Revenue Service Center where you must file your income tax return and pay the amount shown on line 6 below.* **This is not an extension of time for payment of tax.** *You will be charged a penalty for late payment of tax and late filing unless you show reasonable cause for not paying or filing on time (see instructions).*

If you expect to file a gift tax return (Form 709 or Form 709–A) for 1982 due by April 15, 1983, check this box ☐.

I request an automatic 4-month extension of time to August 15, 1983, to file Form 1040 for the calendar year 1982 (or if a fiscal year return to ................................., 19........, for the tax year ending ................................., 19........).

| | | | |
|---|---|---|---|
| 1 | Total income tax liability for 1982 (You may estimate this amount.) . . . . . . .<br>**Note:** You must enter an amount on line 1. If you do not expect to owe tax, enter zero (0). | **1** | |
| 2 | Federal income tax withheld . . . . . . . . . . . . . . . | **2** | |
| 3 | 1982 estimated tax payments (include 1981 overpayment allowed as a credit) . | **3** | |
| 4 | Other payments and credits you expect to show on Form 1040 . . . . . . | **4** | |
| 5 | Add lines 2, 3, and 4 . . . . . . . . . . . . . . | **5** | |
| 6 | Income tax balance due (subtract line 5 from line 1). Pay in full with this form . . . . . . . ▶ | **6** | |
| 7 | Total gift tax you expect to owe for 1982 (see instructions) . . . . . . . . . . . . . ▶ | **7** | |

**If you send only one check for both income and gift tax due, attach a statement showing how much of the check applies to each type of tax.**

### Signature and Verification

**If Prepared by Taxpayer.**—Under penalties of perjury, I declare that I have examined this form, including accompanying schedules and statements, and to the best of my knowledge and belief, it is true, correct, and complete.

Your signature ....................................................................　Date ....................................

Spouse's signature (if filing jointly, BOTH must sign even if only one had income) ...................　Date ....................................

**If Prepared by Someone Other Than Taxpayer.**—Under penalties of perjury, I declare that I have examined this form, including accompanying schedules and statements, and to the best of my knowledge and belief, it is true, correct, and complete; and that I am authorized to prepare this form.

Signature of preparer other than taxpayer ....................................................　Date ....................................

**Note:** *The person who signs this form may be an attorney or certified public accountant qualified to practice before the IRS, a person enrolled to practice before the IRS, or a person holding a power of attorney. If the taxpayer cannot sign because of illness, absence, or other good cause, a person in a close personal or business relationship to the taxpayer may sign this form.*

**For Paperwork Reduction Act Notice, see back of form.**　　　363–193–1　　　Form **4868** (1982)

## General Instructions

**Paperwork Reduction Act Notice.**—The Paperwork Reduction Act of 1980 says we must tell you why we are collecting this information, how we will use it, and whether you have to give it to us. We ask for the information to carry out the Internal Revenue laws of the United States. We need it to ensure that you are complying with these laws and to allow us to figure and collect the right amount of tax. You are required to give us this information.

**Purpose.**—Use Form 4868 to ask for an automatic 4-month extension of time to file Form 1040. Do not request an automatic extension if:

- You want the IRS to figure your tax, or
- You are under a court order to file your return by the regular due date.

The extension will be granted if you complete this form properly, file it on time, **and pay with it the amount of tax shown on line 6.** We will notify you **only** if your request for an extension is denied.

**Note:** *Any extension of time granted for filing your 1982 calendar year income tax return also extends the time for filing a gift tax return for 1982 due by April 15, 1983.*

**When to File.**—File Form 4868 by April 15, 1983. If you are filing a fiscal year return, file Form 4868 by the regular due date of Form 1040. If the due date falls on a Saturday, Sunday, or legal holiday, file by the next regular workday.

You may file Form 1040 any time before the 4-month period ends.

**Filing Form 2688.**—Except in cases of undue hardship, we will not accept Form 2688, Application for Extension of Time to File U.S. Individual Income Tax Return, until you have first used Form 4868.

If you have filed Form 4868 and still need more time, use Form 2688 or write a letter of explanation. You must show reasonable cause. Send Form 2688 or the letter to the Internal Revenue Service Center where you file your Form 1040. (See Where to File, below.)

If you need a further extension, ask for it early so that, if denied, you can still file your return on time.

**Where to File.**—Mail this form to the **Internal Revenue Service Center** for the place where you live.

| | |
|---|---|
| New Jersey, New York City and counties of Nassau, Rockland, Suffolk, and Westchester | Holtsville, NY 00501 |
| New York (all other counties), Connecticut, Maine, Massachusetts, New Hampshire, Rhode Island, Vermont | Andover, MA 05501 |
| Delaware, Maryland, District of Columbia, Pennsylvania | Philadelphia, PA 19255 |
| Alabama, Florida, Georgia, Mississippi, South Carolina | Atlanta, GA 31101 |
| Michigan, Ohio | Cincinnati, OH 45999 |
| Arkansas, Kansas, Louisiana, New Mexico, Oklahoma, Texas | Austin, TX 73301 |

| | |
|---|---|
| Alaska, Arizona, Colorado, Idaho, Minnesota, Montana, Nebraska, Nevada, North Dakota, Oregon, South Dakota, Utah, Washington, Wyoming | Ogden, UT 84201 |
| Illinois, Iowa, Missouri, Wisconsin | Kansas City, MO 64999 |
| California, Hawaii | Fresno, CA 93888 |
| Indiana, Kentucky, North Carolina, Tennessee, Virginia, West Virginia | Memphis, TN 37501 |

| If you are located in: | Use this address: |
|---|---|
| American Samoa | Philadelphia, PA 19255 |
| Guam | Commissioner of Revenue and Taxation Agana, GU 96910 |
| Puerto Rico (or if excluding income under section 933) Virgin Islands: Nonpermanent residents | Philadelphia, PA 19255 |
| Virgin Islands: Permanent residents | Department of Finance, Tax Division Charlotte Amalie, St. Thomas, VI 00801 |
| A.P.O. or F.P.O. address of: | Miami—Atlanta, GA 31101 New York—Holtsville, NY 00501 San Francisco—Fresno, CA 93888 Seattle—Ogden, UT 84201 |
| Foreign country: U.S. citizens and those excluding income under section 911 or 931, or claiming the housing deduction under section 911 | Philadelphia, PA 19255 |

**Penalties.**—You may be charged one or both of the following penalties.

**Late payment penalty.**—Form 4868 does not extend the time to pay income or gift tax. A penalty of ½ of 1% of any tax (other than estimated tax) not paid by the regular due date is charged for each month, or part of a month, that the tax remains unpaid. The penalty will not be charged if you can show reasonable cause for not paying on time. The penalty is limited to 25%.

You are considered to have reasonable cause for the period covered by this automatic extension if the amount you owe on Form 1040, line 71 (minus any estimated tax penalty):

- Is not more than 10% of the amount shown as total tax on Form 1040, line 59, and
- Is paid with Form 1040.

If both of the above conditions are not met, the late payment penalty will apply, unless you show reasonable cause.

If you have reasonable cause, attach a statement to Form 1040 giving your reason.

If you cannot show reasonable cause, figure the penalty on the total tax due on Form 1040, line 71, from the regular due date of Form 1040 to the date of payment.

**Late filing penalty.**—A penalty is charged if your return is filed after the due date (including extensions), unless you can show reasonable cause for filing late. The penalty is 5% of the tax not paid by the regular due date for each month, or part of a month, that your return is late, but not more than 25%. If your return is more than 60 days late, the penalty will not be less than $100 or 100% of the balance of tax due on your return, whichever is smaller. If you file your return late, attach a full explanation with the return.

**Interest.**—Interest is charged from the regular due date of the return until the tax is paid. It will be charged even if:

- You have been granted an extension, or
- You show reasonable cause for not paying the tax.

**When You File Your Form 1040.**—If you owe any interest or penalties when you file your Form 1040, see **Reminders** on page 17 of the Form 1040 instructions for how to report these items.

## Line-by-Line Instructions

At the top of this form, fill in the spaces for your name, address, social security number, and spouse's social security number if you are filing a joint return. If you expect to file a gift tax return (Form 709 or Form 709–A) for 1982 due by April 15, 1983, check the box on the front of this form. Below that, if you are on a fiscal year, fill in the date on which your 4-month extension will end and the date your tax year ends.

We have provided specific instructions for most of the lines on the form. Those lines that do not appear in these instructions are self-explanatory.

**Line 1.**—Enter the amount of income tax you expect to owe for 1982 (the amount you expect to enter on Form 1040, line 59, when you file your return). Be sure to estimate the amount correctly. If you underestimate this amount, you may be charged a penalty as explained earlier under **Penalties**.

**Line 6.**—An extension of time to file your income tax return will not extend the time to pay your income tax. Therefore, you must pay the amount of income tax shown on line 6 in full with this form.

**Line 7.**—If you plan to use the extension of time to file your gift tax return enter the amount of gift tax you expect to owe for 1982. To avoid the failure to pay penalty, you must pay this amount in full with Form 4868 unless you specifically request an extension to pay the gift tax. To request an extension to pay the gift tax only, you must attach a statement to this form that paying the gift tax on the due date would cause you undue hardship (not merely inconvenience).

If your spouse is filing a separate Form 4868, enter on your form only the total gift tax you expect to owe.

If you are filing Form 4868 with your spouse, enter on line 7 the total gift tax the two of you expect to owe. However, if each of you expects to file a gift tax return, also show in the space to the right of line 7 how much gift tax each expects to owe for 1982.

Below line 7, sign and date the form. If someone else prepares the form for you, that person must sign and date the form.

**How to Claim Credit for Payment Made With This Form.**—Enter on Form 1040, line 63, the amount paid (line 6) with this form.

If you and your spouse file a joint Form 4868 for 1982, but file separate income tax returns for the year, you may claim the total tax payment (line 6) on your separate return or on your spouse's separate return or you may divide it in any agreed amounts. Be sure to enter the social security numbers of both spouses on the separate Form 1040 returns.

If you and your spouse file separate Forms 4868 for 1982, but file a joint income tax return for the year, enter on Form 1040, line 63, the total of the amounts paid on the separate Forms 4868. Also enter the social security numbers of both spouses in the spaces on Form 1040.

# B–19 FORM 5695 RESIDENTIAL ENERGY CREDIT

| Form **5695**<br>Department of the Treasury<br>Internal Revenue Service | **Residential Energy Credit**<br>▶ Attach to Form 1040.  ▶ See Instructions on back.<br>For Paperwork Reduction Act Notice, see instructions on back. | OMB No. 1545–0214<br>19**82**<br>33 |
|---|---|---|

Name(s) as shown on Form 1040 | Your social security number

Enter in the space below the address of your principal residence on which the credit is claimed if it is different from the address shown on Form 1040.

If you have an energy credit carryover from a previous tax year and no energy savings costs this year, skip to Part III, line 24.

**Part I**   Fill in your energy conservation costs (but do not include repair or maintenance costs).

1 Was your principal residence substantially completed before April 20, 1977? . . . . . . . ▶ ☐ Yes ☐ No

**Note:** You MUST answer this question. Failure to do so will delay the processing of your return. If you checked the "No" box, you CANNOT claim an energy credit under Part I and you should not fill in lines 2 through 12 of this form.

2 a Insulation . . . . . . . . . . . . . . . . **2a**
  b Storm (or thermal) windows or doors . . . . . . . . . . **2b**
  c Caulking or weatherstripping . . . . . . . . . . . **2c**
  d A replacement burner for your existing furnace that reduces fuel use . . **2d**
  e A device for modifying flue openings to make a heating system more efficient . **2e**
  f An electrical or mechanical furnace ignition system that replaces a gas pilot light . . . . . **2f**
  g A thermostat with an automatic setback . . . . . . . **2g**
  h A meter that shows the cost of energy used . . . . . . . . . **2h**
3 Total (add lines 2a through 2h) . . . . . . . . . **3**
4 Enter the part of expenditures made from nontaxable government grants and subsidized financing . **4**
5 Subtract line 4 from line 3 . . . . . . . . . **5**
6 Maximum amount of cost on which credit can be figured . . . . . . **6** | $2,000 | 00
7 Enter the total energy conservation costs for this residence. Add line 2 of your 1978, 1979, and 1980 Forms 5695 and line 3 of your 1981 Form 5695 . . . . . . . . . **7**
8 Subtract line 7 from line 6 . . . . . . . . . . **8**
9 Enter the total nontaxable grants and subsidized financing used to purchase qualified energy items for this residence. Add the amount on line 4 of this form and the amount on line 4 of your 1981 Form 5695 . **9**
10 Subtract line 9 from line 8. If zero or less, do not complete the rest of this part . . . . . **10**
11 Enter the amount on line 5 or line 10, whichever is less . . . . . **11**
12 Enter 15% of line 11 here and include in amount on line 23 below . . . . . . . . **12**

**Part II**   Fill in your renewable energy source costs (but do not include repair or maintenance costs).

13 a Solar _____ 13 b Geothermal _____ 13 c Wind _____ Total ▶ **13d**
14 Enter the part of expenditures made from nontaxable government grants and subsidized financing . . **14**
15 Subtract line 14 from line 13 . . . . . . . . . **15**
16 Maximum amount of cost on which the credit can be figured . . . . . . **16** | $10,000 | 00
17 Enter the total renewable energy source costs for this residence. Add line 5 of your 1978 Form 5695, line 9 of your 1979 and 1980 Forms 5695, and line 13d of your 1981 Form 5695 . . . . . . **17**
18 Subtract line 17 from line 16 . . . . . . . . . **18**
19 Enter the total nontaxable grants and subsidized financing used to purchase qualified energy items for this residence. Add the amount on line 14 of this form and the amount on line 14 of your 1981 Form 5695 . . . . . . . . **19**
20 Subtract line 19 from line 18. If zero or less, do not complete the rest of this part . . . . . **20**
21 Enter the amount on line 15 or line 20, whichever is less . . . . . **21**
22 Enter 40% of line 21 here and include in amount on line 23 below . . . . . . . **22**

**Part III**   Fill in this part to figure the limitation.

23 Add lines 12 and 22. If less than $10, enter zero . . . . . . . **23**
24 Enter your energy credit carryover from a previous tax year. **Caution**—Do not make an entry on this line if your 1981 Form 1040, line 47, showed an amount of more than zero . . . . . **24**
25 Add lines 23 and 24 . . . . . . . . . . . **25**
26 Enter the amount of tax shown on Form 1040, line 40 . . . . . . **26**
27 Add lines 41 through 46 from Form 1040 and enter the total . . . . . **27**
28 Subtract line 27 from line 26. If zero or less, enter zero . . . . . . **28**
29 Residential energy credit. Enter the amount on line 25 or line 28, whichever is less. Also, enter this amount on Form 1040, line 47. Complete Part IV below if this line is less than line 25 . . . . . **29**

**Part IV**   Fill in this part to figure your carryover to 1983 (Complete only if line 29 is less than line 25).

30 Enter amount from Part III, line 25 . . . . . . . . . **30**
31 Enter amount from Part III, line 29 . . . . . . . . . **31**
32 Credit carryover to 1983 (subtract line 31 from line 30) . . . . . . **32**

363–221–1

## General Instructions

**Paperwork Reduction Act Notice.**—The Paperwork Reduction Act of 1980 says we must tell you why we are collecting this information, how we will use it, and whether you have to give it to us. We ask for the information to carry out the Internal Revenue laws of the United States. We need it to ensure that you are complying with these laws and to allow us to figure and collect the right amount of tax. You are required to give us this information.

Two energy credits make up the residential energy credit, each with its own conditions and limits. These credits are based on: (1) Costs for home energy conservation, and (2) Costs for renewable energy source property.

The credit is based on the cost of items installed in your principal residence after April 19, 1977, and before January 1, 1986.

**Purpose.**—Use this form to figure your residential energy credit if you had qualified energy saving items installed in your principal residence. The instructions below list conditions you must meet to take the credit. If you have an energy credit carryover from the previous tax year and no energy saving costs this year, skip to Part III of the form. Attach Form 5695 to your tax return. For more information, please get Publication 903, Energy Credits for Individuals.

**What is your principal residence?**—To qualify as your principal residence, your residence must be the home in the United States where you live (you may own it or rent it from another person).

A summer or vacation home does not qualify.

For energy conservation items to qualify, your principal residence must have been substantially completed before April 20, 1977. A dwelling unit is considered substantially completed when it can be used as a personal residence even though minor items remain unfinished.

**Special Rules.**—If you live in a condominium, cooperative apartment, occupy a dwelling unit jointly, or share the cost of energy property, see **Publication 903** for more details.

**What are energy saving items?**—You can take the credit for energy conservation and renewable energy source items.

**Energy conservation items** are limited to:

- insulation (fiberglass, cellulose, etc.) for ceilings, walls, floors, roofs, water heaters, etc.
- storm (or thermal) windows or doors for the outside of your residence.
- caulking or weatherstripping for windows or doors for the outside of your residence.
- a replacement burner for your existing furnace that reduces fuel use. The burner must replace an existing burner. It does not qualify if it is acquired as a component of, or for use in, a new furnace or boiler.
- a device for modifying flue openings to make a heating system more efficient.
- an electrical or mechanical furnace ignition system that replaces a gas pilot light.
- a thermostat with an automatic setback.
- a meter that shows the cost of energy used.

To take the credit for an energy conservation item, you must:

- install the item in your principal residence which was substantially completed before April 20, 1977,
- be the first one to use the item, and
- expect it to last at least 3 years.

The maximum credit for energy conservation items cannot be more than $300 ($2,000 × 15%) for each principal residence.

**Renewable energy source items** include solar, wind, and geothermal energy items that heat or cool your principal residence or provide hot water or electricity for it.

Examples of solar energy items that may qualify include:

- collectors;
- rockbeds;
- heat exchangers, and
- solar panels installed on roofs (including those installed as a roof or part of a roof).

An example of an item that uses wind energy is a windmill that produces energy in any form (usually electricity) for your residence.

To take the credit for a renewable energy source item, you must:

- be the first one to use the item, and
- expect it to last at least 5 years.

The maximum credit for renewable energy source items cannot be more than $4,000 ($10,000 × 40%) for each principal residence.

**What items are NOT eligible for the energy credit?**—Do not take credit for:

- carpeting;
- drapes;
- wood paneling;
- wood or peat-burning stoves;
- hydrogen fueled residential equipment;
- siding for the outside of your residence;
- heat pumps (both air and water);
- fluorescent replacement lighting systems;
- replacement boilers and furnaces; and
- swimming pools used to store energy.

**Federal, State, or local government nontaxable grants and subsidized financing.**—Qualified expenditures financed with nontaxable Federal, State, or local government grants cannot be used to figure the energy credit. Also, if Federal, State, or local government programs provide subsidized financing for any part of qualified expenditures, that part cannot be used to figure the energy credit. You must reduce the expenditure limits on energy conservation and renewable energy source property for a dwelling by the part of expenditures financed by Federal, State, or local government subsidized energy financing, as well as by the amount of nontaxable Federal, State, or local government grants used to purchase conservation or renewable energy source property.

**Figuring the credit for more than one principal residence.**—You can take the maximum credit for each principal residence you live in. If you use all of your credit for one residence and then move, you may take the maximum credit amount on your next residence.

To figure your 1982 energy credit for more than one principal residence:

(1) Fill out Part I or II on a separate Form 5695 for each principal residence.

(2) Enter the total of all parts on line 23 of one of the forms.

(3) In the space above line 23, write "More than one principal residence."

(4) Attach all forms to your return.

**Caution:** *You should keep a copy of each Form 5695 that you file for your records. For example, if you sell your principal residence, you will need to know the amount of the credit claimed in prior tax years. If the items for which you took the credit increased the basis of your principal residence, you must reduce the basis by the credit you took.*

**If the credit is more than your tax.**—If your energy credit for this year is more than your tax minus certain other credits, you can carry over the excess energy credit to the following tax year.

## Specific Instructions

**Part I, lines 2a through 2h.**—Enter your energy conservation costs (including expenditures made with nontaxable government grants and subsidized financing) only for this tax year. Count the cost of the item and its installation in or on your principal residence. Do not include the cost of repairs or maintenance for energy conservation items.

**Part I, line 4.**—Enter the amount of nontaxable government grants and subsidized financing used to purchase the energy items. If you do not know the amount, check with the government agency that gave you the grant or subsidized financing.

**Part I, line 7.**—Enter your total energy conservation costs from 1978, 1979, 1980, and 1981 for this principal residence. If you had energy conservation costs in the previous tax year but could not take a credit because it was less than $10, enter zero.

**Part I, line 9.**—Enter the part of nontaxable government grants and subsidized financing received under Federal, State, or local programs to purchase energy items. You must use the amounts received under these programs to reduce the maximum amount of cost used to figure the credit. If you do not know the amount of the nontaxable grant, check with the government agency which gave you the grant or subsidized financing.

**Part II, lines 13a through 13d.**—Enter your renewable energy source costs (including expenditures made with nontaxable government grants and subsidized financing) only for this tax year. Do not include the cost of repairs or maintenance for renewable energy source items.

**Part II, line 14.**—See Part I, line 4 for explanation.

**Part II, line 17.**—Enter your total renewable energy source costs from 1978, 1979, 1980, and 1981 for this principal residence. If you had renewable energy source costs in the previous tax year but could not take a credit because it was less than $10, enter zero.

**Part II, line 19.**—See Part I, line 9 for explanation.

**Part III, line 24.**—Generally, your energy credit carryover will be computed on your prior year Form 5695, Part IV. Exception— If the alternative minimum tax applied, see Publication **909**, Minimum Tax and Alternative Minimum Tax.

**Part IV.**—Complete this part only if line 29 is less than line 25. You can carry over the amount entered on line 32 to your next tax year. Exception—If the alternative minimum tax applies, see Publication **909**.

## B-20 FORM 6251 ALTERNATIVE MINIMUM TAX COMPUTATION

| Form **6251** | **Alternative Minimum Tax Computation** | OMB No. 1545-0227 |
|---|---|---|
| Department of the Treasury<br>Internal Revenue Service | ▶ See instructions on back.<br>▶ Attach to Forms 1040, 1040NR, 1041 or 990–T (Trust). | **1982**<br>34 |

| Name(s) as shown on tax return | Identifying number |
|---|---|

### Part I — Computation of Alternative Minimum Tax

| | | | |
|---|---|---|---|
| 1 | Adjusted gross income from Form 1040 or Form 1040NR, line 33 (see instructions) . . . . . . | **1** | |
| 2 | Deductions (applies to individuals only): | | |
| | **a** Amount from Form 1040, line 34a or 34b, or Form 1040NR, line 36 . | **2a** | |
| | **b** On your 1982 Form 1040, if you checked Filing Status box . { 2 or 5, enter $3,400 / 1 or 4, enter $2,300 / 3, enter $1,700 . . } | **2b** | |
| | **c** Multiply $1,000 by the total number of exemptions on Form 1040, line 6e | **2c** | |
| | **d** Add lines 2a through 2c (estates and trusts, enter zero) . . . . . . | **2d** | |
| 3 | Subtract line 2d from line 1 . . . . . . . . . . . | **3** | |
| 4 | Tax preference items: | | |
| | **a** Adjusted itemized deductions . . . . . . . . . . | **4a** | |
| | **b** Capital gain deduction . . . . . . . . . . . . | **4b** | |
| | **c** Add lines 4a and 4b . . . . . . . . . . . . . | **4c** | |
| 5 | Alternative minimum taxable income (add lines 3 and 4c) . . . . . . | **5** | |
| 6 | Enter $20,000 ($10,000 if married filing separately, or an estate or trust) . . . . . . | **6** | |
| 7 | Subtract line 6 from line 5. If zero or less, do not complete the rest of this form . . . . . | **7** | |
| 8 | Enter the smaller of line 7 or $40,000 ($20,000 if married filing separately, or an estate or trust) . . . . . . | **8** | |
| 9 | Subtract line 8 from line 7 . . . . . . . . | **9** | |
| 10 | Enter 10% of line 8 . . . . . . . . . | **10** | |
| 11 | Enter 20% of line 9 . . . . . . . . . | **11** | |
| 12 | Add lines 10 and 11 . . . . . . . . . | **12** | |
| 13 | Amount from Form 1040, line 50* (estates and trusts—see instructions) . | **13** | |
| 14 | Minimum tax from Form 1040, 1040NR, 1041, or 990–T . . . . . | **14** | |
| 15 | Tax from recapture of investment credit . . . . . . . . | **15** | |
| 16 | Add lines 13 through 15 . . . . . . . . . . . | **16** | |
| 17 | Subtract line 16 from line 12. If zero or less, do not complete the rest of this form . . . . . | **17** | |
| 18 | Foreign tax credit (see instructions) . . . . . . . . . | **18** | |
| 19 | Subtract line 18 from line 17. If line 18 is more than line 17, enter zero . . . . . | **19** | |
| 20 | Credits allowed against alternative minimum tax from Part II, line 27 . . . . . | **20** | |
| 21 | Alternative minimum tax (subtract line 20 from line 19.) If zero or less, enter zero. Enter here and on Form 1040, line 53 or Form 1040NR, line 54 (estates and trusts—see instructions) . . . . . | **21** | |

### Part II — Computation of Credits Allowed Against Alternative Minimum Tax

| | | | |
|---|---|---|---|
| 22 | Enter amount from line 3 above . . . . . . . . . | **22** | |
| 23 | Enter 66⅔% of line 4b . . . . . . . . . . | **23** | |
| 24 | Subtract line 23 from line 22 . . . . . . . . . | **24** | |
| 25 | Figure this line from one of the schedules below on the amount reported in line 24 . . . . | **25** | |
| 26 | Credits, other than Foreign Tax Credit, from Form 1040, line 49. (See instructions.) . . . . | **26** | |
| 27 | Enter line 25 or line 26, whichever is smaller. Enter here and on line 20 above . . . . . | **27** | |

| **Single, Married Filing Jointly, Qualifying Widow(er), or Head of Household** | | | | **Married, Filing Separately, or Estate or Trust** | | | |
|---|---|---|---|---|---|---|---|
| If the amount on line 24 is: | | Enter on line 25: | | If the amount on line 24 is: | | Enter on line 25: | |
| Not over $20,000 | | –0– | | Not over $10,000 | | –0– | |
| Over | But not over | | of the amount over | Over | But not over | | of the amount over |
| $20,000 | $60,000 | 10% | $20,000 | $10,000 | $30,000 | 10% | $10,000 |
| $60,000 | — | $4,000 + 20% | $60,000 | $30,000 | — | $2,000 + 20% | $30,000 |

*Do not include any tax from Form 4970, Form 4972, Form 5544, or any penalty tax under section 72(m)(5).

**For Paperwork Reduction Act Notice, see back of form.**      363–228–1      Form **6251** (1982)

NET· C·G · 0.6 = 20,000·

N L·T·G G = 20,000 / 0·6 = 33,333

# Instructions

(Section References are to the Internal Revenue Code)

**Paperwork Reduction Act Notice**

We ask for the information to carry out the Internal Revenue laws of the United States. We need it to ensure that you are complying with these laws and to allow us to figure and collect the right amount of tax. You are required to give us this information.

**Purpose of Form**

Use this form to figure your alternative minimum tax. Individuals, estates or trusts may be liable if they have: (1) tax preference items for adjusted itemized deductions or capital gain deduction; (2) an entry on Schedule D (Form 1040), line 9a and credits on Form 1040, line 49; or (3) nonbusiness credits for investment credit, WIN credit, or jobs credit.

## Line-by-Line Instructions

**Line 1.**—Do not include in line 1 any alcohol fuel credit included in income.

**Note:** *Line 1 and line 3 can be less than zero. However, when you figure lines 1 and 2, you cannot include a deduction for any loss or expense allowable in figuring a net operating loss that can be carried back or forward.*

If you used the worksheet on page 12 of the Form 1040 instructions or had an entry on Form 1040NR, line 37, enter the amount from line 5 of the worksheet or line 38 of Form 1040NR, on line 1 of Form 6251, instead of the amount from Form 1040 or Form 1040NR, line 33. If you entered your earned income on line 3 of the worksheet, refigure that line using Schedule A (Form 1040), line 28 instead of your earned income.

**Estates and trusts.**—Enter the taxable income from Form 1041, line 25, or Form 990-T, page 1, line 5.

**Line 4a.—Adjusted Itemized Deductions.**

**Individuals—Step 1.**—Subtract the following from your total itemized deductions (Schedule A (Form 1040), line 28):
(1) medical and dental expenses (Schedule A (Form 1040), line 10),
(2) State, local, and foreign taxes (Schedule A (Form 1040), line 15),
(3) casualty and theft losses (Schedule A (Form 1040), line 24), and
(4) any deduction for estate tax allowable under section 691(c).

**Step 2.**—Subtract from your adjusted gross income (Form 1040, line 33), the items in (1) through (4) of step 1. If less than zero, enter zero.

**Step 3.**—Multiply step 2 by 60%.

**Step 4.**—Subtract step 3 from step 1. Enter the result on line 4a. If less than zero, enter zero.

**Estates and Trusts—**

**Step 1.**—Add all deductions except:
(1) those allowable in figuring adjusted gross income,
(2) the deduction for personal exemption,
(3) the deduction for casualty and theft losses,
(4) the deduction for State, local, and foreign taxes,
(5) the deduction allowed for distributions to beneficiaries,
(6) the charitable deduction allowable to a trust to the extent that a corre-

sponding amount is included in the gross income of the beneficiary of the trust, and
(7) any deduction for estate tax allowable under section 691(c).

**Step 2.**—Subtract from adjusted gross income the items in (3) through (7) of step 1. If less than zero, enter zero.

**Step 3.**—Multiply step 2 by 60%.

**Step 4.**—Subtract step 3 from step 1. Enter the result on line 4a. If less than zero, enter zero.

**Note:** *Adjusted gross income for an estate or trust is figured in the same way as for an individual except that the following items are allowed in figuring adjusted gross income:*
(1) *the costs of administration of the estate or trust, and*
(2) *the charitable deduction to the extent provided in section 57(b)(2)(C).*

**Line 4b.—Capital Gain Deduction.**

**Individuals**—Enter one of the following:
(1) The amount from Schedule D (Form 1040), line 21;
(2) The amount from Form 4798, Part I, line 9;
(3) 60% of capital gain distributions if you did not use Schedule D or Form 4798.

**Note:** *Do not include as a tax preference item the capital gain deduction attributable to a sale or exchange of a principal residence.*

**Estates and Trusts—**

Enter the capital gain deduction taken into account on Form 1041 or 990-T. However, an amount paid or permanently set aside for a charitable purpose is not a tax preference item.

**Lines 5 and 12.**—If this is a short period return, use the formula in section 443(d)(1) to determine the amount to enter on these lines.

**Nonresident alien individuals.**—If you disposed of U.S. real property interests at a gain, see Form 1040NR instructions for a special rule in figuring line 10.

**Line 13.**—Estates and trusts, enter the amount from Form 1041, line 30, or Form 990-T, page 1, line 11.

**Line 18.—Foreign Tax Credit.**

If line 17 is more than zero, and you incurred foreign taxes and elect to take them as a credit, enter on line 18 the foreign tax credit allowed against the alternative minimum tax. Use a separate Form 1116 to figure this credit. Do not use the Form 1116 you used to figure the credit on Form 1040, line 42. Figure this credit as follows:
(1) Use and attach a separate Form 1116 for each type of income specified at the top of Form 1116.
(2) Print across the top of each Form 1116 used: "ALT MIN TAX."
(3) **Part I**—Use your alternative minimum taxable income from sources outside the U.S. and items of gross income and deductions used in determining alternative minimum taxable income from sources outside the U.S. Part II need not be completed.
(4) **Part III—**
(a) Skip lines 1 to 4.
(b) Insert on line 5 the result of the following:
(i) the amount from Part III, line 5 of the Form 1116 used

to figure the amount on line 42 of Form 1040, line 27a of Form 1041, or line 9(a) of Form 990-T, minus
(ii) the amount from Part III, line 17 of that Form 1116, plus
(iii) the smaller of (A) the amount from Part III, line 17 of that Form 1116, or (B) Form 6251, line 17 (or if more than one Form 1116 is being used, an allocable portion of Form 6251, line 17).
(c) Complete lines 6 through 8, substituting alternative minimum taxable income from sources outside the U.S. for taxable income from sources outside the U.S. on line 6.
(d) Skip lines 9 and 10.
(e) Line 11—Enter the amount from Form 6251, line 5.
(f) Complete line 12 as indicated in Part III.
(g) Skip lines 13 and 14.
(h) Line 15—Enter the sum of Form 6251, lines 13, 15 and 17.
(i) Complete lines 16 and 17 as indicated in Part III.
(5) **Part IV—**
Enter on line 18, Form 6251, the amount from line 7, Part IV of this Form 1116 (but not more than the amount on Form 6251, line 17).

For more information on how to figure this credit, see **Publication 909**, Minimum Tax and Alternative Minimum Tax.

**Line 21.**—If you are filing Form 1041, enter the amount from this line on Form 1041, line 32. If you are filing Form 990-T, enter the amount from this line on Form 990-T, page 1, line 14.

**Line 23.**—If you had an entry on Schedule D (Form 1040), line 9a, include in line 23 the portion of Schedule D, line 9a included in Form 1040, line 13.

**Line 26.—Credits.**—Enter your credits, other than your foreign tax credit, as they appear on your tax return; Form 1040, line 49, Form 1041, line 29, or Form 990-T, line 10. Include WIN credit only to the extent it is from an active trade or business. Refigure investment credit using another Form 3468. Refigure jobs credit using another Form 5884. Include in such forms, only the credits from an active trade or business. In addition, substitute the amount in Form 6251, line 25 for your tax liability before credits on Forms 3468 and 5884. Print "ALT MIN TAX" across the top of each Form 3468 and Form 5884 you use to refigure these credits. Attach them to this form.

It may be necessary to figure the carryback or carryover of unused credits. See section 55(c)(4).

**Partners, Beneficiaries, etc. If you are a—**
(1) Partner, take into account separately your distributive share of items of income and deductions that enter into the computation of tax preference items.
(2) Beneficiary of an estate or trust, see section 58(c).
(3) Shareholder of an electing small business corporation, see section 58(d).
(4) Participant in a common trust fund, see section 58(e).
(5) Shareholder or holder of beneficial interest in a regulated investment company or a real estate investment trust, see section 58(f).

# APPENDIX C
# GLOSSARY OF TAX TERMS

[NOTE: The words and phrases appearing below have been defined to reflect their conventional use in the field of taxation. Such definitions may, therefore, be incomplete for other purposes.]

## –A–

**A.** See *acquiescence.*

**Accelerated cost recovery system.** A method whereby the cost of a fixed asset is written-off for tax purposes. Instituted by the Economic Recovery Tax Act of 1981, the system places assets into one of four recovery periods (i. e., class life of 3, 5, 10, and 15 years) and prescribes the applicable percentage of cost that can be deducted each year. In this regard, it largely resolves the controversy that used to arise with prior depreciation procedures in determining estimated useful life and in predicting salvage value. § 168.

**Accelerated depreciation.** Various methods of depreciation that yield larger deductions in the earlier years of the life of an asset than the straight-line method. Examples include the double declining-balance and the sum of the years' digits methods of depreciation. § 167(b)(2) and (3).

**Accounting method.** The method under which income and expenses are determined for tax purposes. Major accounting methods are the cash basis and the accrual basis. Special methods are available for the reporting of gain on installment sales, recognition of income on construction projects (i. e., the completed-contract and percentage-of-completion methods), and the valuation of inventories (i. e., last-in first-out and first-in first-out). §§ 446–472. See *accrual basis, cash basis, completed-contract method, percentage-of-completion method,* etc.

**Accounting period.** The period of time, usually a year, used by a taxpayer for the determination of tax liability. Unless a fiscal year is chosen, taxpayers must determine and pay their income tax liability by using the calendar year (i. e., January 1 through December 31) as the period of measurement. An example of a fiscal year is July 1 through June 30. A change in accounting periods (e. g., from a calendar year to a fiscal year) generally requires the consent of the IRS. New taxpayers, such as a newly formed regular corporation or an estate created upon the death of an individual taxpayer, are free to select either a calendar or a fiscal year without the consent of the IRS. §§ 441–443.

**Accrual basis.** A method of accounting that reflects expenses incurred and income earned for any one tax year. In contrast to the cash basis of accounting, expenses do not have to be paid to be deductible nor does income have to be received to be taxable. Unearned income (e. g., prepaid interest and rent) generally is taxed in the year of receipt regardless of the method of accounting used by the taxpayer. § 446(c)(2). See *accounting method, cash basis,* and *unearned income.*

**Accumulated adjustment account.** An account which comprises an S corporation's post-1982 accumulated gross income (less deductible expenses) not previously distributed to the shareholders. § 1368(e)(1).

**Accumulated earnings credit.** A deduction allowed in arriving at accumulated taxable income for purposes of determining the accumulated earnings tax. See *accumulated earnings tax* and *accumulated taxable income.*

**Accumulated earnings tax.** A special tax imposed on corporations that accumulate (rather than distribute) their earnings beyond the reasonable needs of the business. The accumulated earnings tax is imposed on accumulated taxable income (see below) in addition to the corporate income tax. § § 531–537.

**Accumulated taxable income.** The income upon which the accumulated earnings tax is imposed. Basically, it is the taxable income of the corporation as adjusted for certain items (e. g., the Federal income tax, excess charitable contributions, the 85% dividends received deduction) less the dividends paid deduction and the accumulated earnings credit. § 535.

**Accumulating trusts.** See *discretionary trusts.*

**Acq.** See *acquiescence.*

**Acquiescence.** In agreement with the result reached. The IRS follows a policy of either acquiescing (i. e., *A, Acq.*) or non-acquiescing (i. e., *NA, Non-Acq.*) in the results reached in the Regular decisions of the U. S. Tax Court.

**ACRS.** See *accelerated cost recovery system.*

**"Add-on" (or regular) minimum tax.** Prior to the Tax Equity and Fiscal Responsibility Act of 1982, the "add-on" (or regular) minimum tax covered both corporate and noncorporate taxpayers. As applied to individuals, the "add-on" minimum tax was 15 percent of the tax preference items (reduced by the greater of $10,000 or one-half of the income tax liability for the year). For taxable years beginning after 1982, the "add-on" minimum tax is repealed as to individuals. In its place, Congress chose to expand the scope of the alternative minimum tax. As to corporations, however, the "add-on" minimum tax is 15 percent of certain tax preference items in excess of the greater of $10,000 or the regular tax liability. An "add-on" minimum tax is to be distinguished from an alternative minimum tax in that the former is in addition to the regular income tax liability. In the case of an alternative minimum tax, moreover, the tax due is the higher of the regular income or the alternative minimum tax. See *alternative minimum tax*.

**Ad valorem tax.** A tax imposed on the value of property. The more common ad valorem tax is that imposed by states, counties, and cities on real estate. Ad valorem taxes can, however, be imposed on personalty. See *personalty*.

**Adjusted basis.** The cost or other basis of property reduced by depreciation allowed or allowable and increased by capital improvements. Other special adjustments are provided for in § 1016 and the Regulations thereunder. See *basis*.

**Adjusted gross income.** A tax determination peculiar to taxpayers who are individuals. Generally, it represents the gross income of an individual less business expenses and any appropriate capital gain or loss adjustment.

**Adjusted ordinary gross income.** A determination peculiar to the personal holding company tax imposed by § 541. In testing to ascertain whether a corporation is a personal holding company, *personal holding company income divided by adjusted ordinary gross income* must equal 60% or more. Adjusted ordinary gross income is the corporation's gross income less capital gains, § 1231 gains, and certain expenses. Adjusted ordinary gross income is defined in § 543(b)(2) and the Regulations thereunder. See *personal holding company tax* and *personal holding company income*.

**Administration.** The supervision and winding-up of an estate. The administration of an estate runs from the date of an individual's death until all assets have been distributed and liabilities paid. Such administration is conducted by an administrator or an executor. See *administrator* and *executor*.

**Administrator.** A person appointed by the court to administer (i. e., manage or take charge of) the assets and liabilities of a decedent (i. e., the deceased). Such person may be a male (i. e., administrator) or a female (i. e., administratrix). If the person performing these services is named by the decedent's will, he is designated as the executor, or she is designated as the executrix, of the estate.

**AFTR.**  Published by Prentice-Hall, *American Federal Tax Reports* contain all of the Federal tax decisions issued by the U. S. District Courts, U. S. Claims Court, U. S. Court of Appeals, and the U. S. Supreme Court.

**AFTR2d.**  The second series of the *American Federal Tax Reports*. See *AFTR*.

**Alimony payments.**  Alimony and separate maintenance payments are includible in the gross income of the recipient and are deductible by the payor.  The payments must be periodic and made in discharge of a legal obligation arising from a marital or family relationship.  Child support and voluntary payments are not treated as alimony.  § § 62(13) and 71.

**All events test.**  For accrual method taxpayers, income is earned when (1) all the events have occurred which fix the right to receive the income and (2) the amount can be determined with reasonable accuracy.  Accrual of income cannot be postponed simply because a portion of the income may have to be returned in a subsequent period.  The all events test also is utilized to determine when expenses can be deducted by an accrual basis taxpayer.  The application of the test could cause a variation between the treatment of an item for accounting and for tax purposes.  For example, a reserve for warranty expense may be properly accruable pursuant to generally accepted accounting principles but not be deductible under the Federal income tax. Due to the application of the all events test, the deduction becomes available in the year the warranty obligation becomes fixed and the amount is determinable with reasonable certainty. Reg. § § 1.446–1(c)(1)(ii) and 1.461–1(a)(2).

**Alternate valuation date.**  Property passing from a person by death may be valued for death tax purposes as of the date of death or the alternate valuation date.  The alternate valuation date is six months from the date of death or the date the property is disposed of by the estate, whichever comes first.  The use of the alternate valuation date requires an affirmative election on the part of the executor or administrator of the estate.

**Alternative minimum tax.**  For tax years beginning after 1982, individuals (including estates and trusts) will not be subject to an "add-on" minimum tax but, instead, will be covered by a new version of the alternative minimum tax.  Simply stated, the alternative minimum tax is 20 percent of the alternative minimum taxable income (AMTI).  AMTI is the taxpayer's adjusted gross income (1) increased by certain tax preference items; (2) decreased for certain alternative tax itemized deductions; and,

(3) reduced by an exemption amount (e. g., $40,000 on a joint return). The taxpayer must pay the greater of the resulting alternative minimum tax (reduced by the foreign tax credit) or the regular income tax (reduced by all allowable tax credits). See *"add-on" minimum tax*.

**Alternative tax.** An option allowed to corporations in computing the tax on net long-term capital gains. For tax years beginning after 1978, the rate is 28% of the net long-term capital gains. For corporate taxpayers, failure to use the alternative tax means all of the long-term capital gain will be taxed in the appropriate income tax bracket.

**Amortization.** The write-off (or depreciation) for tax purposes of the cost or other basis of an intangible asset over its estimated useful life. Examples of amortizable intangibles include patents, copyrights, and leasehold interests. The intangible goodwill cannot be amortized for income tax purposes because it possesses no estimated useful life. As to tangible assets, see *depreciation*. As to natural resources, see *depletion*.

**Amount realized.** The amount received by a taxpayer upon the sale or exchange of property. The measure of the amount received is the sum of the cash and the fair market value of any property or services received. Determining the amount realized is the starting point for arriving at realized gain or loss. The amount realized is defined in § 1001(b) and the Regulations thereunder. See *realized gain or loss* and *recognized gain or loss*.

**Annual accounting period concept.** In determining a taxpayer's income tax liability, only those transactions taking place during a particular tax year are taken into consideration. For reporting and payment purposes, therefore, the tax life of taxpayers is divided into equal annual accounting periods. See *mitigation of the annual accounting period concept* and *accounting period*.

**Annual exclusion.** In computing the taxable gifts for any one year, each donor may exclude the first $10,000 of a gift to each donee. Usually, the annual exclusion is not available for gifts of future interests. § 2503(b). See *future interest*.

**Annuitant.** The party entitled to receive payments from an annuity contract. See *annuity*.

**Annuity.** A fixed sum of money payable to a person at specified times for a set period of time or for life. If the party making the payment (i. e., the obligor) is regularly engaged in this type of business (e. g., an insurance company), the arrangement is classified as a commercial annuity. A private annuity involves an obligor that is not regularly engaged in selling annuities (e. g., a charity or family member).

**Anticipatory assignment of income.**  See *assignment of income.*

**Appellate court.**  For Federal tax purposes, appellate courts include the Courts of Appeals and the Supreme Court.  If the party losing in the trial (or lower) court is dissatisfied with the result, the dispute may be carried to the appropriate appellate court.  See *trial court.*

**Arm's length.**  The standard under which unrelated parties would carry out a particular transaction.  Suppose, for example, X Corporation sells property to its sole shareholder for $10,000.  In testing whether $10,000 is an "arm's length" price, one would ascertain for how much the corporation could have sold the property to a disinterested third party.

**Articles of incorporation.**  The legal document specifying a corporation's name, period of existence, purpose and powers, authorized number of shares, classes of stock, and other conditions for operation.  These articles are filed by the organizers of the corporation with the state of incorporation.  If the articles are satisfactory and other conditions of the law are satisfied, the state will issue a charter recognizing the organization's status as a corporation.

**Assessment.**  The process whereby the IRS imposes an additional tax liability.  If, for example, the IRS audits a taxpayer's income tax return and finds gross income understated or deductions overstated, it will assess a deficiency in the amount of the tax that should have been paid in light of the adjustments made.

**Assignment of income.**  A procedure whereby a taxpayer attempts to avoid the recognition of income by assigning the property that generates the income to another.  Such a procedure will not avoid the recognition of income by the taxpayer making the assignment if it can be said that the income was earned at the point of the transfer.  In this case, usually referred to as an anticipatory assignment of income, the income will be taxed to the person who earns it.

**Association.**  An organization treated as a corporation for Federal tax purposes even though it may not qualify as such under applicable state law.  What is designated as a trust or a partnership, for example, may be classified as an association if it clearly possesses corporate attributes.  Corporate attributes include: centralized management, continuity of existence, free transferability of interests, and limited liability.  § 7701(a)(3).

**Attribution.** Under certain circumstances, the tax law applies attribution rules to assign to one taxpayer the ownership interest of another taxpayer. If, for example, the stock of X Corporation is held 60% by M and 40% by S, M may be deemed to own 100% of X Corporation if M and S are mother and son. In such a case, the stock owned by S is attributed to M. Stated differently, M has a 60% "direct" and a 40% "indirect" interest in X Corporation. It can also be said that M is the "constructive" owner of S's interest.

**Audit.** Inspection and verification of a taxpayer's return or other transactions possessing tax consequences. See *correspondence audit, field audit,* and *office audit.*

## –B–

**Bargain sale or purchase.** A sale of property for less than the fair market value of such property. The difference between the sale or purchase price and the fair market value of the property will have to be accounted for in terms of its tax consequences. If, for example, a corporation sells property worth $1,000 to one of its shareholders for $700, the $300 difference probably represents a constructive dividend to the shareholder. Suppose, instead, the shareholder sells the property (worth $1,000) to his or her corporation for $700. The $300 difference probably represents a contribution by the shareholder to the corporation's capital. Bargain sales and purchases among members of the same family may lead to gift tax consequences. See *constructive dividends.*

**Basis.** The amount assigned to an asset for income tax purposes. For assets acquired by purchase, basis would be cost [§ 1012]. Special rules govern the basis of property received by virtue of another's death [§ 1014] or by gift [§ 1015], the basis of stock received on a transfer of property to a controlled corporation [§ 358], the basis of the property transferred to the corporation [§ 362], and the basis of property received upon the liquidation of a corporation [§ 334].

**Become of age.** See *legal age.*

**Beneficiary.** A party who will benefit from a transfer of property or other arrangement. Examples include the beneficiary of a trust, the beneficiary of a life insurance policy, and the beneficiary of an estate.

**Bequest.** A transfer by will of personalty. To bequeath is to leave such property by will. See *personalty.*

**Bona fide.** In good faith or real. In tax law, this term is often used in connection with a business purpose for carrying out a transaction. Thus, was there a bona fide business purpose for a share-holder's transfer of a liability to a controlled corporation? § 357(b)(1)(B). See *business purpose.*

**Book value.** The net amount of an asset after reduction by a related reserve. The book value of accounts receivable, for example, would be the amount of the receivables less the reserve for bad debts.

**Boot.** Cash or property of a type not included in the definition of a nontaxable exchange. The receipt of boot will cause an other-wise taxfree transfer to become taxable to the extent of the lesser of: the fair market value of such boot or the realized gain on the transfer. For example, see transfers to controlled corporations under § 351(b) and like-kind exchanges under § 1031(b). See *realized gain or loss.*

**Bribes and illegal payments.** Section 162 denies a deduction for bribes or kickbacks; for fines and penalties paid to a government for violation of law; and two-thirds of the treble damage pay-ments made to claimants under violation of the antitrust law. Denial of a deduction for bribes and illegal payments is based upon the judicially established principle that allowing such pay-ments would be contrary to public policy.

**Brother-sister corporations.** More than one corporation owned by the same shareholders. If, for example, C and D each own one-half of the stock in X Corporation and Y Corporation, X and Y are brother-sister corporations.

**B.T.A.** The Board of Tax Appeals was a trial court which considered Federal tax matters. This Court is now designated as the U. S. Tax Court.

**Bulk sale.** A sale of substantially all the inventory of a trade or business to one person in one transaction. Under certain condi-tions, a corporation making a bulk sale pursuant to a complete liquidation will recognize neither gain nor loss on such sale. § 337(b)(2).

**Burden of proof.** The requirement in a lawsuit to show the weight of evidence and, thereby, gain a favorable decision. Except in cases of tax fraud, the burden of proof in a tax case generally will be on the taxpayer.

**Business bad debts.** A tax deduction allowed for obligations ob-tained in connection with a trade or business which have become either partially or completely worthless. In contrast with non-business bad debts, business bad debts are deductible as business expenses. § 166. See *nonbusiness bad debts.*

**Business purpose.** A justifiable business reason for carrying out a transaction. It has long been established that mere tax avoidance is not a business purpose. The presence of a business purpose is of crucial importance in the area of corporate readjustments.

## –C–

**Calendar year.** See *accounting period*.

**Capital asset.** Broadly speaking, all assets are capital except those specifically excluded. Major categories of *non-capital* assets include: property held for resale in the normal course of business (i. e., inventory), trade accounts and notes receivable, depreciable property and real estate used in a trade or business (i. e., "§ 1231 assets"). § 1221.

**Capital contribution.** Various means by which a shareholder makes additional funds available to the corporation (i. e., placed at the risk of the business) without the receipt of additional stock. Such contributions are added to the basis of the shareholder's existing stock investment and do not generate income to the corporation. § 118.

**Capital expenditure.** An expenditure which should be added to the basis of the property improved. For income tax purposes, this generally precludes a full deduction for the expenditure in the year paid or incurred. Any cost recovery in the form of a tax deduction would have to come in the form of depreciation. § 263.

**Capital gain.** The gain from the sale or exchange of a capital asset. See *capital asset*.

**Capital loss.** The loss from the sale or exchange of a capital asset. See *capital asset*.

**Cash basis.** A method of accounting that reflects deductions as paid and income as received in any one tax year. However, prepaid expenses that benefit more than one tax year (e. g., prepaid rent and prepaid interest) may have to be spread over the period benefited rather than deducted in the year paid. § 446(c)(1). See also, *constructive receipt of income*.

**Cash surrender value.** The amount of money an insurance policy would yield if cashed in with the insurance company that issued the policy.

**Casualty loss.** A casualty is defined as "the complete or partial destruction of property resulting from an identifiable event of a sudden, unexpected or unusual nature" (e. g., floods, storms, fires, auto accidents).

**CCH.** Commerce Clearing House is a publisher of a tax service and of Federal tax decisions (i. e., USTC series).

**Centralized management.** A concentration of authority among certain persons who may make independent business decisions on behalf of the entity without the need for continuing approval by the owners of the entity. It is a characteristic of a corporation since its day-to-day business operations are handled by appointed officers and not by the shareholders. Reg. § 301.7701–2(c). See *association.*

**Cert. den.** By denying the Writ of Certiorari, the U. S. Supreme Court refuses to accept an appeal from a U. S. Court of Appeals. The denial of certiorari does not, however, mean that the U. S. Supreme Court agrees with the result reached by the lower court. See *certiorari.*

**Certiorari.** Appeal from a U. S. Court of Appeals to the U. S. Supreme Court is by Writ of Certiorari. The Supreme Court does not have to accept the appeal and usually does not (i. e., *cert. den.*) unless there is a conflict among the lower courts that needs to be resolved or a constitutional issue is involved. See *cert. den.*

**Cf.** Compare.

**Charitable contributions.** Contributions are deductible (subject to various restrictions and ceiling limitations) if made to qualified nonprofit charitable organizations. A cash basis taxpayer is entitled to a deduction solely in the year of payment. Accrual basis corporations may accrue contributions at year-end if payment is authorized properly prior to the end of the year and payment is made within 2½ months from the end of the year. § 170.

**Civil fraud.** See *fraud.*

**Claims Court.** A trial court (i. e., court of original jurisdiction) which decides litigation involving Federal tax matters. Previously known as the U. S. Court of Claims, appeal from the U. S. Claims Court is to the Court of Appeals for the Federal Circuit.

**Closely-held corporation.** A corporation, the stock ownership of which is not widely dispersed. Instead, a few shareholders are in control of corporate policy and are in a position to benefit personally from such policy.

**Collapsing.** To disregard a transaction or one of a series of steps leading to a result. See *telescoping, substance vs. form,* and *step transaction approach.*

**Common law state.** See *community property.*

**Community property.** The eight states with community property systems are: Louisiana, Texas, New Mexico, Arizona, California, Washington, Idaho, and Nevada. The rest of the states are classified as common law jurisdictions. The difference between common law and community property systems centers around the property rights possessed by married persons. In a common law system, each spouse owns whatever he or she earns. Under a community property system, one-half of the earnings of each spouse is considered owned by the other spouse. Assume, for example, H and W are husband and wife and their only income is the $50,000 annual salary H receives. If they live in New York (a common law state), the $50,000 salary belongs to H. If, however, they live in Texas (a community property state), the $50,000 salary is divided equally, in terms of ownership, between H and W. See *separate property*.

**Completed-contract method.** A method of reporting gain or loss on certain long-term contracts. Under this method of accounting, gross income and expenses are recognized in the tax year in which the contract is completed. Reg. § 1.451–3. For another alternative, see *percentage-of-completion method of accounting*.

**Complex trusts.** Complex trusts are those that are not simple trusts. Such trusts may have charitable beneficiaries, accumulate income, and distribute corpus. § § 661–663. See *simple trusts*.

**Concur.** To agree with the result reached by another, but not necessarily with the reasoning or the logic used in reaching such a result. For example, Judge R agrees with Judges S and T (all being members of the same court) that the income is taxable but for a different reason. Judge R would issue a concurring opinion to the majority opinion issued by Judges S and T.

**Condemnation.** The taking of property by a public authority. The taking is by legal action and the owner of the property is compensated by the public authority. The power to condemn property is known as the right of eminent domain.

**Conduit concept.** An approach the tax law assumes in the tax treatment of certain entities and their owners. The approach permits specified tax characteristics to pass through the entity without losing their identity. Under the conduit concept, for example, long-term capital losses realized by a partnership are passed through as such to the individual partners. The same result does not materialize if the entity is a regular corporation. Varying forms of the conduit concept are applicable in the case of partnerships, trusts, estates, and S corporations.

**Consent dividends.** For purposes of avoiding or reducing the penalty tax on the unreasonable accumulation of earnings or the personal holding company tax, a corporation may declare a consent dividend. In a consent dividend no cash or property is distributed to the shareholders although the corporation obtains a dividends paid deduction. The consent dividend is taxed to the shareholders and increases the basis in their stock investment. § 565.

**Constructive dividends.** A taxable benefit derived by a shareholder from his or her corporation although such benefit was not designated as a dividend. Examples include unreasonable compensation, excessive rent payments, bargain purchases of corporate property, and shareholder use of corporate property. Constructive dividends generally are a problem limited to closely-held corporations. See *closely-held corporations.*

**Constructive ownership.** See *attribution.*

**Constructive receipt of income.** If income is unqualifiedly available, it will be subject to the income tax although not physically in the taxpayer's possession. An example would be accrued interest on a savings account. Under the constructive receipt of income concept, such interest will be taxed to a depositor in the year it is available rather than the year actually withdrawn. The fact that the depositor uses the cash basis of accounting for tax purposes makes no difference. See Reg. § 1.451–2.

**Continuity of life or existence.** The death or other withdrawal of an owner of an entity will not terminate the existence of such entity. This is a characteristic of a corporation since the death or withdrawal of a shareholder will not affect its existence. Reg. § 301.7701–2(b). See *association.*

**Contributions to the capital of a corporation.** See *capital contribution.*

**Contributory qualified pension or profit-sharing plan.** A plan funded with both employer and employee contributions. Since the employee's contributions to the plan will be subject to the income tax, a later distribution of such contributions to the employee will be free of income tax. See *qualified pension or profit-sharing plan.*

**Corpus.** The main body or principal of a trust. Suppose, for example, G transfers an apartment building into a trust, income payable to W for life, remainder to S upon W's death. The corpus of the trust would be the apartment building.

**Correspondence audit.**  An audit conducted by the IRS through the use of the mail.  Typically, the IRS writes to the taxpayer requesting the verification of a particular deduction or exemption.  The completion of a special form or the remittance of copies of records or other support is all that is requested of the taxpayer.  See *field audit* and *office audit*.

**Court of Appeals.**  Any of thirteen Federal courts which consider tax matters appealed from the U. S. Tax Court, a U. S. District Court, or the U. S. Claims Court.  Appeal from a U. S. Court of Appeals is to the U. S. Supreme Court by Writ of Certiorari.  See *appellate court*.

**Criminal fraud.**  See *fraud*.

**Current use valuation.**  See *special use valuation*.

**Curtesy.**  A husband's right under state law to all or part of his wife's property upon her prior death.  See *dower*.


# –D–

**Death benefit.**  A payment made by an employer to the beneficiary or beneficiaries of a deceased employee on account of the death of the employee.  Under certain conditions, the first $5,000 of such payment will not be subject to the income tax.  § 101(b)(1).

**Death tax.**  A tax imposed on property transferred by the death of the owner.  See *estate tax* and *inheritance tax*.

**Decedent.**  A dead person.

**Deductions in respect of a decedent.**  Deductions accrued to the point of death but not recognizable on the final income tax return of a decedent because of the method of accounting used.  Such items are allowed as deductions on the death tax return and on the income tax return of the estate (Form 1041) or the heir (Form 1040).  An example of a deduction in respect of a decedent would be interest expense accrued up to the date of death by a cash basis debtor.

**Deferred compensation.**  Compensation which will be taxed when received and not when earned.  An example would be contributions by an employer to a qualified pension or profit-sharing plan on behalf of an employee.  Such conditions will not be taxed to the employee until they are distributed (e. g., upon retirement).  See *qualified pension or profit-sharing plan*.

**Deficiency.** Additional tax liability owned by a taxpayer and assessed by the IRS. See *assessment* and *statutory notice of deficiency*.

**Deficiency dividends.** Once the IRS has established a corporation's liability for the personal holding company tax in a prior year, the tax may be reduced or avoided by the issuance of a deficiency dividend under § 547. The deficiency dividend procedure is not available in cases where the deficiency was due to fraud with intent to evade tax or to a willful failure to file the appropriate tax return [§ 547(g)]. Nor does the deficiency dividend procedure avoid the usual penalties and interest applicable for failure to file a return or pay a tax.

**Deficit.** A negative balance in the earnings and profits account.

**Depletion.** The process by which the cost or other basis of a natural resource (e. g., an oil and gas interest) is recovered upon extraction and sale of the resource. The two ways to determine the depletion allowance are the cost and percentage (or statutory) methods. Under the cost method, each unit of production sold is assigned a portion of the cost or other basis by the total units expected to be recovered. Under the percentage (or statutory) method the tax law provides a special percentage factor for different types of minerals and other natural resources. This percentage is multiplied by the gross income from the interest to arrive at the depletion allowance. § § 613 and 613A.

**Depreciation.** The write-off for tax purposes of the cost or other basis of a tangible asset over its estimated useful life. As to intangible assets, see *amortization*. As to natural resources, see *depletion*. Also see *estimated useful life*.

**Descent and distribution.** See *intestate*.

**Determination letter.** Upon the request of a taxpayer, a District Director will pass upon the tax status of a completed transaction. Determination letters are most frequently used to clarify employee status, to determine whether a retirement or profit-sharing plan "qualifies" under the Code, and to determine the tax exempt status of certain non-profit organizations.

**Devise.** A transfer by will of real estate. For a transfer of personalty by will see *bequest*.

**Direct charge-off method.** A method of accounting for bad debts whereby a deduction is permitted only when an account becomes partially or completely worthless. See *reserve for bad debts*.

**Disability pay.** A partial exclusion from income is permitted for payments from employers to former employees who are under 65 and are permanently and totally disabled. The exclusion is limited to $100 per week and is reduced on a dollar for dollar basis if the taxpayer's adjusted gross income is more than $15,000. § 105(d).

**Disaster loss.** If a casualty is sustained in an area designated as a disaster area by the President of the U. S., the casualty is designated a disaster loss. In such an event, the disaster loss may be treated as having occurred in the taxable year immediately preceding the year in which the disaster actually occurred. Thus, immediate tax benefits are provided to victims of a disaster. § 165(h). See *casualty loss.*

**Disclaimer.** The rejection, refusal, or renunciation of a claim, power, or property. Code § 2518 sets forth the conditions required to avoid gift tax consequences as the result of a disclaimer.

**Discretionary trusts.** Trusts where the trustee or another party has the right to accumulate (rather than pay out) the income for each year. Depending on the terms of the trust instrument, such income may be accumulated for future distributions to the income beneficiaries or added to corpus for the benefit of the remainderman. See *corpus, income beneficiary,* and *remainderman.*

**Disproportionate.** Not pro rata or ratable. Suppose, for example, S Corporation has two shareholders, C and D, each of whom owns 50% of its stock. If X Corporation distributes a cash dividend of $2,000 to C and only $1,000 to D, the distribution is disproportionate. The distribution would have been proportionate if C and D had received $1,500 each. See *substantially disproportionate* as to stock redemptions.

**Disregard of corporate entity.** To treat a corporation as if it did not exist for tax purposes. In such event, each shareholder would have to account for an allocable share of all corporate transactions possessing tax consequences. See *entity.*

**Dissent.** To disagree with the majority. If, for example, Judge B disagrees with the result reached by Judges C and D (all of whom are members of the same court), Judge B could issue a dissenting opinion.

**Distributable net income (DNI).** The measure that limits the amount of the distributions from estates and trusts that the beneficiaries thereof will have to include in income. Also, DNI limits the amount that estates and trusts can claim as a deduction for such distributions. § 643(a).

**Distributions in kind.** A transfer of property "as is." If, for example, a corporation distributes land to its shareholders, a distribution in kind has taken place. A sale of land followed by a distribution of the cash proceeds would not be a distribution in kind of the land. As to corporate liquidations, see § 336 for one type of distribution in kind.

**District Court.** A Federal District Court is a trial court for purposes of litigating Federal tax matters. It is the only trial court where a jury trial can be obtained. See *trial court.*

**Dividend exclusion.** The $100 exclusion ($200 on a joint return) allowed individuals for dividends received from certain qualifying domestic corporations. § 116. See *domestic corporation.*

**Dividends received deduction.** A deduction allowed a corporate shareholder for dividends received from a domestic corporation. The deduction usually is 85% of the dividends received but could be 100% if an affiliated group is involved. § § 243–246.

**Domestic corporation.** A corporation created or organized in the U. S. or under the law of the U. S. or any state or territory. § § 4920(a)(5) and 7701(a)(4). Only dividends received from domestic corporations qualify for the dividend exclusion [§ 116] and the dividends received deduction [§ 243].

**Domicile.** A person's legal home.

**Donee.** The recipient of a gift.

**Donor.** The maker of a gift.

**Dower.** A wife's right to all or part of her deceased husband's property. It is a concept unique to common law states as opposed to community property jurisdictions.

## –E–

**Earned income.** Income from personal services to be distinguished from income generated by property. See § 911 and the Regulations thereunder.

**Earnings and profits.** A tax concept peculiar to corporate taxpayers which measures economic capacity to make a distribution to shareholders that is not a return of capital. Such a distribution will result in dividend income to the shareholders to the extent of the corporation's current and accumulated earnings and profits.

**Educational assistance payments.** Under prior law, the payment by an employer of the cost of providing additional education (e.g., college course) generally was taxable to the individual employee who benefitted therefrom. Under the Revenue Act of 1978, § 127 enables the employee to exclude these payments from gross income if the employer maintains a qualified educational assistance program. Such a plan must be in writing, be nondiscriminatory in coverage, and not provide the employee with an option to receive some other type of compensation in lieu of the educational assistance benefits. The exclusion applies to tax years beginning after 1978 and ending before 1984. § 127.

**Educational expenses.** Employees may deduct education expenses if such items are incurred either (1) to maintain or improve existing job related skills or (2) to meet the express requirements of the employer or the requirements imposed by law to retain employment status. Such expenses are not deductible if the education is required to meet the minimum educational requirements for the taxpayer's job or the education qualifies the individual for a new trade or business. Reg. § 1.162–5.

**Election to split gifts.** A special election for Federal gift tax purposes whereby husband and wife can treat a gift by one of them to a third party as being made one-half by each. If, for example, H (the husband) makes a gift of $20,000 to S, W (the wife) may elect to treat $10,000 of the gift as coming from her. The major advantage of the election is that it enables the parties to take advantage of the non-owner spouse's (W in this case) annual exclusion. § 2513. See *annual exclusion*.

**Eminent Domain.** See *condemnation*.

**En banc.** The case was considered by the whole court. For example, only one of the nineteen judges of the U. S. Tax Court will hear and decide a tax controversy. However, when the issues involved are unusually novel or of wide impact, the case will be heard and decided by the full Court sitting *en banc*.

**Encumbrance.** A liability, such as a mortgage. If the liability relates to a particular asset, the asset is encumbered.

**Energy Tax Act.** Legislation enacted on November 9, 1978, which provides various income tax credits for certain energy conservation expenditures. See *energy tax credit—business property* and *energy tax credit—residential property*.

**Energy tax credit—business property.** The Energy Tax Act created a 10% tax credit available to businesses that invest in certain energy property. The purpose of the credit is to create incentives for conservation and to penalize the increased use of oil and gas. The business energy tax credit applies to equipment with an estimated useful life of at least three years that uses fuel or feedstock other than oil or natural gas (e. g., solar, wind, coal). If the property also qualifies for the investment tax credit, a total credit of 20% is allowed. Qualifying property must be completed or acquired new after September 30, 1978 and before January 1, 1983. § § 46(a) and 48(e). See *energy tax credit—residential property, estimated useful life,* and *investment tax credit.*

**Energy tax credit—residential property.** The Energy Tax Act provides individual homeowners and renters with two separate tax credits: one for energy conservation expenditures and the other for renewable energy source property. All such expenditures must be made for property installed in or on taxpayer's principal residence. Energy conservation expenditures include insulation, storm windows, and certain other energy-conserving components. The amount of this tax credit is 15% of the first $2,000 of qualifying expenditures (i. e., a maximum credit of $300). Renewable energy source property includes solar, wind, and geothermal energy devices. The amount of the credit is 40% of the first $10,000 of qualifying expenditures (i. e., the ceiling limitation is $4,000). Expenditures made on or after April 20, 1977 and through 1985 will qualify for the credits. § 44C. See *energy tax credit—business property.*

**Entertainment.** Such expenses are deductible only if they are directly related to or associated with a trade or business. Various restrictions and documentation requirements have been imposed upon the deductibility of entertainment expenses to prevent abuses by taxpayers. § 274.

**Entity.** An organization or being that possesses separate existence for tax purposes. Examples would be corporations, partnerships, estates and trusts. But see *disregard of corporate entity.*

**Escrow.** Money or other property placed with a third party as security for an existing or proposed obligation. C, for example, agrees to purchase D's stock in X Corporation but needs time to raise the necessary funds. The stock is placed by D with E (i. e., the escrow agent) with instructions to deliver it to C when the purchase price is paid.

**Estate.** The assets and liabilities of a decedent.

**Estate tax.** A tax imposed on the right to transfer property by death. Thus, an estate tax is levied on the decedent's estate and not on the heir receiving the property. See *inheritance tax.*

**Estimated useful life.** The period over which an asset will be used by a particular taxpayer. Although such period cannot be longer than the estimated physical life of an asset, it could be shorter if the taxpayer does not intend to keep the asset until it wears out. Assets such as goodwill do not have an estimated useful life. The estimated useful life of an asset is essential to measuring the annual tax deduction for depreciation and amortization.

**Estoppel.** The process of being stopped from proving something (even if true) in court due to prior inconsistent action. It is usually invoked as a matter of fairness to prevent one party (either the taxpayer or the IRS) from taking advantage of a prior error.

**Excise tax.** A tax on the manufacture, sale, or use of goods or on the carrying on of an occupation or activity. Also a tax on the transfer of property. Thus, the Federal death and gift taxes, are, theoretically, excise taxes.

**Executor.** A person designated by a will to administer (i. e., manage or take charge of) the assets and liabilities of a decedent. Such party may be a male (i. e., executor), female (i. e., executrix), or a trust company (i. e., executor). See *administrator*.

## –F–

**Fair market value.** The amount at which property would change hands between a willing buyer and a willing seller, neither being under any compulsion to buy or to sell and both having reasonable knowledge of the relevant facts. Reg. § 20.2031–1(b).

**Federal Register.** The first place that the rules and regulations of U. S. administrative agencies (e. g., the U. S. Treasury Department) are published.

**F.2d.** An abbreviation for the Second Series of the *Federal Reporter,* the official series where decisions of the U. S. Claims Court and of the U. S. Courts of Appeals are published.

**F. Supp.** The abbreviation for *Federal Supplement,* the official series where the reported decisions of the U. S. Federal District Courts are published.

**Fiduciary.** A person who manages money or property for another and who must exercise a standard of care in such management activity imposed by law or contract. A trustee, for example, possesses a fiduciary responsibility to the beneficiaries of the trust to follow the terms of the trust and the requirements of applicable state law. A breach of fiduciary responsibility would make the trustee liable to the beneficiaries for any damage caused by such breach.

**Field audit.** An audit by the IRS conducted on the business premises of the taxpayer or in the office of the tax practitioner representing the taxpayer. To be distinguished from a *correspondence audit* or an *office audit* (see these terms). Also see *audit*.

**First-in first-out (FIFO).** An accounting method for determining the cost of inventories. Under this method the inventory on hand is deemed to be the sum of the cost of the most recently acquired units.

**Fiscal year.** See *accounting period*.

**Foreign corporation.** A foreign corporation is one which is not organized under the laws of one of the states or territories of the U. S. § 7701(a)(5). See *domestic corporation*.

**Foreign earned income exclusion.** The foreign earned income exclusion is a relief provision which applies to U. S. citizens working in foreign countries (usually referred to as "expatriates"). To qualify for the exclusion, the taxpayer must be either a bona fide resident of the foreign country or physically present in the country for 330 days during any twelve consecutive months. The exclusion is limited to earned income of $80,000 in 1983 and increases by $5,000 per year until 1986 when it reaches $95,000.

**Foreign tax credit or deduction.** If a U. S. citizen or resident incurs or pays income taxes to a foreign country on income subject to U. S. tax, the taxpayer may be able to claim some of these taxes as a deduction or as a credit against the U. S. income tax. § § 33 and 901–905.

**Form 706.** The U. S. Estate Tax Return. In certain cases this form must be filed for a decedent who was a resident or citizen of the U. S.

**Form 709.** The U. S. Gift Tax Return.

**Form 870.** The signing of Form 870 (Waiver of Restriction on Assessment and Collection of Deficiency in Tax and Acceptance of Overassessments) by a taxpayer permits the IRS to assess a proposed deficiency without the necessity of issuing a statutory notice of deficiency ("90-day letter"). This means the taxpayer must pay the deficiency and cannot file a petition to the U. S. Tax Court. § 6213(d).

**Form 872.** The signing of this form by a taxpayer extends the period of time in which the IRS can make an assessment or collection of a tax. In other words, Form 872 extends the applicable statute of limitations. § 6501(c)(4).

**Form 1041.** U. S. Fiduciary Income Tax Return. The form that is required to be filed by estates and trusts. See Appendix B for a specimen form.

**Form 1065.** U. S. Partnership Return of Income. See Appendix B for a specimen form.

**Form 1120.** U. S. Corporation Income Tax Return. See Appendix B for a specimen form.

**Form 1120S.** U. S. Small Business Corporation Income Tax Return. This form is required to be filed by S corporations. See Appendix B for a specimen form.

**Fraud.** Tax fraud falls into two categories: civil and criminal. Under civil fraud, the IRS may impose as a penalty an amount equal to 50% of the underpayment [§ 6653(b)]. Fines and/or imprisonment are prescribed for conviction of various types of criminal tax fraud [§§ 7201–7207]. Both civil and criminal fraud require a specific intent on the part of the taxpayer to evade the tax; mere negligence will not be enough. Criminal fraud requires the additional element of wilfulness (i. e., done deliberately and with evil purpose). In actual practice, it becomes difficult to distinguish between the degree of intent necessary to support criminal, as opposed to civil, fraud. In both situations, however, the IRS has the burden of proving fraud. See *burden of proof*.

**Free transferability of interest.** The capability of the owner of an entity to transfer his or her ownership interest to another without the consent of the other owners. It is a characteristic of a corporation since a shareholder usually can freely transfer the stock to others without the approval of the existing shareholders. Reg. § 301.7701–2(e). See *association*.

**Fringe benefits.** Compensation or other benefits received by an employee which are not in the form of cash. Some fringe benefits (e. g., accident and health plans, group-term life insurance) may be excluded from the employee's gross income and, therefore, not subject to the Federal income tax.

**Future interest.** An interest that will come into being at some future point in time. It is distinguished from a present interest which is already in existence. Assume, for example, that D transfers securities to a newly created trust. Under the terms of the trust instrument, income from the securities is to be paid each year to W for her life, with the securities passing to S upon her death. W has a present interest in the trust since she is currently entitled to receive the income from the securities. S has a future interest since he must wait for W's death to benefit from the trust. The annual exclusion of $10,000 is not allowed for a gift of a future interest. § 2503(b). See *annual exclusion*.

# –G–

**General partner.** A partner who is fully liable in an individual capacity for the debts of the partnership to third parties. In contrast to a limited partner, a general partner's liability is not limited to the investment in the partnership. See *limited partnership*.

**Gift.** A transfer of property for less than adequate consideration. Gifts usually occur in a personal setting (such as between members of the same family).

**Gift splitting.** See *election to split gifts*.

**Gift tax.** A tax imposed on the transfer of property by gift. Such tax is imposed upon the donor of a gift and is based on the fair market value of the property on the date of the gift.

**Goodwill.** The reputation and built-up business of a company. For accounting purposes, goodwill has no basis unless purchased. In the purchase of a business, goodwill generally is the difference between the purchase price and the value of the assets acquired. The intangible asset goodwill cannot be amortized for tax purposes. Reg. § 1.167(a)–3. See *amortization*.

**Grantor.** A transferor of property. The creator of a trust is usually designated as the grantor of the trust.

**Gross estate.** The property owned or previously transferred by a decedent that will be subject to the Federal death tax. It can be distinguished from the probate estate which is property actually subject to administration by the administrator or executor of an estate. § § 2031–2046.

**Gross income.** Income subject to the Federal income tax. Gross income does not include income such as interest on municipal bonds. In the case of a manufacturing or merchandising business, gross income means gross profit (i. e., gross sales or gross receipts less costs of goods sold). § 61 and Reg. § 1.61–3(a).

**"Gross-up".** To add back to the value of the property or income received the amount of the tax that has been deducted. In the case of gifts made within three years of the gift, any gift tax paid on the transfer is added to the gross estate. § 2035.

**Group-term life insurance.** Life insurance coverage permitted by an employer for a group of employees. Such insurance is renewable on a year-to-year basis and does not accumulate in value (i. e., no cash surrender value is built up). The premiums paid by the employer on such insurance are not taxed to the employees on coverage of up to $50,000 per person. § 79 and Reg. § 1.79–1(b).

**Guardian.** See *guardianship*.

**Guardianship.** A legal arrangement whereby one person (i. e., a guardian) has the legal right and duty to care for another (i. e., the ward) and his or her property. A guardianship is established because of the ward's inability to legally act on his or her own behalf due to minority (i. e., not of age) or mental or physical incapacity.

## –H–

**Head of household.** An unmarried individual who maintains a household for another and satisfies certain conditions set forth in § 2(b). Such status enables the taxpayer to use a set of income tax rates [see § 1(b)] that are lower than those applicable to other unmarried individuals [§ 1(c)] but higher than those applicable to surviving spouses and married persons filing a joint return [§ 1(a)].

**Heir.** A person who inherits property from a decedent.

**Hobby.** An activity not engaged in for profit. § 183.

**Holding period.** The period of time property has been held for income tax purposes. The holding period is of crucial significance in determining whether or not gain or loss from the sale or exchange of a capital asset is long- or short-term. § 1223.

**H.R. 10 plans.** See *Keogh plans*.

**Household effects.** See *personal and household effects*.

## –I–

**Imputed interest.** In the case of certain long-term sales of property, the IRS has the authority to convert some of the gain from the sale into interest income if the contract does not provide for a minimum rate of interest to be paid by the purchaser. The application of this procedure has the effect of forcing the seller to recognize less long-term capital gain and more ordinary income (i. e., interest income). § 483 and the Regulations thereunder.

**Incident of ownership.** An element of ownership or degree of control over a life insurance policy. The retention by an insured of an incident of ownership in a life insurance policy will cause the policy proceeds to be included in his or her gross estate upon death. § 2042(2) and Reg. § 20.2042–1(c). See *gross estate* and *insured*.

**Income averaging.** A special method whereby the income tax for any one year is determined by taking into account the taxable income of the past four years. The income averaging procedure provides relief from the annual accounting period concept where a taxpayer goes from a "rags to riches" income position and has a relatively large amount of income bunched in a particular year. See Schedule G of Form 1040 and § § 1301–1305.

**Income beneficiary.** The party entitled to income from property. A typical example would be a trust where A is to receive the income for life with corpus or principal passing to B upon A's death. In this case, A would be the income beneficiary of the trust.

**Income in respect of a decedent.** Income earned by a decedent at the time of death but not reportable on the final income tax return because of the method of accounting utilized. Such income is included in the gross estate and will be taxed to the eventual recipient (i. e., either the estate or heirs). The recipient will, however, be allowed an income tax deduction for the estate tax attributable to the income. § 691.

**Incomplete transfer.** A transfer made by a decedent during lifetime which, because of certain control or enjoyment retained by the transferor, will not be considered complete for Federal estate tax purposes. Thus, some or all of the fair market value of the property transferred will be included in the transferor's gross estate. § § 2036–2038. See *gross estate*.

**Individual retirement account.** Individuals with earned income are permitted to set aside up to 100% of such income per year (not to exceed $2,000) for a retirement account. The amount so set aside can be deducted by the taxpayer and will be subject to income tax only upon withdrawal. § 219. See *simplified employee pensions*.

**Inheritance tax.** A tax imposed on the right to receive property from a decedent. Thus, an inheritance tax, theoretically, is imposed on the heir. The Federal death tax is imposed on the estate.

**In-kind.** See *distributions in kind*.

**Installment method.**  A method of accounting enabling a taxpayer to spread the recognition of gain on the sale of property over the payout period.  Under this procedure, the seller computes the gross profit percentage from the sale (i. e., the gain divided by the selling price) and applies it to each payment received to arrive at the gain to be recognized.  § 453.

**Insured.**  A person whose life is the subject of an insurance policy. Upon the death of the insured, the life insurance policy matures and the proceeds become payable to the designated beneficiary.

**Intangible drilling and development costs.**  Taxpayers may elect to expense or capitalize (subject to amortization) intangible drilling and development costs.  However, ordinary income recapture provisions now apply to oil and gas properties on a sale or other disposition if the expense method is elected.  § 263(c) and § 1254(a).

**Intangibles.**  Property that is a "right" rather than a physical object.  Examples would be patents, stocks and bonds, goodwill, trademarks, franchises, and copyrights.  See *amortization*.

**Inter vivos transfer.**  A transfer of property during the life of the owner.  To be distinguished from testamentary transfers where the property passes at death.

**Intestate.**  No will exists at the time of death.  Under these circumstances, state law prescribes who will receive the decedent's property.  The laws of intestate succession (also known as the laws of descent and distribution) generally favor the surviving spouse, children, and grandchildren and then move to parents and grandparents and to brothers and sisters.

**Intestate succession.**  See *intestate*.

**Investment indebtedness.**  If funds are borrowed by noncorporate taxpayers for the purpose of purchasing or continuing to hold investment property, some portion of the interest expense deduction may be dissallowed.  Interest is generally limited to $10,000 plus net investment income.  Amounts which are disallowed may be carried forward and treated as investment interest of the succeeding year.  § 163(d).

**Investment tax credit.**  A special tax credit usually equal to 6% or 10% of the qualified investment in tangible personalty used in a trade or business.  § § 38, 46–50.  See *estimated useful life* and *recapture of the investment tax credit*.

**Investment tax credit recapture.**  See *recapture of the investment tax credit*.

**Involuntary conversion.** The loss or destruction of property through theft, casualty, or condemnation. Any gain realized on an involuntary conversion can, at the taxpayer's election, be considered non-recognizable for Federal income tax purposes if the owner reinvests the proceeds within a prescribed period of time in property that is similar or related in service or use. § 1033.

**IRA.** See *individual retirement account.*

**Itemized deductions.** Certain personal expenditures allowed by the Code as deductions from adjusted gross income if they exceed the zero bracket amount. Examples include certain medical expenses, interest on home mortgages, state sales taxes, and charitable contributions. Itemized deductions are reported on Schedule A of Form 1040.

# –J–

**Jeopardy assessment.** If the collection of a tax appears in question, the IRS may assess and collect the tax immediately without the usual formalities. Also, the IRS has the power to terminate a taxpayer's taxable year before the usual date if it feels that the collection of the tax may be in peril because the taxpayer plans to leave the country. § § 6851, 6861–6864.

**Joint and several liability.** Permits the IRS to collect a tax from one or all of several taxpayers. A husband and wife that file a joint income tax return usually are collectively or individually liable for the full amount of the tax liability. § 6013(d)(3).

**Joint tenancy.** The undivided ownership of property by two or more persons with the right of survivorship. Right of survivorship gives the surviving owner full ownership of the property. Suppose, for example, B and C are joint owners of a tract of land. Upon B's prior death, C becomes the sole owner of the property. As to the death tax consequences upon the death of a joint tenant, see § 2041. See *tenancy by the entirety* and *tenancy in common.*

**Joint venture.** A one-time grouping of two or more persons in a business undertaking. Unlike a partnership, a joint venture does not entail a continuing relationship among the parties. A joint venture is treated like a partnership for Federal income tax purposes. § 7701(a)(2).

# –K–

**Keogh plans.** A designation for retirement plans available to self-employed taxpayers. They are also referred to as H.R. 10 plans. Under such plans a taxpayer may deduct each year up to either

15% of net earnings from self-employment or $15,000, whichever is less.

**Kimbell-Diamond rule.**  See *single transaction approach*.

# –L–

**Last-in first-out (LIFO).**  An accounting method for valuing inventories for tax purposes.  Under this method it is assumed that the inventory on hand is valued at the cost of the earliest acquired units.  § 472 and the Regulations thereunder.  See *first-in first-out (FIFO)*.

**Layman.**  Non-member of a specified profession.  For example, a non-lawyer would be a layman to a lawyer.

**Leaseback.**  The transferor of property later leases it back.  In a sale-leaseback situation, for example, R would sell property to S and subsequently lease such property from S.  Thus, R becomes the lessee and S the lessor.

**Legacy.**  A transfer of cash or other property by will.

**Legal representative.**  A person who oversees the legal affairs of another.  Examples include the executor or administrator of an estate and a court appointed guardian of a minor or incompetent person.

**Legatee.**  The recipient of property under a will and transferred by the death of the owner.

**Lessee.**  One who rents property from another.  In the case of real estate, the lessee is also known as the tenant.

**Lessor.**  One who rents property to another.  In the case of real estate, the lessor is also known as the landlord.

**Life estate.**  A legal arrangement whereby the beneficiary (i. e., the life tenant) is entitled to the income from the property for his or her life.  Upon the death of the life tenant, the property will go to the holder of the remainder interest.  See *income beneficiary* and *remainder interest*.

**Life insurance.**  A contract between the holder of a policy and an insurance company (i. e., the carrier) whereby the company agrees in return for premium payments to pay a specified sum (i. e., the face value or maturity value of the policy) to the designated beneficiary upon the death of the insured.  See *insured*.

**Lifetime exemption.**  See *specific exemption*.

**Like-kind exchange.** An exchange of property held for productive use in a trade or business or for investment (except inventory and stocks and bonds) for property of the same type. Unless different property is received (i. e., "boot") the exchange will be nontaxable. § 1031. See *boot.*

**Limited liability.** The liability of an entity and its owners to third parties is limited to the investment in the entity. This is a characteristic of a corporation since shareholders generally are not responsible for the debts of the corporation and, at most, may lose the amount paid-in for the stock issued. Reg. § 301.7701–2(d). See *association.*

**Limited partner.** A partner whose liability to third party creditors of the partnership is limited to the amount invested by such partner in the partnership. See *limited partnership* and *general partner.*

**Limited partnership.** A partnership in which some of the partners are limited partners. At least one of the partners in a limited partnership must be a general partner. See *general partner* and *limited partner.*

**Lump-sum distribution.** Payment of the entire amount due at one time rather than in installments. Such distributions often occur from qualified pension or profit-sharing plans upon the retirement or death of a covered employee.

## –M–

**Malpractice.** Professional misconduct or an unreasonable lack of skill.

**Marital deduction.** A deduction allowed upon the transfer of property from one spouse to another. The deduction is allowed under the Federal gift tax for lifetime (i. e., inter vivos) transfers or under the Federal death tax for death (i. e., testamentary) transfers. § § 2056 and 2523.

**Market value.** See *fair market value.*

**Merger.** The absorption of one corporation by another whereby the corporation being absorbed loses its identity. A corporation is merged into B Corporation and the shareholders of A Corporation receive stock in B Corporation in exchange for their stock in A Corporation. After the merger, A Corporation ceases to exist as a separate legal entity. If a merger meets certain conditions, it will be nontaxable to the parties involved. § 368(a)(1)(A).

**Minimum tax.** See *"add-on" minimum tax* and *alternative minimum tax*.

**Mitigation.** To make less severe in terms of result. See *mitigation of the annual accounting period concept*.

**Mitigation of the annual accounting period concept.** Various tax provisions that provide relief from the effect of the finality of the annual accounting period concept. For example, income averaging provisions provide relief for taxpayers with a large and unusual amount of income concentrated in a single tax year. See *annual accounting period concept*.

**Monetary bequest.** A transfer by will of cash. It is often designated as a pecuniary bequest.

**Mortgagee.** The party who holds the mortgage; the creditor.

**Mortgagor.** The party who mortgages the property; the debtor.

**Moving expenses.** A deduction *for* AGI is permitted to employees and self-employed individuals providing certain tests are met (e. g., the taxpayer's new job must be at least 35 miles farther from the old residence than the old residence was from the former place of work). In addition, an employee must be employed on a full-time basis at the new location for 39 weeks. Ceiling limitations are placed on direct moving expenses (e. g., expenses of moving personal belongings and traveling) and on indirect expenses (e. g., house-hunting trips and temporary living expenses). § 217.

## –N–

**NA.** See *nonacquiescence*.

**Necessary.** Appropriate and helpful in furthering the taxpayer's business or income producing activity. § § 162(a) and 212. See *ordinary*.

**Negligence.** Failure to exercise the reasonable or ordinary degree of care of a prudent person in a situation that results in harm or damage to another. Code § 6653(a) imposes a 5% penalty on taxpayers who show negligence or intentional disregard of rules and Regulations with respect to the underpayment of certain taxes.

**Negligence penalty.** See *negligence*.

**Net operating loss.** In order to mitigate the effect of the annual accounting period concept, § 172 allows taxpayers to use an excess loss of one year as a deduction for certain past or future years. In this regard, a carryback period of three years and a carryforward period of fifteen years is allowed. See *mitigation of the annual accounting period concept.*

**Net worth method.** An approach used by the IRS to reconstruct the income of a taxpayer who fails to maintain adequate records. Under this approach, the gross income for the year is the increase in net worth of the taxpayer (i. e., assets in excess of liabilities) with appropriate adjustment for nontaxable receipts and nondeductible expenditures. The net worth method often is used when tax fraud is suspected.

**Ninety-day letter.** See *statutory notice of deficiency.*

**Non-acq.** See *nonacquiescence.*

**Nonacquiescence.** Disagreement by the IRS on the result reached by the U. S. Tax Court in a Regular Decision. Sometimes abbreviated as *non-acq.* or *NA.* See *acquiescence.*

**Nonbusiness bad debts.** A bad debt loss not incurred in connection with a creditor's trade or business. Such loss is deductible as a short-term capital loss and will only be allowed in the year the debt becomes entirely worthless. In addition to family loans, many investor losses fall into the classification of nonbusiness bad debts. § 166(d). See *business bad debts.*

**Noncontributory qualified pension or profit-sharing plan.** A plan funded entirely by the employer with no contributions being made by the covered employees. See *qualified pension or profit-sharing plans.*

**Nonqualified deferred compensation plans.** Compensation arrangements which are frequently offered to executives. Such plans may include stock options, restricted stock, etc. Often, an executive may defer the recognition of taxable income to future periods. The employer, however, does not receive a tax deduction until the employee is required to include the compensation in income. See *restricted property.*

**Nonrecourse debt.** An obligation on which the endorser is not personally liable. An example of a nonrecourse debt is a mortgage on real estate acquired by a partnership without the assumption of any liability on the mortgage by the partnership or any of the partners. The acquired property generally is pledged as collateral for the loan.

## –O–

**Obligee.** The party to whom someone else is obligated under a contract. Thus, if C loans money to D, C is the obligee and D is the obligor under the loan.

**Obligor.** See *obligee.*

**Office audit.** An audit by the IRS of a taxpayer's return which is conducted in the agent's office. It may be distinguished from a *correspondence audit* or a *field audit* (see these terms).

**Office in home expenses.** Employment and business related expenses attributable to the use of a residence (e. g., den or office) are allowed only if the portion of the residence is exclusively used on a regular basis as the taxpayer's place of business or as a place of business which is used by patients, clients, or customers. If the expenses are employment related, the use must be for the convenience of the employer as opposed to being merely appropriate and helpful. § 280A.

**One-month liquidation.** A special election available to certain shareholders of a corporation which determines how the distributions received in liquidation by the electing shareholders will be treated for Federal income tax purposes. In order to qualify for the election, the corporation must be completely liquidated within the time span of any one calendar month. § § 333, 334(c).

**Ordinary.** Common and accepted in the general industry or type of activity in which the taxpayer is engaged. It comprises one of the tests for the deductibility of expenses incurred or paid in connection with a trade or business; for the production or collection of income; for the management, conservation, or maintenance of property held for the production of income; or in connection with the determination, collection, or refund of any tax. § § 162(a) and 212. See *neccessary.*

**Ordinary and necessary.** See *ordinary* and *necessary.*

**Ordinary gross income.** A concept peculiar to personal holding companies and defined in § 543(b)(1). See *adjusted ordinary gross income.*

# –P–

.**Partner.** See *limited partner* and *general partner.*

**Partnership.** For income tax purposes, a partnership includes a syndicate, group, pool, joint venture, as well as ordinary partnerships. In an ordinary partnership two or more parties combine capital and/or services to carry on as co-owners a business for profit. § 7701(a)(2). See *limited partnership.*

**Passive investment income.** As defined in § 1362(d)(3)(D), "passive investment income" means gross receipts from royalties, certain rents, dividends, interest, annuities, and gains from the sale or exchange of stock and securities. With certain exceptions, if the passive investment income of a corporation exceeds 25 percent of its gross receipts, for three consecutive years, S status is not available or is lost.

**Pecuniary bequest.**  A bequest of money to an heir by a decedent. Also known as a monetary bequest.  See *bequest*.

**Percentage depletion.**  See *depletion*.

**Percentage-of-completion method of accounting.**  A method of reporting gain or loss on certain long-term contracts.  Under this method of accounting the gross contract price is included in income as the contract is completed.  Reg. § 1.451–3.  For another alternative see *completed-contract method of accounting*.

**Personal and dependency exemptions.**  The tax law provides a $1,000 exemption for each individual taxpayer and an additional $1,000 exemption for his or her spouse if a joint return is filed. Additional personal exemptions are provided for old age (65) and blindness.  An individual may also claim a $1,000 dependency exemption for each dependent providing certain tests are met. Prior to 1979 the amount allowed for each personal and dependency exemption was $750.  § 151.

**Personal and household effects.**  Usual reference is to the following items owned by a decedent at the time of death: clothing, furniture, sporting goods, jewelry, stamp and coin collections, silverware, china, crystal, cooking utensils, books, cars, televisions, radios, stereo equipment, etc.

**Personal holding company.**  A corporation that satisfies the requirements of § 542.  Qualification as a personal holding company means a penalty tax of 50% will be imposed on the corporation's undistributed personal holding company income for the year.

**Personal holding company income.**  Income as defined by § 543. Such income includes interest, dividends, rents (in certain cases), royalties (in certain cases), income from the use of corporate property by certain shareholders, income from certain personal service contracts, and distributions from estates and trusts.  Such income is relevant in determining whether a corporation is a personal holding company and is, therefore, subject to the penalty tax on personal holding companies.  See *adjusted ordinary gross income* and *personal holding company*.

**Personal holding company tax.**  See *personal holding company*.

**Personal property.**  Generally, all property other than real estate. It is sometimes designated as personalty when real estate is termed realty. Personal property also can refer to property which is not used in a taxpayer's trade or business or held for the production or collection of income. When used in this sense, personal property could include both realty (e. g., a personal residence) and personalty (e. g., personal effects such as clothing and furniture).

**Personalty.** Personalty is all property not attached to real estate (i. e., realty) that is movable. Examples of personalty are machinery, automobiles, clothing, household furnishings, inventory, and personal effects. See *realty*.

**P-H.** Prentice-Hall is the publisher of a tax service and of Federal tax decisions (i. e., AFTR and AFTR2d series).

**Points.** Loan origination fees which are generally deductible as interest by a buyer of property. A seller of property who pays points is required to reduce the selling price and, therefore, does not receive an interest deduction.

**Political contributions.** Individuals can claim a tax credit equal to one-half of certain qualifying political contributions. The credit is limited to $50 ($100 on a joint return). Prior to 1979 the maximum credit allowed was $25 ($50 on a joint return). The Revenue Act of 1978 eliminated the alternative of allowing the political contribution to be claimed as a deduction (in lieu of a credit). § 41.

**Pollution control facilities.** A certified pollution control facility the cost of which may be amortized over a 60 month period if elected by the taxpayer. § 169.

**Post-1953 securities.** Stock and securities (e. g., bonds) acquired by a corporation after December 31, 1953, and held by such corporation upon its complete liquidation. A shareholder's allocable share of these securities would be a determining factor in the amount of gain (and, in some cases, the nature of such gain) that must be recognized if the one-month liquidation treatment of § 333 has been elected. § § 333(e) and (f). See *one-month liquidation*.

**Prepaid expenses.** Cash basis as well as accrual basis taxpayers usually are required to capitalize prepayments for rent, insurance etc. that cover more than one year. Deductions are taken during the period the benefits are received. See *prepaid interest*.

**Prepaid interest.** In affect, the Tax Reform Act of 1976 placed cash basis taxpayers on an accrual basis for purposes of recognizing a deduction for prepaid interest. Thus, interest paid in advance is

deductible as an interest expense only as it accrues. The one
exception to this rule involves the interest element when a cash
basis taxpayer pays points to obtain financing for the purchase of
a principal residence (or to make improvements thereto) if the
payment of points is an established business practice in the area
in which the indebtedness is incurred and the amount involved is
not excessive.  § 461(g).  See *points* and *prepaid expenses*.

**Present interest.**  See *future interest*.

**Presumption.**  An inference in favor of a particular fact.  If, for example, the IRS issues a notice of deficiency against a taxpayer, a
presumption of correctness attaches to the assessment.  Thus,
the taxpayer has the burden of proof of showing that he or she
does not owe the tax listed in the deficiency notice.

**Previously taxed income.**  Prior to the Subchapter S Revision Act
of 1982, the undistributed taxable income (UTI) of a Subchapter S
corporation was taxed to the shareholders as of the last day of its
tax year.  Because such income was taxed but not received, the
UTI became previously taxed income (PTI) and usually could be
withdrawn by the shareholders without tax consequences at some
later point in time.  The role served by the PTI concept has been
taken over by the new accumulated adjustment account.  See *accumulated adjustment account*.

**Principal.**  Property as opposed to income.  The term is often used to
designate the corpus of a trust.  If, for example, G places real
estate in trust with income payable to A for life and the remainder to B upon A's death, the real estate is the principal or corpus
of the trust.

**Prizes and awards.**  The fair market value of a prize or award generally is includible in gross income.  Certain exceptions are provided where the prize or award is made in recognition of
religious, charitable, scientific, educational, artistic, literary, or
civic achievement and providing certain other requirements are
met.  § 74.

**Pro se.**  In tax litigation a pro se situation is one in which a taxpayer
represents himself or herself before the court.  The taxpayer han-
dles his or her own case without the benefit of counsel.

**Probate.**  The legal process whereby the estate of a decedent is administered.  Generally, the probate process involves collecting a
decedent's assets, liquidating liabilities, paying necessary taxes,
and distributing property to heirs.  These activities are carried
on by the executor or administrator of the estate usually under
the supervision of the state or local court of appropriate jurisdiction.

**Probate court.** The usual designation for the state or local court that supervises the administration (i. e., probate) of a decedent's estate.

**Probate estate.** The property of a decedent that is subject to administration by the executor or administrator of an estate. See *administration* and *probate*.

**Prop. Reg.** An abbreviation for Proposed Regulation. A Regulation may first be issued in proposed form to give interested parties the opportunity for comment. When, and if, a Proposed Regulation is finalized, it is designated as a Regulation (abbreviated "Reg.").

**Pro-rata.** Proportionately. Assume, for example, a corporation has ten shareholders each of whom owns 10% of the stock. A pro-rata dividend distribution of $1,000 would mean that each shareholder would receive $100.

**PTI.** See *previously taxed income*.

**Public policy limitation.** A concept developed by the courts precluding an income tax deduction for certain expenses related to activities which are deemed to be contrary to the public welfare. In this connection, Congress has incorporated into the Code specific disallowance provisions covering such items as illegal bribes, kickbacks, and fines and penalties [§ § 162(c) and (f)].

## –Q–

**Qualified pension or profit-sharing plan.** An employer-sponsored plan that meets the requirements of § 401. If these requirements are met, none of the employer's contributions to the plan will be taxed to the employee until distributed to him or her [§ 402]. The employer will be allowed a deduction in the year the contributions are made [§ 404].

## –R–

**RAR.** A revenue agent's report which reflects any adjustments made by the agent as a result of an audit of the taxpayer. The RAR is mailed to the taxpayer along with the 30-day letter which outlines the appellate procedures available to the taxpayer.

**Realized gain or loss.** The difference between the amount realized upon the sale or other disposition of property and the adjusted basis of such property. § 1001. See *adjusted basis* and *basis*.

**Realty.**  Real estate.

**Reasonable needs of the business.**  The usual justification for avoiding the penalty tax on unreasonable accumulation of earnings.  In determining the amount of taxable income subject to this tax (i. e., accumulated taxable income), §535 allows a deduction for "such part of earnings and profits for the taxable year as are retained for the reasonable needs of the business."  See, further, § 537.

**Rebuttable presumption.**  A presumption that can be overturned upon the showing of sufficient proof.  See *presumption*.

**Recapture.**  To recover the tax benefit of a deduction or a credit previously taken.  See *recapture of depreciation* and *recapture of the investment tax credit*.

**Recapture of depreciation.**  Upon the disposition of depreciable property used in a trade or business, gain or loss is determined measured by the difference between the consideration received (i. e., the amount realized) and the adjusted basis of the property.  Prior to the enactment of the recapture of depreciation provisions of the Code, any such gain recognized could be § 1231 gain and usually qualified for long-term capital gain treatment.  The recapture provisions of the Code (e. g., § § 1245 and 1250) may operate to convert some or all of the previous § 1231 gain into ordinary income.  The justification for recapture of depreciation is that it prevents a taxpayer from converting a dollar of deduction (in the form of depreciation) into forty cents of income (§ 1231 gain taxed as a long-term capital gain).  The recapture of depreciation rules do not apply when the property is disposed of at a loss.  See *Section 1231 gain*.

**Recapture of the investment tax credit.**  When § 38 property is disposed of or ceases to be used in the trade or business of the taxpayer, some of the investment tax credit claimed on such property may be recaptured as additional tax liability.  The amount of the recapture is the difference between the amount of the credit originally claimed and what should have been claimed in light of the length of time the property was actually held or used for qualifying purposes.  § 47.  See *investment tax credit* and *Section 38 property*.

**Recapture potential.**  Reference is to property which, if disposed of in a taxable transaction, would result in the recapture of depreciation (§ § 1245 or 1250) and/or of the investment tax credit (§ 47).

**Recognized gain or loss.**  The portion of realized gain or loss that is subject to income taxation.  See *realized gain or loss*.

**Reg.** An abbreviation for a U. S. Treasury Department Regulation.

**Regulations.** Treasury Department Regulations represent the position of the IRS as to how the Internal Revenue Code is to be interpreted. Their purpose is to provide taxpayers and IRS personnel with rules of general and specific application to the various provisions of the tax law. Regulations are published in the *Federal Register* and in all tax services.

**Rehabilitation expenditures.** A special 5 year amortization election is provided for rehabilitation expenditures on low-income housing. The expenditures must exceed $3,000 per dwelling unit over 2 consecutive years and in the aggregate may not exceed $20,000 per dwelling unit. § 167(k).

**Remainder.** See *remainder interest.*

**Remainder interest.** The property that passes to a beneficiary after the expiration of an intervening income interest. If, for example, G places real estate in trust with income to A for life and remainder to B upon A's death, B has a remainder interest.

**Remainderman.** The holder of a remainder interest (usually as to property held in trust). In a will the remainderman is the party who will receive what is left of the decedent's property after all specific bequests have been satisfied. If, for example, D dies and her will leaves $10,000 in cash to A and the remainder of the estate to B, the remainderman is B.

**Remand.** To send back. An appellate court may remand a case to a lower court, usually for additional fact finding. In other words, the appellate court is not in a position to decide the appeal based on the facts determined by the lower court. Remanding is abbreviated "rem'g."

**Research and experimental expenditures.** Three alternative methods are provided in the Code. The expenditures may be expensed in the year paid or incurred; deferred subject to amortization; or capitalized. If an election is not made to expense such costs or to defer the expenditures subject to amortization (over 60 months), the research and experimental costs must be capitalized. "Incremental" research and experimental expenditures qualify for a 25 percent credit.

**Reserve for bad debts.** A method of accounting whereby an allowance is permitted for estimated uncollectible accounts. Actual write-offs are charged to the reserve and recoveries of amounts previously written-off are credited to the reserve. § 166(c).

**Reserves for estimated expenses.**  Except in the case of bad debts, reserves for estimated expenses (e. g., warranty service costs) are not permitted for tax purposes even though such reserves are appropriate for financial accounting purposes.  See *all events test*.

**Residential energy tax credit.**  See *energy tax credit—residential property*.

**Restricted property.**  An arrangement whereby an employer transfers property (usually stock) to an employee at a bargain price (i. e., for less than its fair market value).  If the transfer is accompanied by a substantial risk of forfeiture and the property is not transferable, then no compensation results to the employee until such restrictions disappear.  An example of a substantial risk of forfeiture would be a requirement that the employee return the property if his or her employment is terminated within a specified period of time.  § 83.  See *nonqualified deferred compensation plans*.

**Retirement of corporate obligations.**  The retirement of corporate and certain government obligations is considered to be a sale or exchange.  Gain or loss, therefore, is treated as capital gain or loss upon the retirement of a corporate obligation rather than ordinary income or loss.  § 1232.

**Return of capital doctrine.**  When a taxable sale or exchange occurs, the seller may be permitted to recover his or her investment (or other adjusted basis) in the property before gain or loss is recognized.  See *open transaction*.

**Revenue Procedure.**  A matter of procedural importance to both taxpayers and the IRS concerning the administration of the tax laws is issued as a Revenue Procedure (abbreviated as "Rev. Proc.").  A Revenue Procedure is first published in an Internal Revenue Bulletin (I. R. B.) and later transferred to the appropriate Cumulative Bulletin (C. B.).  Both the Internal Revenue Bulletins and the Cumulative Bulletins are published by the U. S. Government.

**Revenue Ruling.**  A Revenue Ruling (abbreviated "Rev. Rul.") is issued by the National Office of the IRS to express an official interpretation of the tax law as applied to specific transactions. Unlike a Regulation, it is more limited in application.  A Revenue Ruling is first published in an Internal Revenue Bulletin (I. R. B.) and later transferred to the appropriate Cumulative Bulletin (C. B.).  Both the Internal Revenue Bulletins and the Cumulative Bulletins are published by the U. S. Government.

**Reversed (Rev'd.).**  An indication that a decision of one court has been reversed by a higher court in the same case.

**Reversing (Rev'g.).** An indication that the decision of a higher court is reversing the result reached by a lower court in the same case.

**Reversion.** See *reversionary interest.*

**Revocable transfer.** A transfer of property whereby the transferor retains the right to recover the property. The creation of a revocable trust is an example of a revocable transfer. § 2038. See *incomplete transfers.*

**Rev. Proc.** An abbreviation for an IRS Revenue Procedure. See *Revenue Procedure.*

**Rev. Rul.** An abbreviation for an IRS Revenue Ruling. See *Revenue Ruling.*

**Right of survivorship.** See *joint tenancy.*

## –S–

**Schedule PH.** A tax form required to be filed by corporations that are personal holding companies. The form must be filed in addition to Form 1120 (i. e., U. S. Corporation Income Tax Return).

**S corporation.** The new designation for a Subchapter S corporation.

**Scholarships and fellowships.** Scholarships and fellowships are generally excluded from gross income of the recipient unless the payments are a disguised form of compensation for services rendered. Special rules apply where the payments are for dual motives (i. e., to aid the recipient and to benefit the grantor). § 117.

**Section 38 property.** Property which qualifies for the investment tax credit. Generally, this includes all tangible property (other than real estate) used in a trade or business. § 48.

**Section 1231 assets.** Section 1231 assets are depreciable assets and real estate used in a trade or business and held for more than one year. Under certain circumstances, the classification also includes: timber, coal, domestic iron ore, livestock (held for draft, breeding, dairy, or sporting purposes), and unharvested crops. § 1231(b). See *Section 1231 gains and losses.*

**Section 1231 gains and losses.** If the combined gains and losses from the taxable dispositions of § 1231 assets plus the net gain from involuntary conversions (of both § 1231 assets and long-term capital assets) is a gain, such gains and losses are treated as long-term capital gains and losses. In arriving at § 1231 gains, however, the depreciation recapture provisions (e. g., § § 1245 and 1250) are first applied to produce ordinary income. If the net result of the combination is a loss, such gains and losses from § 1231 assets are treated as ordinary gains and losses. § 1231(a).  See *Section 1231 assets.*

**Section 1244 stock.**  Stock issued under § 1244 by qualifying small business corporations.  If § 1244 stock becomes worthless, the shareholders may claim an ordinary loss rather than the usual capital loss.

**Section 1245 property.**  Property which is subject to the recapture of depreciation under § 1245.  For a definition of § 1245 property see § 1245(a)(3).  See *recapture of depreciation* and *Section 1245 recapture.*

**Section 1245 recapture.**  Upon a taxable disposition of § 1245 property, all depreciation claimed on such property after 1962 will be recaptured as ordinary income (but not to exceed recognized gain from the disposition).

**Section 1250 property.**  Real estate which is subject to the recapture of depreciation under § 1250.  For a definition of § 1250 property see § 1250(c).  See *recapture of depreciation.*

**Separate property.**  In a community property jurisdiction, separate property is that property which belongs entirely to one of the spouses.  Generally, it is property acquired before marriage or acquired after marriage by gift or inheritance.  See *community property.*

**Sham.**  A transaction without substance that will be disregarded for tax purposes.

**Simple trusts.**  Simple trusts are those that are not complex trusts. Such trusts may not have a charitable beneficiary, accumulate income, nor distribute corpus.

**Single-transaction approach.**  An approach developed in the *Kimbell-Diamond* decision which led to the enactment of § 334(b)(2) and later § 338 of the Code.  If one corporation purchases 80% or more of the stock in another corporation and, shortly thereafter, liquidates the acquired corporation, the court concluded that the purchase was of assets and not of stock.  In other words, a single transaction (i. e., the purchase of assets) had occurred and not multiple transactions (i. e., the purchase of stock and the acquisition of assets through liquidation).  Under this assumption, the basis of the subsidiary's assets to the parent corporation would be the cost of the stock and not the subsidiary's basis in such assets.

**Small business corporation.** A corporation which satisfies the definition of § 1361(b), § 1244(c)(2) or both. Satisfaction of § 1361(b) permits an S election, while satisfaction of § 1244 enables the shareholders of the corporation to claim an ordinary loss on the worthlessness of stock.

**Specific bequest.** A bequest of ascertainable property or cash to an heir of a decedent. Thus, if D's will passes his personal residence to W and grants $10,000 in cash to S, both W and S receive specific bequests.

**Specific exemption.** For transfers made prior to 1977, each donor was allowed a specific exemption of $30,000. Available for the lifetime of a donor, the exemption could be used to offset any taxable gifts made. Section 2521 was repealed by the Tax Reform Act of 1976.

**Specific legatee.** The recipient of designated property under a will and transferred by the death of the owner.

**Statute of limitations.** Provisions of the law which specify the maximum period of time in which action may be taken on a past event. Code § § 6501–6504 contain the limitation periods applicable to the IRS for additional assessments while § § 6511–6515 relate to refund claims by taxpayers.

**Statutory depletion.** See *depletion.*

**Statutory notice of deficiency.** Commonly referred to as the 90-day letter, this notice is sent to a taxpayer upon request, upon the expiration of the 30-day letter, or upon exhaustion by the taxpayer of his or her administrative remedies before the IRS. The notice gives the taxpayer 90 days in which to file a petition with the U. S. Tax Court. If such a petition is not filed, the IRS will issue a demand for payment of the assessed deficiency. § § 6211–6216. See *thirty-day letter.*

**Step-down in basis.** A reduction in the income tax basis of property.

**Step-transaction approach.** Disregarding one or more transactions to arrive at the final result.

**Step-up in basis.** An increase in the income tax basis of property. The classic step-up in basis occurs when a decedent dies owning appreciated property. Since the estate or heir acquires a basis in the property equal to its fair market value on the date of death (or alternate valuation date if elected), any appreciation is not subject to the income tax. Thus, a step-up in basis is the result with no income tax consequences.

**Stock attribution.** See *attribution.*

**Straddle sale.** The sale of loss property prior to the adoption of a plan of liquidation. The objective of this approach is to avoid the disallowance of the loss that would result under § 337 (i. e., "12-month liquidation") if the property were sold after the adoption of the plan. See *twelve-month liquidation.*

**Subchapter C corporation.** A regular corporation subject to the rules contained in Subchapter C (§§ 301–385) of the Internal Revenue Code of 1954. To be distinguished from an S corporation which is governed by Subchapter S of the Code.

**Subchapter S.** Sections 1361–1379 of the Internal Revenue Code of 1954. See *Subchapter S corporation.*

**Subchapter S corporation.** An elective provision permitting certain small business corporations and their shareholders to elect to be treated for income tax purposes in accordance with the operating rules of §§ 1361–1379. Of major significance is the fact that Subchapter S status usually avoids the corporate income tax, and corporate losses can be claimed by the shareholders.

**Substance vs. form.** To ascertain the true reality of what has occurred. Suppose, for example, a father sells stock to his daughter for $1,000. If the stock is really worth $50,000 at the time of the transfer, the substance of the transaction is probably a gift of $49,000.

**Substantially disproportionate.** A type of stock redemption that qualifies for exchange treatment under § 302(a). § 302(b)(2).

**Surviving spouse.** When a husband or wife predeceases the other, the survivor is known as a "surviving spouse." Under certain conditions, a surviving spouse may be entitled to use the income tax rates contained in § 1(a) [i. e., those applicable to married persons filing a joint return] for the two years after the year of death of his or her spouse. For the definition of a surviving spouse for this purpose see § 2(a).

**Survivorship.** See *joint tenancy.*

## –T–

**Tangible property.** All property which has form or substance and is not intangible. See *intangibles.*

**Tax benefit rule.** A rule which limits the recognition of income from the recovery of an expense or loss properly deducted in a prior tax year to the amount of the deduction that generated a tax benefit. Assume, for example, that last year T (an individual) has medical expenses of $2,000 and adjusted gross income of $30,000. Due to the 5% limitation, T was able to deduct only $500 of these expenses [i. e., $2,000 − (5% × $30,000)]. If, in this year, T is reimbursed by his insurance company for $600 of these expenses, the tax benefit rule limits the amount of income from the reimbursement to $500 (i. e., the amount previously deducted with a tax benefit).

**Tax Court.** The U. S. Tax Court is one of three trial courts of original jurisdiction which decides litigation involving Federal income, death, or gift taxes. It is the only trial court where the taxpayer must not first pay the deficiency assessed by the IRS. The Tax Court will not have jurisdiction over a case unless the statutory notice of deficiency (i. e., "90-day letter") has been issued by the IRS and the taxpayer files the petition for hearing within the time prescribed.

**Tax credit for elderly.** Elderly taxpayers (age 65 and over) may receive a tax credit amounting to 15 percent of $2,500 or $3,750 for married individuals filing jointly. This amount is reduced by social security benefits, excluded pension benefits and one-half of the taxpayer's adjusted gross income in excess of $7,500 ($10,000 for married taxpayers filing jointly). § 37.

**Tax-free exchange.** Transfers of property specifically exempted from Federal income tax consequences. Examples are a transfer of property to a controlled corporation under § 351(a) and a like-kind exchange under § 1031(a).

**Tax home.** Since travel expenses of an employee are deductible only if the taxpayer is away from home, the deductibility of such expenses rests upon the definition of "tax home". The IRS position is that "tax home" is the business location, post or station of the taxpayer. If an employee is temporarily reassigned to a new post for a period of one year or less, the taxpayer's home should be his or her personal residence and the travel expenses should be deductible. The courts are in conflict regarding what constitutes a person's "home" for tax purposes.

**Tax preference items.** Those items set forth in § 57 which may result in the imposition of the minimum tax. §§ 55–58. See *"Add-on" minimum tax* and *alternative minimum tax.*

**Tax year.** See *accounting period.*

**Taxable estate.** Defined in § 2051, the taxable estate is the gross estate of a decedent reduced by the deductions allowed by

§ § 2053–2056 (e. g., administration expenses, marital and charitable deductions). The taxable estate is the amount that is subject to the unified transfer tax at death. See *gross estate*.

**Taxable gift.** Defined in § 2503, a taxable gift is the amount of the gift that is subject to the unified transfer tax. Thus, a taxable gift has been adjusted by the annual exclusion and other appropriate deductions (e. g., marital and charitable).

**Tax-free exchange.** Transfers of property specifically exempted from income tax consequences by the tax law. Examples are a transfer of property to a controlled corporation under § 351(a) and a like-kind exchange under § 1031(a).

**Tax-option corporation.** See *Subchapter S corporation*.

**Tax rate schedules.** Rate schedules appearing in Appendix A-1 which are used by upper income taxpayers. Separate rate schedules are provided for married individuals filing jointly, unmarried individuals who maintain a household, single taxpayers, and estates and trusts and married individuals filing separate returns.

**Tax table.** A tax table appearing in Appendix A-2 is provided for taxpayers with less than $50,000 of taxable income. Separate columns are provided for single taxpayers, married taxpayers filing jointly, head of household, and married taxpayers filing separately.

**T. C.** An abbreviation for the U. S. Tax Court. It is used to cite a Regular Decision of the U. S. Tax Court.

**T. C. Memo.** An abbreviation used to refer to a Memorandum Decision of the U. S. Tax Court.

**Telescoping.** To look through one or more transactions to arrive at the final result. It is also designated as the *step-transaction approach* or the *substance vs. form* concept (see these terms).

**Tenancy by the entirety.** Essentially, a joint tenancy between husband and wife. See *joint tenancy*.

**Tenancy in common.** A form of ownership whereby each tenant (i. e., owner) holds an undivided interest in property. Unlike a joint tenancy or a tenancy by the entirety, the interest of a tenant in common does not terminate upon his or her prior death (i. e., there is no right of survivorship). Assume, for example, B and C acquire real estate as equal tenants in common, each having furnished one-half of the purchase price. Upon B's prior death, his one-half interest in the property passes to his estate or heirs. For a comparison of results see *joint tenancy*.

**Terminable interest.** An interest in property which terminates upon the death of the holder or upon the occurrence of some other specified event. The transfer of a terminable interest by one spouse to the other spouse may not qualify for the marital deduction. § § 2056(b) and 2523(b). See *marital deduction*.

**Testamentary disposition.** The passing of property to another upon the death of the owner.

**Thin capitalization.** See *thin corporation*.

**Thin corporation.** When debt owed by a corporation to its shareholders becomes too large in relationship to its capital structure (i. e., stock and shareholder equity), the IRS may contend that the corporation is thinly capitalized. In effect, this means that some or all of the debt will be reclassified as equity. The immediate result is to disallow any interest deduction to the corporation on the reclassified debt. To the extent of the corporation's earnings and profits, interest payments and loan repayments are treated as dividends to the shareholders. § 385.

**Thirty-day letter.** A letter which accompanies a revenue agent's report (RAR) issued as a result of an IRS audit of a taxpayer (or the rejection of a taxpayer's claim for refund). The letter outlines the taxpayer's appeal procedure before the IRS. If the taxpayer does not request any such procedures within the 30-day period, the IRS will issue a statutory notice of deficiency (the "90-day letter").

**Transfer tax.** A tax imposed upon the transfer of property. See *unified transfer tax*.

**Transferee liability.** Under certain conditions, if the IRS is unable to collect taxes owed by a transferor of property, it may pursue its claim against the transferee of such property. The transferee's liability for taxes is limited to the extent of the value of the assets transferred. For example, the IRS can force a donee to pay the gift tax when such tax cannot be paid by the donor making the transfer. § § 6901–6905.

**Treasury Regulations.** See *Regulations*.

**Trial court.** The court of original jurisdiction; the first court to consider litigation. In Federal tax controversies trial courts include: U. S. District Courts, the U. S. Tax Court, and the U. S. Claims Court. See *appellate court*.

**Twelve-month liquidation.** A provision of the Code that requires a corporation selling property within the 12-month period from the adoption of a plan of liquidation to its complete liquidation to recognize no gain or loss on such sales. Section 337(b) defines the "property" that qualifies for such treatment. Generally, inventory is not included within the definition unless a bulk sale occurs. See *bulk sale* and *straddle sale*.

## –U–

**Undistributed personal holding company income.** The penalty tax on personal holding companies is imposed on the corporation's undistributed personal holding company income for the year. The adjustment necessary to convert taxable income to undistributed personal holding company income is set forth in § 545.

**Unearned income.** Income that has been received but not yet earned. Normally, such income is taxed when received even in the case of accrual basis taxpayers.

**Unified transfer tax.** A set of tax rates applicable to transfers by gift and death made after 1976. § 2001(c).

**Unified transfer tax credit.** A credit allowed against any unified transfer tax. § § 2010 and 2505.

**Uniform Gift to Minors Act.** A means of transferring property (usually stocks and bonds) to a minor. The designated custodian of the property has the legal right to act on behalf of the minor without the necessity of a guardianship. Generally, the custodian possesses the right to change investments (e. g., sell one type of stock and buy another), apply the income from the custodial property to the minor's support, and even terminate the custodianship. In this regard, however, the custodian is acting in a fiduciary capacity on behalf of the minor. The custodian could not, for example, appropriate the property for his or her own use because it belongs to the minor. During the period of the custodianship, the income from the property is taxed to the minor. The custodianship terminates when the minor reaches legal age. See *guardianship* and *legal age*.

**Unrealized receivables.** Amounts earned by a cash basis taxpayer but not yet received. Because of the method of accounting used by the taxpayer, they have no income tax basis.

**Unreasonable compensation.** Under § 162(a)(1) a deduction is allowed for "reasonable" salaries or other compensation for personal services actually rendered. To the extent compensation is "excessive" (i. e., "unreasonable"), no deduction will be allowed. The problem of unreasonable compensation usually is limited to closely-held corporations where the motivation is to pay out profits in some form deductible to the corporation. Deductible compensation, therefore, becomes an attractive substitute for nondeductible dividends when the shareholders also are employed by the corporation.

**USSC.** An abbreviation for the U. S. Supreme Court.

**U. S. Tax Court.** See *Tax Court.*

**USTC.** Published by Commerce Clearing House, *U. S. Tax Cases* contain all of the Federal tax decisions issued by the U. S. District Courts, U. S. Claims Court, U. S. Courts of Appeals, and the U. S. Supreme Court.

## –V–

**Value.** See *fair market value.*

**Vested.** Absolute and complete. If, for example, a person holds a vested interest in property such interest cannot be taken away or otherwise defeated.

## –W–

**Wash sale.** A loss from the sale of stock or securities which is disallowed because the taxpayer has within 30 days before or after the sale acquired stock or securities substantially identical to those sold. § 1091.

## –Z–

**Zero bracket amount.** A deduction generally available to all individual taxpayers in arriving at taxable income. Unlike the standard deduction which it replaced, the zero bracket amount is not determined as a percentage of adjusted gross income but is a flat amount. For 1979 and thereafter this amount is $2,300 for single persons and head of household, $3,400 for married persons filing jointly, and $1,700 for married persons filing separate returns. The zero bracket amount does not have to be computed separately but is built into the tax rate tables and the tax rate schedules. § 63(d) as amended by the Revenue Act of 1978.

# APPENDIX D-1
# TABLE OF CODE SECTIONS CITED

[See Title 26 U.S.C.A.]

| I.R.C.<br>Sec. | This Work<br>Page |
| --- | --- |
| 1 | 22-5 |
| 1(a) | 2-23, C-23 |
| 1(b) | C-23 |
| 1(c) | C-23 |
| 1(d) | 2-23, 20-5 |
| 1(e) | 20-5 |
| 1-5 | 22-4 |
| 2 | 22-5, 22-6 |
| 2(a) | 2-23, 22-4 |
| 2(a)(1)(A) | 22-4, 22-5 |
| 2(b) | 2-24, C-23 |
| 2(b)(1)(A)(i) | 2-24 |
| 2(b)(1)(B) | 2-24 |
| 3(b) | 2-17 |
| 3(b)(2) | 11-16 |
| 3(b)(3) | 20-5 |
| 5 | 22-4 |
| 6(1) | 17-3 |
| 11 | 22-4 |
| 11-12 | 22-4 |
| 12(d) | 22-5 |
| 31 | 8-17, 8-19 |
| 33 | C-20 |
| 37 | 8-24, 8-25 |
| 38 | 8-7, 8-8, 8-9, 8-11, 8-35, 16-13, 16-23, 16-25, 16-28, 16-29, 16-34, 17-5, 22-33, C-25, E-11 |
| 39 | 8-17 |
| 41(b)(1) | 8-28 |
| 41(c) | 8-28, 8-29 |
| 43 | 8-17 |
| 43(a) | 8-22, 8-23 |
| 43(b) | 8-22, 8-23 |
| 43(c)(2) | 8-22 |
| 44A | 8-26, 8-27, 8-28, 8-33, 8-34 |
| 44C | 8-20, C-18 |
| 44C(a) | 8-20 |

| I.R.C.<br>Sec. | This Work<br>Page |
| --- | --- |
| 44C(b)(2) | 8-20, 8-21 |
| 44F | 8-15, 8-16, 8-17 |
| 44F(a) | 8-16 |
| 44F(d) | 8-17 |
| 44F(g)(1) | 8-17 |
| 44G | 8-18, 8-19 |
| 44G(a)(1) | 8-18 |
| 46(a) | C-18 |
| 46(a)(1)(B) | 8-10 |
| 46(a)(2)(F) | 8-15 |
| 46(a)(3)(B) | 8-5 |
| 46(a)(5) | 8-5 |
| 46(a)(7) | 8-10 |
| 46(b) | 8-5 |
| 46(c) | 8-3 |
| 46(c)(2) | 8-11 |
| 46(c)(8) | 8-11 |
| 46(d) | 8-11 |
| 46-50 | C-25 |
| 47 | 22-33 |
| 47(a)(1) | 8-12 |
| 47(a)(5) | 8-6, 8-15 |
| 47(b) | 17-5 |
| 48(a) | 8-8 |
| 48(c)(2) | 8-3, 8-9 |
| 48(e) | C-18 |
| 48(f) | 20-15 |
| 48(g)(1)(C) | 8-15 |
| 48(g)(2)(B)(i) | 8-15 |
| 48(g)(5)(A) | 8-15 |
| 48(q) | 10-32 |
| 48(q)(1) | 8-4 |
| 48(q)(4) | 8-4 |
| 48(q)(5) | 8-4, 10-25 |
| 51 | 8-12 |
| 51(d) | 8-14 |
| 51(d)(12) | 8-14 |
| 53 | 3-12 |

| I.R.C. Sec. | This Work Page |
|---|---|
| 53(b) | 8-13 |
| 55 | 11-9 |
| 55(c)(2) | 11-13 |
| 55(d) | 11-9 |
| 55(f) | 11-11 |
| 56 | 8-5, 20-5 |
| 57 | 11-9, 11-10 |
| 57(e) | 11-11 |
| 58(i) | 11-11, 11-13 |
| 58(i)(5) | 11-11 |
| 61 | 3-1, 3-2, 4-1, 4-7, 4-16, 5-1, C-22 |
| 61(a) | 2-3, 3-1 |
| 61(a)(1) | 22-37 |
| 61(a)(12) | 19-7, 22-37 |
| 61(a)(3) | 9-4 |
| 62 | 2-4, 5-2 |
| 62(1) | 8-16 |
| 62(13) | C-4 |
| 62(2)(B) | 11-38 |
| 62(2)(C) | 11-36 |
| 62(5) | 5-4, 8-16 |
| 62(8) | 11-40 |
| 63(b) | 5-1 |
| 63(d) | 2-5 |
| 63(i) | 8-26 |
| 66–86 | 3-16 |
| 71 | 3-16, 3-17, C-4 |
| 72(c)(3) | 3-19 |
| 74 | 3-19 |
| 74(b) | 4-2 |
| 79 | 3-20, 3-21, 4-3, 16-22, 17-34, C-23 |
| 82 | 11-40 |
| 83 | 17-6 |
| 85 | 3-21 |
| 101 | 4-1, 4-2 |
| 101(a) | 4-4 |
| 101(a)(2) | 4-4 |
| 101(b) | 4-2, 4-5, 16-22 |
| 101(b)(1) | 17-34, C-13 |
| 101(d) | 4-5 |
| 101(f) | 4-4 |
| 101–129 | 3-1 |
| 102 | 4-2 |

| I.R.C. Sec. | This Work Page |
|---|---|
| 102(a) | 4-3, 9-7 |
| 103 | 4-3 |
| 104 | 4-2 |
| 104(a)(1) | 4-10 |
| 104(a)(2) | 4-9 |
| 104(a)(3) | 4-10 |
| 105 | 4-3, 4-12, 4-15, 16-22, 16-31, 17-34 |
| 105(a) | 4-11 |
| 105(b) | 4-11, 4-12 |
| 105(c) | 4-11, 4-12 |
| 105(d) | 4-11, C-15 |
| 105(d)(1)(5) | 4-13 |
| 105(h) | 4-12 |
| 106 | 4-3, 4-11, 4-12, 4-15, 8-32, 16-22, 16-31, 17-34 |
| 107 | 4-3 |
| 108 | 16-14 |
| 108(b) | 4-23 |
| 108(e)(2) | 4-23 |
| 109 | 4-1, 4-2 |
| 111 | 4-3, 4-22, 4-32, 16-13, 17-15, 22-37 |
| 111(a) | 4-22 |
| 112 | 4-3 |
| 113 | 4-3 |
| 116 | 4-3, 4-19, 4-28, 4-31, 11-10, 11-11, 16-15, 17-15, 20-7, C-16 |
| 117 | 3-19, 4-2, 4-7 |
| 117(a)(2) | 4-7 |
| 118 | C-9 |
| 119 | 3-3, 4-3, 4-13, 16-22, 17-34 |
| 120 | 4-3, 4-15 |
| 121 | 4-3, 9-25, 9-31, 9-32, 9-33, 9-37, 9-38, 9-40, 9-46 |
| 121(a) | 9-31, 9-32, 22-31 |
| 121(b) | 9-31 |
| 121(b)(2) | 9-31 |
| 123 | 4-2 |
| 124 | 4-3, 4-15 |
| 125 | 4-3, 4-15 |
| 127 | 4-3, 4-8, 11-44, 11-60, C-17 |

| I.R.C. Sec. | This Work Page |
|---|---|
| 128 | 4-3, 4-19, 11-10 |
| 129 | 4-1, 4-3, 4-15 |
| 143(b) | 2-34 |
| 151(c) | 2-12 |
| 151(d) | 2-12 |
| 151(d)(3) | 2-12 |
| 151(e) | 2-16 |
| 151(e)(2) | 2-16 |
| 152(a) | 2-15, 2-24 |
| 152(b)(3) | 2-17 |
| 152(b)(5) | 2-15 |
| 152(c) | 2-14 |
| 152(e) | 2-15 |
| 152(e)(2)(A)(i) | 21-33 |
| 152(e)(2)(B)(1) | 2-15 |
| 162 | 4-8, 5-1, 5-2, 5-3, 5-5, 5-7, 5-10, 5-25, 8-9, 8-19, 8-20, 22-18, 22-30, C-8 |
| 162(a) | 5-2, 17-29, 22-16, 22-20, C-29, C-31 |
| 162(a)(1) | 5-6, 21-30, 22-17, 22-22, 22-24 |
| 162(a)(2) | 11-38 |
| 162(c) | 5-7 |
| 162(c)(2) | 22-29 |
| 162(e)(1)(A) | 5-9 |
| 163 | 5-2, 5-11 |
| 163(a) | 8-15 |
| 163(b) | 8-15, 8-19 |
| 163(d) | 8-15, 8-17, 16-14, C-25 |
| 163(d)(4)(C) | 16-24 |
| 164 | 5-2, 8-9, 8-25, 8-35, 22-30 |
| 164(a) | 8-9, 8-11 |
| 164(c)(2) | 8-10 |
| 164(d) | 8-11, 9-2, 9-3 |
| 165 | 5-1, 5-2, 5-3, 5-15 |
| 165(a) | 9-4 |
| 165(c)(3) | 9-23 |
| 165(d) | 16-13, 17-15 |
| 165(g) | 16-24 |
| 165(h) | C-15 |
| 166 | 5-2, 11-20, C-8 |
| 166(d) | 10-37, C-30 |
| 167(b)(2) | C-1 |
| 167(b)(3) | C-1 |

| I.R.C. Sec. | This Work Page |
|---|---|
| 167(g) | 9-9 |
| 167(h) | 20-10 |
| 167(j)(2)(B) | 10-34 |
| 167(k) | 10-34 |
| 168 | C-1 |
| 168(f)(10) | 17-13 |
| 170 | 5-14, 8-19, 8-20, 8-23, 10-31, C-10 |
| 170(a)(1) | 8-20 |
| 170(a)(2) | 8-20, 20-13 |
| 170(b) | 8-21, 8-24 |
| 170(b)(1)(A) | 8-24 |
| 170(b)(1)(B) | 8-24 |
| 170(b)(1)(C)(i) | 8-25 |
| 170(b)(1)(D) | 8-25 |
| 170(b)(1)(E) | 8-21 |
| 170(b)(2) | 8-21 |
| 170(c) | 8-19, 8-20, 17-15 |
| 170(c)(2)(A) | 19-12 |
| 170(c)(5) | 19-12 |
| 170(d)(1) | 8-24, 8-25 |
| 170(d)(1)(A) | 8-25 |
| 170(e) | 10-39 |
| 170(e)(1) | 8-25 |
| 170(e)(1)(A) | 10-31 |
| 170(i) | 8-26 |
| 172 | 16-10, 20-11, C-29 |
| 174 | 5-16, 8-16, 8-17, 8-32, 11-52 |
| 175 | 5-16, 17-15 |
| 179 | 5-16, 10-25, 11-54, 11-55, 11-58, 11-62, 11-63, 16-13, 17-13, E-11 |
| 179(d)(2)(C) | 17-13 |
| 180 | 5-16 |
| 182 | 5-16 |
| 183 | 5-10, 5-11, 5-23, 5-25, 5-26, 16-24, C-23 |
| 183(d) | 5-10 |
| 191 | 8-15 |
| 194 | 16-14 |
| 211 | 17-16, 22-4 |
| 212 | 2-4, 5-1, 5-2, 5-3, 5-4, 5-5, 5-7, 5-10, 5-14, 5-20, 8-9, 11-40, 16-13, 17-15, C-29, C-31 |

| I.R.C. Sec. | This Work Page | I.R.C. Sec. | This Work Page |
|---|---|---|---|
| 212(1) | 22-4 | 274(e) | 11-47 |
| 212(3) | 5-22 | 276 | 5-9 |
| 212(d)(1) | 8-15 | 280A | 5-12, C-31 |
| 213 | 5-14, 8-33, 8-37, 16-22, 17-15, 22-37 | 280A(c)(1) | 11-50 |
| 215 | 3-16, 17-15 | 280A(d) | 5-13 |
| 216 | 17-15 | 280C | 8-13 |
| 217 | 5-14, 9-26, C-29 | 280E | 5-9 |
| 217(a) | 11-40 | 291 | 16-13 |
| 217(b)(3)(A) | 11-43 | 301 | C-12 |
| 217(c) | 11-40 | 301(c) | 4-20 |
| 219 | C-24 | 302 | 16-26 |
| 221 | 2-25, 11-52 | 302(b)(3) | 22-34 |
| 221(b)(2)(A) | 2-25 | 303 | 16-26 |
| 223 | 17-16 | 305(b)(1) | 4-21 |
| 241–250 | 16-10 | 305(e) | 4-3, 4-21 |
| 243 | 16-13, C-16 | 316(a) | 4-20 |
| 243–246 | C-16 | 318 | 10-33, 16-22 |
| 248 | 16-10, 16-12 | 331 | 16-26 |
| 262 | 5-14, 5-22, 22-4 | 332 | 16-26 |
| 263 | 17-29, C-9 | 333 | 16-26, C-31 |
| 263(a) | 5-15 | 334 | C-7 |
| 263(c) | 5-16, 10-35, 16-14, 17-15, C-25 | 334(b)(2) | 22-34 |
| 264 | 8-15 | 334(c) | C-31 |
| 265 | 5-20, 5-21, 5-25, 8-17, 20-16 | 336 | 16-26, C-16 |
| 267 | 5-17, 5-18, 8-15, 8-36, 11-18, 17-28, 20-12, 22-17, 22-19, 22-21, 22-24 | 337 | 16-26, 22-34 |
| 267(a) | 17-28 | 337(b)(2) | C-8 |
| 267(a)(1) | 9-5, 10-33 | 341(e) | 22-19 |
| 267(a)(2) | 8-16, 22-17 | 351 | 11-30, 16-2, 17-7, 17-36, 21-2 |
| 267(b) | 16-24, 20-12 | 351(b) | C-8 |
| 267(c) | 5-18, 17-28 | 351(e) | 17-7 |
| 267(c)(2) | 22-17 | 354 | 21-3 |
| 267(c)(4) | 5-13, 11-11, 17-28, 22-17 | 357(b)(1)(B) | C-8 |
| 267(d) | 17-28 | 357(c) | 17-10 |
| 267(f) | 16-24 | 358 | 21-3, C-7 |
| 274 | 11-46, 21-16, 22-30, C-18, E-6 | 361(a) | 21-3 |
| | | 362 | 21-3, C-7 |
| | | 368(a)(1)(A) | C-28 |
| 274(a)(1)(A) | 11-47 | 368(a)(1)(C) | 21-3 |
| 274(b)(1) | 11-49 | 381 | 16-9 |
| 274(d) | 5-19, 11-49 | 401 | 21-4 |
| | | 401–404 | 17-34 |
| | | 404 | 21-4, 22-16, 22-17 |
| | | 409A | 8-19 |
| | | 415(c)(6)(B)(iii) | 8-19 |

| I.R.C. Sec. | This Work Page | I.R.C. Sec. | This Work Page |
|---|---|---|---|
| 441 | 20-5 | 509(a) | 8-22 |
| 441(a) | 3-4 | 527(e)(1) | 19-7 |
| 441(c) | 11-13 | 531–537 | C-2 |
| 441(f) | 11-13 | 535 | C-2 |
| 441–443 | C-1 | 541 | 22-25, C-3 |
| 442 | 11-14, 20-5 | 542(c)(6) | 16-11 |
| 443 | 17-25 | 543(a)(2) | 22-35 |
| 443(b)(1) | 11-15 | 543(b)(1) | C-31 |
| 443(b)(3) | 11-16 | 543(b)(2) | C-3 |
| 446 | 11-16, 20-5 | 547 | C-14 |
| 446(b) | 1-31, 3-5, 3-10, 11-17 | 547(g) | C-14 |
| 446(c) | 11-20 | 565 | C-12 |
| 446(c)(1) | C-9 | 611 | 17-11, 17-16 |
| 446(c)(2) | C-2 | 611(b)(3) | 20-10 |
| 446(e) | 3-5 | 613 | C-14 |
| 446–472 | C-1 | 613A | C-14 |
| 447 | 10-35 | 613A(c)(13) | 16-24 |
| 451(d) | 3-10 | 615 | 17-15 |
| 453 | 10-45, 11-26, 11-30, 16-29, 20-8, C-25 | 616 | 5-16 |
| 453(a) | 11-26 | 617 | 16-14, 17-15 |
| 453(b)(1) | 11-26 | 641 | 20-1, 20-6 |
| 453(b)(1)(B) | 11-26 | 641(b) | 20-9 |
| 453A | 11-24 | 642(a)(1) | 20-15 |
| 453A(a)(1) | 11-24 | 642(b) | 20-5 |
| 453A(a)(2) | 11-25 | 642(c) | 20-12 |
| 453A(b) | 11-25 | 642(c)(1) | 20-13 |
| 453B | 11-29 | 642(c)(2) | 20-13 |
| 453B(a) | 11-29 | 642(c)(4) | 20-13 |
| 453B(c) | 11-30 | 642(g) | 20-9 |
| 453B(d) | 11-30 | 642(h) | 20-11, 20-24 |
| 453B(f)(1) | 11-30 | 643 | 20-16 |
| 453B(f)(2) | 11-30 | 643(a) | C-15 |
| 454(a) | 3-9 | 643(a)(6) | 20-17 |
| 461(g) | 8-16, 11-19 | 643(b) | 20-17 |
| 461(g)(2) | 8-16, 8-33 | 644 | 20-1, 20-5, 22-38 |
| 464 | 10-35 | 651 | 20-1, 20-14, 20-18 |
| 465 | 8-11, 17-24 | 651(a) | 20-14 |
| 471 | 11-32 | 651(b) | 20-14, 20-16 |
| 472 | C-27 | 652 | 20-1, 20-18 |
| 472(c) | 11-36 | 652(a) | 3-14, 20-16 |
| 472(d) | 11-36 | 652(b) | 20-22 |
| 472(f) | 11-36 | 652(c) | 20-15 |
| 483 | 8-15, 11-28, 11-29, C-23 | 661 | 20-1, 20-21 |
| 501 | 8-20 | 661(a) | 20-14 |
|  |  | 661(c) | 20-16 |

| I.R.C. Sec. | This Work Page |
|---|---|
| 661–663 | C-11 |
| 662 | 20-1, 20-21 |
| 662(a) | 3-14, 20-16 |
| 662(a)(1) | 20-19 |
| 662(a)(2) | 20-19 |
| 662(b) | 20-22 |
| 662(c) | 20-15 |
| 663(c) | 20-21 |
| 665 | 20-1 |
| 667 | 11-9 |
| 668 | 20-1 |
| 671 | 20-1 |
| 673 | 22-38 |
| 674 | 22-38 |
| 677 | 20-2, 22-38 |
| 679 | 20-1 |
| 681 | 20-13 |
| 691 | 22-37, C-24 |
| 691(a)(3) | 20-9 |
| 691(b) | 20-9, 20-10 |
| 691(c) | 20-9 |
| 692 | 20-1 |
| 701 | 17-1, 17-2, 17-13, 17-14 |
| 702 | 16-12 |
| 702(a) | 17-14, 17-16, 17-30 |
| 702(a)(8) | 16-13, 16-32, 16-33, 17-16 |
| 703 | 16-12 |
| 703(a) | 16-13, 17-16 |
| 703(a)(2) | 16-13 |
| 703(a)(2)(E) | 16-22 |
| 704(a) | 17-17, 17-35 |
| 704(b) | 17-17, 20-23, 22-36 |
| 704(c) | 17-21, 17-22 |
| 704(d) | 17-23, 17-24, 17-30 |
| 705 | 16-17, 17-23 |
| 705(a) | 17-11 |
| 705(a)(2) | 17-22 |
| 705(b) | 17-11 |
| 706(a) | 17-24 |
| 706(b) | 17-25 |
| 706(b)(2) | 11-14, 17-25 |
| 706(c)(2)(B) | 22-36 |
| 707(a) | 17-27 |
| 707(b) | 17-27, 17-35 |

| I.R.C. Sec. | This Work Page |
|---|---|
| 707(b)(1) | 17-27, 17-28 |
| 707(b)(1)(A) | 17-28 |
| 707(b)(2) | 17-28 |
| 707(b)(3) | 17-28 |
| 707(c) | 17-29 |
| 708 | 17-13 |
| 708(b)(1) | 17-26 |
| 708(b)(1)(A) | 17-26 |
| 708(b)(1)(B) | 17-26, 17-27 |
| 709 | E-11 |
| 721 | 17-4, 17-5, 17-6, 17-7, 17-10 |
| 721(b) | 17-7 |
| 722 | 17-7 |
| 723 | 17-4, 17-12 |
| 731 | 17-7, 17-10, 17-31 |
| 731(a) | 17-10, 17-31, 17-32 |
| 731(b) | 17-31 |
| 732 | 17-31 |
| 732(c) | 17-31 |
| 733 | 17-23, 17-31 |
| 735(b) | 17-31 |
| 741 | 17-10, 17-31 |
| 742 | 17-10 |
| 751 | 17-31 |
| 751(b) | 17-15 |
| 752 | 17-9, 17-23 |
| 752(a) | 17-9, 17-22 |
| 752(b) | 17-7, 17-9, 17-10, 17-22 |
| 761 | 17-1, 17-34 |
| 761(a) | 17-3, 17-4 |
| 761(b) | 17-4 |
| 901 | 8-35, 20-15 |
| 901–905 | C-20 |
| 904(e)(2) | 8-26 |
| 911 | 4-3, C-16 |
| 911(a) | 4-17 |
| 911(e) | 4-17, 4-18 |
| 1001(a) | 9-1 |
| 1001(b) | C-5 |
| 1001(b)(2) | 8-11, 9-2 |
| 1001(c) | 9-4 |
| 1011 | 9-9 |
| 1011(a) | 9-3 |
| 1012 | 8-11, 9-6, 17-10, C-7 |

| I.R.C. Sec. | This Work Page |
|---|---|
| 1014 | 16-25, 17-11, 20-6, C-7 |
| 1014(a) | 9-10 |
| 1014(b)(6) | 9-10 |
| 1015 | 17-11, 20-6, C-7 |
| 1015(a) | 9-7 |
| 1015(c) | 9-7 |
| 1015(d) | 20-7 |
| 1015(d)(6) | 9-8 |
| 1016 | C-3 |
| 1016(a) | 9-3 |
| 1016(a)(2) | 9-3 |
| 1016(a)(21) | 8-21, 8-22 |
| 1017 | 4-23 |
| 1031 | 9-15, 9-16, 9-17, 9-21, 9-24, 9-33, 9-35, 9-36, 9-42, 10-31, 10-43, 10-46, 17-6, C-28 |
| 1031(a) | 9-15, 9-16, 10-32 |
| 1031(b) | 9-16, C-8 |
| 1031(c) | 9-16 |
| 1031(d) | 9-17, 9-18 |
| 1032 | 9-33 |
| 1033 | 9-19, 9-20, 9-21, 9-23, 9-24, 9-31, 9-32, 9-36, 9-39, 10-31, C-26 |
| 1033(a) | 9-19, 9-20, 9-21 |
| 1033(a)(1) | 9-22 |
| 1033(a)(2)(A) | 9-22 |
| 1033(a)(2)(B) | 9-22 |
| 1033(a)(3) | 9-23 |
| 1033(a)(3)(A) | 9-23 |
| 1033(b) | 9-22, 9-23 |
| 1033(f) | 9-21 |
| 1033(g)(1) | 9-21 |
| 1033(g)(2) | 9-23 |
| 1034 | 2-27, 9-24, 9-25, 9-26, 9-27, 9-28, 9-29, 9-30, 9-31, 9-32, 9-36, 9-37, 9-38, 10-43, 22-31 |
| 1034(a) | 9-25, 9-26, 9-27 |
| 1034(c)(2) | 9-28 |
| 1034(d)(1) | 9-26 |
| 1034(d)(2) | 9-26 |
| 1034(e) | 9-29 |
| 1034(h) | 9-26 |
| 1034(k) | 9-27 |
| 1035 | 9-33 |
| 1036 | 9-33 |
| 1038 | 9-34 |
| 1091 | 9-11, 20-12 |
| 1091(a) | 9-11 |
| 1091(b) | 9-12 |
| 1091(d) | 9-12 |
| 1221 | 2-27, 16-11, C-9 |
| 1221(1) | 22-4 |
| 1222 | 2-28 |
| 1223 | 9-11, C-23 |
| 1223(1) | 9-18 |
| 1223(1)(A) | 9-23 |
| 1223(11) | 20-12 |
| 1223(2) | 9-9, 17-12, 20-7 |
| 1223(4) | 9-12 |
| 1223(7) | 9-29 |
| 1231 | 2-27, 2-28, 5-16, 8-25, 9-7, 9-46, 10-21, 10-22, 10-23, 10-24, 10-25, 10-26, 10-27, 10-28, 10-29, 10-30, 10-31, 10-33, 10-34, 10-35, 10-36, 10-40, 10-41, 10-42, 10-45, 11-28, 16-13, 16-21, 16-25, 16-29, 16-31, 16-32, 16-33, 17-15, 22-33, C-3, C-9 |
| 1231(a) | 10-21 |
| 1239 | 10-32, 10-33, 10-43 |
| 1242 | 10-37 |
| 1244 | 10-37, 16-3, 16-24 |
| 1244(c)(2) | 16-3 |
| 1245 | 8-18, 9-16, 10-25, 10-26, 10-27, 10-28, 10-30, 10-31, 10-32, 10-33, 10-40, 10-41, 10-42, 10-43, 11-11, 11-28, 16-29, 16-31, 16-32, 16-33, 17-5, 17-13, 20-10, 20-11 |
| 1245(a)(1) | 10-30 |
| 1245(a)(5) | 10-30 |
| 1245(b)(1) | 10-31 |
| 1245(b)(2) | 10-41 |
| 1245(b)(4) | 10-31 |
| 1250 | 8-18, 9-16, 10-27, 10-28, 10-29, 10-30, 10-31, 10-32, 10-33, 10-34, 10-40, 10-41, 10-42, 10-43, 10-46, 11-11, 11-28, 11-46, 16-29, 17-5, 20-10, 20-11 |
| 1250(a)(1)(B) | 10-30 |

| I.R.C. Sec. | This Work Page | I.R.C. Sec. | This Work Page |
|---|---|---|---|
| 1250(a)(1)(B)(iii) | 10-34 | 1363(d) | 16-17 |
| 1250(a)(1)(B)(v) | 10-34 | 1366(a) | 16-13 |
| 1250(d)(1) | 10-31 | 1366(a)(1) | 16-13 |
| 1250(d)(2) | 10-41 | 1366(a)(1)(A) | 16-18, 16-23 |
| 1250(d)(4) | 10-31 | 1366(b) | 16-13 |
| 1251 | 10-35 | 1366(d) | 16-19, 17-23 |
| 1252 | 10-35 | 1366(d)(3) | 16-28 |
| 1254 | 11-11 | 1366(e) | 16-24, 16-28 |
| 1254(a) | C-25 | 1367(a) | 16-17 |
| 1254(a)(1) | 10-35 | 1367(b)(2) | 16-17 |
| 1254(a)(2) | 10-36 | 1367(b)(3) | 16-24 |
| 1301 | 11-3, 11-5 | 1368(b) | 16-15 |
| 1301–1305 | C-24 | 1368(c)(1) | 16-15 |
| 1302(a)(1) | 11-4 | 1368(c)(2) | 16-21 |
| 1303 | 11-3 | 1368(e)(1) | 16-15, C-2 |
| 1304(a) | 11-6 | 1368(e)(1)(A) | 16-28 |
| 1361 | 16-2, 16-3 | 1371(b) | 16-14, 16-19 |
| 1361(b)(1) | 16-3 | 1371(c) | 16-21 |
| 1361(b)(1)(A) | 16-4 | 1371(d) | 16-23 |
| 1361(b)(1)(B) | 16-5 | 1371(e) | 16-16 |
| 1361(b)(1)(C) | 16-5 | 1372(a) | 16-22 |
| 1361(b)(1)(D) | 16-5 | 1372(b) | 16-22 |
| 1361(c)(1) | 16-4 | 1372(e)(1) | 16-7 |
| 1361(c)(6) | 16-4 | 1372(e)(1)(A) | 16-7 |
| 1361–1377 | 16-26 | 1373(a) | 16-24 |
| 1361–1379 | 16-1, 22-4 | 1374 | 16-10, 16-20, 16-21, 16-25 |
| 1362(a)(2) | 16-5 | | |
| 1362(b)(1) | 16-6 | 1374(a) | 16-20 |
| 1362(b)(3) | 16-7 | 1374(c) | 16-21 |
| 1362(d)(1) | 16-7 | 1375 | 16-10, 16-21, 16-25, 16-27, 16-31 |
| 1362(d)(1)(B) | 16-7 | | |
| 1362(d)(2)(B) | 16-9 | 1375(a) | 16-9, 16-27 |
| 1362(d)(3)(A)(ii) | 16-9 | 1375(b) | 16-10 |
| 1362(d)(3)(B) | 16-9 | 1375(c)(2) | 16-21 |
| 1362(d)(3)(D) | 16-11, 16-31, 22-35, C-31 | 1375(d) | 16-16 |
| | | 1375(f) | 16-16 |
| 1362(d)(3)(D)(i) | 16-10, 21-16 | 1377(a)(1) | 16-18 |
| 1362(e)(1) | 16-8 | 1377(b) | 16-16, 16-19 |
| 1362(e)(2) | 16-8 | 1378(c) | 16-23 |
| 1362(e)(3) | 16-8 | 1379 | 16-2 |
| 1362(f) | 16-12 | 1379(c) | 16-16 |
| 1362(g) | 16-12, 16-25 | 1504 | 16-4 |
| 1363(b) | 16-12 | 1981 | 8-15 |
| 1363(b)(2) | 16-22 | 2001(b)(2) | 19-6 |

| I.R.C. Sec. | This Work Page |
|---|---|
| 2001(c) | 19-4 |
| 2011 | 19-20 |
| 2014 | 19-20 |
| 2031–2046 | C-22 |
| 2033 | 19-7, 20-9, 22-37 |
| 2035 | 20-4, 22-37, C-22 |
| 2036 | 19-5, 19-6, 22-37 |
| 2036–2038 | C-24 |
| 2038 | 19-5, 19-6 |
| 2040 | 19-9 |
| 2040(a) | 9-11, 19-9 |
| 2041 | C-26 |
| 2042 | 19-10 |
| 2042(2) | 19-8, C-24 |
| 2053 | 20-10, 22-37 |
| 2054 | 20-10, 20-11 |
| 2055 | 19-12 |
| 2055(a)(2) | 19-12 |
| 2056 | 19-13, C-28 |
| 2501(a)(2) | 19-3 |
| 2501(a)(3) | 19-3 |
| 2501(a)(5) | 19-7 |
| 2502(d) | 19-1 |
| 2503 | 19-11, 22-38 |
| 2503(a) | 19-3 |
| 2503(b) | 1-12, 19-3, 19-11, 19-13, C-5, C-22 |
| 2503(c) | 19-14, 19-15 |
| 2505 | 19-13 |
| 2505(a) | 19-15 |
| 2505(b) | 19-15, 19-17 |
| 2505(c) | 19-16 |
| 2511 | 19-3, 19-6 |
| 2511(a) | 19-3 |
| 2512(b) | 19-2 |
| 2513 | 11-32, 19-3, 19-11, 19-17, 19-18, C-17 |
| 2515 | 19-9 |
| 2515(c) | 19-9 |
| 2515A | 19-9 |
| 2516 | 19-11 |
| 2518 | C-15 |
| 2519 | 19-3, 19-6 |
| 2521 | 19-15 |

| I.R.C. Sec. | This Work Page |
|---|---|
| 2522 | 19-3, 19-11, 19-12 |
| 2522(a)(2) | 19-12 |
| 2523 | 19-3, 19-11, 19-18, 19-19, C-28 |
| 2525 | 19-12 |
| 2525(a) | 19-13 |
| 3101–3126 | 1-16 |
| 3301–3311 | 1-17 |
| 3403 | 1-17, 21-20 |
| 3453 | 16-14 |
| 3507 | 8-23 |
| 4041–4998 | 1-9 |
| 4064 | 1-9 |
| 4920(a)(5) | C-16 |
| 4986–4998 | 1-9 |
| 5001–5872 | 1-9 |
| 6001 | 21-20 |
| 6012(a) | 2-20, 20-4 |
| 6012(a)(8) | 8-23, 8-24 |
| 6013 | 22-39 |
| 6013(d)(3) | C-26 |
| 6014 | 8-24 |
| 6019(a)(2) | 19-18 |
| 6031 | 17-2, 17-14 |
| 6041 | 21-19 |
| 6042 | 21-19 |
| 6057(b)(2) | 19-19 |
| 6072(a) | 2-22 |
| 6075(b)(1) | 19-19 |
| 6081 | 19-19 |
| 6103(b)(2) | 21-4 |
| 6110 | 21-2 |
| 6151 | 19-19 |
| 6152(a)(2) | 20-4 |
| 6161(a)(1) | 19-20 |
| 6161(b) | 21-21 |
| 6212 | 21-21 |
| 6213 | 21-21 |
| 6213(d) | C-20 |
| 6303(a) | 21-21 |
| 6321 | 21-21 |
| 6324(b) | 19-1 |
| 6331(b) | 21-21 |
| 6501 | 21-24, 22-39 |

| I.R.C. Sec. | This Work Page | I.R.C. Sec. | This Work Page |
|---|---|---|---|
| 6501(a) | 21-23 | 6655(d) | 21-18 |
| 6501(b)(1) | 21-23 | 6656(a) | 21-20 |
| 6501(c)(4) | C-20 | 6656(b) | 21-20 |
| 6502(a) | 21-24 | 6659 | 21-14 |
| 6503(a)(1) | 21-24 | 6672 | 21-20 |
| 6511(a) | 9-4, 21-25 | 6676 | 21-19 |
| 6511(b) | 21-25 | 6678 | 21-19 |
| 6511(d)(1) | 21-25 | 6682 | 21-18 |
| 6511(d)(2) | 21-26 | 6694(a) | 21-29 |
| 6513(a) | 21-25 | 6694(b) | 21-28 |
| 6532(a)(1) | 21-26 | 6695(a) | 21-29 |
| 6601 | 21-13 | 6695(b) | 21-28, 21-29 |
| 6601(c) | 21-7, 21-12 | 6695(c) | 21-28 |
| 6601(e)(2) | 21-12 | 6695(d) | 21-28 |
| 6601(e)(4) | 21-12 | 6698 | 17-14 |
| 6611 | 21-13 | 6851 | C-26 |
| 6611(e) | 21-12 | 6861 | 21-21 |
| 6621 | 19-20 | 6863(a) | 21-21 |
| 6621(b) | 21-10 | 6901 | 21-21 |
| 6622 | 21-12 | 6905 | 20-4 |
| 6651 | 21-15 | 7121(b) | 21-22 |
| 6651(a)(1) | 19-20, 21-14 | 7122 | 21-22 |
| 6651(a)(2) | 19-20, 21-14 | 7201 | 21-17 |
| 6651(a)(3) | 21-14 | 7201–7207 | C-21 |
| 6651(b) | 21-14 | 7202 | 21-20 |
| 6651(c)(1) | 21-14, 21-15 | 7203 | 21-19 |
| 6652 | 21-19 | 7204 | 21-19 |
| 6652(a) | 21-19 | 7205 | 21-18 |
| 6653 | 21-16 | 7206 | 21-27 |
| 6653(a) | 21-17, 22-20, C-29 | 7216 | 21-27 |
| 6653(a)(1) | 21-16 | 7454(a) | 21-17 |
| 6653(a)(2) | 21-16 | 7602 | 21-20 |
| 6653(b) | C-21 | 7623 | 21-5 |
| 6654 | 21-17 | 7701(a)(2) | 17-3, C-26, C-31 |
| 6654(a) | 21-17 | 7701(a)(3) | C-6 |
| 6654(d) | 21-18 | 7701(a)(4) | C-16 |
| 6654(e)(2) | 21-37 | 7701(a)(5) | C-20 |
| 6655 | 21-17 | 7805 | 22-5 |
| 6655(a) | 21-17 | | |

# APPENDIX D-2
# TABLE OF PROPOSED REGULATIONS AND REGULATIONS CITED

## PROPOSED REGULATIONS

1.2. . . . . . . . . . . . . . . . . . . . . . . 22-6
1.543–9 . . . . . . . . . . . . . . . . . 22-35

## REGULATIONS

| Reg. | This Work Page | Reg. | This Work Page |
|---|---|---|---|
| 1.2. | 22-6 | 1.164–2(e) | 7-10 |
| 1.46–3(d)(1)(ii) | 8-30, 8-31 | 1.164–7 | 9-23 |
| 1.47–2(e) | 22-31 | 1.165–1(a) | 9-4 |
| 1.47–3(f)(1) | 22-33 | 1.165–7(c) | 20-11 |
| 1.47–4(a)(ii) | 16-23 | 1.165–8(b) | 20-11 |
| 1.48–1 | 8-9 | 1.167(a)–(3) | 22-32 |
| 1.61–1(a) | 3-2 | 1.167(a)–3 | 22-34, C-22 |
| 1.61–3(a) | C-22 | 1.167(h)–1(b) | 20-10 |
| 1.61–6(a) | 9-4 | 1.167(h)–1(c) | 20-10 |
| 1.61–9(c) | 3-13 | 1.167(j)–3(b)(1)(i) | 10-34 |
| 1.62–1(f) | 6-36 | 1.170–1(c)(1) | 7-21 |
| 1.72–9 | 3-19 | 1.170–1(c)(3) | 10-31 |
| 1.79–1(b) | C-23 | 1.212–1(f) | 6-51 |
| 1.111–1(a) | 4-22 | 1.213–1(e)(1)(iii) | 22-30 |
| 1.117–3(a) | 4-6 | 1.263(a)–1(b) | 5-16 |
| 1.117–3(c) | 4-7 | 1.441–1(b)(1)(ii) | 11-13 |
| 1.117–4(c) | 4-7 | 1.446–1(c)(1)(ii) | C-4 |
| 1.119–1(d) | 4-14 | 1.451–1(a) | 3-6 |
| 1.121–2(b) | 9-31 | 1.451–2 | C-12 |
| 1.151–3(a) | 2-16 | 1.451–3 | C-11 |
| 1.151–3(b) | 2-16 | 1.451–3(b) | 11-21 |
| 1.152–1(a)(2) | 2-12 | 1.451–5 | 3-11, 3-23 |
| 1.152–1(a)(2)(ii) | 2-13 | 1.461–1(a)(2) | C-4 |
| 1.152–1(c) | 2-13 | 1.471–4(b) | 11-33 |
| 1.152–4 | 2-15 | 1.611–1(c)(4) | 20-10 |
| 1.162–5 | 22-20, C-17 | 1.611–1(c)(5) | 20-10 |
| 1.162–5(d) | 6-57 | 1.641(b)–3(a) | 20-3 |
| 1.162–7(b)(2) | 22-24 | 1.642(c)–1(b) | 20-13 |
| 1.164–1 | 7-9 | 1.642(g)–1 | 20-11 |
| 1.164–2(a) | 7-10 | 1.651(a)–1 | 20-14 |

|                          | This Work Page |
|--------------------------|----------------|
| **Reg.**                 |                |
| 1.652(b)–2(b)            | 20-23          |
| 1.662(b)–1               | 20-22          |
| 1.676(b)–1               | 22-38          |
| 1.677(a)–1(f)            | 22-38          |
| 1.691(a)–1(b)            | 20-8           |
| 1.691(a)–3               | 20-9           |
| 1.691(c)–1               | 20-9           |
| 1.702–1(a)(8)(ii)        | 17-16          |
| 1.704–1(b)(1)            | 17-17          |
| 1.704–1(b)(2)            | 17-17          |
| 1.705–1(a)(2)            | 17-11          |
| 1.706–1(b)               | 17-25          |
| 1.707–1(c)               | 22-36          |
| 1.721–1(a)               | 17-5           |
| 1.721–1(b)(1)            | 17-6           |
| 1.723–1                  | 17-12          |
| 1.731–(a)                | 22-36          |
| 1.1001–1(b)              | 7-11           |
| 1.1002–1(a)              | 9-4            |
| 1.1012–1(b)              | 7-11           |
| 1.1015–1(a)(1)           | 9-7            |
| 1.1015–3(a)              | 9-7            |
| 1.1016–3(a)(1)(ii)       | 9-4            |
| 1.1016–3(a)(2)(i)        | 9-4            |
| 1.1016–5(d)              | 9-29           |
| 1.1031(a)–1(a)           | 9-15           |
| 1.1031(a)–1(b)           | 9-15           |
| 1.1031(b)–1(a)           | 9-16           |
| 1.1031(c)–1              | 9-16           |
| 1.1031(d)–1(a)           | 9-18           |
| 1.1031(d)–1(b)           | 9-18           |
| 1.1031(d)–1(c)           | 9-17           |
| 1.1033(a)–1              | 9-21           |
| 1.1033(a)–1(a)           | 9-20           |
| 1.1033(a)–2(a)           | 9-20           |
| 1.1033(a)–2(b)           | 9-22           |
| 1.1033(a)–2(c)(1)        | 9-22           |
| 1.1033(a)–2(c)(3)        | 9-22           |
| 1.1033(f)–1              | 9-22           |
| 1.1033(f)–1(a)           | 9-21           |
| 1.1033(g)–1(b)           | 9-23           |
| 1.1034–(c)(3)            | 9-27           |
| 1.1034–1(a)              | 9-25           |
| 1.1034–1(b)(1)           | 9-25           |
| 1.1034–1(b)(2)           | 9-25           |
| 1.1034–1(e)              | 9-29           |

|                          | This Work Page |
|--------------------------|----------------|
| **Reg.**                 |                |
| 1,1034–1(g)(1)           | 9-26           |
| 1.1091–1(c)              | 9-12           |
| 1.1223–1(a)              | 9-18, 9-23     |
| 1.1223–1(d)              | 9-12           |
| 1.1223–1(g)              | 9-29           |
| 1.1231–1(e)(1)           | 10-21          |
| 1.1231–1(e)(3)           | 10-21          |
| 1.1245–2(a)(4)           | 10-31          |
| 1.1245–4(a)(1)           | 10-31          |
| 1.1245–4(d)              | 10-31          |
| 1.1245–6(d)              | 16-29          |
| 1.1250–1(c)(6)           | 16-29          |
| 1.1250–1(d)(1)(i)(c)     | 10-34          |
| 1.1250–2(d)(3)           | 10-31          |
| 1.1250–3(a)(1)           | 10-31          |
| 1.1250–3(a)(3)           | 10-31          |
| 1.1250–3(d)(1)           | 10-31          |
| 1.1372–(2)(b)(1)         | 16-6           |
| 1.1375–4(b)              | 16-15          |
| 1.6012–2(a)              | 11-14          |
| 1.6065–1(b)(1)           | 21-27          |
| 1.6081–                  | 21-15          |
| 1.6081–4                 | 2-22           |
| 1.6694–1(b)(2)(i)        | 21-28          |
| 1.6694–3                 | 21-28          |
| 1.6694–4                 | 21-28          |
| 20.2031–1(b)             | C-19           |
| 20.2042–1(c)             | C-24           |
| 25.2511–1(c)             | 22-38          |
| 25.2512–8                | 19-2, 19-6, 19-11 |
| 25.2512–9(f)             | 22-38          |
| 37.3402–1(e)(4)          | 21-18          |
| 301.6402–3               | 21-24          |
| 301.6511(a)–1            | 9-4            |
| 301.6651(c)(3)(i)        | 21-15          |
| 301.7122–1(a)            | 21-22          |
| 301.7623–1               | 21-5           |
| 301.7701–2(a)            | 17-3           |
| 301.7701–2(c)            | C-10           |
| 301.7701–2(d)            | C-28           |
| 301.7701–2(e)            | C-21           |
| 301.7701–3(a)            | 17-4           |
| 301.7701–4(a)            | 20-2           |
| 601.106(d)(1)            | 21-9           |
| 601.106(f)(10)           | 21-9           |

# APPENDIX D–3
# TABLE OF REVENUE PROCEDURES
# AND REVENUE RULINGS CITED

## REVENUE PROCEDURES

| Rev.Proc. | This Work Page | Rev.Proc. | This Work Page |
|---|---|---|---|
| 64–22 | 21-9 | 79–45 | 21-1 |
| 68–16 | 21-22 | 80–32 | 22-25 |
| 72–51 | 11-14, 22-25 | 80–40 | 21-29 |
| 73–13 | 21-21 | 80–51 | 11-36, 11-41 |
| 74–46 | 21-21 | 82–22 | 21-1 |
| 78–9 | 21-10 | | |

## REVENUE RULINGS

| Rev.Rul. | This Work Page | Rev.Rul. | This Work Page |
|---|---|---|---|
| 54–567 | 2-17 | 70–622 | 7-9 |
| 55–273 | 22-28 | 71–287 | 16-6 |
| 57–344 | 2-13 | 71–425 | 4-2 |
| 57–345 | 7-9 | 72–312 | 3-13 |
| 58–418 | 4-9 | 72–545 | 5-15 |
| 58–419 | 2-13 | 73–61 | 22-38 |
| 60–279 | 4-2 | 75–45 | 4-9 |
| 61–112 | 16-11 | 75–169 | 6-49 |
| 64–162 | 16-20 | 75–178 | 22-31 |
| 64–232 | 16-11 | 75–230 | 4-9 |
| 65–34 | 2-17 | 76–514 | 22-33 |
| 65–40 | 16-11 | 80–262 | 21-29 |
| 65–83 | 16-11 | 80–263 | 21-29 |
| 65–91 | 16-11 | 80–264 | 21-29 |
| 66–116 | 16-6 | 80–265 | 21-29 |
| 68–20 | 4-7 | 80–266 | 21-29 |
| 68–139 | 22-36 | 80–325 | 22-25 |
| 68–227 | 16-6 | 80, 1953–1 | 4-13 |
| 68–537 | 16-20 | 81–202 | 22-7 |
| 70–217 | 4-2, 4-3 | 81–269 | 2-22 |

# APPENDIX E
# COMPREHENSIVE TAX
# RETURN PROBLEMS

## Comprehensive Tax Return Problems—Individual

*J. D. McVey*

In December 1981, J. D. McVey graduated from the University of Minnesota (Minneapolis) and immediately accepted employment with Union Valve Corporation, a West Virginia corporation and a manufacturer and distributor of mining and drilling equipment. Under the terms of the employment agreement, J. D. was to assume responsibility (effective February 1, 1982) for the sales region comprising the States of Montana and Wyoming. Since Union Valve Corporation had not yet established an office in the region, J. D. was to conduct all business from his home. J. D. was expected to locate his home in either Montana or Wyoming and he chose Searcy, Wyoming, due to its central location and available housing.

J. D. McVey is 22 years of age and has been a full-time student at the University of Minnesota since his graduation from high school four years ago. He married Gloria, age 25, during his junior year in college. Gloria has one child, named Anthony, age 3, by a former marriage.

During 1982 the McVeys had the following receipts:

(1) Salary of $22,000 from Union Valve Corporation of which $1,474.00 was withheld for FICA and $3,462.39 for Federal income tax purposes (all reflected on Form W–2). Although J. D. received a bonus of $3,500 for his sales in 1982, such bonus was not declared and paid by Union Valve Corporation until February of 1983.

(2) Commissions of $14,300 earned by Gloria from the sale of real estate from early June through December 31, 1982. Gloria operates this business out of her apartment and as a sole proprietor. No taxes have been paid on the amounts earned.

(3) In early 1982 the McVeys won $10,000 in a contest sponsored by a national chain of fast-food franchises. Although the winning ticket was registered in Gloria's name, she placed the proceeds in a savings account with Anthony listed as the owner. Interest on this account for 1982 amounted to $540, none of which was withdrawn.

(4) Receipts of $4,200 from the lessee of property in Ypsilanti, Michigan. The property, a two-story brick house located in a residential area, was acquired by J. D. when his aunt died on December 1, 1981. As executor and sole heir of his aunt's estate, J. D. assumed control over the property on December 15, 1981. On December 16, 1981, he listed the house as being for rent but was not able to find a suitable tenant until late May of 1982. Under the terms of the two-year lease, the lessee was required to pay the following amounts: rent of $500 per month (beginning on June 1, 1982); the last

month's rent of $500 in advance (i. e., the rent for May of 1984); and, a deposit of $200.

The Ypsilanti property had a value of $150,000 and an adjusted basis to the aunt of $50,000 on the date of her death. Gloria, who has had considerable training and experience in matters dealing with real estate, estimates that 20 percent of the value of the property is attributable to the land. (Note: Property acquired by inheritance is *recovery property* eligible for ACRS coverage, even if the property was owned by a related party in 1980.)

(5) Cash of $500 received by Gloria from the estate of J. D.'s aunt. The amount was paid by J. D., acting in his capacity as executor, to Gloria in return for the services she performed in appraising estate assets. Indications are that the charge was reasonable for the services rendered.

(6) Upon the final dissolution of the aunt's estate and after the payment of all expenses and taxes, J. D. received the following:

|  | Fair Market Value on Date of Death | Adjusted Basis to Aunt |
|---|---|---|
| Cash | $ 15,000 | $ 15,000 |
| Household furnishings | 6,000 | ? |
| 1957 Chevrolet convertible | 12,000 | 3,200 |
| Jewelry (mainly gold and silver) | 8,000 | ? |
| Personal effects (e.g., clothing) | 1,200 | ? |

The dissolution and final distribution occurred on March 26, 1982. Under the aunt's will, J. D. was not entitled to any commission for serving as the executor of the estate. As executor, J. D. did not elect the alternate valuation date for the estate.

On June 26, 1982, J. D. received in the mail a check for $5,725.25 from the United Insurance Company. Unknown to him, J. D. was the designated beneficiary of an insurance policy on the life of his aunt. The policy had a maturity value of $5,000 and an enclosed statement from the Company reflected that the aunt had paid premiums thereon of $2,600. Of the amount received, $725.25 was designated as being interest accrued since the date of the aunt's death.

(7) On August 4, 1982, J. D. received $18,200 from the sale of the 1957 Chevrolet [see item (6) above]. Although the car was in good condition when the aunt died, it needed certain repairs to place it in "top" condition for resale. After J. D. received several estimates from mechanics who specialized in such restorations, he decided to do the work himself. In this connection, J. D. spent $2,400 on replacement parts and devoted considerable spare time to their installation. Based on the estimates received from the mechanics, the value of J. D.'s services was $2,100.

(8) On September 25, 1982, J. D. sold his aunt's jewelry for $7,600. For sentimental reasons, J. D. wanted to keep these items but he was concerned about their safekeeping.

(9) Throughout 1982, Gloria received child support of $300 per month (for a total of $3,600) from her ex-husband. Although the divorce decree awards the dependency exemption for Anthony to the ex-husband, the McVeys can prove that they furnished more than 50 percent of the support of the child.

(10) Since beginning employment with Union Valve Corporation, J. D. has been covered under their group-term life insurance policy. The policy applicable to J. D. provides for coverage of $100,000 and designates Gloria as the beneficiary.

(11) Union Valve Corporation follows a policy of allowing its employees to choose between coverage in its noncontributory accident and health care plan *or* the receipt of an annual award of $1,500 in additional wages. For 1982, J. D. chose the medical insurance option. [Note: neither item (10) nor (11) are reflected in the salary information furnished in (1) above.]

(12) Federal income tax refund of $140 received on March 6, 1982. In January of 1982 the McVeys filed a Form 1040A and a State of Minnesota income tax return for 1981 to recover some of the withholdings from Gloria's wages from a part-time job as the tax liabilities proved to be less than the amounts withheld. A refund of $40 was received from the Department of Revenue of the State of Minnesota on March 20, 1982.

(13) Dividends from domestic corporations of $250 and interest on a savings account of $420. The dividends were received on stock owned by Gloria while the interest was from a joint savings account that J. D. established with some of the funds inherited from his aunt. None of the interest was withdrawn by the McVeys.

(14) During 1982 Gloria had the following receipts involving the sales of marketable securities:

| Asset | Date Acquired | Date Sold | Selling Price |
|---|---|---|---|
| 100 shares of common stock in Y Corporation | 3/18/77 | 7/15/82 | $ 5,200 |
| 500 shares of preferred stock in Z Corporation | 7/30/78 | 10/2/82 | 6,500 |

The selling price listed is net of brokerage commissions. In other words, it represents the amount Gloria actually received.

On March 18, 1977, Gloria received as a wedding present from her father 100 shares of common stock in Y Corporation. The stock was acquired by her father on November 10, 1972, had an adjusted basis to him of $3,000, and had a fair market value of $3,800 on the date of the gift. No gift tax was due or paid as a result of the transfer.

Upon the receipt of a cash property settlement from her first husband, Gloria purchased 500 shares of preferred stock in Z Corporation for $10,000. Shortly after purchase, she received a nontaxable two-for-one stock split.

(15) In January J. D. received a check from Union Valve Corporation for $457.28 which represented reimbursement for a trip he made to the home office in West Virginia. The trip for the job interview was made in November of 1981 and led to the offer of employment that J. D. later accepted. It was the understanding of the parties that the company would reimburse J. D. for reasonable expenses actually incurred. The $457.28 was not claimed as a deduction on the McVey's joint return filed for 1981, nor was the reimbursement shown on the Form W–2 (for 1982) sent to J. D. by the employer in early 1983.

(16) A check for $492.17 received on March 19, 1982 from Union Valve Corporation which represented reimbursement for some of the McVey's moving expenses [see item (a) below]. This amount was included in the W–2 sent to J. D. for tax year 1982.

(17) In February of 1982 received a check for $420 from Ajax Casualty Insurance Company which represented the amount due on a policy covering Gloria's 1974 model automobile. In December of 1981, J. D. totalled the automobile on the way to class. When the accident occurred, the car had an adjusted basis of $1,800 and a fair market value of $520.

During 1982 the McVeys had the following disbursements:

(a) On January 12–13, 1982, the McVeys drove to Searcy, Wyoming to find a suitable place to live. After several days of narrowing the alternatives, they leased an apartment [see item (c) below]. The return trip to Minneapolis took place on January 16–17.

On January 30–31, 1982, the McVeys drove to Searcy with their personal belongings. As per the lease agreement, the apartment in Searcy was occupied by them on February 1, 1982.

Expenses incurred in connection with the January 12–17 and the January 30–31 trips are summarized below.

|  | January 12–17 Trip | January 30–31 Trip |
|---|---|---|
| Meals while in transit | $ 36.75 | $ 19.25 |
| Meals in Searcy | 38.23 | 15.40 |
| Lodging while in transit | 48.16 | 24.10 |
| Lodging in Searcy | 76.18 | 24.10 |
| Trailer rental | — | 210.00 |

The distance between Minneapolis and Searcy (one way) is 1,100 miles. In addition, the McVeys drove 140 miles while in Searcy during their January 14–15 stay while looking for an apartment. As noted in item (16), the employer reimbursed the McVeys for $492.17 of the above expenses. Under company policy, however, mileage is not covered under the reimbursement plan in the case of new employees.

(b) As a graduation present from his parents, J. D. received $3,000 for a down payment on a new automobile. On January 2, he purchased a small Buick station wagon for $9,000 through an automobile dealer in Montana with delivery in Detroit. Shortly thereafter, Gloria took a bus to Detroit and picked up the car (the dealer had provided Montana license plates). The reason J. D. used a Montana dealer was to avoid either the Minnesota or the Wyoming sales tax (Montana has no sales tax). The scheme backfired, however, when J. D. registered his car in Wyoming in early March of 1982. On that occasion, he was assessed and had to pay a Wyoming use tax of $400. J. D. estimates that, over the life of the automobile, it will be used approximately 70% for business and 30% for personal use.

Not counting the two trips mentioned in (a) above, the station wagon was used as follows during 1982:

|  | Miles |
|---|---|
| Business | 19,465 |
| Medical | 380 |
| Charitable | 900 |
| Personal | 8,326 |

In addition, J. D. spent $82 on parking while in business travel status.

The station wagon has an estimated useful life to the McVeys of less than three years.

(c) On January 15, 1982, the McVeys leased a three-bedroom apartment in Searcy for one year (occupancy as of February 1). In addition to a $100 damage deposit, they paid the following amounts for this facility during 1982:

| Rent ($400 per month) | $ 4,400.00 |
|---|---|
| Utilities | 1,320.12 |
| Telephone | 1,209.56 |

When they moved in on February 1, J. D. converted one of the bedrooms (approximately 20 percent of the total available floor space) into an office. The office was furnished with office equipment obtained from a local furniture-leasing concern. All lease charges were billed directly to Union Valve Corporation. The office was used exclusively for business, either by J. D. or by Gloria when she began her real estate activities in June.

The McVeys estimate that they use their phone 40 percent of the time for business.

Besides the lease charges on the office furniture, none of these expenses were paid for by J. D.'s employer.

(d) In order to facilitate her real estate operations, in June Gloria leased a used automobile for $210 per month. Lease payments by the McVeys during 1982 totalled $1,260. The car was used 80 percent for business and 20 percent for personal. Operating expenses on the automobile (e. g., gas and oil) were the responsibility of the lessee and amounted to $450.28.

(e) During 1982 the McVeys incurred the following additional expenses in connection with their business activities:

|  | Gloria | J. D. |
|---|---|---|
| Dues to professional organizations | $ 75.00 | $ 110.00 |
| Expenses for attending professional meetings (e. g., business seminars) | 150.00 | — * |
| Subscriptions to professional journals | 48.00 | 95.00 |
| Entertainment (e. g., business lunches) | 140.00 | — * |
| Business gifts | 200.00 | — * |

Except as indicated, none of J. D.'s expenses were reimbursed by his employer. All of these expenses are property substantiated and satisfy the requirements of § 274 of the Code. Prior to Christmas of 1982, Gloria made gifts (worth $40 apiece) to each of five families that had purchased residential property through her during the year. The gifts were of such a nature that none of the cost was attributable to gift wrapping.

(f) During 1982, J. D. paid the following amounts regarding the Ypsilanti rental property [see item (4) above]:

| | |
|---|---|
| Repairs | $ 1,280.00 |
| Management fee | 350.00 |
| Leasing costs (e. g., advertising) | 240.00 |
| Property taxes (not chargeable to the estate) | 1,392.01 |
| Special street-paving assessment | 520.00 |

The special paving assessment was made by the City of Ypsilanti against all property owners in a four block area. The assessment was made in December of 1982 for paving repairs and replacement that would be carried out in early 1983.

(g) During 1982, the McVeys had the interest expense summarized below:

| | |
|---|---|
| Montgomery Ward revolving account | $ 295.86 |
| J. C. Penney revolving account | 121.52 |
| First National Bank of Searcy | 396.39 |

The Montgomery Ward and J. C. Penney accounts were used to purchase clothes, toys, and certain household items.

The interest paid to the First National Bank of Searcy was for amounts J. D. borrowed to help pay for Gloria's dental work [see item (h) below].

(h) Medical expenses paid during 1982 were as follows:

---

[*These items were billed directly to Union Valve Corporation.]

| Payee | Amount |
|-------|--------|
| U of M Memorial Hospital | $ 1,875.00 |
| Dr. Peter Lyons (diagnostician) | 450.00 |
| Dr. Richard Spain (radiologist) | 370.00 |
| Dr. Kenneth Wolford (general dentistry) | 3,500.00 |
| Dr. James Myers (orthodontia) | 2,400.00 |
| Bone and Joint Clinic of Searcy | 750.00 |

The first three charges were incurred in December of 1981 and were the result of J. D.'s automobile accident [item (17) above]. Because J. D. was a student at the University, however, the parties involved allowed him to defer payment until 1982. No interest was charged for the privilege of late payment.

Due to a lack of funds while J. D. was a student, Gloria had been postponing some necessary dental restoration (e. g., crowns, bridges). She also needed braces to improve her oral hygiene. These procedures were initiated and partially carried out in the last half of 1982 by Drs. Wolford and Myers working as a team. Although the orthodontia correction only was 50 percent complete by the end of 1982, the McVeys paid Dr. Myers the full amount that would be due. Full payment for orthodontia work before all of the services are rendered is not an uncommon practice.

As a result of moving from Minneapolis to Searcy, J. D. began experiencing discomfort in his back. Ultimately he went to the Bone and Joint Clinic of Searcy for a series of X-rays and orthopedic therapy. Although the McVeys were under the employer's medical insurance plan [see item (11) above], the expenses resulting from the December automobile accident occurred before J. D. became an employee. Unfortunately, the coverage of the plan does not extend to dental work. In late December, however, J. D. remembered about the plan and promptly filed a claim with Central Insurance Company (the carrier of the Union Valve Corporation plan) for the orthopedic charges. On January 22, 1983, J. D. received a check from the carrier for $650.00 (the policy had a $100 deductible feature for out-patient treatment). The McVeys do not keep a record of their drug expenditures.

(i) Cash charitable contributions for 1982 include: Searcy United Fund Campaign ($450), First Methodist Church of Searcy ($350), and the Italian Red Cross ($100).

Shortly after moving to Searcy, J. D. donated his aunt's personal effects [see item (6)] to the local branch of the Salvation Army.

*Requirements*

Based on the assumptions appearing below, prepare a joint income tax return for the McVeys for calendar year 1982. The return should be in good form and should include all necessary supporting schedules.

*Assumptions and Additional Requirements*

A. The McVeys use the cash method of accounting and the calendar year for tax purposes.

B. Wyoming imposes a 3 percent general sales tax and the City of Searcy another 1 percent. To simplify matters, assume all purchases during the year occurred in Searcy.

C. Wyoming does not impose a state income tax. No state income taxes were paid or are due for 1982 to Minnesota or Michigan.

D. The McVeys do not qualify for income averaging as to tax year 1982.

E. Do not make assumptions not supported by the facts. For example, under (b) you must use the automatic mileage method allowed by the IRS as you cannot determine all of the operating expenses (gasoline purchases are unknown).

F. Allocate the full office in the home expenses to J. D.

G. Prepare a Form 1040–ES for 1983 basing it on the 1982 income tax liability.

H. Other relevant information concerning the McVeys and their affairs is summarized below:

—Gloria's social security number is 371-42-5207.

—J. D.'s social security number is 371-09-7846.

—In Minneapolis the McVeys lived at 1318 Queensbury Street (Apt. 12H), 55440.

In Searcy the McVeys live at 492 Commerce Street (Apt. 4), 82190.

The rental property in Ypsilanti is located at 789 University Drive, 48197.

## Comprehensive Tax Return Problem—Corporation

Plainview Corporation, formed January 1, 1981, sells garden supplies at retail prices. Its address is 1000 10th Street, Anytown, TX 79400. Its employer identification number is 75-1000000. It had the following assets on January 1, 1982:

| | |
|---|---:|
| Cash | $ 10,000 |
| Accounts receivable | 120,000 |
| Inventory | 7,000 |
| Building (salvage, $50,000) | 200,000 |
| Less accumulated depreciation | (24,000) |
| Equipment | 100,000 |
| Less accumulated depreciation | (15,000) |
| Land | 40,000 |

Liabilities were as follows: accounts payable (trade), $20,000; taxes payable, $500; mortgages payable, $205,500 ($50,000 annual installments). It had 100 shares of preferred stock outstanding at $50 par value, and 1,000 shares of common stock outstanding at $100 par value. Paid-in capital was $70,000 and retained earnings (unappropriated) was $37,000.

The building was purchased on January 2, 1981, and the equipment on January 15, 1981.

The corporation's records show the following receipts in 1982:

| | |
|---|---:|
| Gross receipts from sales | $500,000 |
| Receipts paid on accounts | 110,000 |
| Dividends received from domestic corporations (not controlled by Plainview Corporation) | 60,000 |
| Interest income (past-due accounts) | 1,500 |
| | $671,500 |

The following disbursements were made in 1982:

| | |
|---|---:|
| Dividends | $ 60,000 |
| Accounts payable | 20,000 |
| Taxes | 500 |
| Purchases of merchandise for sale | 320,000 |
| Salaries—officers | 45,000 |
| Salaries—salespeople and clerical | 35,000 |
| Interest (due and paid 12-31-82) | 14,500 |
| Payroll taxes | 2,000 |
| Property taxes | 6,000 |
| Repairs | 6,000 |
| Insurance | 2,000 |
| Delivery expense | 2,000 |
| Professional fees | 3,000 |
| Dues | 500 |
| Utilities | 7,000 |
| Telephone expense | 500 |
| Payment on mortgage | 50,000 |
| Payment of estimated tax liability for 1982 | 15,000 |
| | $589,000 |

Officer's salaries of $45,000 were paid as follows: John Plain, president, $30,000 (Social Security number 400-00-1000); John Plain, Jr., secretary-treasurer, $15,000 (Social Security number 500-00-1500). John Plain owns 60 percent of the common stock of the corporation and John Plain, Jr., owns 20 percent. John Plain devotes 40 percent of his time to the business, while John Plain, Jr., devotes 30 percent of his time.

At the end of the year, inventories were $10,000; accounts receivable from sales totaled $70,000; accounts payable for resale merchandise, $15,000; and payroll taxes payable, $500. The corporation uses the accrual method to compute its taxable income. Its net income per books (after deducting Federal income tax liability) was $108,000.

Prepare Form 1120 for Plainview Corporation for taxable year 1982.

## Comprehensive Tax Return Problem—Partnership

The Video Games Company, a cash basis and calendar year partnership, is equally owned by Thomas A. Reese and Victor R. Singleton. The partnership was formed January 15 of the current year with cash contributions of $20,000 from each partner. After arrangements for a three-year lease on suitable space in a local shopping mall, Reese and Singleton purchased four video game machines and signed a two-year lease for eight additional machines. The purchased equipment cost $8,000 per unit. The lease terms of the rental units called for an equal division of all revenues, and the lessor (owner) was obligated to pay for all necessary repairs. All lease agreements were to become effective March 1 of the current year.

On February 21 of the current year, Reese and Singleton had an attorney prepare a partnership agreement to govern the activities of the venture and set forth the duties and obligations of each partner. The agreement provided for an equal division of all profits determined after a guaranteed monthly salary of $500 to be paid to Thomas A. Reese for supervising all daily activities, maintaining all necessary books and records, and completing any required reports for taxing authorities and the leasing companies. The partnership paid $600 to the attorney for drafting the partnership agreement and filing the appropriate application for doing business in Harris County, Texas, under the name "The Video Game Room."

The Video Game Room was opened to the public on March 1 of the current year. As of December 31 of the current year, the accounting records prepared by Thomas Reese reflected the following information before adjustments:

Balance Sheet

| | |
|---|---:|
| Cash | $ 18,500 |
| Certificate of deposit (maturing 1/15 of the year after the next year) | 20,000 |
| Equipment (at cost) | 32,000 |
| Lease deposit | 1,500 |
| Organizational cost | 600 |
| Total assets | $ 72,600 |
| | |
| December profit share due to equipment lessor (payable December 31, of the current year) | $ 2,200 |
| Thomas A. Reese, capital | 20,000 |
| Victor R. Singleton, capital | 20,000 |
| Profits before depreciation and other adjustments | 30,400 |
| Total liabilities and partners' equity | $ 72,600 |

Income and Expenses

| | |
|---|---:|
| Income: | |
| Gross receipts | $ 84,000 |
| Interest collected on Certificates of Deposit | 7,000 |
| Total income | $ 91,000 |
| | |
| Expenses: | |
| Space rental (10 months at $750/month) (does not include required two months' deposit) | 7,500 |
| Equipment lease (includes $2,200 due from December profits) | 22,200 |
| Salary paid to Thomas Reese | 5,000 |
| Utilities | 18,000 |
| Insurance | 4,000 |
| Equipment repairs | 2,300 |
| Advertising cost | 1,600 |
| Total expenses | $ 60,600 |
| | |
| Profits before depreciation and other adjustments | $ 30,400 |

Thomas Reese has asked you to prepare the Federal Partnership Return (Form 1065) and Schedule K–1s for himself and Victor Singleton. After initial discussions regarding your fee and choices of method of accounting and partnership tax year, you conclude the following:

1.  The partnership will be a cash basis taxpayer and file an initial return for the 10-month period ending December 31 of the current year.

2.  Reese mailed a check for $2,200 to the video equipment lessor on December 31 of the current year, resulting in an ending cash balance of $16,300.

3.  The $600 organizational costs are amortizable under § 709 over a period of 60 months beginning on March 1 of the current year.

4.  The purchased video game equipment will qualify as § 38 property with an allowed investment tax credit rate of 6%. The partnership did not elect a § 179 write-off.

5.  The purchased equipment will qualify as three-year recovery property under the new accelerated cost recovery system of depreciation. (For simplicity, use $8,000 as the partnership's depreciation deduction, and do not complete Form 4562).

*Required:*

(a) Determine the partnership's ordinary income for the current year. Preparation of pages 1, 3, and 4 of Form 1065 is required. Questions calling for information not supplied to you should be left blank.

(b) Determine each partner's distributive share of income, loss, deduction, or credit for the current year. Preparation of Schedule K–1s for Thomas Reese and Victor Singleton is required.

## Comprehensive Tax Return Problem—Trust

Prepare the 1982 Fiduciary Income Tax Return (Form 1041) for the Kathryn Anne Thomas Trust. In addition, determine the amount and character of the income and expense items that each beneficiary must report for 1982 and prepare a Schedule K-1 for Harold Thomas.

The 1982 activities of the trust include:

| | |
|---|---:|
| Office building rental income | $600,000 |
| Rental expenses: Management | 85,000 |
| Utilities and maintenance | 375,000 |
| Taxes and insurance | 115,000 |
| Straight-line depreciation | 200,000 |
| Taxable interest income | 100,000 |
| Exempt interest income | 50,000 |
| Net long-term capital gains | 265,000 |
| Fiduciary's fees | 120,000 |

Under the terms of the trust instrument, depreciation, net capital gains and losses, and one-third of the fiduciary's fees are allocable to corpus. The trustee is required to distribute $55,000 to Harold every year. In 1982, the trustee distributed $70,000 to Harold and $60,000 to Patricia Thomas. No other distributions were made.

The trustee, Wisconsin State National Bank, is located at 3100 East Wisconsin Avenue, Milwaukee, WI 53201. Its employer identification number is 84-602487.

Harold still lives at 9880 East North Avenue, Shorewood, WI 53211. His identification number is 498-01-8058.

Patricia lives at 6772 East Oklahoma Avenue, St. Francis, WI 53204. Her identification number is 499-02-6531.

# APPENDIX F
# TABLE OF CASES CITED

## A

Adams, Robert W., 12-38
Affiliated Enterprises, Inc. v. Comm'r, 15-11
Alameda Realty Corp., 14-12
Allen Co., Ivan v. United States, 15-8
American Automobile Association v. United States, 3-11
Anders, Comm'r v., 14-10
Anton, M. G., 3-13
Apollo Indus., Inc. v. Comm'r, 15-6
Arditto, James J., 21-16
Armstrong v. Phinney, 4-13
Armstrong, Dorothy G., 14-31
Arnold v. United States, 4-2
Artukovich, Nick A., 16-6
Automobile Club of Michigan v. United States, 3-11
Axelrod, David, 21-16

## B

Bahan Textile Machinery Co. v. United States, 15-7
Bardahl Int'l Corp., 15-6
Bardahl Mfg. Corp., 15-6, 15-7
Barr's Estate, 18-5
Battelstein Inv. Co. v. United States, 15-22
Berman v. United States, 19-29
Black Motor Co. v. Comm'r, 6-3
Blevins, W. F., 12-39
Bliss Dairy, Inc. v. Comm'r, 14-7
Bone, Thomas E., 16-6
Bramlette Building Corp., Inc., 16-11

Briggs v. United States, 4-13
Byrnes, Inc., Thomas P., 15-14

## C

Camp Wolters Enterprises, Inc. v. Comm'r, 12-25
Campbell, Jr. v. Wheeler, 12-27
Cataphote Corp. of Mississippi v. United States, 15-8
Central Tablet Mfg. Co. v. United States, 14-13
Charbonnet v. United States, 16-23
City Bank of Washington, 14-12
City Markets, Inc. v. Comm'r, 16-11
Cockrell Warehouse Corp., H. C., 15-3
Cohan v. Comm'r, 5-19, 6-49
Cohen, Aaron, 14-10
Collins v. United States, 12-4
Colony, Inc., The v. Comm'r, 21-23
**Commissioner v. ——— (see opposing party)**
Connery v. United States, 14-10
Court Holding Co., Comm'r v., 14-6, 14-9, 14-10, 14-32
Crane v. Comm'r, 4-23, 9-2
Cumberland Public Service Co., United States v., 14-9

## D

D'Angelo Associates, Inc., 12-38
Darrow, Kenneth Farmer, 15-17
Davis, United States v., 3-16, 9-3, 13-18

Dean, J. Simpson, 4-16
Dielectric Materials Co., 15-5
Diedrich v. Comm'r, 4-25
Doak, Comm'r v., 4-13
Dobson v. Comm'r, 4-22
Donruss Co., The United States v., 15-3, 15-24
Doug-Long, Inc., 15-7
Doyle v. Mitchell Brothers Co., 3-3
Duberstein, Comm'r v., 4-4, 7-19
Dustin v. Comm'r, 21-36

**E**

Electric Regulator Corp. v. Comm'r, 15-7
Emeloid Co. v. Comm'r, 15-5
**Estate of (see name of party)**

**F**

Fahs v. Florida Machine & Foundry Co., 12-36
Fausner v. Comm'r, 6-37
Fine Realty, Inc. v. United States, 15-5
Flint v. Stone Tracy Co., 1-2
Fulman v. United States, 15-17

**G**

Garrow, Ralph R., 14-18
Glenshaw Glass Co. v. Comm'r, 4-9
Golconda Mining Corp., 15-2
Goldberg, Harry H., 5-14
Goodman v. Comm'r, 19-10
Goodman v. Granger, 18-13

**H**

Halby Chemicals Co. v. United States, 15-5

Hanco Distributing, Inc. v. United States, 15-18
Hardin v. United States, 15-2
Hardin's Bakeries, Inc. v. Martin, Jr., 15-22
Hardu, W. C. v. United States, 4-16
Hawkins, C. A., 4-8
**Helvering v. ——— (see opposing party)**
Hempt Brothers, Inc. v. United States, 12-24
Hertwig, United States v., 12-38
Hook, Clarence L., 16-29
Horst, Helvering v., 3-13

**I**

Illinois Terminal R. R. Co. v. United States, 5-21
**In re (see name of party)**

**J**

James v. United States, 3-2
Jarvis, Helvering v., 13-22
Johnson, Walter H., 22-13
Jud Plumbing & Heating Co. v. Comm'r, 14-7

**K**

Kimbell-Diamond Milling Co. v. Comm'r, 14-23
Kingsbury Investments, Inc., 15-7
Kintner, United States v., 12-5
Kowalski, Comm'r v., 4-14

**L**

Larson, Phillip G., 12-6
Leck Co. v. United States, 15-18
Lester, Comm'r v., 3-18

Litchfield Securities Corp. v. United States, 15-16

Lucas v. North Texas Lumber Co., 3-6

# M

Magaziner, Martin, 17-17

Magic Mart, Inc., 15-7

Malat v. Riddell, 10-2

Marshall v. Comm'r, 16-11

Martin, Nancy Boyd, 2-15

McCandless Tile Service v. United States, 22-14

McCarthy v. Conley, Jr., 14-5

Mead, Inc., W. L., 15-7

Mills, Jr., United States v., 12-25

Mitchell, Jessie B., 14-12

Moran v. Comm'r, 4-13

Morrissey v. Comm'r, 12-5, 17-3

Motor Fuel Carriers, Inc. v. United States, 15-5

Munter, Estate of David B., 14-10

# N

Nash v. United States, 12-30, 14-11

New Colonial Ice Co. v. Helvering, 5-1

New York Trust Co. v. Eisner, 18-1

Newman, Comm'r v., 22-23

Nicoll Co., R. J., 13-27

Nicodemus v. United States, 21-36

North Valley Metabolic Laboratories, 15-5

# O

O'Connor, John C., 12-36

O'Sullivan Rubber Co. v. Comm'r, 15-11

Old Colony R. R. Co. v. Comm'r, 7-14

Orrisch, Stanley C., 17-17

Otey, John H., 17-5

# P

Papineau, G. A., 4-13

Patterson v. Comm'r, 12-4

Paymer v. Comm'r, 12-4

Peacock, Cassius L., 2-15

Pollock v. Farmers' Loan & Trust Co., 1-2

# R

Rafferty Farms, Inc. v. United States, 12-4

Ray v. United States, 15-23

Riggs, Inc., George L., 14-21

Robinson v. United States, 4-13

Robinson, Lynne T., 2-15

# S

Sauvigne, Donald J., 16-18

Schlude v. Comm'r, 3-11

Schwartz Corp., Henry, 15-17

Shimberg v. United States, 14-30

Simons-Eastern Co. v. United States, 22-13, 22-14, 22-18

Smith, Joe M., 16-20

Smoot Sand & Gravel Corp. v. Comm'r, 15-4, 15-6

Soares, James, 12-29

Standard Paving Co. v. Comm'r, 14-7

Stapf, United States v., 18-19

Sterling Distributors, Inc. v. United States, 15-6

Stuit v. Comm'r, 18-10

Sullivan, Comm'r v., 5-8

# T

Tank Truck Rentals, Inc. v. Comm'r, 5-7

Tax Analysts & Advocates v. Comm'r, 21-2

Tellier, Comm'r v., 5-8

Tennessee-Carolina Transportation, Inc. v. Comm'r, 14-7

Thor Power Tool Co. v. Comm'r, 11-32

Thornton, Joe B., 5-15

Toor, Pir M., 2-17

Tougher v. Comm'r, 4-14

Trico Products v. Comm'r, 15-2

Turnbull, Inc. v. Comm'r, 15-8

Turner v. Comm'r, 12-25

## U

**United States v. ——— (see opposing party)**

## V

Van Hummell, Inc., Henry v. Comm'r, 15-23

Virginia Ice & Freezing Corp., 14-12

## W

Wales, Harold O., 14-12

Ward v. United States, 16-5

Weiss v. United States, 15-11

Welch v. Helvering, 5-6

Wilgard Realty Co. v. Comm'r, 12-26

Wisconsin Cheeseman, Inc., The v. United States, 5-21

## Y

Young's Rubber Corp., 15-5, 15-8

## Z

Zager, Max, 4-16

Zuckman v. United States, 12-6

# SUBJECT INDEX

## A

Abandoned Property, 8-7

Abandoned Spouse Rule, 3-34

Accelerated Cost Recovery System (ACRS)

Antichurning rules, 6-27

Corporations, 12-19, 13-4, 13-23

Deductions and losses, 3-19 to 3-28, 6-52 to 6-55

Depreciable property, 13-12

Depreciation, 6-19 to 6-20, 10-29 to 10-30, 10-41, 17-13

Earnings and profits, 13-4, 13-23

Election to expense assets, 6-26 to 6-27, 6-54 to 6-55

Eligible property, 6-20

General considerations, 6-19 to 6-20

Half-year convention, 6-25 to 6-26

Investment tax credit, 8-3

Net operating loss, 6-55

Partnerships, 17-13

Personal property owned or used during 1980, p. 6-27

Personalty, 6-20 to 6-23

Pre-1981 property, 6-27 to 6-28

Real property owned during 1980, pp. 6-27 to 6-28

Realty, 6-24 to 6-25

Recapture, 10-25, 10-29 to 10-30, 10-41 to 10-42, 12-28

Recapture of the investment tax credit, 13-12

Reconciliation of taxable and financial net income, 12-21

Recovery periods and amounts, 1-20, 6-20 to 6-25

Straight-line depreciation, 6-55

Straight-line election, 6-25 to 6-26, 6-55, 10-41 to 10-42

Tax credits, 8-3

Tax planning, 6-52 to 6-55, 10-41 to 10-42

TEFRA, 6-22 to 6-23

Accelerated Depreciation, *See also* Depreciation and Amortization, 6-18 to 6-19, 17-13

Accident and Health Benefits, *See also* Employee Fringe Benefits, 4-10 to 4-11, 4-26

Accident and Health Plan Exclusion, 16-22

Accounting Methods

Accrual method, 3-6 to 3-7, 7-15 to 7-16, 11-19 to 11-20

Bad debts, 6-3, 6-4

Cash receipts and disbursements method (cash basis), 3-6, 11-17 to 11-19

Change of method, 6-4, 11-20 to 11-21, 11-40 to 11-41

Completed contract method, 11-22 to 11-23

Constructive receipt of income, 11-17 to 11-18

Corporations, 12-7

Deferral of advance payments, 3-11 to 3-12, 3-23

Determination of IRS, 11-17

Electing out of the installment method, 11-30 to 11-31, 11-41

Election, 6-4

Estates, 20-4 to 20-5

Exceptions, 3-5, 11-18

Farming, 10-35

Hybrid method, 11-20

Installment method, 1-28, 11-23 to 11-31, 11-41

Long-term contracts, 11-21 to 11-23

Permissible methods, 11-16 to 11-17

Prepaid expenses, 11-18 to 11-19

Prepaid income, 3-10 to 3-11

Prepaid interest, 7-16, 7-33, 11-18 to 11-19

Reserve for bad debts, 6-3

Special methods, 11-21 to 11-31, 11-40 to 11-41

Straight-line under ACRS, 6-25 to 6-26, 6-55, 10-41 to 10-42

Tax planning, 11-40 to 11-41

Trusts, 20-4 to 20-5

Accounting Periods

Annual accounting period, 1-26 to 1-29, 3-4 to 3-5, 11-2

Annualization of income, 11-15 to 11-16

Changes in accounting period, 11-14 to 11-15

Corporations, 12-7

Election of period, 11-14

Estates, 20-4 to 20-5

Mitigation of annual accounting period concept, 1-26 to 1-29

Partnerships, 11-14

Accounting Periods—Cont'd
　Special, 11-13 to 11-16, 11-40
　Taxable periods of less than one year
　　(short year), 11-15
　Tax planning, 11-40
　Trusts, 20-4 to 20-5
Accrual Basis Corporations, 12-10 to
　12-11
Accrual Method of Accounting
　All-events test, 3-6, 11-19, 11-20
　Deferral of advance payments, 3-11 to
　　3-12, 3-23
　Deferral of income, 3-10 to 3-11, 3-23
　Gross income, 3-6 to 3-7
　Interest deduction, 7-15 to 7-16
　Prepaid income, 3-10 to 3-11
Accumulated Adjustments Account
　(AAA), 16-15, 16-28
Accumulated Earnings Credit, 15-3 to
　15-4, 15-10, 15-11, 15-23, 15-24
Accumulated Earnings and Profit,
　16-15 to 16-16, 16-22, 16-27
Accumulated Earnings Tax, See also
　Penalty Tax; Personal Holding
　Company
　Accumulated taxable earnings, 15-23
　Adjustments, 15-9 to 15-11
　Business needs, 15-3, 15-4 to 15-9
　Deduction for dividends paid, 15-10,
　　15-17 to 15-18, 15-23
　Earnings credit, 15-3 to 15-4, 15-10,
　　15-11, 15-23, 15-24
　Imposition of the tax, 15-3 to 15-4
　Intent, 15-3
　Mechanics of the tax, 15-9 to 15-11
　Tax planning, 15-20 to 15-24
　Tax rates and credit, 15-3 to 15-4,
　　15-23, 15-24
Accumulated Taxable Income (ATI),
　15-9, 15-10, 15-11, 15-23
Accumulation Distribution, see
　Throwback Rule
Accumulation of Earnings, See also
　Accumulated Earnings Tax;
　Penalty Tax; Personal Holding
　Company
　Element of intent, 15-3
　Tax planning, 15-20 to 15-27
Acquiescence (Tax Court Decisions), See
　also Citations—Tax Court, 22-12,
　22-21
ACRS, see Accelerated Cost Recovery
　System
Additions to the Tax Liability, see
　Interest; Penalties
Add-On Minimum Tax, 11-8, 12-18, 12-19

Adequate Records, 5-20
Adjusted Basis, 17-22 to 17-24
Adjusted Gross Income, See also
　Deductions for Gross Income;
　Deductions from Gross Income
　Child and dependent care credit, 8-27
　　to 8-28
　Earned income credit, 8-22 to 8-23
　Elderly taxpayer credit, 8-24 to 8-25
　Itemized deductions, 2-4
　Social Security benefits, 3-21
　Tax credits, 8-1
Adjusted Ordinary Gross Income
　(AOGI)
　Personal holding company, 15-12 to
　　15-16, 15-25, 15-26
　Tax planning, 15-25, 15-26
Adjusted Sales Price, see Sale of
　Principal Residence—Section 1034
Adjusted Taxable Income, 15-16 to
　15-17
Adjustment to Basis—Property Gifted
　or Acquired by Death, 9-8 to 9-9
Administrative Policy, 4-2
Administrative Sources of the Tax Law,
　22-5 to 22-7, 22-16, 22-20 to 22-21
Administrator, 18-4
ADR (Asset Depreciation Range), see
　Depreciation and Amortization
Ad Valorem Tax, 1-5
　Assessed value, 1-7, 1-8
　Intangible property, 1-8
　Personalty, 1-7 to 1-8
　Realty, 1-6 to 1-7
　Tangibles, 1-8
Advance Payments, See also Prepaid
　Income
　Deferral, 3-11 to 3-12, 3-23
Affirmative Refusal, 16-7
Aggregate Concept, see Conduit
　Concept
Alimony, 3-16 to 3-18, 5-5, 6-33, 17-15
　Tax planning, 3-25 to 3-26
All-Events Test, 3-6, 11-19, 11-20
Allocating Partnership Income, 17-17 to
　17-22
Allowance for Bad Debts, see Reserve
　for Bad Debts
Allowance for Depreciation, see
　Glossary
Allowances for Estimated Expenses,
　11-20
All-Savers Certificate, 1-22, 2-21, 4-19,
　5-21, 11-10, 11-11
Alternate Valuation Date, See also
　Federal Estate Tax, 9-10, 19-22

Alternative Minimum Tax, *See also* Minimum Tax
  Alternative minimum taxable income (AMTI), 11-9, 11-10, 11-12
  Capital gains and losses, 11-11, 11-40
  Computation, 11-6 to 11-13
  Corporations, 12-18
  Estates and trusts, 20-5
  Exemption, 11-39
  Exemption amount, 11-11
  Formula for computing tax base, 11-9
  Historical development, 11-8
  Itemized deductions, 11-10, 11-11, 11-12
  Long-term capital gain on lump-sum distributions, 10-4
  Net operating loss deduction, 11-9 to 11-10
  New provisions for computation, 11-11 to 11-13
  New terms, 11-11
  Qualified expenditures, 11-11, 11-13
  Qualified interest, 11-11
  Qualified investment expenses and income, 11-11
  Stock options, 11-10
  Taxable income, 11-9, 11-10, 11-12
  Tax planning, 11-39 to 11-40
  Tax preference items, 11-8, 11-9, 11-10
  TEFRA, 11-8, 11-10, 11-11, 11-13
Alternative Tax Rate, 10-17, 12-9 to 12-10
Amended Tax Return, 2-22, 9-4, 9-24
*American Federal Tax Reports* (AFTR), 22-13, 22-14, 22-15
Amortization, *see* Depreciation and Amortization
Amount Realized, 9-2 to 9-3
AMTI (Alternative Minimum Taxable Income), *see* Alternative Minimum Tax
Annual Accounting Period, 1-26 to 1-29, 3-4 to 3-5, 11-2
Annual Exclusion
  ERTA, 19-3
  Federal gift tax, 19-3, 19-13 to 19-15, 19-25
  In general, 19-13
  Gift splitting, 19-3, 19-17 to 19-18
  Gift tax, 1-12
  Joint ownership, 19-3
  Post-1976 transfers, 19-15 to 19-17
  Pre-1977 exemptions, 19-15
  State gift tax, 19-23
  Trust for minors, 19-14 to 19-15

Annual Exclusion—Cont'd
  Unified transfer tax credit, 19-15 to 19-17
Annualization of Taxable Income, 11-15 to 11-16
Annual Unemployment Tax Return, 1-18
Annuities
  Contributory plan, 18-14 to 18-15
  Employee annuities, 3-25
  Employment arrangements, 18-13 to 18-15
  Noncontributory plan, 18-13 to 18-14
  Nonemployment arrangements, 18-11 to 18-13
  Refund feature, 18-11
  Self and survivor annuity, 18-11
  Tax planning, 3-25
Annuity Starting Date, 3-18 to 3-19
Antichurning Rules, 6-27
Appeal Process, 21-8 to 21-10, 21-11, 21-35 to 21-36
Appellate Courts, *see* Court of Appeals
Appreciated Property, 4-23, 16-17
Arm's Length Concept, 1-33, 13-26
Assessments for Local Benefits, 7-10 to 7-11
Assessments of Tax, *See also* Statute of Limitations
  Deficiency assessment, 21-21
  Statute of limitations, 21-23 to 21-24
  Statutory notice of deficiency (90-day letter), 21-7, 21-9, 21-10, 21-21
Asset Depreciation Range (ADR), *see* Depreciation and Amortization
Assets
  Election to expense, 6-26 to 6-27, 6-54 to 6-55
  Low income-producing, 7-17
  Personalty, 6-14
  Personal use, 9-5 to 9-6, 9-12 to 9-13
  Realty, 6-14
  Straight-line write-off, 6-25 to 6-26, 6-55
  Transfer by corporation in reorganization, 14-28
  Twelve-month liquidation, 14-13 to 14-14
  Write-off, 6-14, 6-19, 6-22, 6-23, 6-25 to 6-26, 6-55
Assignment of Income Doctrine, 13-21, 14-7, 14-24
Assignment of Income from Property, 3-13 to 3-14
Associations, 12-4 to 12-6, 12-35, 17-3 to 17-4

Assumption of Liabilities—Section 357, pp. 12-26 to 12-28

At-Risk Limitation, 8-11 to 8-12, 17-24

Attribution of Stock Ownership, *see* Constructive Ownership of Stock

Audit of Returns
Appeals procedures, 21-8 to 21-10, 21-11, 21-35 to 21-36
Burden of proof, 1-32, 21-17
Demand for payment, 21-21
Discrimination Function System (DIF), 21-4, 21-5
Examination of records, 21-20 to 21-21
Field audit, 21-6 to 21-7, 21-35
Office audit, 21-6
Repeat audits, 21-5
Revenue Agent Report (RAR), 21-7, 21-8, 21-35
Selection of returns, 21-4 to 21-6
Settlement with agent, 21-7, 21-10
Tax planning, 21-35 to 21-36
Verification of returns, 21-6 to 21-7

Automobile Expenses, *see* Transportation Expenses

Averaging, *see* Income Averaging

Avoidance, *see* Tax Avoidance

Awards, *see* Prizes and Awards

**B**

Bad Debts
Allowable methods, 6-3, 6-4
Business versus nonbusiness, 6-4 to 6-5
Deductions, 6-6
Loans between related parties, 6-7, 6-52
Recovery, 16-13, 17-15
Refund claims, 21-25
Reserve addition determination, 6-3 to 6-4
Reserve for bad debts method, 6-3, 6-4
Specific (direct) charge-off method, 6-3, 6-4
Statute of Limitations, 21-25
Summary of provisions, 6-6
Tax benefit rule, 4-22, 14-10 to 14-11, 14-31
Tax planning, 6-52

Bank Credit Cards, *see* Credit Cards

Bankruptcy, 6-2 to 6-3

Bankruptcy Tax Act of 1980, p. 4-23

Banks and Lending Associations, 15-12

Bargain Sale or Rental, *see* Constructive Dividends

Base Period Research Expense, 8-16

Basis, *See also* Cost Basis Considerations
Adjusted, 17-22 to 17-24
Alternative rule for partnership interest, 17-11 to 17-12
Capital additions, 9-3
Capital recoveries, 9-3 to 9-4
Contributed property subject to liability, 17-12 to 17-13
Conversion to business (or income-producing) use, 6-10
Corporate liquidations, 14-15, 14-18 to 14-20, 14-21 to 14-24
Cost basis, *see* Cost Basis Considerations
Distributed property, 17-31 to 17-32
Donee's basis in gift property, 17-12 to 17-13
Excess, 12-27 to 12-28, 13-11, 13-21, 17-9 to 17-10, 17-35
Gifts, 9-7 to 9-10
Income in respect of a decedent, 20-8 to 20-9
Investment tax credit, 8-4, 8-9 to 8-10
Like-kind exchanges, 9-16, 9-17 to 9-19
Liquidation of a subsidiary—Section 332, pp. 14-21 to 14-24
Nontaxable transactions, 12-26, 12-28
Partnership changes in liabilities, 17-11, 17-22
Partnership interest, 17-7 to 17-12, 17-22 to 17-24
Partnership property, 17-31 to 17-32
Personal residence, 9-28, 9-29 to 9-30
Property acquired from a decedent, 9-10 to 9-11
Property contributed to partnership, 17-12 to 17-13
Property distributions to corporate shareholders—special rules, 16-17 to 16-18
Property dividends, 13-6 to 13-8
Property owner's holding period, 10-11
Property received by parent corporation, 14-21 to 14-24
Reduction, 8-4 to 8-5
Shareholder's basis of stock in S corporation, 16-15, 16-17 to 16-18, 6-28
Stock dividends, 13-14
Stock rights, 13-15
Wash sales, 9-11 to 9-12

Basis Rule, 9-11 to 9-12
Beneficiaries, 4-4, 4-5 to 4-6
   Allocation of classes of income, 20-22
      to 20-23
   Deduction for distributions, 20-14
   Distributable net income, 20-16 to
      20-18, 20-25 to 20-27
   Distributions by estates and trusts,
      20-18 to 20-21, 20-25 to 20-27
   Separate share rule, 20-21 to 20-22
   Taxable distributions from simple
      trusts, 20-18 to 20-19
   Tax consequences, 20-2, 20-15 to
      20-16, 20-24 to 20-27
   Tax planning, 20-25 to 20-27
   Tax treatment, 20-15 to 20-22
   Throwback rule, 20-24 to 20-25, 20-27
Bequests, 4-4
Bequests of Property, 9-35 to 9-36,
    18-21 to 18-22, 20-7
Bills, 22-2
Black Motor Company Formula, 6-4
Bona Fide Business Purpose, 12-27,
    12-28
Bonus Depreciation, 6-19, 6-26
Book Value, see Glossary
Book, See also LIke-Kind Exchanges,
    9-16 to 9-17, 9-18, 10-31, 12-23,
    12-24, 12-26, 12-28, 12-39, 12-40,
    14-29 to 14-30
Borrowed Funds, 3-10
Bribes and Illegal Payments, 1-24, 5-3,
    5-7, 5-8
Bulk Sale of Inventory, 14-30, 14-31
Bunching of Deductions, 6-4
Bunching Effects, 1-27, 3-9, 10-1, 11-2,
    11-40, 11-41, 12-38, 17-26, 18-13,
    20-25
Burden of Proof, See also Glossary,
    1-32, 5-10, 7-14, 14-15, 21-17, 22-20
Business Assets, 10-18
Business Bad Debts, 6-4 to 6-5
Business Deductions for Corporations,
    12-7 to 12-8
Business Energy Tax Credit, 8-21 to
    8-22
Business Expenses and Losses
   Bad debts, 6-1 to 6-7
   Criteria for deductibility, 5-2 to 5-3
   Employee, 6-50 to 6-51, 6-55 to 6-56
   Employment expenses, 6-31 to 6-36,
      6-50 to 6-51
   Losses, 5-3
   Reimbursements, 6-56
   S corporations, 16-24
   Substantiation, 5-19 to 5-20
Business Gifts, 6-49 to 6-50

Business Meals, 6-47 to 6-48
Business Operations
   Deductions, 12-7 to 12-8
   Tax planning, 12-33 to 12-35
   Tax treatment, 12-1 to 12-3
Business-Related Tax Credits, 8-2 to
    8-19
Buy and Sell Agreement, 16-27

## C

Cafeteria Plans, 4-15 to 4-16
Calculation of Tax Liability, 2-18 to
    2-20, 2-23
Canons of Taxation, 1-3 to 1-4
Capital Additions, 9-3
Capital Asset Defined, 2-27 to 2-28,
    10-2 to 10-3
Capital Asset Status, 10-38 to 10-39
Capital Assets, See also Sale or
    Exchange of Capital Assets
   Capital gains and losses, 10-2 to 10-3,
      10-38 to 10-39
   Holding period, 10-9 to 10-13
   Patents, 1-21
   Personal use, 10-3
   Property excluded, 10-20
   Property included, 10-19 to 10-20
   Real property, 10-17
   Sale or exchange, 10-5 to 10-9, 17-15
   Statutory expansions, 10-3 to 10-4
Capital Contributions, See also
    Corporations, 4-24, 12-31 to 12-32
Capital Expenditures, 5-15 to 5-17
   For medical purposes, 7-3 to 7-4
Capital Gain Deduction, 2-28 to 2-29
Capital Gain or Loss Holding Period,
    see Holding Period
Capital Gain Property, See also Capital
    Asset Defined: Charitable
    Contributions; Sale or Exchange of
    Capital Assets, 7-22 to 7-23
Capital Gains and Losses, See also
    Long-Term Gains
   Alternative minimum tax, 11-11,
      11-40
   Alternative tax, 2-29, 10-4, 10-17
   Beneficiaries, 20-24
   Capital asset defined, 2-27 to 2-28,
      10-2 to 10-3
   Capital asset status, 10-38 to 10-39
   Capital loss carryover, 10-16, 10-17
   Computation of net capital gains and
      losses, 2-28, 10-20 to 10-25
   Corporations, 2-29, 2-30, 10-17, 12-8
      to 12-10

Capital Gains and Losses—Cont'd
Dealers in securities, 10-3 to 10-4
Distributable net income computation, 20-16
Favorable tax treatment, 10-18 to 10-19
Franchises, 10-8 to 10-9
Holding period, 10-9 to 10-13, 10-20
Involuntary conversions, 10-19, 17-15
Lease cancellation payments, 10-9
Long- or short-term, 2-28 to 2-29
Lump-sum distribution from qualified plans, 10-4
Maximizing benefits, 10-36 to 10-37
Net capital gains and losses, 2-28 to 2-29, 10-13 to 10-16
Nonbusiness bad debts, 10-4
Nontaxable transactions, 10-11
Options, 10-6 to 10-7
Patents, 10-7 to 10-8
Penalty tax, 15-9, 15-10
Personal holding company tax, 15-16
Rationale for favorable capital gain treatment, 10-1
Real property, 10-4
Recapture, 10-25 to 10-36, 10-40 to 10-41
Related-party sales, 10-32 to 10-33
Reporting procedures, 10-17
Retirement of corporate obligations, 10-6
Sale or exchange, 10-5 to 10-9
S corporations, 16-20 to 16-22, 16-25, 16-29
Section 1231, pp. 10-17 to 10-25
Short sales, 10-11 to 10-13
Short-term gain or loss, 2-28 to 2-29
Spreading gains, 10-37
Stock options, 10-6 to 10-7
Stock sales, 10-38
Tax-free exchanges, 10-10
Tax planning, 10-36 to 10-42
Timing of recognition, 10-37 to 10-38
Treatment of capital gains, 10-13 to 10-15
Treatment of capital losses, 2-29 to 2-30, 10-15 to 10-16
Worthless securities, 10-5
Year-end tax planning, 10-37 to 10-38
Capital Improvements, 9-28 to 9-29
Capital Interest in Partnership, 17-5 to 17-6
Capitalization of Expenditures, 5-16 to 5-17
Capital Losses, see Capital Gains and Losses

Capital Recoveries, 9-3 to 9-4
Recovery of capital doctrine, 3-3 to 3-4
Capital Structure of a Corporation
Advantage of debt, 12-32 to 12-33
Capital contributions, 12-31 to 12-32
Debt in the capital structure, 12-32 to 12-33
Reclassification of debt, 12-33
Carryback & Carryover Periods, 6-13 to 6-14
Carrying Charges, 7-19, 11-25
Carryovers
Capital losses, 10-16, 10-17
Charitable contributions, 7-25 to 7-26
ESOPs, 8-19
Investment tax credit, 8-5
S corporations, 16-25 to 16-26, 16-28
Cash Basis Accounting, 11-18
Cash Basis Taxpayers
Bad debts, 6-2
Constructive receipt, 3-6, 3-7 to 3-8, 3-23
Controlling the year of deductions, 3-23 to 3-24
Crop insurance proceeds, 3-9 to 3-10
Prepayment of interest, 7-17, 7-33, 11-18 to 11-19
Repayment obligation, 3-10
Savings bonds, 3-8 to 3-9
State income tax deductions, 7-12
Cash Distributions, 16-15 to 16-16, 16-28
Cash Dividends, see Dividend Income; Dividends
Cash Receipts and Disbursements Method
Constructive receipt, 3-6, 11-17 to 11-18
Deductions, 11-18
Exceptions, 11-18
Prepaid expenses, 11-18 to 11-19
Casualty and Theft Losses
Appraisal, 6-11
Casualty defined, 6-8
Computation of deduction, 6-9 to 6-11
Deductible personal loss, 5-3
Disaster area losses, 6-9, 6-10
Estate tax deduction, 18-21
Events that are not casualties, 6-8
Limitation, 1-32
Reimbursement, 6-9
Tax planning, 6-52
TEFRA, 6-10
Theft Losses, 6-9, 6-52
When to deduct, 6-9
Cattle Feed Costs, 11-19

C.B., see *Cumulative Bulletin*

Certiorari, *see* Writ of Certiorari

CETA, 8-13 to 8-14

Changes in Accounting Method, 11-20 to 11-21, 11-40 to 11-41

Changes in Accounting Period, 11-14 to 11-15

Charge Cards, *see* Credit Cards

Charitable Contributions
  Capital asset status, 10-39
  Ceiling limitations, 7-24 to 7-27
  Contribution of services, 7-23 to 7-24
  Corporations, 12-10 to 12-13
  Criteria for a gift, 7-19 to 7-20
  Deductibility, 7-19
  Deductions, 1-24, 6-33, 18-21 to 18-22, 20-12 to 20-14, 20-16, 20-20 to 20-21, 20-24
  Direct charitable contributions, 7-26 to 7-27
  Documentation, 5-19
  Estates, 18-21 to 18-22, 20-12 to 20-14, 20-16, 20-20 to 20-21, 20-24
  Excess contributions, 7-25 to 7-26
  Excluded as business expense, 5-3
  Filing requirements, 7-27, 7-30
  Gifts, 19-12
  Itemized deductions, 5-5
  Limitations, 7-21 to 7-27, 7-35, 12-12 to 12-13
  Ordinary income property, 12-11 to 12-12
  Partnerships, 17-15, 17-16
  Penalty tax, 15-9, 15-10
  Percentage limitations, 7-24 to 7-27
  Personal holding company tax, 15-16
  Private foundation limitation, 7-24, 7-25
  Property contributions, 7-21 to 7-23, 7-27, 7-28 to 7-29, 7-34 to 7-35, 12-11 to 12-12
  Public charity limitation, 7-24, 7-25 to 7-26
  Qualified organizations, 7-20
  Recapture potential under Section 1245, p. 10-31
  S corporations, 16-13
  Tax planning, 7-34 to 7-35, 10-39 to 10-40
  Tax Reform Act of 1976, p. 7-22
  Time of payment, 7-20 to 7-21
  Trusts, 18-21 to 18-22, 20-12 to 20-14, 20-16, 20-20 to 20-21, 20-24
  Valuation problems, 7-21
  Zero bracket amount, 7-26

Charitable Deduction, 19-12, 19-22

Child and Dependent Care Credit, 1-24, 2-34
  Allowable amounts, 8-27 to 8-28
  Eligible expenses, 8-27
  Employment-related expenses, 8-27
  ERTA, 8-27
  Out-of-the-home expenses, 8-27
  Priority of credits, 8-30
  Tax planning, 8-33 to 8-34

Child Support Payments, 3-17 to 3-18

Churning of Assets, 16-10

Citations, 22-11 to 22-15

Citizenship or Residency Requirement, 2-17

CLADR (same as Asset Depreciation Range), *see* Depreciation and Amortization

Clear Reflection of Income, 3-10 to 3-11

Claim of Right Doctrine, 3-7

Claims Court, 22-7, 22-8, 22-9, 22-10 to 22-11, 22-13 to 22-14

Closely-Held Corporation, *See also* Glossary; Personal Holding Company Tax—Section 541, pp. 6-55, 13-8, 13-20, 13-26, 14-9, 15-10, 15-21, 15-24, 22-24

Closing Agreements, 21-22

Code, *see* Internal Revenue Code

Code of Ethics, Tax Preparers, 21-29 to 21-34

Cohan Rule, 5-19

Collapsible Corporations, 14-25 to 14-26

Commercial Contracts, 18-11 to 18-12

Common Market Countries, 1-12

Community Property, *See also* Separate Property
  Bequests, 9-35
  Classification of income, 3-25
  Gross income, 3-14 to 3-16, 3-25
  Inclusion in gross estate, 18-5 to 18-6, 18-13, 18-16
  Inheritance tax, 19-22
  Marital deduction for gift tax purposes, 18-23, 19-13
  Revenue Act of 1948, p. 1-30
  S corporation, 16-5 to 16-6
  Separate property, 3-15, 3-25
  Tax planning, 2-32, 2-33, 3-25
  Tax returns, 2-23

Commuting Expense, 4-15, 6-36 to 6-37, 6-51

Compensation for Injuries and Sickness, *See also* Employee Fringe Benefits, 4-8 to 4-11, 4-26

Compensation Paid to
    Shareholder-Employees, 13-10
Compensatory Damages, 4-9 to 4-10
Completed Contract Method of
    Accounting, 11-22 to 11-23
Complete Liquidations, *See also*
    Collapsible Corporations;
    Liquidation of a Subsidiary;
    One-Month Liquidations;
    Twelve-Month Liquidations
  Dividend distributions, 14-5 to 14-6
  Exchange treatment, 14-15
  Stock redemptions, 14-5 to 14-6
  Tax consequences to the corporation
    and shareholders, 14-1 to 14-26
Complete Termination of Shareholder's
    Interest Stock Redemptions, 13-20
Complex Trusts, *See also* Throwback
    Rule, 20-14, 20-19 to 20-21, 20-24
    to 20-25, 20-27
Components to Tax Formula
  Adjusted gross income, 2-4
  Deductions for adjusted gross income,
    2-4
  Excess itemized deductions, 2-5
  Exclusions, 2-2 to 2-3
  Exemptions, 2-5
  Gross income, 2-3 to 2-4
  Income (broadly conceived), 2-4 to 2-5
  Itemized deductions, 2-4 to 2-5
  Zero bracket amount, 2-5
Computation of Distributable Net
    Income, 20-16 to 20-18
Computation of Gain under Section
    333, pp. 14-17 to 14-18
Computation of Interest on Unpaid
    Taxes, 21-12
Computation of Investment Credit, 8-4
    to 8-5, 8-8, 8-9 to 8-10, 8-11 to 8-12
Computation of Tax, *see* Special Tax
    Computations; Tax Computation
Condemned Property, 9-20 to 9-22
Conduit Concept
  Partnerships, 12-1, 17-2 to 17-3,
    17-14, 17-16
  S corporations, 16-12
  Trusts and estates, 12-2, 20-5 to 20-6
Constructive Dividends, 13-8 to 13-10
  Tax planning, 13-26 to 13-27
  Unreasonable compensation, 13-10
Constructive Ownership Rules, 16-22
Constructive Ownership of Stock, 5-18
    to 5-19, 13-17, 13-19, 22-17
Constructive Receipt Doctrine, 3-6, 3-7
    to 3-8, 3-23
Contract Price, 11-27 to 11-28
Contracts, 7-19

Contributions to the Capital of a
    Corporation, *see* Capital
    Contributions
Contributions to Partnerships, *see*
    Partnership Taxation
Contribution of Services,
    Nondeductibility, 7-23
Controlled Corporations
  Assumption of liabilities, 12-26 to
    12-28
  Control of transferee corporation,
    12-25 to 12-26
  Recapture, 12-28 to 12-30
  Stocks and securities, 12-23, 12-24 to
    12-25
  Tax benefit rule, 12-30 to 12-31
  Tax planning, 12-36 to 12-40
  Transfer of property, 12-22 to 12-24,
    12-36 to 12-40
Conversions, *see* Involuntary
    Conversions
Copyrights, 5-16
Corporate Accumulation, Chapter 15
  Justifying, 15-20 to 15-22
  Measuring, 15-8 to 15-9
  Penalty tax, *See also* Accumulated
    Earnings Tax; Personal Holding
    Company Tax, 15-11 to 15-20
  Shareholder loans, 15-22 to 15-23
  Tax planning, 15-20 to 15-27
  Unreasonable accumulations, 15-2 to
    15-11
Corporate Advances to Shareholder,
    13-9
Corporation Application for Tentative
    Refund, 21-13 to 21-14
Corporate Deduction for Compensation,
    Disallowance, 13-27
Corporate Distribution
  Complete liquidation, 14-1 to 14-26
  Dividend distributions, *See also*
    Dividend Distributions, 13-1 to
    13-15
  Effect on earnings and profits, 13-12
    to 13-13, 13-22 to 13-23
  Partial liquidations, 13-22
  S corporations, 16-15 to 16-17
  Stock redemptions, 13-16 to 13-22,
    13-27 to 13-28
  Stock and securities distributions,
    13-22
  Tax consequences, 13-22 to 13-24
  Tax effect on the distributing
    corporation, 13-10 to 13-12
  Tax planning, 13-24 to 13-26
Corporate Entity
  Corporate characteristics, 12-5 to 12-6

Corporate Entity—Cont'd
  Disregard of, 12-3 to 12-4
Corporate Form, Advantages and
    Disadvantages, 16-1 to 16-2
Corporations
  Accounting periods and methods,
    12-7
  ACRS, 12-19, 13-4, 13-23
  Affiliated corporations, 6-7
  Associations taxed as corporations,
    12-4 to 12-6
  Business deductions, 12-7 to 12-8
  Capital gains and losses, 2-29, 2-30,
    10-17, 12-8 to 12-10
  Characteristics, 12-5 to 12-6
  Charitable contributions, 12-10 to
    12-13
  Compared with noncorporate forms,
    12-33 to 12-35, 17-33 to 17-34
  Controlled, 12-22 to 12-31
  Deductions available only to
    corporations, 12-14 to 12-17
  Defined, 12-3 to 12-6
  Dissimilarities with individual
    taxpayers, 12-7 to 12-8
  Dividend distributions, 13-1 to 13-15
  Dividends received deductions, 15-10,
    15-16
  ESOPs, 8-19
  Filing requirements, 12-20 to 12-21
  Final tax payment, 12-20
  Income tax liability, 12-17 to 12-22
  Liquidation, *See also* Complete
    Liquidations, 14-1 to 14-26
  Minimum tax, 12-18, 12-19, 15-3
  Net operating losses (NOL), 12-13 to
    12-14
  One-month liquidation, *see*
    One-Month Liquidations
  Reconciliation of taxable income and
    financial net income, 12-21 to
    12-22
  Retirement of corporate obligations,
    10-6
  Shifting deductions, 6-55 to 6-56
  Similarities with individual
    taxpayers, 12-6 to 12-7
  Stock ownership, 6-7
  Structure, 12-31 to 12-33
  Subchapter S status, *see* S
    Corporations
  Taxation, Chapter 12
  Tax credits, 12-7
  Tax liability, 12-17 to 12-22
  Tax planning, 12-33 to 12-40
  Tax preferences, 12-18 to 12-19
  Tax rates, 12-7, 12-17 to 12-18

Corporations—Cont'd
  Tax treatment versus partnership tax
    treatment, 1-25
  Transfers to controlled corporations
    (Section 351), *see* Controlled
    Corporations
  Twelve-month liquidation, *see*
    Twelve-Month Liquidations
Cost Basis Considerations, *See also*
    Basis
  Allocation problems, 9-7
  Determination, 9-6 to 9-7
  Gift basis, 9-7 to 9-10
  Identification problems, 9-6 to 9-7
  Property acquired from a decedent,
    9-10 to 9-11
  Property conversion, 9-12 to 9-13
Cost Depletion, 6-29, 6-55
Cost Identification of Property, 9-35
Cost Recovery, 6-14 to 6-19
  Half-year convention, 6-25 to 6-26
  Investment tax credit, 8-4 to 8-5
Court of Appeals, 22-7, 22-8, 22-9 to
    22-11, 22-13 to 22-14, 22-21
Court of Claims, *see* Claims Court
Courts, *see* Federal Court System
Credit Cards, *See also* Interest Expense,
    7-15, 7-16, 7-18
Credit for the Elderly, *see* Tax Credit
    for the Elderly
Credits, *see* Tax Credits
Credits (Estate Tax)
  Foreign death taxes, 18-28 to 18-29
  Gift taxes, 18-27
  State estate taxes, 18-26, 20-15
  Tax on prior transfers, 18-27 to 18-28
  Unified transfer tax, 18-25 to 18-26,
    18-27, 18-31, 19-15 to 19-17,
    19-22
Crop Insurance Proceeds, 1-22, 3-9 to
    3-10
Crude Oil Windfall Profit Tax Act of
    1980, pp. 1-9
*Cumulative Bulletin* (C.B.), 22-6 to 22-7,
    22-12
Current Tax Payment Act, 1-3
Curtesy Interests, *see* Dower Interests
Customs Duties, 1-18 to 1-19

## D

Damage Deposits, 3-23
Damages, *See also* Compensation for
    Injuries and Sickness, 4-8 to 4-10,
    4-26
Date of Sale of Stock, 10-38

Dealers in Personal Property, *see* Capital Gains and Losses; Installment Method
Death Benefit Exclusion, 16-22
Death Tax Conventions, 18-2, 18-29
Death Tax (Federal), *See also* Credits; Federal Estate Tax; Gross Estate; Marital Deduction; Taxable Estate; Unified Transfer Tax
  Based on fair market value, 18-20 to 18-21
  Compared to inheritance taxes, 1-11
  Computations, 18-24 to 18-30
  Credits, 18-25 to 18-29
  Foreign, 18-28 to 18-29
  Marital deduction, 18-30 to 18-32
  Multiple effect, *see* Credits (Estate Tax), Tax on prior transfers
  Property transfer, 18-27 to 18-28
  Return requirements, 18-20, 18-29 to 18-30
  State, 18-26
  Tax Reform Act of 1976, pp. 18-1, 18-7, 18-25, 18-27
Death Taxes, *See also* Estate Tax
  Administrative expenses, 20-9 to 20-10
  Inheritance taxes, 1-11
  State, 19-21 to 19-23
  Stock redemptions, 13-20 to 13-21, 13-22
  Tax valuation, 20-27
Debt
  Advantages, 12-32 to 12-33
  Reclassification as equity, 12-33, 12-34, 12-39
Debt Versus Equity, *see* Capital Structure of a Corporation
Decedent
  Accrual basis, 20-8
  Annuities, 18-11 to 18-15
  Cash basis, 20-8
  Charitable transfers, 18-21 to 18-22
  Claims against the estate, 18-19 to 18-20
  Estate tax return, 18-29 to 18-30
  Gifts within three years of death, 18-6 to 18-8
  Jurisdiction, 19-23
  Life insurance proceeds, 18-17 to 18-19
  Losses, 18-21
  Marital deduction, 18-22 to 18-24
  Property, 9-10 to 9-11, 18-4 to 18-5, 18-6

Decedent—Cont'd
  Stock redemptions, 13-20 to 13-21
  Tax consequences, 20-8 to 20-9
  Tax on prior transfers, 18-28
Declaration of Estimated Tax, *see* Estimated Tax
Declining-Balance Depreciation, 6-17, 6-18, 6-19, 6-24
Deductible Expenses, 5-4 to 5-5
Deductions (Estate Tax), *See also* Marital Deduction
  Charitable deduction, 18-21 to 18-22
  Expenses, indebtedness, and taxes, 18-19 to 18-20
  Losses during estate's settlement, 18-21
  Mortgages, 18-20
  Taxable estate, 18-19 to 18-24
  Tax planning, 18-30 to 18-32
Deductions *for* Adjusted Gross Income, *See also* Deductions and Losses; Employee Expenses, 2-4, 6-32 to 6-33
  Versus itemized deductions, 5-2, 5-5
Deductions *from* Adjusted Gross Income, *See also* Itemized Deductions, 2-4, 6-32 to 6-33
Deductions Available Only to Corporations
  Dividends received, 12-14 to 12-15
  Organizational expenditures, 12-15 to 12-17
Deductions and Losses, *See also* Itemized Deductions
  ACRS, 3-19 to 3-28, 6-52 to 6-55
  Bad debts, 6-1 to 6-7
  Casualty and theft losses, 6-8 to 6-11, 6-52
  Charitable contributions, 1-24, 6-33, 18-21 to 18-22, 20-12 to 20-14, 20-16, 20-20 to 20-21, 20-24
  Consumption of cost of asset, 6-14
  Cost recovery, 6-14 to 6-19
  Depletion, 6-14 to 6-19, 6-28 to 6-31, 6-55, 16-13, 17-16, 20-10
  Depreciation and amortization, 6-14 to 6-19, 6-52 to 6-54
  Disallowance possibilities, 5-6 to 5-22
  Distributions to beneficiaries, 20-14, 20-26
  Double deductions, 20-10
  Estate income, 20-9 to 20-15
  Expense classifications, 5-2
  Federal gift tax, 19-11 to 19-13
  General tests for deductibility, 5-1 to 5-6

Deductions and Losses—Cont'd
Net operating losses, 6-12 to 6-14
Ordinary and necessary expenses, 20-9 to 20-11
Reporting procedures, 6-31, 6-51
Research and experimental expenditures, 6-11 to 6-12
Shifting deductions in tax planning, 5-23
State inheritance tax, 19-22
Tax planning, 5-22 to 5-24
Tax treatment, 5-1 to 5-5
Trust income, 20-9 to 20-15, 20-23 to 20-24
Deductions Related to Classes of Income, 20-23 to 20-24
Deferral of Advance Payments, 3-11 to 3-12, 3-23
Deferral of Taxes, 3-22 to 3-23, 11-40, 11-41
Deferred Income, 3-8 to 3-9, 3-22, to 3-23
Deferred Pay Contract, 18-13
Deferred Payment Contract, 11-28 to 11-29
Deferred Taxes, 3-22 to 3-23, 11-40, 11-41
Deficiency, *see* Glossary
Deficiency Assessments, 21-12
*De Minimus* Rule, 11-22
Denied Deductions, 5-7
Dependency Exemptions, 1-30, 2-12 to 2-17
Tax planning, 2-31 to 2-34
Depletion, *See also* Glossary
Depletion
Cost depletion, 6-29, 6-55, 16-24
Deductions and losses, 6-14 to 6-19, 6-28 to 6-31, 6-55, 16-13, 17-16, 20-10
Intangible drilling and development costs, 6-28
Methods, 6-28 to 6-31
Partnerships, 17-21
Percentage depletion, 6-29 to 6-31, 6-55, 12-18, 12-19, 16-24
Property held in trust, 20-10
Tax planning, 6-55
Depreciable Property, 9-3 to 9-4, 10-32 to 10-33, 13-12, 13-23, 17-13, 17-15, 17-21, 17-35
Depreciation
ACRS rules, 17-13
Converted property, 9-13
Gift property, 9-9
Investment tax credit, 8-4 to 8-5

Depreciation—Cont'd
Minimizing, 15-26
Original basis of property, 9-3 to 9-4
Property held in trust, 20-10
Real property, 10-26, 10-27
Recapture, 12-28, 13-12, 13-23, 14-23, 17-35, 20-10 to 20-11
Depreciation and Amortization
Accelerated methods, 17-13
Asset Depreciation Range (ADR), 6-19 to 6-20
Deductions and losses, 6-14 to 6-19, 6-52 to 6-54
Methods of depreciation, 6-17 to 6-19
Pre-ERTA, 6-17 to 6-19
Qualifying property, 6-16
Rehabilitation expenditures for low-income housing, 8-9, 10-34 to 10-35
Salvage value, 6-16 to 6-17
Tax planning, 6-52 to 6-54
Determination Letter, 21-3 to 21-4, 21-34
Determination of Tax, *see* Calculation of Tax Liability
DFOR, *see* Deductions *for* Adjusted Gross Income
DFROM, *see* Deductions *from* Adjusted Gross Income
Direct Charge-Off Method (same as Specific Charge-Off Method)
Disability Income, 8-24
Disability and Sick Pay, 4-11, 4-12 to 4-13
Disabled Dependent Care Credit, *see* Child and Dependent Care Credit
Disallowance of Expenses
Capital expenditures, 5-15 to 5-17
Hobby losses, 5-3, 5-4, 5-10 to 5-13
Interest deductions, 5-21 to 5-22
Personal expenditures, 5-14 to 5-15
Public policy limitation, 5-7 to 5-9
Related-party transactions, 5-17 to 5-19, 10-33
Tax-exempt income, 5-20 to 5-22
Unrealized losses, 5-15
Disallowed Losses, 5-6 to 5-22
Estate and trust losses, 20-12
Wash sales, 9-11 to 9-12
Disaster Area Losses, 6-9, 6-10
Discharge of Indebtedness, 4-23 to 4-24, 16-14
Discriminant Function System (DIF), 21-4, 21-5
DISCs, *see* Domestic International Sales Corporations

Distributable Net Income
  Adjustments in computing, 20-16 to 20-17
  Complex trusts and estates, 20-19 to 20-21
  Computation, 20-16 to 20-18
  Computation modifications, 20-18
  Estate and trust beneficiaries, 20-16 to 20-18, 20-25 to 20-27
  Simple trusts, 20-14, 20-18 to 20-19
  Tax planning, 20-26 to 20-27
Distribution of Stock of a Controlled Corporation, *see* Controlled Corporations; Reorganizations
Distributions In Kind—Section 336, *see* In-Kind Distributions
Distributions by a Partnership, 17-30 to 17-32
District Courts, 22-7, 22-8, 22-9, 22-10 to 22-11, 22-13 to 22-14, 22-21
Dividend Distributions
  Carryover, 15-18
  Consequences to corporation, 13-10 to 13-13
  Constructive dividends, 13-8 to 13-10, 13-26 to 13-27
  Dividends paid deduction, 15-10, 15-17 to 15-18, 15-23
  Earnings and profits, 13-2 to 13-6
  Liquidations, 14-5 to 14-6
  Penalty tax, 15-18
  Property dividends, 13-6 to 13-8, 13-10, 13-13
  Source, 13-5
  Stock dividends and stock rights, 13-13 to 13-15, 13-24
  Taxable, 13-1 to 13-2
  Tax planning, 13-24 to 13-27, 15-22 to 15-24, 15-26
Dividend Equivalency Rule, 13-16
Dividend Exclusion, 4-19 to 4-22, 20-7 to 20-8
Dividend Income, 2-18 to 2-19, 2-21
Dividend Reinvestment Plans, 4-21 to 4-22
Dividends
  Corporate deductions, 12-14 to 12-15, 15-17 to 15-18
  Grace period, 15-17
  Gross income, 3-13
  Nonqualifying, 4-20
  Partnerships, 17-15
  Penalty tax, 15-10, 15-11
  Stock and dividend reinvestment plans, 4-21 to 4-22
  Taxable, 13-1 to 13-2, 13-6 to 13-13
  Tax planning, 15-23 to 15-24

Dividends Paid Deduction, 15-10, 15-17 to 15-18, 15-23
Dividends Received Deduction, 12-14 to 12-15, 15-10, 15-16
Divorce, *see* Child and Dependent Care Credit; Child Support Payments; Community Property
Divorce Settlements, *see* Gift Tax (Federal)
Documentation Requirements, 5-19 to 5-20, 6-57, 9-35
Domestic International Sales Corporations (DISCs), 1-22
Donative Intent, 7-19, 19-2, 19-6
Donee, 19-2, 19-23, 19-25, 19-27 to 19-28
Donor, 19-2, 19-20, 19-21, 19-23, 19-25 to 19-27
Double Deductions, 20-10
Double Taxation, 1-5, 8-25, 12-2, 16-2, 18-27, 19-6, 19-21, 20-9
Double-Tax Effect, *see* Multiple Taxation
Dower and Curtesy Interests, 18-5 to 18-6
Drilling Costs, 6-28, 10-35 to 10-36
Dues, 4-16

# E

Earned Income, 2-9
Earned Income Credit, 1-30, 2-34, 8-22 to 8-23, 8-29, 12-7
Earnings and Profits (E & P)
  ACRS, 13-4, 13-23
  Computation, 13-3 to 13-4
  Concept, 13-2 to 13-3
  Current and accumulated E & P, 13-5 to 13-6, 13-25
  Effect of corporate distributions, 13-12 to 13-13, 13-22 to 13-23
  ERTA, 13-4
  Stock redemptions, 13-22
  Tax planning, 13-25 to 13-26
Economic Considerations of the Tax Law, 1-19 to 1-23, 1-34
Economic Recovery Tax Act of 1981 (ERTA)
  Adjusted gross income, 6-33
  All-Savers Certificates, 1-22
  Annual exclusion, 19-3
  At-Risk limitation, 8-11 to 8-12
  Audits, 21-4
  Capital recovery, 9-3
  Child and dependent care expense, 8-27

Economic Recovery Tax Act of 1981
  (ERTA)—Cont'd
  Corporate contributions, 12-11
  Corporate earnings and profits, 13-4
  Earnings and profits, 13-4
  Estate tax, 18-7, 18-16 to 18-17,
    18-25, 18-31
  Federal gift tax, 19-3, 19-9, 19-13
  Foreign income tax breaks, 1-22
  Gross estate, 18-7, 18-16 to 18-17
  Inventories, 11-36
  Investment tax credit, 8-3, 8-8, 8-10
    to 8-11
  Joint ownership, 18-16 to 18-17
  LIFO, 11-36
  Marital deduction, 18-23, 18-31, 19-9
  Marriage penalty, 2-24 to 2-25
  Negligence penalty, 21-16
  Partnership's basis in contributed
    property, 17-13
  Penalties, 21-20
  Property contributions, 17-13
  Purpose, 1-21
  R&D costs, 1-21
  Recapture of investment tax credit,
    12-30
  Recovery periods, 1-20
  Recovery property, 10-25
  Research and experimental
    expenditures, 6-12
  Research and experimentation credit,
    8-18, 8-33
  Residential real property, 9-25 to 9-26
  Tax credits, 8-3, 8-8, 8-10 to 8-11,
    8-18, 8-27, 8-33
  Tax rate reduction, 1-21, 2-17, 2-22 to
    2-23
  Tax Table, 2-17
  Two-earner married couple deduction,
    2-24 to 2-25
  Withholding, 1-31 to 1-32
Educational Assistance Payments, 4-7
    to 4-8
Education Expenses, 4-7 to 4-8
  Classification, 6-46
  Deductibility, 22-20
  Exceptions, 6-45
  General requirements, 6-44 to 6-45
  Maintaining or improving existing
    skills, 6-45 to 6-46
  Retention of employment provision,
    6-45
  Tax planning, 6-56 to 6-57
Elderly Taxpayer Credit, *See also* Social
    Security Benefits, 8-23 to 8-25,
    8-29, 12-7
Electing Out, *see* Installment Method

Election to Expense Assets, 6-26 to
    6-27, 6-54 to 6-55
Employee Annuities, 3-25
Employee Benefits, *see* Employee
    Fringe Benefits
Employee Death Benefits, 4-5 to 4-6
Employee Discounts, 4-16
Employee Expenses
  Dues, 6-51
  Job-seeking expenses, 6-51
  Office in the home, 6-50 to 6-51
  Tax planning, 6-55 to 6-56
  Uniforms (special clothes), 6-51
Employee Fringe Benefits
  Accident and health plan premiums,
    1-23, 4-11 to 4-12, 4-26
  Annuities, 3-25
  Cafeteria plans, 4-15 to 4-16
  Child care, 4-15, 4-26
  Commuting expenses, 4-15
  Death benefits, 4-5 to 4-6
  Disability payments, 4-12 to 4-13
  Discounts, 4-16
  Dues, 4-16
  Educational assistance payments, 4-7
    to 4-8
  Gross income, 4-15 to 4-17, 4-26 to
    4-27
  Group-term life insurance, 1-23, 4-15
  Legal services, 4-15, 4-26
  Loans, 4-16 to 4-17
  Lump-sum distributions, 4-5, 4-6
  Meals and lodging, 4-13 to 4-14, 4-26
    to 4-27
  Medical reimbursement plans, 4-12,
    4-15
  Qualified pension and profit sharing
    plans, 1-24, 3-25
  Supper money, 4-16
Employee Retirement Income Security
    Act of 1974 (ERISA), 12-35, 22-6
Employee Stock Ownership Plan
    (ESOP), 8-10 to 8-11, 8-18 to 8-19,
    8-30
Employment-Related Expenses, *See also*
    Child and Dependent Care Credit;
    Employee Expenses, 5-3, 5-5
Employment Taxes
  FICA, 1-15, 1-16 to 1-17, 8-25, 21-20
  Form 940, p. 1-18
  Form 941, p. 1-17
  FUTA, 1-15, 1-17 to 1-18
Energy Tax Act of 1978, pp. 1-21, 8-9
Energy Tax Credits
  Business energy tax credit, 8-21 to
    8-22
  Priority of credits, 8-30

Energy Tax Credits—Cont'd
  Residential energy tax credit, 8-20 to
    8-21
  Tax planning, 8-32 to 8-33
Entertaining Expenses
  Business gifts, 6-49 to 6-50
  Business meals, 6-47 to 6-48
  Classifications, 6-47
  Facilities, 6-48 to 6-49
  Recordkeeping requirements, 6-49,
    6-57
  Restrictions, 6-46 to 6-50, 6-57
  Substantiation, 5-19 to 5-20
  Tax planning, 6-57 to 6-58
Entity Concept, 17-2 to 17-3
Equity Considerations of the Tax Law,
  1-24 to 1-29, 1-34
ERISA, *see* Employment Retirement
  Income Security Act of 1974
ERTA, *see* Economic Recovery Tax Act
  of 1981
ESOP, *see* Employee Stock Ownership
  Plan
Estates, *see* Death Tax (Federal);
  Federal Estate Tax
Estates—Income Taxation, *See also*
  Beneficiaries; Distributable Net
  Income, Computation; Income in
  Respect of a Decedent
  Basis of property received from
    decedent, 9-10
  Beneficiaries, 20-15 to 20-22
  Capital gain or loss on property
    acquired from decedent, 9-11
  Charitable contribution deduction,
    18-21 to 18-22, 20-12 to 20-14,
    20-16, 20-20 to 20-21, 20-24
  Choice of accounting method and tax
    year, 20-4 to 20-5
  Classes of income, 20-22 to 20-23
  Conduit concept, 20-5 to 20-6
  Deductions, 20-23 to 20-24
  Estate defined, 20-3
  Filing requirements, 20-4
  Gross income, 3-14, 20-6 to 20-8
  Nature of Taxation, 20-3 to 20-6
  Net operating losses, 20-11, 20-24
  Personal exemption, 20-5
  Returns, 18-29 to 18-30
  Taxable income, 20-6 to 20-15, 20-17
  Tax planning, 20-25 to 20-27
  Tax rate, 20-5
  Tax treatment, 12-2
  Throwback rule, 20-24 to 20-25, 20-27
Estate Tax, *See also* Death Taxes
  Computation, 18-24 to 18-30

Estate Tax—Cont'd
  Credit for state death tax, 18-25,
    18-26
  ERTA, 18-7, 18-16 to 18-17, 18-25,
    18-31
  Estates subject to tax, 18-2 to 18-3
  Federal, Chapter 18
  Filing requirements, 18-29 to 18-30
  Formula, 18-3
  Gross estate, 18-4 to 18-19
  Nature of tax, 18-1 to 18-3
  Return, 18-29 to 18-30
  State, 18-24, 18-26, 19-23, 19-24
  Taxable estate, 18-19 to 18-24
  Tax planning, 18-30 to 18-32
  Tax Reform Act of 1976, p. 18-31
  Unified transfer tax credit, 18-25 to
    18-26, 18-27, 18-31, 19-6
Estimated Expenses, 11-20
Estimated Tax, 1-13
  Corporations, 12-19 to 12-20
  Failure to pay, 21-17 to 21-18, 21-36
    to 21-37
  Filing requirements, 2-18
  Individuals, 2-18
  Underpayment penalty, 12-19 to
    12-20, 21-12, 21-18
Ethics, *see* Code of Ethics
Evasion of Tax, 22-23
Excess of Basis, Corporate Property
  Transfers, 12-27 to 12-28
Excess Contributions, 7-25 to 7-26
Excess Employee Stock Ownership
  Credit, 8-19
Excess Investment Interest, 16-24,
  16-27
Excess Itemized Deductions, 2-5, 7-30
Excess Net Passive Income (ENPI),
  16-10
Excess Passive Investment Income,
  16-27
Excess-Profit Tax, 1-13
Excessive Withholding of Taxes, 7-12
Exchange of a Partnership Interest, *see*
  Like-Kind Exchanges
Exchanges, *see* Sale or Exchange of
  Capital Assets; Property
  Transactions
Exchange Treatment, 14-2, 14-5
  Effect on shareholder, 14-15, 14-33
  Tax planning, 14-33
Excise Taxes, 1-9 to 1-10, 1-11, 1-12,
  1-18
Exclusions
  Annual, 19-13 to 19-18
  Federal gift tax, 19-11, 19-13 to 19-18

Exclusions—Cont'd
  Partnership taxation, 17-4
  State inheritance tax, 19-22
Exclusions from Gross Income, 2-2 to
    2-3, Chapter 4
  Accident and health benefits, 4-10 to
    4-11, 4-26
  Accident and health plan premiums,
    1-23, 4-11 to 4-12, 4-26
  Administrative policy, 4-2
  Compensation for injuries, 4-8 to 4-11
  Damages, 4-8 to 4-10, 4-26
  Disability and sick pay, 4-12 to 4-13
  Discharge of indebtedness, 4-23 to
    4-24
  Dividends, 4-19 to 4-22
  Employee death benefits, 4-5 to 4-6
  Employee fringe benefits, 4-15 to
    4-17, 4-26 to 4-27
  Fellowships, 4-6 to 4-8
  Foreign earned income, 4-17 to 4-18
  Gifts, 4-3 to 4-4, 4-25
  Group-term life insurance, 4-26
  Inheritances, 4-3 to 4-4, 4-25
  Injury and sickness compensation, 4-8
    to 4-11, 4-26
  Interest, 4-18 to 4-19
  Interest on state and local
    government obligations, 4-18
  Life insurance proceeds, 4-4 to 4-5,
    4-25
  Meals and lodging, 4-13 to 4-14, 4-26
    to 4-27
  Medical reimbursement, 4-12, 4-15
  Principal exclusions summary, 4-2 to
    4-3
  Scholarships, 4-6 to 4-8
  Social Security benefits, 4-2
  Statutory authority, 4-1 to 4-2
  Tax benefit rule, 4-22
  Tax planning, 4-24 to 4-27
  Workers' compensation, 4-10
Executor, 18-4
Exempt Interest, *see* Tax-Exempt
    Interest; Tax-Exempt Securities
Exemptions
  Alternative minimum tax, 11-11,
    11-39
  Dependency, 2-12 to 2-17, 2-31 to
    2-34
  Estates and trusts, 20-5
  Fiduciary tax liability, 20-5
  Inheritance tax, 19-21, 19-22
  Personal, 2-5, 2-11 to 2-12, 20-5, 20-16
  State gift tax, 19-23
  Tax preference items, 11-39

Expenditures Incurred for Taxpayer's
    Benefit or Taxpayer's Obligation,
    5-13 to 5-14
Expenses
  Business, *see* Business Expenses and
    Losses
  Employee, *see* Employee Expenses
  Illegal business, 5-8 to 5-9
  Liquidation, 14-12 to 14-13
  Ordinary and necessary, 5-1 to 5-2,
    5-5 to 5-6, 5-7, 5-8, 5-14, 20-9 to
    20-11
  Unpaid, 5-18
Expenses Attributable to the
    Production or Collection of Income,
    5-3 to 5-4, 5-5, 5-14
Expenses Relating to Tax-Exempt
    Income, 5-4, 5-20 to 5-22
Extension of Time to File Tax Return,
    2-22, 19-20, 21-15, 21-36
Extension of Time to Pay Taxes, 19-20

**F**

Failure to File or Pay Penalty, 2-22,
    17-14, 21-14 to 21-16, 21-36 to
    21-37
Failure to Make Deposits of Taxes,
    21-20
Failure to Pay Estimated Taxes, 21-17
    to 21-18, 21-36 to 21-37
Fair Market Value (FMV), *See also*
    Federal Estate Tax; Gift Tax
    (Federal)
  Appreciated property, 16-17
  Corporate accumulations, 15-8, 15-9
  Corporate contributions, 12-11, 12-12
  Cost basis of property, 9-6
  Defined, 9-3
  Dividends, 15-17
  Estate tax, 18-20, 18-21
  Gift property, 9-7, 9-8, 9-9, 9-10
  Gross estate, 18-20, 18-21
  Partnership capital, 17-6, 17-34 to
    17-35
  Personal holding company tax, 15-12
  Property acquired from a decedent,
    9-10
  Property contributions, 7-21, 7-22,
    7-27, 7-28 to 7-29, 17-7 to 17-8,
    17-21
  Property distributions, 16-15, 16-16,
    16-17
  Property dividends, 13-6

Farming
  Accounting methods, 10-35
  Cattle feed costs, 11-19
  Crop insurance proceeds, 1-22, 3-9 to 3-10
  Recapture provisions, 10-35
  Special tax treatment, 1-22
  Syndicates, 11-19
Favorable Tax Treatment, 4-4, 5-9
Federal Courts Improvement Act of 1982, p. 22-7
Federal Court System, 1-32 to 1-34
Federal District Court, *see* District Courts
Federal Estate Tax, *See also* Death Tax (Federal)
  Computation, 18-24 to 18-30
  Effect of pre-1977 gifts, 19-5, 19-6
  Formula (exemption, deduction, credits), 18-3
  Gross estate, 18-4 to 18-19
  Inheritance taxes, 8-26
  Joint ownership, 18-15 to 18-17, 19-10, 19-22
  Multiple effect, *see* Credits (Estate Tax), Tax on prior transfers
  Return, 18-29 to 18-30
  Return requirements, 19-19 to 19-20
  Taxable estate, 18-19 to 18-24
  Tax Reform Act of 1976, pp. 18-1, 18-7, 18-25, 18-27
Federal Insurance Contributions Act (FICA), 1-15, 1-16 to 1-17, 8-25, 21-20
Federal Tax Legislation, 22-2 to 22-3
Federal Unemployment Tax Act (FUTA), 1-15, 1-17 to 1-18
Fee, as Distinguished from Tax, 7-9
Fellowships, 4-6 to 4-8
FICA Taxes, *See also* Employment Taxes, 1-15 to 1-17, 8-25, 21-20
Fiduciary Return (Estate), 18-21, 20-4, 20-12
Field Audit, 21-6 to 21-7, 21-35
FIFO, *See also* Inventory Methods, 8-5, 8-6, 9-6, 11-34 to 11-35, 13-23
Filing Requirements
  Charitable contributions, 7-27, 7-30
  Corporations (Form 1120 or 1120S), 12-20 to 12-21
  Estates, 18-29 to 18-30, 20-4
  Estimated tax, 2-18
  Extension of time to file, 2-22, 19-20
  Federal gift tax, 19-18 to 19-20
  Individuals, 2-20 to 2-22
  State inheritance tax, 19-22

Filing Requirements—Cont'd
  State and local taxes, 7-14
  Trusts, 20-4
  Zero bracket amount, 2-5, 2-21
Filing Status, 2-22 to 2-26, 2-34 to 2-35
Finance Charges, 7-15, 7-18
Finance Companies, 15-12
Financial Net Income, Corporations, 12-21 to 12-22
Fines, 1-24, 5-3, 5-7, 5-8
First In, First Out (FIFO), *see* FIFO; Inventory Methods
Fixing-Up Expenses, 9-27 to 9-28, 9-29, 9-30
FMV, *see* Fair Market Value (FMV)
Foreign Charities, 18-22
Foreign Corporations, 15-12
Foreign Corrupt Practices Act, 5-3, 5-7
Foreign Death Tax, 18-28 to 18-29, 19-21
Foreign Earned Income, 4-17 to 4-18
Foreign Tax Credit, 8-5, 8-32
  Computation, 8-25 to 8-26
  Corporations, 12-7
  Estates and trusts, 20-15
  Limitation, 11-13
  Option, 4-17 to 4-18
  Partnerships, 17-15
  Priority of credits, 8-29
  S corporation, 16-13, 16-24
  Tax planning, 8-32
  Unused taxes, 8-26
Foreign Taxes, 16-24, 17-15
Foreign Travel, *see* Travel Expenses
Form 1040EZ, 2-21
Franchises, 10-8 to 10-9
Franchise Tax, 1-19
Fraud, 1-31, 21-16 to 21-17, 21-35 to 21-36, 22-23
Freedom of Information Act, 21-2, 21-4
Fringe Benefits, *See also* Employee Fringe Benefits
  S corporations, 16-22 to 16-23, 16-27
  Tax-sheltered, 17-34
Frivolous Tax Return, 1-32
Functional Use Test, 8-9, 9-21
Funeral Expenses, *See also* Deductions (Estate Tax), 18-19, 18-20
FUTA, *see* Federal Unemployment Tax Act

# G

Gain Requirements, Nonrecognition in Sale of a Residence, 9-27 to 9-28

Gains and Losses
  Capital gains and losses, *see* Capital
    Gains and Losses
  Computation of gain under Section
    333, pp. 14-17 to 14-18
  Determination, 9-1 to 9-6
  Estate income, 20-6 to 20-7, 20-24
  Nonrecognition, 9-5 to 9-6, 9-22 to
    9-24, 9-27 to 9-28, 12-23 to 12-24,
    12-26, 12-38, 17-5 to 17-7
  Property transactions, 2-26 to 2-30,
    9-1 to 9-6, 12-6 to 12-7
  Property transfers, 12-22 to 12-24
  Realized, 2-26 to 2-27, 9-1 to 9-4
  Recognized, 2-26 to 2-27, 9-4 to 9-5
  S corporations, 16-13
  Trust income, 20-6 to 20-7, 20-24
Gas Guzzler Tax, 1-9
Generally Accepted Accounting
  Principles (GAAP), 1-31, 3-11,
  11-32 to 11-33
General Powers of Appointment, *see*
  Gift Tax (Federal)
General Sales Tax, 1-10 to 1-11
  Tables, 7-13 to 7-14
  Tax planning, 7-32 to 7-33
Gifts, *See also* Gift Tax (Federal)
  Adjustment for gift tax, 9-8 to 9-9,
    18-6 to 18-8
  Basis determination, 9-7 to 9-10
  Business, 6-49 to 6-50
  Defined, 4-3
  Depreciation, 9-9
  Elements of completed gift, 19-2 to
    19-3
  Excluded as business expense, 5-3
  Exclusion from income, 4-3 to 4-4
  Holding period, 9-9 to 9-10, 9-11
  Income-producing property, 4-3, 4-25
  Loans between related parties, 19-7
  Recapture potential under Section
    1245, p. 10-31
  Substantiation of expenditure, 5-19 to
    5-20
  Taxable gifts, 19-3 to 19-6, 19-25
  Tax planning, 9-35
Gifts in Contemplation of Death
  (Within Three Years of Death),
  20-4
Gift Splitting, 19-17 to 19-18
Gift Tax (Federal), *See also* Marital
  Deduction (Gift Tax); Unified
  Transfer Tax, 1-12
  Annual exclusion, 19-3, 19-13 to
    19-15, 19-25
  Charitable deduction, 19-12

Gift Tax (Federal)—Cont'd
  Credit, 18-27
  Cumulative aspects, 19-4
  Deductions and expenses, 19-11 to
    19-18
  Donative intent, 19-2, 19-6
  Election for joint tenancies and
    tenancies by the entirety, 19-8 to
    19-10
  Election to split gifts, 19-17 to 19-18
  ERTA, 19-3, 19-9, 19-13
  Estate tax credit, 18-27
  Exemption, 18-3
  General rule, 19-8
  Gift property, 9-8 to 9-9
  Gift splitting, 19-17 to 19-18
  Gift tax conventions, 19-21
  Joint ownership, 19-8 to 19-10
  Life insurance, 19-10 to 19-11
  Loans between relatives, 19-7
  Marital deduction, 19-12 to 19-13
  Minors, 19-14 to 19-15
  Persons subject to the tax, 19-3
  Procedural aspects, 19-18 to 19-20
  Property settlements, 19-11
  Purpose for enactment, 19-1
  Requirements, 19-2 to 19-3
  Returns, 19-19 to 19-20
  Revenue Act of 1948, p. 19-18
  Specific (lifetime) exemption
    (pre-1977), 19-5, 19-15
  State transfer taxes, 19-21 to 19-24
  Tax consequences, 19-25 to 19-28
  Tax planning, 19-25 to 19-30
  Tax Reform Act of 1976, pp. 18-27,
    18-31, 19-1
  Transfer of property, 19-25 to 19-30
  Transfers after 1976, pp. 19-3 to 19-5,
    19-6, 19-15 to 19-17
  Transfers before 1977, pp. 19-5 to
    19-6, 19-15
  Trust for minors and the annual
    exclusion, 19-14 to 19-15
Gift Tax (State), 1-12, 19-23 to
  19-24
Goodwill, 5-16, 6-14, 6-16, 6-57
Government Bonds Issued at a
  Discount, *see* Series E and EE
  Savings Bonds
Government Obligations, State and
  Local, 4-18
Grandfather Fringe Benefits, 16-27
Grease Payments, 5-3
Gross Estate, *See also* Federal Estate
  Tax; Taxable Estate
  Annuities, 18-11 to 18-15

Gross Estate—Cont'd
Dower and curtesy interests, 18-5 to 18-6
ERTA, 18-7, 18-16 to 18-17
Estate tax return, 18-29 to 18-30
Gifts within three years of death, 18-6 to 18-8
Incidents of ownership test, 18-18 to 18-19
Joint interests, 18-15 to 18-17
Life insurance proceeds, 18-17 to 18-19
Property owned by decedent, 18-4 to 18-5, 18-6
Redemption of stock to pay death taxes, 13-20 to 13-21
Revocable transfers, 18-9 to 18-11
Tax credits, 18-25 to 18-29
Tax Reform Act of 1976, p. 18-7
Tax return, 18-29 to 18-30
Transfers with retained life estate, 18-8 to 18-9
Transfers taking effect at death, 18-1 to 18-2
Gross Income, *See also* individual items (e. g., Dividend Income; Interest Income)
Accounting methods, 3-5 to 3-7
Accounting and taxable income compared, 3-2
Accrual basis taxpayers, 3-10 to 3-12, 3-23
Adjusted, 2-4
Alimony and separate maintenance payments, 3-16 to 3-18, 3-25 to 3-26
Annual accounting period, 3-4 to 3-5
Annuities, 3-18 to 3-19, 3-25
Assignment of income from property, 3-13 to 3-14
Capital gains, 2-28 to 2-29, 12-9
Cash basis taxpayers, 3-7 to 3-10
Child support payments, 3-17 to 3-18
Community property, 3-14 to 3-16, 3-25
Commuting expenses, 4-15
Corporations, 12-6, 12-7
Crop insurance proceeds, 1-22, 3-9 to 3-10
Defined, 2-3, 3-1 to 3-2
Dependency exemptions, 2-12, 2-16, 2-32 to 2-33
Educational expenses, 4-7 to 4-8
Employee fringe benefits, 4-15 to 4-17
Estates, 3-14, 20-6 to 20-8
Exclusions, 2-2 to 2-3, Chapter 4

Gross Income—Cont'd
Filing requirements, 2-20, 2-21
Form of receipt, 3-2
Group-term life insurance, 3-20 to 3-21, 4-26
Inclusions, 2-3 to 2-4, Chapter 3
Income sources, 3-12 to 3-16
Not limited to cash received, 3-2
Omission of amount on tax return, 21-23
Partnerships, 3-14
Personal services, 3-12, 3-15, 3-23
Prizes and awards, 3-19 to 3-20
Property settlements, 3-16 to 3-17
Realization of income doctrine, 3-3 to 3-4
Recovery of capital doctrine, 3-3 to 3-4
Repayment obligation, 3-10
Savings bonds, 3-8 to 3-9, 3-23, 3-24
S corporations, 3-14
S corporation shareholders, 16-15, 16-18, 16-21 to 16-22
Shifting income to relatives, 3-23 to 3-24, 16-24, 16-28
Social Security benefits, 3-21
Sources, 3-12 to 3-16
Taxable income, 3-2, 20-6 to 20-8
Tax planning, 3-22 to 3-26, 4-24 to 4-27
Tax preference items, 11-10
Trusts, 3-14, 20-6 to 20-8
Two-earner marital deduction, 3-21
Unemployment benefits, 3-21 to 3-22
Year of inclusion, 3-4 to 3-12
Gross Income Exclusions, 2-2 to 2-3, Chapter 4
Tax planning, 4-24 to 4-27
Gross Income Test, 2-12, 2-16, 2-32 to 2-33
Personal holding company, 15-13 to 15-16, 15-25
Gross-Up Procedure, 14-24, 18-7
Group-Term Life Insurance, 3-20 to 3-21, 16-22, 19-28 to 19-29
Tax planning, 4-26
Guaranteed Payments, 17-29 to 17-30

# H

Half-Year Convention, 6-25 to 6-26
Hardship Area, *see* Foreign Earned Income
Hazards of Litigation, 21-9 to 21-10
Head of Household, 2-24, 2-34

History of U. S. Taxation, 1-1 to 1-3
Hobby Losses, 5-3, 5-4, 5-10 to 5-13
  S corporations, 16-24
  Tax planning, 5-23 to 5-24
Holding Period
  Capital gains and losses, 10-9 to
     10-13, 10-20
  Carryover of basis, 10-10
  Computation, 10-11
  Gifts, 9-9 to 9-10, 9-11
  Inherited property, 9-11
  Like-kind exchanges, 9-18
  Liquidation of a subsidiary, 14-24
  Nontaxable transactions, 10-11
  Partnership property, 17-12 to 17-13
  Property, 10-11 to 10-13
  Replacement property, 9-23
  Review of rules, 10-10 to 10-11
  Sale of a residence, 9-29
  Section 1231 property, 10-20
  Short sales, 10-11 to 10-13
  Stock dividends, 13-14
  Stock rights, 13-15
  Tax-free exchanges, 10-10
  Wash sales, 9-12
Home Office, 6-50 to 6-51
Homestead Laws, 1-6
H.R. 10 (Keogh) Plans, *see* Keogh Plans
Hybrid Accounting Method, 11-20

# I

Illegal Expenses, Deductibility, 5-8 to
  5-9
Imputed Interest, *See also* Installment
  Method, 11-28 to 11-29
Imputed Interest Rules, 1-29
Incidence of Taxation, 1-5
Incidents of Ownership Test, 18-18 to
  18-19
Income, *see* Gross Income; Taxable
  Income
Income Averaging, 1-26 to 1-27
  Averageable income, 11-4 to 11-5
  Computation procedure, 11-5 to 11-6
  Eligible individual, 11-3 to 11-4
  Reporting procedures, 11-6
  Special provisions, 11-6
  Taxable income, 11-2, 11-5, 11-39
  Tax planning, 11-38 to 11-39
Income from Discharge of Indebtedness,
  *see* Discharge of Indebtedness
Income Interest, 20-2
Income-Producing Property, 3-13, 3-23,
  4-3, 6-10, 6-15, 6-16, 9-3, 9-5, 9-12
  to 9-13, 12-8
Income Realization Doctrine, 3-3 to 3-4

Income in Respect of a Decedent, 20-8
  to 20-9
Income Shifting, 2-30, 3-23 to 3-24,
  4-25, 16-2, 16-24, 16-28, 20-27
Income Sources, 3-12 to 3-16
Income Splitting, 17-33, 18-22 to 18-33
Income Tax Act of 1913, p. 4-3
Income Taxation of Trusts, Estates, and
  Beneficiaries, *see* Beneficiaries;
  Estates—Income Taxation; Trusts
Income Taxes (Federal) 1-13 to 1-14
  Audit, *see* Audit of Returns
  Avoidance, *see* Tax Avoidance
  Computation, 2-18 to 2-20
  Corporate, 1-14, 1-15, 12-17 to 12-22
  Interest and penalties, 1-31 to 1-32
  Overpayment, 21-24 to 21-26
  Penalties, *see* Penalties
  Statute of limitations, *see* Statute of
    Limitations
  Tax rates, 1-30
  Withholding, *see* Withholding Tax
Income Taxes (State and Local), 1-14 to
  1-15
Incomplete Transfers, *see* Revocable
  Transfers; Transfers
Incorporated Pocketbooks, 15-11
Individual Retirement Account (IRA),
  5-2, 6-32, 18-13, 18-14
Individual Rulings, 21-1 to 21-3, 21-34
Inheritances, *See also* Basis; Holding
  Period; Property Acquired from a
  Decedent, 4-3 to 4-4, 4-25
Inheritance Taxes, 1-11, 18-2, 18-26,
  19-21 to 19-22, 19-24
In-Kind Distributions, 14-2 to 14-4,
  14-6 to 14-8, 14-14
  Tax planning, 14-30, 14-32
Installment Method of Accounting,
  1-28
  Dealers in personal property, 11-24 to
    11-30, 11-41
  Disposition of installment notes,
    11-29 to 11-30, 11-41
  Electing out, 11-30 to 11-31
  Gain determination, 11-27 to 11-28
  Gross profit, 11-25 to 11-26
  Imputed interest, 11-28 to 11-29
  Installment sales, 11-26
  Installment Sales Revision Act of
    1980, pp. 11-23, 19-26
  Making the election, 11-24 to 11-25
  Nonelective aspect, 11-26
  Payments received, 11-28
  Property other than inventory, 11-26
  Provisions for installment sales,
    11-23 to 11-24

Installment Method of
    Accounting—Cont'd
  Revocation of the election, 11-31
  Tax planning, 11-41
Installment Obligations, 11-29 to 11-30,
    11-41, 13-11, 13-23, 14-10, 14-14,
    19-26
Installment Purchases, 7-19
Installment Sales Provisions, 10-38,
    11-23 to 11-24
Installment Sales Revision Act, 11-23,
    19-26
Installment Tax Method, 16-29
Insurance Premiums, *see* Group-Term
    Life Insurance; Medical Expenses
Insurance Reimbursement, 7-7 to 7-9
Intangible Assets, *see* Depreciation and
    Amortization and specific items
    (e. g., Goodwill; Patents)
Intangible Drilling Costs, 16-14
  Alternative minimum tax, 11-11
  Minimum tax, 12-18, 12-19
  Partnerships, 17-15
  Recapture possibilities, 10-35 to 10-36
Intangible Property, *see* Property,
    Intangible
Interest Assessments, 21-10, 21-12 to
    21-14, 21-36
  Deficiency assessments, 21-21
  Statute of limitations, 21-23 to 21-24
Interest on Bonds and Notes, 4-18
Interest Exclusion, 4-18 to 4-19
Interest Expense
  Allowed interest expense items, 7-14
    to 7-15
  Classification, 7-16 to 7-17
  Credit cards, 7-15, 7-16, 7-18
  Deductible for adjusted gross income,
    7-16
  Disallowed interest items, 7-14 to
    7-15, 7-17 to 7-18
  Finance charges, 7-15, 7-18
  Installment purchases, 7-19
  Interest deductions, 5-21 to 5-22
  Investment indebtedness, 7-17 to
    7-18
  Itemized deduction, 7-14 to 7-19, 7-33
  Limitations on deductibility, 7-15 to
    7-16, 7-17
  Paid for services, 7-18
  Partnerships, 17-15
  Points, 7-18
  Prepaid interest, see Prepaid Interest
  Tax-exempt securities, 7-17
  Tax planning, 7-33
  Time of deduction, 7-15 to 7-16
  Unpaid interest, 5-18

Interest-Free Loans, 3-22
Interest Income, 20-2
  Alternative minimum tax, 11-10,
    11-11
  Form 1040EZ, 2-21
  Series E and EE bonds, 3-8 to 3-9
  Tax-exempt securities, 20-16, 20-18
  Tax refunds, 21-12 to 21-14
  Unreported, 2-18
Interest on Life Insurance Proceeds,
    4-5, 4-25
Interest Penalties, 6-32
Interest Relating to Tax-Exempt
    Income, 5-20 to 5-22
Interest on State and Local
    Government Obligations, 4-18
*Internal Revenue Bulletins* (I.R.B.),
    22-6, 22-7, 22-12
Internal Revenue Code (I.R.C.), 1-2
  Amendment, 1-19 to 1-20
  Capital asset defined, 10-2 to 10-3
  Citing Code sections, 22-4 to 22-5
  Defined, 1-20
  Format, 22-3 to 22-4
  Interpretation, 22-19 to 22-20
  Origin and current formulation, 22-1
    to 22-2
  Regulations, 22-5 to 22-6, 22-18
  Tax law sources, 22-18
  TEFRA, 22-2
Internal Revenue Service
  Accounting period changes, 11-15
  Administrative feasibility, 1-31 to
    1-32
  Administrative powers, 21-20 to
    21-22
  Agent, 21-7
  Audit of returns, *See also* Audit of
    Returns, 1-32
  Commissioner's Annual Report, 1-4
  Influence, 1-30 to 1-32, 1-34
  Procedures, 21-1 to 21-4
  As protector of the revenue, 1-31
  Rulings, 21-1 to 21-3, 21-34
  Special Agent, 21-7, 21-35
Inter Vivos Transfers, 19-1, 19-7
Inventory Methods, 11-32 to 11-38
  Bulk sale, 14-30, 14-31
  Corporations, 13-12 to 13-13, 15-6 to
    15-8
  Determination of inventory cost,
    11-33 to 11-35
  LIFO, 11-34 to 11-38, 13-23
  Lower of cost or market, 11-34
Inventory Pools, 11-37 to 11-38
Investment Company, 17-7
Investment Income, 11-11

Investment Indebtedness, 1-30, 7-17 to
7-18
Investment Interest, 16-14
Investment Interest Deduction, 7-17 to
7-18
Investment-Related Expenses, 5-4 to 5-5
Investment Tax Credit, *See also*
Recapture of the Investment Tax
Credit, 1-29, 6-22 to 6-23, 6-26 to
6-27, 6-54 to 6-55, 8-29
ACRS, 8-3
Amount of credit, 8-3 to 8-4
At-risk limitation, 8-11 to 8-12
Carrybacks and carryovers, 8-5 to
8-6
Computation, 8-4 to 8-5, 8-8, 8-9 to
8-10, 8-11 to 8-12
Corporations, 12-7
Cost recovery, 8-4 to 8-5
Depreciable property, 13-12
Depreciation, 8-4 to 8-5
Energy credits, 8-21 to 8-22
ERTA, 8-3, 8-8, 8-10 to 8-11
Estates and trusts, 20-15
Limitations, 8-5
Maximum allowable, 8-5
Net operating loss, 6-13
Partnership property, 7-16
Pre-ERTA, 8-8, 8-11 to 8-12
Qualifying property, 8-5, 8-8 to 8-9
Public utilities, 8-10 to 8-11
Purpose, 8-2
Recapture, 10-32
Recapture provisions, 8-6 to 8-8, 8-12,
12-29 to 12-30
Reduced credit, 8-31
Reduced credit election, 8-4 to 8-5
S corporation property, 16-13
S corporations, 16-23, 16-25, 16-28 to
16-29
Special rules and exceptions, 8-10 to
8-11
Tax planning, 8-30 to 8-31
TEFRA, 1-20, 8-4 to 8-5
Timing considerations, 8-30 to 8-31
Unused credits, 8-6 to 8-7
Investment Trusts, *see* Trusts
Involuntary Conversions
Capital gains, 10-19, 17-15
Computation of amount realized, 9-20
to 9-21
Defined, 9-20
Earnings and profits, 13-3 to 13-4
General provisions, 9-19 to 9-20
Nonrecognition of gain, 9-22 to 9-24
Nontaxable exchange treatment, 9-14
Personal residence, 9-24

Involuntary Conversions—Cont'd
Recapture potential under Sections
1245 and 1250, pp. 10-31 to
10-32
Replacement property, 9-21, 9-22,
9-23
Reporting procedures, 9-24 to 9-25
Tax planning, 9-36, 14-32
Time (replacement period) limitation,
9-22
Twelve-month liquidation, 14-13
IRA, *see* Individual Retirement
Accounts
I.R.B., see *Internal Revenue Bulletins*
I.R.C., *see* Internal Revenue Code
(I.R.C.)
IRS, *see* Internal Revenue Service (IRS)
Itemized Deductions, *See also*
Deductions and Losses
Adjusted gross income, 2-4 to 2-5
Alternative minimum tax, 11-10,
11-11, 11-12
Charitable contributions, 7-19 to
7-30, 7-34 to 7-35
Classification of expenses, 7-1 to 7-2
Education expenses, 6-44 to 6-46,
6-56 to 6-57
Employee expenses, 6-31 to 6-36, 6-50
to 6-51
Entertainment expenses, 6-46 to 6-50,
6-57 to 6-58
Excess casualty loss, 5-3
Excess deductions, 2-5, 7-30
Interest, 7-14 to 7-19, 7-33
Medical expenses, 7-2 to 7-9, 7-30 to
7-32
Moving expenses, 6-40 to 6-44, 6-56
Partnerships, 17-16
Taxes, 7-9 to 7-14, 7-32 to 7-33
Tax planning, 2-30 to 2-31, 6-52 to
6-58, 7-30 to 7-35
Transportation and travel expenses,
6-32, 6-36 to 6-40
Versus deductions *for* adjusted gross
income, 5-2, 5-5
Zero bracket amount, 2-5

# J

Jeopardy Assessments, *see* Assessments
of Tax
Job-Seeking expenses, 6-51
Joint Ownership, *See also* Community
Property; Joint Tenancy; Tenancy
in Common; Tenancy by the
Entirety

Joint Ownership—Cont'd
  ERTA, 18-16 to 18-17, 19-9
  Exceptions, 19-8 to 19-9
  Federal estate tax, 18-15 to 18-17,
    19-10, 19-22
  Federal gift tax, 19-8 to 19-10
  General rule, 19-8
  Gifts of jointly owned property, 19-3
  Husband-wife situations, 19-9
  Inheritance tax, 19-22
  S corporation shareholder limitation,
    16-4 to 16-5
Joint Return Test, 2-12, 2-16 to 2-17,
  2-31 to 2-32
Joint Tenancy
  ERTA, 19-9
  Federal gift tax, 19-8 to 19-10
  Gross estate, 18-15, 18-16 to 18-17
  Between persons other than spouses,
    18-16, 19-10
  Right of survivorship, 18-15
Judicial Citations, 22-11 to 22-15
Judicial Interpretations of Tax-Exempt
  Income Deduction, 5-21 to 5-22
Judicial Process, 22-7 to 22-8
Judicial Sources of the Tax Law, 22-7
  to 22-15, 22-16, 22-21

## K

Keogh Plans, 1-24, 1-28, 5-2, 6-32,
  12-35, 18-14, 22-2
Keyman Life Insurance, 15-5
Kickbacks, 1-24, 5-3, 5-7, 5-8

## L

Last In, First Out (LIFO), *see* Inventory
  Methods; LIFO; LIFO Property
Lease Cancellation Payments, 10-9
Legal Expenses, 5-7 to 5-8
Legislative Process of Tax Law, 22-2 to
  22-3
Lessee, *see* Glossary
Lessor, *see* Glossary
Liabilities in Excess of Basis, 12-27 to
  12-28, 13-11, 13-21, 17-9 to 17-10,
  17-35
Life Estate, 18-5, 18-8 to 18-9
Life Insurance, 19-10 to 19-11, 19-22
  Group-term policies, 3-20 to 3-21,
    19-28 to 19-29
  Incidents of ownership test, 18-18 to
    18-19

Life Insurance Proceeds
  Gross estate, 18-17 to 18-19
  Interest on life insurance proceeds,
    4-5, 4-25
  Payable to the estate, 18-18
  Tax planning, 4-25
Life Tenant, 18-5, 20-2
Lifetime Transfers, 18-7, 18-8 to 18-11,
  19-1, 19-7, 19-21, 19-25 to 19-30
LIFO, *See also* Inventory Methods;
  LIFO Property, 11-34 to 11-38,
  14-2, 14-6, 14-8, 14-10, 14-24
  Disadvantages, 11-42
  ERTA, 11-36
  Inventory pools, 11-37 to 11-38
  Simplified LIFO, 11-36 to 11-37
  Single pool LIFO, 11-37 to 11-38
  Small business tax benefits, 1-23
  Tax consequences, 13-23
  Tax planning, 11-41 to 11-42
LIFO Property, 13-10 to 13-11, 13-21,
  14-10
Like-Kind Exchanges, 9-14, 10-31,
  12-26
  Basis of property received, 9-16, 9-17
    to 9-19
  Boot, 9-16 to 9-17, 9-18
  Defined, 9-15
  Holding period, 9-18
  Investment tax credit, 8-7, 8-9 to 8-10
  Nontaxability, 1-26
  Qualification, 9-16
  Tax planning, 9-36
Limitations on Charitable
  Contributions, 7-21 to 7-27, 7-35,
  12-12 to 12-13
Liquidating Trusts, *see* Trusts
Liquidation, *see* Complete Liquidations;
  Partial Liquidations
Liquidation of a Corporation, *see*
  Corporations
Liquidation Expenses, 14-12 to 14-13
Liquidation Property, 14-15, 14-18 to
  14-20, 14-21 to 14-24
Liquidation of a Subsidiary, 14-20
  Basis of property received by parent
    corporation—Section 334(b)(1),
    pp. 14-21 to 14-24
  Tax planning, 14-33 to 14-34
Litigation, 3-11, 6-33
Loan Origination Fees, *see* Points
Loans Between Related Parties, 6-7,
  6-52, 7-15, 19-7
Lobbying Expenditures, 5-9
Long-Term Capital Gains, 1-28, 6-32
  Corporations, 12-8 to 12-9

Long-Term Capital Gains—Cont'd
Lump-sum distributions, 10-4
S corporation tax treatment, 16-20 to
16-22, 16-25, 16-29
Long-Term Capital Loss, 10-16
Long-Term Contracts, 11-21 to 11-23
Loopholes, 1-31, 4-18
Losses, *See also* Gains and Losses and
specific items (e.g., Capital Losses,
Casualty and Theft Losses), 5-15
Losses, Estates and Trusts, 18-21, 20-11
to 20-12, 20-24
Losses Between Related Parties, 5-17 to
5-18
Losses on Stock Ownership, 6-7 to 6-8
Lower of Cost or Market, *see* Inventory
Methods
Low-Income Housing, 8-9, 10-34 to
10-35
Lump-Sum Distributions, 4-5, 4-6, 10-4

# M

Machine Hours Depreciation, 6-17
Marital Deduction, *See also* Gift Tax
(Federal)
Allowed for property passing through
estate to spouse, 18-23 to 18-24
Deferral approach, 18-32
Disparity between common-law and
community property states, 18-22
to 18-23
Equalization approach, 18-30 to
18-31, 19-13
ERTA, 18-23, 18-31, 19-9
Estate tax, 18-17
Gift tax, 1-12, 18-17, 19-12 to 19-13
In perspective, 18-30 to 18-31
Purpose of enactment, 18-22 to 18-23
Qualifying property, 18-2
Revenue Act of 1948, p. 18-22
Tax planning, 18-30 to 18-32
Marriage Penalty, 2-24 to 2-26
Mass Tax, 1-3
Matching Concept, 6-19
Meals and Lodging, 4-13 to 4-14, 4-26
to 4-27, 6-43, 7-3, 7-4, 7-23 to 7-24,
16-22
Measuring Partnership Income, 17-14
to 17-17
Medical Expenses, 2-33 to 2-34, 5-5
Capital expenditures, 7-3 to 7-4
Child and dependent care expenses,
8-33 to 8-34

Medical Expenses—Cont'd
General requirements, 7-2 to 7-3
Insurance premiums, 7-4 to 7-5
Medicine and drugs, 7-6 to 7-7, 7-30
to 7-32
Nursing homes, 7-2 to 7-3, 7-32
Reimbursements, 7-7 to 7-9
Special schools, 7-3
Summary and comparison of rules,
7-7
Tax planning, 7-30 to 7-32
TEFRA, 7-2
Transportation expenses, 7-4
Medical Reimbursement Plans, 4-12,
4-15
Medicine and Drugs, *see* Medical
Expenses
Memorandum Decisions, 22-11 to 22-13
Mineral, Oil, and Gas Royalties, 15-13,
15-15
Minimum Tax, 1-29, 8-5, 11-8, 12-18,
12-19, 15-3, 17-6, 20-5
Minimum Tax on Tax Preferences, *See
also* Alternative Minimum Tax,
11-8, 11-9, 11-10
Mining Exploration Expenditures,
16-14
Minors
Estate tax, 18-10 to 18-11
Federal gift tax, 19-14 to 19-15
S corporation stock, 16-6
Mitigation of Annual Accounting Period
Concept, 1-26 to 1-29
Mortgages
Estate tax, 18-20
Interest, 7-15, 7-16
Moving Expenses, 5-2
Allowed expenses, 6-40
Cash basis taxpayer, 6-42
Classification, 6-42 to 6-44
Deductible *for* adjusted gross income,
6-32
Direct expenses, 6-42 to 6-43
Distance test, 6-41
Indirect expenses, 6-43 to 6-44, 6-56
Tax planning, 6-56
Time test, 6-41 to 6-42
When deductible, 6-42
Multiple Assets, 9-7
Multiple Support Agreement, *see*
Personal and Dependency
Exemptions
Multiple Taxation, *See also* Income in
Respect of a Decedent, 1-15, 1-25,
18-27
Multiple Trusts, 20-24 to 20-25

# N

National Sales Tax, 1-12
Negative Income Tax, 8-23
Negligence Penalty, 1-31, 1-32, 21-16, 21-29
Net Capital Gains and Losses
Carryovers, 10-16, 10-17
Computation, 10-13 to 10-15
Corporations, 12-9, 12-10
Deductibility, 10-15 to 10-16
Defined, 10-14
Effective rate, 10-14 to 10-15
Limitation, 10-16
Planning, 10-10
Net Interest Exclusion, 4-19
Net Operating Losses (NOL)
Alternative minimum tax, 11-9 to 11-10
Carryback and carryover periods, 6-13 to 6-14
Computation of net operating loss, 6-14
Corporations, 12-13 to 12-14
Partnerships, 17-16
Penalty tax, 15-10
Personal holding company tax, 15-17
Refund claims, 21-25 to 21-26
S corporations, 16-18 to 16-20, 16-24, 16-25 to 16-26
Statute of limitations, 21-25 to 21-26
Tax planning, 6-55, 16-19 to 16-20
Trusts and estates, 20-11, 20-24
Net Worth Method, *see* Glossary
Ninety-Day Letter, 21-7, 21-9, 21-10, 21-21
NOL, *see* Net Operating Losses
Nonacquiescence (Tax Court decisions), *See also* Citations; Tax Court Decisions, 22-12, 22-21
Nonbusiness Bad Debts, *See also* Bad Debts, 6-4 to 6-5, 10-4
Nonbusiness Expenses, 17-15
Nonbusiness Income or Losses, 5-3, 16-13
Noncommercial Contracts, 18-11
Noncompliance with Tax Laws, 1-32
Noncorporate Shareholders, 13-23
Noncorporate Taxpayer Capital Gains and Losses, 10-13 to 10-17
Noncustodial Parent, 2-15, 2-33
Non-Income Producing Property, 19-28 to 19-29
Nonliquidating Distributions of Partnership Property, 17-31 to 17-32

Nonqualifying Dividends, 4-20
Nonrecourse Debt, 8-11
Nonrecognition of Gains and Losses, 9-5 to 9-6, 9-11 to 9-12, 9-22 to 9-24, 9-27 to 9-28, 12-23 to 12-24, 12-26, 12-38, 17-5 to 17-7
Nonresident Alien Prohibition, 16-15, 16-27
Nonstatutory Fringe Benefits, 4-27
Nonsudden Events, 6-8
Nontaxable Exchanges, 9-13 to 9-15, 14-26, 14-27 to 14-28
Nontaxable Transactions, 12-25 to 12-28
Not Essentially Equivalent to a Dividend Stock Redemption, 13-17 to 13-19
Nursing Home Expenses, 7-2 to 7-3, 7-32

# O

Occupational Taxes, 1-19
Offers in Compromise, 21-22
Office Audit, 21-6
Office in the Home, 6-50 to 6-51
One-Month Liquidations, 14-2, 14-3, 14-4, 14-5, 14-21
Basis of Property received, 14-15, 14-18 to 14-20
Computation of gain, 14-17 to 14-18
Effect on the distributing corporation, 14-20
Effect on the shareholder, 14-15 to 14-16
Effects on shareholder gain recognition, 14-15 to 14-20, 14-33 to 14-34
Making the election, 14-16 to 14-17
One-month requirement, 14-16 to 14-17
Qualifying electing shareholders, 14-16
Tax planning, 14-33 to 14-34
Options
Exercise by grantee, 10-7
Loss from failure to exercise, 10-6 to 10-7
Ordinary Gross Income (OGI) of Personal Holding Company, 15-13, 15-15
Ordinary Income Property, 7-21 to 7-22, 12-11 to 12-12
Ordinary and Necessary Expenses, 4-6, 5-1 to 5-2, 5-5 to 5-6, 5-7, 5-8, 5-14, 6-33, 7-19, 12-7, 20-9 to 20-11, 22-16, 22-20

Organizational Expenditures, 12-15 to 12-17
Out-of-the-Home Expenses, 8-27
Outside Salesperson
 Defined, 6-33 to 6-34
 Expenses, 6-32, 6-50
 Special treatment, 6-33 to 6-34
Overstatements of Deposits, 21-20

# P

Parent Corporations, 14-21 to 14-24
Partial Liquidations, *See also* Distributions In Kind, 13-22
Partners, 17-4
Partnership Agreements, 17-35
Partnership Distributions, 17-30 to 17-32
Partnerships, Chapter 17
 Accounting periods, 11-14
 Association status test, 12-5 to 12-6
 Basis of interest, 17-1 to 17-12
 Capital interest, 17-5 to 17-6
 Conduit (or aggregate) concept, 17-2 to 17-3, 17-14, 17-16
 Contributions, 17-5 to 17-7
 Decision to use partnership form, 17-32 to 17-34
 Defined, 17-3 to 17-4
 Distinguished from other business forms, 12-1 to 12-3, 17-33 to 17-34
 Entity concept, 17-2 to 17-3
 Formation, 17-4 to 17-13, 17-34 to 17-35
 Fringe benefits, rules applying to shareholders, 16-22 to 16-23
 Income, 3-14, 17-17 to 17-22, 17-24, 17-25
 Losses, 17-22 to 17-24
 Measuring partnership income, 17-14 to 17-17
 Nature of partnership taxation, 17-2 to 17-3
 Operation of partnership, 17-13 to 17-30, 17-34 to 17-35
 Partnership interest, 17-5 to 17-6
 Profits interests, 17-6
 Reporting partnership income, 17-14 to 17-17
 Revenue Act of 1978, p. 17-24
 Taxable year, 17-24 to 17-27, 17-33
 Tax-free exchanges, 17-6 to 17-7
 Tax planning, 17-32 to 17-35
 Tax treatment versus corporation tax treatment, 1-25

Partnerships—Cont'd
 Termination, 17-26 to 17-27
 Transactions between partner and partnership, 17-27 to 17-30
Partnership Taxation
 Basis—contributed property subject to liability, 17-12 to 17-13
 Deductions not allowed partnerships, 17-16
 Exclusion from taxation, 17-4
 Guaranteed payments, 17-29 to 17-30
 Limitation on losses deductible, 17-22 to 17-24
 Nature of taxation, 17-2 to 17-3
 Partnership's basis in contributed property, 17-12 to 17-13
 Partnership's tax year, 17-24 to 17-27, 17-33
 Penalty for failure to file, 17-14
 Reportable income, 17-15
 Reporting entity, 17-14 to 17-17
 Special allocation of tax items, 17-17 to 17-22, 17-35
 Taxable income, 17-14, 17-15, 17-16
 Tax return, 17-14, 17-18 to 17-20
Passing Concept, *See also* Marital Deduction, 18-23 to 18-24
Passive Income, *See also* Personal Holding Company, 1-15
Passive Investment Income, *See also* S Corporations; Glossary, 16-7, 16-27
 Capital gain, 16-21
 Compared with personal holding company income, 16-11
 Excess passive investment income, 16-10
 Limitations, 16-9
 Penalty tax, 16-9 to 16-10
 Rents, 16-11
 Sale of securities, 16-11
 S corporations, 16-21
 Taxable income, 16-10
 Types of income, 16-11
Patents, 1-21, 5-16, 10-7 to 10-8, 10-26, 12-38 to 12-39
Pay-As-You-Go Procedures, 1-3, 1-4, 1-13, 1-31 to 1-32, 2-18, 21-18
Payments in Violation of Public Policy, 5-7
Penalties, 1-24, 5-3, 5-7 to 5-8
 ERTA, 21-20
 Estate tax, 18-30
 Extension of time to file, 2-22
 Failure to file and deliver information returns, 21-18 to 21-19

Penalties—Cont'd
Failure to file or pay, 1-31, 1-32, 2-22, 17-14, 19-20, 21-14 to 21-16, 21-36 to 21-37
Failure to make deposits of taxes, 21-20
Failure to make estimated tax payments, 21-17 to 21-18, 21-36 to 21-37
False information on withholding, 1-31 to 1-32, 21-18
Fraud, 1-31, 21-16 to 21-17
Maximum penalty, 21-14
Minimum penalty, 21-15
Negligence penalty, 1-31, 1-32, 21-16, 21-29
Overstatements of deposits, 21-20
Passive investment income penalty tax, 16-9 to 16-10
Tax planning, 21-36 to 21-37
Tax practitioner, 21-27 to 21-29
Tax Reform Act of 1976, pp. 21-28 to 21-29
Treasury Regulations, 22-20
Underpayment by corporations, 12-19 to 12-20
Underpayment of estimated tax, 21-12, 21-18
Penalty Tax, *See also* Accumulated Earnings Tax; Personal Holding Company Tax, 15-9 to 15-11
Penalty Tax on Unreasonable Accumulations, 15-2 to 15-11, 15-24
Pension Plans, *see* Qualified Pension and Profit Sharing Plans
Percentage of Completion Method of Accounting, 11-22 to 11-23
Percentage Depletion, 6-29 to 6-31, 6-55
Perquisites, *see* Employee Fringe Benefits
Personal and Dependency Exemptions
Blindness, 2-12, 2-21
Citizenship or residency test, 2-12, 2-17
Dependency exemption tests, 2-12 to 2-17, 2-31 to 2-34
Determination of marital status, 2-11
Exceptions and special rules, 2-14 to 2-15
Gross income test, 2-12, 2-16, 2-32 to 2-33
Joint return test, 2-12, 2-16 to 2-17, 2-31 to 2-32
For medical expense purposes, 2-12, 2-33 to 2-34
Multiple support agreement, 2-14, 2-33 to 2-34

Personal and Dependency Exemptions—Cont'd
Partnerships, 17-16
Relationship test, 2-12, 2-15 to 2-16, 2-33 to 2-34
65 or over, 2-12, 2-21
Support requirement, 2-12 to 2-15, 2-33
Tax planning, 2-31 to 2-34
Personal Expenditures
Disallowance, 5-14 to 5-15
Tax planning, 5-22
Personal Holding Company, *See also* Personal Holding Company Tax—Section 545
Adjusted ordinary gross income (AOGI), 15-12 to 15-16, 15-25, 15-26
Defined, 15-12 to 15-16
Excluded corporations, 15-11 to 15-12
Mineral, oil, and gas royalties, 15-13, 15-15
Ordinary gross income (OGI), 15-13, 15-15
Personal holding company income, 15-16 to 15-17
Planning model, 15-18 to 15-19
Rental income, 15-12, 15-13, 15-14 to 15-15, 15-26
Rent exclusion test, 15-20
Status, 15-11, 15-16, 15-25 to 15-27
Stock ownership test, 15-12 to 15-13, 15-24, 15-25
Tax planning, 15-24 to 15-27
Personal Holding Company Income, 16-11
Personal Holding Company Tax—Section 545, pp. 15-11 to 15-20
Calculation, 15-16 to 15-20
Dividends paid deduction, 15-17 to 15-18, 15-23
Tax planning, 15-24 to 15-27
Undistributed personal holding company income (UPHC income), 15-16 to 15-17, 15-26 to 15-27
Personal Injury, 4-8 to 4-10, 4-26
Personal Property, *see* Personalty; Glossary
Personal Residence, *see* Involuntary Conversions; Sale of Principal Residence—Section 121; Sale of Principal Residence—Section 1034
Personal Services as Gross Income, 3-12, 3-15, 3-23
Personalty
ACRS, 6-20 to 6-23
Ad valorem taxes, 1-7 to 1-8

Personalty—Cont'd
  Charitable deduction, 7-23
  Recovery periods and methods, 6-20
    to 6-23
Personal Use Assets, 9-5 to 9-6, 9-12 to
    9-13, 10-3, 10-19 to 10-20
Personal Use Taxes, 7-12
Points, 7-15, 7-16, 7-18, 7-33
Political Considerations of the Tax Law,
    1-29 to 1-30, 1-34
Political Contributions, 5-9, 8-28 to 8-29
Postponed Compensation, 5-22
Preferential Tax Treatment, 1-27, 1-29
    to 1-30, 2-28
Prepaid Expenses, 11-18 to 11-19
Prepaid Income, 1-31, 3-3, 3-10 to 3-11,
    11-19
Prepaid Interest, 7-16, 7-33, 11-18 to
    11-19
Preparation of Returns, see Returns;
    Statements on Responsibilities in
    Tax Practice; Tax Return Preparers
Prepayment of Tax, see Estimated Tax
Previously Taxed Income (PTI), 16-15,
    16-28
Principal Exclusions from Gross
    Income, 4-2 to 4-3
Principal Residence, 9-25 to 9-33, 9-36
    to 9-38
Prizes and Awards, 3-19 to 3-20
Probate Estate, 18-4, 18-16
Professional Associations, 17-3 to 17-4
Profitability Tests, 5-10
Profits Interest in Partnership, 17-6
Progressive Tax Rate, 1-4 to 1-5
Property
  Abandonment, 8-7
  Adjusted basis, 2-26, 3-3, 9-3
  Alternative minimum tax, 11-11
  Assessed value, 1-7, 1-8
  Business property as capital asset,
    10-18 to 10-19
  As capital asset, 10-2 to 10-3
  Capital gains and losses, 7-22 to 7-23,
    10-2 to 10-3, 10-4
  Charitable contributions, see Property
    as Charitable Contributions
  Choice of property for tax purposes,
    19-29 to 19-30
  Classification by recovery period, 6-20
    to 6-21
  Community property, see Community
    Property
  Condemned, 9-20 to 9-22
  Conversion, 9-12 to 9-13
  Corporate contributions, 12-11 to
    12-12

Property—Cont'd
  Corporate liquidations, 14-10, 14-21
    to 14-24
  Corporate-owned, 13-9
  Dealers in personal property, 11-24 to
    11-30, 11-41
  Decedent, 9-10 to 9-11, 18-4 to 18-5,
    18-6, 19-23
  Deferred payment contract, 11-28 to
    18-29
  Defined under Section 337, p. 14-10
  Defined under Section 1231, pp. 10-19
    to 10-20
  Depreciable, 10-32 to 10-33, 13-12,
    13-23, 17-13, 17-15, 17-21, 17-35
  Depreciation qualification, 6-16
  Depreciation recapture, 20-10 to
    20-11
  Disclaimers, 18-24
  Dividends, see Property Dividends
  Energy tax credit, 8-20 to 8-22
  Estate, 18-20, 18-21
  Exchange of stock, 9-14, 9-33 to 9-34
  Exclusions, 10-20
  Fair market value, 9-3, 12-11, 12-12,
    18-20, 18-21
  Gift, 9-7 to 9-8, 9-35, 18-27, 19-25 to
    19-30, 20-6 to 20-7
  Gross estate, 18-4 to 18-5, 18-6
  Gross income, 3-13 to 3-14
  Holding period, 10-20
  Imputed interest on sale, 11-28 to
    11-29
  Inclusions, 10-19 to 10-20
  Income-producing, 3-13, 3-23, 4-3,
    6-10, 6-15, 6-16, 9-3, 9-5, 9-12 to
    9-13, 12-8
  Intangible, 6-14, 6-15, 6-16, 8-8, 17-5
  Investment tax credit, 8-4 to 8-5, 8-6
    to 8-12, 8-30 to 8-31, 16-25
  Jurisdiction of decedent's property,
    19-23
  Liability in excess of basis, 13-11,
    13-21, 17-9 to 17-10, 17-35
  LIFO, 13-10 to 13-11, 13-21, 14-10
  LIFO inventory, 14-10
  Like-kind exchanges, 9-15 to 9-16,
    9-17 to 9-19, 9-21
  Marital deduction, 18-23 to 18-24
  Mortgaged, 12-26
  Noncash, 14-6
  Non-income producing, 19-28 to 19-29
  Ordinary income, 12-11 to 12-12
  Other than inventory, 11-26
  Partnership contributions, 17-5 to
    17-7, 17-12 to 17-13, 17-21, 17-35
  Personalty, 10-26

Property—Cont'd
Personal use, 9-12 to 9-13, 9-25
Pre-ERTA, 6-17 to 6-19
Real, 9-34, 17-15
Recapture, 10-26, 13-12
Received in liquidation, 14-15, 14-18
    to 14-20, 14-21 to 14-24
Recovery rates, 6-22
Rental to shareholders, 13-9
Replacement, 9-21, 9-22, 9-23
Sale or other disposition, 9-2
Sale to shareholders, 13-9
S corporations, 16-13, 16-25
Separate, 3-15, 3-25
Subject to a liability, 13-11, 13-21,
    17-8 to 17-12, 17-35
Tangible, 6-14, 6-16, 6-17, 6-18 to
    6-19, 6-20, 6-26, 7-23, 8-8, 8-9,
    12-12, 17-5, 19-23
Tax consequences to donor and donee,
    19-25 to 19-28
Tax planning, 9-35 to 9-36, 19-25 to
    19-30
Transfer, 8-7, 8-30 to 8-31
Trust, 20-7
Property Acquired from a Decedent
Basis, 9-10 to 9-11
General rule, 9-10
Holding period, 9-11
Survivor's share of property, 9-10 to
    9-11
Property as Charitable Contribution,
    7-21 to 7-30, 12-11 to 12-12
Determining deduction, 7-28 to 7-29
Ordinary income property, 7-21 to
    7-22
Tax planning, 7-34 to 7-35
Valuation, 7-21
Property Distributions, 13-23 to 13-24,
    16-28
S corporations, 16-15 to 16-17
Tax effect on the distributing
    corporation, 13-10 to 13-12
Property Dividends, 13-6 to 13-13
Constructive dividends, 13-8 to 13-10
Corporate tax consequences, 13-10 to
    13-13
Depreciable property, 13-12
Earnings and profits, 13-12 to 13-13
Installment obligations, See also
    Installment Obligations, 13-11
Liability in excess of basis, 13-11
LIFO property, 13-10 to 13-11
Property Received by Parent
    Corporation, 14-21 to 14-24
Property Settlements, 3-16 to 3-17,
    19-11

Property Subject to a Liability in
    Excess of Basis, 13-11, 13-21, 17-9
    to 17-10, 17-35
Property Taxes, 1-5
Ad valorem, 1-6 to 1-8
Apportionment of real estate taxes,
    7-11 to 7-12
Assessing value, 1-7, 1-8
Deductibility, 7-10
Estates, 18-19, 20-3 to 20-6
Personalty, 1-7 to 1-8
Realty, 1-6 to 1-7
Trusts, 20-3 to 20-6
Property Transactions, See also
    Involuntary Conversions; Like-Kind
    Exchanges
Basis considerations, 9-6 to 9-13
Capital gains and losses, Chapter 10
Exchange of insurance policies, 9-33
Exchange of stock for property, 9-14,
    9-33
Exchange of stock for stock, 9-14,
    9-33 to 9-34
Gains and losses, 2-26 to 2-30, 9-1 to
    9-6, 12-6 to 12-7
Nonrecognition provisions, 9-33 to
    9-34
Nontaxable exchanges, 9-13 to 9-15,
    14-28
Between partner and partnership,
    16-27 to 16-30
Recapture provisions, Chapter 10
Section 1231, Chapter 10
Tax planning, 9-35 to 9-38
Property Transfers, 12-22 to 12-28,
    12-36 to 12-40, 17-5, 17-7, 19-1,
    19-8, 19-11, 21-21
Tax planning, 12-36 to 12-40, 19-25
    to 19-30
Proportional Tax Rate, 1-4, 1-5
Public Charities, see Charitable
    Contributions
Public Policy Limitation, 5-7 to 5-9
Public Utilities
ESOPs, 8-19
Investment tax credit, 8-10 to 8-11
Punitive Damages, 4-9, 4-26

## Q

Qualified Organizations, see Charitable
    Contributions
Qualified Pension and Profit Sharing
    Plans
Annuities, 3-24 to 3-25, 18-11 to
    18-15

Qualified Pension and Profit Sharing Plans—Cont'd
  Employee stock ownership plan (ESOP), 8-18 to 8-19
  Long-term capital gains, 10-4
  Lump-sum distributions, 4-6, 10-4
  Pension plans, 6-32
Qualifying Electing Shareholders, 14-16
Qualifying Transfers, 18-21 to 18-22
Quarterly Tax Return, 1-17
Quiet Business Meal Rule, 6-47 to 6-48

# R

Railroad Retirement Benefits, 8-25
Realization of Income Doctrine, 3-3 to 3-4
Realized Amount, *see* Amount Realized
Realized Gain or Loss
  Adjusted basis, 9-3
  Amount realized, 9-2 to 9-3
  Capital additions, 9-3
  Capital recovery, 9-3 to 9-4
  Condemned property, 9-22
  Like-kind exchanges, 9-16 to 9-17
  Nonrecognition, 9-11 to 9-12
  Sale of a residence, 9-25, 9-30
Realized Gross Profit Computation, 11-25 to 11-26
Real Property
  ACRS rules for recapture, 10-29 to 10-30
  Depreciable, 10-26, 10-27
  Nonresidential, 10-28 to 10-29, 10-30, 10-41
  Reacquisitions, 9-14, 9-34
Realty
  ACRS, 6-24 to 6-25
  Ad valorem tax, 1-6 to 1-7
  Recovery periods and methods, 6-24 to 6-25
Reasonable Compensation, 16-24, 16-28
Reasonable Needs of the Business, *See also* Glossary, 15-3, 15-4 to 15-9, 15-11, 15-20 to 15-22
Reasonableness Requirement, 5-6, 22-21 to 22-22
  Unreasonable compensation, 5-22, 13-10, 13-27, 22-24
Recapture
  ACRS, 10-25, 10-29 to 10-30, 10-41 to 10-42, 12-28
  Avoiding recapture, 10-41 to 10-42
  Computation, 10-28 to 10-29
  Controlled corporations, 12-28 to 12-30
  Depreciation, 12-28, 13-23, 20-10 to 20-11

Recapture—Cont'd
  Estates and trusts, 20-15
  Farm recapture, 10-35
  Intangible drilling costs, 10-35 to 10-36
  Investment tax credit, *see* Recapture of Investment Tax Credit
  Liquidation of a subsidiary, 14-23 to 14-24
  Postponing recapture, 10-41
  Sales between related parties, 10-32 to 10-33
  Rental housing, 10-33 to 10-35
  S corporations, 16-23
  Section 1245, pp. 10-25 to 10-27, 10-31 to 10-32, 13-21
  Section 1250, pp. 10-27 to 10-29, 10-31 to 10-32, 13-21
  Section 1251, p. 10-35
  Section 1252, pp. 10-35, 13-21
  Shifting recapture, 10-41
  Special provisions, 10-32 to 10-36
  Tax planning, 14-31
  Timing, 10-40 to 10-41
  Twelve-month liquidation, 14-11
Recapture of Investment Tax Credit
  ACRS, 13-12
  Basis reduction, 10-32
  Controlled corporations, 12-29 to 12-30
  Depreciable property, 13-12
  ERTA, 12-30
  Liquidation of a subsidiary, 14-23 to 14-24
  Pre-ERTA rules, 8-8, 8-12
  Property distributions, 13-24
  Qualifying property, 8-5, 8-6 to 8-12
  S corporations, 16-23
Recapture Potential
  Section 1245, pp. 10-26 to 10-27
  Section 1250, pp. 10-27 to 10-28
  Transfers to controlled corporations, 12-28
Recognized Gain or Loss, 9-4 to 9-5
Reconciliation of Taxable and Financial Net Income—Corporations, 12-21 to 12-22
Recordkeeping Requirements, 6-34 to 6-35, 6-49, 6-57
Recovery of Bad Debts, 17-15
Recovery of Capital Doctrine, 3-3 to 3-4, 3-15, 3-18 to 3-19
Recovery Periods and Methods, 17-13, 17-35
Recovery Rates, 6-22
Redemptions of Stock, *see* Stock Redemptions
Reduced Investment Credit, 8-31
Reduction in Basis, 8-4 to 8-5

Reduction of Taxes, 22-23
Refund Claims, 3-6
Refunds of Tax, 2-17, 2-18 to 2-20,
    20-12 to 20-14, 21-5, 21-24 to 21-26
Regular Corporations, 12-2
Regular Decisions, *See also* Citations,
    22-11 to 22-13
Regular Minimum Tax, *see* Minimum
    Tax on Tax Preferences
Regulations, *see* Treasury Department
    Regulations
Rehabilitation Expenditures, Tax
    Credit, 8-14 to 8-15
Rehabilitation Expenditures for
    Low-Income Housing, 8-9, 10-34 to
    10-35
Reimbursements
    Allocation problems, 6-35 to 6-36
    Business expenses, 6-50, 6-56
    Casualty losses, 6-9
    Deductibility, 6-32, 6-56
    Educational expenses, 4-7, 4-8
    Medical expenses, 7-7 to 7-9
    Recordkeeping requirements, 6-34 to
        6-35
    Reporting requirement, 6-51
Related-Party Transactions
    Constructive ownership, 5-18 to 5-19
    Loans, 6-7, 6-52, 7-15, 19-7
    Losses, 5-17 to 5-18, 17-28, 17-35
    Sale of depreciable property, 10-32 to
        10-33
    Unpaid expenses and interest, 5-18
Related Taxpayers, 5-22 to 5-23, 20-12
Remainder Interest in Trust, 18-5, 20-2
Rental Housing, 10-33 to 10-35
Rental Income
    Passive investment income, 16-11
    Personal holding company, 15-12,
        15-13, 15-14 to 15-15, 15-26
    Tax planning, 15-26
Rent Exclusion Test, 15-20
Rents and Royalties, 5-4, 6-32, 6-33,
    7-16, 7-18
Reorganizations, *See also* Controlled
    Corporations, 14-26 to 14-30
Replacement Property, 9-21, 9-22, 9-23
Reporting Partnership Income, 17-14 to
    17-17
Reporting Procedures
    Capital gains and losses, 10-17
    Corporate accumulations, 15-24 to
        15-25
    Income averaging, 11-6
    Involuntary conversions, 9-24 to 9-25
    Sale of a residence, 9-30 to 9-31

Repossessions, *see* Bad Debts;
    Installment Method
Research, *see* Tax Research
Research and Development
    Expenditures, 1-21
Research and Experimental
    Expenditures, 6-11 to 6-12
    Alternative minimum tax, 11-11
    ERTA, 8-18, 8-33
    Limitations, 8-17
    New provisions, 8-33
    Priority of credits, 8-30
    Qualified expenditures, 8-16, 8-17,
        8-18
    Tax credit, 8-15 to 8-18, 8-32 to 8-33
    Tax planning, 8-32 to 8-33
Reserve Additions, 6-3 to 6-4
Reserve for Bad Debts, *See also* Bad
    Debts, 6-3, 6-4
Residence, *see* Sale of Principal
    Residence—Section 121; Sale of
    Principal Residence—Section 1034
Residential Energy Tax Credits, 8-20 to
    8-21
Residential Rental Housing, 10-33 to
    10-34
Retained Life Estate, 18-8 to 18-9,
    18-12
Retirement of Corporate Obligations,
    10-6
Retirement Plans, *See also* Qualified
    Pension and Profit Sharing Plans,
    16-22 to 16-23
Returns
    Audits, 21-4 to 21-6
    Estate tax (death tax), 18-29 to 18-30
    Preparation, 21-27 to 21-34
    Quarterly, 1-17
Revenue Act of 1913, p. 1-2
Revenue Act of 1948, pp. 1-30, 18-22,
    19-18
Revenue Act of 1978
    At-risk limitations, 17-24
    Corporate accumulations, 15-6
    Earned income credit, 8-22
    Investment tax credit, 1-20
    Involuntary conversions, 14-13
    Partnership, 17-24
    Rental income, 5-13
    State and local taxes, 7-9
    Tax rate reduction, 1-20 to 1-21
Revenue Acts, 1-2
Revenue Agent's Report (RAR), 21-7,
    21-8, 21-35
Revenue Procedure (Rev.Proc.), 3-11,
    3-12, 3-23, 21-3

Revenue Rulings (Rev.Rul.), 21-2, 21-34
Revenue Rulings and Revenue
    Procedures, 22-6 to 22-7, 22-20 to
    22-21
Revenue Sources, 1-3, 1-6, 1-11
Revesionary Interest in Trusts, 20-2
Revocable Transfers, 18-9 to 18-11
Ruling Requests, 21-3
Rulings, 21-1 to 21-3, 21-34

# S

Sale or Exchange of Capital Assets,
    17-15
    Franchises, 10-8 to 10-9
    Lease cancellation payments, 10-9
    Options, 10-6 to 10-7
    Patents, 10-7 to 10-8
    Retirement of corporate obligations,
        10-6
    Worthless securities, 10-5
Sale of Principal Residence—Section
    121, pp. 9-31 to 9-33
    Computation procedure, 9-32 to 9-33
    Exclusion for age 55 or over
        taxpayer, 9-31, 9-37
    Relationship to other provisions, 9-32
    Requirements, 9-31 to 9-32
    Tax planning, 9-37 to 9-38
Sale of Principal Residence—Section
    1034, pp. 9-25 to 9-31
    Adjusted sales price, 9-29
    Basis of new residence, 9-29 to 9-30
    Capital improvements, 9-28 to 9-29
    Fixing-up expenses, 9-27 to 9-28,
        9-29, 9-30
    Multiple sales during two-year
        period, 9-26
    Nonrecognition of gain, 9-27 to 9-28
    Principal residence defined, 9-27
    Principal residence requirement, 9-36
        to 9-37
    Replacement period, 9-25 to 9-27
    Reporting procedures, 9-30 to 9-31
    Tax planning, 9-36 to 9-37
Sales by a Liquidating Corporation,
    14-8 to 14-14
Sales of Securities, 9-34, 16-11
Sales Tax, *see* General Sales Tax
Salvage Value, *See also* Depreciation
    and Amortization, 9-4
Savings Bonds, 3-8 to 3-9, 3-23, 3-24
Schedules M-1 and M-2, *See also*
    Reconciliation of Taxable and
    Financial Income—Corporations,
    12-21 to 12-22

Scholarships and Fellowships, 4-6 to 4-8
S Corporations
    Avoidance of corporate income tax,
        1-23
    Capital losses, 16-20 to 16-22, 16-25
    Charitable contributions, 16-13
    Class of stock allowed, 16-5
    Community property, 16-5 to 16-6
    Comparison with partnerships, 17-4
    Conduit concept, *see* Conduit Concept
    Deductions allowed, 16-13
    Disqualification, 16-7, 16-26 to 16-27
    Foreign income, 16-13
    Foreign taxes, 16-24
    Fringe benefits, 16-22 to 16-23, 16-27
    In general, 16-1 to 16-3
    Hobby loss, 5-10
    Ineligible corporation limitation, 16-4
    Installment tax method, 16-29
    Investment tax credit, 16-23, 16-25,
        16-28 to 16-29
    Loans, 16-20, 16-28
    Long-term capital gains, 16-20 to
        16-22, 16-25, 16-29
    Loss of election, 16-7 to 16-12, 16-25,
        16-26
    Making the election, 16-5 to 16-7,
        16-26
    Minor shareholders, 16-6
    Net operating losses, 16-18 to 16-20,
        16-24, 16-25 to 16-26
    Nonresident alien prohibition, 16-5,
        16-27
    Number of shareholders limitation,
        16-4
    Operational rules, 16-12 to 16-24
    Preserving the election, 16-26 to
        16-27
    Previously taxed income (PTI), 16-15,
        16-28
    Qualification, 16-3 to 16-12, 16-26
    Restriction on number of
        shareholders, 16-4
    Restriction on types of shareholders,
        16-5
    Selection of a tax year, 16-23
    Shareholders, *see* Shareholders, S
        Corporations
    Small business corporation
        requirement, 16-3 to 16-9
    Subchapter S Revision Act of 1982,
        pp. 16-12
    Taxable income, *see* Taxable Income,
        S corporations
    Tax planning, 16-24 to 16-29
    Tax year, 16-23

S Corporations—Cont'd
  Type of shareholder limitation, 16-5
  Undistributed taxable income (UTI),
    16-16
Second Job, 6-37
Section 1231
  Computational procedures, 10-20 to
    10-25, 10-36
  Excluded property, 10-20
  Holding period, 10-20
  Included property, 10-19 to 10-20
  Justification for favorable treatment,
    10-18 to 10-19
  Relationship to Section 1221, p. 10-17
    to 10-18
  Tax planning, 10-40
  Timing of gain, 10-40
Section 1244 Stock, 6-8
Section 1245
  Depreciation recapture, 13-12, 13-23
  Exceptions, 10-31 to 10-32
  Included property, 10-25 to 10-26
  Potential, 10-26 to 10-27
  Recapture, 10-25 to 10-27
  Tax planning, 10-41
Section 1250
  Computation of recapture, 10-28 to
    10-29
  Depreciation recapture, 13-12, 13-23
  Exceptions, 10-31 to 10-32
  Potential, 10-27 to 10-28
  Recapture, 10-27 to 10-29
  Tax planning, 10-41
Securities, See also Tax-Exempt
    Securities; Worthless Securities
  Basis rule, 9-11 to 9-12
  Capital gains and losses, 10-3 to
    10-4
  Holding period, 9-12
  Identification problems, 9-6 to 9-7
  Sale or exchange, 9-11, 9-34
  Tax-free reorganizations, 14-27 to
    14-30
  Trust and estate disallowed losses,
    20-12
Self-Employed Business Expenses, 6-31
    to 6-32
Self-Employed Individuals Tax
    Retirement Act of 1962, p. 22-2
Self-Employed Versus Employee Status,
    12-35
Separate Maintenance Payments, See
    also Alimony, 3-16 to 3-18
Separate Property, Sec also Community
    Property, 3-15, 3-25
Separate Share Rule, 20-21 to 20-22

Series E and EE Savings Bonds, 3-8 to
    3-9
  Tax planning, 3-23, 3-24
Series HH Savings Bonds, 3-8 to 3-9,
    3-23
Service Charges, 7-15, 7-18
Services, see Tax Services
Severance Taxes, 1-11
Sham Transactions, 5-17
Shareholder-Employees, 6-55 to 6-56,
    16-22, 16-28
Shareholder Liquidations, 14-2 to 14-4,
    14-15 to 14-20, 14-25 to 14-26
Shareholder Loans, Corporate
    Accumulations, 15-22 to 15-23
Shareholder's Obligation to Third
    Party, 13-9
Shareholders, S Corporations
  Basis in stock, 16-15, 16-17 to 16-18,
    16-28
  Capital gains tax consequences, 16-21
    to 16-22
  Consent to elect, 16-26
  Corporate distributions, 16-15 to
    16-17
  Fringe benefits, 16-22 to 16-23, 16-27
  Membership limitations, 16-4 to 16-5
  Minor shareholders, 16-6
  Net operating loss, 16-18 to 16-20
  Number allowed, 16-26
  Tax brackets, 16-25, 16-28
  Type limitations, 16-5
Shifting Deductions, 5-23, 6-55 to 6-56,
    11-19
Shifting of Income, see Income Shifting
Short Sales, 10-11 to 10-13
Short Year, 11-15
Sick Pay, see Disability and Sick Pay
Simple Trusts, 20-14, 20-18 to 20-19
Simplified LIFO, 11-36 to 11-37
Single Pool LIFO, 11-37 to 11-38
Single Transaction Approach, 14-23
Sixteenth Amendment, 1-2, 4-18
Small Business, 1-22 to 1-23
Small Business Corporations, see Small
    Business Stock; Section 1244 Stock;
    S Corporations
Small Business Investment Companies,
    15-12
Small Business Stock, 6-8, 16-5
Small Claims Division, see Tax Court
Social Considerations of the Tax Law,
    1-23 to 1-24, 1-34
Social Security Benefits, See also Tax
    Credit for the Elderly
  Gross income, 3-21

Social Security Benefits—Cont'd
    Tax credits, 8-24
    Two-earner married couple deduction,
        3-21
Social Security Tax, 1-15, 1-16 to 1-17,
    7-10, 8-24, 21-20
Soil and Water Conservation
    Expenditures, 16-14, 17-15
Sole Proprietors, 6-31, 12-1
Sources of Income, 3-12 to 3-16
Sources of Revenue, 1-3, 1-6, 1-11
Special Accounting Methods, 11-21 to
    11-31, 11-40 to 11-41
Special Interest Legislation, 1-29
Special School Tuition as Medical
    Deduction, 7-3
Special Tax Computations, Chapter 11
    Accounting methods, 11-21 to 11-31,
        11-40 to 11-41
    Accounting periods, 11-13 to 11-16,
        11-40
    Alternative minimum tax, 11-6 to
        11-13, 11-39 to 11-40
    Income averaging, 1-26 to 1-27, 11-2
        to 11-6, 11-38 to 11-39
    Inventories, 11-33 to 11-38
    Tax planning, 11-38 to 11-39
Specific Charge-Off Method, 6-3, 6-4
Spin-Off, 14-28
Split-Off, 14-28
Split-Up, 14-28
Sponge Tax, 18-26
Stamp Tax, 1-10
Standard Deduction, *see* Zero Bracket
    Amount
Start-Up Expenditures, 12-17
State Death Taxes, 19-21 to 19-23
State Gift Tax Law, 19-24
State and Local Influences on Federal
    Tax Law, 1-30
State and Local Taxes, *See also*
    Itemized Deductions; Income Taxes,
    5-5, 7-9, 7-14, 7-32 to 7-33
Statement of Procedural Rules, 21-3
Statement of Responsibilities in Tax
    Practice (SRTP), 21-29 to 21-34
State Transfer Taxes, 19-21 to 19-24
Statute of Limitations, 21-22
    Assessment of tax, 21-23 to 21-24
    Bad debts, 21-25
    Corporate accumulations, 15-25
    Depreciation, 9-4
    Exceptions to three-year limitation,
        21-23 to 21-24, 21-25
    Extensions, 21-24, 21-25, 21-26
    Fraud, 21-23

Statute of Limitations—Cont'd
    Hobby losses, 5-11
    No return filed, 21-23
    Omission of gross income, 21-23
    Refund claims, 21-24 to 21-26
    Special rules, 21-24 to 21-26
    Worthless securities, 21-25
Statutory Authority, 4-1 to 4-2
Statutory Notice of Deficiency
    (Ninety-Day Letter), 21-7, 21-9,
    21-10, 21-21
Statutory Percentages for Real
    Property, 6-24
Statutory Sources of the Tax Law, 22-1
    to 22-5, 22-18 to 22-21
Step-Up in Basis, 9-10, 14-25, 15-27
Stock Attribution Rules, 13-17
Stock Dividends
    Exclusions, 4-21 to 4-22
    Holding period, 13-14
    Proportionate interest concept, 13-13
    Taxability, 13-14
    Tax consequences, 13-24
    Tax-free treatment, 13-13 to 13-14
Stock Options, 10-6 to 10-7, 11-10
Stock Ownership, *see* Constructive
    Ownership of Stock
Stock Ownership Credit, 8-18 to 8-19
Stock Ownership Test, 15-12 to 15-13,
    15-24, 15-25
Stock Redemptions, *See also* Partial
    Liquidations
    Background, 13-16 to 13-17
    Comparison with liquidation, 14-5 to
        14-6, 14-8
    Complete termination of interest,
        13-20
    Dividend equivalence, 13-17 to 13-19
    Effect on earnings and profits, 13-22
    Gain recognized by redeeming
        corporation, 13-21 to 13-22
    Not essentially equivalent to a
        dividend, 13-17 to 13-19
    To pay death taxes, 13-20 to 13-21,
        13-22
    Stock attribution rules, 13-17
    Substantially disproportionate, 13-19
    Tax avoidance, 13-16 to 13-22
    Tax consequences, 13-24
    Tax planning, 13-27 to 13-28
Stock Rights, 13-14 to 13-15, 13-24
Stock Sales, 10-38
Stocks and Securities
    Holding period, 9-12
    Transfers, 12-23, 12-24 to 12-25
    Wash sales, 9-11 to 9-12, 9-34

Straddle Sales, 14-11 to 14-12, 14-32 to 14-33

Straight Debt, 16-27

Straight-Life Annuity, 18-11 to 18-12

Straight-Line Depreciation, 6-17, 6-18, 6-21, 6-24, 6-55, 9-4

Straight-Line Recovery, 6-25 to 6-26, 10-41 to 10-42

Student Loans, *see* Discharge of Indebtedness

Subchapter J, 20-1 to 20-2

Subchapter K, 17-2, 17-34

Subchapter S, *See also* Shareholders, S Corporations; S Corporations, 3-14, 12-2, Chapter 16

Subchapter S Revision Act of 1982, pp. 16-12

Subsidiaries, 14-20 to 14-24

Substantially Disporportionate Stock Redemption, 13-19

Substantiation Requirements, 5-19 to 5-20, 6-57, 7-32

Suddenness Test, 6-8

Summer Youth Employees, 8-14

Sum-of-the-Years' Digits Depreciation, 6-17, 6-18, 6-19

Supper Money, 4-16

Support, *see* Child Support Payments; Personal and Dependency Exemptions

Supreme Court, 22-8, 22-11, 22-14 to 22-15, 22-21

*Supreme Court Reporter* (S.CT.), 22-14, 22-15

Surety Companies, 15-12

Survivorship Annuity, 18-11, 18-12

## T

Tangible Property, *see* Property, Tangible

Targeted Jobs Tax Credit, 8-12 to 8-14, 8-30, 8-31

Tariffs, 1-18 to 1-19

Taxable Dividends, 13-1 to 13-2, 13-6 to 13-13

Taxable Estate, *See also* Gross Estate; Marital Deduction, 13-24, 18-19 to 18-24

Taxable Gifts, 19-25

Taxable Income, 2-21, 11-1
  Accumulated earnings, 15-23
  Alternative minimum tax, 11-9, 11-10, 11-12
  Annualization, 11-15 to 11-16

Taxable Income—Cont'd
  Compared with accounting income, 3-2
  Corporate, 12-21 to 12-22, 15-9, 15-10, 15-11, 15-16 to 15-17, 15-23
  Corporations, 12-8, 16-10
  Deductions, 20-9 to 20-15, 20-23 to 20-24
  Estates and trusts, 20-6 to 20-15, 20-17
  Gross income, 3-2, 20-6 to 20-8
  Income averaging, 11-2, 11-5, 11-39
  Income in respect of a decedent, 20-8 to 20-9
  Liquidation of a subsidiary, 14-24
  Not realized by employees, 3-3
  Partnerships, 17-14 to 17-15, 17-16
  S corporations, 16-10, 16-12 to 16-14, 16-15, 16-20 to 16-21, 16-25, 16-28

Taxable Periods of Less Than One Year, 11-15

Taxable Year, 17-24 to 17-27, 17-33

Tax Administration
  Administrative ruling, 21-34 to 21-35
  Appeals, 21-8 to 21-10, 21-11, 21-35 to 21-36
  Audits, 21-4 to 21-10, 21-35 to 21-36
  Interest, 21-10, 21-12 to 21-14, 21-36
  IRS procedure, 21-1 to 21-4
  Penalties, 21-14 to 21-20, 21-36 to 21-37
  Powers of the IRS, 21-20 to 21-22
  Statute of limitations, 21-22 to 21-26
  Tax planning, 21-34 to 21-37
  Tax practitioners, 21-26 to 21-34, 22-4

Taxation of Corporations, Chapter 12

Taxation, History, 1-1 to 1-3

Tax Avoidance
  Accumulated earnings, 15-23, 15-25
  Bequests, 9-35
  Cash businesses, 21-4
  Collapsible corporations, 14-25 to 14-26
  Constructive dividends, 13-26 to 13-27
  Controlled corporations, 12-27
  Dividends, 15-23, 15-25, 15-26
  Estate tax, 18-6, 18-7, 18-8, 18-31
  Liquidations, 14-9
  Minimum tax, 11-8
  Personal holding company, 15-25 to 15-27

Tax Avoidance—Cont'd
Personal holding company tax, 15-18
Property transfers, 12-36 to 12-40,
18-8
Related taxpayers, 5-18
S corporations, 1-23, 16-2, 16-12,
16-20, 16-21, 16-27, 16-29
State transfer tax, 19-25
Stock redemptions, 13-16 to 13-22,
13-27 to 13-28
Tax planning, 22-23
Tax Base
Adjustments, 1-5
Selection criteria, 1-3 to 1-4
Tax Benefit Rule
Controlled corporations, 12-30 to
12-31
Exclusion from gross income, 4-22
Liquidation of a subsidiary, 14-24
Tax planning, 14-31, 14-32
Twelve-month liquidations, 14-10 to
14-11
Tax Bills, 22-2
Tax Burdens, 1-5
Tax Computation, *See also* Special Tax
Computations, 2-18 to 2-20
Tax Consequences of Operating a
Business, 12-3, 12-34 to 12-35
Tax Court Decisions, 22-11 to 22-13,
22-21
*Tax Court of the United States Report,*
22-12
Tax Credit for the Elderly, *See also*
Social Security Benefits, 8-23 to
8-25, 8-29, 12-7
Tax Credits, 2-19 to 2-20, Chapter 8
ACRS, 8-3
Business-related provisions, 8-2 to
8-19
Child and dependent care expense
credit, 8-26 to 8-28, 8-30, 8-33 to
8-34
Corporations, 12-7
Credit versus deduction, 8-1
Earned income credit, 1-30, 2-34, 8-22
to 8-23
Elderly taxpayer credit, 8-23 to 8-25,
8-29, 12-7
Energy tax credits, 8-20 to 8-22, 8-30,
8-32
ERTA, 8-3, 8-8, 8-10 to 8-11, 8-18,
8-27, 8-33
ESOPs, 8-30
Estates and trusts, 20-15
Foreign tax credit, 8-25 to 8-26, 8-29,
8-32

Tax Credits—Cont'd
Investment tax credit, *See also*
Investment Tax Credit, 8-2 to
8-12, 8-29, 8-30 to 8-31
Nonrefundable, 8-29 to 8-30
Political campaign contributions, 8-28
to 8-29
Priority of credits, 8-29 to 8-30
Refundable, 8-29
Rehabilitation expenditures tax
credit, 8-14 to 8-15
Research and experimentation, 8-15
to 8-18, 8-30, 8-32 to 8-33
Social Security benefits, 8-24
Stock ownership credit, 8-18 to 8-19
Targeted jobs credit, 8-12 to 8-14,
8-30, 8-31
Tax planning, 8-30 to 8-34
Tax policy considerations, 8-1 to 8-2
TEFRA, 8-13 to 8-14
Tax Deductions Substantiation, 5-19 to
5-20
Tax Deferrals, 3-22 to 3-23, 11-40,
11-41
Tax Deficiency, 21-9 to 21-10, 21-36
Tax Determination, 2-17 to 2-20, 11-13
Tax Disputes, 21-8 to 21-10, 21-35 to
21-36
Tax, as Distinguished from Fee, 7-9
Tax Equity and Fiscal Responsibility
Act of 1982 (TEFRA)
ACRS, 6-20 to 6-23
Alternative minimum tax, 11-8,
11-10, 11-11, 11-13
Business expenses, 5-3
Casualty and theft losses, 6-10
Casualty and theft loss limitation,
1-32
Completed contract method of
accounting, 11-22
Corporate income tax, 12-18, 12-19
Depreciation and amortization, 6-15
Depreciation rules, 6-22 to 6-23
Disallowance of tax deduction, 1-24
Dividend and interest income, 2-18
Failure to file penalty, 21-15
Frivolous tax return, 1-32
Illegal business expenses, 5-8
Interest on overpayments, 21-13
Interest on unpaid taxes, 21-10, 21-12
Internal Revenue Code, 22-2
Investment tax credit, 1-20, 8-4 to 8-5
Medical expense deduction, 7-2
Penalties, 1-32, 21-19
Professional associations, 12-35
Recapture, 10-25

Tax Equity and Fiscal Responsibility
    Act of 1982 (TEFRA)—Cont'd
  Targeted jobs credit, 8-13 to 8-14
  Tax preference items, 11-10
  Withholding procedures, 1-31
Taxes
  Ad valorem tax, 1-5, 1-6 to 1-8
  Assessments for local benefits, 7-10 to
    7-11
  Death taxes, 1-11
  Deductibility, 7-9 to 7-10
  Employment taxes, 1-15 to 1-18
  Excise tax, 1-9 to 1-10, 1-11, 1-12,
    1-18
  Franchise tax, 1-19
  General sales tax, 1-10 to 1-11
  Gift tax, 1-12
  Income taxes, 1-12 to 1-15, 7-12
  Occupational taxes, 1-19
  Property taxes, 1-5 to 1-8
  Reduction of taxes, 22-23
  Tariffs, 1-18 to 1-19
  Transaction taxes, 1-9 to 1-11
Tax Evasion, 21-16 to 21-17, 22-23
Tax-Exempt Income, 5-4, 5-20 to 5-22,
  16-13
  All-Savers Certificates, 1-22, 4-19, 5-21
  Interest, 7-15, 17-15
Tax-Exempt Interest, 7-15, 17-15
Tax-Exempt Organizations, 15-12
Tax-Exempt Securities, 7-17, 15-25
  All-Savers Certificates, 5-21
Tax Formula, 6-1
  Application, 2-5 to 2-6
  Components, 2-2 to 2-11
  Zero bracket amount, 2-6 to 2-11
Tax-Free Reorganizations, 14-27 to
  14-30
Tax Holiday, 1-7
Tax Law
  Administrative sources, 22-5 to 22-7,
    22-16, 22-20 to 22-21
  Economic considerations, 1-19 to
    1-23, 1-34
  Equity considerations, 1-24 to 1-29,
    1-34
  Favorable tax treatment, 1-21 to 1-23
  Influence of the courts, 1-32 to 1-34
  Influence of the Internal Revenue
    Service, 1-30 to 1-32
  Judicial sources, 22-7 to 22-15, 22-16,
    22-21
  Political considerations, 1-29 to 1-30,
    1-34
  Research, 22-15 to 22-22
  Selection of tax base, 1-3 to 1-4

Tax Law—Cont'd
  Social considerations, 1-23 to 1-24,
    1-34
  Statutory sources, 22-1 to 22-5, 22-18
    to 22-21
  Tax planning, 22-22 to 22-24
  Tax sources, 22-1 to 22-15
Tax Liability, 2-18 to 2-20, 2-23, 16-13,
  21-36 to 21-37
  Corporations, 12-17 to 12-22
  Energy tax credit, 8-22
  ESOPs, 8-19
  Estates, 18-29 to 18-30
  Investment tax credit, 8-5
  Reduction, 8-5
  Tax credits, 8-5
Taxpayer Appeals Within IRS, *see*
  Appeal Process
Taxpayer Compliance Measurement
  Program (TCMP), 21-5
Taxpayer Identification Number (TIN),
  21-19
Taxpayer Obligations, 7-15
Tax Planning
  Accelerated depreciation, 10-41
  Accounting methods and periods,
    11-40 to 11-41
  Accumulated earnings, 15-20 to
    15-24
  ACRS, 6-52 to 6-55, 10-41 to 10-42
  Alimony, 3-25 to 3-26
  Alternative minimum tax, 11-39 to
    11-40
  Annuities, 3-25
  Associations, 12-35
  Audits, 21-35 to 21-36
  Bad debts, 6-52
  Beneficiaries, 20-25 to 20-27
  Bequests, 9-35 to 9-36
  Capital asset status, 10-38 to 10-39
  Capital gains and losses, 10-36 to
    10-42
  Casualty and theft losses, 6-52
  Charitable contributions, 7-34 to 7-35
  Child and dependent care expenses,
    8-33 to 8-34
  Community property, 2-32, 2-33, 2-35
  Constructive dividends, 13-26 to
    13-27
  Corporate accumulations, 15-20 to
    15-24
  Corporate distributions, 13-24 to
    13-26
  Corporate versus noncorporate
    business organization forms,
    12-33 to 12-35

Tax Planning—Cont'd

Cost identification and documentation considerations, 9-35

Death tax, 18-30 to 18-32

Deductions and losses, 5-22 to 5-24

Deferral of taxes, 3-22 to 3-23, 11-40, 11-41

Dependency exemptions, 2-31 to 2-34

Depletion, 6-55

Depreciation and amortization, 6-52 to 6-54

Distributable net income, 20-26 to 20-27

Dividend distributions, 13-24 to 13-27, 15-22 to 15-24, 15-26

Dividends, 15-23 to 15-24

Education expenses, 6-56 to 6-57

Employee annuities, 3-25

Employee benefits, 4-26 to 4-27

Employee expenses, 6-55 to 6-56

Energy tax credit, 8-32

Entertainment expenses, 6-57 to 6-58

Estate income tax, 18-30 to 18-32

Estates, 20-25 to 20-27

Excess itemized deductions, 7-30

Filing status, 2-34 to 2-35

Follow-up procedures, 22-23 to 22-24

Foreign tax credit, 8-32

Gifts, 4-25, 9-35, 19-25 to 19-30

Gross income, 3-22 to 3-26

Gross income exclusion, 4-24 to 4-27

Group-term life insurance, 4-26

Hobby losses, 5-23 to 5-24

Income averaging, 11-38 to 11-39

Income shifting, 3-23 to 3-24

Inheritances, 4-25

Injury and sickness compensation, 4-26

In-kind distributions, 14-30, 14-32

Interest deduction, 7-33

Interest on life insurance proceeds, 4-25

Investment tax credit, 8-30 to 8-31

Involuntary conversions, 9-36, 14-32

Itemized deductions, 2-30 to 2-31, 6-52 to 6-58, 7-30 to 7-35

Jobs tax credit, 8-31

LIFO, 11-41 to 11-42

Like-kind exchanges, 9-36

Liquidation, 14-30 to 14-34

Marital deduction, 18-30 to 18-32

Maximizing benefits, 10-36 to 10-37

Medical deductions, 2-33 to 2-34, 7-30 to 7-32

Minimum tax, 11-39 to 11-40

Moving expenses, 6-56

Tax Planning—Cont'd

Net operating losses, 6-55, 16-19 to 16-20

Nontax considerations, 22-22 to 22-23

Partnerships, 17-32 to 17-35

Penalties, 21-36 to 21-37

Penalty tax, 15-20 to 15-24

Personal expenditures, 5-22

Personal holding company tax, 15-24 to 15-27

Property transactions, 9-35 to 9-38

Property transfers, 12-36 to 12-40, 19-25 to 19-30

Recapture, 10-40 to 10-41

Reduced investment credit, 8-31

Related taxpayers, 5-22 to 5-23, 6-52

Research and experimental expenditures, 8-32 to 8-33

Sale of a personal residence, 9-36 to 9-38

Sale of securities, 9-34

Sales tax, 7-32 to 7-33

S corporations, 16-24 to 16-29

Series E and EE savings bonds, 3-23, 3-24

Shareholder loans, 15-22 to 15-23

Shifting deductions, 5-23, 6-55 to 6-56

Shifting income, 3-23 to 3-24

Spreading gains, 10-37

Stock redemptions, 13-27 to 13-28

Stock sales, 10-38

Straddle sales, 14-32 to 14-33

Straight-line cost recovery, 10-41 to 10-42

Tax administration, 21-34 to 21-37

Tax avoidance versus tax evasion, 22-23

Tax benefit rule, 14-31, 14-32

Tax credits, 8-30 to 8-34

Tax deferrals, 3-22 to 3-23, 11-40, 11-41

Tax law, 22-22 to 22-24

Tax research, 22-15, 22-22, 22-23, 22-24

Timing of Section 1231 gain, 10-40

Trusts, 20-27

Uniform Gifts to Minors Act, 3-24

Unreasonable compensation, 5-22

Wash sales, 9-34

Year-end, 10-37 to 10-38

Zero bracket amount, 2-30 to 2-31, 2-34, 7-30

Tax Practice

Ethical considerations, 21-29 to 21-34

Penalties, 21-27 to 21-29

Tax Practice—Cont'd
  Rules, 21-27 to 21-28
  Tax practitioner, 21-26 to 21-34
Tax Practitioners, 21-26 to 21-34, 21-35
  to 21-36, 22-4
Tax Preference Items, *See also*
  Minimum Tax on Tax Preferences,
  11-13, 17-16
  Adjustment, 12-18, 12-19
  Corporations, 12-18 to 12-19
  Estates and trusts, 20-5
Tax Rates, 2-29
  Corporations, 12-7, 12-17 to 12-18
  FICA, 1-16
  Progressive, 1-4, 1-5
  Proportional, 1-4, 1-5
Tax Rate Schedules, 2-8 to 2-9, 2-17 to
  2-18, 2-22, 2-23 to 2-24
Tax Rate Structure, 1-20 to 1-21
Tax Reduction, 22-23
Tax Reduction Act of 1975, p. 1-20
Tax Reduction and Simplification Act of
  1977, p. 2-17
Tax Reform, 1-29 to 1-30
Tax Reform Act of 1969, pp. 6-18, 13-21
  Minimum tax, 11-8
Tax Reform Act of 1976
  Charitable contributions, 7-22
  Corporate contributions, 12-11
  Estate tax, 18-1, 18-7, 18-25, 18-27,
    18-31
  Gift tax, 18-27, 18-31, 19-1, 19-15 to
    19-16
  Gross estate, 18-7
  IRS rulings, 21-2
  Nonrecognition of gain, 17-7
  Partnership contributions, 17-7
  Partnership deductions, 17-29
  Partnership losses, 17-24
  Prepaid interest, 7-16, 11-18 to 11-19
  Sports franchises, 10-9
  Tax return preparation, 21-28 to
    21-29
  Unified transfer tax credit, 18-25,
    18-27, 19-15 to 19-16, 19-22
Tax Refunds, 2-17, 2-18 to 2-20, 21-12
  to 21-14, 21-24 to 21-26
Tax Research
  Problem identification, 22-15 to 22-18
  Solutions, 22-21 to 22-22
  Tax law sources, 22-18 to 22-21
  Tax planning, 22-15, 22-22, 22-23,
    22-24
Tax Return Preparers, 21-26, 22-4
  Ethical considerations, 21-29 to 21-34
  Penalties imposed, 21-27 to 21-29

Tax Returns, 2-20 to 2-22, 2-23
Tax Services, 22-18 to 22-19
Tax-Sheltered Annuities, 18-14
Tax-Sheltered Fringe Benefits, 12-35,
  17-34
Tax Shelters, *See also* Depreciation and
  Amortization; Individual
  Retirement Accounts; Tax Planning
  Annuity plans, 18-14
  Audits, 21-5
  Farm losses, 11-19
  Fringe benefits, 12-35, 17-34
  Passive income, 15-11
  Personal holding company, 15-11
  Prepaid cattle feed costs, 11-19
  Real estate investments, 6-18
  Tax-sheltered investments, 1-5
Tax Law Sources, 21-1 to 21-15
Tax Straddles, 14-11 to 14-12, 14-32 to
  14-33
Tax Structure, 1-4 to 1-5
Tax Table, 2-8 to 2-9, 2-17, 2-23 to 2-24
Tax Treatment of Liquidating
  Corporations, 14-9 to 14-10, 14-12
  to 14-13
Tax Versus Fee, 7-9
Tax Year, 16-23
T.D., *see* Treasury Decisions
Technical Advice, 21-3, 21-4, 21-9 to
  21-10, 21-34 to 21-35
TEFRA, *see* Tax Equity and Fiscal
  Responsibility Act of 1982
Temporary Assignments, 6-37 to 6-38
Tenancy in Common, *See also* Joint
  Ownership, 18-15, 18-16
Tenancy by the Entirety, *See also* Joint
  Ownership, 18-15, 18-16 to 18-17,
  19-9, 19-10
Term Certain, 3-19
Termination of S Corporations, 16-7 to
  16-12, 16-25
  Involuntary, 16-7, 16-8 to 16-9, 16-25,
    16-27, 16-29
  Reelection, 16-12
  Voluntary, 16-7 to 16-8, 16-25
Termite Damage, 6-8
Testamentary Transfers, 19-7, 19-26,
  19-27 to 19-28
Theft Losses, *See also* Casualty and
  Theft Losses, 6-9, 6-52
Thin Corporation, *see* Glossary
Thirty-Day Letter, 21-8
Three-Year Rule, 18-6 to 18-8
Throwback Rule, *See also* Complex
  Trusts, 20-24 to 20-25, 20-27
Top-Heavy Plans, 16-23

Trade or Business Expenses, 5-2 to 5-3
Trademarks, 10-8
Transaction in Contemplation of Death,
   *see* Gifts in Contemplation of Death
Transactions Between Partner and
   Partnership, 16-27 to 16-28
Transaction Taxes
   Excise tax, 1-9 to 1-10
   Gas guzzler tax, 1-9
   General sales tax, 1-10 to 1-11
   Severance taxes, 1-11
   Use tax, 1-10 to 1-11
Transfers
   Charitable contributions, 18-21 to
     18-22
   Estate, 18-6 to 18-7
   Post-1976, pp. 19-15 to 19-17
   Pre-1977, p. 19-15
   Prior, 18-27 to 18-28
   Property, 18-8 to 18-11
   Retained life estate, 18-8 to 18-9,
     18-12
   Revocable, 18-9 to 18-11
   Trust for minors exclusion, 19-14 to
     19-15
Transfers to Controlled Corporations,
   *see* Controlled Corporations
Transfers with a Retained Life Estate,
   18-8 to 18-9, 18-12
Transfer Taxes (State), 19-21 to 19-24
Transportation Expenses
   Automobile expenses, 6-38
   Commuting expenses, 6-36 to 6-37
   Medical expense, 7-4
   Qualified expenditures, 6-36 to 6-38
   Second job, 6-37
   Temporary assignments, 6-37 to 6-38
Travel Expenses
   Away-from-home requirement, 6-39
   Combined business and pleasure, 6-39
     to 6-40
   Defined, 6-38
   Foreign conventions, 6-40
   Substantiation, 5-19 to 5-20
Treasury Decisions (T.D.), 22-6
Treasury Department Regulations, 22-5
   to 22-6, 22-18
   Assessing validity, 22-20
Treble Damage Payments, 5-3, 5-7
Trial Courts, 22-8 to 22-9, 22-10
Trusts, *See also* Beneficiaries, Complex
   Trusts; Distributable Net Income
   Computation; Income in Respect of
   a Decedent; Simple Trusts
   Accounting periods and methods, 20-4
     to 20-5

Trusts—Cont'd
   Association status, 12-6
   Beneficiaries, 20-2, 20-15 to 20-22
   Capital gains, 20-24
   Charitable contribution deduction,
     18-21 to 18-22, 20-12 to 20-14,
     20-16, 20-20 to 20-21, 20-24
   Classes of income, 20-22 to 20-23
   Conduit concept application, 12-2,
     20-5 to 20-6
   Deductions, 20-9 to 20-15, 20-23 to
     20-24
   Defined, 20-2
   Distributable net income, 20-16 to
     20-18, 20-21
   Distributions to beneficiaries, 20-14,
     20-25 to 20-27
   Fiduciary income tax return
     requirements, 20-4
   Grantor, 20-2
   Gross income, 3-14, 20-6 to 20-8
   Income tax treatment, 12-2, 20-3 to
     20-6
   Life tenant, 20-2
   Multiple trusts, 20-24 to 20-25
   Nature of taxation, 20-3 to 20-6
   Net operating losses, 20-11, 20-24
   Personal exemption, 20-5
   Separate share rule, 20-21 to 20-22
   Taxable income, 20-6 to 20-15, 20-17
   Tax credits, 20-15
   Tax planning, 20-27
   Tax rates, 20-5
   Throwback rule, 20-24 to 20-25,
     20-27
   Trustee, 20-2
Truth in Lending Act, 7-18
Twelve-Month Liquidations
   Assets retained to pay claims, 14-13
     to 14-14
   Assets sold, 14-9
   Bulk sale of inventory, 14-30, 14-31
   In combination with distributions in
     kind (Section 336), 14-2 to 14-8,
     14-14
   Expenses, 14-12 to 14-13
   Installment sales, 14-14
   Involuntary conversions, 14-13
   Property defined, 14-10
   Recapture, 14-11
   Straddle sales, 14-11 to 14-12, 14-32
     to 14-33
   Tax benefit rule, 14-10 to 14-11
   Tax planning, 14-30 to 14-34
Two-Earner Married Couple Deduction,
   2-25 to 2-26, 3-21, 6-33, 6-52

# U

Underpayment of Estimated Tax Penalty, 12-19 to 12-20, 21-12, 21-18

Undistributed Net Income, *see* Throwback Rule

Undistributed Personal Holding Company Income, 15-16 to 15-17, 15-26 to 15-27

Undistributed Taxable Income (UTI), 16-16

Unearned Income, *See also* Prepaid Income, 2-9, 3-2

Unemployment Compensation, 1-18, 3-21 to 3-22

Unemployment Tax, *see* Federal Unemployment Tax Act

Unified Transfer Tax, *See also* Federal Estate Tax; Gift Tax (Federal) 18-24, 18-25, 18-27, 18-31, 19-5, 19-6

Unified Transfer Tax Credit, 18-25 to 18-26, 18-27, 18-31, 19-15 to 19-17, 19-22

Uniform Gifts to Minors Act, 3-24, 16-6, 18-10, 18-11

Uniform Limited Partnership Act, 17-2

Uniform Partnership Act, 17-2, 17-3

Unit-of-Production Depreciation, 6-17, 6-20, 6-29

Unpaid Expenses and Interest, *See also* Related-Party Transactions, 5-18

Unpaid Interest, 5-18

Unrealized Losses, Disallowance of Deduction, 5-15

Unrealized Receivables, 17-15

Unreasonable Compensation, 5-22, 13-10, 13-27, 22-24

Unrecognized Loss, *see* Nonrecognition of Gains and Losses

Unused Investment Credits, 8-6 to 8-7

Unused Zero Bracket Amount, 2-2, 2-8 to 2-11

*U. S. Board of Tax Appeals Reports* (T.B.A.), 22-12

U. S. Gift Tax Return, 19-19 to 19-20

U. S. Government Bonds, *see* Series E and EE Savings Bonds; Series HH Savings Bonds

*U. S. Reports, Lawyer's Edition* (L.Ed.), 22-14

*U. S. Supreme Court Reports* (U. S.), 22-14

*U. S. Tax Cases* (USTC), 22-13, 22-14, 22-15

U. S. Tax Court, 22-7, 22-8, 22-9, 22-10, 22-11 to 22-13, 22-21

Useful Life, 9-4

Useful Life for Depreciable Asset, 6-17, 6-19, 6-20, 6-52 to 6-53

Use Tax, 1-10 to 1-11

# V

Vacation Homes, 5-12 to 5-13

Valuation, *see* Charitable Contributions

Valuation of Property, *See also* Fair Market Value

Alternate valuation date, 19-22

Estate assets, 20-27

Remainder interests, 18-5, 20-2

Reversionary interests, 20-2

Value Added Tax (VAT), 1-12

Violation of Public Policy, *see* Public Policy Limitation

# W

Waivers, 16-12

Wash Sales, 9-11 to 9-12, 9-34, 12-7, 20-12

Wherewithal to Pay Concept, 1-25 to 1-26, 1-27, 1-28, 2-11

Withholding Tax, 1-4, 1-5, 1-13, 1-17, 1-31 to 1-32, 2-18, 2-23, 7-12, 8-29, 21-18

Workers' Compensation, 4-10, 16-22

Working Capital of Corporation, 15-6 to 15-8

Worthless Securities, 6-7 to 6-8, 10-5, 21-25

Writ of Certiorari, 22-11

# Y

Year-End Tax Planning, 10-37 to 10-38

# Z

Zero Bracket Amount, 1-13 to 1-14, 1-32, 2-5, 2-6 to 2-11

Charitable contributions, 7-26

Dependent child limitation, 2-9 to 2-10

Filing requirements, 2-5, 2-21

Zero Bracket Amount—Cont'd
  Interest expense, 7-16
  Marriage penalty, 2-24
  Married taxpayers filing separately,
    2-10 to 2-11
  Medical deductions, 7-8, 7-9

Zero Bracket Amount—Cont'd
  Outside salesperson, 6-33
  Partnerships, 17-16
  Tax planning, 2-30 to 2-31, 2-34, 7-30
  Tax Table and Schedules, 2-7 to 2-8
  Unused, 2-2, 2-8 to 2-11

†